BIOGRAPHICAL DICTIONARY
OF REPUBLICAN CHINA

VOLUME II: DALAI–MA

BIOGRAPHICAL DICTIONARY OF REPUBLICAN CHINA

HOWARD L. BOORMAN, *Editor*
RICHARD C. HOWARD, *Associate Editor*

VOLUME II: DALAI–MA

COLUMBIA UNIVERSITY PRESS
1968   NEW YORK AND LONDON

COPYRIGHT © 1968 COLUMBIA UNIVERSITY PRESS
LIBRARY OF CONGRESS CATALOG CARD NUMBER: 67-12006
PRINTED IN THE UNITED STATES OF AMERICA

BIOGRAPHICAL DICTIONARY OF REPUBLICAN CHINA

HOWARD L. BOORMAN, Editor
RICHARD C. HOWARD, Associate Editor
O. EDMUND CLUBB
RUSSELL MAETH

STAFF

ANNE B. CLARK

SHEN-YU DAI

LIENCHE TU FANG

PEI-JAN HSIA

YANG-CHIH HUANG

MELVILLE T. KENNEDY, JR.

DONALD W. KLEIN

ROBERT H. G. LEE

BERNADETTE LI

ALBERT LU

SUSAN H. MARSH

YONG SANG NG

LORETTA PAN

A. C. SCOTT

PEI-YI WU

CONTRIBUTORS

John S. Aird
Cyril Birch
Scott A. Boorman
Conrad Brandt
Robert A. Burton
C. M. Chang
K. N. Chang
Kwang-chih Chang
Fu-ts'ung Chiang
Tse-tsung Chow
M. W. Chu
Samuel C. Chu
Wen-djang Chu
James I. Crump, Jr.
John Dardess
James E. Dew
John Philip Emerson
Albert Feuerwerker
Yi-tsi Feuerwerker
Wolfgang Franke
Donald Gillin

Merle Goldman
Jerome B. Grieder
Marus Fang Hao
James P. Harrison
Judy Feldman
    Harrison
David Hawkes
Nicole Hirabayashi
Ping-ti Ho
C. T. Hsia
Ronald Hsia
Kung-chuan Hsiao
Francis C. P. Hsu
Kai-yu Hsu
Chün-tu Hsüeh
Chalmers A. Johnson
Paula S. Johnson
Wiliam R. Johnson
Olga Lang
Kan Lao
Shu-hua Li

C. T. Liang
H. H. Ling
Arthur Link
Chun-jo Liu
Ch'ung-hung Liu
James T. C. Liu
Wu-chi Liu
John T. Ma
Meng Ma
Eduardo Macagno
Robert M. Marsh
Harriet C. Mills
Donald Paragon
Robert W. Rinden
David T. Roy
Harold Schiffrin
Stuart R. Schram
William R. Schultz
T. H. Shen
Tsung-lien Shen
James E. Sheridan

Stanley Spector
E-tu Zen Sun
Rufus Suter
S. Y. Teng
Te-kong Tong
T. H. Tsien
T'ung-ho Tung
Lyman P. Van Slyke
Richard L. Walker
Farrell Phillips
    Wallerstein
Chi-kao Wang
Y. T. Wang
Holmes H. Welch
Hellmut Wilhelm
Hsiang-hsiang Wu
K. T. Wu
William C. C. Wu
William A. Wycoff
Isabella Yen

Editor for the Columbia University Press: Katharine Kyes Leab

EXPLANATORY NOTES

The romanization systems used are the Wade-Giles (with the omission of some diacritical marks) for Chinese and the Hepburn (with the omission of some macrons) for Japanese. The major exception to this rule is Chinese place names for large cities, which are given according to the Chinese Post Office system. In the case of Kwangtung province, Cantonese spellings often have been indicated: Nanhai (Namhoi). For place names in Manchuria and in the case of Peking, we generally have followed contemporary usage. In such outlying areas as Sinkiang, Mongolia, and Tibet, any given place might have several names. For convenience, we have standardized the place names in all outlying areas according to the dictates of common sense.

Chinese personal names are given in the Chinese order, that is, with the surname first. In general, the articles are arranged alphabetically by the Wade-Giles romanization of the subject's surname and given personal name (ming). However, the biographies of Chiang Kai-shek, Eugene Ch'en, H. H. K'ung, T. V. Soong, Sun Yat-sen, and a few others appear under the name most familiar to Western readers. The courtesy, literary, Western, alternate, and common pen names of subjects of biographies are listed at the beginning of each article (*see* ABBREVIATIONS). The reader should note that the ming and the tzu (courtesy name) frequently are confused in modern Chinese sources.

THE CALENDAR

Dates are given according to the Western calendar, converted in many cases from the Chinese calendar. The word sui often is used in referring to age. In China, a person is regarded as being one year old at birth and two years old at the beginning of the next Chinese calendar year. Thus, a person's age by Western calculation will be less than his sui. We have retained the sui form in many articles because of the difficulties of conversion and, frequently, the lack of precise information about month and day of birth.

MEASURES OF MONEY AND LAND

From 1911 to 1949 the values of Chinese monetary units varied so greatly that it is impossible to assign them standard values in Western terms. Until 1933 the official unit of value was the Customs tael (Hai-kuan liang). Other monies, such as silver dollars (yuan), also were current. In 1933 the silver dollar (yuan) became the standard legal tender of China. In 1935, by law, a managed paper currency (fapi) replaced the silver. A gold dollar unit (yuan) was briefly introduced in 1948, but the Chinese monetary system remained unstable until after the establishment of the Central People's Government at Peking in October 1949.

Standard units of land measurement used in this work are li and mu.

1 li = 1/3 mile
1 mu (or mou) = 733 sq. yards
6.6 mu = 1 acre

MILITARY ORGANIZATION

We have used Western military terms to describe the organization of Chinese armies. Thus:

chün = army	ying = battalion
shih = division	lien = company
lü = brigade	p'ai = platoon
t'uan = regiment	

The reader should note that the organization of Chinese armies was not so standardized as that of Western armies, and the size of units varied considerably. During the second phase of the Northern Expedition (1928) armies were combined for field operations to form larger units, although they retained their individual designations (e.g., First Army). The combined forces were known variously as army groups (chün-t'uan) direction armies (fang-mien chün) and route armies (lu-chün). Above this level was that of group army (chi-t'uan-chün). Although these were temporary designations, they achieved the permanence of organizational categories.

PROVINCIAL ADMINISTRATION

The administrative divisions, in ascending order, of each province at the end of the Ch'ing period were:

> hsien = districts or counties
> chou = departments
> fu = prefectures
> tao = circuits composed of
> 2 or more fu

We have used the terms military governor and civil governor in referring to provincial rulers of the 1912–28 period. At the beginning of the republican period the Chinese title for the military governor of a province was tutuh. The official designation was changed to chiang-chün in 1914 and to tuchün in 1916. Beginning about 1925, the title was changed in some areas to tupan, a designation which implied that the governor's primary responsibilities were demilitarization and social rehabilitation.

We have used the term governor in referring to the top-ranking officer of a provincial government after 1928, rather than the more literal rendering of the Chinese (sheng cheng-fu chu-hsi) as chairman.

The term tao-t'ai refers to the official in charge of a circuit. A number of the men who held this office during the Ch'ing period were important in foreign relations because often the tao-t'ai was the highest Chinese official available for negotiations with foreigners.

Mention should be made of the likin, an inland tax on the transit of goods which was introduced by the imperial government at the time of the Taiping Rebellion (1850–64). Likin stations soon proliferated throughout China.

The tax revenues were beyond Peking's control and often were used to finance regional armies. The likin tax on local trade was not suppressed officially until 1933.

THE EXAMINATION SYSTEM

In the Ch'ing period, the official class was defined by statute, and its composition was determined by the results of examinations in literary and classical subjects. Although the examination system was abolished in 1905, a brief discussion of it is necessary because many prominent people in the republican period were members of this class by achievement or purchase and because the examinations and degrees have no Western equivalents.

Preliminary examinations were conducted on three successive levels: the hsien; the fu; and the sheng, which was conducted at the prefectural capital. Successful candidates received the sheng-yuan degree, which entitled them to assume the dress of the scholar and exempted them from forced labor. However, they had no legal right to or opportunity for official appointment. They were subject to sui-k'ao, examinations given regularly in the prefectural capitals under provincial supervision. Success in the sui-k'ao meant that they received a small stipend annually to further their studies. Roughly equivalent to the sheng-yuan degree was the chien-sheng degree, which, however, could be purchased. Accordingly, holders of the chien-sheng degree were not subject to periodic examination. Holders of the chien-sheng and the sheng-yuan degrees, who were neither commoners nor officials, comprised a large and changing group.

Those who wished to qualify for official status took the provincial examinations, composed of a preliminary examination, or k'o-k'ao, and a hsiang-shih, or provincial examination. Successful candidates received the degree of chü-jen, which made the holder eligible for office. The kung-sheng degree was roughly equivalent to the chü-jen, but was acquired by appointment, by examination, or by purchase.

The examinations for the highest degree, the chin-shih, which brought appointment to the middle levels of the imperial bureaucracy, were held at Peking. They were composed of the hui-shih, or metropolitan examination; the tien-shih, or palace examination; and the ch'ao-k'ao, an examination in the presence of the emperor which led to specific appointment. Chin-shih who ranked near the top of their group usually were appointed to the Hanlin Academy, where their duties included drawing up government documents and compiling materials for official histories. Service at the Hanlin Academy frequently afforded access to the highest positions in the imperial government.

Candidates who passed the examinations in the same year were linked in the t'ung-nien (same year) relationship, a bond somewhat similar to that linking, for example, members of the Class of 1928 at Harvard College.

FINAL DATE FOR VOLUME II

The final date for inclusion of information about the subjects of biographies in Volume II was August 1967.

BIBLIOGRAPHY

The final volume of this work will contain a comprehensive bibliography. It will list the published writings, if any, of the subject of each article and the sources, both personal and written, used in preparing the article. A brief bibliography of basic sources for twentieth-century Chinese biography is to be found at the end of each volume.

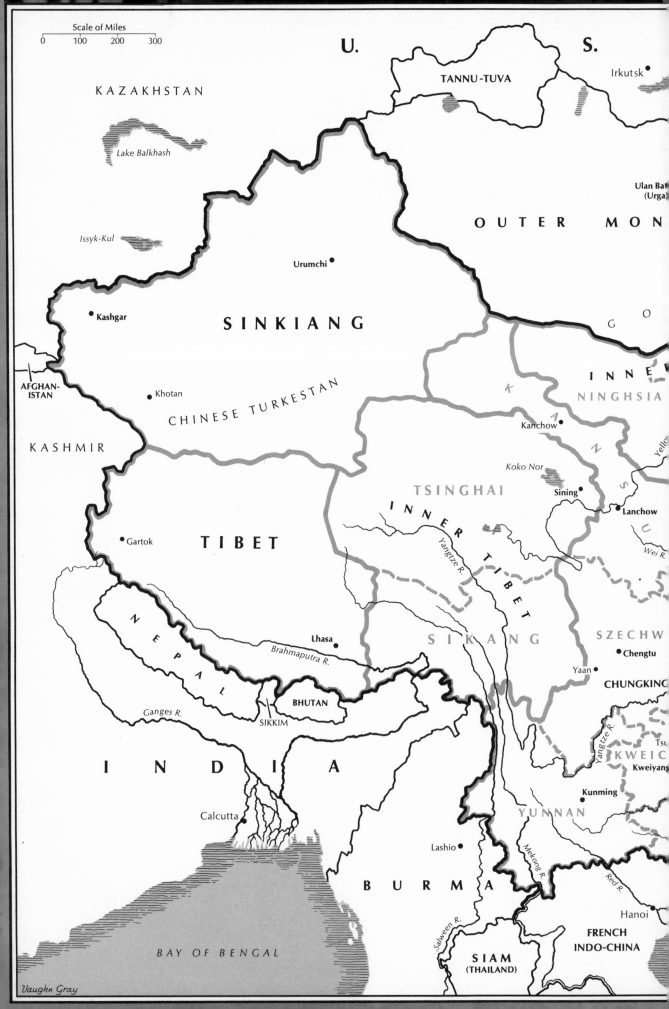

Scale of Miles
0   100   200   300

U.   S.

KAZAKHSTAN   TANNU-TUVA   Irkutsk

Lake Balkhash   OUTER   MON   Ulan Ba
                                                                                          (Urga)

Issyk-Kul   Urumchi   G   O

                        SINKIANG   G
AFGHAN-   Kashgar   INNE
ISTAN   K   NINGHSIA

                    Khotan   CHINESE TURKESTAN   N
                                                                      Kanchow
KASHMIR   S
                                                    Koko Nor   Sining
                                        TSINGHAI   U   Lanchow
                                                                  Wei R.
            Gartok   TIBET   INNER   TIBET

                                        Yangtze R.   SZECHW
                                    SIKANG   Chengtu
                    Lhasa   Yaan
            N   Brahmaputra R.   CHUNGKING
            E
            P   BHUTAN   Yangtze R.   Tsu
            A   SIKKIM   KWEIC
            L   Ganges R.   Kweiyang

    I   N   D   I   A   Kunming

            Calcutta   YUNNAN

                                            Lashio
                                                        Mekong R.
                            BURMA   Red R.

                                                                  Hanoi
                                    Salween R.
    BAY OF BENGAL   SIAM   FRENCH
                                        (THAILAND)   INDO-CHINA
Vaughn Gray

REPUBLICAN CHINA
IN 1928

BIOGRAPHICAL DICTIONARY
OF REPUBLICAN CHINA

VOLUME II: DALAI–MA

ABBREVIATIONS

Alt. = alternate name
H. = hao, a literary name
Orig. = original name
Pen. = pen name

Pseud. = pseudonym
Studio. = pieh-hao (alternate hao)
T. = tzu, courtesy name
West. = Western name

ECCP = *Eminent Chinese of the Ch'ing Period*, ed. by
Arthur W. Hummel. Washington, 1943–44.

Dalai Lama (Thirteenth)

Tibetan. Nga-wang Lop-sang Tup-den
Gya-tso
Secular. Losang Thabkhää Gyaatsho

Dalai Lama (26 June 1876–17 December 1933), spiritual and temporal ruler of Tibet. The thirteenth Dalai was known for his economic and political reforms and for trying to establish independence in Tibet.

Born into a peasant family in an isolated district of Tak-po province in southeastern Tibet, the thirteenth Dalai Lama had several brothers, three of them older than he. After being brought to Lhasa at the age of two, he was confirmed there in 1879 without the participation of the Chinese imperial resident [amban] at Lhasa, who traditionally selected the name of the Dalai Lama from an urn, although with the consent of the emperor. The unusual confirmation proved to be a portent of the later relations between Lhasa and the Ch'ing court at Peking, which had established a protectorate over Tibet in the eighteenth century and thereafter had followed a seclusion policy. The Dalai's mother died when he was three years old. His father, Künga Rincheu, lived at Lhasa and, as was customary for the close relatives of a Dalai Lama, received special honor and political positions in the Tibetan government. Throughout the Dalai's minority a regent ruled at Lhasa.

When the time came for the Dalai's enthronement at the age of 18, the regent and his brother, the prime minister, allegedly plotted to remain in power. An oracle revealed a plan to cause the Dalai's death through the use of a magic diagram inserted into the sole of one of a pair of boots that had been given the Dalai. The diagram was designed to invoke the aid of evil spirits to destroy the wearer of the boots. The regent and the prime minister were arrested and imprisoned.

In 1895, at the age of 20, the Dalai Lama assumed power in Tibet as the incarnation of the Bodhisattva Chen-re-zi, the patron deity of

Tibet. He was the first Dalai Lama to come to power in the nineteenth century, for his predecessors since 1804 had died before reaching maturity, leaving the regents in power. The Dalai Lama immediately began to establish his authority, facing the problem of competition from such rivals as the Ten-gye-ling lamasery, of which his regent had been head, and the Drepung lamasery.

The bypassing of the prerogatives of the imperial resident at the time of the Dalai Lama's confirmation in 1879 had marked Lhasa's initial challenge to the Ch'ing throne. In 1890 Peking had recognized the British protectorate over the neighboring hill state of Sikkim in a convention providing for the demarcation of the Sikkim–Tibet border. In 1893 a new Sino-British agreement on India-Tibet trade through the Chumbi valley had provided for the opening of a new trading market at Yatung in Tibet. The defeat of China by Japan in 1895, the year of the thirteenth Dalai's ascension to power, led to increasing Tibetan defiance of Peking's suzerainty. The Tibetan government did not acknowledge the validity of the Sino-British arrangements, to which it had not been a party, and repulsed moves by the British to open up the projected trade route and to regularize relations with Tibet.

The Dalai Lama was supported in his defiant position by a Buriat Mongol named Dorje, who also was known as Dorjiev. Dorje was a Russian subject who had gone to Tibet in 1880 and who, after winning theological honors at the Drepung lamasery, had become one of the Dalai's tutors and a trusted adviser. In 1898 Dorje returned to Russia to collect funds for the Lama Buddhist religion. The authorities at St. Petersburg, on learning of his mission, engaged him to act as their agent in Tibet, and Dorje returned to Lhasa well supplied with money and gifts for the powerful lamaseries. He then urged the Dalai Lama to seek the support of Russia. The Dalai sent a mission to St. Petersburg in 1901 to establish contact with the court of Tsar Nicholas II. At that time, as a result of the disastrous Boxer Uprising, the Chinese court had been forced to flee from Peking, and Manchuria had been occupied by Russian troops. The situation appeared to favor realization of the Dalai Lama's hopes for independence from China.

The Ch'ing imperial resident at Lhasa strongly opposed the signing of any treaty between Tibet and Russia, as did the Tibetan Grand Council. Dorje then set about to provoke a crisis in Tibetan-British relations in order to create closer contacts with Russia. British fears of Russian expansion increased, and Lord Curzon, the British Viceroy in India, believed that Russian influence, if established in Tibet, would penetrate the Himalayan hill states and threaten India itself. The net result of the Dalai's intransigence, Dorje's scheming, and British suspicion was the dispatching of a British expedition led by Colonel Francis Younghusband and backed by 8,000 troops. That expedition was intended to force the Dalai Lama to comply with the terms of the 1893 Sino-British trade agreement and to forestall anticipated Russian moves.

By March 1904, when the first British-Tibetan engagement was fought on the road to the trade center Gyantse, Russia had become involved in the Russo-Japanese war and, accordingly, paid little attention to the Tibetan situation. At the end of July, as the British forces neared Lhasa, the Dalai Lama, accompanied by Dorje, fled northward to seek refuge in Outer Mongolia. In September 1904 the Tibetan Grand Council was forced by the Younghusband expedition to sign an agreement that, in effect, established a British protectorate. Although the Young-husband convention later was modified, its signature in Lhasa weakened the Dalai Lama's authority. After his flight from Lhasa, the Chinese authorities at Peking invited the ninth Panchen Lama (q.v.) to become regent in Tibet. The Panchen refused, but gave general support to the Ch'ing authorities during the Dalai's absence.

Although his departure from Lhasa had been precipitate, the Dalai Lama nevertheless had traveled in a manner befitting his station. He arrived at Urga (Ulan Bator) in November 1904 with a party of some 700 persons. His host there was the primate of Tibetan Buddhism in Mongolia, the Living Buddha at Urga, or Jebtsun-damba-hutukhtu. While at Urga, the Dalai communicated through Dorje with the Russian Tsar in an attempt to enlist Russian support for the Tibetan independence movement.

In 1906 the Dalai Lama left Urga and traveled to Kokonor in northeastern Tibet. There he stayed in Lama Buddhist lamaseries. During his absence from Tibet proper, the Dalai's hopes of obtaining major assistance from Russia against the Chinese and the British gradually diminished. In 1906 the suzerainty of the Chinese court over Tibet was reasserted and acknowledged in an Anglo-Chinese agreement. In August 1907 Britain and Russia signed a general agreement whereby Russia promised not to interfere in Tibetan political affairs and recognized the British "special interest in the maintenance of the *status quo* in the external relations of Tibet."

Despite these unfavorable developments, the Dalai Lama continued to work for increased independence from China. By an imperial decree of July 1907 he had been invited—actually summoned—to Peking. However, he went instead to the sacred Wu-t'ai mountain in Shansi province, arriving there in the spring of 1908. A Chinese decree of March 1908 announced a program of political reform for Tibet. Nevertheless, the Dalai remained for several months at Wu-t'ai mountain, where he was visited occasionally by diplomats from Peking. He finally arrived at the capital on 20 September 1908 and had an audience with the emperor and the empress dowager in mid-October, just a month before the two Ch'ing rulers died. The attitude of the Chinese court was indicated by the new title bestowed upon the Dalai Lama, "The Sincerely Obedient, Reincarnation-Helping, Most Excellent, Self-Existing Buddha of the West." The Dalai himself, however, had no intention of confirming his subservience by accepting the title. At Peking, he was visited by various foreign diplomats, notably the Russian, British, American, and Japanese envoys. In his meeting with Sir John Jordan, the British minister, the Dalai Lama expressed a desire for peace and friendship between Tibet and India. Since Sir John's response appeared to offer substantial satisfaction, the Dalai turned toward Britain in the hope of obtaining support against China. The visit of the Dalai Lama to Peking in 1908 was described in detail by W. W. Rockhill, the American minister, in an article, "The Dalai Lamas of Lhasa," which appeared in the sinological journal *T'oung Pao* in 1910.

The Dalai Lama left Peking for Lhasa on 21 December 1908. In the meantime, Peking had sent military forces to Tibet. The Chinese general Chao Erh-feng (T. Chi-ho; d. 1911), the brother of Chao Erh-sun (q.v.), had established a base for an advance into Eastern Tibet by conquering Batang in 1906. In 1909, as the Dalai Lama's party traveled westward across China, the Chinese army drove deeper into Tibet. The Dalai Lama reached Lhasa in December 1909. Chao Erh-feng and the Chinese army arrived about a month later. As the Chinese troops neared the holy city, the Dalai negotiated an understanding with the Ch'ing authorities through Wen Tsung-yao, the imperial resident's assistant. Because he was apprehensive about Chinese intentions, however, he decided to flee from his capital a second time. He left Lhasa on 12 February 1910, accompanied by Dorje.

After the Dalai's flight, the Chinese imperial government at Peking issued an edict on 25 February 1910 deposing him as ruler of Tibet. Once again Peking invited the Panchen Lama to assume the Dalai's powers, but the Panchen refused.

The Dalai Lama's party moved toward India, making its way first to Darjeeling in Sikkim. Charles A. Bell, the British official in charge of the relations of the government of India with Sikkim, Bhutan, and Tibet, met with him. The Dalai explained that he had come to seek the assistance of the British government against the Chinese. In March 1910 he went to Calcutta, where he talked with Lord Minto, the Viceroy of India, about the potential Chinese threat, through Tibet, to the Himalayan border states on India's northern frontier. But the Anglo-Chinese treaty of 1906 had acknowledged that Tibet was part of China, and the 1907 Anglo-Russian convention called for mutual abstention from interference in Tibetan affairs. The British policy of that period was, in effect, to admit virtually complete Chinese control over Tibet but to insist that the British would not permit Chinese interference in Nepal, Sikkim, or Bhutan. Throughout the period of over two years that the Dalai Lama and his government in exile remained on the Indian-Tibetan frontier, Charles Bell maintained friendly relations with him, and they frequently had private conversations.

Because he failed to obtain positive assistance from the British, the Dalai Lama turned to Nepal for aid. He also appealed to Russia again, only to have the reply transmitted, much to his discomfiture, through the British government in India. The Russian reply was as non-committal as the British and Nepalese responses had been.

The Chinese revolution that began in October 1911 caused the newly asserted Chinese control over Tibet to collapse. The Chinese military garrison at Lhasa revolted, killed its officers, and turned to looting the city. After the overthrow of the Ch'ing dynasty, the Dalai left Kalimpong in June 1912 to return to Tibet. He was unable to enter Lhasa, however, because Chinese troops still occupied the city. In July 1912 Yuan Shih-k'ai's government at Peking ordered a new expedition from Szechwan for the relief of the Lhasa garrison troops. It was only through British intervention at Peking that the Chinese occupation of Tibet was terminated and that Chinese forces were repatriated through India. The Dalai Lama finally returned to Lhasa in January 1913. In the preceding nine years he had spent only two months in Tibet.

The Dalai Lama was determined to eliminate Chinese authority from Tibet. In July 1912 he had sent Dorje back to Urga to negotiate a treaty with Outer Mongolia. In January 1913 he concluded a treaty with the Living Buddha at Urga which recognized the independence of their respective states. At Lhasa, the Dalai declared the independence of his country, justifying his action in part by saying that China was unable to protect Tibet from foreign aggression. When Yuan Shih-k'ai informed him that the Chinese government had restored his title, the Dalai replied that he desired no rank from the Chinese government, for he planned to exercise both ecclesiastical and temporal authority in Tibet. The new Chinese high commissioner to Tibet, appointed in 1913, was unable to reach Lhasa and remained in India.

The Dalai Lama issued all titles in Tibet on his own authority; formerly, they had been granted only with the sanction of the Chinese emperor. He also began to sound out the opinion of his people on the advisability of Tibet's making a new place for itself in the international community. Peking then endeavored to assert its authority by occupying part of Eastern Tibet. To stabilize the situation and to obtain confirmation of its own interest in the status of Tibet, the British government in 1913 convened the Simla Conference, attended by British, Chinese, and Tibetan representatives. At that conference, the Dalai's representative pressed, for the *de facto* independence of Tibet and the restoration of its original boundaries. By the Simla Convention, as agreed upon and initialed by all three delegates in April 1914, Tibet was divided into two entities, Inner (or Eastern) Tibet and Outer Tibet, with the latter to enjoy full autonomy. Balking at the way the boundaries were drawn and rejecting the grant of autonomy, Peking repudiated its plenipotentiary representative and refused to acknowledge the validity of the convention. Great Britain and Tibet, however, recognized it as binding.

The Dalai Lama also attempted to centralize control over domestic affairs. He began to bypass the consultative assembly at Lhasa on the grounds that that body was obstructive. He improved the efficiency of governmental administration, abolished (for a time) the death penalty as being contrary to the precepts of Buddhism, and undertook measures to improve the government's financial condition. The Dalai gradually reduced the authority of the three great lamaseries of Tibet in the affairs of government. He now claimed sole right to bestow titles, which entailed grants of land, and changed the nature of those titles. They had been hereditary, but he now granted them for the life of the holder only. As supreme ruler of Tibet, he appointed all officials and heads of lamaseries. Recalcitrant ecclesiastics were subjected to heavy fines and to religious sanctions. In fiscal matters, the privileges of the lamaseries, as well as those of the Tibetan nobility, were reduced. Some of the increased tax revenues were used for military development. Near the end of 1917, the Chinese attacked in Eastern Tibet. The Tibetans on that occasion overwhelmingly defeated the Chinese and drove them out of territory they had held previously. The Dalai then proposed that additional troops be recruited yearly and that the Tibetan army be increased by 11,000 men to a total strength of 17,000. His plan was adopted.

The Chinese soon renewed their attempts to restore the relationship between China and Tibet that had existed during the Ch'ing dynasty. To that end they sent missions to Lhasa in 1919 and 1920. Those missions failed, largely, it would appear, because of the support extended by the British to the Dalai's government at that time. In the autumn of 1920 the British government, in response to requests from the Dalai Lama and his government, sent a diplomatic mission to Lhasa, the first from any Western nation. The mission was headed by Charles Bell, and it remained in Lhasa for 11 months. Bell renewed his friendship with the Dalai Lama and expressed the aim of British policy: that Tibet should enjoy internal autonomy and that her freedom would constitute the best defensive buffer to the security of India.

In the early 1920's a schism developed between the Dalai Lama and the Panchen Lama. Because of their exalted natures, they had rarely met. The Dalai had not forgotten that on two occasions, in 1904 and 1910, the Chinese government had invited the Panchen to assume his authority. Although the Panchen had refused both invitations, the overtures had focused attention on him as a possible competitor for authority in Tibet. After the Dalai had returned to Lhasa in January 1913, he had criticized the Panchen for having collaborated with the Chinese during his absence and for having been less than energetic in attempting to oust them from Lhasa after the revolution of 1911. The Dalai Lama was categorically anti-Chinese; he was willing to be either pro-British or pro-Russian for the benefit of Tibet. The Panchen, though opposed to the internal policies of the government at Lhasa, was not actively pro-Chinese. The competition between the Dalai and the Panchen was complicated by the problem of the Dalai's right to collect taxes in the areas controlled by the Tashi-lhunpo lamasery at Shigatse, which was under the jurisdiction of the Panchen. Thus, the Dalai's search for new tax sources to support his programs brought him into conflict with the Panchen Lama, and his efforts to create a regular Tibetan army were opposed by some of his co-religionists. The Dalai's demand that the Panchen pay a large amount of money and grain allegedly owed as taxes caused the Panchen to flee from Tibet in disguise in November 1923. When he arrived at Peking early in 1925, the Chinese authorities welcomed him and promptly undertook to groom him as their candidate for ruler of Tibet. Although the

Dalai at various times entertained the idea of permitting the Panchen to return to Tibet, domestic political considerations in Tibet overruled that plan.

By 1925 the weaknesses of the Dalai Lama's eclectic foreign policy had become evident. He had followed a policy of playing one power against another to buttress Tibet's independent status, and he had never been able to establish a cohesive network of international relations. The Dalai began to reorient Tibetan policy away from Britain and toward China. He appointed an anti-British officer as commander of the army, and British influence at Lhasa declined sharply. There were also reports of Mongol visitors to Lhasa in 1927 and 1928 who were identified by the British as Soviet agents. In 1928 the Panchen Lama sent a delegation to Nanking to pay his respects and to request that the new Chinese authorities take full charge of Tibetan affairs. In 1930 there was a noncommittal exchange of amenities between Nanking and Lhasa through Liu Man-ch'ing, a 23-year-old girl, half Chinese and half Tibetan, who served as an interpreter in the Commission for Mongolian and Tibetan Affairs. On his return to Tibet in 1930, Kung-chueh-chung-ni, a Tibetan lama who had been sent from Lhasa in 1922 to serve at the Yung-ho-kung, or Lama Temple, at Peking, carried with him eight questions from the National Government at Nanking which were designed to elicit the Dalai's terms for reconciliation. The Dalai set forth his proposals, which envisaged a return to the traditional suzerain-vassal relationship, with Tibetan autonomy recognized and Tibet's traditional frontiers restored.

After that exchange, the Dalai Lama sent a representative to Nanking. The National Government, in turn, sent a mission to Lhasa in 1931 with specific proposals for the restoration of "close relations" between Tibet and China. Only one day's march from Lhasa, the Nationalist envoy, Hsieh Kuo-liang, suddenly died. Meanwhile, a new problem had complicated the delicate matter of establishing relations between Lhasa and Nanking. This was the so-called Ta-chin-ssu affair of 1930, a clash between Tibetan lamas and Chinese soldiers at Kantze in Eastern Tibet. It developed into a protracted struggle between the Tibetans and the forces of the Chinese commander in the area, Liu Wen-hui (q.v.), with

Lhasa sending reinforcements to help sustain the Tibetan position. In 1932 and 1933 ceasefire agreements finally were concluded between Lhasa and those two areas of Eastern Tibet which the Chinese National Government had made into the provinces of Sikang and Tsinghai.

The Dalai Lama's health had been weakened by an arduous work schedule, the hardships he had suffered during two extended exiles, and the lack of medical facilities in Tibet. In 1931 the Ne-chung oracle had predicted his early death. He died on 17 December 1933 at Lhasa. His death occurred on the last day of the tenth month of the Tibetan calendar, an evil omen by Tibetan reckoning. In January 1934 the Ra-dreng Hutukhtu, the head of the Ra-dreng lamasery, became regent of Tibet. Immediately after his election, he sent a message to Nanking which not only reported the change of authority but also requested the National Government's confirmation of his appointment. This was the first time since the Chinese revolution of 1911 that an appointment in Tibet had been referred to the Chinese government. Without delay, Nanking granted its confirmation.

The thirteenth incarnation was one of the few Dalai Lamas to exercise real personal authority in Tibet. In this respect, he has been compared to the great fifth Dalai Lama, Lo-zang gya-tso (1617–82), who ruled before the consolidation of Chinese power over the country in the eighteenth century. Despite notable domestic and international difficulties, the thirteenth Dalai succeeded, with the indirect aid of the Chinese revolution in 1911, in eliminating Chinese influence from Tibet for a period and in bringing *de facto* independence to his land.

The fourteenth incarnation of the Dalai Lama succeeded the thirteenth, but he fled into exile in 1959. The thirteenth Dalai Lama may prove to have been the last incarnation of the patron diety of Tibet to reign over that land. He has been sympathetically described by Charles A. Bell, who retired from government service after heading the British mission at Lhasa in 1920–21. Bell (by then Sir Charles Bell) dedicated his book *Tibet Past and Present* (1924) to His Holiness the Dalai Lama. Sir Charles completed his later *Portrait of the Dalai Lama* a few days before his own death, and that work was published in 1946.

Demchukdonggrub
Chinese. Te Wang 德 王

Demchukdonggrub (1902–), Mongolian prince of the West Sunid Banner, was known in China as Te Wang. He led the movement to secure autonomy for Inner Mongolia.

The son of a jassak [prince] of the West Sunid Banner of Mongolia, Te Wang was born in the territory of the Silingol League in Inner Mongolia. He was educated at a Chinese middle school in Suiyuan province and at the Mongolian-Tibetan Academy in Peking. In 1919 he succeeded his father as West Sunid jassak, and in 1921 he became a deputy chieftain of the Silingol League. He also was a leading figure in a nationalist group known as the Young Mongols. Most of the members of this group had been educated in China, and they hoped to establish a self-determined Inner Mongolian government within the framework of the Chinese Nationalist system. After the establishment of the Mongolian People's Republic in Outer Mongolia, another Inner Mongolian nationalist group, the Inner Mongolian People's Revolutionary party, was formed in 1925. Its aim was self-determination through revolution.

When the National Government was established at Nanking in 1928, Te Wang and his reformist group hoped that the right of self-determination promised the minority peoples of China in Sun Yat-sen's *Principles for National Construction* would be granted. The National Government, however, developed a Mongol policy that did little to provide increased political rights for the Mongols of Inner Mongolia. Rather, it transformed the so-called special districts which made up Inner Mongolia into three new provinces—Chahar, Suiyuan, and Ninghsia. At the same time, it encouraged Chinese colonization of Mongol grazing lands. In reaction to Chinese political encroachment and economic exploitation, Inner Mongolian nationalism developed rapidly.

Of the Mongol groups concerned, the Silingol League of northern Chahar was least affected by the Chinese policy; very few Chinese colonists entered its territory. Te Wang became the most influential young leader in Inner Mongolia. By about 1930 he had stirred and intensified anti-Chinese sentiment among the Mongols in the entire area from the grazing lands of western Manchuria to the Ordos desert in Suiyuan.

The Japanese invasion of Manchuria in the autumn of 1931 was a new external military challenge to the Mongols. After the Japanese forces consolidated control in Manchuria, they sponsored the creation there of Manchoukuo, which included three of the six Mongol leagues of Inner Mongolia. Because the National Government made no attempt to counter Japanese aggression, Te Wang and his Young Mongols prepared to defend their territory.

As ruling prince of the West Sunid Banner, Te Wang was a commissioner of the Chahar provincial government, headed by Sung Che-yuan (q.v.). The Mongols had learned that they could expect scant consideration of their views from the Chinese provincial governors. In the winter of 1932, therefore, Te Wang led a small delegation of Mongol dignitaries to Nanking to offer proposals for reforming the National Government's administration of Inner Mongolia. The Mongols were virtually ignored at Nanking, however; and they left the capital in anger, issuing a public protest as they departed and another from Peiping on their way back to Inner Mongolia. The manner of their leaving evidently caused second thoughts at Nanking, for the National Government in December 1932 appointed the Panchen Lama (q.v.) to the Mongolian and Tibetan Affairs Commission and sent him to Pailingmiao in Inner Mongolia as pacification commissioner for the so-called Western Regions. His mission was to mollify the Mongols so that they would remain loyal to Nanking. The Panchen Lama, however, appeared to give qualified support to Te Wang's proposals for self-government in Inner Mongolia. Te was appointed defense commissioner at P'angchiang and was given some responsibility for training Mongolian military forces.

In March 1933 units of the Japanese Kwantung Army occupied Jehol, and at the end of April the Japanese occupied Dolonor in eastern Chahar, on the border of Silingol League territory. The Japanese authorities had organized the Mongols of western Manchuria, or Eastern Inner Mongolia, into a new political division, Hsingan, nominally designed to form an autonomous unit within the political structure of Manchoukuo. That action brought new pressure to bear on the Chinese and on the Silingol League. Nanking, for its part, did not respond to the challenge, and, after the Japanese move into Dolonor, the National Government abandoned a plan, previously approved in response to Te Wang's repeated pleas, to expand the Mongol military training program at P'angchiang.

In the spring of 1933 Te Wang and his associates took steps to achieve autonomy. In addition to being prince of the West Sunid Banner, Te was the most influential figure of the Silingol League, whose titular ruler, Prince So, was over 60 and in poor health. One of Te's close associates was Yun Wang (Prince Yun), chief of the Ulanchap League, whose nephew was a friend of Te Wang and a strong supporter of his demands for self-government in Inner Mongolia. In May 1933 a meeting of Mongol leaders from Western Inner Mongolia was convened at Pailingmiao under the leadership of Prince Yun and Te Wang to discuss the position of Inner Mongolia. Japanese pressure continued. The Tangku Truce of 31 May 1933 left southern Chahar within the Japanese sphere of influence, and the Japanese authorities soon established an autonomous Mongolian district at Dolonor. The Silingol Mongols of northern Chahar were isolated, caught in a pocket between Manchoukuo and the Mongolian People's Republic. A meeting was convened on 26 July 1933 at Pailingmiao to discuss the matter of independence for Western Inner Mongolia. The majority of the Mongol princes were unwilling to declare independence, and the Panchen Lama reportedly exercised a restraining influence. On 14 August, however, the ruling princes of Western Inner Mongolia sent a telegram to Nanking announcing their intention of establishing an autonomous Mongolian government. Prince So's name headed the list of signatories, followed immediately by that of Te Wang.

Huang Shao-hung (q.v.) and Shih Ch'ing-yang, chairman of the Mongolian and Tibetan Affairs Commission, were sent to Inner Mongolia to stop the autonomy movement. Shih Ch'ing-yang failed to calm the Mongol leaders, and Huang Shao-hung was unable even to induce the Mongol leaders to meet with him at Kalgan.

The Mongol leaders had already called a new conference, which met at Pailingmiao in September 1933. From 9 to 24 October, the leaders met to organize an autonomous Mongolian regime in Inner Mongolia. The new government was to remain under the guidance of the National Government at Nanking, but without the interposition of Chinese provincial governors. On 22 October 1933, Prince Yun was elected to head the new regime, and Te Wang was chosen to direct its political affairs bureau.

The Pailingmiao group had sent one of Te Wang's close associates, Pao Yueh-ch'ing, to Kalgan to prepare for a conference with Huang Shao-hung. Nanking then designated Huang to head a special commission to Inner Mongolia; he was assisted by Chao P'i-lien, vice director of the Mongolian and Tibetan Affairs Commission, and by various technical experts. Huang's party left Nanking on 21 October 1933 and, after spending several days at Peiping, arrived at Kweisui in Suiyuan province on 29 October. By that time, the Pailingmiao conference had adjourned.

Huang sent a delegation of ten men to Pailingmiao to talk with Te Wang and his colleagues. Te Wang, in turn, sent an emissary to Kweisui to set forth the Mongol position and to argue that the action regarding autonomy was motivated by a desire to unite the Mongols against the Japanese. The two men then exchanged telegrams, without making any progress toward a mutual understanding. Te Wang suggested that the matter was of sufficient weight and complexity to warrant a meeting between them.

On 10 November Huang Shao-hung went to Pailingmiao, and met with Prince Yun, Te Wang, and the other Mongol leaders. Although Prince Yun nominally headed the Mongol group, Te Wang was the chief Mongol spokesman. Te Wang reported that the Japanese had approached the Mongols and had proposed the creation of a "Mongolia" which would control all territory of Inner Mongolia. He noted reports charging that he was negotiating with Japan, observing that, if he had done so, he would not feel it necessary to petition Nanking regarding the matter. Since three quarters of what had once been Mongolia had been lost to Russia and Japan, he said, it was essential to consider immediate steps for the defense of the remaining quarter. Although Huang Shao-hung made several concessions, he stated categorically that the National Government could not permit the establishment of political autonomy in Inner Mongolia. Finally, after the Panchen Lama had mediated between the two sides, the Mongols dropped their insistence that they have an autonomous government and presented two sets of proposals to Nanking's emissary. Huang accepted one of these.

After Huang Shao-hung and the Panchen Lama had returned to Nanking, the National Government in December 1933 modified the agreement. On 17 January 1934 the Central Political Council of the Kuomintang passed an act that granted the formal framework of what had been agreed upon at Pailingmiao, but omitted the substance. The dispute began again. But this time the Mongols had a stronger bargaining position. P'u-yi was scheduled to be enthroned as emperor of Manchoukuo on 1 March 1934, and there had been new exchanges between the Inner Mongolians and the Japanese. The Mongols then threatened that if Nanking would not accede to their demands, they would be forced to give serious consideration to aligning Inner Mongolia with Manchoukuo.

Nanking repealed the January 1934 act, and on 28 February the Central Political Council of the Kuomintang passed an act establishing the Mongolian Local Autonomous Political Council. On 7 March, Prince Yun was designated to head the Political Council, and Te Wang was made director of its political affairs bureau. The council was inaugurated on 23 April 1934, and on 1 May its officers assumed their duties.

The arrangement soon proved to be unworkable. The Japanese pressure on Inner Mongolia increased. On its eastern border, Li Shou-hsin, a Manchoukuo official with the title of garrison commander of eastern Chahar, moved his headquarters from Dolonor to Kuyuan. At the end of June, Colonel Doihara of the Kwantung Army made a trip to Inner Mongolia to encourage the Mongol leaders to recognize the inevitability and magnanimity of Japanese authority.

Colonel Doihara was not immediately successful. The Mongols still hoped that the agreement with Nanking would give them the autonomy they desired. But the National Government failed to remit the promised funds

for the Political Council and refused to provide arms for the Mongol troops. Then, on 3 September 1934, Nanking agents kidnapped Te Wang's chief of staff in Peiping and shot him, saying that he was a Japanese spy.

By that time, Pailingmiao had begun to interfere with National Government salt traffic and with Chinese trade passing through Mongol territory. The Panchen Lama continued his efforts at mediation, but, as early as August 1934, Te Wang had begun to negotiate openly with the Japanese. He now told an emissary from the Chahar administrative council that Mongol loyalty was dependent upon Nanking's developing a "definite policy" and taking "appropriate measures to help Inner Mongolia."

The National Government, preoccupied with its military campaigns against the Chinese Communists and already moving, under Japanese pressure, toward accepting the establishment of a "friendly" regime in north China, did not aid Inner Mongolia. In November 1934 Prince Yun and Te Wang met with Chiang Kai-shek at Kweisui. However, Chiang at that time was intent on the New Life Movement and other domestic programs, and he gave the Mongol leaders scant encouragement.

In 1935 the Japanese extended their political control of the Tientsin-Peiping-Kalgan sector; in December, the National Government at Nanking in effect legitimized the shift in the power balance in north China by establishing the Hopei-Chahar Political Affairs Council. Te Wang then shifted his allegiance to the Japanese, who had promised the Mongols political autonomy and increased practical support without violent social revolution. Te Wang was not so naive as to ignore the fact that the Japanese had military and strategic interests of their own, but by the winter of 1935 he no longer had any promising alternatives.

In mid-January 1936 Nanking charged that Te Wang had sided with "seditious elements" and had proclaimed the independence of Inner Mongolia. On 21 January, Te Wang sent a formal denial of the report to Nanking. However, the Japanese authorities had given Te Wang the mission of calling a conference of Mongol leaders to proclaim the independence of Inner Mongolia. When that meeting was held at Pailingmiao in February 1936, the participants learned that independence from China would make them entirely dependent upon Japan.

Prince So, leader of the Silingol League, whose banner was immediately adjacent to Jehol province, had previously supported Te Wang at the October 1933 meeting, but had warned Te that if his policies gave rise to an "affair," he would leave the coalition in the name of the Silingol Mongols. Prince So now departed, taking eight of the ten Silingol banners with him. He was accompanied by the leaders and all banners of the Ikechao League (located entirely in that part of Suiyuan province under the jurisdiction of Fu Tso-yi, the governor of Suiyuan), and by two banners of the Ulanchap League. At Kweisui, under the aegis of Fu Tso-yi, they established an opposition political council. Te Wang's supporters now consisted of two Silingol banners (one of them his own), Prince Yun and four Ulanchap banners, and the Chahar aimak.

Te withdrew to Tehua (Coptchil). In April 1936 he and his supporters held a congress at which they decided to establish a military government at Tehua and to cooperate with the Japanese. On 28 June they inaugurated the so-called Inner Mongolian Government at Tehua. The Japanese assigned a military adviser to Te Wang and supplied officers to train his troops. Te and Prince Yun then embarked on a program to expand the Mongolian military forces.

In mid-August 1936 Te Wang returned to Pailingmiao to wind up the affairs of the Political Council. On 13 August an attempt to assassinate him was made. The next day, he returned to his former garrison headquarters at P'angchiang. His antagonism toward the Chinese National Government had increased, and in September he met with his staff and with Japanese officers to plan an invasion of Suiyuan province.

The Suiyuan campaign of November and December 1936 was undertaken by Manchoukuo-Mongol forces with Japanese assistance in the form of military advisers and equipment. Te Wang served as commander of the Mongolian forces, with Li Shou-hsin as his deputy. The combined Manchoukuo-Mongolian forces numbered about 10,000. The Chinese defense of Suiyuan proved to be unexpectedly strong. The Chinese captured Pailingmiao on 19 November. They seized military stores and documents allegedly confirming that the Japanese

planned to extend control throughout Inner Mongolia and even to the predominantly Muslim areas of China's northwest and Sinkiang. On 21 December 1936 Te Wang announced the termination of hostilities. The National Government, in the light of the Chinese successes, instructed Fu Tso-yi, Yen Hsi-shan (q.v.), and Prince Sha of the Ikechao League to establish a new political headquarters at Pailingmiao.

Te Wang was designated a national traitor by the National Government. On 18 January 1937 he proclaimed himself chairman of the Inner Mongolian regime that had been established at Tehua in June 1936.

With the outbreak of the Sino-Japanese war in July 1937, Te Wang's Mongol cavalry forces went into action with Japanese units. The Japanese rapidly extended their military control over Suiyuan province and sponsored a meeting at Kweisui in late October 1937 which proclaimed Suiyuan's independence from China. The Japanese then established a nominally autonomous Mongol government for Suiyuan to parallel similar Mongol regimes which they had already formed in southern Chahar and northern Shansi. In November 1937 they created a Meng-chiang [Mongolian borderlands] joint committee, with headquarters at Kalgan, to act as an administrative and coordinating body for the three Japanese-sponsored Mongolian governments.

In December 1937 the Meng-chiang joint committee became the Mongolian Federated Autonomous Government, with headquarters at Kweisui. Prince Yun was made chairman of that body, with Te Wang as vice chairman and chief of the political affairs bureau. Li Shou-hsin became minister of war. The Kweisui regime adopted a new flag and introduced a new calendar, with chronology reckoned from the reign of Chingis Khan. When Prince Yun died in 1938, Te became chairman of the government. In September 1939 the government headquarters was moved to Kalgan. Te Wang then turned over command of the Mongol cavalry units to Li Shou-hsin and devoted himself to the task of sustaining Mongolian interests as best he could.

The Inner Mongolian regime was nominally on the same administrative level as the so-called provisional Chinese government at Peiping. After the establishment of a new Japanese-sponsored national government at Nanking in

March 1940 (*see* Wang Ching-wei), Te Wang's regime was brought under the authority of that Nanking government. In practice, however, both before and after 1940, the Mongolian Federated Autonomous Government received its main directives from the Japanese. It was noteworthy, however, that the Japanese continued to keep the Mongols of Western Inner Mongolia administratively separated from those of Eastern Inner Mongolia, who continued to be grouped in the Hsingan province of western Manchuria. Te Wang and his adherents were denied the independence they desired.

In 1945 the Kuomintang, the Chinese Communists, the Mongols of Inner Mongolia, and the Mongols of Outer Mongolia all began to jockey for position within the new framework of power created by the demise of Japanese military power and by the entry of Soviet and Outer Mongolian forces into Manchuria and sections of Inner Mongolia. Te Wang escaped to Chungking, but his wife and children were captured and carried away by the invading Soviet-Mongol forces. Te conferred with Chiang Kai-shek about the Kuomintang's postwar plans for Inner Mongolia, but apparently found Chiang no more pliable than he had been earlier with respect to Mongol aspirations. Te was permitted to return to north China, where he lived in retirement in Peiping under the surveillance of Fu Tso-yi (q.v.).

Te Wang remained at Peiping until the end of 1948. Shortly before the Communist occupation of the city, he flew to Tingyuanying in Ninghsia province. There he worked with Ta Wang (Darijaya) in an attempt to mobilize Mongol forces of the Alashan and Etsin Gol Banners to resist the Chinese Communist forces, which were rapidly extending their control of northwest China. Te Wang then flew to Canton, the temporary seat of the National Government, where he proposed that, in order to strengthen the position of Ta Wang and himself, Inner Mongolia be granted autonomy under Chinese Nationalist sovereignty. He conferred with acting President Li Tsung-jen. They reached no agreement, and Te Wang was merely informed that his petition would be made a matter of official record.

Te Wang was forced to return to Inner Mongolia without the political concessions with which he had hoped to rally general Mongol support for resistance to the Communists. He assembled a force of several thousand men and advanced to a point near Paotow in western Suiyuan. There, however, he was confronted by Chinese Nationalist forces under the command of Fu Tso-yi's lieutenant Tung Ch'i-wu (q.v.). The Mongols were forced back to the mountains near Te Wang's former capital of Pailingmiao, where they scattered.

For several years after 1949 there were no reliable reports of Te Wang's whereabouts. It then was learned that he had crossed the border into the Mongolian People's Republic, where his family was living in exile. Te Wang apparently enjoyed a measure of personal freedom during his residence at Ulan Bator (Urga). However, perhaps after the agreement on economic and cultural cooperation concluded in October 1952 between the Mongolian People's Republic and the People's Republic of China, Te Wang was handed over to the Chinese Communist authorities at Peking and was imprisoned for several years as a war criminal. He was pardoned by the Central People's Government at Peking on the occasion of the Chinese New Year celebrations in 1963, and he was released from confinement on 9 April 1963. In 1964 Te Wang was reported to be teaching at the Inner Mongolian University at Huhehot (Kweisui), the capital of the Inner Mongolian Autonomous Region in the People's Republic of China.

Fan Ch'ang-chiang 范長江

Fan Ch'ang-chiang (1908–), a leading Communist journalist who first achieved prominence as a *Ta Kung Pao* correspondent covering northwest China (1933–38). He then became a dominant figure in the Communist news-propaganda services. After 1949 he held such posts at Peking as deputy director of the News Administration and president of the Peking School of Journalism.

Born into a gentry family, Fan Ch'ang-chiang received his early education in his native district of Neichiang, Szechwan, and attended middle school at Chengtu, the provincial capital. He studied in Nanking at the Kuomintang party affairs school, the forerunner of the Central Political Institute, from mid-1927 until 1929.

After leaving Nanking, Fan went north to attend National Peking University. In order to help pay his living and tuition expenses, he wrote articles for the *Ta Kung Pao*, which was becoming popular in north China. He later became a regular reporter on the newspaper and a protégé of Chang Chi-luan (q.v.), then the chief editor of the *Ta Kung Pao*. Japanese aggression in north China during the 1930's turned the attention of the paper to national defense problems, and Fan was assigned to visit the then comparatively unknown provinces of the northwest. His reports from that region to the *Ta Kung Pao* in the years from 1933 to 1935 were published in book form as *Chung-kuo te hsi-pei chiao* [the northwest corner of China]. The book reached its fifth printing within a few months. It described Fan's journey from Chengtu to Lanchow and gave detailed comment on the life and customs of the Muslim and Mongol inhabitants of Kansu and the other northwestern provinces. In a preface written for the fourth printing of the book, Fan commented on the stated Japanese aim of penetrating northwest China in order to prevent the southward expansion of Communism, arguing that Tokyo's true aim was "the malicious expansion of Japanese military aggression against China."

After the Sino-Japanese war began in mid-1937, Fan Ch'ang-chiang became known for his vivid reporting from key battle fronts. He reported on the Chinese defeat in southern Chahar and on the worsening situation at Hankow. After Wuhan fell to the Japanese in the autumn of 1938, Fan left the *Ta Kung Pao*, reportedly as the result of personality clashes. He then went to Changsha, where he joined with some radical newsmen in forming the Young Journalists Society. This group established the International News Agency (Kuo-chi hsin-wen she) and later moved from Changsha to Kweilin, Kwangsi.

In 1941, after the New Fourth Army Incident, Fan Ch'ang-chiang was arrested by the Nationalist authorities for pro-Communist leanings. His news agency was closed. After being released, he fled to Hong Kong and became editor of the pro-Communist *Hua-shang Pao*. When the Japanese occupied the colony in 1942, Fan left for the Communist-controlled areas of the lower Yangtze valley. In the remaining war years he directed the central China branch of the Communist New China News Agency and headed a school of journalism at Huaiyang, Kiangsu, in the Communist-controlled Kiangsu-Anhwei border region.

After the Japanese surrender in 1945, Fan became the spokesman for the Chinese Communist party news office in Shanghai. During the Kuomintang-Communist negotiations of 1946, Fan headed the Nanking branch of the New China News Agency and served in the Communist liaison mission at Nanking. Although Chou En-lai, the senior Communist negotiator, left Nanking in November 1946, a small Communist liaison group headed by Tung Pi-wu (q.v.) remained there. The members of this group, including Fan Ch'ang-chiang, finally left Nationalist territory in March 1947 for northern Shensi. Fan worked in Shensi with Liao Ch'eng-chih (q.v.) and Ch'ien Chun-jui in the party propaganda apparatus.

By the time the Communists gained national power in 1949, Fan Ch'ang-chiang's reputation as an experienced Communist newsman was well established. He was associated with the *Jen-min jih-pao* [people's daily], the organ of the Communist party Central Committee, in Peking; and after Shanghai was taken in the spring of 1949, he helped to establish the *Chieh-fang jih-pao* [liberation daily news] there. After the establishment of the Central People's Government in October 1949, Fan Ch'ang-chiang became deputy director of the News Administration at Peking and president of the Peking School of Journalism. From 1952 to 1954 he was deputy secretary general of the culture and education committee of the Government Administration Council. He later became deputy director of the cultural and educational office of the State Council and vice chairman of the Scientific and Technological Commission.

During the Sino-Japanese war, Fan Ch'ang-chiang married Shen P'u, the daughter of Shen Chün-ju (q.v.).

Fan Wen-lan   范 文 瀾
  T. Chung-yün   仲 雲
  Pen. Wu-po   武 陵

Fan Wen-lan (1891–), the most prominent Marxist historian in Communist China and the director of the institute for the study of modern history of the Chinese Academy of Sciences in Peking.

Little is known of Fan Wen-lan's family background or his childhood except that his native place was Shaohsing, Chekiang, and that he was a poverty-stricken youth when he entered Peking University. Among his teachers were Ch'en Han-chang and Huang K'an (q.v.), both scholars of the traditional school, who guided Fan's study of the Chinese classics. During his student days he absorbed some of the ideas propounded by Ch'en Tu-hsiu and Li Ta-chao (qq.v.), but he did not take an active part in the nationalistic student activities of the period. He was graduated from Peking University in 1919.

Fan went to Japan for further study, but was unable to afford the tuition required for university enrollment. He remained in Tokyo for two years, studying on his own the writings of Kawakami Hajime, Makino Nara, and other Japanese intellectuals who were attracted by Marxism. He returned to China about 1921 and spent the next few years teaching Chinese history and literature at various institutions in north China: Nankai University, Peking University, Peking Normal University, Fu-jen (Catholic) University, and Sino-French University. In 1929 he was named professor of history at the womens college of Peking University. He later became dean of the college.

Fan Wen-lan's reputation as a scholar was established in 1925 with the publication of *Wen-hsin tiao-lung chu* [annotations on the Wen-hsin tiao-lung], which he prepared under the guidance of Huang K'an and which came to be considered one of the best editions of Liu Hsieh's sixth-century classic of literary criticism. It was reprinted in 1936. In 1929 Fan published the *Shui-ching-chu hsieh-ching-wen ch'ao* [selections descriptive of scenic views excerpted from the Shui-ching-chu]. A volume of commentaries on the 25 official Chinese dynastic histories, *Cheng-shih k'ao-lueh*, appeared in 1931; two years later Fan's *Ch'ün-ching kai-lun* [a general discussion of the Confucian classics] was published.

Fan was known among his intimates for his austere personal life and for his generosity toward needy students. A deeply patriotic man, Fan was disturbed by the deteriorating political situation in north China. A major student demonstration against the National Government's foreign and domestic policies took place on 9 December 1935; it was followed by similar demonstrations in other cities. The local authorities at Peiping, saying that the demonstration was Communist-inspired, arrested many of the participants. Fan was arrested that year on the charge of having assisted a colleague who allegedly was involved in the Communist movement. He was imprisoned at Nanking and was brought to trial. University authorities in Peiping attempted to intercede on his behalf, but their representations failed to convince Wang Shih-chieh (q.v.), the minister of education, of Fan's innocence. It was only through the efforts of Ts'ai Yuan-p'ei and Wang Ching-wei that he eventually was released. In very poor health, Fan spent a year in a hospital. He then accepted a professorship at Honan University, for which he had been recommended by the well-known historian of the Ch'ing period Hsiao I-shan.

After the outbreak of the Sino-Japanese war in 1937, Fan began to participate in the Communist underground movement in Honan. In 1940 he went to Yenan, the Chinese Communist wartime capital. He taught at Anti-Japanese University and North Shensi College. In addition, he organized and directed the Chung-kuo li-shih yen-chiu-hui [Chinese historical research association], which sponsored the publication of the *Chung-kuo t'ung-shih chien-pien* [short history of China]. Written by a group of seven historians headed by Fan Wen-lan, the work received official Communist endorsement when it was published at Yenan in 1941 and was widely used in the Communist-controlled areas of China during the war. In 1943 Fan became director of the Central Research Academy at Yenan. Three years later, he was named president of Pei-fang University, and when that institution was reorganized as North China University, he became its vice president. He also served as a deputy in the Shansi-Hopei-Shantung-Honan border area government. In January 1949 he was elected a deputy to the newly established North China People's Government.

Fan Wen-lan's writings of the 1940's were propagandistic in both intent and presentation. They were in the vernacular, in contrast to his pre-1937 volumes, which had been in sedate classical Chinese. The *Chung-kuo t'ung-shih chien-pien* was intended to provide political justification for a revolutionary war directed against both the foreign invader and the regime controlled by the Kuomintang. In this work, Chinese history is presented within the framework set down by Mao Tse-tung and other Chinese Communists in 1939-40, and the great corpus of traditional Chinese history is allotted to the so-called feudal period, defined as beginning with the Chou period and lasting until the mid-nineteenth century. The feudal period is characterized by economic exploitation and political oppression of the mass of the population by the ruling class, headed by the emperor and the landlords. The peasants are described as existing in dire poverty and suffering. The recurrent peasant rebellions through the centuries are shown as notable indicators of the suffering of the great majority of the Chinese people in pre-modern times. Fan held that, although some social progress followed each peasant outburst, the nature of the social and economic system in traditional China blocked reform and prevented progress. *Chung-kuo t'ung-shih chien-pien* was written in 18 months and bore evidences of hasty preparation. Revised editions, less dogmatic in tone and more careful in attention to historical sources, appeared after 1948.

Fan Wen-lan wrote other works designed to apply Chinese Communist doctrinal analysis to problems in modern Chinese history. His 1944 booklet entitled *Han-chien k'uai-tzu-shou Tseng Kuo-fan te i-sheng* [life of the traitorous executioner Tseng Kuo-fan] is a political tract condemning the prominent nineteenth-century Hunanese scholar-general as a traitor because of his actions in suppressing the Taiping Rebellion. By implication, it is an attack on the Kuomintang for glorifying Tseng Kuo-fan as a model statesman and patriot. *T'ai-p'ing t'ien-kuo ko-ming yun-tung* [the revolutionary movement of the Taiping heavenly kingdom], published in 1948, emphasizes the economic and social reforms instituted by the Taiping leaders in spite of ferocious attacks by the imperial Chinese armies, which were aided by the Western nations. The booklet decries the lengths to which the "class enemy" of the peasant masses of China was willing to go in order to perpetuate its own political power; again, the work was an oblique reference to the post-1928 Kuomintang and to its Western supporters.

Work on the *Chung-kuo chin-tai shih* [history of modern China] was begun during the war. It was intended to be a multi-volume study of modern Chinese history, divided into two periods: the era of the old democratic revolution (1840-1919) and that of the new democratic revolution (1919–). The first volume, published at Yenan in 1945, begins with the Opium War (1839–42) and ends with the Boxer Uprising of 1900; it is dominated by the twin themes of class struggle and foreign imperialism.

Fan Wen-lan participated in the Chinese People's Political Consultative Conference in 1949 as a member of the delegation representing the social sciences. In 1950 he was named director of the institute of modern history of the Chinese Academy of Sciences at Peking. In 1951 he became vice president of the China Historical Association. He was a delegate to the National People's Congress in 1954, 1958, and 1964, and he was a member of the Standing Committee of the Chinese People's Political Consultative Conference in 1961. Although Fan Wen-lan presumably had been a member of the Chinese Communist party for some years before 1949, he had not been active in party affairs. His service to the Communist cause in China was rewarded, however, when he was elected an alternate member of the Central Committee at the Eighth National Congress of the Chinese Communist party in September 1956.

After 1949, Fan devoted most of his energies to the work of the institute of modern history of the Academy of Sciences at Peking, the principal national center for the advanced training of Chinese historians and for the compilation and publication of source materials. The institute supported 30 researchers in 1953 and about 200 in 1958. Fan also was a member of the editorial committee that supervised the compilation of the six-volume work on the *Nien-chün* [the Nien army], published in 1953.

Fan Wen-lan's willingness to permit political commitments to influence his interpretation of historical problems is not dissimilar to the didactic outlook of traditional Chinese historiography. In addition to recording data, the official historians of traditional China, in effect, were constructing a body of precedents and ethical standards to guide future generations of bureaucrats. Fan and his disciples also have been devoted to the concept of history as a guide to current policies. Fan Wen-lan's prominence was the result of his ability to bring his training and reputation in traditional Chinese scholarship to the service of a new orthodoxy which blended Marxist-Leninist concepts with the events of modern Chinese history.

Fan Yuan-lien   范 源 濂
T. Ching-sheng   靜 生

Fan Yuan-lien (1875–23 December 1927), a pioneer in the modernization of Chinese education, held such offices as minister of education (1912; 1916–17; 1920–21), president of Peking Normal University (1923–24), and director of the China Foundation for the Promotion of Education and Culture.

A native of Hsiangyin, Hunan, Fan Yuan-lien was orphaned at an early age. His early education was supervised by his maternal uncle. In 1898 Fan was admitted to the Shih-wu hsueh-t'ang [academy of current affairs] at Changsha, which had been established the year before under the auspices of Ch'en Pao-chen, the governor of Hunan. Ts'ai O (q.v.) was also a student at the academy, and Liang Ch'i-ch'ao (q.v.) was its dean of studies. Liang and his colleagues sought to imbue the students with such political concepts as constitutional monarchy and popular sovereignty. The teaching of such concepts aroused a storm of protest from conservative scholars in Hunan. Liang became ill in the spring of 1898 and left for Shanghai. When the Hundred Days Reform collapsed in the early autumn of 1898 and its leaders were either executed or forced into exile, the Shih-wu hsueh-t'ang closed its doors. Of its 40-odd students, 11, including Fan Yuan-lien, left for Japan, where Liang Ch'i-ch'ao had sought refuge.

In Japan, Fan Yuan-lien attended the Ta-t'ung School, established in 1899 by Liang Ch'i-ch'ao and Chinese merchants in Tokyo. Fan later matriculated at the Tokyo Higher Normal School. He noticed that the number of Chinese students in Japan was increasing rapidly, but that many of these students lacked the requisite academic training to be admitted to Japanese schools. Fan suggested to Kano Jigoro, the principal of the Tokyo Higher Normal School, that a special school for Chinese students be established. As a result, the Kobun Academy was established in 1902. The school immediately became popular, for a knowledge of Japanese was not required and it was possible to obtain an education diploma in six months and a law diploma in eighteen months. As

one of the interpreters for the Japanese teachers in the institution, Fan Yuan-lien gained the respect of many of the Chinese students, who helped to make his name known throughout China.

In 1904 Fan returned to Hunan to urge that girls be sent to study in Japan; shortly thereafter, he organized a group of female students and accompanied them on their voyage to Tokyo. In 1905 he was appointed to a minor post as secretary in the ministry of education at Peking, where he was assigned to assist a visiting Japanese scholar in the administration of a new law school. The following year, Fan founded the Chih-pien hsueh-t'ang, a school for the training of Chinese youths for frontier settlement and administration. About 100 students enrolled in the school, which offered courses in Mongolian and Tibetan as well as courses in subjects related to frontier life.

In 1910 Fan became a councillor in the ministry of education. He was assigned to devise a system of standard education for China. During the 1911 revolution he served as a mediator between the government and the republican revolutionaries. After the overthrow of the imperial government, Fan joined the Kuo-min hsieh-chin hui [national advancement association], one of the many small political parties that sprang up in China. It later merged with several other small parties to form the Kung-ho-tang, which in turn became the Chin-pu-tang [progressive party] in 1913. Fan was affiliated with the moderates, headed by Liang Ch'i-ch'ao, who had advocated a constitutional monarchy under the imperial regime and who were willing to cooperate with the Peiyang generals after 1912. In March 1912 Ts'ai Yuan-p'ei, the minister of education in the republican government, appointed Fan Yuan-lien vice minister of education. When Ts'ai Yuan-p'ei resigned in June 1912, Lu Cheng-hsiang appointed Fan minister of education. Because he disagreed with government policies, Fan resigned in January 1913. He then accepted an offer from the Chung-hua Book Company to head its editorial department.

In the autumn of 1915 Fan joined Liang Ch'i-ch'ao and Ts'ai O in the campaign against Yuan Shih-k'ai. When the anti-Yuan forces established a military council at Chaoch'ing, Kwangtung, in 1916, Fan was appointed its representative in Shanghai.

After the death of Yuan Shih-k'ai, Fan Yuan-lien became minister of education in the Tuan Ch'i-jui cabinet. His term of office lasted from July 1916 to June 1917. He also served as minister of interior from January to June 1917. Fan brought Ts'ai Yuan-p'ei back from Europe to be chancellor of Peking University. In May 1917, together with Ts'ai Yuan-p'ei, Liang Ch'i-ch'ao and others, Fan founded the Chung-hua chih-yeh chiao-yü she [China vocational education association].

In 1918 Fan Yuan-lien went to the United States. He and Yen Hsiu, the founder of the Nankai School at Tientsin, toured America to study its educational system. In the wake of the May Fourth Movement of 1919, Fan joined such men as Liang Ch'i-ch'ao, Lin Ch'ang-min, and Chang Tung-sun in organizing the Shang-chih hsueh-hui [aspiration society]. Its leading members arranged for prominent Western scholars, including John Dewey and Bertrand Russell, to visit China. They also sponsored the publication of Chinese translations of Western philosophic works.

In August 1920 Fan Yuan-lien was appointed minister of education for the third time. He resigned in May 1921 and took up biological studies. In the spring of 1922 he made a visit to the United States to study rural education. In November 1922 the ministry of education decided to expand the Peking Higher Normal School into a university, and Fan accepted an invitation to assume the presidency of the new institution in February 1923. Before his inauguration, Fan went to England to discuss with the British government the possibility of remitting to China the British Boxer Indemnity Fund for educational purposes. It was not until his return from Europe in November 1923 that he assumed the duties of his new post. In the year that he was president, such prominent men as Liang Ch'i-ch'ao, Chiang Fang-chen, and Huang Fu lectured at the university. Fan refused the post of minister of education when it was offered to him for the fourth time in 1924.

In September 1924 the Peking government named Fan Yuan-lien to the board of directors of the China Foundation for the Promotion of Education and Culture, which was financed by the American Boxer Indemnity Fund. From 1926 to 1927 he served as the head of the China Foundation. He was also a trustee of Nankai University. He served as a member of the board of managers and then as acting director of the Metropolitan Library of Peking. Fan died at Tientsin on 23 December 1927, at the age of 52 sui. In October 1928 the Shang-chih hsueh-hui and the China Foundation jointly established the Ching-sheng sheng-wu yen-chiu-so [Fan memorial institute of biology] at Peking to commemorate Fan's contributions to modern education in China.

Fang Chih-min   方 志 敏
  Alt. Hsiang-sung   祥 松

Fang Chih-min (1900–6 July 1935), Communist organizer in Kiangsi. He founded the northeast Kiangsi soviet and headed the Red Army's Anti-Japanese Vanguard Unit. He was captured and executed in 1935 by the Nationalists.

Born into a peasant family, Fang Chih-min received his early education in the Chinese classics in his native village of Iyang, Kiangsi. When he was about 15, he went to Nanchang, the provincial capital of Kiangsi, where he attended a modern higher primary school. After studying at the Nanchang Technical School, from which he was expelled for radical activities in 1920, he spent a brief period at a Christian educational institution at Kiukiang, only to be expelled again because of his anti-Christian views. At the end of 1920 he went to Shanghai, where he came into contact with the Chinese Communist youth movement. Official Communist sources state that Fang Chih-min did not join the Chinese Communist party until 1923, but it is probable that he was an active participant in the movement in 1921-22. Because he was convinced that he should devote himself completely to the cause of radical revolution in China, Fang severed relations with his family.

After returning to Kiangsi in 1922, Fang began organizational work among the youth of his native province. He established the New Culture Bookstore (Wen-hua shu-chü), edited and published a periodical, and set up the Li-ming Middle School. Together with Chao Hsing-nung, he organized the Kiangsi Socialist (later Communist) Youth Corps. In 1924 Fang, on Communist party orders, organized peasant associations in the areas around Iyang, Nanchang, and Kiukiang and incited the peasants to resist rent and tax collections. His work in the villages reportedly aided the advance of Northern Expedition units into Kiangsi.

During this period, Fang Chih-min also headed the peasant department in the Kiangsi provincial organization of the Kuomintang. In September 1926 he convened a provincial congress of peasant delegates. In the spring of 1927 he went to a conference on peasant work at Wuhan, where he met Mao Tse-tung and P'eng P'ai.

Fang Chih-min married Miao Min on 12 April 1927. Three days after the wedding, he reportedly had to flee in disguise to avoid arrest. Fang then joined Ho Lung and Yeh T'ing (qq. v.) in the uprising at Nanchang. The new Communist party leadership, after its emergency meeting of 7 August 1927, ordered Fang Chih-min to return to Kiangsi. Working again in the Iyang area, he revived the peasant associations and led the peasants to resist rent and tax collections. In cooperation with Shao Shih-p'ing, he organized guerrilla forces in northeastern Kiangsi, despite continuous pressure from Nationalist military units. During this difficult period in 1927, Fang developed tuberculosis.

In 1928 the Sixth National Congress of the Chinese Communist party, meeting at Moscow, elected Fang *in absentia* to the party's Central Committee. In late 1928 and early 1929 Fang expanded his base of operations in Kiangsi. After a rendezvous with Mao Tse-tung and Chu Teh (q.v.) in the southern part of the province, Fang founded the northeast Kiangsi soviet, also known as the Hsin River area soviet, in September 1929. Fang's guerrilla units became the Tenth Army of the Chinese Red Army in 1930. Two years later, these forces were able to expand their territorial base to include adjacent areas of Fukien and Chekiang. At the First All-China Congress of Soviets, held at Juichin, Kiangsi, in November 1931, Fang was elected to the central executive council of the central soviet government. He was reelected to this body at the Second All-China Congress of Soviets, held in January 1934.

Military pressure from Nationalist units on the Communist areas of Kiangsi increased, and in July 1934 the Chinese Communist party ordered Fang Chih-min to push northward toward the Yangtze. He was appointed commander of the Red Army's Anti-Japanese Vanguard Unit, with Hsün Huai-chou as deputy commander and Su Yü as chief of staff. In September 1934 this unit was halted in southern Anhwei by Nationalist forces, and Hsün Huai-chou was killed in action. By January 1935 Nationalist units had completely encircled Fang's forces. He had lost contact with the central Soviet regime at Juichin and was not aware that the main body of the Communist forces had left Kiangsi and had begun the Long March in October 1934. With the apparent intention of returning to the Kiangsi base, Fang led his troops in an unsuccessful attempt to break through the Nationalist blockade. Fang was captured and was imprisoned at Nanchang for several months. He was executed on 6 July 1935.

Fang wrote two essays in prison. "Simple Life" described his experiences with the Nationalist soldiers and affirmed his devotion to Communism and the Communist party; "Lovely Is China" presented China as an oppressed mother, trampled by the imperialists and unable to feed her children, and praised the immense potential power of a China freed from the "age-old yoke of feudalist and imperialist oppression." These essays, together with letters addressed to Lu Hsün, Soong Ch'ing-ling, and the Chinese Communist party, were smuggled out from the prison in Nanchang and delivered to Lu Hsün in Shanghai for safekeeping. Not until April 1936 did the Chinese Communist party gain possession of Fang's essays, his only known writings, which then were published under the title *Fang Chih-min tzu-chuan*. After the Communist accession to national power, these essays were published in Peking in 1952 under the title *Lovely is China*. Miao Min wrote an account of Fang's career, *Fang Chih-min, Revolutionary Fighter*, which was published in Peking in 1962.

Fang's contributions to the Chinese Communist movement were noted by Mao Tse-tung in an open letter of 5 January 1930 which later was published as "A Single Spark Can Start a Prairie Fire." Mao pointed to Fang Chih-min, Chu Teh, and himself as the three Communist leaders who had followed political policies that were "undoubtedly correct" and stated that Fang's accomplishments were worthy of emulation.

Fei Hsiao-t'ung   費 孝 通

Fei Hsiao-t'ung (2 November 1910–), social anthropologist, became known in China as a pioneer in field research. He applied Western anthropological theories and methods to Chinese data.

Wuchiang, Kiangsu, was the birthplace of Fei Hsiao-t'ung. His family belonged to the local gentry, but was not wealthy. He had two brothers, Fei Ch'ing and Fei Chen-tung. Little is known about his childhood except that he attended a girls school for several years.

Fei attended Yenching University, where he studied under University of Chicago sociologist Robert E. Park. At this time, Chinese data for sociological research were almost nonexistent because so few field studies had been conducted. Visiting professors in China (such as Robert Park and R. H. Tawney, the author of *Land and Labor in China*) deplored this lack and encouraged Fei and other students to conduct field studies. Fei was among the Yenching students who began their field studies under the leadership of Wu Wen-tsao (*see under* Hsieh Wan-ying). After being graduated in 1933, he studied at Tsinghua under S. M. Shirokogoroff, a Manchu specialist. In 1935-36 Fei and his wife, Wang Tung-wei, studied the Yao minority in Kwangsi. On the field trip, Fei fell into a tiger trap, and his wife drowned in a river when trying to get help. The results of their research were published by the Commerical Press in 1936 as *Hua-lan-yao she-hui tsu-chih* — *Kuang-hsi-sheng hsiang-hsien tung-nan hsiang* [the social organization of the Hua-lan-yao, an aboriginal tribe in Kwangsi].

Late in 1936 Fei went to England. He studied under Bronislaw Malinowski at the London School of Economics and received a Ph.D in social anthropology. His thesis was entitled "K'ai-hsien-kung: Economic Life in a Chinese Village." From Malinowski and A. R. Radcliffe-Brown, Fei learned to focus on the functional interrelationships of various "parts" of a community and on the meaning of a culture as seen by its own members. He devised survey methods which incorporated the functional approach and discovered that these new methods elicited far more meaningful responses than the social survey methods used by J. L. Buck and other investigators of rural conditions in China. Fei's methods were demonstrated by his book *Peasant Life in China* (1939).

After returning to China, Fei became a professor of social anthropology at National Yunnan University, a research fellow of the Sino-British Foundation (1939–41), and the director of the Yenching-Yunnan Station for Sociological Research. Between 1939 and 1943 Fei and his colleagues at the research station made studies of selected communities in the Kunming hinterland. In 1943 Fei was invited to visit the United States by the Department of State. He lectured and did research at Harvard University, the University of Chicago, and the Institute of Pacific Relations in New York. At the 1944 Harris Foundation Conference, held at the University of Chicago, he read a paper describing his Yunnan field work. His *Earthbound China* (1945), written with Chang Chih-i, compared three of the hinterland communities, representing three degrees of concentration of land ownership and tenancy. Fei recommended the introduction of rural cooperative industry, with land ownership of small units, but with land management of considerably larger units.

During this period, Fei translated Bronislaw Malinowski's *Theory of Culture* and Raymond W. Firth's *Human Types*. Both were published in 1944. In an essay, "Peasantry and Gentry," published in the *American Journal of Sociology* in July 1946, Fei characterized China as a two-class society, with a large peasantry and a small gentry differentiated from each other by kinship patterns, residence, economic and political roles, attitudes, and values. He showed that the opposition between peasantry and gentry in traditional China had been kept within bounds by economic interdependence, relatively high social mobility, political cooperation in the face of imperial demands, and a common social ethic.

In the 1940's Fei came into conflict with the National Government and the Kuomintang. After the assassination of Wen I-to (q.v.) in July 1946, Fei took refuge in the American consulate at Kunming. Later that year, Fei, who had become professor of anthropology at Tsinghua University, visited England under the auspices of the British Council. He arrived in England in November 1946 and remained there for three months. He spent most of his time at the London School of Economics, but also visited Oxford and spent a brief period in the Oxfordshire village of Kirklington studying aspects of rural life.

After returning to China in 1947, Fei taught at Tsinghua. His *Sheng-yü chih-tu* [systems of child rearing] was published in 1947. It analyzed the institution of child-raising, with particular reference to the Chinese family system. In *Hsiang-t'u Chung-kuo* [rural China], Fei contrasted traditional China, viewed as a rural type of society, and modern society. This book also summarized Fei's views on the village. In 1948 Fei published *Mei-kuo-jen hsing-ko* [first visit to America], *Hsiang-t'u ch'ung-chien* [rural reconstruction], and *Shen-ch'üan yü huang-ch'üan* [gentry power and imperial power].

During this period, Fei also wrote newspaper articles criticizing aspects of traditional Chinese society and, indirectly, the political and social policies of the Kuomintang. At Tsinghua, he came to know Professor Robert Redfield, a University of Chicago anthropologist, and his wife, Margaret Park Redfield. Because Fei hoped to acquaint Western readers with the ideas he had expressed in newspaper articles, in the autumn of 1948 he dictated rough translations of his articles to Mrs. Redfield. After returning to the United States, she revised and edited the translations and supplemented them with six life-histories of Chinese gentry collected by Yung-teh Chow in Yunnan between 1943 and 1946. The resulting book, published at Chicago in 1953 with an introduction by Professor Redfield, was entitled *China's Gentry*.

Immediately after the Communist occupation of north China, Fei was appointed to the university affairs committee which temporarily managed Tsinghua University. From November 1949 until 1954 he was a member of the culture and education committee of the Government Administration Council. Beginning in 1949 he was also a member of the executive committee of the Sino-Soviet Friendship Association, becoming a member of its second executive board in 1954. His other offices included: deputy director of the culture and education department of the central committee of the China Democratic League; member representing the China Democratic League in the Chinese People's Political Consultative Conference; and member of the executive committee of the Chinese People's Institute of Foreign Affairs.

In 1950, as deputy leader of a good-will mission to the national minority groups, Fei went to southwest China to study several remote communities. In 1951 he became a member of the council of the China Political Science and Law Association; in June, he was made vice president of the Central Institute for Nationalities in Peking. From 1953 to 1954 he was a member of the culture and education committee of the Peking Municipal People's Government. He attended the First National People's Congress in August and September 1954 as a deputy representing Kiangsu province and as a member of the Nationalities Affairs Commission. In July 1955 Fei became a member of the executive board of the third session of the Chinese People's Institute of Foreign Affairs. He was elected to the central committee of the China Democratic League in February 1956. In October, he became chief of the specialists bureau of the State Council.

In 1950 Fei had written a number of articles praising the "new democracy." In *Wo che i-nien* [this year of my life] he said that 1949 had been his year for hsueh-hsi, that is, intensive study of Chinese Communist doctrine. He criticized his fellow intellectuals for stinting in their efforts at thought reform and confessed the difficulties that he had encountered in attempting to reach the heights of proletarian consciousness. The same year, at a meeting at Tsinghua University, Fei had joined such professors as Chang Tung-sun, Tseng Chao-lun, Ch'ien Wei-ch'ang, and Ch'ien Tuan-sheng in expressing disapproval of government plans to reorganize Chinese higher education along Soviet lines.

Fei and many other scholars hoped that Chou En-lai's January 1956 speech on a new education policy might mean "re-liberation." During the so-called Hundred Flowers period, Fei said in an article published in the *Jen-min jih-pao* that although the new policies of socialist construction had brought economic improvement in China, they had not freed scholars to pursue research without fear or restraint. Intellectuals, he said, faced the uncertain weather of early spring, not knowing from day to day what to expect. He made a plea for "one room and two books" and freedom for uninterrupted study. As a result of this article and other public pronouncements of the same nature, Fei was severely criticized later in 1957 in the anti-rightist campaign. He was charged with being the leader of the so-called rightist intellectual faction of a group which allegedly was headed by Chang Po-chün and Lo Lung-chi (qq.v.). He also was accused of such intellectual heresies as supporting the so-called idealist sociology of Liang Shu-ming (q.v.) and favoring the revival of capitalism. Fei confessed that his earlier statements reflected "an inaccurate estimate of the intellectuals" and declared that he intended to fight the rightists. The designation of Fei as a rightist was rescinded on 16 September 1959. On 11 April, he had been appointed to the Third Chinese People's Political Consultative Conference as a delegate from the China Democratic League.

In Fei's works of the 1950's, such as *Wo che i-nien*, he retracted his earlier lack of confidence in the Chinese people's potentialities for overcoming such obstacles as low income and capital accumulation, poor technology, and over-population. Under Communist leadership, he said, China could become a modern, industrialized country. His *Min-chu hsien-fa jen-ch'üan* [the people's rights under a democratic constitution] was intended for the average reader who wished to grasp the "correct" meaning of constitutionalism, democracy, and civil rights. Fei's analysis of the Yi people in Liangshan, Kweichow, appeared in his *Hsiung-ti min-tsu tsai Kuei-chou* [a brother nationality in Kweichow].

Fei remarried in 1942 and had one daughter by his second wife.

Feng Ch'eng-chün   馮承鈞
T. Tzu-heng   子衡

Feng Ch'eng-chün (1887–9 February 1946), historian and translator, was best known for introducing Western methods of historiography to the study of Chinese history in China through his translations of the works of European sinologists and Orientalists.

Hsiak'o, Hupeh, was the birthplace of Feng Ch'eng-chün. After receiving a traditional education in the Chinese classics, he went to Europe in 1903 at the age of 17. He studied at the University of Liège in 1905–6 and at the University of Paris from 1906 to 1910, majoring in law. After graduation in 1910, he attended the Collège de France. In Paris, Feng used his spare time to tutor French students of sinology in Chinese. Thus, he became acquainted with several noted sinologists, who gave him copies of their books and articles. These provided the basis for much of his later translation work.

Feng was interested in the history of Chinese legal institutions, and he began to investigate such problems as foreign influences on Chinese cultural and material life and the evolution and development of Chinese institutions. He believed that a knowledge of the foreign institutions and cultures which had influenced China was a prerequisite for the study of the history of Chinese institutions. For instance, he held that the elimination of mutilation as a punishment in the sixth century in China was primarily due to the transmigration and cause-and-effect doctrines of Buddhism.

After spending some eight years in Europe, Feng Ch'eng-chün returned to China in 1911 and served for a year as secretary of diplomatic affairs in the Hupeh provincial government. He then became secretary of the new Parliament when it convened in Peking in 1913. When the Parliament was dissolved in 1914, he was transferred to the ministry of education as an assistant secretary in the bureau of higher and special education at Peking, where he served from 1914 to 1927. He also lectured at National Peking University from 1920 to 1926 and at National Peking Normal University in 1928–29.

Although Feng translated a number of Western works on social and political philosophy, such as Gustave LeBon's *Les opinions et les croyances* (*I-chien yü hsin-liang*), *La déséquilibre du monde* (*Shih-chieh chih fen-luan*), and *La psychologie politique* (*Cheng-chih hsin-li*), his most important work was the translation of Western sinology and Oriental studies, through which he introduced Western methods of historiography to the study of Chinese history in China. The first work he translated was Edouard Chavannes' *Les voyageurs chinois* (*Chung-kuo chih lü-hsing chia*), a booklet about Chinese travelers to foreign lands from the Han to the early Ch'ing periods. When it was presented to him by Chavannes in Paris, Feng paid little attention to it because it was a translation from Chinese sources and thus did not appear to merit careful reading. After he became engaged in teaching and research, however, he was confronted with many difficulties, especially the identification of non-Chinese names which appeared in Chinese histories and literature. Some of these names were identified in Chavannes' work. Feng discovered that some Western studies of Chinese history were not merely translations; rather, they represented a new discipline which could contribute to Chinese scholarship. Thus, he decided to translate this work of Chavannes into Chinese with his comments "to show students an example of methods of research." The translation was published in 1926.

For several years, Feng continued to translate French works, especially those dealing with Chinese intercourse with Southeast Asia and with China's northwestern regions. In 1930 and 1931 he published translations of two articles by Gabriel Ferrand, "Le K'ouen-louen et les anciennes navigations interocéaniques dans les mers du Sud" ("K'un-lun chih Nan-hai ku-tai hang-hsing k'ao") and "L'Empire sumatranais de Crivijaya" ("Su-men-ta-na ku-kuo k'ao"). Others works translated by Feng between 1928 and 1933 were Georges Maspero's La Royaume de Champa (Chan-p'o shih), Gustave Schlegel's "Les peuples étrangers chez les historiens chinois" ("Chung-kuo shih-ch'eng chung wei-hsiang chu-kuo k'ao-cheng"), Victor Segalan's "Premier exposé des résultats archéologiques obtenus dans la Chine occidentale par la Mission Gilbert de Voisins" ("Chung-kuo hsi-pu k'ao-ku chi"), and Joseph Mullie's "Les anciennes villes de l'empire des Grands Leao au royaume mongol de Barin" ("Tung-meng-ku Liao-tai chiu-ch'eng t'an-k'ao chi"). Feng corrected and commented on the Western studies and carefully rendered into Chinese many non-Chinese names which had been identified in them.

Feng's interest in the identification of non-Chinese names in Chinese sources also led him to study Western works on Buddhism, which contain a rich vocabulary of Sanskrit names that are useful for reading Buddhist terms in Chinese. He pointed out that Chinese Buddhist literature frequently had been used by European and Japanese scholars as a source of historical information not available elsewhere, but that it had been neglected by Chinese scholars. Accordingly, in the winter of 1927 he took a month to translate an article on the 16 Lohans by Sylvain Levi and Edouard Chavannes, "Les Seize Archat" ("Fa-chu-chi

chi so-chi O-lou-han k'ao"), after spending more than a year in searching and checking the sources.

Most of Feng's other early translations and writings relate to Buddhism, including the Études Bouddhiques (Fo-hsüeh yen-chiu), by Przyluski, Levi, and Pelliot, which was published in 1928; Li-tai ch'iu-fa fan-ch'ing lu, published in 1934, a collection of 200 biographies of translators of Buddhist sutras from Han to T'ang, based on Chinese sources supplemented by recent Western studies; and Levi's several works on the lankara, mahamayuri, and saddharma smrityupasthana sutras. Feng's interest in the history of other foreign religions in China is indicated by his several books and articles on Manichaeism and Nestorianism and on the Jesuits in China.

Although most of these works were published after 1929, all of the manuscripts were completed before that year. In 1929 Feng suffered a stroke which paralyzed him. He could not move without help and had to give up teaching. When his health improved, he received grants from the China Foundation for the Promotion of Education and Culture (1932–39) to translate a number of Western works on Chinese relations with other countries and on Mongol history. During the period from 1930 to 1936, he produced no fewer than 20 monographs. These included translations of Paul Pelliot's "Deux itinéraires de Chine en Inde à la fin du VIIIe siècle" (Chiao-kuang Yin-tu liang-tao k'ao), Leonard Aurousseau's La première conquete Chinoise des pays Annamites (Ch'in-tai ch'u-p'ing Nan-yüeh k'ao), Edouard Chavannes' Documents sur les Tou-kiue (Turcs) occidentaux (Hsi T'u-chüeh shih liao), sections dealing with the Mongols in René Grousset's Histoire de l'extrême-orient (Meng-ku shih lüeh), D'Ohsson's Histoire des Mongols (Meng-ku shih), Lucien Bouvat's Timour et les Timourides (T'ieh-mu-erh ti-kuo), Pelliot's "Les grandes voyages maritimes chinois au début du XVe siècle" (Cheng Ho hsia hsi-yang k'ao), A. J. H. Charignon's Le livre de Marco Polo (Ma-k'o-po-lo hsing-chi), and the first 50 biographies in Louis Pfister's Notices biographiques et bibliographiques sur les jesuites de l'ancienne mission de Chine (Ju hua yeh-su-hui shih lieh-chuan). He also wrote two books on Mongol history: Yuan tai pai-hua pei (1933), a study of some 30 colloquial versions of Mongolian edicts in stone inscriptions, and the Ch'eng-chi-ssu-han chuan

(1934), a biography of Chingis Khan. His translations of articles on the history and geography of Central Asia and the South Seas were included in two collections, the *Shih-ti ts'ung-k'ao* (1931–33) and the *Hsi-yü nan-hai shih-ti k'ao-cheng i-ts'ung* (1934–56). Almost all of Feng's works were published by the Commerical Press in Shanghai.

After 1936 Feng did not produce many translations, but devoted his time to writing and to collating and editing early Chinese works on foreign travels—the major, sometimes the only, contemporary records of many of the countries of Southeast and South Asia. These include his collation of two texts of early fifteenth-century travels, the *Ying-yai sheng-lan* by Ma Huan and the *Hsing-ch'a sheng-lan* by Fei Hsin, two accounts by men who accompanied Cheng Ho on his famous maritime expeditions to the South Seas between 1405 and 1433. These were published in 1935 and 1936, respectively. He also published editions of the *Chu fan chih* by the thirteenth-century author Chao Ju-kua, which is the most comprehensive account of the foreign countries and of various products traded from abroad during Sung times, and the *Hai lu*, a travel record based on the observations of Hsieh Ch'ing-kao (1765-1821), a Chinese who worked for 14 years on Western ships and who visited several Western countries. Both of these appeared in 1937. Feng also collated several other works, including the *Hsi-yang ch'ao-kung tien-lu*, a record of foreign tribute missions to China, but none of these manuscripts were published.

One of Feng's major compilations during this period was the *Chung-kuo nan-yang chiao-t'ung shih*, published in 1937, a comprehensive treatise on Chinese intercourse with Southeast and South Asia from Han to Ming times and a historical account of individual countries in this area. He also compiled two dictionaries of geographical names. These were the result of his lifelong research in matching foreign names transcribed in European languages with those transliterated in Chinese sources. *Hsi-yü ti-ming*, a bilingual list of place names from Central and Western Asia to Europe and Africa, was published in 1930 by the Sino-Swedish Expedition to the Northwest and again in 1955 from a revised manuscript. Feng's work on the South Seas, "Nan-hai ti-ming," which covers Southeast and South Asia, was not published.

Because of Feng Ch'eng-chün's physical disabilities, after 1931 his translations and writings were dictated by him to his eldest son, Feng Hsien-shu, a graduate of Fu-jen University who died in 1943 after his arrest by the Japanese for participation in anti-Japanese activities. Some of his later writings were dictated to his second son, Feng Hsien-chi, who is mentioned as Shu-yin in his father's books written after 1935. Although many of Feng Ch'eng-chün's friends and several of his children moved to the interior during the war years, he remained in Peiping because of his physical condition. During this period he contributed only a few articles to journals. In 1945, when the universities moved back from west China and a temporary associated university was set up in Peiping, he was appointed a professor of history. He held this position for only a short time; he died of a kidney infection in February 1946 at the age of 60. Feng had ten children, five sons and five daughters.

Feng Chih   馮 至
    Orig. Feng Ch'eng-chih   馮 承 植
    T.   Chün-p'ei   君 培

Feng Chih (1906–), poet, essayist, and professor of German literature. He was one of the most respected poets of the late republican period. Famous for his translations of Rainer Maria Rilke and for his own lyrics in sonnet form, Feng repudiated both after 1949 to become a practitioner of patriotic verse and an ardent and official spokesman for Chinese Communist literary theory and practice.

Little is known of Feng Chih's childhood and youth. He was born in Chohsien, Hopei, a rural community some 45 miles southwest of Peking. His family appears to have been related to a local Feng clan which had been prominent in the district since early Ch'ing times. Feng was probably at school in Peking in the years just before and after 1920. In 1923 he matriculated at Peking University. Except for a journey to Harbin in 1927 he remained in Peking until 1930.

Nothing is known of Feng's start as a poet except that his interest in poetry was awakened early and was stimulated to rapid maturity by contact with the avant-garde vernacular poetry movement centering around Peking University. At the university, Feng commenced the study of German under Yang Ping-cheng and later majored in German literature. This interest seems to have led him into literary circles influenced by then-current German writers. In particular, he joined the staff of *Ch'en-chung* [the sunken bell], a literary periodical which took its title from Gerhart Hauptmann's play *Die Versunkene Glocke*, and in 1925 he became its editor. Feng was writing poetry as early as 1923, when he composed the 16 poems of the cycle *Kuei-hsiang* [back home]. These poems concerned Feng's return to Chohsien for the new year's festivities of January 1923 and expressed his reluctance to leave the excitement of the city for the countryside. The collection was not published until 1929. In 1927 Feng published *Tso-jih chih ko* [songs of yesterday]. Notable in this first volume of verse were his love lyrics "Man-t'ien hsing-kuang" [a skyful of starlight], "Pieh K" [farewell to K], and "Ni" [you] and two narrative poems, "Chang-man" [the curtain] and "Ssu-men chih ch'ien" [by the temple gate]. The narrative poems received much critical acclaim, especially "Chang-man," the retelling of a Chinese folk legend of a pair of lovers who through a misunderstanding entered the life of the cloister. In 1928 Feng Chih published the poem cycle *Pei-yu* [journey to the north], which was based on his Manchurian excursion of the summer of 1927. In *Pei-yu* the narrative mode of such poems as "Chang-man" is replaced by a compelling personal note. The Manchurian poems reveal the despair of the young poet at the decadence of life in the great city and his intense sadness at the passing of youth. Feng's flight, however, seems to have been of little avail, and the cycle ends with a cold and gloomy vision of Harbin in the deep snow. *Pei-yu* was Feng's last major work for many years.

About 1928 Feng was graduated from the German department of Peking University. In the autumn of 1930 he set out for Germany to pursue his literary studies. Feng traveled overland by rail, probably through Siberia. He reported a fragment of this journey in the essay "Ch'ih-t'a i-hsi" [traveling west], which records a discussion on philosophy and religion which he had with two Soviet students and a German missionary. From 1930 to 1935 Feng studied at the University of Berlin and spent some time at Heidelberg. He received a Ph.D. from Berlin in 1935. Feng's writings during this period included a translation of Rilke's *Briefe an den jungen Dichter* (*Letters to a Young Poet*) undertaken in 1931, and "Sai-yin ho-p'ang-ti shao-nü" [the nameless girl by the Seine], which appeared in 1932 in *Ch'en-chung*. In 1932 Feng met Chu Tzu-ch'ing (q.v.) for the first time and was much impressed by the elder poet's candor and humility. Feng returned to China in 1935 and became a member of the German department at Peking University. From 1935 to 1938 he was chiefly concerned with German literature. His translation and discussion of six poems of Friedrich Nietzsche appeared in *Wen-hsüeh* [literature magazine] in 1937.

In 1938 the Sino-Japanese war interrupted Feng's quiet career as scholar and man of letters. He joined the general exodus of intellectuals to the southwest, arriving in Kunming late in the year to take up a teaching post at the newly established Southwest Associated University. The trek to Kunming affected him deeply. He was impressed with both the resilience of traditional Chinese life in the rural areas and the endurance of the average Chinese citizen. In an essay published in 1939, "Tsai Kan-chiang-shang" [on the Kan River], Feng movingly described the age-old practice of fishing by firelight, which, until war removed him from his normal life, he had known only from old books. In another essay written the same year, "I P'ing-lo" [I remember P'ing-lo], Feng described the imperturbable behavior of a tailor in P'inglo, Kiangsi, whose matter-of-fact calmness in getting his job of sewing done on time somehow symbolized the Chinese people bravely going about their business in the face of national crisis. These essays differ considerably in tone from the despair of *Pei-yu*, coupling a serene acceptance of hardship with a Rilke-like respect for "ordinary things."

During his Kunming years (1938–46), Feng Chih continued his professorial career and also wrote what are generally considered to be his best poems. Feng taught German at Southwest Associated University and at T'ung-chi University, where he also acted as dean. His course on Goethe became famous. His translation of Rilke's *Letters to a Young Poet*, begun in Berlin, was published in 1938. Between 1931 and 1939

Feng had written very little poetry. In 1939 or 1940, however, he seems to have had a profound, almost mystical, experience which thawed his frozen creativity. In gratitude for this experience and in an attempt to communicate it, he composed the 27 poems of his *Shih-ssu-hang-shih-chi* [poems in 14 lines], published in 1941. Rilke's influence was quite apparent. Both the form of the poems and the circumstances of their composition recalled the German poet, whose *Sonette an Orpheus* (*Sonnets to Orpheus*) were composed in a brief period after he had produced very little work for over a decade. Like Rilke, Feng gave accurate descriptions of nature a metaphysical overtone. Feng's cavalcades of horses, his rivers, mountains, lonely pines, deserted streets, the utter solitude of lamplight, and the utter freedom of a stringless kite are described not directly for themselves but as occult and premonitory symbols of a world whose beauty can be glimpsed and described only by the poet. Technically, the sonnets demonstrated the possibility of applying a firm metric to vernacular poetry. The form was ideally suited to Feng's materials and allowed much variety and movement within the organizing framework. The poems caused a great stir and were much imitated by younger poets.

In 1941 Feng began to experience the real rigors of war with the inception of regular Japanese bombing of Kunming. One result of the bombings was frequent power failure, which made it impossible for Feng, who had to resort to using a dim lantern, to read any but classical books with large clear type. Accordingly, he devoted the remainder of the war years to the study of classical Chinese poetry. He produced a 1944 essay on the Sung patriot-poet Lu Yu (1125–1209), which centered on the problem of inculcating a sense of duty in the educated man, and he developed an abiding interest in Tu Fu (712–770), a T'ang poet who had written his greatest poems in times of national crisis. The publication in 1942 of a translation by Pien Chih-lin of Rilke's novella *Die Weise von Liebe und Tod des Cornets Christoph Rilke* stimulated Feng to use the same form in retelling the legend of Wu Tzu-hsu, a sixth-century B.C. hero who, rather than yielding to the tyranny of his father's murderer, chose exile and revenge. This work was published in 1944 and, as Feng stated in the preface, was meant to reflect the wartime suffering of the Chinese people and their eventual triumph.

Feng Chih returned to Peiping in the fall of 1946 and resumed teaching. At the same time, he became one of the editors of *Hsien-tai wen-lu* [modern writing]. In November 1946 he published an essay in *Kuan-ch'a* [the observer] entitled "Sha-lung" [salon], which, while seeming merely to detail the history of the European literary salon, was actually a sharp satire on contemporary Chinese letters. In both theme and style this essay marked a new departure in Feng's writing. In 1947 he published long articles on Tu Fu and on Faust in *Wen-hsueh tsa-chih* [literature magazine]. A third article, entitled "Chueh-tuan" [decision] also appeared in *Wen-hsueh tsa-chih* in 1947. In this article Feng examined the existential significance of "decision" as conceived by Kierkegaard, and he concluded with a prophecy of imminent all-encompassing change for China. In 1948 Feng wrote "P'i-p'ing yü lun-chan" [criticism and polemic], which further illustrated his growing preoccupation with the position of the committed writer in a period of political and ideological unrest.

The three articles "Sha-lung," "Chueh-tuan," and "P'i-p'ing yü lun-chan," together with the earlier study of Lu Yu, sketch out Feng Chih's transformation from a scholar and meditative poet to a committed writer of definite political views and prepare for his wholesale acceptance of Marxist literary values after 1949. When Feng joined the new regime is not clear, but in 1950 he went to Europe under Communist auspices as a member of the Wen-lien [the writers union] and revisited many of the places he had known in the 1930's. Out of this trip grew his volume of essays *Tung-ou tsa-chi* [notes on Eastern Europe], published in 1950. In 1952 his long interest in Tu Fu culminated in the publication of his *Tu Fu chuan* [life of Tu Fu], a work of sound scholarship generally regarded as the best piece of biographical writing done in China in recent years. After 1949 Feng continued to publish short patriotic poems in an uncomplicated style and a few translations, notably of Heine. His most famous recent works include "Han Po k'an ch'ai" [Han Po chops wood] of 1952, in which the ghost of a maltreated wood-chopper is avenged by a popular rising against the timber owners, and "Wo ko-ch'ang An-kang"

[I sing of Anshan steel] of 1953–55, in which Chinese steel is hymned as the basis of a new society and lasting peace. In 1953 Feng became secretary of the Union of Chinese Writers. As an official spokesman on literary art, he espoused a doctrinaire position on socialist realism and publicly repudiated his 1941 sonnets and the "decadent" poetry of Rilke. In 1953 he was elected a member of the national committee of the All-China Federation of Literary and Art Circles. In 1954 he was elected a deputy from Honan to the First National People's Congress. The following year, he became a member of the division of philosophy and social sciences of the Academy of Sciences.

Feng Chih's views on the goals and techniques of socialist verse are summed up in "Man-t'an hsin-shih-ti nu-li fang-hsiang" [random observations on the future of the new poetry], which appeared in *Wen-i pao* [literary bulletin] in 1958, and "Kuan-yü hsin-shih-ti hsing-shih wen-t'i" [on the form and structure of the new poetry], published in 1959 in *Wen-i p'ing-lun* [literary critique]. In 1959 Feng also published a volume of new verse, *Shih-nien shih-ch'ao* [poems of the last ten years], and a selection of older writings, *Feng Chih shih-wen hsuan-chi* [selected poems and essays of Feng Chih].

Feng was married to Yao K'o-k'un, who was a translator.

Feng Kuo-chang   馮 國 璋
T. Hua-fu   華 甫

Feng Kuo-chang (7 January 1859–28 December 1919), one of the most powerful officers of Yuan Shih-k'ai's Peiyang military clique, was military governor of Chihli (1912–13) and Kiangsu (1913–17). After Yuan died, he became vice president (1916–17) and acting president (1917–18) of the Peking government. He was the leader of the Chihli clique, which opposed the Anhwei faction of Tuan Ch'i-jui.

A native of Chihli (Hopei), Feng Kuo-chang was the youngest of four sons in a family of farmers in Hochien. Feng and his brothers received training in the Chinese classics, and, in their spare time, they fenced and rode. However, the family fell on hard times, and by the time Feng was ready to attend school all of the family property had been sold to provide his elder brothers with an education. Feng was obliged to earn his own living; reportedly, at one time he played an erh-hu in a local theater to earn money. Feng went with an elder brother to Paoting and enrolled in the Lien-ch'ih Academy, but he was obliged to leave the school soon afterward because he lacked funds.

At the age of 27 sui, Feng went to Taku, where one of his great-uncles was working in the office of a battalion of the Anhwei army. Feng obtained a position as orderly to the battalion commander. When Li Hung-chang (ECCP, I, 464–71) established the Peiyang Military Academy at Tientsin in 1885, Feng's battalion commander recommended him to Li as a promising student. At the academy, Feng did well in his courses. In 1888 he took a leave of absence from the academy and passed the examinations for the sheng-yuan degree. After failing the chü-jen examinations later that year, he returned to the Peiyang Military Academy, from which he was graduated in 1890. He remained at the academy as an instructor until 1891, when he was assigned to serve under Nieh Shih-ch'eng (d. 1900; T. Kung-t'ing) at Port Arthur. As part of his duties, Feng made extensive journeys into Manchuria, and his familiarity with that area was very useful to Nieh and his army during the Sino-Japanese war of 1894–95.

In 1895 Feng Kuo-chang was recommended by Nieh Shih-ch'eng to serve as military attaché to Yü-keng (d. 1905; T. Lang-hsi), the newly appointed Chinese minister to Japan. Feng became acquainted with several Japanese army officers including Fukushima Yasumasa, who later headed the Shikan Gakkō [military academy], and Aoki Nobuzumi, who became a military adviser to Yuan Shih-k'ai during Yuan's presidency. For several months, Feng studied various aspects of Japan's military modernization and recorded his observations in a number of notebooks which he presented to Nieh Shih-ch'eng on his return to China. Nieh forwarded them to Yuan Shih-k'ai, who at that time was building up the Hsin-chien lu-chün [newly created army] at Hsiaochan. Feng's observations on Japanese training methods impressed Yuan, and he made Feng head of the training section of his newly organized staff office.

When Yuan Shih-k'ai was appointed governor of Shantung late in 1899, Feng accompanied him and took part in military operations against the Boxers in that province. At the height of the Boxer Uprising, Feng was stationed at Techou, close to the border of Chihli province, with orders to seal off the area from Boxer incursions. After the suppression of the Boxers by the Eight-Power Allied Army, Yuan became governor general of Chihli province in 1901 and began to organize a new military training center at Paoting. He established a new staff office, the provincial department of military administration. Feng Kuo-chang, by then one of Yuan's chief military assistants, became head of the department's instruction and training section. Feng was in charge of implementing Yuan's military training program, and in the next two years he established a number of military schools at Paoting and founded military primary schools in Chihli.

During the last decade of the Ch'ing dynasty, Feng played a prominent role in the efforts of the central government to reform and reorganize China's military establishment. In December 1903 the Manchu government established a commission for army reorganization, and Feng became head of its military education department. He was responsible for centralizing the administration of military establishments throughout China, standardizing the military training programs in the provinces, and organizing training programs in provinces that did not have them. In the autumn of 1905 he made a brief trip to Japan to observe units of the Japanese Army practice large-scale maneuvers for the first time since the Russo-Japanese war. After his return to China, he reportedly assisted in planning the Peiyang Army maneuvers held in north China in the following years. After the establishment in 1906 of the lu-chün kuei-chou hsueh-t'ang [military school for princes and nobles] to train the sons of Manchu princes and clansmen, Feng was named director of the school (under a Manchu supervisor) with the rank of deputy lieutenant general. In 1907 he also was assigned to the newly created ministry of war as chief of the chancery of the general staff council, a position he retained when the council was reorganized in 1909 as the general staff office.

Little is known of Feng's political attitudes in the years previous to the 1911 revolution. Beginning about 1906, and especially after 1908, the Ch'ing government sought to centralize control of the military forces by adopting a policy of placing Manchus, rather than Chinese, in the top military posts. Yuan Shih-k'ai, Feng's patron and superior officer, was stripped of his command of the Peiyang Army and dismissed in 1909. Feng was said to be unhappy about the way his Manchu superiors in the ministry of war treated him, and he still looked to Yuan Shih-k'ai for leadership. Thus, even before the revolution of 1911, Feng reportedly was ready to follow the orders of his former chief.

After the outbreak of the revolt at Wuchang in October 1911, the Manchu government dispatched two imperial armies to suppress the revolutionists in the Wuhan cities. Yin-ch'ang, the minster of war, was commander in chief and head of the First Army, and Feng Kuo-chang was commander of the Second Army. As his troops were moving southward along the Peking-Hankow railway, Feng stopped to consult Yuan Shih-k'ai at Changte (Anyang) in northern Honan. At Yuan's suggestion, Feng delayed the advance of his troops for several days, allowing the revolutionary movement to spread and thereby increasing the pressure on the desperate Manchu regime to come to terms with Yuan. On 27 October 1911 Yuan took command of Yin-ch'ang's forces as commander in chief of the imperial armies in Hupeh, and Feng became commander of the First Army. The same day, Yuan sent secret orders for an assault on Hankow, which was retaken by imperial forces a few days later. After about two weeks of negotiation between the revolutionary and imperial forces at Wuhan, fighting again broke out. Yuan Shih-k'ai, who was then in Peking, ordered Feng to attack Hanyang. After a week of heavy fighting, the imperial forces under Feng's command retook the city on 27 November. The following day, as a reward for his victory, the Manchu court made Feng a baron of the second class. Yuan, who believed that he was in a good position to bargain with the revolutionaries, ordered Feng not to attack Wuchang and to commence negotiations with Li Yuan-hung (q.v.), the leader of the revolutionary forces. At the end of 1911, after a temporary truce had been negotiated in Wuhan, Feng was ordered to turn over his command to Tuan Ch'i-jui (q.v.) and return to Peking.

Yuan Shih-k'ai moved rapidly to oust the Manchus from important positions in the administration and the army. He forced the Manchu prince Tsai-t'ao to resign as commandant of the chin-wei-chün [guards army], the last remaining stronghold of Manchu military power. Because Feng Kuo-chang, as former director of the lu-chün kuei-chou hsüeh-t'ang, was on good terms with many of the Manchu military officers, he was made the new commandant of the chin-wei-chün. He was instrumental in persuading the younger Manchu officers to accept the terms of the Manchu emperor's abdication. At the same time, Feng appears to have won the good will of his officers by expressing personal regret at the emperor's abdication and by supporting his officers' demands that assurances of good treatment for the imperial house be included in the terms of abdication. For several years thereafter, Feng retained command of the chin-wei-chün, which was to constitute the nucleus of his personal military power.

Feng also was made military lieutenant governor of Chahar in December 1911. After Yuan Shih-k'ai became provisional president, Feng was appointed chief of the military council in the presidential office. In September 1913 he was promoted to the rank of full general and was appointed tutuh [military governor] of Chihli (Hopei) province, acting concurrently as civil governor. Several months later, during the so-called second revolution of 1913, Feng headed one of the two Peiyang armies that Yuan Shih-k'ai had mobilized to crush Kuomintang resistance in the provinces of the lower Yangtze. As pacification commissioner of Kiang-Hwai, in over-all command of the Second Peiyang Army, Feng moved down along the Tientsin-Pukow railway to attack the Kuomintang stronghold at Nanking. After a 50-day siege, the city was taken on 1 September 1913 by the troops of Feng's nominal subordinate Chang Hsün (q.v.), and Chang was made military governor of Kiangsu province. Three months later, in December 1913, Feng was appointed to succeed Chang Hsün.

By the end of 1913 Feng Kuo-chang had become one of the most powerful of Yuan Shih-k'ai's subordinates. Feng's rise to prominence had depended upon Yuan's patronage, and, in turn, the assurance of Feng's military backing had been an important factor in Yuan's successful political maneuvering against the Manchu dynasty in 1911–12 and against the National Assembly in Peking during 1913. However, Feng's appointment as military governor of Kiangsu, with military control over a large and wealthy region out of the immediate reach of Yuan's authority, permitted him a certain degree of independence. After 1913, as Yuan sought to tighten his personal control over the provinces, Feng and other Peiyang military governors, while professing their continued loyalty to Yuan, covertly resisted all his attempts to curtail their powers. This opposition of interests became a source of hidden but persistent friction.

Relations between Feng Kuo-chang and Yuan Shih-k'ai were strained further during the summer of 1915 because of the monarchical movement. Earlier in the year, Feng had become acquainted with Liang Ch'i-ch'ao (q.v.). After hearing from Liang of a scheme to make Yuan monarch, he hurriedly left Nanking for Peking at the end of June to see if such a plan existed. Yuan assured Feng that rumors of his imperial ambitions were groundless. However, soon after Feng returned to Nanking, the monarchist Ch'ou-an-hui [society for national security] was formally established. Because he believed that Yuan had deceived him and that his own future would be seriously jeopardized if Yuan became monarch, Feng refused to take part in the monarchical movement. Yuan sought to win him over to the cause of monarchy by making him a duke in the new order of nobility; he also tried to remove Feng from his base of power in Nanking by ordering him to Peking to be chief of general staff (18 December 1915). Feng countered by indicating that he would assume the new appointment only if he were permitted to remain at Nanking. To support Feng's stand, the military governors of Kiangsi and Hupeh and several prominent citizens of Kiangsu province petitioned Yuan to retain Feng as governor in Nanking. Yuan, for the time being, was obliged to yield.

Late in December 1915 Ts'ai O (q.v.) and other military leaders in Yunnan revolted against Yuan. During the ensuing conflict between Yuan Shih-k'ai and the southern military leaders, Feng withheld his support from Yuan. Early in 1916, when Yuan ordered him to Peking to serve as his chief of general staff and as commander in chief of the anti-Yunnan forces, Feng demurred on the pretext of illness. Moreover, in March, Feng tried to unite the other Peiyang military leaders in opposition to the monarchy and to Yuan himself. Before Feng's activities came to Yuan's attention, he had succeeded in obtaining considerable support from the governors of the Yangtze provinces. In the meantime, Feng also had established contact with the southern military leaders, including Lu Jung-t'ing (q.v.), the military governor of Kwangsi, who on 15 March 1916 joined the revolt against Yuan by declaring his province independent of the central government. Thereafter, as other provinces broke away, Feng became more open in his opposition. On 16 April, he sent Yuan a telegram urging that he bring the war with the south to an end and suggesting that he retire from the presidency. To keep his position ambiguous, he issued a telegram on the next day stating that Yuan should be allowed to complete his four-year term as president.

In the spring of 1916 Feng began a series of political maneuvers designed to secure his own succession to Yuan's position of power as president of the republic and leader of the Peiyang clique. Feng attempted to play the southern military leaders against Yuan's subordinates and, at the same time, to create a new center of political and military influence to support his future candidacy. Early in May, Feng called for a conference of provincial representatives to be held at Nanking to discuss Yuan's resignation and the formation of a new National Assembly. On 18 May, the conference was opened, with Feng as chairman. In spite of strong opposition from Ni Ssu-ch'ung and Chang Hsün, both of whom supported Yuan, Feng secured a recommendation from the conference that Yuan relinquish the presidency. But Feng's proposals for selecting a new president betrayed his ambition to replace Yuan and aroused antagonism among his Peiyang colleagues and the southern military leaders. Feng's hopes were dashed when, after Yuan's death in June, Tuan Ch'i-jui established himself as the *de facto* head of the central government and installed the vice president, Li Yuan-hung, in Yuan's place as president.

Although thwarted in his political ambitions, Feng Kuo-chang wielded considerable power as military governor at Nanking and as one of the most influential leaders of the Peiyang military clique. In seeking to exploit this position, Feng continued to play one political group against another without committing himself. Utilizing Feng's own strategy, certain members of the National Assembly in Peking, hoping to use Feng as a check on Tuan Ch'i-jui's power, nominated him to succeed Li Yuan-hung as vice president. On 30 October 1916, at a joint session of the National Assembly, Feng was elected vice president. Because this position involved little more than prestige, Feng retained his post as military governor of Kiangsu and remained at his headquarters in Nanking. Feng was invited to Peking by Tuan Ch'i-jui in February 1917 to discuss Tuan's proposal that China sever diplomatic relations with Germany. On the German question, as on many others, Tuan was at odds with Li Yuan-hung. By early March, relations between them had become so strained that Tuan threatened to resign and left for Tientsin. Feng assumed the role of mediator between Tuan Ch'i-jui and Li Yuan-hung, and he succeeded in bringing about a truce between the premier and the president. With regard to the German question, Feng remained characteristically noncommittal: though personally opposed to a break with Germany, he gave Tuan the impression that he approved of the latter's policy of breaking with Germany and entering the war on the side of the Allies; but after his return to Nanking (11 March), Feng notified the Peking government of his opposition to China's participation in the war as an enemy of Germany.

In the spring of 1917 the political disagreement between Tuan Ch'i-jui and Li Yuan-hung culminated in a situation from which Feng Kuo-chang emerged as acting president of the republic. After the dismissal of Tuan as premier in May and the dissolution of the National Assembly in June, Chang Hsün attempted to restore the Manchu monarchy. Chang's efforts to involve Feng in this venture were immediately rebuffed by Feng himself; on 2 July, Feng issued a telegram from Nanking denouncing Chang Hsün and denying any connection with Chang's restoration attempt. Shortly afterward, under pressure from the military, Li Yuan-hung announced his intention to retire from the presidency. A telegram, purportedly from Li, requested Feng Kuo-chang, as vice president, to assume the duties of president. On 7 July, when Peking was still in the hands of the monarchists, Feng announced that he would comply with Li's request and called for the organization of a government in Nanking. However, after Tuan Ch'i-jui and his supporters defeated Chang Hsün and regained control of Peking in mid-July, Feng agreed to assume office in the national capital.

Feng Kuo-chang and Tuan Ch'i-jui, as the senior members of the military organization founded by Yuan Shih-k'ai, had vied with one another for leadership of the Peiyang military faction after Yuan's death. Partly as a result of this rivalry, the Peiyang faction itself tended to separate into two major groups, which were subsequently referred to as the Chihli clique (Feng was a native of Chihli province) and the Anhwei clique (Tuan was a native of Anhwei). In 1917 Feng's political and military power was centered in the Yangtze provinces of Kiangsu, Kiangsi, and Hupeh. Before leaving Nanking to assume the presidency, Feng had secured his position there by arranging to have one of his supporters succeed him as military governor of Kiangsu. Feng's chief supporters were officers who had been under his command in the First Army late in 1911 at Hanyang: Li Ch'un, the governor of Kiangsi, who was Feng's choice to succeed him in Nanking; Ch'en Kuang-yuan, who succeeded Li Ch'un as governor in Kiangsi; and Wang Chan-yuan, the governor of Hupeh. Feng retained command of his personal military force, including the former chin-wei-chün, which he had expanded into two divisions. The 16th Division remained at Nanking, and the 15th Division accompanied him to Peking as the presidential guards.

Feng went to Peking on 1 August 1917 to take up his duties as acting president. Almost immediately after assuming office, he came into conflict with Tuan Ch'i-jui, who again was serving as premier. The most important point of disagreement between them was the central government's policy toward the southern military government at Canton. Tuan wanted to suppress this government and subjugate the southern provinces by military force; Feng urged a conciliatory policy toward the southern leaders. After the Peiyang military failures in Hunan and Szechwan in October and November 1917, Tuan resigned as premier, and Feng was able to enforce his policy of peaceful unification for a brief period. However, Tuan soon rallied his supporters behind him; by early February 1918 he was able to exert sufficient pressure on Feng to cause him to abandon his policy of conciliation toward the south. In March, strengthened by the military support of Chang Tso-lin (q.v.), Tuan was in a position to insist that he immediately be reappointed premier.

Because of the superior strength of the Tuan faction, Feng agreed to an arrangement by which he would step aside for a new president when his term of office ended in October 1918. As a face-saving concession, Tuan agreed to resign as premier at the same time. However, although Feng's retirement involved a complete abdication from power, Tuan's resignation in no way impaired his control of the central government. Feng still had sufficient prestige and military support to ensure his freedom from harassment by political enemies in Peking. On 10 October 1918, at the first ceremony of its kind in the history of the young republic, Feng Kuo-chang turned over the office of president to his elected successor, Hsü Shih-ch'ang (q.v.). After his retirement from political life, Feng lived quietly in Peking. On 28 December 1919 he died of pneumonia.

Feng married twice. Nothing is known of his first wife. His second wife, Chou Chih (T. Tao-ju), was a native of Ihsing, Kiangsu. For several years before her marriage to Feng in 1914, she had been the governess of Yuan Shih-k'ai's daughters. Feng was the father of five sons and four daughters. The eldest daughter married Ch'en Chih-chi (T. Shu-liang), a native of Fengjun, Chihli and a member of the T'ung-meng-hui. During the so-called second revolution of 1913, Ch'en, as commander of the 8th Division, was the ranking officer at Nanking for a short time. Feng's eldest son, Chia-sui, served as a member of the National Assembly from Chihli province.

Feng Tzu-k'ai   豐子愷

Feng Tzu-k'ai (1898–), artist, essayist, and calligrapher, was best known for using traditional brush-drawing techniques to depict and comment on the contemporary scene.

A native of Ch'ungte, Chekiang, Feng Tzu-k'ai was one of ten children. His father died when he was a child, and he was brought up by his mother. After attending primary school, he enrolled at the First Normal School in Hangchow, Chekiang. There he came under the influence of a faculty member, Li Shu-t'ung (q.v.), who was a celebrated poet, painter, and calligrapher. Li had studied painting in Japan, and he encouraged his pupil's interest in art. After Li Shu-t'ung decided to become a Buddhist monk in 1918, Feng left the Hangchow school and went to Shanghai. In 1919 he married Hsü Li-ming, also a native of Ch'ungte.

In Shanghai, Feng Tzu-k'ai and Liu Chih-p'ing, another former pupil of Li Shu-t'ung, joined in founding a school to train teachers of art and music, the I-shu ta-hsueh [Shanghai college of art]. Feng later commented on their temerity in launching such an enterprise with little money and less experience. The only similar institution at Shanghai was the Mei-shu hsueh-hsiao [Shanghai art school], established in 1920 by Liu Hai-su (b. 1895), a young Kiangsu painter in the Western style. During this period, Feng read and lectured on Western art and studied Japanese in evening classes.

Because he was aware of his professional limitations and anxious to broaden his experience, Feng Tzu-k'ai in the spring of 1921 left for Japan. His trip was financed by his wife's family, and he spent ten months in Tokyo. Feng became a student at the Hashikawa School of Western Painting. He also studied Japanese, English, and violin. Feng was interested in Western music and theater, and he made an effort to increase his knowledge of Western artistic and dramatic forms. He spent much time visiting museums and art galleries, and he frequented the theater and the cinema.

After his return to China, Feng taught fine arts for a period at the Ch'un-hui Middle School at Shangyu, Chekiang. In 1926 he became an art tutor at Shanghai University and also taught fine arts, music, and aesthetics in middle schools in Shanghai. In addition, he joined the editorial staff of the Kaiming Book Company, which published his *Hsi-yang mei-shu shih* [history of Western art] in 1928.

During the 1920's some of Feng's sketches were published in the Shanghai press. His earliest efforts were tight, stippled panels in the manner favored at the time by some Western illustrators of children's books. But Feng quickly developed a more relaxed manner to express humorous observations of character and human behavior. A series of sketches of mischievous children, for many of which his own children served as models, first made him popular. Feng regularly made rough sketches as he walked the streets of Shanghai. He developed these sketches into drawings depicting everyday life: a family in a railroad station waiting room or a young couple having their baggage examined by customs officers. Two collections of his sketches of children were published by the Kaiming Book Company, *Erh-t'ung man-hua* [sketches of children] in 1925 and *Tzu-k'ai hua-chi* [a collection of Feng Tzu-k'ai's sketches] in 1927. Two years later, the same company issued another collection of his drawings, *Tzu-k'ai man-hua chi* [a collection of Feng Tzu-k'ai's cartoons]. *Jen-chien hsiang* [sketches of this human world] and *Tzu-k'ai man-hua ch'üan-chi* [complete collection of Feng Tzu-k'ai's cartoons] appeared in 1935 and 1946, respectively.

Early in 1929 Feng began collaboration with his former teacher Li Shu-t'ung, who had become one of China's outstanding Buddhist monks and who had adopted the religious name Hung-i. Feng prepared the drawings for the first volume of a collection of fables with Buddhist morals entitled *Hu-sheng hua-chi* [a collection of sketches of the floating life], for which the calligraphic text had been done by Hung-i. The first volume contained 50 drawings. A second volume, containing 60 drawings, was issued in 1940 by the Kaiming Book Company in association with the Fo-hsueh (Buddhist) Book Company. The drawings for the second volume were done at Ishan, Kwangsi, where Feng was teaching at the wartime campus of Chekiang University. Hung-i had been 50 when the first volume was published and 60 when the second appeared; the number of drawings in each equaled his age. In 1940 he wrote to Feng Tzu-k'ai to express his hope that this pattern would continue, with a new volume appearing each decade. Hung-i died in 1942, but Feng honored his teacher's wishes and completed a third volume of 70 drawings at Amoy in 1949–50.

Feng Tzu-k'ai was known in China as one of the most advanced Buddhist disciples of the monk Hung-i and as a painter and calligrapher. In addition to his collections of drawings, he published several volumes of essays and was regarded as a notable stylist. He also published translations of Turgenev's *First Love* in 1932 and Robert Louis Stevenson's *Suicide Club* in 1932, as well as works by Japanese authors.

After the Central People's Government was established in 1949, Feng did no cartooning, though he reportedly continued to prepare drawings for the *Hu-sheng hua-chi* series. In 1955 the People's Fine Arts Publishing Company at Peking reissued his *Tzu-k'ai man-hua chi*, originally published in 1929. In 1956 Feng's study of the Japanese painter Sesshū (1420–1506), *Hsueh-chou ti sheng-yai yü i shu* [the life and art of Sesshū], was published at Shanghai. Two years later he edited and illustrated a collection of essays by Hung-i, *Li Shu-t'ung ko-ch'ü chi* [songs of Li Shu-t'ung].

Feng Tzu-k'ai's importance in the history of twentieth-century Chinese art was that he was a pioneer in using traditional brush drawing to portray the people around him by direct observation. He commented, with a gentle smile born of his Buddhism, on the human foibles that he saw around him. His best drawings achieved sound characterization with skillful economy of line. Good examples are the sketch of a three-year-old child in *Tzu-k'ai hua-chi* (1927) and his portrait of Lu Hsün's famous fictional character Ah Q in *Man-hua Ah Q cheng-chuan*, which he illustrated for the Kaiming Book Company (1939).

Feng Tzu-yu   馮 自 由
   T. Chien-hua   建 華

Feng Tzu-yu (1881–6 April 1958), an early associate of Sun Yat-sen who was prominent in the Hsing-Chung-hui and the T'ung-meng-hui. After the 1924 Kuomintang reorganization, his active political career ended. He later wrote a number of historical works about the revolutionary movement.

A native of Nanhai (Namhoi), Kwangtung, Feng Tzu-yu was born in Japan, where his father, Feng Ching-ju, operated a stationery and printing business. Feng Ching-ju had been born in Hong Kong, and it appears that while residing in the British colony the family had taken the name Kingsell. Thus, the company in Yokohama was known as the Kingsell Company. It dealt in imported stationery, as well as job printing and the printing of books, and the family enjoyed considerable prestige in the growing Chinese community in Yokohama.

The family first came into contact with anti-Manchu political activities when Sun Yat-sen, after founding the Hsing-Chung-hui in Honolulu, passed through Japan in the winter of 1894–95, distributed copies of the new organization's regulations, and enjoined patriotic Chinese to form a branch in Japan. The following year, Sun Yat-sen was again in Japan, and his contact with Feng's family led to the founding of a small branch of the Hsing-Chung-hui in Yokohama. Feng Ching-ju was elected head of the branch organization. His 14-year-old son, Feng Tzu-yu (then known as Feng Mou-lung), was enlisted as its youngest member. In the years following the establishment of the Hsing-Chung-hui, there was considerable controversy within the Chinese community in Japan between those who supported Sun Yat-sen's political views and those who favored the ideas of K'ang Yu-wei and Liang Ch'i-ch'ao (qq.v.). Feng Ching-ju stood aloof from these conflicts. The young Feng Tzu-yu, however, was influenced by the anti-Manchu historical tracts secretly printed and circulated by the Hsing-Chung-hui, and he became an increasingly firm supporter of the objectives of that organization. Feng enrolled at Waseda University in Tokyo in 1900, the year of the Boxer Uprising in China. In the next few years, he became increasingly involved in patriotic activities carried on by Chinese students in Japan. In 1901, in association with Wang Ch'ung-hui (q.v.) and others, Feng helped to found the Kwangtung Independence Association, a group formed to oppose the extension of French influence in their native province. A year later, in collaboration with several other Chinese, including Chang Ping-lin (q.v.) and Ma Chün-wu, he helped to plan a ceremonial meeting to commemorate the death of the last emperor of the Ming dynasty. The interference of the Japanese police prevented them from holding the meeting in Tokyo, but they later held it in Yokohama. Feng also turned his attention to the dissemination of propaganda for Sun Yat-sen's programs and policies. He founded the *Kuo-min-pao* [citizens' newspaper] in 1901 and in 1903 became the Tokyo correspondent of the *Chung-kuo jih-pao* [China daily] of Hong Kong (the organ of the

Hsing-Chung-hui) and of the *Ta-t'ung jih-pao* [Ta-t'ung daily] of San Francisco.

When the T'ung-meng-hui was inaugurated in Tokyo in the autumn of 1905, Feng Tzu-yu was only about 25. However, he had been a member of the Hsing-Chung-hui and had known Sun Yat-sen for a decade. Because he was a Cantonese with family connections in both Hong Kong and Japan, it was decided that he should be sent to direct the organization's affairs in the Hong Kong–Canton-Macao area. He arrived in Hong Kong late in 1905. Headquarters were set up at the office of the *Chung-kuo jih-pao*, then edited by Ch'en Shao-pai, and Feng devoted his attention to both organization and propaganda activities. A year later he was appointed Hong Kong director of the T'ung-meng-hui and director of the *Chung-kuo jih-pao*. This was a period during which anti-Manchu uprisings suffered repeated failures, and Feng was able to continue operations only because of his great persistence.

In 1910 Feng left Hong Kong to become editor of the *Ta-han jih-pao* [great Chinese daily] in Vancouver, British Columbia. The succession of unsuccessful attempts to overthrow the Manchu government in China posed serious financial problems for Sun Yat-sen, and Feng hoped to obtain financial aid for Sun from the overseas Chinese communities in Canada. In the summer of 1911 Sun, who was in the United States on a fund-raising campaign, requested that Feng move to San Francisco to edit the *Ta-t'ung jih-pao* and to secure the cooperation of the Chih-kung-tang, a secret society which, like the T'ung-meng-hui, had been founded with the purpose of overthrowing Manchu rule. The Chih-kung-tang had supported the cause of constitutional monarchy advocated by K'ang Yu-wei. Whether the Chih-kung-tang, which had substantial strength among Chinese in the San Francisco area, would continue to support the constitutional monarchists or would support Sun Yat-sen became a major issue among overseas Chinese, particularly in North America.

In October 1911 the successful revolt at Wuchang brought an abrupt change in the Chinese political scene, and Feng was chosen to help organize the new government at Nanking. Arriving in Shanghai shortly before the end of 1911, Feng brought the records of overseas contributions to the revolutionary cause as well as unused gold script issued by the fund-raising organization. These were presented to Sun Yat-sen as leader of the T'ung-meng-hui. After his election as provisional president of China, Sun Yat-sen made Feng his confidential secretary, and Feng remained in Nanking as long as Sun held the presidency.

After Yuan Shih-k'ai became provisional president, Feng Tzu-yu was appointed director of a newly created organ, the (Ko-ming) Chi-hsün-chü, or Office for Investigation of (Revolutionary) Merits. This relatively unimportant position, the only official governmental post Feng ever held, was established especially for him because of his broad knowledge of the various anti-Manchu revolutionary operations prior to the Wuchang uprising of 1911. Feng held office for a little more than a year. After the outbreak of the so-called second revolution in 1913, he had to flee from Peking.

Following the organization of the Chung-hua ko-ming-tang in 1914, Sun Yat-sen appointed Feng Tzu-yu to take charge of party affairs in the United States. Feng went to San Francisco and published the *Min-kuo tsa-chih* [republican magazine], which functioned as a party organ. In 1917 he was elected to the Senate in Peking as a representative of overseas Chinese. During the next few years, Feng appears to have gradually ceased participation in political activities. In 1923 he was appointed a reserve member of Sun Yat-sen's provisional Central Executive Committee at Canton. In that capacity, he participated in the discussions which paved the way for the reorganization of the Kuomintang the following year. He attended the First National Congress of the Kuomintang in January 1924, but was excluded from the higher councils of the party because he staunchly opposed Sun Yat-sen's policy of cooperation with the Chinese Communists.

Shortly after the First National Congress of the Kuomintang, Feng, together with Teng Tse-ju (q.v.) and other dissident Kuomintang members, independently held a meeting at Canton for the purpose of drafting a resolution warning Li Ta-chao (q.v.) and other Chinese Communist members of the Kuomintang against attempting to seize control of the party. However, before the resolution was circulated, Feng and other participants of this meeting were summoned before Sun Yat-sen on charges by Liao Chung-k'ai (q.v.), Li Ta-chao, and Borodin that they had violated party discipline and had incited discord between the Kuomintang and the Chinese Communist party. Feng later claimed that these charges were dismissed by Sun, but the details of the case remain obscure.

After the death of Sun Yat-sen, Feng, in the latter part of 1925, took a leading part in setting up the so-called Kuomintang Comrades Club in Peking. This group, according to some sources, was on friendly terms with militarists and politicians in the northern capital. On the eve of the Western Hills conference, Feng was involved in the assault on and abduction of Tai Chi-t'ao (q.v.) and Shen Ting-i, two prominent Kuomintang members who had come to Peking to attend the conference.

Feng Tzu-yu earned the disfavor of the Kuomintang leadership, and he never again wielded significant influence in either party or government. Although he was appointed a member of the Legislative Yuan at Nanking in 1932 and was named to membership on the National Government Council in 1943, these positions had little political importance. In 1949, after the removal of the Nationalists to Taiwan, Feng became national policy adviser to Chiang Kai-shek, a title which he held until his death of apoplexy in the spring of 1958, at the age of 77 sui.

After the mid-1920's, Feng's interests had turned from politics to history, and he made a major contribution in the field of party history. Early in 1928 Feng began to gather together reports, correspondence, and other personal papers, as well as the recollections of his former colleagues within the party. Using these materials and relying upon his own extensive knowledge of the people and events of the pre-republican period, he began to compile a history of the revolutionary party and its activities before the revolution of 1911. In November 1928 the first volume was published as the *Chung-hua min-kuo k'ai-kuo ch'ien ko-ming shih* [history of the revolutionary movement before the founding of the republic]; a second volume appeared two years later, and the third and final volume was published in 1944. Observing the traditional distinction in Chinese historiography between the formal history (cheng-shih) and the informal history (yeh-shih or i-shih), Feng planned this book as a formal history of the revolutionary party, as a supplement to which he subsequently compiled an informal history, using materials which he considered to be more intimate than official, such

as personal reminiscences and anecdotes about events and personalities in the early revolutionary movement. Entitled *Ko-ming i-shih* [an unauthorized history of the revolution], this latter work was published in five volumes (1939–47). Feng was also the author of three other histories of the revolutionary movement, the *Hua-ch'iao ko-ming k'ai-kuo shih* [the role of overseas Chinese in the revolution and in the founding of the republic], the *Chung-kuo ko-ming yün-tung erh-shih-liu nien tsu-chih shih* [a history of the organization of China's revolutionary movement of twenty-six years], and the *Hua-ch'iao ko-ming tsu-chih shih-hua* [history of the revolutionary organization of the overseas Chinese]. These were published, respectively, in 1946, 1948, and 1954.

A versatile writer and keen observer, Feng Tzu-yu was one of the earliest Chinese revolutionaries to perceive the similarities between Sun Yat-sen's "principle of the people's livelihood" and Western socialism. In 1906 he wrote an article for the *Chung-kuo jih-pao* entitled "Ming-sheng chu-i yü Chung-kuo cheng-chih ko-ming chih ch'ien-t'u" [the principle of the people's livelihood and the future of the Chinese political revolution], in which he enjoined members of the T'ung-meng-hui to devote particular attention to Sun's economic concepts, especially land nationalization and the single tax theory. This article was reprinted on 1 May 1906 in the fourth issue of the *Min Pao* [people's journal]. In 1920 Feng published a work entitled *She-hui chu-i yü Chung-kuo* [socialism and China], which purported to be a study of the various schools of socialism and of their implications for China.

Feng Yu-lan   馮友蘭
Alt. Fung Yu-lan

Feng Yu-lan (1895–), noted philosopher, best known for his *Chung-kuo che-hsueh-shih* [history of Chinese philosophy] and for his philosophical system, which combined Neo-Confucianism of the Ch'eng-Chu school with Western realism and logic and with elements of Taoist thought. After 1950, he publicly committed himself to interpreting Chinese philosophy according to the tenets of Marxism-Leninism.

A native of T'angho, Honan, Feng Yu-lan was born into a landlord family. He received his early education from his parents, especially his mother, and from private tutors. In 1910 he entered the Chung-chou Institute at Kaifeng, the provincial capital of Honan, where he came under the influence of teachers who exposed him to nationalistic and revolutionary ideas. Feng then was awarded a provincial scholarship which enabled him to study at the Chung-kuo kung-hsueh [China academy] at Shanghai. At that time, Western political and social thought was being introduced into China through the translations of Yen Fu (q.v.). The Chung-kuo kung-hsueh, one of the more progressive schools of that period, offered its students a course in logic, using Yen Fu's Chinese version of William Stanley Jevons' *Primer of Logic* as the textbook. However, the teachers were not capable of teaching the course. Feng related that one teacher made the students recite the text word by word and that another teacher resigned because he could not solve one of the problems in the book. In 1915, when Feng heard that a department of Western philosophy was to be established at National Peking University, he immediately applied for admission. But the professor who was to teach Western philosophy died, and Feng entered the department of Chinese philosophy instead.

After graduation from Peking University in 1918, Feng returned to Kaifeng and edited a bi-weekly paper devoted to current events. In 1919 he was granted a scholarship by the ministry of education in Peking to continue his studies abroad. After arriving in New York in December 1919, he was admitted to the graduate school of Columbia University. He received instruction from two of America's most eminent philosophers of that period, John Dewey and Frederick J. E. Woodbridge, and obtained the Ph.D. degree in 1923. His dissertation was entitled "A Comparative Study of Life Ideals: the Way of Decrease and Increase, with Interpretations and Illustrations from the Philosophies of the East and West."

After returning to China in the latter part of 1923, Feng was appointed professor of philosophy at the newly founded Chung-chou University at Kaifeng. That winter he gave a lecture, "A Conception of Life," to the students of the Shantung First Provincial Middle School. In that lecture, later published as a booklet, he touched on some of the topics then being debated by Chinese intellectuals. In 1926 he

published his *Jen-sheng che-hsueh* [philosophy of life], which was based on his doctoral dissertation, but which incorporated some of the points made in the 1923 lecture. The publication of *Jen-sheng che-hsueh* coincided with heated debates among Chinese intellectuals about the comparative value of Western and Oriental civilizations and about the superiority of a scientific or a metaphysical view of life. In general, the conservative camp, including such men as Carsun Chang (Chang Chia-sen), Liang Ch'i-ch'ao, and Liang Shu-ming (qq.v.), argued for the superiority of Oriental civilization because of its dominant concern for the spiritual aspects of man's existence, as opposed to the materialistic preoccupation of the West. The liberal camp, including such men as Shu Hsin-ch'eng, V. K. Ting (Ting Wen-chiang), and Hu Shih (qq.v.) emphasized the material foundation of moral values and the importance of scientific method in achieving that material progress which is the indispensable basis for a moral life. Thus, Feng's book was another manifestation of the general concern in China about the validity of the Chinese way of life.

Feng stated in his book that the material world is real and that the universe exists independently of human purpose. The laws of nature, which are immutable, can be discovered through scientific experiments and logical reasoning. But human norms and values are relative: their validity is dependent upon their ability to harmonize the greatest number of conflicting human desires. Because human societies are not static, human values also change in accordance with changes in the social system. Feng adhered to the traditional Chinese view that the achievement of social harmony is the chief criterion for judging the worth of a particular social system. In this regard, he made the following statement: "For example, at present we all consider a socialist social system superior to a capitalist social system. Why? It is just because many of the human desires that can be satisfied by a socialist social system cannot be satisfied by a capitalist social system, while many of those human desires that can be satisfied by a capitalist social system can be satisfied by a socialist social system. The relative superiority of the socialist social system is due precisely to its ability to obtain a greater measure of 'harmony'."

In 1927 Feng was appointed professor of

philosophy at Tsinghua University. That year, he and his associates founded the *Che-hsueh p'ing-lun* [philosophical review], a journal which continued publication until the outbreak of the Sino-Japanese war in 1937. Feng was promoted in 1933 to chairman of the department of philosophy and dean of the college of arts at Tsinghua. Two years later, he helped to organize the Chung-kuo che-hsueh hui [philosophical society of China], which held its first meeting in Peiping.

Feng's major contribution to the history of philosophy was the two-volume *Chung-kuo che-hsueh-shih* [history of Chinese philosophy]. The first volume, published by the Shen-chou Publishing Company in Shanghai in 1931, covered what is perhaps the most brilliant period of Chinese philosophy—its beginnings to about 100 B.C. The first volume was reprinted by the Commercial Press in Shanghai in 1934, and a second volume, which covered the subject from about 100 B.C. to the twentieth century, was published. A separate supplement to the work appeared in 1936. The most complete work on the subject, Feng's *Chung-kuo che-hsueh-shih* won him acclaim in China. It became known in the West through the English translation of Derk Bodde, who attended Feng's class on Chinese philosophy in 1934–35 and undertook the task of translating the work shortly thereafter. The translation of the first volume was published in Peiping by Henri Vetch in the summer of 1937.

In his preface, Feng stated that his approach to the writing of the history of Chinese philosophy was influenced by the methodology of modern Western historiography. He asserted that up to the end of the Ch'ing dynasty China had had only ancient and medieval philosophies. He attributed the absence of modern philosophies to the fundamental stability of Chinese political, social, and economic institutions since the establishment of the Ch'in empire in the third century B.C. During the post-Ch'in period—which Feng called the Period of Classical Learning, as distinguished from the pre-Ch'in or ancient period, which he called the Period of Philosophers—philosophical discussions were essentially medieval in spirit because the philosophers expounded their views within the framework of the ancient systems. However, according to Feng, history is progressive, advancing from the simple to the complex. Therefore, although the

scholars of the Period of Classical Learning did not formulate completely new philosophical theories, they nevertheless refined, expanded, and modified the old concepts. But the intellectual and social changes in twentieth-century China were so great that the classical philosophies no longer sufficed for the needs of the modern generation, and the Period of Classical Learning finally came to an end.

Feng's *Chung-kuo che-hsueh-shih* was completed at a time when the methods of Chinese historical study were changing. The traditional writing of history by separate dynasties, with its obligatory categories of praise and blame and its cyclical interpretation of human events, had been discredited. In its place appeared histories written to present the linear progress of human societies and the interrelatedness of political, economic, and intellectual trends. Some historians subjected ancient documents and writings to searching criticism, questioning their reliability and authenticity, and others attempted to reconstruct the early history of China with the aid of modern archaeological discoveries. As the problems of political reform, economic reconstruction, war, and revolution increasingly claimed the attention of the nation's intellectuals, historians became involved in ideological disputes. Scholars often reconstructed the past to make a point about the present. Though stressing the philosophical thought of the past, Feng was also seeking inspiration for the construction of his own philosophical system, which he hoped would provide guidance to the Chinese people at a time of national crisis.

The Sino-Japanese war began in 1937. Peiping was lost to the Japanese soon after the beginning of hostilities. The three famous northern universities—Tsinghua, Peking, and Nankai—moved from the enemy-occupied zone to Changsha in Hunan province, where they combined their resources. The college of arts was located at Heng-shan, one of the five sacred mountains of China. During the four months that Feng was there, he drafted most of *Hsin li-hsueh* [new Neo-Confucianism]. The manuscript was finished in the summer of 1938 in Yunnan and the book was published in 1939. *Hsin shih-lun* [new culture and society] and *Hsin shih-hsun* [new self] were published in 1940, followed by *Hsin yuan jen* [new morality] in 1943, *Hsin yuan tao* [new philosophy] in 1944, and *Hsin chih yen* [new scholarship] in 1946.

Together with *Hsin li-hsueh*, these works constitute a complete philosophical system. Feng called them a "series written at a time of national rebirth" as an affirmation of his faith in China's ability to survive its gravest modern crisis.

The war touched Feng deeply. He saw his beloved country ravaged by an enemy, and he sent his eldest son to the Salween front in 1943. He returned in 1944 to his ancestral home in Honan, which he had not seen for some 20 years, to bury his mother in an enemy-infested province.

Feng's wartime series was reprinted many times during the 1940's. The metaphysical features of *Hsin li-hsueh* were summarized by Feng himself in the last chapter of *The Spirit of Chinese Philosophy* (the English translation of the *Hsin yuan tao* by E. R. Hughes, London, 1947). This work was basically a new development of the Neo-Confucianism of the Ch'eng-Chu school. The rationalist Neo-Confucian element was combined with Western realism and logic and with elements of negativism and transcendentalism found in Taoism. In a sense, Feng's philosophical system was in the mainstream of the Chinese philosophical tradition, although he modified tradition to suit the requirements of modern times. Of particular interest, in view of his later conversion to Marxism-Leninism, was his assertion that the economic foundation of a society determines its moral values. For this reason, he declared, neither parliamentary democracy nor Communism could be effective in contemporary China until the nation had been industrialized. The energy expended on ideological disputation, he concluded, might better be spent on economic construction.

At the end of the war, Feng went to the United States on a Rockefeller grant as a visiting professor at the University of Pennsylvania for the academic year 1946–47. He spent 1947–48 at the University of Hawaii. In April 1947 he participated in a colloquium on China held at Princeton University during its bicentennial celebrations. Princeton awarded him an honorary Doctor of Laws degree. During the year in Philadelphia, while he was collaborating with Derk Bodde on the English translation of the second volume of the *Chung-kuo che-hsueh-shih*, he decided to write, with Bodde's assistance, a brief version of his work for Western readers. This version also embodied a number of conclusions and interpretations

arrived at by Feng after the original publication of his work in China. In 1948 *A Short History of Chinese Philosophy* was published in New York. Although not an objective historical summary, it is a stimulating interpretation of Chinese philosophical history. The disproportionate emphasis placed on Sung Neo-Confucianism and on the Confucian way of spiritual development is in accordance with Feng's assertion that the history of Chinese philosophy is a continuous effort to discover the way of "sageness within and kingliness without."

After returning to China in the summer of 1948, Feng resumed his teaching post at Tsinghua University. During 1948–49 Professor Bodde, who was in China on a Fulbright fellowship, continued to work with Feng on the translation of the second volume of the *Chung-kuo che-hsueh-shih* despite the tensions that accompanied the final period of Nationalist rule in north China. (The English translation of the second volume was published in 1953 by the Princeton University Press, which also reissued the translation of the first volume.) In December 1948 troops of the Communist Fourth Field Army reached the Tsinghua campus, located just west of Peiping. Feng Yu-lan remained at the university during and after the takeover.

The Central People's Government, which was inaugurated on 1 October 1949, demanded intellectual conformity. As early as 11 October 1949, the Peking government promulgated a set of provisional regulations governing the teaching of humanities in institutions of higher learning. According to them, the teaching of philosophy was aimed at guiding students to a deeper understanding of the theory of dialectical materialism. They also required that the history of Chinese philosophy be interpreted in accordance with the tenets of Marxism-Leninism. Feng, together with other non-Communist intellectuals, was to undergo the process of thought reform.

The Communist revolution, by its very boldness and energy in tackling the problems of postwar China, was attractive to many Chinese intellectuals. Feng was particularly impressed by the agrarian reform program. In 1950 he wrote a letter to Mao Tse-tung saying that he was "unwilling to be a remnant of a bygone age in a time of greatness" and offering to participate in the remolding of his own ideas. Mao replied immediately, welcoming his decision. Subsequently, Feng went to a village and took part for a time in land reform.

Later in 1950 Feng wrote for the editors of the *Bol'shaia sovetskaia entsiklopediia* [great Soviet encyclopedia] an article on the development of Chinese philosophy in which he attempted for the first time to explain the history of Chinese thought in Marxist terms. The article ended with a tribute to Mao Tse-tung's *On Practice*, which, according to Feng's article, had solved the traditional Chinese philosophical problem of the relationship between "knowledge" and "practice" within the framework of Marxism-Leninism, thus showing the way for the present and future development of Chinese philosophy.

In 1952 the Central People's Government completed the reorganization of the country's institutions of higher education. Tsinghua became a polytechnical university. Its department of philosophy was transferred to Peking University, and Feng went to teach there. In 1956 he was appointed to the Chinese People's Political Consultative Conference. In keeping with the spirit of the Hundred Flowers Campaign, Feng was sent to Europe in the autumn to attend the Geneva meeting of intellectuals on the problem of tradition and innovation in the modern world. Then Feng went to Venice to attend a conference sponsored by the European Cultural Association. In his report on these meetings, he asserted that the preoccupation of the Western intellectuals with the "cultural crisis" of the modern world reflected the contradiction between advanced methods of production and backward social systems in the Western nations.

The Hundred Flowers Campaign and its attendant relaxation of ideological control did not last long. In 1957 an anti-rightist campaign was launched when the Communists came to realize the extent of the opposition to their policies despite years of indoctrination and government control of all public expression. Feng was not ostracized as a rightist, but official guardians of political orthodoxy regarded his former confessions of ideological errors as being insufficiently thorough, and his writing came under a barrage of criticism.

On 8 January 1957 Feng had published an article in the *Kuang-ming jih-pao* entitled "The Problem of Inheriting the Philosophical Heritage of China." He deplored the fact that the Peking authorities, by negating the relevance of much of China's philosophical tradition on the grounds that it was idealistic and feudalistic, hampered the teaching of the history of Chinese philosophy. He argued that such teaching had been unfruitful in meeting Mao Tse-tung's stated desire for a thorough reexamination of China's cultural heritage, "retaining its essence and discarding its dregs." Feng therefore proposed that certain traditional philosophical concepts and propositions be accepted as valid by abstracting them from their concrete, practical meaning as understood in traditional Chinese society. In other words, he argued that there are concepts and propositions which transcend the confines of class and time and can be applied equally well to feudal, bourgeois, or socialist societies. His Marxist critics declared that his position was essentially the same as the one advanced in his *Hsin li-hsueh* and that he had attempted to resuscitate the idealistic philosophies of traditional China under a new guise. From 1957 to 1959 Feng's philosophical ideas again became the target of criticism.

By 1960 the fury of the anti-rightist campaign had spent itself, and the intellectual atmosphere had become more relaxed. It was perhaps at this time that Feng began to write a new history of Chinese philosophy in accordance with Marxist theories as he understood them. In 1962 he published *Chung-kuo che-hsueh-shih shih-liao-hsueh ch'u-kao* [a provisional study of the materials for a history of Chinese philosophy] in which he reviewed and criticized the resources in the field. In 1964 *Chung-kuo che-hsueh-shih hsin-pien* [new history of Chinese philosophy] appeared. It covered the period from Shang to Eastern Han.

Feng's *Chung-kuo che-hsueh-shih* was reprinted in 1961. Perhaps its reprinting was an acknowledgment by the authorities that the book had no peer and that the author was deemed ideologically reliable. In any event, Feng pointed out in a new introduction that the principal value of the book was to serve as an example of how the history of Chinese philosophy was erroneously written from the standpoint of the bourgeois class and in accordance with the methodology of bourgeois historiography.

Feng's *Chung-kuo che-hsueh-shih* successfully utilized the methodology of modern historiography to systematically present the story of Chinese philosophy from the ancient period to the beginning of the twentieth century. His own philosophical system represents, to date, probably the most successful effort in modern times to revive Neo-Confucianism. In a period when different ideologies competed for the allegiance of the Chinese people, it was a great tribute to Feng that the voice of a philosopher, not identified with any political faction or party, was both heard and respected.

Feng Yu-lan had a younger brother, Feng Ching-lan, who was a scientist. His younger sister, Feng Shu-lan (1902–), better known as Feng Yuan-chün, was a graduate of the Women's Normal University at Peking who obtained the D.Litt. degree at the Sorbonne. She married Lu K'an-ju, and both she and her husband taught Chinese literature at Shantung University. In 1935 the couple collaborated on *Chung-kuo shih-shih* [history of Chinese poetry]. One of Feng Yuan-chün's major interests in the 1940's was the traditional theater, and in 1947 she published *Ku-chü shuo hui* [on the classical Chinese drama]. In 1957 she and Lu K'an-ju produced another joint work, *Chung-kuo ku-tien wen-hsueh chien-shih*, which was republished in English translation in 1958 by the Foreign Language Press at Peking as *A Short History of Classical Chinese Literature.*

Feng Yü-hsiang　　馮御香 (馮玉祥)
　Orig. Feng Chi-shan　馮基善
　T.　　Huan-chang　　煥章

Feng Yü-hsiang (1882–1 September 1948), military leader known as the Christian General, built up a formidable personal army, the Kuominchün, and dominated much of north China until his power was broken in 1930.

Although his native place was Chaohsien, Anhwei, Feng Yü-hsiang was born at Hsing-chi-chen, Chihli (Hopei), where his father, Feng Yü-mou, was serving as a minor army officer. He was the second of five sons. Feng attended school for about 15 months. Then, when he was ten years old, his name was entered on the rolls of a battalion of the Huai Army so that he could earn money to help support the family. When the first Sino-Japanese war broke out in 1894, Feng Yü-mou's battalion was sent to Taku, and Feng Yü-hsiang went with his father. After the unit returned to Paoting in 1896,

Feng became a full-fledged soldier in the Huai Army, and his formal military training began.

Although he was almost illiterate, Feng had a high regard for learning and began a program of self-education which would continue throughout his life. He gradually acquired the ability to read vernacular literature, and he read most of the famous Chinese novels. He studied a few historical and philosophical works, but had difficulty understanding the literary language in which such works were written.

After Li Hung-chang (ECCP, I, 464–71) died in 1901, Yuan Shih-k'ai succeeded him as the governor general of Chihli and began to expand his military forces. In 1902 Feng joined Yuan's guards unit and began to associate with better-educated officers in Yuan's army. One of the officers in the guards unit (which later became the 6th Division) was Lu Chien-chang. Feng married Lu's niece, probably in 1907. From the time of his marriage until Lu's murder in 1918, Feng profited from Lu's protection and influence.

Feng rose steadily in rank, becoming a company commander. In 1907 his unit was transferred to Manchuria for garrison duty at Hsinmin under Hsü Shih-ch'ang (q.v.). Feng became associated with a number of anti-Manchu officers, and in 1909 he participated in the formation of a so-called military study society. Another member of the society was Chang Chih-chiang (q.v.), who continued to be associated with Feng for a number of years. Feng later said that the objective of the society was the overthrow of the Ch'ing dynasty.

After the Wuchang revolt of October 1911, Feng was involved with a group of Peiyang Army officers who planned an uprising at Luanchou, Chihli, during the scheduled autumn maneuvers there. This group also included Lu Chung-lin, Han Fu-chü (qq.v.), and Chang Chih-chiang. Feng was imprisoned and dismissed from military service for using the regimental printing machine to print revolutionary broadsides before the uprising took place. Although the other conspirators carried out the uprising in December 1911, they were betrayed, and some of them were captured and executed. Feng was released after Lu Chien-chang interceded on his behalf and guaranteed his good behavior.

In 1912, on the recommendation of Lu Chien-chang, Feng was restored to the rolls of the Peiyang Army. He served as a battalion commander under Lu, with the assignment of recruiting and training troops in central-south Chihli. His unit grew steadily, and in 1913 it became a regiment. In October 1914 Feng's force was designated the 16th Mixed Brigade. The brigade became an independent unit which received orders directly from the central government. However, in a large operation it would come under the command of the over-all commanding officer.

In 1914 Feng became a Christian and joined the Methodist Church. As his military fame increased, he became known as the Christian General.

In the four years after the creation of the 16th Mixed Brigade, Feng and his men had few periods of inaction. In December 1915 Ts'ai O and T'ang Chi-yao (qq.v.), who opposed Yuan Shih-k'ai's plan to become monarch, began a rebellion in southwest China. Feng's brigade, which had been sent to Szechwan on a bandit-suppression mission, was assigned to resist the invasion of that province by Ts'ai O's forces and to assist Ch'en Huan, the military governor, in maintaining order. Feng came to sympathize with the rebels, although he clashed with them on several occasions, and on 22 May 1916 he forced Ch'en Huan to declare Szechwan independent. After Yuan Shih-k'ai died in June 1916, Feng was ordered to station his troops in the vicinity of Langfang, between Peking and Tientsin. He remained at Langfang until the spring of 1917, reorganizing and training his troops. Then, after objecting to a proposal by Tuan Ch'i-jui (q.v.) that would have divided the 16th Mixed Brigade, Feng was dismissed from his command and given a sinecure post. The officers of his brigade protested his removal, and Peking finally allowed the brigade to remain intact.

At Peking, the conflict between Li Yuan-hung (q.v.), the president, and Tuan Ch'i-jui, the premier, resulted in the restoration attempt of Chang Hsün (q.v.). Tuan Ch'i-jui called on the 16th Mixed Brigade to be the vanguard of the anti-restoration army. It became clear that only Feng Yü-hsiang could order the brigade into action, and his rank was restored. The 16th Mixed Brigade was one of the first units to enter Peking and defeat Chang Hsün's troops. After winning control at Peking in early

1918, Tuan Ch'i-jui attempted to unify China by military means. Feng Yü-hsiang and his brigade were ordered into action in Hupeh. In February, Feng reached Wuhsueh, Hupeh, but he then refused to accept further orders from Peking and issued a public statement advocating a truce between north and south China and the settlement of outstanding issues at a peace conference. Feng was stripped of his command by order of Feng Kuo-chang (q.v.), then the president, and his case was referred to Ts'ao K'un (q.v.) for investigation. Ts'ao intervened on Feng's behalf, and Feng was permitted to remain in his post under Ts'ao's command.

In June 1918 Feng Yü-hsiang was restored to rank by Tuan Ch'i-jui and was made defense commissioner of Ch'angte. He remained there for nearly two years, devoting his energies to the training and indoctrination of his troops. Although the principles and methods of training employed at this time later were modified in detail, they remained characteristic of Feng's training programs throughout his career. He stressed physical fitness, which was achieved through hard military training and competitive athletics; the forced march became the army's forte. He permitted no corruption or favoritism in his army. Officers were chosen on the basis of merit, and they shared the life of the men and led them in battle. Feng maintained close personal contact with his officers and men. Above all, he subjected his troops to intensive moral indoctrination. Until late 1926, when Feng joined the Kuomintang, this indoctrination involved a combination of Christian and traditional Chinese values which stressed the individual's moral obligations to society, to himself, and to God. After 1926, some of the Christian elements of Feng's indoctrination program were replaced by Sun Yat-sen's Three People's Principles. However, the change was not great: both before and after 1926 Feng's men were taught that they were the servants of the common people and that moral value was attached to their behaving as such. Feng himself remained the final arbiter of what acts were good for the people, and of what behavior was moral. In this fashion, he maintained close and complete control over his army.

As defense commissioner, Feng also was responsible for the civil administration of

Ch'angte and the surrounding vicinity. His reforms reflected his philosophy of civil government. These included: the establishment of peace and order by vigorous suppression of bandits and other disorderly elements; the promotion of public education; the prohibition of such vices as gambling, prostitution, and the use of opium; the establishment of institutions of social welfare, such as rehabilitation centers for beggars, sanitaria for narcotics addicts, and orphanages; the prohibition of such traditional practices as foot-binding; and the use of his troops for such tasks as repairing city walls, building roads, and planting trees.

The years from 1918 to 1920 were marked by constant strife between the Anhwei faction of Tuan Ch'i-jui and Hsü Shu-cheng (qq.v.) and the Chihli group, in which Ts'ao K'un and Wu P'ei-fu (q.v.) were prominent. Feng's association with the Chihli group had begun in the spring of 1918. Tuan Ch'i-jui and his supporters were overthrown at Peking after the Chihli-Anhwei war of 1920, and a number of changes were made in provincial administrations. In July, Feng Yü-hsiang and his men left Ch'angte and went to southern Honan, where they remained until the spring of 1921. His brigade then was ordered, on the recommendation of Wu P'ei-fu, to assist the newly appointed tuchün [military governor] of Shensi, Yen Hsiang-wen (T. Huan-chang), in ousting Ch'en Shu-fan, who had refused to leave his post as governor. As a reward for his success in that undertaking, Feng was ordered on 5 August to reorganize his brigade as the 11th Division. Shortly thereafter Yen Hsiang-wen committed suicide, and on 25 August 1921 Feng was appointed military governor of Shensi.

Feng remained in Shensi until April 1922, when he marched into Honan to support Wu P'ei-fu in the first Chihli-Fengtien war. One of Feng's brigades, led by Li Ming-chung, fought in Chihli province and was instrumental in the victory that initiated the rout of Chang Tso-lin. Feng himself led troops to suppress a rebellion by the military governor of Honan. On 10 May, he became military governor of that province. He expanded his forces, filling out his division and creating three new mixed brigades. However, on 31 October he was ordered to Peking as inspecting commissioner of the army. Although the appointment

supposedly was a promotion, it diminished Feng's power by depriving him of a regional base and of access to tax revenues. Feng's transfer was largely the result of friction between him and Wu P'ei-fu. Relations between the two men worsened in the spring and summer of 1923, when Feng cooperated with anti-Wu (and pro-Ts'ao K'un) factions to oust Li Yuan-hung from the presidency. On 5 October, Ts'ao K'un was elected president. Feng's financial situation improved because he was able to gain control of the octroi, a tax on merchandise coming into Peking.

Later that year, Feng Yü-hsiang's personal life underwent an important change. On 17 December 1923 his wife died. On 19 February 1924, Feng married Li Te-ch'uan (q.v.), who, unlike his first wife, was educated, active in Christian church-work, and able to assist Feng in social and educational projects.

After the second Chihli-Fengtien war began in the autumn of 1924, Wu P'ei-fu assigned Feng Yü-hsiang to the Jehol front, in spite of rumors that Feng would declare his neutrality. To insure Feng's reliability, Wu assigned two officers, Hu Ching-i (d.1925; T. Li-seng) and Wang Ch'eng-pin (b. 1873; T. Hsiao-po) to keep watch on Feng's movements. However, Hu, Wang, and Sun Yüeh (1878–1928; T. Yü-hsing), the garrison commander at Peking, had joined with Feng in a conspiracy against Wu. Feng and his cohorts occupied Peking on 23 October 1924. Ts'ao K'un was forced to dismiss Wu P'ei-fu from his posts and to call for a cessation of hostilities. Wu, though cut off from reinforcements in central China and badly defeated by Chang Tso-lin's forces at Shanhaikuan, hastened to Tientsin with a small contingent of troops. He was defeated, and the war came to an end.

Immediately after the coup, Feng Yü-hsiang, Hu Ching-i, and Sun Yüeh had reorganized their armies as the First, Second, and Third armies of the Kuominchün, or People's Army. Feng was named commander in chief.

On 2 November 1924 Feng forced Ts'ao K'un to resign the presidency and set up an interim regency government under Huang Fu (q.v.). On 5 November, he forced P'u-yi (q.v.), the last Manchu emperor, to leave the Forbidden City at Peking. Feng, Chang Tso-lin, and Lu Yung-hsiang met at Tientsin on 10 November for a series of conferences with Tuan Ch'i-jui to organize a new government. Tuan became provisional chief executive. However, not one of Feng's supporters was included in his cabinet.

At the beginning of 1925 Feng established headquarters in Kalgan. His supporters Chang Chih-chiang and Li Ming-chung were now the military governors of Chahar and Suiyuan, respectively. Feng came to control Kansu in August. Throughout this period, Feng and Chang Tso-lin contended for political control of the government at Peking. In the Northwest, Chang's control of the north China coast meant that there was no access to the sea from the regions under Feng's control. Feng had to look to the Soviet Union for military supplies. Since Soviet advisers then were guiding the Kuomintang, Feng could hardly resist Russian-Kuomintang overtures. Also, one of Feng's political advisers was Hsü Ch'ien (q.v.), who had supported Sun Yat-sen's cause for years. In April 1925 Feng, in return for Russian instructors and military aid, agreed to permit Kuomintang political work in his army. However, Feng severely limited Kuomintang and Russian political activity in the Kuominchün and expanded his program of Christian indoctrination.

Chang Tso-lin was determined to extend his influence to Peking and north China, as well as to the Yangtze provinces. Late in 1925, therefore, the long anticipated war between Feng Yü-hsiang, on one side, and Chang Tso-lin and Wu P'ei-fu, on the other, broke out. Feng had come to a covert arrangement with Kuo Sung-ling, a leading Fengtien general, and he counted heavily on Kuo's defection to undermine Chang Tso-lin's position. Kuo, however, was defeated and executed in December 1925; and, at the same time, Feng's Kuominchün troops suffered heavy casualties when taking Tientsin from the Fengtien forces. Caught between his two antagonists, Feng sought to arrange a compromise settlement. He announced that he was resigning all his posts and declared that he would take a trip abroad.

The armies, however, showed no inclination to end hostilities. On 8 March 1926 Feng's Kuominchün mined and blockaded the harbor at Taku, near Tientsin, against Chang Tso-lin's naval force. The blockade was challenged at once by the Japanese, who accused the government at Peking of violating the provisions of the Boxer Protocol. The Japanese also enlisted the support of the foreign diplomatic corps at Peking, which on 16 March issued an ultimatum to the Peking government calling for an immediate withdrawal of the blockade. The next day, representatives of various organizations and student groups in Peking, under joint Kuomintang-Communist leadership, petitioned Tuan Ch'i-jui to reject the foreign ultimatum. The protest delegation was met by government guards, who opened fire and injured several petitioners. On 18 March, a mass protest meeting was held in the square at T'ien-an-men, the south gate of the Forbidden City. The demonstrators then headed for Tuan's office where they were confronted by government guards, who reportedly killed more than 40 of the demonstrators. The next day, Tuan Ch'i-jui ordered the arrest of four prominent Kuomintang members—Hsü Ch'ien, Li Shih-tseng, Ku Meng-yü, and Yi P'ei-chi—and of the Communist leader Li Ta-chao. They were charged with instigating the 18 March incident and with disseminating Communist propaganda.

Hsü Ch'ien and his associates, protected by Lu Chung-lin, then the Kuominchün commander of the Peking garrison, were temporarily safe from arrest. Within a month, however, Chang Tso-lin and Wu P'ei-fu pressed their attack, and Lu Chung-lin was forced to evacuate Peking on 15 April. Hsü Ch'ien fled to Kalgan and then joined Feng Yü-hsiang at Urga (Ulan Bator).

After his troops had been defeated at Tientsin, Feng had gone to Suiyuan. Near the end of March 1926, he had left Suiyuan to go to Urga, where he awaited the arrival af Hsü Ch'ien. After discussions at Urga with Hsü Ch'ien and Borodin, Feng finally agreed to join the Kuomintang. Accompanied by Hsü, he then traveled overland to Moscow. He arrived there on 9 May 1926 and remained in the Soviet Union for about three months. During that time he visited various institutions, talked with a number of Soviet leaders, obtained agreements for the delivery of military supplies to his forces, and received some indoctrination in the precepts of Marxism-Leninism.

Hsü Ch'ien left Moscow in July 1926 after hearing that the Northern Expedition had been launched. Feng himself departed on 17 August for Outer Mongolia and China. One month later he reached Wuyuan, Suiyuan, where he resumed command of the Kuominchün. On 16 September 1926 he issued a long statement on his political position. He formally accepted membership in the Kuomintang, stated that he would accept the decisions of the First and Second National congresses of the Kuomintang, and stressed his support of the party's anti-imperialist stand.

By the time Feng made his formal public declaration of allegiance to the Kuomintang, the forces of the National Revolutionary Army had made good progress on their drive northward from Canton. Feng then led his troops into Shensi; he consolidated control of the province before the end of 1926. He then moved into Honan. Although his troops were fatigued, Feng's leadership spurred the drive to seize Chengchow, the provincial capital. He consolidated control of northern Honan in the spring of 1927.

Feng then held an important position between the contending regimes at Wuhan and Nanking, and both factions sought his support. He conferred with representatives of the Wuhan group at Chengchow from 10 to 13 June 1927. The Wuhan delegation included Wang Ching-wei, T'ang Sheng-chih, T'an Yen-k'ai, Hsü Ch'ien, Sun Fo, and Yü Yu-jen. They agreed to give Feng control of Honan and acceded to his other demands, but he did not commit himself. Then, from 19 to 21 June, Feng conferred with Chiang Kai-shek at Hsuchow. He decided to cast his lot with Nanking. After returning from Hsuchow, Feng began to purge the Communist political workers in areas under his control. His decision to join Chiang and his subsequent actions shattered the political plans of the Wuhan regime and ended the effectiveness of the Russian advisers in China.

For the second stage of the Northern Expedition, beginning in 1928, Feng's armies (he then had about 30 divisions) comprised the Second Army Group, with Feng as commander in chief. His troops played an important part in the final drive northward, and his subordinate generals, notably Sun Liang-ch'eng, Lu Chung-lin, and Han Fu-chü, were prominent field commanders.

After the fall of Peking on 8 June 1928, the question of troop disbandment arose. In July, the commanders of the four army groups—Chiang Kai-shek, Feng Yü-hsiang, Yen Hsi-shan, and Li Tsung-jen—met to discuss this question. Feng and Yen disagreed about the principles that should guide this process, and the problem was left to be solved after the reorganization of the National Government.

In October 1928, when the new National Government was established at Nanking, Feng Yü-hsiang was named minister of war and vice chairman of the Executive Yuan. He retained regional power through his control of Honan, Shensi, Kansu, and part of Shantung.

The troops disbandment conference was held in January 1929, and formal agreement was reached on disbandment and military reorganization; however, the decisions of the conference were not implemented. Relations between Feng Yü-hsiang and Chiang Kai-shek became strained. Feng held that Chiang's plan for troop disbandment was designed to concentrate military power in the hands of Chiang's close associates. In April, Chiang took control of Shantung, thus depriving Feng of direct access to the sea. Feng accused Chiang of packing the Third National Congress of the Kuomintang and of favoring the troops under his direct command in the distribution of military funds. On 20 May 1929 Feng in effect declared his independence of the National Government. He was dismissed from all government and party offices, and a punitive expedition was ordered.

Feng had concentrated his forces in Honan and Shensi, and in challenging Chiang Kai-shek's power he planned to rely heavily on the strength of Han Fu-chü (q.v.) in Honan. However, in late May 1929, as the opposing forces were being deployed, Han, Shih Yü-san, Ma Hung-k'uei (q.v.), and thousands of troops defected to the National Government side. The defections deprived Feng of some of his most experienced soldiers and of economic and strategic control of Honan.

On 10 October 1929 leading Kuominchün officers addressed a public telegram to Feng Yü-hsiang and Yen Hsi-shan denouncing the policies of the National Government and asking them to rectify the situation. Chiang Kai-shek ordered an expedition against the Kuominchün, and the fighting began in western Honan in mid-October. Yen Hsi-shan did not take part in the conflict, and the campaign ended when the Kuominchün withdrew from Honan in late November.

In February 1930 Yen Hsi-shan finally indicated that he had joined with Feng Yü-hsiang in opposing Chiang Kai-shek. They formed what came to be known as the northern coalition or the Yen-Feng movement. They received some support from Li Tsung-jen, Pai Ch'ung-hsi, and Chang Fa-k'uei (qq.v.), who conferred about coordinating their military plans with those of the northern coalition and decided to abandon Kwangsi in favor of a drive toward Wuhan. On 10 May Feng Yü-hsiang issued orders for a general offensive, and fighting began the next day. The Kwangsi forces advanced quickly, but were defeated near Hengyang in mid-June (see Huang Shao-hung) and eliminated from the campaign. However, Yen Hsi-shan and Feng Yü-hsiang won the support of Wang Ching-wei and the so-called Reorganizationist faction of the Kuomintang and of other groups opposed to Chiang Kai-shek. They met in the so-called enlarged conference in July and August to organize an opposition government at Peiping. In the meantime, heavy fighting had begun in Shantung and Honan.

At the beginning of September 1930 the northerners lost Shantung. At this point, the northern coalition could be saved only by the intervention of Chang Hsueh-liang (q.v.) and his Manchurian forces. Both sides had courted Chang throughout the campaign, but he had remained neutral. However, he doomed the northerners when, on 18 September, he intervened as a neutral and sent troops to north China. By early October, the war had ended. Feng was forced to relinquish control of his forces, which subsequently were reorganized as National Government troops.

The collapse of the northern coalition and the dispersion of his troops marked the end of Feng Yü-hsiang as a military and political force in China. From 1931 until his death in 1948, Feng held posts in the National Government and the Kuomintang, but he never again wielded power.

In December 1931 Feng was reinstated as a member of the Central Executive Committee of the Kuomintang and was made a member of the State Council. He was appointed minister of interior in February 1932, but he did not take up the duties of that office. He formally resigned two months later. In October, he went to Kalgan; he remained there until the spring of 1933 when the Japanese, having occupied Jehol province, began to advance into Chahar. Then, on 26 May 1933, Feng appointed himself commander in chief of the so-called People's Allied Anti-Japanese Army. He vigorously denounced the National Government for failing to resist Japanese aggression and hastily began to assemble troops. However, both Nanking and Tokyo opposed his action, and he was forced to retire in early August. He went to Shantung and lived in seclusion on the sacred mountain T'ai-shan for about two years.

Feng accepted an appointment as vice chairman of the Military Affairs Commission on 6 January 1936 and took up residence at Nanking. He gave many speeches urging national resistance to Japan. After the Sino-Japanese war broke out and the National Government moved to Chungking, he held such posts as minister of water conservancy and member of the Supreme National Defense Council. However, he was not permitted to play an active role in directing wartime activities.

In September 1946 the National Government announced that Feng would head a mission to the United States to study irrigation and conservation facilities. Accompanied by his wife, Feng sailed from Shanghai in late September. The United States government had arranged a comprehensive tour of water control and other engineering projects. Feng followed about the first third of the planned itinerary, but then discontinued the tour. From mid-1947 on, he devoted himself mainly to public lectures, delivered through an interpreter, in which he attacked Chiang Kai-shek as the man responsible for the existing chaos in China. He soon was ordered to return to China, on the grounds that his study of water conservation in the United States had been completed, but he demurred, explaining in a public speech that his life would be forfeit if he returned to Chinese Nationalist jurisdiction.

At the beginning of January 1948, Feng was elected to the central committee of the Revolutionary Committee of the Kuomintang, founded by Li Chi-shen (q.v.) and others at Hong Kong with the announced intention of opposing the central political apparatus of the party dominated by Chiang Kai-shek. On 7 January, the Central Supervisory Committee of the Kuomintang at Nanking formally expelled him from the party for disloyalty. In April, Feng registered with the United States Department of Justice as an agent of the Revolutionary Committee of the Kuomintang. In July, he and his wife sailed from New York aboard a Russian ship, the Pobeda, bound for Odessa. On 1 September, just before the ship reached Odessa, a fire broke out on board. Feng was caught in the fire and died, apparently of asphyxiation or a heart attack. The circumstances of Feng's death naturally gave rise to much comment and speculation, but no evidence was discovered to indicate that it was anything other than an accident. On 15 October 1953, in a special commemorative ceremony held in China, his ashes were buried at T'ai-shan in Shantung province. Feng's widow, Li Te-ch'uan, landed at Odessa in 1948 and then traveled through the Soviet Union to Manchuria.

Feng Yü-hsiang was known to have had ten children. Five of these, two sons and three daughters, were by his first wife. He and Li Te-ch'uan had two sons and three daughters.

Feng Yü-hsiang's important publications include *Wo-ti sheng-huo* [my life], an autobiographical account of his life up to 1928, and *Wo so jen-shih ti Chiang Chieh-shih* [the Chiang Kai-shek I knew], his highly critical recollection of Chiang Kai-shek; these were published in Shanghai in 1947 and 1949 respectively. Among his earlier works are his diary covering the period from 25 November 1920 to the end of 1927, *Feng Yü-hsiang jih-chi*, published in 1932; and several volumes of speeches and reports delivered in 1936 and 1937, *Feng tsai Nan-ching chiang-yen chi*, *Feng tsai Nan-ching pao-kao chi*, *Feng tsai Nan-ching ti-i nien*, and *Feng tsai Nan-ching ti-erh nien*. A collection of his 1938–39 speeches entitled *Feng fu-wei-yüan-chang k'ang-chan yen-lun chi* [vice chairman Feng's collected speeches on the war of resistance] appeared in 1940. Feng also wrote poetry. When in seclusion at T'ai-shan in 1933, he wrote the poems that accompany Chao Wang-yün's sketches in *Chao Wang-yün nung-ts'un hsieh-sheng chi* [Chao Wang-yün's drawings of village life], published in 1934. A collection of verse, *Feng Yü-hsiang shih ko hsüan chi* [selected poems by Feng Yü-hsiang]

was published in Shanghai in 1957. A comprehensive biography, *Chinese Warlord: The Career of Feng Yü-hsiang*, by James E. Sheridan, appeared in 1966.

Fong Sec: *see* K'UANG FU-CHO.

Fu Ssu-nien	傅 斯 年
T. Meng-chen	孟 眞

Fu Ssu-nien (26 March 1896–20 December 1950), a leader in the May Fourth Movement who became an historian and an administrator of historical scholarship. He organized the Academia Sinica's institute of history and philology and served as its director for more than 20 years. He acted as director of the Academia Sinica during the Sino-Japanese war. In Taiwan, he served as chancellor of National Taiwan University.

Born into a scholarly family in Liaoch'eng, Shantung, which boasted descent from Fu I-chien (ECCP, I, 253), who was the first scholar to receive a degree of chuang-yüan or optimus in the Ch'ing dynasty and who later became a grand secretary, Fu Ssu-nien was orphaned at the age of eight. He was brought up by his paternal grandfather, a senior licentiate and sometime director of studies. Between 1905 and 1908 Fu attended primary school in Liaoch'eng, and he also was tutored in the Chinese classics by his grandfather. In 1909 he entered the Prefectural Middle School in Tientsin, from which he was graduated in the winter of 1912. In the summer of 1913 Fu entered the preparatory department of Peking University. In 1916, having made a brilliant academic record, he was admitted to the department of Chinese literature. He was graduated from Peking University late in 1919.

In the autumn of 1917 Fu Ssu-nien, together with his roommate Ku Chieh-kang (q.v.) and Hsü Yen-chih, discussed the idea of starting a magazine to support the new thought and literature movements. With the aid of Ch'en Tu-hsiu and Li Ta-chao (qq.v.), Fu and his friends obtained funds and a meeting place in the Peking University library. Hu Shih was their faculty adviser. On 13 October 1918 the first preparatory meeting was held. Lo Chia-lun (q.v.) suggested the title *Hsin-ch'ao* [new tide] and Hsü Yen-chih proposed the English subtitle "Renaissance" for the new magazine. The students, who formed the Hsin-ch'ao Society, also adopted a platform stressing critical analysis of ideas and events, scientific thinking, and revolutionary, or vernacular, language. The first issue of the magazine appeared on 1 January 1919. Before it ceased publication in March 1922, the *Hsin-ch'ao* had carried articles by such writers as Yü P'ing-po, Yeh Sheng-t'ao, Feng Yu-lan, Chu Tzu-ch'ing, and Mao Tzu-shui. In the first issue, Fu expressed agreement with Lo Chia-lun's contention that the "new tide" of the twentieth century was social revolution on the Russian model, and added that Russia would soon "annex" the world, not in territory but in thought. Fu's attitude was typical of the members of the Hsin-ch'ao Society, who tended at that time to be more radical than Ch'en Tu-hsiu, Hu Shih, or Li Ta-chao. The Hsin-ch'ao Society was not merely a literary club, but an active political group. Lo Chia-lun, the editor of the magazine, was one of the four student representatives who entered the American legation at Peking on 4 May 1919 to present a memorandum of grievances concerning the Paris Peace Conference decision on Shantung. Fu himself was "marshal" of the historic demonstration. Fu Ssu-yen, Fu Ssu-nien's younger brother, received credit for having been the first of a band of five students to storm the mansion of Ts'ao Ju-lin (q.v.). Fu Ssu-nien published articles in the vernacular in defense of the new literature and produced poems in the new medium in imitation of Hu Shih. He was also one of the first to recognize the talents of Mao Tse-tung; he said that Mao's shortlived magazine *Hsiang River Review* was one of the six best publications in China. Fu's association with the Hsin-ch'ao Society ended in late 1919 when he sailed for England on a scholarship provided by the Shantung provincial government. Yü P'ing-po and Lo Chia-lun also went abroad to study, and other members of the Hsin-ch'ao Society began to drift away from Peking University. The heyday of the Hsin-ch'ao Society had been short, and the group had never numbered more than about 40 members, but most of them, like Fu, were leaders in the May Fourth Movement and subsequently played important roles in the intellectual and social development of China.

Fu Ssu-nien spent almost seven years in Europe. He arrived in England in January 1920. Yü P'ing-po, who was with him, soon succumbed to homesickness and returned to China, but not before Fu had followed him to Paris and Marseilles in a vain effort to dissuade him. From 1920 to 1922 Fu studied history at the University of London and attended lectures in mathematics and experimental psychology. From September 1923 to October 1926 he studied philosophy and history at Berlin University. None of his studies led to a degree. However, Fu made the acquaintance of Yü Ta-wei (q.v.), and Yü introduced him to Yü Ta-ts'ai, whom he later married.

Fu returned to China and joined the faculty of National Chungshan University in Canton in January 1927. He became head of the departments of Chinese and history, and for a time he served as acting dean of its college of arts. In the summer of 1927 Fu established a research institute for history and philology at Chungshan. During this period, Fu was active not only as an administrator but also as a scholar. His long correspondence (carried on from Europe) with Ku Chieh-kang about early Chinese history was published at this time in the weekly bulletin of the new history and philology institute.

Fu's growing reputation as a scholar and his success as an administrator led in August 1928 to his appointment as research fellow and director of the institute of history and philology in the newly established Academia Sinica, a position he was to hold for 22 years. At that time the institute had three sections: history, headed by Ch'en Yin-k'o (q.v.); philology, headed by Chao Yuen-ren (q.v.); and archeology, headed by Li Chi (q.v.). Fu Ssu-nien was fortunate in his subordinates and highly successful in coordinating their efforts as well as in procuring adequate government support for them. In October 1928 he supervised the publication of the first issue of *Collected Studies in History and Philology (Chi-k'an)*, the new institute's journal. In the first issue, Fu, in imitation of the *Historische Zeitschrift* (1859), defined the objective of the institute as progress in all fields of study to be achieved by research in primary sources, by enlargement of the fields of research through the discovery and investigation of new primary sources, and by the development of new research tools. In carrying out these resolves, Fu's achievements of the next two decades were impressive. Perhaps the institute's most important work during this period was the excavations at Anyang, which established the historicity of the Shang dynasty (c.1523–1028 B.C.). The institute also supervised the digging of the neolithic site at Ch'eng-tzu-yai in Shantung, the type site for the Black Pottery culture. The department of philology undertook a valuable series of dialect surveys, including tribal languages of the southwest, and the history department published a series of studies on sources of Ming and Ch'ing history. Fu moved the institute to Peiping in 1929 and began collecting a library which by 1937 totaled 150,000 volumes. In January 1936 Fu became *de facto* head of the Academia Sinica by succeeding V. K. Ting as secretary general at a time when the president, Ts'ai Yuan-p'ei, was incapacitated by illness. In 1937, to insure the safety of the institute and its collections, notably the Central Museum, Fu supervised its evacuation to Nanking. In 1938 he organized the evacuation of the Academia Sinica to Kunming by way of Changsha and Kweilin, and he moved it to Szechwan in 1941.

In 1930 Fu became professor of history at Peking University. He published a summary of his methods, "Shih-hsueh fang-fa t'ao-lun chiang-i kao" [provisional syllabus on historiography], in the sixth issue of *Chi-k'an*. As a historian, he made significant contributions to the study of the Shang and Chou dynasties and to the study of Chinese intellectual history. In 1930 he published an article, "Hsin-huo pu-tz'u hsieh-pen hou-chi pa" [notes on a newly discovered oracle-bone inscription], in which he applied epigraphic evidence to the problem of the relationship between the Shang and Chou states and to the origin of the Ch'u state. In 1932, after the Japanese occupation of Manchuria, Fu published the first volume of his projected *Tung-pei shih-kang* [outline of Manchurian history]. He submitted it as a memorandum to the Lytton Commission, which was investigating the Mukden Incident on behalf of the League of Nations. This hastily prepared volume was severely criticized by such historians as Miao Feng-lin, and Fu decided to give up the project. In 1937–38 he prepared for publication the *Hsing-ming ku-hsun pien-cheng*

[studies on the ancient meanings of "nature" and "destiny"], which appeared in 1940. In the 1932–36 period he also wrote a number of current events articles for the *Tu-li p'ing-lun* [independent critic] and for the Tientsin *Ta Kung Pao*.

From 1938 to 1948 Fu was a prominent member of the People's Political Council, and he participated in political consultations between the National Government and the Communists. He visited Yenan and returned thoroughly disillusioned with the Chinese Communists. Nevertheless, he was a fearless critic of administrative defects in the Nationalist regime. In 1945 he was appointed acting chancellor of Peking University. He served in the post for three years and added colleges of engineering, agriculture, and medicine to the existing colleges of arts, science, and law. In 1946 he supervised the return of the institute of history and philology from Lichuang, Szechwan, to Nanking. In 1947, exhausted by his wartime and postwar activities and suffering from chronic high blood pressure, he went to the United States for treatment and rest. He spent almost a year in New Haven, Connecticut.

In the spring of 1948 Fu was elected *in absentia* to the Legislative Yuan and was appointed an academician of the Academia Sinica. After he returned to China in August, he was asked by Chu Chia-hua, the president of the Academia Sinica, to organize its evacuation to Taiwan. Because of the bulkiness of its equipment, the institute of science and engineering could not be moved, but the institute of history and philology and the mathematical research department of the institute of science and engineering were moved safely. The invaluable library of the institute of history and philology was transported to Taiwan without appreciable loss.

In January 1949 Fu became chancellor of Taiwan University. In December 1950, while reporting on conditions at the university to the Taiwan provincial assembly, he suffered an attack of high blood pressure and died. In commemoration of his services to the university, Fu's remains were interred on campus in a specially constructed Greek-style mausoleum. His collected works, *Fu Meng-chen hsien-sheng chi*, in six volumes, were published in Taipei in 1951, with a preface by Hu Shih.

Fu Ssu-nien married twice. His first wife, whom he married in 1911, was Ting Fu-ts'ui. They were divorced in 1934, and Fu then married Yü Ta-ts'ai.

Fu Tseng-hsiang   傅 增 湘
T. Shu-ho   叔 和
H. Yuan-shu   沅 叔

Fu Tseng-hsiang (1872–1950), scholar-official and bibliophile, introduced educational reforms and established schools in Chihli (Hopei) during the last decade of the Ch'ing period. After holding such posts as minister of education (1917–19) he withdrew from public life and became a noted bibliophile.

Little is known of Fu Tseng-hsiang's early years except that he was born in Chiangan, Szechwan, and that in 1872 his family left that province for north China. He became a chü-jen in 1888, and three years later he moved to Paoting, Chihli (Hopei), where he studied under Wu Ju-lun (ECCP, II, 870–72) at the Lien-ch'ih Academy. For the next six years he served on the staff of Lao Nai-hsuan at the Ch'iu-shih Academy at Hangchow. Fu won the chin-shih degree in 1898.

Fu became an adviser to Yuan Shih-k'ai. In the last years of the Ch'ing period, he was responsible for a number of educational reforms in Chihli and served as commissioner of education. In 1903, together with Ying Lien-chih (q.v.) and Yao Hsi-kuang (b. 1870; T. Shih-ch'üan), he founded one of the first schools for girls in north China. Lu Ching (1856–1948; T. Mien-chih), a chü-jen of 1885 who in 1929 donated both books and money for a library at Nankai University in Tientsin, was also associated with the school. In 1905 Yuan Shih-k'ai directed Fu Tseng-hsiang to establish the Peiyang nü-tzu shih-fan hsueh-t'ang [Peiyang girls normal school] at Tientsin; that school was managed by Wu Ting-ch'ang and by the wife of Wang Chih-ming. In June 1908 Fu was asked to establish another normal school for girls at Peking, the Ching-shih nü-tzu shih-fan hsueh-t'ang. Hu Yü-jen (1866–1920), who later was responsible for the establishment of many modern schools in Shanghai and Wusih, was appointed to direct the Peking school. During his term as commissioner of education in Chihli, Fu made a tour of the province, at the conclusion of which he proposed a plan to establish junior normal schools at Paoting, Tientsin, Luanchou, and Hsingt'ai. However, the outbreak of the revolution of 1911 forced him to abandon the project.

After the revolution, Fu Tseng-hsiang was appointed an adviser to T'ang Shao-yi, who represented Yuan Shih-k'ai in peace negotiations with the provisional government of Sun Yat-sen. In 1917 Fu accepted an invitation to become minister of education at Peking under Wang Shih-chen, the premier, and he held that office until May 1919. In 1922 Fu was assigned to prepare a detailed report on loans, both domestic and international, that had been made to the Peking government. He worked on that task for more than a year and compiled a comprehensive report in five volumes. He then withdrew from official life and devoted his time to bibliographical studies and to travel in China.

Fu Tseng-hsiang had inherited from his grandfather a rare Hsing-wen-shu edition of the famous *Tzu-chih t'ung-chien* [comprehensive mirror for aid in government], prepared in the Sung dynasty by Ssu-ma Kuang (1018–1086). He acquired another complete set of that massive work from the private library of Tuan-fang (ECCP, II, 780–82). Since he possessed two copies of the *Tzu-chih t'ung-chien*, Fu named his personal library the Shuang-chien-lou. In his early years, Fu had made the acquaintance of such prominent bibliophiles as Miao Ch'uan-sun, Tung K'ang (qq.v), and Ts'ao Yuan-chung (d. 1927; T. K'uei-i); after 1911 he met Chang Yuan-chi, Yang Shou-ching (qq.v), and other scholars specializing in bibliographical studies. Fu Tseng-hsiang was able to acquire on the open market many works from private collections, notably those of Pao-hsi (b. 1871; T. Jui-ch'en) and Sheng-yü (ECCP, II, 648–50). In 20 years he collected more than 66,000 chüan of rare Chinese books, including 3,600 chüan of Sung, Liao, and Chin editions; 2,500 chüan of Yuan editions; and 30,000 chüan of Ming editions; as well as manuscripts which had been collated by renowned Chinese scholars. In 1918 Fu Tseng-hsiang added a new wing, which he called the Ts'ang-yuan, to his private library in Peking, and there he did most of the work of collating bibliographical notes on books in his collection. The most important of these works were the *Shuang-chien-lou shan-pen shu-mu* [catalogue of rare books in the Shuang-chien-lou], with a supplement issued in 1919, and the *Ts'ang-yuan chün-shu t'i-chi ch'u-chi* [preliminary listing of books in the Ts'ang-yuan collection], with supplements issued in 1938 and 1943. Fu was consulted by Japanese sinologists and librarians engaged in purchasing Chinese classical books in Tientsin and Peking. He served as an adviser to Hashikawa Tokio in his educational and literary activities for the Japanese occupation authorities. Fu wrote the preface to Hashikawa's *Chūgoku bunkakai jimbutsu sōkan*, a biographical dictionary of more than 4,000 Chinese leaders in the fields of education, art, and letters who were alive after 1912. The book was published in Peking in 1940.

Fu Tseng-hsiang compared the books in his possession with other editions and exchanged items with other collectors. Unlike some other collectors, he was willing to publish editions of rare books in his collection. Of his books thus published, one was a portion of the great Ming compendium, the *Yung-lo ta-tien* [encyclopedia of the Yung-lo period]; Fu published two manuscripts of the original volumes 2,610 and 2,611. He also published such works as the *Liu Pin-k'o wen-chi* [literary works of Liu Pin-k'o], the *Chou-i cheng-i* [annotated text of the Book of Changes], the *Fang-yen* [dictionary of dialects in north and central China], and the *K'un-hsueh chi-wen* [book of miscellaneous notes by Wang Ying-lin]. Fu was interested in the Taoist canon and published parts of it from collections which were in his library. When serving as minister of education at Peking, he had made arrangements with the Commercial Press in Shanghai to prepare a photographic reproduction of the complete canon, which was the property of the Pai-yun-kuan [white cloud temple] of Peking. That task was completed between 1924 and 1926, with the assistance of Hsü Shih-ch'ang (q.v.).

Fu Tseng-hsiang also edited and published the *Sung-tai Shu-wen chi-yao* [collection of Shu Han literature compiled in the Sung dynasty], a compendium of 2,100 literary items by 380 authors. His *Ch'ing-tai tien-shih k'ao-lueh* [brief account of the system of imperial examinations during the Ch'ing dynasty] appeared in 1933.

In 1915 Fu wrote a travel book with Yuan Kuan-lan (1866–1930; T. Hsi-t'ao), who had served as his deputy when he was commissioner of education for Chihli province. Later works, most of them published in the 1930's, record Fu's journeys to some of the five sacred mountains of China (notably T'ai-shan in Shantung and Heng-shan in Hunan), to Shensi province, and to other historic spots. In 1931 he prepared the *Ts'ang-yuan chü-shih liu-shih tzu-shu*, an autobiographical memoir to mark his sixtieth year of life; it was photographically reproduced in Fu's calligraphy.

Fu Tseng-hsiang spent his later years in retirement and died in 1950.

Fu Tso-yi   傅 作 義
T. I-sheng   宜 生

Fu Tso-yi (1895–), military officer who, as top commander in north China after 1947, negotiated the surrender agreement under which the Chinese Communist forces entered Peiping in 1949. He began his career under Yen Hsi-shan (q.v.) and served as governor of Suiyuan in 1931–47. In 1949 he became minister of water conservancy in the Central People's Government.

A native of Shansi, Fu Tso-yi was born in Anchang village, Jungho hsien. At the time of the 1911 revolution, he was a student at the Shansi Military Primary School in Taiyuan. He received a brief introduction to military life during the late months of 1911, when he served as platoon commander in a military unit organized by the Shansi students. After the Ch'ing dynasty had been overthrown, he returned to his studies. In 1913 he went to Peking to enter the Ch'ing-ho Officers Preparatory School. On completion of the course, he enrolled in the Paoting Military Academy; he was graduated in 1918 as a member of the fifth class.

Fu then returned to Shansi and entered the military service of Yen Hsi-shan (q.v.). He served successively as company, battalion, and regimental commander. When stationed at Tienchen in northern Shansi in 1926, Fu and his regiment were attacked by a force of Feng Yü-hsiang's Kuominchün. Although the attacking force was three times the size of his regiment, Fu held Tienchen. Then he struck his opponent in a flank attack and raised the siege. He was promoted to brigade commander for his performance. In June 1926 he was assigned to command the 4th Shansi Division.

In 1927 Yen Hsi-shan declared his allegiance to the Nationalists. Yen was assigned to make a flank attack on the Fengtien forces to support Nationalist advances along the rail lines from the Yangtze valley to north China. Fu Tso-yi's 4th Division was assigned to capture and hold the walled town of Chochow, midway between Paoting and Peking on the Peking-Hankow rail line. He took Chochow on 12 October 1927. Although Fu's assignment proceeded according to schedule, the Nationalist advance from the south did not. Fu, isolated at Chochow, found himself confronting substantial Fengtien forces commanded by Wan Fu-lin and supported by reserve troops under Chang Hsueh-liang (q.v.) at Paoting. Fu reported his position to Yen Hsi-shan and requested assistance. None was forthcoming. After the 4th Division had lost some of its men in battle, Fu stationed all of his remaining forces inside the town walls of Chochow.

The tactical position favored the defense, and the 4th Division successfully repulsed a series of enemy assaults. After a month, the attackers prepared to starve Fu Tso-yi and his unit into submission. As the weeks passed, the food supply for the troops and for the civilian population ran out. Telegraphic messages from both Yen Hsi-shan and the National Government lauded the 4th Division's brave defense; however, no troops were sent. The defenders were subsisting on steamed bread made from inferior grain. After other food supplies had been exhausted, they found that they could survive for a few additional days by eating fermented grain refuse from the local wine distillery. On 25 December 1927 they received a report from Yen Hsi-shan which stated that the Nationalist units were advancing, and on 28 December Fu Tso-yi was named to the Military Affairs Commission. Fu called a conference of his officers to consider attempting a breakout. They decided that the troops, half-starved and with limbs swollen from the diet of grain refuse, would not be able to make the effort.

Fu Tso-yi had asked his men to hold out for a final period of 15 days. That period expired on 5 January 1928, and Fu then had no alternative to surrender. On 12 January 1928 the 7,000 survivors of the 4th Division left Chochow, and Wan Fu-lin's Fengtien forces occupied the town. Fu was placed under the surveillance of Chang Hsueh-liang at Paoting, and his 4th Division was reorganized. Fu Tso-yi's defense of Chochow for a full three months, isolated and without prospect of relief, was recognized throughout China as an outstanding accomplishment in the best military tradition.

Fu Tso-yi regained his freedom when Fengtien power in north China collapsed. He was released in May 1928 after promising Chang Hsueh-liang that he would not participate in the final stages of the military action in north China. Yen Hsi-shan's troops entered Peking on 8 June 1928, and Yen appointed Fu Tso-yi garrison commander at Tientsin. After the last Fengtien troops left Tientsin on 12 June, Fu entered the city at the head of the 4th Division and assumed his duties as garrison commander. He continued to hold commands under Yen Hsi-shan and in 1929 led the 43rd Shansi Division. Thus, he was associated with the 1929–30 coalition of Feng Yü-hsiang, Yen Hsi-shan, and Wang Ching-wei against the growing authority of Chiang Kai-shek at Nanking. In February 1930 he was promoted commander of the Tenth Army of Yen's Third Group Army. The northern coalition issued orders on 10 May for a general offensive against Nanking, and Fu was assigned to advance south along the Tientsin-Pukow rail line. On 25 June, he captured Tsinan, the capital of Shantung province. The National Government, after shifting forces from other fronts, launched a strong drive northward on 1 August and deployed ten divisions against the smaller force of Fu Tso-yi at Tsinan. National Government forces recaptured Tsinan on 15 August 1930, and Fu's retreat turned into a rout because his troops could not cross the Yellow River, which was in flood. This defeat contributed substantially to the failure of the northern coalition.

Fu Tso-yi then became associated with Chang Hsueh-liang, who had become the dominant figure in north China. In March 1931 Fu's army was reorganized, and he became commander of the Seventh Army; in July, he received command of the Thirty-fifth Army, with concurrent command of the

73rd Division. With the tacit approval of Chang Hsueh-liang, he helped Hsü Yung-ch'ang (q.v.) take over the provincial chairmanship of Shansi from Shang Chen (q.v.) in August and became acting governor of Suiyuan province. Later that year, he became governor of Suiyuan.

In February 1933 Japanese forces began to advance into Jehol province. On the eve of the Jehol campaign, Fu Tso-yi, after a visit to Yen Hsi-shan in Taiyuan, went to Peiping to announce that the Shansi and Suiyuan forces were prepared to participate in the defense against the Japanese invasion. However, Jehol fell so rapidly that there was no opportunity to accept the Shansi-Suiyuan offer. The immediate result of that debacle was the resignation of Chang Hsueh-liang, whose Northeastern forces then were placed under the command of Ho Ying-ch'in (q.v.). In the reorganization that followed, Fu Tso-yi was appointed defense commander of Chahar province. He continued to serve as governor of Suiyuan.

At the end of April 1933 Japanese forces took Dolonor, in eastern Chahar. The Japanese planned to extend their influence and control westwards from Manchoukuo into the provinces of Chahar, Suiyuan, Ninghsia, Kansu, and Sinkiang with the aid of Mongols. In Suiyuan, Fu Tso-yi soon found himself pitted against the Mongol Te Wang (Demchukdonggrub, q.v.), the leader of a movement for Inner Mongolian autonomy.

Under Te Wang's leadership and with Nanking's approval, the Mongolian Political Affairs Council was established at Pailingmiao, Suiyuan, in April 1934. Fu had no sympathy with Inner Mongolian aspirations for independence. He believed that Chinese rule was quite suitable for Mongol needs and that so-called independence movements of the Mongols served the purposes of the invading Japanese.

Within months after the establishment of the council, Te Wang, for a variety of reasons, established close relations with the Japanese, and their support of the Inner Mongolian independence movement increased. Fu Tso-yi employed the Tumet Mongol Communist Ulanfu (q.v.) and mobilized Mongols of the Ikechao League to attempt to counter the activities of Te Wang and his supporters. The contest culminated in the breaking apart of Te Wang's council in February 1936, the establishment of a rival political council at Kweisui under Fu Tso-yi's direction, and the occupation of Pailingmiao by Suiyuan forces in November 1936. Despite Japanese protests, Fu continued his drive against Te Wang's forces and pressed them back into eastern Chahar. He was decorated in 1936 by the National Government. In 1935 he had been elected to the Central Executive Committee of the Kuomintang.

At the outbreak of the Sino-Japanese war in July 1937, the defending forces in Suiyuan were composed of the forces under Fu's personal command, three cavalry divisions, a Nationalist division, several units that had defected from the Manchoukuo forces in Jehol and Inner Mongolia, and a cavalry brigade of the Northeastern Vanguard Army of Ma Chan-shan (q.v.).

The Japanese had indicated their strong interest in Chahar and Suiyuan; if they captured that sector, they could command the vital northwest China plateau and maintain a force against the flank of the Mongolian People's Republic and the Soviet Union. They now drove in that direction with a combined Manchoukuo-Mongol force, supported by a Japanese contingent. The Chinese position in north China crumbled rapidly. Kalgan soon was abandoned; Tat'ung was given up without a fight; and the approaches to Inner Mongolia were left undefended. Fu Tso-yi's defense preparations in Suiyuan were of no use because the Chinese units there were outnumbered. The Japanese-sponsored invaders captured Kweisui on 13 October 1937 and then drove on to Paotow.

Fu Tso-yi was transferred to northern Shansi. The Japanese soon broke through the northern and eastern defenses of Shansi and took the provincial capital of Taiyuan in November. Fu remained in the Second War Area until 1939, when he was appointed deputy commander of the Eighth War Area, under Chu Shao-liang (q.v.).

Because they hoped to terminate the war through a political settlement with the National Government, the Japanese did not press on past Paotow. In the winter of 1939, after becoming deputy commander in that sector, Fu Tso-yi deployed his forces against the

Japanese position at Paotow, but the attack did not succeed. The Japanese brought in reinforcements, and in January 1940 they drove westwards to occupy Wuyuan. They continued on to Linho and Shanpa, but then met Chinese resistance. The Japanese attacked again in March, but they were defeated. At the beginning of April 1940, the Chinese reoccupied Wuyuan and went on to reestablish their original battle positions. Fu Tso-yi again was decorated by the National Government.

In July 1945 the National Government converted Suiyuan and Ninghsia into the Twelfth War Area, with Fu Tso-yi as commander. Fu was charged with recovering Suiyuan after the Japanese surrender. His forces occupied Paotow and Kweisui on 11 August, just after Tokyo announced Japan's willingness to surrender. By early October, the disarming of the Japanese units in Suiyuan had been completed.

Fu's haste was motivated by more than a general desire to restore his primacy in Suiyuan. One of his wartime functions in the Suiyuan-Shensi-Ninghsia area had been to contain the military and political operations of the Communist commander Ho Lung (q.v.), who had established a territorial base in Suiyuan. The Communist objective in the Chahar-Suiyuan area was to hold a corridor through which Communist troops could pass from northwest and north China into Manchuria. Once that mission had been accomplished, the Communists relaxed their pressure on Suiyuan.

When political negotiations between the Nationalists and the Communists broke down in the summer of 1946, the Chinese civil war resumed. Fu Tso-yi's forces lost, but then recaptured, several points on the Peiping-Suiyuan railroad, and they succeeded in lifting the siege of Tat'ung in Shansi. On 11 October 1946 Fu took Kalgan from the Communists. That move constituted the basis for the Communists' repeated charge that the Nationalists were taking "provocative" action. Fu Tso-yi nevertheless retained Kalgan, and in November 1946 he was appointed governor of Chahar province. In March 1947 the Twelfth War Area became the Kalgan pacification headquarters, with Fu as its chairman. In August 1947 he was named commander in chief of the newly established bandit-suppression headquarters in north China.

North China was relatively quiet; most of the Communist forces were concentrated in Manchuria and elsewhere in China. On 24 September 1948, however, the Nationalist garrison at Tsinan, Shantung, surrendered with hardly a fight, thus isolating north China from the Nationalist stronghold in the Hsuchow sector to the south. Fu Tso-yi was assigned to reinforce the Nationalist troops at Chinchow in the Liaoning corridor. Manchuria was taken by the Communists at the beginning of November, and the Nationalists lost troops and large stores of munitions that might have been used to strengthen Fu Tso-yi's line of defense along the Great Wall. When the Hwai-Hai battle began in the Kiangsu-Anhwei sector in early November 1948, the National Government at Nanking was so hard-pressed that it could not provide support for Fu in north China.

Fu Tso-yi controlled a strategically important zone extending from Shanhaikuan and Tangku on the east to Ninghsia province on the west. This zone included such important cities as Tientsin, Peiping, Kalgan, Tat'ung, and Chengteh in Jehol, commanding the Kupeikow pass. There were more than 500,000 fighting men under Fu's general command. Immediately after the capture of the Manchurian port of Yingkow on 5 November 1948, the combined Communist forces of Lin Piao and Nieh Jung-chen (qq.v.) began to threaten Fu's positions. Fu realized that the war had been lost in Manchuria and that the massive Hwai-Hai battle would probably mark the end of organized Nationalist military strength on the mainland. Accordingly, he did not take the field against the advancing Chinese Communist forces, but limited himself to delaying actions and planned retreats.

Nieh Jung-chen's forces took Chengteh on 9 November 1948; Lin Piao occupied Shanhaikuan on 18 November; and Communist forces took Kupeikow on 2 December. Lin Piao's Fourth Field Army then launched a general offensive along a front extending from Tangku to Kalgan. By 7 December the Fourth Field Army was within 30 miles of Peiping. The Communists then broke through Fu Tso-yi's front and isolated Peiping, Tientsin, and Kalgan from each other. By mid-December, Peiping, guarded by some 25 infantry divisions, had been encircled. The Communist occupation of Kalgan on 23 December isolated Fu Tso-yi from his base in Suiyuan. The Hwai-Hai battle, a debacle for the Nationalists, ended in early January 1949, and Tientsin fell, after sharp fighting, on 15 January. When the military situation disintegrated, Chiang Kai-shek called a conference of his military commanders at Nanking. That meeting confirmed the obvious: that a coordinated Nationalist military effort was no longer possible and that each military commander should put up the best fight he could. Fu Tso-yi, recognizing that the Nationalist cause was lost, did not attend the Nanking conference and began to make independent arrangements for peace.

As early as December 1948 Fu had established informal contact with the field headquarters of the attacking Communist forces under the command of Lin Piao. That covert liaison was reportedly arranged by Chi Ch'ao-ting (q.v.), a fellow native of Shansi who served in Peiping as economic adviser to Fu Tso-yi, and by Yenching University professor Chang Tung-sun (q.v.), a prominent figure in the China Democratic League. Fu Tso-yi still held a relatively strong bargaining position. His military forces were largely intact and were based in the Peiping area and in Suiyuan, where they were in a position to join with the Muslim generals of northwest China. The Peiping garrison force alone numbered more than 200,000 men, supported by a substantial artillery force, and Fu was known for his determination in holding beseiged points against strong attacking forces. The Communists had an interest in arranging a peaceful entry into the ancient capital and in avoiding a battle which would threaten the historical monuments and national treasures of the city.

An arrangement was made whereby Fu Tso-yi could save face by nominally fulfilling his duties as a Nationalist military officer. On 22 January 1949, the day after Chiang Kai-shek retired from the presidency, Fu signed an agreement with his Communist opponents in north China. He surrendered with the Peiping garrison, and, on 31 January, troops of the Communist Fourth Field Army began to enter Peiping. The agreement negotiated by Fu Tso-yi protected the city's treasures and even guaranteed the safety of foreign consular officers stationed there. It also protected Fu's personal position. It later became evident that the agreement had made provision for the preservation of Fu's troops in Suiyuan, where two of his subordinate generals, Tung Ch'i-wu and Sun Lan-feng (qq.v.), retained command of some of his troops. The Communists permitted Tung Ch'i-wu to remain in office as governor of Suiyuan after that province was surrendered to them. The Kuomintang responded to the agreement by expelling Fu Tso-yi from its ranks.

As one of the most senior Nationalist generals to make a separate peace with the Communists, Fu Tso-yi was rewarded with senior offices when the Central People's Government was established in October 1949. He became minister of water conservancy, a member of the National Committee of the Chinese People's Political Consultative Conference, and a member of the People's Revolutionary Military Council. When the government at Peking was reorganized in 1954, Fu continued to be minister of water conservancy and became a vice chairman of the National Defense Council. In September 1955 he was awarded the Liberation Medal, first class. He visited Europe in the spring of 1956 as a special delegate from China to the meeting of the World Peace Council at Stockholm, and he also headed a Chinese delegation which visited the Soviet Union to inspect flood control methods. In February 1958, he became minister of water conservancy and electric power at Peking.

Fu Tso-yi was married to Liu Yun-sheng.

Fung Yu-lan: *see* FENG YU-LAN.

Han Fu-chü   韓 復 榘
 T. Hsiang-fang   向 方

Han Fu-chü (1890–24 January 1938), served under Feng Yü-hsiang until May 1929, when he gave allegiance to Chiang Kai-shek. He served as governor of Shantung from 1930 to 1938. After his troops failed to resist the Japanese invasion of Shantung, he was arrested and executed.

Pahsien, Chihli (Hopei), was the birthplace of Han Fu-chü. He received his early education in an old-style military school and then began his career in the army. At the time of the 1911 revolution, he participated in a military uprising at Luanchow, Chihli (Hopei), with such Peiyang Army officers as Feng Yü-hsiang (q.v.). After that revolt against Manchu authority had been crushed, Han made his way back to his native district. In 1912, when Feng Yü-hsiang returned to the Peiyang Army of Yuan Shih-k'ai as a battalion commander, Han visited Feng, recalled their former ties, and was taken into Feng's service.

Han served as an orderly and then, successively, as a platoon, company, and battalion commander. He was closely associated with Feng Yü-hsiang's leadership of the 16th Mixed Brigade in the next few years. Han also was associated with one of Feng's captains who later gained national prominence, Sung Che-yuan (q.v.). After Feng Yü-hsiang's successful coup at Peking during the second Chihli-Fengtien war of 1924, Han became a brigade commander in Feng's new Kuominchün [people's army]. In 1925 he visited Japan to observe military maneuvers, but soon returned to China to join Feng's new fight for power. Han was given command of the 1st Division.

After the expulsion of Feng's forces from Peking in early 1926, however, Han did not remain with the Kuominchün. Instead, he joined a division commanded by Shang Chen (q.v.) in Shansi. When Shang Chen was made military governor of Suiyuan, Han was assigned to garrison duty in Suiyuan as commander of the Shansi 13th Division.

Feng Yü-hsiang returned to China from Moscow in September 1926 and announced that he intended to support the Northern Expedition forces then striking northward from Canton. Han Fu-chü soon rejoined his former chief and returned to active service under Feng's command. In 1927 he was made a commander when Feng's forces were reorganized as the Second Army Group of the National Revolutionary Army. Han played an important role in the drive on north China in 1928 which comprised the second stage of the Northern Expedition. His forces participated in the actions at Hsuchow and at Changho and then struck into Hopei province in the final thrust toward Peking.

After Feng Yü-hsiang became minister of war in the National Government established at Nanking in 1928, Han Fu-chü was ap-

pointed governor of Honan, and he went there with his army in 1928. At the fifth plenum of the second Central Executive Committee of the Kuomintang, held in August, he was elected to the State Council.

Han Fu-chü was an able general, and he now held an important position. Feng Yü-hsiang, when he concentrated his forces in Honan and challenged Chiang Kai-shek's growing power in the late spring of 1929, planned to rely heavily on the strength of Han Fu-chü. However, in May 1929, as the opposing forces were being deployed, Han Fu-chü defected to the National Government side, taking with him three division commanders, including Shih Yü-san and Ma Hung-k'uei (q.v.), and thousands of troops. The battle between Feng Yü-hsiang and Chiang Kai-shek was fought in the autumn, and Feng lost the campaign.

Han Fu-chü was appropriately rewarded by Chiang Kai-shek. He was given command of the First Army and was assigned to stabilize the provinces of Honan and Shantung. He fought against the Shansi forces in Shantung province in 1930 to help break up the so-called northern coalition, led by Feng Yü-hsiang and Yen Hsi-shan. In September 1930, after the defeat of Yen's forces in Shantung and the collapse of the coalition, Han was named governor of Shantung.

Han Fu-chü's administration of Shantung represented a notable improvement over that of Chang Tsung-ch'ang (q.v.). Han reduced taxes and delivered a substantial portion of the tax revenues to the National Government at Nanking. He tightened administrative and military discipline, restricted the cultivation and consumption of opium, and established equitable qualifying examinations for Shantung students who wished to go abroad to study. In his personal life, Han Fu-chü followed the regimen that he had learned under Feng Yü-hsiang: wearing a plain uniform, eating the same food as his troops, and sleeping on a board bed.

In July 1931, when Han's former Kuominchün associate Shih Yü-san took action against the National Government, Chang Hsueh-liang and Chiang Kai-shek called upon Han to use his influence to bring the revolt to an end. Han took no action, and Shih finally was defeated by the combined forces of Chang Hsueh-liang, Liu Chih (q.v.), and Yen Hsi-shan.

Liu and Yen were, respectively, the governors of Honan and Shansi. However, when Shih Yü-san announced his political retirement in August 1931, he turned over his troops to Han Fu-chü for "reorganization." That action antagonized the National Government authorities at Nanking.

Han Fu-chü faced internal problems in Shantung. When he became governor, a militarist named Liu Chen-nien, who had been a follower of Chang Tsung-ch'ang, still controlled a large area of eastern Shantung. Liu's military presence in Shantung was condoned at least nominally by the authorities at Nanking. In September 1932 Han Fu-chü's forces and Liu Chen-nien's troops clashed. In a telegram to Chiang Kai-shek, Han charged that Liu had been guilty of illegal exactions from the populace and of connivance in banditry. After negotiations between Han and the National Government, Ho Ying-ch'in, the minister of war at Nanking, announced on 1 November 1932 that the Shantung dispute had been settled. Later that month, "in accordance with orders," Liu Chen-nien and his forces moved to Chekiang province.

Han Fu-chü's control of Shantung now was complete. To maintain it, he commanded a military force of about 75,000 men. As governor of Shantung, Han held a key position with respect to Sino-Japanese relations in north China. Han took an active part in an important conference of north China military leaders which was held at Peiping on 27 December under the chairmanship of Chang Hsueh-liang.

The crisis that developed in Jehol at the beginning of 1933 did not involve Shantung directly. After the Japanese had taken Jehol and had gained control of the Great Wall passes, fighting was brought to a close with the signature of the Tangku truce of 31 May 1933. Although Han Fu-chü had remained in Shantung and had taken no action against the Japanese, it was generally assumed that if the Japanese should thrust at Shantung, Han's military forces would have no difficulty in withstanding the attack.

Sung Che-yuan, also a former Kuominchün officer, came to power at Peiping in late 1935. He and Han Fu-chü joined together to halt the Japanese drive to convert the five provinces of north China, including Shantung, into a Japanese-sponsored autonomous region. Japanese Ambassador Kawagoe, on his way to Nanking in August 1935 after conferences with other Japanese officials in north China, stopped off at Tsinan and reportedly outlined the political position and demands of Japan to Han Fu-chü. In the spring of 1937 Major General Kita Seiichi became military attaché of the Japanese embassy at Nanking. Shortly after arriving at his new post, General Kita, in the course of a tour of central and north China, visited Han Fu-chü.

Neither Han Fu-chü nor Sung Che-yuan attended the special conference of senior Chinese officials that was convened at Lushan in early July. After the Lukouchiao Incident of 7 July 1937 began the Sino-Japanese war, Han sent a representative to see Chiang Kai-shek at Lushan. Han conferred with Hu Tsung-nan and Liu Chih at Hsuchow and then went to Nanking for a conference with Chiang Kai-shek and Feng Yü-hsiang. On 1 August 1937 he returned to Tsinan.

The Japanese navy landed at Tsingtao on 14 August, and ground forces drove into Shantung from the north at the beginning of October. Doubts about Han Fu-chü's attitude toward the war were raised in both China and Japan. On 3 October 1937 the Japanese took Techow from Chinese defending forces composed of units of Sung Che-yuan's Twenty-ninth Army and one division of Han's Shantung forces. Japanese troops then advanced on the provincial capital, Tsinan. Han Fu-chü made various public gestures to demonstrate his patriotism and on 10 October directed his subordinates to resist Japanese aggression to the end. In the critical test, however, Han Fu-chü's troops, which had been presumed to be a formidable combat force, offered little resistance to the Japanese. The invaders occupied Tsinan on 25 December, with only minor losses. Han had concentrated a large force at T'aian, but the Japanese advanced to take that point on 1 January 1938. On 5 January, they captured Tsining.

Chiang Kai-shek notified Han Fu-chü on 6 January that he was not to withdraw further unless ordered to do so. But the Chinese retreat in Shantung continued. In the meantime, Li Tsung-jen (q.v.), who had been assigned to defend the Hsuchow sector, was massing troops there in an effort to halt the Japanese, who had already landed at Haichow. On 11 January 1938, acting on orders from Chiang Kai-shek, Li Tsung-jen arrested Han Fu-chü on charges of dereliction of duty.

Han was sent to Hankow, where Ho Ying-ch'in presided over his court martial, which was conducted in secret. The other judges were Ho Ch'eng-chün (q.v.), the governor of Hupeh province, and Lu Chung-lin, under whom Han had served during the Northern Expedition. The formal charges included repeatedly disobeying orders and retreating at his own volition; forcing opium upon the people of his province; extracting excessive taxes and levies, pilfering public funds; and depriving the people of Shantung of their firearms. Although most of the charges could not be substantiated, Han was convicted and sentenced to death. He was executed at Hankow on 24 January 1938, along with nine other military officers who had been convicted of dereliction of duty.

Han Fu-chü's wife, Kao I-chen, also came from Pahsien. She was the granddaughter of Kao Pu-ying (b. 1875), a chü-jen of 1894 who headed the department of social (adult) education in the ministry of education at Peking during the early republican period and who edited several compilations of traditional Chinese literary works.

Ho Ch'eng-chün   何 成 濬
T. Hsueh-chu   雪 竹

Ho Ch'eng-chün (20 June 1882–7 May 1961), a military officer and protégé of Huang Hsing who became a leading intermediary in negotiations with independent generals and among competing factions in the Kuomintang. He held such posts as governor of Hupeh (1929–32; 1937–38), director of the Generalissimo's Wuhan headquarters, and director general of the courts martial (1939–46).

Little is known of Ho Ch'eng-chün's background or childhood except that he was born into a prosperous family in Suihsien, Hupeh. At the age of 14 he applied to a military preparatory school in Hupeh, but was rejected because he was too young and because he could not meet the required physical standards. At the age of 19 he won first place in the examinations for the district school, and the educational

commissioner of Hupeh province recommended him for study at the Ching-hsin Academy. After the imperial examination system was abolished in 1905, the Ching-hsin and the Liang-hu academies were merged to form a new institution. When Ho was a student there, he was influenced by Huang Hsing (q.v.), who had returned from Japan to attempt to convert students and army officers to the anti-Manchu revolutionary cause.

In 1907 Ho Ch'eng-chün won a Hupeh government scholarship for study in Japan. He enrolled at the Shimbu Gakkō in Tokyo. After graduation, he was admitted to the infantry course at the Shikan Gakkō [military academy], where he was a member of the fifth class. He joined the T'ung-meng-hui under the sponsorship of Huang Hsing.

After graduation in 1909, Ho Ch'eng-chün returned to China, where he planned to join the staff of Wu Lu-chen, who was serving as border defense commissioner at Yenki in Manchuria. However, government-sponsored scholars returning from abroad were required to serve in their native provinces, and Ho therefore went to the Hupeh training bureau at Wuchang. In 1910 Wu Lu-chen, then commanding the 6th Brigade, which was stationed at Paoting, Chihli (Hopei), requested that Ho be assigned to head a regiment under his command. The request was refused, and Ho was assigned instead to the personnel division of the Board of War at Peking. While serving in that key office in the highest military organ of the imperial government, he established new contacts with anti-Manchu revolutionaries in north China.

After the Wuchang revolt in October 1911, Ho Ch'eng-chün served in the First Army, commanded by Yin-ch'ang, the minister of war. Ho sought to leave the government forces but friends dissuaded him, saying that his resignation would be regarded as a sign that he intended to join the rebels. He reluctantly returned to Peking, where he learned that Wu Lu-chen had been appointed governor of Shansi. He decided to join Wu and was making travel arrangements when word came that Wu had been assassinated. Fearing for his own safety, Ho immediately went to Tientsin and then joined Huang Hsing at Shanghai. Huang sent him to Nanking to assist the revolutionaries in establishing a provisional central government.

After Sun Yat-sen's inauguration as provisional president on 1 January 1912, Huang Hsing was made minister of war. Huang named Ho Ch'eng-chün his chief adjutant. When Yuan Shih-k'ai assumed the presidency and the provisional government was moved to Peking, Huang Hsing remained at Nanking in charge of the rear headquarters of the revolutionary armies in central China. Ho continued to be Huang's chief subordinate. The rear headquarters at Nanking was abolished in June, and Ho went to Hupeh. In November, when Huang Hsing was named director general of the Hankow-Canton and Szechwan railroads, he sent Ho to Peking to serve as his liaison officer. Ho remained at Peking after Huang resigned in January 1913.

Ho left north China in March 1913 and went to Shanghai, where he served Huang Hsing as chief of staff during the so-called second revolution. When that move against Yuan Shih-k'ai failed, he was among those who fled to Japan. In the summer of 1914, after Sun Yat-sen had reorganized the revolutionary party as the Chung-hua ko-ming-tang, Ho Ch'eng-chün covertly returned to China to organize a new uprising against Yuan Shih-k'ai; he went to Shanghai. Ch'en Ch'i-mei (q.v.) arrived shortly thereafter, and the two men became close associates. Yuan Shih-k'ai died in June 1916, and Li Yuan-hung succeeded to the presidency. When Li invited Huang Hsing to visit Peking, Huang sent Ho to north China to assess the situation. He remained there for a few weeks, but then returned to Shanghai at the end of October 1916 because Huang Hsing had died.

In 1917, after Sun Yat-sen's military government was organized in south China, Ho Ch'eng-chün went to Canton. Sun ordered him to mobilize support in the Yangtze valley. Ho went secretly to Shasi, Hupeh, but he was prevented from carrying out his mission by Wang Chan-yuan, the military governor of Hupeh. Ho and his troops marched to Ch'angte, where he joined Li Shu-ch'eng, the commissioner of western Hunan. In March 1918, when Peiyang forces from north China moved into Hunan, Ch'eng Ch'ien (q.v.), the commander in chief of the Hunan army, called on Li Shu-ch'eng and Ho Ch'eng-chün for assistance. They complied, but Ho was outflanked by Peiyang forces. In May 1918 he left Hunan and went to Canton.

He then went to Shanghai, where Sun Yat-sen had moved.

Ho remained at Shanghai until the Peiyang forces were expelled from Hunan in October 1920. Sun Yat-sen then sent him to Hunan, where he gained the political support of T'an Yen-k'ai. However, T'an soon was forced from power by Chao Heng-t'i. Ho went to Hunan again in mid-1921 to participate in a military drive against Wang Chan-yuan in Hupeh. That move failed when Wu P'ei-fu (q.v.) came to the aid of Wang Chan-yuan.

Sun Yat-sen, as a part of his attempt to strengthen his political alliances in the south, employed Ho Ch'eng-chün as a personal emissary to gain support for the Kuomintang, sending him first to Yunnan province, where T'ang Chi-yao, a schoolmate of Ho in Japan, had consolidated control early in 1922. Although Ho spent three months in Kunming, the provincial capital, he failed to win support for Sun. He was more successful in Fukien, where he helped to prepare the way for the establishment of a temporary base of power for the Kuomintang. In 1923 and 1924 Ho held several military commands under Hsü Ch'ung-chih and T'an Yen-k'ai. In August 1925, after the death of Sun Yat-sen, he returned to Canton and assisted Chiang Kai-shek in the eastern expedition against Ch'en Chiung-ming. After the expeditionary forces had occupied Waichow, Ch'en's principal base in eastern Kwangtung, Ho returned to Shanghai.

The Northern Expedition was launched in July 1926, and Chiang Kai-shek sent Ho to Shanghai in an attempt to gain the support of Sun Ch'uan-fang (q.v.), who then controlled the lower Yangtze provinces. Ho, who had been a schoolmate of Sun Ch'uan-fang at the Shikan Gakkō, urged Sun to ally himself with the National Revolutionary Army of Chiang Kai-shek for a joint attack on Wu P'ei-fu, Sun's sometime superior officer. Sun believed that his position was vulnerable because of the geographical proximity of the northern generals, and he decided not to join forces with Chiang Kai-shek.

After the Nationalist forces had captured Wuhan in October 1926, Chiang Kai-shek assigned Ho to help organize the Hupeh Political Council. For a time, Ho served as a member of that body and as pacification commissioner of northern Hupeh, but he came into conflict with the Hunanese general T'ang Sheng-chih (q.v.) and was forced to withdraw from the area. After Chiang Kai-shek broke relations with Wuhan and established a regime at Nanking, Ho Ch'eng-chün became a member of the Military Affairs Commission at Nanking and senior adviser in the general headquarters of the National Revolutionary Army.

In the early summer of 1927 Ho was assigned to win the support of Yen Hsi-shan (q.v.) in Shansi province. Although the northern sections of the Peking-Hankow railroad were then under the control of the Fengtien forces (*see* Chang Tso-lin), Ho succeeded in reaching Tientsin. Han Lun-ch'ün, a Fengtien army commander who had been a schoolmate of Ho, arranged for him to meet Chang Hsueh-liang (q.v.) and others at Peking. Chang Hsueh-liang lent Ho his private railway car for the trip to see Yen at Taiyuan. Yen already had shown an equivocal attitude toward his alliance with Chang Tso-lin, and Ho Ch'eng-chün's negotiations with Yen proceeded smoothly. Soon after the discussions, Yen became northern commander of the National Revolutionary Army. After receiving news of Chiang Kai-shek's temporary retirement, Ho returned to central China, stopping at Peking to confer with Chang Hsueh-liang and Han Lun-ch'ün about Manchuria's possible acceptance of Nationalist rule.

When the Northern Expedition was resumed in April 1928, Ho Ch'eng-chün, as director of Chiang Kai-shek's Hsuchow headquarters, utilized his ties with officers in the opposition forces of Sun Ch'uan-fang and Chang Tsung-ch'ang to contribute substantially to the Nationalist campaign in the Hsuchow sector.

After Chiang Kai-shek's First Group Army clashed with the Japanese in the Tsinan Incident of May 1928, Chiang sent Hsiung Shih-hui to negotiate with the Japanese, but Hsiung made little headway. On 9 May, Ho replaced Hsiung in the negotiations. The Japanese commander, after presenting terms which Ho found unacceptable, detained him until 12 May. After going to Yenchow for discussions with Chiang Kai-shek, Ho returned to Hsuchow.

The Northern Expedition bypassed Tsinan; Ho Ch'eng-chün was ordered to proceed from Hsuchow by sea to Tientsin and Peking. He negotiated with Wang Shih-chen, Hsiung Hsi-ling, Yen Hsi-shan, and representatives of the Fengtien Army to save Peking from the ravages of war. In the end, the Fengtien forces withdrew eastward. Yen Hsi-shan maintained order in the evacuated areas, and on 6 June his Shansi army occupied Peking. On 8 July 1928 Ho accompanied representatives of Chang Hsueh-liang to a meeting with Chiang Kai-shek to discuss Manchuria's possible acceptance of Nationalist rule. Arrangements were made, and in December 1928 the Nationalist flag was raised over Manchuria.

After Chiang Kai-shek assumed the chairmanship of the National Government at Nanking in 1928, Ho Ch'eng-chün became chief military counselor. His efforts to induce Liu Hsiang in Szechwan and the Kweichow generals to support the National Government met with little success.

When the Kwangsi military officers threatened Chiang Kai-shek's authority in February 1929, Ho was ordered to go to Peiping, where the Kwangsi general Pai Ch'ung-hsi (q.v.) was based. Ho persuaded divisional commanders in north China to remain loyal to Nanking. Chang Hsueh-liang assisted him by ordering troops under Yü Hsueh-chung to threaten Pai Ch'ung-hsi's positions in the area. Pai was forced out of north China.

Ho Ch'eng-chün was elected a member of the Central Executive Committee of the Kuomintang at the Third National Congress in March 1929. In April he was appointed provincial governor of Hupeh. New crises arose, and Ho had to contend with political maneuvers in both north China and Manchuria. Yen Hsi-shan regarded the presence of Ho Ch'eng-chün and T'ang Sheng-chih in north China as a barrier to the expansion of his own power. Ho visited Yen Hsi-shan at Taiyuan in August 1929 and satisfied Yen's demands regarding control and distribution of personnel in both Shansi and Hopei. In Manchuria, China and the Soviet Union were involved in a dispute about Chang Hsueh-liang's seizure of the Chinese Eastern Railway. Chang invited Ho to come to Manchuria for consultation so that he could coordinate his moves with those of Nanking. With Chiang Kai-shek's consent, Ho left for Mukden on 17 August and remained with Chang Hsueh-liang for two weeks before returning to Peiping. But he was unable to affect the outcome of the Manchurian situation; Soviet military action led to restoration of the *status quo ante* on the rail line.

Ho Ch'eng-chün visited Shansi in September 1929 to report on the Manchurian situation to Yen Hsi-shan. Yen seemed to be somewhat evasive in dealing with him. The reason became clear in October, when the possibility of alliance between Yen Hsi-shan and Feng Yü-hsiang (q.v.) became known. Ho then went to Cheng-chow to win the support of T'ang Sheng-chih's forces, reported to Chiang Kai-shek at Nanking, and on 20 October went to Kaifeng to direct operations against Feng Yü-hsiang's forces. After Feng's troops had been defeated, T'ang Sheng-chih on 5 December 1929 announced his intention to oppose Chiang Kai-shek. Ho escaped from Kaifeng, made his way to Hsu-chow, and then went to Tsingtao and Nanking.

In February 1930 Ho finally went to Wuchang to assume the governorship of Hupeh province, to which he had been appointed ten months earlier. He also became director of Chiang Kai-shek's Wuhan headquarters. Two months later, Li Tsung-jen joined the northern coalition of Feng Yü-hsiang and Yen Hsi-shan in opposing Chiang Kai-shek. Chiang appointed Ho Ying-ch'in to succeed Ho Ch'eng-chün as director of the Wuhan headquarters, and Ho Ch'eng-chün was assigned responsibility for operations along the Peking-Hankow rail line. He assumed over-all command of several armies in that sector. These armies had not been under Nationalist command for long, and their loyalty to Chiang Kai-shek was uncertain. Because Ho Ch'eng-chün had long-standing associations with their commanders, he was successful in holding these armies on Chiang's side. Ho's assignment was to defeat Feng Yü-hsiang's forces along the rail line and to join the National Government forces at Chengchow. His armies began their attack in May 1930, with some initial success. However, Feng's and Ho's troops soon reached a stalemate. In mid-August, National Government forces on the eastern front captured Tsinan, enabling Chiang Kai-shek to shift troops to the Peking-Hankow railroad front. With Ho Ch'eng-chün holding a major command, the Nationalists began a general offensive on 11 September 1930, and by the end of that month the armies of Feng Yü-hsiang and Yen Hsi-shan were in retreat.

In the meantime, however, the Chinese Communists had seized the opportunity to expand their territorial bases in the central Yangtze provinces. By the time Ho returned to his provincial post at Wuchang, they had established themselves in almost half of Hupeh's 70 hsien. Campaigns against the Communists in 1930–31 had little success in Hupeh. In 1931 a severe flood inundated much of the province. Ho Ch'eng-chün held both civil and military responsibility in Hupeh; he now requested that he be relieved of one of his functions. In March 1932 Hsia Tou-yin was named to succeed him as provincial governor. In June, the military structure in central China was reorganized, with Ho becoming pacification commissioner of Hupeh and commander in chief for military operations against the Communists in the Hupeh-Anhwei area. He held the latter post until 1937 and participated in anti-Communist campaigns in the Hupeh-Anhwei area, in Hunan, and in Kiangsi.

In March 1933, when the Japanese attacked the Great Wall passes, Chiang Kai-shek sent Ho to Paoting to assume charge of the headquarters there. After the Tangku truce was signed on 31 May, Ho returned to Wuchang. In 1935 Ho Ch'eng-chün was reelected to the Central Executive Committee of the Kuomintang. He also became pacification commissioner for the Honan-Hupeh border district. In the winter of 1936 the office of the Hupeh pacification commissioner was renamed the Generalissimo's headquarters. Ho continued to be its director.

After the outbreak of war with Japan in 1937, the National Government moved from Nanking to Wuhan in October. The provincial governments of the Yangtze region were reorganized in November, and Ho again became governor of Hupeh. In June 1938 he was succeeded as provincial governor by Ch'en Ch'eng (q.v.). The National Government was forced to evacuate the Wuhan cities in October 1938, and the Generalissimo's Wuhan headquarters was abolished. In January 1939, at the Nationalist wartime capital of Chungking, Ho was appointed director general of the courts martial. He held that post throughout the remaining war years.

In 1946, at the age of 64, Ho Ch'eng-chün retired from military service. He returned to Hupeh, where he was elected speaker of the provincial assembly. In the winter of 1948 he was injured in a fall and underwent medical treatment in Shanghai. He moved to Hong Kong in the spring of 1949 and to Taiwan in

December. In March 1960 he was given the honor of transmitting the certificate of election to Vice President Ch'en Ch'eng. On 7 May 1961 he died at Taipei. His book, *Pa-shih hui-i* [reminiscences at eighty] was published at Taipei in 1961.

Ho Ch'i-fang   何其芳

Ho Ch'i-fang (1910–), poet, journalist, and literary critic, was a prize-winning poet in his youth and an admirer of Western literature. He later became a leading figure in the Chinese Communist cultural hierarchy and a close associate of Chou Yang (q.v.).

Little is known about Ho Ch'i-fang's family or early life except that he was born in Szechwan. He studied classical Chinese as a child, becoming familiar with the poetry of the *Shih-ching* [book of poetry] and the *Ch'u-tz'u* [elegies of Ch'u] and with the romantic mysticism of the *Chuang-tzu*. At the age of 15, he was sent to a modern middle school in Chengtu. He remained there for about five years, during which time he absorbed the elements of Western learning. He began reading Western literature, especially the romantic English poets of the nineteenth century, and he was introduced to the ideas of such Western innovators as Darwin, Kropotkin, Dewey, and Marx. Ho was exposed to the political realities of early republican China when a number of his fellow students were arrested or forced to flee for joining demonstrations sympathetic to the Nationalist cause.

At the age of 20, Ho entered the philosophy department of Peking University, from which he was graduated in 1936. Much of his time, however, seems to have been devoted to literature, and as early as 1931 he was active as a poet. He composed "Yü-yen" [prophecy], an invocation to his personal muse, whose coming had been revealed some time earlier in a moment of prophetic intuition. The poem concludes on a note of anxiety, the fear that the "youthful god with the voice of a silver bell" will desert the poet as suddenly as he had appeared. In organization and imagery the poem is reminiscent of certain sections of the "Chiu-ko" [nine songs] in the *Ch'u-tz'u*, in which poet-priests draw down gods and goddesses from heaven with a kind of erotic liturgy, only to lament the brevity of their ecstatic contact with the divine. In tone and feeling, "Yü-yen" has reminded many Western readers of the subdued melancholy of Keats and of his anxiety about his poetic gift. This early poem also evidences Ho Ch'i-fang's major artistic excellence, a smooth vernacular style with much of the grace, elegance, and restraint of the older classical idiom.

In January 1934 Ho joined such writers as Yeh Sheng-t'ao (Yen Shao-chün), Hsieh Wan-ying (Ping Hsin), Wan Chia-pao (Ts'ao Yü), Li Shu-hua, and Wu Tsu-hsiang in contributing to the newly founded *Literary Quarterly*, which was edited by Cheng Chen-to (q.v.) and Chin I. In 1936 Pa Chin (Li Fei-kan, q.v.) replaced Cheng as co-editor. This appointment was providential both politically and professionally for Ho. Pa Chin enjoyed the attention of the Communist literary circles in which Ho was later to move; he also became editor in chief of the Wen-hua sheng-huo ch'u-pan she [cultural life publishing company], which subsequently published a number of Ho's books. While somewhat leftist in sentiment, the *Literary Quarterly* (known in later issues as *Wen-chi yueh-k'an*) and Ho Ch'i-fang avoided extremes.

As a student at Peking University, Ho befriended and lived with Li Kuang-t'ien and Pien Chih-lin, both of whom were enrolled in the department of Western languages. Pien had already acquired a reputation as a translator of Baudelaire and Mallarmé and as a stream-of-consciousness poet. Li had published a number of poems in a more conventional style which depicted the life and hardships of the peasants in his native Shantung. Pien and Li stimulated Ho's interest in the technical aspects of poetry and deepened his understanding of Western literature. In 1936 the three young men published a volume of poetry, *Han-yuan chi* [the garden of Han], which was acclaimed by the critics.

In 1934 Shen Ts'ung-wen (q.v.) had become editor of the weekly literary supplement of the *Ta Kung Pao*. He soon made it one of the most respected literary periodicals of the day. Ho Ch'i-fang, Hsiao Ch'ien, Lu Fen, and Li Ni were frequent contributors to the supplement. In 1936 Ho was awarded the *Ta Kung Pao* poetry prize for a volume of prose poems, *Hua-meng lu* [dream sketches]. The themes of *Hua-meng lu*—youthful longing for perfect love, the transience of youth and beauty, and the loneliness of the artist—were not new to Chinese readers, but, embodied in Ho's disciplined yet rich imagery and diction, they made a novel impression.

After graduation, Ho returned to Szechwan, where he taught at a middle school. In 1937 he wrote two more books: *K'o-i chi* [words to remember] consisted of essays and poems that had appeared in various newspapers and magazines; *Huan-hsiang jih-chi* [home again], recounted Ho's experiences as a successful writer and Westernized intellectual returning to the narrow provincialism of Chengtu. With its blend of exasperation with an old order still stubbornly clinging to life and unfeigned admiration for the positive strength inherent in the lives of the peasant and the villager, *Huan-hsiang jih-chi* is reminiscent of such stories by Lu Hsün (Chou Shu-jen, q.v.) as "Ku-hsiang" [my native place] and "Tsai chiu-lou-shang" [in the wineshop]. Ho's shift in allegiance from the quiet humanism of Chou Tso-jen to the trenchant militancy of Chou's older brother marks a break in his development as a writer. He now moved toward realism, social protest, and, ultimately, revolutionary commitment.

Late in 1937, at the urging of his friend Pien Chih-lin, Ho left Chengtu for Yenan, the Chinese Communist capital, where Pien was engaged in propaganda activity. Although Ho's stay there was brief, the Yenan journey had a powerful effect on him. Soon after his return, Ho wrote: "No more clouds! no more moon! no more stars without number! Give me only a room of thatch, and a voice to stir the world!" In 1940 Ho made his way north to Yenan to join the Communists.

Full details of Ho Ch'i-fang's career from 1940 to 1945 are lacking, but it is known that he was welcomed by the Communists and that he, in turn, became a dedicated party member and worker. In 1940 and 1941 Ho spent several months with a guerrilla band as a reporter in a deliberate effort to obtain "experience of life." Though the experience overtaxed him physically and he returned to Yenan with only one story written, his months with the guerrilla fighters completed his conversion to Communism. At Yenan, Ho taught literature in the Lu Hsün i-shu hsueh-yuan [Lu Hsün institute of arts] and soon became its head. He also served as chairman of the Yenan branch of the All-China Federation of Writers and Artists and as editor of *Ta-chung wen-i* [masses' literature and art], the official organ of the federation. As a leading member of the Yenan cultural establishment, Ho played an important role in applying Communist dogma to the creation and evaluation of literature after Mao Tse-tung's 1942 *Talks at the Yenan Literary Conference*. In a "confession" published that year, Ho admitted to intellectual errors ranging from overemphasis on bourgeois Western literature and neglect of the Chinese tradition, especially folk literature and art, to inability to apply a mass viewpoint to the solution of problems of literature and art. Ho's conclusion was that he and all other "culture workers" should perform all tasks in strict conformity with Mao's policy, the gist of which was that the proper role of the artist in revolutionary times was as propagandist to revolutionary action. Mao's *Talks* and the confessions of Ho and others diminished the freedom of the writer and the artist in Communist-controlled areas and presaged the thought-control policies of the 1950's. Only a few independent men, such as Hu Feng (q.v.), dared to protest. Ho, together with Liu Pai-yü, a reporter and writer of stories, visited Hu in 1944 and attempted to compel him, without success, to conform to the policy set forth in the *Talks*. By these and similar activities Ho consolidated his position in the new cultural hierarchy and became a close associate of the arch-advocate of the Maoist line, Chou Yang (q.v.).

Shortly after his arrival in the north, Ho Ch'i-fang had begun a series of poems embodying his new experiences and outlook. He completed and published this series in 1945 as *Yeh-ko* [songs in the night]. *Yeh-ko*, which focused on the wartime lives of workers, peasants, and soldiers, satisfied the objective criteria set forth by Mao, but, as a whole, failed to carry conviction. Part of the fault lay in Ho's "classic" and Europeanized diction, a carry-over from *Han-yuan chi* and *Hua-meng lu*. Ho once again confessed his errors and resolved to learn anew from the masses. Little opportunity was afforded, however, to pursue these new insights, for Ho was sent soon after to Chungking, where he remained until 1947 as editor of the literary page of the *Hsin-hua jih-pao* [new China daily], the official Communist party organ in Szechwan.

After the Communists came to power in 1949, Ho continued to play a leading role in cultural affairs and in the application of party dictates to literature and the arts. Ho participated in the formation of the All-China Federation of Literary and Arts Circles and became a member of its national committee. In December 1951 he published an influential article, "Improve our Work by Means of the Literary and Artistic Theories of Mao Tse-tung," which denounced both literary and art workers who still clung to outmoded bourgeois aesthetics and literary and art workers, who, while accepting Marxism, were "confused" about its applications to the special problems of their professions. The "correct" line for any culture worker in any field, according to Ho, was the line set forth by the party. In 1953 Ho became deputy chairman of the classical literature department of the Union of Chinese Writers, and in 1954 he was made a member of the Chinese People's Society for Cultural Relations with Foreign Countries. He attended the second national congress of the Sino-Soviet Friendship Association in 1954, and in 1955 he was appointed a member of the standing committee of the Philosophy and Social Science Institute of China. Beginning in 1951 he taught at the Marxist-Leninist Institute, and in 1953 he published a series of lectures on literature entitled *Kuan-yü hsien-shih chu-i* [realism in art].

The capstone of Ho Ch'i-fang's career as a Communist arbiter of the arts was his participation in the so-called Hu Feng affair. Hu, whom Ho had tried to compel to orthodoxy ten years earlier, took occasion in November 1954 to indict the entire Maoist literary establishment, particularly Chou Yang and Ho Ch'i-fang, for what he termed the total abortion of literature since 1949. Blind worship of authority, dogmatic Marxism, and the persecution of young progressive writers were but a few of the charges Hu leveled at Chou and Ho in the two tense days of denunciation. Chou replied to the charges with equal bitterness in an address entitled "We Must Fight," which launched a nation-wide attack on Hu in which Ho Ch'i-fang played a prominent role. Subsequent to Hu's arrest and disap-

pearance in June 1955, Ho continued to attack Hu's position in a series of books, including *Kuan-yü hsieh-shih ho tu-shih* [writing poetry and reading poetry], published in 1956; *Mei-yu p'i-ping chiu mei-yu ch'ien-pu* [without criticism there are no steps forward], published in 1958; *Shih-ko hsin-shang* [the appreciation of poetry], published in 1962; and *Wen-hsueh i-shu ti ch'un-t'ien* [the springtime of literary art], published in 1964.

Ho Ch'i-fang continued to write poetry and essays after 1945. In 1946 he published *Hsing-huo chi* [star fire], a collection of essays. He published a collection of poems, *Yü-yen*, in 1947. *Hsi-yuan chi* [western park], a second collection of essays, appeared in 1952. In 1951 in another attempt at "re-education," Ho traveled extensively in north China, studying folk songs from northern Shansi. Such post-1955 poems as "Wo hao-hsiang t'ing-chien-le po-t'ao ti hu-hsiao" [I seem to hear the roar of the waves], which celebrates the success of water conservancy measures at Hankow, have dealt with "correct" themes, but most of them were written in the polished idiom of Ho's early works, a distinctive style which was unaffected by the Maoist line and Ho's own studies in folk poetry.

Ho Chien   何 鍵
    T. Yün-ch'iao   芸 樵
    H. Jung-yuan   容 園

Ho Chien (10 April 1887–25 April 1956), Hunanese military leader, served as governor of Hunan from March 1929 to November 1937.

The Liling district of Hunan was the birthplace of Ho Chien. He attended the Chu-tzu Primary School in his native village and then entered the Hunan government school. After the revolution began in 1911, he joined the Nanking student corps. In 1912 he enrolled at the Second Army Preparatory School at Wuchang. He then went to north China to enter the third class at the Paoting Military Academy. One of his classmates at Paoting was Pai Ch'ung-hsi (q.v.). Ho was graduated from the cavalry course in 1916. He then received field training with the 1st Hunan Division. In 1917 he became a platoon commander, and then he was made deputy commander of the 9th Company, 2nd Regiment, of that division.

The Peiyang general Chang Ching-yao was appointed military governor of Hunan in 1918, and the Hunan forces were compelled to retreat to Pinhsien. Ho Chien was assigned to the Liuyang-Liling area with the mission of harassing the rearguard of the northern forces. In the following year, he expanded his force and divided it into two units. In 1920 Chao Heng-t'i and T'an Yen-k'ai (qq.v.) simultaneously attacked Chang Ching-yao and forced him from power. Wu Kuang-hsin, a relative of Tuan Ch'i-jui (q.v.), was named governor of Hunan.

During the campaign against Chang Ching-yao, Ho Chien was made commander of the cavalry regiment of the Hunan 1st Division. He then become commander of the 9th Regiment. In 1924 Ho accompanied T'ang Sheng-chih (q.v.) to Loyang for a conference with Wu P'ei-fu. In May 1926, when T'ang Sheng-chih became commander of the Eighth Army of the National Revolutionary Army, Ho Chien received command of its 2nd Division. Ho participated in the military operations that led to the capture of Wuchang in October 1926. After the April 1927 split between the left-wing Kuomintang at Wuhan and Chiang Kai-shek's faction at Nanking, T'ang Sheng-chih became commander of the Fourth Front Army, and Ho Chien was made commander of the Thirty-fifth Army of the Fourth Front Army.

In the areas under Wuhan's jurisdiction, and especially in Hunan, members of the Communist-led workers and peasants movement confiscated land and killed landlords. Although Ho Chien pointed out the dangers of the radical program for redistributing land, Wang Ching-wei and T'ang Sheng-chih accepted it on 22 April 1927. At the end of April, T'ang led his armies northward to attack the northern generals. Ho Chien's Thirty-fifth Army, with the exception of a few units ordered to remain in Hunan, was assigned to the expedition as a reserve force. Before leaving Wuhan, Ho Chien sent instructions to Hsü K'o-hsiang, the commander of the 33rd Regiment, and to the other commanding officers of the units remaining in Hunan.

On 19 May 1927 elements of the Thirty-fifth Army in Hunan clashed with the General Labor Union in Changsha. Ho Chien's residence was ransacked by the union's "inspection brigade," and his father was arrested. On 21 May, Hsü K'o-hsiang's 33rd Regiment took action against the union, the peasants associations, and the Communists. By the next morning, Hsü had suppressed and disarmed the opposition forces. This action was called the Ma Jih Incident because the code name for 21 May was Ma Jih. T'ang Sheng-chih ordered that the rifles taken from the workers and peasants be returned to them. Ho Chien, who was then in Hsinyang, Honan, acceded to this demand. On 5 June, he informed Wuhan that his troops in Hunan had been instructed to await settlement of the affair by government investigators from Wuhan.

T'ang Sheng-chih returned to Changsha on 25 June 1927. His forces had been withdrawn from Honan after the conference between Wang Ching-wei and Feng Yü-hsiang (q.v.) at Chengchow. T'ang discovered that his subordinates and supporters in Hunan had become strongly anti-Communist, and his own attitude began to change. Ho Chien and his Thirty-fifth Army were sent to Wuhan. On 28 June, while Li P'in-hsien and his Eighth Army disarmed the picket corps of the Wuhan General Labor Union, units of Ho's army occupied the headquarters of labor unions in Hankow and Hanyang. On 15 July the political council at Wuhan passed a resolution expelling the Communists from the Kuomintang. Two days later, Li P'in-hsien and Ho Chien placed Hankow and Hanyang under military control and rapidly suppressed Communist, workers, and peasants organizations.

Chang Fa-k'uei, Chu P'ei-te (qq.v.), and T'ang Sheng-chih then deployed their forces against Nanking. By September 1927 Ho Chien and his troops had reached Anking, the provincial capital of Anhwei, and Liu Hsing's Thirty-sixth Army had arrived at Wuhu. On the recommendation of T'ang Sheng-chih, Ho Chien was appointed acting governor of Anhwei.

By this time, the Kuomintang leaders at Nanking and Wuhan were discussing reunification. On 20 October 1927 the Nanking authorities announced plans for an expedition against T'ang Sheng-chih and issued an order removing him from his official posts. A week later, Ho Chien, whose lines of communication were being threatened by Chu P'ei-te at Kiukiang, withdrew from Anking without a fight. Immediately, the city was occupied by the forces of Li Tsung-jen (q.v.). On 11 November, an emissary from the Nanking Military Affairs Commission met with Ho Chien at T'uanfeng, and Ho agreed to return to Wuhan and urge T'ang Sheng-chih to retire. The next day, because other commanders refused to accept his orders and because his front-line forces had failed to fight, T'ang announced his retirement.

Nanking's forces reached Hankow on 15 November. Ho Chien, Liu Hsing, and Li P'in-hsien retreated to Hunan, where they attempted to consolidate their position. On 3 January 1928, after Li Tsung-jen at Nanking had expressed the hope that Chiang Kai-shek would resume office as commander in chief of the Nationalist armies, Ho and his colleagues telegraphed Chiang to urge him to return to his posts. However, this gesture did not save their position. Nanking forces led by Pai Ch'ung-hsi and Ch'eng Ch'ien advanced into Hunan and defeated the Hunan forces in a battle fought on 21–23 January. Changsha was occupied on 25 January, and Ho Chien retreated into western Hunan. On 23 May, the National Government appointed Lu Ti-p'ing governor of Hunan and director of rural pacification. On 1 January 1929 he was appointed commander in chief of bandit suppression for Hunan and Kiangsi, with headquarters at Pinghsiang, Kiangsi. At the end of January, his forces occupied the Communist base at Chingkang-shan.

In the meantime, the struggle between Chiang Kai-shek and the Kwangsi faction, led by Pai Ch'ung-hsi, Huang Shao-hung (q.v.), and Li Tsung-jen, was coming to a climax. On 21 February 1929 the Wuhan branch of the Political Council, which was dominated by the Kwangsi generals, sent an army under Yeh Ch'i to Hunan to oust Lu Ti-p'ing. The council also announced the reorganization of the Hunan provincial government and appointed Ho Chien governor. The National Government temporarily acquiesced and designated Ho acting provincial governor. He assumed office on 2 March 1929. He also took over Lu Ti-p'ing's post as director of rural pacification, and Yeh Ch'i became his deputy. Because the National Government then was mobilizing its forces, Ho asked to be relieved of his posts on 11 March.

However, he maintained his connections with the Kwangsi leaders, and he was assigned an important command in the Kwangsi forces.

After the National Government armies went into action against the Kwangsi forces in the Wuhan area, Ho Chien sent a message to Huang Shao-hung on 29 March that indicated his abandonment of the Kwangsi cause. Ho also sent a representative to Nanking to announce his support of the National Government. He was appointed commander of the Fourth Route of the Punitive Army and was confirmed as governor of Hunan. By the end of April, Kwangsi power in central China had been broken.

Ho Chien participated in the troop disbandment conference at Nanking in August 1929. The conference, however, served only to increase resistance of regional commanders to National Government authority. In September, Chang Fa-k'uei, then at Ichang, Hupeh, demanded safe passage through western Hunan to join his allies in south China. Ho Chien, on instructions from Nanking, deployed troops to intercept Chang. However, when Ho discovered that Chang's field headquarters was at Shaoyang, a short distance southwest of the provincial capital, he allowed Chang to pass through western Hunan to Kwangsi without serious difficulty.

The National Government then directed its attention to meeting the threat to its power in Honan, where Feng Yü-hsiang's armies held control. T'ang Sheng-chih participated in the campaign against Feng's troops. In December 1929, however, T'ang announced that he would oppose the National Government and named Ho Chien as one of his supporters. After talking with Nanking's representative Liu Wen-tao, Ho decided to remain loyal to the National Government. Thus, T'ang Sheng-chih's move failed.

In 1930 Feng Yü-hsiang and Yen Hsi-shan reached agreement with the Kwangsi armies on a joint military action against the National Government. When the Kwangsi forces and Chang Fa-k'uei's army drove northward in late May, Ho Chien evacuated Hengyang and Shaoyang without a fight. Chiang Kai-shek ordered Ho into battle and sent reinforcements from Wuhan and Nanking. However, the Kwangsi forces captured Changsha on 3 June and Yochow on 6 June. A force from Kwang-tung then cut off the Kwangsi rearguard. The Kwangsi forces turned back to extricate the rearguard, but were defeated near Hengyang. Ho Chien occupied Changsha and then pro-ceeded to Hengyang.

Ho Chien was ordered to join the Kwangtung forces in a drive on Kwangsi. In July 1930, however, the Communist commander P'eng Te-huai (q.v.) advanced from the Hunan-Kwangsi border toward Changsha. Ho hastily returned to his capital. The Communist forces captured Yochow on 5 July and turned to surround Changsha. Although Ho deployed four regiments against them and recalled troops from southern Hunan, the Communists took Changsha on 27 July. The National Govern-ment sent forces commanded by Ho Ying-ch'in to Hunan, and American and Japanese gun-boats attacked Changsha. The Communists finally evacuated the city on 5 August. Although Ho Chien was severely criticized for failing to prevent the occupation of Changsha, he con-tinued to serve as governor of Hunan, and he became a member of the State Council.

Ho's chief concern as governor of Hunan was the maintenance of public order. Relying principally on police power, he strengthened the local pao-chia system and brought local military groups, particularly the Ai-hu-t'uan, under the control of the provincial government. He also sponsored modest educational reforms and developed Hunan's road system.

By mid-1933 Nationalist forces had encircled and blockaded the main Communist forces in southern Kiangsi. When a new campaign against the Communists was launched in October, Ho Chien received command of the West Route Army. The only strong Communist forces in Hunan were in the north and north-western regions; Ho systematically set out to fight them, dividing his area of operations into four districts. When the Communists in the Kiangsi-Fukien base area broke through the Nationalist blockade in October 1934 to begin the Long March, Ho Chien, on orders from the National Government, led ten divisions to intercept the Communists as they passed through southern Hunan. However, he missed the rapidly moving Communists by one day.

In 1935 Ho was appointed commander of the First Army of the so-called bandit-suppression forces, and he was elected to the Central Executive Committee of the Kuomintang. In 1936 he was made Changsha pacification direc-tor for a new campaign against the Communists. The Kwangtung-Kwangsi combine was elimi-nated as an independent political and military force, and Ho Chien lost much of his power, for he no longer was in a position to bargain with both the National Government and the Kwangsi-Kwangtung leaders. After the Sino-Japanese war broke out in July 1937, the National Government undertook a series of political re-organizations designed to centralize authority. On 20 November 1937, with the reorganization of several provincial governments in the Yangtze valley, Ho Chien was succeeded as governor of Hunan by Chiang Kai-shek's trusted lieutenant Chang Chih-chung (q.v.). Ho be-came minister of interior in the National Government (which then was located at Wuhan). He served as minister of interior for about 18 months, during which time the ministry produced important draft proposals for a new hsien system and for the mutual transfer of central and local government officials. In May 1939 he was made chairman of the pensions committee of the Military Affairs Commission. He held that post for about six years.

In 1945 Ho Chien resigned on grounds of illness and retired to Nanyueh, on one of China's five sacred mountains, in his native Hunan. In the spring of 1949, as the Chinese Communists approached Changsha, Ho went to Hong Kong. He joined the National Govern-ment in Taiwan in the summer of 1950. He was appointed adviser on strategy and state policy in the office of President Chiang Kai-shek. Ho Chien died in Taipei on 25 April 1956, only a year short of his seventieth birth-day.

Among the prominent Hunanese military officers of the republican period, Ho Chien was roughly of the same generation as Ho Yao-tsu, Lu Ti-p'ing, and T'ang Sheng-chih and several years junior to Chao Heng-t'i and Ch'eng Ch'ien. His ability as a political general was demonstrated by his success in maintaining himself as governor of Hunan from March 1929 to November 1937, a record surpassed only by Yen Hsi-shan in Shansi province and by Yang Tseng-hsin in Sinkiang.

Ho Chung-han   賀 衷 寒
T. Chün-shan   君 山

Ho Chung-han (5 January 1900–), directed political training in the Nationalist armies (1931–38) and headed the labor bureau of the ministry of social affairs (1942–47). In Taiwan, he served as minister of communications (1950–54) and chairman of the Kuomintang's Central Planning Committee (1962–).

Yochow (Yoyang), Hunan, was the birthplace of Ho Chung-han. After receiving his early education in his native place, he went to Wuchang in 1916 to enter a special middle school for Hunan provincials. From 1917 to 1919 he also worked as a student reporter for a news agency at Wuchang, and he participated in student activities at the time of the May Fourth Movement of 1919. In the winter of 1920, when Tung Pi-wu and Ch'en T'an-ch'iu (qq.v.) organized a small Marxist study group at Wuchang, Ho joined it.

Ho Chung-han went to Shanghai in the spring of 1921 to study Russian. In September 1921 he was elected a delegate to the Congress of the Toilers of the East, and he went to Moscow late in that year with Chang Kuo-t'ao (q.v.), one of the founders of the Chinese Communist party. Ho remained in the Soviet Union for about seven months, but he did not join the Chinese Communist party.

Ho Chung-han returned to China in the spring of 1922 and became a reporter for the People's News Agency at Wuchang. After the agency was forced to close in 1923, he went to Changsha to establish a news agency. At that time, T'an Yen-k'ai (q.v.) was preparing to oust Chao Heng-t'i (q.v.), the governor of Hunan. The initial success of T'an's campaign and Chao's withdrawal from Changsha enabled Ho Chung-han to spread nationalistic propaganda. But the venture proved to be short-lived. Wu P'ei-fu soon intervened in the area and restored Chao Heng-t'i to power. Although Chao closed the news agency, Ho continued to be active in youth affairs at Changsha and became a special correspondent for a Shanghai paper.

In the spring of 1924 Ho Chung-han applied for admission to the Whampoa Military Academy. He entered the academy in May 1924 as a member of its first class. After being graduated in November, he was assigned to work in the political department of a recently established branch of the academy at Canton. His classmate Li Chih-lung was assigned to similar duties.

In 1925–26 the Kuomintang and the Communists competed for political control of the Whampoa cadets. In January 1925, Soviet adviser Borodin and the Chinese Communists established the Young Soldiers Association to bring the cadets under Communist direction. Ho Chung-han, then the chief editor of the *Kuo-min ko-ming chou-k'an* [national revolutionary weekly], objected to the criticism of Sun Yat-sen which appeared in publications of the Young Soldiers Association after Sun's death in March 1925; he proposed that the young officers of China pay more attention to the ideas of Sun Yat-sen than to alien ideas propounded by Marx, John Dewey, Bertrand Russell, and others. Together with Miao Pin (q.v.) and others, he suggested that the Sun Yat-sen Study Society be formed. Chiang Kai-shek and Liao Chung-k'ai, the senior Kuomintang representative in charge of political affairs at Whampoa, approved the idea.

The formation of the new society was postponed for a time, however, because Ho Chung-han and Miao Pin were assigned to participate in the Kuomintang's campaign against the forces of Ch'en Chiung-ming (q.v.) in eastern Kwangtung. Despite personal and political disagreements during the period of preparation, plans for the formation of the society moved forward steadily. The organization was established on 29 December 1925, with its headquarters at Canton. Ho Chung-han was its chairman.

Ho Chung-han was serving as party representative in the 1st Regiment of the 1st Division of the National Revolutionary Army. However, he had passed the examinations given at Whampoa for study in the Soviet Union. Despite the continuing friction between the Sun Yat-sen Study Society and the Communist-influenced Young Soldiers Association at Canton, Ho went to Moscow in early 1926 and enrolled at the Frunze Military Academy. On 20 March, Chang Kai-shek took action against both the Chinese Communists and the Soviet advisers in China as a result of the Chung-shan incident, in which Li Chih-lung was implicated. On 21 May 1926, on orders from Chiang Kai-shek, both the Sun Yat-sen Study Society and the Young Soldiers Association were dissolved.

After graduation from the Frunze Academy, Ho returned to China in January 1928. Chiang Kai-shek assigned him to command the cadets unit at the military training center at Hang-chow, which had been established to accommodate cadets from the later classes at Whampoa who had fled from Canton during the disorders of late 1927.

After the inauguration of the National Government at Nanking in October 1928, Ho, who had been relieved of his training responsibilities at Hangchow, was assigned to the Kuomintang headquarters for the Nanking municipality. In the spring of 1929 he requested Chiang Kai-shek's permission to go to Japan to study military and political affairs. The request was approved, and Ho moved to Tokyo. In addition to observing developments in Japan, he produced two books criticizing Wang Ching-wei and his so-called Reorganization faction, a group within the Kuomintang which strongly opposed the growing personal power of Chiang Kai-shek.

Ho Chung-han was ordered to return to China in February 1931 and was assigned to direct the office in charge of political propaganda in the Nationalist military headquarters at Nanking. The 1927 break with the Chinese Communists had been followed by wars within the Nationalist camp in 1929 and 1931. The Communists, by exploiting the situation, presented new problems to the Nationalist political workers. Ho Chung-han called his organization the "bandit-suppression propaganda office," and he proceeded to standardize that name: thereafter, Nationalist anti-Communist campaigns were called "bandit-suppression" campaigns. On Chiang Kai-shek's orders, the Central Military Academy at Nanking provided a special training class of some 200 senior students for a two-week course, after which they were assigned to Ho's new office.

In the winter of 1931, the bandit-suppression propaganda office became the political training office of bandit-suppression troops, under the inspectorate general of military training. In June 1932, after a conference of Nationalist officials at Lushan, it was decided that there should be separate political training offices for the bandit-suppression commands of Honan-Hupeh-Anhwei and Kiangsi-Kwangtung-Fukien. Ho was placed in charge of the first of these two offices, which was established on 28 June at Hankow. He established an official motion picture studio, and he transferred to Hankow the Nationalist army newspaper that he had launched in 1931 at Nanchang, then the field headquarters for the campaigns against the Communists in Kiangsi. This paper was the well-known and strongly anti-Communist Sao-tang pao [mopping-up journal], which continued to publish under that name even during the interlude of Nationalist-Communist collaboration in the early part of the Sino-Japanese war. The paper later was directed at Chungking by Huang Shao-ku (q.v.).

In the early 1930's Ho was elected to membership on the Kuomintang's Central Executive Committee. The National Government's organizational structure for political work at the time was rather complex. The two political training offices designed for anti-Communist operations in the field were, in practice, independent of the political training office of the Military Affairs Commission at Nanking. In February 1933 the local offices were merged with the central political training office at Nanking, and Ho Chung-han was given responsibility for centralized direction of political training and propaganda work as the head of the political training office at Nanking. He now had control over political work in the military forces, in government offices, and in schools throughout the Nationalist-controlled areas of China.

In May 1933, at Ho Chung-han's request, a political work conference was convened at Nanchang. The conference formulated a political training order which defined the tasks, duties, and powers of political workers in the Nationalist army. It also drew up plans to guide the development of political work in the so-called bandit-suppression campaigns. Ho also headed a political training office in the Nanchang headquarters of the Military Affairs Commission.

The advance of the Japanese in north China in the spring of 1933 had increased the tasks of the political workers. In April, a special north China propaganda column was organized to carry on political work in the Chinese military forces in north China, most of which were not directly controlled by Nanking. On 1 August 1933 the column was reorganized as the political training bureau of the Peiping branch of the Military Council.

In March 1934, again under Ho's direction, a second political work conference was convened at Nanchang to readjust work plans. In October, the Communist forces broke out of the encirclement of their Kiangsi base and began the Long March. In January 1935, in conjunction with the pursuit of the Communists, the Military Affairs Commission set up a Chungking staff corps, with a political training office under it, as a device for extending Nanking's political authority over military forces in Szechwan and Sikang. Ho's deputy Yuan Shou-ch'ien went to Chungking to direct operations.

In 1935 Ho Chung-han was reelected to the Kuomintang Central Executive Committee and was made a member of its standing committee. He also became a member of the organization department of the Kuomintang and chief of the army party affairs group.

In April 1935, at Ho's request, a third political work conference was held, this time at Hankow. That gathering worked to coordinate the efforts of political organs with the army reorganization plan proposed by the Military Affairs Commission. Nationalist political work was directed toward the extension of Nanking's control over provincial armies in west and northwest China and toward the task of resisting the Japanese advance.

The Japanese opposed the expansion of Nationalist political activity in north China; they were working to detach north China from Nanking's direct jurisdiction. When the political training bureau of the Peiping branch of the Military Council in June 1935 undertook to enroll students in a military training program, the Japanese brought pressure on the National Government at Nanking to withdraw its political and party organs from Hopei and Chahar and, in particular, to remove its political workers immediately. On 24 June 1935 the National Government complied with the Japanese demand; all Kuomintang political workers in north China were ordered to withdraw to Wuchang. The north China group then was reassigned to Sian, where a northwest

branch of the political training office was established in August 1935. Its mission was to prevent the Northeast Army units of Chang Hsueh-liang (q.v.) from being influenced by Communist propaganda, which then called for a national united front to oppose Japanese aggression.

In 1936 Ho was assigned several additional positions at Nanking: secretary general of the political affairs department of the Military Affairs Commission; head of the censorship bureau of the Central News Agency; and executive secretary of the provisional standing committee of the San Min Chu I Youth Corps.

In June 1937 Chiang Kai-shek granted Ho permission to visit Europe and the United States to inspect military and political conditions. When he took leave of Chiang at Lushan on 22 June, Ho presented a plan, later implemented, for reorganization of the San Min Chu I Youth Corps. Ho was in Bombay on his way to Europe when Japanese and Chinese forces clashed in the Lukouchiao Incident of 7 July 1937. He went on to Europe and had spent four weeks in Germany when the Sino-Japanese conflict spread to Shanghai. On 14 August Chiang Kai-shek recalled him to China. In October, Ho Ching-han resumed his duties as director of the political training office at Nanking.

In February 1938 the Military Affairs Commission established a political department to consolidate the work of the political training office and other governmental organs. Ch'en Ch'eng (q.v.) was named director, with Chou En-lai and the Kwangtung military man Huang Ch'i-hsiang as his deputies. Ho Chung-han received only a subordinate position as chief of the first bureau of the political department. His authority had been reduced and restricted, although he remained in charge of political training in the Nationalist armies and military academies and was later given the concurrent assignment of secretary general of the political department. In April 1939 Ho spent a period in the field as chief of a Nationalist "comfort" mission to northwest China. He visited Yenan, the Communist wartime capital, where he talked with Mao Tse-tung.

When he assumed control of the political department of the Military Affairs Commission, Ch'en Ch'eng succeeded Ho Chung-han as secretary general of the San Min Chu I Youth Corps. Ho retained a position in the central executive apparatus of the corps. By early 1940, friction between Ho Chung-han and Ch'en Ch'eng had increased to such an extent that Ho resigned from the political department.

In the spring of 1941 Ho Chung-han was named director of the manpower section of the National General Mobilization Council. In 1942 he became director of the labor bureau of the ministry of social affairs of the National Government. He held that position for five years, during which he confronted many serious problems, notably the control of wage levels and the settlement of labor disputes under the skyrocketing inflation which gripped Nationalist-controlled areas of China. He also made efforts to plan and implement a program, based on the writings of Sun Yat-sen, of voluntary labor service. His 1947 lectures on the subject, given at Wuchang to a special training class for labor service cadres, were published in book form as *Chung-kuo te ping-ken* [the root of China's evils]. Ho Chung-han continued to play an active role in the Kuomintang. He was reelected to the Central Executive Committee at the Sixth National Congress in 1945, and he was executive secretary of the central organizational apparatus of the San Min Chu I Youth Corps from 1944 to 1947.

In 1947 Ho was made political vice minister of the ministry of social affairs at Nanking. He also was elected a delegate, representing Yo-yang, to the National Assembly. In January 1949, when Chiang Kai-shek retired from the presidency, Ho resigned his government position in the ministry of social affairs to devote himself to lecturing and writing on the national crisis. Ho did not return to political office until after the Nationalist withdrawal from the mainland. In March 1950, when Chiang Kai-shek resumed leadership of the National Government in Taiwan, Ho was appointed minister of communications. Ch'en Ch'eng, who became president of the Executive Yuan, was again his superior. Ho Chung-han served as minister of communications for slightly more than four years. In May 1954, after Ch'en Ch'eng had been elected to the vice presidency, all members of his cabinet, including Ho, submitted their resignations. In 1962 Ho became chairman of the Central Planning Committee of the Kuomintang.

Ho Hsiang-ning   何香凝

Ho Hsiang-ning (1880–), the wife of Liao Chung-k'ai (q.v.), was the first woman to join the T'ung-meng-hui (1905). A member of the Kuomintang's Central Executive Committee (1926–31), she left the party and helped to found the Kuomintang Revolutionary Committee. She served the Central People's Government as chairman of the Overseas Chinese Affairs Commission (1949–59).

Although her native place was Nanhai (Namhoi) hsien, Kwangtung, Ho Hsiang-ning spent her early years in the British colony of Hong Kong, where her family was in the tea business. Little is known of her childhood. In 1897 she married Liao Chung-k'ai (q.v.) in Canton. Ho Hsiang-ning's family gave them money so that they could go to Japan to study.

In 1902 Ho and Liao arrived in Tokyo. Liao Chung-k'ai studied at Waseda University, and Ho studied painting at the Tokyo Girls Art School. They met other Chinese students, many of whom were sympathetic to the anti-Manchu movement led by Sun Yat-sen. Ho Hsiang-ning and her husband met Sun in the summer of 1903, and they soon became active supporters of his plans for a revolution. In 1905 they joined the T'ung-meng-hui, of which Ho was the first female member. To avert the suspicion of the Japanese police, their residence in Tokyo was used as the T'ung-meng-hui headquarters. Ho did the housework even though it was unusual at this time for Chinese women from well-to-do families to concern themselves with domestic chores.

In 1911, a year after Ho's graduation from the Tokyo Girls Art School, she and Liao returned to Canton. She worked to recruit women for the revolutionary cause. After the failure of the so-called second revolution in 1913, she and Liao followed Sun Yat-sen to Japan. For the next decade Ho spent much of her time in Tokyo with her two children. Liao Meng-hsing (Cynthia Liao), who had been born in Japan in 1903, attended school in Tokyo; Liao Ch'eng-chih (q.v.), born in Tokyo in 1908, received his early education there, and then returned to Canton in 1919 for middle school.

Liao Chung-k'ai returned to Canton in March 1923, taking Ho and Liao Meng-hsing with him. Ho took an active role in political affairs at Canton. She was one of three Chinese women who took part in the First National Congress of the Kuomintang, held in January 1924 at Canton. The others were Soong Ch'ing-ling, the wife of Sun Yat-sen, and Ch'en Pi-chün, the wife of Wang Ching-wei. Ho was appointed director of the women's department of the Kuomintang. In 1924 she was a member of the party that accompanied Sun Yat-sen to north China, and she was among those who witnessed his will in 1925.

After the death of Sun Yat-sen in March 1925, Liao Chung-k'ai became one of the most powerful political figures at Canton. He and his wife strongly supported Sun's policies of alignment with the Chinese Communists and the Soviet Union to achieve national unification in China. Conservative elements within the Kuomintang opposed the alliance, and on 20 August 1925 Liao was assassinated at Canton. Ho Hsiang-ning, who was with him at the time, was not injured.

In January 1926 Ho and Soong Ch'ing-ling became the first women to be elected to the Central Executive Committee of the Kuomintang. In the winter of 1926 she moved to Wuhan, where Teng Ying-ch'ao, the wife of Chou En-lai, served for a time as her assistant.

In 1927 Chiang Kai-shek broke with the Communists and began a vigorous campaign to eliminate Communists in the areas of China under his effective control. That action led to the destruction of the women's department, and many girls and women working under Ho Hsiang-ning were imprisoned, tortured, and executed. Ho resigned her posts in the Kuomintang and moved to Hong Kong. For some 20 years, she actively opposed the Kuomintang under the personal domination of Chiang Kai-shek. Although she was reelected to the Central Executive Committee of the Kuomintang in 1931, she did not take part in Kuomintang affairs. She and Soong Ch'ing-ling attempted to promote civil liberties in China and to defend political prisoners of the Kuomintang. For the most part, Ho lived quietly in Hong Kong with

her daughter or traveled. During the Sino-Japanese war, she contributed to war relief work among refugees and troops in west China.

In 1948 Ho Hsiang-ning participated in the establishment of the Kuomintang Revolutionary Committee, one of the minor parties opposing the Nationalists and indirectly supporting the Chinese Communists during the final stages of the civil war. Li Chi-shen (q.v.) headed the organization, and Ho was elected to its standing committee.

Ho Hsiang-ning left Hong Kong for north China in April 1949. When the Central People's Government was established at Peking in October, she was elected to the Central People's Government Council and was made chairman of the Overseas Chinese Affairs Commission and a member of the People's Procurator-General's Office. She served as chairman of the Overseas Chinese Affairs Commission until 1959, although much of the administrative work was done by her son, Liao Ch'eng-chih, who was one of the vice chairmen. In August 1960, at the age of 80, Ho was elected chairman of the central committee of the Kuomintang Revolutionary Committee. She also held the office of honorary chairman of the China Women's Federation.

Ho Hsiang-ning was one of the first women of her generation to take an active role in the attempt to liberate women from the constraints imposed on them by traditional Chinese conservatism and superstition. Photographs taken at Peking in the 1960's showed Ho wearing her hair in the short, straight cut that she had worn at Canton 40 years earlier, when such a style had been considered a reliable indicator of social radicalism and dangerous thoughts.

Ho Hsiang-ning was also known in China as a poet-painter in the classical tradition. A collection of her paintings was published as *Ho Hsiang-ning hua-chi*. In 1957 she published a book of reminiscences about Sun Yat-sen and Liao Chung-k'ai called *Hui-i Sun Chung-shan ho Liao Chung-k'ai*. At the fiftieth anniversary celebrations of the 1911 revolution in Peking, Ho was a featured speaker, and she wrote a lengthy article which appeared in the Peking *People's Daily* on 7 October 1961 and which gave a moving, if not always precise, account of the death of Sun Yat-sen.

Ho Kuei-yen: *see* HO YAO-TSU.

Ho Lung　　　　賀　龍
　T. Yün-ch'ing　　雲　卿

Ho Lung (11 March 1896–), Hunanese military leader who, with Yeh T'ing (q.v.) staged the Nanchang uprising of 1 August 1927. He helped build the Chinese Communist military establishment in the 1930's and 1940's. After 1949 he served the Central People's Government in such posts as commander of the Southwest Military District (1950–52), head of the National Physical Culture and Sports Commission (1952–), and officer of the State and National Defense councils.

A native of Tayung in western Hunan, Ho Lung was the son of a poor, but locally prominent officer of the Ch'ing military forces. He received little formal education. His father, an influential member of the Ko-lao-hui [elder brother society], encouraged him to become a military man. In the spring of 1912 there was a famine in western Hunan. Ho Lung participated in a peasant rebellion in the neighboring hsien of Sangchih; he often was referred to in later years as a native of that district. Starting with a few followers, Ho built an armed force of several thousand men, and he gradually extended his raids into bordering districts of Kweichow, Szechwan, and Hupeh. Because it was unable to defeat him, the government of Hunan in 1918 gave him a commission in the provincial army.

From 1918 to 1925 Ho Lung gained practical experience as a military officer and rose to the rank of regimental commander under Wu P'ei-fu (q.v.). Early in 1925 he was associated for a time with the Szechwanese general Hsiung K'o-wu (q.v.) and was given command of a unit in the Szechwan National Construction Army. Ho then transferred his loyalties to the Hunanese general Chao Heng-t'i (q.v.), who made him garrison commander of Lichou, with jurisdiction over some ten hsien of western Hunan, a territory through which opium caravans passed on the way from Yunnan to Hankow. Ho maintained himself comfortably by levying taxes on the opium trade.

As plans developed for the Northern Expedition, Ho Lung was induced to join the Kuomintang and to support the Nationalist effort to unify China. When the National Revolutionary Army reached Hunan in 1926, Ho Lung joined it, and he established a program of political indoctrination in the unit under his command. His unit then was reorganized as the Independent 5th Division, and his relative Chou I-ch'un was named to head its political department. Chou I-ch'un, a Communist, was a graduate of the first class at the Whampoa Military Academy. He had served as a political instructor under Chou En-lai after graduation. In the campaign in Honan, the Independent 5th Division distinguished itself, capturing the sedan chair of Chao Jung-chen, an army commander under Chang Tso-lin. Ho Lung's division then was enlarged to become the Twentieth Army of the National Revolutionary Army.

When the Kuomintang factions at Wuhan and Nanking split in the spring of 1927, Ho Lung remained loyal to the authorities at Wuhan. When Wang Ching-wei, the dominant Kuomintang figure at Wuhan, began to suppress the Communists there in July 1927, Ho Lung was ordered to move his forces to Kiukiang in Kiangsi province. However, Ho did not stop at Kiukiang, but moved on to Nanchang. Forces of his Twentieth Army joined with units of the Eleventh Army under Yeh T'ing (q.v.) to stage an uprising in the early morning hours of 1 August 1927. Although it was suppressed a few days later, the Nanchang uprising later came to be celebrated by the Chinese Communists as the birth of the Red Army in China.

After their defeat at Nanchang, Ho Lung, Yeh T'ing, Chu Teh, and other military officers associated with the action marched southward. On 10 August 1927 Ho Lung joined the Chinese Communist party. In late September, the Communist forces occupied Swatow, but they were driven out a few days later. Under sustained attack, Ho Lung and his forces retreated to Haifeng, Kwangtung, where he was captured. He escaped and fled to Hong Kong. Chou En-lai, then recovering in Hong Kong from a bout with malaria, gave him formal indoctrination in Marxism-Leninism. Ho Lung then went to Shanghai to establish contact with the central authorities of the Chinese Communist party.

Ho Lung was assigned to western Hunan to organize a new base. Accompanied by a few political workers, he traveled secretly to Wuhan and thence to the Sangchih district of Hunan. His assistants included Chou I-ch'un, who had served with him in the Twentieth Army, and his sister Ho Hsiang-ku. Ho Lung began to mobilize political support among the poor peasants and to organize military forces. The resulting Hunan-Hupeh soviet area soon developed into an important Communist base area in central China. In 1930, Ho Lung's troops were designated the Second Red Army. In the next year, the unit was expanded to include three Red armies, the Second, Sixth, and Ninth, with Ho in over-all command.

The Chinese Communist party top command, then underground at Shanghai, assigned Teng Chung-hsia (q.v.), who had recently returned to China from the Soviet Union, to the soviet area as Ho Lung's political commissar. Teng soon returned to Shanghai. In 1931 Teng was succeeded by Hsia Hsi, a Hunanese Communist who had been an original member of the Hsin-min hsueh-hui [new people's study society] at Changsha in the period after the First World War. Through Hsia Hsi, Ho Lung met Mao Tse-tung. In November 1931, when the first All-China Soviet Congress met at Juichin, Kiangsi, a central soviet government was formed and Ho Lung was elected to membership on its executive council. In 1932 Kuan Hsiang-ying (q.v.) was assigned to Ho Lung's base area as political commissar. Kuan and Ho became close friends.

Because of increasing Nationalist military pressure in 1932–33, Ho Lung was forced to abandon his original base area in the Hung Lake area west of Wuhan and to seek refuge in the remote Hunan-Kweichow border area. In November 1934 Communist forces under Hsiao K'o and Jen Pi-shih (qq.v.), which had been operating along the Kiangsi-Hunan border, joined forces with Ho Lung at Yenho. Hsiao K'o had succeeded Chou I-ch'un (who had been killed) as commander of the Sixth Red Army. The Second Army and the Sixth Army were merged to form the Second Front Army, with Ho Lung as commander. Ho then began work to establish a new Communist

territorial base, the Hunan-Hupeh-Szechwan-Kweichow border area.

Although Nationalist military encirclement forced the bulk of the Chinese Communist forces in Kiangsi to begin the Long March in October 1934, Ho Lung and his Second Front Army remained in their base area until the autumn of 1935, when they began a separate retreat. After moving through Kweichow and Yunnan, Ho Lung led his men on an arduous march into Sikang, where they succeeded in making a rendezvous in June 1936 with the Fourth Front Army of Chang Kuo-t'ao and Hsü Hsiang-ch'ien (qq.v.). These forces then decided to march northward. Ho Lung and his troops finally arrived at the new Communist base in northern Shensi in October 1936.

After the Sian Incident and the outbreak of the Sino-Japanese war in the summer of 1937, the Communists and the Kuomintang reached agreement on the formation of a united front against Japan. Under the terms of that agreement, Communist forces were reorganized as the Eighth Route Army, composed of three divisions, under the nominal authority of the National Government. Ho Lung was named to command the 120th Division of the Eighth Route Army, with Kuan Hsiang-ying as political commissar and Hsiao K'o as deputy commander. In the autumn of 1937 Ho's division thrust into northwestern Shansi to create an anti-Japanese base along the Shansi-Suiyuan border. In 1938 the main force of the 120th Division moved eastward into Hopei to support the efforts of Nieh Jung-chen (q.v.) to build a Communist base on the central Hopei plain. In 1940 Ho Lung returned to the Shansi-Suiyuan border area to command the Communist military district which had been established there. From 1940 until the Japanese surrender in 1945, he held responsibility for the military security of the principal Shensi-Kansu-Ninghsia Border Region and for Communist operations in western Shansi designed to control the important railroad linking Taiyuan, the provincial capital, with Peiping. Ho became one of the best known and most colorful of the Communist military commanders in China. In 1945, when the Chinese Communists held their Seventh National Congress at Yenan, Ho Lung was elected to the Central Committee of the party.

After the Japanese surrender, Ho continued to hold primary military responsibility in the Communist-controlled Shensi-Kansu-Ninghsia Border Region and in the Shansi-Suiyuan area. In the early autumn of 1945 he was assigned to hold open a corridor through which Communist troops could move from northwest and north China into Manchuria, which was to be a vital theater of military operations in the Chinese civil war. In Suiyuan, where his principal Nationalist adversary was Fu Tso-yi (q.v.), Ho Lung laid siege to Paotow and Kweisui in November and December 1945. After the Communist troop movement to Manchuria had been completed, Ho Lung withdrew his forces and Suiyuan became relatively peaceful for a time. In March 1947 the Communists evacuated their wartime capital of Yenan, Shensi, in the face of an advance by Hu Tsung-nan (q.v.), but Ho Lung soon returned to defeat Hu's forces at Ich'uan. In 1948 Ho Lung continued to act as the senior Communist commander of what was called the northwest China military district. In 1949 he led his troops in a slashing move from western Shensi into Szechwan, where he joined forces with the Communist Second Field Army, commanded by Liu Po-ch'eng (q.v.).

Between 1949 and 1952, one prominent feature of the pattern of control established by the Communists in China was the creation of administrative regions. To a great extent, the jurisdiction of these administrative regions reflected the pattern of military control in China at the end of the civil war. The southwest region, with headquarters at Chungking, was established in July 1950 with jurisdiction over Szechwan, Yunnan, Kweichow, and Sikang. Authority over this vast and populous area of southwest China lay, practically speaking, in the hands of three senior Communists: Ho Lung, Liu Po-ch'eng, and Teng Hsiao-p'ing (q.v.). Ho Lung commanded the Southwest Military District, with Teng Hsiao-p'ing as political commissar; and he served as a senior vice chairman of the Southwest Military and Administrative Committee, which was headed by Liu Po-ch'eng.

In 1949 Ho Lung attended the Chinese People's Political Consultative Conference as a representative of the First Field Army of the People's Liberation Army. He became a member of the Central People's Government Council and of the People's Revolutionary Military Council. With the reorganization of the Central People's Government in 1954, Ho Lung became a vice premier of the State Council and a vice chairman of the National Defense Council. In September 1955 Ho Lung's military contributions to the Communist cause were recognized when he was awarded the rank of Marshal of the People's Republic of China. At the Eighth National Congress of the Chinese Communist party, held in September 1956, Ho Lung was reelected to the Central Committee. He also was elected to the Political Bureau. On 1 August 1965, observed as Army Day in the People's Republic of China, a lengthy article by Ho Lung embodying official doctrine regarding party-military relations in the Chinese Communist military forces was published in all Peking newspapers. The article stressed the continued relevance of the basic experience and methods outlined by Mao Tse-tung before 1949, praised the development of the revolutionary tradition under Lin Piao, and argued that the armed services of Communist China should remain under the firm political control of the Chinese Communist party.

Aside from a brief stay as a political refugee in the British colony of Hong Kong in 1927, Ho Lung had never traveled outside China before 1953, when he headed a delegation to visit Chinese Communist troops stationed in North Korea. He went to the Soviet Union in 1954 to attend the Soviet Sports Festival at Moscow. In the summer of 1955 he flew to Warsaw to head the Chinese Communist delegation at the tenth anniversary celebrations of the government of Poland, and in March 1956 he attended the celebrations that marked the independence of Pakistan. In November 1956 Ho accompanied Chou En-lai on a tour of Viet Nam, Cambodia, India, Burma, and Pakistan. Because of the growing unrest in Eastern Europe, Chou En-lai and Ho Lung returned to Peking at the beginning of January 1957. They then flew to Moscow, Warsaw, and Budapest. After returning to Moscow to issue a Sino-Soviet declaration stressing the need for "socialist solidarity," they left Russia for India, Nepal, and Ceylon. In March 1957 Ho Lung accompanied Chou En-lai to Kunming for a meeting with Burmese statesman U Nu to discuss Sino-Burmese border problems. Ho served as the representative of the Central People's Government Council at

the inauguration of the Kwangsi-Chuang Autonomous Region in March 1958. He headed the
delegation from the Central Committee of the
Chinese Communist party and the State Council
which flew to Urumchi in the autumn of 1965
for the celebrations which marked the tenth
anniversary of the establishment of the Sinkiang
Uighur Autonomous Region.

In 1952 Ho was named to head the National
Physical Culture and Sports Commission at
Peking, the principal organ devoted to making
China a sports-conscious nation and to raising
China's athletic accomplishments to recognized
world levels. The commission's program,
patterned after the Soviet Union's program of
sports for the masses, made rapid progress. The
People's Republic of China held its First
National Games in 1959 and its Second National
Games in 1965.

Because of the relative novelty of athletic
competition in China and the lack of sustained
international competition, Chinese performances in such major sports as track and field and
swimming generally were below world standards. However, the Chinese demonstrated outstanding proficiency in other events: archery,
cycling, gymnastics, parachuting, shooting, soc-
cer, speed skating, wrestling, and weight-lifting.
And Chinese players gained international
supremacy in table tennis. At the Twenty-
eighth World Table Tennis Championships in
1965, players from the People's Republic of
China won several world titles in the singles
competition and won both the Swaythling and
the Corbillon Cups for team events. In an
official message from Peking, Ho Lung saluted
the major victory scored by the Chinese in both
men's and women's events.

Almost all of Ho Lung's immediate family
died in the Communist revolution in China. A
brother died in prison in Shanghai. Of his
three sisters, two were active Communists who
were killed in the late 1920's. Ho Lung's first
wife was imprisoned and executed in the
1920's. He later remarried.

Ho Meng-hsiung 何夢雄

Ho Meng-hsiung (1903–7 February 1931),
Chinese Communist labor organizer who
opposed Li Li-san's policies. He was expelled
from the Chinese Communist party in 1931

after opposing the leadership of Chen Shao-yü.
He was executed by the Nationalists. Mao
Tse-tung later praised him as a "noble
martyr."

Little is known of Ho Meng-hsiung's early
life except that he was born in Hunan province
in Hsiangt'an hsien, Mao Tse-tung's native
district, and was graduated from a higher
primary school there at the age of 16. He then
went to Peking to live with an uncle who was
a member of the Parliament. Ho audited
classes at Peking University and became active
in the Marxist study group formed by Li Ta-
chao (q.v.). He also participated in early
attempts to carry the message of Marxism to the
railroad workers in north China.

In 1922 the Comintern decided that the
Chinese Communists should join the Kuomintang in pursuing the anti-imperialist revolution. The Comintern policy provoked divergent
reactions within the Chinese Communist party
regarding the extent of cooperation with non-
Communist groups and individuals. Ho Meng-
hsiung agreed with Chang Kuo-t'ao (q.v.) who,
although favoring the establishment of a united
front with the Kuomintang, opposed the idea
of having members of the Chinese Communist
party join the Kuomintang and work on its
behalf. Ho Meng-hsiung continued to work as
a Communist organizer, but the nature of his
activities is not known.

In 1927 Ho was a member of the Kiangsu
provincial committee of the Chinese Communist party and a leader of the Communist-
controlled general labor union at Shanghai. By
1930 he had become secretary of the Kiangsu
provincial committee and an alternate member
of the Central Committee of the Chinese Communist party.

From 1928 to 1930 Li Li-san (q.v.) was the
most influential man in the central apparatus
of the Chinese Communist party, then based
at Shanghai. Together with Lo Chang-lung,
Ho Meng-hsiung led a faction, composed
largely of labor organizers, which opposed
Li's leadership. This so-called labor union
faction believed that Li Li-san disregarded the
practical interests of the workers and that
official Communist political policies had a
damaging effect on the Communist-led unions.

In opposing Li Li-san, the labor union group
in the Chinese Communist party organization

at Shanghai found itself in temporary alliance with the so-called 28 Bolsheviks (*see* Ch'en Shao-yü), who had returned in the summer of 1930 from study in Moscow together with Pavel Mif, the Comintern representative assigned to China. At the third plenum of the sixth Central Committee of the Chinese Communist party in September 1930, Chou En-lai, who then supported the Li Li-san position, castigated Ho Meng-hsiung and Lo Chang-lung as right deviationists. Chou accused the labor union faction of being opportunistic in pressing for greater emphasis on improving working conditions at the expense of more important political programs. Ho Meng-hsiung wrote a series of letters to the Political Bureau to justify his position. After affirming that he was a loyal Communist and that he accepted the perspective of armed uprisings set by the Comintern in Moscow, Ho stated that relations between the Communist party and the Chinese masses were tenuous and argued that the party should strive to establish a solid proletarian base. To gain this objective, Ho concluded, emphasis should be placed on strikes designed to improve the economic position of urban industrial workers.

At a meeting of the Political Bureau of the Communist party on 25 November 1930 Pavel Mif attacked both the so-called Li Li-san line and the views of Ho Meng-hsiung and his supporters. In particular, he accused Ho and Lo Chang-lung of a tendency to compromise the goals of the revolutionary movement because of their lack of enthusiasm for politically inspired strikes. Li Li-san was forced to resign from the Political Bureau, but friction soon developed between the two groups that had joined in opposition to Li. Because the labor union faction viewed the 28 Bolsheviks as Moscow-trained intellectuals who had not been hardened by practical organizational activity in China, it was determined to prevent them from dominating the central apparatus of the party. However, at the fourth plenum of the sixth Central Committee in January 1931, Ch'en Shao-yü and his associates gained control of the Political Bureau.

Ho Meng-hsiung and Lo Chang-lung refused to accept the decisions of that plenum. They withdrew and formed a so-called emergency committee to make plans for a separatist movement. Accordingly, the central apparatus

of the Chinese Communist party expelled Ho and his associates from the party. On 17 January 1931 a meeting of the emergency committee was raided by the British police, and Ho Meng-hsiung and the other participants were arrested. They were extradited by the Chinese authorities at Shanghai and were executed at Lunghua on 7 February 1931.

In editions of the *Selected Works* of Mao Tse-tung published after 1949, Ho Meng-hsiung, Lin Yu-nan, and Li Ch'iu-shih were praised as Communists who did useful work for the Communist party and the Chinese people, maintained close connections with the masses, and, when arrested, "stood up firmly to the enemy and became noble martyrs." A summary of the letters to the Political Bureau written by Ho Meng-hsiung in September-October 1930 was released by the central party authorities in January 1931 under the title *Ho Meng-hsiung i-chien shu* [a statement of the views of Ho Meng-hsiung].

Ho Shu-heng   何 叔 衡

Ho Shu-heng (1874– February 1935), an early colleague of Mao Tse-tung and the oldest of the original members of the Hsin-min hsüeh-hui and the Chinese Communist party, was prominent in the party's attempts to use the Hunan school system to spread Marxist-Leninist ideas and in the establishment of the party's branch in Hunan.

A native of Ninghsiang, Hunan, Ho Shu-heng was born into a moderately prosperous peasant family. He attended the Yunshan Primary School, where his schoolmates included Hsieh Chueh-tsai (q.v.), Chiang Meng-chou, and Wang Ling-po, all of whom later became Communists in Hunan. As students, they favored the study of science and other practical subjects which would encourage modernization and reform and strongly opposed the attitudes of conservative members of the provincial gentry.

After 1912, Ho Shu-heng studied at the Hunan First Normal School at Changsha, where he first met Mao Tse-tung. After graduation in 1914, Ho went to teach at the Ch'u-i School in Changsha, one of the better known private schools of that period. Ho and his friends, including Mao Tse-tung, Ts'ai Ho-sen (q.v.), and other students from the normal school, often met at the Ch'u-i School in Changsha to discuss political problems. The Hsin-min hsueh-hui (New People's Study Society) was formed by Mao and Ts'ai in April 1918, and Ho Shu-heng was the oldest member of the initial group invited to join the organization. Ho participated in the local movement which opposed Chang Ching-yao, the Peiyang warlord who governed Hunan from 1918 to 1920, and thus was drawn into increasingly close association with Mao. When Mao and Ts'ai Ho-sen went to Peking to investigate the possibility of participating in the work-study program in France, Ho Shu-heng took charge of the New People's Study Society and its 70-odd members.

In 1920 Ho Shu-heng was appointed by the provincial education council to the post of director of the bureau of education in Hunan. He also took over direction of the *T'ung-su-pao* [commoners' newspaper], published by the bureau to promote popular education in the province. The paper had been established shortly after 1911, but it had no clearly defined editorial policy or objective. Ho and the group associated with him in planning and editing the paper had little experience with popular journalism, but were determined to use the paper to spread their political ideas. This undertaking coincided with Ho Shu-heng's conversion to Marxism, probably through the personal influence of Mao Tse-tung. The *T'ung-su-pao* soon assumed a new aspect, opposing warlordism and advocating social reform, and it increased in circulation and influence among the students and the peasants of Hunan. In 1920, after Mao Tse-tung returned from his second trip to Peking, the provincial bureau of education at Changsha, along with the New People's Study Society, became an active center of political discussion and planning. Disturbed by the radicalism of the *T'ung-su-pao*, the provincial authorities dismissed Ho Shu-heng from his post in May 1921. All those on the staff of the newspaper who were members of the New People's Study Society resigned, and several of them went to teach under Mao Tse-tung at the primary school of the First Normal School. In the summer of 1921 Mao and Ho Shu-heng went to Shanghai, where they represented Hunan at the founding meeting of the Chinese Communist party organization in July. Ho was the oldest member of the small group which attended that historic gathering.

Ho Shu-heng then returned to Changsha, where he worked with Mao in developing a branch of the Communist party in Hunan. The activities of the New People's Study Society came to an end, and the radical members of that group joined the Communist party branch. Ho remained in Hunan until 1927. During these years he was a member, and later the director, of the Wang Fu-chih Study Society, an institute which had been established at Changsha in the early years of the republican period to study the works of the seventeenth-century Hunanese nationalist and classical scholar (*see* ECCP, II, 817–19). In the early twentieth century, Chinese revolutionaries had used the writings of Wang Fu-chih to support the anti-Manchu movement. Ho Shu-heng was also responsible for Communist political activities in the primary schools of the province. Many of the Hunanese Communists were teachers, and the school system was an important channel for organization and propaganda.

In 1928, after the split between the Kuomintang and the Communists, Ho Shu-heng went to the Soviet Union, where he studied at the University for Toilers of the East. In Moscow, he was a close associate of the Hunanese Communist Hsü T'e-li (q.v.). Both of them were considerably older than most of the other Chinese then studying in Russia. Ho returned to China in the summer of 1930 and went to the Communist area in Kiangsi. When the central soviet government was formed at Juichin in 1931, Ho became head of the workers and peasants inspection committee of the regime. In 1931, and again in 1934, he was elected to the central executive council of the central soviet government in Kiangsi.

In the autumn of 1934, when the Communists were forced to retreat from the Kiangsi base, Ho Shu-heng, who was then about 60, stayed at the base to assist the remnant units that remained there. Early in 1935 he moved from Kiangsi into Fukien with a group which also included Ch'ü Ch'iu-pai and Teng Tzu-hui (qq.v.). At the end of February, Nationalist forces surrounded this group and captured Ch'ü Ch'iu-pai and some of the others. When Nationalist forces encircled the remaining

Communists near Ch'angt'ing, Fukien, Ho Shu-heng jumped off a cliff and ended his life.

Ho-tung   何 東
T. Hsiao-sheng   曉 生
West. Robert Hotung

Ho-tung (2 December 1862–26 April 1956), internationally known entrepreneur and philanthropist, became Hong Kong's largest property owner and one of its wealthiest citizens. He was knighted (1915) by King George V for his patriotic generosity.

Born in a small house off d'Aguilar Street in Hong Kong, Ho-tung began life in unpromising circumstances. He was the eldest son in a large family of moderate means and had strikingly handsome European features. He received his early education in a private Chinese school. At the age of 12 he was admitted to the British Central School (later renamed Queen's College), operated by the colonial government in Hong Kong. At this school, English was the language of instruction.

In 1878 Ho-tung passed a competitive examination for the staff of the Chinese Maritime Customs service at Canton, and he worked there for two years. Because that position did not seem promising, he returned to Hong Kong. Through personal connections, he became an office assistant at the British firm of Jardine, Matheson and Company, long known on the China coast as the "princely hong." In 1882 he was made Chinese agent of the Hong Kong Fire Insurance Company and the Canton Fire Insurance Company, both subsidiaries of Jardine's. In 1898 he resigned and was succeeded by his brother Ho Kom-tong. Ho-tung himself remained actively associated with Jardine's for another two years as a Chinese adviser to the firm. Although he resigned from the company again in 1900, his association with it continued throughout his life. Later, he became a member of the board of directors of several enterprises in the Jardine group, including those in which he had worked.

During the latter part of his 20-year direct association with Jardine's, Ho-tung launched his own enterprises. He entered the sugar trade, dealing with the Philippines and the Netherlands East Indies, and gradually expanded his business interests both in Hong Kong and in the Yangtze ports. He also entered and greatly developed the real estate business in Hong Kong. By 1896 he had become a millionaire. In 1898 he was elected chairman of the Tung Wah Group of Hospitals, the colony's leading Chinese charity organization. In 1899 he was named a justice of the peace by the Hong Kong government, an appointment that indicated his acceptance by British social circles in the colony.

In 1898 K'ang Yu-wei (q.v.) fled to Hong Kong after the unsuccessful reform effort of that year. His close friends and relatives were anxious to avoid him, but Ho-tung gave him shelter and treated him as an honored guest. Ho-tung also gave financial aid to members of K'ang's family and to some of his other dependents.

In 1900 Ho-tung made his debut as a public benefactor in Hong Kong by establishing the Kowloon British School. The first school for children of European parentage in the colony, it later was renamed the King George V School. At the same time, he established a scholarship at Queen's College. Ho-tung was one of the founders of Hong Kong University, and his accumulated donations to the institution reached HK$260 thousand by 1941.

Ho-tung became Hong Kong's largest property owner and was generally thought to be the colony's wealthiest citizen. He was a director of many companies and a shareholder in many more. His interests included the Hongkong and Shanghai Banking Corporation, the Hongkong and Whampoa Dock Company, the Hongkong Electric Company, the Hongkong Tramway Company, the Hongkong Land Investment Company, and other shipping, insurance, investment, and manufacturing companies. During the First World War, Ho-tung contributed HK$100 thousand to the Prince of Wales War Fund and donated ambulances and airplanes to the British government. When a war emergency surcharge was imposed by the government, he paid not only his share of the tax, but that of all the tenants of his extensive properties in the colony. Because of his patriotic generosity, he was knighted by King George V in 1915, becoming Sir Robert Ho-tung.

In 1920 Sir Robert Ho-tung served as chairman of the Chinese industries section of an economic planning board set up by the Hong Kong government. In 1922 he acted as a mediator during the great strike which paralyzed Hong Kong. The same year, he acquired the controlling interest in the Chinese-language newspaper *Kung Sheng Daily News*. That paper suspended publication during the Japanese occupation; after the Second World War it was noted for its consistently anti-Communist stand.

Although Sir Robert Ho-tung's primary loyalty was to the British government, he showed genuine concern for republican China. His concern did not lead to direct involvement in Chinese politics, but in 1923 he sponsored a proposal for a round-table conference to settle the differences between the several contending factions in China. After the establishment of the National Government at Nanking in 1928, Sir Robert made such major financial contributions to China as a donation of HK$30 thousand to the fund for additional buildings for the Sun Yat-sen Mausoleum at Nanking.

In 1935, as a memorial to his wife Clara, Sir Robert built one of the finest Buddhist temples in Hong Kong, the Tung-lien-chueh-yuan, located in Happy Valley. The building also housed a vocational school for young women, with a primary school for poor children as an annex. Sir Robert paid the operating expenses of all these institutions. After the Second World War, the temple became a leading center for the study of Buddhism, with regular lectures given by monks and lay Buddhist leaders.

In December 1941 Sir Robert and Lady Ho-tung (Margaret) celebrated their sixtieth wedding anniversary. After the event, Sir Robert took a trip to Macao. Thus, he was not in Hong Kong when the War in the Pacific broke out. He remained in Macao for the duration of the war and refused many invitations from the Japanese occupation authorities to return to Hong Kong. Lady Ho-tung, however, lived in Hong Kong during the war, and she died there in 1944. At the end of the war, Sir Robert returned to Hong Kong with Admiral Sir Cecil Harcourt, the military governor. In 1948 Sir Robert made his largest single contribution, HK$1 million, for the construction of the Lady Ho-tung Hostel for women students at the University of Hong Kong.

In 1947, at the age of 85, Sir Robert visited the United States. In 1949 he went to Europe, where he was received by the royal families of England, Norway, Sweden, and Denmark and by President of France Vincent Auriol. In England, Sir Robert called on George Bernard Shaw, who had visited him in Hong Kong in 1935. He brought Shaw a Chinese gown, which so pleased the playwright that he immediately put it on and had his photograph taken with Sir Robert. Sir Robert was then 87, and Shaw was 93. On his ninetieth birthday in 1952 Sir Robert Ho-tung was honored by Hong Kong. Jardine, Matheson and Company noted that his association with the firm and with the Keswick family, who ran it, had lasted for more than three generations. Thus, Hong Kong paid tribute to one of its most distinguished citizens. In addition to honors received from the British government, Sir Robert Ho-tung had been decorated by the governments of China, Portugal, France, Germany, Italy, Belgium, and Annam.

Sir Robert Ho-tung's eldest son, Ho Sai-wing, was actually a nephew whom he adopted; Ho died shortly after the war, having served as an agent of the Hongkong and Shanghai Banking Corporation. The second son, Ho Sai-san, died in childhood. Edward Ho-tung, the elder of the two brothers surviving him, was a successful businessman, and Ho Sai-lai was the first Chinese cadet to be admitted to Woolwich Military Academy in England and had a distinguished army career in the service of the Chinese National Government. General Ho Sai-lai served for a period as Chinese representative on the United Nations Military Staff Committee. Sir Robert's eight daughters were: Lady Lo (wife of Sir Man-kam Lo, a prominent Hong Kong solicitor); Mrs. Daisy Au-yeung; Mrs. Mary Wong; Dr. Eva Ho; Irene Cheng; Mrs. Jean Gittens; Mrs. Grace Lo; and Mrs. Florence Yeo.

In 1955 Queen Elizabeth II, in recognition of Sir Robert Ho-tung's service in the colony of Hong Kong, made him a Knight Commander of the Order of the British Empire. Despite his age and feeble health, he flew to London to receive the honor. It was his last public appearance. He was baptized a Christian on his deathbed, an example followed three years later by Sir Shouson Chow (Chou Ch'ang-ling, q.v.), and he died on 26 April 1956.

Ho Yao-tsu   賀 耀 祖
T. Kuei-yen   貴 嚴

Ho Yao-tsu (1859–16 July 1961), Hunanese military leader, participated in the May Third Incident at Tsinan (1928) and later served Chiang Kai-shek in such posts as minister to Turkey (1934–36), special envoy to the Soviet Union (1938–40), director of the attendance office (1941–42), and mayor of Chungking. After 1949 he lived in Peking.

Ninghsiang, a thriving hsien in Hunan province, produced several prominent military leaders in the republican period, one of whom was Ho Yao-tsu. Little is known about his family background or his childhood. He studied at a preparatory school for cadets in Hunan and then enrolled at the military academy at Wuchang, Hupeh. Ho was sent to Japan to complete his military training at the Shikan Gakkō [military academy]. Among the Hunan provincial military group that academy was especially well known, and study there was useful in gaining promotion in the military hierarchy.

T'an Yen-k'ai (q.v.) was the recognized senior figure in the Hunanese hierarchy, with Chao Heng-t'i and Ch'eng Ch'ien (qq.v.) next in importance. Ho Yao-tsu was regarded as a contemporary of such officers as Ho Chien, Lu Ti-p'ing, T'ang Sheng-chih, and Yeh K'ai-hsin. In the post-1912 period, armed clashes between rival factions were recurrent in Hunan. During the early 1920's the principal antagonists in that province were Chao Heng-t'i, who was allied with Wu P'ei-fu (q.v.) and his northern military forces, and T'an Yen-k'ai, who supported Sun Yat-sen and his cause. Ho Yao-tsu served under Chao Heng-t'i. In time, he was promoted to the rank of division commander.

On the eve of the Northern Expedition in mid-1926, T'ang Sheng-chih (q.v.) defected from Chao's camp to join the Nationalist regime at Canton. T'ang then was appointed commander of the Eighth Army and was assigned to lead an expeditionary force against Chao Heng-t'i and Wu P'ei-fu. Ho Yao-tsu was made front-line commander of the Hu-Hsiang-chün [Hunan protection army] and was assigned to stem the advance of T'ang's units. Ho soon recognized that he was fighting on the losing side. When the vanguard units of the Nationalist forces entered Changsha, the provincial capital, in August 1926, Ho immediately petitioned the Kuomintang authorities in Hunan to intercede on his behalf with Chiang Kai-shek. The petition was accepted, and Ho Yao-tsu's army was reorganized as the 1st and 2nd Independent divisions of the National Revolutionary Army.

After rapid victories in Hunan and Hupeh, Chiang Kai-shek turned his attention in the autumn of 1926 to Kiangsi, where the Nationalists confronted the forces of Sun Ch'uan-fang (q.v.). On 5 November 1926 Ho Yao-tsu's forces, which had been assigned to the northern Kiangsi front, captured Kiukiang, enabling the Nationalists to take Nanchang three days later. As a result of this victory, Ho Yao-tsu was promoted to commander of the Fortieth Army. Early in 1927 he led his army to the vicinity of Nanking and captured it from Sun Ch'uan-fang's forces on 24 March. After the incident involving the destruction of property and the killing of foreigners by Nationalist soldiers (later alleged to have been members of the Communist-infiltrated Sixth Army under the command of Ch'eng Ch'ien), Ho Yao-tsu, Ho Ying-ch'in (q.v.), Lu Ti-p'ing, and Ch'eng Ch'ien were assigned responsibility for restoring order at Nanking.

In the summer of 1927 the Nationalists suffered a serious military reverse when a surprise counterattack launched by the joint forces of Sun Ch'uan-fang and Chang Tsung-ch'ang (q.v.) imperiled Nanking. Chiang Kai-shek resigned in mid-August to aid the reconciliation of the Kuomintang factions at Wuhan and Nanking, and he went to Japan. By the end of 1927 he had returned to China. The Kuomintang leaders at Nanking urged him to resume the post of commander in chief. Ho Yao-tsu, then the garrison commander for the Nanking-Shanghai sector, offered his full support to Chiang. This gesture, made at a crucial time, won him Chiang's confidence.

Early in 1928 the National Government at Nanking decided to resume the Northern Expedition and to advance against the forces of Chang Tsung-ch'ang and Chang Tso-lin (q.v.) in the north. The First Route Army under Ho Ying-ch'in was reorganized as the

First Group Army; it was commanded personally by Chiang Kai-shek, with Ch'en Tiao-yuan, Ho Yao-tsu, and Liu Chih (q.v.) as commanders. Late in April, Ho's forces routed the Shantung troops of Chang Tsung-ch'ang in T'aian and captured Tsinan. Chiang Kai-shek arrived there on 2 May to plan the crossing of the Yellow River. However, the Japanese, making use of their large garrison in the provincial capital of Shantung, took steps to safeguard their interests. The result was the May Third Incident at Tsinan. Clashes on that date between Chinese and Japanese units caused many deaths, including that of the Chinese foreign-affairs commissioner, and resulted in serious damage to property. The May Third Incident aroused nation-wide indignation in China. Because of superior Japanese military power, however, Chiang Kai-shek desired to avoid an international conflict. Accordingly, Ho Yao-tsu, whose troops had been directly involved in the incident, was relieved of his military command, and the Nationalist forces detoured to move northward along the Peking-Hankow rail line.

From 1929 to 1934 Ho Yao-tsu was at Nanking, where he held a sinecure post as aide-de-camp to Chiang Kai-shek. In 1931 he was elected to membership on the Central Executive Committee of the Kuomintang (he was reelected to that organ at later Kuomintang party congresses until 1949). From 1932 to 1934 he also served as deputy chief of the general staff.

During the early 1930's Chiang Kai-shek developed great interest in the rise of Turkey. Knowing of this interest, Ho Yao-tsu submitted to Chiang a memorandum assessing the situation in Turkey and suggesting that closer relations be established between the two countries. Some observers have suggested that the memorandum was written by two of Ho Yao-tsu's fellow-provincials, Wang P'eng-sheng (q.v.) and Ho Feng-shan. In any event, Ho Yao-tsu became minister to Ankara in November 1934 and spent two years in the Turkish capital. Wang P'eng-sheng and Ho Feng-shan accompanied him as advisers.

Ho Yao-tsu was named governor of Kansu in 1937. After the outbreak of war between China and Japan, the National Government sought to strengthen ties with the Soviet Union. In 1938 T. F. Tsiang (Chiang T'ing-fu, q.v.),

the Chinese ambassador to Moscow, returned to China. Ho Yao-tsu was sent to Russia as special envoy—on the assumption that he understood the military requirements of wartime China better than any civilian or career diplomat. His tour of duty at Moscow was marked by the signing of a commercial treaty between the two countries and by the conclusion of several barter agreements which bolstered China's war effort. He was recalled from the Soviet capital in 1940, when Shao Li-tzu (q.v.) was named ambassador.

At Chungking, Ho Yao-tsu was rewarded with an appointment as director of the Generalissimo's attendance office. That post, which Ho held in 1941–42, was a position of the highest trust, and Ho became one of Chiang's most influential deputies. He had access to the most vital information and plans of the National Government; all documents destined for Chiang Kai-shek went first to Ho. He also served as secretary general of the National Economic Council. Toward the end of 1942 Ho was appointed mayor of Chungking, succeeding K. C. Wu, who had been appointed vice minister of foreign affairs. Ho held that office until the end of the war in 1945.

After the Japanese surrender, Ho Yao-tsu returned to Nanking. Using his connections with Wang P'eng-sheng, who had been director of the wartime Institute of International Affairs under Chiang Kai-shek, Ho organized the New Asia Association in Shanghai, a group which published a monthly magazine analyzing Asian international relations. Other leading members of the association were P'eng Hsueh-p'ei, a former vice minister of communications and an able pamphleteer, and Shao Yü-lin, an expert on Japan who later served as Chinese Nationalist ambassador to Korea (1949–51). The New Asia Association asserted that the proper international role for China was to serve as a bridge between the United States and the Soviet Union. As the military and economic position of the National Government worsened in the civil war with the Chinese Communists, Ho became increasingly critical of Chiang Kai-shek and his policies.

When Ho Ying-ch'in was appointed president of the Executive Yuan in 1949, Ho Yao-tsu became minister without portfolio in the last Kuomintang cabinet on the mainland. He left Shanghai in the spring of 1949 for Hong Kong, where a group of former Kuomintang officials had assembled. Among them was Huang Shao-hung (q.v.), who had visited Peiping on a mission to discuss peace terms with the Communists in 1948. The Hong Kong group, numbering 44 persons, signed a statement declaring their allegiance to the Communist cause and denouncing Chiang Kai-shek. The signatures of Huang Shao-hung and Ho Yao-tsu headed the list. Ho then went to Peiping and attended the Chinese People's Political Conference in September 1949. He was appointed a member and a director of the department of communications of the Central-South Military and Administrative Committee. After 1949 Ho Yao-tsu consistently used his courtesy name, Ho Kuei-yen. He died in Peking on 16 July 1961.

Little is known about Ho's first wife. Ni Fei-chün, his second wife, had been a nurse in Chungking before Ho Yao-tsu met and married her. There were reports of her leftist political sympathies in Chungking even when Ho Yao-tsu was the Generalissimo's confidant and the mayor of Chungking, but no action was taken by the Nationalist security authorities because of Ho's favored position. After 1945 Ni was associated with Madame Sun Yat-sen (Soong Ch'ing-ling, q.v.) at Shanghai. After 1949 she served as deputy secretary general of the Red Cross Society of China. She also represented the Central People's Government at peace congresses and other international gatherings.

Ho Ying-ch'in 何 應 欽
T. Ching-chih 敬 之

Ho Ying-ch'in (1890–), one of Chiang Kai-shek's most trusted military officers. As minister of war (1930–44), he negotiated the 1935 Ho-Umezu agreement, by which China capitulated to Japanese demands in north China. He was chief of staff in 1938–44, commander in chief of the Chinese army in 1944–46, and chief Chinese delegate to the United Nations Military Advisory Committee in 1946–48. He became chairman of the Strategy Advisory Committee in Taiwan in 1950.

The ancestral home of Ho Ying-ch'in's family had been in Kiangsi, but some of his forebears had moved westward at the turn of the

eighteenth century to settle in Kweichow and had made their home in Hsingyi in southwestern Kweichow. The family began as cattle dealers, prospered during the later Ch'ing period, and acquired both land and influence. Ho's father, Ho Ch'i-min, was a respected citizen who represented his village in the hsien defense corps.

Following the occupation of Peking by foreign military forces after the Boxer Uprising of 1900, Ho Ying-ch'in went to the provincial capital, Kweiyang. He enrolled in the Kweichow Army Primary School in 1901. After graduation, Ho went to Wuchang, where he studied at the Third Army Middle School. He passed an examination for study abroad, and in 1908 he was sent by the ministry of war to Japan, where he enrolled at the Shimbu Gakkō and later served as a student recruit in the 59th Infantry Company of the Japanese Army. A year later, he enrolled as an infantry cadet at the Shikan Gakkō [military academy]. He also joined the T'ung-meng-hui.

After the Wuchang revolt broke out in October 1911, Ho Ying-ch'in returned to China, where he joined the headquarters of Ch'en Ch'i-mei (q.v.) in Shanghai. In 1913 he served as commander of an infantry battalion in the 1st Division of the Kiangsu Army. That August, after the failure of the so-called second revolution, he went to Japan to complete his studies.

After graduation from the Shikan Gakkō, Ho Ying-ch'in returned to Kweichow in the autumn of 1916. On the recommendation of Liu Hsien-shih, the provincial governor, he was given command of the 4th Infantry Regiment in the 1st Division of the Kweichow Army. In July 1917 he was made dean of studies at the Kweichow Military Academy and chief of staff in the headquarters of the commander of the academy. In 1919 he received command of the 2nd Mixed Brigade of the Kweichow Army. In 1920 he held several military and police posts in Kweichow, and in 1921 he became chief of staff to the commander of the Kweichow Army. Because Ho Ying-ch'in was well aware of the relative backwardness of Kweichow province, he organized the so-called Young Kweichow Society, patterned after Mazzini's Young Italy Movement, to fight conservatism and to bring genuine republican government to his province. Many Kweichow military men and politicians became hostile to him because of his reform work, and in the summer of 1922 he was forced to flee to Yunnan. T'ang Chi-yao (q.v.) gave him protection, and Ho became dean of studies at the Yunnan Military Academy at Kunming. The Kweichow generals sent assassins after Ho. He was shot in the chest, but emergency surgery by a French doctor at Kunming saved his life. With the help of Fan Shih-sheng, a Yunnan army commander, Ho left Yunnan and went to Shanghai.

Ho lived in Shanghai for more than a year before completely recovering from his wound. In January 1924 he went to Canton, where he was appointed a military staff officer in Sun Yat-sen's headquarters. In June, he was named chief instructor in tactics at the Whampoa Military Academy, with the rank of brigadier general. That appointment brought Ho into close association with Chiang Kai-shek. At the beginning of September, Ho was ordered to create a training regiment, and on 12 October, he was assigned to command it. The following day, Chiang Kai-shek appointed him acting director of the training department of the Whampoa Military Academy.

There were then two training regiments at Whampoa, the 1st, commanded by Ho Ying-ch'in, and the 2nd, commanded by Wang Po-ling, his friend and fellow-graduate of the Shikan Gakkō. Sun Yat-sen's headquarters at Canton assigned these two units to the expeditionary force being sent to break the power of Ch'en Chiung-ming (q.v.) in eastern Kwangtung. On 1 February 1925 they left Whampoa under the over-all command of Chiang Kai-shek. In April, when they were still in the field, the two training regiments were combined to form the 1st Brigade, with Ho Ying-ch'in as brigade commander.

After the National Government was established at Canton in July 1925, the Nationalist armed forces were transformed into the National Revolutionary Army. The Whampoa cadet units became part of the First Army, with Chiang Kai-shek as its commander. The former 1st Brigade became the 1st Division of the First Army, with Ho Ying-ch'in as its commanding general. At that time, the Kuomintang and the Chinese Communists were allied, and the political representative in the 1st Division was Chou En-lai. In September 1925 the Nationalists mounted a second eastern expedition in Kwangtung. Chiang Kai-shek deployed the

expeditionary force in three columns commanded, respectively, by Ho Ying-ch'in, Li Chi-shen (q.v.), and Ch'eng Ch'ien (q.v.). Ho's column distinguished itself in actions at Waichow and Haifeng. The last remnants of Ch'en Chiung-ming's military power in Kwangtung had been eliminated by late November.

In January 1926 Chiang Kai-shek was relieved of command of the First Army so that he could devote himself to the work of the Whampoa Military Academy. Ho Ying-ch'in succeeded Chiang as commander of the First Army, and Wang Po-ling became commander of its 1st Division. In April, after the Chungshan gunboat incident (*see* Chiang Kai-shek), Ho was named dean of the Whampoa Military Academy.

The Northern Expedition was launched in July 1926. At the end of the month, Chiang Kai-shek appointed Ho Ying-ch'in garrison commander responsible for securing the Chaochow-Meihsien sector in eastern Kwangtung. In September, after initial victories in Hunan, the National Revolutionary Army attacked the forces of Sun Ch'uan-fang (q.v.), who controlled the five lower Yangtze and coastal provinces. Ho Ying-ch'in defeated the forces of Chou Yin-jen, the Fukien governor, in a surprise attack on Yungting. Ho then drove on to capture Foochow on 2 December 1926 and to extend Nationalist control into northern Fukien. In the meantime, Nationalist forces to the west had seized Nanchang, the capital of Kiangsi. In January 1927 the National Revolutionary Army launched a campaign against Sun Ch'uan-fang's positions, with Ho Ying-ch'in driving northward into Chekiang. By the end of March 1927, both Shanghai and Nanking had been captured, and Sun Ch'uan-fang's remaining troops had retreated northward.

In April 1927 Chiang Kai-shek broke with the Nationalist authorities at Wuhan and established an opposition regime at Nanking. Chiang then decided to continue the northward drive on three routes commanded, respectively, by Chiang himself, Li Tsung-jen (q.v.), and Ho Ying-ch'in. Ho was assigned to advance on the right wing. By the beginning of June, he had reached Ihsien in southern Shantung, and Li Tsung-jen had captured Hsuchow. The combined strength of Sun Ch'uan-fang and the Chihli-Shantung armies then were thrown into counterattack. Weakened by the political conflict with Wuhan and put into reverse motion by Chiang Kai-shek's order for a general retreat, the Nationalists fell back toward the Yangtze. In August, Chiang Kai-shek resigned his posts and went to Japan.

After Chiang's retirement, the headquarters of the commander in chief of the National Revolutionary Army was reorganized as the Military Affairs Commission, with Ho Ying-ch'in, Li Tsung-jen, and Pai Ch'ung-hsi (q.v.) constituting the standing committee. It was then rumored that Li Tsung-jen would join with T'ang Sheng-chih (q.v.), the dominant military figure in the Wuhan regime, to eliminate Ho Ying-ch'in's First Army, which was viewed as an important source of support for Chiang Kai-shek. Ho remained at Nanking, but sent his army eastward into Kiangsu and Chekiang.

Taking advantage of the disarray of the Nanking forces, Sun Ch'uan-fang in August 1927 crossed the Yangtze. The armies of Ho Ying-ch'in and Li Tsung-jen united to defeat him in the battle of Lungtan and then pursued the remnants of his forces across the Yangtze. T'ang Sheng-chih took this opportunity to drive eastward against Nanking, and Li Tsung-jen moved his forces to deal with that new threat. In October 1927, as Li repulsed the attack from the west, Ho Ying-ch'in cleared the area south of the Hwai River and occupied Pengpu. T'ang Sheng-chih then retired, and members of the contending factions of the Kuomintang, including Ho Ying-ch'in, met at Chiang Kai-shek's residence at Shanghai on 24 November to discuss the problem of party unity.

Early in December 1927 the forces of Sun Ch'uan-fang and Chang Tsung-ch'ang, the governor of Shantung, after administering a defeat to Feng Yü-hsiang on the Lunghai rail line, moved southward along the Tientsin-Pukow railroad. Ho Ying-ch'in led the First Army northward to counter the threat and captured Hsuchow on 16 December 1927. Four days later, Ho and other Nationalist generals in the field issued a statement that was, in effect, a proclamation of support for Chiang Kai-shek. After Chiang resumed his military and political posts in January 1928, Ho was named governor of Chekiang. In mid-February, the First Route Army was reorganized as the First Group Army, with Chiang Kai-shek as commander and Ho Ying-ch'in as chief of staff.

After the overthrow of the Peking government in June 1928, the problem of military reorganization gained new importance. Ho Ying-ch'in was named inspector general of military training in October. A month later, he was named to head a committee to prepare for a national meeting on troop disbandment. That conference, which met in January 1929, achieved no practical results, however, because the senior Nationalist generals were intent upon preserving their personal and regional power.

After the formal establishment of the National Government at Nanking in October 1928, Ho Ying-ch'in became a member of the State Council. In 1929, at the Third National Congress of the Kuomintang, he was elected to the Central Executive Committee and was made a member of the Central Political Council. That year, he also was appointed chief of staff of the national army, navy, and air force headquarters. In 1929 and 1930, as the authorities at Nanking confronted a series of threats to Chiang Kai-shek's power, Ho served successively as director of Chiang's field headquarters at Kaifeng, Canton, Chengchow, and Wuhan. On 10 March 1930 he was appointed minister of war in the National Government.

One of Ho Ying-ch'in's most important tasks was the elimination of Communist power in the rural areas. He was assigned to command the Nationalist forces charged with the so-called bandit-suppression campaigns. The first attack, launched in December 1930, failed. In February 1931 Chiang Kai-shek made Ho director of his Nanchang headquarters and assigned him to direct a campaign against the Communist forces in Kiangsi and Hunan. By June, Ho's campaign against the enemy had failed, and Chiang Kai-shek personally assumed command. Ho then was given the post of field commander of the Bandit-Supression Army. There was some sharp but inconclusive fighting against the Communist forces in Kiangsi, with a northward advance by forces of the dissident Kuomintang regime at Canton providing an unwelcome distraction. After the Mukden Incident of September 1931, which marked the beginning of the Japanese occupation of Manchuria, both the bandit-suppression campaigns and the controversy with Canton were shelved.

In 1932 Ho Ying-ch'in was made a member of the special affairs committee of the Central Political Council. In January 1933 the Japanese undertook the invasion of Jehol and the breaching of the Great Wall defense line. Ho Ying-ch'in was sent to Peiping to help Chang Hsueh-liang check the invaders. Chang then resigned his military and political posts, and on 12 March 1933 Ho was appointed acting chairman of the Peiping branch of the Military Affairs Commission. He collaborated with Huang Fu (q.v.) in attempting to check the Japanese advance by political negotiation. On 31 May 1933, chiefly through their efforts, the Tangku truce was signed.

There was much popular resistance to this new arrangement with the Japanese, which many believed to be tantamount to a surrender of Chinese national interests. Feng Yü-hsiang (q.v.) gave expression to the popular resentment by mobilizing the Anti-Japanese Allied Army, which went into action against Japanese positions in Chahar. Huang Fu and Feng's veteran associate Sung Che-yuan negotiated with Feng, and Ho Ying-ch'in threatened Feng's forces by massing troops south of the Peiping-Suiyuan railway. In mid-August Feng turned over his military and administrative authority in Chahar to Sung Che-yuan and retired. Ho Ying-ch'in then dispersed his forces.

In November 1933 Major General Okamura, the deputy chief of staff of the Japanese Kwantung Army, presented Ho Ying-ch'in and Huang Fu with a provisional plan for what he termed the rehabilitation of north China. The subsequent negotiations led to the resumption of rail traffic and of mail and telegraph services between north China and the area which had become the puppet state of Manchoukuo.

By 1935 it had become evident that Japan was working toward the establishment of autonomous status for the five northern provinces of China proper. On 10 June 1935 Ho Ying-ch'in and Lieutenant General Umezu Yoshijiro, the commander of the Japanese north China garrison, concluded the so-called Ho-Umezu agreement, by which the Chinese committed themselves to transfer Yü Hsueh-chung (q.v.) and his troops out of Hopei, to abolish Kuomintang party organs and the political training department of the Peiping branch of the Military Affairs Commission, to dissolve the Blue Shirts and other secret anti-Japanese societies, and to prohibit anti-Japanese and anti-foreign activities throughout China. On 6 July, Ho

signed a document incorporating the substance of that agreement.

At Peiping, Ho Ying-ch'in, in addition to being minister of war and chairman of the Peiping branch of the Military Affairs Commission, was the resident representative of the Executive Yuan. Accordingly, he was a prime target of the increasing resentment of the National Government's Japan policies. The Ho-Umezu agreement was secret, but its existence inevitably became known. In the autumn of 1935 student demonstrations and popular opposition to the trend toward autonomy in north China increased. Nevertheless, Nanking abolished the Peiping branch of the Military Affairs Commission in November. Shortly afterwards, chief authority in north China was transferred from Ho Ying-ch'in to Sung Che-yuan, the chairman of the newly created Hopei-Chahar Political Affairs Council.

Throughout this period, Ho had continued to perform his duties as minister of war at Nanking. Much had been done to strengthen China's military establishment, especially in the field of aviation. Now Ho was able to give his full attention to the task of developing China's defenses.

The Sian Incident of December 1936, in which Chiang Kai-shek and other leading Nationalist military and political figures were detained by Chang Hsueh-liang (q.v.) and Yang Hu-ch'eng, who demanded that the National Government renounce civil war in favor of resisting Japan, introduced a new, critical factor into the Chinese situation. Ho Ying-ch'in was in Nanking, and by authority of the National Government he assumed the duties of supreme military commander in Chiang Kai-shek's absence. Ho proposed to launch prompt punitive action, including bombing. A series of fortuitous circumstances and the strenuous efforts of Madame Chiang Kai-shek, W. H. Donald, and T. V. Soong prevented Ho from taking such action.

Ho Ying-ch'in's hard attitude may have contributed indirectly to the peaceful solution of the Sian Incident; and, in any event, the outbreak of the Sino-Japanese war in July 1937 resulted in his political rehabilitation. In August, he was appointed commanding officer of the Fourth War Area, with headquarters at Canton. In January 1938 he also was appointed chief of the general staff of the Military Affairs

Commission. From that time on, the duties of wartime military administration, planning, and direction were his, although Chiang Kai-shek remained in over-all command.

The National Government's contest with the Communists continued, in spite of their formal alliance against Japan. Ho Ying-ch'in reportedly was a prime mover in the Nationalist action that led to a military clash involving the Communist-led New Fourth Army in January 1941 (see Yeh T'ing).

In December 1941, after the Japanese had attacked the American naval base at Pearl Harbor, the United States entered the war. Shortly thereafter, Lieutenant General Joseph W. Stilwell arrived in China in the dual role of commander of United States forces in the China-Burma-India theater and chief of staff to Chiang Kai-shek. The official United States military history of the theater later noted that: "General Ho's actions soon suggested to Stilwell that he saw in the arrival of an American as chief of staff to the Generalissimo's joint staff the introduction of a rival center of power and influence and a direct challenge to his own position."

Sharp rivalry soon developed between Ho Ying-ch'in and Stilwell. One American view of Ho, as summarized in a letter written by General George C. Marshall, then Chief of Staff of the United States Army, to President Franklin D. Roosevelt in March 1943, was that he represented a "school of thought now existing in the Chinese Army that a military 'watch and wait' policy should be followed." Stilwell pressed for the overhaul of the ineffective command structure of the Chinese army and for the training of Chinese ground forces. Many United States representatives in China believed that the Chinese Nationalists were continuing to allot a major portion of their ground forces to contain the Chinese Communists in the northwest and that they consistently refrained from aggressive action against the Japanese in China.

Although Stilwell was joint (Allied) chief of staff to Chiang Kai-shek, the commander of the China theater, Ho Ying-ch'in was chief of staff of the Chinese army. To Chiang Kai-shek, the latter position was the more important. In February 1943 Ho accompanied Stilwell to India to inspect Chinese troops, most of which had been sent there as a result of the disastrous first Burma campaign of 1942. After that trip,

it was agreed that Chinese troops would be trained by American officers, and Stilwell's hopes for improved and expanded training of Chinese ground forces rose. On 1 September 1943 Ho Ying-ch'in presented a plan for establishing a training force of 45 divisions. A program was launched for the training and equipment of 36 Chinese divisions. In April 1944 Ho Ying-ch'in, by authority of Chiang Kai-shek, gave formal approval for Chinese crossing of the Salween River in the second Burma campaign.

At that point, the Japanese, who had not carried out a major military campaign in China since 1938, drove southward in central China in the so-called Operation Ichi-go, with disastrous results for the Chinese Nationalist forces. On 3 July 1944 Stilwell wrote to General Marshall in Washington to report that the desperate situation in China required desperate remedies. Stilwell requested that he be recommended for the top command post in the Chinese Nationalist Army and that Ho Ying-ch'in be asked to resign as chief of staff. In September, President Roosevelt proposed to Chiang Kai-shek that Stilwell be placed "in unrestricted command of all your forces." A few days later, Stilwell submitted detailed proposals to Chiang for supplying arms to the Chinese Communists. Stilwell was recalled from China in October.

Ho Ying-ch'in, after 14 years as minister of war in the National Government, was removed from that post in November 1944 under strong urging from the United States government. In December, Chiang Kai-shek named Ho commander in chief of the Chinese army. Lieutenant General Albert C. Wedemeyer, Stilwell's successor in China, had evolved a plan which called for the concentration and training of Chinese forces south and east of Kunming, with a command structure that would permit coordinated defense. Wedemeyer had recommended that Ch'en Ch'eng (q.v.) be assigned to carry out the plan, but Chiang Kai-shek, in an order of 11 December 1944, designated Ho Ying-ch'in.

It had been agreed that orders for field operations by the Nationalist forces would be referred to the Sino-American combined staff. On 6 May 1945, however, as the War in the Pacific was coming to an end, Chiang Kai-shek, without referring either to Wedemeyer or to the

Chinese combat command, instructed Ho Ying-ch'in to occupy Hengyang, deep in Japanese-held territory. After Wedemeyer protested, Chiang said that his message to Ho had been merely an opinion, but that it had been issued in the form of an order due to a misunderstanding on the part of his staff. Nevertheless, on 8 May, Ho ordered a general attack on the western Hunan front. The offensive achieved limited success; but Ho failed to occupy Hengyang.

The Japanese surrendered on 14 August 1945, and the next day Ho Ying-ch'in transferred the army headquarters from Kunming to Chih-chiang in western Hunan. He delivered to the Japanese representative a memorandum on surrender procedure, and, on 8 September, he established his advance headquarters in Nanking. On 9 September, Ho Ying-ch'in, as Chiang Kai-shek's representative, received the formal Japanese surrender from General Okamura, the commander in chief of the Japanese expeditionary force in China. Ho also worked out arrangements whereby the Japanese forces in China would temporarily maintain their stations and perform certain garrison duties pending the arrival of Chinese Nationalist forces.

Even before open civil war with the Communists erupted, the position of Ho Ying-ch'in in the top Nationalist command changed. The shifts arose primarily because Ho had powerful enemies, including such senior Nationalist generals as Ch'en Ch'eng and Hu Tsung-nan (q.v.) and such key figures in the central political apparatus of the Kuomintang as Ch'en Kuo-fu and Ch'en Li-fu (qq.v.). In May 1946 the wartime Military Affairs Commission, of which Ho Ying-ch'in had been chief of staff, was replaced by a new ministry of national defense. Pai Ch'ung-hsi was appointed the first minister of national defense, and Ch'en Ch'eng was named chief of staff. Ho Ying-ch'in was then assigned to head Chiang Kai-shek's headquarters at Chungking, but that appointment hardly compensated for his loss of the key posts of chief of staff and commander in chief of the Chinese army.

In October 1946 Ho Ying-ch'in was sent abroad to serve as chief Chinese delegate to the Military Staff Committee of the United Nations and chief of the Chinese Military Mission to the United States. The National Government issued an official statement commending his service to the nation. In March 1948 he was ordered to return to Nanking. In May, when the Nationalist situation was rapidly deteriorating as a result of the civil war with the Communists, Ho Ying-ch'in was named to succeed Pai Ch'ung-hsi as minister of national defense. In the wake of a new series of Nationalist military disasters, Chiang Kai-shek retired from the presidency on 21 January 1949, and Li Tsung-jen became acting President. In March 1949, when Sun Fo resigned as president of the Executive Yuan, Li Tsung-jen invited Ho Ying-ch'in to become premier. After privately consulting Chiang Kai-shek, Ho Ying-ch'in assumed office at Nanking on 23 March. He played an important role in bringing about the rejection of harsh Communist peace terms in April. After the Communist forces crossed the Yangtze and occupied Nanking, Ho resigned as premier on 30 May. He flew to Taiwan late in 1949.

In May 1950 Ho Ying-ch'in was named chairman of the Strategy Advisory Commission. He also became a member of the Central Advisory Committee of the Kuomintang, which was established to reorganize the central organs of the party.

In his later years, Ho Ying-ch'in became active in the Moral Rearmament Movement and, in connection with the work of that organization, made several trips to Japan, Europe, and the United States. He has been credited with authorship of the following publications: *Pa-nien k'ang-chan chih ching-kuo* [eight years of the war of resistance], *Jih-pen fang-wen chiang-yen hsüan-chi* [selected speeches during a visit to Japan], and *Tao-te ch'ung-cheng yun-tung yen-chiang chi* [collected speeches on the moral rearmament movement].

Hou Te-pang　　　侯 德 榜
T. Chih-pen　　　　致 本

Hou Te-pang (1890–), the foremost Chinese chemical engineer of his generation, was chief engineer (1921–49) and general manager (1945–49) of China's leading chemical works, the Yungli Chemical Industry Company at Tientsin. After 1949 he held important technical posts at Peking, where he became vice minister of chemical industry in 1958.

Born in Minhou, Fukien, Hou Te-pang received his early education in his native province. He then went to Shanghai, where he enrolled in the Fukien-Anhwei Railroad School. After being graduated from that institution in 1908, he worked for two years as a construction supervisor on the Tientsin-Pukow railway.

In 1910 Hou passed a government examination for a Boxer Indemnity Fund scholarship and entered Tsinghua College to prepare for study in the United States. He went to Cambridge, Massachusetts, in 1913 and received a B.S. in chemical engineering from the Massachusetts Institute of Technology in 1917. He then went to New York, where he studied tanning methods at the Pratt Institute in Brooklyn in 1917–18 and did graduate work at Columbia University. Hou received the M.S. in 1919 and the Ph.D. degree in 1921. His thesis, dealing with iron tannage, was printed in the *Journal of the American Leather Chemists Association* in 1921.

Hou Te-pang returned to China in 1921 and became chief engineer of the Yungli Soda Company at Tangku, Hopei. The company had been founded by Fan Hsü-tung (1892–1945), a cousin of Fan Yuan-lien and one of the most prominent industrial pioneers of that period. In 1922 Hou put the company's soda plant into operation, utilizing the Solvay process. In 1933 the Yungli Soda Company was renamed the Yungli Chemical Industry Company, and it began to produce ammonium sulphate. Hou Te-pang visited the United States to prepare designs for the establishment of a chemical fertilizer plant near Nanking and to recruit young Chinese engineers for the company. He returned to China in 1935 to supervise construction of a plant to produce nitrogen-bearing chemical fertilizers. The plant was ready for operation by the end of 1936. In recognition of Hou Te-pang's outstanding work, the Chinese Engineering Society gave him a special award at its annual meeting in 1935.

In 1937 the Japanese occupied the Yungli plants near Tientsin and Nanking. Fan Hsü-tung then decided to establish a new plant in west China. Because the site selected for the plant at Wu-t'ung-ch'iao, Szechwan, presented special engineering and design problems, Hou Te-pang went to Germany late in 1938 to seek technical assistance. However, Sino-German relations were deteriorating, and the German engineers were not cooperative. Hou Te-pang and his assistants then went to the United States. Hou's research in the United States during this period, with his technicians in Szechwan carrying on necessary experiments under his long-distance direction, led to improvements in the process used by Yungli in manufacturing industrial soda. The Yungli workers named it the Hou process.

Hou Te-pang's work in the field of chemical engineering brought him international recognition during the Second World War. In 1943 he was made a fellow of the institute of chemistry of the Academia Sinica. In 1944 the National Government conferred a special award on him for his assistance in designing small chemical plants for military use during the war. Hou again visited the United States, where he received an honorary D.Sc. degree from Columbia University. His book, *The Manufacture of Soda, with Special Reference to the Ammonia Process*, originally published in English by the American Chemical Society in 1933, appeared in a revised edition in 1942. Hou was elected to honorary membership in the American Chemical Society and in the Society of Chemical Industry in London. During the war years, he also designd a soda plant for the government of Brazil. In 1945 the Tata Chemical Works in India retained him as an engineering consultant. However, other duties permitted him to make only one trip to India under that arrangement, in 1947.

In 1945, after the death of Fan Hsü-tung, Hou became general manager of the Yungli Chemical Industry Company, and he continued to serve as its chief engineer. Hou went to the United States in 1946 for discussions with the Export-Import Bank in Washington, D.C., about a loan for the construction of a new plant in Hunan province. Yungli was the only Chinese industrial enterprise to obtain approval for a loan from the United States government in the postwar period. However, the continuing political and military instability in China prevented implementation of the agreement. In 1948 Hou became the first recipient of the Fan Hsü-tung memorial award. He donated the proceeds from the award to the library of the Chinese Chemical Industry Society at Shanghai. The same year, Hou visited the United States as a counselor of the National Government's ministry of industry. While abroad, he submitted a paper, "Postwar Developments in the Synthetic Ammonia

Industry in the United States," to the annual meeting of the China Engineering Society.

After spending more than 25 years in private business as China's foremost chemical engineer, Hou Te-pang began a new career in the People's Republic of China at the age of 59. He was elected vice chairman of the All-China Federation of Scientific Societies in 1950, and he continued to hold that post after the organization became the Scientific and Technical Association of China in 1958. He also served as chairman of the China Chemical Society and of the preparatory committee of the China Chemical Engineering Society. He was named to the standing committee, technical sciences department, of the Chinese Academy of Sciences in 1955 and to membership on the Scientific Planning Commission of the State Council in 1957. In 1958 he was appointed vice minister of chemical industry in the Central People's Government at Peking.

Hou Te-pang was active in the affairs of the All-China Federation of Industry and Commerce and of the Democratic National Construction Association. He also was a delegate to the National People's Congress. Hou represented the People's Republic of China at scientific meetings in India and Pakistan in 1954–55 and headed the Chinese delegation of chemical fertilizer specialists that visited Japan in the winter of 1957. He was elected a member of the World Peace Council by the World Peace Congress in 1955, and he attended its meetings at Stockholm in 1956 and at Colombo in 1957. After the 1956 meeting in Sweden, Hou headed a Chinese cultural delegation which visited Italy, Switzerland, France, and Belgium during the spring of that year. He also served as a member of the board of directors of the China-Pakistan and Sino-Iraq Friendship associations.

Hsia Yen: *see* SHEN TUAN-HSIEN.

Hsiang Ching-yü   向 警 子

Hsiang Ching-yü (1895–1 May 1928), the wife of Ts'ai Ho-sen (q.v.) and an early member of the Chinese Communist party, was known for her work in organizing women for the party's cause. She was executed by the Nationalist authorities.

Little is known of Hsiang Ching-yü's childhood except that she was born into a well-to-do merchant family in Hsup'u, Hunan. About 1910 she entered the Chou-nan nü-hsiao [Chou-nan girls school] in Changsha. Three of her brothers had gone to Japan in pursuit of a modern education. At school, she was a student leader and acquired the nickname of "Mo-tzu" because this humanitarian philosopher was her chief interest at that time. She came to know Ts'ai Ho-sen (q.v.) and Mao Tse-tung; and when the two men organized the Hsin-min hsüeh-hui [new people's study society] in 1918, she became a member. After graduation in 1918, Hsiang Ching-yü returned to Hsup'u and founded a girls' primary school, of which she became principal. She also traveled to other cities in Hunan to promote women's education.

Hsiang Ching-yü was about 24 at the time of the May Fourth Movement, and in the spring of 1919 she was active in patriotic demonstrations. Some members of the Hsin-min hsüeh-hui at Changsha were then making plans to go to France under the work-study plan. Hsiang Ching-yü and Ts'ai Ch'ang (q.v.), who was also a graduate of the Chou-nan nü-hsiao, organized a group of young women to join them. On the voyage to France, Ts'ai was accompanied by her mother and her elder brother, Ts'ai Ho-sen. Hsiang and Ts'ai Ho-sen were married in 1921. In France, Hsiang Ching-yü worked in a factory, studied French intensively, and began to read Marxist literature. She and her husband were leading figures in the work-study movement. In the spring of 1921 they helped organize the Chung-kuo ch'ing-nien kung-ch'an-t'uan [young Chinese Communist corps], which in 1922 became the French branch of the Chinese Communist party. In 1921 Hsiang Ching-yü and her husband were leaders of the 8 February demonstrations against the anarchists, in which they were joined by Chou En-lai, Ch'en Yen-nien, and Chao Shih-yen (qq.v.). The French government deported Ts'ai Ho-sen in the winter of 1921 because of his political activities. He returned to China, where he made contact with the central apparatus of the infant Chinese Communist party at Shanghai. Hsiang Ching-yü joined him in Shanghai in the spring of 1922.

Both Hsiang and Ts'ai attended the Second National Congress of the Chinese Communist party, held in July 1922, and both were elected to the Central Committee. Hsiang Ching-yü was appointed director of the newly created women's department of the Central Committee, and she played a leading role in expanding Communist influence among women. In 1924 she helped organize the strikes in the silk factories and at the Nanyang Tobacco Company in Shanghai, enterprises staffed largely by women and girls. During the period of the May Thirtieth Incident of 1925, when police fired on demonstrators in Shanghai, both Hsiang and Ts'ai were active in Shanghai, attempting to direct the political unrest resulting from the incident into channels useful to the Chinese Communist party.

Toward the end of 1925 Hsiang accompanied Ts'ai to Moscow to attend the sixth plenum of the Executive Committee of the Comintern. Ts'ai then served as Chinese Communist delegate to the Comintern, and Hsiang studied at the Communist University for Toilers of the East. They remained in the Soviet Union until May 1927, when they returned to China to attend the Fifth National Congress of the Chinese Communist party. Hsiang Ching-yü then served in the propaganda department of the Wuhan general labor union. Later, she took charge of party propaganda work in Hankow while her husband was working in the propaganda department of the Central Committee.

After the left-Kuomintang group at Wuhan broke with the Communists in July 1927, Hsiang Ching-yü worked underground as a labor organizer in Hankow. The rigors of this existence affected her health. In April 1928 she was arrested and imprisoned by the French concession police in Hankow. In prison, she led her cellmates in a hunger strike to demand better treatment. She was extradited to the Chinese authorities and was executed on 1 May 1928. Large crowds of workers accompanied her to the execution ground, where she made a speech and shouted slogans before facing the firing squad. Three years later, her husband also was captured and executed.

Hsiang Ching-yü was the most prominent woman in the Chinese Communist party during its formative years. Because she believed that the emancipation of Chinese women could be attained only through radical change in the Chinese social system, she saw the Chinese Communist party as the most effective

channel through which to achieve that objective. Her most important contribution to the Chinese Communist movement was the organized political mobilization, for the first time, of worker and peasant women. Her only surviving writings are contained in *Hsiang-shang t'ung-meng* [toward a brighter day], a collection of love poems she exchanged with Ts'ai Ho-sen during their voyage to France. An official biography, *Lieh-shih Hsiang Ching-yü* [Hsiang Ching-yü, revolutionary martyr], was published in Peking in 1958.

Hsiang Chung-fa   向 忠 發

Hsiang Chung-fa (1888–23 June 1931), Communist labor organizer. He became general secretary of the Chinese Communist party in 1928 and held that post until his arrest and execution in 1931.

Little is known of Hsiang Chung-fa's background or early life except that he was born in Hupeh. Hsiang worked as a coolie on the ore barges of the Han-yeh-p'ing Company in central China. He became a Communist through the influence of Shih Yang, a Hupeh lawyer. Shih established workers schools at Wuhan about 1920 and directed the Hupeh bureau of the China Trade Union Secretariat in 1921–22. Under his tutelage, Hsiang became a labor organizer. Shih Yang, who served as counselor for much of the early Communist labor organizational work in Hupeh, was seized and put to death in the 7 February 1923 affair, when Wu P'ei-fu (q.v.) moved to suppress the formation of a labor union of Peking-Hankow railroad workers.

Hsiang Chung-fa worked to organize miners of the Han-yeh-p'ing Company and soon rose to be general secretary of the Han-yeh-p'ing labor union. In 1925, in recognition of his contributions in the labor field, Hsiang, who had received little formal education, was selected by the Chinese Communist party to study in the Soviet Union. He probably traveled to Moscow with a group of young Chinese Communists who later became known as the 28 Bolsheviks (*see* Ch'en Shao-yü). He returned to China in 1926 and became chairman of the Communist-directed Hupeh General Labor Union. In the spring of 1927 he was elected to the Central Committee of the Chinese

Communist party at the Fifth National Congress, which was held at Wuhan.

Hsiang Chung-fa commanded a substantial following among the workers and labor organizers of Hupeh, where the influence of Ch'en Tu-hsiu, then the leader of the Communist party, was negligible. When an insurgent group within the Chinese Communist party headed by Ch'ü Ch'iu-pai (q.v.) attempted to wrest the party leadership from Ch'en Tu-hsiu, it sought the cooperation of Hsiang Chung-fa. Hsiang was one of the very few members of the Central Committee invited to attend the emergency meeting of 7 August 1927 at which Ch'en was deposed as general secretary of the party on orders of the Comintern.

After the collapse of the Wuhan government in the summer of 1927, the Kuomintang inaugurated a vigorous suppression campaign against the Communists, and Hsiang went to the Soviet Union. At the Sixth National Congress of the Chinese Communist party, held at Moscow in the summer of 1928, he was elected to succeed Ch'ü Ch'iu-pai as general secretary of the party. His proletarian background, combined with his flair for public speaking, reportedly helped to win Russian support for his election.

Hsiang Chung-fa held the post of general secretary of the Chinese Communist party from 1928 until 1931, the period during which the major lines of political policy were dominated by Li Li-san (q.v.) and then, after Li was removed from the Political Bureau in November 1930, by the so-called 28 Bolsheviks. In 1929 and 1930 Hsiang's views on contemporary political matters appeared in *Hung-ch'i* [red flag], the official organ of the party, and he presented the Political Bureau report at the fourth plenum of the sixth Central Committee, which met at Shanghai in January 1931.

In the spring of 1931 Ku Shun-chang, a member of the central apparatus of the Chinese Communist party, was arrested at Wuhan by the Kuomintang authorities. After his arrest, he gave the police the names and addresses of most of the prominent Central Committee members at Shanghai. Hsiang Chung-fa was seized by the authorities in the International Settlement at Shanghai on 21 June 1931. He was extradited to Chinese territory and was executed on 23 June. His obituary was published by the official *International Press Correspondence* in Moscow on 1 August 1931. Although Hsiang Chung-fa was the only man of working-class background to hold the position of general secretary of the Chinese Communist party in the pre-1949 period, he had relatively little impact on the political history of the movement and was not listed as a martyr in official Communist party histories published after 1950.

Hsiang Ying   項 英

Hsiang Ying (1897– January 1941), Chinese Communist labor organizer and military leader, was one of the two vice chairmen of the central soviet government headed by Mao Tse-tung (1931–34) and became deputy commander and political commissar of the New Fourth Army. He was killed in the January 1941 clash with Nationalist forces in Anhwei.

Born into a poor family in Huangp'i, Hupeh, Hsiang Ying was orphaned at an early age. After serving as an apprentice in a pawnshop, he worked as a laborer on the Peking-Hankow railway. About this time, the Communist-led China Trade Union Secretariat moved to Peking. The secretariat concentrated on organizing the Peking-Hankow railroad workers, and Hsiang became one of the local labor leaders. After the incident of 7 February 1923, when Wu P'ei-fu (q.v.) took action to prevent the formation of a labor union among the railroad workers, Hsiang joined the Chinese Communist party.

For the next two years, Hsiang worked as a labor organizer in his native Hupeh. By May 1925 he had become sufficiently prominent to be chosen to represent the Wuhan workers at the Second All-China Labor Congress in Canton, which established the All-China Federation of Labor. He also was elected to the 25-man executive committee of the All-China Federation of Labor. In 1926 he became Communist party secretary at the Hupeh general labor union and head of the union's organization department. In 1927 he became party secretary at the Shanghai general labor union. In this capacity he worked with Chou En-lai, who was one of the principal organizers of a general uprising in the spring of 1927 which was intended to facilitate the seizure of Shanghai by the National Revolutionary Army.

After the Kuomintang-Communist split in mid-1927, Hsiang Ying went to the Soviet Union, where he reportedly received military training. In the summer of 1928 he attended the Sixth Congress of the Chinese Communist party, held at Moscow, at which the leadership of Ch'ü Ch'iu-pai (q.v.) was repudiated. Hsiang Chung-fa (q.v.) was elected general secretary of the party, and Hsiang Ying was elected to the Central Committee and the Political Bureau. After returning to China, Hsiang Ying became chairman of the All-China Federation of Labor at its fifth congress, which was held secretly in Shanghai. At that time, Li Li-san (q.v.) was very active in party and labor work in Shanghai, and Hsiang Ying reportedly was one of his trusted supporters.

Little is known of Hsiang Ying's role in the Chinese Communist party from 1928 to 1931. After the political downfall of Li Li-san in late 1930 and the capture and execution of Hsiang Chung-fa in mid-1931, Ch'en Shao-yü (q.v.) became the general secretary of the party. Some sources suggest that Ch'en Shao-yü's group, in cooperation with Chou En-lai, sent Hsiang Ying to Kiangsi as a representative of the Political Bureau to establish contact with the rural areas under Communist control, where the influence of Mao Tse-tung and his associates was increasing steadily. In any event, when the First All-China Congress of Soviets met in Juichin, Kiangsi, in November 1931 to establish a central soviet government, Mao Tse-tung was elected chairman, and Hsiang Ying and Chang Kuo-t'ao (q.v.) became vice chairmen. Hsiang Ying also served as a member of the military committee, commander of the Eighth Red Army, and chairman of the supervisory committee.

When the main Communist armies left Kiangsi on the Long March in the autumn of 1934, Hsiang Ying remained behind to cover the retreat and to attempt to develop a new base of operations in the area. He took charge of party affairs in what had been the central soviet area. His guerrilla troops fought savagely to escape annihilation by the Nationalist armies; by mid-1936 they had been driven east to the Kiangsi-Fukien border. Hsiang divided the remnants of his forces into smaller units which dispersed through the rural area of central China into Kiangsi, Fukien, Hunan, Chekiang, and Anhwei. After the outbreak of the war with Japan in July 1937, the Nationalist armies were forced to halt their campaigns against the Communists, and, gradually, the guerrilla units began to reassemble. In September 1937 Hsiang Ying met with Hsiung Shih-hui (q.v.), the representative of Ho Ying-ch'in (q.v.), the Nationalist war minister. They agreed to cease hostilities in central China. Tentative plans were made for reorganizing the Communist troops in the area and for incorporating them into the Nationalist military establishment. It appears that Hsiang Ying visited Yenan after this meeting. When he returned to central China in January 1938, negotiations had been completed for the creation of the Communist New Fourth Army, named for the Fourth Red Army, which had been organized when Chu Teh (q.v.) and Mao Tse-tung joined forces at Chingkangshan in 1928.

On 4 January 1938 the New Fourth Army, numbering about 12,000 troops, established headquarters at Nanchang, Kiangsi. It was assigned a territory of operations along the Yangtze in central China about 50 miles wide and 150 miles long. Yeh T'ing (q.v.), who had achieved prominence on the Northern Expedition and who later had broken with the Communist party, was appointed commander; Hsiang Ying became deputy commander and political commissar. In addition to his military responsibilities, Hsiang served as secretary of the southeast bureau of the Chinese Communist party.

In April 1938 the New Fourth Army established headquarters in Anhwei and began to extend its territory of operation. Guerrilla raids were made along the Nanking-Shanghai and the Wuhu-Nanking railways and along the Nanking-Hangchow highway. When Hsüchow in northern Kiangsu fell to the Japanese in May 1938, the Communist forces moved northward. From that time on, the New Fourth Army maintained two detachments north of the Yangtze. Between the spring of 1938 and the autumn of 1939 the Chinese Communist guerrillas won in several engagements with the Japanese. The Communists were more successful in areas north of the Yangtze than in the areas to the south; by 1940 almost four-fifths of their troops were north of the river.

In the autumn of 1940, Nationalist elements began to agitate for the removal of all Communist troops to bases north of the Yangtze and the Yellow rivers. An ultimatum to that effect was issued in December. However, the Communist forces moved in a direction more to the east than to the north. In January 1941 units of the New Fourth Army came into sharp conflict with Nationalist forces at Maolin in southern Anhwei. The ensuing battle (6–14 January 1941), which resulted in an almost total rout of the Communists, is known in Communist literature as the New Fourth Army Incident. Yeh T'ing, the commander, was captured by the Nationalists; and Hsiang Ying was killed.

Of the leaders of the New Fourth Army, it was Hsiang Ying who was blamed in Yenan for the destruction of the army. Specifically, he was accused of entertaining rightist ideas and of failing to implement a series of directives drafted for the Central Committee of the Chinese Communist party by Mao Tse-tung on 4 May 1940, thereby exposing the New Fourth Army to attack by Nationalist forces.

This criticism notwithstanding, Hsiang Ying was known throughout his career as an effective agitator and guerrilla commander. According to the renegade Communist Li Ang (Chu Ch'i-hua, q.v.), Hsiang also was a formidable figure in intraparty disagreements, far more vigorous and outspoken than was Ch'ü Ch'iu-pai. Hsiang's speeches and instructions to the cadres of the New Fourth Army, some of which were collected and published in a small volume entitled *Hsiang Ying chiang-chün yen-lun chi* (1939), suggest that he was a persuasive speaker and that his knowledge of contemporary affairs was quite extensive.

Hsiang's wife was arrested in Fukien in February 1935, together with Ch'ü Ch'iu-pai. Nothing further is known of her.

Hsiao Fo-ch'eng   蕭 佛 成
T.   T'ieh-ch'iao   鐵 橋
Alt. Siu Fat-sing

Hsiao Fo-ch'eng (1862–1939) headed the T'ung-meng-hui branch in Siam, edited the Chinese edition of the *Hua-hsien jih-pao* [Sino-Siam daily], and worked to improve the lot of overseas Chinese. He was a leader of the 1931 secession movement at Canton.

Bangkok, Siam, was the birthplace of Hsiao Fo-ch'eng. His family's native place was in southern Fukien, but an ancestor had opposed the Manchus toward the end of the Ming dynasty and had fled to Taiwan. Later, members of the family had emigrated to Malacca, and early in the nineteenth century some had moved to Siam, where they had prospered in business. Hsiao received a traditional education in the Chinese classics.

Hsiao's tutor, Kao Chuan-pai, had served as a staff officer in the Taiping Rebellion and had escaped to Siam when that movement failed. Thus, the young Hsiao became an ardent nationalist and revolutionary. He also qualified as a lawyer. In 1888, at the age of 27 sui, Hsiao joined the local Triad Society, or San-ho Hui. That group had originated as an organization pledged to the overthrow of the Manchus and the restoration of the Ming dynasty, but it had become a secret society, and some of its members had been implicated in crimes of violence. Nevertheless, some of the traditional objectives of the society had been kept alive, and there were branches of the organization throughout Southeast Asia. Recognizing the need for a more effective organization, Hsiao Fo-ch'eng formed the Kuang-fu Club [club for the restoration of the nation] with a number of other revolutionaries.

Meanwhile, Sun Yat-sen had organized the Hsing-Chung-hui, the predecessor of the T'ung-meng-hui. That organization established the newspaper *Chung-kuo jih-pao* [China daily] at Hong Kong in 1899. This was the first newspaper published by the anti-Manchu revolutionaries, and it gradually increased its circulation in the overseas Chinese communities of Southeast Asia. In 1905 Hsiao Fo-ch'eng established contact with staff members of the newspaper and began to make plans for establishing a revolutionary newspaper at Bangkok. With the help of Ch'en Ching-hua, a former district magistrate in Kwangsi who had been forced to flee after incurring the displeasure of Ts'en Ch'un-hsuan (q.v.), the governor general, Hsiao founded a Chinese newspaper in Bangkok in 1906. Control of that newspaper soon fell into the hands of local Chinese supporters of the constitutional monarchy movement led by K'ang Yu-wei (q.v.). Hsiao Fo-ch'eng, Ch'en Ching-hua, and other republican revolutionaries then founded the *Hua-hsien jih-pao* [Sino-Siam daily] in 1907. Hsiao edited the Chinese edition and his daughter edited the Siamese edition. The *Hua-hsien jih-pao* continued publication until the Japanese occupied Siam in 1942.

In 1908 Sun Yat-sen, accompanied by Hu Han-min (q.v.) and others, visited Bangkok. The Siamese authorities would not permit Sun to pursue his political activities openly, but revolutionary supporters met secretly and organized the Siamese branch of the T'ung-meng-hui. Hsiao Fo-ch'eng was elected head of the branch. He and Hu Han-min became friends during this time. Thereafter, Hsiao remained loyal to Sun Yat-sen and helped Sun in many fund-raising campaigns.

In 1926 Hsiao Fo-ch'eng attended the Second National Congress of the Kuomintang, held at Canton, and was elected to the Central Executive Committee. At that meeting he advocated that the government adopt a vigorous policy for the protection of Chinese abroad.

In March 1927 Hsiao attended a preparatory meeting for the fourth plenary session of the Kuomintang Central Executive Committee. Hu Han-min presided at the meeting, and Hsiao presented a proposal which contained provisions for affirmation of Nanking as the national capital, abolition of the illegal central party headquarters, abolition of the Wuhan government, expulsion of party members who had dual party membership, arrest of rebels, restoration of the authority of the commander in chief as decided in July 1926, use of armed force against rebels, and publication of a formal announcement embodying the program. The proposal was, in effect, a public declaration of the legitimacy of the Nanking government.

For a time, Hsiao served as head of the overseas Chinese department of the Kuomintang at Nanking. In 1928 he returned to Siam, where he became involved in the movement among overseas Chinese, resulting from the May Third Incident at Tsinan (*see* Ho Yao-tsu), to boycott Japanese goods. The Siamese government, which opposed political activism, took steps to suppress the movement. Hsiao had sufficient influence to convince the Siamese authorities to limit their action to

deporting a few men convicted of attempting to kill the boycott-breakers. The Chinese community in Bangkok contributed a substantial amount of money to aid victims of the May Third Incident.

In 1929, when the Third National Congress of the Kuomintang met at Nanking, Hsiao was elected to the Central Supervisory Committee of the party. On behalf of the National Government, he undertook negotiations with the Siamese authorities for a treaty which would improve the lot of the Chinese residents in Siam. He repeated his efforts in 1933, and other representatives were sent by the National Government in the intervening years.

In February 1931 Hu Han-min, then president of the Legislative Yuan, was detained by Chiang Kai-shek because of political differences and later was imprisoned. On 30 April, Hsiao Fo-ch'eng, in his capacity as a member of the Kuomintang Central Supervisory Committee, joined three other members of that body, Ku Ying-fen, Lin Sen, and Teng Tse-ju (qq.v.), in proposing the impeachment of Chiang Kai-shek, who was accused of "implicating comrades to build up his personal position."

The proposal precipitated a secession movement at Canton. Ch'en Chi-t'ang (q.v.), who then held military power in Kwangtung, supported the group from the Central Supervisory Committee, as did Wang Ching-wei, Sun Fo, Eugene Ch'en, and T'ang Shao-yi (qq.v.). An extraordinary session of all members of the first, second, and third central committees of the Kuomintang met at Canton, and a rival national government was founded there.

Impending civil war was averted by the Mukden Incident of 18 September 1931. The Japanese invasion restored unity to the Kuomintang ranks. The Canton secession movement was called off, and the National Government was reorganized toward the end of 1931. Hsiao Fo-ch'eng was elected a member of the State Council.

A state of semi-independence continued to prevail in the provinces of Kwangtung and Kwangsi with the creation of the Southwest Executive Headquarters of the Kuomintang and the Southwest Political Council. The leaders of the 1931 secession movement remaining at Canton, other than the militarists Ch'en Chi-t'ang and Li Tsung-jen (qq.v.), included only Hsiao Fo-ch'eng, T'ang Shao-yi, and Teng Tse-ju. In the party hierarchy, both Hsiao Fo-ch'eng and Teng Tse-ju ranked higher than T'ang Shao-yi.

After the deaths of Teng Tse-ju (1934) and Hu Han-min (early 1936), Hsiao Fo-ch'eng was the only remaining party elder at Canton. However, he had no real authority, and his health had begun to deteriorate. He spent much of his leisure playing Chinese chess and often entertained professional chess players.

After the Sino-Japanese war broke out in the summer of 1937, Hsiao returned to his home in Siam. He died at Bangkok in June 1939.

Hsiao Hua 萧 華

Hsiao Hua (c.1915–), served as a Communist political officer in north China during the Sino-Japanese war. After 1949 he served as a deputy director and then as director of the general political department of the People's Liberation Army.

The date and place of Hsiao Hua's birth are uncertain, but available evidence indicates that he was born during the early part of the First World War and that he was a native of either Hunan or Kiangsi. After joining the Chinese Communist party through the youth movement when in his late teens, Hsiao became an officer in the Chinese Communist military forces. In 1934–35 he participated in the Long March, in the course of which he was associated with Lin Piao, Liu Po-ch'eng, Yang Yung, and other commanders.

After the Sino-Japanese war began in 1937, Hsiao was assigned to political work with the Communist forces in north China. Throughout the early 1940's he was active in the Communist-controlled areas of Hopei and Shantung, where he was associated with Nieh Jung-chen (q.v.) and other Communist officers in developing bases of political and military strength in areas nominally under Japanese jurisdiction. In 1945 he became the director of the political department of what the Communists called the Shantung military district. In 1946 he was assigned to southern Manchuria, and he commanded the Liaotung military district in 1947 and 1948.

Shortly after the Communists advanced from Manchuria into north China in the winter of 1948, Hsiao became active in the Communist-directed program to mobilize young people for national political purposes. In 1949 he was elected to the national committee of the China Democratic Youth Federation, and in August of that year he led a delegation to the World Youth and Student Festival held at Budapest. He was elected a member of the executive committee of the World Federation of Democratic Youth, and in the autumn of 1949 he visited youth organizations in Eastern Europe and the Soviet Union. In 1949 Hsiao was elected a member of the central committee of the New Democratic Youth League, the principal national organization established by the Chinese Communist party to train future party members, and from 1951 to 1953 he was a member of its standing committee.

Hsiao was appointed a deputy director of the general political department of the People's Liberation Army in 1950. Lo Jung-huan (q.v.) headed the department, which was responsible for the political command and control system which operated at all levels in the Chinese Communist forces. Hsiao represented the Northeast People's Liberation Army at the National People's Congress in 1954. He was promoted to the rank of colonel general in September 1955 and was awarded all top military decorations given by the Central People's Government. In September 1956 he was elected to the Central Committee of the Chinese Communist party at the Eighth National Congress. He also became a member and a deputy secretary of the Control Commission, the central organization responsible for party discipline.

Hsiao Hua continued to hold important positions in the military command structure at Peking. In December 1956 he was named director of the general cadres department, the headquarters unit responsible for personnel control in the armed forces. Hsiao was a member of a military delegation, led by P'eng Te-huai (q.v.), which toured the Soviet Union, Eastern Europe, and the Mongolian People's Republic in the spring of 1959. The general political department absorbed the cadres department headed by Hsiao Hua in 1960. Hsiao presented major reports on political work in the People's Liberation Army during the early 1960's and was one of the leading staff officers attached to the military affairs committee of the Central Committee of the Chinese Communist party. After the death of Lo Jung-huan in December 1963, Hsiao Hua was named to succeed him as director of the general political department in September 1964.

Hsiao K'o 蕭 克

Hsiao K'o (August 1909–), Chinese Communist army officer, served under Yeh T'ing and Chu Teh in the 1920's and under Ho Lung in the 1930's and 1940's. After 1949 he held office as director of the general training department of the Chinese Communist military forces.

Chiaho hsien, Hunan, was the birthplace of Hsiao K'o. His father was a scholar who had received the sheng-yuan degree. Hsiao K'o received a conventional Chinese education in his native village. About 1921 his elder brother participated in a local peasant uprising, and his father was imprisoned soon afterward. Although the family's finances became straitened, Hsiao K'o was able to continue his education. He studied at a provincial normal school in Hunan after his graduation from higher primary school.

In 1926 Hsiao went to Canton, where he joined Chiang Kai-shek's 65th Gendarme Regiment. When the Northern Expedition began, Hsiao was assigned as a company-level political officer in the 24th Division, commanded by Yeh T'ing (q.v.), of Chang Fa-k'uei's Fourth Army. He joined the Chinese Communist party in the summer of 1927 and participated in the uprising at Nanchang in August as a company commander. After the failure of the action at Nanchang, Hsiao K'o joined the forces commanded by Chu Teh (q.v.) which moved southward toward Kwangtung. However, Hsiao's unit soon was defeated and dispersed. He then served with Chiang Kai-shek's Thirteenth Army for a brief period and returned to his native village in Hunan.

At the beginning of 1928 Communist troops under Chu Teh moved into southern Hunan, and in the spring they succeeded in joining forces with Mao Tse-tung in the Ching-kang mountains. Hsiao, who had been organizing a peasant insurrection at Ichang, led a small group of men to join Chu and Mao. He became a company commander in the newly created Fourth Red Army.

In 1929 Hsiao was promoted to regimental commander. After fighting in Kiangsi, Fukien, and Kwangtung, he became a division commander. He assumed command of the Sixth Red Army in September 1932, after the death of Chou I-ch'un. Jen Pi-shih (q.v.) joined Hsiao as political commissar in 1933. Hsiao's troops began the Long March in the early autumn of 1934, before the main Communist forces under Chu Teh and Mao Tse-tung evacuated the central soviet base area in Kiangsi. In October 1934 the Sixth Red Army joined forces in Kweichow with the Second Red Army under Ho Lung and Kuan Hsiang-ying to form the Second Front Army, with Ho Lung as over-all commander and Jen Pi-shih as political commissar.

Hsiao K'o remained in the Szechwan-Hunan-Hupeh-Kweichow base area from late 1934 until November 1935, when the Second Front Army began a separate retreat. Hsiao and his associates reached Kantzu, Sikang, on the eastern edge of the Tibetan plateau, in June 1936 and joined forces with the Fourth Front Army under Chang Kuo-t'ao and Hsü Hsiang-ch'ien (qq.v.). Hsiao K'o and his troops finally arrived at the Communist base area in northern Shensi in October 1936. He then was assigned to command the Thirty-first Army.

After the Sino-Japanese war began in the summer of 1937, the Eighth Route Army, composed of three Communist divisions, was organized. Hsiao K'o was named deputy commander of the 120th Division, led by his fellow-provincial Ho Lung. In 1938 the main force of the 120th Division moved eastward from Shansi into Hopei province, where Hsiao spent the remaining war years helping to mobilize support for the Chinese Communists in the rural areas around Peiping and in Jehol province.

After the Japanese surrender in 1945, Hsiao K'o continued to be active in the Communist military command structure, with jurisdiction over portions of north China, including Hopei and Shansi; Inner Mongolia, notably Jehol and Chahar; and Liaoning in southern Manchuria. In 1949 he became chief of staff to Lin Piao (q.v.), who commanded the Fourth

Field Army. From 1949 to 1951 Hsiao served as chief of staff of the Central-South Military District; he also was a member of the Central-South Military and Administrative Committee, the regional government structure established by the Communists to consolidate political control.

In 1953 Hsiao K'o was named director of the general training department of the People's Revolutionary Military Council. He represented the North China Military District at the first National People's Congress in 1954. With the reorganization of the Central People's Government in that year, Hsiao became a vice minister of national defense, deputy director of the general training department, and a member of the National Defense Council. In June 1955 he led a Chinese delegation to Prague, Czechoslovakia. Hsiao K'o was raised to the rank of colonel general in September 1955 and was awarded all top military decorations given by the Central People's Government. At the Eighth National Congress of the Chinese Communist party, he was elected to the Central Committee. In November 1957 he was named director of the general training department, succeeding Liu Po-ch'eng (q.v.), who had held that post from 1954 to 1957.

In the government reorganization of 1959 Hsiao K'o became a vice minister in the ministry of state farms and land reclamation, headed by Wang Chen (q.v.), a veteran Communist general with whom Hsiao had been associated in the Hunan-Hupeh soviet area in the 1930's. Hsiao was reappointed to the National Defense Council in April 1959. He succeeded Wang Chen as acting minister of state farms and land reclamation in 1963.

Hsiao T'ung-tzu   蕭 同 茲
   West. T. T. Hsiao

Hsiao T'ung-tzu (1894–), director of the Central News Agency from 1932 to 1950.

Ch'angning, Hunan, was the birthplace of Hsiao T'ung-tzu. Little is known of his early life. He was graduated from Hunan Industrial College in Changsha in 1917. His first known activities were in connection with the Hunan labor movement in the winter of 1920. At that time, Hsiao was associated with

Huang Ai and P'ang Jen-ch'uan, who were shot in January 1921 in connection with the strike at the Hua-shih Cotton Mill in Changsha. Hsiao was not a labor organizer; he appears to have restricted his activities to such propaganda work as the preparation of posters and handbills. Nevertheless, he was forced to flee Changsha in 1921.

Hsiao went to Canton and became associated with the Kuomintang. He reportedly prepared propaganda for the Northern Expedition. After the National Government was established at Nanking in 1928, he became a secretary attached to the Kuomintang's central propaganda apparatus.

In 1932 Hsiao T'ung-tzu was named director of the Central News Agency (Chung-yang t'ung-hsün she), which had been established at Canton in April 1924 as a subsidiary of the central propaganda department of the Kuomintang. Before Hsiao became its director, there was no long-term planning with regard to the operations of the agency except for the vague stipulation that Kuomintang branches and members should furnish news to the central party apparatus. For domestic news, the private Kuo-wen News Service of the *Ta Kung Pao* and the Shun-shih News Service in Shanghai were the leading news sources. Foreign news services dominated the dissemination of international news in China.

Hsiao expanded and developed the Central News Agency into a respected news service. He realized at the outset that the agency, to be effective, had to achieve a more independent status. Hsiao's first step was to move the Central News Agency office out of the Kuomintang headquarters building at Nanking. Although he continued to receive party directives, he was given a free hand in establishing a news collection and distribution service. Hsiao opened branch offices in all the important cities of China, organized a wire service with its own telegraphic facilities, and arranged for the exchange of news with foreign news agencies operating in China.

By 1937 the Central News Agency had 10 bureaus and 21 staff correspondents. A total of 159 Chinese newspapers subscribed to the service, which handled 15,000 words of incoming news and 20,000 words of outgoing news daily. The success of the Central News Agency forced the Kuo-wen News Service to close. In 1936, when Sino-Japanese relations were entering a crucial stage, Hsiao recruited Ch'en Po-sheng, a veteran journalist who was known as a Japan specialist, to open a Tokyo bureau, the first overseas branch of the Central News Agency. The same year, Feng Yü-chen, the chief reporter of the agency, was sent to Berlin to cover the Olympic Games.

After the Sino-Japanese war broke out, the Central News Agency was forced to close its bureaus in areas of China occupied by the Japanese. Hsiao moved his headquarters to Chungking. Despite the difficulties of wartime operation, he maintained 18 domestic news bureaus in China and a staff of field correspondents. A new photographic department was established to provide pictorial coverage of the war. When Japanese bombing of Chungking was heavy, the central staff worked underground in deep dugouts. By this time the principal foreign news agencies, notably Reuters and the United Press, had concluded arrangements with the Central News Agency by which their dispatches were issued under a joint dateline with the Central News Agency. This development reflected the growth of the agency's English-language department, which served the foreign press. The first Central News Agency office outside the Far East was established at Washington in 1940; within five years bureaus had been opened in New York, London, Moscow, New Delhi, Calcutta, and Paris. The agency's reporters were attached as war correspondents to major commands in the Pacific theater.

At Chungking, Hsiao was elected president of the Chinese National Press Association. He worked closely with Hollington Tong (Tung Hsien-kuang, q.v.), who handled relations with the foreign press corps and distributed official news. After 1938 Ch'en Po-sheng served as chief editor of the Central News Agency and handled much of the technical work of the enterprise.

Hsiao served as director of the Central News Agency until 1950. He then relinquished his post to Tseng Hsü-pai, but remained chairman of the supervisory board. In 1954 he became an adviser to Chiang Kai-shek in Taipei. Hsiao was never regarded as being active in party affairs; however, he was a member of the Central Executive Committee of the Kuomintang after 1934.

Hsieh Ch'ih
T. Hui-sheng

謝 持
慧 生

Hsieh Ch'ih (18 January 1876–16 April 1939), anti-Manchu revolutionary and official in Sun Yat-sen's Canton government, was a member of the first Central Supervisory Committee of the Kuomintang. He became associated with the Western Hills faction of the Kuomintang and participated in the so-called enlarged conference movement of 1930.

Born into a merchant family in Fushun, Szechwan, Hsieh Ch'ih was adopted three days after birth by a childless paternal uncle. His parents and his adopted parents lived together in the same house until Hsieh was 12 years old. He was a sickly and accident-prone child, and his education frequently was interrupted by illness. In the spring of 1898 he entered the Chiang-yang Academy, where he encountered the literature of the reform movement. In the winter of that year his father died, and the funeral expenses caused his adopted father to go into debt. Hsieh had to forego his schooling to help in his adopted father's shop. Nevertheless, he took the hsien examination in the summer of 1899 and earned the sheng-yuan degree.

In the summer of 1900, Hsieh passed the entrance examinations of the Ching-wei Academy at Ipin, Szechwan. He studied under Chou Shan-p'ei, and, after graduation in 1902, he followed Chou to Chengtu. In the spring of 1903 Chou, who was then an official in the Szechwan provincial government, appointed Hsieh a physical education instructor in a police academy. Hsieh soon became a superintendant of school construction for the Szechwan office of education. In the summer of 1903 Chou Shan-p'ei was transferred to Kwangtung; Hsieh accompanied him, but returned to Szechwan after only a short stay. In 1904 he became a teacher at the Shu-jen School. Hsieh returned to his native place in the spring of 1905 to organize the Fushun Second Primary School. Because of disagreements with influential people in the town, Hsieh was forced to leave Fushun after only a few months. In 1906 he taught at the primary school and the school of sericulture in Junghsien.

In February 1907 the Fushun Second Primary School again invited him to serve on its faculty. About that time, Hsieh joined the T'ung-meng-hui. He headed the Fushun branch of that organization.

In June 1907 Chou Shan-p'ei was appointed superintendant of trade by the Szechwan government. Hsieh Ch'ih accepted Chou's invitation to become his assistant as a secretary in the bureau of trade, and he arrived at Chengtu in September. He plotted a revolutionary takeover of the city on 2 October, but the plan failed. On 28 October, Hsieh asked for leave to return to Fushun to celebrate his mother's birthday. That night the government arrested several of his comrades. Hsieh was warned of this action by friends. He returned to Chengtu on 20 November in an effort to rescue the imprisoned men. However, he had to flee for his life the next day. He hid at the home of a friend in Luhsien for several months. During this time he used the name Chu Hui-sheng. He left Szechwan in February 1908 for Shanghai.

In the spring of 1909 Hsieh went to Chungking, where he joined a T'ung-meng-hui group composed of graduates of the higher school at Chengtu and the provincial normal school. Because it was dangerous for him to stay in Chungking, his comrades insisted that he leave for the coast. Accordingly, he returned to Shanghai, were he served as provost at the new Chung-kuo Kung-hsueh. In the summer of 1909 he was sent by the T'ung-meng-hui group to Honan and Shensi. He stayed at Fenghsiang, Shensi, where he and other revolutionaries worked as shepherds and engaged in anti-Manchu activities.

In December 1910 Hsieh's adopted mother died in Fushun. After attending her funeral, Hsieh decided to remain in Szechwan to care for his adopted father. He accepted a teaching post at the Pahsien Girls School near Chungking. In May 1911 public demonstrations against the Ch'ing government's plan for nationalization of the railroads broke out in Szechwan. Hsieh Ch'ih and his comrades plotted to take over Chungking. Upon hearing that Tuan-fang (ECCP, II, 780–82), the newly appointed governor general of Szechwan, was leading Hupeh troops into Szechwan, the revolutionaries decided to ambush boats carrying weapons at Ch'angshou, a river port. The scheme failed,

and Hsieh returned to Chungking. That city declared its independence on 22 November; government troops joined the revolutionaries and took over the city without bloodshed. Hsieh Ch'ih was elected director of the general affairs bureau of the new military government at Chungking. After the fall of Chengtu to the revolutionaries on 27 November, the military governments of the two cities were amalgamated in February 1912 to form the military government of Szechwan. Hsieh was appointed vice director of the general affairs bureau of the new government. Later that year, he also was appointed to the post of counselor.

In the parliamentary election of February 1913 Hsieh Ch'ih was elected to the Senate. In March, when he heard that Sung Chiao-jen (q.v.) had been murdered, Hsieh Ch'ih joined a group plotting to assassinate Yuan Shih-k'ai. The group also included Chao T'ieh-ch'iao, Cheng Yü-hsiu, Chou Yu-chueh, and Huang Fu-sheng. The plot was discovered by Yuan's agents, and Hsieh was arrested on 17 May 1913. Because of the lack of evidence and the support of fellow-senators, he escaped indictment. Because he feared for his life, he moved to the Legation Quarter in Peking and then fled by way of Tientsin to Japan.

In Japan, Hsieh Ch'ih assisted Sun Yat-sen in organizing the Chung-hua ko-ming-tang and assumed the post of vice director of its general affairs department. Since the director of that department, Ch'en Ch'i-mei (q.v.), often was absent from Japan, Hsieh was responsible for carrying out the duties of his department. He did not return to China until the Parliament reconvened after the death of Yuan Shih-k'ai in June 1916.

Hsieh left Peking in June 1917 after the dissolution of the Parliament by Li Yuan-hung (q.v.). Thereafter he served Sun Yat-sen in the Canton government as vice minister of justice (1918–19), vice minister of interior (1919–21), and secretary general of the presidential office (1921–22). Hsieh was elected director of the department of party affairs in October 1919 when the Chung-hua ko-ming-tang was renamed the Kuomintang. Because the party was ineffective as a political organ, Sun Yat-sen began to prepare for a radical transformation of the Kuomintang. In 1922 Sun called a series of meetings of Kuomintang members to announce his intention to reorganize the party and to discuss with his followers the revision of the party constitution. On 1 January 1923 the process of reorganization formally began. On 21 January, Hsieh Ch'ih was named one of the 20 counselors to participate in the formation of new party policies. A year later, in January 1924, he was elected one of the five members of the Central Supervisory Committee by the First National Congress of the reorganized Kuomintang.

Despite his personal loyalty to Sun Yat-sen's cause, Hsieh Ch'ih opposed the Kuomintang's new policy of alliance with the Russians and the Chinese Communists. His antagonism was expressed as early as June 1924, when he joined two other members of the Central Supervisory Committee, Chang Chi and Teng Tse-ju (qq.v.), in submitting a memorandum to Sun which stated that the political activities of Li Ta-chao (q.v.) and the Communists were certain to undermine the political integrity of the Kuomintang. In November 1924 Hsieh, who was then in Shanghai, joined Sun Yat-sen's entourage and went to Peking for the much publicized conference with Tuan Ch'i-jui (q.v.) and the men holding power in north China. After Sun's death in Peking in March 1925, the issue of Communist subversion within the party organization caused a serious split within the Kuomintang. Hsieh remained in Shanghai after Sun's funeral. In August 1925 he went to Canton to confer with the anti-Communist faction of the Kuomintang, headed by Hu Han-min, Teng Tse-ju, C. C. Wu (Wu Ch'ao-shu), and Tsou Lu (qq.v.). They discussed ways of countering the growth of Communist influence within the Kuomintang and the domination of the revolutionary government at Canton by Wang Ching-wei and left-wing groups. On 21 August 1925 Liao Chung-k'ai (q.v.), a prominent left-Kuomintang leader, was assassinated at Canton. The murder gave Wang Ching-wei and the Communists an excellent opportunity to attack the rightist faction. Hsieh Ch'ih, Teng Tse-ju, and Tsou Lu were forced to leave Canton.

In November 1925 Hsieh participated in the so-called Western Hills Conference held near Peking. Anti-Communist members of the Central Executive Committee and the Central Supervisory Committee declared their firm opposition to Communism and to the Wang Ching-wei government at Canton. The leftist faction, in turn, convened the Second National Congress of the Kuomintang at Canton in January 1926 and formally expelled Hsieh Ch'ih and Tsou Lu from the Kuomintang. The Western Hills faction held a national congress at Shanghai on 1 April 1926 and elected Hsieh Ch'ih and others to a 25-man central executive committee.

After the 1927 purge of the Communists, the major Kuomintang factions held a series of meetings in Shanghai from 11 to 13 November. A special committee composed of thirty-two regular and nine alternate members drawn from the three factions was organized to provide unified direction of party affairs. Hsieh Ch'ih was named to the special committee by the Western Hills group. The National Government was reorganized under the aegis of the special committee. Since Nanking was then under the military control of Li Tsung-jen (q.v.) and other Kwangsi generals who were friendly to the Western Hills faction, Hsieh was given the important post of director of the organization department of the Kuomintang.

This effort at unification, however, was more apparent than real. The Wuhan faction under Wang Ching-wei was dissatisfied, and one of its military supporters, T'ang Sheng-chih (q.v.), soon rebelled against Nanking. T'ang's revolt was quelled by Li Tsung-jen. After a celebration of Li's victory resulted in two deaths and several injuries, members of the Western Hills group were criticized by organizations in Nanking. Hsieh withdrew from the government and retired to Shanghai.

In 1930 the northern generals Feng Yü-hsiang and Yen Hsi-shan (qq.v.) decided to challenge the supremacy of the National Government, then dominated by Chiang Kai-shek. Feng and Yen were supported by Wang Ching-wei, the erstwhile foe of the Western Hills clique. Suppressing former animosities, the Western Hills leaders, including T'an Chen (q.v.), Hsieh Ch'ih, and Tsou Lu, organized a group in Peiping which cooperated in forming an alliance against Chiang Kai-shek. The political organ of the alliance was the so-called enlarged conference, formally established on 9 July 1930 in Peiping to serve as the decision-making organ of the Kuomintang, in opposition to the party apparatus functioning at Nanking. Hsieh Ch'ih was elected to the standing committee of the enlarged conference. The Yen-Feng coalition soon suffered defeats and began to collapse. In September, the enlarged conference moved to Taiyuan; it was dissolved the following month. Hsieh Ch'ih left Taiyuan in November and sought safety in the Japanese concession in Tientsin.

In May 1931 Hsieh Ch'ih suffered a stroke which kept him bed-ridden for three months and which left his right side paralyzed. By that time, the persistent antagonism between Nanking and Canton had led to the organization of a new dissident government at Canton. Hsieh was listed by the Canton leaders as a member of their government council even though he was in Tientsin. The split between Nanking and Canton was healed temporarily by the crisis created by the Japanese invasion of Manchuria. When the Japanese occupied Mukden in September 1931, Hsieh immediately left Tientsin for Peiping. After the peace meeting between the Nanking and Canton leaders had been successfully concluded in November, he went to Shanghai. Soon after his arrival in Shanghai, Hsieh suffered another paralytic stroke. He was bed-ridden for several years.

In August 1937, after the outbreak of the Sino-Japanese war, Hsieh left Shanghai to return to his native Szechwan. He remained at Chengtu until his death on 16 April 1939. The National Government honored him with a state funeral on 29 July 1939.

Hsieh Chüeh-tsai   謝 覺 哉

Hsieh Chueh-tsai (1881–), Chinese Communist leader, held important party offices in the 1930's and 1940's. He served the Central People's Government as minister of interior (1949–59) and was president of the Supreme People's Court (1959–64).

Born into the family of a landholder in the Ninghsiang district of Hunan province, Hsieh Chueh-tsai received his early education in the Chinese classics and passed the examinations for the sheng-yuan degree. In the late 1890's he became associated with other young Hunanese who were agitating for modernization. Hunan, which had provided important anti-Taiping leadership in the mid-nineteenth

century, gave equal support to the reform programs advocated by K'ang Yu-wei (q.v.) and his followers. Hsieh came under the influence of Ho Shu-heng (q.v.), Wang Ling-po, and Chiang Meng-chou, leaders of the young Hunanese radical nationalists, all of whom became Communists in later years. For a time, Hsieh also served as an adviser to the prominent scholar-official T'an Yen-k'ai (q.v.).

Little is known about Hsieh's activities during the early years of the century, but he apparently earned his living as a schoolmaster. From 1921 to 1924 he taught in schools in Hunan organized by Ho Shu-heng and Mao Tse-tung. Although his life-long friendship with Ho Shu-heng had been formed in late Ch'ing times, Hsieh seems to have been unaware of Ho's connection with the infant Chinese Communist party and of the fact that the schools had been established to disseminate Marxist ideas. After T'an Yen-k'ai joined the Kuomintang at Canton, Hsieh became a member of that party in 1924.

Together with Li Wei-han (q.v.), Chiang Meng-chou, and others, Hsieh founded the Hsiang-chiang Middle School, where he taught Chinese. In addition to teaching at the school, he wrote for and later edited the *T'ung-su jih-pao* [popular daily] at Changsha. It was while working for this paper that Hsieh had his first personal contact with Mao Tse-tung, who took time from his other activities to give the paper ideological direction.

When the Northern Expedition forces reached Hunan in 1926, Hsieh became a member of the provincial committee of the Kuomintang, editor of the Kuomintang newspaper *Min-pao* [people's journal] in Hunan, and counsel to the Special Court. At that time, Hsieh was identified as a member of the left-Kuomintang, but in 1925 he had joined the Chinese Communist party. He had kept his membership a secret, but when Hsü K'o-hsiang began the mass arrest and execution of Communists and leftists in Hunan in May 1927, he went into hiding. In December 1927 he went to Hankow and then to Shanghai. Possibly following in the footsteps of Liu Shao-ch'i (q.v.), who had also fled from Hankow and who subsequently was assigned to take charge of Communist party affairs in Manchuria, Hsieh traveled from Shanghai to Mukden, where he remained for about two years.

In 1931 Hsieh left Shanghai for the Hunan-Hupeh region to help Ho Lung (q.v.) develop a Communist base at Sangchih in western Hunan. He edited the *Kung-nung-pao* [workers' and peasants' paper], and taught at the Communist party school where junior cadres were indoctrinated and trained. In 1932 when this soviet area was encircled by National Government troops, Hsieh went with Ho Lung's army to the Hung Lake area to establish a new base. This new soviet was besieged, and Hsieh was arrested by Kuomintang troops. He was released, however, allegedly because he looked like a traditional Chinese scholar rather than a Communist. He went to Shanghai, where, at the height of the Nationalist suppression drive, he worked in the secretariat of the All-China Federation of Labor, under the leadership of Lo Teng-hsien. When Lo was arrested in March 1933, this Communist-led labor organization disintegrated, and Hsieh left Shanghai for Kiangsi, where he was made secretary of the central soviet government at Juichin.

Hsieh Chueh-tsai made the Long March at the age of 53 and arrived in good health in Shensi late in 1935. He continued to hold the post of secretary of the soviet government at Paoan and Yenan until 1937. Then, after a brief stay in Lanchow as Communist party representative, he became secretary general of the Shensi-Kansu-Ninghsia Border Region government for a short time. In 1938 Hsieh lived quietly near Hengyang, Hunan. He was not known locally as a Communist; he may have been doing secret work for the party. It soon became impossible for Communists to work in Hunan, however; and he returned to Yenan to head the central party school.

At Yenan, Hsieh served as second secretary of the northwest bureau of the Chinese Communist party and vice chairman of the people's political council of the Shensi-Kansu-Ninghsia Border Region. Hsieh was a close friend of Hsü T'e-li (q.v.), and Western observers in northern Shensi often noted the two elders walking arm-in-arm down the primitive main street of the Communist wartime capital. Hsieh remained in Shensi after the Japanese surrender in 1945. In August 1948, when the Communists established the North China People's Government in Hopei under the chairmanship of Tung Pi-wu (q.v.), Hsieh

became its minister of justice and a member of the government council.

In October 1949 the Central People's Government was established at Peking, and Hsieh became a member of the Government Administration Council, a member of its committee on political and legal affairs, and minister of interior. As the Communists consolidated nation-wide political control and assigned more responsibilities to younger men, Hsieh was gradually relieved of duties in the legal field. His principal concern was the ministry of interior, which he headed until April 1959. He became a vice chairman of the China People's Relief Committee, headed by Madame Sun Yat-sen (Soong Ch'ing-ling, q.v.), in April 1950. From April 1953 to March 1956 he was vice chairman of the Chinese political and legal society. In 1953 he was on the committee for drafting the constitution and the central government election committee which prepared for the National People's Congress. In July 1954 he became vice president of the central political-legal cadres school. He attended the National People's Congress in 1954 as a representative from Shantung. At the Eighth National Congress of the Chinese Communist party, held in 1956, Hsieh was elected to alternate membership on the Central Committee. His last substantive position at Peking was that of president of the Supreme People's Court; he succeeded Tung Pi-wu and served from April 1959 until December 1964.

Hsieh Chueh-tsai attained ministerial rank at Peking and was regarded as one of the senior figures of the Chinese Communist party. His career was marked more by durability than by brilliance. He was often referred to as a mild and scholarly man, trained in the classical tradition and known for his essays and poetry. He maintained an interest in political movements devoted to the modernization of China—the reform movement at the turn of the century, the beginnings of the Kuomintang, and the Chinese Communist party. Perhaps more significant is the fact that he belonged to that small coterie of Hunanese Communists who had long been associated with Mao Tse-tung.

Hsieh Chueh-tsai was the author of a number of articles on revolutionary theory and practice which were published in Communist newspapers and in memorial volumes dedicated to Communist comrades. His writings include *San-san chih-tu li-lun yü shih-chi* [theory and practice of the three-three system], which appeared in 1945; an outline of Communist study methods and Communist ethics, published in 1957; and a collection of essays, *Pu-huo-chi* [no doubts]. He also contributed to *Kuan-yü jen-min min-chu chien-cheng* [concerning the establishment of a democratic government], published in 1951, and to *Mao Tse-tung ti ku-shih* [stories of Mao Tse-tung], published in 1954.

Hsieh Chueh-tsai was married and had two children, a son and a daughter. His son, Hsieh Hsuan-ch'ü, was a graduate of the Whampoa Military Academy. He became a Communist, but left the party in 1928. During the Sino-Japanese war, Hsieh Hsuan-ch'ü served under Ho Chung-han (q.v.) doing political work in the National Government military forces. Hsieh Chueh-tsai's daughter became a nurse.

Hsieh Hung-lai   謝 洪 賚
   T.   Ch'ang-hou   鬯 侯
   West. H. L. Zia

Hsieh Hung-lai (9 May 1873–2 September 1916), Chinese Christian author and publicist, known as H. L. Zia, was secretary of the national committee and director of the publications department of the YMCA in China (1904–1916). Under his direction, the Association Press in China became one of the most influential YMCA publishing efforts in the world.

The son of a Presbyterian minister, H. L. Zia was born, the eldest of two brothers and four sisters, in Shaohsing, Chekiang. His father, an early convert of the Presbyterian mission in northern Chekiang, had shown such talent as a youth that he had been sent to Hangchow College for three years of study. After graduation, he had established two small schools near his home before deciding to prepare for the ministry. His theological training consisted of private tutoring with the Reverend Samuel Dodd, during the course of which he reportedly copied several volumes of his tutor's lectures.

H. L. Zia received early training in the Chinese classics. In 1892, at the age of 19, he entered Buffington Institute in Soochow, which had been established 20 years earlier by the Methodist mission. (Later, it was merged with other schools to become Soochow University.) After three years of study, he was graduated in 1895. He then began teaching physics and chemistry at Anglo-Chinese College in Shanghai (also a forerunner of Soochow University). Zia soon showed himself to be a gifted teacher, interested equally in the intellectual and ethical development of his students. He maintained friendships with many of them throughout his life, and even during periods of strain and overwork he devoted long hours to correspondence with former students.

In 1900 H. L. Zia, in addition to his teaching, undertook part-time editorial and translation work at the Commercial Press in Shanghai. At the same time, he began editing materials for the National Committee of the Young Men's Christian Association for use in high schools and colleges throughout the country. He also taught in a YMCA night school. After deciding in 1904 to devote full time to the YMCA, H. L. Zia became a secretary of its national committee and director of the publication department in China. In the next 12 years he became possibly the foremost Christian publicist and author in China and made the YMCA publication department in China one of the most influential YMCA publishing efforts in the world.

H. L. Zia believed that there was a need for an "easy wen-li" style in written Chinese which would command the respect of the literati as well as being more intelligible to the average reader than the terse and elliptical style of traditional literary Chinese. Because he was writing mainly for Chinese students who were being introduced to Western literature and ideas, Zia had an incentive, as translator and interpreter, to develop a dignified, but direct and interesting style. It has been suggested that his success as a stylist in vernacular Chinese helped to prepare the Chinese literary world for the pai-hua [vernacular] movement later advocated by Ch'en Tu-hsiu, Hu Shih (qq.v.), and others.

H. L. Zia contracted tuberculosis in 1907. In January 1909 he went to the United States and spent a few months in the mountains of Colorado. After returning to China in October 1909, he went to the mountains at Kuling, Kiangsi, to seek relief from the advancing illness. Zia made a thorough study of the causes, prevention, and cure of tuberculosis and wrote one of the best-known lay treatises on the disease in China, *Consumption: Its Nature, Prevention, and Cure.* In 1910, aware that there was no hope for recovery, Zia moved to his home near West Lake in Hangchow to devote his remaining years to the work he loved best. He continued to serve as editor in chief of the YMCA Association Press, administering a staff of 12 men in Shanghai. He edited three magazines and supervised an immense output of books, pamphlets, and tracts, many of which he wrote himself.

Zia was a charter member of the board of directors of the Hangchow YMCA. One of his close associates remarked that "no man understood the YMCA more clearly than Mr. Zia." As a key member of the joint union evangelical committee of the Hangchow churches, he created a vital program for the committee and showed his devotion to the church by participating actively in its work long after he had given up his other activities.

When Sherwood Eddy, one of the leaders of the World Student Christian Movement, visited Hangchow in October 1914 in the course of an evangelistic campaign in China, H. L. Zia prepared a corps of Bible-study leaders beforehand and directed the follow-up program after his visit. He also wrote a series of study courses for general use throughout the Eddy conferences. Near the end of his life, when two prominent Hangchow citizens sought his help in organizing an informal circle of friends to discuss philosophical and ethical problems, H. L. Zia established the Fortnightly Club in cooperation with Eugene E. Barnett, the American YMCA secretary. Although his strength was failing, he met regularly with the group, his broad knowledge and his forthright Christian outlook drawing together a varied group of officials, lawyers, educators, and businessmen.

H. L. Zia worked intensively throughout his life. During his last week, when suffering severe pain and in a state of semi-consciousness, he kept his writing equipment at hand to make occasional notes. After his death in September 1916, at the age of 43, more than 20 memorial services in his honor were held in the leading cities of China.

In the course of his brief career as an author, an editor, and a translator, H. L. Zia, through unflagging industry, produced more than 200 books, pamphlets, and articles in English and Chinese. While working with the Commercial Press, he published textbooks on physics, chemistry, general science, biology, and geography. He also prepared texts in the main branches of mathematics from algebra through calculus.

As the director of YMCA publications in China, H. L. Zia produced large quantities of consistently excellent materials. He compiled the first edition of the YMCA hymnbook. Most of his writings, however, dealt with the practical application of the Christian faith. The term, "social service," long identified in China with the YMCA, was first used and was made current by H. L. Zia when he was editor of the Association Press. In 1918 Paul Hutchinson, in later years editor of the *Christian Century* in the United States, said of Mr. Zia that he "made the imprint of the YMCA known throughout China, and it is largely due to him . . . that the publications of the YMCA are today making a real impression on the thinking men of China—something that can be said of no other [Christian] publications."

Men instinctively trusted H. L. Zia's wisdom and judgment, responded to his sympathy, and sought his counsel and assistance. Great as the impact of his writing was, his more enduring influence probably lay in the "depth, vitality, and multiplying power" of his personal relations, through which he was able to inspire many Chinese to significant achievement and strong faith. For the YMCA, Eugene Barnett summarized the results of H. L. Zia's work: "No man has been more influential in shaping the Association movement in China during the formative years and in informing it with lofty ideals and enduring principles."

One of H. L. Zia's children, Grace Zia Chu, wrote *The Pleasures of Chinese Cooking* (1962) and conducted classes in cooking in New York. A grandson, Samuel C. Chu, received his Ph.D. at Columbia University and wrote *Reformer in Modern China: Chang Chien, 1853–1926*, published in 1965.

Hsieh Ping-ying   謝 冰 瑩
Pen. Ping Ying   冰 瑩

Hsieh Ping-ying (1903–), writer and feminist, best known for her *Ts'ung-chün jih-chi* (*War Diary*) which described her experiences with the National Revolutionary Army during the Northern Expedition.

The youngest of six children, Hsieh Ping-ying came from an isolated and backward village in the Hsinhua district of Hunan. Her father, a classical scholar who held the chü-jen degree, was the principal of the Hsinhua Middle School for more than 25 years and was known by his students as the "K'ang-hsi Dictionary" because of his ability to quote classical texts. He gave Hsieh Ping-ying initial instruction in the traditional Chinese texts and in poetry. Her mother was a forceful personality who demanded strict obedience of her children. By her own account, Hsieh Ping-ying was a rebellious child who refused to have her feet bound or her ears pierced in accordance with tradition. Her mother made her do both, however, and betrothed her when she was still a child. Later, her feet were unbound because of her vigorous protests.

Hsieh Ping-ying succeeded in defying her mother's wishes by entering an old-style school for boys at the age of ten. She then studied at schools for girls in her native district and at the Hsin-yi Girls School, a missionary institution at Iyang, Hunan. She organized a student demonstration against Japanese imperialism in May 1922, an act which led to her expulsion from the institution. In the autumn of 1922 she entered the Hunan First Normal School for Girls at Changsha, where her interest in literature developed rapidly. By her own account, she read Chinese translations of works by such European authors as Maupassant, Zola, Dumas, and Dostoyevsky, as well as the traditional Chinese novels, particularly the *San-kuo-chih yen-i* [romance of the three kingdoms] and the *Shui-hu-chuan* [water margin]. She also was interested in the works of members of the Creation Society, notably Kuo Mo-jo, Yü Ta-fu (qq.v.), and Ch'eng Fang-wu. She wrote a short story, "A Moment's Impression," which was published in the literary supplement of the *Ta Kung Pao*.

After graduation from normal school at Changsha in 1926, Hsieh decided to pursue a literary career and to escape from the marriage arranged by her family. Acting on the suggestion of one of her elder brothers, she went to Wuhan in the winter of 1926 and entered the military academy which had been established there after the occupation of the area by the forces of the Northern Expedition. After receiving strict political-military training, she joined the National Revolutionary Army in 1927 and saw service at the front with a corps comprised of some 50 girls. While serving in the army, she wrote *Ts'ung-chün jih-chi* (*War Diary*), which was published under her pen name, Ping Ying, in the *Chung-yang jih-pao* (Central Daily News) in 1928. An English translation, prepared by Lin Yü-t'ang (q.v.), was published simultaneously in the same paper. *War Diary* later was translated into French, German, Russian, Japanese, and Esperanto, and it attracted the attention of such prominent literary figures as the French writer Romain Rolland.

After the girls corps was disbanded, Hsieh Ping-ying returned to Hunan to attempt to break her long-standing engagement. Her parents eventually forced her into marriage, but she left her husband immediately and fled to Shanghai. She lived in poverty, attempting to support herself by selling her writings. She received some financial help from Sun Fu-yuan, the former editor of the *Central Daily News* at Wuhan. In 1928, with financial assistance from an elder brother, she entered National Normal University for Women at Peiping. She studied Chinese literature until 1931, supporting herself, after her brother's financial support ceased, by teaching part time at two middle schools in the city. After leaving the university in 1931, Hsieh returned to Shanghai, where she completed two works, *Ch'ing-nien Wang Kuo-ts'ai* [young Wang Kuo-ts'ai] and *Ch'ing-nien shu-hsin* [youth's letters], a collection of correspondence. Advance payment for these manuscripts enabled her to make a brief trip to Japan in September 1931, the very month of the Japanese attack at Mukden. After the Japanese advance on Shanghai in January 1932, she returned to China, where she participated actively in a variety of efforts to mobilize Chinese women to support the war effort. She then went to Changsha to complete the first volume of her autobiographical work, *I-ko nü-ping te tzu-chuan* [autobiography of a woman soldier].

In 1935 Hsieh Ping-ying made a second trip to Japan, where she enrolled at Waseda University in Tokyo to study Western literature. While arrangements were being made with a Japanese publisher to bring out a collection of her writings, she was arrested on 12 April 1936 and was imprisoned for three weeks. She returned to China that summer and went to Kweilin, Kwangsi, to rest. In the autumn, she took a teaching position at a middle school in Nanning, but had to resign after a semester because of ill health.

After the Sino-Japanese war began in July 1937, Hsieh Ping-ying again devoted herself to writing and war work. In 1937 she organized a war area service corps for women in Hunan. In December she went to Chungking, where she became editor of the literary supplement of the *Hsin-min pao*. During 1937 and 1938 she wrote prolifically on the early stages of the war. In the spring of 1938 she visited the Hsuchow front as a war correspondent attached to the headquarters of the Fifth War Area at Wuhan. She returned to Chungking that autumn and became an editor in the ministry of education of the National Government.

The year 1940 was marked by the appearance of an English translation of Hsieh's 1936 work, *Girl Rebel: The Autobiography of a Woman Soldier*, translated by Adet and Anor Lin (Lin Yü-t'ang's daughters) and published by the John Day Company in New York. From 1940 to 1943 Hsieh edited the *Huang-ho* [yellow river] monthly at Sian in Shensi province. She then returned to Szechwan, where she spent the remaining war years teaching at Chengtu.

After the Japanese surrender in 1945, Hsieh went to Hankow, where she edited the literary supplement of the *Ho-p'ing jih-pao* [peace daily]. She then moved to Peiping, where she lectured on contemporary Chinese literature at the National Normal College and served as an editor of *Wen-i yü sheng-huo* [literature and life]. An English translation by Ts'ui Chi of her 1928 book entitled *Autobiography of a Chinese Girl* appeared in London in 1948. When the Chinese Communists took power, Hsieh went to Taiwan and taught at the Taipei Normal School for

Women. Her *Wo-tsen-yang hsieh-tso* [how I write], was published at Taipei in 1964.

As Lin Yü-t'ang pointed out in his introduction to *Girl Rebel: Autobiography of a Woman Soldier*, Hsieh won prominence by recording her personal experience during a period of social upheaval in China. Her outspoken patriotism, her relentless attack on political corruption, her indomitable struggle against poverty and persecution, and her rebellion against the traditional Chinese discrimination against women typified the social idealism of young China after the May Fourth Movement. Her works constitute an important literary record of the participation of an emancipated Chinese woman in the modern Chinese social revolution.

Hsieh Wan-ying　　謝 婉 瑩
Pen. Ping Hsin　　　冰 心

Hsieh Wan-ying (5 October 1900–), known as Ping Hsin, poet, essayist, and short story writer.

A native of Minhou, Fukien, Hsieh Wan-ying was born into a prosperous family in Foochow. Her father, Hsieh Pao-chang, was an officer in the Chinese naval service. When Hsieh Wan-ying was only a few months old, her mother took her to Shanghai, where her father was serving. In 1903 the family moved to Yent'ai (Chefoo), Shantung, where Hsieh Pao-chang was assigned to head a naval training school.

Hsieh Wan-ying spent her childhood on the Shantung coast, where she received her early education and her first impressions of natural beauty. A solitary child, she spent much of her time at home. Adult relatives told her stories, taught her to read, and developed in her an enthusiasm for traditional Chinese literature. When she was ten, her mother's cousin became her tutor. Hsieh read Chinese literature and classical texts, and she was permitted to attend meetings of a Chinese poetry club to which her father and his friends belonged. At an early age she began to write stories and verses. At the time of the 1911 revolution, she and her family went to the home of her paternal grandfather in Fukien. For several months, Hsieh attended the Foochow Normal School for Girls. She also spent much time reading in her grandfather's home library.

In 1913 Hsieh Pao-chang took his family to Peking. Hsieh Wan-ying did not attend school that year. She continued to read at home and enjoyed such magazines as the *Fu-nü tsa-chih* [women's magazine] and the *Hsiao-shuo yueh-pao* [short story magazine], which her mother read regularly. Her interest in poetry was broadened through exposure to the tz'u form, which she learned of from the literary columns of contemporary magazines. She drew on her reading to tell stories to her three younger brothers when they returned home from school. She also wrote a few short stories in the traditional Chinese style, but left them unfinished.

In the autumn of 1914 Hsieh Wan-ying entered the girls school of the Bridgman Academy, a middle school run by American Congregational missionaries in Peking. Later, both she and her mother became Christians. Because standards in the school were high and competition was keen, she had little time to read Chinese literature during her years at Bridgman.

After graduation in 1918, Hsieh Wan-ying entered Peking Union College for Women, which later was incorporated into Yenching University. Despite her retiring nature, she was drawn into the student activities associated with the May Fourth Movement of 1919. She was called on to serve as secretary of the student association at the Women's College and was also chosen to head the propaganda section of the students' union in Peking. Hsieh Wan-ying's cousin Liu Fang-yuan was editing the literary supplement of the Peking newspaper *Ch'en Pao* [morning post]. Hsieh made her first serious attempt at writing in the vernacular style and succeeded in having an article published in the supplement. Her cousin encouraged her and sent her copies of new Chinese magazines, including *Hsin ch'ing-nien* [new youth], *Hsin-ch'ao* [renaissance], and *Kai-tsao* [reconstruction]. In these and other journals of the period Hsieh read Chinese translations of some of the writings of Leo Tolstoy, Rabindranath Tagore, Bertrand Russell, John Dewey, and other non-Chinese authors. Her discovery that it was possible to blend serious philosophy with fiction led her to begin writing stories again.

Soon, Hsieh's short story *Liang-ke chia-t'ing* [two families] was published in the *Ch'en Pao*

literary supplement under the pen name Ping Hsin, meaning pure in heart. Encouraged by this success, she began writing poems and essays as well as short stories. Many of these appeared in the *Ch'en Pao* supplement. Hsieh joined the Literary Research Society (*see* Cheng Chen-to) when it was formed at Peking in 1921 and published some of her early work in its *Short Story Magazine*. By the early 1920's, though still a college student at Yenching, Hsieh had established herself as a pioneer among modern Chinese women writers. Two collections of poetry, *Fan-hsing* [myriad stars] and *Ch'un-shui* [spring water] appeared in 1923. The verses—lyrical, unrhymed, and exquisite in diction—created a vogue for the short verse. *Ch'un-shui* later was translated into English by Hsieh's friend Grace M. Boynton of the Yenching English department and was published at Peiping in 1929. *Fan-hsing* was written in imitation of Tagore's "Flying Birds." In 1923 Hsieh published a collection of short stories entitled *Ch'ao-jen* [superman], which marked the high point of her youthful writing career. In a lucid and distinctive style, she depicted with tenderness and sympathy the loneliness of childhood and the melancholy of youth in China.

Hsieh soon began to receive quantities of mail from impressionable and admiring contemporaries. Her fluency in English attracted the attention of an American visitor to Peking, Candace Stimson, sister of Henry L. Stimson, who was looking for a talented Chinese girl to send to Wellesley for graduate work. Hsieh received her B.A. degree at Yenching in the summer of 1923. In August, she sailed from Shanghai on the President Jackson for the United States. She entered Wellesley, but became ill with tuberculosis and was forced to spend six months in a Massachusetts sanitorium. At this time, she composed some of her *Chi hsiao-tu-che* [letters to young readers], which were published serially in the literary supplement of the *Ch'en Pao*. They were collected and published in book form in 1926. In these letters, Hsieh demonstrated a talent for writing for children and a notable capacity for describing scenery. She later returned to Wellesley and received the M.A. degree in 1926.

After returning to China in the summer of 1926, Hsieh joined the faculty of Yenching University and taught literature there. She journeyed frequently to Shanghai, where her family was living. In June 1929 at Peiping, Hsieh married Wu Wen-tsao, whom she had met in the United States. Wu had received his Ph.D. in sociology at Columbia University. Shortly after their marriage, Hsieh's mother, who had been an invalid for some years, died. After her trip to Shanghai to settle family affairs, Hsieh wrote an essay, *Nan-kuei* [returning south], to commemorate her mother.

Hsieh continued to teach at Yenching. Because she was busy with domestic affairs, she produced only a Chinese translation of Kahlil Gibran's *The Prophet*, published in 1931 as *Hsien-chih*, and a few short stories in which she attempted, with limited success, to write of adult life. In 1933 Wu Wen-tsao became chairman of the sociology department at Yenching.

In 1936 Hsieh accompanied her husband to the United States, where he represented Yenching University at Harvard's tercentenary celebrations. They then visited Europe and returned to the Far East by way of the Soviet Union, arriving at Peiping only a week before the outbreak of the Sino-Japanese war in July 1937. After the hostilities began, they went to west China, arriving at Kunming in August 1938. Wu Wen-tsao organized a sociology department for Yunnan University. They went to Chungking in 1940, and Wu served on the Supreme National Defense Council. Hsieh continued to write intermittently and produced *Hsü chi hsiao-tu-che* [more letters to young readers]. In 1943, writing under a new pen name, Nan-shih, she published a book of essays entitled *Kuan-yü nü-jen* [about women]. These essays were brief portraits of prominent Chinese women, written in an informal style. During the war years, Hsieh served as a member of the People's Political Council and had considerable contact with Wellesley alumna Soong Mei-ling. Hsieh returned briefly to Peiping in the spring of 1946 and then went on to Tokyo, where Wu Wen-tsao had been appointed an adviser on the staff of the Chinese Mission in Japan. She gave weekly lectures on modern Chinese literature at Tokyo University, did some writing, and was active in the Wellesley alumnae group in Tokyo.

Late in 1951 Hsieh and her husband returned to China. Many of their friends were unaware of their decision until after they had arrived at Peking. Hsieh became a member of the national committee of the All-China Federation of Literary and Arts Circles and a council member of the Union of Chinese Writers. She was named to membership on the executive committees of the Chinese People's Association for Cultural Relations with Foreign Countries and of the China Women's Federation and was elected a deputy from Fukien to the National People's Congress in 1954 and 1959. In the winter of 1953 Hsieh was a member of a Chinese friendship delegation to India which was led by Ting Hsi-lin (q.v.). In the next few years she represented the People's Republic of China at meetings held in New Delhi, Lausanne, Tokyo, Cairo, Tashkent, and Moscow. In the spring of 1958 she was a member of the delegation led by Hsü Ti-hsin that visited Italy and England. Her activities left little time for creative writing. However, in the 1950's two volumes of stories for children, *T'ao Ch'i te shu-ch'i jih-ch'i* [T'ao Ch'i's summer schedule] and *Yin-tu t'ung-hua chi* [Indian fairy tales] appeared, and in 1964 a volume of essays written between 1959 and 1963 was published at Peking under the title *Shih-sui hsiao-ch'a* [miscellaneous essays].

Hsieh Wan-ying enjoyed great popularity in China in the early 1920's. Her forte was the ability to write movingly of such subjects and emotions as mother love, the joys and sorrows of childhood and adolescence, and the beauties of nature. Her later writing was influenced by Western literature and by Christianity, which contributed a certain didacticism and pseudo-mysticism to her literary efforts. Because of these limitations, Hsieh's work had come to be regarded as escapist and outdated by the 1930's. A three-volume collection of her best writings, *Ping Hsin ch'üan-chi*, was published by the Pei-hsin Book Company in 1932–33. A revised edition of her works, with some additions, was edited by Pa Chin (Li Fei-kan, q.v.) and was published in 1943 by the K'ai-ming Book Company at Kweilin. It was reprinted in 1947. A volume of essays about her work, *Lun Ping Hsin*, edited by Li Hsi-t'ung, was published by the Pei-hsin Book Company in 1932.

Hsieh Wan-ying had three children. Her two daughters were born in 1935 and 1938. Her son, Wu Tsung-sheng, born in February 1931, was graduated from the department of architecture of Tsinghua University in 1952.

Hsien Hsing-hai　　　　洗 星 海

Hsien Hsing-hai (1905–30 September 1945), French-trained composer. He combined music and leftist politics in such compositions as the *National Symphony* and *War in a Noble Cause*.

The son of a Cantonese boat worker, Hsien Hsing-hai was born in P'anyü, Kwangtung. His father died before Hsien was born, and in 1911 Hsien's mother emigrated with her son to Malaya. Hsien received his early education there; he studied at Chinese schools and for one year (1915–16) at a British school where he learned some English.

Hsien returned to Canton in 1918 and entered the middle school attached to Lingnan University. By working at various jobs he managed to support himself while studying in the music department at Lingnan, and he was graduated in 1924. He then taught at Lingnan until 1926, maintaining his part-time jobs. In 1926 he went north to Peking University, where he specialized in violin and theory of composition. He held a part-time job in the library. In 1927 he enrolled in the new Shanghai Conservatory of Music, but was expelled on political grounds. At that time, he was associated with the Nan-kuo-she, led by T'ien Han (q.v.). In 1930, under the sponsorship of Sitson Ma (Ma Ssu-ts'ung), a Cantonese violinist who had then recently returned from study in France, Hsien Hsing-hai went to Paris. There, despite continuing financial difficulties, he continued his musical studies under such teachers as Vincent d'Indy and Paul Dukas.

After returning to China in 1935, Hsien worked for two film companies and began to compose songs. Among his early efforts were "The Athletic Meet" and "Far-away Siberia," both with words by T'ien Han; "War Song," with words by Fu Shih; and "Midnight Music" and "Youth Advances," both composed while working for the Hsin-hua Film Company in 1936. During this period he also started work on his first symphonic composition.

After the outbreak of the Sino-Japanese war in 1937, Hsien Hsing-hai joined a patriotic group that was touring China to boost morale and mobilize support for the war effort. In 1938

he went to Yenan, the Chinese Communist wartime capital, and became the director of the music department of the Lu Hsün Academy. In 1938 Hsien composed an opera, *Chün-min chin-hsing ch'ü* [army and people advance]. In 1939 he produced *Huang-ho ta-ho-ch'ang* [yellow river cantata] and *Sheng-ch'an ta-ho-chang* [production cantata]. The second composition was a combination of song, dance, and drama, and it drew heavily on Chinese folk sources. It was written as part of a major production campaign launched in the Communist-controlled areas of China in 1939.

In 1940 Hsien Hsing-hai left Yenan for Russia to continue his musical studies. There he completed his *National Symphony*, which he had begun in 1936. The German invasion of the Soviet Union in the summer of 1941 inspired Hsien's final work, a symphony which he called *War in a Noble Cause*. He died of tuberculosis at Moscow in 1945. Hsien Hsing-hai's second symphony was given its premiere at Peking in 1960 to commemorate the fifteenth anniversary of his death. It was played by the student orchestra of the Central Conservatory of Music, conducted by Huang Fei-li. Despite increasing tension between the Communist party leaders at Peking and Moscow, Hsien's symphony was lauded as an effective musical portrayal of the surge of Soviet national resistance in the face of the Nazi invasion. The work is a typical example of music written in accordance with the political requirements laid down in the Chinese Communist artistic manifesto proclaimed in 1942 at Yenan, and its performance at Peking in 1960 was hailed as an important musical event.

Hsien Hsing-hai was one of a small group of composers in the Western idiom to achieve some reputation in China before the Sino-Japanese war. His name was generally linked in China with that of Nieh Erh (q.v.), the two men being assigned to the category of "pioneers of proletarian music."

Hsiung Fo-hsi　　　　熊 佛 西
Alt. Hsiung Fu-hsi　　熊 福 熙

Hsiung Fo-hsi (1900–26 October 1965), playwright, educator, and critic, was a leading creator of "popular drama," plays written to educate the peasantry.

Fengch'eng, Kiangsi, was the birthplace of Hsiung Fo-hsi. At the time of the 1911 revolution, Hsiung's father took him to Hankow, where he completed his primary and middle school education. He evinced an interest in drama during his student days, directing and acting in school productions as well as writing two plays which were published in 1919. He entered Yenching University at Peking in 1919 and specialized in literature and education. In May 1921 he helped to found the *Min-chung hsi-chü she* [people's dramatic society], together with Ch'en Ta-pei, Mao Tun (Shen Yen-ping), and Ou-yang Yü-ch'ien (qq.v.). He was graduated from Yenching in 1923.

Hsiung then went to the United States for graduate work. He studied dramatic art at Columbia University in New York from 1923 to 1926 and received an M.A. degree. After returning to China in 1926, he was appointed professor and chairman of the department of dramatic arts in the school of fine arts at Peking University. He also lectured at Yenching and taught in the department of dramatic arts of the Peking Academy of Fine Arts. In 1930 he became chief editor of the periodical *Hsi-chü yü wen-i* [drama and literature], a bi-monthly magazine which published plays and articles on the new drama.

In 1932 Hsiung became the director of the rural theater of Tinghsien, Hopei, under the auspices of the National Association for the Advancement of Mass Education. The founder of that association and pioneer of the mass education movement in China, James Yen (Yen Yang-ch'u, q.v.), enlisted Hsiung in an attempt to produce popular drama as a means of educating the peasants of north China. To achieve this end, the dramatist went to rural areas and lived among the peasants so that he could create plays they could understand. Hsiung's role in this rural experiment won him renown. He wrote a book about his experiences entitled *An Experiment in Popularizing Drama* (1937).

After the outbreak of the Sino-Japanese war in July 1937, Hsiung moved with the National Association for the Advancement of Mass Education to Hankow and then to Changsha. When the association was forced to suspend its activities, he and his troupe, now called the Farmers' Resistance Dramatic Corps, went to Chengtu, Szechwan, where they gave a series of performances to huge audiences. Because of their success, the provincial government established the Szechwan Provincial College of Dramatic Arts in 1942 and made Hsiung Fo-hsi president of the institution. The Chungking authorities named him to head the central youth dramatic club under the auspices of the San Min Chu I Youth Corps. About this time, however, a play that Hsiung wrote about Yuan Shih-k'ai was banned by the government. Increasing censorship distressed Hsiung. He moved to Kweilin, where he founded two wartime literary magazines, *Tang-tai wen-hsueh* [contemporary literature] and *Wen-hsueh ch'uang-tsao* [literary creation], and wrote fiction, short stories, and travel articles. His first novel, *T'ieh-miao* [iron anchor], was published in 1946. He then wrote a sequel entitled *T'ieh-hua* [iron flower]. After returning to east China in 1946, Hsiung became president of the Shanghai Experimental School of Dramatic Art.

In the summer of 1949 Hsiung was a delegate to the meeting at Peiping that established the All-China Federation of Literary and Arts Circles. He continued to be prominent in that organization after 1949; he was elected to its national committee in 1953 and again in 1960. He became a member of the standing committee of the All-China Association of Dramatic Workers, the national organization responsible for coordinating work in the theater. He also served on the culture and education committee of the East China regional government apparatus from 1949 until 1954. In June 1955 he was named president of the east China branch at Shanghai of the Central Academy of Dramatic Arts. He also became a member of the National Committee of the Chinese People's Political Consultative Conference, representing the All-China Federation of Literary and Arts Circles. He died in Shanghai on 26 October 1965.

Hsiung Fo-hsi is generally regarded as a leading playwright of the so-called popular drama, as distinguished from the literary drama, of which Hung Shen and T'ien Han (qq.v.) were leading representatives. In his work for the theater Hsiung often experimented with Western methods and emphasized stage effects. He specialized in comedy, often with a satirical twist, and attempted to cater to the tastes of the uneducated Chinese playgoer. Many of Hsiung's plays originally were published in the *Ch'en Pao* [morning post] literary supplement, the *Tung-fang tsa-chih* [eastern miscellany], and *Drama and*

Literature. They were collected and published by the Commercial Press in four volumes, which appeared from 1930 to 1932. Hsiung also published a volume of essays on the drama, *Fo-hsi lun-chü* and a book on the principles of play writing, *Hsieh-chü yuan-li*.

Hsiung Fo-hsi married Yeh Chung-yin (Yeh-tzu), a graduate of the National Drama School who worked at the Szechwan Provincial College of Dramatic Arts in Chengtu when Hsiung was president of that institution.

Hsiung Hsi-ling　　熊 希 齡
T. Ping-san　　秉 三

Hsiung Hsi-ling (1870–1942), government official, is best known as the premier of the "first caliber cabinet" of 1913–14. Hsiung all but retired from public life in 1914. He later achieved considerable reputation as a philanthropist and sponsor of charitable works.

A native of Fenghuang hsien, Hunan, Hsiung Hsi-ling was the son of a military officer who held the rank of tsung-ping [brigadier]. Hsiung was a brilliant student, and in 1895 he obtained the chin-shih degree at the remarkably early age of 24. Seven years before, he had married Chu Ch'i-hui, the sister of Chu Ch'i-yi (*see* Chu Ching-nung), then the magistrate of Hsiung's native district. Chu Ch'i-yi was greatly impressed by the young scholar, even then referred to as the "boy genius of Hunan." Hsiung's wife proved to be highly talented and was a great help to her husband in his career.

In 1894 Hsiung Hsi-ling entered the political life of the capital with a three-year appointment to the Hanlin Academy. His series of memorials opposing peace with Japan during the Sino-Japanese war of 1894–95 cost him this place, however, and he was obliged to return to his native Hunan. Hsiung worked with such reform leaders as T'an Ssu-t'ung (ECCP, II, 702–5), T'ang Ts'ai-ch'ang (ECCP, I, 30; II, 769), and Liang Ch'i-ch'ao (q.v.) in the Nan-hsueh-hui [south China academic society] and in the Changsha Shih-wu Hsueh-t'ang [contemporary affairs school]. In the aftermath of the Hundred Days Reform, Hsiung was cashiered and permanently barred from office, but soon he gained the favorable attention of Tuan-fang (ECCP, II, 780–82) and of Chao Erh-sun (q.v.), who

were successive incumbents in the governorship of Hunan, and his name was reentered on the civil list; appointment as a tao-t'ai in Kiangsu followed.

In 1905 Hsiung accompanied his patron, Tuan-fang, on a tour of Europe and the United States to study constitutional government. Although the tour bore little fruit for the reform of the Manchu government, it did open the way for Hsiung's active and successful official career. Most notably, he won the favor of Tsai-tse (ECCP, II, 781, 968), one of the most powerful figures in the Manchu court, who appointed him a financial superintendent and later a salt commissioner in Manchuria, both lucrative posts and ones which enabled Hsiung to become familiar with the intricacies of fiscal administration.

Despite his official and personal ties with the Manchu establishment, Hsiung maintained and soon enhanced his political position when the republic was established, emerging in March 1912 as minister of finance in the Chin-pu tang (Progressive party) cabinet headed by T'ang Shao-yi (q.v.). When T'ang resigned some three months later, Hsiung also left office. Almost immediately, he was appointed tut'ung [lieutenant governor] of Jehol. A scandal occurred in Jehol which permanently attached itself to Hsiung's name, the pilfering of certain Manchu treasures stored in the summer palace. Although Hsiung was thought to be guilty of complicity in the thefts, the affair remained obscure and no official action against him was taken. Many people believed, however, that his involvement, whatever it was, secured him the premiership a few months later when the necessity of appointing a progressive yet malleable premier impressed itself on Yuan Shih-k'ai. In the late summer of 1913 Yuan turned his attention to the political suppression of the Kuomintang and to the dissolution of the Parliament, where the Progressive party had succeeded in gaining control after the murder of Sung Chiao-jen (q.v.) and the splitting of the Kuomintang into factions. Hsiung Hsi-ling, long associated with reform ideas, a leader of the Progressive party, and a native of Hunan, which was a center of anti-Yuan sentiment, was a logical choice for the office of premier. Yuan accordingly recommended Hsiung to the Parliament late in July, and on 31 July, with the concurrence of both houses, Hsiung was appointed premier.

The appointment came as something of a surprise to Yuan, who half expected that his first choice would be rejected. The moderate wing of the Kuomintang, however, was totally opposed to Hsü Shih-ch'ang (q.v.), a member of the Peiyang clique who was his second choice, and cooperated with the Progressive party in supporting Hsiung. The Parliament's approval must also have surprised Hsiung, for he hesitated in accepting, arriving in Peking on 28 August only after the repeated urging of Liang Ch'i-ch'ao.

Progressive party demands for an all-Progressive cabinet and Yuan Shih-k'ai's insistence on picking all important ministers himself delayed formation of the government for nearly two weeks. Hsiung Hsi-ling, however, had determined to appoint the best cabinet he could, starting with Liang Ch'i-ch'ao, who was not a member of the Progressive party, as minister of finance. After much negotiation, Hsiung, who had characterized Yuan's slate as being only "second caliber," prevailed, and on 11 September he appointed a cabinet that he justly described as "first caliber." Liang Ch'i-ch'ao was named as minister of justice, Chang Chien (q.v.) as minister of agriculture and commerce, Sun Pao-ch'i (q.v.) as minister of foreign affairs, and Chu Ch'i-ch'ien as minister of the interior. Hsiung himself served as premier and as minister of finance.

The formation of the "first caliber" cabinet marked not only the apogee of Hsiung's political career but also the end of responsible parliamentary rule in early republican China. A speaker of great fluency, Hsiung impressed his contemporaries with his sincere resolve to preserve the parliamentary system. In particular, he proposed such financial reforms as the abolition of the likin tax, the institution of an income tax, the standardization of currency, and the balancing of the national budget. However, on 4 November, Yuan issued an order, which Hsiung co-signed, for the dissolution of the Kuomintang and the cancellation of its membership in the Parliament. In all, 438 persons affiliated in one way or another with the Kuomintang were dismissed from the Parliament. On 5 November, there were not enough members left in either house to form a quorum, and on 10 January 1914 the Parliament was dissolved. A short time before, Hsiung had answered two long letters of in-

quiry from the remaining members of the two houses by stating that Yuan had been forced to dissolve the Parliament because of the exigencies of the times and that he therefore was not bound by ordinary parliamentary procedure. Hsiung's "first caliber" cabinet did not benefit from its compliance in the destruction of the Parliament. Chronically short of funds, split over deploying Peiyang forces in Hunan, and secretly ridiculed for proposing a master unification scheme which would have abolished all special provincial interests, the cabinet fell apart in February 1914 with the resignation of Liang Ch'i-ch'ao and others.

Hsiung gave up the premiership. He was appointed director of the national petroleum bureau, and he also headed the river conservancy bureau. In 1915 Yuan appointed him pacification commissioner of western Hunan, where it was hoped that Hsiung's influence would prove useful in winning popular support for Yuan's attempt to become monarch. In 1917, after Yuan had died and Li Yuan-hung (q.v.) had become president, Hsiung was named head of the P'ing-cheng-yuan [political consultative board]. Hsiung joined with Chang Chien, Ts'ai Yuan-p'ei (q.v.), and others in 1919 to promote the Shanghai peace conference, which, however, was a total failure. In the 1920's Hsiung became a popular advocate of federalism, possibly as a result of the Shanghai failure of 1919 and his own earlier failure as premier in 1913–14 to put across his plan for consolidation of power in a strong central government. Hsiung's last important political appointment was as a delegate to a national crisis conference held at Loyang in 1932 to cope with the situation resulting from the Mukden Incident of 18 September 1931. Hsiung also served as part of a delegation from Shanghai to persuade Chang Hsueh-liang (q.v.) to take up arms against the Japanese.

After 1914 Hsiung Hsi-ling ceased to be of major political importance in China. But as his political stature waned, Hsiung began earning a reputation for philanthrophy and charitable works. He gained prominence for his direction of famine relief activities in north China after the tragic flood of 1917 in Chihli (Hopei). In 1918 he founded a home for orphaned children, the Tz'u-yu-yuan, which was directed for a time by Ying Lien-chih (q.v.), a prominent Catholic layman. That orphanage, located in the Western Hills near Peking, became widely and favorably known. Hsiung also organized or joined many other philanthropic organizations and in 1929 served on the executive board of the National Famine Relief Commission. His charities were private and personal as well as public. For example, in 1931 he paid for the funeral of his former patron Tsai-tse and provided for his family.

In 1935, having lived as a widower for several years, Hsiung Hsi-ling married Mao Yen-wen (Helen Hsiung), a young and attractive graduate of Ginling College who had assisted him in running the Tz'u-yu-yuan. Hsiung's marriage to a woman half his age stirred great controversy at the time, but did not disturb Hsiung, who went so far as to shave off his twenty-year-old mustache at his bride's request. The second marriage was as happy as the first. In 1937 the Hsiungs moved from Shanghai to Hong Kong. In 1942, shortly after the Japanese occupation of that colony, Hsiung Hsi-ling died. His widow resided in Taiwan after 1950.

Hsiung had three children by his first wife. The son, stricken by disease in childhood, was an invalid and died early. The second child was Nora Hsiung, the wife of Lin Chu; she was a prominent educator who became the president of the Women's Normal College in Taipei, Taiwan. The third child, Rose Hsiung, was well known in Peking before the war; she remained in China after 1949.

A biographical article on Hsiung Hsi-ling, written by his relative Chu Ching-nung (q.v.), appeared in the *Tung-fang tsa-chih* [eastern miscellany] in January 1947.

Hsiung K'o-wu 熊 克 武
T. Chin-fan 錦 帆

Hsiung K'o-wu (1881–), anti-Manchu revolutionary and senior Szechwanese military leader, was one of the very few active commanders elected to the Central Executive Committee of the Kuomintang in 1924. He later became a member of the party's Central Supervisory Committee and of the Government Council. In 1950–54 he served Peking as a vice chairman of the Southeast Military and Administrative Committee.

Chingyen hsien, Szechwan, was the native place of Hsiung K'o-wu. Little is known of his family or his childhood. After receiving his early education in Szechwan, he went to Japan for advanced study and enrolled in the Shikan Gakkō [military academy]. He also joined the T'ung-meng-hui and took part in its activities.

After completing his military studies in Japan in 1906, Hsiung K'o-wu returned to Szechwan early in 1907. That was a year of scattered anti-Manchu insurrections in various parts of China, and Hsiung led an uprising at Hsuchow, Szechwan. It failed, and he had to flee the area. He reportedly participated in the uprising at Canton in 1911, later referred to as the 29 March Insurrection, which was led by the prominent revolutionary. Huang Hsing (q.v.).

After the republic was established in 1912, Hsiung K'o-wu returned to Szechwan and took command of a division stationed at Chungking. In August 1913 he joined the so-called second revolution against Yuan Shih-k'ai. Hsiung hoped to lead his troops down the Yangtze to join forces with revolutionaries marching northward from Hunan. Yuan Shih-k'ai, however, had the situation well in hand, and Hsiung's forces were defeated near Chungking in early September.

Hsiung K'o-wu was among those who sought refuge in Japan after the second revolution. When Sun Yat-sen set forth a plan to reorganize the Kuomintang which stipulated that all members take an oath of personal obedience to the party leader, Hsiung and many other members of the party adamantly opposed the stipulation. In 1914, after the outbreak of war in Europe, Hsiung and other Chinese leaders organized the Ou-shih yen-chiu-hui [European affairs research society].

In 1915, as Yuan Shih-k'ai's monarchical aspirations became increasingly apparent, many revolutionary leaders returned from abroad to their home districts in China to raise armed opposition to him. Hsiung K'o-wu left Japan in October 1915. After arriving in Shanghai, he went to Hong Kong and accompanied Li Lieh-chün (q.v.) to Yunnan, where Li was to join T'ang Chi-yao and Ts'ai O (q.v.) in a new campaign against Yuan. When the expeditionary forces from Yunnan began operations in 1916, Hsiung K'o-wu accompanied the army of Ts'ai O into Szechwan. He rallied the troops that had served under him in the Hsuchow area and soon gathered an army of more than 5,000 men. Liu Tsun-hou, the commander of the native Szechwan forces, defected to the republican cause. Yuan Shih-k'ai's forces were defeated, and Ch'en Huan, the Szechwan governor, had to declare independence to avoid further fighting.

The campaign against Yuan soon ended; Yuan died at Peking in June 1916. The local Szechwan troops were reorganized into five divisions, and Hsiung K'o-wu was named to command the First Division. Hsiung remained in the Chungking area, where he also served as defense commissioner. In 1917 the Szechwan and the Yunnan-Kweichow armies came into conflict on several occasions. The Szechwanese, although they claimed victory, did not achieve their objective of expelling the Yunnan-Kweichow armies from the province. Hsiung K'o-wu remained neutral throughout these campaigns and, through his presence there, protected the Chungking area from the ravages of war.

The northern government at Peking and the southern military government at Canton vied for the support of the Szechwanese army commanders because the province was rich in natural resources and important strategically. Liu Tsun-hou, who had commanded a Szechwanese division in 1917, supported the northern government, which appointed him military governor of Szechwan. Although the Peking government appointed Hsiung K'o-wu border defense commissioner of Szechwan, he remained loyal to the southern government. In 1918 he ousted Liu Tsun-hou and became military governor.

Hsiung hoped to bring stability to his province. However, T'ang Chi-yao (q.v.) hoped to dominate Szechwan as part of his plan to become the overlord of southwest China. T'ang then controlled both Yunnan and Kweichow and had stationed military forces in Szechwan. The people of Szechwan resented the intrusion from Yunnan, and in May 1920 Hsiung K'o-wu assumed leadership of the Szechwanese military commanders in demanding the evacuation of the Yunnan and Kweichow armies from the province. Fighting broke out, and the Yunnan and Kweichow troops finally left Szechwan. In December 1920 the military leaders of Szechwan declared it an independent and autonomous region. Hsiung resigned as military governor of Szechwan on 31 December

1920, thereby fulfilling a promise he had made when leading the Szechwan armies in the movement to oust the Yunnan and Kweichow troops.

At a rehabilitation conference, Liu Hsiang was elected commander in chief of all Szechwan armies and civil administrator of the province. Liu reiterated the autonomy of Szechwan and the refusal of the provincial authorities to accept orders or appointments from the Peking government. In May 1921 Liu Hsiang took action against Hsiung K'o-wu, who was forced to flee the province. Liu Hsiang's subsequent efforts to establish himself as the supreme authority in Szechwan resulted in a period of civil war in the province.

Little is known of Hsiung K'o-wu's activities from the time of his departure from Szechwan in 1921 to his return in 1923. In May 1923 Hsiung and his troops occupied Chengtu. In June, Sun Yat-sen appointed him commander in chief for "bandit suppression" in Szechwan. At that time, Yang Sen (q.v.), supported by Wu P'ei-fu, held power in Szechwan. In October, Hsiung captured Chungking. In mid-December, however, Yang Sen recaptured that city. Yang pursued Hsiung and drove him out of Chengtu in February 1924. Liu Hsiang, then allied with Yang Sen, also gave pursuit to Hsiung, who was forced to retreat into Kweichow with his men.

In the meantime, however, Hsiung's support of the republican cause had been rewarded by the Kuomintang. At the First National Congress, held at Canton in January 1924, Hsiung K'o-wu was one of the very few military commanders elected to the 24-man Central Executive Committee of the Kuomintang. Sun Yat-sen then was preparing for his long-delayed northern expedition, and revolutionary armies from several provinces were being assembled at Canton. Hsiung planned to move his troops from Kweichow through Hunan to Canton, but when his forces reached Hunan in 1925, Chao Heng-t'i (q.v.), the governor, ordered their immediate departure. Hsiung also was troubled by dissension in his own ranks. In April 1925, Ho Lung (q.v.), who had followed him on the march out of Szechwan, defected.

Hsiung K'o-wu brought the remnants of his Szechwan army to Canton. When he arrived there on 3 October 1925, he was placed under arrest by Chiang Kai-shek, who charged him with collaborating with Ch'en Chiung-ming (q.v.), who still commanded troops in eastern Kwangtung. Hsiung was detained at the military fort at Humen, and his army was disbanded. He remained a prisoner for about two years.

In September 1927, Hsiung K'o-wu was elected to the 47-member National Government Council at Nanking. In 1931, when a separatist movement started at Canton as the result of Chiang Kai-shek's detention of Hu Han-min (q.v.), Hsiung K'o-wu attended the meeting of the Kuomintang central committees which was called by the Canton leaders to form an opposition government. After the settlement of the Nanking-Canton dispute, Hsiung was among those elected to the Central Executive Committee of the Kuomintang in 1932. Although he continued to serve as a member of the National Government Council, he took no part in political life and spent most of his time in Shanghai.

After 1934 Hsiung also maintained a home in Hong Kong, where he spent much of his time. In November 1935, at the Fifth National Congress of the Kuomintang, Hsiung was elected to the Central Supervisory Committee, a mark of his having entered the ranks of the party elders. From 1937 through 1945, Hsiung lived in Szechwan. In 1945, at the Sixth National Congress of the Kuomintang, held at Chungking, he was reelected to the Central Supervisory Committee. In 1946 he was a delegate to the National Assembly at Nanking.

In December 1949, as the Chinese Communist forces advanced into Szechwan after sweeping over most of the mainland, Hsiung K'o-wu, along with Liu Wen-hui and Teng Hsi-hou (qq.v.), publicly declared support of the People's Republic of China. In 1950, Hsiung K'o-wu was named a vice chairman of the Southwest Military and Administrative Committee, the principal regional authority in southwest China, and he continued to hold that post until the regional regimes were abolished in 1954. Although he was not one of the original members of the Chinese People's Political Consultative Conference, he later became a member of its first National Committee. In 1954 and in 1958 he was a delegate to the National People's Congress, and in December 1958 he was elected a vice chairman of the central committee of the Kuomintang Revolutionary Committee.

Hsiung Shih-hui   熊 式 輝
T. T'ien-i   天 翼

Hsiung Shih-hui (1894–) served Chiang Kai-shek as an officer on the Northern Expedition, governor of Kiangsi (1931–41), head of a military mission to the United States (1942–43), and head of the Northeast headquarters of the Military Affairs Commission (1945–47). He then lived in Hong Kong, Macao, and Bangkok before moving to Taiwan in 1954.

Born in an agricultural village in Anyi hsien, Kiangsi, Hsiung Shih-hui was the sixth of seven children. His father was active in military affairs and often acted as instructor for the local militia. Hsiung received his early education in a private school in his native village. In 1908 his father enrolled him in the Kiangsi Army Primary School, and in the spring of 1911 he transferred to the Fourth Army Middle School at Nanking. About this time, he secretly joined the T'ung-meng-hui.

After the outbreak of the Wuchang revolt in October 1911, Hsiung joined the revolutionary forces. Feng Kuo-chang (q.v.) defeated the republican troops, and Hsiung returned to Nanking in December. He then became a staff officer under the republican tutuh [military governor] Ch'eng Te-ch'uan.

In the spring of 1913 Hsiung resigned from his post and went to north China, where he entered the Ch'ing-ho Army Preparatory School. After completing the course, he enrolled at the Paoting Military Academy as a member of the second class. He was graduated in the summer of 1915. In December, when Ts'ai O (q.v.) and others took action against Yuan Shih-k'ai, Hsiung went to Yunnan province and became executive officer in the 38th Regiment of the 4th Division of the Second Army, commanded by Li Lieh-chün (q.v.). A number of other officers who later became prominent in the Nationalist military establishment—notably Chang Chih-chung, Chu P'ei-te (qq.v.), and Wang Chün—also served in the 4th Division.

In the spring of 1920 Hsiung Shih-hui, along with Chu P'ei-te and other officers of the 4th Division, supported Li Lieh-chün's attempt to wrest control of the Yunnan troops in

Kwangtung from Li Ken-yuan (q.v.). The attempt was unsuccessful, and Hsiung went to Tokyo, where he enrolled at the Shikan Gakkō [military academy] in 1920. After graduation in 1924, he returned to Canton, where Sun Yat-sen was attempting to consolidate a Nationalist base. Hsiung became chief instructor at the Yunnan Army Military Officers School, which came under the jurisdiction of the Third Army, commanded by Chu P'ei-te.

When the Northern Expedition was launched in July 1926, Hsiung Shih-hui was given the assignment of subverting Lai Shih-huang, the commander of the 4th Kiangsi Division. At the beginning of August, Hsiung met with Lai, who was a personal friend, at Juichin. Through Lai Shih-huang, Hsiung gained regular access to the war plans of Sun Ch'uan-fang (q.v.). He relayed the information to Ho Ying-ch'in (q.v.) for transmittal to Chiang Kai-shek. In mid-August, Lai received command of the Fourteenth Army, and Hsiung Shih-hui became the Kuomintang representative in that unit.

In September 1926 the Fourteenth Army began to advance against Teng Ju-cho, the Kiangsi tuchün [military governor]. Kanchow was occupied on 6 September, and on orders from Li Chi-shen and Ho Ying-ch'in in Canton, Lai Shih-huang proceeded to garrison the city. Hsiung Shih-hui led two regiments northward in conjunction with the Fifth Division of the Second Army. The advance through southern Kiangsi assisted the revolutionary forces besieging Nanchang, the provincial capital. Hsiung's forces arrived in northern Kiangsi in time to join that battle, and Nanchang was occupied on 8 November 1926.

Toward the end of November, the victorious Nationalists established a Kiangsi provincial political committee, and Hsiung Shih-hui was appointed to it. In the meantime, Ho Ying-ch'in had begun to advance into Fukien. After Ho had captured Changchow and Chuanchow in November, Lai Shih-huang's Fourteenth Army was ordered to that front. The forces of Ho Ying-ch'in captured Foochow at the beginning of December, and the Fourteenth Army was assigned to eastern Kiangsi to prepare for an attack on Chekiang. Hsiung Shih-hui then received command of the 1st Division of the Fourteenth Army, retaining his position as party representative.

After the Nationalists consolidated control of the Shanghai-Nanking area in March 1927, Hsiung and his forces were stationed at Kiangyin on garrison duty. In May, the Fourteenth Army resumed its northward march as part of the forces under the general command of Ho Ying-ch'in. Hsiung's division crossed the Yangtze, drove northward, and prepared for an attack on Shantung. But news of the advance on Nanking by T'ang Sheng-chih (q.v.) caused Nationalist commander Pai Ch'ung-hsi to order a general retreat. Hsiung withdrew to Yangchow in August 1927 and then took up garrison duties at Wusih and Kiangyin.

At the end of August 1927, when the Chihli-Shantung forces met the Nationalist forces in a critical battle at Lungtan, the Fourteenth Army was ordered to advance from Kiangyin and cut off the enemy's line of retreat. Lai Shih-huang delayed too long, and, although the Nationalists won the battle of Lungtan, he was charged with dereliction in the performance of duty and was executed by a firing squad on 31 December. The Fourteenth Army was reorganized as the Thirteenth Army, with Hsiung Shih-hui as deputy commander. Hsiung retained command of the 1st Division, which was redesignated the 37th Division.

In January 1928 Pai Ch'ung-hsi, then the Woosung-Shanghai garrison commander, took the field in a campaign against T'ang Sheng-chih's remnant forces in Hunan province. Hsiung was assigned as acting garrison commander at Shanghai. When plans were made for the final stage of the Northern Expedition in early 1928, Hsiung Shih-hui's 37th Division was designated a reserve force for the First Group Army commanded by Chiang Kai-shek. On 1 April 1928 Hsiung turned over the Woosung-Shanghai garrison force to Ch'ien Ta-chün (q.v.).

When Japanese resistance to the northward advance of the Nationalist forces through Shantung led to the Tsinan Incident in May 1928, Chiang Kai-shek named Hsiung Shih-hui and Lo Chia-lun (q.v.) to meet with the Japanese and work out a peaceful settlement of the affair. The Japanese rejected the two delegates on the grounds that they were too junior in rank. Ho Ch'eng-chün (q.v.) was assigned to handle the negotiations, and Hsiung went to Nanking. After the successful conclusion of the Northern Expedition in mid-1928, Hsiung was reappointed Woosung-Shanghai garrison commander in October.

In the military regroupings of 1929 Hsiung received command of the Eight Army, which, however, was reorganized soon thereafter as the 5th Division. In May 1930, when the Nationalists began so-called bandit-suppression campaigns against Communist forces in rural areas, Hsiung was assigned to direct military operations in the Kiangsu-Chekiang-Anhwei area. In December, he was ordered to Nanchang for consultation with Chiang Kai-shek. The plane in which he was traveling, however, crashed as it was taking off at Shanghai, and Hsiung received a foot injury. It took him several months to recover, but in June 1931 he finally reported to Nanchang, where Chiang Kai-shek appointed him chief of staff in his field headquarters. In that capacity, he participated in the 1931 campaign against the Communists.

In December 1931 Hsiung Shih-hui was named governor of Kiangsi. The Chinese Communists under Mao Tse-tung had established a central soviet government at Juichin, with its territorial base in the south-central part of the province. Hsiung was given responsibility for civil affairs, education, and peace preservation in the province. He also became a member of the provincial branch of the Kuomintang. In May 1933 he was given the additional office of chief of staff in Chiang Kai-shek's Nanchang headquarters. In 1933 and 1934 Hsiung Shih-hui and Yang Yung-t'ai (q.v.) were regarded as being the two most influential men in the Generalissimo's headquarters at Nanchang. Yang Yung-t'ai, whom Hsiung had introduced to Chiang Kai-shek, served as chief secretary at the Nanchang headquarters, which was a major administrative center for political, military, and party affairs not only for Kiangsi but also for the provinces of Honan, Hupeh, and Anhwei. Both Hsiung and Yang were active in promoting the New Life Movement (*see* Chiang Kai-shek). And both men were regarded as pillars of the so-called political science faction, which was composed of senior officials who exercised major influence in the National Government in the 1930's and 1940's.

After the Nationalist encirclement campaigns had forced the Communists to evacuate their base area in southern Kiangsi in the autumn of 1934, Hsiung Shih-hui enjoyed an interlude of relative tranquility in the province. He remained on good terms with the top Nationalist authorities at Nanking, and in November 1935 he was elected to the Central Executive Committee of the Kuomintang. Shortly after the Sino-Japanese war began in 1937, Hsiung proposed to Chiang Kai-shek that his son Chiang Ching-kuo (q.v.), who had returned from the Soviet Union in April, be sent to Kiangsi to work under him. Chiang Kai-shek approved the plan, and Chiang Ching-kuo went to Nanchang in January 1938. After the Japanese military advance up the Yangtze valley, Hsiung removed the seat of the provincial government to T'aiho in the spring of 1939.

After a decade of service as governor of his native province, Hsiung was assigned to new responsibilities after the United States entered the war in December 1941. He was appointed to the Supreme National Defense Council, and in March 1942 he was named chief of a Chinese military mission to the United States. Shortly after the appointment was announced, Hsiung publicly warned the embattled Allies of Japanese military strength and predicted that the Japanese would attack the Soviet Union. He then flew to Washington, where he worked to obtain for China the largest possible amount of United States aid.

The Chinese military mission at Washington was not admitted into the top-secret inner councils of the early wartime strategy conferences, and the United States was unable to allot to China the quantities of military supplies that the Chinese wanted. In July 1942, on the occasion of the fifth anniversary of the outbreak of the Sino-Japanese war, Hsiung Shih-hui gave a speech in New York in which he accused the United States of having failed to fulfill its pledges to China and stated that the series of defeats suffered by the Allies after Pearl Harbor had led to "the most critical and dangerous crisis in China's history." China, he continued, was still waiting for large-scale American aid. If China were defeated, he warned, Japan might be able to wage war for a hundred years. Because of Chinese dissatisfaction with Allied war strategy, which gave first priority to the European theater, Hsiung and his mission were recalled to Chungking at the end of 1942. On 31

December 1942, just before departing, he met with President Franklin D. Roosevelt. Hsiung returned to China in April 1943, after stopping in London for the announced purpose of studying the war situation.

In August 1943, Hsiung Shih-hui was appointed secretary general of the Central Planning Board, the organ responsible for wartime and postwar reconstruction. He held that office until the summer of 1945, when he was called upon to accompany T. V. Soong (q.v.) to Moscow for the negotiations which finally resulted in the signature, on 14 August, of the Sino-Soviet Treaty of Friendship and Alliance.

Shortly thereafter, Hsiung Shih-hui was given a new assignment. On 31 August 1945 the National Government announced that, in connection with projected reestablishment of its authority in Manchuria, it planned to create a Northeast headquarters of the Military Affairs Commission, with Hsiung Shih-hui as director. A few days later, Hsiung was also given the post of chairman of the political affairs commission of the headquarters. His close ties with Chiang Kai-shek and Ho Ying-ch'in may well have played a part in determining his assignment to the top military-political position in what was clearly to become a key post in the postwar competition for power in the Far East. Chang Kia-ngau (Chang Chia-ao, q.v.) was assigned responsibility for economic affairs in Manchuria, and Chiang Ching-kuo was named special foreign affairs commissioner. A substantial number of Hsiung Shih-hui's associates were named to posts in Manchuria.

Hsiung proceeded to his post at Changchun, which had been known as Hsinking while it had been the capital of Manchoukuo. Other Nationalist officials began to gather there to plan the reassertion of Chinese Nationalist authority in the area. Hsiung's initial task was to establish liaison with Marshal Rodion Ya. Malinovsky, the commander of the Soviet military forces which had entered Manchuria in August 1945. After Hsiung informed Malinovsky that the United States Navy was preparing to disembark Chinese Nationalist troops at the port of Dairen, the Soviet ambassador at Chungking on 6 October 1945 informed the Chinese ministry of foreign affairs that the Soviet government objected to the planned operation. Hsiung clashed with Malinovsky over the issue and made unsuccessful attempts to designate alternative ports in southern Manchuria at which the Chinese Nationalist troops could land. Hsiung then pressed for the use of airfield facilities at major Manchurian cities to enable the Nationalists to land both troops and civilian officials at these points from United States military aircraft. Malinovsky again demurred, and in October and early November 1945, Chinese Communist forces, which had moved rapidly to Manchuria from north China after the Japanese surrender, seized the airfield at Changchun and occupied the city.

The Chinese Communists established a local government at Changchun and confined the Nationalist officials there, about 500 men, to the South Manchurian Railway building which had been their headquarters. Malinovsky's forces did not assist the beleaguered Nationalists. On 9 November 1945, Hsiung Shih-hui flew to Nanking to report on the serious situation that had already developed in Manchuria. The National Government ordered its officials at Changchun to withdraw to Peiping in north China, and on 17 November they left Changchun by air. Chiang Ching-kuo and a few other officials remained behind for a period to maintain liaison with Malinovsky's headquarters.

In 1946–47 Manchuria was a major theater in the conflict between the Nationalists and the Communists. Although the Nationalists scored some initial successes, a Communist offensive directed by Lin Piao (q.v.) in May and June 1947 gave the Communists the initiative. In July, the National Government at Nanking ordered nation-wide military mobilization, and, at the end of August, Chiang Kai-shek was forced to reorganize the Nationalist political and military command structure in Manchuria. Ch'en Ch'eng (q.v.), chief of the general staff, was assigned to replace Hsiung Shih-hui as director of the Northeast headquarters and of its political affairs commission. After his dismissal from the Manchurian command in the autumn of 1947, Hsiung was given a sinecure post as a strategy adviser at Nanking.

When Nationalist power on the mainland collapsed in 1949, Hsiung Shih-hui did not follow Chiang Kai-shek and the National Government to Taiwan. He lived for a time in Hong Kong and Macao. Hsiung believed that the tiny Portuguese colony of Macao would retain its immunity, as it had during the Second World War. He lived there quietly and entertained some of the Portuguese officials of the colony. A border incident in the early 1950's apparently shocked Hsiung into the realization that Macao was not as secure a place of retirement as he had thought. He then moved to Bangkok, Thailand, where he reportedly suffered heavy financial losses after investing in a cotton mill. In 1954 Hsiung Shih-hui moved to Taiwan, where he lived in retirement at Taichung.

Hsiung Shih-li   熊 十 力

Hsiung Shih-li (1885–), philosopher. As expressed in his most important work, *Hsin wei-shih lun* [new doctrine of consciousness only], Hsiung's system combined elements of the *I-ching*, the Lu-Wang school of Neo-Confucianism, and the wei-shih school of Mahayana Buddhism.

A native of Huangkang, Hupeh, Hsiung Shih-li was the third in a family of six boys. Only he and his eldest brother received any education. Apparently, their mother died when they were small children. Their father, Hsiung Ch'i-hsiang, was a poverty-stricken scholar who adhered to the Ch'eng-Chu school of Neo-Confucianism. As a boy, Hsiung Shih-li herded cattle for his neighbors. When he was ten, his father, who was ill with a lung ailment, forced himself to take on students so that Hsiung could learn to read and write. Endowed with an unusually good memory, the boy learned to recite the *San-tzu-ching* [three-character classic] in one day. Later, he studied the Confucian classics under his father's guidance. Hsiung Ch'i-hsiang died about 1896. On his deathbed, he told Hsiung Shih-li that fate had terminated the boy's schooling and that, since the boy was weak and sickly, it would be best for him to become a tailor. Hsiung Shih-li swore to his father that he would continue his education despite all obstacles. His brother Hsiung Chung-fu, who had attended school until he was 15, often brought along books to read while working in the fields, and Hsiung Shih-li followed his example. Hsiung Shih-li's formal education was limited to a few months of study with a country teacher named Ho. Hsiung read books on science and other modern subjects which he borrowed from a chü-jen scholar in a neighboring district. He also read essays and memorials written by contemporary reformers and the works of Wang Fu-chih (ECCP, II, 817–19) and Ku Yen-wu (ECCP, I, 421–26), whose patriotic sentiments made their writings popular in the decades immediately preceding the overthrow of the Manchus.

In 1902, when he was 18, Hsiung Shih-li and two other young men from his district in Hupeh, Wang Han and Ho Tzu-hsin, went to Wuchang, the provincial capital, in search of political adventure. Wang and Ho joined an anti-Manchu revolutionary society called the K'o-hsueh pu-hsi [science study club], and Hsiung enlisted as a private in the army. In 1904 Wang Han committed suicide in Changte, Honan, after failing in an attempt to assassinate the vice minister of finance, T'ieh-liang (ECCP, II, 952). That year, Hsiung Shih-li and Ho Tzu-hsin joined another revolutionary society. Its members met in the newspaper reading room of the Wuchang Sheng-kung-hui [Episcopal church]. Hsiung was admitted to the Army Special School. In 1906 he helped organize a military study group as a cover for anti-Manchu activities. His revolutionary agitation in the army soon came to the notice of Chang Piao, the commanding general of the garrison force, and he fled Wuchang. On returning to his native village, he found that his brothers were living in dire poverty. When they learned that the Nanchang-Kiukiang railway in Kiangsi was about to be built and that virgin land was available in Tean, a district lying between the two terminal cities, the brothers decided to try their luck as agricultural settlers.

After the 1911 revolution broke out, Huang-kang was seized by the republican army. Hsiung Shih-li became a staff officer in the local military government. But when Yuan Shih-k'ai became provisional president of the new republic in 1912 and began to persecute Kuomintang members in Hupeh, Hsiung temporarily withdrew from politics. After Yuan's death and during the ensuing struggle for power between the Peking government of Tuan Ch'i-jui (q.v.) and the Canton government of Sun Yat-sen, Hsiung joined the southern forces and participated in the Kwangsi military expedition against Hunan in 1917–18. He then went to live in Canton and resolved to devote himself to an academic life. About this time, his eldest brother and his two youngest brothers died in succession in bleak poverty. Hsiung sought consolation in Buddhism, studying for more than a year under Ou-yang Ching-wu (q.v.), who was the organizer of the China Buddhist Association and the founder of the China Institute of Inner Learning at Nanking. He studied the rationalistic wei-shih, or "consciousness-only," school of Mahayana Buddhism. However, he soon became dissatisfied with Buddhist thought and began to construct his own philosophical system.

In 1922 Hsiung Shih-li accepted an offer to teach at National Péking University. He lectured on his philosophy of "new consciousness-only" and became a close friend of Liang Shu-ming (q.v.) and Lin Tsai-p'ing. In the early 1930's Hsiung became ill. He convalesced at Hangchow and returned to Peking University in 1935.

In the spring of 1938, after the outbreak of the Sino-Japanese war, Hsiung made his way to Pishan, Szechwan. In the summer of 1939 he accepted an offer to lecture at the Fu-hsing Academy at Loshan. Some of his manuscripts were destroyed and he was wounded during an air raid there. Hsiung's stay at the academy was cut short by illness, and he returned to Pishan in the autumn of 1939. Shortly thereafter, he moved to Peip'ei, where he lived at the Mien-jen Academy, founded by his friend Liang Shu-ming.

In 1944 Hsiung Shih-li obtained the support of Chü Cheng, T'ao Hsi-sheng (qq.v.), and T'ao Chun in organizing the Research Institute for Chinese Philosophy at Peip'ei, with Chü as chairman of the board of trustees and Hsiung as director. The building was donated by Lu Tzu-ying, the mayor of Peip'ei. The only student was Chü Cheng's son Chü Hao-jan, and Hsiung soon completed his *Tu-ching shih-yao* [essence of the classics]. In 1945 he lectured for a brief period at a school maintained by the Yellow Sea Chemical Industry Research Association. He then returned to Hupeh. In 1948 he taught at the National Chekiang University for a semester. He moved to Canton in the spring of 1949, but returned to Hupeh at the end of the year. The Central People's Govern-

ment apparently reappointed him to Peking University in 1950. In 1956 Hsiung published a two-volume study of Confucianism entitled *Yuan-ju* [on Confucianism] dealing with the Confucian concepts of "kingliness without and sageness within."

Hsiung's major work, *Hsin wei-shih lun* [the new theory of consciousness-only], was written in classical Chinese in 1923. After many revisions, it was privately published in October 1932. Beginning in the spring of 1938, with the assistance of Ch'ien Hsueh-hsi and Han Yü-wen, Hsiung rewrote it in the vernacular and published it in three volumes (1940, 1941, and 1944). The central thesis of Hsiung's system is the perpetual transformation of reality which he describes as the "closing" and "opening" of the "original substance." In its closing aspect, the original substance tends to integrate, the result of which may temporarily be called mind. This mind itself is one part of the "original mind," which in its various aspects is mind, will, and consciousness. Elements of the *I-ching*, the Lu-Wang school of Neo-Confucianism (so named because of the dominant influence of the writings of Lu Hsiang-shan, 1139–1193, and Wang Yang-ming, 1472–1529), and the "consciousness-only" school of Mahayana Buddhist thought are synthesized in Hsiung's work.

Extracts from Hsiung Shih-li's letters, lectures, and conversations were collected by students and friends and published in four volumes between 1935 and 1947. Entitled *Shih-li yü-yao* [the essence of Hsiung Shih-li], the work contains comments by the author on a variety of topics, mostly philosophical but also historical, political, and personal. A supplement was published in 1949. Hsiung's other publications included *P'o p'o wei-shih-lun* [refutation of consciousness-only], *Fo-chia ming hsiang t'ung-shih* [comprehensive explication of the Buddhist theory of phenomena], and *Yin-ming ta-shu shan-ju* [notes on higher Buddhist logic].

Hsiung Shih-li's philosophy reflects the influence of two important intellectual trends in modern China prior to 1949: Buddhist idealism and the revival and reinterpretation of Neo-Confucianism. Even under the new Communist orthodoxy, Hsiung refused to alter his philosophy. His important study of Confucianism published in 1956 did not pay even lip service to Marxism-Leninism.

Hsü Ch'ien　　　　徐　謙
T.　　Chi-lung　　　季　龍
West. George Hsu

Hsü Ch'ien (26 June 1871–26 September 1940), scholar and legal expert who helped reform the judicial system (1907) and who became one of the most prominent leaders in the Wuhan regime (1926–27).

Although his native place was Shehsien, Anhwei, Hsü Ch'ien was born in Nanchang, Kiangsi. He had one brother, Hsü Sun (T. Feng-jen). His father died when he was four, and his mother brought up her sons in straitened circumstances. Hsü Ch'ien, while preparing for the imperial examinations, taught school to help support the family. He passed the examination for the chü-jen degree in 1902 at Nanking and obtained the chin-shih degree in 1904. In the palace examination for the chin-shih, held at Peking, he ranked eighth in the second division; the first division was limited to the three top scholars. Hsü then entered the Shih-hsüeh-kuan in Peking and studied there for one year. In 1905 the Shih-hsüeh-kuan was merged with the Ching-shih ta-hsüeh-t'ang [metropolitan university] in Peking to form the Chin-shih-kuan. From 1905 to 1907 Hsü studied law and government at the Chin-shih-kuan, the forerunner of the college of law of Peking University.

In 1907 Hsü was appointed a Hanlin compiler. He became head of the Law Codification Bureau of the ministry of justice and drew up regulations for the reform and modernization of the traditional judicial system which were approved and put into effect by the imperial government. The regulations provided for a four-level court system, procedure for appeals, a fixed schedule of legal fees, standard petition forms for civil and criminal suits, and the appointment of public prosecutors. These provisions laid the foundation for an independent judiciary in China.

In 1908 Hsü Ch'ien was appointed judge of the Peking local court. Within a year he had disposed of more than 1,000 cases, most of which had accumulated in the court because corrupt officials had demanded bribes to process them. Hsü won public favor through his vigorous actions, and he soon was named attorney general

for the Peking higher court. In 1910 he and Hsü Shih-ying (q.v.) represented China at the Eighth International Conference on Prison Reform, which was held in Washington, D.C. On their way to the United States, they visited Moscow, Berlin, Rome, Paris, and London to study foreign judicial systems.

Hsü Ch'ien returned to Peking after the Wuchang revolt of October 1911. He immediately resigned from office and called for the abdication of the emperor. He and his brother helped to organize the Kuo-min kung-chin-hui at Tientsin, a society that advocated the establishment in China of a federal republic in which the legislative and judicial branches of the government would be centralized, but the executive branch would be decentralized. Although the plan received little public notice at the time, by 1917 the idea of federalism had come to be supported by a number of Chinese political figures and intellectuals; Hsü's essay on the subject, "Kung-ho lien-pang che-chung shang-chueh-shu" [analysis of republican federations], was reprinted by Tai Chi-t'ao in his *Chung-hua min-kuo yü lien-pang tsu-chih* [the Chinese republic and federal organization].

In spite of Hsü's support of the republican cause, the imperial government, attempting to prolong its own life, pressed him to accept an appointment to the Supreme Court late in 1911. Hsü refused. In March 1912 he accepted the post of vice minister of justice in the first republican cabinet, headed by T'ang Shao-yi. When T'ang left the government in 1912 because of a disagreement with Yuan Shih-k'ai about the constitutional role of the president, Hsü Ch'ien also resigned. In August 1912 the Kuo-min kung-chin-hui and other societies merged with the T'ung-meng-hui to form the Kuomintang, and Hsü was elected a councillor of the new party. He went to Shanghai and joined the staff of Sun Yat-sen, who had charge of national railroad development. Because the so-called second revolution of 1913 failed to dislodge Yuan Shih-k'ai from power, Hsü remained in Shanghai and practiced law there for three years.

Hsü Sun, noting his brother's low spirits after the failure of the second revolution, advised him to seek solace in Christianity. Hsü Ch'ien vowed that he would become a Christian if his prayers for Yuan Shih-k'ai's death were answered. After Yuan died in June 1916, Hsü joined the Episcopal Church. Thereafter, he maintained that his conversion to Christianity had originated in a desire to save China.

Hsü returned to Peking in 1916 and resumed office as vice minister of justice. At that time the Peking government was dominated by Tuan Ch'i-jui (q.v.), the premier, whose relationship with Li Yuan-hung (q.v.), the president, was far from cordial. The two men disagreed sharply on the question of China's participation in the First World War. In May 1917 Li Yuan-hung dismissed Tuan from the premiership. The Peiyang military leaders, who supported Tuan Ch'i-jui, then forced Li to dissolve the Parliament on 29 May. Hsü tried to dissuade Li Yuan-hung from issuing the dissolution order and advised C. T. Wang (Wang Cheng-t'ing, q.v.), the acting premier, not to countersign it. When Li refused to follow his advice, Hsü resigned from the cabinet and went to Shanghai.

Earlier, when Hsü was in Peking, Chinese Protestants and Catholics had united to form the General Association for Religious Freedom to lobby for the adoption of a clause guaranteeing religious freedom in the national constitition then being drafted. The association elected Hsü Ch'ien its president, with Ch'eng Ching-i and Ma Liang (qq.v.) heading the Protestant and Catholic groups, respectively. Later, Chinese Muslims under the leadership of Sun Sheng-wu joined the association, and Buddhist and Taoist organizations also pledged their support. This unprecedented unity among Chinese religious groups helped to secure the passage of the religious freedom clause. In 1918, at a joint meeting of Chinese and foreign Protestants held under American missionary auspices at Kuling, Hsü Ch'ien proposed the formation of a Christian National Salvation Association. The proposal was adopted, and Hsü was chosen to lead the Christian National Salvation movement.

In the meantime, Tuan Ch'i-jui had strengthened his political position at Peking, after the collapse of the attempt to restore the Manchu emperor by Chang Hsün (q.v.) in July 1917. Tuan announced his plans to convene a provisional senate to draft a new constitution and to install a new parliament. Sun Yat-sen accused Tuan of violating the existing constitution and in September 1917 organized a military government at Canton with himself as Generalissimo. Sun appointed Hsü Ch'ien secretary general of his office.

In the spring of 1918 the office of Generalissimo was abolished, and control of the Canton government was entrusted to a seven-man directorate. Sun, who refused to participate in the reorganization, assigned Hsü Ch'ien to represent his interests and departed in May for Shanghai. Hsü's mission was to help maintain the military strength of Ch'en Chiung-ming (q.v.), Sun's only source of military support in Kwangtung, and to oppose any suggestion of compromise with the Peking government on the constitution issue. In September 1918 Hsü was named minister of justice by the Canton government.

At the end of the First World War, Hsü Ch'ien, Tsou Lu, and Lin Sen suggested that Sun Yat-sen represent China at the Paris Peace Conference. Sun rejected the idea, saying that the European powers recognized only the Peking government and that he would not serve as the spokesman of that regime. In January 1919 Hsü visited Sun Yat-sen in Shanghai. Sun agreed to allow Hsü and Eugene Ch'en to go to the Paris Peace Conference as unofficial observers. In Paris, Hsü was among those who opposed China's signing of the Treaty of Versailles because of the settlement of the Shantung question.

Hsü returned to China. However, he did not return to Canton because Ts'en Ch'un-hsuan (q.v.) then held power there. Instead, Hsü served as editor in chief of the popular Catholic newspaper *Yi-shih pao* [social welfare newspaper], which was published at Peking and Tientsin. He resigned from that position in May 1920. In September, after Feng Yü-hsiang (q.v.) had led his 16th Mixed Brigade to southern Honan from Hunan, Hsü Ch'ien and Niu Yung-chien, on instructions from Sun Yat-sen, met with Feng at Hankow. According to Feng, this meeting led him to a favorable view of Sun Yat-sen's cause, and in later years Hsü frequently acted as intermediary between Sun and Feng. In November 1920 Ts'en Ch'un-hsuan was forced out of the government at Canton. Hsü Ch'ien then returned to Canton, where he was named minister of justice once again. In May 1921 the military government was dissolved, and Sun Yat-sen was elected provisional president at Canton. Hsü Ch'ien was appointed head of the supreme court.

In August 1922 Sun Yat-sen had to leave Canton for Shanghai after Ch'en Chiung-ming's revolt against his authority. Sun then sent

Hsü Ch'ien to see Wu P'ei-fu (q.v.) in Honan, perhaps to seek political accommodation with Wu, who was then the dominant military figure in north China. That mission led to Hsü's appointment in September as minister of justice at Peking in the so-called good-man cabinet of Wang Ch'ung-hui (q.v.). However, both Wang and Hsü resigned in 1922 after the arrest of Lo Wen-kan (q.v.), the minister of finance, by Li Yuan-hung, the president.

In January 1923 Sun Yat-sen returned to Canton. At the end of February, Sun sent Hsü Ch'ien, Hu Han-min (q.v.), Wang Ching-wei, and Sun Hung-i to Shanghai to make arrangements for the peaceful unification of China. The mission failed, and in the summer of 1923 Hsü returned to Canton and accepted an invitation to teach Chinese literature at Lingnan University.

In 1924 Hsü went to Shanghai and founded a newspaper, the *P'ing-i jih-pao* [deliberation daily]. He also established the Fa-cheng ta-hsueh [school of law and government]. In September, the conflict between Wu P'ei-fu and Chang Tso-lin known as the second Chihli-Fengtien war broke out in north China. At a critical moment, Wu's subordinate general Feng Yü-hsiang renounced his allegiance to Wu, removed his troops from the front, and occupied Peking on 23–24 October. After that coup, Feng invited Hsü Ch'ien to Peking as his adviser. Some observers stated that Hsü had encouraged Feng to undertake the coup. Hsü's official post at Peking was that of principal of the Russian Language School of Law and Government.

In Peking, Hsü Ch'ien, who actively supported Sun Yat-sen's alliance with the Communists, helped to maintain friendly relations between the Kuomintang and the Communists, both Russian and Chinese. In the period from October 1924 to April 1926 when Peking was controlled by Feng Yü-hsiang, Kuomintang and Communist activities were permitted to increase rapidly. After the May Thirtieth Incident of 1925, when Chinese students were killed by British police at Shanghai, a wave of anti-imperialist sentiment swept China. Hsü Ch'ien seized the opportunity to organize a political section in the Peking headquarters of the Kuominchün to disseminate Kuomintang propaganda among Feng's officers. In July 1925 Hsü was named chairman of the Peking branch council of the Kuomintang and was elected to

the 16-man Government Council of the National Government at Canton. The Peking government appointed him chancellor of Sino-Russian University, which incorporated the Russian Language School of Law and Government, and named him chairman of the commission in charge of the Russian Boxer Indemnity Fund remission. In January 1926 the Second National Congress of the Kuomintang, meeting at Canton, elected Hsü to membership on the Central Executive Committee. He received 224 of a possible 256 votes.

After the incident at the Taku harbor on 8 March and the demonstration at Peking on 18 March in which more than 40 people were killed (for details, *see* Feng Yü-hsiang), Tuan Ch'i-jui (q.v.) ordered the arrest of four prominent Kuomintang leaders—Hsü Ch'ien, Li Shih-tseng, Ku Meng-yü, and Yi P'ei-chi—and the Communist leader Li Ta-chao. These men were charged with instigating the 18 March demonstration and with disseminating Communist propaganda. Hsü was protected from arrest by Lu Chung-lin, the Kuominchün commander of the Peking garrison. According to Chang I-lin (q.v.), Hsü left Peking just before Chang Tso-lin's forces entered the capital and went to Kalgan. He then received an invitation from Feng Yü-hsiang to go to Urga (Ulan Bator) in Outer Mongolia, where Feng had been since late March. Other sources state that Hsü left Peking earlier with Eugene Ch'en, Ku Meng-yü, the Soviet adviser Borodin, and others, and arrived at Urga by way of Kalgan on 3 April. In any event, Hsü remained in Urga with Feng when the Borodin party left for Vladivostok and Canton. According to his own account, Feng decided to join the Kuomintang after talking at some length with Hsü about the matter.

Feng and Hsü traveled to Moscow and met many Russian leaders. Hsü left Moscow on 15 July 1926 after receiving news of the launching of the Northern Expedition. He went to Canton and formally assumed his responsibilities as a member of the Central Executive Committee and as minister of justice. Feng Yü-hsiang left Moscow in mid-August and, after his arrival in Suiyuan, announced his intention to join the Northern Expedition. Hsü acted as Feng's intermediary in obtaining National Government funds for the Kuominchün.

The Nationalist forces took Wuchang in October 1926 and Nanchang in November.

Chiang Kai-shek, then commander in chief of the National Revolutionary Army, suggested moving the National Government from Canton to the Yangtze valley, and Hsü Ch'ien, Soong Ch'ing-ling, and Borodin left Canton on 28 November 1926 to confer with Chiang at Nanchang about this matter. Hsü Ch'ien was an outspoken member of the Kuomintang left wing, which was still allied with the Communists. After the Nanchang meeting with Chiang Kai-shek, Hsü and his party went to Hankow, where, on 13 December 1926, they held a meeting attended by left-wing members of the Kuomintang. Hsü Ch'ien was elected chairman of the provisional joint session of the Kuomintang Central Executive Committee and the National Government Council, which was to act as the supreme party and government authority until a central government was established at Wuhan.

The creation of the joint session widened the split between the left and right wings of the Kuomintang. After a prolonged tug-of-war between the Wuhan and Nanchang factions, the third plenum of the second Central Executive Committee of the Kuomintang was held at Hankow from 10 to 17 March 1927. Hsü Ch'ien, Wang Ching-wei (in absentia), T'an Yen-k'ai, Sun Fo, and T. V. Soong were elected members of the standing committee of the 28-man Government Council. Hsü was also elected to the nine-man standing committee of the Kuomintang Political Council and to the presidium of the 15-man Military Council. At the end of the meeting, the headquarters of the Kuomintang and of the National Government were formally established at Wuhan.

Hsü was now at the peak of his power. However, the Wuhan regime was unable to dominate the entire Nationalist movement. It was weaker than Chiang Kai-shek's faction both militarily and financially. Also, the Communist elements at Wuhan were a divisive factor in internal operations there. Wang Ching-wei returned from Europe at the beginning of April and issued a joint declaration at Shanghai with Ch'en Tu-hsiu (q.v.) reiterating the alliance between the Kuomintang and the Chinese Communist party. Wang then went to Hankow. On 12 April 1927 Chiang Kai-shek began a purge of Communists in the areas under his control. Hsü Ch'ien and other members of the Wuhan regime were put on the "wanted" list of Communists and fellow-travelers.

Hsü Ch'ien's position at Wuhan derived in part from his close friendship with Feng Yü-hsiang, who then held the balance of power between the rival Kuomintang factions. Feng's troops controlled northern Honan. From 10 to 13 June 1927 a Wuhan delegation which included Hsü Ch'ien, other Kuomintang military and political leaders, and Russian military adviser Bluecher (Galen), conferred with Feng at Chengchow. In return for Feng's support, the Wuhan leaders withdrew their troops from Honan province and appointed Feng chairman of the Honan provincial government.

Hsü Ch'ien did not return to Wuhan with the rest of the delegation. His ostensible reason for remaining in Honan was his membership in the Kaifeng branch of the Political Council, but apparently he was dissatisfied with the situation at Wuhan and complained to Feng Yü-hsiang about the deterioration of public order there. Hsü may have influenced Feng's decision to give his support to Chiang Kai-shek. On 8 July 1927 Feng began a purge of Communists in areas under his control and dismissed all political workers who had been sent to him from Wuhan. A week later, Wang Ching-wei and the Wuhan regime also broke with the Communists, providing the necessary precondition to the reconciliation of the Kuomintang factions.

Hsü Ch'ien had antagonized both factions of the Kuomintang and the Communists as well. Each group accused him of betraying its trust. He went to Shanghai in September 1927 and publicly declared on 17 November that he was retiring from public life. After living in Shanghai for some time, Hsü moved to Hong Kong and settled in Kowloon.

In 1933 Ch'en Ming-shu (q.v.) and other Nationalist leaders opposed to Chiang Kai-shek persuaded Hsü Ch'ien to participate in their plan to form a rival government in Fukien. On 10 November 1933 Hsü attended a meeting at Foochow at which the authority of the National Government was repudiated and a so-called people's government was established. He was elected a member of its government council. Chiang Kai-shek, in a telegram issued from Nanchang on 23 November, named Hsü Ch'ien and Huang Ch'i-hsiang as leaders of this movement. The Fukien government collapsed in January 1934, and Hsü Ch'ien returned to Hong Kong.

After the outbreak of the Sino-Japanese war in July 1937, Hsü went to Nanking, where he was given a sinecure post on the National Defense Council. In October 1939 he flew to Hong Kong for surgery. On 26 September 1940 he died in Hong Kong.

Hsü Ch'ien's publications included *Shih-tz'u-hsueh* [studies of shih and tz'u], *Hsing-fa tsung-pien* [a collection of penal laws], *Tsung-chiao wen-hsueh* [religious literature], *Pi-fa t'an-wei* [a glimpse into calligraphy], and *Lao-tzu ho-i* [unity of capital and labor]. A collection of his poems, the *Hsü Chi-lung hsien-sheng i-shih*, was printed privately by his widow in 1943. Hsü was also known as a good calligrapher and a diligent correspondent.

Hsü Ch'ien married twice. His first wife, *née* Yu, a native of Shantung, died in 1920. His second wife, Shen I-pin, was from Shaohsing, Chekiang. Hsü had two sons and three daughters.

Hsü Chih-mo		徐志摩
Orig.	Hsü Yu-sen	徐槱森
T.	Chih-mo	志摩
	Yu-shen	又申
Alt.	Hsü Chang-hsü	徐章垿
Pen.	Nan-hu	南湖
	Shih-che	詩哲

Hsü Chih-mo (1896–19 November 1931), poet. His poetic experiments in form, meter, and theme and his essays increased Chinese understanding and awareness of Western poetry and of the potentialities of the modern Chinese language.

Hsiashih, Chekiang, was the birthplace of Hsü Chih-mo. His father, Hsü Shen-ju, was a prominent banker and a friend of the noted entrepreneur Chang Chien (q.v.). Hsü Chih-mo received traditional training in the Chinese classics and then attended a Western-style college in Shanghai. He entered Peking University in the autumn of 1916. During this period, his ambition was to become the Alexander Hamilton of China, and he even adopted the Western name Hamilton for a time.

In the summer of 1918, after graduation from Peking University, Hsü went to the United States for further study. On the trip, he composed a long pledge in classical Chinese to his parents, vowing to devote his life to the well-being of his country. He studied economics and sociology at Clark University in Worcester, Massachusetts, and then transferred to Columbia University to study political science. Finding life in the United States incompatible with his temperament, he went to England in 1920.

In England, Hsü studied at Cambridge University, which had an important influence on him. From reading Swinburne he acquired a taste for alliterative cadence and impressionism, and from the Bloomsbury group, ideas on the poetic use of images. He also met Katherine Mansfield and her associates. He soon began to write poetry and decided to pursue a literary career.

After returning to China in October 1922, Hsü Chih-mo went to Peking. He wrote poems and essays in the new vernacular style, and became a cherished protégé of Liang Ch'i-ch'ao (q.v.) because of his command of classical Chinese. Hsü came to know many of the leading intellectuals of the period and in 1924 taught literature at National Peking University. A new dimension was added to Hsü's literary development in the same year, when Rabindranath Tagore visited China. Hsü Chih-mo served as interpreter for the prominent Indian poet and philosopher, accompanying him on his lecture tour through China and on his short visit to Japan. His renderings of Tagore's words into Chinese were praised for their spontaneous artistry.

In March 1925 Hsü again went abroad. Traveling by way of the Soviet Union, he went to Germany and then toured Italy and France, where he paid tribute at the graves of a number of famous literary men. He also spent some time in London, where he had a brief interview with the English novelist and poet Thomas Hardy.

After five months in Europe, Hsü Chih-mo returned to China and entered upon his most productive period as a poet. Then only in his early thirties, he had established a literary position that enabled him to play a leading role in the so-called modern poetry movement. The poets of Hsü's circle attempted to write according to the literary standards of the modern West rather than those of traditional China. Their aim was to develop a new style in Chinese poetry by combining vernacular Chinese and Western poetic forms. The poems of Hsü Chih-mo and those of Wen I-to and Chu Hsiang (qq.v.) are good examples of this pioneering, self-conscious attempt to follow Western rhythmic and metrical forms. The approach marked a complete break with classical Chinese style, and conservative critics viewed it as an heretical deviation.

Hsü Chih-mo also influenced literature in China as an editor and as a teacher. In October 1925 he assumed the editorship of the literary supplement of the *Ch'en Pao* [morning post] in Peking. The *Ch'en Pao* supplement was a major literary organ in the post-1919 era in north China, and Hsü did much to increase its prestige by obtaining poems, stories, and articles from such leading intellectuals as Chang Tung-sun, Y. R. Chao (Chao Yuen-ren), Ch'en Heng-che, Kuo Mo-jo, Liang Ch'i-ch'ao, Wen I-to, and Wong Wen-hao. Hsü extended the supplement's influence by devoting regular and specific attention to the fields of poetry and drama. He also served as chief editor of *Shih-k'an* [poetry magazine], another supplement to the *Ch'en Pao*, from its appearance on 1 April 1926 until its suspension on 10 June. At that time, he was in close contact with members of the literary group known as Hsin-yueh-she [crescent moon society], which had been organized in Peking earlier in 1926 by a group including Hu Shih, Liang Shih-ch'iu, Lo Lung-chi, P'an Kuang-tan(qq.v.), and Wen I-to. Some members of this group had studied in the United States or England; others were poets connected with the *Ch'en Pao* supplement.

When the Northern Expedition forces reached the Yangtze in 1927, Hsü Chih-mo left Peking and went to Shanghai, where he taught English at Kuang Hua University, Soochow University Law School, and later at Ta Hsia University. In the spring of 1928 Hsü, Hu Shih, and Shao Hsun-mei organized the Hsin-yueh shu-tien [crescent moon book company] in Shanghai. The following year, this book company began publishing the *Hsin-yueh yueh-k'an* [crescent moon monthly], the literary journal of the Hsin-yueh-she, which was influential in introducing Western literature to Chinese readers and in promoting an appreciation of the aesthetic aspects of literature. Hsü Chih-mo was one of three editors, the other two being Wen I-to and Jao Meng-k'an.

After a brief trip to Europe with Wang Wen-po in the autumn of 1928, Hsü returned to China and in 1929 taught English at National Central University in Nanking. He continued to teach at Kuang Hua University in Shanghai and joined the Chunghua Book Company, one of the

leading publishers in Shanghai, as an editor. In 1930 Hsü resigned from National Central University to resume teaching at National Peking University at the invitation of Hu Shih, then the dean of studies. At the beginning of 1931 Hsü was a leading figure in the group which launched the first independent periodical in China devoted to modern Chinese poetry. The magazine was entitled *Shih-k'an* [poetry] and is to be distinguished from the earlier poetry supplement to the *Ch'en Pao*.

During 1931 Hsü Chih-mo often commuted by airplane between Peiping and Shanghai; the exhilaration of flying delighted him. However, air travel in China in that period was still risky. When Hsü was flying from Shanghai to Peiping on 19 November 1931, the plane encountered fog over Shantung and crashed near Tsinan, killing all aboard.

Hsü left four collections of verse. These are *Chih-mo ti shih* [poems of Chih-mo], of 1925; *Feng-lang-ts'ui ti i-yeh* [one night in Florence], of 1927; *Meng-hu chi* [fierce tiger], of 1931; and *Yun-yu* [cloud wanderings], of 1932. He also left four volumes of essays: *Lo-yeh chi* [fallen leaves], of 1926; *Pa-li ti lin-chao* [Parisian trifles], of 1927; *Tzu-p'ou chi* [self-dissection], of 1928; and *Ch'iu* [autumn], of 1931. Hsü was also an able translator. His important translations include *Undine*, published in 1923, and Katherine Mansfield's short stories, published in 1927. He also published translations of Voltaire's *Candide* and of James Stephens' *The Charwoman's Daughter* in 1927. A number of Hsü's poems were set to music by Y. R. Chao and made the Shanghai "hit parade," notably one entitled "Yun-hai" [sea of rhyme].

Hsü Chih-mo married twice. His first wife, Chang Yü-i, was the younger sister of Carsun Chang (Chang Chia-sen, q.v.) and Chang Kia-ngau (Chang Chia-ao, q.v.). They were married in Hsiashih in 1915 and had two sons, Hsü Pi-te and Hsü Ju-sun. During his Cambridge days, Hsü had come to believe that the free pursuit of adventure by the soul was the highest ideal in life. In March 1922 he wrote his wife that they must be divorced. In the summer of 1924 Hsü met Lu Hsiao-man, a talented and beautiful Peking socialite who was married to a high-ranking Chinese army officer. After a stormy romance and a period of separation in 1925 when Hsü went to Europe, she divorced her husband. They were married in

1926 at a ceremony which was memorable because Liang Ch'i-ch'ao delivered a blistering public speech chastising Hsü. Herself a writer and painter, Lu Hsiao-man collaborated with Hsü in writing *Pien K'un-kang* (1928), a five-act play applauded by contemporary critics for its atmosphere, characterization, and dialogue. The letters exchanged between Hsü Chih-mo and Lu Hsiao-man were published in *Chih-mo jih-chi* in 1947, 16 years after Hsü's death. Lu died in Shanghai on 2 April 1965, at the age of 64 sui.

Hsü Chih-mo was generally regarded by his contemporaries as the first fully successful modern poet in the Chinese language. His experiments in form, meter, and theme, had a far-reaching influence. His poems and essays on poetry did much to raise the level of Chinese understanding of Western poetry and to increase awareness of the potentialities of the modern Chinese language. His ingenious use of Peking speech dialect, together with his native Hsiashih dialect and English, produced a refreshing, individual style. Poetry, he believed, should aspire to the beauty of music in its rhythm, the beauty of painting in its diction, and the beauty of architecture in its style; and he strove, with considerable success, to achieve these ends in his own poems.

Hsü Ch'ung-chih   許 崇 智
T. Ju-wei   汝 爲

Hsü Ch'ung-chih (26 October 1887–25 January 1965), as chief aide to Ch'en Chiung-ming, helped to build Sun Yat-sen's military establishment, becoming commander in chief of Sun's Kwangtung forces in 1923. He reached the peak of his career in 1925, when he served briefly as minister of war and governor of Kwangtung. After 1945, he made his home in Hong Kong.

A native of P'anyü, Kwangtung, Hsü Ch'ung-chih was born in Canton. Little is known about his parents. His paternal grandfather, Hsü Ying-k'uei, an anti-reform leader who was particularly critical of the views of K'ang Yu-wei (q.v.), served as governor general of Fukien-Chekiang from 1898 until 1903.

Hsü Ch'ung-chih received a classical education at Canton and then went to Japan, where he enrolled at the Shikan Gakkō. He was graduated as a member of the second class. After returning to China in 1907, he became a staff officer of the 10th Brigade of the New Army at Foochow and chief instructor at the Fukien Provincial Military School. He later was given command of the 20th Brigade of the Fukien forces.

After the Wuchang revolt of October 1911, Hsü Ch'ung-chih led the Foochow movement to declare the independence of Fukien from the Manchus and became commander in chief of the Fukien revolutionary forces. Sun Tao-jen, the divisional commander in Fukien, was elected governor of the province. Early in 1912 Hsü led an army northward from Fukien. By the time he reached Shanghai the emperor had abdicated and the republic had been established. He then led his army back to Fukien, where it was reorganized as the 14th Division. He joined the Kuomintang when it was established in 1912.

In 1913 the republican revolutionaries launched the so-called second revolution against Yuan Shih-k'ai. The provinces then under Kuomintang governors, led by Li Lieh-chün (q.v.) in Kiangsi, declared their independence. Hsü Ch'ung-chih tried to persuade Sun Tao-jen to join the revolutionary side in July. However, the second revolution was suppressed within a few weeks, and Hsü was forced to flee to Japan.

In 1914 Sun Yat-sen reorganized the Kuomintang as the Chung-hua ko-ming-tang and required its members to take an oath of personal allegiance to him. Some of Sun's close associates, notably Huang Hsing (q.v.), opposed the reorganization because of this requirement. Hsü Ch'ung-chih, however, was among Sun's most ardent supporters; and when the Chung-hua ko-ming-tang was formally established in Tokyo on 8 July 1914, he was named to head the military affairs department, with Teng K'eng (q.v.) as his deputy.

In March 1915 Hsü Ch'ung-chih was sent to Malaya by Sun Yat-sen to promote the cause of party unity and to counter the anti-Sun efforts of Ch'en Chiung-ming (q.v.). Hsü's trip apparently was successful, and he returned to Tokyo in June to report to Sun. Almost immediately, he was sent to Malaya again to raise funds for the anti-Yuan Shih-k'ai campaign.

After Yuan Shih-k'ai's monarchical aspirations became known in 1915, many of the revolutionary leaders in Japan returned to China to direct anti-Yuan forces in their native provinces. Ch'en Chiung-ming, Hsü Ch'ung-chih, and others returned to Kwangtung. The struggle ended with Yuan Shih-k'ai's death in June 1916.

In 1917 Sun Yat-sen launched the so-called constitution protection movement. A rump parliament met at Canton in August 1917 and formed a military government, headed by Sun Yat-sen. Hsü Ch'ung-chih became adjutant general at Sun's headquarters. Because of the military strength of the Kwangsi generals, led by Lu Jung-t'ing (q.v.), Sun Yat-sen decided to build a military establishment of his own. With the help of Chu Ch'ing-lan, the Kwangtung civil governor, he organized an army. Ch'en Chiung-ming was named commander in chief, and Hsü Ch'ung-chih was appointed his chief aide. To avoid open conflict with the Kwangsi leaders, Sun sent the newly organized army into Fukien in December 1917. Ch'en Chiung-ming and Hsü Ch'ung-chih established a base at Changchow and undertook a military training program. In September 1918 the Kwangtung forces were divided into two armies, with Ch'en Chiung-ming as over-all commander in chief and commander of the First Army and Hsü Ch'ung-chih as commander of the Second Army.

In August 1920 Sun Yat-sen, who had retired to Shanghai, ordered Ch'en Chiung-ming and Hsü Ch'ung-chih to return to Kwangtung and attempt to dislodge the Kwangsi warlords entrenched at Canton. The campaign was successful, and Sun Yat-sen returned to Canton. In 1921 the rump parliament elected Sun president extraordinary, and he assumed office on 5 May. On Sun's orders, Hsü Ch'ung-chih marched his Second Army into Kwangsi and eventually captured Kweilin. Sun himself established his field headquarters at Kweilin and made plans to launch a northern expedition through Hunan.

Early in 1922 Sun changed his plans and decided to march northward by way of Kiangsi. He moved his field headquarters to Shaokuan in northern Kwangtung and ordered Hsü Ch'ung-chih to lead the Second Army into Kiangsi. Ch'en Chiung-ming, who opposed Sun Yat-sen's northern expedition plans, was

becoming restive, and on 16 June 1922 Ch'en's troops openly revolted and attacked Sun's presidential headquarters at Canton. Sun himself managed to escape to the gunboat Yung-feng. Hsü Ch'ung-chih's Second Army and other units which had entered Kiangsi were ordered to Canton to counter Ch'en Chiung-ming's move, but Ch'en defeated these forces in northern Kwangtung in August. Hsü then moved his army into Fukien. Sun Yat-sen retired to Shanghai and issued an order naming Hsü commander in chief of the East Route Anti-Rebel Army, with Chiang Kai-shek as chief of staff. Hsü then expanded his forces into three armies, with Huang Ta-wei commanding the First Army, himself commanding the Second Army, and Li Fu-lin commanding the Third Army.

In December 1922 Sun Yat-sen won the support of the Yunnan army commanded by Liu Hsi-min, and the Kwangsi army commanded by Liu Chen-huan. In February 1923 Sun ordered Hsü Ch'ung-chih to take his forces back to Kwangtung, and Hsü occupied the Swatow area. The Yunnan and Kwangsi armies were approaching Canton, and many units of the Kwangtung forces rose in support of these armies and ousted Ch'en Chiung-ming from Canton. However, Ch'en still held control of the East River area, between Canton and Swatow, with headquarters at Huichou (Waichow). At this time, Sun Yat-sen appointed Hsü Ch'ung-chih commander in chief of all the Kwangtung forces, the post previously held by Ch'en Chiung-ming.

Sun Yat-sen returned to Canton, resumed control of the southern government, and proceeded with plans for the reorganization of the Kuomintang. At the First National Congress of the Kuomintang, held in January 1924, Hsü Ch'ung-chih was elected to the Central Supervisory Committee, which then was composed of only five full members and five alternates. He was appointed director of the military affairs department of the Kuomintang headquarters. He also served Sun's government as acting minister of war in the absence of Ch'eng Ch'ien (q.v.), who had been sent to his native Hunan province to raise an army.

Late in 1924 Sun Yat-sen went to Peking to discuss major national issues with the northern authorities, leaving Hu Han-min (q.v.) with full authority at Canton. After Sun's death at

Peking in March 1925, the most pressing problem at Canton was the threat of open revolt of the Yunnan and Kwangsi armies of Yang Hsi-min and Liu Chen-huan. Hu Han-min handled the issue with decisive firmness. After consultation with Hsü Ch'ung-chih and Chiang Kai-shek, then commandant of the Whampoa Military Academy and garrison commander, Hu determined to use force against the unruly troops. In May, Hsü's army, aided by the Whampoa cadets, suppressed the revolt in two weeks.

Hsü Ch'ung-chih reached the peak of his public career in the summer of 1925. When the National Government was inaugurated at Canton on 1 July 1925, he was elected to the sixteen-man Government Council and to its five-man standing committee, which also included Hu Han-min, Liao Chung-k'ai, T'an Yen-k'ai, and Wang Ching-wei. He was named minister of war and a member of the military council, of which Chiang Kai-shek was the senior member. He also was appointed chairman of the reorganized Kwangtung provincial council, or governor.

In August 1925 a new crisis arose at Canton with the assassination of Liao Chung-k'ai. At first, the only prominent official involved was Hu Han-min, whose cousin was suspected as a principal figure in plotting the murder. As time passed, however, more suspects were arrested, including ranking officers of the Kwangtung armies. As senior commander of these forces, Hsü Ch'ung-chih could not be completely absolved from blame. On 20 September 1925 he was relieved of all his posts. That very night, Chiang Kai-shek sent Ch'en Ming-shu (q.v.) to escort Hsü on board a steamer bound for Shanghai.

In November 1925 a group of veteran Kuomintang leaders who held anti-Communist views convened a meeting, later known as the Western Hills conference, at Peking. Although Hsü Ch'ung-chih was not present at that meeting, he participated in the group's activities in Shanghai when the Western Hills leaders moved their headquarters there and convened a second congress of the Kuomintang. Subsequently, when the Kuomintang authorities at Nanking and Wuhan expelled the Communists, the dissident factions of the party were reunited temporarily, with Hsü representing the Western Hills group. He then left on a mission for Europe and the United States to "inspect party affairs." After returning to China, he lived in Shanghai. On 12 December 1929 the Nanking authorities ordered the arrest of Hsü and such other Western Hills leaders as Chü Cheng, Hsieh Ch'ih, and Tsou Lu (qq.v.). The reasons for the order were never clarified, but it was generally assumed in China that these men were regarded as having been responsible for encouraging the revolts staged by various Kuomintang factions against the central authority at Nanking during 1928 and 1929. Of those named, Chü Cheng was the only one to be arrested and imprisoned.

In 1931, when a secessionist government was formed at Canton after Chiang Kai-shek had Hu Han-min arrested, Hsü Ch'ung-chih joined the southern coalition. However, the Japanese invasion of Manchuria in September brought an end to the secessionist movement. At the Fourth National Congress of the Kuomintang, held to end internal feuding, Hsü was elected to the Central Supervisory Committee and was appointed vice president of the Control Yuan. His positions were confirmed at the Fifth National Congress of the Kuomintang, held at Nanking in November 1935. However, he continued to reside in Shanghai and took no active part in either party or government affairs.

After the outbreak of the Sino-Japanese war in 1937 and the organization of the Japanese-sponsored puppet regime under Wang Ching-wei (q.v.) at Nanking in 1940, Hsü left Shanghai for Hong Kong and then proceeded to Chungking. Tu Yueh-sheng (q.v.) helped effect a reconciliation between Hsü Ch'ung-chih and Chiang Kai-shek. Hsü remained in Chungking throughout the war years. He was reelected to the Central Supervisory Committee of the Kuomintang at the Sixth National Congress, held in May 1945.

After the Japanese defeat in 1945, Hsü Ch'ung-chih made his home in Hong Kong. Former Cantonese military officers who were residing in the colony addressed the elderly gentleman as lao-tsung [the chief] when they met. Hsü enjoyed good health and played mahjongg for relaxation until a few days before his death. He died on 25 January 1965, at the age of 78 sui. He was survived by six sons, five of whom were in Hong Kong at the time of his death, and by six daughters, all married.

Hsü Hai-tung   徐 海 東

Hsü Hai-tung (1900–), Chinese Communist guerrilla leader in Hupeh whose peasant self-defense corps grew to become the Fourth Front Army.

The Huangp'i district of Hupeh was the birthplace of Hsü Hai-tung. His father and his five elder brothers were potters. Hsü attended a local primary school for about three years. At the age of 11 he became an apprentice in the local pottery works. He worked there for ten years and became one of the most skillful potters in the factory. In 1920, after a family dispute, he left home and traveled through central China, working occasionally in such cities as Hankow, Kiukiang, and Nanchang. After two years of this itinerant existence, Hsü decided to return to Hupeh, but he became ill with cholera and had to spend all of his money for treatment. Because he was unwilling to return home in destitution, he enlisted in the Kiangsi provincial army.

After serving as a soldier in the Kiangsi army for about three years, Hsü deserted and went to Kwangtung. He joined the 12th Division, commanded by Chang Fa-k'uei (q.v.), of the Fourth Army and participated in the early campaigns of the Northern Expedition. By the spring of 1927 he had become a platoon leader.

Communist cadres in Chang Fa-k'uei's division persuaded Hsü to join the Chinese Communist party. In the summer of 1927 he returned to his native district in Hupeh, set up a party branch, and began to organize workers and peasants in the area. Later that year, he formed a peasant self-defense corps which boasted a force of thirteen peasants, two potters, and one student and an arsenal of one rifle. Hsü worked to expand the corps, and it soon became large enough to be designated the 32nd Division of the Workers and Peasants Red Army. He continued to recruit men in the Hupeh-Honan border area, and in the summer of 1929, after Hsü Hsiang-ch'ien (q.v.) had arrived in the border area, the 31st Division was created. In 1931 Chang Kuo-t'ao (q.v.) was assigned to establish a Communist border region administration for the Hupeh-Honan-Anhwei soviet (also known as the O-yu-wan

soviet), and Hsü Hai-tung came under his jurisdiction. By this time, Hsü's peasant self-defense corps had grown to become the Fourth Front Army.

In the early 1930's the National Government worked to combat Communist activities in central China, and several members of Hsü Hai-tung's family were imprisoned or executed during anti-Communist campaigns. By November 1932 the Communists in the Hupeh-Honan-Anhwei border area had been forced to evacuate their base. Chang Kuo-t'ao and Hsü Hsiang-ch'ien led the Fourth Front Army into Shensi and Szechwan. Hsü Hai-tung, who had been wounded when the march began, remained behind to cover the retreat as commander of the Twenty-fifth Army.

Hsü directed guerrilla activities in the Hupeh-Anhwei border region for almost two years before being forced to withdraw at the time of the Long March. Late in 1934 his troops marched into Shensi with the apparent intention of rejoining the Fourth Front Army, then based on the Shensi-Szechwan border. Hsü failed to locate his former associates and decided to march northward. Because of this decision, his was the first Communist force from outside Shensi to reach the Communist base area in the north. The Twenty-fifth Army reached Paoan in February 1935 and joined forces with two local Communist units: the Twenty-sixth Army of Kao Kang (q.v.) and the Twenty-seventh Army of Liu Chih-tan (q.v.). In September, the three armies were reorganized as the Fifteenth Army Group, with Hsü Hai-tung as commander. Hsü established headquarters in the Yuwang district of Ninghsia.

After the Sino-Japanese war began in 1937, Hsü was assigned to the Shantung-Hopei aare, where he served under Hsü Hsiang-ch'ien. In 1939 he became a member of the Chinese Communist party's Shantung bureau, and he directed Communist forces in the Shantung-Kiangsu border area in support of the New Fourth Army's operations in northern Kiangsu. By 1944 he had become the commander of the Communists' Shantung-Kiangsu-Honan military district.

After 1945 Hsü's importance in Chinese Communist affairs declined, and he received no new posts for almost ten years. Reports indicated that Hsü was in very poor health during this period. His long and dedicated service to the Chinese Communist movement was not forgotten by its leaders. In 1954 he was appointed to the National Defense Council at Peking, and in 1955 he was made a general in the People's Liberation Army and was awarded all of the top military honors of the People's Republic of China. He was elected to the Central Committee of the Chinese Communist party at the Eighth National Congress, held in September 1956. Although he had been confined to a wheel chair, Hsü managed to attend the August 1957 ceremonies which marked the thirtieth anniversary of the establishment of the Chinese Red Army, and in 1959 he served as a member of the presidium for the tenth-anniversary celebrations of the establishment of the People's Republic of China. In October 1964 he attended a national meeting called by the general political department of the People's Liberation Army in Peking.

Hsü Hsiang-ch'ien   徐 向 前

Hsü Hsiang-ch'ien (1902–), Communist military commander, served under Chang Kuo-t'ao in the Hupeh-Honan-Anhwei soviet area (1931–32)´ and in Szechwan and Sikang (1932–36).

Wut'ai, Shansi, was the birthplace of Hsü Hsiang-ch'ien. Little is known about his background except that his father was a sheng-yuan. Hsü received a primary education in the Chinese classics and then enrolled at the Taiyuan Normal School. After graduation, he became a teacher in his native town.

In 1924 Hsü joined the Kuomintang and went to Canton, where he enrolled at the Whampoa Military Academy as a member of the first class. After serving as a squad leader in the 1925 eastern expedition against Ch'en Chiung-ming (q.v.), he joined the forces of Feng Yü-hsiang (q.v.) in north China as a political officer. By 1927 he had been promoted to regimental commander. When a branch of the Central Military Academy was established at Wuhan, he served on its staff as an instructor, with the rank of captain. About this time, he joined the Second Front Army of Chang Fa-k'uei (q.v.) as a staff officer and became a member of the Chinese Communist party. After marching with Chang's army to Canton, he participated in the Canton Commune of 11 December 1927 (*see*

Chang T'ai-lei). After the uprising failed, he went to Hailufeng in eastern Kwangtung, where he served under P'eng P'ai (q.v.) as chief of staff of the 4th Division of the Chinese Communist forces in the Hailufeng soviet area. When the Hailufeng base was crushed in February 1928, Hsü escaped to Shanghai.

In June 1929 Hsü Hsiang-ch'ien was assigned to Hupeh, where Hsü Hai-tung (q.v.) had been working since 1927 to develop a Communist guerrilla force. The force had been designated the 32nd Division of the Workers and Peasants Red Army. Hsü Hsiang-ch'ien helped organize the 31st Division, with K'uang Chi-hsün as commander. The new division was based in the Huangan and Mach'eng districts. By the end of 1929 the Hupeh-Honan soviet had been established. In 1930 the Communists enlarged their base area to include four adjacent districts of Anhwei and created the Hupeh-Honan-Anhwei soviet, also known as the O-yu-wan soviet. Hsü Hsiang-ch'ien's troops, now part of the Fourth Front Army, successfully repulsed forces led by Hsia Tou-yin and others in the Nationalist campaigns to annihilate the Communists. In 1931 Chang Kuo-t'ao (q.v.) was assigned to create a border region administration for the area and to serve as political commissar of the Fourth Front Army.

In July 1932 Chiang Kai-shek sent a large force to annihilate the Chinese Communists in the Hupeh-Honan-Anhwei border area. K'uang Chi-hsün, then the commander of the Fourth Front Army, was relieved of his command on charges of ineffective performance, and Hsü Hsiang-ch'ien succeeded him. The Nationalist forces continued to press the Communists, forcing Chang Kuo-t'ao to issue an evacuation order. On 25 November, Chang and Hsü led the Fourth Front Army into Shensi. They encountered little resistance until they came within 30 miles of Sian. Instead of attempting to fight their way to the provincial capital, they crossed the Tapa mountains and entered Szechwan. Because T'ien Sung-yao, the garrison commander of that sector, had withdrawn most of his forces from northern Szechwan to fight Liu Wen-hui (q.v.), the Communists were able to establish a Szechwan-Shensi border area in February 1933. They set up a soviet government in the Pachung district, with Chang Kuo-t'ao as chairman and Hsü Hsiang-ch'ien as senior military commander.

Hsü and Chang worked to rehabilitate their forces and to bring more territory under their control. Their efforts were successful for a time because the Szechwan generals were fighting among themselves. In the autumn of 1933 Hsü led his army southward and defeated forces led by Yang Sen (q.v.). The Communists also used political means to achieve their ends. Among other things, they persuaded men serving under the senior Szechwan general Liu Ts'un-hou to join the Fourth Front Army. Hsü soon reorganized the five divisions of his growing Fourth Front Army into four armies.

Hsü's basic mission during this period was to maintain the security of the border area. He made good use of the natural features of the region in setting up defenses and used positional warfare tactics to stave off the forays of Szechwanese troops. Although his methods differed greatly from the tactics of high mobility and swift action usually associated with Chinese Communist operations of this period (*see* Ho Lung), they were admirably suited to the requirements of his mission.

Late in 1934 National Government forces under the command of Hu Tsung-nan (q.v.), who had been a Whampoa classmate of Hsü Hsiang-ch'ien, were assigned to join with Szechwanese provincial troops in an attempt to destroy the Communist base in the Szechwan-Shensi border area. By February 1935 Hsü Hsiang-ch'ien and Chang Kuo-t'ao had been forced to retreat from the base area. They crossed the Chialing river and moved along the Szechwan-Sikang border to establish a new base. They had formed the so-called northwest revolutionary military council, with Chang Kuo-t'ao as chairman, Hsü Hsiang-ch'ien as military commander, and Ch'en Ch'ang-hao as political commissar, to extend Communist control into the areas of China's northwestern provinces inhabited by non-Chinese minority groups.

In the summer of 1935 the Communist forces which had begun the Long March in Kiangsi in October 1934 reached the Szechwan-Sikang border. Chang Kuo-t'ao and Mao Tse-tung soon came into conflict with regard to future plans. Chang and Hsü wished to move west and establish a new base in Sikang; Mao favored moving northward to the existing Communist base in Shensi. In the end, Hsü, Chang, and the Fourth Front Army remained in Sikang, and Mao moved the First Front Army on to Shensi.

In October 1935 Chang and Hsü established a headquarters at K'angting and made plans to mobilize the non-Chinese minorities in the area. A few months later, National Government forces under Hsueh Yueh (q.v.) and Szechwanese provincial armies moved westward from Chengtu and forced the Communists to evacuate the new base area. By March 1936 the Fourth Front Army had retreated to Kantz'u. The food supply in that region was barely adequate, and, after being joined by Ho Lung's Second Front Army in June, the Communists abandoned Sikang. Hsü reached southern Kansu in July and attempted to move toward Sinkiang, but his ragged forces were pushed back by the vigorous Muslim cavalry of Ma Pu-fang. The survivors of this defeat marched to the central Communist base in northern Shensi. Western reporters who interviewed Hsü in Shensi at the end of the year found him to be reserved and gaunt.

After the Sino-Japanese war began in the summer of 1937, the Chinese Communist forces were reorganized as the Eighth Route Army, composed of three divisions. Hsü Hsiang-ch'ien became deputy commander of Liu Po-ch'eng's 129th Division and played an active role in creating Communist bases behind the Japanese lines in Shantung and Hopei. After being wounded in 1941, he was assigned to Shensi. From 1942 to 1946 he served under Ho Lung as deputy commander of the defense headquarters for the Shensi-Kansu-Ninghsia and Shansi-Suiyuan regions. In 1945 he succeeded Lin Piao as president of Anti-Japanese Military and Political University in Yenan.

In the civil war between the Nationalists and the Chinese Communists Hsü first served as commander of the Shansi-Hopei-Shantung-Honan military district. In 1948 he became deputy commander of the north China military district and headed Communist military operations in the Taiyuan area of Shansi.

After the Central People's Government was established at Peking in October 1949, Hsü became a member of the Government Council. Although he was appointed chief of staff of the Chinese Communist forces, he remained in Shansi and did not assume that post. In 1954 he represented the People's Liberation Army at the National People's Congress and became a member of the Standing Committee. He also was appointed a vice chairman of the National Defense Council. In September 1955 Hsü was one of ten generals named to the rank of Marshal of the People's Republic of China.

Hsü had become a member of the Central Committee of the Chinese Communist party about 1940, and he was reelected to it in 1945 and 1956. He also served on the influential standing committee of the party's Military Affairs Committee. In the 1960's, despite reports that he was in ill health, Hsü continued to participate in public ceremonies. He was a prominent figure on the reviewing stand at the celebrations in October 1965 to commemorate the establishment of the People's Republic of China. In January 1967 he became head of a new committee which had charge of the so-called cultural revolution.

Hsü Hsin-liu　　　徐 新 六
T.　Chen-fei　　振 飛
West. Singloh Hsu

Hsü Hsin-liu (1890–24 August 1938), banker, used Western banking methods to transform the conservative National Commercial Bank of Shanghai into one of the three leading commercial banks in that city. As the bank's general manager (1925–38), he also helped to form the Tai-shan Insurance Company.

The son of a prominent classical scholar who was an official of the Commercial Press at Shanghai, Hsü Hsin-liu was born into an affluent family in Hangchow. His native place was Yühang, Chekiang. A precocious child, he reportedly was adept at literary composition at the age of 11 sui. After being graduated from the Yangcheng School in Hangchow, he spent six years in Shanghai at the Nanyang kung-hsueh, the institution which later became Chiaotung University.

Hsü Hsin-liu received a Chekiang government scholarship for advanced study in Europe. After arriving in England in 1908, he took a four-year course in metallurgy at Birmingham University and received a B.Sc. degree in 1912. He read economics at the Victoria University of Manchester, where he received a B.A. degree in 1913, and then went to France to study public finance at the Ecole des Sciences Politiques.

After returning to China in 1914 and passing the competitive examination for senior civil servants, Hsü was assigned to the ministry of finance at Peking. He also held a teaching post at Peking University. When Liang Ch'i-ch'ao (q.v.) was named minister of finance in the summer of 1917, Hsü entered his service as an assistant. At that time, Liang was concentrating on the problem of currency reform. However, public opinion was against him, and he resigned in November of 1917. Hsü Hsin-liu left government service at the same time and joined the staff of the Bank of China. He served as assistant treasurer and later as assistant manager of the bank's branch office at Peking. For a time, he also served as chief accountant of the Han-yeh-p'ing Company at Hankow.

Liang Ch'i-ch'ao emerged from retirement shortly after the end of the First World War and took an extended trip to Europe to acquaint himself with conditions in the West, traveling in the capacity of an unofficial delegate to the Paris Peace Conference. Hsü Hsin-liu was invited to become a member of Liang's entourage, which also included Carsun Chang (Chang Chia-sen), V. K. Ting (Ting Wen-chiang), and Chiang Fang-chen (qq.v.). After the group arrived in France, Hsü was appointed a member of the Chinese delegation on the reparations committee of the Paris Peace Conference.

On his return from Europe, Hsü Hsin-liu began his long association with the National Commercial Bank of Shanghai. The bank had been founded by the Chekiang Railway Company in 1907, with its head office at Hangchow. After the inauguration of the republic in 1912, the railway company had been nationalized and the bank had been reorganized as a private enterprise. By 1918 the bank's capital had grown from CN$250 thousand to CN$1 million. Yeh Ching-kuei, who had been superintendent of the Ta Ch'ing Bank, was its general manager. To compete more efficiently with such modern banks as the Shanghai Commercial and Savings Bank and the National Industrial Bank of China, both of which were managed by men who had received Western training, the directors of the National Commercial Bank decided to obtain Hsü Hsin-liu's services as secretary of the board of directors. He served as assistant general manager of the bank from 1923 to 1925 and as general manager from 1925 until his death in 1938.

Hsü instituted important reforms in the operations of the National Commercial Bank. New men were hired to train the staff, and new business methods were adopted to expand the bank's operations. Hsü favored gradual streamlining rather than drastic reform. By 1929 the bank had set up an independent savings department, with separate capital and unlimited responsibility to depositors. A year later, a realty and trust department was launched, also with separate capital. In 1932 the National Commercial Bank, collaborating with C. V. Starr and Company, an American insurance company, formed the Tai-shan Insurance Company (capitalized at CN$1 million) to engage in life, fire, and casualty insurance business. By 1931 the National Commercial Bank had increased its capital to CN$4 million. The bank had become one of the three most prominent commercial banks in Shanghai, the other two being the Shanghai Commercial and Savings Bank and the National Industrial Bank of China. Hsü Hsin-liu also served as a member of the board of directors of the Shanghai Municipal Bank, the *China Times* (*Shih-shih hsin-pao*), and the *China Press* of Shanghai.

During Hsü Hsin-liu's long career in Shanghai, he also played an active role in public affairs. He was particularly concerned with furthering the interests of the Chinese residents of the International Settlement. The Shanghai Municipal Council (SMC), which was dominated by its British and American members, administered the International Settlement. Representing the Chinese Ratepayers Association of Shanghai, Hsü began to participate in the work of the SMC after the First World War. When a post for a Chinese member was created on the SMC, Hsü Hsin-liu was elected to it by the Ratepayers Association. He served on the council for a decade, during which he worked consistently to protect the interests of his Chinese fellow citizens and to support Sino-Western cooperation in Shanghai. In 1936 the SMC appointed Hsü chairman of its library committee. He was the first Chinese to hold a chairmanship in the council.

Through the years, Hsü Hsin-liu often had been asked by the National Government to undertake official assignments involving financial matters. He had declined all such offers, though he expressed his opinions to the government authorities when consulted. In the summer of 1938, when the Japanese were concentrating their military operations against the Wuhan cities, the problem of foreign assistance to China became critical. The only significant aid that China had received from friendly governments in the first year of the war came from the Soviet Union, which gave credits and "volunteers," and from the United States, which undertook the purchase of Chinese silver. At the end of July 1938 word was received from the United States that Secretary of the Treasury Henry Morgenthau, Jr. had indicated that, although he could make no promises, it might be well for China to send K. P. Ch'en (Ch'en Kuang-fu, q.v.) to Washington to investigate the possibility of obtaining American credits. Hsü Hsin-liu was made a member of the Chinese delegation, and the National Government considered sending Hsü as chief representative instead of K. P. Ch'en because of Ch'en's uncertain health. Hsü, who was then in Hong Kong, was summoned to Chungking for urgent consultation with H. H. K'ung, the minister of finance. He left Hong Kong on the regular commercial flight of the China National Aviation Corporation passenger plane Kweilin on 24 August 1938. One of the other passengers was the banker Hu Yün. The plane never reached its destination. It was intercepted and shot down by Japanese military aircraft. As a war casualty, Hsü Hsin-liu was honored by the National Government. The *Times* of London eulogized him as "a great gentleman," and Mr. Arthur N. Young, then financial adviser to the Chinese government, described him as "a man of high character and ability and a real patriot."

Hsü Kuang-p'ing   許 廣 平
T. Shu-yuan   漱 園

Hsü Kuang-p'ing (1907–), the wife of Lu Hsün (Chou Shu-jen, q.v.). After his death in 1936 she began to collate and edit his unpublished works and to write articles about him. After 1949 she served the Central People's Government as a member of many committees and delegations.

Little is known about Hsü Kuang-p'ing's background or childhood except that she was a native of P'anyü, Kwangtung. After being graduated from a junior normal school in Canton, she became a teacher. To further her education and to avoid an arranged marriage, she left Canton and went to Peking.

In 1923 Hsü Kuang-p'ing entered the Peking Women's Higher Normal School, where she majored in literature. At this time, Lu Hsün (Chou Shu-jen, q.v.) was teaching at the school and at National Peking University. In March 1925 Hsü wrote to Lu Hsün asking for advice and guidance. Thus began a regular correspondence, which later was collected and published as *Liang-ti shu*. As a student, Hsü's chief interests were literature and politics. She contributed essays to the magazine *Mang-yuan* [thicket], of which Lu Hsün was the chief editor; and she served as chairman of the students association at the school. In May 1925 she led a student movement to oust the principal. As a result, she was suspended from school. Lu Hsün also participated in the movement, and he was dismissed temporarily from his ministry of education post.

After being graduated from the Women's Higher Normal School, Hsü Kuang-p'ing left Peking in May 1926 to teach at the Women's Normal School in Canton, where she also was in charge of student discipline. She resigned about six months later because of student disturbances. After Lu Hsün became head of the Chinese literature department and academic dean at Sun Yat-sen University, Hsü Kuang-p'ing became his assistant and common-law wife. In April 1927 Lu Hsün resigned, protesting the Kuomintang's persecution of leftist students at Sun Yat-sen University. He and Hsü remained in Canton for a few months, and on 27 September a boy was born to them. They named him Hai-ying.

In October 1927 Hsü Kuang-p'ing, Lu Hsün, and their child left Canton and went to live in Shanghai. Their life was not peaceful: after 1930 Lu Hsün was under constant threat of arrest because of his leftist activities and his hostility to the Kuomintang. Hsü Kuang-p'ing was his constant companion and provided him with a family life that undoubtedly was his refuge and consolation.

After Lu Hsün died in 1936, Hsü remained in Shanghai. She began to edit and collate Lu Hsün's unpublished works and to write articles of reminiscence. After the Sino-Japanese war broke out in 1937, she and Cheng Chen-to (q.v.) organized the Fu She [recovery society] to promote the anti-Japanese movement. She was arrested by the Japanese on 15 December 1941 and imprisoned for two months. She remained in Shanghai throughout the period of Japanese occupation.

When the war ended, Hsü Kuang-p'ing became the editor of the *Min-chu* [democratic weekly] and a delegate to the National Assembly. She also was active in women's organizations, serving as chairman of the Shanghai Women's Fellowship Society and the Shanghai branch of the China Women's Federation.

After 1949, Hsü Kuang-p'ing served the Central People's Government in such positions as: member of the standing committee of the National Committee of the Chinese People's Political Consultative Conference; vice chairman of the All-China Federation of Democratic Women; board member of the Chinese People's Society for Cultural Relations with Foreign Countries; and member of the standing committee of the China Association for Promoting Democracy. However, there is no evidence that she became a member of the Chinese Communist party. She served as head or a member of many delegations to foreign countries, including those to: the anniversary of the October Revolution in Moscow (1948, 1953); the fifth council meeting of the Women's International Democratic Federation in Geneva (1955); the Second World Conference for the Prohibition of Nuclear Bombs in Nagasaki and Tokyo (1956); the Congress on Disarmament and International Cooperation in Sweden (1958); and the Afro-Asian Writers Conference in Tashkent (1958).

Hsü Kuang-p'ing's chief contributions to Chinese literature were her work in editing and collating Lu Hsün's work and her writings about him. Among her important publications is her edition of the *Lu Hsün shu-chien* [letters of Lu Hsün], originally published in 1946. She also contributed to the *Lu Hsün ch'uan-chi* [complete works of Lu Hsün], published at Peking in 1957.

Hsü Mo   徐 謨
T. Shu-mo   叔 謨

Hsü Mo (1893–28 June 1956), lawyer and political scientist, played a key role in the planning and administration of Chinese foreign policy from 1932 to 1941 and served on the International Court of Justice from 1946 until his death.

Born into a family of modest means in Soochow, Kiangsu, Hsü Mo received his early education at home under the guidance of his father, who was a teacher, and then attended a local middle school. In 1912 he enrolled at Peiyang University, where he became known as the most gifted student of English literature and composition to attend the university since Wang Ch'ung-hui (q.v.) had studied there, and he gained a notable reputation as an excellent public speaker in both Chinese and English. He also studied Chinese and Western law and received an LL.B. degree from Peiyang in 1916.

After graduation, Hsü returned to Kiangsu and taught English at the Yangchow Middle School. In 1919 he ranked first in the government examinations for the diplomatic service. He was sent to the United States for a tour of duty in the Chinese legation, and he served as a secretary to the Chinese delegation at the Washington Conference in 1921–22. He also took law courses at George Washington University and received an LL.M. degree in 1922. At this time, he came to the attention of C. T. Wang (Wang Cheng-t'ing, q.v.), who was the head of the Chinese delegation to the Washington Conference.

After returning to China in 1922, Hsü Mo became professor of law and political science at Nankai University. He gave political science, comparative constitution, and international law courses. During the academic year 1925–26 he also served as dean of the university's college of arts. In 1926 he was made a member of the Chinese Bar Association in Tientsin. He also served as chief editor of the *I Shih Pao*, an influential Catholic newspaper at Tientsin, and wrote special articles on international affairs for it.

Late in 1926 Hsü Mo resigned from Nankai and moved to Shanghai, where he established a private law practice. In January 1927 the Provisional Court of the International Settlement was inaugurated at Shanghai as a concession to Chinese demands for judicial sovereignty. Because of his legal training and his familiarity with Anglo-American law and jurisprudence, Hsü was appointed to the court as a judge. He accepted the position eagerly, for he viewed the establishment of the Shanghai Provisional Court as a preliminary step toward the reassertion of China's legal independence,

the abolition of extraterritoriality, and the abrogation of the unequal treaties. In late 1927 he became president of the district court at Sungkiang, Kiangsu.

With the emergence of a center of political authority at Nanking in the spring of 1928, new opportunities arose in the field of foreign affairs. Through the introduction of Wunsz King (Chin Wen-ssu), who had been one class ahead of him at Peiyang University, Hsü Mo entered the ministry of foreign affairs as a counselor. In June 1928 C. T. Wang was made minister of foreign affairs. At Wang's request, Hsü became his chief aide. In the following six months, he helped Wang to conclude twelve new tariff agreements with as many countries. From January 1929 until January 1932 Hsü served as chief of the ministry's European and American affairs department. In 1929 he served briefly as special commissioner of foreign affairs to deal with the abolition of extraterritorial rights in Shanghai. He also assisted C. T. Wang in gaining the restitution to China of Weihaiwei, reaching an agreement with France regarding Tonkin, signing a new tariff agreement with Japan, and concluding commercial treaties with Greece, Poland, and Czechoslovakia.

Japanese aggression in Manchuria in September 1931 and the attack at Shanghai in January 1932 shifted the focus of Chinese diplomatic attention to the Japanese threat. During the latter part of 1931 Hsü Mo served as acting chief of the Asian affairs department of the ministry of foreign affairs. In January 1932 he became administrative vice minister. He was promoted to political vice minister in June, succeeding Kuo T'ai-ch'i (q.v.). From 1932 to 1941 Hsü played a key role in molding, stabilizing, and administering Chinese foreign policy.

In 1941, at his own request, Hsü Mo was appointed minister to Australia, with the rank of ambassador, although his seniority and record of service qualified him for more prominent posts. He served there during the remaining war years until 1945. The Australians thought him an eloquent public speaker, and Melbourne University awarded him an honorary LL.D. degree.

As the war drew to a close, Hsü Mo, as one of China's most experienced diplomats, was drawn into the postwar planning. Early in 1945 he participated in the work of the Committee of Jurists, which met in Washington from 9 to 20

April to prepare the draft statute of the International Court of Justice. At the United Nations Conference on International Organization in San Francisco, Hsü played an active and constructive role as the Chinese representative on the committee which drafted the section of the United Nations Charter dealing with the settlement of disputes. He also served as ambassador to Turkey in 1945–46.

On 6 February 1946 Hsü was one of thirteen men elected to the International Court of Justice on the first ballot. After three years of service at The Hague, he was reelected for a second term of nine years. Hsü suffered a heart attack and died on 28 June 1956 in the Netherlands.

Hsü Pei-hung   徐 悲 鴻
West. Péon Ju

Hsü Pei-hung (19 July 1895–26 September 1953), artist, was best known for his mastery of both Chinese and Western painting techniques and for his powerful studies of galloping horses.

A native of the Ihsing district of Kiangsu, Hsü Pei-hung was the eldest of six children; he had two brothers and three sisters. His father, Hsü Ta-chang, was a village schoolmaster and craftsman who also taught painting. Hsü Pei-hung began learning to paint at an early age. By the time he was 17, he was helping to support his family by teaching art at several schools in his native district. After his father died in 1914, the young artist went to Shanghai. At first he led a hand-to-mouth existence, and at one point he was forced to return home. But he soon went back to the city and managed to sell a few paintings. By 1916 his work had begun to attract some notice. About this time, he began to study French.

In 1917 Hsü spent nine months studying in Japan. He then secured a post in the newly organized art department at Peking Normal College. In the spring of 1919, through the recommendation of Ts'ai Yuan-p'ei (q.v.), the chancellor of Peking University, the ministry of education awarded him a scholarship for study in France. He went to Paris and studied for a time at the Academie Julien. He then enrolled at L'Ecole des Beaux Arts, which was under the direction of Paul Albert Besnard.

Hsü received much encouragement and advice from Pascal Adolphe-Jean Dagnan-Bouveret, a fashionable portrait painter of the period. During his first two years in Paris, Hsü exhibited his work at the Salon des Artistes Français and the Societé National des Beaux Arts. However, he sold only one painting, for which he received F.1,000. His financial situation became difficult when the Chinese government, because of political complications, defaulted in its payment of scholarship money to Chinese students abroad.

Hsü went to Berlin in 1921 and remained there until 1923. He then went back to Paris. In the winter of 1925 he returned to China, visiting Malaya on the way. He made a second trip to Europe in 1926 and finally returned to Shanghai in the autumn of 1927.

Hsü Pei-hung was appointed professor in the newly opened art department of National Central University at Nanking in 1927. He also became head of the art section of Nan-kuo Academy of Fine Arts at Shanghai, which had been founded by T'ien Han (q.v.) to promote a new Western-style drama. That institution was a center of the bohemianism then fashionable in Shanghai, and Hsü Pei-hung affected the long hair, flowing tie, and Parisian mannerisms of the Quartier Latin. In 1929 he was appointed head of the department of fine arts at Peking University, but he resigned in the autumn and resumed direction of the department at Nanking. He soon abandoned European dress for the Chinese gown, an outward change which coincided with a new, and essentially Chinese, development in his painting. He laid aside his palette and oils and took up the Chinese brush again. His painting now combined the free style of the Chinese brush and ink with a Western knowledge of anatomy and academic form. With Hsü Pei-hung as its presiding spirit, Nanking became a flourishing center of the new art in China.

In 1931 a highly successful exhibition of Hsü Pei-hung's paintings was held at Brussels; it was the first showing of modern Chinese art in that city. In May 1933 Hsü was invited to Paris as his country's representative to an exhibition of modern Chinese paintings held in the Musée Nationale des Ecoles Etrangères. In November, the Berlin Artists' Association invited him to show his own work. He accompanied the modern Chinese painting exhibition to

Frankfurt, Brussels, and Milan. Early in 1934 he was invited to take it to Moscow and Leningrad. He returned to China that summer.

In 1935 Hsü went to Kweilin to organize the Kwangsi Provincial College of Art, which later was headed by his student Chang An-chih. In 1937 Hsü's work was exhibited at Canton, Hong Kong, and Changsha. After the Sino-Japanese war broke out, his department at Nanking moved with the university to Chungking, the wartime capital. In 1938 he made a tour of Indonesia and Malaya, where an exhibition of his work was held in Singapore. The proceeds were donated to famine relief in China. In 1939 he went to India at the invitation of Rabindranath Tagore, and in 1940 he exhibited his paintings in Santiniketan and Calcutta. The following year, he held exhibitions in Kuala Lumpur and Penang, and on both occasions the sales proceeds were given to Chinese famine relief.

Hsü Pei-hung returned to Chungking in 1942, where he became director of the National Art Research Institute founded by the Academia Sinica. In 1944 he became seriously ill; he never regained his health completely. He returned to Peking in 1946 as director of the Academy of Fine Arts. He refused to be evacuated when the Nationalist authorities fled south in the winter of 1948 and retained his Peking post until his death in 1953. He had to conform to the Communist pattern in the arts, but his work was easily reconciled with the new tenets. In addition to his direction of the freshly named Central Institute of Fine Arts at Peking, he was elected chairman of the China Artists' Association and a delegate to the Chinese People's Political Consultative Conference. But Hsü Pei-hung was by then a sick man, and in 1951 he suffered a stroke which virtually put an end to his working life. After his death, he was extolled as one of the great artists of modern China, and his house was turned into a memorial museum.

Hsü married three times. The first two unions were dissolved. He had four children, two by his second wife and two by his third wife.

Hsü Pei-hung was an artist who could adapt his impeccable technique to any medium and who painted a wide variety of subjects in several styles. His many works included portraits and landscapes in the Western academic manner, figure drawings, animal studies, and large narrative compositions, as well as a series of flower, tree, and bird studies in traditional Chinese style. He mastered the realistic technique of European oil painting and draftmanship to a degree attained by no other Chinese artist of the period. That mastery was typified by two of the large compositions with almost life-size figures which Hsü painted at Nanking between 1930 and 1933. One of them, "The Five Hundred Retainers of T'ien Heng," depicts a group of more than 20 people listening in sorrow to the news of a messenger who has just dismounted from his horse. The central figure in the group is a self-portrait of the artist. The arrangement is in the best academic tradition; the drawing is sound; and the anatomy is impeccable. However, to the Western observer there is little to set it apart from hundreds of narrative canvases painted in the art schools of Europe during the early years of this century. The same may be said of "Waiting for Our Liberator," which shows a group of country people in a landscape with trees and a grazing buffalo. The scene epitomizes the studied grouping of the life classes, and the fact that the figures are Chinese seems only to emphasize the contrived effect. An extension of this method may be seen in a much later composition entitled "Yu Kung Moves the Mountain," a mythological work of 1940. In this painting, the artist has again experimented by attempting to combine large-scale Western narrative style with Chinese method and subject, a constant preoccupation throughout his career.

Hsü Pei-hung's exhaustive exploration of Western academism had deep influence on the traditional Chinese-style paintings which were his most important contribution to the art of his time. Among both Chinese and Western art lovers, Hsü's name is most readily associated with his powerful studies of galloping horses. Hsü Pei-hung's horses are wholly Chinese in conception, but reflect the strong influence of Western visual naturalism. The group of chalk and wash life drawings of horses he made in 1939 demonstrates how much his Chinese paintings owed to his entirely Western grasp of form and anatomy. Horses also appear in many of his earlier narrative compositions in the Western style. In the purely Chinese studies, the sheer verve of Hsü Pei-hung's handling of this traditional medium transmutes the

Western realism of the prancing and snorting animals.

Trees and birds also were among Hsü's favorite subjects. The indirect effect of Western naturalism may also be seen in these paintings, although many of them are completely Oriental. His "Black Pig" of 1935 and his "Eagle" of 1940 show Hsü's direct descent from the masters of the past, but in a number of his compositions of animals, birds, and trees he used a new approach to pictorial design, combining a fresh element of representation with the bold simplicity of the old literati painters. Some of his most successful works were portrait drawings. A pencil drawing of Gandhi done about 1940, chalk drawings of a woman's head done in 1942, and two sensitive brush drawings of his wife done in 1943 all bear eloquent testimony to his skill in portraiture.

Collections of Hsü's paintings include: *Hsü Pei-hung hua-fan* [model paintings by Hsü Pei-hung], Shanghai, 1939; *Hsü Pei-hung hua hsuan-chi* [selected paintings of Hsü Pei-hung], Peking, 1954; *Hsü Pei-hung ti ts'ai-mo hua* [Hsü Pei-hung's watercolor paintings], Peking, 1956; and *Hsü Pei-hung yu-hua* [oil paintings by Hsü Pei-hung], Peking, 1960.

Hsü Shih-ch'ang   徐 世 昌
T. Chü-jen   菊 人
H. Tung-hai   東 海

Hsü Shih-ch'ang (23 October 1855–6 June 1939), protégé of Yuan Shih-k'ai who in 1918 became the only man of civilian background to hold the presidency at Peking. After his retirement in June 1922, he devoted himself to literary and cultural pursuits.

Little is known of Hsü Shih-ch'ang's origins or early life. His forebears had been registered as natives of Tientsin, but for generations they had served as minor officials in Honan province, where Hsü probably was born and where he spent much of his youth. Although his family was poor, he received a traditional education. For a time, he made his living as a tutor in the family of a district magistrate in Honan. It was during this period that he made the aquaintance of Yuan Shih-k'ai; the two men became life-long friends. Financial assistance from Yuan enabled Hsü to go to Peking and take the

imperial examinations. He became a chü-jen in 1882, a chin-shih in 1886, and a compiler in the Hanlin Academy in 1889.

After a decade of routine service in the metropolitan bureaucracy, Hsü returned to Honan in 1896 when his mother died. At that time Yuan Shih-k'ai was in charge of training the Hsin-chien lu-chün [newly created army] at Hsiaochan, Chihli (Hopei). Hsü Shih-ch'ang, despite his civilian background, became chief of staff in Yuan's new military organization, thus beginning his long and intimate association with the Peiyang military clique. In 1901, after Yuan was appointed governor general of Chihli province, he established a military training center at Paoting and made Hsü the head of its staff organization. Two years later, when the imperial government established a commission for army reorganization (*see* Yuan Shih-k'ai), Hsü was appointed its senior administrative officer, with the rank of lieutenant general. In 1904 he was promoted to vice president of the Board of War, and early in 1905 he was made probationary grand councillor and acting president of the Board of War.

In July 1905 Hsü was appointed to a five-man special commission, which also included Tuan-fang (1861–1911; ECCP, II, 780–82), Tsai-tse, Shao-ying, and Tai Hung-tzu (1853–1910; T. Kuang-ju; H. Shao-huai, I-an), to study systems of government in the West. On 20 September, the group assembled at the Peking railroad station to embark on their mission. A bomb carried by the revolutionary assassin Wu Yueh exploded in the station, killing Wu and wounding two members of the commission. The trip was postponed, and Hsü was reassigned to new duties. He became president of the newly established Board of Police and, by the end of the year, a full member of the Grand Council.

In December 1906 Hsü Shih-ch'ang was sent on a special mission to Manchuria. The Ch'ing court viewed the presence of Russian military units in Manchuria after the Boxer Uprising and of Japanese troops during and after the Russo-Japanese war of 1904–5 as possible threats to China. The purpose of Hsü's mission was to survey the situation and to propose measures that would strengthen the influence of China in that region. Hsü proposed reorganizing the civil and military administration and instituting other far-reaching reforms in the Northeast. He also proposed various means by which

Japanese and Russian influence in Manchuria might be checked: official encouragement of Chinese settlement in areas that had formerly been the exclusive preserve of the Manchus; the construction of railroads and other Chinese-owned enterprises to compete with Russian and Japanese interests in the region; and the opening of Manchuria to foreign investment by nations other than Russia and Japan. An imperial edict of 20 April 1907 effected a comprehensive reorganization in Manchuria. The military governors, or chiang-chün, were abolished, and civil governors, or hsun-fu, were appointed in the provinces of Fengtien, Kirin, and Heilungkiang. All were under a governor general, or tsung-tu, of the Three Eastern Provinces. Hsü Shih-ch'ang became governor general, with T'ango Sha-yi (q.v.) as governor of Fengtien, Chu Chia-pao (d. 1923; T. Ching-t'ien) as governor of Kirin, and Ch'eng Te-ch'üan (d. 1930; T.H sueh-lou) as governor of Heilungkiang.

Hsü Shih-ch'ang proceeded to carry out many of the measures he had proposed in his report. A detailed record of his administration, published in 1911 as the *Tung-san-sheng cheng-lueh*, contained his official papers and reports on a number of subjects that engaged his attention: frontier affairs, Mongolian affairs, foreign relations, military affairs, civil administration, finance, education, the judicial system, agriculture, industry, commerce, and resolutions of the provincial assemblies in Manchuria. Hsü was assisted by several civilian protégés who were to become prominent in the republican period: Ch'ien Neng-hsün (1870–1924; T. Kan-ch'en), who later served in Peking as minister of interior (1913, 1917–19) and premier (1918–19); Chou Shu-mou (1865–1925; T. Shao-p'u), who became governor of Heilungkiang in 1909 and later served as president of the p'ing-cheng-yuan [administrative court] under Yuan Shih-k'ai; and Chu Ch'i-chien (b. 1872; T. Kuei-hsin), who later served as minister of communications (1912) and minister of interior (1914–16) in Yuan's government.

After the accession to the throne of the Hsuan-t'ung emperor, P'u-yi (q.v.), and the dismissal of Yuan Shih-k'ai early in 1909, Hsü Shih-ch'ang was replaced as governor general by the Mongol Hsi-liang and was recalled to Peking. Although he had been closely associated with Yuan for many years, Hsü continued to enjoy the favor of the court. In the final years of the Ch'ing dynasty, when members of the imperial clan were seeking to reassert direct control over all branches of the imperial administration, he held several top positions in the metropolitan bureaucracy. In 1909 he was appointed president of the Board of Posts and Communications and director of the Tientsin-Pukow railway. In the following year he was promoted to the office of grand secretary and to renewed membership on the Grand Council. In May 1911, as a result of growing pressure from the newly convened Parliament in Peking, the imperial court announced the formation of a cabinet to replace the Grand Council. The cabinet, headed by Prince Ch'ing, was dominated by Manchu princes and nobles. Hsü, as one of two associate premiers, was the ranking Chinese member.

Throughout this period, Hsü Shih-ch'ang continued to associate with his colleagues in the Peiyang group and to correspond with Yuan Shih-k'ai. After the outbreak of the revolt at Wuchang in October 1911, Hsü was instrumental in persuading the Manchu regent, Prince Ch'un, to recall Yuan from his enforced retirement; and it was also through Hsü that Yuan presented the six conditions on which he would consent to resume office. However, after helping Yuan to establish himself as the *de facto* ruler at Peking and to complete the arrangements for the abdication of the Manchus, Hsü resigned from office as a gesture of loyalty to the dynasty. He withdrew from public life to live in Tsingtao. With the help of a group of his former assistants in the government, he compiled a volume of his official papers (memorials, official correspondence, and official telegrams) for the years from 1904 to 1911 and published it in 1914 as the *T'ui-keng-t'ang cheng-shu*.

In 1914 Yuan Shih-k'ai finally induced Hsü to accept a position in his government at Peking. By that time, Yuan had dissolved the National Assembly and had reorganized the cabinet as the Cheng-shih-t'ang [office of government affairs]. To head this body, Yuan created the office of Kuo-wu-ch'ing [secretary of state]; it was this post which he persuaded his old friend to accept (1 May 1914). Hsü Shih-ch'ang enjoyed the prestige of being Yuan's first minister, but he wielded no real power. In 1915, when Yuan's monarchical plans became known, Hsü withdrew to his estate at Shui-chu-ts'un in Honan. In making preparations to ascend the throne late in 1915, Yuan accorded Hsü the distinction of being one of the Sung-shan ssu-yu [four friends of Sung-shan]—the others being Chang Chien, Chao Erh-sun (qq.v), and Li Ching-hsi—a group given the special privilege of treating Yuan as their personal friend rather than as their monarch. Despite this and other inducements, Hsü remained in retirement until Yuan, because of the revolt of the southwestern provinces, agreed in March 1916 to abolish the monarchy. Hsü then resumed office as Kuo-wu-ch'ing. Because he failed to bring about a reconciliation between Yuan and the southern leaders, he resigned in favor of Tuan Ch'i-jui (q.v.) after only a month in office and returned to Honan. On 5 June 1916, the day before Yuan's death, Hsü was summoned to Peking for a final conference, and, as Yuan's oldest friend, he was entrusted with the management of Yuan's family affairs.

In November 1916 Hsü went to Peking to bring about a reconciliation between Tuan Ch'i-jui, the premier, and Li Yuan-hung (q.v.), the president. During the attempt to restore the Manchu dynasty in the summer of 1917 (*see* Chang Hsün) and the ensuing rivalry between Tuan Ch'i-jui and Feng Kuo-chang (q.v.), Hsü refused to take sides. Because of his reputation as a mediator and his neutral position in politics, he had come to be regarded as an impartial elder statesman. When Feng and Tuan resigned from their positions as president and premier in 1918, many people hoped that Hsü would become president, for they believed that he would be able to resolve the differences between the Peiyang factions and between the northern and southern governments. The pro-Tuan Anhwei faction urged Hsü's election to the presidency, believing it to be a convenient means of neutralizing Feng Kuo-chang's power without impairing its own control of political affairs. Accordingly, on 4 September 1918 the National Assembly elected Hsü to succeed Feng Kuo-chang as president. He assumed office on 10 October 1918.

Hsü Shih-ch'ang was able to wield a certain degree of influence within the Peking government through several former protégés, including Ch'ien Neng-hsün, the new premier; Ts'ao Ju-lin (q.v.), the minister of communications; and Wang I-t'ang (q.v.), the titular head of the pro-Tuan Anfu Club. However, Hsü soon found that he was powerless to implement his policies of conciliation between north and south and that he was, in fact, little more than a puppet of Tuan Ch'i-jui and his supporters. His efforts to achieve a settlement at a peace conference held in Shanghai early in 1919 were thwarted by the refusal of Tuan and his followers to consider the southern government's demands that the "old National Assembly" be restored in Peking. Hsü's position as mediator was further undermined because his election to office was not recognized by the southern leaders, who contested the legitimacy of the "new National Assembly," which had elected him president.

Hsü Shih-ch'ang soon was confronted by popular reaction to the terms of the Treaty of Versailles, which awarded former German concessions in Shantung to Japan. Hsü believed that China should sign the treaty; and following the May Fourth demonstrations in 1919 he issued orders for the arrest of the students involved in the attacks made on Ts'ao Ju-lin and other pro-Japanese officials, and publicly praised these officials for their service to the nation. It was only with great reluctance that he sent belated instructions to Paris in June 1919 to cancel his orders to sign the treaty and that he accepted the resignations of Ts'ao Ju-lin and his colleagues. Because of these actions, Hsü aroused the anger of the Canton government and of students and young intellectuals throughout China.

The steady encroachment upon his already limited authority by his powerful military colleagues in the Peiyang group left Hsü little scope for the exercise of authority. To improve his political position, he resorted to a tactic formerly employed to advantage by Yuan Shih-k'ai—playing one faction against another. Thus, when Tuan Ch'i-jui and the Anhwei faction were in power, he sought to counter the influence of Tuan's right-hand man, Hsü Shu-cheng (q.v.), by supporting another of Tuan's lieutenants, Chin Yun-p'eng, for the position of premier. At the same time, he secretly intrigued with Chang Tso-lin (q.v.) and the leaders of the Chihli clique in an attempt to break the Anhwei clique's monopoly of power in Peking. After Tuan Ch'i-jui was defeated in the Chihli-Anhwei war of 1920, Hsü sought to extract maximum political advantage from the rift between Chang Tso-lin and the Chihli leaders, Ts'ao K'un and Wu P'ei-fu (qq.v.).

Despite his deftness in the art of political manipulation, Hsü was unable to diminish the power of the militarists. After the defeat of Chang Tso-lin in the first Chihli-Fengtien war of 1922 he became an obstacle to the ambitions of the victorious Chihli leaders, who demanded his resignation. On 2 June 1922 Hsü stepped down from the presidency, to be succeeded a few days later by Li Yuan-hung, the candidate of the Chihli faction. Hsü Shih-ch'ang left Peking for Tientsin, where he lived quietly.

After the Japanese seized the Northeast in 1931, Hsü was among the members of the Pei-yang group who were approached by Japanese agents who tried to persuade them to participate in the puppet regime of Manchoukuo. He refused their offer. From 1931 until his death in June 1939 he continued to resist the Japanese, who made several attempts to win his co-operation.

Hsü Shih-ch'ang maintained a strong interest in Chinese cultural traditions throughout his life, and he became an important patron and entrepreneur in the field of Chinese letters. Although he had spent most of his early life in Honan, he considered himself a native of Chihli. Moved, perhaps, by the traditionally strong feeling among Chinese for their ancestral locality, he sought to publicize the cultural heritage of his native province by compiling a number of works by and about earlier scholars of the area. In 1915 he published the *Ta-Ch'ing Chi-fu shu-cheng*, which was a bibliography of works by Chihli authors of the Ch'ing period. He developed a particular interest in two pragmatist philosophers of the early Ch'ing period, Yen Yuan (1635–1704; ECCP, II, 912–15) and Li Kung (1659–1733; ECCP, I, 475–79). Among Hsü's works concerning these men were the *Yen Li i-shu*, a collection of their writings, and the *Yen Li yü-yao*, a selection of important passages from their works. His biographies of these scholars and their disciples were published under the title *Yen Li shih-ch'eng chi*. In 1919 Hsü issued a presidential order adding Yen and Li to the sages honored in the Temple of Confucius. In 1920 a society, the Ssu-ts'un hsüeh-hui, was formed to promote interest in their teachings and in the reissuing of their works.

Hsü Shih-ch'ang sponsored the compilation of other works on the philosophy and literature of the Ch'ing period, the most significant of which was the *Ch'ing-ju hsüeh-an* (which was not published until 1940), containing biographies of some 1,690 Ch'ing scholars. This work emulated the *Sung Yuan hsüeh-an* and the *Ming-ju hsüeh-an*, compiled early in the Ch'ing dynasty by Huang Tsung-hsi (1610–95; ECCP, I, 351–54). With complete disregard for the vernacular literature movement, Hsü set up within the presidential palace the Wan-ch'ing-i shih-she (Wan-ch'ing-i being Hsü's studio name during his presidency), a literary society devoted to the study and writing of poetry in the traditional style. An important product of this society was a compilation of Ch'ing poetry, the *Wan-ch'ing-i shih-hui*, which was published at Tientsin in 1929.

Hsü Shih-ch'ang's poems and essays appeared in a number of collections, the earliest of which, the *T'ui-keng-t'ang chi*, was published at Tientsin in 1914. The *Shui-chu-ts'un-jen shih-chi* appeared in 1920, and the *Shui-chu-ts'un-jen chi* in 1928. The *Kuei-yun-lou t'i-hua shih* appeared in the fortnightly magazine *Yi Lin Shuen Kan* between 1928 and 1929 and later was published as a book. Several issues of this periodical contained reproductions of Hsü's paintings, most of which were landscapes.

Despite his political involvements, Hsü was a serious student of Taoism, and it was largely because of his financial backing that the so-called White Cloud edition of the complete Taoist canon (*Tao-tsang*), the first new edition to appear since the Ming dynasty, was published by the Commercial Press from 1923 to 1926. A survey of economic and educational conditions in China after the European war entitled *Ou-chan-hou chih Chung-kuo ching-chi yü chiao-yü* (translated into French and published in Paris in 1922 as *La Chine après la guerre*) appeared in Hsü's name in 1920. A rather mild exposition of China's postwar aspirations, this work, as a declaration of policy, lacked both force and precision. It later became known that Huang Fu (q.v.) had written it for Hsü. Before then, Hsü was awarded an honorary D.Litt. degree by the University of Paris.

Hsü Shih-ch'ang married twice, and both of his wives were daughters of officials in Honan. He had one daughter; because he had no son, he adopted as his heir Hsü Hsü-chih, one of the sons of his younger brother, Hsü Shih-kuang (d. 1924; T. Yu-mei, H. Shao-ch'ing). Hsü

Shih-kuang had served as prefect of Tsinan when Yuan Shih-k'ai was governor of that province. Another brother, Hsü Shih-chang (b. 1888; T. Tuan-fu), had been managing director of the Tientsin-Pukow railway, vice minister of communications (1920–22), and director general of the currency bureau (1922).

Hsü Shih-ying
T. Ching-jen

許 世 英
靜 仁

Hsü Shih-ying (1872–13 October 1964), official in the Ch'ing, Peiyang, and National governments whose most important posts were those of premier (December 1925–March 1926) and Chinese ambassador to Japan (February 1936–January 1938). He was also known for his famine-relief activities.

Chiupu (Chihteh), Anhwei, was the birthplace of Hsü Shih-ying. He received his primary education at a local school established by his clan, where he was the youngest of ten students. When he was 12, his father sent him to study under a tutor, T'ung Wen-ch'ü, in Wangchiang hsien. Hsü studied under T'ung for 12 years and established himself as a classical scholar by passing the examinations for the chü-jen and pakung degrees. In 1897 he was appointed to the Board of Punishments at Peking, with the rank of seventh grade junior metropolitan official.

Hsü reported for duty in Peking in May 1898, shortly before the beginning of the Hundred Days Reform (see K'ang Yu-wei). He became assistant departmental keeper of drafts in the Chekiang division of the Board of Punishments, working under Liu Kuang-ti. Hsü and Liu soon became friends. Liu, however, was among the reformers who were executed in 1898 after the Hundred Days Reform ended with the empress dowager's coup against the Kuang-hsu emperor. Hsü developed a distaste for the work of the Board of Punishments, and although he was promoted to departmental keeper of drafts in the Chihli division, he left Peking in the spring of 1900 and went to Szechwan, where his father's friend Chou Fu was provincial treasurer. Hsü hoped to obtain a post as a hsien magistrate. He nearly drowned when the junk on which he was traveling sank in the Yangtze rapids, and he arrived in Chengtu in June only to be advised that, although he could be a hsien magistrate if he chose, the rapid spread of the Boxer Uprising would create better opportunities for him in Peking. He accepted this advice and began the long journey back to Peking.

When he reached Hankow, Hsü learned that the Eight-Power international expedition was nearing Peking and that the empress dowager and the Kuang-hsu emperor had fled the capital. He then went to his home in Anhwei. About a month later he received a telegram informing him that the Board of Punishments needed personnel and asking him to proceed promptly to Sian. Hsü arrived at Sian in October. In addition to his job as departmental keeper of drafts in the Chihli division, he received the equivalent post for Szechwan, where some 4,000 cases were outstanding. He won a reputation as an able official by clearing up all of these cases before the imperial government returned to Peking in 1902. He was promoted to the rank of sixth grade assistant in 1902.

Because Hsü failed to pass the 1903 special examinations for the chin-shih degree, he continued to work in the Board of Punishments. In October 1905 the Bureau of Police Affairs was organized, and Hsü became senior assistant in the bureau's administrative section. He also continued to handle special cases for the Board of Punishments. By the end of 1906 he had become a fourth grade official.

When Hsü Shih-ch'ang (q.v.) became viceroy of the newly established Three Eastern Provinces of Manchuria in April 1907, he requested the services of Hsü Shih-ying in setting up the needed legal organs in the Northeast. Hsü Shih-ying was named to the high court at Mukden and was assigned to formulate proposals for judicial organization. In the autumn of 1908 he became associate chief justice of that court. At Mukden, Hsü came to know the Japanese consul, Hirota Koki, and the vice consul, Arita Hachiro. Their friendship with Hsü was to become important in Sino-Japanese relations.

In 1910 Hsü accompanied Hsü Ch'ien (q.v.) on a mission to Europe and the United States to study judicial structures and prison conditions. He attended the Eighth International Congress on Prison Reform, held at Washington, D.C. The mission returned to China in the spring of 1911. That November, Hsü Shih-ying was appointed judicial commissioner of Shansi, then under the governorship of Chang Hsi-luan. A few months later, he became provincial treasurer. Hsü joined Chang in urging the Manchu court to give way to the early establishment of the republic. In 1912, after the republic had been established, Chang was appointed tutuh [military governor] of Chihli (Hopei) province. On his recommendation, Hsü was made chief justice of the Supreme Court at Peking in May. In July, Hsü became minister of justice in the cabinet of Lu Cheng-hsiang, and Chang Tsung-hsiang (q.v.) succeeded him as chief justice.

Hsü Shih-ying, Hsü Ch'ien, Ch'en Lu, and Ch'en Chin-t'ao had organized the Kuo-min kung-chin hui, one of the many small political parties that had sprung up after the Wuchang revolt of October 1911. In August 1912 the Kuo-min kung-chin hui and two other parties were merged with the T'ung-meng-hui to become the Kuomintang. However, when Kuomintang leader Sung Chiao-jen (q.v.) was assassinated in March 1913 by adherents of Yuan Shih-k'ai, Hsü Shih-ying refused to permit the Kuomintang at Shanghai to establish a special court to try the case, insisting that the local court had jurisdiction. The case became a political rather than a judicial cause, and one of the alleged killers, Ying Kuei-hsing, was assassinated in January 1914 after escaping from jail.

In September 1913 Hsü was replaced as minister of justice by Liang Ch'i-ch'ao (q.v.), a member of the Progressive party, which was supporting Yuan against the Kuomintang in the so-called second revolution. Hsü was appointed civil governor of Fengtien in November, and on 4 January 1914 Yuan Shih-k'ai named him to the newly established Political Council, which had been formed to replace the Parliament (dissolved on 10 January). After Hsü helped draft a new constitution, he became civil governor of Fukien on 3 May.

After the death of Yuan Shih-k'ai in 1916, Tuan Ch'i-jui (q.v.) formed a cabinet on 30 June in which Hsü was minister of interior. However, on 12 July Hsü was replaced by Sung Heng-i and was named minister of communications. In 1917 he was forced to resign after being implicated in a bribery case which concerned the purchase of rolling-stock for the Tientsin-Pukow railway. He was brought before a Peking court, but was acquitted of the charges. In 1918 he became managing director of the Hua Yi Bank, a Sino-Italian enterprise.

Hsü returned to public office in September 1921 as civil governor and director general of famine relief for Anhwei. However, he was forced to resign because of public opposition. In November 1922 he was named minister of justice in Wang Ta-hsieh's cabinet, but the cabinet was dissolved before Hsü reached Peking. He became director of the bureau of aeronautics in February 1923, but was relieved of that post when Ts'ao K'un became president in November. Hsü spent much of the next year representing Tuan Ch'i-jui in negotiations between Sun Yat-sen and the northern factions of Tuan and Chang Tso-lin (q.v.) for the formation of a tripartite alliance against Ts'ao K'un and Wu P'ei-fu in Peking. Hsü Shu-cheng (q.v.) also represented Tuan at these meetings. Hsü Shih-ying met with Sun Yat-sen at Shaokuan on 4 October 1924 and reached a tentative agreement. Shortly after Hsü returned to Tientsin, Feng Yü-hsiang (q.v.) staged a coup against Wu P'ei-fu, occupying Peking and forcing Ts'ao K'un from the presidency, and Tuan Ch'i-jui emerged from retirement at Tientsin to assume leadership of the new provisional government. On 2 November, Sun Yat-sen announced that he had accepted an invitation to go to Peking and participate in negotiations for a new government. On 24 November, Hsü Shih-ying, now Tuan Ch'i-jui's confidential political strategist, received the post of secretary general in Tuan's government. By the time Sun Yat-sen arrived at Tientsin on 4 December, Tuan's cabinet had formulated principles to govern the organization of the projected Rehabilitation Conference which he could not accept, and he had announced a "minimum program" for the Kuomintang which Tuan could not accept. On 4 December, Hsü, as secretary general of the conference's preparatory committee, and Yeh Kung-cho went to Tientsin to confer with Sun, but no agreement was reached. Sun left Tientsin for Peking on 31 December. The conference, with Hsü serving as its secretary general, convened on 1 February 1925, but Sun Yat-sen and the Kuomintang refused to participate in it. Sun died in Peking on 12 March.

On 26 December 1925 Tuan Ch'i-jui appointed Hsü Shih-ying premier. Hsü's

Kuomintang-oriented cabinet included Kuomintang member Yü Yu-jen (q.v.) as minister of interior, C. T. Wang (Wang Cheng-t'ing) as minister of foreign affairs, Ch'en Chin-t'ao as minister of finance, and Chia Te-yao as minister of war. Hsü, to enlist Kuomintang support for Tuan, drafted a telegram for Tuan's signature in which he was to announce the handing over of his authority to Yü Yu-jen as of 16 January 1926. The telegram was not issued. Some of Tuan's supporters rose against Hsü, and he was forced to flee to the Legation Quarter for safety. Yü Yu-jen refused to take up the post of minister of interior.

By this time, Feng Yü-hsiang was in retreat before the forces of Chang Tso-lin, and Tuan's hold on power at Peking was becoming shaky. Hsü Shih-ying returned to office, but he submitted his resignation on 15 February 1926. Tuan granted him a leave of absence and appointed Chia Te-yao acting premier. On 4 March he accepted the resignations of Hsü and his cabinet, and about a month later his regime fell.

Hsü soon went to Shanghai and helped organize the Kiangsu-Chekiang-Anhwei Joint Society to oppose Sun Ch'uan-fang (q.v.) and to support local autonomy. For security reasons, the society's headquarters was established in the International Settlement. In early January 1927 Sun issued orders for the arrest of Hsü and his group and requested the foreign authorities to halt his activities. Hsü went to Hong Kong for safety, but returned to Shanghai in March, after Sun's forces had been defeated.

In the spring of 1928 the National Government gave Hsü a modest appointment as chairman of a relief committee for Chihli and Shantung. He became chairman of the National Famine Relief Commission in January 1930, and he also served as chairman of the National Government's financial affairs commission. Relief matters, notably in connection with the Yangtze flood of 1931, kept him busy and necessitated frequent travel during the next five years. In 1932 he formed the Shanghai War Zone Refugee Relief Association to give relief to persons afflicted by the fighting between Japanese and Chinese forces in January.

In February 1936, when the National Government was making a new attempt to settle the problem of north China, Hsü Shih-ying was sent to Tokyo as ambassador. Arita Hachiro became Japan's foreign minister in April 1936, and Hirota Koki, his predecessor in that post, became premier. Hsü had only a secondary role to play in the Sino-Japanese negotiations. He renewed the friendship that he had established with Arita and Hirota at Mukden some 30 years earlier. After the signing in November of the Anti-Comintern agreement between Japan and Germany, Arita spoke to Hsü and implied that China's participation in the pact would be welcomed. Hsü, on instructions from Nanking, gave China's refusal. After the Sian Incident (see Chiang Kai-shek) in December, the National Government's Japan policy became rigid and resistant. In March 1937 Hsü was called to Nanking for consultation with Wang Ch'ung-hui (q.v.), who had become foreign minister. Hsü was still consulting with Wang about ways to improve Sino-Japanese relations when the Lukouchiao Incident of 7 July began the Sino-Japanese war. Hsü hurriedly returned to Tokyo and called on Hirota in an attempt to ensure the preservation of Chinese rights in the settlement of the north China "incident." Hirota responded by requesting non-interference by the National Government, and Japanese aggression continued. When China signed a non-aggression pact with the Soviet Union in August, Hsü undertook to explain this "purely pacific instrument" to Hirota, informing him that China was "ready to conclude a similar treaty with Japan if Japan wishes."

War was not declared, but peace was not forthcoming. The intervention of the League of Nations, the attempted mediation of German Ambassador to China Oskar Trautmann, and the efforts of Hsü Shih-ying at Tokyo were equally fruitless. Hsü was recalled from Japan in January 1938. After arriving in Wuhan, he predicted that China would win the war. In June, he was appointed to the People's Political Council, created by the National Government to rally support for the struggle against the Japanese. He also became acting chairman of the National Famine Relief Commission and chairman of the Air-Raid Salvage Committee. He was confirmed as chairman of the Famine Relief Commission in December 1944. Hsü, who had tried to refuse the Tokyo ambassadorship on the grounds of advancing years, neither sought nor received major political appointments. In February 1945 he was given the title of senior adviser to the National Government.

From April 1947 to March 1949 Hsü served the National Government as member of the State Council and as chairman of the Mongolian and Tibetan Affairs Commission. In the summer of 1950 he went to Taiwan, where he was named high adviser in the presidential office. After the alleged discovery in August 1955 of espionage activities among the subordinates of Sun Li-jen, Hsü was appointed to the commission charged with investigating the matter. He lived quietly in Taiwan and died in Taipei, at the age of 91, on 13 October 1964.

Hsü and his wife, Shen Yi-jen, had three sons and two daughters.

Hsü Shu-cheng　　徐樹錚
T. Yu-cheng　　又錚

Hsü Shu-cheng (4 November 1880–30 December 1925), held many important offices in Peking as the most powerful deputy of Tuan Ch'i-jui (q.v.) in the period from 1912 to 1920 and co-founder of the Anfu Club. His actions in extending Chinese authority in Outer Mongolia after 1918 turned the Mongols against China and were a chief cause of the Chihli-Anhwei conflict of 1920. He was assassinated at Langfang in December 1925.

The youngest of seven children, Hsü Shu-cheng was born in Hsiaohsien, Kiangsu. His father, Hsü Chung-ching, held the pa-kung-sheng degree (similar to the chü-jen) and taught school in the village. The young Hsü proved to be a gifted student, and he was sent to Hsuchow to study in 1889. He enrolled at the district school and passed the examinations for the sheng-yuan degree in 1892. Four years later, he became a salaried sheng-yuan.

In 1901 Hsü went to Tsinan and sent a memorial on current affairs and troop-training to Yuan Shih-k'ai, then the governor of Shantung. Although Yuan did not receive him or give him an appointment, his trip to Tsinan was not fruitless, for he came to the attention of Tuan Ch'i-jui (q.v.). At the end of the year Hsü joined Tuan's staff as a clerk. In 1905, with Tuan's support, he went to Japan to prepare for entrance into the Shikan Gakkō [military academy] as a government student.

He enrolled in the infantry course at the Shikan Gakkō in 1908 as a member of the seventh class. After being graduated in 1909, he returned to China and reportedly received a commission in Tuan Ch'i-jui's 6th Division. When Tuan received command of the First Army at the end of 1911, Hsü became his chief of staff.

After the republic was established, Tuan was appointed minister of war in Yuan Shih-k'ai's government at Peking. Hsü Shu-cheng acted as chief of the ministry's military studies office. In September 1912 he was appointed chief of the remount depot and was assigned to handle matters pertaining to the general affairs office. He came to be known as "the spirit of Tuan Ch'i-jui." In May 1914 Hsü was appointed vice minister of war. Tuan Ch'i-jui decided to oppose Yuan's plan to become monarch, and he resigned on 31 May 1915. Soon after Tuan departed, Hsü, who supported Tuan's stand, was impeached for allegedly padding the cost of foreign munitions in his reports. He was relieved of his post on 26 June. Hsü remained in Peking and established the Cheng-chih Middle School. When Ts'ai O and T'ang Chi-yao (qq.v.) took action against Yuan Shih-k'ai in December 1915, Hsü wrote Yuan a letter advising him to abandon his monarchical plan.

In April 1916 Yuan Shih-k'ai appointed Tuan Ch'i-jui premier and minister of war. Tuan proposed that Hsü Shu-cheng be made secretary general of the cabinet, but Yuan installed one of his own men, Wang Shih-t'ung, in that office and made Hsü deputy secretary general. After Yuan died in June and Li Yuan-hung (q.v.) succeeded to the presidency, Tuan again proposed that his trusted supporter be appointed secretary general of the cabinet. Li opposed the appointment, but he submitted to Tuan's wishes after Hsü Shih-ch'ang (q.v.) intervened in the matter.

The Peiyang faction began to split into the Chihli clique, led by Feng Kuo-chang (q.v.), and the Anhwei clique, led by Tuan Ch'i-jui. Hsü worked to increase the power of the premiership and to strip the presidency of all authority. He conferred on himself the right to speak at cabinet meetings and the power to initiate action. Hsü soon came into conflict with Sun Hung-i, the minister of interior, who sought to increase Li's power in order to curb Tuan. Hsü Shih-ch'ang was called upon to mediate their dispute. In November 1916, on Hsü Shih-ch'ang's recommendation, both men were removed from office.

Hsü Shu-cheng's power and influence were not diminished greatly by his removal from office. He played a major role in Tuan Ch'i-jui's action to break relations with Germany in March 1917. The question of whether China should oppose Germany and participate in the First World War assumed such proportions that Tuan Ch'i-jui was forced out of the premiership in May. However, after Chang Hsün (q.v.) carried out his monarchical plot, Li Yuan-hung issued an order on 2 July 1917 by which Tuan was restored to the premiership and was made minister of war. Li also ordered Feng Kuo-chang to assume the duties of the presidency. In August, Hsü Shu-cheng became vice minister of war, and China declared war on Germany. Hsü was a prime mover in the 1917–18 negotiations with the Japanese for the Nishihara loans, which supposedly were designed to enable China to create a model army. The increased antagonism of the Chihli faction toward the Anhwei faction forced Tuan and Hsü to resign from office in November.

Hsü Shu-cheng, hoping to restore his chief to power, went to Mukden and received from Chang Tso-lin (q.v.) the loan of some Fengtien forces and the title of vice commander in chief of the Fengtien Army within the Great Wall. He established headquarters at Chünliangcheng, near Tientsin, and began to apply political pressure on Feng Kuo-chang. On 7 March 1918 he and Wang I-t'ang (q.v.) established the Anfu Club, which came to control the National Assembly. On 23 March, Feng issued a mandate reappointing Tuan Ch'i-jui premier.

Feng Kuo-chang and Tuan Ch'i-jui had come into conflict over the question of how to deal with Sun Yat-sen's government at Canton. Feng had proposed that negotiations be held, but Tuan and Hsü thought military force to be a better solution to the problem. In May 1918 Hsü ordered three Fengtien divisions to Hunan. However, Chang Tso-lin would not permit Hsü to act as if these troops were his own and ordered the three divisions to return to Manchuria. In mid-June, Hsü caused the assassination of Lu Chien-chang, a former military governor of Shensi who had opposed him. The action was to have repercussions, for Lu was

the uncle by marriage of Feng Yü-hsiang (q.v.). The Peking government had relieved Feng Yü-hsiang of command of the 16th Mixed Brigade in February. Tuan Ch'i-jui restored Feng to his post and made him defense commissioner of Ch'angte. Feng did not comment on the assassination or the appointment. At the end of July, Hsü incurred the wrath of Chang Tso-lin once again, this time for using funds appropriated to the Fengtien forces for other purposes. Chang rescinded Hsü's title as vice commander in chief of the Fengtien Army within the Great Wall.

The war participation bureau, with Tuan Ch'i-jui as its director, had been established to prepare China for war with Germany. In September 1918 Hsü succeeded Chin Yun-p'eng as co-director of the war participation bureau. After Hsü Shih-ch'ang assumed the presidency in October, Tuan resigned as premier, but retained his post as director of the bureau. Hsü became Tuan's chief of general staff. The following month, Hsü Shu-cheng, with the brevet rank of general, was sent to Japan for the ostensible purpose of observing the autumn military maneuvers. It has been reported that the real purpose of his mission was to discuss with high officials at Tokyo the matter of closer cooperation between the two nations in such areas as Manchuria. Hsü returned to China in mid-December 1918.

Hsü Shu-cheng then turned his attention to the problem of reasserting Chinese authority in Manchuria and Outer Mongolia. At Tuan's suggestion, in April 1919 he proposed a plan for "frontier pacification." A presidential mandate of 24 June abolished the war participation bureau and established a frontier defense bureau, with Tuan Ch'i-jui as its director general. Hsü was appointed high commissioner for northwestern frontier development and commander in chief of the Northwest Frontier Defense Army. The Chinese resident commissioner at Urga (Ulan Bator), Ch'en Yi, was instructed that he would continue to conduct negotiations with the Mongols and that Hsü would have authority only in military matters. Hsü arrived in Urga in late October determined to abolish Mongolian autonomy, which had been recognized by a Sino-Russian agreement in 1913 and reaffirmed in 1915. He disregarded the resident commissioner and presented his proposals directly to the Mongolian government.

When he encountered Mongol opposition, he threatened to arrest both the premier and the Hutukhtu. Under this pressure, the Mongol princes and ministers signed a petition for the abolition of autonomy. On 22 November 1919 Hsü Shih-ch'ang proclaimed the end of Outer Mongolian autonomy. Hsü Shu-cheng arrived in Peking two days later. At his urging, the post of resident commissioner was abolished and he was appointed rehabilitation commissioner of Outer Mongolia on 1 December. The following day, he was given the title of special envoy, with power to confer titles or withhold privileges. He then returned to Urga, arriving there on 27 December.

Hsü Shu-cheng began to consolidate personal power in Outer Mongolia by disarming Mongol forces, transferring the functions of government to his office, and filling important posts with his own men. He placed the financial burden of supporting Chinese garrison troops on the Mongols and obtained two large Japanese loans to develop the region, one of them for the purpose of constructing a railway between Kalgan and Kiakhta. In February 1920 he went to Peking for formal appointment as director of the projected railway. He returned to Urga soon afterwards.

By this time, Chang Tso-lin had become outraged by what he considered to be Hsü's usurpation of territory and authority that was rightfully in his sphere of influence. In March 1920 Chang informed Tuan Ch'i-jui that if Hsü and the Anfu Club did not make policy modifications, he would terminate his alliance with Tuan. In April, Chang formed an alliance with the Chihli generals led by Ts'ao K'un against Tuan and the Anfu Club. Hsü returned to Peking on 17 June. He was removed from office, with the consent of Tuan Ch'i-jui, on 4 July, after his dismissal had been demanded by Ts'ao K'un, Chang Tso-lin, and Li Ch'un. On 6 July, Tuan announced the formation of the National Pacification Army. Five days later, the situation erupted again when Hsü Shih-ch'ang yielded to pressure from Tuan's camp, censured Ts'ao K'un, and removed Wu P'ei-fu (q.v.) from command of the 3rd Division. Chang Tso-lin, Ts'ao K'un, and their allies then charged that Tuan Ch'i-jui and his followers had declared war on the Chihli forces. Chang began to move Fengtien troops southward, and Chihli forces marched north from Paoting. Hsü

Shu-cheng's forces fought well on the eastern front, but units of the National Pacification Army under Tuan Chih-kuei were defeated near Paoting on 17 July. Tuan Ch'i-jui then asked to be dismissed from his posts for failure to accomplish his mission. On 19 July, Hsü Shih-ch'ang issued a mandate ordering the cessation of Chihli-Anhwei hostilities. Hsü Shu-cheng was deprived of all honors and posts, and an order was issued for his arrest on 29 July. He took refuge in the Japanese legation at Peking and remained there until mid-November, when he went to Shanghai. The Anfu Club was dissolved by government mandate on 4 August.

Hsü Shu-cheng's Mongolian policies also served to turn the Mongols against the Chinese government at Peking. Some of them collaborated with Baron von Ungern-Sternberg and his White Russian forces. A provisional people's government of Mongolia was established at Urga in March 1921. The Russian Red Army and Mongol forces occupied Urga on 6 June and established a people's revolutionary government of Mongolia.

From December 1921 to February 1922 Hsü Shu-cheng represented Tuan Ch'i-jui in Canton at discussions concerning an alliance of the Anhwei faction and Sun Yat-sen's supporters against the Chihli faction in control at Peking. Liao Chung-k'ai, Wang Ching-wei, and Chiang Kai-shek represented Sun in these talks. After Chang Tso-lin sent Li Shao-pai to Kweilin to discuss the matter of alliance with Sun, Hsü was replaced by Chou Shan-p'ei, presumably because of Chang's objections to him.

In the autumn of 1922 Hsü allied himself with Wang Yung-ch'uan, with aid from Hsü Ch'ung-chih, against Li Hou-chi, the governor of Fukien. He announced that he would establish a provisional military government and, on 2 October, ordered Li Hou-chi to evacuate Foochow within 24 hours. On 12 October, Li was forced to take refuge on a warship in the harbor. Six days later, Hsü proclaimed himself head of the new government and designated Wang Yung-ch'uan pacification commissioner. Because the people of Fukien refused to support the new regime, Hsü changed Wang Yung-ch'uan's designation to commander in chief and appointed Lin Sen (q.v.) provincial chairman on 31 October. However, these changes did not win him the support of the people. The

Peking government sent Sa Chen-ping (q.v.) to assume charge of military affairs in Fukien, and Hsü fled to Shanghai on 2 November.

In the early autumn of 1923 Hsü made a trip to Japan. He returned to Shanghai before the second Chihli-Fengtien war began in 1924. He attempted to use the International Settlement as a base and to gain control of the remnant forces of Lu Yung-hsiang, the governor of Chekiang. In October, the International Settlement authorities charged him with violating settlement regulations and forced him to leave Shanghai on a British ship. He was told to remain on board until the ship reached London. However, when the ship reached Hong Kong the British authorities, having learned of Feng Yü-hsiang's coup at Peking, informed Hsü that he was free to remain in China. He decided to go to Europe and arrived in Paris in late December. On 4 January 1925 Tuan Ch'i-jui, who had become provisional chief executive of the new government at Peking, appointed Hsü special commissioner to study political conditions in Europe, America, and Japan. After visiting eight European countries, the United States, and Japan, he returned to China at the end of the year, arriving in Peking on 23 December. Five days later, he paid a formal call on Tuan Ch'i-jui, but he received no official appointment from Tuan.

Hsü Shu-cheng left Peking for Shanghai on 29 December 1925. The next day, when his train passed through Langfang, then occupied by a unit of Feng Yü-hsiang's Kuominchün, he was taken from it and shot. The assassination was reputed to be the work of Lu Ch'eng-wu, the son of Lu Chien-chang, and a public telegram issued in his name stated that he had killed Hsü to avenge his father's death. Hsü was survived by his first wife, his second wife, four sons, and two daughters. His first wife, born in 1878, died on the mainland in 1956. His second wife was Shen Ting-lan, whom he married in 1913. One of his daughters, Hsü Ying, married the linguist Li Fang-kuei (q.v.).

In 1921 Hsü wrote *Chien-kuo ch'uan-chen* [true commentary on national construction]. One of his sons, Hsü Tao-lin (Dau-lin), published *Hsü Shu-cheng hsien-sheng wen-chi nien-p'u ho-k'an* [the collected writings and chronological biography of Hsü Shu-cheng] in 1962.

Hsü T'e-li 徐 特 立
T. Mao-hsün 懋 循

Hsü T'e-li (1876–), educator, Chinese Communist party elder, and one-time teacher of Mao Tse-tung. He served the Communist governments at Juichin and Yenan as an educational administrator. In 1947 he became deputy director of the propaganda department of the Chinese Communist party's Central Committee.

Changsha, Hunan, was the birthplace of Hsü T'e-li. From 1885 to 1891 he attended an old-style school and received a traditional education in the Chinese classics. He taught Chinese at Changsha from 1891 until 1905. During the late Ch'ing period, many Hunanese became interested in modernization through educational reform. Hsü, then nearly 30, enrolled in the Hunan First Normal School, a "new-style" institution at Changsha, and studied there from 1905 to 1907. After graduation, he taught mathematics at a girls school for a year before going to Shanghai, where he worked with the Kiangsu Educational Association from 1908 to 1910. He then returned to Hunan, where he worked to promote opposition to the Ch'ing government's program of nationalizing the railroads. He also supported the movement to convene a national parliament.

In 1911 Hsü T'e-li spent several months in Japan studying the Japanese educational system. He came to know republican revolutionaries in Japan, and he joined the T'ung-meng-hui shortly after returning to Hunan. After the Wuchang revolt of October 1911 and the proclamation of the republic, Hsü became a member of the short-lived provincial assembly in Hunan. From 1912 to 1919 he was principal of the Chou-nan Girls School at Changsha, and among his students were Hsiang Ching-yü and Ts'ai Ch'ang (qq.v.), who later became prominent in the Chinese Communist party. During this period, Hsü also taught mathematics at the Hunan First Normal School, where Mao Tse-tung was a student.

Hsü's career as a teacher was interrupted again in 1919. Several of his students, including Ts'ai Ho-sen (q.v.) and Mao Tse-tung, were active in the work-study program (*see* Li

Shih-tseng), and some of them were about to set out for France. Hsü T'e-li, though 43, decided to join the program and went to France with a group of Hunanese students in 1919. He studied at Lyon and worked part-time in a factory to earn money. By tutoring Chinese students in mathematics and doing factory work, he was able to support himself while studying at the University of Paris from 1920 to 1923. He did not participate in the radical and nationalist political activities of the younger Chinese students.

After returning to China in 1923 by way of Germany, where he spent six months, Hsü T'e-li established two normal schools at Changsha. From 1923 to 1925 he served as principal of the Hunan First (also known as Tao-t'ien) Girls Normal School. He also joined the Kuomintang.

In 1925 Hsü read Stalin's *Problems of Leninism* in Chinese translation. He read Mao Tse-tung's *Report of an Investigation into the Peasant Movement in Hunan* in 1927 and became particularly interested in the organization of peasant associations in rural areas. After Chiang Kai-shek's anti-Communist coup, Hsü K'o-hsiang, a regimental commander in the Hunanese army of T'ang Sheng-chih (q.v.), carried out a vigorous purge of Communists and suspected radicals at Changsha on 21 May 1927. Incensed by the brutality of the executions, Hsü T'e-li determined to join the Chinese Communist party. He went to Wuhan in July to see Mao Tse-tung, and shortly thereafter he joined the party.

Hsü T'e-li went to the Soviet Union in 1928 and studied at the Communist University for Toilers of the East until 1930. His stay in Moscow coincided with that of Ch'ü Ch'iu-pai (q.v.), who was serving as a Chinese delegate to the Comintern. Ch'ü also was continuing studies on the romanization of the Chinese language which he had begun about 1921 during an earlier visit to Moscow. Hsü T'e-li soon came to share Ch'ü's belief that simplifying the Chinese written language was essential to the process of extending literacy and expanding education in China. In mid-1930 Hsü returned to China, probably with Ch'ü Ch'iu-pai, and went to the Communist-controlled area in Kiangsi. He did educational work in the soviet government headed by Mao Tse-tung at Juichin, serving in 1934 as deputy commissioner of education under Ch'ü Ch'iu-pai.

Although he was in his late fifties, Hsü T'e-li left Kiangsi in October 1934 and made the Long March to northern Shensi. When the news that Ch'ü Ch'iu-pai had been captured and executed in Fukien in the summer of 1935 reached Shensi, Hsü was named to head the educational section of the Communist government in the northwest. In 1936, on the occasion of Hsü's sixtieth birthday, Mao Tse-tung honored him by stating that: "Twenty years ago you were my teacher. You are my teacher now, and it is certain that in the future you will continue to be my teacher."

After the outbreak of the Sino-Japanese war in 1937, Hsü was assigned to return to Hunan and stir the people to support the united front (*see* Chiang Kai-shek) against the Japanese. From 1938 to 1945 he served as director of education in the government of the Shensi-Kansu-Ninghsia Border Region. In 1940, despite the lack of basic texts and laboratory equipment, he undertook the task of establishing the Yenan College of Natural Sciences, the predecessor of Peking Industrial College, and served as its first president. At Yenan, Hsü was closely associated with Hsieh Chueh-tsai (q.v.), another party elder who also had been a teacher in Hunan.

In 1945 the Seventh National Congress of the Chinese Communist party, meeting at Yenan, elected Hsü T'e-li to the party's Central Committee. He became a deputy director of the propaganda department of the Central Committee in 1947. In the autumn of 1949 he was named a member of the official delegation of the Chinese Communist party to the Chinese People's Political Consultative Conference. Soon afterwards, he was elected to the Central People's Government Council. He attended the National People's Congress in 1954 as a delegate representing Hunan and became a member of the Standing Committee of the congress. He was reelected to the Central Committee at the Eighth National Congress of the Chinese Communist party, held in September 1956. Hsü also became honorary chairman of the China Geographical Society in 1956. He was reelected to the Standing Committee of the National People's Congress in 1959 and 1965.

Hsü T'e-li's primary concern, both in his years as a teacher in Hunan before 1927 and in his post-1927 career as Communist, was education. He never sought or gained positions of political authority. He wrote many textbooks and essays on Chinese educational problems, including articles on the use of romanized Chinese as an aid in teaching illiterates. Because he admired the abilities and contributions of the prominent Anhwei educator and promoter of popular education T'ao Hsing-chih, for a time he adopted Shih-t'ao [learning from T'ao] as his alternate name. Throughout his active career as a teacher, Hsü T'e-li was known for his genuine interest in young people and their problems, qualities which eventually earned him an affectionate nickname, wai-p'o [granny].

Hsü, when still a boy, submitted to an arranged marriage, and he and his wife had four children.

Hsü Ti-shan 許 地 山
Pen. Lo-hua-sheng 落 華 生

Hsü Ti-shan (1893–4 August 1941), a founding member of the Literary Research Society and a noted writer of short stories, became the first professor of Chinese at the University of Hong Kong in 1936.

Tainan, Taiwan, was the birthplace of Hsü Ti-shan. His father, Hsü Nan-ying, was a native of Taiwan and a junior official at Tainan. He went to Fukien when Taiwan was ceded to the Japanese in 1895, and he later went to Singapore and Siam. He returned to China in 1902, when he was appointed magistrate of Hsuwen hsien in Kwangtung. A while later, he was transferred to Sanshui hsien, and in 1906 he resigned to make his home in Kwangtung. In 1911 the Hsü family moved to Fukien again, and Hsü Nan-ying became a middle school teacher. He went to Rangoon to teach in 1914 and to Sumatra in 1916, where he died in 1919. Because of these early travels Hsü Ti-shan grew up speaking Fukienese as well as Cantonese and Mandarin. While at middle school, he became closely associated with activities of the London Mission Society and was converted to Christianity. In 1918 he entered Yenching University in Peking. After receiving the B.A. degree in 1920, he entered the School of Religion and received the B.Div. degree in 1922. Hsü went to study abroad, first at Columbia University in New York, where he received an

M.A. degree in 1925, the title of this thesis being "A Study of Certain Chinese Texts Relating to Manichaeism," and then to Oxford, where he received a B.A. After returning to China in 1926, he joined the Yenching University faculty as a professor of theology and history. In the years following, he also lectured at Tsinghua and Peking universities and served as a member of the ministry of education's commission for the promotion of the unification of the national language.

In 1936 Hsü resigned from Yenching to go to Hong Kong, where the university was attempting to remedy the backward state of Chinese studies in its curriculum by creating a new chair of Chinese. The post was first offered to Hu Shih. He turned it down, but recommended Hsü Ti-shan. At first Hsü was reluctant to work in such a cultural backwater as colonial Hong Kong, but, after considerable discussion, he was persuaded to go. He remained in this post until his death and commanded a loyal following as a teacher.

Hsü Ti-shan had a wide range of scholarly interests. Literature was only one of his many activities, and he was as much an anthropologist as a writer. He did extensive research on comparative religion and was a specialist in Taoism and Buddhism. He was also a serious student of Sanskrit. He published frequent articles on Buddhism and Taoism in Chinese journals, and in 1934 the Commercial Press published the first volume of his *Tao-chiao-shih* [history of Chinese Taoism], which, unfortunately, he never completed. He also compiled the *Combined Indices to the Authors and Titles of Books and Chapters in Four Collections of Buddhistic Literature* (Harvard-Yenching Sinological Index Series, 1933), an invaluable research tool for all scholars of Chinese Buddhism. During his years in Hong Kong, Hsü also published a series of articles in the *Ta Kung Pao* on the history of Chinese women's costume.

It was as a writer, however, that Hsü claimed his place in the history of republican China. When he was still a student at Yenching, he became prominent in contemporary literary developments. He was one of the 12 sponsors elected to the Literary Association, set up under Cheng Chen-to's direction on 29 November 1920. After the inauguration of the society in January 1921, Hsü became a regular contributor to *Hsiao-shuo yueh-pao* [the short story]. Most of his writings were published under the pseudonym Lo-hua-sheng. Hsü's early tales were romantic and showed the influence of both Buddhist stories and Christian legends. In 1925 he published his first collection of stories under the title *Chiu-wang lao-chu* [the vain labours of a spider]. In 1928 a second collection, *Wu fa-t'ou ti yu-chien* [letters that could not be sent anywhere], was published. Both collections show Hsü's basic concern with religious love and charity and his attempt to recover spiritual values for his time. His plots are complicated, and many of his characters are conceived allegorically. This is most noticeable in "Yü kuan," in which disinterested goodness as a touchstone for conduct is explored through the experiences of a Chinese Christian convert, Yü-kuan. Unlike much of the fiction of the time, which was preoccupied with ideology and propaganda, Hsü's story achieves the level of pure moral exploration. Alone of his contemporaries, and most perfectly in "Yü-kuan," Hsü argued for a spiritual, as opposed to a material and revolutionary, solution to the problems of life in China.

Hsü Ti-shan married twice. His first wife died very young after bearing him a daughter, Fan-hsin. In 1929 he married Chou Sun-sung, a graduate of Peking Normal College. They had a daughter, Yen-chi, and a son, Lin-ch'ung.

Hsü Yung-ch'ang   徐 永 昌
T. Tz'u-ch'en   次 辰

Hsü Yung-ch'ang (23 November 1869–12 July 1959), military man who served under Feng Yü-hsiang and Yen Hsi-shan. He was governor of Suiyuan (1928–29), and Shansi (1931–35). In August 1945 he represented China at the formal Japanese surrender aboard the U.S.S. Missouri. As dean of the National Military Academy (1946–51), he supervised its transfer to Taiwan.

A native of Yenkout'sun, Kuohsien, Shansi, Hsü Yung-ch'ang was the youngest of four children. A few years after his birth, his father, Hsü Ch'ing, moved the family to Tat'ung. The boy began his studies at a private school in 1897. Tragedy soon shattered the family: first, Hsü's two sisters and his brother died and then, in 1900, his parents died. Later that year, the

orphaned boy attracted the attention of a battalion clerk in Ma Yü-k'un's army, which passed through Tat'ung with the fleeing empress dowager and emperor. Hsü followed these troops to Shensi and then to their headquarters at Liuliho, Chihli (Hopei). In 1901 he settled down to regular studies under the direction of his protector, the battalion clerk Hsü Ch'un-ling.

Hsü Yung-ch'ang became a soldier in Ma Yü-k'un's I-chün (*see under* Sung Ch'ing, ECCP, II, 686–88) in 1906. Two years later, he won admission to the battalion school. After being graduated in 1911, he became deputy commander of a company. During this period, he came into contact with anti-Manchu revolutionaries at Peking and attended their meetings. After the revolution began, his unit was sent to the Tat'ung front to fight the rebels. Hsü asked to be transferred, saying that he could not bear to fight in his native region. He then became a company commander in a new battalion of the I-chün.

After the republic was established, Hsü enrolled at the new institute for officer training. In 1913 he was appointed a company commander at the Military Officers Preparatory School at Nanking. A year later, he enrolled at the Peking Military Academy. When Chü Cheng (q.v.) began to move against Yuan Shih-k'ai in the spring of 1916, Hsü interrupted his studies and went to Shantung to organize a staff corps for Chü. Although Chü's troops were defeated, Yuan was unable to effect his plan to become emperor. After Yuan died in June, Hsü returned to the Peking Military Academy. He was graduated at the head of the fourth class.

Hsü then worked as an editor in the inspectorate general of military training at Peking, where he was associated with Hsü T'ung-ch'i and Sun Yueh. In the winter of 1917 Sun founded the Chihli Officers Educational Corps at Lanfeng, with Hsü Yung-ch'ang as its director. The corps, which was to become the officers cadre for Sun's Third Army of the Kuominchün, moved to Paoting in 1918. Hsü later served under Sun as a battalion commander in the Chihli Protection force and as chief of staff of the 15th Mixed Brigade.

In the first Chihli-Fengtien war of 1922, the 15th Mixed Brigade fought a critical battle in the Lianghsiang area and helped thrust the

Fengtien forces back to Peking. It then was sent to fight in Honan, and Hsü received command of the 2nd Regiment. When the war ended, the brigade assumed garrison duties at Taming. In May 1924 Hsü was given command of the 1st Regiment and was stationed at Tinghsien.

After the October 1924 coup at Peking of Feng Yü-hsiang (q.v.), Sun Yueh's force became the Third Army of the Kuominchün, and Hsü was promoted to commander of its 1st Mixed Brigade. In January 1925 he became deputy peace preservation commander for Shensi. His troops arrived in southern Shensi in mid-July. When Sun Yueh became military governor of the province in August, he appointed Hsü commander of the 1st Division and garrison commander of Shensi. About this time, Hsü was promoted to the rank of full general.

In the winter of 1925, when war broke out between the Kuominchün and the Fengtien-Chihli-Shantung forces, Hsü's division was among those which left Tungkuan in early December to drive north. He participated in the battle with Li Chang-lin's forces on the Tientsin-Pukow rail line and in the occupation of Tientsin. In January 1926 the Fengtien-Shantung forces counterattacked in the Tientsin sector, and Sun Yueh's army was forced to retreat into Suiyuan and Chahar. In March, Hsü succeeded the ailing Sun as commander of the Third Army. In the massive Kuominchün withdrawal from the Nankow-Kalgan area, he led his forces to Paotow and then to northern Shensi. In early 1927 his army marched into Shansi to garrison the Fenyang-Yützu area. By this time, his troops had come under the influence of Yen Hsi-shan (q.v.), and when Yen entered into a formal alliance with the Nationalists in June, Hsü's forces were designated the Third Shansi Army. In the Shansi-Fengtien conflicts of 1927 his army forced the Fengtien troops to withdraw from Shihchiachuang in early October, but were defeated later that month. They then established a defensive position along the eastern edge of the Chinghsing mountains.

In the military reorganization that followed Chiang Kai-shek's return to power in January 1928 Yen Hsi-shan became commander in chief of the Third Group Army and Hsü became commander in chief of the Twelfth Route Army. In April, Hsü led the eastern route of Yen's army

in support of Nationalist forces advancing north along the rail lines. His men captured Paoting on 30 May, and he was ordered to garrison the city. The Nationalists captured Peking six days later.

Soon after the fall of Peking, Hsü was appointed a provincial commissioner of Hopei. When Suiyuan province was created on 12 October 1928, he was named its governor. He remained in that post until 10 August 1929, when he was appointed to succeed Shang Chen as governor of Hopei. He assumed office on 9 September. When the northern coalition of Feng Yü-hsiang and Yen Hsi-shan was formed in 1930, Hsü went to Shansi and played an important role in the so-called enlarged conference movement against the National Government, serving as deputy field commander under Lu Chung-lin. Lu and Hsü formally assumed their posts on 5 May at Lanfeng and led the northern coalition armies in the drive eastward. When the rebellion failed, Lu Chung-lin renounced allegiance to Feng Yü-hsiang, and Yen Hsi-shan announced his retirement. Hsü, whose force had made a successful retreat from Honan back to Shansi, did not suffer as a result of participating in the rebellion. His force was designated the Fifth Army, and he was appointed Shansi-Suiyuan defense commander in chief. In June 1931 he was appointed to the State Council, and his army was designated the Thirty-third Army. That August, he was named to succeed Shang Chen as governor of Shansi.

About 1934 Hsü contracted tuberculosis and underwent treatment at Peiping. He continued to perform his administrative tasks, however; and in 1935 he was elected to the Central Supervisory Committee of the Kuomintang. In January 1936 he went to Kweisui to help organize a Mongolian political affairs council in opposition to an autonomous political council at Pailingmiao which was headed by Te Wang (Demchukdonggrub, q.v.). When Chinese Communists invaded Shansi from the west in late February, Hsü hastened back to assume charge of provincial defense. By May, the Communists had been expelled from the province. Hsü then resigned the governorship because of his ill health, but he accepted the post of pacification commissioner for the Shansi-Honan-Shensi border.

In March 1937 Hsü was appointed officer in charge of the Military Affairs Commission.

After the Sino-Japanese war began, he became director of the commission's executive office. He also helped direct operations in the First War Area. When the Military Affairs Commission was reorganized in January 1938, Hsü became minister of military operations, heading the board which functioned as the general staff of the Nationalist military establishment. He also continued to serve as a liaison between the National Government and Yen Hsi-shan. In 1945, as the representative of China, he participated in the formal ceremony aboard the U.S.S. Missouri in Tokyo Bay which marked the Japanese surrender and signed the surrender document. In June 1946 he became dean of the National Military Academy. He served as minister of defense in Sun Fo's cabinet of December 1948 and in Ho Ying-ch'in's cabinet of early 1949 and as minister without portfolio in the June 1949 cabinet of Yen Hsi-shan. In the autumn, he led the faculty and student body of the National Military Academy to Taiwan.

Hsü resigned from the cabinet in 1950 and from the National Military Academy in the spring of 1951. In 1952 he became a general first class and a member of the new Kuomintang Central Advisory Committee. From 1952 to 1956 he served as a political adviser to Chiang Kai-shek, and in 1954 he was appointed assistant director of the planning committee for recovery of the mainland. He died in Taipei on 12 July 1959, at the age of 69.

Hsü Yung-chang had three wives, two sons, and three daughters. One of his sons, Hsü Yuan-teh, became an examiner at the Bank of Taiwan. His other son died in childhood.

In July 1941 Hsü published a report entitled "General Review of the Strategy and Tactics of the Enemy and Ourselves in the Past Four Years," which analyzed Japan's failure to conquer China. He also kept a diary from 1 January 1916 to 7 July 1959.

Hsueh Min-lao   薛 敏 老
West. Albino Z. SyCip

Hsueh Min-lao (1887–), known as Albino SyCip, banker and civic leader in the Philippines, helped found the China Banking Corporation and became its president in 1939. He was noted for his strenuous efforts to improve economic and social conditions in the Philippines.

Although Albino SyCip's ancestral home was Amoy, Fukien, he was born in Manila, where his father was a general merchandise merchant. He attended the Anglo-Chinese School of Foochow and in 1905 entered Ann Arbor High School in Ann Arbor, Michigan. After graduation from high school in 1908, he entered the Law School of the University of Michigan. He maintained an "A" average, and in his final year he was elected associate editor of the Michigan *Law Review*. After being graduated in 1912, he returned to Manila, passed the bar examination with a superior rating, and began to practice law.

In 1921 Albino SyCip went to the United States on an important mission for the Chinese business community in the Philippines concerning the so-called Philippines Bookkeeping Law—Act No. 2972 entitled "An Act to Provide in What Language Account Books Shall Be Kept, and to Establish Penalties for Its Violation." Chinese merchants in the Philippines deemed the act harsh and unjust and thought it would be detrimental to business. On behalf of the Chinese Chamber of Commerce in Manila SyCip prepared a petition for the repeal of this law; it was forwarded to the Philippines Legislature by Governor General Leonard Wood together with Wood's recommendation for the postponement of the effective date of this law to 1 January 1923 (instead of 1 November 1920). It was during this period of postponement that SyCip went to the United States on behalf of the Chinese businessmen in the Philippines. Because he had no direct contact with high officials in Washington, he called on Dean Henry M. Bates of the Law School of the University of Michigan and requested his help. Dean Bates wrote letters of introduction for him to Secretary of Navy Edwin Denby and Attorney General Harry M. Daugherty and obtained a list of interested congressmen for SyCip to see. In Washington, SyCip conferred with the Secretary of War, the chief of the Bureau of Insular Affairs, and the chairmen of the Senate and House committees on Insular Affairs about the "harsh and unreasonable" features of the Philippines Bookkeeping Law. According to SyCip, these men were all convinced by him of the justice of the Chinese merchants' case, and they assured him that they would do all they could to have this law repealed. SyCip had written a memorandum about the case, and he sent copies of it to high officials in Washington. He described his trip as a success in a letter to Dean Bates, and in 1922 he sent Dean Bates from the Philippines a carved mahogany chair for his office as a token of appreciation for his help.

In 1920 Li Ch'ing-ch'üan (Dee C. Chuan), a prominent timber merchant and president of the Chinese Chamber of Commerce in Manila observed that the business community there needed a domestic bank, and he decided to set up the China Banking Corporation with an authorized capital of ₱10 million. Albino SyCip was asked to help in the establishment of this bank. He became vice president, with Li as president. The China Banking Corporation opened on 16 August 1920. In 1925 it opened a branch in Amoy, and in 1929 it established a branch in Shanghai to serve overseas Chinese in the transfer of funds to China. Li Ch'ing-ch'üan died in 1939, and Albino SyCip succeeded him as president. SyCip held this office from 1940 to 1951 and then became general manager and chairman of the board. The steady progress of the China Banking Corporation led to the establishment of several domestically-owned private commercial banks in the Philippines.

During the Japanese occupation of Manila, Albino SyCip refused to cooperate with the Japanese. As a result, his bank was taken over by them, and all of its available assets were confiscated. He was arrested by the Japanese in 1942 and condemned to death, but that sentence was later reduced to a prison term of 20 years. However, he was actually imprisoned for less than two years because of an amnesty granted by the Japanese to political prisoners. After the liberation of the Philippines, SyCip was confronted with the problem of reestablishing the China Banking Corporation. In a few years the bank again rose to a position of leadership among local financial institutions.

In managing the bank, SyCip worked to create equal employment opportunities for all people of the Philippines by providing credit facilities in every area of commercial, agricultural, and industrial enterprise. Not long after the reopening of his bank, SyCip, responding to the call of the business community, placed his banking resources at the disposal of a great number of businessmen and firms, both large and small, in postwar rehabilitation. He was voted "Banker of the Year" in 1947 and 1952 by the Business Writers Association of the Philippines. In support of the 1952 government policy of encouraging private investment in industries which used domestic raw materials, the China Banking Corporation extended needed credit to new and necessary industries. In 1959 Albino SyCip was given an award for "leadership in the banking industry" by the Philippine Council of Industrial Editors.

The success of the China Banking Corporation was largely the result of the sound management of Albino SyCip and his predecessor. SyCip himself set an example for his colleagues. He was a man of great integrity and dedication, and his management policies did much to establish a solid tradition of private banking in the Philippines.

SyCip also worked to promote social welfare and economic development in the Philippines. Rice production was one of the nation's major problems. In 1953 SyCip headed the Benitez Memorial Rice Committee and, in cooperation with the Department of Agriculture and Natural Resources, conducted the first national rice production contest, which encouraged the nation's farmers to improve yields. The contest became a regular feature of the nation's agricultural life. Clean drinking water was in short supply in the Philippines. In support of President Ramón Magsaysay's appeal for creation of artesian wells in all barrios [villages] of the country, Albino SyCip founded the Liberty Wells Association in 1954. Any person who donated an amount sufficient to build an artesian well could have the well dedicated to the memory of a loved one, with a suitable inscription. SyCip also took keen interest in civic improvement. He was an active supporter of such organizations as the Manila Police Trust Fund, the Philippines National Red Cross, the Community Chest for Greater Manila, the Masonic Hospital for Crippled Children, and the YMCA. He also served as a trustee of Silliman University.

To justify requests from the Philippines for more economic aid from the United States and to facilitate an early settlement of the Philippines financial claims against the United States as a result of the Second World War, Albino SyCip published two pamphlets, "American Economic

Help to the Philippines" in 1950 and "U.S. Aid and Philippine Claims" in 1959.

Albino SyCip's efforts to improve economic and social conditions in the Philippines benefited both the Chinese and the Filipino inhabitants of the islands and resulted in increasingly harmonious relations between the two groups. SyCip became the first Chinese in the Philippines to receive an honorary Doctor of Laws degree when St. John's University in Shanghai awarded him this degree in December 1929. He was similarly honored by the University of Michigan in 1955.

Hsueh Yueh 薛 岳
T. Po-ling 伯 陵

Hsueh Yueh (17 December 1896–), Nationalist military commander who was known for his pursuit of the Communist Long March forces in 1935 and for his brilliant defense of Changsha (1939) and Ch'angte (1943) against the Japanese. He served as governor of Hunan (1939–45) and Kwangtung (1949).

Lochang hsien, Kwangtung, was the birthplace of Hsueh Yueh. In 1907, at the age of 11, he went to Canton and enrolled at the Whampoa Military Primary School, where his schoolmates included Teng Yen-ta and Yeh T'ing. He was graduated from the school in 1910. During this period, Chu Chih-hsin (q.v.) and other T'ung-meng-hui revolutionaries were planning and preparing revolutionary uprisings in the area, and Hsueh became active in the T'ung-meng-hui when he was still at school.

In 1914 Hsueh went to Wuchang and enrolled at the Army Second Preparatory School. He spent two years at the school and six months in the army before entering the sixth class of the Paoting Military Academy in 1916. He left the academy in 1918 to join the Yuan-Min Yueh-chün [Kwangtung army to assist Fukien], commanded by Ch'en Chiung-ming (q.v.). Hsueh served as a staff officer under Teng K'eng (q.v.). In August 1920, when the Yuan-Min Yueh-chün marched back to Kwangtung to oust the Kwangsi militarists, he became a company commander, with the rank of major.

In 1921 Teng K'eng was ordered to organize a garrison regiment to guard Sun Yat-sen's presidential headquarters. Hsueh Yueh, Yeh T'ing, and Chang Fa-k'uei commanded the three battalions comprising this regiment, with Ch'en Ko-yu in over-all command. On 16 June 1922, when Ch'en Chiung-ming's troops besieged the presidential headquarters, the stubborn resistance of Hsueh Yueh, Yeh T'ing, and their men enabled Sun Yat-sen and his wife to escape safely to a gunboat in the Pearl River. After arriving in Shanghai, Sun issued an order naming Hsü Ch'ung-chih (q.v.) commander in chief of the East Route Anti-Rebel Army, with Chiang Kai-shek as chief of staff. Hsueh became a staff officer in this army. He was promoted to regimental commander in 1923, after Ch'en Chiung-ming had been driven from Canton.

The National Government established in Canton in 1925, after the death of Sun Yat-sen, reorganized the Kuomintang armed forces in Kwangtung as the National Revolutionary Army, with Chiang Kai-shek as commander of the First Army. Hsueh Yueh commanded a regiment in the First Army, and during the second eastern expedition of October 1925 he also served as vice commander of the 14th Division. His courage and ability were rewarded when, in the spring of 1926, he was made vice commander of the 1st Division and commander of its 3rd Regiment, with the rank of major general. When the Northern Expedition was launched in the summer of 1926, Hsueh's forces first served as a general reserve. In September, his men were ordered from Hunan into Kiangsi, where they defeated Sun Ch'uan-fang (q.v.) and continued their advance into Chekiang. On 20 March 1927 they participated in the occupation of Shanghai.

At this point, Hsueh Yueh and Pai Ch'ung-hsi (q.v.), then commander in chief of the vanguard force on the Shanghai front, had a difference of opinion which led to Hsueh's resignation. Hsueh returned to Canton, and at the invitation of Li Chi-shen (q.v.) he became commander of Li's newly organized 2nd Division. In October 1927 Chang Fa-k'uei (q.v.) brought his Fourth Army back to Canton and issued a message opposing the authorities at Nanking. Li Chi-shen left Canton, and Chang became chairman of the military committee. He reorganized the armies in Kwangtung, and Hsueh's division became the 1st Model Division of the Fourth Army.

In December 1927 the Chinese Communists staged the Canton Commune (see Chang

T'ai-lei), and Hsueh's division helped to suppress the uprising. Chang Fa-k'uei was relieved of his duties after this incident, and Miao Pei-nan became commander of the Fourth Army, with Hsueh as his deputy. In January 1928 the army battled its former companion unit, the Eleventh Army, commanded by Ch'en Ming-shu. On 9 January, Chiang Kai-shek ordered the hostilities to cease. The Fourth Army was ordered to proceed north, and it contributed to the capture of Peking and Tientsin. In July, the reduction of the National Revolutionary Army was discussed, and the Fourth Army set an example by requesting to be reorganized first. Hsueh declined an offer to serve as chief of staff of the new 4th Division and returned to Kowloon.

In February 1930, after the Fourth Army had been restored to its original size and designation, Hsueh returned to duty as commander of its 35th Division and participated in an unsuccessful campaign against Ch'en Chi-t'ang and Chiang Kuang-nai (qq.v.). He then retreated to Kwangsi. In May, Chang Fa-k'uei and Li Tsung-jen (q.v.), supporting the Yen-Feng coalition in the north, marched into Hunan. After the rearguard had been held back at Hengyang and Chiyang, Hsueh proposed that they proceed to Kiangsi and then to Chekiang. However, he was overruled by the other generals, who marched southward to defeat in a brutal battle near Henyang with the forces of Chiang Kuang-nai and Tsai T'ing-k'ai (q.v.). The remnants of the Fourth Army retreated to Kweilin. On 14 July, Li Tsung-jen appointed Hsueh Yueh commander of the 10th Division of the Fourth Army.

After the Yunnan Army entered Kwangsi in October 1930, Hsueh's division went to fight it. He was wounded on 25 October and gave up command of his division on 15 December to become head of the Central Military Academy branch at Liuchow. When the Canton secessionist movement took form in May 1931, Hsueh resigned and went to live in Kowloon.

Hsueh remained inactive until May 1933, when he was summoned by Chiang Kai-shek to take command of the Fifth Army. In the autumn of 1933 he became director general of the Sixth Route of the northern front in the fifth anti-Communist campaign. His forces included the Fourth Army, commanded by Wu

Ch'i-hui, and his task was to advance on the Communist armies in Kiangsi. In March 1934 the Nationalist forces launched their campaign. Hsueh led his men in many battles against such formidable opponents as Lin Piao and P'eng Te-huai (qq.v.).

In October 1934 the Chinese Communists, unable to withstand the onslaughts of the Nationalists any longer, broke through the encircling blockades and began their Long March westward. Hsueh was assigned to pursue the Communists, and he followed them into Hunan, passed through Kwangsi, and went on to Kweichow. His was the first Nationalist force to enter Kweichow province since the establishment of the National Government in Nanking in 1927.

On 7 January 1935 the Chinese Communists captured Tsunyi and threatened the provincial capital of Kweiyang. Hsueh and his Fourth Army rushed to the outskirts of Kweiyang on 8 January and saved the city from occupation. Because Chiang Kai-shek feared that the Communists would use Tsunyi as a base, he ordered the armies in Szechwan and Kweichow to recapture the city. On 12 March, the Fourth Army and a Szechwanese force recaptured Tsunyi. The Communist forces then entered Yunnan.

The support of the Yunnanese governor Lung Yun (q.v.) was essential to the continued pursuit of the Communists; accordingly, Chiang Kai-shek named Lung commander in chief of the Second Route Army and appointed Hsueh director general of operations in the front of the Second Route Army, with control of all other units in Kweichow and Yunnan. Hsueh's army entered Yunnan and established front-line headquarters in Kunming on 4 May 1935. The Communists, on learning of his position, turned north toward Szechwan. Hsueh continued to pursue them.

On 11 July 1935 Chiang Kai-shek, during a meeting at Chengtu, pointed out that Hsueh's forces had pursued the enemy on foot over difficult terrain for more than 20,000 li, an unprecedented feat. After reaching Chengtu, Hsueh's forces proceeded northward in August. On new orders from Chiang, he moved most of his forces to Nanch'ung in September while the rest pushed forward to Wutu to complete the encirclement of the north Szechwan–south Shensi area.

As part of an attempt to establish a Szechwan-Yunnan-Kweichow border area, Communist forces occupied Jungcheng on 23 November 1935 and attempted to move east to Chengtu and south to meet the forces of Ho Lung (q.v.). Szechwanese troops were unable to stop this advance, and Hsueh Yueh was ordered to come to their aid. He sent some of his men to defend Chengtu and led the rest to victory at Jungcheng on 15 December. On 14 February 1936 he recaptured Tienchuan from the Communists, a victory which assured the safety of Chengtu and Chungking.

Hsueh spent part of 1936 planning the construction of a Szechwan-Sikang highway to facilitate military operations. He then was ordered to lead his men to Kweichow, and in May 1937 he became governor of that province. When the Sino-Japanese war broke out in July, he was appointed deputy commander of the Third Reserve Army. After repeated appeals to be sent to the front, he received command of the Nineteenth Group Army in September. After the Shanghai, Nanking, and Hangchow areas had been lost and evacuated, he was appointed director general of the vanguard forces in the Third War Area, two of his tasks being the defense of southern Anhwei and the reorganization of defeated troops. In May 1938 he was sent to Honan, where he directed the battle at Lanfeng and dealt a severe blow to the Japanese. He then served briefly as commander in chief on the front lines of the First War Area. On 4 June he sent troops to breach the Yellow River dikes at Huang-tao-k'ou; the resulting floods checked the Japanese advance westward. On 10 June, Hsueh relinquished his duties in the First War Area and went to Kiangsi to help defend Wuhan. Although his troops fought well, the Japanese captured Wuhan on 25 October.

On 12 November 1938 Chang Chih-chung (q.v.), the governor of Hunan, caused Changsha to be set ablaze after hearing a false report that the Japanese were approaching the city. Chiang Kai-shek then ordered Hsueh Yueh to take control of the Ninth War Area, with headquarters at Changsha. In April 1939 he also was appointed governor of Hunan. He successfully repulsed major Japanese attacks on Changsha in September 1939, September 1941, and December 1941, thereby increasing his military renown. In November 1943 the Japanese launched an offensive against Ch'angte.

Although this city was part of the Sixth War Area and thus was out of Hsueh's military jurisdiction, it was part of Hunan, and thus was his responsibility as governor. He rushed his forces to the area and forced the Japanese to withdraw. General Claire Chennault later praised Hsueh's handling of this engagement and administration of the Ninth War Area in *Way of a Fighter*, stating that Hsueh was superior to General Stilwell both in strategy and in the direction of combat operations. Despite Hsueh's efforts, the Japanese captured Changsha on 18 June 1944 and Hengyang on 8 August.

In May 1946, less than a year after the war had ended, Hsueh was appointed head of the Hsuchow pacification bureau, succeeding Ku Chu-t'ung (q.v.). Hsuchow faced increasing threats from Communist forces under Ch'en Yi and Liu Po-ch'eng (qq.v.). Within nine months Hsueh Yueh had destroyed Ch'en Yi's base at Linyi, Shantung, and had forced him to retreat into the mountains. Liu Po-ch'eng was driven back across the Yellow River. Before Hsueh could complete the restoration of Shantung, he was relieved of his post for political reasons and was succeeded by Ku Chu-t'ung. Hsueh then became personal chief of staff to Chiang Kai-shek.

Early in 1949 Hsueh Yueh was appointed governor of Kwangtung in the hope that he could preserve the area as a Nationalist base. However, the situation was beyond his control, and Kwangtung fell to the Chinese Communists in October 1949. Hsueh then went to Taiwan, where he became a member of Chiang Kai-shek's strategic advisory council. In 1958 he was appointed to the Executive Yuan as minister without portfolio. He was generally regarded as the senior Cantonese general in Taiwan.

Hu Cheng-chih: *see* HU LIN.

Hu Feng   胡 風
  Orig. Chang Ku-fei   張 谷 非

Hu Feng (1903–), Marxist literary critic, essayist, and poet. Because of his independent approach to Marxism and his affirmation that the artist is entitled to an individual vision of truth, he was singled out for attack in the 1955 campaign for ideological purity, which was led by Chou Yang (q.v.).

Although Hu Feng's father was an unskilled laborer in a Hupeh village, he managed to earn enough money to send his son to school. Hu learned little about Chinese culture, but he responded quickly to the Western ideas which were affecting China at the time. While at a school in Nanking in 1923–25 he joined the Communist Youth League, participated in the May Thirtieth Movement of 1925, and joined the revolutionary movement which was developing in the south. It appears, however, that he never became a member of the Chinese Communist party. During this period, he also began to write poetry.

In 1928 Hu went to Japan, where he wrote essays expressing his active interest in political and social developments. He was expelled from Japan in 1933 for participating in a leftist demonstration. After returning to Shanghai in 1934, he began to work as a professional writer and editor and joined the League of Left-Wing Writers, led by Lu Hsün (Chou Shu-jen, q.v.). Hu Feng soon became one of Lu Hsün's leading disciples.

At this time Hu defined his political and aesthetic ideas more precisely. Although a Marxist, he did not conform to Communist party doctrine; rather, he attempted to fuse certain Marxist beliefs with his own ideas about literary creativity. According to orthodox Communist theory, environment determines realism in art. Hu believed that a writer achieved realism by combining emotional intensity and spontaneity, which he called the "subjective struggling spirit," with objective reality, which he frequently equated with the demands of the people for a livelihood and a democratic government. In assimilating objective reality into his consciousness, a writer moved closer to Marxism.

Although Hu used his concept of the "subjective struggling spirit" to explain the individual personality and the creative process, he used Marxist dialectic to explain social and political trends. Nevertheless, his contentions that a person may adopt a political ideology through his own experience without coercion and that party discipline should control a writer's political life but not his creativity were bound to bring him into conflict with party officials.

Hu's unorthodox beliefs and the backing of Lu Hsün and a devoted coterie gradually brought him prominence in left-wing literary circles in Shanghai. Even at this time, his group contended with more orthodox factions in a struggle for preeminence which came to be motivated as much by personal antagonisms as by aesthetic differences. Hu fought his most vehement battles with Chou Yang (q.v.), a close associate of Mao Tse-tung. According to Chou, politics and ideology were the foremost concern of literature; Hu believed that they were secondary to literary value. This basic conflict underlay all of Hu's controversies with more orthodox Communist writers. In the factional squabbles of the 1930's Hu was charged with unorthodoxy and subversion. A major subject of debate was the problem of "typical characters" in literary creation. Chou held that literary characters should be representative of certain groups; in the period of national liberation, writers should create types of national heroes and national traitors. Hu believed that characters should have universal characteristics, but should not be stereotypes. Throughout his controversies with more orthodox Communist writers, both sides quoted Soviet literary critics in citing the theoretical bases of their arguments. Because no authoritative interpretation had been formulated to support Chou Yang's views, Hu's more analytical arguments triumphed. During these debates Chou tried to win Lu Hsün to his side, but Lu Hsün supported Hu. This development marked the beginning of a rivalry between Hu Feng and Chou Yang for superiority in left-wing literary circles in China.

A far more caustic debate between the two antagonists took place in July 1937. At the outset of the Sino-Japanese war, "Literature for National Defense" took the place of proletarian literature in left-wing circles. The shift coincided with the formation of the united front (*see* Chiang Kai-shek) against the Japanese. One group of leftist writers, however, suggested the slogan "People's Literature for the National Revolutionary Struggle." The leader of the Communist literary movement was Chou Yang, with Hsü Mo-yung as his deputy, and the leader of the leftist writers was Lu Hsün, with Hu Feng as his chief aide. Chou published essays calling for a united literary front, and "Literature for National Defense." After several articles had been published on the subject, Hu came forth with an article entitled "What Do the Masses Want from Literature?" in which he formally proposed the slogan "People's Literature for the National Revolutionary Struggle" and attacked Chou.

At this juncture, Hsü Mo-yung wrote to Lu Hsün and warned him that Hu Feng and his group were carrying on divisive activities arising from their own selfish ambitions. He accused them of extreme sectarianism and controversial theories. Lu Hsün replied that it was he who had requested Hu to propose the slogan. Lu Hsün looked upon these accusations as a challenge to Hu and others who had not joined the Writers' Association, which was being organized by Chou Yang to advance the concept of "Literature for National Defense." Such accusations were expected to provoke retaliation, thus creating a pretext for charging Hu and others with the crime of being "traitors to the united front." Lu Hsün further stated that various people had informed him that Hu was a traitor sent by the Nationalists to sabotage the Chinese Communist party. Lu Hsün insisted that Hu had never opposed the united front. The disputes subsided when Chou and his associates followed Mao Tse-tung to the Communist areas in Yenan; Hu and his followers remained in Nationalist-controlled territory. They helped to prepare for the eventual triumph of the Chinese Communist party, although their writings continued to be unorthodox.

Mao Tse-tung's Yenan talks of 1942, which set forth the doctrine that literature must be an instrument of political utility, aroused Hu Feng and his group to a concerted campaign of opposition. Because they were safe from direct Communist pressure, they were able to insist on independent aesthetic values and to criticize Communist literary theory in public. In January 1945 Hu established a magazine, *Hsi-wang* [hope], as a sounding board for his ideas and a weapon with which to fight the opposing faction. A colleague's article, "On Subjectivism," in the first issue, provoked a literary controversy which raged for nine years. Hu was investigated by the Chinese Communist party, which attempted to interfere with the publishing of his journal. Nonetheless, he was able to preserve a degree of independence in the period before the Communists came to power.

From 1949 to 1951 Hu Feng's expression of the proper political sentiments overbalanced his remarks on literature, and his poetry lauded Mao Tse-tung in superhuman terms. He did not condemn the political leadership, although he charged those responsible for literary policy with distorting the leadership's program. He sought to break the literary monopoly of his old enemies and to gain party sanction for his own literary ideas. Hu no longer was allowed to debate freely, nor was he equal to his opponents. Because he was still influential in literary circles and praised for his revolutionary activities, he was appointed to the councils of two writers associations. However, he was given no real authority. Doctrinal interpretation of literature continued to be the province of Chou Yang, then deputy chairman of the All-China Federation of Writers and Artists. Although Hu's posts were nominal, they indicated that the Communists still wanted his cooperation. Hu's plan seems to have been to comply with party directives so that he could gain a position in the Communist party hierarchy which would enable him to influence the content of such directives.

During the ideological remolding movement begun in 1951 Chou Yang engineered formal attacks on Hu and his colleagues. Although the attempts to reform Hu's thinking failed, he was not condemned beyond reprieve. By the beginning of 1954 Hu's position in Communist party circles had improved. He was made a representative to the National People's Congress and was appointed to the editorial board of *Jen-min wen-hsueh* [people's literature], an important party literary magazine. At that point, he apparently assumed that his position had risen to the point where an open struggle could result in victory.

In July 1954 Hu Feng presented a report to the Central Committee of the Chinese Communist party in which he blamed the failure of literary development on the literary authorities. He hoped to weaken their control by setting forth his criticisms of their policies. Hu expressed opposition to Marxist indoctrination of writers and suggested that writers would come closer to true Communism if they accepted his principle that the "subjective struggling spirit" relates itself to objective reality and if they participated in the practical daily problems of the people. He opposed the idea that writers should draw their material solely from the concerns of peasants, workers, and soldiers. Literature, he held, should not merely portray certain classes, but should describe the daily struggles of all men. He denounced thought reform imposed from without on the grounds that it kept writers and artists from being in touch with the realities of daily life. Hu believed that each writer should reform his own thoughts. He rejected the evaluation of literature according to its subject matter, and he objected to making the literary form of the past the national literary standard. Having set forth the causes of artistic stagnation, Hu went on to present a program designed to eliminate rigid controls over writers and to create an atmosphere conducive to the production of valid literary works. He proposed the creation of several writers organizations which would edit their own publications. Free competition in creative work, he asserted, would lead to ever high standards and achievements. In Hu's opinion, his report merely demanded a greater degree of freedom for writers to develop their individual talents within the Communist system.

Since no action was taken against him after the presentation of his report, Hu believed that the time had come to ask for party sanction of his theories. At a meeting in November 1954 he again outlined his view of literature and then openly accused the literary authorities of the same charges that had been brought against him: sectarianism, distortion of Marxism, and surrender to bourgeois thought. The rapidity with which the emphasis of the meeting suddenly switched to an attack on Hu seemed to indicate that he had been invited to participate in the meeting so that others could attack him.

The intensity and the nation-wide scope of the subsequent campaign may be explained by examining Communist internal policy at the end of 1954. As the Chinese Communists moved into a period of intensive socialist reorganization of society and the economy, it became imperative for them to combat all heterodoxy. One of the chief forces behind the drive for ideological purity was Hu's old enemy Chou Yang, who attempted to make Hu Feng a symbol of heterodoxy. Although the campaign was not free from personal vindictiveness, it must be considered as another phase in the

continuing program of thought reform in the People's Republic of China. The 1955 campaign was different from the previous attacks on Hu; he now was regarded not as a deviationist guilty of "subjectivism, emotionalism and aestheticism," but as a counterrevolutionary leader. However, though the charge that he disagreed with official literary-political rulings could be substantiated, there was no evidence to show that his ideas were anti-Marxist in principle or that he intended to subvert political authority.

The campaign reached a climax on 13 May 1955, when Hu's published self-criticism was rejected as being false. Although he had begged his followers to break away from him, most of them resisted the campaign against their old master. On 18 July 1955 Hu was arrested and imprisoned. The campaign did not end with his arrest, but became broader in scope and more intense, proving that it had a function beyond neutralizing a single disturbing influence.

After the inauguration in 1956 of the period of the "Hundred Flowers," many of Hu Feng's views, as previously presented in his report to the Central Committee, were supported openly by several intellectuals. Opinions which had been denounced as heresy a year earlier were publicly debated. Such terms as "vulgar sociology" and "mechanized literature," coined by Hu to describe China's current literature, were used by Communist leaders. Not only Hu's ideas but also his example of defiance of the Communist authorities inspired many of those who expressed disagreement with the regime at this time. Among them, his name became a symbol of protest against control of intellectual and artistic activity. There were reports of student meetings at which speakers declared that history would judge Hu as a hero of the age, and there was a movement to demand a reexamination of the charges against him. Several writers who had published sharp criticisms of Hu now insisted that Chinese culture would have been less backward if some of his reforms had been accepted. However, when the party launched its anti-rightist drive in the latter half of 1957, discussion of Hu's ideas and praise for his courage was silenced. Those who had voiced beliefs similar to Hu's were rebuked and were branded as supporters of Hu.

Hu Fu: *see* LIU SHAO-CH'I.

Hu Han-min　　　　　胡 漢 民
　Orig.　Hu Yen-kuan　　胡 衍 鶴
　Alt.　Hu Yen-hung　　胡 衍 鴻
　T.　　Chan-t'ang　　　展 堂
　H.　　Pu-k'uei shih-chu　不 匱 室 主

Hu Han-min (9 December 1879–12 May 1936), revolutionary leader and close associate of Sun Yat-sen, was the first republican governor of Kwangtung. In 1924 he became the top-ranking member of the Central Executive Committee of the Kuomintang and one of the seven members of the Central Political Council. He was president of the Legislative Yuan (September 1928–February 1931). His arrest in 1931 precipitated the successionist movement at Canton.

The ancestral home of Hu Han-min's family was Luling hsien, Kiangsi province. His paternal grandfather, Hu Hsieh-san, had moved to Kwangtung as a private secretary to an official of the imperial civil service and had decided to establish a new family home there. At the time of Hu's birth, his father, Hu Wen-chao, was employed as a legal secretary to various prefects and district officials, with the result that the family moved frequently to different parts of Kwangtung. Hu Wen-chao's wife, *née* Wen, was the daughter of a scholarly family from P'inghsiang hsien in Kiangsi. Hu Han-min was born in P'anyü hsien, the district of which Canton is the chief city. He was the fourth of seven children, with two elder brothers, two younger brothers, one elder sister, and one younger sister. Only three of the children survived to adulthood: the eldest brother, the younger sister, and Hu Han-min himself.

By the age of 11 sui, Hu had completed his basic reading of the Chinese classics and had shown talent as an essayist. His father died in the autumn of 1891 when the boy was only 13 sui, and his mother died two years later. To help support the family, Hu and his elder brother Hu Ch'ing-jui became tutors in 1894. Hu Han-min was then only 16 sui, and many of his pupils were older than he.

The defeat of China in the Sino-Japanese war of 1894–95 aroused the youth of China and prepared them for acceptance of revolutionary ideas. At that time, Hu was reading Chinese historical writings. He was particularly impressed by the works of the great seventeenth-century Ming loyalists and patriots Ku Yen-wu (ECCP, I, 421–26) and Wang Fu-chih (ECCP, II, 817–19) and came to resent the Manchu dynasty. The young Hu learned of Sun Yat-sen from Chinese Christians at Canton.

After learning more about the anti-Manchu revolutionary movement, Hu determined to go to Japan to join it. To raise money for the trip, he went to work for a Canton newspaper in 1898 and soon gained a reputation as an able writer. He also decided to take the imperial examinations as a substitute for wealthy men who desired degrees which they were unable to obtain through their own efforts. To carry out this plan, he had to become a degree-holder. Accordingly, in 1900 Hu took and passed the provincial examinations for the degree of chü-jen. He then put his plan into action and raised the funds he needed.

Hu Han-min went to Japan early in 1902 and enrolled in the normal department of the Kobun Institute in Tokyo. He had been there only a few months, however, when an incident involving Wu Chih-hui (q.v.) and Ts'ai Chun, the Chinese minister to Japan, disrupted his schooling. In July 1902 the Chinese embassy refused to recommend Ts'ai O (q.v.) and two other Chinese students for study at a Japanese military school. Wu Chih-hui led a movement to protest this refusal. Hu Han-min was one of the leaders of the campaign and was forced to withdraw from school as a result.

Hu returned to Canton at the end of 1902 and worked on the Canton newspaper *Ling-hai pao* as an editor. He engaged in a war of words with another Canton paper, the *Yang-ch'eng pao*, which supported the monarchist cause of K'ang Yu-wei (q.v.). Hu's activities soon attracted the attention of the authorities, and he was listed as an active revolutionary. He therefore left Canton and went to Kwangsi, where he served as an instructor at the Wuchow Middle School. He was popular with the students, and he disseminated revolutionary ideas. Many of these Wuchow students later participated in the revolution of 1911 and supported Sun Yat-sen's nationalist cause.

In 1904 Hu Han-min, who had just married Ch'en Shu-tzu, went to Japan a second time, traveling with a group of students which included Wang Ching-wei (q.v.). Hu and Wang became close friends; both of them enrolled at Tokyo Law College in the autumn of 1904. The following summer, Hu returned to Canton for the summer vacation. When he went back to Japan, he took his wife, his younger sister, and Liao Chung-k'ai (q.v.) with him. On 20 August 1905 the T'ung-meng-hui was established in Tokyo. Hu and Liao arrived in Tokyo ten days later. They immediately joined the new revolutionary organization. Wang Ching-wei headed one of the three major committees of the T'ung-meng-hui, and Hu became a member of the committee. Soon afterwards, Sun Yat-sen named Hu secretary of the party headquarters.

Hu Han-min's earliest contributions to the revolutionary movement were his writings in the *Min-pao* [people's journal], the official organ of the T'ung-meng-hui, which began publication in Tokyo in November 1905. He first used the name Han-min in signing these articles. Hu also continued to study at Tokyo Law College; he was graduated in 1906. The inauguration of the T'ung-meng-hui raised the hopes of its members for revolutionary action. In 1906 many of its members returned to China and participated in unsuccessful uprisings. Sun Yat-sen visited French Indo-China and Malaya, and branches of the revolutionary party were organized in those areas.

After the Peking government demanded Sun Yat-sen's expulsion from Japan, he left for Indo-China in March 1907. Accompanied by Hu Han-min, Wang Ching-wei, and others, he went to Hanoi to establish a new base from which to direct operations planned for the southern provinces of Kwangtung, Kwangsi, and Yunnan. He and his followers also began to train a small revolutionary force and arranged for supplies of arms and ammunition to be sent to them from the T'ung-meng-hui office in Japan. In April 1907 Hu Han-min was sent to Hong Kong to help foment uprisings in eastern Kwangtung. Insurrections near Swatow in May and at Huichou (Waichow) in June were crushed by government troops. Another unsuccessful uprising took place in September at Ch'inchow (Yamchow) in western Kwangtung.

Late in September 1907 Hu Han-min returned to Hanoi. In December, a revolt broke out on the Kwangsi border, and Sun Yat-sen, accompanied by Huang Hsing (q.v.) and Hu Han-min, hastened from Hanoi to join an insurgent group which had succeeded in capturing the frontier outpost at Chen-nan-kuan. But imperial government forces commanded by Lu Jung-t'ing (q.v.) drove the revolutionaries out after a day, and they were forced to retire into French territory. Sun, Hu, and Huang then returned to Hanoi. The French authorities had been persuaded by the Peking government to expel Sun from Indo-China. In March 1908 he was forced to leave Hanoi for Singapore, where he planned to raise funds for munitions to send to Huang Hsing, who again entered Kwangsi to organize uprisings, and to Hu Han-min, who remained at Hanoi. To escape detection by the French authorities, particularly after the unsuccessful revolts at Ch'inchow and Hokow, Hu lived on the top floor of a tailor shop in Hanoi which the revolutionaries used as their headquarters and for two months did not venture into the street.

Hu Han-min left Hanoi and went to Singapore in July 1908 to join Sun Yat-sen. By that time the fortunes of the revolutionary organization were at a low ebb. Repeated military failures in south China had disheartened the remnant revolutionary forces in Malaya and had seriously damaged the prestige of the T'ung-meng-hui among the overseas Chinese of Southeast Asia. The Chinese communities there became reluctant to contribute to Sun Yat-sen's cause. Sun and his followers nevertheless attempted to expand the T'ung-meng-hui organization in Southeast Asia and to enlist support wherever possible. Sun Yat-sen established a new general branch of the T'ung-meng-hui at Singapore to control activities in Southeast Asia and appointed Hu Han-min its director. A newspaper, the *Chung-hsing jih-pao*, was also established at Singapore, and Hu and Wang Ching-wei became two of its most forceful contributors. In the campaign to raise funds, the revolutionaries found a capable supporter in Teng Tse-ju (q.v.), who was to become a close friend of Hu Han-min. The T'ung-meng-hui also extended its activities to Siam, where a devoted supporter was Hsiao Fo-ch'eng (q.v.).

Sun Yat-sen then decided to leave for Europe with the intention of obtaining a loan in France. In May 1909 he established a new south China bureau of the T'ung-meng-hui at Hong Kong to plan revolutionary activities in the southern provinces. It was then that Ch'en Chiung-ming and Tsou Lu (qq.v.) joined the revolutionary movement through the introduction of Chu Chih-hsin (q.v.), another close associate of Sun Yat-sen. Hu Han-min was named chief of the south China bureau of the T'ung-meng-hui, and Wang Ching-wei was appointed secretary. Wang, however, had become discouraged by the repeated failures of the revolutionary movement and had resolved to assassinate the Manchu prince regent. Because he was secretly making plans toward that goal, he contributed little to the bureau's work. Hu attempted to dissuade him. The immediate objective of the bureau was to foment a revolt in the ranks of the New Army at Canton. Working with Hu at Hong Kong was Chao Sheng (1881–1911; T. Po-hsien), a former regimental officer in the New Army who had been relieved of his command on suspicion of revolutionary sympathies. Because the plans for the uprising became known, it was staged two weeks ahead of schedule, on 12 February 1910, but it ended in failure.

Hu Han-min, together with Huang Hsing and Chao Sheng, left Hong Kong in March for Singapore to raise funds for renewed action. Hu arrived in Singapore on 28 March 1910 and a few days later received news of Wang Ching-wei's arrest at Peking following his unsuccessful attack on the life of the Manchu prince regent. Hu assumed that Wang Ching-wei would be executed and was greatly upset about the fate of his friend. When he learned that Wang had received a life sentence, Hu Han-min joined with Ch'en Pi-chün (q.v.), who later married Wang, in an attempt to rescue him. Hu even thought of going to Peking himself, but Ch'en Pi-chün checked that obviously fruitless venture.

Sun Yat-sen arrived in Singapore from Europe in July 1910. He then proceeded to Penang, where he called a strategy conference on 13 November. The group in attendance at Penang included Hu Han-min, Huang Hsing, Chao Sheng, Teng Tse-ju, and leaders of the overseas Chinese community in Malaya. Plans were made for an all-out attack at Canton. Because of the restrictions placed on his movements by government and colonial authorities in Southeast Asia, Sun returned to Europe to raise funds. Huang Hsing and Chao Sheng went to Hong Kong to make preparations for the uprising. Hu Han-min joined them in March 1911.

On the afternoon of 27 April 1911 the Huang-hua-kang uprising, personally led by Huang Hsing, was launched in Canton. That evening, Hu Han-min, Chao Sheng, Ch'en Pi-chün, and more than 200 other revolutionaries who had been unable to go to Canton earlier, took the night boat from Hong Kong to Canton. On arrival the following morning they found that the insurrection had already failed. Hu returned to Hong Kong that night.

Although unsuccessful, the Huang-hua-kang uprising aroused nation-wide attention and led to the Wuchang revolt of 10 October 1911. After the uprising at Wuchang, revolutionaries in other parts of China rose against the Manchus. In Kwangtung, Ch'en Chiung-ming, Chu Chih-hsin, a cousin of Hu Han-min named Hu I-sheng, and other supporters of the revolutionary cause gathered forces to march on Canton. Hu Han-min was then in Hanoi. On hearing the news, he returned to Hong Kong, leading a number of Chinese youths from overseas who had volunteered for military service. The imperial authorities at Canton capitulated. At a public meeting on 9 November 1911 Hu Han-min was elected, *in absentia*, tutuh [military governor] of the Kwangtung provisional government. He arrived at Canton on 12 November to assume the post, and Ch'en Chiung-ming was elected his deputy.

Sun Yat-sen, returning from abroad, reached Hong Kong on 21 December 1911 on his way to Shanghai. The Kwangtung leaders had decided to invite Sun to form his government at Canton; accordingly, Hu Han-min and Liao Chung-k'ai went to Hong Kong to greet Sun and to convey their proposal to him. Sun Yat-sen vetoed the plan, however, and called upon Hu Han-min to go north with him. Hu accompanied Sun to Shanghai, sending Liao Chung-k'ai back to Canton and delegating governmental authority at Canton to Ch'en Chiung-ming.

Sun Yat-sen and Hu Han-min arrived at Shanghai on 25 December 1911. They were met by Ch'en Ch'i-mei (q.v.), who had been elected military governor of Shanghai. Huang Hsing and Wang Ching-wei, who had been released from prison at Peking, also welcomed them. On 29 December 1911 Sun Yat-sen was elected provisional president of the Republic of

China. When he assumed office at Nanking on 1 January 1912, he named Hu Han-min his chief secretary. Before going to Nanking, Hu had raised some China $700,000 among the Kwangtung residents of Shanghai to help finance the new government.

In February 1912 Sun Yat-sen relinquished the provisional presidency to Yuan Shih-k'ai (q.v.). At the end of April, Hu Han-min returned to Canton and resumed his duties as tutuh of Kwangtung. By 1913 Yuan Shih-k'ai had launched his campaign to suppress the Kuomintang, the successor to the T'ung-meng-hui. In June 1913 Yuan appointed Ch'en Chiung-ming to succeed Hu as Kwangtung tutuh. Earlier, Li Lieh-chün (q.v.) had been dismissed as governor of Kiangsi. The Kuomintang leaders then launched a campaign against Yuan Shih-k'ai which became known as the second revolution. The well-trained Peiyang forces were too strong for the republican revolutionaries, and the campaign was suppressed quickly. Sun Yat-sen and many of his political supporters, including Hu Han-min, were forced to flee to Japan.

In 1915, when Yuan Shih-k'ai's monarchical aspirations became apparent, Sun Yat-sen and his supporters launched a new campaign against him. Hu Han-min spent the greater part of the year in the Philippines raising funds for the campaign. By early 1916 Ch'en Ch'i-mei had returned to Shanghai to direct operations in that area. Hu Han-min, after spending a short period in Tokyo following his visit to the Philippines, soon arrived in Shanghai to join Ch'en. When Ch'en Ch'i-mei was assassinated in May 1916, Hu Han-min was living in the same house and was on the upper floor of the building when the murder was committed.

After Yuan Shih-k'ai died in June 1916, Li Yuan-hung (q.v.) succeeded to the presidency at Peking. In September 1916 Hu Han-min visited Peking on behalf of Sun Yat-sen to discuss national problems with Li Yuan-hung and Tuan Ch'i-jui (q.v.), the premier. A more important goal of Hu's trip, however, was to promote unity among members of the revolutionary party in north China, particularly those who were members of the Parliament.

The rebellion of the northern group of military governors against Li Yuan-hung in May 1917 and the forcible dissolution of the Parliament in June led to the movement launched by Sun Yat-sen for "protection of the constitution." With the support of the navy, a rump parliament met at Canton in July 1917 and established a military government headed by Sun Yat-sen. Hu Han-min was named minister of communications in that government. However, Kwangtung province was then under the control of the Kwangsi military faction headed by Lu Jung-t'ing and Ts'en Ch'un-hsuan (q.v.), and Sun found it impossible to exercise real authority. In May 1918 he left Canton for Shanghai.

Hu Han-min followed Sun to Shanghai. For the next two years he devoted himself to disseminating Sun's ideas on national reconstruction and to popularizing Sun's political and social concepts. In August 1919, together with Chu Chih-hsin, Liao Chung-k'ai, and Tai Chi-t'ao (q.v.), Hu Han-min established the *Chien-she tsa-chih* [reconstruction magazine] and published many of his more systematic articles on political theory, including socialism, in it. Although Sun Yat-sen and most of his disciples had never accepted Marxism, some of his close followers, notably Hu Han-min and Tai Chi-t'ao, defended some of its concepts from the conservative and nationalist standpoint. Hu and Tai both believed that China's most important political problem was how to become a strong and independent national state. By underplaying the element of class struggle and accenting the nationalist implications of the Leninist theory of imperialism, they argued that Marxism-Leninism might serve as an acceptable doctrinal base for their nationalist political program. They accepted the materialist conception of history and the ideal of equal distribution of wealth, and they suggested that similar theories were to be found in the writings of the ancient Chinese philosophers.

During this period, Hu Han-min also attempted to assess Chinese history, philosophy, and institutions in the light of historical materialism. His "Materialistic Study of the History of Chinese Philosophy," which appeared in the third issue of the *Chien-she tsa-chih* in October 1919, attempted to find precedents for Marxism-Leninism in traditional Chinese thought. In the fifth issue of the journal (December 1919), Hu Han-min published a lengthy article entitled "A Criticism of the Criticism of Historical Materialism." This article was a point-by-point rebuttal of the article by Li Ta-chao (q.v.) entitled "My Views on Marxism" in the 19 May special issue on Marxism of *Hsin ch'ing-nien* [new youth].

When Sun Yat-sen returned to office in Canton on 5 May 1921, Hu Han-min was appointed chief counselor, head of the civil affairs bureau, and head of the political department of the government. After a successful campaign against the Kwangsi leaders, who fled westward to their own province, Sun Yat-sen in 1922 turned again to his cherished plan for a northern expedition against the Peking government. That plan was vigorously opposed by Ch'en Chiung-ming, who took action against Sun in June 1922 and forced him to take refuge on a gunboat in the Pearl River.

At the time of Ch'en Chiung-ming's coup, Hu Han-min was at Sun Yat-sen's field headquarters at Shaokuan in northern Kwangtung. An advance unit of the northern expedition had already entered Kiangsi and captured Kanchow. On hearing of the coup, Hu Han-min, who was in tactical command at the field headquarters, decided to bring the men back from Kanchow to march on Canton against Ch'en Chiung-ming. Ch'en had won over a portion of the Kwangtung troops and soon defeated another portion in an engagement near Shaokuan. The units of the Kwangtung army which remained loyal to Sun Yat-sen were commanded by Hsü Ch'ung-chih (q.v.); Hunan, Kiangsi, and Yunnan armies also supported Sun. It was decided that Hu Han-min and Hsü Ch'ung-chih should lead the Kwangtung units into Fukien while Li Lieh-chün led the other units into Hunan with the objective of reaching Kwangsi. Hu Han-min came to a peaceful arrangement with a local army commander in Fukien which enabled Hsü Ch'ung-chih to bring his army into Fukien for rest and regrouping. When in Fukien, Hu Han-min heard of Sun Yat-sen's safe arrival in Shanghai and hastened to join him there.

In September 1922 Sun Yat-sen called a meeting of the Kuomintang members in Shanghai at which he announced his intention to reorganize the party and named a committee to study the problem. In November, the committee elected Hu Han-min and Wang Ching-wei to draft a declaration on party reform. That document was published on 1 January 1923. With the help of Yunnan and Kwangsi armies, Sun's forces were successful in ousting Ch'en Chiung-ming from Canton in February 1923, and Sun reestablished the military government; Hu Han-min relinquished the governorship and became chief counselor in Sun Yat-sen's office.

When the First National Congress of the Kuomintang met at Canton in January 1924 under the personal direction of Sun Yat-sen, one major objective was to reorganize the party on Leninist lines. At that congress, Hu Han-min was elected top-ranking member of the Central Executive Committee. When the Whampoa Military Academy was established in May 1924, Hu was appointed one of its political instructors. In July 1924 he became one of the seven members of the Central Political Council of the Kuomintang.

In September 1924 Sun Yat-sen again turned to planning a northern expedition and moved his headquarters to Shaokuan. Hu Han-min was ordered to remain at Canton to act on behalf of Sun and was named governor of Kwangtung province once again. As soon as Hu assumed these duties, he had to confront the armed defiance of the Canton Merchant Corps, supported by conservative British interests in Shameen and Hong Kong and by Ch'en Chiung-ming. Hu Han-min deployed all the armed forces available at Canton under the command of the garrison commander, Chiang Kai-shek. By mid-October, the uprising had been quelled.

The death of Sun Yat-sen in March 1925 had far-reaching consequences for the Kuomintang and for China. The most pressing problem confronting Hu Han-min at Canton was the threat of revolt by the Yunnan and Kwangsi armies of Yang Hsi-min and Liu Chen-huan. Hu Han-min handled the issue with the same firmness he had shown in dealing with the Canton merchants corps. After consultation with Hsü Ch'ung-chih and Chiang Kai-shek, Hu determined to use force against the unruly troops. Michael Borodin, the Russian adviser to the Central Political Council, strongly opposed such action. Hu Han-min overruled Borodin's protest and vindicated his judgment by suppressing the revolt in two weeks during May 1925.

The Kuomintang leaders then confronted the thorny succession problem. The major aspirants were generally assumed to be Hu Han-min,

Wang Ching-wei, and Liao Chung-k'ai, in that order. All were T'ung-meng-hui veterans who had been associated with Sun Yat-sen for many years and who had enjoyed his personal confidence. However, it was obvious that no single individual could hope to occupy Sun Yat-sen's position and command the same obedience from his associates. The Central Political Council, with Hu Han-min as *de facto* chairman, held a series of meetings in July 1925 and decided on the organization of a new national government. That government was officially inaugurated on 1 July 1925, with a government committee of 16 members. Five of these formed the standing committee: Hu Han-min, Wang Ching-wei, Liao Chung-k'ai, Hsü Ch'ung-chih, and T'an Yen-k'ai (q.v.). Wang Ching-wei was elected chairman of the government, and Hu was named minister of foreign affairs. This development led to a rift between Hu and Wang.

On 30 August 1925 the still unsettled foundations of the new Kuomintang leadership were shaken when Liao Chung-k'ai, who had been elected minister of finance, was assassinated. The mystery surrounding Liao's death has never been penetrated. However, Hu Han-min's cousin Hu I-sheng, himself a veteran revolutionary, was thought to be a principal figure behind the planning of the murder because he had publicly denounced Liao Chung-k'ai for his pro-Communist views. Hu I-sheng fled the city. Although Hu Han-min was absolved from complicity in the crime, he was obliged to retire from active political life. The Kuomintang sent him on a mission to the Soviet Union to study party organization and political and economic conditions. Hu left Canton on 22 August 1925 and reached Moscow on 18 October, where he was accorded a civil reception and was given the opportunity to make several speeches. In February 1926 he attended the Third Congress of the Comintern and presented an application from the Kuomintang for membership in that organization. That act led to an interview with Stalin, but the matter of Kuomintang admission was tabled.

While Hu Han-min was in the Soviet Union, the Kuomintang held its Second National Congress at Canton in January 1926. That meeting was dominated by Wang Ching-wei, and a substantial group of Wang's supporters were elected to the central apparatus of the party. Hu Han-min was reelected to the Central Executive Committee and the Central Political Council. He also was made a member of the standing committee of the Central Executive Committee and director of the workers department of the central party headquarters.

Hu Han-min returned to China in April 1926, but remained inactive in Shanghai until the spring of 1927. Then, after the anti-Communist Kuomintang leaders broke with the Kuomintang regime at Wuhan and established a national government at Nanking on 18 April 1927, Hu was elected chairman of that government. His first official act was to order the arrest of Borodin and nearly 200 members of the Chinese Communist party, including Ch'en Tu-hsiu (q.v.), its general secretary. Hu held the chairmanship for only four months, however; he left Nanking for Shanghai in August 1927. By that time the Wuhan leaders had also taken action against the Communists. In September, the two factions of the Kuomintang reunited.

In January 1928 Hu Han-min left China on a trip to Europe, accompanied by his daughter, Hu Mu-lan. Sun Fo (q.v.) and C. C. Wu (Wu Ch'ao-shu, q.v.) also traveled with him. On the way, the party stopped at Singapore to attend receptions given them by the local Chinese community. On his way to one of the receptions on 8 February, C. C. Wu was wounded when an attempt was made to kill him. It was later discovered that the assassins, allegedly Communist agents, had intended to kill Hu Han-min, who had been prevented from attending the reception by another engagement. Hu Han-min then traveled to Turkey. He had great admiration for that country's modernization programs, directed by Mustafa Kemal (Ataturk). In Ankara, he had a long discussion with Ismet (Inonu), the prime minister. Hu was greatly impressed by the achievements of the Turkish republic. He also visited France, Germany, Italy, England, and other European countries before returning to China in August 1928.

Hu Han-min arrived at Nanking in September 1928. The following month, when the new National Government was established, he was appointed president of the Legislative Yuan, one of the five principal organs of government. After the collapse of the 1930 revolt against Nanking led by Feng Yü-hsiang (q.v.), Wang Ching-wei, and Yen Hsi-shan (the so-called enlarged conference movement), the National Government decided to convoke a national assembly and adopt a provisional constitution. These had been among the demands made by the enlarged conference rebels, and they possessed some political appeal. Hu Han-min, however, held strong views on political development in China and adamantly opposed the creation of a constitution. Hu's stand, derived from the concepts of Sun Yat-sen, was that a single-party dictatorship under the Kuomintang and a period of political tutelage were necessary. After tutelage had been effective, a constitutional era could be inaugurated. His uncompromising stand brought him into open conflict with Chiang Kai-shek.

Hu resigned the presidency of the Legislative Yuan on 28 February 1931. Almost immediately, he was placed under house arrest by Chiang Kai-shek and sent to T'angshan near Nanking. Hu's confinement precipitated another major crisis in the Kuomintang. On 30 April, four senior members of the Central Supervisory Committee of the Kuomintang issued a statement impeaching Chiang Kai-shek for the illegal arrest of Hu Han-min. The four were: Lin Sen, who had succeeded Hu as president of the Legislative Yuan; Ku Ying-fen (q.v.), who had joined the T'ung-meng-hui at its inception in 1905; and Hsiao Fo-ch'eng and Teng Tse-ju, the two overseas Chinese leaders who were old and close friends of Hu. Military officers in Kwangtung, led by Ch'en Chi-t'ang (q.v.), immediately announced their support of the statement. Kuomintang leaders who were opposed to the authority exercised by Chiang Kai-shek assembled at Canton on 27 May 1931 in an extraordinary conference of members of successive central committees of the party. Among the prominent Kuomintang leaders present were Wang Ching-wei, Sun Fo, T'ang Shao-yi, Eugene Ch'en, Ch'en Chi-t'ang, and Li Tsung-jen.

The extraordinary conference led to the formation on 28 May 1931 of an opposition national government at Canton. Civil war threatened. The situation was saved by the national crisis precipitated by the Japanese invasion of Manchuria in September 1931. In the face of that grave threat the leaders at Nanking and Canton held peace talks. Hu Han-min was released, and the feuding party and government factions were reunited. After his release, Hu Han-min paid a visit to Canton in late November 1931, partly to attend to funeral arrangements for his friend Ku Ying-fen, who had died in October. Hu then took up residence in Hong Kong. Although the secessionist government at Canton had been abolished, new organs were created through which the provinces of Kwangtung and Kwangsi continued to maintain a state of virtual autonomy. These organs were the Southwest Executive Headquarters of the Kuomintang and the Southwest Political Council. Although Hu Han-min remained in Hong Kong, he gave moral support to the leaders of the southern provinces, Ch'en Chi-t'ang and Li Tsung-jen, whose course of action sometimes was incompatible with Nanking's policies and orders.

In February 1933 Hu Han-min founded the *San-min-chu-i yueh-k'an* [Three People's Principles monthly], in which he published many of his writings on the political thought of Sun Yat-sen. Hu considered himself the inheritor and legitimate interpreter of Sun's political legacy, and he had edited a five-volume collection of Sun's writings, the *Tsung-li ch'uan-chi*, which had been published in 1930. In March 1933, when Wang Ching-wei passed through Hong Kong on his way back to China from France, he called on Hu Han-min and tried to persuade him of the validity of some of his views on the national situation. However, this meeting of the two former friends, which proved to be the last, was not a success.

In November 1933, when Ch'en Ming-shu and Li Chi-shen (qq.v.), with the support of the Nineteenth Route Army, staged the Fukien revolt and organized a short-lived people's government at Foochow, Hu's name was linked with the movement. Hu set the record straight by joining the leaders at Canton in a message to the Fukien insurgents which condemned their action. He also issued a personal statement on the general political situation which, while condemning the Fukien uprising, stated in categorical terms his disapproval of Chiang Kai-shek's policies and associates.

In June 1935 Hu Han-min left Hong Kong on a trip to Italy, Switzerland, Germany, and France. He left France toward the end of 1935 and arrived in Hong Kong on 19 January 1936. In the meantime, the Fifth National Congress of the Kuomintang, held at Nanking in November 1935, had reelected him to the Central

Executive Committee. Two veteran Kuomintang leaders, Chü Cheng and Yeh Ch'u-ts'ang (qq.v.), were sent to Hong Kong in early 1936 to invite Hu to return to Nanking and be welcomed into the central organization of the party. Hu replied that he would do so later in the spring. He went to Canton, where he died of apoplexy on 12 May 1936, at the age of 56. He was given a state funeral and was buried on 13 July 1936 in the northeastern suburb of Canton. He was survived by his wife, Ch'en Shu-tzu, and his daughter, Hu Mu-lan, who had been his traveling companion on most of his trips outside China after 1925.

The most complete account of Hu Han-min's career is Chiang Yung-ching's *Hu Han-min hsien-sheng nien-p'u-kao* [chronological biography of Hu Han-min], published in Taipei in 1961.

Hu Lin 胡 霖
Hu Cheng-chih 胡 政 之

Hu Lin (1893–1949), chief editor of the *Ta Kung Pao* (1916–25), who became general manager of the newspaper and related enterprises of the Hai-chi Company in 1926. He also served as a resident member of the People's Political Council (1942–45) and as a non-partisan member of the Chinese delegation to the United Nations Conference on International Organization at San Francisco in 1945.

Little is known of Hu Lin's background or childhood except that he was born and educated in Szechwan and that he received a college education in Japan, majoring in law and science. After returning to China in 1911, he passed the bar examinations in Shanghai. He served briefly as a private tutor and then joined the staff of the *Ta-kung-ho pao* [great republican paper] as a translator of Japanese news items. Hu wrote so well that he soon was asked to contribute articles to the *Ta-kung-ho pao* and other Shanghai newspapers.

About 1914 Hu Lin left Shanghai to serve as judge of the Chinkiang branch of the Kiangsu provincial high court. In 1915 he went to Peking, where he combined his two major interests by teaching at Peking Law College and serving as Peking correspondent for the *Ta-kung-ho pao* and other Shanghai newspapers.

When Japan presented the Twenty-one Demands in 1915, there was a complete news blackout on the matter in China, and Chinese reporters could not gain access to any of the high officials who took part in the negotiations. Because he knew both Japanese and English, Hu was able to glean some information about the negotiations and the Japanese terms from foreign correspondents in Peking, notably Frederick Moore of the Associated Press and William Giles of the London *Daily Mail* and the Chicago *Tribune*. Thus, he was able to write exclusive stories for his Shanghai papers.

In mid-1915, after the *Ta-kung-ho pao* suspended publication, Hu went to Kirin to serve as counselor of the provincial government in charge of financial affairs and foreign relations. He returned to Peking in 1916 to become a counselor in the ministry of interior. About the same time, he became chief editor of the *Ta Kung Pao*. This newspaper, founded in 1902 by Ying Lien-chih (q.v.), had built up a large circulation in the Tientsin-Peking area and a reputation as a constructive and impartial journal. After Ying had relinquished the chief editorship in 1913, the paper had suffered from lack of management and policy. Hu, on assuming the chief editorship, determined to restore the *Ta Kung Pao* to its former eminence. In 1918 he undertook a two-year tour of more than twenty countries to increase his knowledge of world affairs and to broaden the coverage of the *Ta Kung Pao*. His dispatches from abroad, especially those from the Paris Peace Conference, were read avidly in China.

After returning to China in 1920, Hu founded the *Hsin-she-hui pao* [new society daily] in Peking. The following year, he went to Shanghai to establish the Kuo-wen News Service, which was the foremost news agency in China for many years. He also founded the *Kuo-wen Weekly* and served as director and general manager of both enterprises.

Ying Lien-chih died in 1926, and the *Ta Kung Pao* suspended publication for a brief period. It was reorganized in September under a holding company, the Hai-chi Company, which was directed by Wu Ting-ch'ang (q.v.). Hu Lin became general manager, and Chang Chi-luan (q.v.) was appointed editor in chief. The new company also assumed direction of the Kuo-wen enterprises.

The reorganization of the *Ta Kung Pao* coincided with the Northern Expedition. The paper supported the aims of the Kuomintang, and it was vehemently anti-imperialist and anti-warlord. Although Hu Lin did not join the Kuomintang, he supported the Northern Expedition and Chiang Kai-shek's leadership in the National Government. As the Kuomintang consolidated power, the *Ta Kung Pao's* influence and circulation increased commensurately. Because the *Ta Kung Pao* was based in Tientsin, its editorial freedom in criticizing government policies was greater than that of newspapers in the Nanking-Shanghai area. It became known as a liberal newspaper.

In April 1936 a Shanghai edition of the *Ta Kung Pao* was established, partly because of the increasing threat to north China by Japan. By September 1936, the tenth anniversary of its reorganization, the *Ta Kung Pao* had a staff of 700 and a combined circulation of about 100,000, and the *Kuo-wen Weekly* had attained a circulation of about 20,000. These achievements reflected the managerial and journalistic abilities of Hu Lin.

In 1937, after the Sino-Japanese war began, both editions of the *Ta Kung Pao* had to suspend publication. Hu went to Hong Kong to establish a new edition, using machinery evacuated from Tientsin. The Shanghai plant was moved to Hankow in September and to Chunking in October, where a new edition was established. Although the Chungking edition of the *Ta Kung Pao* endorsed the war policies of the National Government, it became sharply critical of many government policies. The Hong Kong edition began publication on 13 August 1938.

After Hong Kong fell, Hu went to Chungking. From 1942 to 1946 he served as a resident member of the People's Political Council. In November 1943 he was appointed to a mission to England headed by Wang Shih-chieh. The delegation arrived in London on 3 December and returned to Chungking, by way of the United States, on 27 March 1944. Hu participated in the 1945 United Nations Conference on International Organization at San Francisco as a non-partisan member of the Chinese delegation. He also utilized his second overseas trip to talk and correspond with manufacturers about the purchase of printing machinery for postwar expansion of the *Ta Kung Pao*.

When the war ended in 1945, the *Ta Kung Pao* quickly reestablished its Tientsin, Shanghai, and Hong Kong editions. It now was the most formidable newspaper complex in China. During the struggle between the Kuomintang and the Chinese Communists for control of the mainland, the *Ta Kung Pao* moved steadily toward endorsement of the Communists.

Hu Lin became ill and died in 1949. Although the *Ta Kung Pao* continued to publish after his death (in Peking and Hong Kong), its traditional policies and viewpoints died with him, and the paper became a news channel for the Central People's Government.

Hu Shih   胡 適
T. Shih-chih   適 之

Hu Shih (1891–24 February 1962), leading member of the Peking University galaxy of intellectuals. His efforts to promote the use of pai-hua [the vernacular] in writing sparked the literary and cultural movements of the 1920's. A disciple of John Dewey, he utilized Western philosophical terminology and methodology in reinterpreting classical Chinese thought. His historical studies of pai-hua literature were important works. From 1937 until his death, he spent only six years in China. He lived in the United States, serving as Chinese ambassador from 1938 to 1942. He became president of the Academia Sinica in Taiwan in 1958.

A native of Chihsi hsien, Anhwei, Hu Shih was born in Shanghai. At the time of his birth, his father, Hu Ch'uan (1841–1895; T. T'ieh-hua), was serving as inspector of the likin barriers in the Shanghai area. His mother, Feng Shun-ti (1873–1918), was Hu Ch'uan's third wife, and Hu Shih was their only child. In 1892 Hu Ch'uan was transferred to Taiwan, and his family joined him there in 1893. Hu Shih and his mother returned to the family home in Chihsi in early 1895, but Hu Ch'uan remained in Taitung, where he was serving as prefectural magistrate and garrison commander, until summer. He sailed from Taiwan in the middle of August. Shortly after landing at Amoy, he died, probably of beri-beri. The four-year-old Hu Shih was left in the care of his mother and his paternal uncles. The family's economic position declined steadily, partly because Feng Shun-ti had to care for Hu Ch'uan's children by earlier marriages as well as for Hu Shih. The domestic tensions and financial anxieties of those years formed some of Hu Shih's most vivid childhood memories.

From 1895 to 1904 Hu Shih was educated by uncles and cousins in the family school in Chihsi. He was, by his own account, a precocious student, having learned a thousand characters before entering school at the age of four. He received a classical primary education and read a good deal of history. He also devoured the popular fiction which was part of every Chinese schoolboy's informal education. In 1904 he accompanied one of his older half-brothers to Shanghai in search of a "modern" education. He remained in the city for six years and attended several of the so-called new schools, which taught English, Western mathematics, and rudimentary natural science in addition to more traditional subjects. Among these was the China National Institute [Chung-kuo kung-hsueh], a radical institution established in 1905 by Chinese students who had studied in Japan, most of whom were avowed supporters of the revolutionary movement. Hu studied at the institute from 1906 to 1908. Although he did not become active in the revolutionary movement, he participated in student politics and served as editor of a student-sponsored newspaper called *Ching-yeh hsun pao* [the struggle]. By 1908, however, he no longer could afford to go to school. He remained in Shanghai, supporting himself by teaching English and by doing editorial work.

Hu's frustrating financial difficulties led him to mild dissipation. In the spring of 1910 he was jailed after having a drunken scrap with the police. At this point, he resolved to reform his ways. After two months of diligent preparation, he went to Peking to take the examinations for the Boxer Indemnity Scholarship. He was one of seventy successful candidates who sailed for the United States in August.

Hu Shih enrolled at the College of Agriculture at Cornell University because he then subscribed to the popular belief that China's greatest need was men with technical expertise. However, he failed to develop any interest in his studies, and early in 1912 he transferred to the College of Arts and Sciences, where he majored in philosophy. He was an excellent student, though by his own estimate somewhat too bookish, and in 1913 he was elected to Phi Beta Kappa. After receiving a B.A. degree in June 1914, he remained at Cornell for another year to begin graduate work in philosophy. During this period, he became a close friend of Y. R. Chao (Chao Yuen-ren, q.v.), who was one of his classmates. In the summer of 1915 Hu discovered John Dewey's writings on experimentalism, and in September he entered Columbia University and began working for his Ph.D. under Dewey. His doctoral dissertation, "The Development of the Logical Method in Ancient China," completed in 1917, was designed to discover "pragmatic" tendencies in early Chinese philosophy. It foreshadowed the scholarly uses to which Hu would put his understanding of experimentalist methodology. In June 1917 he left the United States, and in July, nearly seven years after his departure, he landed in Shanghai.

Hu Shih's education in Shanghai and America led him to become, in many respects, thoroughly untraditional in his opinions. Many of his contemporaries regarded him as the epitome of the Westernized Chinese. However, it is apparent that traditional ideas and attitudes had influenced his intellect and temperament. Hu Ch'uan had been a Confucian in the rationalist tradition of Chu Hsi. He had written some poems expressing these convictions, which were among the first writings that Hu Shih had read as a child. The environment in which the boy grew up, however, had been colored by the Buddhist faith of his mother and the other women of the household. Hu's first intellectual adventure began when, at the age of ten or eleven, he stumbled upon anti-Buddhist passages in the *Tzu-chih t'ung-chien* and the writings of Chu Hsi. The scepticism thus stimulated, supplemented in later years by ideas drawn from T. H. Huxley and others, became one of Hu's chief weapons in his struggle to free the Chinese mind from the bonds of habit and tradition. In Shanghai, he had read Yen Fu's translations of Huxley's *Evolution and Ethics*, Mill's *On Liberty*, and Montesquieu's *L'Espirit des lois*. Liang Ch'i-ch'ao's essays in the *Hsin-min ts'ung-pao* had given him at least a general understanding of Western historical and intellectual development, and Liang was also responsible for bringing other aspects of Chinese thought to Hu's attention. The Shanghai years had laid the foundations for Hu's later acceptance of Western values, but, at the same time, it was in Shanghai that he had come to share with other intellectuals of his own generation the common burden of their nation's failing strength and the common commitment to the mission of "enlightenment."

Hu Shih's intellectual development in the United States was influenced at least as much by the extracurricular concerns of his undergraduate years as by his formal courses of study. He was active in several Chinese student groups, but he did not limit his social and intellectual friendships to the Chinese student community. He was a member of the Cornell Cosmopolitan Club, through which he became involved in the International Federation of Students and in several of the pacifist organizations that flourished before and during the First World War. Woodrow Wilson's idealistic internationalism made a profound impression on him. In 1915, when Japan presented her Twenty-one Demands to Yuan Shih-k'ai's government, Hu stood by his pacifist convictions, urging "patriotic sanity" and arguing against a militant Chinese response.

Hu's enthusiastic acceptance of experimentalism after 1915 did not necessitate a fundamental revision of his intellectual position. The great appeal of Dewey's experimentalist philosophy, as Hu interpreted it, was that it provided a methodological scheme for social and cultural reconstruction which harmonized with his own moderate convictions. He was better prepared, by temperament as well as experience, to understand the implications of experimentalism than were most of those to whom he preached its tenets after his return to China.

In the autumn of 1917 Hu Shih became a professor of philosophy at Peking University, thus beginning an association with China's most renowned center of higher education which was to endure, despite several lengthy interruptions, for more than three decades. He remained in Peking, except for brief absences, until 1926. Then, following his appointment to the British Boxer Indemnity Fund committee, he traveled to London (by way of Manchuria, the Soviet Union, and Europe), and thence to the United States. After returning to China in the spring of 1927, he spent three years in Shanghai teaching philosophy at Kuanghua University. From April 1928 to May 1930 he also served as president of the China National Institute, his old school, which had become a private university at Woosung. Hu attempted to obtain official recognition of the institute as a

university, but he failed because he had antagonized a number of Nanking officials by criticizing National Government policies. In 1930 he made an arrangement with Chiang Monlin (Chiang Meng-lin, q.v.), the minister of education and an old friend, to resign in return for official recognition and registration of the school.

Hu returned to Peking to head the compilation and translation bureau of the China Foundation for the Promotion of Education and Culture. He had been a member of the board of the foundation since 1926. Early in 1931 he was appointed dean of the college of arts at Peking University by Chiang Monlin, who had become chancellor of the university. Hu remained at Peking until the outbreak of the Sino-Japanese war in 1937, making only one brief excursion abroad, in 1933, to deliver the Haskell Lectures at the University of Chicago (collected and published as *The Chinese Renaissance* in 1934). In July 1937 Hu attended the Lushan Conference in Kiangsi. Shortly thereafter, he set out on a government-sponsored goodwill tour of the United States and Europe.

Hu Shih's intellectual activities and influence reached their peak in the 20 years between his return to China in 1917 and his departure in 1937. His reputation as an intellectual rebel and a leader in the movement to replace the classical written language with pai-hua [the vernacular] had been established during his years of study in the United States. In January 1917 his "Wen-hsueh kai-liang ch'u-i" [tentative proposals for literary reform] was published in Ch'en Tu-hsiu's influential review, *Hsin ch'ing-nien* [new youth]. It was followed by other essays arguing the same case, most notably "Li-shih-ti wen-hsueh kuan-nien lun" [on the genetic concept of literature] and "Chien-she ti wen-hsueh ko-ming lun" [on a constructive revolution in literature]. These essays appeared in May 1917 and April 1918, respectively. His principal contributions to the literary revolution were, like these, essays on problems of style and content in a historical context. He was not a creative writer, and his only efforts in that direction, except for translations of a few short stories, were poems in the vernacular style published in 1919 as *Ch'ang-shih chi* [a collection of experiments]. He was, however, a master of straight-forward and lucid prose.

In Peking, Hu belonged to the small group of avant-garde intellectuals who gathered around the *Hsin ch'ing-nien*—Ch'en Tu-hsiu, Li Ta-chao, Ch'ien Hsuan-t'ung, Chou Tso-jen and his brother Chou Shu-jen (Lu Hsün), Kao I-han, T'ao Meng-ho, Liu Fu, and others. The Literary Revolution was only one of their causes, a single aspect of a broader campaign directed against the whole structure of traditional values. Hu published a number of essays in the *Hsin ch'ing-nien* on aspects of the general problem of cultural regeneration and intellectual reform: "I-pu-sheng-chu-i," a paper on Ibsenism which involved a discussion of the relationship between the individual and his society and of individual responsibilities, in June 1918; "Chen-ts'ao wen-t'i" [the question of chastity] in July 1918, and "Mei-kuo ti fu-nü" [American women], in September 1918, concerning the emancipation of women; "Pu-hsiu" [immortality], a summation of his own philosophy of life, in February 1919; and "Shih-yeh chu-i" [experimentalism], an exposition of the fundamentals of pragmatism, published on the eve of John Dewey's arrival in China in 1919.

As John Dewey's most illustrious Chinese disciple, Hu was active during the two years of Dewey's lecture tour (1919–21) in China, serving as his interpreter for lectures in Peking and elsewhere and doing what he could to exploit the interest in experimentalist philosophy which Dewey's presence stimulated. Hu repeatedly affirmed that the scientific method of experimentalism—initial scepticism, clear definition of specific and concrete problems, a process of logical reasoning to hypothetic conclusions or solutions, and careful attention to final results—represented a universally applicable approach to the solution of social and political problems. Above all else, he strove to impart to his audience a respect for this methodology and its uses.

Much of Hu's time and energy was devoted to using experimentalist methods to reevaluate various aspects of Chinese tradition. In a number of essays, reviews, and prefaces he discussed the intent of such scholarship. Among these were "Kuo-hsueh chi-k'an fa-k'an hsuan-yen" [inaugural announcement of the *Chinese Studies Quarterly*], which appeared in 1923, and "Chih-hsueh ti fang-fa yü ts'ai-liao" [the methods and materials of scholarship], which appeared in 1928. Hu also wrote about specific aspects of Chinese philosophy. In 1919 he had published the first volume of a work, based on his dissertation, which dealt with the sources of texts traditionally ascribed to the classical philosophers. He never completed the *Chung-kuo che-hsueh shih ta-kang* [outline of the history of Chinese philosophy]. However, his "Ch'ing-tai hsueh-che ti chih-hsueh fang-fa" [the intellectual methodology of Ch'ing dynasty scholars] of 1921 and his "Chi-ko fan-li-hsueh ti ssu-hsiang-chia" [some anti-li-hsueh thinkers] of 1928 discussed the writings of Ch'ing dynasty scholars who, according to Hu, had a "scientific" point of view. These studies of the history of Chinese thought were intended to substantiate Hu's conviction that the methods of modern scientific thought had Chinese antecedents and could therefore be appropriated as something not entirely alien to traditional inclinations.

In other areas of scholarly endeavor, Hu sought to demonstrate the usefulness of experimentalist methodology in clarifying hitherto confused issues of cultural history. Among the results of such research were several studies of the lineage of the great pai-hua novels, starting with the *Shui-hu chuan* (*The Water Margin*) and the *Hung-lou meng* (*Dream of the Red Chamber*), which shed new light on questions of authorship and textual continuity. Hu's interest in vernacular literature also led him to undertake a history of its development, the first volume of which, covering the period through the T'ang dynasty, was published in 1928 as *Pai-hua wen-hsueh-shih, shang-chüan*. Like his history of philosophy, this work remained unfinished, but a number of lectures on related topics were collected and published separately as the *Kuo-yü wen-hsueh-shih* in 1927.

Hu Shih proclaimed himself an experimentalist in politics as well as in scholarship. He argued that the attitudes and methods of experimentalist analysis were essential to the examination of contemporary social and political problems and that by isolating and attacking specific problems, gradual but certain progress could be assured. The logic of this particularistic approach brought him into conflict with many other reform-minded intellectuals. Although he remained strongly iconoclastic in his opinions concerning China's traditional culture and its place in the modern world, he consistently opposed any attempt to solve China's problems by revolutionary means. He was, moreover, profoundly distrustful of political activity on the part of intellectuals, and he repeatedly affirmed his belief that no genuine solution to the immediate problems of Chinese politics would be possible until new social and intellectual attitudes had been implanted and cultivated over a period of years or decades.

In spite of his beliefs, Hu Shih frequently felt compelled to speak out on questions of political concern, particularly in response to the spread of Marxism and militant nationalism. In the summer of 1919 Hu had attacked the tendency of his fellow intellectuals to accept vague and ready-made analyses of China's situation and all-embracing solutions to its problems in an article entitled "Wen-t'i yü chu-i" [problems and -isms]. The immediate target of his displeasure was Marxism, toward which Li Ta-chao and Ch'en Tu-hsiu (qq.v.), together with many students and younger intellectuals, already were gravitating. Hu's rejection of Marxism stemmed from his belief that it was intellectually dogmatic and founded on assumptions that could not withstand critical examination. He was not initially fearful of its political and social implications, and when he saw Communism in practice in the Soviet Union in 1926 he was greatly impressed by the purposefulness of its programs and the willingness of Soviet leaders to experiment. As late as the mid-1930's he continued to think of Soviet Communism as a logical continuation of the course of Western political development. But he did not believe that its underlying premises could be applied to the Chinese situation, and he asserted unequivocally that evolutionary progress, not revolutionary change, was China's best hope. Addressing himself as much to the Kuomintang as to the Chinese Communist party, Hu argued his case against revolution in these terms: revolution accomplishes its aims with speed and efficiency, but is blind and unreasoning in its course and too often diverted from its original intent; evolution (or, as he sometimes qualified it, "conscious evolution"), though slower and in certain ways more wasteful, is more easily controlled and less likely to do unnecessary damage. He recorded these views in such articles as "Wo-men tsou na-i t'iao-lu?" [which road shall we follow], of 1929, and "Chieh-shao wo tzu-chi ti ssu-hsiang" [introducing my own thought], of 1930.

Hu Shih's aversion to revolution and his concern for social continuity were shared by Liang Ch'i-ch'ao (q.v.) and other spokesmen of the neo-conservative viewpoint that took form in the 1920's. In May 1922 Hu, together with V. K. Ting, Chiang Wei-tz'u, and others, began to publish the magazine *Nu-li chou pao* [endeavor]. In its second issue was a manifesto entitled "Wo-men ti cheng-chih chu-chang" [our political proposals], written by Hu Shih and signed by 16 leading intellectuals, including men of such divergent opinions as Liang Shu-ming, Li Ta-chao, Ts'ai Yuan-pei, and Hu. The purpose of this document was to define good government in terms general enough to elicit further discussion and thus to arouse "a militant and decisive public opinion" to press for political reforms. However, in more important respects Hu Shih's ideas and those of the neo-conservatives conflicted. Liang Ch'i-ch'ao, together with Carsun Chang (Chang Chia-sen), and Liang Shu-ming (qq.v.), directly challenged Hu's system of values by declaring that Chinese traditional values were more humane than those of the West and more beneficial to the spiritual life of man, by emphasizing the superiority of intuition to Western reason, and by attacking what they termed the materialistic and legalistic basis of Western civilization. Hu, in defending science and Western civilization, contended that the distinction drawn between "spiritual" and "material" development was a false one. He urged his fellow intellectuals not to deceive themselves by seeking grounds for the belief that China occupies a unique position in the world. Instead, he argued, they should become thoroughly "modernized" and sufficiently tough-minded to accept the unflattering position assigned to China when her accomplishments are measured on the scale of world history.

The debates on the place of scientific values in civilization raged throughout 1923, with Liang Shu-ming, Liang Ch'i-ch'ao, and Carsun Chang on one side, and V. K. Ting and Hu Shih on the other. *Nu-li chou pao* and its monthly supplement, *Tu-shu tsa-chih* [study], were made to serve the defenders of science and Western culture until they ceased publication in October after having opposed Ts'ao K'un's attempt to secure the presidency.

Hu Shih wrote a lengthy preface to a collection of essays, *K'o-hsueh yü jen-sheng-kuan* [science and the philosophy of life], published at the end of 1923. His other writings on the so-called science-philosophy controversy include "Tu Liang Shu-ming hsien-sheng ti Tung Hsi wen-hua chi ch'i che-hsueh" [after reading Liang Shu-ming's "The Culture of East and West and Their Philosophies"], published in 1923; "Women tui-yü Hsi-yang chin-tai wen-ming ti t'ai-tu" [our attitude toward modern Western civilization], published in 1926; and "Shih-p'ing so-wei 'Chung-kuo pen-wei ti wen-hua chien-she' " [a critique of "Cultural Reconstruction on a Chinese Basis"], published in 1935.

The nature of Hu Shih's relationship to the Kuomintang is somewhat obscure. During the early 1920's his contact with the party was minimal, and there is reason to believe that he did not hold a high opinion of Sun Yat-sen or of his prospects as a revolutionary leader. Hu was abroad during the Northern Expedition. By the time he returned to Shanghai in May 1927, Chiang Kai-shek had established firm control of the city. During the next several years, Hu Shih wrote some of his most perceptive political commentaries, most of which were published in *Hsin-yueh* [the crescent moon], a review devoted chiefly to literature and literary criticism which he established in 1928 together with Hsü Chih-mo, Liang Shih-ch'iu, Lo Lung-chi (qq.v.), and several others. Hu's criticisms of the Kuomintang concentrated on two major issues: its position on the questions of political tutelage and constitutionalism and its attitude toward cultural innovation and reform. As in his earlier political writings, Hu emphasized the importance of "the proper organs of government" and the educational responsibilities of the government. He attacked with vigor Sun Yat-sen's doctrine of the difficulty of knowledge, upon which rested the justification for party tutelage. He accused the Kuomintang of maintaining a "reactionary" attitude toward the purposes and accomplishments of the New Culture Movement because of the narrowly nationalistic aims of the revolution. The National Government replied to these criticisms with the charge that Hu was speaking irresponsibly and warned him about the consequences of thus "misleading" the people.

Throughout his life, Hu remained a proud representative of the "no party, no faction" intellectuals. In the *Tu-li p'ing-lun* [independent critic], which he edited in Peking from 1932 to 1937, he continued to speak out against Chinese culturalism, a cause which had revived some-

what as a result of the tradition-oriented New Life Movement launched by the National Government as a means of counteracting the appeal of Communist ideology. Nevertheless, the changing problems of the 1930's drew Hu closer to the Nationalist position on a number of issues, a reconciliation made easier by the fact that many of Hu's friends of former years had found places for themselves in the Nationalist camp. Hu was among the last to abandon the hope that a *modus vivendi* with Japan might be achieved, primarily because he was convinced that war would destroy everything that had been accomplished in the areas of institutional and intellectual reform over the preceding decades. He also was out of sympathy with the temper of student politics during these years.

When Hu left China in 1937, the years of his greatest influence were behind him. All but six of the remaining years of his life were spent in the United States, and as his contact with events in China lessened, so also did his ability to comment significantly on them.

In September 1938, upon arriving in France after an extended stay in the United States, Hu received notification of his appointment as Chinese ambassador to the United States. In that time of deepening crisis in Japanese-American relations Hu was in many respects an ideal representative of the Chinese cause in the United States—a man Americans knew and respected and who, in turn, liked and respected the American way of life. The years of his ambassadorship were devoted to publicly promoting the Chinese cause, the kind of work in which Hu was most effective. Even before December 1941 much of the burden of diplomatic negotiations designed to secure tangible American aid for the Chinese war effort was entrusted to others, notably T. V. Soong. The entry of the United States into the war radically changed the character of the National Government's aims in Washington. In September 1942 Hu was relieved of his post without explanation and replaced by Wei Tao-ming (q.v.). Hu subsequently was made a special adviser to the Executive Yuan, but he remained in the United States until 1946, writing and lecturing. In May 1943 he contributed a laudatory preface to the first volume of *Eminent Chinese of the Ch'ing Period (1644–1912)*, edited by Arthur W. Hummel. The second volume of the Hummel work contained an extended note by Hu Shih on the results of his intensive research on collated and emended texts of the *Shui-ching chu* [commentary on the book of waterways]. In April–June 1945 he was a member of the Chinese delegation to the United Nations Conference on International Organization in San Francisco, and later that year he served, in the absence of Chu Chia-hua (q.v.), as acting head of the Chinese delegation to the first UNESCO conference in London.

In June 1945 Chiang Monlin resigned the chancellorship of Peking University to become the secretary general of the Executive Yuan. Hu Shih was appointed to succeed his old friend, but he did not return to China immediately to assume this new post. Fu Ssu-nien (q.v.) served as acting chancellor of the university until Hu arrived in mid-1946. Hu remained at Peking University for two-and-a-half years. In November 1946 he served as a nonpartisan delegate to the tempestous constitutional convention of the National Assembly in Nanking held to draft a constitution that would bring to a close the period of political tutelage and one-party dictatorship. The following year he was elected to the first National Assembly under the new constitutional regime. Although Hu lent his support to the National Government in this fashion, he refused to become closely linked with it. In March 1948 he was invited to stand for election to the presidency by Chiang Kai-shek himself, but he declined. A few months later, he was suggested for the premiership. He declined the offer, reportedly remarking that a scholar who could not keep his desk in order was hardly suited to undertake the task of managing a government.

When Chinese Communist forces encircled Peiping in mid-1948, Hu Shih flew to Nanking, leaving behind a large part of his personal library and many manuscripts and letters. From Nanking he went to Shanghai, and thence to the United States. Except for a brief period of service as curator of the Gest Oriental Library at Princeton, he lived in semi-retirement in New York. He wrote articles for *Foreign Affairs* and other journals in which he lamented the expansion of Stalinist authority in China. In his 1954 introduction to John Leighton Stuart's *Fifty Years in China* Hu commented on the role of the United States in the Nationalist-Communist conflict of the 1940's by recounting his reaction to Secretary of State Dean Acheson's letter of transmittal which accompanied the official report *United States Relations with China, 1944–1949*. Hu had made the marginal notation "Matthew 27:24" by Acheson's statement that "nothing that this country did or could have done within the reasonable limits of its capabilities could have changed the result; nothing that was left undone by this country has contributed to it." The Bible verse reads: "When Pilate saw that he could prevail nothing, but that a tumult was made, he took water, and washed his hands before the multitude, saying I am innocent of the blood of this just man: see ye to it."

A collection of learned articles entitled *Ch'ing-chu Hu Shih hsien-sheng liu-shih-wu sui lun-wen-chi* [symposium in honor of Hu Shih on his sixty-fifth birthday] was published in Taiwan under the auspices of the Academia Sinica in 1957. In the autumn of 1958 Hu went to Taiwan and assumed the presidency of the Academia Sinica. Although he retained some influence because of his early, pioneering work, his late writings had little effect on younger Chinese intellectuals. He was among the older literati who supported the magazine *Tzu-yu Chung-kuo* [free China fortnightly], which was published by Lei Chen and others until 1960, when it was forced to suspend publication after Lei was arrested and imprisoned on charges of subversion. The magazine had been highly critical of National Government policies and had published a considerable number of outspoken articles about inefficiency and corruption in the government and the military. It has been noted that many of the older intellectuals guiding the magazine often referred to John Dewey and Bertrand Russell, using the terms they had used in the 1920's, as the culmination of Western scientific enlightenment and seemed to be unaware of later Western works produced in reaction to Dewey's philosophy or of Russell's later writings.

On 24 February 1962, during a reception for new members at the Nankang headquarters of the Academia Sinica, Hu Shih suffered a heart attack and died. He was survived by Chiang Tung-hsiu, whom he had married in 1917, and by two sons.

In his later years, Hu Shih was lionized by Westerners, attacked by Chinese Communists as an agent of "American cultural aggression" and a "lackey of the Chiang Kai-shek regime," and relegated to the history books by many younger Chinese intellectuals. Because of his early work, however, his place in modern Chinese intellectual history is secure. The critic C. T. Hsia has called Hu Shih "the father of the Literary Revolution" because his efforts to promote the use of pai-hua resulted in the literary and cultural movements of the 1920's, which wrought a radical change in the course and content of Chinese literature. His other important contributions to intellectual life in China were his historical works on pai-hua literature and his utilization of Western philosophical terminology and methodology in reinterpreting classical Chinese thought.

Hu Tieh   胡 蝶
West. Butterfly Wu

Hu Tieh (1907–), actress. As Butterfly Wu, she achieved international recognition as the star of Chinese films of the 1920's and early 1930's. She abandoned her career after her marriage to P'an Yu-sheng (Eugene Penn) in 1936, but returned to the screen after his death in 1958.

Little is known about Hu Tieh's childhood. She was the only child of Hu Li-chen, a Cantonese who had migrated to north China as a youth and who had been employed by the railways until he moved to Shanghai. His daughter began her stage career in the small tea-house theaters of Shanghai, where her beauty and stage presence attracted the attention of promoters looking for potential film actresses. She assumed the name Hu Tieh, a pun on the homophonous word for "butterfly." In 1924 she studied at the Chung Hua film company's training school for nine months. She made her screen debut in *Ch'iu-shan yüan* [a deserted wife's hatred], made by the Yu-lien film company. Then she joined the T'ien-i company and made several films, including *Fu-ch'i chih pi-mi* [a husband and wife's secret], *Tien-ying nü-ming-hsing* [a woman film star], and *Pai-she chuan* [the story of the white snake]. All of these were produced in 1926. Hu Tieh then joined the Hsing-p'ien kung-ssu (Star Motion Picture Company), which had been founded in 1922. Under the management of Chang Shih-ch'uan it grew so rapidly that in 1928 it absorbed five other companies. Hu Tieh was an important factor in the rising fortunes of the company. At the height of her fame, Hu received China $500 a month, a considerable salary for those days, particularly for a woman. When the company studios were equipped for sound in 1931, Hu was given the leading role in a film called *Ko-nü hung-mu-tan* [singing peony], which had its premiere at the Strand Theatre in Shanghai on 15 March 1931. The story was by Hung Shen (q.v.), then the chief script-writer for the company, and it concerned the domestic tribulations of a singer. This film shared the distinction of being a pioneer Chinese sound film with a picture called *Yü-kuo t'ien-ch'ing* [clear sky after rain], made by the T'ien-i company. *Yü-kuo t'ien-ch'ing* was severely criticized by one Peiping reviewer who, among other technical deficiencies, found fault with Hu Tieh's pronunciation of Mandarin. Few of the film stars of the time were natives of north China, and most of the film companies employed teachers to improve their accents, passages of dialogue being rehearsed on the sets between "takes." Hu Tieh, who originally had a Shanghai accent, was no exception to the rule, but she conquered the northern accent sufficiently to win the critics' praise for the majority of her films. During this period, Hu acquired the English stage names of Butterfly Wu and Miss Butterfly.

Altogether, Hu Tieh played in more than 20 films for the Star Motion Picture Company. Her most famous role was in the picture *Mei-mei hua* [two sisters], which brought her a citation as Movie Queen of China. Its two-month run in a Shanghai cinema in 1935 marked the first time that a Chinese film exceeded the records of foreign films for long runs. *Mei-mei hua* was essentially an exposé of the Chinese family system, although it was scarcely original in theme or constructive in message. The action centered around two sisters who had been separated in childhood and who were brought together again in later life, unrecognized by each other. One had become the concubine of a wealthy warlord, the other, her servant. The latter was caught stealing from her sister-employer and was sent to jail. Hu Tieh played the double role of rich and poor sister in this film. Although such films were leftist in sentiment to some extent, they made no attempt to portray the dignity of labor, but rather submerged their themes in an overwhelming atmosphere of melodramatic tragedy.

In February 1935 Hu Tieh sailed for Russia as a member of a cultural group led by W. W. Yen (Yen Hui-ch'ing, q.v.), the Chinese ambassador to Moscow. The actor Mei Lan-fang and his troupe were also in this group. The visit was arranged under the auspices of VOKS, the Soviet Society for Cultural Relations with Foreign Countries. The Chinese party traveled by sea to avoid passing through Japanese-occupied territory in north China. Hu Tieh's visit to Moscow was arranged to coincide with an international film congress being held there, and the group arrived in the Russian capital on 12 March. After an official banquet given by the Commissariat for Foreign Affairs in the government mansion Spiridonovika, Hu Tieh entertained the assembled company with a concert of Chinese folk songs sung in the Cantonese, Shanghai, and Szechwan dialects.

Mei Lan-fang and Hu Tieh left Russia for Warsaw on 20 April 1935 and then visited Germany, France, Italy, and England. In London, Hu Tieh visited English film studios and, in particular, spent time on the sets with the London stars Jessie Matthews and Sonnie Hale. She then returned to China. In 1936 she married P'an Yu-sheng (Eugene Penn), a Shanghai businessman who ran his own manufacturing firm. His company later specialized in the making of enamelware with the trademark "Butterfly." After the Sino-Japanese war began in 1937, Hu Tieh and her husband went to Hong Kong. They were living there when the Japanese occupied the British colony in 1942. Mei Lan-fang was also a refugee in Hong Kong at this time. The Japanese approached both artists on a number of occasions, requesting Hu Tieh to make films under their sponsorship and Mei to return to the stage. Both artists declined the Japanese proposals; Mei grew a luxuriant mustache, which effectively debarred him from playing his usual roles. In August 1943 Hu Tieh and her husband escaped from Hong Kong aboard a junk and made their way to Chungking, where they remained for the rest of the war. During this time Hu Tieh appeared in one film, *Chien-kuo chih lu* [the way of a nation], made in the autumn of 1944. In Chungking, she also gave a song recital to aid the war effort.

After the war, Hu Tieh and her husband returned to Shanghai, only to leave again in 1948 for Hong Kong. In 1958 her husband died, and in the following year rumors which had circulated for some time were confirmed when Hu Tieh signed a film contract with the Shaw Brother Studios. Her first picture was called *Hou-men* [back door], a story about the love of a middle-aged couple for an adopted child. The setting was the nostalgic no-man's land created in the minds of the Shanghai exiles in Hong Kong. Hu Tieh was awarded the best actress award at the Asian Film Festival of 1960.

Hu Tieh became a symbol of an era. Through the new medium of the film she rose to social prominence and professional independence in the face of deep-rooted public prejudice against women in the world of entertainment. Her achievements marked a new stage in the emancipation of Chinese women. Even though most of the films she made have been forgotten, her attainments encouraged other women to embark on careers in the arts. Hu Tieh had one son, P'an Chia-mo, and a daughter, P'an Chia-li, who studied in Edinburgh.

Hu Tsung-nan　　　　胡 宗 南
T. Shou-shan　　　　　壽 山

Hu Tsung-nan (1895–14 February 1962), Nationalist army commander who became known as the "King of the Northwest." During the Sino-Japanese war he commanded the First Army, the Seventeenth Army Group, and the Thirty-fourth Group Army. In 1943 he received command of the First War Area. He served the National Government in Taiwan as commander of the guerrilla forces on Tach'eng Island, governor of Chekiang, and commander of the Pescadores.

Hsiaofeng, Chekiang, was the birthplace of Hu Tsung-nan. After receiving a primary education in the Chinese classics, in 1911 he enrolled at the Wuhsing Middle School. After graduation, he became a primary-school teacher in his native town.

In 1924 Hu went south to enroll at the newly founded Whampoa Military Academy. Chiang Kai-shek, the commandant of the academy, and his associates had planned to select a class of 324 cadets, but they finally chose 499 young men from among 2,000 candidates. Hu was almost rejected because he was thin and short, but Wang Po-ling, the chief instructor, successfully argued for his admission. Hu was graduated from the academy on 30 October 1924. Soon afterwards, he was appointed a section leader in a cadre regiment which served in the first eastern expedition against Ch'en Chiung-ming (q.v.) in January 1925. The regiment then was ordered to Canton to suppress a revolt led by Yunnan and Kwangsi militarists. Hu's distinguished performance in this campaign earned him a promotion to platoon commander. During the second eastern expedition, launched in October, Hu again performed bravely and gained the notice of Chiang Kai-shek. As a result, he was promoted to deputy battalion commander.

By the time the Northern Expedition began in July 1926, Hu had become the commander of the 2nd Regiment of the 1st Division of the First Army. His troops marched through Hunan, Kiangsi, and Chekiang and then participated in the occupation of Shanghai and Nanking in the spring of 1927. At the end of the year, Hu was made commander of the 22nd Division, and when the Northern Expedition forces were reorganized in 1928, he received command of the 2nd Brigade of the 1st Division.

From 1928 to 1931 Hu fought many battles in support of Chiang Kai-shek's authority. In the spring of 1928 he led the 2nd Brigade to Hankow after defeating the Kwangsi army in that area. He marched north in May to fight Feng Yü-hsiang's army in Honan. In January 1929 he crushed the rebellion of T'ang Sheng-chih (q.v.) at Chengchow. Hu also participated in the successful 1930 campaign against the coalition of Feng Yü-hsiang and Yen Hsi-shan (qq.v.). He then received command of the 1st Division.

From late 1930 until mid-1932 Hu and his division fought Chinese Communist troops in Kiangsi, Anhwei, and Honan. In September 1932 the Communists serving under Chang Kuo-t'ao and Hsü Hsiang-ch'ien (qq.v.) were forced by the Nationalist units of Wei Li-huang to abandon their base in the Honan-Hupeh-Anhwei border area. The Communists attempted to reach northern Szechwan by marching through Shensi. To keep them from moving farther north, the 1st Division was transferred from Chenchow to T'ienshui, Kansu, where it served to contain the Communists and to ensure the loyalty of local warlords.

As commander of the only Nationalist force in the northwest, Hu Tsung-nan was in a difficult position. He was cut off from his main supplies and from trustworthy allies. Accord-

ingly, he set up the Northwest Officer Training Corps and worked to expand the 1st Division, which had become known in China as a model force. Hu's men were well-disciplined, and they established harmonious relations with the inhabitants of the area.

In October 1934 the main Communist forces in Kiangsi began the Long March. They broke through Nationalist blockades in Hunan, Kweichow, Yunnan, Szechwan, and Sikang and advanced toward northern Shensi. Hu was ordered to rush his division to the barren Sungfan, Lifan, and Maohsien districts in northwest Szechwan to halt the Communist march. In the winter of 1935 the Communists bypassed Sungfan by crossing the grasslands at Mao-erh-kai. Hu moved his division to Mao-erh-kai and engaged the Communists in battle. Both sides suffered heavy casualties in the bitter fighting. The Communists managed to cross the almost impassable grassland and eventually reached northern Shensi by way of Kansu.

By 1936 Hu had become the commander of the First Army. In June, a good part of his army was ordered to reinforce Nationalist troops engaged in suppressing an armed revolt by Ch'en Chi-t'ang (q.v.) in Kwangtung. Hu suffered his first serious defeat in November, when his troops in the north fought the Communists at Shan-ch'eng-pao, a small city on the Shensi-Kansu-Ninghsia border. The battle lasted for two days, and the First Army lost two brigades. Casualties in the 1st Division were particularly high, and the remaining troops were exhausted from their pursuit of the Communists through the hinterland.

After the Sian Incident of December 1936 (see Chiang Kai-shek) and the outbreak of the Sino-Japanese war in July 1937, the Nationalists and the Chinese Communists united to fight the Japanese. Hu's First Army was moved to Shanghai to reinforce Chinese units in the area. Although the First Army suffered heavy losses, it succeeded in delaying the Japanese advance for six weeks.

In 1938 Hu received command of the Seventeenth Army Group and returned to Shensi to reorganize his forces. He was assigned to establish a branch of the Central Military Academy at Wangchu, a small suburb of Sian. As commandant of the branch academy, which opened on 29 March, he was responsible for military training in northwest China. He also headed the Wartime Political Cadre Training Corps, the Northwest Labor Corps, and an education guidance center for youth from occupied areas. Under his sponsorship, a primary school and two middle schools were established for the children of his officers. Because of his widespread authority in the area, he came to be known as the "King of the Northwest."

In 1939 Hu Tsung-nan received command of the Thirty-fourth Group Army. He had the dual task of resisting the Japanese in north China and containing the Communists in northern Shensi. Many high-ranking government officials sent their sons to serve under him. Chiang Wei-kuo (q.v.), the second son of Chiang Kai-shek, was among the young men who joined Hu's forces during this period. In 1943 Hu became the commander of the First War Area, which included Kansu, Tsinghai, Ninghsia, Sinkiang, Honan, Shantung, Hopei, and parts of Kiangsu, Anhwei, and Shansi. Hu's training organizations operated in six provinces, with headquarters at Sian. At one point, the number of cadets and political cadres in training exceeded 30,000.

In the spring of 1944 the Japanese launched an offensive in south and west Honan. After more than a month of hard fighting, Hu's troops were forced to withdraw. However, they held T'ungkwan and Hsiping on the Honan-Shensi border and prevented the Japanese from advancing into Shensi. In 1945, at the war's end, Hu went to Chengchow to accept the surrender of the Japanese forces in Honan.

In the general reorganization of Nationalist armies after the war, Hu's forces were reduced by about 40 percent. Some of his units were transferred to Peiping and Shih-chia-chuang, and forces remaining under his command were deployed to Kansu, Shensi, Shansi, and Honan. The struggle between the Nationalists and the Chinese Communists for control of the mainland put an end to the National Government's plans for demobilization and rehabilitation. Skirmishes between Hu's troops and Communist units mounted in intensity. Chu Teh and Ho Lung (qq.v.) sent a telegram demanding that Hu withdraw his troops from central Shensi. In 1946 Communist forces under Li Hsien-nien broke through Nationalist barricades in the Honan-Hupeh border area and fought their way to northern Shensi. When the National Govern-

ment, after American mediation efforts had failed, officially ordered the suppression of the Communists, Hu marched into northern Shensi and captured Yenan in March 1947.

As Hu's forces advanced into the Communist areas of Shensi, however, they became increasingly isolated from other Nationalist troops and supplies. The Communists split their armies into small columns and harrassed Hu's divisions one-by-one. Hu eventually was forced to retreat to central Shensi. His army was routed in 1949 when the Communists launched an attack with heavy artillery brought from Shansi. He retreated to southern Shensi and then to Szechwan. In December, most of his army was annihilated by the Communists. Hu and a small group of aides escaped to Hainan Island. He sought and received permission from Chiang Kai-shek, who had gone to Taiwan, to fly to Hsichang and attempt to regroup Nationalist troops on the Szechwan-Sikang border which had managed to break through Communist lines. After putting up a brief but desperate resistance, with fewer than 30,000 troops and no supplies, Hu escaped to Hainan in March 1950 and then went to Taiwan.

In 1951 Hu was appointed commander of the guerrilla forces on Tach'eng Island and governor of Chekiang. After Tach'eng was evacuated in 1954 he received command of the Pescadores. He held that post until the end of 1959. He died in Taipei on 14 February 1962.

Hu Tsung-nan married twice. His first wife lived with and cared for his mother in Hsiaofeng. During the Sino-Japanese war his family, with the exception of his mother, was killed in an air raid. In 1947 Hu married Yeh Hsia-ti, an American-educated sociologist who was a lecturer at Nanking University. They had two sons and two daughters.

Hu Tzu-ching: *see* HU YUAN-T'AN.

Hu Wen-hu   胡文虎
Burmese. Aw Boon Haw

Hu Wen-hu (16 January 1893–4 September 1954), known as Aw Boon Haw, overseas Chinese entrepreneur, newspaper publisher, and philanthropist who made a fortune in pharmaceuticals.

Although Aw Boon Haw was born in Rangoon, his native place was Yungting hsien, a Hakka-speaking district in western Fukien. In 1862 his father, Aw Chi Ching (Hu Tzu-ch'in), had migrated to Burma. He practiced traditional Chinese medicine and operated a store in Rangoon which stocked Chinese medicinal herbs and other pharmaceuticals. The store was called Eng Aun Tong. Aw Chi Ching married a Chinese girl named Li in Burma. They had three sons. Aw Boon Haw, the second son, was sent to Fukien at the age of 10 for a traditional Chinese education. His younger brother, Aw Boon Par, who later served as his junior partner, received an English education in Burma.

Aw Boon Haw studied in his native district for four years. He then was recalled to Rangoon. He immediately began to study his father's profession and learned to manage the family business. After his father died in 1908, he took over the store. Assisted by his younger brother, he greatly increased the family fortune. He traveled extensively in China, Japan, and Siam, investigating the pharmaceutical market and developing trade connections.

By 1923 Aw's business had grown to such an extent that he decided to transfer his headquarters to Singapore, leaving his younger brother to take charge of their interests at Rangoon. From Singapore, his operations branched out to Malaya, the Netherlands East Indies, and Siam. As the business developed, Aw made it his policy to take an active part in philanthropic work in each area.

Aw Boon Haw had not been identified with the many overseas Chinese figures who had energetically and generously supported the anti-Manchu revolutionary movement in the pre-republican era. Both his age and his circumstances at the time had prevented him from playing any significant role then. His first known support of Sun Yat-sen was reported in 1924, when he was stated to have contributed a substantial sum to Sun during the final eastern expedition against Ch'en Chiung-ming (q.v.), who had moved to oppose Sun in 1922. That support was the more remarkable because Ch'en, himself a Hakka-speaking person, then had a considerable following in Southeast Asia.

In 1927 Aw Boon Haw was reported to have made large contributions to the Northern Expedition and to the relief of refugees from natural disasters in Kwangtung province. By then he had qualified as a member of the Singapore Chinese "millionaires club" and had become one of the targets of the numerous fund-raising missions which Chinese educational institutions sent to Southeast Asia. In 1929 he gave SS$10,000 to Ta-hsia University in Shanghai and SS$50,000 to National Chung-shan University in Canton. In 1932 he visited Hong Kong and Canton. At that time, he made a donation to Lingnan University in Canton.

Aw Boon Haw's pharmaceutical business continued to grow. Tiger Balm and other products were firmly established in various areas of Southeast Asia, and Hu had also achieved the remarkable feat of marketing his proprietary medicines in China. He now planned further expansion and decided to transfer his headquarters to Hong Kong. He made this move gradually and maintained his connections in Singapore because of its importance as a distribution center for Southeast Asia.

Aw Boon Haw led the Malayan Chinese contingent to the Chinese National Olympic Meet held at Shanghai in 1935. He then went to his native province, where he donated SS$10,000 to Fukien College in Foochow and an identical sum to Amoy University. In addition to these larger gifts, Aw made generous contributions to schools in various Chinese cities and in Singapore, Malaya, and the Netherlands East Indies. About this time, he also drew up a grandiose and extensively publicized plan for eliminating illiteracy in China which called for the establishment of 1,000 primary schools in various parts of the country. He promised personal donations if the provincial authorities would accept the plan. He received widespread publicity, but his offer was not accepted.

Earlier, in 1928, Aw Boon Haw had launched the second important business venture of his career when he established in Singapore the *Sing-chew jit-po*, which was to become the first of a chain of newspapers. The second paper of the chain was the Swatow *Sing-hua jit-po*, established in 1931; the third was the *Amoy Singkwong jit-po*, first published in 1935. Later that year, a Singapore afternoon paper, the *Sing-chung jit-po*, also began publication. Aw also planned to establish a large and modern daily paper in Canton which would be called *Sing-yuet jit-po*. He acquired offices for the paper and began installation of a printing plant, but the deteriorating situation in south China delayed the project. In 1938 Canton was occupied by the Japanese before the paper could begin publication. It was in 1938, however, that Aw Boon Haw established what was probably his most important, and certainly his most successful, newspaper, the Hong Kong *Sing-tao jih-pao*. In 1941, before the outbreak of the War in the Pacific, Aw added another paper in Southeast Asia to his chain, the Penang *Sing-ping jit-po*.

When the National Government moved to Chungking after the Sino-Japanese war began in 1937, Aw Boon Haw was appointed to the People's Political Council as an overseas Chinese representative. In the latter part of 1941 he traveled from Singapore to Chungking by way of Burma to attend a meeting of the council. At the wartime capital, he was received by Chiang Kai-shek. He then left Chungking for Hong Kong, where he had just finished building a mansion, and arrived there just as the War in the Pacific broke out. When the Japanese forces occupied Hong Kong late in December 1941, Aw Boon Haw was detained in custody for three days at the Gloucester Hotel. After his release, he remained in Hong Kong.

In 1943 Aw made several trips from Hong Kong to Shanghai and met Wang Ching-wei (q.v.), who was serving as head of the Japanese-sponsored government at Nanking. He made at least one trip to Tokyo, where he met Premier Tojo, reportedly to speak on behalf of Hong Kong merchants regarding the conduct of the Japanese occupation troops. In 1944 Aw was elected chairman of the Hong Kong Chinese Association. He was quoted as saying that he would do all in his power as an Asian to cooperate in the Japanese plans for a "Greater Asia Co-Prosperity Sphere." From 1940 to 1945 Aw was listed as chairman of the board of directors of the Singapore Tsun Tsin Association, a Hakka organization with branches in most major overseas Chinese centers. He was active in both the Singapore and the Hong Kong branches of the organization.

At the end of the Second World War, Aw Boon Haw resumed his business operations. He visited Singapore in 1946 to supervise the restoration of his interests in that area and in other parts of Southeast Asia. At that time, he also drew up a scheme for a large enterprise to promote the economic development of Fukien province by raising funds among prominent Malayan Chinese. That scheme, however, never advanced beyond the proposal stage.

Aw soon turned his attention to the further expansion of the newspaper empire he was building. Most of his pre-war newspapers resumed publication. In 1946 he began publishing an English-language paper, the *Hong Kong Tiger Standard*, in direct competition with the established British papers in the colony. He also announced plans (never realized) for a Foochow daily to be called *Sing-ming jit-po* and a Shanghai daily to be called *Sing-woo jit-po*. Papers were also contemplated for Peiping, Hankow, Mukden, and Taiwan. He met with no success in his attempt to recover the printing plant which he had installed in Canton, the machinery having been moved to Taiwan by the Japanese during the war. Hu was more successful in Southeast Asia, where he soon established the Bangkok *Sing-sian jit-po*. In 1950 Aw began publishing a second English-language daily, the *Singapore Tiger Standard*. That paper suspended publication in 1959.

In 1949 Aw criticized the Singapore government's policy toward the Chinese population in the 16 February issue of his paper *Sing-chew jit-po*. When he visited Singapore later that year, he was detained at the airport, a ban on his entry having been ordered. He was released on the payment of bail. A similar ban was applied by the Federation of Malaya.

After occupying Canton in 1949, the Chinese Communists seized Aw's considerable assets in that city in 1951 and claimed large arrears of tax payments. Aw wrote a personal letter to Yeh Chien-ying (q.v.), then head of the Chinese Communist administration in Canton, asking for the release of his property, but his letter was ignored. During the early days of the Communist rise to power in China, some of Aw's papers, particularly the Hong Kong *Sing-tao jit-po*, expressed a tolerant attitude toward the new regime, but after Aw's Canton property was confiscated, his papers became strongly anti-Communist. In 1953 Aw Boon Haw affirmed his support of the Chinese Nationalists by making a visit to Taiwan.

During the postwar years, Aw undertook new philanthropic activities in Hong Kong. Those benefiting from his donations included hospitals, orphanages, and old people's homes. He also made generous contributions to the St. John's Ambulance Brigade, a voluntary British organization, and for several years he celebrated his birthday by distributing food parcels and cash gifts to the aged poor. Aw left Hong Kong for the United States in 1954 to undergo an operation in a Boston hospital. On the return journey, he died of a heart attack in Honolulu in September 1954.

Aw Boon Haw was the first Chinese businessman to use Western publicity methods in Eastern trading. His shrewd perception of the power of the press in business promotion was demonstrated by his own chain of newspapers. As his fortune grew, his philanthropy increased accordingly, and he was sometimes called the "Rockefeller of China." He had large estates in Singapore and Hong Kong, and their elaborate gardens became tourist attractions.

Aw Boon Haw had four wives. He married the first one, *née* Cheng, in 1917 in Rangoon, and she lived in Singapore. His second wife, Ch'en Chin-chih, played an important social role in Hong Kong. Her daughter, Aw Sian, better known as Sally Aw, came to control Aw Boon Haw's newspaper in Hong Kong. A second daughter, Aw Sin, studied in the United States. Aw Boon Haw had five sons. The eldest, Aw Kow, took charge of the family interests in Malaya. The second, Aw San, also known as Aw Swan, assumed direction of the Rangoon interests after the death of Aw Boon Haw's younger brother Aw Boon Par in 1944. The third son, Aw Haw, also known as Aw Hoe, a sportsman and playboy, was killed in an air crash in Malaya in 1951. The fourth son, Aw It Haw, also known as Aw One, studied in the United States. The fifth son, Aw Sai Haw, was a small child at the time of his father's death.

Hu Yeh-p'in　　　　　　　胡 也 頻
　Orig. Hu Ch'ung-hsüan　胡 崇 軒
　Pen. Yeh-p'in　　　　　也 頻
　　　P'in　　　　　　　頻
　　　Shen-mo　　　　　沈 默
　　　Ho I-p'ing　　　　何 一 平
　　　Hung Hsiao　　　　紅 笑

Hu Yeh-p'in (1907–7 February 1931), writer and companion of Ting Ling (q.v.). He became an ardent Communist and an official of the League of Left-Wing Writers. After his arrest and execution by the Nationalists, he became known as one of the five martyrs of the League of Left-Wing Writers.

Foochow, Fukien, was the birthplace of Hu Yeh-p'in. His father ran a Peking opera troupe which had been organized by his grandfather, a native of Kiangsi. Hu had four younger brothers and a younger sister. He was enrolled at an old-style private school at the age of four, but had to leave school four years later because his father's troupe disbanded. Two years later, the family's financial situation improved when his father rented a theater and arranged for other troupes to appear there. Hu then went to the Ch'ungte Primary School, which was run by foreign missionaries. At school, he participated in oratorical contests and theatrical events. Because his mother, a devout Buddhist, opposed his participation in the school's Christian religious services, he spent only one year at the Ch'ungte Primary School. He then was sent to a private school, where he studied the Chinese classics for three years.

In 1918 the family's financial situation again became straitened, and Hu Yeh-p'in had to leave school. At the age of 14, he became an apprentice in a Foochow jewelry store. In 1920 he rebelled and ran away to Shanghai, where he enrolled at the P'u-tung Middle School under the name Hu Ch'ung-hsien. About a year later, he was admitted to the tuition-free Navy School at Ta-ku-k'ou on the recommendation of a relative working in the naval ministry, and he studied mechanical engineering. Hu soon had to leave school because he lacked funds. He went to Peking, where he held a variety of jobs and spent many hours listening to young intellectuals discuss literature. These discussions led him to begin reading fiction and poetry, and he soon decided to become a writer.

In 1924 Hu Yeh-p'in and two friends established a literary supplement to the *Ching-pao* [Peking news] called *Min-chung wen-i chou-k'an* [masses literature weekly], and its first issue appeared in December. In this enterprise he was closely associated with Lu Hsün (Chou Shu-jen, q.v.) and with Shen Ts'ung-wen (q.v.), who was a frequent contributor to the supplement. Although the magazine ceased publication in May 1925, it gave Hu Yeh-p'in the opportunity to publish 15 pieces, including short stories and essays, under the name Hu Ch'ung-hsien.

In the spring of 1925 Hu Yeh-p'in met Ting Ling (q.v.). Before long, they began to lead a secluded existence in a small cottage in the

Western Hills near Peking. He wrote poetry and in 1926 contributed regularly to the literary supplement of the *Ch'en Pao* [morning post], using the pen names Yeh-p'in and P'in. His work also appeared in *Hsien-tai p'ing-lun* [contemporary review], *Hsiao-shuo yueh-pao* [short story magazine], and *Tung-fang tsa-chih* [eastern miscellany]. In 1926 his poems were collected and published as *Yuan-wang* [expectations]. However, only a few of his writings were published, and he tried unsuccessfully to found a new magazine. According to Ting Ling, he "contracted the diseases of melancholy and nihilism. The poems he wrote at that time were filled with such deplorable emotions."

When Ting Ling's writings became popular, Hu Yeh-p'in's depression increased. They moved to Shanghai, where, on Shen Ts'ung-wen's recommendation, Hu Yeh-p'in became the editor of a literary supplement of the *Central Daily News*. The first issue of the supplement appeared on 19 June 1928, and it ceased publication with the issue of 31 October. Hu Yeh-p'in, Ting Ling, and Shen Ts'ung-wen then established *Hung-hei yueh-k'an* [red and black] and *Jen-chien yueh-k'an* [mankind], which began publication on 20 January 1929. The venture soon ended in bankruptcy: the last issue of *Jen-chien yueh-k'an* appeared in April, and the last issue of *Hung-hei yueh-k'an*, in August.

During this period, Hu Yeh-p'in had become interested in Marxist literary and political theories. His radical tendencies first were reflected in a novel about class struggle, *Tao Mo-ssu-k'o ch'ü* [to Moscow], which he completed in May 1929. It tells of a woman whose Communist lover is killed by her husband, a government official. The book ends with the heroine's departure for Moscow and a new life. In early 1930 Hu Yeh-p'in wrote *Kuang-ming tsai wo-men ti ch'ien-mien* [light is ahead of us], which was intended to illustrate the impact of the May Thirtieth Movement of 1925 on writers of "art for art's sake," anarchists, and Communist intellectuals. Part of this novel was published in May 1930 in the first issue of *Jih-ch'u* [sunrise], which was fined and forced to close as a result.

As Hu Yeh-p'in became more outspoken in his political beliefs, the market for his writings dwindled. Because he needed money, in the spring of 1930 he accepted a teaching position at the Tsinan Middle School. He was very popular with the students. He lectured on proletarian literature and formed a literary club which soon had a membership of more than 400 students. The principal of the school and the proctor also joined. On 9 May, at the commemoration ceremonies of the humiliating Twenty-one Demands on China by the Japanese, the students became excited and almost rioted. Hu Yeh-p'in did not know how to lead a crowd to mass demonstration. He attempted to find the Communist party organization in Tsinan so that one of its members could channel the agitation to mass movement, but failed. He was about to try and contact the Communists in Shanghai when the principal of the school informed him that government authorities had become apprehensive about the upheaval at the school and that he should leave Tsinan. Hu went to Tsingtao and then to Shanghai, where he devoted himself to political activity.

Hu Yeh-p'in joined the newly formed League of Left-Wing Writers (*see* Chou Shu-jen) and soon became a member of its executive committee and chairman of its board of correspondence with workers, peasants, and soldiers. He also taught at a summer school organized by Feng Hsueh-feng and other Communists. In November 1930 he joined the Chinese Communist party. On 17 January 1931, during a preparatory meeting for the All-China Congress of Soviets, he and other participants were arrested by the Nationalist authorities. Ting Ling and Shen Ts'ung-wen tried to secure his release, but he and 23 others were executed on 7 February 1931. Hu Yeh-p'in, Jou Shih, Feng K'eng, Yiu Fu, and Li Wei-sen became known as the five martyrs of the League of Left-Wing Writers, and the mass execution, publicized by such Western writers as Nym Wales, Agnes Smedley, and Edgar Snow, became a scandal.

In 1951 *Hu Yeh-p'in hsuan-chi* [selections from Hu Yeh-p'in], which included two novels and some stories and essays, was published by the Communist Hsin-wen-hsueh hsuan-chi pien-chi wei-yuan-hui [editorial committee for the anthologization of progressive literature]. The novels received special commendation from the committee as exceptionally good examples of proletarian literature in content, ideology, and technique.

Hu Yuan-t'an 胡 元 倓
  T. Tzu-ching 子 靖
  H. Nai-an 耐 菴

Hu Yuan-t'an (1872–November 1940), educator. He founded and devoted his life to the development of the Ming-te schools in Changsha.

A native of Hsiangt'an, Hunan, Hu Yuan-t'an was born into a scholar-gentry family. His grandfather, Hu Yun-fan, was magistrate of Nanhai (Namhoi), Kwangtung. His father, Hu T'ung-sheng, and his uncle, Hu Chi-men, had followed their father to Nanhai and had studied under the noted Kwangtung scholar Ch'en Feng (ECCP, I, 90). They specialized in the study of the *Shih-ching* and the *Tzu-chih t'ung-chien*, and both of them wrote books on these texts. Hu Yuan-t'an's eldest brother, Hu Yuan-i, studied the *Shih-ching* and the *Hsün-tzu*, and his writings on these texts were collected by Wang Hsien-ch'ien (q.v.) and included in the *Huang-Ch'ing ching-chieh hsu-pien* [Ch'ing annotations to the classics, continued]. Another brother, Hu Yuan-yu, was also a recognized scholar. Hu Yuan-t'an was the ninth son born to the family. As was common for persons of his background, Hu received his early education entirely along classical lines. He was known to be assiduous and earnest, and when modern Western ideas became known to students and scholars in his province, he became avidly interested in these new areas of knowledge. He qualified for the degree of senior licentiate. In 1903 a government scholarship enabled him to go to Japan to attend Kōbun Normal College. The training he received in Japan, though brief, opened new vistas to the young scholar.

One of the most eminent Japanese educators of that time was Fukuzawa Yukichi, the founder of Keio University. His educational emphasis was moral and inspirational, geared to training for strength of character. Hu Yuan-t'an, having been inculcated with Confucian precepts and ethics, was at once attracted to this significant approach to education. After returning to Changsha later in 1903, he set out at once to found the Ming-te School, with the active support of such Hunanese leaders as Lung Chan-lin and T'an Yen-k'ai (q.v.). The school

consisted of a normal school for training in pedagogy and a middle school. Later, it was expanded to include a special normal class and a preparatory school. A middle-school affiliate of Ming-te was founded in Chingcheng, and the Ming-te Higher School of Commerce was established in Nanking. The Ming-te schools became comparable in fame to the Nankai school system in Tientsin, founded under the sponsorship of Yen Hsiu and Chang Po-ling (q.v.).

Although Hu himself had never been a revolutionist, the early history of Ming-te was closely associated with a number of leaders of the republican revolution of 1911, notably Huang Hsing and Chang Chi (qq.v.). Huang accepted an invitation from Hu Yuan-t'an to head the normal department, and Chang accepted an invitation to teach history. Other members of the Ming-te faculty were Su Man-shu (q.v.), a poet and writer who was later to become a Buddhist abbot, and Wang Cheng-t'ing (q.v.), a future diplomat and Kuomintang statesman. The presence of such talents in a middle school made a strong impression on the people of Hunan and its neighboring provinces.

Soon after Huang Hsing joined the Ming-te faculty, it became evident that his real purpose was to engage in clandestine revolutionary activities. Huang hatched a plot to murder the prominent leaders of the province, both Chinese and Manchu, when they assembled to celebrate the seventieth birthday anniversary of the empress dowager. The plot was discovered, and a thorough search for Huang was conducted by provincial officials. During the crisis, Huang managed to escape by taking refuge in the home of Lung Chan-lin, probably through arrangements made by Hu Yuan-t'an. Hu attempted to persuade Chang Ho-ling, then the director of educational affairs in Hunan, to be lenient with the plotters. In so doing, Hu endangered his own life. It was largely through his plea for leniency that the search for the culprits was eased. Huang Hsing and Chang Chi were allowed to escape, first to Hankow and then to Japan. In subsequent years, the valiant deed of Hu Yuan-t'an bolstered the prestige and popularity of Ming-te as the home of revolutionary tradition in Hunan.

Hu Yuan-t'an constantly sought to expand Ming-te to include a college. Following the establishment of the republic in 1912, Ming-te College was inaugurated in Peking. This expansion increased financial needs, and Hu made fund-raising trips to Peking, Tientsin, Shanghai, Nanking, and even as far north as Mukden and Kirin. When contributions from domestic sources proved inadequate, he made trips to Southeast Asia, where large Chinese communities thrived. Contributions never quite equaled expenses, however; and in 1915 Ming-te College was closed. In 1919 the college department was revived in Hankow, but it was discontinued seven years later. At Ming-te College business courses were emphasized. A working arrangement was made between the school authorities and certain commercial banks to employ Ming-te graduates. A notable associate in this enterprise was the Continental Bank in Tientsin and Hankow.

Among those who supported Ming-te consistently and loyally were Huang Hsing and T'an Yen-k'ai, who also became Hu's closest associates and mentors. At one time, Hu was so distressed by the lack of response to his fund-raising campaign in Shanghai that he wrote to T'an Yen-k'ai, saying that he might as well commit suicide as a gesture of devotion to Ming-te. T'an pleaded with Hu to return to Changsha at once and promised to be personally responsible for Ming-te's financial support. The Hunanese statesman is said to have counseled Hu that "to die is not difficult, but not to die is."

After 1925, Hu began to concentrate his energies on developing Ming-te solely as a middle school. He made a point of using former professors from his college to augment the staff of his middle school, thereby offering a more comprehensive curriculum than did other schools in Changsha. According to Tso Shunsheng, "private schools exercised pivotal influence on Hunan's educational mode and climate, and they trained more talents than government-sponsored schools. Under the crisis of foreign aggression, the people of Hunan took the initiative of establishing schools without government assistance. Mr. Hu was a representative figure in this endeavor."

After the Sino-Japanese war began in 1937, Hu Yuan-t'an followed the National Government to Hankow and Chungking. He was invited to be a member of the People's Political Council in 1938 on the strength of his reputation as a dedicated educator. He accepted the post and lived in the suburbs of the wartime capital until his death in November 1940, at the age of 69 sui.

Hu Yuan-t'an moved among high government officials and millionaires and fraternized good-humoredly and unobtrusively with his numerous students and colleagues. He was always simply dressed. He was fond of little pleasures: a cup of wine, a movie, or a Chinese opera. He was meticulous in preserving his personal health: whenever he visited friends, a personal servant followed him about with an extra jacket of padded silk which Hu might put on if he felt a chill. That was his only luxury. He was inordinately proud of his students, especially those who had made their mark in life. Among these were Ch'en Kuo-fu, Huang Shao-ku, and Jen Pi-shih (qq.v.).

Hu Yuan-t'an was an excellent calligrapher and a good classical poet. Most of his poems, which were collected in a volume entitled *Nai-an yen-chih*, concern his ambitions, strifes, and struggles in the cause of education.

Hu Yün　　　　　　胡 筼
　T. Pi-chiang　　　　筆 江

Hu Yün (1881–24 August 1938), banker. After serving as general manager of the Bank of Communications from 1915 to 1920, he organized and directed the operations of the China and South Seas Bank. When the National Government centralized the management and control of Chinese banking in the 1930's, he became chairman of the board of the Bank of Communications.

Chinkiang, Kiangsu, was the birthplace of Hu Yün. Because he was a sickly child, he received no schooling until he was 8 years old. Three years later, in 1892, his family engaged a tutor to help him prepare for the imperial examinations. In 1896 he abandoned this avenue of advancement and became an apprentice in a native bank. He undertook increasingly important tasks at the bank and soon mastered the intricacies of the traditional banking system. When the bank failed in 1907, Hu decided to go to Peking.

In 1908, at the age of 27, Hu became assistant manager of the Kung-i Bank (Kung-i yin-hang), where he learned Western banking procedures. Two years later, his reputation as a talented banker won him the post of chief auditor at the Bank of Communications (Chiao-t'ung yin-hang). In 1911 he was promoted to assistant manager of the bank's head office, and in 1915 he was appointed general manager.

After the death of Yuan Shih-k'ai in 1916, political turmoil engulfed north China, and the practice of banking became increasingly precarious. Accordingly, Hu Yün resigned from the Bank of Communications in 1920 and moved to Shanghai. He soon was offered the opportunity to create a modern banking corporation in Peking and Shanghai by Y. S. Oei (Hung I-chu), who had become wealthy in the sugar business in Java and who owned most of the public utilities at Amoy. Hu accepted Oei's offer, and they went to Peking to confer with Tuan Ch'i-jui (q.v.), then the premier. Tuan authorized the chartering of the China and South Seas Bank (Chung-nan yin-hang), and the Peking government took the unusual action of granting the power of note issue to the new bank. Hu and Oei then returned to Shanghai to establish the head office, which opened for business in July 1920.

The bank was an immediate success, and it helped to set new standards of efficiency and integrity in Chinese banking. By law, a bank with the power of issue had to have a reserve equivalent to the banknotes issued. In practice, banknotes had sometimes been issued without adequate reserves, causing the worth of the banknotes and the confidence of the public to decline. Hu backed the China and South Seas Bank currency in strict accordance with the law. The bank soon established offices in Peking, Tientsin, Hankow, and Wusih. The addresses of the bank's offices were printed on each banknote, and people soon learned that they could confidently expect to redeem any note for silver at any of the bank's offices.

In the early 1920's Chinese banks seldom dealt in foreign exchange transactions. Under Hu's direction, the China and South Seas Bank established foreign remittance operations and began dealing with Europe, the United States, and Southeast Asia.

Hu soon joined with Chou Tso-min (q.v.) and other bankers in establishing a reserve system which emulated the Federal Reserve System of the United States. Banknotes would be backed by a reserve which would be 60 percent cash bullion and 40 percent government bonds and negotiable securities. In 1923 the China and South Seas Bank, the Kincheng Banking Corporation (Chin-ch'eng yin-hang), the Continental Bank (Ta-lu yin-hang), and the Yien-yieh Commercial Bank (Yen-yeh yin-hang) pooled their resources to establish the Joint Treasury and the Joint Savings Society. The Joint Treasury issued banknotes and assumed responsibility for the maintenance of the required reserves. The Joint Savings Society encouraged people to save, and it became a highly profitable operation. Through the society, the participating banks made substantial investments in Shanghai real estate and in domestic and foreign bonds. The four participating banks became known collectively as the four northern banks.

In 1932 Hu became interested in reviving the moribund Chinese silk and tung oil industries. As a result of his efforts, two schools with laboratory facilities were established in his native district of Chinkiang. The school of sericulture developed new techniques of larva incubation, reeling, and mulberry cultivation which came to be used throughout China. The other school helped to stimulate the production of tung oil.

In 1934 the China and South Seas Bank established new branches in Hong Kong and Canton. Its foreign remittance business with the Philippines, Singapore, Malaya, and the Netherlands East Indies increased greatly. The bank provided its overseas clientele with market and commodity information as well as regular services. Domestic business increased when the Nanking branch initiated an installment plan for government employees who wished to build homes. This plan caused a real estate boom in the Nanking area.

In the meantime, the National Government had begun to take steps to strengthen the financial structure of China and to initiate currency reform. One of the measures called for the revoking of the power of issue of non-government banks. The Central Bank of China (Chung-yang yin-hang) was to be the only bank empowered to issue the newly introduced fapi. In the final auditing of banknotes issued, it was confirmed that the China and South Seas Bank had used its power of issue in strict conformity with government reserve regulations.

It was also in 1934 that the China and South Seas Bank, under Hu Yün's direction, entered the cotton business in direct competition with Japanese interests. Japanese entrepreneurs had long since established cotton mills in Shanghai, Tientsin, and Tsingtao. In 1929 and 1930 these operations were expanded and modernized. By 1933 most of the Chinese cotton mills, burdened with obsolete machinery and an ill-trained labor force, had been forced to the edge of bankruptcy. The large unsecured loans made to mills by Shanghai, Wusih, and Nanking banks seemed to be uncollectable. The China and South Seas Bank was virtually supporting the large Pu Yih and Min Sen mills in Shanghai. By 1934 Hu Yün had realized that the situation demanded action. He joined with other bankers to assume charge of the ailing mills. Hu then undertook detailed studies of Japanese-run mills to determine the nature of their competitive advantage. He soon discovered that unit costs in Chinese mills were much higher because of technological and operational backwardness. Hu employed highly trained textile experts to solve the technical problems and reorganized the financial operations of the mills. By 1935 the Chinese mills had begun to show a profit, the first in many years, and by 1938, with an assist from war production demands, they had retired their bank loans.

In the meantime, the National Government had continued to centralize the management and control of banks in preparation for war with Japan. Private banks were absorbed into the centrally managed system. Hu Yün assumed the post of chairman of the board of the newly centralized Bank of Communications and became a key figure in the handling of China's defense finances and war economy. He set up branch offices of the Bank of Communications in other cities so that liquid assets would not be concentrated in Shanghai alone. When the Japanese invaded Shanghai in 1937, Hu supervised the transfer of funds and operations of his and other banks to Hong Kong and later to Chungking and Kunming.

In the summer of 1938 Hu, then in Hong Kong, was summoned by the National Government to an urgent financial conference in Chungking. On the morning of 24 August he boarded a Chinese National Aviation Corporation plane, the Kweilin, to fly to Chungking. The plane was intercepted and forced down in the sea near Tang Kai bay. Hu Yün and 18 of the 21 other passengers, including the banker Hsü Hsin-liu (q.v.), perished. He was officially mourned by the National Government, which issued an order commending him and awarding him its highest civilian honors.

Hua Lo-keng   華 羅 庚
Alt. Hua Loo-keng

Hua Lo-keng (11 October 1909–), mathematician. His papers dealing with number theory and with the geometry of matrices won him international recognition. After serving as professor of mathematics at Southwest Associated University, he went to the United States and worked at the Institute for Advanced Study at Princeton and the University of Illinois. In 1950 he resumed teaching and became head of the institute of mathematics of the Academy of Sciences at Peking.

Chint'an, Kiangsu, was the birthplace of Hua Lo-keng. During his school years he spent his spare time working in his father's small shop. In 1923 he was graduated from the junior division of the Chint'an district middle school. He then went to Shanghai and enrolled at the Chung-hua Vocational School to prepare for a business career. Financial difficulties forced him to leave that institution in 1924, only a few months before graduation. He returned home, worked in his father's shop, and studied mathematics. When he was 20, he contracted rheumatic fever, which left him lame. His physical disability barred him from many activities, and mathematics became his consuming interest.

About 1929 Hua Lo-keng began to contribute independent papers to mathematical journals at Shanghai. His work attracted the attention of Hsiung Ch'ing-lai (Hiong King-lai), then professor and chairman of the department of mathematics at Tsinghua University in Peking. Hsiung paid him a visit and in 1931 persuaded him to come to Tsinghua to work as an assistant in the mathematics department. Hua served as departmental librarian and acted as research assistant to Hsiung. He used the opportunity to audit courses at Tsinghua and began to study foreign languages. As a protégé of Hsiung Ch'ing-lai, he participated in all the activities of the mathematics department. Within five years he had become a lecturer at Tsinghua. After 1934 he began to publish papers on algebra, number theory, and functions of several complex variables in such mathematical journals as the *Transactions of the Science Society of China*, the *Tōhoku Mathematical Journal*, the *Bulletin of the Calcutta Mathematical Society*, *Mathematische Zeitschrift*, the *Journal of the London Mathematical Society*, and the *Doklady Akademii Nauk SSSR*.

In 1936 Hua Lo-keng received a research fellowship from the China Foundation for the Promotion of Education and Culture and went to England to study under G. H. Hardy at Cambridge. He returned to China in 1938 to become professor of mathematics at Southwest Associated University in Kunming. During the war years, Hua devoted much attention to problems of number theory, and in 1941 he completed an important manuscript on the additive theory of prime numbers. Because of the war, however, the study could not be published at that time.

In 1945 Hua Lo-keng, by invitation, went to the Soviet Union for a two-month visit, during which he gave lectures and held discussions with prominent Russian mathematicians and scientists. In the spring of 1946 he was invited to visit the United States by the Department of State. He accepted the invitation and became a member of the Institute for Advanced Study at Princeton, New Jersey. He moved to Urbana, Illinois, in 1948 to serve as a visiting research professor in mathematics at the University of Illinois.

Shortly after the Communist military victory on the mainland of China, Hua returned to Peking, where he was appointed professor of mathematics at Tsinghua University. In 1950 he became director of the institute of mathematics of the Academy of Sciences and president of the China Mathematics Society at Peking. A year later he became professor of mathematics at Peking University. Hua visited the Soviet Union as a member of the delegation sent by the Chinese Academy of Sciences in 1953. During the 1950's he also visited Stockholm, East Berlin, New Delhi, and other cities. In 1956 he wrote a monograph entitled *Harmonic Analysis of Functions of Several Complex Variables in the Classical Domains* which won a prize from the Academy of Sciences. This important work was translated into Russian in 1959 and into English

in 1963. Hua was criticized in 1957 for contributing to an article published in the *Kuang-ming jih-pao* which dealt with "Problems of Scientific Systems for China" and which allegedly expressed anti-socialist views. He was "rehabilitated" soon thereafter, and he served as a delegate to the First and Second National People's congresses.

In 1960 Hua was named chairman of the department of applied mathematics at the Scientific and Technical University in Peking. A year later, he became vice president of the institution. In 1964 he was elected a delegate to the Third National People's Congress.

Throughout his career Hua Lo-keng published papers which won international recognition. From 1934 to 1944 he dealt almost exclusively with number theory. His important treatise in this field, completed in 1941, did not appear until 1947, when it was published in Leningrad after being translated into Russian. This work was translated from Russian into English and published in 1965 by the American Mathematical Society as *Additive Theory of Prime Numbers*. The work is a detailed exposition of the Waring-Goldbach problem of representing positive integers as sums of a given number of kth powers of primes. He improved the Vinogradov mean-value theorem and extended the Waring problem to the representation of integers as sums of polynomials with integral coefficients. After 1944, Hua concentrated on the geometry of matrices. He also contributed a supplement to Jean Dieudonné's *On the Automorphisms of the Classical Groups*, which was published by the American Mathematical Society in 1951.

After 1960 many of Hua's writings linked theoretical mathematics with practical production problems in China. An example was his "Notes on Experimental Work in Methods of Over-all Planning," an analytical exposition of the application of abstract concepts to industrial planning and engineering. Another interesting example of Hua's later work was the booklet *Ts'ung Sun-tzu te shen-ch'i miao-suan t'an-ch'i* [talks on the ingenious mathematical calculations of Sun-tzu], which embodies Hua's successful attempt to solve a problem in number theory posed in the *Sun-tzu suan-ching*, one of the earliest extant Chinese mathematical texts. The appearance of Hua's booklet in 1964 reflected the emphasis placed by the Communist authorities at Peking on the importance of popularizing mathematical modes of reasoning among young Chinese and on the specific importance of the text as one of the earliest Chinese contributions to the history of mathematics. The Sun-tzu theorem, also known as the Chinese remainder theorem, has long held an important place in the history of mathematics. It has also had an influence on the development of electronic computers.

Huang Chieh 黃節
Orig. Huang P'ei-wen 黃佩文
T. Hui-wen 晦聞

Huang Chieh (1874–January 1935), poet, scholar known for his studies of the Six Dynasties period, and teacher. Although he was one of the founders of the Nan-she (1908), he preferred the Sung style to that of T'ang.

A native of Shunte, Kwangtung, Huang Chieh received his early classical training from Chien Ch'ao-liang, a disciple of the renowned Cantonese scholar Chu Tz'u-ch'i, and distinguished himself as a student at the Kuang-ya Academy in Canton. Because the possibility of China's being partitioned after the Boxer Uprising worried him, Huang left Kwangtung for Shanghai, where, together with Teng Shih and Liu Shih-p'ei (q.v.) he founded in 1905 the Kuo-hsueh pao-ts'un-hui [association for the preservation of classical Chinese learning], to which he contributed money and 4,000 books and for which he made special efforts to find books outlawed by the Ch'ing government. He wrote many articles for the journal *Kuo-ts'ui hsueh-pao* [national essence]. In addition, he was one of the founders of the Nan-she [the southern association], established in Soochow in 1908, which was supported by a group of prominent poets with strong nationalist sentiments.

In the early years of the republican era, Huang Chieh returned to Kwangtung as director of Provincial High College, but he soon left for north China to teach at National Peking University. When Yuan Shih-k'ai was about to proclaim himself monarch, Huang left Peking for Kwangtung, where he served briefly as provincial minister of education. He advocated a coeducational system, but this reform proved premature. Consequently, he resigned and returned to his teaching position in Peking. By happy coincidence, two girl students were admitted to National Peking University in February 1920. This innovation was adopted by Kwangtung public schools in 1921.

Huang Chieh is best remembered as a poet. He preferred the Sung style to that of T'ang, and he had highest regard for the elegant style of Ch'en Shih-tao (1053–1101) and for the work of Ku Yen-wu (ECCP, I, 421–26). In this particular respect he differed from his cofounders of the Nan-she, most of whom were faithful followers of Kung Tzu-chen (ECCP, I, 431–34). Huang's collected poems were published as *Chien-chia-lou shih*. The majority of the poems were first published in chronological sequence in the *Hsueh-heng* [critical review]. Huang is also known for his studies of the poetry of the Six Dynasties period. He annotated and collated the poetic works of Ts'ao Ts'ao (150–220), Ts'ao P'ei (190–252), and Ts'ao Jui (205–239) in *Wei Wen-Wu-Ming-ti shih chu*. He performed similar labors for Juan Chi (210–263) in *Juan Pu-ping yung-huai-shih chu*, Hsieh Ling-yün (385–433) in *Hsieh K'ang-lo shih chu*, and Pao Chao (421–465) in *Pao Ts'an-chün shih chu*. In addition, Huang selected and collated popular songs of the Han-Wei period (206 B.C.–265 A.D.) in his *Han-Wei yüeh-fu feng chien*.

Huang Chieh died in Peiping in January 1935.

Huang Fu 黃郛
Orig. Huang Shao-lin 黃紹麟
T. Ying-pai 膺白
H. Chao-fu 昭甫

Huang Fu (8 March 1880–6 December 1936), government official, was a friend and adviser of Chiang Kai-shek and Feng Yü-hsiang. In the early 1920's he held such posts in Peking as acting foreign minister and minister of education. From 3 to 24 November 1924 he functioned as premier, president, and minister of interior. He served the National Government as minister of foreign affairs (1928) and as chairman of the Peiping political affairs council (1933–35).

Paikuanchen, Shaohsing, Chekiang province, was the birthplace of Huang Fu. His father, Huang Wen-chih, came from a once-prosperous family in Chiahsing, Chekiang. He had been forced to leave Chiahsing during the Taiping Rebellion and had gone to live with an uncle in Paikuanchen. Huang Wen-chih, a man of scholarly accomplishments and a hou-pu chou-hsien [expectant magistrate], died in Hanghsien in 1886. His widow, *née* Lu, thereupon moved with her four sons (of whom Huang Fu, then seven sui, was the second) to Hangchow, where she sent Huang Fu to a charity-supported local school, the Cheng-meng i-shu, for a classical primary education. When Huang was 17 sui (1896), he took the provincial examinations and received an invitation to study under the Hangchow prefect. Because he had to help support his family, he was forced to refuse the invitation.

During the Hundred Days Reform period of 1898 Huang came upon Liang Ch'i-ch'ao's essay "Shang wu lun" [on the martial spirit] and was so strongly affected by it that he began to consider a military career. In 1903, when teaching literature and mathematics in the Anchi hsien school, he took the entrance examinations for the newly established Chekiang Military School. Because he doubted his abilities, he used the name Huang Fu. He ranked first on the list of successful candidates and in 1904 embarked upon his new studies at Hangchow. Thereafter, he went by the name Huang Fu.

In 1905 Huang was sent by the provincial government to Japan for advanced study. He matriculated at the Shimbu Gakkō [military preparatory school] and joined the T'ung-meng-hui. His enthusiasm for the revolutionary cause led him to organize a group of some 25 Chinese military students in Japan which included Li Lieh-chün, Yen Hsi-shan, and Chang Ch'ün. During his stay in Tokyo, Huang collaborated with Chiang Kai-shek and others in publishing the periodical *Wu-hsueh tsa-chih* [military studies magazine]. He contributed articles to Chinese and Japanese publications under the pen names Ming-ch'ih and K'u-k'uei.

After Huang completed his course of study at the Shimbu Gakkō in 1908, he went to the Military Survey Academy in Tokyo. After being graduated with honors in 1910, he returned to China and became a topographer in the military advisory bureau at Peking. He also translated a Japanese book on the 1904 battle of Port Arthur into Chinese under the title *Jou-tan* [bullets of flesh].

At the time of the Wuchang revolt in October 1911, Huang Fu was participating in military maneuvers near Shanhaikuan, charged with the care of foreign guests. The Peking government sent him to Shanghai as a "military investigator." He promptly resigned and joined the staff of Ch'en Ch'i-mei (q.v.). When Ch'en assumed office as Shanghai tutuh [military governor], Huang became his chief of staff. He also organized the 2nd Division (later designated the 23rd Division) and became its commander. That unit participated in the capture of Nanking by the revolutionaries in December. Among its regimental commanders was Chiang Kai-shek, Huang's associate of Tokyo days. Huang, Ch'en, and Chiang became sworn brothers at this time.

After the provisional government was established at Nanking in January 1912, Huang became superintendent of the base headquarters of the northern expeditionary forces. In February, he was transferred to the headquarters of the newly appointed Kiangsu military governor, Ch'eng Te-ch'uan. His first task was to disband the northern expeditionary forces.

At the end of 1912 Huang was ordered to go abroad for further military study. He and Chang Ch'ün were to join Ch'en Ch'i-mei in Japan and proceed to Europe. In mid-March, Ch'en changed his mind about the trip and was already in communication with Huang when, on 20 March, the revolutionary leader Sung Chiao-jen (q.v.) was assassinated by agents of Yuan Shih-k'ai. Ch'en Ch'i-mei then cancelled all plans for a European trip. Sun Yat-sen returned to Shanghai from Japan, and he, Ch'en Ch'i-mei, and Huang Hsing joined in opposition to Yuan Shih-k'ai. Although Huang Hsing counseled delay because of the strength of Yuan's forces, the so-called second revolution began in May. Ch'en's forces failed in an attempt to take the Shanghai arsenal; in mid-August, they were compelled to evacuate the Woosung fort. After Yuan Shih-k'ai ordered the arrest of Huang Hsing and other revolutionaries, Huang Fu fled to Japan in August. He was joined there by Ch'en Ch'i-mei.

Ch'en Ch'i-mei and Huang Fu soon came to a parting of ways over the question of tactics. When Ch'en in January 1914 proposed going to Manchuria to carry on revolutionary activities, Huang argued strongly with him, holding that it would only mean the dissipation of scarce resources, without benefit to anyone. Because Ch'en did not heed his advice, Huang set forth his ideas in a letter to his old comrade and boarded a ship for Singapore; he did not communicate with Ch'en for three months. In June, Sun Yat-sen endeavored to strengthen his position by organizing, in Japan, the Chung-kuo ko-ming-tang, with Ch'en Ch'i-mei as director of general affairs. However, his requirement that members swear personal allegiance to him created dissension among his followers. Among the dissenters was Huang Fu, who broke with Sun's group and never rejoined it.

In 1914, using the pen name Yi-t'ai, Huang published an analysis of the conflict in Europe in the Singapore *Kuo-min jih-pao* on 9–12 August. He forecast that Germany and Austria would be defeated and stated that China should seize the opportunity to recover Tsingtao. At that time, the Japanese were moving to occupy the German concession in Shantung. In the spring of 1915, he went by way of Japan to the United States, where he took up residence in Oakland, California. He visited a number of West Coast cities and participated in meetings at the American headquarters of the Kuomintang.

After the outbreak of the rebellion against Yuan Shih-k'ai in the southwest, Huang went by Japanese freighter to Hong Kong in December 1915. In response to the summons of revolutionary comrades, he went to Shanghai in January 1916 to help plan military action in Chekiang and to assume the post of military commissioner for the revolutionary troops in that province. His efforts were crowned with success in mid-April when Chekiang declared independence. After the death of Yuan Shih-k'ai in June, Huang made a short trip to Peking as a representative of the Chekiang military government.

On 14 August 1917 the Peking government, then dominated by Tuan Ch'i-jui (q.v.), formally announced its decision to enter the First World War on the side of the Allies. Huang Fu reiterated his belief that China should seize the opportunity to recover Tsingtao and urged Wang Ta-hsieh, the foreign minister, to take appropriate action. Wang refused his request, saying that no such action could be taken so long as national unity was lacking. Soon afterwards, Huang went to live in Tientsin, where he busied himself with study and writing. At Tientsin, he made the acquaintance of such

important political figures as Chang Yao-tseng and Hsü Shih-ch'ang (q.v.). In collaboration with Chang, he organized the National Peace Association and helped spread the "peace movement" to Shanghai, with the purpose of frustrating Tuan Ch'i-jui's program of unifying the country by military force. In 1918 and 1919 he published two of his most important works: *Ou-chan chih chiao-hsun yü Chung-kuo chih chiang-lai* [lessons of the European war and the future of China] and *Chan-hou chih shih-chieh* [the postwar world].

Late in 1919 Huang Fu gave a series of nine lectures in Tientsin which later were published as *Chan-hou chih hsin-chieh* [the postwar new world]. Hsü Shih-ch'ang, who held the presidency from 1918 to 1922, in 1920 commissioned Huang to write a book for him and gave him the title of consultant in the presidential office. Hsü also made him director of the Chinese economic investigation bureau. The book was published in 1920 as *Ou-chan hou Chung-kuo, ching-chi yü chiao-yü* [China after the European war: economics and education]. That Huang had written it was not disclosed until his death.

In February 1921 Huang was sent on a semi-official mission to the United States and Europe to study economic conditions. He reached New York in early summer. When the Washington Conference was scheduled, he and Yuan T'ung-li (q.v.) wrote an article entitled "Hua-sheng-tun hui-i fa-ch'i chih nei-jung chih chiang-lai chih ch'ü-shih" [the beginning of the Washington Conference and its future tendencies], which was published in the Shanghai *Hsin-wen-pao* at the beginning of September. The Peking authorities promptly made him an adviser to the Chinese delegation, then already in Washington. When the conference opened in November, Huang served as Hsü Shih-ch'ang's personal representative at the meeting. However, on 7 December, Huang resigned from the Chinese delegation, and shortly afterwards he left for Europe. After a brief stopover in London, he traveled in France, Belgium, Holland, Czechoslovakia, Italy, Hungary, Switzerland, and Germany collecting cartographic materials and surveying military affairs. In the autumn of 1922 he returned to Tientsin.

In September 1922 Huang Fu was appointed by Li Yuan-hung (q.v.), who had assumed the presidency at Peking, to organize and direct a finance commission. In November, he was appointed high commissioner of a national conference on finance. His friend Chang Shao-tseng formed a new cabinet in December, and Huang became acting foreign minister two months later. After the Peking government's envoys to foreign countries, long unpaid, submitted their resignations, Huang resigned on 22 March 1923. His resignation was accepted ten days later, when it became obvious that he would not reconsider his decision. He then agreed to serve as a member of the foreign affairs committee.

During the 1922–24 period, Huang lectured at Peking University and National Normal University on military institutions, world political geography, and world politics; he became known as a vigorous and learned speaker. In September 1923 he was appointed minister of education. He left office when the entire cabinet resigned in January 1924, but was returned to the post in September, when W. W. Yen (Yen Hui-ch'ing, q.v.) formed a new cabinet.

Huang had become a close associate of Feng Yü-hsiang (q.v.) and had lectured to the officers at Feng's headquarters near Peking. In mid-October 1924 Feng secretly sent an agent from Langfang to Peking to contact Huang. On 18 October, Huang sent Feng a message which said "this is the juncture to determine to save the country." After Huang met with Feng at Kuoliying on 21 October, Feng and Sun Yueh turned against Wu P'ei-fu and Ts'ao K'un (qq.v.) and occupied Peking on 23 October. Huang then returned to Peking. He was the only member of the W. W. Yen cabinet who had collaborated with Feng in the coup. After the resignation of the Yen cabinet at the end of the month, he assumed the post of acting premier. And when Ts'ao K'un, under detention, resigned on 3 November, Huang announced that he was performing presidential functions *ad interim*. He also assumed the burdens of another post, that of minister of interior. When Feng forcibly ousted P'u-yi (q.v.) from his palace and stripped him of most of his perquisites, Huang Fu legitimized the action by adding a unilateral "amendment" to the Articles of Favorable Treatment of 1912. In mid-November 1924 Tuan Ch'i-jui (q.v.) assumed the post of provisional chief executive, and on 24 November, the Huang Fu cabinet was

dissolved. Huang became a member, and then vice chairman, of a new financial rehabilitation commission.

In October 1925 Huang was made a delegate to the customs tariff conference in Peking. He was appointed ambassador to Germany, but was unable to proceed to his new post because the work of the customs tariff conference was unfinished and because he was acting as a political intermediary between Tuan Ch'i-jui and Feng Yü-hsiang. In January 1926 the tariff conference began to hold sessions again. Huang tried, without success, to convince the Japanese that China and Japan should aid each other and that Japan ought to be the first of the treaty powers to renounce its tariff privileges. When the Kuominchün evacuated Peking in April, Huang retired to Tientsin.

By October 1926 Northern Expedition forces had reached the Yangtze. In November, Feng Yü-hsiang wrote to Huang asking advice regarding his future course of action. Later that month, Chiang Kai-shek sent a message and then sent Chang Ch'ün to Huang, asking him to join the Nationalists. Huang finally agreed and left Tientsin for Nanchang in early January. Shortly afterwards, for the first time in more than ten years, he met with Chiang Kai-shek. Chiang left for the critical party meetings at Wuhan on 11 January 1927, and Huang followed. The right wing faction of the Kuomintang suffered setbacks at the Wuhan conferences. Huang departed about two weeks later to reside temporarily at Lushan. He was invited to join the Kuomintang, with Chiang Kai-shek as one of his sponsors, but declined. Huang held a number of strategy discussions with Chiang and other Kuomintang officials, proposing, among other things, alliance with Feng Yü-hsiang and Yen Hsi-shan. Of immediate importance to Chiang Kai-shek was the situation at Shanghai (*see* Sun Ch'uan-fang). Huang was sent to Shanghai with the mission of doing all he could to achieve Nationalist victory. Shanghai was captured on 22 March 1927.

The break between the right and left wings of the Kuomintang occurred in mid-April 1927, and Chiang Kai-shek established his opposition government at Nanking. Feng Yü-hsiang now held the balance of power between Chiang Kai-shek at Nanking and Wang Ching-wei at Wuhan. Huang Fu and Ku Chung-hsiu acted as Nanking's representatives to Feng and Yen

Hsi-shan. Huang also participated in the conference held by Feng Yü-hsiang and Chiang Kai-shek at Hsuchow from 19 to 21 June, after which Feng chose to side with Chiang against the Wuhan regime. Feng's telegram of 21 June announcing his decision to the Wuhan authorities was drafted by Huang Fu.

On 7 July 1927 Huang took office as mayor of Shanghai. In accordance with plans made by Sun Yat-sen, the boundaries of Shanghai had been extended and it had been designated a special municipality under the direct jurisdiction of the National Government. Huang began the task of creating a legal and administrative framework for the new municipality, but he resigned a few days after Chiang Kai-shek retired from office on 12 August.

In February 1928, Chiang Kai-shek having resumed control of the National Government, Huang Fu was made a member of the State Council and minister of foreign affairs. He inherited the task of settling claims made as a result of the incident at Nanking of March 1927 (*see* Chiang Kai-shek) when a number of foreigners had been killed and foreign property had been destroyed by Nationalist forces. He brought the matter to a successful conclusion in April. In the meantime, Huang had sent an envoy to Tokyo to dissuade the Japanese from interfering with the advance of the Northern Expedition forces. However, the Japanese sent troops to Shantung in April which clashed with Nationalist troops at Tsinan on 3 May. Chiang Kai-shek and Huang Fu, who were in Tsinan at the time, immediately returned to Nanking. Huang's protests to the Japanese and appeals to the League of Nations for intervention were unsuccessful. On 21 May, he went to Shanghai and wired his resignation to Nanking.

Huang retired to Mokanshan, a Chekiang mountain resort, and lived in seclusion for three years. He declined offers of diplomatic posts in London and Berlin and refused to assume office as vice chairman of the Hwai River conservancy board in June 1929, although he took part in the ceremonies to inaugurate the board. Huang studied Buddhism and became interested in the cultural and economic problems of the Mokanshan villagers. Ch'en Kuo-fu (q.v.), then the acting director of the organization department of the Kuomintang, frequently intruded upon Huang's pastoral existence to seek advice on party organization. In October 1930, when the

bloody fighting between the troops of the National Government and those of the northern coalition (*see* Feng Yü-hsiang; Yen Hsi-shan) came to an end, Huang's "Prayer for Peace" was published as an editorial in all Shanghai newspapers. In April 1931 he was appointed to the Peiping cultural guidance committee, but he again refused to leave Mokanshan.

After the Japanese Kwantung Army began its advance in the north with the Mukden Incident of 18 September 1931, Huang Fu found it impossible to remain apart from political life in China. He went to Shanghai and helped organize the New China Reconstruction Society as a forum for the discussion of public affairs. The society soon began to publish a monthly, the *Fu-hsing yueh-k'an*. Huang did not forget the people of Mokanshan, however; he established the Mokan Elementary School and organized the Mokan Countryside Improvement Association in March 1933. Huang's resumption of public activity led to his appointment in May 1933 as chairman of the Peiping political affairs council, which had jurisdiction over the five northern provinces of China. The Japanese had begun to work toward the establishment of an autonomous regime in those same provinces, and Huang soon was called upon to negotiate with them. The result of his efforts was the Tangku Truce of 31 May, which many Chinese regarded as being tantamount to surrender. Huang Fu, for his part in the matter, was attacked as a "pro-Japanese traitor."

In the meantime, Feng Yü-hsiang, who also had descended from a mountain retreat to meet the Japanese threat to China, had appointed himself commander in chief of what he called the People's Allied Anti-Japanese Army and had begun to assemble troops. Huang Fu and Sung Che-yuan (q.v.), acting as representatives of the National Government, finally persuaded Feng to abandon his plans; Feng disbanded his army in August and returned to his mountain retreat at T'ai-shan. At the time of his retirement, the north China railway lines resumed operations. After going to Nanking to report on his mission, Huang visited Feng at T'ai-shan in October.

Huang Fu returned to Peiping and energetically applied himself to strengthening the political affairs council. He refused an invitation from Ch'en Ming-shu (q.v.) to join the Fukien revolt against Chiang Kai-shek and declined offers from Chiang of higher posts in the National Government. In April 1934 he went to Nanchang and met with Chiang, who was directing the fifth campaign against the Chinese Communists. After returning north in September, he concluded negotiations for the restoration of postal service with Manchuria—then Manchoukuo—in December. Popular dissatisfaction with Huang increased, and impassioned nationalists charged that the working arrangements he had reached with the Japanese-sponsored regime in the Northeast constituted *de facto* recognition of Manchoukuo. Huang was appointed minister of interior, but he remained in Peiping.

In January 1935 a new crisis arose in north China with the Japanese occupation of Kuyuan in eastern Chahar. Although a new compromise agreement was signed, Japanese political, military, and economic pressure continued to increase. Huang Fu requested sick leave and returned to Mokanshan. The Peiping political affairs council was abolished on 28 August. Huang resigned as minister of interior on 10 September; he had not assumed the duties of that office. He participated in political discussions at Nanking in early December and then went to Shanghai. In February 1936 he returned to Mokanshan.

Huang Fu, who had suffered from a liver ailment for some time, became quite ill in the spring of 1936. In August, he was taken to a Shanghai hospital, where his illness was diagnosed as cancer of the liver. The following month, he was made an alternate member of the State Council. He died in Shanghai on 6 December 1936.

Huang Fu married twice. His first marriage, in 1898, ended in divorce in 1910. About 1912 he married Shen Yi-yun. Huang was survived by his second wife and by two married daughters, Hsi-wen and Hsi-chih.

In 1937 a collection of commemorative articles and messages was published under the title *Huang Ying-pai hsien-sheng ku-chin kan-i-lu* [collection of articles in memory of Huang Fu]. Shen Yi-yun, who later moved to the United States, wrote a biographical article entitled "Huang Ying-pai hsien-sheng chia-chuan." A detailed chronological biography of Huang Fu was prepared by Shen Yün-lung under the title "Huang Ying-pai hsien-sheng nien-p'u ch'u-k'ao."

Huang Hsing　　黃　興
　Orig. Huang Chen　黃　軫
　T.　K'o-ch'iang　克　強
　H.　Chin-wu　厪　午

Huang Hsing (28 October 1874–31 October 1916), revolutionary who founded the Hua-hsing-hui [society for the revival of China], which merged with other groups in 1905 to form the T'ung-meng-hui. Huang directed such uprisings as the Canton revolt of 27 April 1911. He continued to act as one of Sun Yat-sen's most important deputies until 1914, when he broke with Sun over party reorganization.

A native of Changsha, Hunan, Huang Hsing was the son of a school teacher who held the honorary position of tu-tsung, or head of a district subdivision. After receiving a traditional education in the Chinese classics at the Yo-lo shu-yuan, he passed the examinations for the sheng-yuan degree in 1892. He enrolled at the Liang-hu shu-yuan in Wuchang in 1897 and studied there for five years. This academy had been founded by Chang Chih-tung (ECCP, I, 27–32) to put into practice his belief in "Chinese learning for fundamental principles, Western learning for practical application." After being graduated with distinction in 1902, Huang was among the students chosen by Chang Chih-tung to study normal school education in Japan.

Huang Hsing arrived in Tokyo in May 1902 and enrolled at the Kobun Institute, which offered Chinese students short-term courses in law, physics, political science, and normal-school training. Huang became interested in military education and spent much of his leisure time in target practice and military drill. That autumn, Huang, Yang Tu (q.v.), and other Hunanese students established a monthly magazine, *Yu-hsüeh i-pien*, to publish translations of Japanese and Western writings on government and politics. Huang came to share the anti-Manchu sentiments of many Chinese students in Japan, and in May 1903 he helped form the Chün-kuo-min chiao-yü-hui [society for the promotion of military education]. Although organized ostensibly to protest Russian encroachment in Manchuria, the real purpose of the society was to overthrow the Manchu dynasty. Members returning to China were to further the cause of revolution in their native provinces through propaganda, armed revolt, and assassination.

Huang Hsing left Tokyo to return to China on 4 June 1903. After arriving at Shanghai, he accepted an appointment at the Ming-te School in Changsha, headed by Hu Yuan-t'an (q.v.). That autumn, he made full use of his position to spread revolutionary propaganda among the students. These activities soon led to his resignation from the school.

In late 1903 or early 1904 Huang founded the revolutionary society Hua-hsing-hui [society for the revival of China] in Hunan. Among its members were Sung Chiao-jen, Chang Chi, Chang Shih-chao (qq.v.), Liu Kuei-i, and Ma Fu-i, a local leader of the Ko-lao-hui [society of elders and brothers]. Huang also established the T'ung-ch'ou-hui [association against the common enemy] to maintain liaison between the secret societies in Hunan and the Hua-hsing-hui. He and his associates made elaborate plans for simultaneous uprisings at Changsha, Yochow, Hengchow, Paoking, and Ch'angte to be touched off by the bombing of leading provincials as they gathered at Changsha in November 1904 to celebrate the empress dowager's seventieth birthday. The plot was discovered, however, and Huang was forced to flee. He reached Shanghai on 20 November, but was arrested a few days later on suspicion of involvement in an attempt to assassinate Wang Chih-ch'un, a former governor of Kwangsi. After being released four days later, he fled to Japan. In early 1905 he returned to Hunan with firearms to be used in an uprising by Ma Fu-i and the secret societies of western Hunan. However, the firearms were discovered and Ma was captured by government troops. Huang took refuge in Japan once again.

Huang Hsing soon became a popular leader of the Chinese revolutionary movement in Japan. In the spring and summer of 1905 he was visited in Tokyo by many young Chinese revolutionaries and by Japanese sympathizers, including Miyazaki Torazō, a close friend and admirer of Sun Yat-sen. Through Miyazaki, Huang met Sun immediately after his return to Japan in July 1905. The two men held preliminary discussions and agreed that it was necessary to unify the various revolutionary groups in China and Japan. On 30 July, at a meeting of the revolutionaries in Tokyo, it was decided to form a new revolutionary organization, the Chung-kuo T'ung-meng-hui. The T'ung-meng-hui was formally inaugurated on 20 August 1905, with Sun Yat-sen as its head. Huang Hsing was second in command, and many of his close associates in the Hua-hsing-hui, such as Chang Chi, Sung Chiao-jen, and Liu Kuei-i, also held important posts in the new party. A magazine founded by Sung Chiao-jen was renamed the *Min-pao* [people's journal]; it became the party's official organ.

In the autumn of 1905, following Sun Yat-sen's departure for Saigon, Huang Hsing and other members of the T'ung-meng-hui left Japan for China to set up branch organizations and to seek support for the revolutionary movement among the people. From past experience, Huang realized that, even with the help of the secret societies, the T'ung-meng-hui had little prospect of success without support from the Chinese army. It was with the aim of converting army officers to the revolutionary cause that Huang traveled in secret to Kwangsi and other parts of the country. However, he had little success, and, after consulting briefly with Sun in Singapore and spending a few months in Hong Kong, he returned to Japan in September 1906. Three months later, news of uprisings in Hunan and Kiangsi reached T'ung-meng-hui headquarters in Tokyo. In January 1907 Huang went to Kwangtung to establish contact with the rebels, but the alertness of the government authorities there obliged him to return to Japan.

The renewed vigilance of the Manchu authorities had led to the arrest and execution of many T'ung-meng-hui agents in the Yangtze provinces. Discouraged by the successive misfortunes of the revolutionary party in central China and the failure of Sung Chiao-jen's venture in Manchuria (planned by Sung, Huang, and others in March 1907), Huang Hsing turned his attention to Kwangtung and Kwangsi. He left Japan in the summer of 1907 and went to Hanoi, where he helped Sun Yat-sen and Hu Han-min (q.v.) to make preparations for insurrections in western Kwangtung. Early in September, Huang took part in an unsuccessful assault on Ch'inchow. Three months later, with Sun Yat-sen, Hu Han-min, and a small force of adventurers, he advanced from Annam a few miles into Kwangsi province in an effort to assist a band of local guerrillas, led by Huang

Ming-t'an, which had captured the mountain fort at Chen-nan-kuan. After this futile venture, Sun decided to return to Hanoi. However, the French authorities discovered his identity and expelled him from Indo-China in March 1908, leaving Huang and Hu Han-min to carry on the work in Hanoi. Huang advanced with a force of 200 men into the western Kwangtung districts of Ch'inchow and Lienchow. After an inconclusive 40-day campaign, his men, out of ammunition and demoralized by the tropical climate, returned across the Kwangtung border into Indo-China. After returning to Hanoi early in May, Huang left immediately by train for the Yunnan border, where a revolt had broken out at Hokow. A few days later, he returned to Hanoi for a conference with Hu Han-min. On the trip back to Hokow, his identity was discovered by the French frontier police. He was deported from Indo-China.

Huang went to Singapore and remained there for several months. In the autumn of 1908 he went to Japan, where he lived with Chang Ping-lin (q.v.), then the editor of the *Min-pao*. In Tokyo, Huang found that the repeated failures of the revolts in China during 1907–8 not only had exhausted the finances of the T'ung-meng-hui but also had seriously impaired the morale of the party. An increasing number of party members began to favor terrorism and assassination instead of the hitherto unsuccessful strategy of armed revolt. Although personally averse to this course, Huang agreed to set up a secret cell in Tokyo to experiment with the making of explosives. These years of adversity had also increased personal friction among party members. Sun's leadership had been attacked at the party headquarters in Tokyo by Chang Ping-lin, Chang Chi, Sung Chiao-jen, and others. In the summer of 1908, after the failure of Sun's efforts in Kwangtung and Kwangsi, a movement had begun in Tokyo to oust Sun from chairmanship of the T'ung-meng-hui and to replace him with Huang Hsing. Huang, however, was anxious to avoid dissension within the party, and he urged his supporters to cease their attacks on Sun.

Although Huang Hsing and other revolutionaries had sought to infiltrate the regular army and to persuade army officers and their men to join in the anti-Manchu cause, they had not been successful. By the end of 1909,

however, conditions for subversion in the army seemed more favorable. In the modernized New Army division then being formed at Canton, more than 2,000 officers and men were said to have secretly joined the T'ung-meng-hui. In the autumn of 1909, a south China bureau of the T'ung-meng-hui, headed by Hu Han-min, was set up in Hong Kong with the immediate purpose of organizing a revolt of the troops in Canton. Working with Hu was Chao Sheng (1881–1911; T. Po-hsien), a former regimental officer in the New Army who had been deprived of his command on suspicion of revolutionary sympathies. Preparations for the coup were well under way when Huang Hsing arrived in Hong Kong from Tokyo on 29 January 1910 to take charge of military operations. But several days before the scheduled date of the revolt, a mutiny broke out among the troops of the New Army which was soon put down by forces loyal to the Manchu government, and the plans for the coup were thwarted. Although this venture was disappointing to the revolutionaries in its outcome, it marked the first occasion on which Huang and his associates succeeded in inciting government troops to take action against the government itself.

The T'ung-meng-hui still had many secret sympathizers in the government forces at Canton. For this reason, Huang Hsing believed that Canton was the best place to stage a new revolutionary uprising; and during the remainder of the year he worked to mobilize funds and men for another revolt. Late in March 1910 he left Hong Kong for Singapore with Chao Sheng, Hu Han-min, and others to raise money for the new venture, but soon hastened back to confer with a secret Japanese military mission which had arrived in Hong Kong. He then left for Japan, where he consulted briefly with Sun Yat-sen in Yokohama on 10 June. After receiving funds collected by Sun in the United States, he went to Burma to organize a revolt in Yunnan province. This attempt was soon abandoned, however; and Huang left Rangoon for Malaya to attend a conference of T'ung-meng-hui leaders in Penang on 13 November. At this meeting, attended by Huang, Sun Yat-sen, Chao Sheng, Hu Han-min, Teng Tse-ju (q.v.), and leaders of the overseas Chinese community in Malaya, plans were made for an all-out assault on Canton. The military initiative was to be taken by 500 volunteers from the T'ung-meng-hui, aided by revolutionary sympathizers among the troops of the New Army in Canton. In the next two months, Huang and his colleagues succeeded in gathering more than HK$180,000 from overseas Chinese in Southeast Asia, the Netherlands East Indies, Canada, and the United States to finance the revolt. On 18 January 1911 Huang returned to Hong Kong from Singapore and set up an elaborate headquarters with himself as chief of staff, Chao Sheng as his assistant, and Ch'en Chiung-ming (q.v.) acting as chief of the secretariat during the absence of Hu Han-min.

The uprising was originally scheduled for 13 April 1911, but it had to be postponed to await the arrival of more guns and men in Hong Kong and Canton. In the meantime, government authorities learned of the plot and instituted new security measures in Canton. On 23 April, Huang left Hong Kong for Canton. Because he feared that further postponement would delay the revolt indefinitely and thereby destroy the confidence of overseas Chinese financial backers of the T'ung-meng-hui, he decided to attack on 27 April. Partly because of lack of coordination among the various units and partly because some of the participants lost their nerve at the last minute, only the group led by Huang Hsing carried out the attack as planned. He and his unit stormed and set fire to the governor general's residence. In the street fighting that ensued the insurgents were defeated and about 85 people were killed. Huang lost one of the fingers of his right hand. He fled to the countryside south of the city, where he was hidden by Hsü Tsung-han, a widow who had been active in the revolutionary underground. On 30 April, Huang and Hsü escaped to Hong Kong. She subsequently became Huang's secondary wife.

More than for any other contribution he made to the Chinese revolutionary movement, Huang Hsing was known for his role as leader of the Canton revolt of 27 April 1911. The most ambitious and costly military operation organized by the T'ung-meng-hui up to that time, it has been celebrated in the annals of the Chinese Nationalists as the "Three Twenty-nine Revolution" (according to the Chinese lunar calendar, the uprising occurred on the twenty-ninth day of the third moon). Unlike the previous revolutionary attempts, it took place in one of the most important cities in China.

In 1918, six years after the establishment of the republic, a magnificent memorial was erected north of Canton at Huang-hua-kang [yellow-flower mound] on the site where the bodies of 72 "revolutionary martyrs" were buried shortly after the uprising.

When organizing the Canton revolt, Huang had sent T'an Jen-feng to organize uprisings in Hunan and Hupeh. Huang had come to agree with the T'ung-meng-hui members of Hunan and Hupeh origin, including T'an Jen-feng and Sung Chiao-jen, who pressed for more action in central China. They were not satisfied with the party's military strategy, which had been focused on the provinces on China's southern border. Huang had promised to act in their support if funds were available. It was one of the secret groups set up with funds given by Huang which was responsible for the bomb explosion that precipitated the Wuchang revolt in October 1911.

While Huang was brooding over the death of his comrades in Hong Kong after the failure of the Canton revolt in April, T'an Jen-feng, Sung Chiao-jen and others formed the central China bureau of the T'ung-meng-hui in Shanghai on 31 July 1911 to instigate revolution in the Yangtze area. Meanwhile, the local revolutionaries in the New Army of Hupeh had become very active. When the revolution was imminent, they and the central China bureau leaders repeatedly requested Huang to assume leadership. After the outbreak of the Wuchang revolt on 10 October, Huang left Hong Kong hurriedly and arrived in Shanghai on 24 October. Huang, Sung Chiao-jen, and a number of other T'ung-meng-hui leaders proceeded upriver to Hankow disguised as Red Cross workers.

When Huang arrived in the Wuhan area, the revolutionary forces had been fighting for more than two weeks without over-all military leadership. After a brief interview with Li Yuan-hung (q.v.), a former imperial military officer who had been forced to join the revolt and who became the military governor of Hupeh, Huang was designated commander in chief of the revolutionary army, which then was defending Hankow against imperial army units of Feng Kuo-chang (q.v.). By the time of Huang's arrival, however, street fighting had broken out within the city. On 2 November 1911 Huang's forces were defeated; they retreated across the

Yangtze to Wuchang, leaving Hankow in the hands of the imperial troops. The same day, at an emergency meeting of the new military government at Wuchang, Huang was put in charge of the defense of the city of Hanyang. Huang and his forces held the city against overwhelming odds for more than three weeks, thus giving revolutionaries in other parts of the country adequate time to organize uprisings. By the time Hanyang fell to imperial troops on 27 November, more than ten provinces had declared their independence of imperial rule.

After retiring with his battered army from Hanyang to Wuchang, Huang decided to leave for Shanghai, which had fallen to the republican revolutionaries early in November. On 2 December 1911, the day after his arrival in Shanghai, revolutionary forces captured Nanking. A representative body of delegates from 14 provinces met at Nanking, named Huang generalissimo in charge of organizing a provisional government, and gave him the authority to act as provisional president until elections could be held. By this time, the military situation in Wuchang had been stabilized, and Li Yuan-hung was ready to make a bid for power. Huang knew that the military commanders who had recently defected from the Manchu government and who were responsible for the capture of Nanking wanted Li Yuan-hung to take charge at Nanking. Accordingly, he tactfully declined the post in Li's favor. Li, however, insisted that Huang accept the post, and the resulting impasse delayed the formation of a provisional government until Sun Yat-sen returned from abroad.

On 1 January 1912, a week after his arrival in Shanghai, Sun Yat-sen was inaugurated provisional president in Nanking. Huang Hsing became minister of war. Later, he also served as chief of general staff. He seems to have exercised predominant power in the provisional government except in matters of finance and diplomacy, which were handled personally by Sun Yat-sen. After Sun's resignation in March in favor of Yuan Shih-k'ai and the subsequent transfer of the provisional government from Nanking to Peking, Huang remained in Nanking as resident general (with the title of liu-shou, an ancient title given to an official left in charge of civil and military affairs during the emperor's absence from the capital) in command of the revolutionary forces and civil

affairs in south China. Partly because of financial difficulties in maintaining these forces and partly as a gesture of sincerity in support of the central government at Peking, Huang asked to be relieved of his command. On 14 June, the post was abolished, and Huang disbanded his troops.

The T'ung-meng-hui had become an open party early in 1912, with Sun Yat-sen as chairman and Huang Hsing as vice chairman. After the establishment of the republican government at Peking, uneasy relations developed between Yuan Shih-k'ai and the provisional National Assembly, then controlled by the T'ung-meng-hui. On 25 August 1912 the T'ung-meng-hui was reorganized as a parliamentary political party, the Kuomintang, through amalgamation with four other parties. Sun Yat-sen, Huang Hsing, and seven others served as its directors. Sun Yat-sen was the titular head of the new party, with Sung Chiao-jen in charge of the party headquarters. With a view to ending political differences between north and south, both Sun and Huang accepted Yuan Shih-k'ai's invitation to come to Peking for a discussion of national affairs. In Peking (11 September–5 October), Huang sought to stabilize the political situation by bringing the cabinet ministers of the new republican government into the Kuomintang and by impressing upon Yuan Shih-k'ai the importance of adhering to the principles of parliamentary government. He refused offers of the premiership and other honors, including the title General of the Army. Huang then turned his attention to the economic reconstruction of China. While making plans for the development of mines in Hunan, he was appointed by Yuan on 28 November as director general of the Hankow-Canton and Szechwan railways. He resigned at the end of January 1913.

As a result of the national elections held early in 1913, the Kuomintang was returned to the new National Assembly as the majority party, but it did not plan to challenge Yuan Shih-k'ai's hold on the presidency. It aimed instead to capture control of the cabinet. The assassination of Sung Chiao-jen on 20 March 1913 and the opposition of the Kuomintang to the "reorganization loan" (*see* Yuan Shih-k'ai) led to increasing hostility between Yuan and the Kuomintang. Huang was reluctant to resort to force or to break with Yuan. He was firmly convinced that in a democracy political differ-ences should be settled by legal and political means rather than by force. However, he also wished to gain time to make military prepa-rations in case legal or political methods failed, for he was well aware of the military weakness of the Kuomintang.

In June 1913 the Kuomintang military gov-ernors of Kiangsi, Kwangtung, and Anhwei were dismissed from their posts by Yuan, whose intention to crush the Kuomintang now became unmistakably clear. Resistance to Yuan's move by Li Lieh-chün (q.v.), the military governor of Kiangsi, and by Huang Hsing and other provincial Kuomintang leaders marked the out-break of the so-called second revolution in July. After hastening to Nanking on 15 July, Huang assumed command of the anti-Yuan forces in Kiangsu and compelled Ch'eng Te-ch'üan (1860–1930; T. Hsueh-lou), the military gov-ernor, to declare war against Yuan. But Yuan's armies, which were superior to those of his adversaries, moved rapidly southward, and Huang became convinced that further resistance would be useless. He left Nanking on 28 July and sailed from Shanghai in mid-August to seek asylum in Japan.

After the failure of the second revolution, Huang was criticized in Tokyo by Sun Yat-sen and other party associates for his hesitation in moving against Yuan Shih-k'ai. The constant bickering between their supporters in the Kuomintang placed an increasing strain upon the relationship between Sun and Huang. Sun, in an attempt to strengthen party discipline, announced his intention to reorganize the Kuomintang as the Chung-hua ko-ming-tang and demanded that members take an oath of personal loyalty to him and seal the pledge with their thumbprints. Huang Hsing and many other important Kuomintang leaders refused to comply because they considered this demand a violation of the spirit of the republican revolu-tion. When the reorganized party was formally inaugurated in June 1914 with only eight provinces represented, Huang was already on his way to the United States. The vice chair-manship of the new party was left vacant in Huang's absence.

Huang Hsing remained in the United States for almost two years, and devoted much of his time to propaganda and fund-raising activities directed against Yuan Shih-k'ai's plan to make himself monarch. In April 1916 he left the United States for Japan so that he could main-tain closer contact with political developments in China. Yuan Shih-k'ai died on 16 June, and Huang returned to Shanghai in early July. He reconciled his differences with Sun Yat-sen, who had quietly dropped the requirement of personal obedience. Three months later, on the fifth anniversary of the Wuchang revolt, Huang became ill when an old stomach ailment re-curred. He died, at the age of only 42, on 31 October 1916.

Huang Hsing was survived by his wife, *née* Liao Tan-ju (1873–1939), also a native of Changsha; his secondary wife, Hsü Tsung-han (1876–1944), who had helped him escape from Canton to Hong Kong in April 1911 after the Huang-hua-kang uprising; and his five sons and two daughters. His eldest son by Liao, Huang I-ou (1893–), later served as a member of the Legislative Yuan, and their eldest daughter, Huang Chen-hua (1896–), became a member of the Legislative Yuan in 1948. Huang Te-hua, their youngest daughter, married Chün-tu Hsüeh, who later taught at the University of Maryland and who wrote *Huang Hsing and the Chinese Revolution*, which was published by the Stanford University Press in 1961. Huang Hsing's sons by Hsü Tsung-han were Huang I-mei (1913–1949), who married a daughter of Chang Chi, and Huang I-chiu, who married a daughter of Ch'eng Ch'ien (q.v.).

Huang K'an 黃 侃
T. Chi-kang 季 剛

Huang K'an (1886–8 October 1935), philologist and poet, noted for his studies of the *Wen-hsin tiao-lung* of Liu Hsieh and the *Jih-chih-lu* of Ku Yen-wu.

Ch'ich'un, Hupeh, was the birthplace of Huang K'an. He was the youngest son of Huang Yun-ku, the salt and tea intendant, and later the acting judicial commissioner, of Szechwan province. He died when Huang K'an was 13 sui. Little is known about Huang K'an's childhood. At about the age of 20, he was interviewed by Chang Chih-tung (ECCP, I, 27–32), then the governor general of Hupeh and Hunan, and Chang sent him to study in Japan. Huang soon met Chang Ping-lin (q.v.), who had assumed the editorship of the *Min-pao* [people's journal] in Japan. Huang became one of Chang's pupils and wrote anti-Manchu articles for his paper under the name Yun-pi.

After the establishment of the republic in 1912, Huang K'an returned to China and served briefly as secretary general to Chao Ping-chün (1865–1914). After Chao's death in February 1914, Huang was invited to teach at National Peking University, where he subsequently became a follower of Liu Shih-p'ei (q.v.). During the May Fourth Movement of 1919, he resigned from Peking University to protest the policies advocated by the movement's leaders, Ch'en Tu-hsiu and Hu Shih (qq.v.), and went to Wuchang to teach at the Normal College. In 1927 Wang Tung, who also had been a student of Chang Ping-lin, became chairman of the department of Chinese at National Southeastern (later Central) University in Nanking and persuaded Huang to join his teaching staff. Huang remained at the university until his death in October 1935.

Huang K'an's chief scholarly contributions were made in the field of philology. He held that there were no third or fourth tones in ancient Chinese phonetics and that there should be no fewer than 72 basic sounds in modern phonetics. Among Huang's major works in this field was *Chi-yun sheng-lei piao* (published in 1936), a study of the noted eleventh-century phonetic dictionary *Chi-yun*. Another important study was his *Wen-hsin tiao-lung cha-chi* (published in 1934) dealing with the *Wen-hsin tiao-lung*, a famous work on literary criticism by Liu Hsieh. Huang's work contained 20 essays in which he corrected many of the errors made by Huang Shu-lin (ECCP, I, 344–45) in his popular edition of the *Wen-hsin tiao-lung*. In *Wen-hsin tiao-lung Huang-chu pu-cheng*, Huang quoted notes written by Sun I-jang (ECCP, II, 677–79) and Li Hsiang (ECCP, II, 782). Huang's work was expanded by his pupil Fan Wen-lan (q.v.) into the *Wen-hsin tiao-lung chu* [annotations on the *Wen-hsin tiao-lung*], which was published in 1925.

Huang K'an devoted considerable attention to the text of the *Jih-chih-lu* of Ku Yen-wu (ECCP, I, 421–26). Although a standard edition of the *Jih-chih-lu* had been prepared and printed in 1695 by P'an Lei (ECCP, II, 606–7), Chang Ping-lin had long suspected the existence of a variant manuscript version of this work. In 1931 Chang Chi (q.v.) discovered a rare copy of the *Jih-chih-lu*, possibly dating from the early years of the Ch'ing dynasty, which contained more entries than the P'an Lei edition and which observed the taboo rules in such a way as to indicate that the author was a loyal subject of the Ming dynasty. After obtaining this manuscript, Huang compared the texts of the two editions and compiled the *Jih-chih-lu chiao-chi* (published in 1933), in which he noted the alterations made in the P'an Lei version. Other writings of Huang K'an were collected by his students in Nanking and published in 1937 as the *Huang hsien-sheng chi-nien ts'e*.

Like Chang Ping-lin, Huang K'an was known for his quick temper. Once, while teaching at Peking University, he is said to have threatened his colleague Ch'en Han-chang (b. 1874) with violence during a dispute over a philological interpretation. The two men later became good friends and, as members of the same literary club, exchanged poems.

In his poetry, Huang was said to have followed the style of Wang K'ai-yun (q.v.), which, in turn, had been influenced strongly by the third-century poets of the Wei-Chin period. Three small collections of Huang K'an's verse were published: *Hsi-ch'iu-hua-shih*, including poems written between 1906 and 1915; *Shih-ch'iao chi;* and *Yu Lung-shan shih*, a collection of 37 poems with a preface by Chang Ping-lin, which appeared in 1927.

Huang K'o-ch'eng   黃克誠

Huang K'o-ch'eng (1902–), Communist military officer who served under P'eng Te-huai in the early 1930's and the early 1950's. He held important posts in the People's Republic of China and in 1958 became chief of staff of the People's Liberation Army. He was dismissed from his party and government offices in 1959 on the grounds that he had been a participant in an anti-party group headed by P'eng Te-huai.

Yunghsing hsien, Hunan, was the native place of Huang K'o-ch'eng. Little is known of his family background and early life. After being graduated from middle school, he enrolled in May 1924 at the Whampoa Military Academy as a member of the first class. He presumably served as an officer of the National Revolutionary Army in the Northern Expedition, which began in 1926.

After the Nationalist-Communist split in 1927, Huang, who had joined the Chinese Communist party, took part in the so-called autumn harvest uprising in Hunan (*see* Mao Tse-tung). In the spring of 1928 he was among the Communist refugees who followed Mao Tse-tung to Chingkangshan. From 1930 until 1934 he served as a divisional commander in the Communist forces in Kiangsi and engaged in campaigns against the Nationalist forces. He served under P'eng Te-huai (q.v.) as an officer of the First Front Army during the Long March of 1934–35. After the Communist forces reached their new base in northern Shensi, Huang received staff and training assignments at Yenan, where he remained until the outbreak of the Sino-Japanese war.

In the summer of 1937 Huang was assigned to command units of the Communist Eighth Route Army. His forces moved southward from Shensi to penetrate areas behind the Japanese lines. After Nationalist and Chinese Communist forces clashed in southern Anhwei (*see* Yeh T'ing) in January 1941, Huang was ordered to reorganize his forces; they became the 3rd Division of the New Fourth Army, which was led by Ch'en Yi (q.v.). From 1941 until 1945, Huang commanded that division in operations in northern Kiangsu. He also served as military commander and secretary of the Chinese Communist party committee in northern Kiangsu. In 1945, at the Seventh National Congress of the Chinese Communist party, he was elected an alternate member of the Central Committee.

After the Japanese surrender in August 1945, Huang K'o-ch'eng was ordered to lead his troops into Manchuria, where Communist military operations were under the over-all direction of Lin Piao (q.v.). From 1946 to 1948 Huang served as a military commander in the important campaigns against the Nationalists in the Northeast. By 1948 he had become commander of Communist field operations in the Jehol-Liaoning district.

Huang continued to serve under Lin Piao when the Communist forces in Manchuria, then designated the Fourth Field Army, moved through the Shanhaikuan pass into north China. After the Communist victory at Tientsin in January 1949, Huang was named chairman of the military control commission which was responsible for consolidating Communist authority there. However, he soon moved south with the Twelfth Army Group of the Communist Fourth Field Army. Huang K'o-ch'eng and Hsiao Ching-kuang accepted the surrender of the Nationalist forces under Ch'eng Ch'ien (q.v.) and Ch'en Ming-jen in Hunan. Huang became secretary of the Hunan provincial committee of the Chinese Communist party, political commissar of the Hunan military district, and vice chairman of the military control commission for Changsha. In February 1950 he was made a member of the newly established Central-South Military and Administrative Committee, the principal governing authority for the provinces of that region. In April, he was named to the provincial government council in Hunan.

In 1949 Huang became a member of the National Committee of the Chinese People's Political Consultative Conference. After the death of Jen Pi-shih in 1950, he was elevated to full membership on the Central Committee of the Chinese Communist party. When the Chinese intervened in the Korean war in October-November 1950, Huang returned to active duty and led the Twelfth Army Group across the Yalu as part of the Communist drive against the United Nations forces. From 1952 to 1954 he was a member of the State Planning Commission and deputy chief of staff of the People's Revolutionary Military Council.

After the reorganization of the government structure at Peking in 1954, Huang served as a delegate, representing the Central-South Military District and the Fourth Field Army, to the First National People's Congress. In September, he was elected to the membership on the Standing Committee of the National People's Congress. At the same time, he was made a vice minister of national defense and a member of the National Defense Council. He served in the central military command of the People's Liberation Army as director of the general rear services department from 1954 until 1956. In 1955 he was promoted to the rank of general in the Chinese Communist armed forces and was awarded all top military decorations of the People's Republic of China. At the Eighth National Congress of the Chinese Communist party in September 1956, Huang K'o-ch'eng was elected to both the Central Committee and the Secretariat.

In October 1958 Huang was named chief of staff of the People's Liberation Army, succeeding Su Yü (q.v.). He held this office and continued to serve as a vice minister of national defense until September 1959. Then he was removed from all official positions at Peking, and P'eng Te-huai was forced to resign as minister of national defense. Huang was identified as one of the principals in an "anti-party group" allegedly headed by P'eng Te-huai. He later was named a vice governor of Shansi.

Huang Kuang-jui 黃 光 瑞

Huang Kuang-jui (5 June 1898–), aviator, participated in the first long-distance flight made in China (1928). As commander of the Kwangtung Air Force, he helped end the 1936 revolt of Ch'en Chi-t'ang (q.v.) by turning over his men and their planes to the National Government. After holding such posts as the presidency of the Aviation Research Institute and the vice chairmanship of the Air Force Commission, he retired in 1946.

Although he was born in Toishan, Kwangtung, Huang was taken to the United States as a child and was educated in San Francisco's Chinatown. In 1917 he was one of a group of young Chinese selected by Yang Hsien-i to train as pilots. Yang was the leader of a group sent by Sun Yat-sen to the United States to study aviation and to recruit personnel for a new air force. He purchased two training planes and engaged an American instructor. The group of trainees included Lin Wei-ch'eng, a future commander of the Kwangsi Provincial Air Force; Ch'en Tso-lin, who became a chief staff member of the Eurasia Aviation Corporation; and Yang Kuan-yu, who, with Huang, took part in China's first long-distance flight and later became commander of the air transport corps of the Chinese air force. Because official funds had run out, the trainees had to buy fuel for the planes and pay the instructor's salary.

After a year's rudimentary training in flying and mechanics, Huang Kuang-jui was attached to the T'ung-meng-hui headquarters in California, where he acted as chief technician of an armaments purchasing commission. By staging exhibitions of flying, he and his colleagues raised funds for the purchase of six old Jennie-type planes, which were dismantled and shipped back to Canton. In 1922 Sun Yat-sen established military headquarters in Canton, and Huang was ordered home to become a pilot in the flying corps, which consisted of the six old planes sent from America. They were used in Sun's numerous campaigns against the Kwangtung and Kwangsi military factions. Sometimes the aviators dropped a few hand-made bombs on the enemy, but often they simply relied on the roar of the engines to demoralize their opponents' troops. Huang Kuang-jui was made leader of this squadron in 1923, and in 1924 he became director of the Aviation Bureau. He had constant personal contact with Sun Yat-sen, who rewarded him for his services with citations and cash bonuses.

In 1926, after the death of Sun Yat-sen, Chiang Kai-shek made Huang president of the new aviation academy at Ta-sha-t'ou. Early in 1927 Huang was sent to purchase planes in the Soviet Union. He was unable to carry out his mission, but he took advantage of the opportunity afforded him by attending the Second Aviation Academy, where he studied military flying for six months. On returning to China, Huang became leader of the First Squadron of the Kwangtung Air Force, which was controlled by the provincial government authorities even though it was under the jurisdiction of the new National Government in Nanking.

In 1928, Chang Hui-ch'ang, the director of the aviation office of the Eighth Route Army in Kwangtung, decided to publicize flying activities by undertaking a long-distance flight. Huang Kuang-jui and Yang Kuan-yu accompanied Chang on this mission. The three aviators left Canton on 11 November at 8:30 a.m. in a monoplane which various reports credit with the names Pearl River and Spirit of Canton. They arrived at Hankow at 4 p.m. to receive an enthusiastic welcome. Bad weather postponed their departure for Nanking until 9:50 a.m. on 15 November. They arrived at Nanking at 1:30 p.m., where they were met by an official welcoming party which included Feng Yü-hsiang, Ho Ying-ch'in, Sun Fo, and other dignitaries. The aviators left Nanking on 20 November and flew to Peking. They went to Mukden on 26 November and then to Tientsin, which they left on 4 December at 9 a.m. They arrived in Shanghai less than six hours later. In a mandate issued on 7 December, the three aviators were commended and awarded medals for a feat which, at a time when airfields were crude and radio and weather reports were non-existent, had required great courage.

In 1928 Huang became chief of the aviation office of the Eighth Route Army, where he served under Chen Chi-t'ang (q.v.). At that time Huang held the rank of major general. In July 1931 the Kwangtung Air Force was made an independent command by the Kwangtung government, and Huang was made chief of staff. In July 1932 he was made commander of the Second Squadron. The Kwangtung Air Force was integrated with the First Army Group in 1933, and Huang was appointed to command it.

In 1934 Huang was sent to France, Italy, Great Britain, and the United States to study military aviation. His experiences abroad convinced him that China must be unified to achieve strength and independence. In 1936 Chen Chi-t'ang, the leader of the Kwangtung military faction, joined forces with the Kwangsi leaders Li Tsung-jen and Pai Ch'ung-hsi (qq.v.) in opposition to the National Government. In early July, Huang Kuang-jui assembled the 160 fliers of the Kwangtung Air Force and ordered them to fly 62 planes from Canton to the Shaokuan airfield. On arrival, he ordered his men to fly 58 planes to Nanchang to join the National Government forces. He took the four remaining planes and their crews to Hong Kong, where he issued a statement declaring allegiance to Nanking. His action was instrumental in quelling the Kwangtung-Kwangsi revolt, for its leaders realized the futility of operating without an air force.

In September 1936 Huang assumed the presidency of the Central Aviation Academy at Hangchow. Three months later, he was made a member of the Aviation Commission. In March 1938 he became vice chairman of the Air Force Commission and air force commander at Chengtu, Szechwan. When the commission was reorganized in April 1941, Huang was placed in charge of military aviation administration and was made president of the Aviation Research Institute. The Air Force Commission was reorganized a second time in February 1943; Huang was reappointed vice chairman

and was made vice president of the Aviation Research Institute. He was promoted lieutenant general of the air force on January 1946 and was placed, at his request, on the retired list. Later that year, he was elected to serve as a delegate to the National Assembly. He moved to Canton and later went to live in Hong Kong.

Huang and his wife, *née* Tsai, had two sons, Wei-chiu and Wei-chih, and four daughters, Pi-hsia, Pi-yun, Pi-tsui, and Pi-chan. All of his children were educated in the United States.

Huang Lu-yin   黃 廬 隱
  Orig. Huang Ying   黃 英
  Pen. Lu-yin   廬 隱

Huang Lu-yin (1898–13 May 1934), writer whose short stories and novels enjoyed great popularity after 1925. Many of her writings depicted young Chinese in their search for new standards and values during the May Fourth era.

A native of Fukien, Huang Lu-yin was born into a gentry family. On the day of her birth, her maternal grandmother died; for this reason, Huang's uneducated mother considered her a sinister baby and refused to feed her. She was sent away with a wet nurse to be reared in the country. After being brought home at the age of three, she went with her family to Hunan, where her father had been appointed magistrate at Changsha. He died three years later, leaving his widow with four children. At the invitation of Huang's uncle (her mother's brother), a physician at the imperial court, the family moved north from Changsha, reaching Peking in 1907. Huang's mother continued to be harsh, and the other adult relatives in the household thought Huang backward. She was beaten for her reluctance to study, forced to sleep with the illiterate maidservants of the household, and locked in the garden when guests came.

At the age of nine, Huang was sent briefly to a missionary boarding school in Peking, where she was bullied by other pupils because she was the youngest student. She also was forced to perform disagreeable tasks which were beyond her capacities. The experiences of these early years filled her with resentment, and she sought comfort in Christianity.

After the outbreak of the 1911 revolution, Huang's eldest brother returned home from Fukien and began to assist her in studying Chinese composition. To the surprise of her mother and other relatives, she made rapid progress, first in primary school, and later, from 1912 to 1917, at a girls normal school. During her last year in normal school she developed a keen interest in literature. She read widely, devouring popular Chinese novels as well as Western fiction translated by Lin Shu (q.v.), and acquired the nickname "novel addict." At the age of 17 she defied her mother by becoming engaged to a young relative.

After graduation from normal school at the age of 18, Huang, under renewed pressure from her mother, turned to teaching to help support the household. From 1917 to 1919 she taught at several schools in Anhwei, Honan, and other places, staying only briefly at each school. As a result, her cousins called her a "one-semester teacher."

By 1919 Huang Lu-yin had saved enough money to be able to continue her education. She enrolled at the Peking Women's Higher Normal School. Entering in the same class in the autumn of 1919 was another young woman who was to gain prominence as a writer, Su Hsueh-lin (q.v.), whom Huang had known when they had taught together in Anking, Anhwei. New literary and political theories were rapidly taking hold in China, and Huang Lu-yin entered with enthusiasm into the stimulating intellectual atmosphere of the May Fourth Movement. Although a newcomer, she was elected head of the student association. Her energy, combined with her eloquent command of the Peking dialect, led her schoolmates to dub her "big sister" because of her leadership abilities. She soon rejected the fiancé to whom she had been engaged for three years, declaring that she found his intellect "too mediocre." She joined a small organization called Social Reform and met Kuo Meng-liang, whom she later married. In 1922 she and her classmates took a trip to Japan, where she was impressed by the "good order and good government" of the Japanese.

After graduation in 1922, Huang Lu-yin returned to middle-school teaching. In 1925 she worked for a year preparing thousand-character readers for the National Association for the Advancement of Mass Education at

Peking, headed by James Yen (Yen Yang-ch'u, q.v.). For a time, she ran the Hua-yen Bookstore in Peking and edited its monthly magazine, *Hua-yen pan-yueh-k'an*. She also taught modern Chinese literature and served as principal of a girls school at Peking until the Nationalist troops arrived in north China in 1928.

Huang Lu-yin's writing career began when she was still a college student. During her freshman year she came under the influence of Hu Shih (q.v.), who was then beginning his career at Peking University. In 1919–20 she attended Hu Shih's lectures on the history of Chinese philosophy and responded to his advocacy of pai-hua [the vernacular] as a medium for creative writing. She submitted her first pai-hua attempt, *I-ko chu-tso chia* [a writer], to Mao Tun (Shen Yen-ping, q.v.), the editor of the *Hsiao-shuo yueh-pao* [short story magazine], and its publication in 1921 greatly strengthened her self-confidence. From 1920 to 1922 she wrote more than 100,000 words: short stories, essays, and travel sketches. Her first successful short story, *Hai-pin ku-jen* [friend by the sea], was published in 1925. Like most of her stories, it is autobiographical, with Huang herself portrayed as one of a group of five college classmates who, as they move down the conventional path of marriage, become aware of the gap between dream and reality. The tone is melancholic; the mood, bitter and cynical. Love among women and between the sexes is the subject, but the deeper theme is the quest for the meaning of human existence. *Ling-hai ch'ao-hsi* [mental tides], *Man-li* [Mary], *Nü-jen ti hsin* [a woman's heart], and *Hsiang-ya chieh-chih* [ivory ring] all depict young Chinese in the May Fourth era as they seek new values and new standards to give meaning to the twentieth-century world. The essential value of Huang Lu-yin's work, according to Mao Tun, lies in its reflection of the psychology of young people of her period. The heroines in her stories, most of them projections of personal experience, are fighters against destiny. They struggle to overcome misfortunes and take a courageous stand against outmoded social conventions. Huang Lu-yin's essential range, however, is the individual and his private tensions; and her creative writing, like her life, was largely confined to three elements: passion, suffering, and the conflict between reason and emotion. She said of herself: "I was born of and perished from contradiction. There can be no relief for my sufferings." She advocated unlimited development of individuality. Although her stories are often loose in structure and ornate in diction, they are redeemed by their earnestness and flowing style. Her writings appealed especially to girl students in China, and she enjoyed about nine years of popularity after the publication of *Hai-pin ku-jen* in 1925. She and Hsieh Wan-ying (q.v.) shared the prestige of being the two foremost women writers in the early period of the new literary movement. Both women belonged to the Literary Research Society and were individualistic idealists, stressing spiritual life and love of nature.

Huang Lu-yin's early writings, sentimental tales about love and the struggle against destiny, reflected the influence of traditional Chinese poetry and popular novels. In the later stage of her career, she turned her attention to social problems. She produced the bulk of her work under pressure, writing in the spare time afforded by her teaching tasks. She was capable of intense concentration and rapid production.

Huang Lu-yin married twice. Her first romance, with Kuo Meng-liang, an intellectual who had turned from studies in Chinese classical literature to espouse socialism, caused widespread criticism, for Kuo was married. He divorced his first wife to marry Huang Lu-yin in 1923. That union, reportedly unsatisfactory, ended with Kuo's death two years later. Later, Huang fell in love with Li Wei-chien, a young Tsinghua student and poet. This romance, like the first, encountered stern public disapproval, for she was several years older than Li. They were married in 1930, went to Tokyo on their honeymoon, and remained in Japan for about a year. They then returned to China to live at Hangchow. In the spring of 1934 Huang, then 37 sui, died in childbirth at the Great China Hospital at Shanghai. Before her death she had begun to write "Huo-yen" [flame], a novel about the anti-Japanese resistance of the Nineteenth Route Army at Shanghai in January 1932.

In her autobiography, *Lu-yin tzu-chuan*, published at Shanghai in 1934, Huang Lu-yin traced the development of her thinking in the preceding decade, dividing it into three stages: sorrowful, transitional, and broadening. The first stage, during which she was under the influence of Schopenhauer and viewed life as a sea of bitterness, lasted longest. The deaths of her close relatives and friends contributed to her feeling of sadness and emptiness. She resorted to drinking and smoking ("slow suicide") to ease her sorrow. *Hai-pin ku-jen* (1925), *Ling-hai ch'ao-hsi*, and *Man-li* (1927) were products of this stage. When suffering from an illness, she came to better understanding of sorrow and began to develop sympathy for others. Her romance with Li Wei-chien, which revived her dead passion and enabled her to achieve a better understanding of herself, was also a major cause of her transition. *Kuei-yen* [the home-coming swan] of 1930 and *Yün-ou ch'ing-shu chi* [love letters of Yün Ou] of 1931 were produced in the second stage. Huang Lu-yin triumphed over sorrow and no longer thought only of herself when she wrote. In *Nü-jen ti hsin*, for instance, she denounced feudal traditions and opposed the idea that chastity is expected of women but not of men. This novel, together with *Ch'ing-fu jih-chi* [the diary of a paramour], represents her thinking in the third stage.

Huang Mu-sung　　　黃 慕 松

Huang Mu-sung (1885–20 March 1937), military man who served as dean of the Paoting Military Academy and deputy commander of the cadet corps of the Whampoa Military Academy. He represented the National Government on special missions to Sinkiang (1933) and Tibet (1934) and became chairman of the Mongolian and Tibetan Affairs Commission in 1935. He became governor of Kwangtung in 1936.

Meihsien, Kwangtung, was the birthplace of Huang Mu-sung. His parents were prosperous landholders of Hakka extraction. After receiving a traditional education in the Chinese classics at local schools, he enrolled at the Peking Military Academy in 1903. Four years later he was sent as a government-sponsored student to the Shikan Gakkō [military academy] in Japan, where he majored in military engineering. After graduation in November 1908, he returned to China and became an instructor at the Peking Military Academy. Huang soon transferred to the newly established Paoting Military Academy. He eventually became dean of the academy, and in 1919 he attained the rank of major general. After participating in a Sino-Russian conference at Moscow in 1920, he served as a staff officer in the Peking military office which was responsible for Sino-Russian affairs.

In 1924 Huang Mu-sung declared allegiance to the Kuomintang and moved to Canton, where he joined the staff of the Whampoa Military Academy, headed by Chiang Kai-shek. When the Northern Expedition was launched in 1926, Huang was assigned to remain at Whampoa as deputy commander of the cadet corps and Kuomintang political commissar. After the Nationalist military forces consolidated control of the lower Yangtze valley, Huang was sent to Nanking, where he served as commander of the Third Army for several months. He then returned to Kwangtung as commander of the Third Army.

After Chang Hsueh-liang (q.v.) pledged allegiance to the National Government on 29 December 1928, Huang Mu-sung served for a few months as president of the military college at Peking. In January 1930 he was made chief of the survey bureau of the Nationalist army's general staff. In that capacity, he participated in international conferences on problems of land survey and aerial photography. He also served on the Chinese delegation to the preparatory commission for general disarmament which met (1926–31) under the auspices of the League of Nations at Geneva, Switzerland. In December 1931 he was elected to alternate membership on the Central Executive Committee of the Kuomintang. When the World Disarmament Conference convened at Geneva in February 1932, Huang attended the meetings as plenipotentiary representative of China. The conference was adjourned in March 1933, and Huang returned to Nanking to become deputy chief of army general staff and chief of the border affairs section.

In the spring of 1933, after Sheng Shih-ts'ai (q.v.) seized power in Sinkiang and clashed with the Muslim forces of Ma Chung-ying (q.v.), Huang Mu-sung received a special appointment as pacification commissioner of Sinkiang. He arrived at Urumchi on 10 June 1933 to find the troops of Sheng and Ma ready to do battle again. He immediately issued a directive forbidding military action, but Sheng and Ma ignored it. Sheng emerged victorious from the

ensuing battle. Soon afterwards, he accused Huang Mu-sung of plotting to overthrow him and placed Huang under house arrest. On 4 July, Sheng had three National Government officials (also alleged plotters) shot within sight of the house in which Huang was being held. Sheng and Liu Wen-lung, then the acting governor of Sinkiang, informed the National Government of the supposed plot and requested a full investigation of the matter. Chiang Kai-shek and Wang Ching-wei replied by telegram with a warning to Sheng to exercise caution in pursuing the matter, and the Executive Yuan ordered Huang Mu-sung to return to Nanking immediately to report on the matter. Sheng permitted Huang to leave Sinkiang only after he had wired Nanking recommending that the authority of Sheng Shih-ts'ai and Liu Wen-lung in Sinkiang be confirmed. Huang reached Nanking on 21 July, and the National Government confirmed the authority of Sheng Shih-ts'ai on 1 August.

In January 1934, a month after the death of the Thirteenth Dalai Lama (q.v.), the National Government appointed Huang Mu-sung Chinese high commissioner in Tibet. At that time, the National Government was seeking to restore Chinese authority in Tibet. After arriving in Lhasa in April, Huang represented the National Government at a memorial service for the Dalai, issued a proclamation exhorting the Tibetans to place their trust in the National Government as the sole source of lasting prosperity and happiness, and began to negotiate with the Ka-dreng Hutukhtu, who had become the regent of Tibet. Huang Mu-sung proposed that China and Tibet resume full relations and that the pro-Chinese Panchen Lama (q.v.) be permitted to return to Tibet. The Ka-dreng Hutukhtu agreed in principle to the establishment of a Chinese commissioner's office in Tibet; the Panchen Lama would be allowed to return if he did not bring a large Chinese entourage with him and if he would not attempt to exercise any political authority at Lhasa.

After returning to Nanking in October 1934, Huang reported that British influence continued to be the dominant external force in Tibetan affairs. He then proposed that the National Government provide the Panchen Lama, who had been given the title of pacification commissioner of the Western Regions in December 1932, with a military force for his return to

China. In February 1935 the Panchen was assigned a military escort of some 500 Chinese troops. He established headquarters in the Alashan region of Ninghsia province. In March, Huang Mu-sung was made chairman of the Mongolian and Tibetan Affairs Commission. He soon persuaded the Executive Yuan to recognize the autonomy of Inner Mongolian tribes to improve relations between Inner Mongolia and the National Government. On 2 April, he received the rank of lieutenant general. He was elected to membership on the Central Executive Committee of the Kuomintang in November.

On 28 July 1936 Huang Mu-sung was appointed governor of Kwangtung, succeeding Ch'en Ch'i-tang (q.v.). Many observers believed that the appointment reflected Chiang Kai-shek's personal confidence in Huang as a man who could consolidate National Government authority in south China. Huang reportedly had been one of the men who had recommended Chiang for study in Japan in 1908, and Chiang had revered him as a teacher. Huang assumed office at Canton in August 1936, with Yü Han-mou (q.v) as his pacification commissioner. He died on 20 March 1937, at the age of 52. He was survived by his wife, five sons, three daughters, and his 82-year-old mother.

Huang Shao-hung 黃 紹竑
 Alt. Shao-hsiung 紹 雄
 T. Chi-k'uan 季 寬

Huang Shao-hung (1895–), military leader who joined with Li Tsung-jen and Pai Ch'ung-hsi to form the so-called Kwangsi clique. After breaking with Li and Pai in 1930, he served the National Government in such posts as minister of communications, governor of Chekiang, governor of Hupeh, and deputy commander of the First and Third War areas. In the 1950's he held minor posts in the Central People's Government at Peking.

Junghsien, Kwangsi, the birthplace of Huang Shao-hung, had been the ancestral home of the Huang family since the late years of the Ming dynasty. His father, Huang Shao-tien, brought two progressive teachers from Canton into their native village after the Boxer Uprising of 1900.

Huang Shao-hung received his early education in the primary school organized by his father.

In the spring of 1911 Huang Shao-hung enrolled at the Kwangsi Army Primary School. Among his schoolmates were Li Tsung-jen and Pai Ch'ung-hsi (qq.v.). After the Wuchang revolt and the declaration of independence in Kwangsi, a group of students of which Huang was a member organized the Students Army Dare-to-Die Corps. Huang became a squad commander. The Dare-to-Die Corps went to the Wuchang area, but the military stage of the revolution ended without the corps having seen any fighting. The unit was transferred to Nanking for enrollment in the Officers' Academy. Huang entered the cavalry section of the Nanking Enlistment Corps, but resigned shortly afterwards. Later, the corps was removed to Wuchang and transformed into the Second Military Preparatory School. Huang then rejoined the group. He was graduated in the winter of 1914 and was ordered to Peking for duty. Upon arrival, he was assigned to Lu Yung-hsiang's 10th Division, stationed at Peiyuan. In June 1915 he entered the third class of the Paoting Military Academy. Among his classmates were Pai Ch'ung-hsi and Hsia Wei. After graduation in late 1916, Huang returned to Kwangsi and joined the 1st Kwangsi Division. In the summer of 1917 the provincial government established the Kwangsi Model Battalion under the command of Ma Hsiao-chün, a recent graduate of the Shikan Gakkō [military academy] in Japan. Huang became a deputy commander under Huang Hsu-ch'u. Other deputy commanders in the battalion were Pai Ch'ung-hsi and Hsia Wei.

In the autumn of 1917 the Model Battalion was ordered to Hunan to fight in the so-called constitution protection movement. It was assigned as a guard unit to the headquarters of T'an Hao-ming, Kwangsi tuchün [military governor] and commander in chief of the Hunan-Kwangtung-Kwangsi Constitution-Protection Army. When a machine-gun company was added to the Model Battalion, Huang Shao-hung, Pai Ch'ung-hsi, and Hsia Wei all volunteered as deputy commanders. Because the company had no commander, the three received joint command. After Wu P'ei-fu (q.v.) defeated T'an Hao-ming's forces, T'an reorganized the Model Battalion. Huang and Pai each received command of a company.

In early 1919 the Kwangsi forces returned home. The Model Battalion was transferred to Nanning, where it took part in the so-called bandit-suppression campaigns. That winter, Ma Hsiao-chün received command of the Model Battalion. The battalion was ordered to Chaoch'ing, Kwangtung, for garrison duty early in 1920.

Sun Yat-sen established a government at Canton in the winter of 1920 and engineered an attack on the Kwangsi forces, using the combined armies of Kwangtung, Kweichow, and Yunnan. The Kwangsi forces, after a defeat in October, were forced to retreat along the West River to Kwangsi. The Model Battalion and troops under Li Tsung-jen served as the rear guard.

Ma Hsiao-chün strove to keep his forces intact by assuming a semi-independent, or neutral, position. Huang Shao-hung and Pai Ch'ung-hsi accompanied him to Paise (Poseh) in western Kwangsi in February 1921. The Kwangtung-Kwangsi conflict resumed in June, and the Kwangtung troops of Ch'en Chiung-ming (q.v.) soon occupied all of Kwangsi. The Model Battalion continued to garrison Paise. Men from other armies were recruited, and the battalion soon was reorganized as an army of five battalions, with Huang Shao-hung commanding the 1st Battalion. That summer, the army was surrounded by Liu Jih-fu's Kwangsi Autonomous Army. Huang Shao-hung escaped with many of his men and recruited new troops. Ma Hsiao-chün then appointed him commander of the 1st Regiment. Later that year, when Pai Ch'ung-hsi, then commanding the 2nd Regiment, was injured in a fall from a cliff, Huang received command of the 2nd Regiment.

In the spring of 1922 Ma Hsiao-chün retired and gave Huang command of his army. Huang then joined Li Tsung-jen's forces in Yülin as commander of the third column. When Li reorganized his forces as the 5th Independent Brigade, Huang became commander of its 3rd Regiment. After spending about nine months at Yülin, Huang was ordered to garrison Junghsien. About that time, Shen Hung-ying became administrator of Kwangtung military affairs. Early in the summer of 1923 Huang brought a small force to Shen's headquarters at Wuchow and accepted an appointment from him. However, Pai Ch'ung-hsi soon returned secretly from Canton and persuaded Huang to accept an appointment from Sun Yat-sen as com-

mander in chief of the Kwangsi Anti-Rebel Army. After Sun's troops defeated Shen's expeditionary force in Kwangtung in the autumn, Huang seized Wuchow. Units of the Kwangtung Revolutionary Army soon arrived in Wuchow, and Huang began to organize the Kwangsi Anti-Rebel Army, with Pai Ch'ung-hsi as his chief of staff.

Huang then undertook the double task of expanding his influence in Kwangsi and strengthening his ties with the Kwangtung group. He joined forces with Li Tsung-jen's Kwangsi Pacification Army and began a campaign to unify Kwangsi. In June 1924 the joint force occupied Nanning. In July, the two armies were consolidated by establishment of the joint headquarters of the Kwangsi Pacification Anti-Rebel Army, with Li Tsung-jen as commander in chief, Huang Shao-hung as his deputy, and Pai Ch'ung-hsi as chief of staff and field commander. The army took the field in August to help the armies of Shen Hung-ying defeat Lu Jung-t'ing (q.v.).

In November 1924 Huang Shao-hung went to Canton as Li Tsung-jen's representative to discuss unification of Kwangtung and Kwangsi. He joined the Kuomintang at this time. On 1 December, the Kwangsi Pacification Anti-Rebel Army was abolished, and Huang became commander of the Second Kwangsi Army and deputy pacification commissioner of Kwangsi, serving under Li Tsung-jen. After defeating Shen Hung-ying in February 1925, they turned to meet the troops of T'ang Chi-yao (q.v.), the military governor of Yunnan. T'ang, following the death of Sun Yat-sen on 12 March, attempted to send forces through Kwangsi to Canton so that he could become Sun's successor. T'ang's forces took Nanning, and Huang Shao-hung lost the first battle to recover it. However, the Yunnan forces soon were defeated, and they retreated from Kwangsi with only a fraction of their original strength.

Negotiations for the closer cooperation of Kwangsi and Kwangtung began late in 1925. On 24 March 1926 the Kwangsi forces became the Seventh Army of the National Revolutionary Army, with Huang Shao-hung as party representative, Li Tsung-jen as commander, and Pai Ch'ung-hsi as chief of staff. In June, Huang became governor of Kwangsi.

Huang Shao-hung returned to the field in 1927. At the request of Li Chi-shen (q.v.), he organized the Fifteenth Army and helped defeat

Chinese Communist forces under Ho Lung and Yeh T'ing (qq.v.) at Swatow and Chaochow. Huang had become a member of the Canton branch of the Political Council in April, and he stationed some of his troops at Canton. On 17 November, Chang Fa-k'uei (q.v.) staged a coup at Canton and captured some of Huang's men. Huang escaped and organized his forces to attack Canton. In the meantime, Li Chi-shen, who was in Shanghai, ordered forces loyal to him, including those of Ch'en Ming-shu (q.v.), to oust Chang Fa-k'uei. Although Huang's army suffered heavy casualties, it defeated Chang's Fourth Army. Huang returned to Kwangsi in April 1928.

In 1929 the so-called Kwangsi clique of Huang Shao-hung, Li Tsung-jen, and Pai Ch'ung-hsi broke with the National Government. Huang and Pai launched an unsuccessful attack on Kwangtung. They then were attacked from Hunan by Liu Chien-hsü, who occupied Kweilin. The National Government had appointed Yü Tso-po to succeed Huang as provincial governor, and Yü's forces occupied Nanning on 27 June. Huang and Pai entrusted their forces to subordinates and went to Indo-China. They then went to Hong Kong and joined Li Tsung-jen. The three men returned to Kwangsi in November and established the Party-Protecting National Salvation Army at Nanning, with Li as commander in chief, Huang as deputy commander and Kwangsi governor, and Pai as field commander.

In January 1930 the Kwangsi forces united with Chang Fa-k'uei's Fourth Army in an attempt to capture Canton. However, they were defeated and forced back to Kwangsi. After Feng Yü-hsiang and Yen Hsi-shan (qq.v.) formed a coalition in April 1930 to oppose the National Government, Li, Pai, and Chang Fa-k'uei met in conference and decided to support the Yen-Feng coalition by invading Hunan and capturing Wuhan. Although Huang did not participate in the conference, he agreed with its decisions. The armies had reached Changsha when Kwangtung forces led by Chiang Kuang-nai and Ts'ai T'ing-k'ai (qq.v.) occupied Hengyang, cutting off Huang Shao-hung's rearguard troops from the rest of the Kwangsi forces. Li and Chang turned back to extricate Huang, but their troops were defeated at Hungchiao. The remnants of the Kwangsi forces returned home to regroup.

At this point Huang broke away from the Kwangsi clique because he opposed the policy of continuing the civil war. Without formally resigning his posts, Huang retired and left Kwangsi in the winter of 1930. He went to Nanking and called on Chiang Kai-shek, who offered to appoint him rehabilitation commissioner for Kwangsi. Huang refused, went to Hong Kong, and then took a trip to the Philippines.

In May 1932 Huang Shao-hung became minister of interior at Nanking. A few months later, he succeeded Ch'en Ming-shu as minister of communications. After the Japanese invaded Jehol in February 1933, Chiang Kai-shek made Huang chief of staff to Ho Ying-ch'in (q.v.), who had been appointed director of the Peiping branch of the Military Council. He accompanied Ho and T. V. Soong to north China for negotiations with the Japanese. After the signature of the Tangku Truce in May 1933, Mongols of Inner Mongolia led by Te Wang (Demchukdonggrub, q.v.) and Prince Yun increased their demands for autonomy. Huang was sent to Suiyuan in late October. He conferred with Fu Tso-yi (q.v.) at Kweisui and then went to Pailingmiao. After more than 20 days of negotiations, he reached agreement with the Mongols and returned to Nanking.

In January 1934 Huang proposed that Nanking undertake an expedition to pacify Sinkiang. He was given money and was ordered to plan the expedition in secrecy. Huang made arrangements and flew to Lanchow in mid-April to confer with Chu Shao-liang, the pacification commissioner of Kansu. However, he soon received a telegram from Nanking cancelling the expedition and recalling him to Nanking.

Huang went to Lushan to rest, for he had contracted beri-beri in Lanchow. In October 1934 Chiang Kai-shek asked him to become governor of Chekiang. He accepted the appointment and assumed office in December. In 1935 he was elected to the Kuomintang's Central Supervisory Committee. Chiang Kai-shek summoned him in July to Lushan. On his way there, Huang learned that the National Government had appointed Li Tsung-jen and Pai Ch'ung-hsi to posts outside of Kwangsi and had appointed Huang military affairs rehabilitation commissioner for Kwangsi. At Lushan, Huang refused the appointment and wired Li and Pai that he had done so. He then went to Shanghai. After the Kwangtung position collapsed (*see* Ch'en Chi-t'ang), Chiang Kai-shek went to Canton and prepared to subdue the Kwangsi generals by force. He summoned Huang to Canton and tried to persuade him to accept command of the punitive army. Huang, however, thought it possible to negotiate a settlement and requested an opportunity to do so. Supported by Ch'eng Ch'ien (q.v.) he held negotiations with his former associates and established a basis for agreement. He and Ch'eng then accompanied Li Tsung-jen to Canton for meetings with Chiang Kai-shek. Li and Chiang resolved their differences, and Kwangsi acceded to the authority of the National Government. Huang then returned to Chekiang.

In January 1937 Huang Shao-hung succeeded Yang Yung-t'ai, who had been assassinated in November 1936, as governor of Hupeh. After the Sino-Japanese war broke out, he went to Nanking on 6 August 1937 to take charge of war planning in the Military Affairs Commission's first section. He then served under Yen Hsi-shan as deputy commander in chief of the Second War Area. In October, he took charge of the Niangtzukuan sector, blocking Japanese entry into Shansi from the east. However, the Japanese forced Huang's troops and those defending Hsinkow to retreat and then took Taiyuan. Huang Shao-hung returned to Nanking.

In December 1937 Huang again became governor of Chekiang. After Nanking fell in mid-December, he removed the provincial capital from Hangchow. The provincial administration moved several times, and, although the Japanese occupied several cities and large towns in the province, Huang's government remained intact throughout the war. In 1943 Huang also became deputy commander of the Third War Area.

Huang Shao-hung continued to serve as governor of Chekiang until 1947, when he became vice president of the Control Yuan and a member of the strategic advisory committee. In 1948 he was elected to the Legislative Yuan. In March 1949, after Li Tsung-jen became acting President, Huang was made a member of the Kuomintang's Central Political Council. That spring, Li sent a peace delegation to Peking. When Huang learned that the peace mission had failed, he went to Hong Kong, where he publicly urged Kuomintang members to support the Chinese Communist party and

to denounce Chiang Kai-shek. He was formally expelled from the Kuomintang in August 1949.

Huang participated in the Chinese People's Political Consultative Conference, held in Peking in September 1949, and served the Central People's Government as a member of the Government Administration Council. He attended the 1954 National People's Congress as a delegate from Kwangsi. He was elected to the Standing Committee of the congress. In 1956 he became a member of the Kuomintang Revolutionary Committee's central committee. That November, he served on the National People's Congress delegation that went to the Soviet Union and Eastern Europe, returning to China in January 1957. During the Hundred Flowers Campaign (*see* Mao Tse-tung) Huang criticized the National People's Congress, saying that it served merely as a rubber stamp for the Chinese Communist party. In January 1958 he was censured as a rightist and removed from his posts. Nevertheless, he was elected to the National Committee of the Chinese People's Political Consultative Conference in April 1959. His name was removed from the list of rightists in November 1960.

Huang Shao-ku   黃 少 谷

Huang Shao-ku (24 July 1901–), journalist and politician, was secretary general in Feng Yü-hsiang's headquarters in 1928 and Feng's representative at the so-called enlarged conference of 1930. He served under Chang Chih-chung as an administrative commissioner in Hunan and as chief of the third office of the Military Council's political department. From 1943 to 1948 he was the publisher of the newspaper *Sao-tang pao*. In Taiwan, he held such offices as vice president of the Executive Yuan, foreign minister, and ambassador to Spain.

Nanhsien, which borders on the Tungt'ing Lake in northern Hunan, was the birthplace of Huang Shao-ku. Although his father had little money, he did all he could to ensure that Huang would receive a good education. In 1919 Huang was admitted to the Ming-te Middle School in Changsha. It was the year of the May Fourth Movement, and student agitation soon began in Hunan. When a student-led movement to oust Chang Ching-yao, the northern warlord in control of the province, was launched, Huang became a leader in the campaign.

After completing his secondary education toward the end of 1929, Huang Shao-ku decided to apply to National Peking University, which provided scholarships. He succeeded in gaining admission to the university in 1923. He soon found, however, that it was necessary to find part-time work because of the erratic nature of government appropriations to educational institutions. In the summer of 1925 he was given a job at the *Shih-chieh wan-pao* [world evening news], the evening edition of the well-known newspaper *Shih-chieh jih-pao* [world daily news]. He soon became chief editor of the evening paper.

The death of Sun Yat-sen early in 1925 greatly spurred Kuomintang development in north China, and Huang Shao-ku was one of the many enthusiastic young people who joined the revolutionary party at that time. Chang Tso-lin (q.v.), then in control at Peking, ordered the summary arrest of Communists and Kuomintang members, for the two parties were working together in the Northern Expedition. Huang Shao-ku was forced to flee Peking. With an introduction from the Communist leader Li Ta-chao (q.v.), he went to Sian to join the army of Feng Yü-hsiang (q.v.).

Feng Yü-hsiang had announced his support of the Northern Expedition, and on 1 May 1927 he assumed the post of commander in chief of the Second Group Army of the National Revolutionary Army. Huang Shao-ku was appointed to serve as a secretary under Ho Chih-kung, the secretary general in Feng's headquarters. The young man of 26 made such an impression on Feng that he soon was made head of the propaganda office for the three provinces of Shensi, Kansu, and Honan and head of the peasants training institute for those provinces. When Ho Chih-kung resigned as secretary general, Feng bypassed many of his older subordinates and appointed Huang to succeed Ho.

After the Northern Expedition was brought to a successful conclusion in 1928, Feng Yü-hsiang became minister of war in the National Government. For a time, Huang Shao-ku lived in Shanghai and held no official posts. Feng soon joined the Kwangsi clique (*see* Pai Ch'ung-hsi; Li Tsung-jen; Huang Shao-hung) in opposition to Chiang Kai-shek. After Feng's departure from Nanking for the north in 1929, Huang Shao-ku served as his deputy in the Nanking-Shanghai area. In 1930 Yen Hsi-shan (q.v.) joined with Feng in what became known as the Yen-Feng coalition or the enlarged conference movement. The group also included the Kwangsi clique, Wang Ching-wei and his Reorganizationist clique, and the Western Hills group. Although hostilities between the rebels and the Nanking government troops broke out in May 1930, the so-called enlarged conference of the second central committees of the Kuomintang was not convened until early in July. Feng Yü-hsiang was represented by Huang Shao-ku throughout the important deliberations. The movement soon was suppressed, chiefly because Chang Hsueh-liang (q.v.) gave his support to the National Government.

The collapse of the Yen-Feng coalition sent Huang Shao-ku into political retirement once again. By early 1932 he had decided that he wished to go abroad for further education. Ch'en Kung-po, the minister of industry, offered Huang an appointment as investigator of industrial conditions abroad so that he could take a trip overseas, but Huang declined the appointment. Instead, he accepted the offer of Ku Meng-yü, the minister of railways, of a scholarship from that ministry. In the summer of 1934 Huang left China for England, where he attended lectures at the School of Economics and Political Science of the University of London.

When the Sino-Japanese war broke out in the summer of 1937, Huang Shao-ku returned to China from England. Chang Chih-chung (q.v.), then governor of Hunan, appointed Huang administrative commissioner of the eighth special district of Hunan and magistrate of Nanhsien. It happened that there was a poor harvest that season, and the superstitious gentry blamed it on Huang, saying that "Shao-ku," meaning "deficiency in grain," was a bad omen and had brought about the bad fortune. Huang immediately resigned.

Huang Shao-ku went to Chungking in the summer of 1938 and met Yü Yu-jen (q.v.), head of the Control Yuan, who had thought highly of Huang when he first went to serve Feng Yü-hsiang at Sian in 1927. Yü appointed him to the Control Yuan. In 1939 Huang also became councillor of the secretariat of the Supreme National Defense Council.

In October 1940 Chang Chih-chung succeeded Ch'en Ch'eng (q.v.) as chief of the political department of the Military Council.

At Chang's invitation, Huang resigned from the Control Yuan and the Supreme National Defense Council to assume the post of chairman of the planning committee of the political department. In 1941 Huang became chief of the third office of the political department, in charge of cultural and propaganda activities in the army. The importance of this appointment may be gauged from the fact that his predecessor as head of the third office had been Kuo Mo-jo (q.v.). In 1943 Huang Shao-ku was made publisher of *Sao-tang pao* [mopping-up journal], the newspaper of the Nationalist army. He held this post until early 1948 and was continually embroiled in ideological and political debates with the Chinese Communist paper *Hsin-hua jih-pao*. After the war ended in 1945, the paper, renamed *Ho-p'ing jih-pao* [peace daily], moved its headquarters from Chungking to Nanking. It soon became a huge newspaper chain, with editions printed in Nanking, Shanghai, Hankow, Chungking, Lanchow, and Canton.

In 1947, with the adoption of a new constitution and the holding of the first popular elections for national offices, Huang Shao-ku became a member of the Legislative Yuan as a representative from Hunan. In 1948 he was appointed minister of propaganda of the Kuomintang headquarters. He had been elected a full member of the Central Supervisory Committee of the party in 1945.

After Chiang Kai-shek retired from the presidency in January 1949 and Li Tsung-jen became acting President, Ho Ying-ch'in (q.v.) was appointed president of the Executive Yuan, and Huang Shao-ku was made secretary general of the yuan. The collapse of the peace talks with the Chinese Communists led to the launching of the general offensive against Nanking by the Communists. On 22 April, Huang accompanied Li Tsung-jen and Ho Ying-ch'in to Hangchow for a conference with Chiang Kai-shek. Their return to Nanking from Hangchow was the signal for the abandonment of Nanking by the Nationalists. On the morning of 23 April, Li, Ho, and Huang emplaned for Canton, the new seat of the National Government. Ho Ying-ch'in resigned as president of the Executive Yuan on 30 May; he was succeeded by Yen Hsi-shan. Huang was made a minister without portfolio in the new cabinet.

In August 1949 Chiang Kai-shek established in Taipei the office of the tsung-ts'ai [leader] of the Kuomintang and appointed Huang chief secretary. Earlier, in July 1949, Huang had been a member of Chiang Kai-shek's entourage during the Generalissimo's visit with President Quirino of the Philippines at Baguio. Huang was also in Chiang's party when he visited with President Syngman Rhee of South Korea at Chinhai in August. Chiang Kai-shek returned to office in March 1950 as President in Taiwan, and Ch'en Ch'eng was appointed president of the Executive Yuan. Huang Shao-ku became minister without portfolio and secretary general of the Executive Yuan. In June 1954, when O. K. Yui (Yü Hung-chün, q.v.) assumed the presidency of the Executive Yuan, Huang was made its vice president. Yui resigned in July 1958, and Ch'en Ch'eng was reappointed head of the Executive Yuan. In this cabinet, Huang Shao-ku served as foreign minister. He also served as the National Government's special envoy to the inauguration of President Arduro Frondize of Argentina, the coronation of Pope John XXIII, and the inauguration of President Adolfo Lopez Mateos of Mexico.

In Taiwan, Huang continued to be active in the Kuomintang. In 1952 and 1957 he was elected to the Central Executive Committee and to its standing committee. He also served as chairman of the propaganda work guidance committee of central party headquarters.

Huang Shao-ku served as foreign minister until July 1960, when he was appointed ambassador to Spain. In June 1962 he was succeeded by Chou Shu-kai.

Huang Yen-p'ei   黃 炎 培
T. Jen-chih   任 之

Huang Yen-p'ei (6 September 1878–21 December 1965), known as an early advocate of vocational education in China, founded the China Vocational Education Society and such industrial schools as the China Vocational Institute. In the 1940's he became active in anti-Kuomintang groups which advocated constitutional government in China. He helped found (1945) and served as chairman of the China Democratic National Construction Association. After 1949, he held office in the Central People's Government, serving as minister of light industries until 1954.

Born at Ch'uansha, a district near Shanghai, Huang Yen-p'ei was orphaned at an early age and was brought up by relatives. He received a traditional education, and by 1902 he had obtained the prestigious chü-jen degree. He then entered Nanyang College in Shanghai and supported himself by teaching at the P'utung Middle School, where one of his students was Fan Wen-lan (q.v.), who later became a leading Communist historian.

In 1903 Huang returned to Ch'uansha, where he founded a primary school and helped form a study club to arouse interest in mass education. The activities of the group soon involved Huang in a crisis of the first magnitude. On the denunciation of a relative, he was arrested by the Manchu authorities for violating ordinances prohibiting the spread of revolutionary ideas. Huang was sentenced to death. He avoided that penalty only through the intervention of a missionary, William Burke. After being released, Huang immediately set out for Japan, then the refuge of many Chinese who had come into conflict with the Manchu government.

In Japan, Huang concentrated on the study of education and developed an interest in the field of vocational education. He took part in many of the political activities which enlivened Chinese student life in Japan at that time and became an advocate of constitutional government. After returning to China, he served as a district school inspector in Kiangsu and then as a member of the staff of the Kiangsu provincial assembly. He also became director of the Kiangsu branch of the Hsien-yu-hui [friends of the constitution party]. This party, which was tolerated by the Manchu government, advocated a mild program of reform through constitutional monarchy which was far removed from the revolutionary doctrines of the proscribed T'ung-meng-hui.

After the Wuchang revolt of October 1911, Kiangsu declared its independence of Manchu rule. Soon afterward, Huang was appointed commissioner of education for Kiangsu, a post which he held for three years. Huang effected the complete reorganization of the Kiangsu school system along modern lines. He personally supervised the preparation of new school laws and regulations as well as of new curricula for all levels. His report on educational administration in the province from October 1911 through July 1913 summarized his reforms and

probably constituted the first post-Manchu report on education in China. It was published in 1914.

In 1914 Huang left his Kiangsu post to become a correspondent for the Shanghai *Shun-pao* with the special assignment of reporting on the state of education in China. His articles, published serially as *Huang Yen-p'ei k'ao-ch'a chiao-yü jih-chi* [diary of a tour of education inspection], appeared in 1914–15 and recorded his impressions of school administration in six provinces—Kiangsu, Anhwei, Kiangsi, Chekiang, Shantung, and Chihli (Hopei). The reports played an important part in the formulation of national education policy and enhanced Huang's reputation as an expert in education. As a result, he was appointed secretary of a Chinese industrial mission to the United States, in which capacity he visited Japan and the United States in 1915.

Following the death of Yuan Shih-k'ai in 1916, Huang won new attention by writing an article which castigated Yuan as a traitor. Also in 1916 he became a member of the Kiangsu provincial assembly and vice chairman of the Kiangsu provincial education association. By 1917, however, his interest in provincial politics had waned. He resigned from his posts and departed for Japan to make a thorough study of vocational education, which he had come to believe was the primary educational need of China. In Tokyo, Huang conferred with Tejima Seiichi, then president of the Tokyo Higher Technological School and a leader in Japanese vocational education. After several months of study and inspection of facilities in Japan, Huang returned to China. In 1917 he also completed a critical survey of China's foreign trade situation, with special reference to the status and administration of its customs service, which was published as *Chung-kuo shang-yeh shih-pai shih* [a history of the ruin of Chinese commerce]. In 1918 Huang founded the China Vocational Education Society, with himself as chairman, and established the China Vocational Institute.

Because Huang wished to devote himself to furthering vocational education, he refused appointment as commissioner of education for Kiangsu province and also declined to serve as educational adviser to the governor, Li Shun. In 1921 and again in 1922 Huang succeeded in having his appointment rescinded as minister of education in the cabinets of Liang Shih-i and W. W. Yen. In 1923 he received an honorary doctorate from St. John's University in Shanghai and consented to become a member of the Educational Sinking Fund Commission. He also took charge of the planning section of the *Shun-pao* and served as co-editor of its fiftieth-anniversary supplement, *Tsui-chin chih wu-shih-nien* [the past 50 years]. Such eminent men as Shih Liang-ts'ai, Sun Yat-sen, Liang Ch'i-ch'ao, Ts'ai Yuan-p'ei, Hu Shih, and Huang contributed reminiscences to the supplement.

During the late 1920's and the early 1930's Huang continued to develop the China Vocational Education Society and the China Vocational Institute. In 1930 he published the *Chung-kuo chiao-yü shih-yao* [brief history of Chinese education]. Soon afterwards, he was drawn into political activity again. Tsou T'ao-fen (q.v.), the editor of the China Vocational Education Society's monthly journal and later of the magazine *Sheng-huo chou-k'an* [life weekly], reportedly influenced Huang's views, and Huang became prominent in anti-Kuomintang front organizations in educational circles. In the early 1930's Huang was active in the Society for the Improvement of Chinese Education, of which T'ao Hsing-chih (q.v.) was executive secretary. Both T'ao and Tsou were active in the so-called people's front, and Huang, by association as well as interest, was drawn into this group.

In 1937 Huang consented to become a member of the Defense Advisory Council. In July 1938, after the first year of the Sino-Japanese war, Huang became a member of the standing committee of the People's Political Council. In February 1939 he was appointed commissioner in charge of unifying guerrilla activities in the Hunan-Hupeh area. He also was made a member of the Supreme National Defense Council.

In 1940 Huang was dispatched to Manila to supervise the sale of Chinese war bonds there. After returning to Chungking in 1941, he participated in the formation of the League of Chinese Democratic Political Groups. The Vocational Education Society was accepted as a member group, and Huang became a vice chairman of the federation. In 1943 he was made chairman of the national sales committee for Chinese war bonds. During these years at Chungking, Huang continued to take an active

interest in the practical details of vocational education, and he established schools in Chungking, Kunming, and Kweilin, including the China Industrial and Commercial Technological School.

In 1944 the League of Chinese Democratic Political Groups was reorganized as the China Democratic League, and it began to accept individual citizens as members. As a result of the reorganization, Huang became chairman of its committee for industrial and commercial movements. This appointment marked the first time that Huang had assumed leadership of important industrial and commercial interests. He also accepted membership in the economic reconstruction committee of the People's Political Council. Also in 1944 Huang founded the *Hsien-cheng yüeh-k'an* [constitutional government monthly] at Chungking with the dual purpose of promoting constitutional democratic rule in China after the war and of staving off civil war between the National Government and the Chinese Communists. He published the *Chung-kuo fu-hsing shih-chiang* [the rebirth of China: ten lectures], in which he outlined his vision of the democratic and prosperous future possible for China under a popularly elected constitutional government. Perhaps because of these views, Huang was one of the representatives of the People's Political Council sent to Yenan in July 1945 to solicit Communist participation in the Political Consultative Conference. His *Yen-an kuei-lai* [to Yenan and back] tells of this trip.

After the war ended, tension between the National Government and the Communists increased, and Huang became active in movements seeking to promote a peaceful solution to China's political dilemma. In August 1945 he rallied his followers from the committee for industrial and commercial movements of the China Democratic League and, together with friends and associates representing various intellectual groups, organized the China Democratic National Construction Association, with himself as chairman. The political program of the association stressed protection of civil liberties, nationalization of big businesses, cooperative ownership of small businesses, tax reform, improvement of agriculture, and implementation of welfare measures. In 1946 the association moved its headquarters to Shanghai, where it began publication of the *Chan-wang chou-k'an* [expectations weekly], a journal considered by some Western observers to be virtually a Communist propaganda organ. The association and the Chinese Communist party agreed on many issues, and the *Chan-wang chou-k'an* was vociferous in demanding the withdrawal of American troops from China. In January 1946 Huang participated in the Political Consultative Conference as a delegate from the China Vocational Education Society. After the suppression of the China Democratic League in 1947, Huang lived quietly in Shanghai until February 1949, when he left for north China. He arrived at Peiping, which had come under Communist control, in March. Three months later, he was named to membership on the standing committee of the Chinese People's Political Consultative Conference preparatory committee and the All-China Conference of Educational Workers preparatory committee.

Huang attended the meetings of the Chinese People's Political Consultative Conference in September 1949 as a representative of the China Democratic National Construction Association. He was elected to the National Committee of the conference. After the Central People's Government was formally established, Huang was appointed to the Government Council, the Government Administration Council, and the financial and economic committee. He served as minister of light industries from 1949 until 1954, when the Government Administration Council was reorganized as the State Council. He then was replaced by Chia T'o-fu. Huang also assisted in the founding of the Sino-Soviet Friendship Association and became a vice chairman of that organization.

Under the new regime the China Vocational Education Society continued to flourish. Huang's concept of nation-wide vocational training received official encouragement. In 1951, on the occasion of the thirty-fourth anniversary of the society, Huang called upon its members and the alumni of the China Vocational Institute to work for the development of vocational and technological education in secondary schools. In October 1953 Huang, as the representative of the China Democratic National Construction Association, delivered a speech to the congress of the All-China Federation of Industrial and Commercial Circles. As minister of light industries, he spoke on behalf of the government program for develop-

ment of light industries and the need for state capitalism in order to accomplish the ends desired. In 1954 Huang became a vice chairman of the All-China Conference of Education Workers and a member of the board of the Association for the Reform of the Chinese Written Script. He also attended the First National People's Congress as a deputy from Kiangsu and became vice chairman of its Standing Committee. In 1955 he was appointed to the executive committee of the People's Parliamentary Group for Joining the Inter-Parliamentary Union. He attended the Second National People's Congress in 1958 as a delegate from Kiangsu, again serving on the Standing Committee. By that time, the 80-year-old Huang had become a respected elder statesman, but one to whom little real power had been entrusted since 1954. He died at Peking on 21 December 1965.

Huang married twice. He and his first wife are known to have had two sons and two daughters. The two daughters attended Tsinghua University, and one of them studied in the United States. Huang's son Huang Fang-kang studied at Harvard, became a professor at Wuhan University, and died in Szechwan during the Sino-Japanese war. His brother, Huang Ching-wu, was a banker in Shanghai who became associated with the China Democratic League and who was killed by agents of the National Government during the evacuation of Shanghai in 1949. Huang Yen-p'ei married Yao Wei-chün in 1942. Two daughters were born of this union.

Hung Shen   洪 深
    T. Po-chün   伯 駿
    H. Ch'ien-tsai   淺 哉

Hung Shen (1893–29 August 1955), playwright, director, and drama critic. He used Western techniques in his stage productions and played an important part in the development of sound films in China. After 1949 he was prominent in cultural administration at Peking, and he served as vice chairman of the Chinese Stage Artists.

A native of Wuchin, Kiangsu, Hung Shen was born into a gentry family. His father was a supporter of Yuan Shih-k'ai and a minor figure in the Ch'ou-an hui, which supported Yuan's monarchical aims in 1915. After graduation from Tsinghua College, Hung went to the United States in 1916 and studied ceramics at Ohio State University until 1919. He then went to Harvard, where he received an M.A. degree in 1922.

After returning to China, Hung taught dramatic arts and Western literature in Shanghai at Ta-hsia, Chinan, and Futan universities. In the autumn of 1923, on the recommendation of Ou-yang Yü-ch'ien (q.v.), he was invited to join the Shanghai hsi-chü hsieh-she [Shanghai dramatic society], which had been founded in the winter of 1922. He soon became its principal director. The society presented Ou-yang Yü-ch'ien's *P'o-fu* [the screw] and Hu Shih's *Chung-shen ta-shih* [a major event in one's life]. It departed from traditional stage practice by using both men and women in its productions. Hung Shen also directed the Futan University Dramatic Club and acted the title role in *Chao-yen-wang* [Chao, the king of Hades], which he wrote in the winter of 1922. The central character was a soldier, a victim of the conflict between Chinese warlords. Hung Shen's next successes were productions in 1924 of his translations of Oscar Wilde's *Lady Windermere's Fan* and J. M. Barrie's *Dear Brutus*. Hung soon became interested in T'ien Han (q.v.) and his Nan-kuo-she, which he joined in 1928. T'ien Han's *Death of a Famous Actor*, in which Hung Shen played the leading role, was acclaimed by critics and audiences.

During this period, Hung Shen's political sympathies gradually moved toward the left. His plays *Wu-k'uei-ch'iao* [Wu-k'uei bridge] and *Hsiang-tao-mi*, published in 1933, portrayed the conflict between landlord and peasant in Chinese society and revealed Hung Shen's sympathy for the peasants. In 1930 Hung Shen was the central figure in an incident which took place at the Grand Theatre in the International Settlement in Shanghai. During the showing of a Harold Lloyd film which portrayed the Chinese as sinister figures, Hung stood up and made a violent protest, an act which required considerable courage.

In 1930 Hung Shen went to work for the celebrated Hsing-p'ien kung-ssu (Star Motion Picture Company) and produced one of the first Chinese sound films. This was *Ko-nü hung-mu-tan* [singing peony], starring Hu Tieh (q.v.), which

was shown in Shanghai and Peking in 1931. In 1932 the company sent Hung Shen to Hollywood to study technique and methods. After his return, restraining censorship on anti-Japanese films was abolished, and Chinese films imbued with vigor and national consciousness began to be produced. Hung produced *Chieh-hou t'ao-hua* [peach blossoms after the storm], an anti-Japanese film which enjoyed great success.

Hung Shen was one of the leading members of the Tso-i hsi-chü-chia lien-meng [left-wing dramatists league], which sprang out of the League of Left-Wing Writers. His response to the slogan "National Defense Drama" was the publication of a volume of plays entitled *Tsou-ssu* [smuggling], which contained *Hsien-yü chu-i* [salt fish doctrine], *To-nien ti hsi-fu* [many years a daughter-in-law], and the title piece.

After the outbreak of the Sino-Japanese war in 1937, Hung Shen directed touring dramatic troupes which performed patriotic plays in the interior. When the National Government established the third department of the ministry of political training in 1939, Hung Shen was appointed director of its dramatic branch. He taught at Sun Yat-sen University, the College of Dramatic Art in Kiangsu, the Social Education Institute at Pishan, and the refugee campus of Futan University at Peip'ei in Szechwan. When the war ended, he returned to Shanghai with Futan University and became chairman of the motion picture department of the Shanghai Experimental School of Dramatic Arts. He left Shanghai to teach at Amoy University, and in 1948 he went to Hong Kong.

Hung Shen went to Peking in 1949. After the Central People's Government was established, he played a prominent part in official cultural administration, serving as director of the ministry of culture's liaison department for cultural relations with foreign countries and as one of three vice presidents of the Chinese People's Association for Cultural Relations with Foreign Countries. He was active in the national theater movement and served as vice chairman of the Chinese Stage Artists. He died at Peking on 29 August 1955.

Hung Shen was a careful craftsman with a sound sense of construction; he was a methodical writer rather than one who wrote in the heat of inspiration. His American training had a deep influence on his later work. He had a talent for handling large casts in his productions, and he successfully experimented on the stage with the use of dialects, notably that of Szechwan. Hung also published a number of technical books on film and drama, as well as critical essays. At one time, he edited the drama and motion picture weekly published by the *Ta Kung Pao* in Shanghai.

Hung Shen married a daughter of T'ao Lan-ch'üan, a former governor of the Bank of China, but the union ended in divorce.

Jao Shu-shih   饒漱石

Jao Shu-shih (1901–), Communist official who served as political commissar of the New Fourth Army after October 1942. With the establishment of the Central People's Government in 1949, he received a number of important posts in east China. In 1953 he became a member of the State Planning Committee and director of the Chinese Communist party's central organization department. In 1954–55 he and Kao Kang (q.v.) were accused of forming an "anti-party alliance," and Jao was stripped of his posts.

Linchuan hsien, Kiangsi, was the birthplace of Jao Shu-shih. Little is known about his childhood or his family background except that his father was a scholar who taught at the Nanchang First Provincial Middle School. According to one source, he went to France in 1919 to participate in the work-study movement (*see* Li Shih-tseng). He was graduated from the Nanchang First Provincial Middle School about 1923.

Jao Shu-shih enrolled at Shanghai University, where he came under the influence of such radicals as Ch'ü Ch'iu-pai, Teng Chung-hsia, Shih Ts'un-t'ung, and Yün Tai-ying. In 1925 he joined the Chinese Communist party. He was active in the May Thirtieth Movement and worked as a labor organizer in the Shanghai area. In the spring of 1927 he worked under Chao Shih-yen, Ch'en Yun, and Chou En-lai (q.v.) in organizing the workers' uprising that facilitated the entry of the National Revolutionary Army into Shanghai.

There is little clear information about Jao's activities during the next decade. He reportedly served as head of the Communist Youth League in Manchuria in 1929–30, and he apparently lived in Moscow for a time. He may have worked for the *Chiu-kuo shih-pao* [national salvation news], which was published in the Soviet Union from 1931 to 1935 under the editorship of Wu Yü-chang (q.v.). In any event, when the *Chiu-kuo shih-pao* began publication in Paris in 1935, it listed Jao Shu-shih as a contributor. Other sources indicate that Jao visited the United States in the 1930's and worked on the staff of a Chinese-language newspaper in New York.

In 1936 Jao was assigned to work under Liu Shao-ch'i (q.v.) in the Communist political mobilization programs in north China. After the Sino-Japanese war broke out in the summer of 1937, he worked at the Communist base in Yenan. In the winter of 1939 he was made deputy to Liu Shao-ch'i, who then headed the party's central China bureau. He also served as head of the bureau's propaganda department. When the New Fourth Army was organized at Nanchang in January 1938, Jao was assigned to serve under Yeh T'ing and Hsiang Ying (qq.v.) and was given responsibility for political training.

In the so-called New Fourth Army Incident of January 1941 Hsiang Ying was killed by the Nationalists; Yeh T'ing and Jao Shu-shih were captured. Because the Nationalists failed to recognize Jao, he was able to escape and make his way to northern Kiangsu. He then became deputy commissar of the New Fourth Army, once again serving under Liu Shao-ch'i. In October 1942 he succeeded Liu as political commissar of the New Fourth Army, secretary of the central China bureau, and head of the party's central China school. The New Fourth Army spent most of the next two years in areas that were behind the Japanese lines, and it performed well. In recognition of his wartime service, Jao Shu-shih was elected to the Central Committee of the Chinese Communist party at the Seventh National Congress in 1945.

After the Japanese surrendered, the Nationalists and the Communists resumed their struggle for power. As a result of American mediation efforts, a truce agreement was signed by Chou En-lai and Chang Ch'ün (q.v.) in January 1946. An executive headquarters for the implementation of the agreement was established at Peiping, and the Communists appointed Yeh Chien-ying (q.v.) their representative to the headquarters. Jao was assigned to Yeh's staff as political adviser, and he traveled regularly between Peiping and the Communist headquarters at Yenan. Control of Manchuria soon became a prime issue between the Nationalists and the Communists, and in June 1946 an advance section of the executive headquarters was established at Changchun, with Jao as the Chinese Communist representative. When the truce agreement expired on 30 June, the civil war resumed, and Jao returned to Yenan with Yeh Chien-ying. He then went to northern Kiangsu to resume the post of political commissar of the New Fourth Army, now called the East China People's Liberation Army. He was one of the first Communist leaders to enter Shanghai after its capture in May 1949.

With the establishment of the Central People's Government, Jao became a member of the Government Council and the Military Council. He also served in east China as political commissar of the military district, chairman of the military and administrative committee, first secretary of the party's regional bureau, secretary of the party's Shanghai municipal committee, and a member of the standing committee of the Shanghai General Labor Union.

In October 1952 Jao Shu-shih and Liu Shao-ch'i went to Moscow for the Soviet Communist party's Nineteenth Congress. At the end of the year, Jao resigned from most of his posts in east China and went to Peking, where he became a member of the State Planning Committee, headed by Kao Kang (q.v.), and of the committee assigned to draft a new constitution. In the spring of 1953 he was appointed director of the party's central organization department.

Jao's promising political career came to a sudden halt in 1954 when he and Kao Kang mysteriously disappeared from public view. There was no further word of him until 4 April 1955, when Peking issued a report on what it termed the Kao Kang–Jao Shu-shih anti-party alliance. Kao Kang committed suicide. Jao refused to confess to alleged anti-party crimes. Most of the charges against him were based on the testimony of one of his former subordinates in east China, Hsiang Ming. A national conference of the Chinese Communist party had passed the following resolution on 31 March: "It was fully established that in the ten years between 1943 and 1953 Jao on many occasions resorted to shameless deceit in the party to seize

power. During his tenure of office in east China, he did his utmost to adopt a rightist policy of surrender to the capitalists, landlords, and rich peasants in the cities and countryside. At the same time he did everything possible to protect counterrevolutionaries in defiance of the Central Committee's policy of suppressing them. After his transfer to the Central Committee in 1953, he thought that Kao Kang was on the point of success in his activities to seize power in the Central Committee. Therefore, he formed an anti-party alliance with Kao Kang and used his office as director of the organization department of the Central Committee to start a struggle aimed at opposing leading members of the Central Committee and actively carried out activities to split the party. From the fourth plenary session of the Seventh Central Committee [held in February 1954] to the present, Jao has never shown any signs of repentance and now persists in an attitude of attacking the party." Jao Shu-shih was stripped of his many posts. Nothing further is known of him.

Jao's wife, Lu Ts'ui, was educated in France. In September 1952 she became secretary of the China branch of the International Federations of Democratic Women. Her last recorded public appearance was made in 1954, when she attended sessions of the Chinese People's Political Consultative Conference and the Sino-Soviet Friendship Association.

Jeme, Tien Yow: *see* CHAN T'IEN-YU.

Jen Cho-hsuan   任 卓 宣
Alt. Yeh Ch'ing   葉 青

see esp Winston Hsieh JAS Vol 31 No 3 the p 620-21

Jen Cho-hsuan (4 April 1896–), Chinese Communist youth leader who severed relations with the Chinese Communist party in 1928 to launch a new career as a publisher and writer of philosophical and polemical works. After 1937 he worked to further understanding of and adherence to Sun Yat-sen's Three People's Principles. After 1950, he taught at the Political Cadres College in Taiwan, directed the Pamir Bookstore, and published the magazine *Cheng-chih p'ing-lun* [political review].

A native of Nanch'ung, Szechwan, Jen Cho-hsuan was the eldest of five children in a poor peasant family. After studying the Chinese classics at a village school, he attended the Nanch'ung District Middle School. At that time, the principal of the school was Chang Lan (q.v.). After graduation, Jen taught at a primary school for about six months. Then, on the recommendation of Chang Lan, he was admitted to the French language school at Peking to prepare for participation in the work-study program (*see* Li Shih-tseng) in France. He also audited some courses at Peking University. Jen organized the Work-Study Mutual Assistance Society, which operated a small restaurant to support its members. It was during his stay in Peking, Jen later reminisced, that he first was exposed to socialist ideas.

In 1920, a special grant from the Szechwan government enabled Jen Cho-hsuan to sail for France. He worked as an apprentice in an iron factory near Lyon and then as a technician in a factory near Paris. He came to know some French Communists and began to learn about Marxism. About 1921 he joined both the French Communist party and the Chinese Socialist Youth Corps. He became a member of the Kuomintang in 1922 because the Chinese Communist party, on Comintern instructions, had allied itself with the Kuomintang in Europe as well as in China. Jen also served as one of four permanent secretaries of the General Association of the Students on the Work-Study Program, an organization of Chinese students in France which had been established at the end of 1921 with the financial support of the Peking government. Jen proved to be an efficient organizer, and he became the most important officer of the association, partly because he was the only secretary who lived in Paris. Together with Chao Shih-yen and Ch'en Yen-nien, a son of Ch'en Tu-hsiu (q.v.), he engaged in an animated controversy with the anarchists and state socialists. Some of his polemical essays were published in *Shao-nien* [youth], a mimeographed periodical of the Chinese Socialist Youth Corps. Jen's political activities left little time for study. His formal education during his five years in France consisted of six-months study as a language student at a school in Paris.

In early 1923 Jen Cho-hsuan emerged as the Chinese Communist party's chief secretary in France. Chao Shih-yen and Ch'en Yen-nien had left France for Moscow at the end of 1922. When the Kuomintang established a European

headquarters at Paris in March 1924, Jen became head of the propaganda bureau. Chou En-lai (q.v.) took charge of the bureau of organization. Working closely with Chou and Li Fu-ch'un (q.v.), Jen skilfully conducted campaigns of persuasion and agitation among Chinese students and workers in France.

In the summer of 1925, after hearing of the May Thirtieth Incident, Jen attempted to organize Chinese nationals to stage "a demonstration against imperialism" as a response to the movement in China, but his plan was thwarted by the French police. On 21 June, he led a group of some 100 men into the Chinese legation in Paris; the group compelled Ch'en Lu (q.v.), the Chinese minister to France, to sign a document demanding that the French government renounce its privileges in China. As a result of this incident, more than 30 Chinese students were deported immediately and another 20, including Jen Cho-hsuan, were arrested by the French authorities. Jen was released four months later, but was ordered to leave France. He went to Russia, where he studied briefly at Sun Yat-sen University in Moscow.

Toward the end of 1926 Jen Cho-hsuan returned to China. He was assigned to work in the Kwangtung regional committee of the Chinese Communist party. In 1927, having become a member of the Hunan regional committee, he led underground party activities in Changsha. That winter, he was arrested by the provincial authorities, imprisoned in Changsha, and sentenced to death. He somehow emerged alive from the execution, and he continued to direct Communist activities while recuperating in Hsiang-ya Hospital in Changsha. These activities produced many small-scale uprisings in 1928 in Changsha, P'ingchiang, Liuyang, and Liling. The provincial authorities soon realized that Jen was alive. After being arrested again, he renounced his affiliation with the Chinese Communist party and worked briefly as a political instructor for the Kuomintang, training anti-Communist cadres in Hunan.

In the latter part of 1928 Jen Cho-hsuan went to Chengtu, where he established and edited a magazine called *K'o-hsueh ssu-hsiang* [scientific thought]. He found it difficult to stay in Szechwan because of his Communist background, and in the autumn of 1929 he went to Shanghai. There he reportedly shared a small room with T'ao Hsi-sheng and Chu Ch'i-hua (qq.v.), and the three were in close touch with Chou Fo-hai, Kuo Mo-jo, Liu Ya-tzu, Lu Hsün, and Mao Tun. Probably through the assistance of these friends, Jen established a bookstore, the Hsin-k'en shu-tien, the name of which was derived from the English word "think." The name of the bookstore as well as the books it published reflect Jen's strong interest in philosophy during that period. Among the philosophical treatises published by the bookstore were works by French materialists of the eighteenth century, including la Mattrie, d'Holback, Helvetius, Condillac, and Diderot; by the Greek philosophers Heraclitus, Democritus, and Epicurus; by the Marxists Plekhanov, Deborin, Bogdanov, and la Fargue; and by the scientific synthesists Planck, Jeans, Eddington, Huxley, Pearson, and Einstein.

Jen Cho-hsuan was also an active polemicist. In such journals as *Erh-shih shih-chi* [the twentieth century] and *Yen-chiu yü p'i-p'an* [research and criticism], which he founded and edited, he wrote voluminously under various pen names, notably Yeh Ch'ing. As a Marxist, he strongly criticized such anti-Marxist intellectuals as Hu Shih and Chang Tung-sun (qq.v.) in *Hu Shih p'i-p'an* [criticism of Hu Shih], *Tung-sun che-hsueh p'i-p'an* [criticisms of Chang Tung-sun's philosophy], and *Che-hsueh lun-chan* [philosophical controversy]. The first two works were published in 1934, and the third appeared in 1935. Jen also attacked such Chinese Communists as Ch'en Po-ta and Ai Ssu-ch'i, who, in turn, bitterly denounced him as an heretical Marxist. Because of the antagonisms aroused by the controversies, Jen was compelled to leave the Hsin-k'en shu-tien in 1936. The following year, he organized the Chen-li ch'u-pan she [truth publishing house] to carry on the debates. Jen's anti-Communist essays of 1936 and 1937 are contained in *Hsin che-hsueh lun-chan chi* [the controversies of the new philosophy] and *Wei fa-chan hsin che-hsueh erh-chan* [struggle for the development of the new philosophy]. Ironically, his books attacking the Communists were banned by the Kuomintang authorities.

Jen Cho-hsuan's own philosophical position at this time was set forth in two of his books: *Che-hsueh tao ho ch'u-ch'ü* [whither philosophy], published in 1934; and *Che-hsueh wen-t'i* [problems of philosophy], published in 1936. In the first book, taking up the thesis of two obscure

Russian philosophers, Minin and Enchumen, he announced the forthcoming extinction of philosophy. Jen asserted that philosophy had brought about the disappearance of religion by disclaiming it. Therefore, science, because it had broken with philosophy to become an independent field of study, would bring about the decline of philosophy. In the second book, Jen declared that because idealism and materialism each contain a part of the truth, they must be amalgamated. Marx himself effected a synthesis of Hegelian idealism with the materialism of Feuerbach. In consequence of this higher synthesis, the eternal conflict between idealism and materialism vanished. "Since the opposition is resolved, and opposition was the motivating force of its development, the history of philosophy stops. Is this the end of philosophy? Obviously. That is a natural and inevitable conclusion." The system that resulted from this definitive synthesis has changed its nature, and now there is only the "science of thought," concluded Jen.

The outbreak of the Sino-Japanese war in 1937 caused a dramatic change in Jen Cho-hsuan's thinking and career. According to his own account, his political outlook prior to the war had been that of an internationalist-socialist, but in facing the vital question of national survival, he realized that what China needed most was nationalism. Consequently, he began to study the Three People's Principles, and he arrived at the conclusion that Sun Yat-sen's doctrine was the key to solving China's problems.

In September 1937 Jen Cho-hsuan left Shanghai for Wanhsien, Szechwan, where he became a senior instructor of the special training class of the Central Military Academy. In 1938 he spent three months in Sian lecturing to the Shensi wartime administrative personnel training class. Together with Wu Man-chün and others, he founded a magazine called *K'ang-chan hsiang-tao* [guide to the war of resistance], which stressed adherence to the Three People's Principles. In 1939, through the introduction of P'an Kung-chan and Yeh Ch'u-ts'ang (qq.v.), Jen rejoined the Kuomintang, from which he had been estranged since the mid-1920's. He also founded *Shih-tai ssu-ch'ao* [thought currents], a magazine which was devoted exclusively to the study of Kuomintang ideology. In 1940, at the invitation of Hsiung Shih-hui (q.v.), then acting governor of Kiangsi province, he went to Kiangsi, where he worked with Chiang Ching-kuo (q.v.) to promote the study of the Three People's Principles by soldiers and students. He also lectured at Chung-cheng University. In the spring of 1942 he left Kiangsi to teach at Ch'ao-yang College in Chungking. Shortly afterwards, he was appointed head of the research section of the organization department of the Kuomintang.

At the first congress of the San Min Chu I Youth Corps in March 1943, Jen was elected an executive secretary of the organization. He also was appointed a professor at the Central Cadres School established under the auspices of the corps. In September 1944 he became a member of the organization's central standing committee. He was a delegate from the corps to the Sixth National Congress of the Kuomintang, held in April 1945, at which he was elected an alternate member of the party's Central Executive Committee. In 1945 he was awarded a medal by the National Government in recognition of his zealous efforts in promoting the study of the Three People's Principles during the war.

In late 1945, Jen Cho-hsuan and T'ang Ju-yen founded *Cheng-chih hsiang-tao* [political guide], a magazine published every ten days. The first issue of the journal appeared in Chungking on 11 December. Jen also took an active part in the reform movement led by Liang Han-ts'ao and helped edit the movement's *Ko-hsin chou-k'an* [reform weekly]. In July 1946 Jen went to Nanking, where he wrote articles for several newspapers and lectured at Cheng-chih University. He was a delegate to the National Assembly in November 1946.

In 1948 Jen unsuccessfully campaigned for a seat in the Legislative Yuan. He then founded the Pamir Bookstore, which published his *Wu-ch'üan hsien-fa yü min-chu cheng-chih* [the constitution of five powers and democratic polity] and *Kuo-fu i-chiao ta-kang* [basic principles of the inherited teachings of Sun Yat-sen]. When the Chinese Communists pushed southward in late 1948, Jen went to Shanghai, where he stayed until April 1949. The Kuomintang appointed him vice chairman of its propaganda department in July, and he soon became acting chairman. In this capacity, he delivered a series of anti-Communist speeches at major cities in southwestern China.

In 1950 Jen Cho-hsuan went to live in Taipei, Taiwan, and resigned from the propaganda department. He taught at the Political Cadres College, directed the Pamir Bookstore, and published the bi-monthly *Cheng-chih p'ing-lun* [political review]. He also continued to write voluminously and to lecture on the Three People's Principles. In 1957 and 1965 he received awards from the National Government in Taiwan for his efforts to promote adherence to the Three People's Principles.

Jen Cho-hsuan married Wei Su-ch'iu, a teacher of Chinese literature, in Shanghai in 1935.

Jen Hung-chün　　　任 鴻 雋
　T.　Shu-yung　　　叔 永
　West. H. C. Zen

Jen Hung-chün (20 December 1886–9 November 1961), known as H. C. Zen, educational administrator and a pioneer in the effort to promote modern scientific learning in China. He held such positions as president of the Science Society of China (1914–23, 1934–36, 1947–50), executive director of the China Foundation for the Promotion of Education and Culture (1929–34, 1942–48), head of National Szechwan University (1935–37), and secretary general of the Academia Sinica (1939–42). After 1949 he served the Central People's Government as a member of the Government Council's Commission on Culture and Education. He was married to Ch'en Heng-che (q.v.).

Although his native place was Wuhsing, Chekiang, H. C. Zen was born into a gentry family in Pahsien, Szechwan. He attended the first modern public school established in Pahsien, where he received training in classical studies as well as the rudiments of a Western education. In 1904 he entered the newly established Prefectural Middle School of Chungking, where he began to study world history and geography. He also read the translations of Yen Fu (q.v.), gleaning from them vivid, if fragmentary, conceptions of Western thought. His English teacher, Yang Ch'ang-pai, introduced him to contemporary Chinese revolutionary propaganda. Like many other schoolboys of his generation, Zen became an avid reader of the officially banned *Hsin-min ts'ung-pao*, published in Tokyo by Liang Ch'i-ch'ao (q.v.), and others, which advocated the establishment of a constitutional monarchy. While pursuing these diverse trends of thought, Zen did not neglect his preparations for the district examination in Pahsien, which he passed in 1904.

In 1906, after being graduated from middle school, H. C. Zen taught school in Chungking. Early in 1908 he left China for Japan to further his education at the Higher Technical College of Tokyo. He soon joined the T'ung-meng-hui and became the chairman of its Szechwan branch. In Japan, he often met with other members of the T'ung-meng-hui at the home of Miyazaki Torazō, a close associate of Sun Yat-sen.

When the revolution broke out in 1911, H. C. Zen returned to China to serve as secretary in the presidential office of the provisional government at Nanking. It was perhaps then that he met Sun Yat-sen, whom he admired greatly. Sun's manifesto to the nation, which was issued after his assumption of the presidency, was drafted by Zen. After the dissolution of the provisional government in 1912, Zen served in the cabinet of T'ang Shao-yi (q.v.) as recording secretary until T'ang resigned in June 1912 because of a disagreement with Yuan Shih-k'ai. Zen edited the anti-Yuan *Min-i Pao* in Tientsin and then left China to study in the United States.

H. C. Zen was a student at Cornell University from 1912 to 1916 and a graduate student at Columbia University in 1917, receiving his B.A. and M.A. in chemistry. He participated in Chinese student affairs, wrote for the *Chinese Students Quarterly*, and engaged in heated discussion with Hu Shih on the desirability of employing the Chinese vernacular language as a medium of literary expression. During this period, he courted Sophia H. Chen (Ch'en Heng-che, q.v.). They were married in Peking in 1920.

In 1914 Zen and other Chinese students at Cornell organized the Science Society of China. The stated aims of the society were the diffusion of scientific knowledge among the Chinese people, the encouragement of scientific research by the members, and the promotion of industrial progress of the nation. As the first step toward the realization of these goals, the society published in 1915 the first issue of its magazine, *K'o-hsueh* [science]. For several years the maga-

zine was printed in Shanghai but edited in the United States, first in Ithaca, then in Cambridge. It continued publication until 1950. When its leaders began to return home, the society was removed to China, where its main office was established in Nanking. It came to have branches in Shanghai, Peking, and Canton.

H. C. Zen served three terms as president of the Science Society of China (1914–23, 1934–36, 1947–50) and sat on the board of directors almost from its inception. The society published many scientific monographs and translations, supported the Biological Research Institute in Nanking and a science library in Shanghai, and held lectures and exhibits in various cities. Until the organization of the Academia Sinica in 1927, the Science Society was probably the most influential scientific body in China. For this reason, Zen and his associates in the society—such as V. K. Ting (Ting Wen-chiang), Chu K'o-chen, Yang Ch'uan, and Wong Wen-hao (qq.v.)—must be considered pioneers in the development of modern science in China. Zen was also an early member of the Chinese Engineering Society, which was founded in the United States.

In 1919, two years after his return to China from the United States, H. C. Zen was asked by the Szechwan authorities to draw up plans for the creation of an iron and steel works in the province. In connection with this project, he made a trip to the United States in 1919–20 to purchase machinery. In 1920 he taught science at Peking University. He served from 1920 to 1922 as chief of the technical education section in the ministry of education, from 1922 to 1923 as editor of the Commercial Press in Shanghai, and from 1923 to 1925 as vice chancellor of National Southeast University in Nanking. Many of the founders of the Science Society taught at Southeast University, and Zen's appointment further strengthened the relationship between the two institutions.

On 16 July 1925 the American government announced the remittance to China of the balance of the American Boxer Indemnity Fund. The money was to be used, at the discretion of the President of the United States, for educational and cultural activities in China. A board of trustees consisting of ten Chinese and five American members would decide which organizations were to receive grants. The China Foundation for the Promotion of Education and

Culture was organized to receive and administer the funds. H. C. Zen was among the first appointees to the foundation. As executive director from 1929 to 1935, he devoted much of his energy to the realization of the foundation's basic aim, the promotion of scientific research and education in China. In reply to the criticism that the foundation's funds were controlled by a small group of men instead of being administered by the national authorities, Zen stated in 1932 that the foundation had been established to prevent government officials from misappropriating the money for civil war purposes.

H. C. Zen also helped to propagate the scientific achievements of China abroad. He was a member of the Chinese delegation to the Third Pan-Pacific Science Congress, held in 1927 in Tokyo, where he obtained recognition of the Science Society as the official body representing Chinese scientists. In 1931 he wrote a chapter on science for the *Symposium on Chinese Culture*, edited by his wife.

Although Zen had been a member of the T'ung-meng-hui, he never joined its successor, the Kuomintang. He had shared the enthusiasm of many progressive Chinese for the Northern Expedition, which put the Kuomintang into power and which was regarded as a step toward the elimination of warlords and the modernization of the nation, but he was also a trenchant critic of the conduct of the Kuomintang government. He was a co-founder of the *Tu-li p'ing-lun* [independent critic], an influential journal of liberal opinion which flourished in the 1930's. In an article opposing the advocates of tang-hua chiao-yü ["partyization" of education], which meant strict party control of education and political indoctrination of the students, he declared that such a concept violated the very purpose of education, which is the development of the intellectual curiosity of individuals, and would prove dangerous to the party itself because it would deprive party doctrines of the opportunity to compete with other systems of thought in an open forum. Without such competition, the party would lose its intellectual vitality.

In 1935 H. C. Zen accepted an offer to head National Szechwan University at Chengtu. As a result of years of civil war and misrule by provincial warlords, Szechwan had become one of the more backward provinces in China. The

assignment was a challenge to Zen, who met it with characteristic candor and determination. His initial dislike of Chengtu was reinforced when slanderous attacks on his wife appeared in the local newspapers. Everyone should visit Chengtu at least once, he angrily remarked, and stay for at least a year in order to really understand to what great depth a culture can decline. He believed that there were at least two major obstacles in the path of academic progress in Szechwan: the belief that the university was just another government bureau and the psychological resistance to criticism of any sort. In spite of these obstacles, he was able to bring a number of highly qualified scholars to National Szechwan University and to strengthen its colleges of science and agriculture, especially the research facilities. The agricultural faculty contributed to the important improvements made in grain production in southwest China during the war years. After leaving the university in 1937, he assumed office as chairman of the Commission of Editing and Translation, which was an offshoot of the China Foundation.

The outbreak of the war compelled the National Government to search for means for widening its basis of political support. In 1937 H. C. Zen was summoned by Chiang Kai-shek to the Lushan conference. The following year, when the National Government established the People's Political Council, a consultative body composed of delegates from various walks of life and from the minor political parties, Zen was appointed to the council as an academic representative.

In 1939 Zen became secretary general of the Academia Sinica and director of its research institute of chemistry. He moved to Kunming, where the institute was located, to direct the unspectacular but vital task of keeping alive the spirit of scientific experiment at a time when the scientists had difficulty in keeping themselves alive in an economy beset by inflation. In 1942 he resigned from the Academia Sinica to resume office as executive director of the China Foundation for the Promotion of Education and Culture. At that time, the foundation was critically short of funds. In 1939 Boxer Indemnity Fund payments had been suspended, and the foundation, deprived of its regular income, had to depend upon bank loans to maintain its activities. In January 1942 an emergency committee was formed in Chungking, with Wong Wen-hao as chairman, Y. T. Tsur (Chou I-ch'un, q.v.) as honorary secretary, and Arthur N. Young and H. C. Zen as assistant treasurers. The executive committee was composed of Sun Fo, Chiang Monlin, and Arthur N. Young. Because of the efforts of these men, the foundation was able to continue its program of granting research professorships and fellowships, subsidizing scientific and educational institutions, and maintaining the Division of Soils of the National Geographical Survey of China. At the end of the war in 1945, the office of the foundation was removed to Shanghai.

In 1946–47 Zen was in the United States. After his return, he lived in Shanghai. He remained in the city after it fell to the Communist armies. On 21 September 1949 he participated in the Chinese People's Political Consultative Conference, held in Peking, as a specially invited delegate. After the establishment of the People's Republic of China, he devoted much of his time to the activities of the All-China Federation of Natural Science Societies and became a member of its standing committee. The Science Society ceased to exist, and its function as a national organization of scientists was assumed by the federation. From 1950 to 1954 Jen was a member of the Commission on Culture and Education of the Government Administration Council. After 1954, except for his membership in the Chinese People's Political Consultative Conference, he did not serve the government in any active capacity. However, he continued to work for the federation until his death on 9 November 1961.

H. C. Zen and Ch'en Heng-che had three children: a daughter, E-tu (Mrs. S. C. Sun); a son, E-an, who went to live in the United States; and another daughter, E-su (Mrs. Shu-ming Cheng), who remained in China. Zen had three brothers and three sisters. His eldest brother, Jen Hung-hsi, served as the magistrate of two counties. Another brother, Jen Hung-tse, was in business. The youngest brother, Jen Hung-nien, of whom Zen was particularly fond, served as editor of a revolutionary newspaper in Chengtu in 1912. He committed suicide in 1913 to protest the assassination of Sung Chiao-jen (q.v.).

H. C. Zen was a talented calligrapher and poet, though most of his poems, written in the classical style, have not been published. His hobbies included stamp-collecting and photog-

raphy. A connoisseur of Chinese art, he served from 1932 to 1937 as an adviser to the Palace Museum in Peiping.

Jen Pi-shih   任弼時

Jen Pi-shih (1904–27 October 1950), Chinese Communist political worker and close associate of Mao Tse-tung, rose to the top rank of the Chinese Communist party hierarchy in the early 1940's as a member of the Political Bureau and the Secretariat and head of the Central Committee's organization department.

Hsiangyin, Hunan, was the birthplace of Jen Pi-shih. Little is known about his family background or his childhood. After receiving his primary and secondary education in Changsha, he went to Shanghai. In 1920 Jen, then 16 years old, began to learn Russian and joined the Socialist Youth League, which was established in August under Comintern guidance to disseminate Marxist concepts in China. That winter, he and a few other students, among them Liu Shao-ch'i (q.v.), were sent to the Soviet Union under Comintern auspices to the Communist University for Toilers of the East. They arrived in Moscow in the spring of 1921. Liu Shao-ch'i returned to China in 1922, but Jen remained in the Soviet Union for two more years, improving his Russian and studying Marxism. In 1922 he became a member of the Chinese Communist party.

After returning to Shanghai in 1924, Jen Pi-shih was assigned to work in the Communist Youth League (formerly the Socialist Youth League). In 1925 he was made the director of its organization department and a member of its central committee. He became general secretary of the Communist Youth League in 1926 and a member of the Central Committee of the Chinese Communist party in 1927.

After the Kuomintang split with the Chinese Communist party in 1927, Jen Pi-shih was assigned to work under cover in Nationalist-controlled areas of the Yangtze valley. In the summer of 1928 he was reelected (*in absentia*) to the Central Committee of the Chinese Communist party at the Sixth National Congress, held in Moscow. Jen was arrested in Nanling hsien, Anhwei, in October 1928 and was imprisoned at Anking, but he was released in

March 1929. After returning to Shanghai, he was arrested again in September 1929 and held for two months. At the end of the year, the central apparatus of the Chinese Communist party, then operating secretly in Shanghai, sent him to Wuhan as a member of the Yangtze bureau of the Central Committee. During 1930 he also served as secretary of the party's Wuhan municipal committee and Hupeh provincial committee.

Jen Pi-shih was elected to the Political Bureau of the Chinese Communist party in January 1931 and was sent in March to the central soviet area in Kiangsi, where he headed the bureau's organization department for two years. In May 1933 he was assigned to the Hunan-Kiangsi border area as secretary of the party committee, political commissar of the military district, and head of the political committee of the Sixth Red Army. Nationalist military forces surrounded the base area, but the Sixth Red Army, commanded by Hsiao K'o (q.v.) managed to break through the encirclement in July 1934. The Communist troops moved southwest and joined forces in eastern Kweichow with the Second Army Group of Ho Lung and Kuan Hsiang-ying (qq.v.). In October the combined force was designated the Second Front Army, with Ho Lung as commander and Jen Pi-shih as political commissar. Ho and Jen soon established a new Communist base in the Hunan-Hupeh-Szechwan-Kweichow border area.

The Second Front Army remained in its base area until November 1935, when Nationalist military pressure forced it to make a retreat. After an arduous march through Kweichow and Yunnan and into Sikang, it joined the Fourth Front Army of Chang Kuo-t'ao, Chu Teh, and Hsü Hsiang-ch'ien (qq.v.) at Kantzu in June 1936. Jen Pi-shih reportedly was intrumental in the decision to rejoin Mao Tse-tung at the Communist base in northern Shensi. After arriving in the Yenan area in November, Jen Pi-shih became political commissar of the front-line general headquarters, serving under P'eng Te-huai (q.v.).

After the Sian Incident of December 1936 (*see* Chiang Kai-shek) and the outbreak of the Sino-Japanese war in July 1937, some Communist forces were reorganized as the Eighth Route Army, with Chu Teh as commander in chief, P'eng Te-huai as deputy commander, and Jen Pi-shih as director of the general political department. The army went to Shansi, where Jen worked to rouse the peasants of north China against the Japanese and to spread Communist influence. He helped formulate Communist political policy in the north and traveled to Sinkiang, where Sheng Shih-ts'ai (q.v.) was permitting Communist organizations to work openly in the united front effort against Japan.

After 1940 Jen Pi-shih remained at Yenan, the seat of Mao Tse-tung's soviet government. He became a member of the Chinese Communist party's Secretariat and head of the Central Committee's organization department. Thus, by his fortieth birthday, he had risen to the top rank of the party hierarchy. In April 1945 he gave the opening address at the party's Seventh National Congress. He was reelected to the Central Committee (of which he was the fourth-ranking member), the Political Bureau, and the Secretariat.

In March 1947, when Nationalist forces drove the Chinese Communists from Yenan, Mao Tse-tung decided to divide the party leaders into two groups for safety. Jen remained in Shensi with Mao and Chou En-lai; an alternate working committee under Liu Shao-ch'i and Chu Teh moved to the Shansi-Chahar-Hopei area. Jen was given the additional assignment of formulating policy for Communist activities in the rural areas of China. In January 1948 he produced a notable report entitled "Some Problems of Agrarian Reform." During this period he also acted as guardian for Liu Shao-ch'i's son. The two groups of party leaders were reunited in May 1948 at Shih-chia-chuang in southern Hopei.

Although their control of the mainland was not yet complete, the Chinese Communist leaders had begun preparations for the establishment of a nation-wide training organization for young people. In April 1949 the first congress of the New Democratic Youth League (later renamed the Young Communist League) was convened. The importance placed on this organization by the Communist leadership was indicated by the fact that Jen Pi-shih made a speech at its first meeting which was a major statement of national political policy. His speech, which reflected decisions made at the March 1949 meeting of the Central Committee, marked an important shift in the "center of gravity of the revolution" from the rural areas to the cities and outlined a long-term program for national industrialization. At the congress, Jen was elected honorary chairman of the new organization.

Jen Pi-shih's April 1949 speech proved to be his last significant public appearance. Because of his poor health, he was unable to participate in the ceremonies held to inaugurate the Central People's Government of the People's Republic of China in October 1949. He went to Moscow in January 1950 and received medical treatment for six months. He returned to China and gradually resumed work during the summer, but on 27 October he suffered a cerebral hemorrhage and died, at the age of only 46. Mao Tse-tung and virtually all of the top party leaders were present at his funeral, and his coffin was attended to by Liu Shao-ch'i, Chou En-lai, Chu Teh, and P'eng Chen. The official accounts of his career published at Peking identified him as one of the "closest comrades-in-arms of Mao Tse-tung." A booklet, *Hsueh-hsi Jen Pi-shih t'ung-chih* [study comrade Jen Pi-shih], was published at Canton in 1950.

Jen was survived by his wife, Ch'en Tsung-ying, and by three daughters and one son.

Ju, Péon: *see* Hsü Pei-hung.

Kahn, Ida: *see* K'ang Ch'eng

Kan Nai-kuang   甘 乃 光
　T. Tzu-ming   自 明

Kan Nai-kuang (1897-September 1956), protégé of Liao Chung-k'ai and early adherent of Wang Ching-wei, served the National Government as deputy secretary general of the Supreme National Defense Council (1942–44), vice minister of foreign affairs (1945–47), secretary general of the Executive Yuan (1947), and ambassador to Australia (1948–49).

Little is known of Kan Nai-kuang's background or childhood except that he was a native of Ts'ench'i, Kwangsi. He attended Lingnan University at Canton, where he studied political science and economics and became active in student politics. After graduation in

1920, he remained at Lingnan as a member of the faculty.

Canton was then the principal operating base of the Kuomintang, and Kan joined the party about the time of its reorganization in 1924. Kan's energy and ability attracted the attention of Liao Chung-k'ai (q.v.), then a leading figure in the top command of the Kuomintang. He employed Kan as a secretary and apparently did much to advance his career. In 1925 Kan Nai-kuang was assigned to the Whampoa Military Academy as English secretary. He also managed two influential newspapers at Canton, the *Kuo-min hsin-wen* [citizens news] and the *Min-kuo jih-pao* [republican daily]. By the time Liao Chung-k'ai was assassinated in August 1925, Kan Nai-kuang had become identified with Wang Ching-wei and Ch'en Kung-po (q.v.) in the Kuomintang. At the Second National Congress of the Kuomintang in January 1926, which was dominated by Wang Ching-wei's supporters, Kan was elected to membership on the Central Executive Committee. He also became one of the three secretaries of the party secretariat and director of the youth department of the Kuomintang. In May 1926, after Wang Ching-wei left Canton, Kan was relieved of the youth department post and was appointed to succeed the Communist Lin Po-ch'ü (q.v.) as director of the peasants department.

During the Nanking-Wuhan schism in the early months of 1927, Kan worked in Nanking with the Kuomintang faction led by Chiang Kai-shek. However, he came to the support of Wang Ching-wei when Wang began to purge the Communists at Wuhan in August. After serving as a representative of the Wuhan faction at the unsuccessful party reunification meetings that were held at Shanghai in September, he accompanied Wang to Canton in late October. Chang Fa-k'uei (q.v.) and his troops returned from Wuhan to Kwangtung in November and ousted Li Chi-shen (q.v.). Soon afterwards, Kan was appointed mayor of Canton. It was during his administration that the Chinese Communists staged the December 1927 uprising which became known as the Canton Commune (*see* Chang T'ai-lei). After the return of Li Chi-shen to power in Canton, the central Kuomintang authorities at Nanking relieved Kan of his post in December 1927. Nanking charged him with "tolerating and protecting" Communist rioters at Canton and censured him for alleged misappropriation of municipal funds. Kan Nai-kuang spent 1928–29 as a political exile. He went to the United States, where he studied political science at the University of Chicago. Later, on the way back to China, he visited England and Western Europe to observe public administration procedures.

The Third National Congress of the Kuomintang, held in March 1929, again took strong action against left-wing elements in the party. Kan Nai-kuang and Ch'en Kung-po were "permanently" dismissed from the Kuomintang, and Wang Ching-wei was sent a written warning for alleged collusion with the Kwangsi clique of Li Tsung-jen and Pai Ch'ung-hsi in "anti-Nanking" activities. In later years, Kan, although remaining on friendly terms with Wang Ching-wei and Ch'en Kung-po, gradually extricated himself from his political connections with them and began to devote himself increasingly to the technical aspects of the government administration in China.

Japanese aggression in Manchuria, beginning in 1931, forced some realignment of political factions in the Kuomintang. Kan Nai-kuang was readmitted to the party and was elected to the Central Executive Committee by the Fourth National Congress of the Kuomintang. He held administrative posts in the ministry of interior beginning in 1932, and he served as vice minister, under Huang Shao-hung (q.v.), in 1934–35. He also became a standing member of the committee on administrative efficiency of the Executive Yuan at Nanking.

After the Sino-Japanese war began, Kan moved westward to Chungking with the National Government. From 1938 to 1942 he was deputy secretary general of the central headquarters of the Kuomintang, serving under Chu Chia-hua, Yeh Ch'u-ts'ang, and Wu T'ieh-ch'eng (qq.v.), successively. From 1942 to 1945 he was deputy secretary general of the Supreme National Defense Council, serving under Wang Ch'ung-hui (q.v.). These positions were essentially administrative, and Kan had no voice in major political decisions at Chungking.

After the Japanese surrender, Kan Nai-kuang became political vice minister in the ministry of foreign affairs. He assumed office in the autumn of 1945 and retained that post until mid-1947. When Chang Ch'ün (q.v.) became premier in

1947, Kan was appointed secretary general of the Executive Yuan. The following year, Kan was appointed ambassador to Australia. He held that post from 1948 until 1950, when he resigned. He continued to reside in Australia until his death, after a brief illness, at Sydney in September 1956.

Kan Nai-kuang wrote a number of works on problems of public administration and questions of administrative efficiency and personnel policy. Perhaps his best known work in this field is *Chung-kuo hsing-cheng hsin-lun* [new treatise on Chinese administration], published in 1947. Earlier works include *Sun Wen chu-i chih li-lun yü shih-chi* [the theory and practice of Sun Yat-senism], which appeared in 1926, and *Hsien-Ch'in ching-chi ssu-hsiang shih* [history of economic thought in the former Ch'in dynasty], published in 1930.

K'ang Ch'eng   康 成
West. Ida Kahn

K'ang Ch'eng (1873–1930), known as Ida Kahn, prominent physician who introduced modern medical practices and facilities to Nanchang, where she worked from 1903 until her death in 1930. A devout Methodist, she was a strong advocate of religious education and social welfare programs.

The birth of Ida Kahn, the sixth girl in a Kiukiang, Kiangsi, family of very limited means, was a disappointment to her parents, for they had hoped for a son. Accordingly, when Gertrude Howe of the Methodist Mission at Kiukiang offered to relieve the K'ang family of some financial burdens by adopting the infant, they accepted her offer.

A few years later, Ida Kahn began her education at the Rulison-Fish Memorial School at Kiukiang, which had been founded by Miss Howe. Mary Stone (Shih Mei-yü, q.v.), who became her close friend and associate, also attended this school. At the age of 9, Ida Kahn accompanied Miss Howe on a trip to the United States, where she attended a home-mission school for Chinese children in San Francisco. After a brief stay in Japan and another change of school, they returned to China in 1884 and spent two years in Chungking, where Miss Howe worked to develop a new Methodist mission center. When they returned to Kiukiang in 1886, Ida Kahn resumed her formal education.

In 1892 Miss Howe took Ida Kahn and Mary Stone to the United States. Both girls had decided to study medicine, and they had been accepted as students by the University of Michigan Medical School. After graduation in the spring of 1896, they spent two months observing medical techniques and hospital procedures in Chicago; they returned to China in the autumn to serve as medical missionaries under the sponsorship of the Women's Foreign Missionary Society of the Methodist Episcopal Church.

Soon after their arrival in Kiukiang, Dr. Kahn and Dr. Stone won the confidence of the local residents and persuaded them to accept modern medical treatment. In their first ten months of practice, they treated more than two thousand patients at their one-room dispensary. In 1898 Dr. Isaac Newton Danforth, a Chicago physician who had befriended Dr. Stone, provided funds for the construction of a hospital. At the time of the Boxer Uprising of 1900, the two doctors were forced to abandon the newly completed building and seek refuge in Japan. They returned to Kiukiang in 1901 and formally opened the Elizabeth Skelton Danforth Hospital on 7 December.

In 1903 Ida Kahn left Kiukiang and went to Nanchang to establish a modern medical program. By the end of 1905, a new dispensary building had been completed and a site for a new hospital had been acquired. Medical facilities and services increased steadily. More than 8,000 patients had received treatment by the end of 1907. Despite these claims on her attention and energies, Dr. Kahn found time to develop evangelical and social reform programs and to plead for improved education in China; in 1905 she addressed the fifth triennial meeting of the Educational Association of China at Shanghai on the subject of medical education.

In 1908 Ida Kahn went to the United States on leave and enrolled at Northwestern University to study literature. She completed three years' work in two years. In the spring of 1910 she went to Berlin as a delegate to a world conference of the Young Women's Christian Association. After the conference, she went to London for six months to study tropical diseases. While in London, she completed her course

work at Northwestern by correspondence and received a B.A. degree in January 1911. The following month, she returned to Nanchang.

By the time of the Wuchang revolt in October 1911, a new 40-bed hospital had been completed and put into service at Nanchang. The hospital remained open throughout the revolution and gave treatment to all who required it. The hospital was constantly in debt because many patients were treated free of charge. Dr. Kahn accepted a lucrative position in Tientsin so that she could pay the hospital's creditors. Within three years, she had discharged the debt and had returned to Nanchang. When she resumed work, the Kiangsi provincial government made two financial grants to the hospital as an indication of its esteem for her and its appreciation of her contributions to the life of the province. Later, it gave periodic subsidies to ensure the hospital's continuing operation.

In 1926 the Nanchang hospital gave extensive aid to casualties of the Northern Expedition only to be repaid with valueless notes. Dr. Kahn, who was in poor health, sold her personal belongings to help the hospital meet its financial obligations. She then went to Shanghai, where she died a short time later.

Throughout her career, Ida Kahn was a strong advocate of religious education, social welfare programs, and modern medical training in China. In pursuit of these ends, she wrote articles for such publications as the *Atlantic Monthly*, *Asia*, and the *China Press*. All of her activities reflected her deep personal concern for the physical, social, and spiritual well-being of all Chinese people.

K'ang Sheng 康生
Orig. Chao Jung 趙容 (～榮)

K'ang Sheng (1899–), Chinese Communist leader in security and intelligence work in Shanghai and at Yenan.

Chuch'eng, a small city in eastern Shantung, was the birthplace of K'ang Sheng. His father was a moderately wealthy landholder. Little is known about K'ang's childhood or primary education. About 1920 he went to Shanghai to attend the Shanghai University Middle School. He then enrolled at Shanghai University, where he studied under Ch'ü Chiu-pai (q.v.). In the early 1920's, he joined the Communist Youth League and the Chinese Communist party. From 1925 to 1928 he worked under Hsiang Ying (q.v.), then the secretary of the party's Shanghai district committee, as a labor organizer. He soon became the director of the district committee's organization department, and he also undertook intelligence work for the political security bureau of the party.

After the split between the Kuomintang and the Communists in August 1927, the Kuomintang intensified police surveillance in Shanghai, forcing Communists and other radicals to carry on their activities secretly or to leave the area. Little information concerning K'ang Sheng's activities in 1928–30 is available. It has been reported that he was elected to the Central Committee of the Chinese Communist party at the Sixth National Congress, held at Moscow in 1928. However, because no official list of the 1928 Central Committee has been published, K'ang's election cannot be documented. It is certain that K'ang had reached the Soviet Union by 1933. He and Ch'en Shao-yü (q.v.) wrote a tract called *Revolutionary China Today* in 1934, and he was a delegate to the Seventh Congress of the Comintern in 1935, at which he became a candidate member of the Presidium and of the Executive Committee. In 1937 he returned to China with Ch'en Shao-yü and Ch'en Yun.

K'ang Sheng went to Yenan, where he worked in the organization department of the Chinese Communist party under Ch'en Yün and took charge of many of the party's security operations. He later served as a member of the Central Committee's organization department and as director of the central social department. He also became vice president of the Central Party School in Yenan. At the party's Seventh National Congress, held at Yenan in April 1945, K'ang was elected to the Central Committee and the Political Bureau.

When the Central People's Government was established in 1949, K'ang was appointed to the Government Council and to the executive board of the Sino-Soviet Friendship Association. He held these posts until 1954. During this period, he also served as chairman of the Shantung Provincial People's Government and as secretary of the Shantung sub-bureau of the Central Committee. In 1950 he became a member of the East China Military and Administrative Committee; he served on this committee and on its successor, the East China Administrative Committee, until 1954. After the adoption of a new constitution in 1954 and the reorganization of the Central People's Government, he became less prominent in government affairs.

In December 1954 K'ang Sheng was elected to the National Committee of the Chinese People's Political Consultative Conference and to its standing committee. He led a delegation to the Third Congress of the United Socialist party in East Germany in 1956. At the Eighth National Congress of the Chinese Communist party, held in September 1956, he was reelected to the Central Committee, but was made an alternate member of the Political Bureau, of which he had been a full member.

In February 1956 K'ang was appointed a vice chairman of the Central Working Committee for the Popularization of Common Spoken Language, headed by Ch'en Yi (1901–; q.v.). After June 1958 he was a professor at Peking People's University. He represented Shantung at the Second and Third National People's congresses, held in 1958 and 1964. In late January 1959 K'ang accompanied Chou En-lai to Moscow for the Twenty-first Congress of the Communist party of the Soviet Union. He made another trip to Moscow that September to sign the Sino-Soviet Economic Cooperation Agreement. In February 1960 he attended the Political Consultative Conference of the Warsaw Treaty Nations as an observer. That autumn, he served on a Chinese delegation to the October Revolution celebrations in Moscow. He also served on the Chinese delegation to the Third Congress of the Rumanian Workers party. In 1961 he went to North Korea in September to attend the Fourth Congress of the Korean Workers' party. He went to Moscow in April to attend the Twenty-second Congress of the Communist party of the Soviet Union. In November 1964 he accompanied Chou En-lai to Moscow for the October Revolution celebrations.

After the so-called Cultural Revolution began in 1966, K'ang's political status appeared to rise. He reportedly was restored to full membership on the Political Bureau in August 1966.

K'ang married Ts'ao I-yu, and they had two children.

K'ang Yu-wei 康有爲
Orig. K'ang Tsu-i 康祖詒
T. Kuang-hsia 廣厦
H. Ch'ang-su 長素

K'ang Yu-wei (19 March 1858–31 March 1927), leader of the reform movement that culminated in the ill-fated Hundred Days Reform of 1898 and prominent scholar of the chin-wen [new text] school of the Confucian classics.

The elder son of an expectant district magistrate, K'ang Yu-wei was born in a village in Nanhai (Namhoi), a district southwest of Canton. The K'ang family was prosperous and had gained local prominence in the mid-nineteenth century, largely as a result of its activities on behalf of the Ch'ing dynasty during the Taiping Rebellion. One of K'ang's great-uncles, K'ang Kuo-ch'i (1815–1892), by virtue of his military exploits under Tso Tsung-t'ang (ECCP, II, 762–67), had risen to the position of provincial treasurer and acting governor of Kwangsi. K'ang Yu-wei's grandfather, a chü-jen of 1846, had served in several educational posts in Kwangtung and taken part in the compilation of the 1872 revision of the *Nan-hai hsien-chih*. His father died shortly before K'ang's tenth birthday.

K'ang Yu-wei received thorough training in the Chinese classics from his grandfather and his uncles. After failing the examinations for the chü-jen degree in 1876, he became a student of Chu Tz'u-ch'i (ECCP, I, 91), a friend of the family and one of the leading Cantonese scholars of the time. Initially, K'ang was an enthusiastic student. Chu stressed the importance of the moral doctrines of Sung Neo-Confucianism and the scholarly techniques of the school of Han Learning. After the death of his grandfather, however, the young K'ang underwent a severe emotional crisis during which he experienced a revulsion against book learning. He withdrew to the Hsi-ch'iao hills and spent several months in meditation and in the study of Taoism and Buddhism.

It apparently was during this time that K'ang conceived the ambition of becoming a sage who would devote his life to delivering the world from its sufferings. In preparation for this role he began to study government, history, and geography as well as Buddhism. He came across certain works that aroused his interest in the West. In 1879 he visited Hong Kong, and in 1882 he traveled to the foreign concessions in Shanghai, where he purchased translations published by the Kiangnan Arsenal and the missionary press in China and began to study Western civilization. Having been stimulated by his studies and by what seems to have been a mystic experience late in 1884, K'ang began to write down some of his ideas about a world utopia.

After the Sino-French hostilities of 1884–85, K'ang Yu-wei grew increasingly disturbed by China's weakness in dealing with the Western powers. While in Peking in 1888, he was shocked by the complacency and corruption of the ruling bureaucracy. He promptly sent a memorial to the Kuang-hsü emperor in which he pointed to the dangers of foreign invasion, criticized the incompetence and irresponsibility of high officials, and urged the empress dowager and the emperor to undertake reforms in the imperial administration. Although his petition did not reach the emperor, his outspoken criticisms earned him the enmity of such highly-placed conservatives as Li Wen-t'ien (ECCP, I, 494–95) and Hsü T'ung (ECCP, I, 407). However, K'ang won the sympathy of several metropolitan officials, including the Manchu Sheng-yü (ECCP, II, 648–50) and Shen Tseng-chih (1850–1922), who assisted him in his reform efforts.

Because the political climate in Peking did not favor reform, K'ang, on the advice of his friends, gave up his political activities. He then turned to epigraphy. In 1889 he completed the *Kuang-i-chou shuang chi*, a short work in which he developed the theories of Pao Shih-ch'en (ECCP, II, 610-11) on the evolution of calligraphy. The study of ancient inscriptions led K'ang to the problem of the authenticity of the Confucian classics. Early in 1890, after leaving Peking, he met the Szechwanese scholar Liao P'ing (q.v.). Liao was a scholar of the Kung-yang school of classical interpretation, which held that the officially recognized ku-wen [old text] versions of the classics were less authentic than the chin-wen [new text] versions current during the Former Han dynasty. A few years before his meeting with K'ang, he had found evidence that many of the ku-wen versions were actually the work of the Han dynasty scholar Liu Hsin and that the chin-wen versions of the classics revealed Confucius as a man who had favored a periodic change of institutions. In 1891, less than two years after his encounter with Liao P'ing, K'ang published the *Hsin-hsueh wei-ching k'ao* [the forged classics of the Wang Mang period], in which he claimed as his own the discovery that the ku-wen versions of the classics were all falsifications of Liu Hsin. This attack upon the authenticity of the accepted classical tradition provoked a storm of protest from scholars throughout China, and in 1894 the book was banned by imperial decree. The ban failed to discourage K'ang. In 1897 he published the *K'ung-tzu kai-chih k'ao* [a study of Confucius as a reformer], which developed the idea that Confucius had been an advocate of institutional change.

In compiling these two works K'ang was assisted by his pupils at a school called the Wan-mu ts'ao-t'ang, which he had founded in Canton in 1891 at the urging of such young admirers as Liang Ch'i-ch'ao (q.v.). The curriculum K'ang drew up for his school owed much to the course of studies he had followed under Chu Tz'u-ch'i. However, he also included such modern subjects as mathematics, music, military drill, and the study of Western learning. Needless to say, he imbued his pupils with his own theories about the Confucian classics and his ideas about institutional reform. Many of these students became his most active supporters in later reform campaigns.

In 1893, while teaching in Canton, K'ang succeeded in becoming a chü-jen. In 1895, after passing the examinations for the chin-shih degree at Peking, he was appointed secretary second class in the Board of Works. At that time, as a result of the disastrous war with Japan, the Ch'ing court was compelled to negotiate the Treaty of Shimonoseki, by which Taiwan was ceded to Japan. When K'ang learned of the humiliating treaty terms, he sent a memorial to the emperor urging the rejection of the treaty, the removal of the capital inland to Shensi province, the continuation of the war, and the adoption of extensive reforms. However, this petition, known as the "Kung-ch'e shang-shu" [candidates' memorial] because it bore the signatures of several hundred examination candidates then in the capital, failed to prevent the treaty from being ratified by the imperial court. A few months later, K'ang sent two memorials

urging the inauguration of a systematic program of administrative, educational, economic, and military reform. One of these petitions reached the emperor, who praised it highly, but K'ang's proposals were not adopted. K'ang then began a campaign to mobilize support among the educated elite of China for his reform ideas. In the summer of 1895 he and Liang Ch'i-ch'ao founded a reform newspaper, the *Chung-wai chi-wen*, in Peking, and he and a few friends organized a reform association, the Ch'iang-hsueh hui [society for the study of national strengthening], which soon won the support of several prominent officials. However, K'ang's activities also aroused the hostility of powerful conservatives. He prudently heeded the advice of his friends and left for Canton.

By the time that the Ch'iang-hsueh hui and the reform newspaper were suppressed early in 1896, K'ang had succeeded in arousing widespread enthusiasm for his ideas. Reform associations sprang up in several provinces during 1896 and 1897. The Kiaochow incident of 1897, the seizure of Port Arthur and Dairen by Russia, and the demands of other foreign powers for territorial concessions led many Chinese to believe that partition of China was imminent. Taking advantage of the atmosphere of crisis, K'ang submitted a succession of memorials to the emperor which called for a radical overhauling of the administrative system. In April 1898 he organized the Pao kuo-hui [society for protecting the nation]. At its first meeting he gave an impassioned speech about the mortal dangers which confronted the empire and pleaded for prompt reform of the outmoded institutions and practices which had made China a helpless victim of foreign aggression.

Although repeated attacks by K'ang's conservative opponents soon frightened away many of his reform sympathizers and deprived his movement of widespread support among scholar-officials, a few prominent officials, including Weng T'ung-ho (ECCP, II, 860–61), the imperial tutor, recommended K'ang to the emperor, who was keenly interested in reform. On 16 June 1898, five days after an edict had formally inaugurated the Hundred Days Reform, K'ang was summoned to an imperial audience. Although this apparently was his only meeting with the emperor, K'ang became one of the chief advisers to the throne. In the next three months he wrote detailed recommendations for reform. Influenced by these and other writings, the emperor issued a series of decrees ordering the abolition of the eight-part essay in the official examinations, the establishment of a university in Peking and Western-style schools in the provinces, the institution of a budget system, the modernization of the army and navy, the complete revision of administrative regulations, the abolition of sinecure offices, and many other innovations.

K'ang relied upon the emperor's enthusiasm to implement his reform program and tended to underestimate the opposition of many officials to the reform measures. Provincial officials either ignored the decrees or made little effort to carry them out; Peking officials whose interests were adversely affected by the program beseeched the aging empress dowager, Tz'u-hsi (ECCP, I, 295–300), to intercede for them. Although she had retired as regent in 1889, she had never relinquished her political ambitions. The reform controversy gave her an opportunity to reassert her authority. K'ang and his associates sought to enlist the military support of Yuan Shih-k'ai, but because all other military forces near the capital were firmly under the control of the empress dowager's supporters, Yuan was neither willing nor able to help the reformers. On 21 September, Tz'u-hsi placed the emperor in confinement, rescinded all of his reform decrees, and imprisoned several of the reformers. One week later, six of the reform leaders were executed, including T'an Ssu-t'ung (ECCP, II, 702–4) and K'ang's younger brother, K'ang Kuang-jen (1867–1898). K'ang Yu-wei had left Peking the day before the coup. The emperor, who had learned of Tz'u-hsi's plans, had dispatched him to Shanghai to take charge of the *Shih-wu pao*, the official organ of the reform movement. After narrowly escaping arrest in Shanghai, K'ang was taken by a British gunboat to Hong Kong.

K'ang Yu-wei claimed that before leaving Peking he had received a secret edict instructing him to devise means of rescuing the emperor from the empress dowager and her party. On the strength of this supposed edict, K'ang went first to Japan and then to Great Britain in an unsuccessful attempt to enlist the aid of these countries in securing the imprisoned emperor's release and restoration to power. K'ang then went to Canada and began to organize the overseas Chinese communities in support of a movement to rescue the Kuang-hsü emperor. In July 1899 he founded the Pao-huang hui [society to protect the emperor] in Victoria, British Columbia. Within a year, several branches of this society had been formed in Chinese communities in the United States, Latin America, Hawaii, Japan, and Southeast Asia. After returning to Hong Kong in 1899, he prompted his followers in the Pao-huang hui to deluge the imperial government with telegrams expressing opposition to the empress dowager's scheme to depose the Kuang-hsü emperor. During the confusion of the Boxer Uprising of 1900, K'ang plotted with other expatriate reform leaders to oust the empress dowager. However, the plot was discovered by governor general Chang Chih-tung. He arrested and executed T'ang Ts'ai-ch'ang, who had been chosen to lead the armed revolt, and several of his comrades in Wuhan.

K'ang Yu-wei withdrew from political activity and spent a year in semi-seclusion at Penang. He then went to India, where he remained for some time at Darjeeling. Between 1900 and 1903 he wrote commentaries, the *Chung-yung chu*, the *Ch'un-ch'iu pi-hsiao ta-i wei-yen k'ao*, the *Lun-yü chu*, the *Ta-hsueh chu*, and the *Meng-tzu wei*, in which he brought to completion the reinterpretation of the Confucian classics that he had begun more than a decade earlier. His most important writing of this period, however, was the *Ta-t'ung shu*, a work which embodied the final expression of the utopian ideas he had first formulated during the 1880's.

K'ang Yu-wei left India and went to Hong Kong in the spring of 1903. Because he believed that the Kuang-hsü emperor was no longer in personal danger and that sentiment in China had begun to favor reform, he decided to change the name of the overseas Chinese reform organization from Pao-huang hui to Hsien-cheng hui [society for constitutional government]. In political tracts such as his *Kuan-chih i* [on systems of government], published in 1903, and his *Wu-chih chiu-kuo lun* [national salvation through material upbuilding], published in 1905, he began to advocate the adoption in China of a constitutional monarchy similar to the British system.

Ever since the founding of his monarchist

organization in 1899, K'ang had been a bitter
political enemy of Sun Yat-sen. K'ang's
efforts to advance the cause of constitutional
monarchy soon brought him into conflict with
the T'ung-meng-hui, the revolutionary party
organized in 1905 under Sun's leadership.
Initially, K'ang's organization was the stronger.
In the competition for overseas Chinese allegiance, however, it steadily lost ground to the
revolutionary party as the Manchu regime's
prestige declined.

The latter part of K'ang's long exile was spent
in almost continual wandering in Europe and
the United States, with occasional visits to
Penang and Hong Kong. These travels were
occasioned in part by the affairs of his monarchist
organization, but they also gave K'ang an
opportunity to study Western culture. His
impressions, set down in such works as his
Ou-chou shih-i kuo yu-chi [record of travels in
eleven European nations] of 1904, reveal that
his earlier admiration for the West had been
modified by growing awareness of the short-
comings of Western civilization and by renewed
appreciation of the traditional values of Confucian China.

When the 1911 revolution broke out, K'ang
was in Japan. He soon launched a campaign
against republicanism. In his *Chiu-wang lun*
[on salvation from disaster] and *Kung-ho
cheng-t'i lun* [on the republican system of govern-
ment], both written late in 1911, he argued
that only by adopting constitutional monarchy
could China avoid prolonged and disastrous
chaos. After the establishment of the republic,
K'ang remained a loyal partisan of the fallen
dynasty and a resolute advocate of Confucianism as the national doctrine of China. He
enthusiastically supported the founding of the
K'ung-chiao hui [Confucian association] and
wrote an opening statement for the new organization in the autumn of 1912. His views were so
unpopular that he deemed it prudent to remain
in Japan. Because he could not find a publisher
for his writings, he had some of his followers in
China start a monthly magazine, the *Pu-jen
tsa-chih*, eight issues of which appeared between
the spring and autumn of 1913. The new
magazine, devoted exclusively to the publication
of K'ang's writings, presented many of his
hitherto unpublished political tracts and serial-
ized parts of the *Ta-t'ung-shu* and some of his
earlier writings which had been banned and

destroyed by order of the empress dowager in
1898 and 1900.

Late in 1913 K'ang Yu-wei left Japan for
Hong Kong. In December, he returned to his
native village in Kwangtung to bury his mother
—the first time he had set foot in China in 15
years. In the summer of 1914 he took up
residence in Shanghai, where he lived quietly
until the end of 1915. At that time he joined
his former pupil Liang Ch'i-ch'ao in the movement to resist Yuan Shih-k'ai's monarchical
ambitions, not because he opposed monarchy
as such, but because he believed that Yuan, as
the betrayer of the Manchu dynasty, was unfit
to assume the imperial dignity. After Yuan's
death in 1916, K'ang grew increasingly dissatisfied with the conduct of the republican
government in Peking and once again took
action on behalf of the Manchu dynasty. In
the spring of 1917 he wrote several letters to
Chang Hsün (q.v.), the military governor of
Anhwei, urging him to use his military forces to
restore the former Hsuan-t'ung emperor, P'u-
yi (q.v.), to the throne. Chang, a diehard
royalist, also looked forward to the restoration
of the Manchus. In making plans to this end,
he readily accepted the support of K'ang and
other Manchu loyalists.

Several days after Chang Hsün's entry into
Peking with the vanguard of his troops, K'ang
left Shanghai for the capital, arriving on 27
June. He was escorted to Chang's quarters for
a secret conference, and three days later, on 1
July 1917, the reenthronement of the Hsuan-
t'ung emperor was announced. K'ang had
drafted several edicts designed to formalize the
restoration of the emperor and the imperial
administration, but they were ignored by the
new regime. His disenchantment with the
restoration became complete when he discovered that the autocratic Chang Hsün had
no use for his proposals for a constitutional
monarchy. On 17 July, following the termination of the short-lived restoration, the republican
government issued orders for the arrest of the
royalist leaders. By that time, however, K'ang
had taken asylum in the United States legation
in Peking. Five months later, he left Peking,
escorted by legation guards, and went to
Shanghai. In a final issue of his *Pu-jen tsa-chih*,
he published a number of his later political
writings, including a critique of the republican
government (*Kung-ho p'ing-i*) that he had

drafted in the United States legation. In March 1918 the Peking government granted a general amnesty to the participants in the restoration movement.

Despite the debacle of 1917 K'ang's political convictions remained unshaken. In the spring of 1923 he visited Wu P'ei-fu (q.v.) and other militarists in a vain attempt to enlist their support in reviving the Ch'ing dynasty. Meanwhile, he continued to condemn indiscriminate Westernization, to plead for the preservation of the "national heritage," and to urge the establishment of a Confucian "state religion" as a bulwark against moral and intellectual degeneration. However, after the patriotic May Fourth Movement in 1919 and the ensuing intellectual revolution, K'ang's voice all but ceased to be heard by his countrymen.

In his final years, K'ang turned to the study of cosmology, a subject which had interested him since the 1880's. In 1924 he established the T'ien-yu hsueh-yuan [academy for celestial peregrination] in Shanghai, where he lectured to a small group of students. His lectures, published after his death as *Chu-t'ien chiang* [lectures on the heavens], were an intriguing combination of scientific knowledge, philosophical speculation, and poetic fancy. In March 1927 he celebrated his seventieth sui in Shanghai. A few weeks later he died at Tsingtao. He was buried by his family on a nearby hill with the official regalia bestowed upon him by P'u-yi in 1917 in recognition for his services to the dynasty.

A collection of K'ang Yu-wei's memorials of 1898 appeared in 1911 as the *Wu-hsu tsou-kao*. A collection of his pre-1899 verse was published in 1911 as *Nan-hai hsien-sheng shih-chi*; the calligraphy was done by Liang Ch'i-ch'ao. Another collection bearing the same title but including verses written both before and after 1898 was published in four volumes in 1940 by the Commercial Press in Changsha.

Among K'ang's writings, three stand out as works of special importance. In the first of these, the *Hsin-hsueh wei-ching k'ao*, he claimed to have uncovered evidence that the ku-wen versions of the Confucian classics were all products of an elaborate program of falsification conducted by Liu Hsin in order to legitimize the claims of Wang Mang's short-lived Hsin dynasty as the successor to the Former Han. K'ang stated that in suppressing or perverting the chin-wen

versions of the classics, particularly the Kung-yang commentary on the *Ch'un-ch'iu*, Liu Hsin had successfully hoodwinked scholars for almost 2,000 years into believing that the spurious ku-wen classics were the repository of the teachings of Confucius.

In the *K'ung-tzu kai-chih k'ao* K'ang went on to assert that Confucius himself was the author of the genuine (i.e., chin-wen) classics, rather than merely the transmitter of the teachings of the ancient sage kings; but, in order to gain general acceptance of his teachings, Confucius had resorted to the device of ascribing his teachings to the mythical culture-heroes of antiquity. According to K'ang, Confucius's purpose in writing the classics was to devise institutional systems to meet the requirements of societies in all ages.

In picturing Confucius as a far-sighted reformer, K'ang laid the groundwork for a theory of progress based on the chin-wen concept of the Three Ages: as society advanced from the age of "disorder" through the age of "minor tranquility" to the age of "great peace," government advanced from autocratic government through constitutional monarchy to the "rule of the people." The final age of "great peace," which K'ang equated with the "grand unity" (ta-t'ung) described in the *Li-yün* chapter of the *Li-chi* [book of rites], served as the subject of his third major work, the *Ta-t'ung-shu*. Although some of the ideas in this treatise were conceived as early as the 1880's, the work was not completed until 1902. The first two of its ten sections appeared in the *Pu-jen tsa-chih* in 1913, but the entire work was not published until 1935, eight years after Kang's death. In the *Ta-t'ung shu* K'ang described at length his vision of the future world of the "grand unity." Human society would be organized into thousands of small, democratic communities, each equally represented in a world parliament. Within each community, property would be owned communally, and all inhabitants would share equally in the means of livelihood. Moreover, with the institution of sexual equality, freedom of mating, and the raising of children at public expense in nurseries and schools, the family system would no longer be necessary and would disappear. In this utopian world there would be full political, economic, and social equality, regardless of race, sex, or occupation.

In these theoretical works K'ang's chief purpose was to recast Confucianism into a system of doctrine which could meet the challenge of the new ideologies from the West. But so radical were his revisions of the accepted tradition that they served to undermine the very Confucian values he had set out to preserve. It was presumably in reference to the initial reaction of shock and outrage from even the more progressive of K'ang's contemporaries that Liang Ch'i-ch'ao compared the *Hsin-hsueh wei-chin k'ao* to a typhoon, the *K'ung-tzu kai-chih k'ao* to a volcano, and the *Ta-t'ung shu* to an earthquake. However, when Liang made this assessment in 1920, K'ang no longer exerted any significant intellectual influence, although some scholars, such as Ch'ien Hsuan-t'ung and Ku Chieh-kang (qq.v.), acknowledged him as their predecessor in their own critical re-examinations of China's traditions of ancient history. But during the latter part of his life K'ang was more often reviled or ridiculed as a hopeless reactionary by intellectual leaders. Paradoxically, with the advent of Communist supremacy in China, K'ang's ideas were re-evaluated and praised. Before 1915 Mao Tse-tung had been an admirer of the reform efforts of K'ang Yu-wei and Liang Ch'i-ch'ao. Mao later referred to K'ang as one of a group of early progressives who sought truth from the West and as the author of a book on world Communism.

Kao Kang   高 崗

Kao Kang (1902–1954?), Chinese Communist guerrilla leader who helped establish the northern Shensi base area. From 1949 to 1953 he was the senior Communist official in the Northeast. He disappeared in 1954, and he and Jao Shu-shih (q.v.) were charged in 1955 with having formed an "anti-party alliance."

The son of a landholder in Hengshan, Shensi, Kao Kang received his early education in his native district and then attended the Yülin Middle School. One of his schoolmates was Liu Chih-tan (q.v.) with whom he was to be associated for more than a decade. Kao came under the influence of liberal teachers at Yülin, and he soon joined the Socialist Youth League. In 1926 he enrolled at the Chungshan Military Academy, which had been established by Feng Yü-hsiang at Sanyuan, Shensi. Among his instructors at the academy were Liu Chih-tan and Teng Hsiao-p'ing. By the end of the year, Kao had joined the Chinese Communist party.

When the Nationalists broke with the Chinese Communists and began a campaign against them in 1927, Liu Chih-tan and other radical instructors were dismissed from the academy at Sanyuan, and the cadet corps of the academy was reorganized and was placed under close surveillance. In the spring of 1928 Liu Chih-tan and others led an insurrection in the Weinan-Huayin area which became known as the Wei-hua uprising. Kao was among the cadets who participated in the insurrection. After it was quelled by the Nationalists, Kao Kang, Liu Chih-tan, and other surviving cadres were assigned by the Chinese Communist authorities in Shensi to spread propaganda and to subvert Nationalist military units in Shensi and Kansu.

The famine conditions then prevailing in the northwestern provinces of China facilitated Kao Kang's efforts to organize peasant uprisings and to form a guerrilla force in Shensi. Although the uprisings he led at Hsi-hua-ch'ih and in other areas of central Shensi were unsuccessful, he won the support of many of the starving peasants. In the autumn of 1931 Kao and his followers joined forces with guerrilla units led by Liu Chih-tan and Hsieh Tzu-ch'ang. After this combined force and remnants of the Twenty-fourth Red Army united to form the so-called Anti-Imperialist Allied Army, Kao served as Liu's political commissar. At the end of 1932, when the army was designated the Twenty-sixth Red Army, Kao was replaced as political commissar by Tu Heng. Kao retained membership on the provincial military affairs committee of the Chinese Communist party, but he was given no new assignments. Accordingly, he went to Yuehhsien and organized a small guerrilla force.

After the Twenty-sixth Red Army, which had moved to the Weinan area, had been defeated and disbanded, Liu Chih-tan and some of his men made their way back to central Shensi and joined forces with Kao Kang. By the end of 1933 Kao and Liu had organized a new Twenty-sixth Red Army of more than 1,000 men. Using Lang-chia-chai as a base, they worked to extend their control of central Shensi to the Kansu border. After encountering formidable opposition from the warlords of Shensi and Kansu, however, they decided to move to northern Shensi, which was loosely controlled by the independent and unpopular warlord Ching Yueh-hsiu. In the autumn of 1934 the Twenty-sixth Red Army was divided into three columns and was sent into action in central, eastern, and northern Shensi with all units moving northward. By the spring of 1935 a Shensi-Kansu soviet regime had been established in northern Shensi, with headquarters at Wa-yao-pao. The National Government had sent Kao Kuei-tzu to northern Shensi to smash the Communist stronghold. However, the Twenty-sixth Red Army and the newly formed Twenty-seventh Red Army soon consolidated control of the area surrounding the base by defeating the Nationalist troops and by conducting a successful campaign against Ching Yueh-hsiu's army.

In the meantime, the Chinese Communist forces which had left the central Soviet district to begin the Long March in October 1934 had been working their way north. In the summer of 1935 the Twenty-fifth Red Army of Hsü Hai-tung (q.v.) arrived in Shensi from the Hupeh-Hunan-Anhwei (O-yu-wan) soviet area and joined with the Shensi forces to form the Fifteenth Army Group, with Hsü in over-all command. In August, after some members of the Central Committee of the Chinese Communist party had arrived at Wa-yao-pao, Kao Kang, Liu Chih-tan and a number of local cadres were arrested and imprisoned on charges of deviation from the party line. When Mao Tse-tung reached northern Shensi in October, he ordered their release. An official Communist version of this incident blamed the imprisonment of Kao and Liu on the "subjectivism" and "sectarianism" of some ambitious party leaders. Kao Kang was made political commissar of the Fifteenth Army Group. In the spring of 1936 he accompanied Liu Chih-tan on a campaign in Shansi. Their long association ended in April, when Liu was fatally wounded in battle.

Beginning in 1937 Kao Kang held important posts in Mao Tse-tung's government at Yenan. He became chairman of the people's council of the government in 1939. An indication of Kao's standing during the Yenan period is to be found in pre-1956 editions of *Mao Tse-tung hsuan-chi* (*Selected Works of Mao Tse-tung*): "I came to northern Shensi five or six years ago, yet I cannot compare with comrades like Kao Kang in my knowledge of conditions here or in relations with people of this region. No matter what progress I make in investigation and research, I shall always be somewhat inferior to our northern Shensi cadres." Kao Kang also held important posts in the Chinese Communist party during this period. He was made political commissar of the Shensi-Kansu-Ninghsia Border Region military district in the late 1930's and secretary of the party's northwest bureau a few years later. In November 1942 he presented a major address at a conference held at Yenan to discuss the Chinese Communist party's first rectification movement, which had been inaugurated in February by Mao Tse-tung. Kao's report, "Pien-ch'ü tang ti li-shih wen-t'i chien-t'ao" [examination and discussion of problems concerning party history in the border region], was a detailed analysis of past political disagreements between the central party authorities and the local Shensi Communists and a justification of the guerrilla strategy used by Kao and Liu Chih-tan. In the early 1940's Kao was elected to regular membership in the party's Central Committee.

After the Japanese surrender in 1945, Mao Tse-tung sent such Communist leaders as Kao Kang, Lin Piao, Ch'en Yun, and P'eng Chen to the Northeast, for he was well aware of its crucial importance to all who sought control of China. Kao served as commander of the Kirin-Heilungkiang military district, with responsibility for political mobilization in rural areas, organization of cavalry units, and work among non-Chinese minority groups. It is interesting to note that a Mongol cavalry unit joined the People's Liberation Army during the battles between the Chinese Communists and the Nationalists in the spring of 1947.

At the end of 1948 Lin Piao's forces left Manchuria, which had come under Communist control, and moved into north China. Kao Kang remained at Mukden as the senior party, government, and military official in the Northeast. By mid-1949 he had become secretary of the party's Northeast bureau, commander and political commissar of the Northeast military district, and chairman of the Northeast Administrative Council. In July 1949 he headed a delegation to Moscow which negotiated a trade agreement between the Chinese Communist regime in the Northeast and the Soviet Union. In August, he assumed the chairmanship of the newly created Northeast People's Government.

When the Central People's Government was established at Peking in October 1949, Kao Kang became one of its six vice chairmen and a member of the People's Revolutionary Military Council. Beginning in November 1951 he served as vice chairman of the Military Council. Although his posts at Peking were of high importance, he remained in Mukden from 1949 to 1953, for Manchuria was crucial to both the domestic and foreign affairs of the People's Republic of China. Because the region had achieved a relatively high level of political and economic development, it served as a testing area for political campaigns, industrial and agricultural innovations, and economic development programs. Its geographical location made it an important supply and staging area during the Korean conflict.

In the early 1950's Kao Kang was considered to be one of the ten most important men in the Chinese Communist party. In November 1952 he was appointed chairman of the State Planning Committee at Peking, which had been established to direct the first five-year plan for the economic and industrial development of the People's Republic of China. He was transferred to Peking early in 1953. Soon afterwards, Jao Shu-shih (q.v.) became a member of the State Planning Committee. A year later, however, both men mysteriously dropped from view. Kao made his last recorded public appearance in January 1954, at which time he was identified as a member of the Political Bureau of the Chinese Communist party.

In February 1954, at a plenary session of the Central Committee, Liu Shao-ch'i (q.v.) called for party unity and made scathing reference to those who "regarded the region or department under their leadership as their individual inheritance or independent kingdom." This reference was not given full explanation until 4 April 1955, when Peking issued a report on the so-called anti-party alliance of Kao Kang and Jao Shu-shih; it incorporated a resolution on the alleged alliance which had been passed at a national conference of the Chinese Communist party. The two men and a number of their subordinates had been expelled from the party for anti-party activities. According to the report, Kao Kang had "engaged in conspiratorial activities" with the aim of seizing the leadership of the party and the government. He had "created and spread many rumors" designed to slander the Central Committee and to enhance his personal position. His "anti-party faction" in Manchuria had created discord and dissension and had attempted to make the Northeast "the independent kingdom of Kao Kang." After his transfer to Peking in 1953, he had tried to instigate party members "to support his conspiracy" against the Central Committee and had argued that as the representative of the "party of the revolutionary bases and the army" he should become vice chairman of the party's Central Committee and premier of the State Council. The report stated that although serious warning was given him in February 1954, "Kao Kang not only did not admit his guilt but even committed suicide as an expression of the ultimate betrayal of the party." Thus, Kao Kang, who had been known as an "ever-correct comrade" and a trusted associate of Mao Tse-tung, ended his long career in the Chinese Communist party by becoming the central figure in the first major upheaval to jar the party and government structure of the People's Republic of China.

Kao Lun   高　崙
  T. Chien-fu   劍　父

Kao Lun (12 October 1879–22 June 1951), known as Kao Chien-fu, artist. He was a leader of the Lingnan-p'ai [Lingnan school] of painting, which combined Japanese, Western, and Chinese painting techniques and which placed new emphasis on realism.

P'anyü, Kwangtung, was the birthplace of Kao Chien-fu. He was the fourth of six sons to be born to Kao Pao-hsiang, a physician interested in art. Kao Chien-fu's two younger brothers were Kao Ch'i-feng (Kao Weng, q.v.) and Kao Chen-wei (T. Chien-tseng). At the age of five, Kao Chien-fu began his primary education in the Chinese classics. A few years later, after both of his parents died, he went to live with an uncle who was a physician and a painter. Kao worked in his uncle's medicine shop and learned the rudiments of painting.

When he was 12, he was sent to study under the well-known Cantonese artist Chü Lien (1828–1904). He lived in the Chü household, but his relations with some members of the family were far from cordial. A year later, he went to live with an uncle who was a military physician at the Whampoa Naval Academy. He enrolled at the academy, but had to drop out because of illness.

In 1894 Kao Chien-fu returned to Canton to study under Chü Lien. He came to know Wu Te-i (T. I-chuang), a wealthy trader and art collector who also was studying under Chü Lien. Kao increased his knowledge of painting by copying many Sung and Yüan works in Wu's collection. In 1895, with financial support from the Wu family, he studied Western painting under a French artist at Canton Christian College, the predecessor of Lingnan University. He then became an art teacher in an elementary school, where one of his colleagues was the Japanese artist Yamamoto Baigai, who taught him Japanese.

In 1898, at the age of 19, Kao Chien-fu went to Japan, where he studied Japanese painting techniques and joined such organizations as the White Horse Society, the Pacific Painting Society, and the Watercolor Study Association. He managed to sell enough paintings to support himself. In 1902 he returned to China and taught drawing at the Kwangtung-Kwangsi Advanced Institute of Technology. He made a second trip to Japan in 1904 to study at the Tokyo Academy of Fine Arts. He joined the T'ung-meng-hui and helped to establish a branch of the party at Canton after returning there in 1906. His firm support of the anti-Manchu revolution led him to stage mock funerals to smuggle ammunition into Canton.

After 1911, Kao Chien-fu and his brother Kao Ch'i-feng established such enterprises in Shanghai as the Sheng-mei shu-kuan, which was an art publishing house, and the *Chen-hsiang hua-pao* (*Revue Artistique de la Realité*), which was the first photographic magazine to be published in China. During this period, Kao Chien-fu's paintings were exhibited in Tokyo, Kobe, Seoul, Shanghai, Nanking, Hong Kong, and Canton. In 1916 he established the Ch'un-shui School of Painting in Canton. In 1921 he organized a provincial art exhibit, the first of its kind, at Canton; and eight years later he directed China's first national art exhibit, which was held at Nanking.

About 1931 Kao traveled to Burma, India, Ceylon, Persia, and Egypt. In the Himalayas he received leg injuries during a snow storm and eye injuries from glare. After returning to China, he wrote several books about his travels abroad, including *Fo-kuo chi* [an account of the Buddhist countries], *Yin-tu i-shu* [the art of India], and *Hsi-ma-la-ya-shan ti yen-chiu* [a study of the Himalayas]. Beginning in the 1930's he taught at National Sun Yat-sen University and headed the Municipal Academy of Fine Arts in Canton. In addition, he continued to direct the Ch'un-shui School of Painting. In 1935 he took a leave of absence to teach at National Central University in Nanking, where he founded the Ya-feng-she [Asian wind society]. During the Sino-Japanese war, he journeyed through west China and painted many landscapes and war scenes.

Kao Chien-fu, Kao Ch'i-feng and their associates and students came to be referred to as the Lingnan-p'ai, or Lingnan school. Among the many students who studied at the Ch'un-shui School of Painting under Kao Chien-fu were Li Hsiung-ts'ai, Fang Jen-tung (1903–), Kuan Shan-yüeh (1910–), and Yu Yüan-shan. Kao exempted poor students from tuition, and even provided some of them with lodgings, food, and pocket money. Painters of the Lingnan School combined traditional composition and brushwork with Japanese and Western techniques. In *Wo-ti hsien-tai kuo-hua-kuan* [my views on modern Chinese painting], a lecture delivered at Nanking in 1935 and published in 1955, Kao Chien-fu stated that foreign influences had affected the development of traditional Chinese painting and that modern Chinese artists should combine the brush techniques and the vitality of spirit of Chinese painting with such Western ideas as shading, perspective, and atmosphere. The new Chinese painting, which Kao termed hsin-kuo-hua, should emphasize not only form and technique but also the subject matter and motive for painting. To achieve this goal, such modern objects as airplanes, railroads, telephone poles, and human figures in modern dress should be depicted. For example, in 1915 he had painted a traditional-style hanging scroll, "Two Monsters of Heaven and Earth," which depicted an airplane and a tank. He considered this commentary on the First World War to embody revolutionary spirit. During the 1920's Kao sought to revitalize Chinese art by advocating a fresh study of the art of Sung and Yüan times and of the wen-jen-hua [gentlemen's painting], establishing in turn the Hsin Sung Yüan p'ai [new school of Sung and Yüan painting] and the Hsin wen-jen-hua p'ai or [new school of gentlemen's painting]. During the Sino-Japanese war, Kao and his students emphasized realism, painting war scenes of bombing, refugees, and city ruins. Two published collections of Kao's paintings are *Wa-sheng chi* and *Chien-fu hua chi*.

Working in the tradition of Chinese painting, Kao Chien-fu and his followers of the Lingnan school were notable for three distinguishing characteristics: most of them were connected with Canton revolutionaries; almost all had studied at one time in Japan; and almost all aimed at a synthesis of traditional, Japanese, and Western values in painting. In technique, the Lingnan school's handling of perspective, atmosphere, and chiaroscuro derived from Western practice. Their brushwork was Chinese, while a tendency to purely decorative effect and a smooth, oily surface texture revealed Japanese influences. The ultimate aim of the Lingnan painters was to bring a new kind of subject matter within the orbit of the traditional medium, and the major effort of the Lingnan school was to effect an intellectual synthesis of traditional and international values. The results were often labored, and Kao's precepts cannot be said to have solved the problems of content and form for modern Chinese painters. Nonetheless, Kao Chien-fu's work as both artist and teacher had a considerable influence on Chinese art. He died in Macao on 22 June 1951. He was survived by his second wife, Weng Hsiu-chih; his son, Kao Li-chieh; and his daughter, Kao Li-hua (Diana Kao). His first wife, Sung Ming-huang, died in Hong Kong in 1938.

Kao Weng   高嵡
  T. Ch'i-feng   奇峰

Kao Weng (3 July 1889–2 November 1933), known as Kao Ch'i-feng, artist. A leading painter of the Lingnan-p'ai [Lingnan school], he worked to combine the excellences of Chinese and Western painting.

The fifth son of Kao Pao-hsiang, a physician who was interested in art, Kao Ch'i-feng was born in P'anyü, Kwangtung. He was ten years younger than Kao Chien-fu (for details of their early life, *see* Kao Lun). After receiving a primary education in the Chinese classics, Kao Ch'i-feng went to Canton, where he studied under his brother's former teacher Chü Lien. In 1905, at the age of 16, he went to Japan to study Western art. Before returning to China in 1911, he joined the T'ung-meng-hui.

After 1911, Kao Ch'i-feng and Kao Chien-fu established such enterprises as the Sheng-mei shu-kuan, a publishing house which specialized in art works. In 1918 Kao Ch'i-feng went to Canton, where he taught drawing at the Kwangtung Institute of Technology and established the Mei-hsueh-kuan, an art institute which later became the T'ien-feng Academy of Art. Beginning in 1925 he taught Chinese art at Lingnan University. He was commissioned in 1926 to do several large paintings for the Sun Yat-sen Memorial Hall at Canton. These works, which included "The Lone Eagle," "The White Horse," and "The Fierce Lion," were said to symbolize the revolutionary spirit of the new China.

In 1929 Kao Ch'i-feng built a studio, the T'ien-feng-lou, on the shore of the Pearl River in Canton. He lived a quiet life of teaching there with his adopted daughter and favorite pupil, Chang K'un-i, who cared for him after he became ill with tuberculosis.

Kao Ch'i-feng and Kao Chien-fu belonged to a group of artists which was referred to as the Lingnan-p'ai, or Lingnan school. Another prominent exponent of this school was Ch'en Shu-jen (q.v.). The Lingnan artists combined Japanese, Western, and Chinese painting techniques and placed new emphasis on realism. In a lecture delivered at Lingnan University Kao Ch'i-feng described his experience and his artistic credo. He told of his gradual realization that traditional Chinese paintings, though excellent in many respects, were overly metaphysical, illusive, and imaginary. Accordingly, he had turned to the study of Western art, paying particular attention to portrait painting, geometrical drawing, shading, and perspective. He then had made his first attempts to combine some Western methods with Chinese techniques of brush work, inking, and composition. "In short," he said, "I tried to retain what was exquisite in the Chinese art of painting and at the same time to adopt the best methods of composition which the world's art school had to offer, thereby blending the East and the West into a harmonious whole, taking for my guidance beauty, naturalness, and my own creative power and taste. The result is my paintings of today." The paintings of Kao's students also reflected his beliefs. Among his pupils were Chao Shao-ang (1904–), who became known for his studies of insects and flowers, and Chang K'un-i, noted for her animals and landscapes.

In 1933 Kao Ch'i-feng went to Shanghai to embark on a trip to Berlin, where he planned to participate in a Sino-German art exhibition. However, he fell ill and died on 2 November in Shanghai. He was given a state funeral in recognition of his artistic accomplishment and his early association with the revolutionary movement in China.

Kao Ch'i-feng's publications included *Hsin hua hsüeh* [new theories of painting], *Mei-shu-shih* [a history of art], and *Ch'i-feng hua-fan* [a manual of painting]. In 1935 a collection of Kao's lectures, paintings, and poems, *Kao Ch'i-feng hsien-sheng jung-ai-lu*, was published in Nanking as a memorial volume. Kao's works have been exhibited in Japan, Italy, Belgium, France, and the United States as well as in China. In 1944 an exhibition of works by Kao and Chang K'un-i was held at the Metropolitan Museum of Art in New York. Seven volumes of Kao Ch'i-feng's paintings have been published since 1935 under the title *Ch'i-feng hua-chi*.

Kaung, Z. T.: *see* CHIANG CH'ANG-CH'UAN.

Kiang K'ang-hu: *see* CHIANG K'ANG-HU.

Ko Kung-chen 戈 公 振
   Orig. Ko Shao-fa 戈 紹 發
   T.   Ch'un-t'ing 春 霆

Ko Kung-chen (16 October 1890–22 October 1935), editor of the Shanghai newspapers *Shih-pao* and *Shun-pao* and historian of journalism.

Tungt'ai, Kiangsu, a small town near Shanghai, was the birthplace of Ko Kung-chen. He received a primary education in the Chinese classics at a clan school which had been established by his great-aunt. At the age of 14, he enrolled at a semi-modern school; he studied there until 1908 and then entered the Tungt'ai

Higher School. After being graduated in 1912, he worked as an apprentice at a small local newspaper, the *Tung-t'ai jih-pao* [Tung-t'ai daily news]. He passed the entrance examination for Nant'ung Teachers College in 1913, but was unable to enroll there because he lacked funds. He soon left home and went to Shanghai.

Ko went to work in 1913 for the Yu-cheng shu-chü [Yu-cheng book company], which published both traditional and modern books and which was famous for its editions of Chinese paintings and calligraphy. Its owner, Ti Ch'u-ch'ing, had founded the influential Shanghai newspaper *Shih-pao* [the Eastern times] in 1904. Ko won Ti's trust, and he soon was transferred to the staff of the *Shih-pao*. He also entered the Shen-chou Law School, where he studied jurisprudence, history, and economics.

Ko worked for the *Shih-pao* for about 13 years, during which time he rose from proofreader to chief editor and made a number of contributions to the modernization of journalism in China. Ko's principal innovations were the pictorial section (beginning in 1920), the regular publication of supplements, and the use of color printing. He also instituted expert and extensive sports reporting. Under Ko's editorship, the *Shih-pao* became the most Americanized of the Shanghai dailies and, according to Hu Shih (q.v.), the favorite newspaper of intellectuals and students.

As the successful editor of the *Shih-pao*, Ko was invited to teach journalism in a number of Shanghai colleges. This activity, in turn, led him to write books about practical journalism and the history of the profession. When the Hsin-wen chi-che lien-ho-hui [journalists association] was organized at Shanghai in 1920, Ko became its first president. In 1924 he translated and adapted *The Handbook of Journalism* by F. N. Clark as *Hsin-wen ts'o-yao* [essentials of journalism]. It was published in 1925 and reprinted in 1929. Ko was invited to teach journalism in Kuo-min University in 1925. At this time, he began to collect materials for a definitive history of journalism in China. The completed work, *Chung-kuo pao-hsueh shih* [history of Chinese journalism] was published in 1927, and, despite certain inaccuracies, was generally regarded as the pioneering work in the field. In 1925 Ko also helped organize the Shang-hai pao-hsueh she [Shanghai journalism society] to advance the study of journalism.

In 1927 Ko resigned the editorship of the *Shih-pao* to embark on a two-year stint of foreign travel and reportage. In January, under the auspices of the central propaganda department of the Kuomintang, but probably at his own expense, Ko left China to make a reporting tour and to study journalistic practices in Japan, Europe, and the United States. He attended the League of Nations Journalists Conference, held in August 1927 at Geneva, as the official representative of the Shanghai Daily Newspapers Guild. As a reporter, he also attended the International Labor Conference, the Conference for the Limitation of Naval Armaments, the International Conference for Communications and Transit, and the Universal Theaters Conference. He interviewed such prominent statesmen as Sir Austen Chamberlain, Aristide Briand, and Benito Mussolini. Ko attracted a good deal of attention as the first Chinese correspondent ever seen in the capitals of Europe. His frequent dispatches, which appeared in the *Shih-pao*, gave the Chinese reading public new insight into world events. During this period, Ko continued to collect data on the history of journalism in China, visiting libraries in England and France to locate copies of rare foreign journals published in China.

After returning to China in the winter of 1929, Ko was invited by Shih Liang-ts'ai (q.v.), the owner of the *Shun-pao* [Shanghai news daily], to join that enterprise as co-director of its planning department with Huang Yen-p'ei (q.v.). Ko accepted the position and introduced a number of new enterprises, including the monthly *Shun-pao yueh-k'an*, a pictorial, a book-rental program, and a correspondence school. Ko was in great demand as a teacher of journalism, and between 1929 and 1932 he taught courses at Nan-fang University, Ta-hsia University, and Futan University. He also worked on the draft of his *Shih-chieh pao-yeh k'ao-ch'a chi* [survey of the world's press industry]. Unhappily, the manuscript of this work was destroyed in the Japanese bombardment of the Commerical Press during the battle of Shanghai in 1932. In 1931 Ko finished writing *Hsin-wen-hsueh* [journalism], but it was not published until 1940.

After the Japanese attacked Mukden on 18 September 1931, Ko actively participated in the anti-Japanese movement. In the autumn of 1932 he accompanied the Lytton Commission to Manchuria, and in Mukden he was arrested and detained briefly by Japanese authorities. After being released, he went with the commission to Geneva in September, where he attended and reported on the special sessions of the League of Nations which discussed the problem of Japanese intervention in China. In his reports Ko expressed disappointment in the League's compromise solution and warned of the dangers of further encroachment and aggression if the Chinese people did not unite and resist Japan. After the meetings, Ko went to Madrid, where he attended the International Conference of Press Experts. He also visited and sent dispatches from Italy, Germany, France, Austria, Czechoslovakia, and the Soviet Union.

The Soviet Union, along with the writings of Marx and Lenin, had become one of Ko's preoccupations after the events of 1931–32. Diplomatic relations with the Soviet Union had been restored in December 1932. Ko arrived in the Soviet Union in 1933 and remained there until the autumn of 1935. During this period, he traveled extensively and wrote a large number of articles sympathetically detailing the political, cultural, and economic strides which the Soviet Union was making. These articles later were collected by Tsou T'ao-fen (q.v.) and published as *Ts'ung Tung-pei tao Su-lien* [from Manchuria to the Soviet Union]. In the autumn of 1935, Ko became ill shortly after his arrival in Shanghai on 15 October. He died on 22 October of peritonitis caused by a ruptured appendix.

Ko's brother, Ko Shao-lung, a minor literary figure, was a physician who practiced in Shanghai. He oversaw the publication of his brother's *Hsin-wen-hsueh* in 1940.

K'o Ch'ing-shih   柯慶施

K'o Ch'ing-shih (1902–9 April 1965), Chinese Communist administrator who became the most important official at Shanghai in 1955, serving as head of the party's Shanghai bureau and chairman of the Shanghai municipal government.

A native of Wuhu, Anhwei, K'o Ch'ing-shih was born into a landowning family at Huangshan. After being graduated from the South

Anhwei Normal School, he taught school in Anhwei for a time. He reportedly joined the Socialist Youth League in Shanghai in August 1920 and the Chinese Communist party in 1922.

From about 1920 to 1937 K'o engaged in underground party work in the Shanghai, Nanking, and Wuhan areas. He also held such offices in the Chinese Communist party as secretary of the Anhwei provincial committee, director of the political department of the Eighth Army of the Chinese Workers and Peasants Red Army, secretary of the front committee of the Hopei provincial committee, and director of the organization department of the front committee.

After the Sino-Japanese war began in 1937, K'o was called to Yenan, where he became a deputy director of the united front work department, serving under Ch'en Shao-yü (q.v.). In 1944 Ch'en was replaced by Li Wei-han (q.v.). Because Li's duties as secretary general of the Shensi-Kansu-Ninghsia Border Region government occupied most of his time, K'o became acting director of the department.

In 1947 K'o Ch'ing-shih was appointed deputy director of the financial committee of the Shansi-Chahar-Hopei Border Region. Near the end of that year he was named mayor of Shih-chia-chuang, Hopei, which the Chinese Communists had occupied in November and which was the largest city under Communist control at that time. K'o held that post for about a year. After the Communists took Nanking in May 1949, K'o was moved there to serve as deputy mayor under Liu Po-ch'eng (q.v.). Liu soon moved his Second Field Army to the south, and in 1951 K'o became mayor of Nanking. He also served as secretary of the Nanking municipal committee of the Chinese Communist party.

In 1952, as the Central People's Government began to consolidate its control of the mainland, party and civil administrative posts were reorganized. In November, K'o was appointed secretary of the party committee for Kiangsu province, political commissioner of the Kiangsu Military District, and vice chairman of the Kiangsu People's Government. His immediate superior was T'an Chen-lin (q.v.), whose chief responsibility was the party's east China bureau. T'an delegated most of the duties involved in directing party affairs in Kiangsu to K'o Ch'ing-shih. In 1954 K'o attended the National People's Congress as a deputy from Kiangsu. In November, he was appointed to the committee of the party's east China bureau. However, the regional governments and their civil bureaus were abolished soon afterward.

K'o Ch'ing-shih was named to head the newly established Shanghai bureau of the Chinese Communist party in January 1955. He also became first secretary of the party's Shanghai committee. These positions were important because Shanghai had become one of three special municipalities in the People's Republic of China. Its civil affairs were administered directly by bureaus of the State Council rather than by the provincial authorities. Similarly, the Chinese Communist party's Shanghai bureau was responsible to the Political Bureau rather than to the provincial committee. K'o's Shanghai bureau also controlled party affairs in Kiangsu and Chekiang.

K'o became a member of the Shanghai municipal council in February 1955. About three months later, he was elected chairman of the party's Shanghai municipal committee and president of the Shanghai branch of the Sino-Soviet Friendship Association. At this time, he relinquished his posts in the Kiangsu provincial administration. In June, he served as a deputy to the National People's Congress.

K'o was elected to the Central Committee of the Chinese Communist party at the Eighth National Congress, held in 1956. He received the highest number of votes cast for a new committee member, and ranked thirty-fifth (of 97) in total number of votes received. In May 1958 he was made a full member of the Political Bureau even though several higher-ranking members of the party had not yet achieved that distinction.

In March 1958 K'o had accepted an invitation to lecture at the former Catholic Futan University in Shanghai. His acceptance reflected the party's interest in having prominent officials join the faculties of leading Chinese universities. That autumn, he succeeded Ch'en Yi as chairman of the Shanghai municipal government, or mayor. He now held the most important post in the civil administration of Shanghai. K'o became vice premier of the State Council and first political commissar of the Nanking Military District early in 1965. He soon became ill, however, and died at Ch'engtu, Szechwan, on 9 April 1965.

The career of K'o Ch'ing-shih is interesting in that, although he served the Chinese Communist movement almost from its beginnings, he did not begin to emerge as an important leader until the end of the Sino-Japanese war. Then, as the party began to move from its rural headquarters in north China into the important industrial and agricultural centers of the mainland, the need for capable administrators increased greatly. This shift in party needs was reflected in the changing composition of its Central Committee. In 1945 most of the new members of the Central Committee were military men; in 1956, when K'o was elected to the Central Committee, most of the new committee members were administrators.

K'o Shao-min   柯 劭 忞
   T. Feng-sun   鳳 孫
     Feng-sheng   鳳 笙
   H. Liao-yuan   蓼 園

K'o Shao-min (1850-1933), historian and classical scholar, known for his monumental history of the Yüan dynasty, the *Hsin Yüan-shih*.

A native of Liaohsien, Shantung, K'o Shao-min was the son of K'o Heng, a historian who wrote supplementary notes to the seven tables in the *Han-shu* which were known as the *Han-shu ch'i-piao chiao-pu*. K'o Shao-min's mother, Li Ch'ang-hsia, was the daughter of Li Ch'ang-po and was known as a poet. K'o Shao-min's precocity attracted the attention of Li Tz'u-ming (ECCP, II, 493), who recorded his impressions of K'o's early writings in his diary on 5 October 1872. K'o is said to have been a serious student of mathematics and traditional medicine, as well as of classical studies.

K'o Shao-min enjoyed a smooth and prosperous career both as a scholar and an official. He became a chü-jen in 1870 and a chin-shih in 1886. For a short time, he was at the Hanlin Academy. Between 1901 and 1906 he twice held the post of commissioner of education, first of Hunan and then of Kweichow. During this period, he also served in the Imperial Academy of Learning (Kuo-tzu-chien) and in the Hanlin Academy, where he achieved the rank of sub-expositor. Subsequently, he was sent to Japan to study that country's educational

system, and upon his return in 1909 he was appointed to the ministry of education. He also became associate dean of classics and then acting chancellor of the Ching-shih ta-hsüeh-t'ang, the predecessor of Peking University. In December 1911, when the Ch'ing court was on the verge of complete collapse, the regent, Prince Ch'un, appointed K'o and 11 other popular and respected officials to visit their respective home provinces in a last attempt to win popular support for the tottering dynasty.

As an elder statesman loyal to the Ch'ing, K'o Shao-min declined all political appointments offered him by the republican government, including membership in the National Assembly. However, he agreed to take part in compiling the history of the Manchu dynasty. Thus, in 1914 he joined the Ch'ing-shih-kuan [Ch'ing history bureau] headed by Chao Erh-sun (q.v.). Among other things, he completed the treatises on astronomy, calendrical reckoning, and portents. After Chao Erh-sun's death in September 1927, K'o Shao-min became head of the Ch'ing-shih-kuan and supervised publication of the *Ch'ing-shih kao*, which appeared in 1928.

Because Japanese scholars held him in high esteem, K'o Shao-min was appointed in May 1925 as China's chief delegate to the ill-fated Sino-Japanese Joint Committee on Oriental Cultural Studies, which was to be financed by the reimbursement of the Japanese portion of the Boxer Indemnity Fund. Many meetings were held, but all adjourned in disagreement. In December 1929 the National Government ordered the dissolution of the committee.

During the Ch'ing period, many prominent scholars had devoted themselves to the study of the history of the Mongol (Yüan) dynasty. However, they produced works which were fragmentary or inadequately documented, and they neglected non-Chinese source materials. In any case, their works did not in any sense supersede the standard *Yüan-shih*, a hurriedly compiled work of the early Ming dynasty which had been accepted as one of the twenty-four dynastic histories despite the fact that it was riddled with errors, some of them ludicrous. K'o Shao-min therefore spent nearly 50 years studying Chinese, Japanese, and European materials and writing a completely new history of the Yüan dynasty which, when published for the first time in 1922 as *Hsin Yüan-shih*, consisted of 257 chüan. This monumental work was well received in Japan, and, on the recommendation of Yanai Wataru, Tokyo Imperial University in 1923 awarded K'o an honorary D.L.H. degree. Somewhat earlier, Hsü Shih-ch'ang (q.v.), who had received the chin-shih degree in the same year as K'o Shao-min and who belonged to the same poetry society, by an executive decree of December 1919 formally accepted the *Hsin Yüan-shih* in manuscript as one of the standard histories, thus increasing the total number from 24 to 25. K'o Shao-min received less favorable criticism from contemporary Chinese scholars. Ch'en Yüan (q.v.), for example, expressed the opinion that K'o Shao-min should have written a commentary to the original *Yüan-shih* instead of a new history. Liang Ch'i-ch'ao (q.v.) criticized K'o for arbitrarily selecting some documents on a given topic and rejecting others which disagreed, without interpreting or even mentioning the contradictions. The latter criticism was partially answered, however, by K'o Shao-min's *Hsin Yüan-shih k'ao-cheng* [evidential basis for the new history of the Yüan dynasty], published in 1935.

K'o was also interested in the *Ku-liang*, the commentary to the *Ch'un-ch'iu* which had been least studied by Ch'ing scholars. He therefore wrote the *Ch'un-ch'iu Ku-liang-chuan chu* [annotations to the Ku-liang commentary on the *Ch'un-ch'iu*], which was published in 1917 and reprinted with corrections in 1935.

K'o's poems were collected and published in 1924 as *Liao-yüan shih-ch'ao* [selected poems from the smartweed garden—smartweed (liao) being a pun on the name of K'o's native district]. In style they were held comparable to those of Wu Wei-yeh (ECCP, II, 882–83) and Wang Shih-chen (q.v.).

After the death of his first wife, K'o Shao-min married the third daughter of Wu Ju-lun (ECCP, II, 870–72), an accomplished scholar with whom he had exchanged poems. K'o died in 1933, at the age of 83.

Koo, V. K. Wellington: *see* KU WEI-CHÜN.

Ku Cheng-lun   谷正倫
T. Chi-ch'ang   紀常

Ku Cheng-lun (23 September 1890–3 November 1953), known as "the father of the Chinese

military police." He also served the National Government as governor of Kansu (1941–46), minister of food (1947), and governor of Kweichow (1948–49).

A native of Anshun, Kweichow, Ku Cheng-lun was the eldest son of Ku Yung-ch'ien, a scholar who held the chü-jen degree. Two of his younger brothers were Ku Cheng-kang and Ku Cheng-ting (q.v.). After being graduated from the Kweichow Military Primary School in 1905, he attended the Wuchang Military Middle School for three years. In 1908 he went to Japan, where he studied at the Shimbu Gakkō [military preparatory academy] and the Shikan Gakkō [military academy], specializing in artillery.

When news of the Wuchang revolt of October 1911 reached Japan, Ku immediately returned to China to join the revolutionary forces. He served as an aide to Huang Hsing (q.v.) in the Hanyang general headquarters and received the rank of major. After the republic was established in 1912, he served under Huang in the ministry of war. Huang remained in Nanking as commander in chief of the southern forces when the provisional government was moved to Peking, and Ku continued to serve as his aide. He soon received the rank of lieutenant colonel. In the autumn of 1913 when the so-called second revolution against Yuan Shih-k'ai failed, Ku followed Huang to Japan and returned to his studies at the Shikan Gakkō. He was graduated in 1915 as a member of the eleventh artillery class, and he returned to Kweichow in September 1916 to command the artillery regiment in the 1st Division of the Kweichow army. In August 1920 he was promoted commander of the Second Mixed Brigade.

After hostilities broke out between Canton and Peking in 1920, Ku, fighting on the side of Canton, led his Kweichow troops into Szechwan, but soon returned to his native province. In April 1921 he was named commander of forces guarding Kweichow's southern route. In May, Sun Yat-sen, who was campaigning against Lu Jung-t'ing (q.v.) in Kwangsi, appointed Ku commander in chief of the Kweichow forces. In cooperation with the troops under the command of Li Lieh-chün and Ch'en Chiung-ming (qq.v.), these forces inflicted a crushing defeat on Lu Jung-t'ing. Sun Yat-sen established headquarters in Kweilin in December and assumed personal direction of a northern expedition. Ku's troops were ordered to march into Hunan in the spring of 1922. However, the expedition was halted by the revolt of Ch'en Chiung-ming in Kwangtung. Ku's troops, cut off from rear support and stranded in southern Hunan, soon dispersed.

In July 1925, on the recommendation of Ho Yao-tsu (q.v.), his classmate at Shikan Gakkō, Ku was appointed an adviser to the 1st Division of the Hunan army and dean of the Officer Training School. Chiang Kai-shek launched the Northern Expedition from Canton in July 1926. In September, after being defeated in battle by the troops of T'ang Sheng-chih and Li Tsung-jen (qq.v.), Ho Yao-tsu decided to join the revolutionary cause. He received command of the Independent 2nd Division of the National Revolutionary Army, with Ku Cheng-lun as his deputy commander. During the incident at Nanking of 24 March 1927, the Independent 2nd Division was expanded into the Fortieth Army and was assigned the task of maintaining order in Nanking. On 17 February 1928 Ku Cheng-lun was appointed commandant of Nanking, which was under martial law. He became vice commandant of the capital garrison on 10 May. When the National Government established a military police system in January 1932, Ku was named provost marshal and commandant of the Nanking garrison. During the 1930's Ku devoted most of his attention to the organization and training of the military police force, which later developed into one of the major organs responsible for internal security. He organized a training center for police cadets and drew up a set of regulations governing the power and responsibilities of the military police. As a result of his efforts, the force was expanded from two regiments in 1932 to thirty regiments in 1935. He thus earned the title of "father of the Chinese military police."

In November 1935 Ku Cheng-lun and his two younger brothers Ku Cheng-kang and Ku Cheng-ting were elected by the Kuomintang Fifth National Congress to the Central Executive Committee. On 11 September 1937, after the outbreak of the Sino-Japanese war, Ku Cheng-lun was appointed vice supervisor of military law, a post which was directly under the jurisdiction of the Military Affairs Council. As the Japanese approached Nanking in November, he and his military police evacuated the city.

After serving in Wuchang and Chihchiang, he became director of the Hupeh-Hunan-Szechwan-Kweichow border area pacification bureau on 28 February 1939. He soon rid the district of the bandits who long had plagued it. His efforts were rewarded on 1 December 1940, when he received the governorship of Kansu.

During the more than six years that he governed Kansu, Ku worked to reorganize and increase the efficiency of the local administrative structures below the hsien level, especially the village and town governments. At the same time, he forcibly broke the alliance of corrupt politicians, bandits, and opium smugglers in southern Kansu. Ku's arrival at Kansu coincided with the completion of the Huang-hui canal, which could irrigate 30,000 mou of land. To enable peasant farmers to benefit from this project, he bought all lands in the irrigated district in the name of the provincial government and then sold them to the peasants on a 15-year mortgage plan. This project was the first "land to the tiller" program to be put into effect in Nationalist-controlled territory. Ku also reorganized the grain transportation system in the province, which greatly reduced the cost of transport, enriched the provincial treasury, and made the food price index of Kansu the most stable of all the provinces of wartime China.

Ku was also responsible for a rapid increase in school and college enrollment in Kansu, which had been known as one of China's most backward provinces. According to provincial statistics, the number of college students in Kansu in 1945 was 30 times the 1937 figure; the number of middle school students had quadrupled; and the number of primary school students had doubled.

In recognition of his achievements in Kansu, Ku was appointed minister of food and a member of the administrative council of the Executive Yuan in May 1947. A year later, he became governor of Kweichow. By this time, he was in poor health, and the anxiety caused by the civil war with the Communists aggravated his stomach condition. As the Communists approached Kweiyang in November 1949, Ku managed to escape and fly to Hong Kong, but he had to leave behind his mother and his younger brother Ku Cheng-k'ai. Ku Cheng-lun died in Taipei on 3 November 1953.

Ku Cheng-ting 谷 正 鼎

Ku Cheng-ting (24 October 1903–), member of Wang Ching-wei's Reorganizationist faction who, beginning in 1937, was director of the bureau in Chiang Kai-shek's Sian headquarters that had jurisdiction over military and political affairs in the northwestern provinces and responsibility for combatting Chinese Communist influence. He became vice director (1946) and director (1948) of the Kuomintang's organization department and a member of the Legislative Yuan (1947). In Taiwan, he devoted his time to the Legislative Yuan.

The fourth son of the scholar Ku Yung-ch'ien and the younger brother of Ku Cheng-lun (q.v.), Ku Cheng-ting was born in Anshun, Kweichow. He and his elder brother Ku Cheng-kang attended various schools together until 1927. After receiving their primary education in the Chinese classics at a village school, they attended a modern higher primary school and the Kweiyang Provincial Lower Normal School. Ku Cheng-ting participated in student-led demonstrations during the May Fourth Movement of 1919 and became chairman of the Kweichow Federation of Student Associations.

In 1922 the two brothers left Kweichow and went to Germany, where they studied political economy at Berlin University. They joined the German branch of the Kuomintang in 1924, and Ku Cheng-ting was elected to its executive committee. After news of the May Thirtieth Incident of 1925 reached Berlin, Ku made a number of speeches in various German cities to protest the presence of foreign powers in China. After graduation from Berlin University in 1925, the two brothers went to Moscow, where they studied at Sun Yat-sen University and spent much of their time in debate with Chinese Communist students. In 1926 Ku Cheng-ting met and married P'i I-shu (1908–), a native of Nanch'uan Szechwan, who was a member of the Kuomintang and chairman of the women's department of the Federation of Peking Students. In August 1927 Ku and his wife left the Soviet Union and went to Nanking, where he became director of the political department of the Twenty-sixth Army.

Ku Cheng-ting became secretary of the Kuomintang's central propaganda department and a member of the Central People's Training Committee in February 1928. After the successful conclusion of the Northern Expedition in June, he was made a member of the standing committee of the Peiping Party Affairs Guidance Committee. Both he and Ku Cheng-kang opposed the leadership of Chiang Kai-shek, and in the winter of 1928 they joined the Reorganizationist faction of Wang Ching-wei (q.v.). After participating in the unsuccessful enlarged conference movement of 1930 (see Feng Yü-hsiang; Yen Hsi-shan), they went into hiding. Little is known of their activities during 1931.

When Wang Ching-wei assumed the premiership in January 1932, Ku Cheng-ting became a councillor in the Executive Yuan. He soon was transferred to the ministry of railways, serving first as a councillor and then as director of its general affairs office. In September, he was elected to the executive committee of the Nanking branch of the Kuomintang. He evidently overcame many of his objections to Chiang Kai-shek as a leader, for he was elected to the Central Executive Committee of the Kuomintang in November 1935, as were his brothers Ku Cheng-lun and Ku Cheng-kang.

After the Sino-Japanese war began, Ku Cheng-ting was sent to Sian in the winter of 1937 as director of the bureau in Chiang Kai-shek's headquarters that had jurisdiction over the military and political affairs of Shensi, Kansu, Tsinghai, and Ninghsia. Because Chinese Communist influence was increasing in Shensi and Kansu, Ku was ordered to suppress Communist organizations in the areas under his jurisdiction. In 1938 he established a branch of the Central Military Academy, a battalion for the training of youths who had escaped from Japanese-occupied territory and who wished to become military or political cadres, and the Northwest Youth Labor Camp for the indoctrinating of young Communists who had been captured by National Government forces. Kuomintang ideology was stressed in the schools of the region, and people who lived near the Communist Shensi-Kansu-Ninghsia Border Region were ordered to construct fortifications and to organize militia units as means of curbing the expansion of Communist military power. P'i I-shu, who was chairman of the women's committee of the Shensi headquarters, established homes for refugee children and workshops for the dependents of Nationalist servicemen. With the 1939 redesignation of the Sian headquarters as the T'ienshui headquarters and the extension of its jurisdiction to include the First, Fifth, and Eighth War areas, Ku became responsible for combatting the Communist challenge in Honan, Shansi, northern Anhwei, northern Hupeh, and Sinkiang, as well as in the northwestern regions.

In February 1939 Ku was entrusted with the delicate mission of securing the return to Chungking of Wang Ching-wei, who had fled the wartime capital and had gone to Hanoi in December 1938. Wang refused Ku's offers and requested diplomatic passports for himself and his entourage so that they could go to Europe. Ku returned to Hanoi with the passports and money for traveling expenses early in March. On 21 March, the day after Ku left Hanoi, his efforts to appease Wang Ching-wei were ruined by the assassination of Wang's adviser Tseng Chung-ming (q.v.). Because Wang believed that the shooting was a Nationalist plot with himself as the intended victim, he decided to collaborate with the Japanese.

When the T'ienshui headquarters was reorganized as the Sian office of the Military Affairs Commission in 1940, Ku Cheng-ting was named its vice director. Four years later, he became chairman of the Kuomintang's Shensi provincial headquarters. Thus, Ku was a key figure in the National Government's political campaign against Japanese and Chinese Communist influence throughout the Sino-Japanese war.

In 1946 Ku Cheng-ting became vice director of the organization department of the Kuomintang. He was elected to the Legislative Yuan in 1947 as a representative of Kweichow and was made director of the organization department in the autumn of 1948. His department, along with other party and government organs, was forced by the advancing Communists to move from Nanking to Taiwan, by way of Canton and Chungking, in 1949.

In Taiwan, Ku Cheng-ting resigned from the organization department in 1950 to devote all of his time to the Legislative Yuan, of which his wife also was a member. Ku's brother Ku Cheng-kang, who had served the National Government as minister of social affairs from 1940 to 1949, also held important posts in Taiwan.

Ku Chieh-kang   顧 頡 剛

Ku Chieh-kang (1895–), a professor and historian known for his critically analytic investigations of Chinese antiquity. His best known work, the *Ku-shih pien* [discussions on Chinese ancient history], was published in seven volumes between 1926 and 1941.

Born into a scholarly Soochow family, Ku Chieh-kang was exposed to the study of classical texts at a very early age. From his grandfather, a student of Han-hsüeh, the rigorous discipline of Ch'ing philology, Ku learned the rudiments of the classical curriculum. His grandmother taught him the vivid folklore of Soochow, which was later to turn his interest to the classical Chinese stage and which gave him many valuable insights into the development and transmission of oral traditions, insights which he later applied to the corpus of Chinese canonical texts. Even as a boy, Ku evidenced an interest in history, the *Tso-chuan* being his favorite classic. He also began to fill notebooks with lists of discrepancies discovered in the classics and his own juvenile efforts to resolve these conundrums. On one occasion, Ku's questioning cost him dearly: he lost a high-school scholarship for criticizing the Han commentator Cheng Hsuan (127–200). This experience merely intensified Ku's devotion to his special studies and his distaste for hypocrisy and ignorance.

In 1906 Ku had entered the newly founded primary school in Soochow. He then went to middle school, where he remained until 1913. Most of his teachers were unimpressive, and the curriculum was ordinary. However, Ku's studies of the classics under his grandfather's direction continued. At school, he became a close friend of Yeh Sheng-t'ao (q.v.), who, years later when he was editor in chief of the K'ai-ming Book Company, published a number of Ku's works. Not all of Ku's time was devoted to study. For a short time he participated in politics as a member of the She-hui-tang [socialist party]. However, the lure of classical and historical research, combined with the natural skepticism of the historian and the diffidence imposed on him by a speech defect, soon obliged him to drop politics.

In 1913 Ku enrolled at the preparatory school of National Peking University, but he seems to have spent more time attending the theater than studying. Theater did, however, revive his interest in folklore, and he soon began to gather material on the history of the Chinese theater and on different versions of plays performed by various companies. From such researches, combined with his early experience of folklore, Ku developed a feeling for the mechanism of the transmission of oral tradition. He later applied these ideas about the accretion of material around a theme in the traditional drama with great brilliance to the classical accounts of Chinese history, notably the stories of Yao, Shun, Yü, and their predecessors.

At Peking University, Ku came under the influence of Chang Ping-lin (q.v.), then recognized as the greatest living philologist and a leading exponent of the ku-wen [old text] school. Chang's lectures introduced him to the complexities of the controversy between the ku-wen school and the chin-wen [new text] school. Ku found Chang a disappointing teacher. He was much more impressed by the *K'ung-tzu kai-chih k'ao* of K'ang Yu-wei (q.v.), the leader of the chin-wen school, who dared speculate that the old texts were, in fact, Han forgeries. Ku did not, however, espouse the chin-wen school, for he considered that school too willing to "twist the past in favor of present changes."

In 1917 Hu Shih (q.v.) returned from the United States, and in him Ku found a mentor and a friend. A circle of scholars formed about the two men to engage in critical discussions and lively correspondence concerning history and the classics. The fruits of these interchanges were published between 1926 and 1941 in the series *Ku-shih pien* [discussions on Chinese ancient history]. At the university, Ku also made a number of other friends who were to distinguish themselves in later years, including Mao Chun and Fu Ssu-nien (q.v.).

After graduation in 1920, and a brief stint as a cataloguer in the university library, Ku was appointed an instructor in Chinese on the recommendation of two of his teachers, Ma Yü-tsao and Shen Chien-shih. His career was interrupted, however, when in 1922 he found it necessary to return to Soochow to care for his ailing grandmother. Thanks to Hu Shih, he was put on the payroll of the Commercial Press in nearby Shanghai as an editor in Chinese history. In the spring of 1924 he returned to Peking, where he worked in the research institute of National Peking University. These were years of joy for Ku, who for the first time had literally at his fingertips all the rare books necessary for his researches. In his "autobiography" of 1926 Ku remarks that he won his colleagues' admiration for frequently remaining all night in the reading room, but adds that he did it for only one reason, his own pleasure. Unfortunately for Ku, the worsening political situation and personal problems obliged him to give up this ideal post, and in 1926, on the recommendation of Shen Chien-shih and Lin Yü-t'ang (q.v.), he went to Amoy University as a research professor. However, he ran afoul of Lu Hsün (Chou Shu-jen, q.v.) and was obliged to depart. Lu Hsün commemorated the incident by caricaturing Ku as a stammering, red-nosed pedant in his story "Li-shui" [controlling the waters], in which Ku, identified as Niao-t'ou hsien-sheng ("Mr. Birdhead," an obscure structural pun on the character for Ku's surname) is represented as arguing against the historicity of Yü the Great on the grounds that Yü contains the graphic element meaning "insect" and that insects generally do not engage in works of water conservancy. The satire has a basis in fact, for in 1924 Ku had argued on such grounds that Yü was a mythic and not a historical character. Ku's ill-fated theory had received immediate and sarcastic criticism, and even such staunch supporters as Hu Shih and Ch'ien Hsuan-t'ung (q.v.) came to his help only as peacemakers.

From Amoy, Ku moved on to National Chung-shan University in Canton. In 1929 he went north to Yenching University, where he was appointed professor of Chinese history. At Yenching, Ku directed the Pei-p'ing yen-chiu-yuan li-shih-tsu [history division of the national Peiping research institute] and also served as director general of the Yü-kung hsüeh-hui [Yü-kung society], a learned organization devoted to the study of Chinese historical geography and deriving its name from the "Yü-kung" [tribute of Yü] chapter of the *Book of History*. Ku edited and contributed frequently to its official publication, *Yü-kung*. Ku was also the editor of the militantly nationalistic and anti-Japanese journal *T'ung-su tu-wu* [the popular reader]. In addition, he organized a group to study China's borderlands, the Pien-chiang yen-chiu-hui [borderlands research association]. Ku had to flee Peiping after the Marco Polo Bridge Incident and the subsequent Japanese occupation of north China. He was invited by the Sino-British Cultural and Educational Endowment Fund to study educational problems in China's northwest. He left Peiping in July 1937 and went as far as Kansu and Tsinghai before arriving at Chungking in September 1938.

During the war years, Ku headed the Institute of Chinese Cultural Studies of the refugee Ch'i-lu University in Chungking. He founded the Chung-kuo shih-hsüeh-hui [Chinese history research society] in 1943 and served as editor in chief of its journal, *Shih-hsüeh tsa-chih* [history magazine]. After the war, he appears to have spent some time teaching at Chen-tan University in Shanghai. In December 1954 he took part in the second session of the Chinese People's Political Consultative Conference. In 1956 he apparently participated in meetings of the League for Democratic Action.

Ku was the author or editor of many articles and books. The best known among the latter is the seven-volume *Ku-shih pien* (1926–41), written and compiled under the encouragement of Hu Shih. Ku edited the first three volumes and the fifth volume. The *Ku-shih pien* amounted to a reevaluation of China's traditional history and of traditional methods of historical investigation and interpretation. Perhaps Ku's most striking contribution was his analysis of how, as one advanced through time, traditions pertaining to ever more ancient times made their appearance much as latecomers to the theater have to take seats farther and farther back in proportion to the tardiness of their arrival. His autobiographical preface to this work was translated by Arthur W. Hummel for his doctoral dissertation at the University of Leiden and was published in 1931 as *The Autobiography of a Chinese Historian*. Among Ku's other works are the *Han-tai hsüeh-shu shih-lüeh* [a brief intellectual history of the Han dynasty], published at Chengtu in 1944 and reprinted in Shanghai in 1955 as *Ch'in-Han ti fang-shih yü ju-sheng* [magicians and literati of Ch'in and Han], notable for its close study of the inception and later development of the "Five Elements"

theory; and *Ch'in Shih-huang-ti* (the first emperor of unified China, 221–207 B.C.). He also edited the unpublished manuscripts of the skeptical Ch'ing historian Ts'ui Shu (ECCP, II, 770–77), which appeared under the title *Ts'ui Tung-pi i-shu* in 1936. Ku collaborated with a number of other scholars in joint works. These include the *Chung-kuo chiang-yü yen-ko shih* [history of China's borderlands], written with T'an Ch'i-hsiang and Shih Nien-hai, and the *Pen-kuo shih* [history of China], written with Wang Chung-ch'i. In 1955 he and a number of other historians produced the *Chung-kuo shang-ku shih yen-i* [the saga of ancient Chinese history]. A series of Ku's addresses, essays, and lectures called *Shih-lin tsa-chih* [miscellaneous notes on history] was begun in 1963. Ku also took the humble position of punctuator and annotator of the by now familiar "Yü-kung" chapter of the *Book of History* as a part of the anthology *Chung-kuo ku-tai ti-li hsüeh ming-chu hsuan-tu* [selected masterpieces of ancient Chinese geographical writing], prepared under the supervision of one of his former disciples, Hou Jen-chih.

Ku Chu-t'ung   顧 祝 同
  T. Mo-san   墨 三

Ku Chu-t'ung (9 January 1893–), Kuomintang military leader whose many important posts included: commander of the Third War Area (1937–45), commander in chief of the Chinese Nationalist army (1946–47; 1949), chief of general staff in the ministry of national defense (1948–49). In Taiwan, he became secretary general of the National Defense Council in 1959 and deputy secretary general of the National Security Council in 1967.

A native of Kiangsu province, Ku Chu-t'ung was born into a gentry family in Lienshui hsien. At the age of six, he began to study the Chinese classics under the guidance of a paternal uncle. He entered the Lienshui Higher Primary School in 1908 and studied there for two years before being selected for the fifth class of the Kiangsu Army Primary School at Nanking. The school temporarily closed after the Wuchang revolt of October 1911, and Ku joined the republican forces, serving as a platoon commander in the 34th Regiment of the 9th

Division, stationed at Hsuchow. He returned to school in 1912, and he joined the Kuomintang later that year.

After graduation in 1913, Ku participated in the so-called second revolution as a staff officer in the Nanking defense headquarters. When the second revolution ended with the fall of Nanking on 1 September 1913 to Peiyang troops led by Chang Hsün (q.v.), Ku fled to Shanghai, where he continued to work for the overthrow of Yuan Shih-k'ai. In 1914 he went to Wuchang when southern graduates of army primary schools were called upon to enter the Hupeh Second Army Preparatory School. Because close restrictions were placed on all cadets after Yuan Shih-k'ai launched his monarchical movement in 1915, Ku left Wuchang and did not return to school until June 1916, when Yuan died. After graduation in December 1916, he enrolled at the Paoting Military Academy as a member of the sixth class, infantry division. In the spring of 1919, having completed his military education, he returned to active service as a company commander in central China.

Late in 1921 Ku Chu-t'ung went to Kweilin and joined the Second Kwangtung Army as an adjutant in the headquarters of Hsü Ch'ung-chih (q.v.). He was assigned to the officers training corps as district corps commander. He soon came to know Chiang Kai-shek, who was drafting plans for Sun Yat-sen's proposed northern expedition, and the two men became friends. In 1922 Ku took part in the Kwangsi campaign and in the Fukien campaign which culminated in the capture of Foochow on 12 October. When Chiang Kai-shek was appointed chief of staff of Hsü Ch'ung-chih's army on 20 October, he immediately recommended Ku's promotion to chief adjutant.

In June 1924 Ku Chu-t'ung became an instructor in military tactics at the Whampoa Military Academy. Chiang Kai-shek soon promoted him to director of administration and gave him command of the 1st Battalion of the 2nd Training Regiment. In March 1925 Ku led his cadet troops on the first expedition against Ch'en Chiung-ming (q.v.).

When the National Revolutionary Army was organized in August 1925, Ku Chu-t'ung was designated chief of staff of the 2nd Regiment in the 1st Division of the First Army, which was commanded by Ho Ying-ch'in (q.v.). After participating in the second eastern expedition

in October, Ku rose to become deputy commander of the 3rd Division of the First Army. During the Northern Expedition, Ku was promoted to commander of the 3rd Division after the capture of Foochow late in 1926 and to commander of the Ninth Army, comprising the 3rd, 14th, and 21st divisions, in October 1927. He was named to the Military Affairs Commission at the end of 1927.

In the military reorganization that followed the completion of the Northern Expedition in 1928, the Ninth Army was redesignated the 2nd Division and was stationed at Pengpu, with Ku still in command. He participated in the 1929 campaign against the Kwangsi forces in Hupeh and became commander of the First Army in October of that year. In 1930 he led his army in battle against the northern coalition forces of Feng Yü-hsiang and Yen Hsi-shan (qq.v.). From the end of May until September, he engaged in a hard-fought campaign on the Honan front. After the northern coalition collapsed in the autumn of 1930, he occupied Loyang and became director of Chiang Kai-shek's headquarters there. At the end of the year, he was made director of the T'ungkuan headquarters, with the mission of containing Feng Yü-hsiang's remnant forces in northwest China.

In July 1931 Ku was appointed commander of the National Government Guards Army at Nanking. This crack force was beginning to receive modern training from the officers of the German military advisory group in China, and Ku assumed his new duties enthusiastically. Before long, however, Ku was sent into the field again, this time to battle Shih Yu-shan in Hopei. He led the Second Group Army, which was composed of the Guards Army and other forces, into Hopei in July and easily quelled Shih's revolt.

At the Fourth National Congress of the Kuomintang, held in December 1931, Ku was elected to the Central Executive Committee. He held membership in this body until 1950. Also in December 1931, he was appointed governor of Kiangsu. He was removed from this post on 3 October 1933 after having caused the execution of several Chinese journalists. Three weeks later, he was appointed commander in chief of the northern route forces in the fifth so-called bandit suppression campaign against the Chinese Communists in Kiangsi. After the Communists broke through the Nationalist encirclement in October 1934 to begin their Long March to Shensi, Ku was named pacification commissioner of Kiangsi and deputy minister of war for political affairs in December.

In 1935 and 1936 Ku worked to increase National Government control of Kweichow, Szechwan, and Sikang. He was appointed pacification commissioner of Kweichow in April 1935. Under his supervision, the Kweichow military forces were transferred to other provinces and the provincial government was reorganized. He then carried out a similar reorganization in Szechwan, where he became director of the Chungking headquarters of the Military Affairs Commission in November. On 2 August 1936 he was given the concurrent post of governor of Kweichow.

During the Sian Incident of December 1936 (*see* Chiang Kai-shek) Ku went to Nanking to confer with Ho Ying-ch'in about launching an attack on Sian and prepared to serve under Ho as deputy commander of the so-called anti-rebel forces. The crisis ended with the release of Chiang Kai-shek on 25 December. In the northwest, however, the Manchurian forces and troops commanded by Yang Hu-ch'eng (q.v.) refused to support National Government policies. Accordingly, Ku Chu-t'ung was sent to the northwest in January 1937 as director of Chiang Kai-shek's Sian headquarters and commander in chief of five group armies. After holding unsuccessful negotiations with the dissidents at Loyang, Ku moved to T'ungkuan and ordered his troops to prepare for battle. On 29 January, Yang and the Manchurian commanders indicated their willingness to compromise. They agreed to troop reorganization, and Yang decided to take a trip abroad. Accordingly, Ku Chu-t'ung led his forces into Sian on 8 February 1937 and began the work of reorganizing the northwestern forces.

After the Sino-Japanese war began in July 1937, Ku was appointed commander in chief of the Ninth Group Army. He became deputy commander, under Chiang Kai-shek, of the Third War Area in August. Its headquarters, established at Soochow, was assigned responsibility for directing operations on the Woosung-Shanghai front. The Chinese managed to resist all attacks in that area until 5 November, when the Japanese outflanked them by making a successful landing in Hangchow bay. Three

weeks later, Ku was appointed governor of Kiangsu, a post he held until 1939. When the war area system was reorganized after the 12 December 1937 evacuation of Nanking, he was designated commanding officer of the Third War Area, then composed of southern Kiangsu, southern Anhwei, northeastern Kiangsi, Chekiang, and Fukien. He held this post throughout the remainder of the war. His problems in administering the area were complicated by the presence of the New Fourth Army, led by the Communists Yeh T'ing and Hsiang Ying (qq.v.). Friction between Nationalist and Communist units in the Third War Area finally resulted in the so-called New Fourth Army Incident. In January 1941 New Fourth Army units and Nationalist troops came into conflict at Maolin in southern Anhwei. The ensuing battle (6–14 January) ended in disaster for the Communists: Hsiang Ying was killed; Yeh T'ing was captured and imprisoned; and Communist military influence was virtually eliminated from the areas south of the Yangtze for the remainder of the war.

In the autumn of 1945 Ku Chu-t'ung accepted the surrender of Japanese forces in the Third War Area. When the war area administrations were abolished in January 1946, he became pacification commissioner at Hsuchow, with responsibility for Shantung, Kiangsu, Honan, and Anhwei. He assumed new duties on 18 May as commander in chief of the Chinese army. On 14 September, he assumed the concurrent post of pacification commissioner at Chengchow in an effort to strengthen Nationalist defenses against the operations of the Communist Liu Po-ch'eng (q.v.). Ku undertook a campaign against the Communists in Shantung in 1947 and succeeded in restoring much of the province to Nationalist control. In May 1948 he became chief of general staff in the ministry of national defense, serving under Ho Ying-ch'in. Although he worked hard to turn the tide of the civil war, the Communists continued to advance and Nationalist military positions continued to disintegrate.

When Nanking fell to the Communists on 22 April 1949, Ku flew to Shanghai and resumed the post of commander in chief of the Nationalist army. He went to Canton and continued to be active in military planning. On 14 October, he flew to Taipei to confer with Chiang Kai-shek. The Nationalists abandoned

Canton on 15 October and moved the remnant National Government to Chungking. After meeting with Chiang Kai-shek, Ku flew to Chungking to direct military operations in southwest China.

On 7 December 1949 the Executive Yuan of the National Government confirmed Ku's status as commanding officer in southwest China and designated Hu Tsung-nan as his deputy. At about the same time, Chang Ch'ün (q.v.) went to Kunming to try to dissuade Lu Han (q.v.), who controlled Yunnan, from declaring allegiance to the Communists. Ku Chu-t'ung took action against the forces of Liu Wen-hui (q.v.) in the immediate vicinity of Chengtu and provided a shield for the officials of the National Government as they prepared to depart for Taiwan. On 10 December, at Ku's urging, Chiang Kai-shek went to Taiwan. When Lu Han declared allegiance to the Communists on 11 December, Ku made an unsuccessful attempt to block his action. At this point, Ku was unable to provide any effective defense against the rapidly advancing Communist forces. On 25 December, he flew from Szechwan to Hainan Island. After making a brief trip to Taiwan, he flew to Yunnan on 13 January 1950 in a desperate but unsuccessful effort to rescue the remnants of the Nationalist Eighth and Twenty-sixth armies.

When Chiang Kai-shek resumed the presidency of the Republic of China in Taiwan on 1 March 1950, Ku Chu-t'ung became deputy director of the military strategy advisory committee in the presidential office. In July 1959 he was appointed secretary general of the National Defense Council. When that body was superseded by the National Security Council in January 1967, he became deputy secretary general of the new organ, serving under Huang Shao-ku (q.v.).

Ku Hung-ming 辜 鴻 銘
Orig. Ku T'ang-sheng 辜 湯 生
H.　Han-pin tu-i-che 漢 濱 讀 易 者

Ku Hung-ming (1857–30 April 1928), European-educated scholar and long-time subordinate of Chang Chih-tung who was known as a trenchant critic of the Westernization of China and a staunch defender of traditional Confucian values.

The ancestors of Ku Hung-ming had come from T'ungan, Fukien, near Amoy. However, his family had resided for generations before his birth in the state of Kedah in northern Malaya. Ku's great-grandfather, Ku Li-huan, had served in Kedah while that state was still under the rule of Siam. When the British extended their influence further into the Malay peninsula, Ku Li-huan moved from Kedah to Penang, where he was appointed by the British to a post in the local government. He died in 1862 leaving eight children, of whom the third son was Ku Ling-ch'ih, Ku Hung-ming's grandfather. Ku's father, also of Penang, was Ku Hsia-feng, who was the manager of a British-owned rubber plantation. Ku himself was born in Penang.

Little is known of Ku's early life. At about the age of ten, after his father's death, he was taken to Edinburgh by a Scottish friend of the family. He subsequently matriculated at the University of Edinburgh, from which he received the M.A. degree in April 1877. As preparation for the degree, he had studied and mastered the complete classical university curriculum of the time, including Latin, Greek, mathematics, metaphysics, moral philosophy, natural philosophy, rhetoric, and English literature. Before returning to Malaya, Ku studied in Leipzig, where he appears to have obtained a diploma in civil engineering, and lived for several months in Paris. About 1880 he returned to Penang.

Ku found employment in the government of the Straits Settlements. At this time, at the urging of a high official of the China Merchants Steam Navigation Company, Ku began to study classical Chinese and to wear a queue and Chinese clothes. In 1881–82 he served the British explorers Mahab and Colquhoun as an interpreter. He accompanied them on their journey from Canton to Mandalay, but abandoned them in Yunnan when their progress became difficult. Little is known of Ku's activities in the next two years, except that he went to live in Hong Kong.

In 1885 Ku met Yang Yü-shu, a subordinate of Chang Chih-tung (ECCP, I, 27–32). Chang, probably impressed by Yang's account of Ku's knowledge of Western affairs, made Ku a member of his personal staff. Ku remained an associate of Chang for 20 years, until 1905, during which time he never seems to have risen beyond the status of private secretary and adviser. He did much interpreting and translating, but his relations with Chang were never intimate. He was not admitted to Chang's inner circle of advisers until 1898, and he frequently complained that Chang never followed any of his suggestions. Chang considered Ku generally correct in principle, but lacking in common sense. However, certain of Chang Chih-tung's ideas about Europe and America probably were derived from Ku's thought. Among these are the notions, expressed in Chang's *Ch'üan-hsüeh-p'ien* [exhortation to study] of 1898, that the absence of a wealthy middle class in China vitiated the idea of popular legislative assemblies and that democracy was a bad thing. Both of these ideas had been vigorously developed by Ku in a letter to Chang in 1896.

While serving Chang, Ku had occasion to engage in a number of polemical disputes with resident European and American missionaries and businessmen through the medium of the treaty-port English-language press. In 1891, when anti-missionary riots were disturbing the Yangtze valley, Ku wrote an article attacking missionary enterprise entitled "Defensio populi ad populos," which was published in the *North China Daily News*. The article dispassionately analyzed the avowed objectives of missionary endeavor, which Ku defined as: "I. The moral elevation of the people, II. The intellectual enlightenment of the people, III. Works of charity." Ku observed that, far from attracting the "morally higher, better and nobler" Chinese, it was an open secret that "only the worst, the weak, the ignorant, the needy, and the vicious" were "what the missionaries call converted." He pointed out that for missionaries to pose as champions of the cause of science and enlightenment against the background of the religious persecutions of Europe was an hypocrisy which made "the educated Chinese intellectually despise the foreigner." He attacked missionary orphanages and hospitals as inefficient and concluded by appealing to the "common sense, the sense of justice among disinterested foreigners, to say whether the time is not come . . . to undertake, if not the entire withdrawal, at least some modification of the missionary enterprise in China." Ku's appeal to reason, which was summarized and commented on at length in the London *Times*, was answered during the subsequent months by numerous

letters to the editor, almost all of them expressing outrage and shock.

In 1900 Ku broadened his attack to include the eight anti-Boxer powers, whom he denounced as wanting in wisdom, morality, and justice in a series of articles in the Yokohama *Japan Mail*, which he published in 1901 as *Papers from a Viceroy's Yamen*. During the Boxer troubles Ku also had occasion to exercise his pen in defense of the empress dowager, Prince Tuan, and the Boxers themselves. In a poem of several stanzas called "Prince Tuan and His Brave, Braw, Bonnie Laddies," Ku wrote: "To the lords of convention 'twas Prince Tuan who spoke:/ E're the King's crown go down there are crowns to be broke;/ Then each Boxer lad who loves fighting and fun,/ Let him follow the bonnets of bonnie Prince Tuan/ . . . . Then away to the hills, to the lea, to the rocks,/ E're I own a usurper I'll crouch with the fox;/ And tremble, ye de'ils in the midst of your glee,/ Ye hae no seen the last of my bonnets and me." Another series of articles by Ku was carried in the *Japan Mail* in 1904 under the title "Et Nunc, Reges, Intellegite! The Moral Causes of the Russo-Japanese War." Ku attributed the Allies' mistakes in Asian policy to their attempts to substitute force for reason in dealing with Chinese and Japanese.

During this period, Ku also published translations of Chinese classics, including *The Discourses and Sayings of Confucius: A Special Translation, Illustrated with Quotations from Goethe and Other Writers*, published in 1898, and a translation of the *Chung-yung* [doctrine of the mean] entitled *The Conduct of Life*, which was published in 1906 after serialization in the *Japan Mail* two years earlier.

In 1905 Ku Hung-ming was appointed a secretary in the ministry of foreign affairs at Peking. Shortly afterwards, he was made director of the Huang-p'u-chiang chün-hsieh chü [Whangpoo conservancy board] in Shanghai, in which capacity he served until 1908. He exposed certain misappropriations connected with dredging work performed by Dutch contractors, and, during the subsequent scandal, he proved his charges and won high praise from Chou Fu, then governor general at Nanking. In 1908 Ku left Shanghai for service in Peking as an assistant department director in the ministry of foreign affairs. While serving in this capacity, Ku sent a long memorial to the throne urging extreme caution in modernization and stressing the need for fixed rules of government to guarantee governmental stability. In 1909 Chang Chih-tung died, and Ku received the degree of chin-shih by special decree. Ku then wrote *The Story of a Chinese Oxford Movement*, in which he compared Cardinal Newman's fight against "liberalism" in the Church of England with Chang's fight against "the intensely materialistic civilization of modern Europe" in China, regretting the failure of both movements and expressing the fear that immoral force would triumph in both China and Europe. The book was translated into German by Richard Wilhelm in 1911 as *Chinas Verteidigung gegen europäische Ideen: Kristische Aufsätze*. It made a deep impression on neo-Kantians at the University of Göttingen, where it became required reading in the faculty of philosophy. In 1910 Ku composed and published anonymously *Chang Wen-hsiang mu-fu chi-wen* [reminiscences of a secretary to Chang Chih-tung].

Ku resigned from office in 1910 and served the following year as principal of Nanyang College in Shanghai. During the revolution of 1911 he proclaimed his loyalty to the Manchu cause. After the emperor abdicated, Ku retired. He lived in Shanghai and then moved to Peking. He retained his queue and remained loyal to the Manchu cause. In 1914 an English translation of the *Chang Wen-hsiang mu-fu chi-wen* appeared in the *Journal of the North China Branch of the Royal Asiatic Society*, evidently written by Ku under the curious pseudonym Ardsheal. In 1915 Ku published *The Spirit of the Chinese People*, in which he defined the Chinese people as deep, broad, and simple, and possessed of a "Divine Duty of Loyalty," above all to the king, but also to the head of a family. He believed that the "Divine Duty" was perfectly expressed in the philosophy of Confucius, which he recommended to Europe, then in the throes of the First World War, as a cure for British "mob-worship" and German "might-worship" and as a substitute for Christianity, which, Ku averred, "has become ineffective as a moral force."

Ku played a role in the abortive restoration of July 1917 (*see* Chang Hsün), when he accepted an appointment as senior undersecretary of foreign affairs under Liang Tun-yen. The restoration lasted a scant two weeks, however, after which Ku returned to more pedestrian pursuits, including a stint of Latin teaching at Peking University.

In 1919 Ku wrote two articles for *Millard's Review of the Far East* denouncing the vernacular literature movement (*see* Ch'en Tu-hsiu; Hu Shih). His attitude was shared by Lin Shu and Yen Fu (qq.v.). He was particularly violent and bitter in his references to students just back from Europe and the United States who were, in his view, destroying overnight the world's oldest civilization. Ku also wrote weekly pieces for the *North China Standard*. In 1924 he went to Japan to deliver a series of lectures for the Daitō bunka kyōkai [eastern culture association]. In 1927 he returned to China to serve as an adviser to Chang Tso-lin (q.v.), and in 1928 he was nominated principal of Shantung University. He died at Peking on 30 April 1928.

About 1887 Ku married a Japanese girl, Yoshida Sadakō, a geisha then serving in a Canton teahouse. Ku was devoted to her, and she bore him several children before she died in 1905. He later remarried, and at his death he left his second wife and their three children in utter poverty. Word portraits of Ku appear in W. Somerset Maugham's *On a Chinese Screen* (1922), in which Ku figures in the story "The Philosopher," and in Francis Barrey's *Un sage chinois Kou Hong Ming; notes bibliographiques*. Maugham described Ku as "an old man, tall, with a thin grey queue, and bright large eyes under which there were heavy bags. His teeth were broken and discoloured. He was exceedingly thin, and his hands, fine and small, were withered and claw-like . . . . There was in him none of the repose of the sage. He was a polemicist and a fighter." In 1922 Lo Chen-yü (q.v.), a fellow Manchu loyalist, published a collection of Ku's literary works under the title *Tu'i ts'ao-t'ang wen-chi*.

Ku Meng-yü　　　顧 孟 餘
Orig. Ku Chao-hsiung　　顧 兆 熊

Ku Meng-yü (1889–), German-trained economist and professor at Peking University who joined the Kuomintang in the 1920's. He was a political associate of Wang Ching-wei until 1933. After 1949 he participated in the so-called third force movement in Hong Kong. He went to the United States in the mid-1950's, where he reentered academic life.

The son of Ku Chia-hsiang, a writer and artist, Ku Meng-yü was born in Wanp'ing, Chihli (Hopei). After receiving a traditional education in the Chinese classics, he studied at the Imperial University of Peking from 1903 to 1906, specializing in German language and literature. In 1906 he received a government grant for advanced study in Germany. He studied at the University of Leipzig from 1906 to 1908 and at Berlin University from 1908 to 1911.

After returning to Peking in 1911, Ku accepted an appointment as an assistant professor of economics at the university (which was renamed Peking University after the republic was established in 1912). He became a full professor in 1915 and chairman of the economics department in 1918. He was among the young intellectuals who contributed articles to the magazine *Hsin ch'ing-nien* [new youth] and who were prominent in the May Fourth Movement of 1919 (*see* Ch'en Tu-hsiu).

In 1924 Ku Meng-yü reportedly joined the Shih-ch'ien she, a Kuomintang affiliate in Peking. About 1925 he left Peking and went to Canton. At the Second National Congress of the Kuomintang, held in January 1926, he was elected to the Central Executive Committee by a vote of 222 to 34. He became identified with the faction of the Kuomintang led by Wang Ching-wei (q.v.), which supported the policy of collaboration with the Communists begun in 1924. After returning to Peking, he participated in the incident of 18 March (for details, *see* Feng Yü-hsiang). On 19 March, Tuan Ch'i-jui ordered the arrest of Ku Meng-yü, Hsü Ch'ien, Li Shih-tseng, and Yi P'ei-chi, charging that they had instigated the incident and had disseminated Communist propaganda. Ku and his associates were shielded from arrest by the Kuominchün commander of the Peking garrison, Lu Chung-lin. Ku and a party which included Eugene Ch'en and the Soviet adviser Borodin left Peking and went to Urga (Ulan Bator), arriving there on 3 April, traveling by way of Vladivostok.

In the spring of 1926 the left wing of the Kuomintang found itself without a leader, for Wang Ching-wei resigned his posts after the incident of 20 March, when Chiang Kai-shek declared martial law in Canton and arrested a number of Communists without consulting him. Soon afterwards, Wang left for Europe. Chiang Kai-shek then was able to move toward domination of the party and the government. On 15 May, the Central Executive Committee of the Kuomintang acted on Chiang's proposals to curtail Communist influence in the party. Mao Tse-tung, who had been acting head of the propaganda department, was replaced by Ku Meng-yü.

In July 1926 the Northern Expedition forces began to move northward, and by 10 October the Wuhan cities had been captured. A month later, the National Government was moved from Canton to Wuhan. Ku Meng-yü served on the joint council which was established to run the government until the main body of party and government leaders arrived in Wuhan to take control. Other members of the council were Hsü Ch'ien, Sun Fo, Eugene Ch'en, Teng Yen-ta, and the Communists Wu Yü-chang and Lin Po-ch'ü. A split in the Kuomintang was imminent, for Chiang Kai-shek and his right wing faction favored Nanchang, and later Nanking, as the seat of the government. When the Central Executive Committee met at Wuhan in March 1927, the left-wing faction dominated the proceedings. Chiang Kai-shek's authority was diminished by the establishment of a seven-man presidium of the Central Political Council and the revival of the Military Council. Ku Meng-yü was elected to both bodies and was confirmed as head of the propaganda department. In April, Wang Ching-wei returned from Europe to assume control of the Wuhan regime, and Chiang Kai-shek established a rival government at Nanking. Ku Meng-yü remained at Wuhan and supported Wang's decision of 15 July to break with the Communists in the interests of Kuomintang reunification.

On 29 August 1927, eight days after Chiang Kai-shek retired from office, Ku Meng-yü and other Wuhan leaders accompanied Wang Ching-wei to a conference with Li Tsung-jen (q.v.) at Lushan, Kiangsi. A result of this meeting was the 11 September conference, held in Shanghai, at which representatives from the various factions of the Kuomintang drew up an agreement for party unity. Four days later they created the Special Central Committee of the Kuomintang to function as an interim government. Ku Meng-yü, who shared Wang Ching-wei's objections to the composition of the committee, returned to Wuhan and joined with T'ang Sheng-chih (q.v.) in forming the Wuhan branch of the Political Council, which denounced the Special Central Committee as an illegal body. In late October, Li Tsung-jen led a punitive expedition against the Wuhan dissidents and forced Ku and T'ang to abandon Wuhan. Ku then went to Canton, where he worked with Ch'en Kung-po and Kan Nai-kuang (qq.v.) in making preparations for the 17 November coup of Chang Fa-k'uei (q.v.). After taking control of Canton, Chang declared opposition to the Special Central Committee. This effort soon collapsed, however, and Wang Ching-wei, having failed to undermine Nanking's authority, left for France on 17 December. His departure brought Ku Meng-yü's political career to a halt.

In the winter of 1928 Ku Meng-yü, Ch'en Kung-po, and other members of the Kuomintang left wing who were in Shanghai organized the Kuomintang kai-tsu t'ung-chih hui [society of comrades for Kuomintang reorganization], sometimes known as the Reorganizationist faction. In the spring of 1929 they established the *Min-hsin chou-k'an* [public opinion weekly], in which they exhorted the Kuomintang to return to the spirit of the 1924 reorganization. In response, the Kuomintang headquarters in Nanking decided to convene a third party congress from which most of the left-wing members would be excluded. On 12 March 1929 Ku Meng-yü joined Wang Ching-wei, who had returned to China, and 12 other prominent members of the party in issuing a manifesto which declared the meeting to be illegal. Three days later, the congress convened. Its members voted to removed Ku Meng-yü from the Central Executive Committee and to expel Ch'en Kung-po from the party. The Reorganizationist faction responded to this action by initiating a search for military allies who would join with it in attempting to overthrow the Nanking regime.

In the spring of 1930 Wang Ching-wei formed an anti-Chiang Kai-shek alliance with Feng Yü-hsiang and Yen Hsi-shan (qq.v.). Preparations were made for the so-called enlarged conference of the Kuomintang, which would include representatives of the Reorganizationist faction, the Yen-Feng coalition, the Western Hills faction, and other dissident groups. The conference, which began on 7 August at Peiping, established a national government, headed by Yen Hsi-shan, and a Kuomin-

tang organization, headed by Wang Ching-wei. Ku Meng-yü was appointed to direct the propaganda department of the new party organization. After the movement collapsed in September 1930, Ku Meng-yü disappeared from public view for more than a year.

After Wang Ching-wei became president of the Executive Yuan in January 1932, he appointed Ku Meng-yü to his cabinet as minister of railways. He held this post until August, when Wang and the entire cabinet resigned. The National Government refused Wang's resignation and granted him a leave of absence. As a result, most of the cabinet members withdrew their resignations, but Ku insisted on resigning.

Little is known about Ku Meng-yü's activities during the middle and late 1930's. After the Sino-Japanese war broke out, he moved to Chungking with the National Government. When Wang Ching-wei established a Japanese-sponsored regime at Nanking in 1939, Ku chose not to join him and remained in Chungking. From 1941 to 1943 he held the presidency of National Central University. However, he generally remained aloof from politics.

Civil war between the Chinese Communists and the Nationalists began soon after the victory over the Japanese. In May 1948 Ku Meng-yü rejected an offer to serve in the cabinet of Wong Wen-hao (q.v.) as vice president of the Executive Yuan. According to Ku, he refused the post because he believed that the cabinet's chief function would be to undertake peace negotiations with the Communists and that the undertaking would surely fail because of the intransigence of the Communists and the divided counsel among the Nationalist leaders. In 1949, when Chiang Kai-shek and his associates moved to Taiwan and the Chinese Communists took full control of the mainland, Ku went to Hong Kong. His past opposition to Chiang Kai-shek and his aloofness from wartime and postwar politics were deemed political assets by anti-Communist and anti-Chiang Kai-shek politicians and intellectuals in Hong Kong who tried to form the so-called third force movement. Ku Meng-yü and Chang Fa-k'uei reportedly became leaders in this attempt to give the Chinese people an option to choose neither the nationalism of Chiang Kai-shek nor the ideology of the Chinese Communists. The movement aroused some interest in 1950, but faded away when the United States came to the support of Chiang Kai-shek's government in Taiwan.

In the mid-1950's Ku Meng-yü went to the United States and established residence in Berkeley, California. Beginning in 1959, he was a consultant to an agricultural project and a language and cultural project on the People's Republic of China which was sponsored by the Center for Chinese Studies at the University of California. Thus, after many years of political involvement, much of which was distasteful to him, Ku Meng-yü returned to his chosen career as an academic.

Ku Wei-chün   顧 維 鈞
T.   Shao-ch'uan   少 川
West. V. K. Wellington Koo

Ku Wei-chün (1887–), known as V. K. Wellington Koo, distinguished diplomat who made significant contributions to the formation and early years of the League of Nations and the United Nations and who also represented China as ambassador to France, Great Britain, and the United States. From 1957 to 1967 he served on the International Court of Justice at The Hague.

Chiating, Kiangsu, was the birthplace of V. K. Wellington Koo. His father, a tax collector who owned property in Chiating and Soochow and a mansion in the International Settlement at Shanghai, reportedly named the boy Wellington, or Wei-chün, because of his admiration for the Duke of Wellington. After studying at Anglo-Chinese College (1899–1900) and the Yü Ts'ai School (1900–1) in Shanghai, he enrolled at St. John's University, where he completed the four-year course of study in three years and served as literary editor of the student paper *The Dragon*. After receiving B.A. and M.A. degrees from St. John's in 1904, Wellington Koo went to the United States with a group of Hupeh students led by Sao-ke Alfred Sze (Shih Chao-chi, q.v.). He spent a year at the Cook Academy in Ithaca, New York and matriculated at Columbia College in 1905. He became a member of the debating team and of several student societies and served as editor of the *Columbia Daily Spectator* and manager of the *Columbian*, the yearbook. He won the Columbia Philolescean Literary Prize and the Columbia-Cornell Debating Medal. He also served as president of the Chinese Students Alliance of the Eastern States. After graduation in 1908, he became a graduate student in political science at Columbia University. He received the M.A. degree in 1909 and the Ph.D. degree in 1912, and his dissertation was published in 1912 by the Columbia University Press as *The Status of Aliens in China*. During this period, Koo also served for a time as editor of the *Chinese Students' Monthly* and the *Chinese Students' Annual*.

Wellington Koo returned to China in April 1912, and became secretary of the cabinet and secretary in the presidential office. Soon afterwards, he married the eldest daughter of T'ang Shao-yi (q.v.). He became secretary to the ministry of foreign affairs in August, retaining his post in the presidential office, and vice chairman of the Commission for International Claims Resulting from the Revolution. In October 1912 Wellington Koo was promoted to the post of councillor in the ministry of foreign affairs.

In July 1915, at the age of 27, Wellington Koo was appointed Chinese minister to Mexico. His assignment was changed three months later, and he became minister to the United States and Cuba. His distinguished performances as a diplomat in the United States was recognized by Yale University in 1916 when it awarded him an honorary LL.D. degree. At the end of 1918, his wife having died in an influenza epidemic, he returned to China on leave. In January 1919, he went to France as a member of the Chinese delegation to the Paris Peace Conference. He played a prominent role in the delegation's handling of the Shantung question and in the decision not to sign the Treaty of Versailles because it provided for the transfer to Japan of Germany's treaty rights in Shantung. In September, Koo signed, on behalf of the Chinese government, peace treaties with Hungary and Bulgaria.

During this period, Wellington Koo also served as a delegate to the International Labor Conference, which produced the International Labor Organisation. In addition, he was elected one of five members representing "minor states" on the Paris Peace Conference's League of of Nations Commission, which devoloped the League Covenant, and the chief delegate from China to the first meeting of the League Assembly, which convened in November

1920. By that time, Koo had been appointed minister to the Court of St. James's.

On 14 November 1920, the day before the League Assembly convened at Geneva, Wellington Koo married Oei Hui-lan. Her father, Oei Tiong Ham, an overseas Chinese whose native place was Amoy, had become the "sugar-king" of Java. The newly wed couple's life in Geneva was a combination of diplomatic activity and glittering social events. Koo overcame formidable obstacles to have China elected a non-permanent member of the League Council. In so doing, he developed the principle of geographical representation that subsequently became an accepted policy for international organization. He served as China's first representative on the League Council, and in September 1921, when he again represented China at the Assembly and Council meeting, he became president of the Council for the fourteenth session.

In October 1921, Wellington Koo was made a member of the Chinese delegation, headed by Sao-ke Alfred Sze, to the Washington Conference. At the conference, Koo, as Sze's chief collaborator, presented China's "Ten Points" which included a definition of China, its territorial and administrative entity, and its right to participate in international conferences affecting its interests. The Nine-Power treaty signed in February 1922 and the settlement of the Shantung issue constituted an important diplomatic success for the Chinese delegation.

After the Washington Conference ended, Wellington Koo returned to China amidst rumors that he was to replace W. W. Yen (Yen Hui-ch'ing, q.v.) as minister of foreign affairs. Although frugal by nature, he and his wife moved into the Ch'en Yuan Yuan, a palace which the famous Ming general Wu San-kuei had built for his favorite concubine. At the urging of Oei Hui-lan, Oei Tiong Ham bought the palace for them. Koo was appointed head of a commission for the discussion of national financial questions in June and was named minister of foreign affairs in August when Wang Ch'ung-hui (q.v.) formed a new cabinet.

Wellington Koo's first task as foreign minister was to hold negotiations with the Soviet Union in an attempt to establish full diplomatic relations, settle the Chinese Eastern Railway question, and reach agreement on the political status of Outer Mongolia. On 2 September,

Adolf Joffe, the new Soviet representative, proposed that the Karakhan declarations of 1919 and 1920 be used as the basis of the discussions. Koo demanded that the Red Army forces in Outer Mongolia be withdrawn before negotiations began. Joffe objected to the then current administration of the Chinese Eastern Railway in disregard of Soviet treaty rights, and Koo replied that "the best solution of this problem would be the complete restoration of the railway to China." Soon after these exchanges took place, the Wang Ch'ung-hui cabinet fell, and Koo was forced to resign as foreign minister. Joffe went to Shanghai to meet with Sun Yat-sen, and Koo became chief of a commission to prepare for a special tariff conference which had been requested by China at both the Paris and the Washington conferences.

In March 1923 the Peking government gave C. T. Wang (Wang Cheng-t'ing, q.v.) responsibility for handling Sino-Soviet relations. After Huang Fu (q.v.) resigned in early April, Wellington Koo became acting foreign minister in Kao Ling-wei's cabinet. Ts'ao K'un (q.v.) and his supporters forced Li Yuan-hung (q.v.) to abdicate the presidency in June so that Ts'ao could assume office. Koo retained his post and worked to negotiate a settlement of the so-called Lincheng Incident, during which a number of Westerners had been kidnapped by train robbers in Shantung. After weeks of patient negotiation resulting in a compromise settlement of the issue, Koo turned his attention to negotiations with Soviet envoy Leo M. Karakhan. He soon assigned direct responsibility for these negotiations to C. T. Wang.

Beginning in January 1924, Wellington Koo served as minister of foreign affairs in the cabinet of Sun Pao-ch'i (q.v.). In March, C. T. Wang signed an agreement with Karakhan which provided for the immediate establishment of diplomatic relations but which contained no provisions for the cancellation of Soviet-Mongol treaties or the withdrawal of Red Army forces from Outer Mongolia. The cabinet refused to ratify the agreement, and Koo repudiated Wang's signature and dismissed him from office. On 31 May, however, Koo signed a similar agreement under strong Soviet pressure. He became acting premier in July, after Sun Pao-ch'i resigned, but he was forced to resign in October, when Feng Yü-hsiang (q.v.) staged a coup at Peking. Koo helped Ts'ao K'un and his family to escape to a foreign concession in Tientsin, surrendered his seal of office to C. T. Wang, and retreated to Weihaiwei. His wife remained in Peking at the foreign-run Hotel de Pekin. Later, on the advice of Chang Tso-lin and Chang Hsueh-liang (qq.v.), she went to a foreign concession in Tientsin, where Koo joined her. In their absence, Sun Yat-sen died in their Peking palace in March 1925.

After a year of political inactivity, during which he served as a trustee of the China Foundation for the Promotion of Education and Culture, Wellington Koo returned to Peking in May 1926 to become minister of finance in the cabinet of W. W. Yen. Chang Tso-lin, who had driven Feng Yü-hsiang's forces from Peking, opposed the appointment of Yen and forced the cabinet to flee Peking. A new cabinet was formed by Tu Hsi-k'uei in late June. Koo served as minister of finance until October, when he became acting premier and minister of foreign affairs. He attempted to resign three times in the next two months, but Chang Tso-lin refused his requests. After assuming the post of commander in chief of the Ankuochün [national pacification army] and moving to Peking in December 1926, Chang confirmed the appointments of Koo and his colleagues in the cabinet in January 1927. Chang's raid on the Soviet embassy in April created new problems for Koo, who resigned in June and retired to a villa in the Western Hills.

As the Northern Expedition forces approached Peking in June 1928, Chang Tso-lin and his entourage left the ancient capital. Wellington Koo went to Peking and accompanied his friend as far as Tientsin. The special train continued on to Manchuria only to be blown up near Mukden by the Japanese. Chang Tso-lin died in the explosion. Soon afterwards, the Nationalists at Peking issued an order for the arrest of Wellington Koo as a prominent supporter of Chang Tso-lin's regime. After taking refuge in Weihaiwei, Koo went to France and then went on a fishing trip in Canada.

Wellington Koo returned to China in 1929 and went to Mukden, where he was associated with Chang Hsueh-liang. After Chang caused the collapse of the northern coalition of Feng Yü-hsiang and Yen Hsi-shan (q.v.) that threatened Chiang Kai-shek's National Government in 1930, he prevailed on Chiang to rescind the order for Koo's arrest and to restore

his property to him. Koo remained in Mukden, where he constantly warned Chang Hsueh-liang that his foreign policy was aiding the Japanese and urged Chang to change it. Chang, however, did not heed Koo's counsel. In 1931 Koo became chairman of the reform commission for Manchuria and a member of the foreign affairs commission of the Kuomintang Central Political Council.

The occupation of Manchuria by the Japanese, beginning with the Mukden Incident of 18 September 1931, resulted in Wellington Koo's return to national politics and international diplomacy. C. T. Wang resigned as minister of foreign affairs; Sao-ke Alfred Sze refused the post; and Koo became officiating minister of foreign affairs in December. At the end of the year, Chiang Kai-shek was forced into temporary retirement, and Koo was replaced by Eugene Ch'en (q.v.). After serving as chairman of the commission for the recovery of the lost territory of the Northeast, Koo was attached to the Lytton Commission, which had been sent to Manchuria by the League of Nations to investigate the Sino-Japanese dispute, as China's assessor. He filled that role from February to August 1932, despite personal danger, and presented a lengthy memorandum on Japanese aggression to the commission. He was appointed minister to France that summer and China's delegate to the League of Nations in October. He sailed from Shanghai with the members of the Lytton Commission and went to Geneva, where he cogently argued China's case before the League Assembly. Both China and Japan rejected the Lytton Commission's recomendations, and Japan withdrew from the League of Nations in March 1933.

In March 1933 Wellington Koo served as the Chinese delegate to the Conference on Reduction and Limitation of Armaments at Geneva; in May he was the Chinese delegate to the World Monetary and Economic Conference at London; and in July he helped T. V. Soong (q.v.), the minister of finance, obtain technical cooperation from the League of Nations in such fields as public health in China. He served as China's representative on the League Council until mid-1934 and as a delegate to the League Assembly. In January 1934 he was appointed an assessor on the Permanent Court of Arbitration at The Hague. In 1935–36 he was China's chief delegate to the League Assembly. These and other assignments left him little time for his duties as minister to France.

Upon returning to Paris in April 1936 after spending several months in China on home leave, Wellington Koo was raised to the rank of ambassador to France. After the Sino-Japanese war began, he served once again as China's chief delegate to the League of Nations and presided over the ninety-sixth session of the League Council. In November 1937 he attended the Brussels Conference of the Washington Treaty powers, convened to consider the Sino-Japanese conflict, as China's chief representative. He continued to work on China's behalf at the League of Nations sessions of 1938 and 1939, but with little success. His ambassadorial duties presented many problems, especially when, under Japanese pressure, the French authorities refused his requests concerning the free transportation of arms on the Indo-China–Yunnan railway. He negotiated and signed a treaty of friendship with Liberia in December 1937, and he presented China's claim to the Paracel Islands when French forces occupied them in mid-1938. The following year, he took time off from his duties in France to serve as China's envoy to the coronation of Pope Pius XII.

The Koos were in Paris when the Second World War began. They soon moved to Bordeaux and then to Saint-Jean-de-Luz. Koo represented China at the eight-hundredth anniversary of the founding of Portugal in 1940. By the time he returned to Saint-Jean-de-Luz, it was under Nazi occupation. He spent a short time at Vichy before going to London to replace Quo Tai-chi (Kuo T'ai-ch'i, q.v.), who had been named minister of foreign affairs, as ambassador to the Court of St. James's. Because he feared for his wife's safety, he sent her to the United States. Koo helped effect and signed a Sino-British agreement regarding Chinese seamen in 1942; he was prominent in the negotiations which led to the exchange of parliamentary missions at the end of 1942 and in late 1943, the relinquishment of British extraterritorial rights in China in 1943, and the Sino-British Lend-Lease Agreements of May 1944. He was the chief Chinese delegate to the second phase of the Dumbarton Oaks Conversations, held from 29 September to 7 October 1944.

In March 1945 Wellington Koo was named to the Chinese delegation to the United Nations

Conference on International Organization at San Francisco. He represented China at the signing ceremony, held at the Veterans War Memorial Building in San Francisco on 26 June 1945, at which China was accorded the honor of being the first nation to sign the Charter of the United Nations. Subsequently, he served as the chief Chinese delegate to the United Nations Preparatory Commission.

Wellington Koo was transferred to Washington as Chinese ambassador to the United States in May 1946. He made strenuous efforts to secure American aid for the Nationalists during the civil war with the Chinese Communists. In addition to his ambassadorial duties, he served as chairman (1946) and then acting chairman (1947) of the Chinese delegation to the United Nations. In 1948 he played a prominent role in submitting the National Government's request for US$3 billion in American aid to be supplied over a three-year period. He also participated in the Nationalist effort of January 1949 to achieve a peace settlement with the Communists through American mediation, but this effort was completely unsuccessful. After the Communists won control of the mainland and the National Government moved to Taiwan, he continued his efforts to obtain American economic and military aid for the Nationalists. In 1954, after a trip to Taiwan for consultation with National Government officials, he accompanied George K. C. Yeh (Yeh Kung-ch'ao, q.v.), the minister of foreign affairs, to Washington and helped negotiate a Sino-American defense pact, which was signed on 2 December. In March 1956, after Koo had made another brief trip to Taipei, the National Government in Taiwan announced his resignation from the ambassadorship. Two months later, he was named senior adviser, residing in the United States, to Chiang Kai-shek.

In January 1957 Wellington Koo was elected to complete the term of Hsü Mo (q.v.), who had died on 28 June 1956, on the International Court of Justice. He assumed office at The Hague in mid-May, and he was reelected for a full ten-year term in October. He served as vice president of the court from 1964 until 1967. When his term expired on 5 February 1967, he returned to the United States to live in New York.

Wellington Koo and Oei Hui-lan were divorced after the Second World War, and Koo later married the widow of Clarence Kuangson Young. He had four children, two by his marriage to the daughter of T'ang Shao-yi and two, Wellington and Freeman, by his marriage to Oei Hui-lan.

In addition to *The Status of Aliens in China* and the Lytton Commission memorandum, Wellington Koo wrote a number of articles during his long diplomatic career. An analysis by Wunsz King of some aspects of Koo's pre-1931 career, *V. K. Wellington Koo's Foreign Policy*, was published in Shanghai in 1931. In October 1963 Koo presented his collection of diplomatic papers to Columbia University, including files of correspondence, telegrams, speeches, records of conversations with many world leaders and 35 dual-language diaries. He stipulated that the collection not be made available for use until his death and that copies of certain documents be deposited in the archives of the Academia Sinica in Taiwan. In announcing the receipt of the collection Grayson Kirk, the president of Columbia University, said that it "provides an accurate and detailed account of a career filled with significant assignments, executed in a truly effective and distinguished manner."

V. K. Wellington Koo's accomplishments in the field of international diplomacy won him many honors, including honorary degrees from such universities as Columbia, St. John's, Aberdeen, Birmingham, and Manchester. He made significant contributions to the formation and early years of the League of Nations and the United Nations, and he helped strengthen the international position of China, a particularly notable accomplishment in the pre-Nationalist era, when the power of the Peking government fluctuated greatly. He was known for his brilliance as a public speaker, and, although his methods and actions were criticized from time to time, even his enemies recognized that he was, above all, a patriot whose loyalty to China was unshakable.

Ku Ying-fen   古 應 芬
　T. Hsiang-ch'in   湘 芹

Ku Ying-fen (1873–28 October 1931), prominent T'ung-meng-hui revolutionary in Kwangtung who became minister of finance in Sun Yat-sen's military government, commissioner of finance of Kwangtung, and superintendent of

supplies at Canton. After the National Government was established, he held less important posts, and in 1931 he helped establish an opposition government at Canton.

Canton was the birthplace of Ku Ying-fen. His father, Ku Chieh-nan, was a merchant who had scholarly as well as commercial interests. The young Ku was encouraged to study the Chinese classics, and in 1902 he passed the examinations for the sheng-yuan degree. Two years later, he won a government scholarship for study in Japan. He went to Japan in the winter of 1904 and enrolled at Tokyo Law College. In July 1905 he participated in the organizational meeting of the T'ung-meng-hui. By the end of 1907 the Japanese authorities had forced the T'ung-meng-hui to suspend most of its activities. Ku then returned to south China with Chu Chih-hsin (q.v.) to promote anti-Manchu activities and to teach at the Kwangtung fa-cheng hsueh-t'ang [college of law and government]. Among his students were Ch'en Chiung-ming and Tsou Lu (qq.v.), who soon joined the T'ung-meng-hui. Ku's revolutionary activities escaped the notice of the Kwangtung authorities, who appointed him secretary to the provincial assembly.

Early in 1911 Ku Ying-fen went to Hong Kong to assist Huang Hsing and Hu Han-min (qq.v.) in planning an uprising at Canton. The uprising took place in April, but it was not a success. When the imperial authorities at Canton were overthrown on 9 November 1911, the republican revolutionaries elected Hu Han-min governor of Kwangtung, with Ku Ying-fen as secretary general of the military government. Ku became ch'iung-yai tupan [governor of Hainan island] in 1912. After the collapse of the so-called second revolution in 1913, he fled to Hong Kong. The following year, he returned to Kwangtung and worked with Chu Chih-hsin and Teng K'eng (q.v.) to induce the outlaw bands known as min-ping [militia men] to rise against Lung Chi-kuang (q.v.), the governor of Kwangtung. Ku also made three trips to Southeast Asia to raise funds in overseas Chinese communities for the campaign against Yuan Shih-k'ai. The campaign ended with Yuan's death in June 1916.

Beginning in November 1918, Ku Ying-fen served under Ch'en Chiung-ming at Changchow, Fukien. He participated in Ch'en's 1920 campaign to wrest control of Kwangtung from the Kwangsi militarists and served as commissioner of political affairs for Kwantung after Ch'en became governor of Kwangtung in November. By the middle of 1921 Ch'en Chiung-ming's personal ambitions had begun to conflict with Sun Yat-sen's plans to unify China. Ku attempted to curb Ch'en's efforts to impede Sun's northern campaign, but without success. After the assassination of Teng K'eng at Canton in March 1922, Ku resigned from Ch'en's staff and went to Shanghai. Ch'en Chiung-ming's forces took control of Canton in June. Acting on orders from Sun Yat-sen, Ku helped Teng Tse-ju (q.v.) and others to form an anti-Ch'en coalition. Troops from Yunnan and Kwangsi joined with Kwangtung forces which had remained loyal to Sun Yat-sen and drove Ch'en from Canton. In February 1923 Sun Yat-sen returned to Canton to reestablish his government.

On 24 February 1923 the Kwangsi commander Shen Hung-ying staged an attempt to assassinate a number of Kuomintang leaders at Canton. Ku Ying-fen immediately went to Chiangmen, where he established a command post and mobilized loyal Kwangtung Army forces. His decisive action prevented the Kwangsi forces from making any further attempts to take control of Canton and unified the Kuomintang military forces in Kwangtung. In August, Sun Yat-sen appointed Ku secretary general of the expeditionary headquarters for operations against Ch'en Chiung-ming, who was regrouping his forces in eastern Kwangtung. In November, Ch'en attacked Canton, but he was driven back to his stronghold in the East River Area.

On 23 September 1924 Sun Yat-sen appointed Ku Ying-fen minister of finance of the military government, commissioner of finance of Kwangtung province, and superintendent of military supplies at Canton. Ku's financial tasks were difficult and complex because a large part of Kwangtung was controlled by Yunnan, Hunan, and Kwangsi troops whose commanders appropriated the local tax revenues.

When the National Government was established at Canton in July 1925, Ku Ying-fen was elected to the Government Council, headed by Wang Ching-wei (q.v.). He also became commissioner of political affairs. The growing influence of the Communists, both Chinese and

Russian, within the Kuomintang distressed Ku, and when the Nationalist authorities at Canton sent him to Kiangsi in October 1926 to bolster the morale of the Northern Expedition forces, he met with Chiang Kai-shek to discuss the possibilities of ending the Kuomintang alliance with the Communists. In March 1927 he went to Shanghai, where he participated in the Central Supervisory Committee meeting of 2 April which led to a drive against the Communists by the conservative wing of the Kuomintang. When Chiang Kai-shek established a national government at Nanking in opposition to the left-Kuomintang government at Wuhan, Ku was made minister of finance and a member of the government's standing committee, headed by Hu Han-min (q.v.). To help finance the Northern Expedition, he issued government bonds, which had a face value of China $20 million. He also established criteria for the imposition of local and national taxes. When Chiang Kai-shek retired from office in August 1927, Ku resigned from his posts and went to Japan with Teng Tse-ju. On his return, he settled in Hong Kong. On 16 December, he and Teng were asked by the Nationalist authorities to investigate Wang Ching-wei's role in the Canton Commune (see Chang T'ai-lei). Despite their long-standing friendship with Wang, they submitted a report which was highly critical of him.

Ku Ying-fen was appointed wen-kuan-chang [chief of civilian officials] in the new National Government which was inaugurated at Nanking on 10 October 1928. His chief task was to act as a mediator in disagreements between party factions. He endured the frustrations of this job until December 1930, when he announced that he was going to Canton for back surgery and left Nanking.

On 28 February 1931 Ku's friend and longtime associate Hu Han-min was placed under house arrest by Chiang Kai-shek. Ku and three other members of the Central Supervisory Committee of the Kuomintang—Lin Sen, Hsiao Fo-ch'eng, and Teng Tse-ju—issued a statement in April which called for the impeachment of Chiang Kai-shek. In May, Ku joined such political leaders as Sun Fo, Eugene Ch'en, T'ang Shao-yi (qq.v.), and Wang Ching-wei in establishing an opposition government at Canton. Ku served on both the government council and the standing committee at Canton.

The Canton regime was dissolved after the Japanese attack on Mukden in September created a national emergency. Hu Han-min was released on 14 October, and delegates from Canton and Nanking met in Shanghai later that month for peace talks. Although Ku had been named to the Canton delegation, he was prevented from going to Shanghai by illness. He died at Canton on 28 October 1931.

Kuan Hsiang-ying   關 向 應

Kuan Hsiang-ying (1902-July 1946), Chinese Communist who became general secretary of the Communist Youth League in 1928. A close associate of Ho Lung, he served as Ho's political commissar at the Hunan-Hupeh soviet base (1932–33) and in the 120th Division of the Eighth Route Army (1937–40). Although in poor health after 1941, Kuan headed the Communists' Shansi-Suiyuan organization in 1942–45.

Born into a poor family in Manchuria, Kuan Hsiang-ying received only a few years of formal education before being apprenticed to a printer. After completing his apprenticeship, he went to Shanghai and worked in a printing shop. He soon began to participate in activities sponsored by the Socialist Youth League, which had been established in August 1920 under Comintern guidance. About 1922 he joined the league. In 1924 he was among those chosen by the league to study at the Communist University for Toilers of the East in Moscow. He joined the Moscow branch of the Chinese Communist party in 1925.

After returning to China in the summer of 1925, Kuan Hsiang-ying worked in the Communist party organization at Shanghai for a short time before being sent to Honan as secretary of the party's Honan provincial committee. When Jen Pi-shih (q.v.) succeeded Yün Tai-ying (q.v.) as general secretary of the Communist (formerly Socialist) Youth League in 1926, Kuan was recalled to Shanghai to succeed Jen as head of the league's organization department. In 1927 he helped organize a strike of Shanghai textile workers.

In 1928 Kuan Hsiang-ying succeeded Jen Pi-shih as general secretary of the Communist Youth League. At the Sixth National Congress of the Chinese Communist party, held at Moscow in the summer of 1928, he was elected to the Central Committee. After returning to China from the congress, he was assigned to work undercover in Shanghai. In 1930 he served on the military committee and the Yangtze bureau of the Central Committee, utilizing his early training to plan the printing and distributing of Communist propaganda. He also became secretary of the Shanghai Industrial Workers Association.

For reasons that are unclear, Kuan Hsiang-ying was arrested and imprisoned in 1931. It is known, however, that his Shanghai captors were not aware that he was an important Communist leader. Kuan spent about a year in jail, studying Chinese literature and cultivating a taste for T'ang poetry.

After his release from prison in 1932, Kuan went to the Hunan-Hupeh border district, where Ho Lung (q.v.) was establishing a soviet base, to serve as political commissar of Ho's Second Red Army. The two men became close friends and often were referred to as "Ho-Kuan." In 1933 Nationalist units forced Ho and Kuan to abandon their soviet area and make a circuitous retreat to the Hunan-Kweichow border. They joined forces with the Sixth Red Army, led by Hsiao K'o (q.v.), in October to form the Second Front Army, with Ho Lung as commander and Jen Pi-shih as political commissar. The Second Front Army established a base in the Szechwan-Hunan-Hupeh-Kweichow border area, but Nationalist units forced it to abandon the base and move northward in 1935. After joining the Fourth Front Army (see Chang Kuo-t'ao) at Kantzu in June 1936, it completed the Long March to northern Shensi in November.

When the Eighth Route Army was organized after the Sino-Japanese war began in 1937, Ho Lung received command of its 120th Division, with Kuan Hsiang-ying as political commissar. In the autumn of 1937 the 120th Division marched into northwestern Shansi and began to create a base area along the Shansi-Suiyuan border. In 1938 Ho and Kuan marched the division into central Hopei to assist Nieh Jung-chen (q.v.) and Lü Cheng-ts'ao in guerrilla operations. They returned to northwestern Shansi to assume command of the Shansi-Suiyuan military district in 1940.

In 1941 Kuan Hsiang-ying, who had contracted tuberculosis in the late 1930's, was
bedridden for a time. In 1942 he became
secretary of the Shansi-Suiyuan sub-bureau of
the Chinese Communist party. Although his
health did not improve, he continued to perform his party and Central Committee duties
for three years before being confined to bed at
Yenan in 1946. He died in July 1946, at the
age of 44.

Kuan Hsiang-ying devoted himself completely to the Chinese Communist cause, and
he never married. Next to Ho Lung, his closest
friend was Hsü Fan-t'ing, whose defection from
the Shansi forces of Chao Ch'eng-shou in 1937
had helped Ho Lung and Kuan Hsiang-ying
to establish a base in northwestern Shansi
quickly. Kuan is known to have composed a
number of verses. He reportedly was fond of
Sung poems, particularly those of Lu Yu.

K'uang Fu-cho   鄺 富 灼
  T.   Yao-hsi   耀 西
  West. Fong F. Sec

K'uang Fu-cho (1869–October 1938), known as
Fong Sec, chief editor of the English department
of the Commerical Press (1908–29), noted for
his English-language textbooks. He won almost
comparable distinction as a leader in Christian,
civic, and philanthropic activities in Shanghai.

Born into a peasant family in the Sunning
(Hsinning, later Toishan) district of Kwangtung,
Fong Sec began his primary education at the
age of eight in a village school. Four years
later he decided to join an uncle who had gone
to the United States to work on railroad construction crews. On his first trip to Shanghai
Fong Sec failed to secure passage, but the
following year he was successful. In 1882, at the
age of 13, he found himself a friendless immigrant
in San Francisco at a time when anti-Chinese
sentiment on the West Coast of the United
States was high. Exclusion laws barring Chinese
immigrants had been passed in 1881, but had
not been enforced.

Through his uncle's efforts, Fong went to
live with a family in Sacramento, California,
where he worked for his maintenance and
pocket money. He also studied English in a
Chinese night school. Fong soon was befriended
by Chin Toy, the pastor of a local Chinese
mission, who converted him to Christianity
and encouraged his interest in study and self-
improvement.

Fong Sec joined the Salvation Army in 1889,
at the age of 20. For the next seven years he
worked with the Salvation Army along the
length of the West Coast, attracting attention as
"a Chinese Christian speaking English." During the latter part of this period Fong, who had
learned shorthand in night school, served as
secretary to the chief officer of the Salvation
Army on the West Coast. This position gave
him a wide range of social contacts, rapidly
improved his English, strengthened his self-
assurance, and stirred his desire for further
education.

In 1897 Fong met young Edwin Hahn, a
student at Pomona College, to whom he
confided his desire for formal education. Hahn,
the son of a prominent Pasadena businessman,
introduced Fong to Cyrus G. Baldwin, then the
president of Pomona College, who arranged for
him to enter a preparatory academy and to earn
his way through school. (Fong named his first
son "Baldwin" in recognition of all that Cyrus
Baldwin had done for him.) After five years at
Pomona, during which he completed high
school and first-year college courses, Fong
transferred to the University of California for
three years of study, receiving his B.A. degree
in 1905. He then went to New York, where he
studied at Teachers College, Columbia University, and received an M.A. in 1906.

As Fong Sec prepared to return to China,
Liang Ch'eng, then the Chinese minister at
Washington, recommended him as a teacher to
the Kwangtung Provincial College at Canton.
On arriving in Canton, Fong joined the staff
of that college as professor of English in its
school of foreign languages. After teaching for
a year, he secured a government post at Peking
and served for a year in the ministry of communications. In 1908 he resigned his post and
moved to Shanghai. He soon was appointed
chief editor of the English department of the
Commercial Press, a post which he was to hold
for 21 years.

The Commercial Press had been established
in 1897 to meet the acute need for new textbooks
throughout China. Because of the rapid transition from the traditional Chinese educational
system to a modern curriculum incorporating

new fields of Western knowledge, Chinese schools at all levels required large numbers of textbooks on a wide variety of subjects. Most of the new texts were in Chinese (*see* Chang Yuan-chi). After a time, however, a significant number of English-language books were published because English had become a required second language for advanced students in modern schools.

The Commercial Press was distinguished among the larger Chinese business firms in Shanghai by the fact that its founders were Protestant Christians. Many of the staff had received technical training in publishing in the Presbyterian and Methodist mission presses in Shanghai. In addition, they had grasped the importance of efficient business management. Fong Sec's long tenure at the Commercial Press coincided with the period of most rapid expansion in textbook publishing in republican China and with the development of branches of the Commercial Press in many cities. In addition to writing on problems of modern education in China, he prepared many English textbooks himself and supervised the production of others. During most of this period, Fong Sec and Chou Yueh-jan of the Chung Hwa Book Company, the chief competitor of the Commercial Press, were the most prominent writers of English textbooks in China.

Fong Sec also became a respected member of the Shanghai business and social community. He was active in many Christian, civic, and philanthropic organizations. He served on the national committee of the YMCA in China for 30 years, first as a member of its executive committee and later (1919–25) as its chairman. During these years, the YMCA grew rapidly in membership and in the variety of its activities. Fong also served as chairman of the Shanghai YMCA for more than ten years.

An enthusiastic Rotarian, Fong Sec became a director of Rotary International and succeeded C. T. Wang (Wang Cheng-t'ing, q.v.) as governor of the district comprising China and Hong Kong. In 1922 he was a delegate to an international Rotary convention held at Los Angeles. While in the United States in 1922, he received an honorary LL.D. degree from Pomona College which had previously granted the degree to only two other men, the founder of the college and the president of the University of California. That summer, Fong Sec went to

New York and took courses at Teachers College "to keep abreast of modern educational movement."

Among the other civic and educational institutions in which Fong Sec was active and held positions of leadership were the China Christian Education Association, the Pan-Pacific Association, the Red Cross Society, the National Child Welfare Association, the Institute for the Chinese Blind, and the Chinese Mission to Lepers. He was a member of the boards of Shantung Christian University and the Nanyang Commerical Academy. He was also a member of the China Continuation Committee, later the National Christian Council, and an elder of the Cantonese Union Church in Shanghai. Fong Sec devoted much time and energy to the direction of these many private organizations. Following his retirement from the Commercial Press in 1929, he devoted all of his attention to these activities. He died in October 1938 at the Dah Wha Hospital in Shanghai.

K'ung, H. H.

Orig. K'ung Hsiang-hsi 孔 祥 熙
T.   Yung-chih   庸 之
H.   Tzu-yüan   子 淵

H. H. K'ung (1881–15 August 1967), banker and businessman who married Soong Ai-ling and who entered the service of the new National Government in 1928 as minister of industry and commerce. As minister of finance (1933–44) he was responsible for the currency reform of November 1935 and for the major financial programs undertaken by the National Government during the Sino-Japanese war. He was also known as a staunch Christian and as the founder of the Oberlin-Shansi Memorial Schools.

The Ch'üfu district of Shantung was the original home of the K'ung family, who were regarded as lineal descendants of Confucius. During the Wan-li period (1573–1620) of the Ming dynasty, the family moved to Shansi. In the late Ch'ing period, K'ung Hsun-ch'ang enjoined his heirs from accepting government service. His son, K'ung Ch'ing-lin (T. Jui-t'ang) laid the foundation of the family fortune by establishing and successfully managing remittance shops (p'iao-hao), centered at T'aiku,

Shansi. He came to have business correspondents in Peking, Canton, and Japan. His third son, K'ung Fan-tz'u, served as chief clerk of the remittance business at Peking and later returned to T'aiku to manage the family interests. Near the end of the Ch'ing dynasty, the domestic remittance business was gradually displaced by semi-modern banking institutions. Accordingly, the K'ung family obtained from the British Asiatic Petroleum Company its general agency for Shansi, established the Hsiang-chi Company, and handled shipments and sales of petroleum products, as well as candles, dye stuffs, and related imports.

H. H. K'ung, the son of K'ung Fan-tz'u, was born at T'aiku. His sister, Hsiang-chen, was born three years later. His mother, *née* Chia, who came from a prosperous Shansi family, died when he was only eight sui. K'ung attended a primary school in T'aiku which had been established by Dr. Charles Tenney, who had been sent by the American Board of Commissioners for Foreign Missions to begin missionary and educational work in Shansi in 1883. In addition to introducing K'ung to Christianity, to which he became a convert, the American Protestant teachers at the school taught him English and provided him with the rudiments of a Western education.

From 1896 to 1900 K'ung studied at another missionary institution, North China Union College, which was located at T'ungchow near Peking. At this time, demands for imperial government reforms were increasing steadily, and K'ung soon joined with a classmate, Li Chin-fan, in organizing a secret society, the Wen-yu hui, which supported the republican revolutionary efforts of Sun Yat-sen.

When the Boxer Uprising erupted in the summer of 1900, K'ung was at home in T'aiku on vacation. Yü-hsien, the governor of Shansi, executed 159 foreigners in Shansi, of whom 137 were Protestant missionaries or their children. K'ung used personal influence and family influence to shelter Western missionaries in the T'aiku area. His activities at T'aiku during that crisis later were recounted by the American missionary Luella S. Miner in *Two Heroes of Cathay*. K'ung then went to Peking, where Li Hung-chang (ECCP, I, 464–71) was negotiating with the Allied expeditionary forces that had occupied Peking. Through his friendship with Dr. H. E. Edwards, an English

missionary, K'ung helped secure the reduction of the Allied demands on his native province. In recognition of these services, Li provided K'ung with a passport and honorary titles so that he could leave China in 1901 to study in the United States. Li also gave him a letter of introduction to Wu T'ing-fang (q.v.), then the Chinese minister to Washington.

In the United States, H. H. K'ung worked to improve his English and then enrolled at Oberlin College in Ohio. In 1905 he met Sun Yat-sen, who was traveling through the United States, in Cleveland. After being graduated from Oberlin in 1906, K'ung went to Yale University, where he received an M.A. in economics in 1907.

Because Shansi lacked modern educational facilities and because K'ung was an advocate of American Christian education, he returned to T'aiku in 1908 as a representative of the Oberlin-Shansi Memorial Association and established the Ming-hsien School, which provided both primary and secondary education for students from north China. Although K'ung maintained an active interest in the family businesses, he devoted much of his attention to the affairs of the Ming-hsien School.

Although K'ung is known to have been a supporter of Sun Yat-sen's revolutionary cause before 1911, the extent of his participation in the revolutionary movement has not been determined. In 1911 his cousin K'ung Ping-chih was killed in the fighting in Shansi, and H. H. K'ung served for a time under Yen Hsi-shan (q.v.), who led the anti-Manchu uprising in Shansi. In 1913, after the republic had been established, he went to Japan to serve as secretary of the Chinese YMCA in Tokyo. Thus, he was in Japan when Sun Yat-sen and other Kuomintang leaders sought refuge there after the so-called second revolution of 1913 collapsed. At that time he met Soong Ai-ling (*see* article on Soong family), the eldest daughter of Charles Jones Soong. She had accompanied Sun Yat-sen to Tokyo and was serving as his English secretary. K'ung, whose first wife, North China Women's College graduate Han Shu-mei, had died of tuberculosis, married Soong Ai-ling in 1914.

The death of Yuan Shih-k'ai in 1916 brought the period of Kuomintang exile to an end. H. H. K'ung and his wife went to his family home in Shansi, where they remained until

1918, when they embarked on a trip to England, France, and the United States. Early in 1919 they went to Ohio, where K'ung made formal arrangements for cooperation between Oberlin College and the Ming-hsien School. American graduates of Oberlin volunteered to teach at Ming-hsien, or Oberlin-in-China, and outstanding Ming-hsien graduates were selected for study in the United States.

H. H. K'ung returned to Shansi in 1919. He continued to divide his time between the prospering family business and the Ming-hsien School until 1922. As a result of the Washington Conference of 1921–22 and attendant Sino-Japanese negotiations, Japan agreed to return its interests in Shantung to China. The Peking government gave C. T. Wang (Wang Cheng-t'ing, q.v.) responsibility for the transfer of authority in Shantung and named H. H. K'ung as his deputy. In 1923–24 K'ung's brother-in-law, Sun Yat-sen, who had married Soong Ch'ing-ling (q.v.) in 1914, enlisted K'ung's help in his efforts to reorganize the Kuomintang and to achieve national unification. K'ung served as a channel of communication with such north China leaders as Chang Tso-lin, Feng Yü-hsiang (qq.v.), and Yen Hsi-shan. K'ung presented Feng with a calligraphic copy of Sun's *Chien-kuo ta-kang* [outline of national reconstruction], and Feng recorded his favorable impressions of that work in his diary. K'ung went to Canton in 1924 and joined the newly organized Kuomintang. He accompanied Sun to Peking in 1925, served as a witness to his political will, and remained in Peking after Sun's death in March to make arrangements for the private funeral. He went to Shansi to attend the commencement exercises of Ming-hsien, or the Oberlin Shansi Memorial Schools, and then embarked on a journey to the United States, where he received an honorary LL.D. degree from Oberlin College.

During the period of the Northern Expedition, H. H. K'ung became associated with Chiang Kai-shek and his rise to political prominence. After serving as director of the Kwangtung provincial finance bureau and as acting minister of finance in the National Government at Canton and Wuhan, he joined Chiang Kai-shek's opposition government at Nanking in the spring of 1927. He played an important role in inducing Feng Yü-hsiang to come to

Chiang's support in June and in smoothing the way for Chiang's marriage to Soong Mei-ling (q.v.) in December. Soong Ai-ling advocated the union; Soong Ch'ing-ling opposed it; and their mother finally gave her consent to the marriage on the condition that Chiang Kai-shek investigate Christianity.

When the new National Government was inaugurated at Nanking in 1928, H. H. K'ung became minister of industry and commerce. In accordance with Sun Yat-sen's Principle of the People's Livelihood, he introduced labor arbitration and insurance systems, established a bureau of trade, and appointed commercial attachés to serve in Chinese missions abroad. He was elected to the Central Executive Committee of the Kuomintang in 1929. K'ung continued to hold office after the ministry of industry and commerce was merged with the ministry of agriculture and mining in 1931 to form the ministry of industries. However, when Chiang Kai-shek temporarily retired from office in the winter of 1931 to conciliate dissident Kuomintang leaders, K'ung, as Chiang's close associate and brother-in-law, resigned from office.

In April 1932 H. H. K'ung was appointed special commissioner to study European industrial conditions. One of his most important assignments was to secure foreign aid for the development of an adequate national defense system in China. K'ung went to Italy, where Mussolini agreed to sell planes and send technicians to China to strengthen the Chinese air force. These negotiations also resulted in the establishing of the Central Aviation Academy at Hangchow and an aircraft factory at Nanchang. K'ung's mission then took him to Germany and Czechoslovakia, where he made arrangements for procuring arms and engaging military advisers, and to England, where he met with financial experts to discuss economic reform measures for China.

After returning to China in April 1933, H. H. K'ung was appointed governor of the Bank of China. In October, he became minister of finance and, for a brief interlude, vice president of the Executive Yuan, serving under Wang Ching-wei (q.v.). He thus succeeded his brother-in-law T. V. Soong (q.v.) in the top financial post of the National Government, which Soong had occupied almost continuously since 1926. Almost immediately, K'ung began work on a comprehensive program designed to increase the National Government's financial control of the modern sector of the economy.

H. H. K'ung began by holding a national financial conference at Nanking in 1934 to deal with the problems created by the more than 7,000 varieties of local taxes then extant in China. As a result of that conference and of action taking during the next three years, 25 provinces had abolished local taxes by the time the Sino-Japanese war began in 1937. K'ung also increased the ratio of government-owned shares in the principal semi-governmental banks. In March 1935 increases in the capital of the Central Bank of China (from CN$20 million to CN$100 million), the Bank of China (from CN$20 million to CN$40 million), and the Bank of Communications (from CN$12 million to CN$20 million) were made. The increase of government shares in these banks was designed to bolster the capacity of the treasury to float bond issues and make loans and to increase government control of credit. K'ung's action was criticized by private bankers associated with the Bank of China and the Bank of Communications, for their institutions antedated the National Government, and they prided themselves on their reputations for fiscal responsibility and independence of judgment.

These and other measures paved the way for the monetary reform of November 1935, when the National Government abandoned the silver standard in favor of a managed paper currency. That reform required the nationalization of silver, the withdrawal of silver dollars from circulation, and the creation of a foreign exchange reserve for the Chinese currency. The reform had been precipitated by the American silver-buying program, the National Government's defense requirements, and the need for a standard legal tender in China. The American program had increased China's depression problems and had resulted in widespread smuggling of silver to foreign countries. The National Government had enacted a silver-export tax and an equilibrium tax, but they had not been effective. Furthermore, China still lacked a standard legal tender. Although some progress had been made in that direction, a wide variety of provincial or regional currencies were still in use, particularly in the northwestern and southwestern provinces. The new system of paper currency, called fapi, was introduced on

3 November 1935. Holders of silver dollars were required to exchange them for the new currency. The notes of the four government banks—the Central Bank of China, the Bank of China, the Bank of Communications, and the Farmers Bank of China—were declared legal tender for payment of taxes. The Central Bank became a central reserve bank, with responsibility for preserving the stability of the national currency system and foreign exchange. The foreign exchange rate of the Chinese dollar was fixed at CN$100 to US$33. The currency reform, although its long-term effects have been a subject of much debate, strengthened the economic position of the National Government and enabled China to survive the early stages of the Sino-Japanese war without a serious inflation and to build a national banking system that was independent of foreign powers. However, the success of the reform depended largely on the ability of China to convert its silver stocks into foreign exchange by selling silver to the United States. In 1936 the Chinese Silver Mission, headed by K. P. Ch'en (Ch'en Kuang-fu, q.v.) successfully negotiated the purchase of 75,000,000 ounces of silver by the United States. H. H. K'ung also helped increase confidence in the new currency by ordering his own Hsiang-chi Company to convert its deposits with the Asiatic Petroleum Company, amounting to some £25 thousand, into fapi at the official exchange rate.

In December 1935 Chiang Kai-shek succeeded Wang Ching-wei, who had been wounded in an assassination attempt, as president of the Executive Yuan. H. H. K'ung continued to serve in the cabinet, and during the Sian Incident of December 1936 (see Chiang Kai-shek) he assumed political authority at Nanking by order of the Central Political Council. Ho Ying-ch'in (q.v.), who had been assigned responsibility for military affairs during the crisis, advocated attacking Sian, but K'ung and his associates persuaded him that this course of action would endanger Chiang Kai-shek's life. The ensuing negotiations at Sian resulted in Chiang's release on 25 December and in the formation of a Kuomintang-Communist united front against the Japanese.

In April 1937 H. H. K'ung was sent abroad as a special envoy of the National Government. His stated mission was to represent China at the coronation of King George VI, but the chief purpose of his journey was the procurement of war matériel and financial aid in Europe and the United States. K'ung's chief secretary on this mission was Wong Wen-hao (q.v.), then secretary general of the National Defense Advisory Council. After arriving in England, K'ung held conferences with British officials and attended the coronation on 12 May. He made a brief trip to France, Belgium, and Germany before going to the United States, where he discussed China's financial requirements with President Franklin D. Roosevelt and Secretary of State Cordell Hull. He also received an honorary degree from Yale University in recognition of his achievements in education and finance.

H. H. K'ung returned to Europe soon after the Sino-Japanese war began in July 1937. He was aided in his renewed attempts to obtain armaments by Yü Ta-wei (q.v.), the director of the Chinese army ordnance bureau. K'ung remained in Europe, spending most of his time in Germany and Italy, until October. Germany, which had sent a number of officers to China to train Chiang Kai-shek's troops in the early 1930's, continued to maintain a military advisory group in China until 1938, despite the fact that the German government had signed the Anti-Comintern pact of November 1936 and thus was an ally of Japan.

After returning to China, K'ung instituted a series of emergency financial controls. He limited withdrawals of private bank deposits to curb the flight of capital. To support government economic progress a special loan committee was established under the Joint Administration of the four government banks and three adjustment committees were created for agricultural products, industries and mining, and foreign trade. The industrial and mining committee was responsible for the removal of factories from the coastal cities to the interior, and the foreign trade committee supervised essential exports of tung oil, bristles, tea, silk, and other natural products.

When Chiang Kai-shek resigned the presidency of the Executive Yuan in 1938 so that he could devote all of his time to military affairs, H. H. K'ung succeeded him. The cabinet came to include Chang Kia-ngau (Chang Chia-ao, q.v.) as minister of communications, Wong Wen-hao as minister of economic affairs, and Ch'en Li-fu (q.v.) as minister of education.

Among other things, the Sino-Japanese war stimulated the development of an industrial cooperatives movement in China. The idea, first developed in conversations in Shanghai in the spring of 1938, attracted the attention of the British ambassador to China, Sir Archibald Clark-Kerr, who made a personal appeal to Madame Chiang Kai-shek. On the strength of the ambassador's interest, H. H. K'ung allocated CN$5 million to the cooperative movement. The Chinese Industrial Cooperative Association was established at Hankow on 5 August 1938, with K'ung as chairman of the board of directors. During the next year, the movement spread rapidly in the provinces of northwest China. The personal interest and prestige of Madame Chiang and H. H. K'ung were especially helpful during the initial stage of the cooperative movement, which continued to expand during the war years.

Although Chiang Kai-shek formally resumed office as president of the Executive Yuan on 11 December 1939, H. H. K'ung, who resumed the vice presidency, continued to serve as his surrogate until the autumn of 1944. During this period, he also served as president of the Chinese-American Institute of Cultural Relations, of which Ch'en Li-fu (q.v.) was the vice president. At the same time, as minister of finance, he bore the responsibility for foreign-exchange control and for securing credits from Western governments to support the war effort. Such financiers as T. V. Soong and K. P. Ch'en also played important roles in directing China's financial programs. In February 1939 the United States agreed to grant China a loan of US$ 25 million, to be secured by shipments of tung oil. A second agreement, concluded in April 1940, provided for an American credit of US$20 million against tin exports from Yunnan, and a third granted US$25 million against tungsten shipments. Also in April 1940 the United States government and the British government granted credits of US$50 million and £5 million, respectively, to the Central Bank of China. These and other funds subscribed by Chinese banks were administered by an American-British-Chinese currency stabilization board, with K. P. Ch'en as its chairman. In February 1942, as a result of negotiations initiated by H. H. K'ung, the United States, which had entered the war against Japan, granted China a loan of US$500 million; in

July, a British loan of £50 million was secured. A portion of the American loan was used to purchase gold bullion in the United States in an attempt to support the fapi.

A celebration in honor of H. H. K'ung's tenth anniversary as minister of finance was held at Chungking on 1 November 1943. This event received international attention, for no other National Government official had held a cabinet-level office for so long a period as had K'ung. More than 500 government officials and friends took part in the ceremonies, and laudatory messages came from Chiang Kai-shek, who had recently become Chairman of the National Government, and from such eminent Westerners as United States Secretary of War Henry L. Stimson. Such leading Chinese newspapers as the *Ta Kung Pao*, which often had critized K'ung's policies and actions, praised his achievements.

In June 1944 H. H. K'ung went to the United States as head of the Chinese delegation to the United Nations Monetary and Financial Conference at Bretton Woods, New Hampshire. Chi Ch'ao-ting (q.v.) accompanied him as his personal assistant and secretary general of the Chinese delegation to the Bretton Woods Conference. As the personal representative of Chiang Kai-shek, K'ung met three times with President Roosevelt in Washington.

When the Executive Yuan was reorganized in May 1945, T. V. Soong, who had become its acting president in November 1944, was named president of the yuan and minister of finance. H. H. K'ung retired from political life in June and, at war's end, went to live in Shanghai. In the spring of 1947 he made a trip to north China, where he visited the Oberlin Shansi Memorial Schools. Its staff had returned to T'aiku after having spent the war years at Chint'ang, Szechwan. Early in 1948, before the civil war between the Nationalists and the Chinese Communists reached a critical stage, he and his wife moved to the United States because she was ill. K'ung went to Taiwan for a brief visit in 1962. He later went to Taiwan for a longer stay, but returned to the United States in December 1966 and established residence in Locust Valley, Long Island, New York. He died on 15 August 1967.

H. H. K'ung and his wife had four children. Rosamonde (Ling-i) was born in T'aiku; David (Ling-k'an), Jeannette (Ling-wei), and Louis (Ling-chieh) were born in Shanghai. David L. K. K'ung later served as director of the Central Trust of China, a wartime purchasing agency. In 1948 his cousin Chiang Ching-kuo (q.v.), then deputy economic control supervisor for the Shanghai area, ordered his arrest, but Madame Chiang Kai-shek intervened and sent David to Hong Kong. Louis K'ung served as secretary general of his aunt's official party during her trip to the United States in 1943.

Throughout his public career, H. H. K'ung was a controversial figure. His personal wealth alone was sufficient to make his political position a matter for national and international debate. Such Chinese Communist spokesmen as Ch'en Po-ta (q.v.) were particularly outspoken in condemning K'ung and his relationships with the Soongs and Chiang Kai-shek, and, indeed, there was general agreement that his public eminence was largely the result of these relationships. Economists argued about whether the monetary reform of November 1935 had saved the Chinese economy or had caused the postwar hyperinflation that ruined it. However controversial K'ung's financial and political activities may have been, his educational activities, which received less public attention, were acknowledged to be a reflection of his concern with modern education as an instrument of social progress. K'ung was a staunch Christian, a one-time YMCA secretary, and a friend and supporter of many Protestant missionaries in China. For many years, he helped finance and maintained close contact with the school he had founded at T'aiku. He also had a sustained interest in the affairs of Yenching University, the successor of North China Union College. He was chairman of its board of managers for many years and became its chancellor on 17 June 1937. Because of the burden imposed on K'ung by the Sino-Japanese war, J. Leighton Stuart, the president of Yenching, assumed the duties of the chancellorship. After the university was forced to close, K'ung presided over a meeting of members and former members of the Yenching board on 8 February 1942 at which it was decided to re-open Yenching at Chengtu, Szechwan. Y. P. Mei (Mei Yi-pao, q.v.) served as acting chancellor and acting president at Chengtu. After the university reopened at Peiping in 1946, K'ung continued to head its board of managers until 1949.

A laudatory biography by Yu Liang, *K'ung Hsiang-hsi*, was published in Hong Kong in 1955. An English-language version of this work was published in the United States by the Alumni Club of Oberlin Shansi Memorial College in 1957. Arthur N. Young's *China and the Helping Hand 1937–1945*, published in 1963, contains more professional information about K'ung as wartime minister of finance.

K'ung Te-ch'eng   孔 德 成
T. Ta-sheng   達 生

K'ung Te-ch'eng (22 February 1920–), the seventy-seventh lineal descendant of Confucius. A scholar, he held office in the National Government as officer in charge of making sacrifices to Confucius. In Taiwan, he directed the Joint Administration of the National Palace and Central Museums in 1950–63.

The seventy-seventh lineal descendant of Confucius, K'ung Te-ch'eng, was born in Ch'üfu, Shantung, three months after the death of his father, K'ung Ling-i (1872–1919). At his death, K'ung Ling-i had two daughters, but he had no son to inherit the title of Yen-sheng kung [holy duke]. The fate of the 900-year-old title depended on the sex of the child that Ku's wife, *née* Wang, was carrying. Hsü Shih-ch'ang, who held the presidency at Peking, sent Ch'ü Ying-kuang, the governor of Shantung, to Ch'üfu to supervise the birth. K'ung Te-ch'eng's arrival was greeted by a city-wide celebration. Because his mother died 17 days after his birth, he was raised by his father's secondary wife, *née* T'ao. In accordance with tradition, the young Yen-sheng kung received his education from private tutors. His first tutor, Wang Tzu-ying, assumed responsibility for K'ung's upbringing after his stepmother died in 1929. K'ung later received instruction from Lü Chin-shou. Because his education was confined to the study of the Chinese classics, K'ung was unaware of and unaffected by the many literary, cultural, and political upheavals that took place in China during his childhood.

In March 1934 Chiang Kai-shek launched the New Life Movement, which emphasized moral reform through a return to traditional Chinese virtues. On 31 May, the standing committee of the Kuomintang's Central Executive Committee designated 28 September as the official birthday anniversary of Confucius, and the National Government sent Yeh Ch'u-ts'ang (q.v.) to Ch'üfu to offer sacrifices during the nation-wide observances. Respect for Confucius was demonstrated once again in September, when the Central Executive Committee adopted the section on universal justice in the *Li-yün* chapter of the *Li-chi* [book of rites] as the official song dedicated to the memory of Confucius. K'ung Te-ch'eng's life was directly affected by this Confucian revival in the spring of 1935, when the National Government decided to abolish his hereditary title and create the new rank and position of officer in charge of making sacrifices to Confucius, the Great Sage. On 8 July, K'ung, then only 15 sui, assumed his new post at Nanking.

After the Sino-Japanese war began in 1937, K'ung Te-ch'eng moved with the National Government to the wartime capital of Chungking, where he was appointed to the People's Political Council in 1938. K'ung was exposed to modern scholarship at Chungking, and he devoted most of his time to study and to discussion with other scholars. He became a devout Buddhist and rejected the idea that Confucianism is a religion. In May 1946, the war having ended, he followed the National Government back to Nanking and then went home to Ch'üfu. In 1948 he went to the United States on a National Government scholarship and spent a year in New Haven as an honorary research fellow of Yale University. After returning to China in March 1949 he gave anti-Communist lectures in Canton, Hong Kong, and Macao, urging the Chinese people to revive the traditional Confucian spirit of morality. He gave these lectures at the behest of Han (Hang) Li-wu, the minister of education.

K'ung Te-ch'eng moved to Taiwan in 1950, where he taught at National Taiwan University, Taiwan Provincial Normal University, and Taiwan Provincial Chunghsiu University and served as director of the Joint Administration of the National Palace and Central Museums. He published *Li-chi shih-i* [interpretations of *Li-chi*] and did research on bronze inscriptions of the Shang and Chou dynasties. He also continued to serve in his official capacity as officer in charge of making sacrifices to Confucius. In 1957 he gave a series of lectures in Japan under the sponsorship of the Morality and

Science Research Institute of Japan. He was received by the Japanese people with great respect and was made an honorary citizen of Tokyo. The following year, he traveled to South Viet Nam at the invitation of the Vietnamese Confucian Society and lectured in Saigon and other cities. He and President Ngo Dinh Diem discussed the idea of reviving Confucian ethics to strengthen anti-Communist spirit. K'ung received an honorary degree from a university in Seoul, South Korea, in 1959. He lectured in Seoul and met with President Syngmann Rhee. In 1961 and 1962 ancient Chinese art objects from the collections under K'ung's care were exhibited in Washington, New York, Chicago, and San Francisco. He resigned from the Joint Administration of the National Palace and Central Museums in 1963, but the ministry of education did not accept his resignation until 1964.

K'ung Te-ch'eng married a great-granddaughter of the prominent Ch'ing scholar-official Sun Chia-nai (ECCP, II, 673–75) in 1935. They had two daughters, Wei-o (1935–) and Wei-lai (1941–), and two sons, Wei-yi (1939–) and Wei-ning (1947–).

Kuo Hua-jo   郭 化 若

Kuo Hua-jo (1907–), Chinese Communist military commentator, political officer, and military historian known for his studies of the *Sun-tzu ping-fa* [Sun-tzu on the art of war].

Little is known about Kuo Hua-jo's background or early years except that he was a native of Fukien and a graduate of the Whampoa Military Academy. He reportedly joined the Chinese Communist party at the time of the Kuomintang-Communist schism in 1927 and was a staff officer in the headquarters of the Red Army in Kiangsi in 1931.

Kuo Hua-jo first attracted notice as a military commentator during the Sino-Japanese war. He published an article on tactics in the 11 January 1938 issue of *Chieh-fang* [liberation] at Yenan. On 7 July, the Society for the Study of the Anti-Japanese War at Yenan published *K'ang-Jih yu-chi chan-cheng ti i-pan wen-t'i* [on all the problems of the anti-Japanese guerrilla war]. In addition to Mao Tse-tung's "Questions of Strategy in the Anti-Japanese Guerrilla

War," the book contained six chapters that were written jointly by Kuo Hua-jo, Ch'en Ch'ang-hao, Hsiao Ching-kuang, and Liu Ya-lou. Later in 1938, Kuo went to the Shansi-Chahar-Hopei (Chin-ch'a-chi) base area, which had been established by Nieh Jung-chen (q.v.). Kuo's "Experiences and Lessons of the Ch'in-ch'a-chi Border Region in Smashing the Japanese Bandit Large-scale Encirclement Attack" appeared in the 25 December 1938 issue of *Chieh-fang*. He also wrote articles for the *Chün-cheng tsa-chih* [military-political magazine] of the Communist Eighth Route Army.

Information about Kuo's career as a Communist political officer during the decade after 1938 is sparse. He reportedly served under Ch'en Yi (1901–; q.v.) in the New Fourth Army, and he was identified as the political commissar of an army group in accounts of the Communist campaign that culminated in the capture of Shanghai in the spring of 1949. He served on the Shanghai Military Control Commission and became political commissar of the Woosung-Shanghai garrison headquarters in May and commander of the Woosung-Shanghai garrison area in October.

After the Central People's Government was established, Kuo served until 1953 as a member of the East China Military and Administrative Commission, the regional authority for the important coastal provinces of east China. He published *Chün-shih pien-cheng fa* [military dialectics] in 1950 and wrote an article for the *Jen-min jih-pao* [people's daily] of 3 June 1953 on the occasion of the fifteenth anniversay of Mao Tse-tung's "On the Protracted War," a series of lectures which Mao had delivered between 26 May and 3 June 1938 before the Society for the Study of the Anti-Japanese War and had published in *Chieh-fang* in July 1938.

In 1955 Kuo was appointed to the Shanghai Municipal People's Council and was given the rank of lieutenant general of the People's Liberation Army. Two years later, he became a deputy commander of the Nanking military district, which included the provinces of Kiangsu, Chekiang, and Anhwei, and a member of the National Defense Council. He served as a delegate to the Chinese People's Political Consultative Conference, and in April 1959 he was elected to the National Committee and the Standing Committee of that body. He was reelected to those committees in December 1964.

Kuo Hua-jo is best known for his work on the venerable Chinese military text *Sun-tzu ping-fa* [Sun-tzu on the art of war]. The Chinese Communists began to take great interest in the maxims of Sun Tzu (fl. 500 B.C.) in the 1930's, and Mao Tse-tung became an admirer of his thought. Kuo was the author of one of the earliest Communist articles on Sun Tzu, the "Sun-tzu ping-fa ch'u-pu yen-chiu" [preliminary research on the *Sun-tzu ping-fa*], which appeared in the *Chün-cheng tsa-chih* of the Eighth Route Army in 1939. He continued to study the text for almost 20 years, and in 1957 he published *Chin-i hsin-pien Sun-tzu ping-fa* [modern translation and new edition of *Sun-tzu ping-fa*], which contained a rendering of the classical text into modern Chinese and an introduction which dealt with some textual and interpretive problems.

Kuo Hua-jo was selected to write the introduction to a handsome reprint of the Sung edition of commentaries on Sun Tzu which was published at Shanghai in 1961 by the Chung-hua Book Company. His introduction provides a useful summary of official Chinese Communist attitudes toward the "oldest and greatest book on the art of war in ancient China." He subscribed to the view that the work was written by Sun Tzu (Sun Wu) and that it was based on the wars of the Spring and Autumn period (722–481 B.C.) and on Sun's own military experience. The work later was revised by Sun Pin, a direct descendant of Sun Tzu. By the time of the Han dynasty, much of the original text had been lost. During the Three Kingdoms period, however, Ts'ao Ts'ao (155–200) collated and edited the available texts and produced a 13-chapter edition of the *Sun-tzu ping-fa*. (This edition, with notes by Ts'ao Ts'ao and ten other commentators, is the one that was photographically reproduced in 1961.)

According to Kuo Hua-jo, the essence of Sun Tzu's philosophy is to be found in his materialist view of war and his military dialectics, which are similar to the tenets of Marxism-Leninism. He asserted that Sun Tzu pioneered in pointing out that military operations are governed by definite laws and in perceiving that if one can control the laws governing war, he may be certain of ultimate victory. However, Sun Tzu's outlook was limited by the social environment of the age in which he lived. Because he was related by blood to a ruling class which used war as a means of economic exploitation, he made no distinction between just and unjust wars. He advocated offensive strategy designed to end a war quickly rather than the indirect approach of protracted war. Finally, he emphasized the importance of command decision, but neglected the matters of military education and study programs for the troops. Kuo concluded that the strategic thought of Mao Tse-tung was superior to that of Sun Tzu because Mao's thought eliminated these feudal elements.

Kuo Mo-jo

Kuo Mo-jo	郭 沫 若
Orig. Kuo K'ai-chen	郭 開 貞
Pen. Ting-t'ang	鼎 堂
Shih-t'o	石 沱
Tu K'an	杜 衎
Mai-k'o Ang	麥 克 昂
I K'an Jen	易 坎 人

Kuo Mo-jo (October 1892–), poet, playwright, novelist, essayist, translator, historian, paleographer, Creation Society leader, and Chinese Communist propagandist. After 1949 this versatile intellectual served the People's Republic of China as chairman of the All-China Federation of Writers and Artists and president of the Chinese Academy of Sciences.

A native of Loshan, Szechwan, Kuo Mo-jo was born into a merchant-landlord family. From 1897 to 1905 he received a traditional education in the Chinese classics, designed to prepare him for the civil service examinations. When the examination system was abolished in 1905 and modern schools were established in the prefectural town of Chiating, Kuo Mo-jo studied at one of them from 1906 to 1909. He then went to Chengtu, the provincial capital, to complete his secondary education. In 1914, at the age of 22, he went to Japan and enrolled in the preparatory class for Chinese students at the First Higher School in Tokyo. He soon became acquainted with Chang Tzu-p'ing and Yü Ta-fu (qq.v.), who later joined with him in founding the Ch'uang-tsao she (Creation Society).

In 1915 Kuo enrolled in the pre-medical department of the Sixth Higher School at Okayama. He went to Tokyo in the summer of 1916 to visit a sick friend at an American mission hospital. At the hospital, he met and fell in love with Satō Tomiko, the daughter of a Japanese Protestant minister from Sendai. After Kuo returned to school, they kept up a regular and impassioned correspondence until December, when Satō joined him in Okayama. Because Kuo had submitted to an arranged marriage in the spring of 1912 and was afraid of offending his parents by divorcing his Chinese wife, he and Satō had no formal marriage ceremony. She became his common-law wife and bore him five children.

In addition to his medical work, Kuo Mo-jo studied the writings of the sixteenth-century Neo-Confucian philosopher Wang Yang-ming and the Bengali poet Rabindranath Tagore. In 1917–18 he became interested in Goethe and Spinoza and proclaimed himself a believer in pantheism, which he saw as an element common to the philosophies of Wang Yang-ming, Tagore, Goethe, and Spinoza. After graduation from the Sixth Higher School in 1918, he entered the medical school of Kyushu Imperial University at Fukuoka.

In the early autumn of 1919 some of Kuo Mo-jo's poems were published in the literary supplement of the *Shih-shih hsin-pao* (*China Times*) in Shanghai. His pride in seeing his poems in print for the first time produced an explosion of poetic activity. About this time, he discovered and immersed himself in the poems of Walt Whitman. Kuo Mo-jo's most famous poems were written in this period of frenzied poetic activity of 1920.

In April 1921 Kuo Mo-jo suddenly left school and went to Shanghai with Ch'eng Fang-wu, who had been one of his schoolmates at Okayama. Through Ch'eng's efforts, he obtained a position on the editorial staff of the T'ai-tung Publishing Company. During the next three months he compiled the *Nü-shen* [goddesses], a collection of his poems which soon brought him fame, and persuaded Chao Nan-kung, the manager of the T'ai-tung Publishing Company, to undertake the publication of a new literary magazine to be edited by Kuo Mo-jo and his friends. He returned to Japan in July and, together with such friends as Chang Tzu-p'ing, Yü Ta-fu, and T'ien Han (q.v.), founded the Creation Society.

Between 1922 and 1924 Kuo Mo-jo and his associates founded and edited the *Ch'uang-tsao chi-k'an* (*Creation Quarterly*), the *Ch'uang-tsao chou-k'an* (*Creation Weekly*), and the *Ch'uang-tsao jih-pao* (*Creation Daily*). Through these magazines they helped popularize the concepts of romanticism and "art for art's sake" in China. By the autumn of 1923, however, personal friction within the society had begun to shake its foundations. The last issue of the *Creation Weekly*, published in May 1924, marked the end of the original Creation Society. During this period, in addition to producing literary works of his own and editing Creation Society publications, Kuo Mo-jo translated Goethe's *The Sorrows of Young Werther* and part of *Faust*, *The Rubaiyat of Omar Khayyam*, the first book of Nietzsche's *Thus Spake Zarathustra*, and a number of poems by English and German Romantic poets. He also translated classical Chinese poetry into pai-hua [the vernacular].

From 1921 to 1924 Kuo Mo-jo made a number of trips between Fukuoka and Shanghai. During the academic year he continued his medical studies at Kyushu Imperial University and produced a constant stream of material for the various publications of the Creation Society. He spent the summers working for the T'ai-tung Publishing Company in Shanghai. After graduation from medical school in April 1923, he moved his family to Shanghai. However, his wife and children were unhappy in China, and his wife became angry when he refused to practice medicine. In February 1924 she insisted on returning to Japan with the children, whether he came with them or not. Kuo Mo-jo saw them off and promised to join them in Japan as soon as he had wound up the affairs of the Creation Society.

Kuo Mo-jo returned to Japan in April 1924 and began to translate *Social Organization and Social Revolution*, by the Japanese Marxist Kawakami Hajime, into Chinese. By the end of May he had announced his conversion to Marxism-Leninism. He did not reject romanticism, but projected it into the future as being characteristic of the Communist utopia to come. In July and August he translated Turgenev's *Virgin Soil* into Chinese. He later claimed that these two works caused him to decide to return to China and devote himself to the task of furthering the social revolution. This determination may well have been reinforced by the offer of a position on the liberal arts faculty of Wuchang Normal College. However, when a civil war between the rulers of Chekiang and

Kiangsu broke out in late August, Kuo Mo-jo decided to postpone his return to China until the hostilities ended. He then wrote his most famous novel, *Lo-yeh* [fallen leaves], a work in epistolary form which commemorates the first few months of his love affair with Satō Tomiko.

In mid-November 1924 Kuo Mo-jo and his family went to Shanghai and established residence in the International Settlement. Since 1921 he had been associated with the Chung-hua hsueh-i she [Chinese association of arts and sciences], and since 1923 he had served as one of the two managing editors of its journal, *Hsueh-i*. He also was associated with the Ku-chün she [lone force association], a smaller organization composed mainly of members of the Chung-hua hsueh-i she who worked in the editorial offices of the Commercial Press. It was headed by Ho Kung-kan, who had given Kuo Mo-jo the book by Kawakami Hajime that had helped effect his conversion to Marxism. The Ku-chün she supported moderate reforms and the restoration of constitutional law. Kuo Mo-jo was accepted as a member because he had many friends in the organization and because he had persuaded the T'ai-tung Publishing Company to publish the organization's magazine, *Ku-chün*. In Shanghai, Kuo Mo-jo endeavored to persuade the other members of the *Ku-chün* that China should adopt a policy of state capitalism, which was what he understood the New Economic Policy of the Soviet Union to be. The Chung-hua hsueh-i she soon appointed Kuo Mo-jo to the planning committee for the establishment of the Hsueh-i ta-hsueh, or Arts and Sciences College, and promised him the post of chairman of the department of literature when the college opened in the autumn of 1925.

In the spring of 1925 Kuo Mo-jo wrote a number of poems and translated Gerhart Hauptmann's novel *Der Ketzer von Soana*, John Galsworthy's drama *Strife*, and several plays of J. M. Synge. Beginning in April, he gave two lectures a week at Ta Hsia University on the theory of literature. The lecture series came to an end with the May Thirtieth Incident. Kuo Mo-jo devoted much of his time during the summer to the national movement of protest that resulted from this incident. His dedication to Marxism-Leninism, especially the Leninist theory of imperialism, and his devotion to literature as a political weapon both increased.

The rebirth of the Creation Society was marked by the appearance in September 1925 of a new fortnightly review entitled *Hung-shui* [the flood]. The editing of this magazine and of the *Ch'uang-tsao yueh-k'an* (*Creation Monthly*), which began publication in March 1926, was largely the work of the so-called junior Creationists—including Chou Ch'üan-p'ing, Ching Yin-yü, and Ni I-te—but they were supported and advised by such members of the original Creation Society as Kuo Mo-jo and Ch'eng Fang-wu.

During the fall term of 1925 Kuo Mo-jo taught at the newly established Arts and Sciences College. However, the new institution was not a successful venture, and Kuo Mo-jo resigned in December after engaging in a heated dispute with a prominent member of the board of directors. That winter, Kuo Mo-jo was introduced to Ch'ü Ch'iu-pai (q.v.), who went to Canton shortly after their meeting. In February 1926 Kuo Mo-jo was invited to become chairman of the department of literature at Sun Yat-sen University in Canton. He later learned that the offer had been made at the suggestion of Ch'ü Ch'iu-pai. He accepted the post on the condition that Yü Ta-fu and Wang Ta-ch'ing be given positions at the university. His terms were accepted, and the three men set out for Canton on 18 March, arriving there on 23 March.

In July 1926, just before the Northern Expedition was launched, Kuo Mo-jo was appointed to the staff of Teng Yen-ta (q.v.) as chief of the propaganda section of the National Revolutionary Army's general political department. He had been recommended for the post by Teng Yen-ta's secretary, Sun Ping-wen. Kuo Mo-jo left Canton at the end of July and arrived in the Wuchang area on 1 September. Eight days later, Teng Yen-ta ordered him to proceed to Hankow and set up headquarters for the general political department. From 9 September until the fall of Wuchang on 10 October Kuo Mo-jo was virtually in charge of the department. On 12 October its offices were moved to Wuchang. The following month, Kuo Mo-jo was promoted to vice chairman of the general political department and was sent to Nanchang, the field headquarters of Chiang Kai-shek, to establish a department office. This assignment put Kuo Mo-jo in a delicate position: he supported the policies of the Wuhan leaders, but he was working in

Nanchang for Chiang Kai-shek at a time when the split between the Wuhan leaders and the Nanchang leaders was imminent. On 1 March 1927 Chiang Kai-shek appointed him chairman of the political department of the Generalissimo's field headquarters, but stipulated that the appointment should be kept secret until Nanking and Shanghai had fallen. Before accepting the post, Kuo Mo-jo secretly sent a telegram to Wuhan and received orders to accept Chiang's offer. On 16 March, he and his department set out for the front. He went as far as Anking, Anhwei, waited until Chiang left the city, and then sent the staff of the political department to Wuhan. He returned to Nanchang on 30 March and moved into the home of Chu Teh, where he spent an entire day writing a vitriolic attack on Chiang Kai-shek in which he called Chiang a reactionary counterrevolutionary and demanded that he be executed. The publication of this essay may well have been a cause of Chiang's 12 April purge of Communists.

Kuo Mo-jo returned to Wuhan in mid-April. From 10 to 13 June 1927 he participated in the unsuccessful Chengchow conference between the Wuhan leaders and Feng Yü-hsiang (q.v.). Soon afterwards, he became chief of the political department of the Second Front Army, which was commanded by Chang Fa-k'uei (q.v.). After the Nanchang uprising of 1 August (*see* Yeh T'ing), later celebrated as the birth of the Chinese Communist army, the leaders of the insurrection published a list of the members of their revolutionary committee which included Kuo Mo-jo and Chang Fa-k'uei, both of whom were in Kiukiang. On 3 August, Chang Fa-k'uei asked Kuo Mo-jo to disband the political department and to become his private secretary. Kuo Mo-jo agreed to the first request, but asked permission to go to Nanchang. Chang agreed to let him go if he would have Chang's name removed from the membership list of the revolutionary committee. Kuo Mo-jo arrived in Nanchang on 4 August and became chairman of the political department of the revolutionary committee. In the meantime, Chang Fa-k'uei had rallied his forces to suppress the insurgents. On 5 August, Kuo Mo-jo and the Communist forces withdrew from Nanchang and headed south. He participated in an unsuccessful uprising at Swatow in September and hid in the hills during the first three weeks of October. After reaching Shanghai, he rejoined his family

and went into hiding in the International Settlement.

In November 1927 Kuo Mo-jo made plans to revive the Creation Society. He hoped to secure the cooperation of Lu Hsün (Chou Shu-jen, q.v.) in reestablishing the *Creation Weekly* and persuaded his friends Cheng Po-ch'i and Chiang Kuang-tz'u to discuss the matter with Lu Hsün. Tentative agreement was reached, but the matter was dropped when Ch'eng Fang-wu returned from Japan with a group of young radicals who opposed the idea of cooperating with Lu Hsün. In January 1928 the young men began to publish several new magazines in which they called for the creation of a proletarian literature and attacked Lu Hsün as being too conservative.

Kuo Mo-jo could not remain in Shanghai indefinitely, for the National Government had put a price on his head. At the end of 1927 he made arrangements to go to the Soviet Union with his family, but he was stricken with typhoid fever and was hospitalized for a month. He then decided to go to Japan, a decision which was approved by the Chinese Communist party. Such prominent Communists as Chou En-lai visited him at home during his recuperation. On 24 February 1928 Kuo Mo-jo and his family left Shanghai for Japan on separate ships.

For the next ten years Kuo Mo-jo and his family lived in Ichikawa, a suburb to the east of Tokyo. He devoted most of his time to the study of ancient Chinese history and paleography. In 1930 he published the controversial *Chung-kuo ku-tai she-hui yen-chiu*, a Marxist interpretation of ancient Chinese history. The following year he published *Chia-ku wen-tzu yen-chiu* [studies of oracle-bone inscriptions]. He also made important contributions to the study of bronze inscriptions. During his ten years in Japan he wrote about fifteen scholarly works, seven autobiographical works, and a number of scholarly articles, short stories, and comments on topical issues. He translated three novels by Upton Sinclair, a German history of archaeology, Marx's *A Contribution to the Critique of Political Economy* and *The German Ideology*, and part of Tolstoy's *War and Peace*.

In June 1936 Kuo Mo-jo joined the Writers' Association (*see* Chou Yang). In the following months he played a significant role in the controversy over the slogan "Literature for National Defense." In October 1936 he was listed as one of the twenty-one signatories of the proclamation of unity which ended the controversy.

In November 1936 Yü Ta-fu went to Tokyo, where he resumed his friendship with Kuo Mo-jo. Yü agreed to try to pave the way for Kuo Mo-jo's return to China, and in the spring of 1937 he persuaded such prominent men as Chang Ch'ün, Ch'ien Ta-chün, Shao Li-tzu, and Ho Lien to intercede with Chiang Kai-shek on Kuo Mo-jo's behalf. In May, Yü informed Kuo Mo-jo that he could return to China. On 27 July, he landed in Shanghai. His wife and children remained in Japan.

In August 1937 Kuo Mo-jo's name was removed from the list of enemies of the National Government. He began writing anti-Japanese propaganda and helped found the *Chiu-wang jih-pao* [salvation daily], an influential left-wing newspaper. At the end of September, he went to Nanking, where he was received by Chiang Kai-shek. Chiang asked him to remain in Nanking and offered him a position. Kuo Mo-jo refused Chiang's offer, but promised that he would continue to write anti-Japanese propaganda. He then returned to Shanghai.

On 12 November 1937 Shanghai fell to the Japanese, and Kuo Mo-jo went into hiding in the French concession. On 27 November, he escaped aboard a French ship bound for Hong Kong. Among his fellow passengers were Ho Hsiang-ning and Tsou T'ao-fen (qq.v.). In mid-December, he went from Hong Kong to Canton in search of financial backing for the *Chiu-wang jih-pao*. Tseng Yang-fu, the mayor of Canton, and Wu T'ieh-ch'eng, the governor of Kwangtung, refused to help him, but Yü Han-mou (q.v.) offered his support. The newspaper resumed publication on 1 January 1938.

In response to a telegram from Ch'en Ch'eng (q.v.), Kuo Mo-jo went to Hankow in January 1938. Ch'en was organizing the political department of the Military Affairs Commission. He was to be the director, with Chou En-lai and Huang Ch'i-hsiang as his deputies. Kuo Mo-jo was asked to head the literary propaganda section of the department. He retired to Changsha to consider the offer. On 28 February he returned to Hankow, accepted the position, and promised to have his section in operation by 1 April. About this time, he set up housekeeping with Yü Li-ch'ün, the younger sister of a Chinese newspaper correspondent whom he had known in Tokyo. He had met her soon after his return to Shanghai in 1937.

In October 1938 Wuhan fell to the Japanese, and the political department was evacuated to Changsha. On 13 November, Kuo Mo-jo witnessed the great fire that destroyed most of the city (*see* Chang Chih-chung). Because he participated in relief work after this catastrophe he did not rejoin the staff of his section, which had moved to Kweilin, until 3 December. At the end of the month, he and Yü Li-ch'ün flew to Chungking, where they remained until the spring of 1946.

Early in 1939 Kuo Mo-jo's staff was reduced. He was replaced by Huang Shao-ku (q.v.) in the autumn of 1940, when the National Government decided to remove radicals from important posts, and was given a sinecure post as head of a newly created cultural works committee. Thus, he was able to pursue his own interests in comparatively comfortable circumstances until the committee was suppressed on 30 March 1945.

In 1942 and 1943 Kuo Mo-jo wrote five historical plays. The most popular of these was *Ch'ü Yuan*, an imaginative reconstruction and interpretation of the life of the earliest great Chinese poet about whom anything is known. Kuo Mo-jo's fascination with Ch'ü Yuan also manifested itself in scholarly articles and in his translations of Ch'ü Yuan's poems into pai-hua. From 1943 to 1945 he made a critical reevaluation of the intellectual history of ancient China. His *Ch'ing-t'ung shih-tai* [the bronze age] and *Shih p'i-p'an shu* [ten critiques], published in 1945, were among his most important and influential works.

In May 1945 Kuo Mo-jo was invited to the anniversary celebration of the Russian Academy of Sciences, to be held in Moscow and Leningrad from 16 to 28 June. He left Chungking on 9 June, but did not arrive in Leningrad until 26 June. He remained in the Soviet Union until 16 August, spending most of his time in Moscow, but also making a brief trip to Stalingrad, Tashkent, and Samarkand. He then flew back to Chungking with the Chinese delegation which had come to Moscow to complete negotiations for the Sino-Soviet friendship treaty which had been signed on 14 August.

In January 1946 Kuo Mo-jo participated in the Political Consultative Conference as one of nine nonpartisan delegates. On 10 February, he and two other speakers were injured in a riot which took place during a public meeting held to explain the accomplishments of the conference. At the end of June, he participated in the efforts of the so-called third force movement at Nanking to bring about an agreement between the Kuomintang and the Chinese Communist party. When truce negotiations broke down in July, he began to write anti-American propaganda. In 1947 he devoted himself to scholarly writing and to the preparation of new editions of his earlier works. He moved to Hong Kong that winter and began work on a series of autobiographical sketches. On 24 November 1948 he left Hong Kong and went to join the Chinese Communists in Shih-chia-chung, Hopei.

On 22 March 1949 the North China Cultural and Art Working Committee and the North China Writers Union held a tea party in Peking for writers and artists. Kuo Mo-jo attended the gathering and proposed the formation of a new national organization of writers and artists. This suggestion received unanimous approval, and a preparatory committee, headed by Kuo Mo-jo, was established. The All-China Congress of Writers and Artists, meeting in Peking in July, established the All-China Federation of Writers and Artists, with Kuo Mo-jo as its chairman. In September, Kuo Mo-jo was elected to the Chinese People's Political Consultative Conference. After the Central People's Government was established, he became a vice president of the Government Administration Council, chairman of the Committee on Cultural and Educational Affairs, and president of the Chinese Academy of Sciences. These honors were the well-earned reward of long years of service to the Communist cause. In 1966, however, Kuo Mo-jo reportedly was removed from his posts during the so-called Cultural Revolution. He declared that his works should be burned because he had failed to understand the Thought of Mao Tse-tung.

Kuo Ping-wen 郭 秉 文
T. Hung-sheng 鴻 聲

Kuo Ping-wen (1880–), educator who was president of Tung-nan University and director of the China Institute in America. After 1930 he served the National Government in trade and financial posts. He was deputy director general and chief of secretariat of the United Nations Relief and Rehabilitation Administration from 1944 to 1947.

A native of Shanghai, Kuo Ping-wen attended, from 1893 to 1896, Lowrie Institute in Shanghai, where he received a Western-style education. After graduation he taught at the institute for a year and then served in the customs and postal services in Shanghai, Kashing, and Hangchow.

In 1906 Kuo left China to continue his education in the United States. He majored in science at the College of Wooster in Ohio and was graduated in 1911 with a Ph.B. degree. He received an M.A. from Columbia University in 1912 and a Ph.D. in 1914. His dissertation, *The Chinese System of Public Education*, was published by Teachers College in 1915.

Kuo was an active student leader. He served as the editor in chief of the *Chinese Students' Monthly* (1908–9), editor of the *Wooster Voice* (1909–10), and general secretary of the Chinese Students' Alliance (1911–12). A brilliant scholar, he was elected to Phi Beta Kappa and Phi Delta Kappa and was awarded the Livingston Fellowship in education by Teachers College.

After returning to China in 1914, Kuo became an editor at the Commercial Press. In 1915 he was appointed dean of the Nanking Higher Normal School. The following year, he served as president of the Lowrie Institute and of Chekiang Provincial College. In 1917 he headed an educational commission to Japan and the Philippines to study their educational systems. He then rejoined the Commercial Press as an editor and director and edited two English-Chinese dictionaries.

In 1918 Kuo was appointed president of the Nanking Higher Normal School. He also led an educational mission abroad to study postwar educational problems in America and Europe. The Nanking Higher Normal School was one of the outstanding teachers colleges in China. Its predecessor, the Liang-kiang Normal School, founded by Chang Chih-tung (ECCP, I, 27–32) in 1902 for the training of primary and middle school teachers, had been the first institution of its kind in China. In 1914 the Nanking Higher Normal School had been founded on the campus of the Liang-kiang Normal School. When Kuo assumed the presidency, the school had already expanded from an initial enrollment of 126 students to 416 students.

In 1920 the school administration, under Kuo's leadership, proposed the establishment of a national university. The proposal received the support of Ts'ai Yuan-p'ei (q.v.) and other prominent educators and was presented for consideration by the ministry of education in Peking. Fan Yuan-lien, the minister of education, was sympathetic to the proposal and obtained the cabinet's approval. On 6 December 1920 the preparatory office of Tung-nan University, or National Southeastern University, began operations, and in July 1921 the ministry of education approved the university's organic laws. The Shanghai College of Commerce was founded as a component unit of the new university. Examinations for incoming students were held in August. A month later, Kuo was appointed president of Tung-nan University and of the Nanking Higher Normal School. The two institutions shared a campus until 1923, when the school was absorbed into the university.

From 1918 to 1925 appropriations for public schools and national universities often were in arrears. Fortunately for Kuo, the military governor of Kiangsu, Ch'i Hsieh-yuan (q.v.), was sympathetic to local educational needs. Tung-nan University thus enjoyed a greater degree of financial stability than other universities under the jurisdiction of the Peking government. This state of affairs may be attributed partly to Kuo's diplomatic skill in adjusting himself to contemporary political realities. He established friendly relations with the provincial authorities, with Peking government officials, and with prominent educators. On the other hand, such political flexibility won him the enmity of some Kuomintang partisans, such as Yang Ch'üan (q.v.), a professor in the university who instigated a campaign to oust Kuo from the presidency.

In 1924 Kuo Ping-wen was appointed by the Peking government to the first board of trustees of the China Foundation for the Promotion of Education and Culture, which was supported by the Boxer Indemnity funds returned by the United States (see Jen Hung-chün). Kuo was a member of the board until 1927, and it was he who proposed the establishment of the China Institute in America to provide assistance to Chinese students in American universities and to function as a channel for Sino-American cultural relations. The institute was inaugurated in 1925, and Kuo resigned from Tung-nan University to become its first director, a post which he held until 1930. From 1928 to 1930 he also served as a special commissioner to the United States and Europe for the National Government.

Kuo returned to China in 1931 to become the managing director of the Shanghai Trust Company, a director of the National Industrial Bank, and a supervisor of the Savings Society of the Central Trust of China. He held all these positions until the outbreak of the Sino-Japanese war in 1937. He also served as director of the bureau of foreign trade in the ministry of industries and commerce in 1931 and 1936. In 1932 he served as director general of the Chinese customs administration. He was elected president of the Pan-Pacific Association and the director of the Institute of International Affairs.

From 1938 to 1944 Kuo was stationed at London as the director of the Chinese Government Trading Commission to Great Britain and financial counsellor in the Chinese embassy. He played an important part in procuring war matériel and financial aid for China. In 1944 he was appointed (in absentia) vice minister of finance.

In 1943 Kuo led the Chinese delegation to the United Nations Conference on Food and Agriculture held in Hot Springs, Virginia, and to the United Nations Preliminary Monetary Conference in Washington, D.C. He was a member of the Chinese delegation, headed by H. H. K'ung, to the 1944 United Nations Monetary and Financial Conference at Bretton Woods, New Hampshire.

Kuo Ping-wen resided in the United States from 1944 to 1947 as the deputy director general and chief of secretariat of the United Nations Relief and Rehabilitation Administration. After 1947, he remained in the United States, serving in various capacities as an adviser of Chinese students and as a promoter of Sino-American cultural relations and residing in Washington, D.C. He was appointed chairman of the National Government's cultural and educational enterprises advisory committee in 1957.

Kuo T'ai-ch'i   郭 泰 祺
T.   Fu-ch'u   復 初
West. Quo Tai-chi

Kuo T'ai-ch'i (1889–29 February 1952), known as Quo Tai-chi, government official and diplomat who was best known as China's envoy to Great Britain (1932–41) and as a delegate to the League of Nations (1932–38). He bore much of the responsibility for formulating foreign policy at Chungking from 1941 to 1946. After serving as a delegate to the United Nations (1946–47) and as ambassador to Brazil (1947–49), he retired from public life and went to California.

The son of a well-known scholar, Quo Tai-chi was born in Wuhsueh, Hupeh. After receiving his primary education in the Chinese classics, he enrolled at a modern school in Wuchang. In 1904 he was sent by the Chinese government to study in the United States. He attended the Easthampton (Massachusetts) High School from the autumn of 1904 until the summer of 1907 and the Williston Academy in Easthampton in the academic year 1907–8. After completing secondary school, he enrolled at the University of Pennsylvania, where he majored in political science. He was elected to Phi Beta Kappa in March 1911 and was awarded a scholarship for graduate study in sociology in June of that year. Quo led an active social life in Philadelphia and joined such groups as the Philomathean Literary Society and the Cosmopolitan Club. He worked for a few months in 1911 as a reporter for the *Philadelphia Press* and later served as an editor of the student paper *Pennsylvanian.*

After learning of the republican revolution touched off by the Wuchang revolt of October 1911, Quo left the United States and returned to China in March 1912. He soon became a secretary to Li Yuan-hung (q.v.), who was serving as tutuh [military governor] of Hupeh and who had been elected vice president of the provisional republican government. Li remained in Wuchang until December 1913, when Yuan Shih-k'ai prevailed upon him to take an active part in government affairs in Peking. Quo accompanied Li to Peking and continued to serve under him. After Li assumed the presidency on 7 June 1916, Quo became chief

English secretary in the presidential office and a councillor in the ministry of foreign affairs. He left Peking after Li's forced retirement from office in July 1917 (*see* Chang Hsün; Tuan Ch'i-jui) and became a councillor in Sun Yat-sen's headquarters at Canton. Quo had joined the Kuomintang soon after its formation in 1912.

In the summer of 1918 Quo Tai-chi, Eugene Ch'en, and C. T. Wang were sent to the United States in an attempt to win American support for the new military government which had been formed at Canton, but their efforts were unsuccessful. The following year, Quo served as a technical expert to the southern group, headed by C. C. Wu (Wu Ch'ao-shu, q.v.) of the Chinese delegation to the Paris Peace Conference. He returned to China in early 1920 by way of the United States.

When Sun Yat-sen returned to Canton from Shanghai and assumed office as president extraordinary in May 1921, Quo Tai-chi became a councillor in the presidential office and head of the information bureau. In April 1922 he became chief of the administrative department of the Kwangtung provincial government when the dissident Ch'en Chiung-ming (q.v.) was replaced as governor by Wu T'ing-fang. Quo was forced to flee Canton after Ch'en's coup of 16 June, but he returned with the government in early 1923 to become vice minister of foreign affairs, serving under C. C. Wu. After the National Government was established at Canton in July 1925 and Hu Han-min became minister of foreign affairs, Quo Tai-chi resigned from office to become president of a commercial college at Wuhan.

After the Kuomintang split into two factions and Chiang Kai-shek established a national government at Nanking in opposition to the regime headed by Wang Ching-wei at Wuhan, Quo Tai-chi went to Shanghai to serve Chiang as foreign affairs commissioner for Kiangsu and as a member of the Shanghai branch of the Kuomintang's Central Political Council. He soon became vice minister of foreign affairs, under C. C. Wu, and chief of the international section of the Kuomintang's Shanghai information bureau. His attitude toward one foreign power was demonstrated in December 1927, when he was appointed chairman of a committee on Sino-Soviet relations. He immediately undertook the liquidation of Soviet commercial enterprises in Shanghai and the compulsory registration of all Russians residing in the city. C. C. Wu resigned at the end of 1927, and Quo became acting foreign minister. However, after Huang Fu (q.v.) succeeded Wu in February 1928, Quo was dismissed from his government and party offices.

When the new National Government was inaugurated at Nanking in the autumn of 1928, Quo Tai-chi was named to the Legislative Yuan. He was appointed ambassador to Italy in March 1929, but did not assume that post. In 1930 he joined the so-called northern coalition of Feng Yü-hsiang and Yen Hsi-shan (qq.v.) and participated in the so-called enlarged conference movement. After the movement collapsed in October, Quo went south. In 1931 he joined the secessionist government formed at Canton by Wang Ching-wei, T'ang Shao-yi, Ch'en Chi-t'ang (qq.v.) and others.

After Wang Ching-wei became president of the Executive Yuan at Nanking in January 1932, with Lo Wen-kan (q.v.) as minister of foreign affairs, Quo Tai-chi was appointed political vice minister of foreign affairs. He also became a member of the foreign affairs committee of the Kuomintang's Central Political Council. At the time Quo assumed office, Japanese and Chinese forces were fighting for control of Shanghai. Truce negotiations began at Shanghai in March, with Quo as the senior representative of the National Government delegation. Because he disagreed with the Japan policy formulated by Lo Wen-kan, he resigned from the ministry of foreign affairs.

Quo was appointed minister to Great Britain in April 1932, but, at the request of the National Government, he continued to function as political vice minister of foreign affairs until a successor could be appointed. On 3 May, following a report that the terms of the truce agreement worked out at Shanghai were favorable to the Japanese, a "national salvation" group at Shanghai set upon Quo and beat him. Thus, the signing of the truce agreement that put an end to the Shanghai embroglio with Japan took place in a Shanghai hospital on 5 May. After recovering from his injuries, Quo left China for London in the summer of 1932. In addition to performing his duties in London, he served as a Chinese delegate to the League of Nations until 1938. Both before and after Japan withdrew from the League of Nations in

1933, he regularly raised the issue of Japanese aggression in China and fought against recognition of Manchoukuo, He reiterated these accusations and called for joint Anglo-American action in support of China at the World Economic and Monetary Conference held in London in May 1933. Also in May, the Chinese mission at London was raised to embassy status, and on 22 May, Quo became China's first ambassador to the Court of St. James's. He spent some of the remaining months of 1933 as a Chinese delegate to the Disarmament Conference at Geneva. He was the senior Chinese delegate to the League of Nations Assembly in 1934 and the senior representative to the League Council in 1936. Quo, who had strongly opposed Sino-Russian cooperation in 1927, responded to changes in the world political situation by welcoming the 1934 entry of the Soviet Union into the League of Nations. China, he said, was "the cornerstone of Asia," and the Soviet Union was "a bridge between Europe and Asia."

After the Sino-Japanese war broke out in July 1937, Quo Tai-chi and V. K. Wellington Koo (Ku Wei-chün, q.v.) made intense efforts to enlist foreign support for China. They appealed to the League of Nations for aid and attended the Brussels Conference of the Washington Treaty powers in November 1937. Although they urged economic sanctions against Japan and aid to China, they received no support. British sympathy was not fully committed to China in the struggle, and on 3 May 1938 an Anglo-Japanese agreement on Chinese Maritime Customs funds accruing in Japanese-occupied ports was signed. On 6 May, Quo protested these arrangements, and they never came into full effect. A happier note was sounded in the British communication of 14 January 1939, which stated the readiness of the British government to negotiate with China, after the conclusion of peace, the abolition of extraterritoriality and the revision of treaties for better equality. However, Quo protested another British policy decision in August 1939, when the British authorities at Tientsin allowed the Japanese to take custody of four Chinese suspected of murdering a bank manager on 9 April. Quo also was unable to prevent the British from closing the Burma Road for three months in 1940, but he did manage to secure some British credits for China when the road was reopened in October.

In April 1941 the National Government, then at Chungking, appointed Quo minister of foreign affairs and designated V. K. Wellington Koo to succeed him as ambassador. Quo had served with distinction in London for more than nine years, and Oxford University had recognized his achievements by awarding him an honorary D.C.L. degree in 1938. He returned to China by way of the United States, where he appealed for American aid to China. In an exchange of notes in May 1941, Secretary of State Cordell Hull rejected Quo's policy suggestions, but promised the relinquishing of American extraterritorial rights in China when peace returned. After assuming office at Chungking in July, Quo was appointed to the standing committee of the Supreme National Defense Council. He worked to prevent foreign recognition of Wang Ching-wei's Japanese-sponsored government at Nanking, severed relations with countries which recognized Wang's government, supported the Atlantic Charter, and established diplomatic ties with the Czech government in exile. After the Japanese attacked Pearl Harbor in December 1941 and China declared war on Japan, Germany, and Italy, Quo stressed the mutual responsibilities of the Allies. Although he was replaced as foreign minister by T. V. Soong (q.v.) late in December and was made chairman of the foreign affairs committee of the Supreme National Defense Council, he continued to bear much of the responsibility for the formulation of foreign policy because Soong spent most of his time in the United States.

In February 1946 Quo Tai-chi was appointed representative for China on the Security Council of the United Nations. After chairing the Security Council from mid-March to mid-April, he also became a member of the United Nations Atomic Energy Commission. In June, he received an honorary LL.D. degree from the University of Pennsylvania. He was named to membership on the United Nations Commission for Conventional Armaments in March 1947, but resigned in December to become Chinese ambassador to Brazil. When the Chinese Communists came to power in 1949, he left Rio de Janeiro and retired to Santa Barbara, California, where his wife and two sons had been living since 1939. Quo died at Santa Barbara, after a long illness, on 29 February 1952.

Lao Nai-hsuan	勞 乃 宣
T. Chi-hsuan	季 瑄
H. Yü-ch'u	玉 初

Lao Nai-hsuan (1843–21 July 1921), government official, Neo-Confucian scholar, and historian known for his scholarly account of the origins of the Boxer movement.

Although T'unghsiang, Chekiang, is often given as Lao Nai-hsuan's native place, his family had lived in Soochow, Kiangsu, since his paternal grandfather's day. Lao was born in the home of his maternal grandfather, Shen Hsi-yung, then the prefect of Kuangp'ing, Chihli (Hopei). Soon after his birth, he was designated heir to his paternal uncle, Lao Kung-fu. His family stayed in Kuangp'ing until 1846 and then moved south to live with Lao's maternal uncle, who was the magistrate of Wuchiang in Kiangsu. From 1848 to 1850 they lived in Wusih, where the uncle had been transferred.

In 1851 Lao's father, Lao Ts'ang-ts'ao, was appointed Ts'ang ta-shih [granary keeper] in the office of the financial commissioner of Nanking. In 1853, during the Taiping Rebellion, the family fled to Soochow. In 1856, while the elder Lao was serving in Chenchiang with the army of Liu Ts'un-hou, the imperial troops suffered a crushing defeat at the hands of the rebels. Liu died in battle and the elder Lao attempted suicide by throwing himself into a river. Although rescued from drowning, he died later that year. In consideration of his services to the imperial cause, one of his heirs was granted the status of chien-sheng. The honor was given to Lao Nai-hsuan because his elder brother had already passed the provincial examinations.

When Taiping forces took Soochow in 1860, Lao's family fled to T'aichou to live with his maternal uncle. The following year Lao was betrothed to a girl of the K'ung clan of Ch'üfu, descendants of Confucius. He began to devote himself to the philosophy of Sung Neo-Confucianism. In 1863 he went to Ch'üfu, where he remained until 1865, when he went to Hangchow and passed the provincial examinations. Lao won the chin-shih degree in 1871 after having failed the examinations in 1868.

In 1873 Li Hung-chang (ECCP, I, 464–71), then the governor general of Chihli (Hopei), sponsored the compilation of a new gazetteer for the province, the *Chi-fu t'ung-chih*. Lao was among the many noted scholars invited to take part in the project in Paoting, where his family had been living for several years.

In 1877 the household servants of a Manchu prince in a village near Peking joined with local bullies in seizing the lands of the villagers on the grounds that they belonged to the estate of the prince. The resulting litigation lasted for years, and many villagers were imprisoned by timid magistrates. Lao was delegated by the provincial financial commissioner to join with the current magistrate in investigating the matter together with the magistrate. They discovered the truth, punished the servants, and reported the case to their superiors, recommending a thorough trial at the provincial level. The recommendation was not heeded. The matter was solved through mediation, with the burdens of the villagers lightened by the reduction of rents and the forgiving of debts. In 1879 Lao became acting magistrate at Linyu near Shanhaikuan. He showed unusual resourcefulness, energy, and interest in education. When his term ended in 1880, Tseng Kuo-ch'üan (ECCP, II, 749–51), who was leading an army to Shanhaikuan to reinforce border defenses during the period of Sino-Russian conflict over Ili, asked Lao to be his private secretary. Tseng's forces were withdrawn in the spring of 1881, and Lao then was appointed to the magistracy of Nanp'i, Chihli. After assuming office at the beginning of 1882, Lao suppressed a robber band that had been terrorizing the district for some time.

Lao's mother died in the spring of 1882, and he resigned from office to observe the traditional mourning period. That autumn, Chou Fu (ECCP, I, 471), then superintendent of customs at Tientsin, invited Lao to be his secretary in charge of foreign affairs. Lao went to Tientsin and remained there until 1884, when he was appointed magistrate of Wanhsien. He was transferred to Lihsien in 1888, where his wife died, and to Wuch'iao in 1891. After taking a year of sick leave in 1895, he served as magistrate of Ch'ingyuan and acting prefect of Paoting.

In the summer of 1898 Lao began his second magistracy at Wuch'iao. Here he encountered the Boxers for the first time. Through his own researches, he found that the cult of Boxers originated from the Eight Trigrams Sect, which, in turn, was a branch of the rebellious White Lotus Sect that the government had suppressed with great bloodshed in the first years of the Chia-ch'ing reign (1796–1820). Lao published his findings in 1899 as *I-ho-ch'üan chiao-men yuan-liu k'ao*. He distributed this work in territories under his jurisdiction together with notices prohibiting Boxer activity. Later in the winter, Boxers from Techow in Shantung crossed into Wuch'iao and incited a mob to riot. A church and six houses belonging to Chinese Christians were destroyed, and one man was killed. Lao immediately sent troops to quell the riot and succeeded in capturing a score of Boxers. On 5 January 1900, when a band of several hundred Boxers invaded Wuch'iao, Lao's troops defeated them with ease, killing nine and capturing twenty. Among the captured was the deputy commander of the band. Lao demonstrated the falseness of the Boxer's claim of invulnerability by having the leader flogged and executed in public. The families of the Boxers were ordered to pay for the damage to the church and the houses. Lao then presented his book on the Boxers to his superiors and recommended means by which the cult could be eradicated. Unfortunately, his views were not shared by powerful court officials, who advocated the employment of the Boxers to expel foreigners. Lao resigned. He was appointed secretary in the Board of Civil Appointments, but he asked for and was granted a leave of absence.

After returning to Soochow in the autumn of 1900, Lao accepted an invitation from Yu Tsu-i, governor of Chekiang, to serve on his private staff and declined a similar but later invitation from Chang Chih-tung (ECCP, I, 27–32), then the governor of Hupeh and Hunan. When Yu left his post early in 1901, Lao accepted a second invitation from Chang. Before his planned departure for Hupeh, he received a telegram from Ts'en Ch'un-hsuan (q.v.), the governor of Shansi, who had obtained court permission to avail himself of Lao's services. Lao then declined both offers on the grounds of ill health. After serving reluctantly for two months as director of the Nanyang School in Shanghai at the insistance of Sheng Hsuan-huai (q.v.), he went to Hangchow. At that time, the Chekiang government planned to

transform the Ch'iu-shih Academy, a traditional Confucian school in Hangchow, into a
modern college. At the request of Jen Tao-
jung, then the governor of Chekiang, Lao took
charge of the reorganization. In the spring of
1903 a student demonstration caused by the
dismissal of six students for insubordination
was decisively quelled by Lao. He resigned that
autumn because of ill health and lived quietly
until September 1904 when the acting governor
general of Kiangsu and Chekiang, Li Hsing-jui,
persuaded him to join his private staff at
Nanking. When Li died a month later, Lao
continued in his post at the request of Li's
successors, Chou Fu and Tuan-fang (ECCP, II,
780–82).

Lao was summoned to Peking on 1 December
1907 for an imperial audience, but he was
granted a delay of several months because of his
health. He arrived at Peking in May 1908 for
an audience with the Empress Dowager Tz'u-
hsi (ECCP, I, 295–300) at the Summer Palace.
Subsequently, he was appointed counsellor at
the Hsien-chien pien-ch'a kuan [constitution
drafting office] and assistant proctor of the
Nei-ko hui-i cheng-wu-ch'u [committee of
ministers].

In 1910 Lao was appointed to a seat reserved
for eminent scholars in the Tzu-cheng yuan, or
National Assembly. He also acted as consultant
to the Li-fan pu [ministry of dependencies].
From October 1910 to January 1911 he participated in the first session of the National
Assembly and took the lead in the controversy
over the draft of a new criminal code because
he thought that some of its provisions disregarded traditional Chinese values. The documents in this controversy were collected by Lao
in a book entitled *Hsin hsing-lü hsiu-cheng-an
hui-lu* [collected records concerning the bill to
reform criminal statutes].

In the spring of 1911 Lao left Peking to assume
office as education commissioner at Nanking.
He had been appointed to this post in July 1910,
but had remained in Peking at the request of the
constitution drafting office. During the summer
he inspected educational facilities in northern
Kiangsu. He resigned in September so that he
could attend the National Assembly meetings
scheduled to be held in October and could
participate in the drafting of regulations governing the reorganization of provincial governments. By the time he arrived at Peking, the

revolution had broken out and Nanking had
been lost to the revolutionaries. In November,
he was appointed president of Peking University, and in December he became vice minister
of education. When he heard that the emperor
had decided to abdicate, a course which he
opposed, he resigned from all his posts.

In November 1913 Lao accepted an invitation from the German Sinologist Richard
Wilhelm to preside over the Confucius Society,
founded by Wilhelm and a number of former
imperial officials in the German-leased territory
of Tsingtao. The two men became close
friends, and their mutual interest in the *I-ching*
(*Book of Changes*) resulted in a new edition of
that text by Lao entitled *Chou-i tsun Ch'eng* [the
book of changes according to the Ch'eng school]
and a German rendering of the classic by
Wilhelm, the *I-Ging, das Buch der Wandlungen*,
published at Jena in 1924.

When the Japanese seized Tsingtao in 1914,
Lao and his family moved to Tsinan and then
to Ch'üfu. Earlier in the year he had refused to
accept an official post offered him by Yuan
Shih-k'ai; now he publicly advised Yuan to
restore the Ch'ing monarchy. During the July
1917 restoration attempt by Chang Hsün (q.v.),
Lao was appointed minister of justice, but the
restoration failed before his memorial declining
the honor on account of age could reach Peking.
On the advice of the Ch'üfu magistrate, Lao
again moved his family to Tsingtao. He resumed his collaboration with Wilhelm on the
I-ching and began work, at the request of Liu
Chin-ts'ao, on the *Huang-ch'ao hsü wen-hsien
t'ung-k'ao* [documentary records of the Ch'ing
dynasty, continued], particularly on the period
from 1877 to 1911. Lao died on 21 July 1921
in his Tsingtao home.

Lao was a staunch Confucianist of the Ch'eng-
Chu School. Among Ch'ing scholars, he
expressed admiration for Ku Yen-wu (ECCP, I,
421–26) and Wang Fu-chih (ECCP, II, 817–
19), but his hero was Tseng Kuo-fan (ECCP,
II, 751–56). Although he was a supporter of
the Ch'ing dynasty, Lao favored institutional
changes in keeping with the times. After the
overthrow of the dynasty, Lao wrote an essay,
"Kung-ho cheng-chieh" [the true meaning of
the term "republic"], in which he pointed out
that historically the term had no republican
connotations but stood for a caretaker situation
in a monarchical context. In a continuation

of this essay written in 1914, he tried to impress his interpretation on Yuan Shih-k'ai, suggesting that Yuan should return power to the deposed emperor, P'u-yi (q.v.), once the latter came of age.

In his educational programs, Lao favored indoctrination with the principles of Sung Confucianism combined with modern scientific and technical learning. He was a firm believer in universal education as a means of strengthening the country, to be promoted and supported by the government and private individuals. As an aid to universal education he advocated the use of phonetic symbols in place of characters. He adopted the phonetic symbols devised by Wang Chao for the Mandarin dialect and created additional symbols for the dialects of the southern provinces. In the 1904–6 period he established a training school in Nanking for the popularization of his phonetic script. He also presented his ideas to the imperial court in a number of memorials.

Lao's favorite discipline, particularly in his middle years, was mathematics. From 1883 to 1900 he wrote at least seven treatises on mathematical problems and on the explication of ancient books of Chinese mathematics. Lao's miscellaneous writings—including letters, poems, and official documents—were collected by his disciple Lu Hsueh-p'u and published in 1927 as *T'ung-hsiang Lao hsien-sheng i-kao*. Lao's autobiography, *Jen-shou tzu-ting nien-p'u*, was begun in 1915, finished in 1920, and published without alteration in 1922.

Lao She: *see* SHU CH'ING-CH'UN.

Lebbe, Vincent: *see* LEI MING-YUAN.

Lee, Dai-ming: *see* LI TA-MING.

Lee, K. C.: *see* LI KUANG-CH'IEN.

Lei Hai-tsung   雷 海 宗
  T. Po-lun   伯 倫

Lei Hai-tsung (1902–25 December 1962), historian known for his cyclic theory of Chinese

history and his studies of ancient Chinese culture. He taught at Tsinghua University from 1932 until 1952, when the Central People's Government transferred him to Nankai University. Although he remained at Nankai until his death, after 1957 he was forbidden to teach Chinese history because of his outspoken criticism of the Communists during the Hundred Flowers campaign.

The eldest of five brothers, Lei Hai-tsung was born into a scholarly Christian family in the Yungch'ing district of Chihli (Hopei). A number of his forebears had been prominent residents of T'ungchou (near Peking), but his father, Lei Ming-hsia, an Anglican priest, had been assigned to Ta-wang-chuang, outside the walled city of Yungch'ing, sometime before Lei Hai-tsung was born. His father became an intimate friend of and lived with Chu Chiu-tan, a leading local scholar, bibliophile, and connoisseur. It was in the Chu household that Lei Hai-tsung received his early training in Chinese classics. Lei received his formal education first at the Ts'unshih School in Yungch'ing and then at the Ch'ungte Middle School in Peking, both of which were Anglican mission schools. In 1919 he enrolled at Tsinghua Junior College, from which he was graduated in 1922. He then went to the United States, where he completed his undergraduate work at the University of Chicago in 1924. He received a Ph.D. from the same institution in 1927 after writing a dissertation entitled "The Political Ideas of Turgot" and studying under the eminent medievalist James Westfall Thompson.

After returning to China in 1927, Lei Hai-tsung became a professor of history at National Central University in Nanking. In 1931 he joined the faculty of Wuhan University and published the results of his investigation of the Chou conquest of Shang, fixing its date as 1027 B.C. His conclusions were supported by the later inquiries of William Hung (Hung Yeh) at Yenching University and of the Swedish scholar Bernhard Karlgren. In 1932 T. F. Tsiang (Chiang T'ing-fu, q.v.) persuaded Lei to join the history department of Tsinghua University. At this point, Lei turned away from European history and devoted himself to developing a general theory of Chinese history and to studying ancient Chinese history. For use in teaching, he compiled and edited a six-volume source book of Chinese history, *Chung-kuo t'ung-shih hsuan-tu*, which was privately printed at Tsinghua. Between 1932 and 1937 he published important articles in the *Ch'ing-hua hsueh-pao* [Tsinghua journal] and the *She-hui k'e-hsueh* [the social sciences] on such subjects as the periodicity of Chinese history, the rules and practices of imperial succession in pre-modern empires, the evolution of the Chinese family and kinship system from ancient to medieval times, and the evolution of the Chinese army in terms of social composition and morale. These studies were revised and published in 1940 as *Chung-kuo wen-hua yü Chung-kuo ti ping* [Chinese culture and the Chinese soldier].

The core of Lei's approach to Chinese history was his theory of periodicity. Using philosophy and religion as his main criteria, he divided Chinese history into two long cycles, each within five stages. The stages of the first cycle (c.1300 B.C.–383 A.D.) were: (1) the period of Sinitic religion based on ancestor worship (c.1300–771 B.C.); (2) the rise of creative philosophy to its culmination in the thought of Confucius (770–473 B.C.), a period also characterized by the decline of the royal house of Chou, the emergence of feudal hegemonies and a balance of power among them, and the gradual disintegration of feudal social order; (3) the decline of creative philosophy into sectarianism (473–221 B.C.), accompanied by the transformation to "unitary" states, the passing of chivalry, the emancipation of serfs, the development of a universally conscripted army, and a prolonged internecine military struggle; (4) the period of merger and stagnation of thought (221 B.C.–88 A.D.); and (5) the period of cultural disintegration (89–383 A.D.), which coincided with political disintegration, barbarian conquest of north China, and the introduction of Buddhism. The second cycle in the history of China comprised: (1) the period of Buddhist domination of Chinese life and thought (383–960); (2) the rise of Neo-Confucianism (960–1279); (3) the decline of Neo-Confucianism into sectarian conflict (1279–1518); (4) the death of creative philosophy, leading to the rise of textual and historical criticism (1528–1839); and (5) the disintegration of traditional culture and institutions and the widespread introduction of Western thought and culture (1839–), a period similar to the final stage of the first cycle.

Lei's studies of the changing social composition and quality of the traditional Chinese army also had a bearing on his cyclical theory. In his opinion, much of the dynamism of the period of Warring States and the early empires was accounted for by the development of a conscripted army of free commoners. After the decline of this form of universal military service in the Later Han period, the Chinese army came to be composed of recruits from the lowest stratum of Chinese society. Service as a soldier left an indelible social stigma. Because China then had what Lei termed a "soldierless civilization," during the second cycle of Chinese history the nation was conquered, either partially or totally, several times.

In the late 1930's, the Sino-Japanese war having begun, Lei Hai-tsung moved with Tsinghua University to Changsha and then to Kunming, where it merged with Peking and Nankai universities to form Southwest Associated University. From the summer of 1940 to the summer of 1946 Lei served as chairman of the combined university's history department and taught medieval European history as well as Chinese history. In 1940 he and Lin T'ung-chi, a political scientist, began publishing a fortnightly review called *Chan-kuo ts'e*. Its name was derived from the title of the annals of the Warring States. For a few months in 1941 the *Chan-kuo ts'e* also appeared monthly in Shanghai. Soon afterwards, the magazine ceased independent publication and became the *Chan-kuo* supplement of the leading newspaper *Ta Kung Pao*. Through this organ, Lei's cyclic theory of Chinese history and his studies of Chinese culture reached a large audience. He and Lin T'ung-chi collected and published a number of their *Chan-kuo* articles in 1946 under the title *Wen-hua hsing-t'ai shih-kuan* [historical views of cultural configurations].

Lei Hai-tsung served as chairman of the Tsinghua history department after the university returned to its Peiping campus in the summer of 1946. During the academic year 1946–47 he also served as acting dean of the faculty of arts and letters. Because Lei had opposed Marxism and had consistently supported the National Government as a unifying force in China, he was respected by such high-ranking Kuomintang officials as Chu Chia-hua (q.v.). In 1948 Chu, then the minister of education, persuaded Lei to launch a new magazine, the *Chou-lun* [weekly review]. That year, 44 issues of the magazine appeared.

After the Chinese Communists gained full control of the mainland in 1949, Lei remained in Peking. In 1952 the Central People's Government transferred him to Nankai University in Tientsin. Lei's only comments on the new regime were made in his occasional reports on land reform, in which he was required to examine his past. He stated that it would be difficult for him to cast away his pre-Communist Chinese cultural heritage and his Western education. During the Hundred Flowers campaign, when intellectuals were encouraged to speak their minds, Lei did so at a conference of professors in the Tientsin area on 14 April 1957. He argued that genuine social sciences can flourish only in a capitalist society and that the "new social sciences" of Marx, Engels, Lenin, and Stalin were only applications of "capitalist" social sciences to the specific problems of the working class. He went on to say that Marxism and its offshoots had suffered from intellectual stagnation since the passing of Engels in 1895 and that, as a result, the "new social sciences" had degenerated into dogmatic creeds. Finally, he challenged the historical accuracy of Marx and Engels with reference to their view of ancient "slave society." Official reaction to Lei's attack on Communist ideology was swift and condemnatory. He was criticized in newspapers, scholarly magazines, and popular magazines and was forbidden to teach Chinese history. Although he was permitted to remain at Nankai University, his teaching activities were limited to one course in foreign historiography.

Lei Hai-tsung died of a kidney ailment on 25 December 1962. He was survived by his wife, *née* Chang Ching-fo, and his daughter, Lei Ch'ung-lei, who was a lecturer in English literature at Peking University.

Lei Ming-yuan   雷 鳴 遠
Orig.   Frederick Lebbe
Ordination. Vincent

Lei Ming-yuan (19 August 1877–24 June 1940), also known as Father Vincent Lebbe, a Belgian priest and Roman Catholic missionary who became a Chinese citizen in 1927. From 1901 until his death he worked for the Sinification of the liturgy and the clerical hierarchy in China, his motto being "La Chine aux Chinois, et les Chinois au Christ."

Ghent, Belgium, was the birthplace of Frederick Lebbe, the eldest of six children of a Belgian lawyer. His maternal grandparents were of English extraction, and his mother was a convert to Catholicism. Young Frederick showed early evidence of piety and interest in China. He wrote and played a leading role in a play, presented at his secondary school commencement exercises, about St. John Gabriel Perboyre, who had been martyred in China in 1840. In December 1895 he joined the Congregation of the Mission (generally known as the Lazarists or, in English-speaking countries, the Vincentians) in Paris and took the name Vincent.

The Vincentians had been entrusted with the China mission in Peking in 1773 when Pope Clement XIV dissolved the Society of Jesus. The young Belgian missionary sailed for China on 10 February 1901, reaching Shanghai on 16 March. Soon after his arrival, he observed Indian policemen beating a Chinese coolie. This cruelty outraged him and strengthened his desire to improve the lot of the Chinese people. He soon left Shanghai and went to Peking, where he was ordained a priest on 28 October.

In 1902 Father Lebbe began missionary work in such places as Ta-k'ou-t'an, Huang-hou-tien, and Chochow. He became pastor director of Tientsin in 1906. Father Lebbe soon developed a deep affection for Chinese ways and worked hard to assimilate Chinese culture. He wore Chinese dress and a queue, smoked a waterpipe, studied the Four Books, became a good calligrapher, and developed great fluency in the Tientsin dialect. He proposed the Sinification of the liturgy and the clerical hierarchy, recommended the use of double genuflection on entering a church, and even suggested the adoption of the Confucian "three kneelings and nine kowtows." His motto was "La Chine aux Chinois, et les Chinois au Christ." His proposals, particularly those involving the appointment of Chinese bishops, were regarded as absurdities by many of his missionary colleagues.

In 1909 Father Lebbe founded the Ch'uan-tao-hui [propagation of the truth society] in Yenshan, Tientsin. The following year, he joined the Red Cross and founded the Fa-cheng hsueh-hui, where he taught sociology and wrote *Lectures on Sociology*. He opened nine missionary centers in Tientsin in 1911. He also helped Father Wang Chih-yuan and others to establish the Society of Catholic Action in Han-lo-yen, Hungting, Shansi. This organization opened headquarters in Tientsin as a result of Father Lebbe's zealous promotion of its cause. Soon afterwards, Father Lebbe assumed the chief editorship of the recently discontinued *Bulletin of Catholicism*, which had been founded by Wang Yao-hua, a Catholic from Yenshan, to promote better understanding between Catholics and non-Catholics. Father Lebbe renamed the publication *Kuang-i lu*, later changed to *Kuang-i pao*.

In June 1913 Father Lebbe traveled to Europe to raise money for the establishment of a normal school in Tientsin. He returned with the needed funds in the spring of 1914 and proceeded to open the school. He later used graduates of this school to found more than 70 primary schools. The manifestations of his concern for the Chinese people became increasingly varied. In May 1915, after the Chinese government had accepted the humiliating terms of Japan's Twenty-One Demands, he convened a conference in Tientsin in an attempt to raise funds to save the country from submitting to the agreement. He also decided that China needed a propaganda organ to give voice to the people's views and to promote national spirit. Accordingly, he founded the *I-shih pao*, which began publication on the Double Tenth holiday (10 October) in 1915 and which became one of the most influential papers in China.

Father Lebbe's efforts on behalf of the Chinese people brought him into conflict with the French authorities in China in 1916. On 18 October, the French ambassador demanded that the French concession be enlarged by 30 mou of land in Lao-k'ai-hsi by 20 October. Two days later, the French authorities occupied the land in question. Father Lebbe opposed this demand by sending telegrams to government officials and by publicizing the matter in the Tientsin *I-shih chu-jih pao* (formerly the *Kuang-i pao*) and the Peking *Social Welfare Newspaper*. The French authorities responded by securing his expulsion from Tientsin. He was transferred to Chengting and then to Hochia, where he served as vice pastor. In

March 1917 the superior general of the Congregation of the Mission ordered an investigation of the incident. On 25 March, Father Lebbe was ordered to establish temporary residence in Chiahsien, Chekiang. A month later, the apostolic vicar of Ningpo, Monsignor Paul Renaud, appointed him pastor of Shaohsing.

Since 1914 Father Lebbe and his friend and supporter Father Anthony Cotta had been advocating reforms in Catholic methods in China in a series of remarkable letters and memoranda. A number of their suggestions were incorporated in the encyclical *Maximum Illud*, issued by Pope Benedict XV on 30 November 1919. Early in 1920 Monsignor Jean Baptiste Budes de Guebriant, the apostolic visitor of Catholic churches in China, convened a conference in Shanghai at which it was revealed that Father Lebbe was to return to Europe with him to oversee Chinese students in Europe. They arrived in France on 14 April. Father Lebbe's superiors instructed him to refrain from writing for the *I-shih pao* and from going to Rome. In July, Désiré Joseph Cardinal Mercier read Father Lebbe's reports and asked to see him. When they met in August, Father Lebbe urged that the Curia Romana appoint Chinese priests to the dignity of apostolic vicar as soon as possible. On 16 December William-Martin Cardinal Van Rossum summoned Father Lebbe to Rome and asked him to recommend suitable candidates for appointment. Father Lebbe also explained the necessity of appointing a permanent apostolic delegate to China to Cardinal Gasparri, the Secretary of State, who agreed with him and arranged an audience with Pope Benedict XV. The Pope received Father Lebbe on 28 July 1920. He was impressed by Father Lebbe's grasp of missionary problems in China, and he promised that the recommended appointments would be made as soon as the opportunity arose.

On 27 January 1921, five days after the death of Pope Benedict XV, Father Lebbe left Rome. On 12 August, Pope Pius XI appointed Celso Constantini the first apostolic delegate to China. Father Lebbe's efforts again bore fruit when Father Odoric Ch'eng was appointed apostolic prefect of Puchi on 12 December 1923 and Father Melchior Sun was appointed apostolic prefect of Ankuo on 15 April 1924.

After the work-study program (*see* Li Shih-tseng) was discontinued in 1921, many of the Chinese students in France went to Father Lebbe. During the next five years, despite the fact that the program had espoused an anti-religious attitude, Father Lebbe helped a number of these students to learn French so that they could attend school, and arranged factory jobs for them. He also worked to obtain scholarships for them and asked Catholic families to house them. More than 200 students matriculated at European colleges and universities because of Father Lebbe's efforts, and he constantly journeyed through France, Belgium, Germany, England, and the Netherlands on their behalf.

China remained Father Lebbe's prime concern, and he never ceased to hope that he would be permitted to return. Catholics in Tientsin petitioned the Curia Romana to allow his return, but foreign missionaries in Tientsin and the Congregation of the Mission voiced considerable opposition to it. In April 1926 Cardinal Van Rossum summoned Father Lebbe to Rome and informed him that the Curia Romana had decided to appoint Father Philip Chao apostolic vicar of Hsuanhua. On learning of the appointment, Father Lebbe reportedly remarked, "My Lord, Your servant may now die in peace." On 28 October, six Chinese apostolic vicars were consecrated by the Pope. Father Lebbe wept with joy during the ceremony. At the request of Monsignor Melchior Sun, the superior general of the Congregation of the Mission finally granted Father Lebbe permission to return to China, though not to Tientsin.

On 11 February 1927 Father Lebbe set off from Marseilles. After arriving in China, he proceeded to Kao-chia-chuang. At this time, the Kuomintang was divided into two major factions, with rival governments at Wuhan and Nanking. On 1 August, the Curia Romana sent a telegram to Chinese Catholics, ordering them to obey the existing government and indirectly implying recognition of Chiang Kai-shek's regime at Nanking. Father Lebbe gave aid to the National Revolutionary Army in October, when he and Monsignor Philip Chao established a medical corps and refugee reception center in Hsuanhua. In 1927 Father Lebbe became a Chinese citizen, taking the Chinese name Lei Ming-yuan. On 19 December, he founded the Society of Theresian Sisters. He established the Congregation of St. John the Baptist a year later.

When the League of Nations sent the Lytton Commission to China in 1932 to investigate the Mukden Incident of 18 September 1931 and subsequent charges of Japanese aggression, the governor of Hopei (Chihli) asked Father Lebbe to receive the commission. Because his Vincentian superiors prohibited him from undertaking the task, the six Chinese apostolic vicars met the commission. In August 1933 Father Lebbe resigned from the Congregation of the Mission; on 24 December he joined the Congregation of St. John the Baptist, which he had founded five years earlier.

The remainder of Father Lebbe's active life was devoted largely to the organization and administration of medical units. His first such effort was on behalf of the 29th Division of Sung Che-yuan (q.v.), which fought Japanese troops along the Great Wall in 1933. On 20 March, 260 men who had been recruited, trained, and equipped by Father Lebbe joined the Chinese Red Cross and went to work at Hsi-feng-kou, Ku-pei-k'ou, and Lengk'ou. In December 1936, at the request of Fu Tso-yi (q.v.), Father Lebbe took charge of the medical units serving on the Suiyuan front. When the Sino-Japanese war began in the summer of 1937, he mobilized his order to serve as stretcher bearers in the Ihsien area. He also served as a company commander in charge of medical aid for the 12th Division of the Third Army. The commander of the division, T'ang Hui-yuan, later said that "it was mainly due to the efforts of Father Lebbe and other Catholics that our people were able to remain calm, that the morale of our troops was high." In July 1938 the National Government awarded him a medal. Chiang Kai-shek received him on 4 September at Wuchang and appointed him director of special medical and educational services for the north China theater. Although Father Lebbe was in poor health, he worked vigorously to carry out educational programs and to build medical facilities in the region under his jurisdiction.

In February 1940 Father Lebbe, who was then in southwestern Hopei, was obliged to retreat from the area because of the Chinese Communist military threat. On 17 March, he and two other members of the Congregation of St. John the Baptist were captured by the

Chinese Communists and taken to Shih-chia-kang. He was subjected to interrogations and was forced to move with the Communists to Shehsien and Liaohsien. His release finally was secured on 14 April. He arrived at Loyang on 8 May, having crossed the intervening Japanese-occupied territory at night and on foot. By this time, he was seriously ill. On the morning of 13 June, he was flown to Chungking on a special plane dispatched by Chiang Kai-shek. He died on the evening of 24 June 1940, the centennial anniversary of the martyrdom of St. John Gabriel Perboyre. On 18 July, the National Government issued a statement of tribute and decreed a national day of mourning for Father Lebbe.

Lew, Timothy: *see* LIU T'ING-FANG.

Li Ang: *see* CHU CH'I-HUA.

Li Chao-lin 李兆麟
Pseud. Chang Shou-chien 張壽錢

Li Chao-lin (1908–9 March 1946), Chinese Communist political worker who became commander of the Third Route Army in Manchuria in the late 1930's. He scattered his troops, hid them, and carried on guerrilla warfare until August 1945.

Hsiaojunghuan village, Liaoyang hsien, in Liaoning, Manchuria, was the birthplace of Li Chao-lin. His father died when Li was a small boy, and Li was forced to go to work after completing his primary education. He continued to study in his spare time and went to Peiping in search of further education in 1930. Soon after arriving in Peiping, he joined the Chinese Communist party.

After the Japanese invaded Mukden on 18 September 1931, Li Chao-lin joined the Peiping Anti-Japanese National Salvation Society and returned to Manchuria to join anti-Japanese forces led by Keng Chi-chou. Keng's troops were defeated after a series of engagements near Hsinmin, west of Mukden, and Li went back to Peiping. Early in 1932 he was sent to the Liaohsi region to serve with the forces of Li Ch'un-lun. After these forces were defeated

and dispersed, Li Chao-lin went to Mukden. The Chinese Communist party's special commission for Fengtien sent him to Penhsihu to organize the coal miners of the area into an anti-Japanese unit. He worked as a coal miner for about eight months and created a unit of about 300 coal miners. In the spring of 1933, he was forced to leave Penhsihu because of his organizing activities. He returned to Mukden and became a member of the Chinese Communist special military affairs committee for Fengtien. Before long, he was forced to flee again, this time to Harbin, because of Japanese military action in the Mukden area. He participated in the anti-Japanese campaigns of so-called people's revolutionary forces in the winter of 1933.

In 1934 Li Chao-lin was sent to northeastern Manchuria to serve as a political worker in the Third Anti-Japanese Allied Army of Chao Shang-chih. By this time, he had assumed the pseudonym Chang Shou-chien. Seven people's revolutionary units came into existence in Manchuria. On orders from the Chinese Communist party, they were reorganized into three route armies of the Anti-Japanese Allied Army in July 1936, with Chao's unit as the Third Route Army. After the 1938 Kwantung Army campaign against these armies, the Third Route Army, which had suffered heavy losses, was ordered to northwestern Manchuria. By this time, Li Chao-lin had become commander in chief of the remnant forces, and he led the Third Route Army to its new station in the dead of winter. Food and medicine were in short supply, and the army was in constant danger of Japanese attack. Li established a base in the Amur River plain and the Nun River valley and carried on guerrilla warfare against the Japanese.

By 1941, because of the buildup of Japanese troop strength in Manchuria, Li had scattered his troops and hidden them in order to survive. When troops from the Soviet Union invaded Manchuria in August 1945, the surviving underground fighters emerged from their hiding places and resumed military operations. Li, in accordance with the Chinese Communist program formulated at Yenan, worked to increase Communist influence in Manchuria. The Chinese Communists appointed him vice chairman of Sungkiang province. After the National Government appointed a governor of Sungkiang in January 1946, Li resigned to become head of the Sino-Soviet Friendship Association at Harbin. On 9 March, he was stabbed to death by two unknown assassins.

Li Chi   李 濟
T. Chi-chih   濟 之

Li Chi (1896–), archaeologist who became head of the archaeology section of the Academia Sinica's institute of history and philology in 1928 and director of that institute in Taiwan in 1955. He was best known to Westerners for his direction of the excavations at Anyang.

A native of Chunghsiang, Hupeh, Li Chi was born into a scholarly family. His father, Li Hsün-fu, served in the Ch'ing government in Peking, where Li Chi received his childhood education. When the Tsinghua Academy was established in 1911 to prepare students for higher education in the United States on Boxer Indemnity Fund scholarships, Li took and passed its first entrance examination. After being graduated in 1918 he went to the United States, where he studied psychology and sociology at Clark University in Massachusetts. He received the B.A. in 1919 and the M.A. in 1920.

In the fall of 1920 Li began graduate work at Harvard in anthropology and archaeology. He received the Ph.D. in 1923. His doctoral dissertation was *The Formation of the Chinese People: An Anthropological Inquiry.* An abridged Chinese translation by Lei Pao-hua appeared in the journal *K'o-hsueh* [science], in 1925. Li later expanded the dissertation, and it was published by the Harvard University Press in 1928.

After returning to China in the autumn of 1923, Li accepted an appointment as lecturer at Nankai University in Tientsin. He soon met V. K. Ting (Ting Wen-chiang, q.v.), who was then general manager of the Pei-p'iao Coal Company. Later, when Ting heard that a large number of ancient bronze vessels had been discovered in Hsincheng, Honan, he sent Li and a member of the China Geological Survey to investigate the site of discovery, but, because of the uncooperative attitude of the local populace and a rumor of banditry, nothing came of the effort.

In 1925 Tsinghua Academy was reorganized as a university. A research institute for Sinological studies was established with the aim of applying modern research methods to the study of traditional Chinese culture. Li was asked to join its faculty in company with such eminent scholars as Liang Ch'i-ch'ao, Wang Kuo-wei, and Chao Yuen-ren (qq.v.). In the meantime, the Freer Art Gallery, through its representative Carl W. Bishop, had invited Li to join its field archaeology staff. Because of his obligation to Chang Po-ling (q.v.), the chancellor of Nankai University, Li found it difficult to decide which offer to accept. On the advice of V. K. Ting, Li accepted the Tsinghua appointment and advanced two conditions for participating in the Freer venture: that excavations must be done in cooperation with Chinese academic organizations and that all cultural relics must remain in China. Two months later, he received a letter from Carl Bishop which stated that the Freer Gallery would never ask a patriotic man to do what he did not want to do. Li was satisfied with the answer. Subsequently, an agreement was made between Bishop and the Tsinghua Research Institute by which the Freer Gallery would finance an expedition directed by Li and sponsored by the university. Li and Yuan Fu-li, a geologist, then undertook the Hsia-hsien expedition in Shansi. Excavation was begun in the spring of 1926 at the village of Hsi-yin-ts'un, and numerous prehistoric painted potsherds and some silkworm cocoons were found. The result of this expedition was reported in Li's *Hsi-yin-ts'un shih-ch'ien ti i-ts'un* [prehistoric remains at Hsi-yin-ts'un], published by Tsinghua University in 1929.

In 1928 the research institute at Tsinghua was discontinued. Li then went briefly to the United States to discuss with officials of the Freer Gallery the possibility of continuing his excavating work. The Freer Gallery agreed to give Li complete freedom to collaborate with any Chinese academic institution he chose. When the institute of history and philology of the Academia Sinica was formally established in Canton in November 1928 under the direction of Fu Ssu-nien (q.v.), Fu wired Li Chi asking him to head the archaeology section of the institute. In December, Li met Fu in Canton, where the two men came to an understanding on Li's status with the Academia Sinica and with the Freer Gallery. Li was to undertake a planned excavation of the Yin site at Anyang,

Honan, for both the Academia Sinica and the Freer Gallery, with the latter providing the financial support. Soon after, in the spring of 1929, the institute of history and philology was transferred to Peiping; Li remained in Peiping until 1934.

Previously, in October 1928, before Li had been appointed to his new post, Fu Ssu-nien had sent Tung Tso-pin (q.v.), a member of the institute, to make a preliminary survey of the Anyang site. The excavation under Li's direction which began on 7 March and which lasted until 10 May 1929, was the second of a series of fifteen digs undertaken at Anyang prior to the Japanese invasion. A great quantity of potsherds, some bronzes, and 684 inscribed oracle bones and tortoise shells were uncovered. Work at the site was interrupted by civil war between Feng Yü-hsiang (q.v.) and Chiang Kai-shek, but excavations were resumed in the autumn. From 7 October to 12 December an unprecedented number of inscribed oracle bones and shells, some pottery and bronze vessels, and two inscribed oracle bones and skulls were unearthed. A unique fragment of painted pottery was also discovered at the site. This discovery created the possibility of identifying for the first time the chronological relationship between the prehistoric painted pottery culture of Yangshao, discovered in 1921 by J. G. Andersson, a Swedish geologist, and the historic Shang-Yin culture.

Disputes with the Honan provincial authorities and unauthorized diggings carried on under their auspices caused suspension of the Anyang excavations. Li tendered his resignation to the Freer Gallery on 22 February 1930. The burden of the financial support for the operation was then assumed by the China Foundation for the Promotion of Education and Culture, which presented the institute with a chair in archaeology with an annual salary of 6,000 yuan for five years and an annual grant of 10,000 yuan for three years for field work to begin in 1931.

With the Anyang excavations halted and the financial question waiting to be settled, Li devoted his time to writing and editing the reports of the Anyang finds. In May, he went to Nanking to investigate the site of Six Dynasties tombs and then to Shantung province where Wu Chin-ting, an assistant at the institute, had discovered a black-pottery site at Ch'eng-tzu-yai

in Lich'eng. Realizing the importance of the find, Li decided to start excavating there on 7 November 1930. After 30 days of digging, the expedition confirmed the existence of a new culture complex, which Li designated the Lungshan culture in honor of the township in which Ch'eng-tzu-yai is located.

The excavations at Anyang were resumed on 21 March 1931, with the support of the Honan government, and lasted until 11 May. Li was joined by two other trained archaeologists, Liang Ssu-yung (q.v.) and Kuo Pao-chun. At Houkang, the fifth series of excavations, from 7 November to 9 December, unearthed Yin, Lungshan, and Yangshao strata in clear stratigraphic sequence. This was the first time that strata representing these three culture complexes had been found in a single site.

The Japanese invasion of Manchuria on 18 September 1931 aroused Li's patriotism. A group of scholars, including Fu Ssu-nien and T. F. Tsiang (Chiang T'ing-fu, q.v.), had written *Tung-pei shih-kang* [outline history of the Northeast], an historical account of China's relationship with the northeastern provinces, designed to refute Japanese propaganda saying that Manchuria had never been a part of China. Li took time out from his archaeological work to abridge and translate this work into English. It was published in Peiping in 1932 as *Manchuria in History: A Summary*.

The deepening national crisis lent a sense of urgency to the task of completing the Anyang excavations. The sixth series of excavations was carried out from 12 April to 31 May 1932, the seventh from 19 October to 15 December 1932, and the eighth from 20 October to 25 December 1933. In 1934 the institute of history and philology was moved from Peiping to Nanking. The ninth series of excavations, from 9 March to 31 May, shifted the base of operations from Hsiao-t'un on the south bank of the Huai River to Hou-chia-chuang on the north bank. In the tenth series, from 3 October to 29 December, four large tombs were opened, in which more than a thousand stone implements were discovered. Li agreed with Liang Ssu-yung, who was the field director, that Hou-chia-chuang was undoubtedly the burial ground of the Yin capital unearthed at Hsiao-t'un. Since it was known that the Yin people paid much attention to the dead, it was decided that a large-scale excavation of the new site was justified.

By that time Li had succeeded Fu Ssu-nien as the director of the preparatory office of National Central Museum, which was organized in April 1933 with the support of the British Boxer Indemnity Fund. V. K. Ting, the director general of the Academia Sinica, was a member of the museum's board of directors. Since additional financial support was needed to finance the Hou-chia-chuang excavation, Li proposed that the museum assume part of the expenses. Ting readily gave his consent. In March 1935 work began on the burial site. A great variety of bronze, jade, ivory, and pottery remains were uncovered before digging ceased on 15 June. After a summer recess, the excavation was resumed with a force of 500 workmen. In the period from 5 September to 16 December, 8 large tombs and 785 small tombs were opened. Beginning with the thirteenth series of excavations, from 18 March to 24 June 1936, the operation was shifted back to the Hsiao-t'un site, where an unprecedented number of inscribed oracle bones and tortoise shells were found.

The Anyang and Lungshan discoveries gained world-wide attention through the reports issued by the institute and the writings of such noted scholars as Paul Pelliot, Bernard Karlgren, and W. P. Yetts. In the spring of 1936 some of the Anyang bronzes were displayed at the Chinese Art Exhibition held in London. That winter, Li was invited by the English Association of Universities and the Swedish heir apparent, later King Gustav VI, to lecture at London and Stockholm.

The fifteenth series of excavations were undertaken from 16 March to 10 June 1937. Several weeks later, the Sino-Japanese war broke out. Li, who had just returned from Europe, supervised the removal of all the records and remains of the Anyang excavations from Nanking to Changsha, Hunan, where the institute of history and philology found a temporary home. When the Japanese advanced toward Hankow, the institute was evacuated farther inland to Kunming, Yunnan. In 1938, in recognition of his contributions to the development of archaeology in China, the Royal Anthropological Institute of Great Britain and Ireland elected Li an Honorary Fellow.

Li soon resumed field investigations. Expeditions were dispatched to Shensi, and to Tali and Kunming in Yunnan. In 1939 the institute was moved to Lichuang, a village in Nanch'i, Szechwan, where it remained until the end of the war. In the spring of 1946 the institute returned to Nanking. Soon afterwards, Li was appointed a member of the Chinese delegation stationed in occupied Japan. His task was to trace and recover cultural objects pillaged from China by Japanese soldiers and civilians during the war. In March 1948 Li Chi was among the 81 scientists and scholars elected to the Academia Sinica. These men were to be responsible for the direction of the scientific development of postwar China. Liang Ssu-yung, Tung Tso-pin, and Kuo Mo-jo (q.v.) were also elected to represent the field of archaeology.

By the winter of 1948 the tide of civil war was turning against the National Government. The Academia Sinica had to be evacuated to Taiwan. Li aided in removing the art treasures and archaeological specimens of the institute of history and philology, the Central Museum, and the Palace Museum from the mainland to Taiwan. In February 1949 he was appointed professor of history at National Taiwan University. In August, he became the chairman of the university's department of archaeology and anthropology.

Li led a Chinese delegation to the Eighth Pacific Science Conference and the Fourth Far Eastern Prehistory Conference held in the Philippines in 1953. He accepted a Rockefeller grant in 1954 to lecture at the Escuela Nacional de Antropologia e Historia in Mexico. In 1955 the University of Washington at Seattle invited him to lecture on ancient Chinese culture. The three lectures he gave there were published in 1957 as *The Beginnings of Chinese Civilization*.

After returning to Taipei in the summer of 1955, Li was appointed director of the institute of history and philology. He left Taiwan for the United States on 20 October 1959 to do research and lecture at Harvard. In June 1960 he visited the Museum of Natural History in Washington, D.C., and later, the Toronto University Museum in Canada to advise on the display of their collections of ancient Chinese artifacts. In July, he attended the Sino-American Conference on Intellectual Cooperation held at Seattle, Washington. He then returned to Taiwan, arriving there on 3 September.

As an advocate of new methodology Li Chi succeeded through his writings and field work in making systematic excavation, stratigraphy, and typology essential to the scientific study of China's past history. He demonstrated that modern archaeology and the traditional study of ancient artifacts enhance each other. In this respect the *An-yang fa-chueh pao-kao* [report on the An-yang excavations] for 1928 edited by Li is epoch-making. Under his leadership Chinese archaeologists, with limited financial backing and working in a time of political turmoil, carried out significant excavations. Many leading Chinese archaeologists, such as Yin Ta, Hsia Nai, Yin Huang-chang, Shih Chang-yu, and Kao Chu-hsun received their practical training under Li.

As a student of China's ancient history Li wrote the pioneering study of the formation of the Chinese people, contributed significant studies of Shang artifacts, and formulated a precise and workable terminology for the description of ancient artifacts. His interpretations of the ancient cultures of north China, based on his intensive knowledge of many prehistoric and historic sites and collections as well as his wide acquaintance of archaeological developments in other parts of the world, greatly increased understanding of a still dimly known period of China's past. In these areas his most significant publications were *The Formation of the Chinese People, Hsi-yin-ts'un shih-ch'ien ti i-ts'un*, and *Ch'eng-tzu-yai* (1934), in which Li hypothesized a Lungshan culture complex extending over eastern China during the neolithic period and indicated its relationship to the civilization of Shang; the *An-yang fa-chueh pai-kao* for 1929–33, also edited by Li; "Yin-ch'ü t'ung-ch'i wu-chung chi ch'i hsiang-kuan wen-t'i" [five bronze objects from Anyang and problems related to them], an article of 1933; and "Chi Hsiao-t'un ch'u-t'u chi ch'ing-t'ung-ch'i" [Hsiao-t'un and the bronzes discovered there], an article which appeared in *Chung-kuo k'ao-ku hsueh-pao* [Chinese archaeology] in 1948–49 and which established a precise and well-organized terminology for bronzes and the details of their decor.

Li Chi-shen　　　李 濟 深
　T. Jen-ch'ao　　　任 潮
　Alt. Li Chai-sum

Li Chi-shen (1886–9 October 1959), commander of the Fourth Army (1925–26) who served during the Northern Expedition as governor of Kwangtung, military affairs commissioner, and acting president of the Whampoa Military Academy. He became the top-ranking military and political officer at Canton. He later participated in several movements which opposed Chiang Kai-shek. After being expelled from the Kuomintang in 1947, he became chairman of the Kuomintang Revolutionary Committee (1948) and an official of the Central People's Government.

A native of Kiangsu, Li Chi-shen was born into a scholar-gentry family in Hushents'un, Ts'angwu hsien (Wuchow), Kwangsi. His mother died when he was four years old. In 1903, after receiving a primary education in the Chinese classics, Li enrolled at the Wuchow Middle School, where one of his teachers was Hu Han-min (q.v.). In 1904 he transferred to the Liang-kuang Military Middle School in Canton. Three years later, he was selected for advanced study in Peking at the Officers Military Academy, run by the Board of War. He interrupted his studies after the Wuchang revolt of October 1911 to serve as chief of staff of the 22nd Division of the revolutionary army in Kiangsu. After the republic had been established, he returned to the academy, now called the Military Staff College. After being graduated, he remained at the college as an instructor. He also served as an editor in the research bureau of the ministry of war.

In 1921 Li went to Canton at the invitation of Teng K'eng (q.v.), who was chief of staff of the Kwangtung Army and commander of the 1st Division. Teng appointed him chief of staff of the 1st Division. Teng was assassinated in March 1922, and Ch'en Chiung-ming (q.v.) staged a coup in Canton on 16 June. Li Chi-shen participated in the campaign that drove Ch'en from Canton in the spring of 1923. He then received command of the 1st Division.

In 1924 Li served briefly as commissioner of reconstruction of the West River–Wuchow area and Wuchow garrison commander. When the Whampoa Military Academy was established in May 1924, Li became deputy dean, serving under Chiang Kai-shek. After Sun Yat-sen's death in March 1925, the Canton government was reorganized as the National Government. Hsü Ch'ung-chih (q.v.), the commander of the Kwangtung Army, became minister of war, and he relinquished command of the army on 1 August 1925. The National Revolutionary Army was created in August, and Li was appointed commander of the Fourth Army (formerly the Kwangtung Army). Among the men who served under him in that army were Chang Fa-k'uei, Ch'en Ming-shu, Ts'ai T'ing-k'ai, and Ch'en Chi-t'ang. (qq.v.).

Because Ch'en Chiung-ming's forces still maintained a strong position along the East River, a second eastern expedition was organized. Li's Fourth Army formed the second column of the expeditionary forces which destroyed Ch'en's remaining power in October-November 1925. In the final phase of this campaign Li led his troops into southern Kwangtung to destroy the power of Ch'en's supporter Teng Pen-yin.

When the Northern Expedition began in July 1926, the divisions of the Fourth Army led by Chang Fa-k'uei and Ch'en Ming-shu participated in the drive northward. Li Chi-shen and the Fourth Army divisions under Ch'en Chi-t'ang and Hsü Ching-t'ang remained behind to garrison the Canton area. Li also served as governor of Kwangtung, military affairs commissioner, and acting president of the Whampoa Military Academy. In 1927 he was elected to the Central Executive Committee of the Kuomintang.

In 1927 Chang Fa-k'uei's division was expanded and was given the designation of Fourth Army. Some of his forces, commanded by Ho Lung and Yeh T'ing (qq.v.) took part in the Communist-led uprising at Nanchang on 1 August. At Li Chi-shen's request, Huang Shao-hung (q.v.) organized the Fifteenth Army and defeated the Chinese Communist forces at Swatow and Chaochow. In the meantime, the Kuomintang factions at Wuhan and Nanking were attempting to resolve their differences. Such Wuhan leaders as Wang Ching-wei, Ho Hsiang-ning, and Ch'en Kung-po went to Canton and conferred with Li Chi-shen. In early November, Li and Wang left Canton and went to Shanghai to attend a plenary session of the Central Executive Committee. The purpose of the meeting was the restoration of party unity.

On 17 November 1927 Chang Fa-k'uei, taking advantage of Li's absence, staged a coup at Canton. Li promptly ordered forces loyal to him to oust Chang. He directed Ch'en Ming-shu, then in Fukien, to return with his men to Canton. Huang Shao-hung's Kwangsi forces soon converged on Canton. Chang Fa-k'uei deployed forces along the East and West rivers to defend his position. However, few of his troops remained in Canton, and on 11 December some of his troops, led by Huang Ch'i-hsiang, joined with Communist elements to stage the Canton Commune (see Chang T'ai-lei). Chang's forces suppressed these rebels two days later. When Ch'en Ming-shu and Huang Shao-hung moved against Chang from two directions and caused heavy casualties among his troops, Chang Fa-k'uei announced that he had been relieved of his posts and requested an opportunity to redeem himself. Li Chi-shen returned to Canton on 4 January 1928.

Li was made a member of the standing committee of the Military Affairs Commission on 7 February 1928. He also became commander in chief of the newly established Eighth Route Army, which was composed of the military forces stationed in Kwangtung. On 1 March, the Central Executive Committee of the Kuomintang issued regulations governing branch political councils, and Li Chi-shen became chairman of the important Canton branch. On 30 March, he was named chief of the general staff of the Northern Expedition. He joined other Kuomintang leaders in Peking for meetings in July, and after Chiang Kai-shek returned to Nanking, he served as acting commander in chief of the Nationalist forces. However, he soon left Peking and returned to Canton. Li was appointed to the State Council on 8 October, and he relinquished the post of governor of Kwangtung to Ch'en Ming-shu in November.

In 1929 the so-called Kwangsi clique of Li Tsung-jen, Pai Ch'ung-hsi (qq.v.), and Huang Shao-hung broke with the National Government. Li Chi-shen went to Nanking in mid-March to attend the Third National Congress of the Kuomintang and to mediate the dispute between Chiang Kai-shek and the Kwangsi clique. On 20 March, Chiang Kai-shek made a statement in which he specifically rejected mediation as a means of ending the dispute. The following day, Li Chi-shen was placed under detention. On 27 March, Li Tsung-jen, Pai Ch'ung-hsi, and Li Chi-shen were expelled from the Kuomintang. After the Japanese attacked Mukden on 18 September 1931, the opposing factions were reunited, and Chiang

Kai-shek was forced to retire from office. The Kwangsi leaders were restored to party membership in October, and Li Chi-shen was freed. He was appointed inspector general of military training in December.

After Chiang Kai-shek returned to power, Li remained at Canton, although he did not resign from office. He was a member of the Southwest Political Council and an *ex officio* member of the Military Affairs Commission, but he had no real function at Nanking or Canton. About 1933 he left Canton for Hong Kong.

In 1933 Ch'en Ming-shu (q.v.), urged on by members of his Social Democratic party, decided to actively oppose Nanking's authority. After meeting with Li Chi-shen and others, Ch'en launched the Fukien revolt. On 20 November, Ch'en and his associates proclaimed the establishment of a people's revolutionary government at Foochow, with Li Chi-shen as chairman. Li assumed office on 21 November. However, Ch'en made the important decisions, and Li was only a figurehead. Nanking moved quickly to suppress the revolt, and the government at Foochow was dissolved in January 1934. Li Chi-shen fled to Hong Kong. The National Government ordered his arrest, expelled him from the Kuomintang, and dismissed him from his official post.

In 1935 Li, along with some of his Fukien associates and Feng Yü-hsiang, founded the Chinese People's Revolutionary League to unite China in resistance to Japan and to work for "overthrow of the traitor government and establishment of the people's state power." The league sought alliance with other groups, but had little success. In 1936 Li went to Kwangsi to help plan a joint Kwangtung-Kwangsi revolt against Nanking. The revolt began in June, but it received a fatal blow in early July when the Kwangtung air force (*see* Ch'en Chi-t'ang) defected to the National Government side. On 30 July, Li Tsung-jen and Pai Ch'ung-hsi organized a military government in Kwangsi, with Li Chi-shen as its chairman. However, the mediation efforts of Huang Shao-hung and Ch'eng Ch'ien (q.v.) led to an agreement between Li Tsung-jen and Chiang Kai-shek by which Kwangsi accepted the authority of the National Government. Although the order for Li Chi-shen's arrest was rescinded, he took refuge in Hong Kong.

After the Sino-Japanese war began in 1937, Li dissolved the Chinese People's Revolutionary League, saying that it had accomplished its mission of mobilizing the nation to fight Japan. In 1938 he was restored to membership in the Kuomintang. He also became a member of the Military Affairs Commission and the State Council. In 1941, when the Japanese began to threaten Kwangsi, Li was appointed director of the Kweilin field headquarters of the Military Affairs Commission and vice chairman of the war areas party and political affairs commission. The culmination of the Japanese offensive known as Operation Ichi-go was the occupation of Kweilin in mid-November 1944. Li then was appointed president of the Military Advisory Council but he refused to go to Chungking to assume office. Instead he organized a people's mobilization committee in southern Kwangsi and worked to consolidate resistance to the Japanese. The National Government disapproved of Li's unauthorized program but took no action against him. In May 1945 at the Sixth National Congress of the Kuomintang, Li Chi-shen was elected to the Central Supervisory Committee of the Kuomintang. The following year he was a Kuomintang delegate to the National Assembly.

Li went to Hong Kong in early 1947 and issued a statement (8 March) urging that the Nationalists and the Communists settle their differences and end the civil war. On 6 August, he was expelled from the Kuomintang on the grounds that he had made unwarranted statements and had incited the people to riot. Li soon joined the Democracy Promotion Association and the International League for the Promotion of Human Rights. He also worked to unite Kuomintang members and former members who opposed the policies of the National Government. His activities resulted in a conference, convened on 12 November, which, in turn, led to the formation of the Kuomintang Revolutionary Committee. That group was inaugurated in January 1948 with Madame Sun Yat-sen (Soong Ch'ing-ling) as its honorary chairman and Li Chi-shen as its chairman. The founding members of the committee included Feng Yü-hsiang Ho Hsiang-ning, Liu Ya-tzu, and T'an P'ing-shan. The two basic aims of the Kuomintang Revolutionary Committee, as set forth in its inaugural declaration, were the implementation of Sun Yat-sen's policies and the completion of the anti-feudal and anti-imperialist missions of the "Chinese Revolution."

In early 1949 Li Chi-shen left Hong Kong and journeyed north. He arrived in Peiping in February, shortly after the Chinese Communists occupied the city. As the chief representative of the Kuomintang Revolutionary Committee, he was appointed to the preparatory committee for the Chinese People's Political Consultative Conference. When the conference convened in September 1949, Li was elected vice chairman of its Standing Committee. The work of the conference laid the foundation of a new political regime in China, and the Central People's Government was inaugurated on 1 October 1949. Li became one of the six vice chairmen of the Central People's Government and vice president of the Sino-Soviet Friendship Association.

In January 1953 Li was made a member of the committee assigned to draft a constitution. He served as a delegate from Kwangsi to the National People's Conference in September 1954. The 1954 constitution reduced the number of government vice chairmen from six to two, and Li gave up his post. He then became a vice chairman of the Standing Committee of the National People's Congress. In 1955 he was appointed to the executive committee of the People's Parliamentary Group for Joining the Inter-Parliamentary Union. From November 1956 to January 1957 he served as deputy leader of a National People's Congress delegation which visited the Soviet Union and Eastern Europe. He participated in the National People's Congress of 1958 as a delegate from Kwangsi, and he was reelected vice chairman of the Standing Committee of the congress in April 1959. Also in April, he was elected vice chairman of the National Committee of the Chinese People's Political Consultative Conference and vice president of the executive board of the Sino-Soviet Friendship Association. Throughout this period, he continued to head the central committee of the Kuomintang Revolutionary Committee. On 9 October 1959 he died at Peking of stomach cancer and a cerebral thrombosis.

Li Chi-shen married several times and had a number of children. One of his sons became dean of the agricultural college of Lingnan University in the early 1940's. His eldest son,

Li Hao-hsuan, was given a 12-year prison sentence in 1952 for exploiting the peasantry. Three daughters—Li Hsiao-chu, Li Hsiao-lien, and Li Hsiao-tao—reportedly were students at Yenching University in 1950.

Li Fang-kuei   李方桂

Li Fang-kuei (20 August 1902–), anthropologist and linguist whose scholarly interests ranged from the study of Archaic and Ancient Chinese to the languages and cultures of American Indian tribes.

Although his native place was Hsiyang, Shansi, Li Fang-kuei was born in Canton. He was the fifth child of Li Kuang-yü, an expectant taot'ai who had received the chin-shih degree in 1880. When Li Kuang-yü retired to Shansi in 1910, he left his wife, née Ho Chao-ying, in Peking to supervise the education of their children. In 1915, after several years of elementary school supplemented by private tutoring, Li Fang-kuei entered the Shih-ta fu chung [normal university middle school], where he soon demonstrated exceptional ability in all subjects. Upon graduation, Li passed the Tsinghua College entrance examinations and enrolled in its pre-medical program. In 1924 his outstanding academic record at Tsinghua won him a fellowship for advanced study in the United States.

Li enrolled at the University of Michigan in the autumn of 1924. Because Latin and German had fascinated him as a pre-medical student, he decided to change his field of concentration to linguistics. He was elected to Phi Beta Kappa and was graduated *magna cum laude* in June 1926. That autumn, he began graduate work in linguistics at the University of Chicago, where he studied under the eminent linguists Edward Sapir and Leonard Bloomfield. Li made significant contributions to the study of American Indian languages, applying the theories and modern techniques of descriptive linguistics to this almost untouched field. He received the M.A. degree in 1927 and the Ph.D. in 1928. His Master's thesis, "A Study of Sarcee Verb Stems," was published in the *International Journal of American Linguistics* in June 1930, and his dissertation, "Mattole, an

Athabaskan Language," became an indispensable reference for the study of Athabaskan linguistics. After spending the academic year 1928–29 at Harvard University as a Harvard-Yenching fellow, he returned to China on a Social Science Research Council fellowship to study Chinese dialects.

In 1929 Li joined the staff of the Academia Sinica's institute of history and philology, which included Y. R. Chao (Chao Yuen-ren), Fu Ssu-nien, Li Chi, and Ch'en Yin-k'o (qq.v.). Research on the island of Hainan led Li to the study of ancient phonology. The Swedish scholar Bernhard Karlgren had argued a few years earlier that all varieties of modern Chinese derive from a single T'ang prototype, which he called Ancient Chinese. In the course of his dialect studies, Li had discovered evidence that contradicted certain aspects of Karlgren's reconstruction of this prototype. Beginning with "The Sources of the Ancient Chinese Vowel â" of 1932, he demonstrated his solid approach to Chinese historical phonology in a series of articles which appeared in the Academia Sinica's *Bulletin of the Institute of History and Philology*. Some of his criticisms of Karlgren's theory were accepted by Karlgren himself. In 1935 Li and Y. R. Chao did pioneering field work in Kwangtung, Kwangsi, and Hunan, recording and investigating dialects. Li also worked with Y. R. Chao and Lo Ch'ang-p'ei (q.v.) on a Chinese translation of Karlgren's monumental work, *Etudes sur la phonologie chinoise*, which was published in 1940 under the title *Chung-kuo yin-yün-hsüeh yen-chiu*.

Li Fang-kuei moved from his study of Ancient Chinese to a consideration of Archaic Chinese, Karlgren's term for the language of the *Shih ching* [book of odes]. He then began an investigation of non-Chinese languages of the Sino-Tibetan family to provide more external evidence to substantiate his reconstruction of Archaic Chinese. As early as 1929 he had studied such languages on Hainan, and in 1933 he had spent three months in Thailand studying Tai languages. His 1935 investigations in Kwangsi had included studies of non-Chinese dialects, and in 1936 he had studied the Pai-yu dialect.

Li Fang-kuei's field work was interrupted in 1937 when he went to the United States to spend two years at Yale University as a visiting professor. After returning to China, he spent 1940–45 investigating non-Chinese languages in Yunnan, Kweichow, and Szechwan. During this period he collected a vast amount of data, more than could be analyzed at the time. His monographs *The Tai Dialect of Lungchow* and *Notes on the Mak Languages* appeared in 1940 and 1943, respectively. Li also found time to serve as visiting professor of Chinese linguistics at Yenching University from 1944 to 1946.

In the autumn of 1946 Li Fang-kuei went to the United States as a visiting lecturer in Chinese linguistics at Harvard University. In 1948 he left Harvard to assume a similar post at Yale. The following year he moved to the University of Washington at Seattle, and in 1950 he became a permanent member of the Washington faculty. He also became vice president of the Linguistic Society of America (1950) and an associate editor of the *International Journal of American Linguistics*.

Li's departure from China did not disrupt his scholarly activities in comparative Tai, Chinese, Tibetan, and American Indian languages. He resumed his inquiries into Athabaskan linguistics and wrote such articles as "Some Problems in Comparative Athabaskan," which appeared in the *Canadian Journal of Linguistics* in 1965. His writings on Tibetan included "The Study of Sino-Tibetan Languages," which was published in *K'o-hsueh chi-k'an* in 1951; "Tibetan Globa-'dring," which appeared in the 1959 volume *Studia Serica Bernard Karlgren Dedicata*; and "A Sino-Tibetan Glossary from Tun-huang," published in the *T'oung Pao* in 1963. Li fostered Tibetan studies at the University of Washington and invited a number of Tibetan refugees to participate in the university's program, thus creating a center of Tibetology in Seattle. The majority of Li's publications were in the area of comparative Tai studies, with special concentration on Tai, Kam-sui, and T'en. His researches into these languages and the related Mak language indicated that they had branched off from Tai. With this relationship as a basis, Li reconstructed the tones of Ancient Tai, demonstrated their close resemblance to the tones of Ancient Chinese, and suggested that other over-all resemblances between the two languages could be established. Although Li published little on Chinese linguistics after 1946, all of his research was relevant to his work toward the reconstruction of Archaic Chinese. For example, "Some Fundamental Ideas of

Chinese Grammar," which appeared in the *Memoir of the Tenth Anniversary of Taiwan National University* (1956), showed how the results of comparative studies could be used in solving problems of reconstruction.

Li married Hsü Ying, a daughter of Hsü Shu-cheng (q.v.), on 21 August 1932. One son, Peter, and two daughters, Lindy and Anne, were born to them.

Li Fei-kan   李 芾 甘
Pen. Pa Chin   巴 金

Li Fei-kan (1904–), anarchist writer known as Pa Chin, whose novels and short stories achieved popularity in the 1930's and 1940's.

Born in Chengtu, Szechwan, Li Fei-kan came from a wealthy and educated gentry family. His early childhood was spent in Chengtu except for three years in Kuangyuan, where his father was magistrate from 1906 to 1911. Li's mother died when he was ten, and two years later his father died. His life was also darkened by the deaths of an elder sister and of a maid-servant who had been his playmate. The remainder of his childhood and youth were spent in his grandfather's house in Chengtu, an extensive establishment which Li later described as "a despotic kingdom." From his early experiences in this household grew Li's lifelong detestation of the traditional Chinese family system.

After several years of traditional Chinese studies under the supervision of a tutor, Li entered a modern school in Chengtu which emphasized the study of foreign languages. He remained there until 1923 and acquired a knowledge of English and French. He also became aware of social problems. Li's interests in foreign literature and social reform soon led him to explore the radical writings then available to Chinese readers. He was impressed by the anarchist writers Peter Kropotkin and Emma Goldman, by Leopold Kamf's play *On the Eve* (which depicted Russian revolutionaries of 1905 and which Li and his friends staged several times), and by magazines published by partisans of the May Fourth Movement. Li's socialist convictions began to take form at this time, and he also began to write. He joined a youth group, participated in agitation against the local warlord, and contributed articles to socialist and anarchist publications. This period of Li's life provided the main material for his autobiographical trilogy *Chi-liu* [turbulent stream]. About this time, he adopted the pen name Pa Chin, in honor of the eminent anarchists *Ba*kunin and Kropo*tkin*.

In 1923 Pa Chin and his elder brother went to Shanghai and then to Nanking, where he entered the middle school of Southeastern University. He was graduated in 1925. His strongest impressions of this period—the Shanghai demonstrations of 30 May 1925 and the political developments that followed—were recorded in the novel *Ssu-ch'ü-ti t'ai-yang* [the dying sun], published in 1930. From 1925 to 1927 Pa Chin lived in Shanghai as a freelance political writer. At this time, he identified himself with the anarchist movement, writing articles on anarchism and corresponding with Emma Goldman.

Pa Chin left China for France in 1927. His journey from Canton to Marseilles by way of Indo-China, Ceylon, and the Suez Canal is described in his book *Hai-hsing tsa-chi* [notes of a sea voyage], published in 1932. He spent two years in Paris and its environs, with occasional trips to London. He studied French (language and literature), philosophy, economics, political science, Russian literature, and the history of the French Revolution and of the anarchist movement. He also studied the Russian "populist" movement of the nineteenth and early twentieth centuries. His life and acquaintances in France provided him with the material for a number of short stories. He also continued to correspond with prominent anarchists. The execution, on 23 August 1927, of Sacco and Vanzetti in the United States shocked him deeply. The articles collected in 1929 as *Tuan-t'ou t'ai-shang* [on the scaffold] were written in this period, as were the biographies of several Russian women revolutionaries, a number of theoretical treatises on the ideology of anarchism, and a Chinese translation of Peter Kropotkin's *Ethics*. He also wrote a novel based on his experiences in China just before his departure. *Mieh-wang* [destruction] was completed in 1929 and published the same year in *Hsiao-shuo yueh-pao (Short Story Magazine)*. The novel was a great success, and when Pa Chin returned to China in 1929, he found himself famous.

From 1929 to 1934 Pa Chin lived in Shanghai. He continued to work on translations and to write on social problems for anarchist periodicals, but his main concern was the writing of novels and short stories. During this period his great success was the novel *Chia* [family] of 1931, the first volume of the autobiographical trilogy *Chi-liu*. He also wrote *Ssu-ch'ü-ti t'ai-yang; Hsin-sheng* [new life], published in 1931; *Hai-ti meng* [sea dream], published in 1932; *Ch'un-t'ien-li ti ch'iu-t'ien* [autumn in the midst of spring], published in 1932; and *Ai-ti san-pu ch'ü* [three songs of love]. Most of these works describe the life of the Chinese intelligentsia. During a trip to north China, he had an opportunity to observe the life of Chinese coal miners. In 1933 he published a novel exposing their plight, *Hsueh* [snow]. It clearly emulated Zola's *Germinal;* in fact, its original title was *Meng-ya* [young shoots]. Li wrote a similar novel about the antimony miners of south China, *Sha-ting* [toilers in the sand]. During this period, he wrote with enthusiasm about his literary work as a mission; he felt "an inner urge to describe my life, feelings and ideas of Chinese youth and to influence life by my writings." His dedication to his political and social dreams, what he called "something which has a more perennial value than art," led him on more than one occasion to shun the striving for excellence which characterized his contemporary Mao Tun (Shen Yen-ping, q.v.) and to pursue immediate propagandistic ends. Pa Chin refused to acknowledge himself as an artist, depicting his process of creation as a kind of frenzy or daemonic possession in which he figured merely as an instrument through which overmastering passions were channeled. For all his political fervor, he did not align himself with any of the literary groups of the time. Unlike the majority of left-wing writers, who sympathized with the Communists, he continued to belong to the small group of Chinese anarchists.

In January 1932 Pa Chin saw the destruction of his home and property during the looting and burning of Chapei. This experience and the Japanese occupation of Manchuria made him acutely aware of the danger of Japanese aggression and led him to participate in the struggle against the Japanese. Perhaps as a result of renewed Kuomintang pressure on Communists and other left-wing elements in 1933, he found it prudent to leave China. Although he was an outspoken foe of Japanese policy in China, he went to Japan and remained there from October 1934 to July 1935. His impressions were reflected in the stories collected under the title *Shen, kuei, jen* [gods, demons, and men] and in the collection of essays called *Tien-ti* [drips and drops].

After returning to Shanghai in 1935, Pa Chin devoted most of his time to editorial work and to the writing of essays and book reviews. He was chief editor of the series *Wen-hua sheng-huo* [culture and life], which published translations of works by foreign writers as well as original Chinese works. He and the novelist Chang Chin-i established the *Wen-hsueh yueh-k'an* [literary monthly], which was suspended after only seven weeks by government order.

Despite his writings and activities on behalf of the left, Pa Chin was attacked by the Communists and their supporters. His opponents called his works "politically wrong and artistically inadequate," and he was reproached for his "vague humanitarianism" and for his continued adherence to the anarchist movement. His defense of the Spanish anarchists during the Spanish civil war also made him the target of Communist attack. Through all this, he defended his point of view, proclaimed his opposition to historical materialism, and asserted his right to dissent. As early as 1935 he unswervingly supported the united-front movement; and in October 1936, together with Lu Hsün (Chou Shu-jen, q.v.), Mao Tun, Kuo Mo-jo and others, he signed the "Manifesto for Consolidation of the Whole Literary World in Resistance to the External Enemy and for the Freedom of Speech."

The outbreak of the Sino-Japanese war in 1937 obliged Pa Chin to leave Shanghai; he spent the next eight years moving from one city to another, visiting Canton, Kunming, Kweilin and Chungking in the course of his wartime travels. In 1941 he visited Chengtu for the first time in 18 years. On 8 May 1944 he paused from his journeyings long enough to marry Ch'en Yun-chen.

During the war Pa Chin was active as a polemicist and as a creative writer. On 19 October 1937 he wrote an open letter to Yamakawa Hitoshi asserting the Chinese people's determination to resist the Japanese menace. He also was one of the leaders of the All-China Association of Artists and Writers to Resist Aggression and, at one time or another, served as co-editor of the militantly anti-Japanese magazines *Na-han* [call to arms], *Feng-huo* [the beacon], and *Wen-tsung* [literature]. He also continued to edit the *Wen-hua sheng-huo* series. The novels *Ch'un* [spring] and *Ch'iu* [autumn] appeared in 1938 and 1940 respectively, completing the trilogy *Chi-liu*. He also wrote *Huo* [fire] a novel in three volumes which appeared in 1940, 1942, and 1945. *Chieh-yuan* [garden of rest] and *Ti-ssu ping-shih* [ward four] were published in 1946. He also found time to write short stories and essays and to translate two novels of Turgenev and some of Kropotkin's treatises.

After the war, Pa Chin returned to Shanghai, where he finished *Han-yeh* [wintry night]. In 1947 he wrote *Huai-nien* [reminiscences], in which he recalled those of his friends who had fallen in the struggle against Japan. He continued to edit the *Wen-hua sheng-huo* series.

After the People's Republic of China was established, reprints of Pa Chin's works began to appear, evidence of his good standing with the new Communist regime. Chang Chin-i and he established a magazine called *Shou-huo* [harvest]. Pa Chin did not join the Chinese Communist party, but he repeatedly expressed his sympathy with its aims. Even before the Central People's Government had been inaugurated, he had been elected a member of the national committee of the All-China Federation of Literary and Art Circles. In October 1949 he was made a member of the culture and education committee of the Government Administration Council. In 1953 he became vice chairman of the Union of Chinese Writers and a member of the presidium of the All-China Federation of Literary and Art Circles. In 1952–53 he visited Korea as a member of the writers delegation and spent some time at the front. His 1953 collection of stories, *Ying-hsiung-ti ku-shih* [tales about heroes], is based on his Korean experiences. He was elected a deputy from Szechwan to the first and second sessions of the National People's Congress, which met in 1954 and 1959. After the Hundred Flowers campaign of 1957, Pa Chin was sharply criticized several times for his utterances during this period, but his "deviations" did not appear to injure his standing with the Communist authorities.

Pa Chin renounced his anarchist ideas, and, when preparing a new edition of his works in the late 1950's, he deleted every sympathetic reference to anarchism that he had written.

Pa Chin owed his generally acknowledged popularity among young Chinese readers in the 1930's and 1940's mainly to the fact that they identified themselves with his heroes. In his novels they saw the reflection of their own lives, sufferings, and struggles. A particular target of attack in his works was the Chinese family system, which deprived the youth of their freedom of action and of their right to love and to marry people of their own choice. The young heroes of his novels and short stories feel their social responsibilities deeply; they fight for freedom, for a better future for humanity. He shared the national aspirations of his people and resented the dominant position of foreigners in China. But, except in times of acute crisis, the struggle for political freedom and social justice figures more prominently in his works than does the national struggle. His simple, emotional, and often poetic language also contributed to Pa Chin's success and helped his readers to disregard the poor organization of many of his novels. An important study, *Pa Chin and His Writings*, by Olga Lang, was published in 1967.

Li Fu-ch'un　　　李 富 春

Li Fu-ch'un (1901–), Chinese Communist from Hunan who served under Ch'en Yun (q.v.) in economic and financial posts for more than a decade after 1937. In 1954 he became chairman of the State Planning Commission at Peking.

Little is known about Li Fu-ch'un's background or early education except that he was born into an impoverished scholar-gentry family in Changsha, Hunan. About 1916, after being graduated from a normal school in Changsha, he joined the Hsin-min hsueh-hsi [new people's study society], which had been established by Mao Tse-tung and Ts'ai Ho-sen (q.v.). Thus, he came to know Ts'ai Ho-sen and his younger sister, Ts'ai Ch'ang (q.v.). About 1919 Li went to France on the work-study program (*see* Li Shih-tseng). He studied at the Collège de Montargis and worked at the Renault plant in Billancourt and at the Creusot munitions factory. In 1923 he married Ts'ai Ch'ang in Paris. After the overseas branches of the Chinese Communist party and the Kuomintang had adopted the policy of their parent organizations and had formed an alliance, Li became a member of the executive committee of the Kuomintang branch in Paris in March 1924. He also joined the Chinese Communist party. He and his wife then made a brief trip to Moscow to study at the Communist University for Toilers of the East.

Li Fu-ch'un and his wife returned to China in late 1924. Chou En-lai (q.v.), who had been in France with Li and who was serving as deputy director of the political department of the Whampoa Military Academy, made Li a political instructor at the academy. When the Northern Expedition began in mid-1926, Li became head of the political department of the Second Army of the National Revolutionary Army.

After the Kuomintang split with the Chinese Communist party in 1927, Li Fu-ch'un went to Shanghai and disappeared from view until mid-1931, when he went to the central soviet area in Kiangsi and became secretary of the Kiangsi provincial committee of the Chinese Communist party and an officer in the political department of the Red Army. He was elected to the Central Committee of the Chinese Communist party in January 1934. After making the Long March from Kiangsi to Shensi in 1934–35, he headed the organization department of the Central Committee until mid-1937, when Ch'en Yun (q.v.) returned from Moscow. Thereafter, Li served under Ch'en as deputy director of the organization department and, beginning in 1940, as a member of the economic-financial committee of the Shensi-Kansu-Ninghsia Border Region. In 1945, after the Japanese surrender, he and such other Central Committee members as Kao Kang, Lin Piao, and P'eng Chen (qq.v.) were sent to Manchuria under the direction of Ch'en Yun. Li became a member and then vice chairman (1948) of the Northeast bureau of the Chinese Communist party, deputy political commissar of the Northeast military district, and vice chairman of the economic-financial committee of the Northeast Administrative Committee. When the Northeast People's Government was established at Mukden in August 1949, he became a vice chairman of that regime.

Beginning in 1950, Li Fu-ch'un held office in the Central People's Government at Peking as minister of heavy industry and as a member of the Government Administration Council and vice chairman of its economic-financial committee. He was a member of the Chinese delegation which went to Moscow and negotiated the Sino-Soviet treaty of February 1950, and he remained in Moscow until mid-April to work out details of a Sino-Soviet trade agreement. In the autumn of 1952 he accompanied Chou En-lai and Ch'en Yun to Moscow for negotiations on issues left unresolved by the February 1950 treaty. By this time, he had become a member of the State Planning Commission at Peking. He also took part in the negotiations concerning the extent and types of Soviet technical and economic assistance which would be given the People's Republic of China during the period of its first Five-Year Plan (1953–57). He returned to China in mid-1953 and became vice chairman of the State Planning Commission.

In the governmental reorganization of 1954, Li Fu-ch'un became chairman of the State Planning Commission and a vice premier of the State Council. Together with Ch'en Yun and Po I-po, he was considered to be one of the most important economic planners at Peking. Throughout the period of the first Five-Year Plan, he was responsible for delivering major reports on the progress made by the People's Republic of China towards its goal of integrated national economic development. In September 1956, at the Eighth National Congress of the Chinese Communist party, he was elected to the Political Bureau, and two years later, he was made a member of the Secretariat. He was a delegate from Hunan to the National People's congresses in 1958 and 1964. As director of the industry and communications office of the State Council, a post he held in 1959–61, he made a report on national economic planning to the second session of the Second National People's Congress in 1960.

Li Hsien-nien   李 先 念

Li Hsien-nien (1907–), Chinese Communist guerrilla leader who became increasingly important in the establishing and expanding of Communist authority in central China after

1937. From 1949 to 1954 his primary responsibility was to consolidate control of Hupeh and the Central-South region. He then became minister of finance and a vice premier of the State Council at Peking.

Born into a working-class family in Huangan, Hupeh, Li Hsien-nien received no formal education. Little is known about his background or early years except that he became a carpenter. After Hsü Hai-tung (q.v.) returned to Hupeh in 1927 to work as an organizer for the Chinese Communist party, Li joined the party and became secretary of its Huangan committee. He also created a small guerrilla force.

After Chang Kuo-t'ao and Hsü Hsiang-ch'ien (qq.v.) established a formal military and political administration for the Hupeh-Honan-Anhwei soviet (also known as the O-yü-wan soviet), Li Hsien-nien's unit became part of the Fourth Front Army. In November 1932 Li moved with the army into Shensi and Szechwan. After 1934 he served as political commissar in the Thirtieth Army and participated in the Long March. The Thirtieth Army was one of the units under Hsü Hsiang-ch'ien which, when marching up the Kansu corridor toward Sinkiang in the autumn of 1936, was attacked and decimated by the cavalry forces of Ma Pu-fang (q.v.). Li Hsien-nien fled to Sinkiang and eventually reached the Communist base in northern Shensi in 1937.

After the Sino-Japanese war began in July 1937, Li Hsien-nien was assigned to work with Wang Chen (q.v.) in Shansi and Hopei. Their troops were the nuclei around which were formed local units which fought the Japanese and worked to extend Communist territorial control. Late in 1938 Li and a small group of cadres moved southward to develop new Communist bases. By uniting local guerrilla units in central and eastern Hupeh, Li's group was able to establish an anti-Japanese base in the Tapieh mountain area along the Hupeh-Honan border. By the end of 1940 that base had grown to support about 10,000 men, who formed a column of the New Fourth Army. In 1941 Li's forces were reorganized as the 5th Division of the New Fourth Army, with Li as divisional commander. The following year, he narrowly escaped capture when Japanese surrounded his headquarters in Hupeh, forcing him to retreat northward to an area occupied by troops under Liu Po-ch'eng (q.v.).

Li Hsien-nien returned to Hupeh in 1942 to direct Communist military and political operations in the central plain area. The 5th Division extended its guerrilla operations into southern Hupeh and harried Japanese garrisons in the Wuhan area and along the rail lines. Li gradually carved out the Hupeh-Honan-Anhwei-Hunan-Kiangsi (O-yü-wan-hsiang-kan) border area, one of the largest areas held by the Chinese Communists before 1945.

At the Seventh National Congress of the Chinese Communist party, held in Yenan just before the Japanese surrender in 1945, Li Hsien-nien was elected to the Central Committee. He then served as commander of the central plain military district and deputy secretary of the party's central China bureau. Although Nationalist military pressure forced him to move northward in 1946, he returned to Hupeh in 1947. He became deputy commander, under Liu Po-ch'eng, of the main body of Communist forces in central China in 1948 and deputy commander, under Lin Piao (q.v.), of the Fourth Field Army in 1949.

With the establishment of the Central People's Government at Peking in October 1949, Li Hsien-nien became a member of the People's Revolutionary Military Council. Between 1949 and 1954, however, his primary responsibility was to consolidate Communist control of Hupeh province and the Central-South region. He dominated the Communist party, government, and military hierarchies in Hupeh as secretary of the party's provincial committee, chairman of the provincial government, and commander and political commissar of the provincial military district. From 1952 to 1954 he was mayor of Wuhan, the principal urban industrial center of central China. At the regional level, he was a member (1949–52) and later deputy chairman (1952–54) of the Central-South Military and Administrative Committee, with particular responsibility for economic affairs. He also served as third deputy secretary of the Central-South bureau of the Chinese Communist party in 1953–54.

In mid-1954 Li Hsien-nien resigned the chairmanship of the Hupeh provincial government and moved to Peking, where he became minister of finance and deputy chairman of the financial-economic committee of the Government

Administration Council. In the autumn he attended the First National People's Congress as a delegate from Hupeh, where he was elected to the presidium. He ·continued to serve as minister of finance after the governmental reorganization of 1954 and became one of the twelve vice premiers of the State Council and a member of the National Defense Council. From 1954 to 1959 he was director of the fifth general office of the State Council. In November 1954 he was made director of the finance and trade office of the State Council, and he was reappointed in September 1959. He was appointed vice chairman of the State Planning Commission in 1962.

Li's prominence was confirmed at the Eighth National Congress of the Chinese Communist party in September 1956, by his election as the 24th-ranking member of the Central Committee and as a member of the Political Bureau. In May 1958 he was elected to the Secretariat of the Central Committee.

Li Hsien-nien traveled abroad several times as a representative of the People's Republic of China. In November 1954 he headed a Chinese delegation which visited Tirana to attend the tenth anniversary celebration of the Communist regime in Albania, and in July 1956 he led a delegation to the thirty-fifth anniversary celebrations of the Mongolian People's Republic. He was a member of a Chinese delegation to the Soviet Union for the celebration of the October Revolution in 1957. He led delegations to Albania in February 1961 and November 1964 and one to Rumania in August 1964.

Li married Lin Chia-mei, who served from 1954 to 1958 as deputy section chief of the department of child and maternity care in the ministry of public health of the Central People's Government.

Li Huang　　　　　李　璜
T. Yu-ch'un　　　　幼　椿
H. Hsueh-tun　　　學　鈍

Li Huang (14 January 1895–), scholar who joined with Tseng Ch'i (q.v.) in founding the China Youth party. It became part of the so-called third force movement, which endeavored to avert the possibility of civil war between the Kuomintang and the Chinese Communist party.

The son of a prosperous Szechwanese merchant, Li Huang was born in Chengtu. After receiving a primary education in the Chinese classics, he studied at the government foreign-language school in Chengtu from 1908 to 1912. The following year, he entered Aurora University, a French Jesuit institution in Shanghai. His three years at Aurora gave him a good knowledge of the culture and language of France and a distaste for missionary institutions. Among his friends in Shanghai were Tseng Ch'i (q.v.) and Tso Shun-sheng.

After participating in the founding of the Young China Association in June 1918, Li Huang left China for France in December to continue his studies. He sailed with Li Shih-tseng (q.v.), a founder of the work-study program in France, and in February 1919 he took charge of a group of students in the program who were entering the Collège de Montargis. That autumn, he entered the Sorbonne, where he spent the next five years studying European history, sociology, and comparative religion.

Because Li did not have to earn a living while pursuing his studies, he had sufficient leisure to engage in many outside activities. He held French classes for students in the work-study program and joined with Chou T'ai-hsuan in founding a news agency, the Pa-li t'ung-hsin-she, to cover the Paris Peace Conference. After the conference ended, the agency continued to supply Chinese publications with European news. Li wrote a number of articles for Chinese educational journals and acquired a reputation as an authority on Western educational methods. From December 1922 to June 1923 he toured Germany with Tseng Ch'i.

By the time Li and Tseng returned to France, the Kuomintang and the Communists in France had followed the example of their parties in China and had formed an alliance. Other Chinese students had formed a counter-alliance dedicated to the upholding of kuo-chia-chu-i [nationalism] in opposition to the internationalism of the Kuomintang-Communist bloc. In December 1923 Tseng and Li became the two principal founders of the Young China party, which was composed of supporters of kuo-chia-chu-i.

After completing his studies at the Sorbonne in 1924, Li Huang returned to China, where he taught courses in European history, French literature, and education at Wuchang University (1924–25), Peking University (1925–26), and Szechwan University (1926–27). During this period, he worked to win support for the China Youth party, but had little success. In 1929 he decided to move to the French concession in Shanghai. The matter of his personal safety played a part in this decision, for his outspoken criticisms of Chiang Kai-shek and of his methods of governing had angered several government leaders at Nanking. Li remained in the French concession for three years, teaching at Futan University, Chiangnan College, and Chihhsing College.

In 1932 Li Huang went to Peiping, then held by troops of Chang Hsueh-liang (q.v.), who had allowed the Young China party much more freedom in Manchuria than had been permitted it in areas controlled by the Kuomintang. Chang had appointed a Young China party member, Weng (Ong) Chao-yuan, to command a division which guarded the gateway to China proper at Shanhaikuan. Li joined with Weng and his subordinate officers Miao K'o-hsin and Teng T'ieh-mei, who also were Young China party members, in establishing a base from which Weng could direct guerrilla harassment of the Japanese. This base area, located between Chinchow and the Great Wall, was a center of guerrilla operations until mid-1933, when the Japanese attacked it. Li and Weng then sought refuge in Tsingtao.

Li Huang returned to his native Szechwan. After Chinese Communist troops entered Szechwan on their Long March to northwest China, a number of prominent citizens of Chengtu, some of whom were sympathetic to the Young China party, formed a pacification committee and began a campaign to exterminate the Communists. The committee, in the hope of inducing the provincial troops to fight vigorously, appointed Li Huang its representative to the headquarters of the provincial army commander, Liu Hsiang (q.v.). Li's standing at the headquarters was enhanced by his long-time friendship with Liu Hsiang's chief of staff, Chang Chün-yu. He lived with the provincial army until mid-1935, and, although the Szechwanese troops did not annihilate the Communist forces, they prevented them from advancing into central Szechwan.

After the Sian Incident of December 1936 (*see* Chiang Kai-shek) and the outbreak of the Sino-Japanese war in July 1937, the Young China party modified its policies with respect to the Chinese Communist party and supported the united front. It became part of the so-called third force movement in Chinese politics, which endeavored to avert the possibility of civil war between the Kuomintang and the Chinese Communist party. When political parties of the third force movement formed the League of Chinese Democratic Political Groups (later the China Democratic League, *see* Chang Lan) in 1941, Li became deputy chairman of its central committee and chairman of its branch in Chengtu. From 1938 until 1945 he also served as co-chairman of the People's Political Council at Chungking.

In 1945 Li Huang went to the United States as a member of the Chinese delegation to the United Nations Conference on International Organization at San Francisco. After returning to China, he took part in the Kuomintang-Communist peace negotiations initiated by General George C. Marshall in 1946. The third force movement's efforts to avert or end civil war had no success, and some of its constituent parties, including one wing of the Young China party, struck bargains with the Kuomintang and came to support the National Government. Chiang Kai-shek offered Li Huang the post of minister of economic affairs in 1947, but Li refused the offer. Later that year, the National Government outlawed the China Democratic League. Li declined an invitation to become a political adviser to Chiang Kai-shek in 1948. After the Chinese Communists won control of the mainland in 1949, he established residence in Hong Kong, where he and Tso Shun-sheng continued to speak for that faction of the Young China party which remained critical of both the Kuomintang and the Chinese Communists. He also taught European history at Chinese colleges in Hong Kong and wrote articles for journals which supported the third force movement.

Among Li Huang's most important scholarly works were *Fa-kuo wen-hsueh shih* [history of French literature], published in 1920; *Kuo-chia-chu-i ti chiao-yü* [nationalist education], written with Yü Chia-chü and published in 1923; and *Li-shih hsueh yü she-hui k'o-hsueh* [history and the social sciences], published in 1932.

Li Huang married Wang En-hui in 1916. They had two sons, Li Yin-yuan and Li

Yin-chang, and two daughters, Li Yin-lien and Li Yin-t'ang.

Li I-chih
T. Hsieh

李儀祉
協

Li I-chih (c.1882–1938), the foremost advocate of water conservation in republican China. A German-trained hydraulic engineer, he planned and supervised the construction of eight irrigation systems in Shensi and directed conservation commissions for the Huai and Yellow rivers. He was president of the Chinese Hydraulic Engineering Society from 1931 to 1938.

A native of P'uch'eng, Shensi, Li I-chih was the son of Li T'ung-hsien (1860–1932), a teacher who later became deputy chairman of the Shensi provincial government council. After passing the examinations for the sheng-yuan degree about 1899, the young Li, after submitting to an arranged marriage, went to Ching-yang to study at the Ch'ung-shih Academy. In 1905 he received a provincial scholarship and enrolled at the Imperial University of Peking, where he majored in German, took science courses, and served as president of the senior class. After graduation in 1909, he received a scholarship from the Hsi-t'ung railway administration of Shensi for study in Germany. He cut off his queue, the traditional symbol of loyalty to the Manchus, before sailing. On arrival in Germany, Li enrolled at the engineering school of Berlin University, where he studied for two years before returning to China to participate in the republican revolution. He soon became convinced that he could serve his country best by becoming expert in hydraulic engineering and soil conservation. Accordingly, he returned to Germany in 1913 and studied under eminent conservationists at the University of Danzig for three years.

From 1916 to 1922 Li I-chih taught hydraulic engineering and related subjects at the Ho-hai kung-ch'eng hsueh-hsiao [college of conservation] in Nanking, which had been established in 1915 by the provinces of Hopei, Shantung, Kiangsu, and Chekiang to train personnel for conservation projects. From 1922 to 1927 he served as head of the Shensi provincial water conservation bureau. He began by making a thorough study of the incidences of natural

calamities in Shensi from 1136 B.C. to 1912 A.D. and discovered that the province had suffered a severe drought every ten years. Accordingly, he devoted his energies to planning a modern irrigation system for the plains north of the Wei River, where much of the province's cotton and wheat was grown. As provincial commissioner of reconstruction (1928–32) and chief engineer of the Wei-pei conservation bureau (1934–37), Li built eight irrigation systems, the most important projects being the Ching-hui and Wei-hui canals along the Wei River and the Lo-hui canal along the Lo River. In 1935 he also began work on a ten-year conservation program designed to eliminate drought and famine in Shensi.

During this period, Li I-chih held a number of water conservation posts outside of Shensi. He served as chairman of the north China conservation commission in 1927, chief engineer of the Huai River conservation commission in 1929, and chairman of the Yellow River conservation commission in 1932–35. When the Chinese Hydraulic Engineering Society was founded in 1931, Li was elected its first president, a post he retained until his death in the spring of 1938.

The writings of Li I-chih were collected and published in Taiwan by the Chinese Hydraulic Engineering Society in 1956 as *Li I-chih ch'üan-chi* [collected works of Li I-chih]. His comprehensive approach to the problems of conservation is exemplified by his reports, included in the compendium, on the first and second phases of construction of the Ching River canal, "Shensi Wei-pei shui-li kung-ch'eng chu ying Ching ti-i ch'i pao-kao-shu" and "ti-erh ch'i pao-kao-shu." These reports discuss the history and methods of conservation, preparations for work, survey organizations, topography, rainfall, water flow, and the volume of water to be made available by the irrigation system. Among the other valuable essays in this collection are those on the Yellow and Yangtze rivers.

Because Li I-chih's chief concern as a hydraulic engineer was the practical problem of soil improvement through the proper management of water supply, he came to view China as a nation of farmers which would achieve national salvation through agricultural, not political, improvement. He believed that water conservation was the key to agricultural progress. In *Chung-nung chiu-kuo-ts'e* [national salvation by emphasis on agriculture], he developed these ideas. According to Li, all of the great leaders of ancient China had been exceptionally competent farmers. Throughout the history of China, the nation had enjoyed social order and prosperity whenever agriculture had been a primary concern and had fallen into chaos in periods when agricultural problems had been ignored. In setting forth his plan for national salvation, Li suggested emphasizing the importance of agriculture by calling the head of state "Nung-shou" [chief farmer] and changing the designation of provincial governor to "Shih-nung" [agricultural ministers]. He drafted a "Nung-hsien" [agricultural constitution] to provide a framework for the new agricultural state. All elections, educational activities, military affairs, and industrial developments would be based on and derived from agriculture, and all the people would be obligated to serve as either regular farmers [shang-nung] or occasional farmers [hsi-nung]. Existing armies would be replaced by a peasant army [nung-chün]. According to Li, programs of this nature would bring prosperity and strong social order to China.

Li I-chih's conservation work improved the lot of many Chinese farmers. When he was buried at Chingyang in the spring of 1938, more than 5,000 farmers came to pay their respects at his grave and the National Government issued a special mandate honoring Li on 28 March. His achievements were recognized and honored by Nationalists and Communists alike.

Li Ken-yuan	李 根 源
T. Yin-ch'üan	印 泉
Hsueh-sheng	雪 生
H. Li-kung shan-jen	黎 貢 山 人

Li Ken-yuan (6 June 1879–6 July 1965), Yunnanese T'ung-meng-hui and Kuomintang leader who participated in the so-called second revolution in 1913 and who commanded the Yunnan Army in Kwangtung from February 1918 to October 1920. After serving as minister of agriculture in the Peking government from November 1921 to June 1923, he retired from political life. He had some influence on government policy after 1928 through his association with the Political Science Group.

A native of T'engyueh (T'engchung), Yunnan, Li Ken-yuan was the son of Li Ta-mou, a military officer with the rank of chien-tsung [lieutenant]. In 1884, at the age of six sui, the young Li began to receive a traditional education under the guidance of his grandmother. He studied under a succession of tutors, all of whom were well-known scholars. In 1899, at the age of 21 sui, Li married Hsü Pao-chuang; their first son, Hsi-mu, was born a year later. In 1904, after spending a year at a modern school in Kunming, Li won a provincial scholarship for study in Japan. He went to Tokyo and, having decided on a military career, entered the Shimbu Gakkō [military preparatory academy].

Li Ken-yuan met Sun Yat-sen in 1905 and joined the T'ung-meng-hui when it was established later that year. He worked to interest other students in the revolutionary society and became known as a student leader. In 1906 he was elected chairman of the Association of Yunnan Students in Japan. After graduation from the Shimbu Gakkō in 1906, he spent a year with a Japanese regiment before entering the Shikan Gakkō [military academy] as a member of the sixth class. His fellow graduates in 1907 included Sun Ch'uan-fang, Yen Hsi-shan, T'ang Chi-yao, Chao Heng-t'i, and Li Lieh-chün. After receiving further training in a Japanese army unit, Li returned to Yunnan in 1909 to become superintendant of the Chiang-wu-t'ang [military school] and an instructor in the infantry department.

In 1910, after a number of incidents had taken place in the Yunnan-Burma border area, Li was sent there for defense work and negotiations with the British authorities. He helped plan the successful revolution in Yunnan that followed the Wuchang revolt of October 1911. A republican government was established in Yunnan on 1 December 1911, with Ts'ai O (q.v.) as tutuh [military governor], Li Ken-yuan as head of the military department, and Li Yueh-kai and T'ang Chi-yao (q.v.) as Li's deputies. When the Kuomintang was established in 1912, Li became head of that party's Yunnan branch headquarters. He was promoted to lieutenant general in October 1912 and was elected to the National Assembly in January 1913. Although Yuan Shih-k'ai, who held the presidency at Peking, attempted to win Li's support by offering him a high advisory post, Li refused his offer. After the Parliament convened on 8 April 1913, Li was elected chairman of the Kuomintang Parliamentarians Club. The Kuomintang leader Sung Chiao-jen (q.v.) was assassinated in March 1913, and Li went to Shanghai to confer with Sun Yat-sen and Huang Hsing (q.v.).

In June 1913 Yuan Shih-k'ai dismissed the governors of Kiangsi, Kwangtung, and Anhwei, an unmistakably anti-Kuomintang action. In response, Li Lieh-chün and other provincial Kuomintang leaders launched the so-called second revolution. In the meantime, Li Ken-yuan had been dismissed from his government posts by Yuan Shih-k'ai. Li accompanied Ts'en Ch'un-hsuan (q.v.) to Canton to help the revolutionaries there. When the forces of Lung Chi-kuang (q.v.) captured Canton in August, Li and Ts'en escaped to Macao and then went to Hong Kong. Li finally had to seek refuge in Tokyo, for Lung Chi-kuang sent agents to Hong Kong in an attempt to capture Li and claim the reward that Yuan Shih-k'ai had offered for his arrest. The fall of Nanking on 1 September ended the anti-Yuan attempt and caused scores of other Kuomintang leaders to flee to Japan.

Li Ken-yuan enrolled at Waseda University to study political economy. When Sun Yat-sen reorganized the Kuomintang in 1914 as the Chung-hua ko-ming-tang and required each member to swear an oath of personal allegiance to him, Huang Hsing and some other Kuomintang leaders objected to the oath. Li and Chü Cheng attempted to placate the dissenters, but had little success. In August 1914 Li and others founded the Ou-shih yen-chiu-hui [European affairs research society], the forerunner of the Political Science Group. Its membership included Li Lieh-chün, Ch'eng Ch'ien, and Hsiung K'o-wu. When Yuan Shih-k'ai accepted Japan's Twenty-one Demands in 1915 and launched his monarchical plot, the revolutionaries determined to return to China in a renewed campaign against Yuan. Li arrived in Shanghai in October to help plan the campaign. In 1916 he went to Kwangsi and served under Liang Ch'i-ch'ao (q.v.). A military council was formed, with T'ang Chi-yao as its head, Tsen Ch'un-hsuan as acting head, Liang Ch'i-chao as chief of the political committee, and Li Ken-yuan as staff officer to the allied northern expeditionary forces and liaison officer in Shanghai. On 8 May at Chaoching, Kwangtung, the council announced its intention to act as the legitimate government of China until Yuan Shih-k'ai retired from public life, the 1912 constitution was restored, and the 1913 Parliament was reconvened.

Yuan Shih-k'ai died and Li Yuan-hung (q.v.) assumed the presidency in June 1916. Li Ken-yuan went to Peking and urged the election to the vice presidency of either Ts'en Ch'un-hsuan or Lu Jung-t'ing (q.v.) so that both northern and southern interests would be represented in the government. When Feng Kuo-chang (q.v.) was elected vice president, Li and his associates organized the Political Science Group, with Li, Ku Chung-hsiu, Chang Yao-tseng, and Niu Yung-chien as its secretaries. Li also resigned from the Parliament. On 20 February 1917 he assumed office as governor of Shensi. He was imprisoned by Ch'en Shu-fan, the provincial military governor, three months later when he refused to join other northern governors in supporting the plans of Tuan Ch'i-jui (q.v.) and his associates to oust Li Yuan-hung. He was released in October, by which time Li Yuan-hung had retired to Tientsin and Feng Kuo-chang had assumed the duties of the presidency.

In February 1918 Li Ken-yuan went to Canton to become commander in chief of the Yunnan Army in Kwangtung, which was an independent force. He served under Li Lieh-chün, then chief of staff in Sun Yat-sen's military government, in a successful campaign against Lung Chi-kuang, who was attempting to recover Kwangtung. After the campaign ended, Li served as chief administrator for the 15 hsien in the North River area. Early in 1920 several leaders, including T'ang Chi-yao and Li Lieh-chün, attempted to win control of the Yunnan Army in Kwangtung. The Canton government, then controlled by the Kwangsi militarists, ordered Li and his men to Hainan Island, where they remained for about six months. After Ch'en Chiung-ming (q.v.) defeated the Kwangsi armies and their supporting troops in October 1920, the Yunnan Army in Kwangtung forced Li to resign his command. On 24 October, he went to Shanghai with Ts'en Ch'un-hsuan and Ch'eng Ch'ien. An attempt was made on Li's life on 29 November, but the assassin's bullet hit another man, who was visiting Li.

In November 1921, after a year of political inactivity, Li Ken-yuan was appointed acting minister of agriculture in the cabinet of Wang Ta-hsieh at Peking. He was confirmed in this post when Chang Shao-tseng succeeded Wang as premier in January 1923. Soon afterwards, Li appointed a committee for the formulation of agricultural and commercial laws, which drafted 29 laws, including one for the protection of trade marks. He also helped found a national compilation and translation bureau. Chang Shao-tseng was forced out of the premiership in 1923, and the entire cabinet resigned on 6 June. After Li Yuan-huang assumed the presidency on 11 June, he appointed Li Ken-yuan acting premier, pending the arrival of T'ang Shao-yi. However, the Chihli leader Ts'ao K'un (q.v.) and his supporters soon ousted Li Yuan-hung from the presidency. Li left Peking and went to Tientsin and Shanghai in the company of Li Ken-yuan.

Li Ken-yuan retired from public life to his home in Soochow. After the death of his mother in 1927, he became an increasingly devout Buddhist. However, it was generally believed that he indirectly served the National Government through his association with the Political Science Group, which became a powerful influence in party and government affairs under the leadership of such younger men as Chang Ch'ün, Chang Kia-ngau (Chang Chia-ao), Hsiung Shih-hui, Ch'en Yi, and Wu Ting-ch'ang, some of whom consulted Li frequently.

In 1949, as the civil war between the Nationalists and the Chinese Communists neared its end, Li Ken-yuan, then 71, left Soochow and established residence at Kunming in his native province of Yunnan. When Chang Ch'ün, a leader of the Political Science Group, and Li's nephew Li Mi were detained by Lu Han (q.v.), the governor of Yunnan, Li Ken-yuan helped to secure their release. After Lu Han declared allegiance to the Chinese Communists, Li returned to his home in Soochow. In 1954 and 1958 he was named to the National Committee of the Chinese People's Political Consultative Conference. He died on 6 July 1965, at the age of 86.

Li K'o-nung   李 克 農

Li K'o-nung (1907–9 February 1962), Chinese Communist known for his intelligence and security work. A long-time associate of Chou En-lai, he served under Chou as deputy minister of foreign affairs in 1949–54. He became deputy chief of staff of the People's Liberation Army in 1955.

Little is known about Li K'o-nung's early life and education except that he was born in Hofei, Anhwei, and that he studied in Shanghai after completing middle school. About 1927 he joined the Chinese Communist party. For about five years he worked in the party intelligence apparatus in the Shanghai area, where his associates included Chou En-lai (q.v.) and Ku Shun-chang. In the spring of 1931 Ku surrendered to the Kuomintang authorities at Wuhan and gave them information which enabled them to arrest Hsiang Chung-fa (q.v.), the general secretary of the Chinese Communist party. Increased Kuomintang surveillance made it difficult for Communists in Shanghai to carry on their party activities, and by mid-1932 many of them, including Li K'o-nung, had been forced to escape to the newly established central soviet area in Kiangsu.

At Juichin, Li continued to work in such areas of intelligence as cryptography. He became chief of the investigation department in the political security bureau of the First Front Army and secretary general of the party's united front department. After participating in the Long March to Shensi, he continued to direct police and other security operations in association with K'ang Sheng (q.v.). Beginning in 1936 he also served as director of the communications department of the Chinese Communist foreign affairs office, with headquarters at Paoan. In December, he accompanied Chou En-lai to Sian at the time of the Sian Incident (see Chang Hsueh-liang) and participated in the negotiations that led to the release of Chiang Kai-shek and the establishment of a united front against the Japanese. He also accompanied Chou En-lai to Hankow in 1937 for negotiations concerning the Kuomintang-Communist military alliance.

After the Sino-Japanese war began in July 1937, Li K'o-nung became head of the Kweilin liaison office of the Eighth Route Army, one of the two Communist forces which had been reorganized under the terms of the Kuomintang-Communist alliance. He served under K'ang Sheng as deputy director of the social affairs department of the Chinese Communist party from 1938 to 1946. He then joined the staff of Yeh Chien-ying (q.v.) at the Peiping Executive

Headquarters, which was established as a result of the mediation efforts of General George C. Marshall. When the Kuomintang-Communist negotiations collapsed in 1947, Li returned to northwest China. About 1949 he became director of the party social affairs department, but it is not known how long he held this post. That year, he also served as a member of the founders committee of the New China Jurisprudence Research Institute and as a party representative to the Chinese People's Political Consultative Conference.

After the Central People's Government was inaugurated, Chou En-lai, who had become foreign minister and who had been an associate of Li K'o-nung since 1927, appointed Li a vice minister of foreign affairs. Li held this post until the government was reorganized in 1954. During this period, he also served on the executive board of the Sino-Soviet Friendship Association. He accompanied Chou En-lai to the Geneva Conference of 1954 and represented Chou at the meeting with Vaslav David, the foreign minister of Czechoslovakia, on his way back to China. In 1954 and 1958 he represented Anhwei at the National People's Congress. He received the rank of colonel general and the post of deputy chief of staff of the People's Liberation Army in 1955. At the Eighth National Congress of the Chinese Communist party, held in September 1956, he was elected to the Central Committee. Two years later, he became a member of the Standing Committee of the Chinese People's Political Consultative Conference. He died at Peking on 9 February 1962.

Li Kuang-ch'ien   李 光 前
West. K. C. Lee

Li Kuang-ch'ien (1894–2 June 1967), known as K. C. Lee, Fukienese entrepreneur who became a multi-millionaire in Singapore. His many business and financial interests in Singapore, Malaya, Thailand, and Indonesia included the Lee Rubber Company, which controlled about one-eighth of the total world trade in natural rubber in the 1950's.

Nanan, Fukien, was the birthplace of K. C. Lee. In the late 1890's his father, Li Kuo-chuan, moved to Singapore to establish a business, leaving him in Nanan for elementary training in the Chinese classics. He joined his father in Singapore in 1904, and thereafter he attended both English schools and Chinese schools with modern curricula. In 1908 he went to Nanking on a Ch'ing government scholarship to study at the Chinan School, which had been established to provide advanced education for overseas Chinese students. After graduation, he became a scholarship student at T'ang-shan Engineering College, near Tientsin. However, his studies were interrupted by the republican revolution of 1911, and he returned to Singapore.

After spending five years in the Singapore civil service as a student surveyor, K. C. Lee decided to enter the rubber manufacturing business, which was booming as a result of the First World War. He joined the staff of the rubber company that had been established in 1915 by Tan Kah Kee (Ch'en Chia-keng, q.v.). Tan, who was greatly impressed by K. C. Lee's character and talents, arranged the marriage of his eldest daughter, Alice Tan (Tan Ah Lay) to Lee in 1920 and appointed him general manager of his Singapore enterprises.

In 1927 K. C. Lee founded the Lee Rubber Company. By 1939 he had established companies in Indonesia and Thailand and had helped effect the merger of the Chinese Commercial Bank, the Ho Hung Bank, and the Overseas Chinese Bank to form the Overseas-Chinese Banking Corporation, of which he became chairman in 1938. In the meantime, Tan Kah Kee's economic position waned because of the fire which had destroyed his main rubber plant in 1928 and because of the world economic depression, which struck Malaya's speculative rubber business in 1929–30. His enterprises were liquidated in 1934, but Lee bought some of his interests so that they would remain in the family. Lee also made a large donation to Tan's beloved Amoy University. Tan had been the sole supporter of the university since its creation in 1921; and it was only because of the donations made by K. C. Lee and Tan's relative Tan Lark Sye that Amoy University was able to continue operations until the Chinese ministry of education assumed responsibility for its finances in 1937. Lee's succession to Tan's economic position in Singapore was marked by his election to the chairmanship of the Singapore Chinese Chamber of Commerce in 1939 for a two-year term.

K. C. Lee went to the United States in 1941 as a member of a delegation which was sent to Washington, D.C., to discuss the maintenance of rubber supplies to the United States from Eastern Asia. When the War in the Pacific began, Li decided to remain in the United States. He established residence in New York, where he lectured at Columbia University and acted as a consultant on economic affairs. He returned to Singapore after the war and began to reconstruct his enterprises. Although most of his Malayan and Indonesian factories and their equipment had been destroyed during the Japanese occupation, he managed to restore them to full operation by 1948.

By the mid-1950's K. C. Lee controlled about one-eighth of total world trade in natural rubber. He owned such enterprises as the Lee Rubber Company, with about 15 factories; the Lee Rubber Estates, which totaled about 18,500 acres; the Lee Pineapple Company; the Lee Sawmills; the Lee Oilmills, which processed palm oil; Lee Biscuits; the Lee Printing Company; and the Lee Produce Company. His foreign holdings included the Hok Tong Company, established in Indonesia in 1932; the Siam Paktai Company, which began operations in Thailand in 1934; and the South Asia Corporation, which was organized in New York in 1938. In addition, Lee was either a controlling or a major shareholder in such public corporations as the Overseas Chinese Bank and Association, the Great Eastern Life Assurance Company (a joint Sino-European enterprise), the Fraser and Neane Corporation, the Sime, Darby Company, and the *Straits Times* Corporation. In sum, he became by far the most important Chinese entrepreneur and investor in Southeast Asia.

Although K. C. Lee usually sought to avoid publicity, he took an active part in community and educational activities in Singapore. From 1939 to 1954 he was president of the Chinese Swimming Club, an important position because Asians were excluded from European recreational facilities and the creation and maintenance of facilities equal to those of the most exclusive European ones became a matter of honor among Singapore Chinese. From 1931 to 1957 he served as chairman of the management Committee of the Singapore Chinese High School, which became one of the best and most modern private high schools in Southeast Asia, although it sometimes drew criticism as a center of radical student activity. Lee's contributions to educational institutions, either directly or through the Lee Foundations, amounted to millions of dollars. In 1958 he assumed the chairmanship of the Singapore Council of Social Service, the central organization for directing and coordinating social service, charity, and relief work in Singapore. A citizen of the State of Singapore, he supported the efforts of the Singapore government to promote the Malayanization of the Chinese residents of the area. In 1961 the Singapore government and the Federation of Malaya agreed to change the name of the University of Malaya, at Singapore, to the University of Singapore, paving the way for the establishment of the National University of Malaya at Kuala Lumpur. K. C. Lee was named as the first chancellor of the University of Singapore on 25 January 1962, and he formally assumed office on 12 June. In November 1965 he resigned because of ill health. He died in Singapore on 2 June 1967.

Throughout his life, K. C. Lee lived quietly and modestly, earning a well-deserved reputation as a hard and serious worker who was more interested in the processes of business than in money. He had three sons, Seng Gee, Seng Tee, and Seng Wee, and three daughters, Siok Kheng, Siok Tin, and Siok Chee. Seng Gee, who became managing director of the Lee Rubber Company, and Seng Tee, who became managing director of the Lee Pineapple Company, were graduates of the University of Pennsylvania. Seng Wee, a graduate of the University of Ontario who majored in electrical engineering and economics, became a director of the Lee Rubber Company. Siok Kheng, a graduate in medicine of the University of Melbourne, became a doctor at the general hospital in Singapore; Siok Tin became a teacher at the University of Singapore; and Siok Chee, a graduate of Teachers College, Columbia University, became a lecturer at Nanyang University in Singapore. K. C. Lee's younger brother George Lee Giok Eng (1898–) owned and controlled George Lee Motors and Nanyang Printers, which owned several important newspapers in Southeast Asia.

Li Li-san　　　　　李 立 三
　Orig. Li Lung-chih　　李 隆 郅
　Alt.　Li Min-jan　　　李 敏 然
　Pen.　Po-shan　　　　伯 山

Li Li-san (c.1900–), leading Chinese Communist labor organizer who became *de facto* head of the party in 1928. After being removed from office in 1930 and censured by the Comintern, he spent 15 years in exile in the Soviet Union. He returned to China in 1946, having been restored to membership in the Central Committee, and served under Lin Piao in the Northeast. After holding office as vice chairman of the All-China Federation of Labor (1948–53) and minister of labor in the Central People's Government (1949–54), he made a lengthy confession of his past errors at the party's Eighth National Congress in 1956.

Little is known about Li Li-san's family background or early life except that he was the son of a poor rural teacher in Liling hsien, Hunan, and that he attended the First Provincial Normal School in Changsha. The first public mention of him was in reference to a meeting with Mao Tse-tung which took place in 1917, after Mao advertised in a Changsha newspaper for patriotic young men with whom he might exchange ideas. According to Mao, there were "three-and-a-half" replies, the half reply being that of Li Li-san, who met with Mao and listened to his views, but went away without commenting on them or otherwise committing himself. About 1919 Li went to France on the work-study program (*see* Li Shih-tseng). According to one source, he attended the College de Montargis, worked in a factory to support himself, and formed a socialist study group with Chao Shih-yen. In 1921 Li and Chao went to Paris, where they joined with Chou En-lai, Ch'en Yen-nien, and Ch'en Ch'iao-nien in organizing the Chinese Communist Youth party. Li Li-san headed the propaganda department and edited the party newspaper, *Shao-nien* [youth]. According to Li Ang (Chu Ch'i-hua, q.v.), Li Li-san was the most active member of the organization. Although founded as an independent group, the Chinese Communist Youth party soon became a branch of the Chinese Communist party.

Li Li-san returned to China early in 1922, after being expelled from France for participating in a demonstration to protest a French loan to the Peking government in China. He began work as a labor organizer for the newly established China Trade Union Secretariat in Shanghai, headed by Chang Kuo-t'ao. Soon afterwards, he and his subordinate Liu Shao-ch'i (q.v.) were sent to Anyuan, Kiangsi, to organize coal workers in the Han-yeh-p'ing mines. He started a part-time school for workmen which grew to become the Anyuan Mine Workers Club and then the Anyuan Coal Mine Labor Union. He also established the Han-yeh-p'ing Workers Union for employees of the mining company in Hanyang, Tayeh, and P'inghsiang. The three-day strike at Anyuan and the strike on the Canton-Hankow railroad in September 1922 were organized by Li and such co-workers as Liu Shao-ch'i and Mao Tse-tung. Li reportedly made a trip to Peking in 1923. That he was an effective organizer and agitator was demonstrated in 1924, when the Han-yeh-p'ing Company was forced to close because of strikes. When troops were brought into Anyuan to control the mines, Li returned to Shanghai.

Li Li-san was a leading figure in the May Thirtieth Incident of 1925. On the evening of 30 May, at a meeting of the Association of Shanghai Labor Unions, he proposed the organization of the Shanghai General Labor Union, a federation of trade unions and students, to give unified direction to the strikes. The proposal was accepted, and Li was elected president of the new union. On 1 June he ordered a general strike. In the ensuing months the Chinese Communists, through manipulation of the Shanghai General Labor Union, controlled almost all of the strikes in Shanghai, of which there were 75 in 1925 and 257 in 1926. Li also worked for the enactment of laws to protect labor unions, but he had to flee to Canton after a warrant was issued for his arrest on 19 September 1925.

In March 1926 the All-China Federation of Labor sent Li Li-san to Moscow to attend the fourth session of the Communist International Federation of Trade Unions. After returning to China, he was elected vice president of the All-China Federation of Labor at its third congress, held at Canton in May 1926. He spent most of his time doing union work in Hupeh. In May

1927 he made a report on the Chinese labor movement at the Pan-Pacific Trade Union Conference in Hankow, and he was elected to the secretariat of that body. After the Kuomintang-Communist split, Li met at Kiukiang with T'an P'ing-shan, Ch'ü Ch'iu-pai (qq.v.), and others to plan a revolt by Nationalist units stationed at Nanchang. After the Central Committee of the Chinese Communist party approved the plan, Li made his way to Nanchang, where he helped organize the ill-fated uprising of 1 August (*see* Chang Kuo-t'ao). Li had been elected to the Political Bureau of the Chinese Communist party at the Fifth National Congress, and he participated in the emergency conference at Kiukiang on 7 August which elected Ch'ü Ch'iu-pai to replace Ch'en Tu-hsiu (q.v.) as general secretary of the party. He then joined the forces of Ho Lung and Yeh T'ing (qq.v.), which had abandoned Nanchang on 3 August and were moving southward. In September, Li took part in the unsuccessful attempt to capture Swatow and then fled to Hong Kong with Chang Kuo-t'ao, Chou En-lai, and other Communist leaders. He succeeded Chang T'ai-lei (q.v.) as chairman of the Chinese Communist party's Kwangtung provincial committee after Chang died in the Canton Commune of December 1927.

After 1928 Li Li-san rose rapidly in the Chinese Communist party. At the Sixth National Congress, held in Moscow in 1928, he was reelected to the Political Bureau and was made head of the propaganda department. He also was elected to the Communist International Federation of Trade Unions in April. After returning to China, he worked to extend his influence in many areas of party activity. At that time, Hsiang Chung-fa (q.v.) was the general secretary of the party, but Li Li-san soon began to dominate political policy.

Beginning in 1929 Li proposed a series of policy changes which later became known as the "Li Li-san line." His plan to organize the urban proletariat to lead military uprisings, aided by the Red Army, was formulated at a time when the percentage of urban workers in the Chinese Communist party was rapidly declining because the Kuomintang authorities had driven the Communists into hiding in the cities and in rural areas. To revitalize the Chinese Communist movement the Central Committee, meeting at Shanghai in June 1929,

confirmed Li's *de facto* leadership and advocated a revolutionary upsurge, a vigorous labor policy, and the expansion of rural soviets under urban leadership. In May 1930, under Li's direction, the National Conference of Delegates from the Soviet Areas was held in Shanghai. The conference adopted a political program, a land law, and a labor law; it called upon the masses "to win preliminary successes in one or more provinces and establish a national soviet regime as soon as possible." Li's policies were expounded further in a Political Bureau resolution of 11 June 1930. (An English translation of this document is to be found in Conrad Brandt, Benjamin Schwartz, and John K. Fairbank, *A Documentary History of Chinese Communism*.) In this document Li, working on the assumption that conditions were ripe for revolution in China, maintained that large-scale uprisings in key cities would lead to nation-wide revolution. These events in China would lead, in turn, to "world revolution and the final decisive class war of the world." The immediate objective of the Communists would be to take Wuhan, the strategic center of China. According to Li, the struggles of workers in urban areas, rather than peasant uprisings and Red Army assaults, would be the decisive factor in the revolutionary movement, and he condemned Mao Tse-tung's rural emphasis and "stubborn adherence to the military concept of guerrilla warfare." The extreme sinocentrism of Li's theories angered some Comintern officials in Moscow, but no immediate action was taken against him.

Li Li-san was eager to put his theories into practice. He already had created a revolutionary council in Shanghai to bring together party, union, and youth corps members. The Fourth Red Army, with Chu Teh (q.v.) as commander in chief and Mao Tse-tung as political commissar, attacked Nanchang, but soon abandoned their efforts. On 5 July 1930, P'eng Te-huai (q.v.) captured Yochow and made plans to surround Changsha. His forces captured Changsha on 27 July, established a soviet government, and proclaimed Li Li-san its chairman *in absentia*. The occupation of the Hunan capital, which marked the height of Li Li-san's power, lasted only until 5 August. The Communists were driven out by Nationalist forces under Ho Ying-ch'in (q.v.). Li contended that the occupation had failed because the broad masses had not supported the uprising with large-scale demonstrations and political strikes. His hopes for realizing his revolutionary plans were dashed in September when a second attempt to occupy Changsha failed. It had become apparent that the Communists would have to shift the focus of their work to the rural areas.

The Central Committee of the Chinese Communist party met in September 1930 to reconsider Li Li-san's policies. Chou En-lai, presumably on Comintern instructions, criticized Li's policies, but argued that although Li had deviated from Comintern policy in tactics, he had adhered to its basic aims. Li was sent to Moscow to answer Comintern charges of deviating from its doctrines, and he made confessions of guilt on all counts. On 25 November 1930 his effective political career came to an end with his expulsion from the Political Bureau of the Chinese Communist party. He spent the next 15 years in exile in the Soviet Union. In 1931 the Comintern ordered him to study at the Lenin Institute "to learn the substance of his errors." He was associated with the Communist International Federation of Trade Unions in 1933–34, and he became director of the translation department of the Moscow Foreign Languages Publishing House. Little else is known about his period of exile.

In 1945 Li Li-san was elected *in absentia* to the Central Committee of the Chinese Communist party. After returning to China early in 1946, he served under Lin Piao (q.v.) as an adviser and political commissar in Harbin, where he handled negotiations regarding the distribution in Manchuria of supplies provided by the United Nations Relief and Rehabilitation Administration. He also became a member of the Northeast bureau of the Chinese Communist party. Soon afterwards, he went briefly to Yenan to pay a call on Mao Tse-tung and effect a reconciliation. He reported in 1956 that after their meeting he had begun to read, for the first time, "the more important works of Comrade Mao Tse-tung."

Li Li-san became a member of the executive committee of the Northeast General Labor Union and a vice chairman of the All-China Federation of Labor in 1948. After the Central People's Government was inaugurated in 1949, he was appointed minister of labor. He abandoned orthodox Marxist economics and formulated a Maoist labor policy of "taking care of the interest of both labor and capital and benefiting both the public and private interest." He also held such posts and titles as member of the Central People's Government Council, member of the finance and economics committee and the labor employment committee of the Government Administration Council, member of the executive board of the Sino-Soviet Friendship Association, director of the department of wages and president of the Cadre Officers School of the All-China Federation of Labor, and member of the cinema guidance committee of the ministry of culture.

Li apparently came into conflict with the Peking leaders at some point, for he resigned as vice chairman of the All-China Federation of Labor in 1953 and relinquished his post as minister of labor in 1954. He was reported to be "resting" in 1955. Although he was re-elected to the Central Committee of the Chinese Communist party at the Eighth National Congress, held in September 1956, only eight members of the committee were ranked below him. At that congress he made a lengthy confession of his past errors and endorsed the 1945 Central Committee "resolution on certain historical questions," which had condemned the Li Li-san line as a "left deviation." He attributed his mistakes in leading the party in 1930 and the All-China Federation of Labor in 1950 to sectarianism, subjectivism, and other "foul traits of the petty bourgeoisie." After his appearance at the congress, Li disappeared from public view for six years. In 1962 he was identified as a secretary of the Central Committee's north China bureau.

Li Li-san married three times; his third wife was a Russian women named Liza. He had one son, Li Jen-tsun, who was born about 1930.

Although Li Li-san was best known for the ideological controversy caused by the "Li Li-san line," his most significant contributions to the Chinese Communist cause were his early accomplishments in organizing and developing the Chinese labor movement in the 1920's.

Li Lieh-chün   李 烈 鈞
  Orig. Li Lieh-hsün   李 烈 訓
  T. Hsieh-ho   協 和
  H. Hsia-huang   俠 黃

Li Lieh-chün (1882–1946), T'ung-meng-hui military man who commanded troops at

Kiukiang, Anking, and Wuchang during the 1911 revolution. As military governor of Kiangsi, he led the Kuomintang's so-called second revolution of 1913. He joined with Ts'ai O and T'ang Chi-yao in leading the 1915–16 campaign against Yuan Shih-k'ai. After serving as Sun Yat-sen's chief of staff in the 1917–23 period, he became an active supporter of Chiang Kai-shek and held important posts at Nanking in 1927.

The forebears of Li Lieh-chün had been farmers in northern Kiangsi until the time of the Taiping Rebellion, when his father and his uncles had joined the insurgent forces. After the rebellion ended, they engaged in transporting tea from Nanchang to Kiukiang. The business prospered, and Li Lieh-chün spent his boyhood in comfortable circumstances. After receiving a traditional education in the Chinese classics, he decided to pursue a military career. Accordingly, he was one of the first students to enroll at the Kiangsi Wu-pei hsueh-t'ang [military preparatory school] when it was established in 1902. After graduation in 1904, he was sent to Japan for further study. He enrolled at the Shimbu Gakkō [military preparatory academy] in Tokyo, where his classmates included Li Ken-yuan and T'ang Chi-yao (qq.v.). He came to know a number of Chinese revolutionaries in Japan, and in June 1906 he joined the T'ung-meng-hui. After completing the training course at the Shimbu Gakkō, he received a year's field training with an artillery unit. In 1907 he enrolled at the Shikan Gakkō [military academy] as a member of the sixth class, which included such future military leaders as Sun Ch'uan-fang and Yen Hsi-shan (qq.v.) as well as his former classmates Li Ken-yuan and T'ang Chi-yao.

After completing his studies at the Shikan Gakkō in December 1908, Li Lieh-chün returned to China, where he received command of a battalion in the 54th Regiment, stationed in Kiangsi. Early in 1910 he went to Kunming and served as an instructor and then as the director of a provincial military school. Li Ken-yuan and T'ang Chi-yao also taught at the military school, and Li Lieh-chün worked with Li Ken-yuan, who was head of the Yunnan branch of the T'ung-meng-hui, to win student support for the revolutionary movement. In 1911 Li Lieh-chün was ordered to participate in the imperial army's autumn military ma-

neuvers at T'aihu. He reached Hankow in mid-October, only three days after the Wuchang revolt had begun. After surveying the Wuhan situation, he went to Peking and met with several republican revolutionaries who had studied with him in Japan.

At the end of October 1911 Li responded to a call from revolutionaries in his native province and left Peking for Kiukiang, where he became chief of staff to Chiang Ch'ün, who then resigned in his favor. With the help of Wu T'ieh-ch'eng (q.v.) and others, he negotiated with Huang Chung-ying, the commander of an imperial navy fleet, and gained control of Huang's ships and their crews. Ma Yu-pao, the tutuh [military governor] of Kiukiang, named Li commander in chief of all army and navy units in the area. By this time, fighting had broken out among the republican forces in Anhwei. When the people of Anhwei appealed to Li to restore order to their province, he sent some of his land units to Anking and sailed with his naval forces to join them. Upon arrival at Anking he was chosen tutuh of Anhwei, but he soon relinquished this office and sailed upriver to aid the republican troops at Wuchang, who were being attacked by the imperial army of Feng Kuo-chang (q.v.).

Li Lieh-chün remained in Wuchang until March 1912, when he was elected tutuh of Kiangsi. He went to Nanchang, assumed office, and began the work of restoring political and economic stability to the province. He also reorganized the Kiangsi military forces.

In May 1913, after the assassination of the Kuomintang leader Sung Chiao-jen (q.v.), Li Lieh-chün joined with Hu Han-min, T'an Yen-k'ai (qq.v.), and Po Wen-wei, the Kuomintang governors of Kwangtung, Hunan, and Anhwei, in a public denunciation of Yuan's government at Peking. On 9 June, Yuan responded by dismissing Li as governor of Kiangsi. Soon afterwards, Hu Han-min and Po Wen-wei were also dismissed. Yuan then ordered the Peiyang Army to move southward toward the Yangtze, with Li Lieh-chün's base in Kiangsi as a principal target of military operations. As the First Peiyang Army of Tuan Chih-kuei and the Second Peiyang Army of Feng Kuo-chang advanced in a two-pronged drive on Kiukiang and Nanking, Li Lieh-chün went to Shanghai to consult with Sun Yat-sen and other Kuomintang leaders. Li insisted that the Kuomintang declare war on

Yuan Shih-k'ai, and, with Sun's approval, he returned to Kiangsi early in July to mobilize his forces. Because Kiukiang had already fallen to Yuan's forces, Li concentrated his troops downriver from Kiukiang at Huk'ou. On 12 July, he declared Kiangsi's independence and assumed the title of commander in chief of the Kiangsi Anti-Yuan Army [T'ao-Yuan-chün], thereby initiating the so-called second revolution.

Although Kuomintang leaders in Kwangtung, Anhwei, Fukien, Hunan, Nanking, Shanghai, and Chungking followed Li's lead in declaring independence from Yuan's regime, most of them were unable to give Li military assistance, and others were unwilling to do so. Thus, Li's troops at Huk'ou and the Kuomintang forces at Nanking were left to bear the brunt of the Peiyang offensive. Li's troops could not resist the onslaught of the larger and better trained First Peiyang Army, and on 25 July 1913 they retreated from Huk'ou to Nanchang. By 19 August, the Kiangsi Anti-Yuan Army had been routed and scattered, and Nanchang had fallen to Yuan's forces. Li Lieh-chün took refuge in Hunan, hid on a river steamer bound for Shanghai, and sailed from Shanghai for Japan. The fall of Nanking on 1 September 1913 signified the end of the second revolution and the triumph of Yuan Shih-k'ai.

Early in 1914 Li Lieh-chün went to France and spent several months at the home of Chang Chi (q.v.) in the Paris suburbs. In October, he decided to return to China in the hope of organizing resistance to Yuan Shih-k'ai. His destination was Yunnan province, for his old friend and classmate T'ang Chi-yao had become its governor. When Li's ship reached Indo-China, the French authorities refused him permission to land, and he was obliged to spend several months in Singapore. In the summer of 1915, after learning of the campaign to make Yuan Shih-k'ai monarch, Li sent some of his associates to Yunnan, where, with the tacit consent of T'ang Chi-yao, they began to organize anti-Yuan groups within the Yunnan army. Li also established contact with Ts'ai O (q.v.), a former governor of Yunnan who was working to organize resistance to Yuan Shih-k'ai.

In November 1915 Li Lieh-chün was allowed to pass through Indo-China. He arrived in Kunming on 17 December, and Ts'ai O joined him two days later. The two men and T'ang Chi-yao's military subordinates prevailed upon T'ang to send Yuan Shih-k'ai an ultimatum which demanded that the monarchical enterprise be abandoned and that those who had promoted it be punished. Yuan did not reply, and T'ang declared Yunnan's independence on 25 December 1915. Military leaders in Yunnan held a council of war at which they organized the National Protection Army [Hu-kuo-chün]. It was composed of the First Army, led by Ts'ai O, which was ordered to attack Szechwan; the Second Army, commanded by Li Lieh-chün, which was ordered to pass through Kwangsi and Kwangtung to Kiangsi; and the Third Army, nominally under T'ang Chi-yao but led by Tai K'an, which was ordered to march into Kweichow.

Early in 1916 the First Army and the Third Army moved north from Kunming, and Li Lieh-chün's Second Army moved east into Kwangsi. Lu Jung-ting (q.v.), the governor of Kwangsi, allowed Li's forces free passage through the province. Despite stiff resistance from the forces of Lung Chin-kuang, a brother of the pro-Yuan governor of Kwangtung, Lung Chi-kuang (q.v.), Li's army won control of several cities in northern and central Kwangtung and advanced eastward to Nanhsiung (Namyung), near the Kiangsi border.

By the end of March 1916 Kweichow and Kwangsi had declared themselves independent of Yuan's government. Lu Jung-t'ing's forces joined those of Li Lieh-chün in invading Kwangtung, and they forced Lung Chi-kuang to declare Kwangtung's independence in April. Soon afterwards, several other provinces followed suit. Yuan Shih-k'ai had sought to stem the rising tide of opposition by announcing his abandonment of the monarchical plan, but this gesture had failed to appease the leaders of the National Protection Army. In mid-April, Li Lieh-chün, Ts'ai O, and T'ang Chi-yao demanded that Yuan resign from the presidency in favor of Li Yuan-hung and that the National Assembly of 1913 be restored. Because Yuan did not accede to their demands, they formed a military council at Chaoch'ing (Kaoyao) on 8 May. The stated purpose of the council was to act as the legitimate government of China until such time as Li Yuan-hung replaced Yuan Shih-k'ai as president.

The death of Yuan Shih-k'ai on 6 June 1916 and the passing of the presidency to Li Yuan-hung brought the National Protection Army's campaign to an end. Their military council was dissolved on 14 July. In northern Kwangtung, however, the fighting between Li Lieh-chün and Lung Chi-kuang continued. Li soon forced Lung's forces to withdraw to Canton, whereupon Lung's allies among the Peiyang militarists called for a campaign against Li Lieh-chün. Under heavy pressure from the Peiyang leader Tuan Ch'i-jui (q.v.), the premier of the Peking government, Li relinquished command of his forces, then known as the Yunnan Army in Kwangtung, and went to Shanghai.

When Sun Yat-sen formed a military government at Canton in 1917, Li Lieh-chün became chief of staff in the new regime. In the spring of 1918 Li led an expedition against Lung Chi-kuang, who was attempting to recover Kwangtung, and defeated Lung's forces in May. Soon afterwards, the government at Canton was reorganized in accordance with the wishes of the Kwangsi militarists in Kwangtung, and Sun Yat-sen retired to Shanghai. Li Lieh-chün continued to serve as chief of staff at Canton, but the dominant Kwangsi faction severely limited his military authority because of his association with Sun Yat-sen.

In June 1920 the Kuomintang broke with the Kwangsi militarists, and Sun Yat-sen sent Li Lieh-chün to Yunnan to confer with T'ang Chi-yao. T'ang, who was engaged in a struggle for power in Szechwan, gave Li command of two battalions. Li's forces soon were driven from Szechwan into Kweichow, where they remained for about a year. When Sun Yat-sen established a new government at Canton in May 1921, he named Li chief of staff and ordered him to lead a combined force from Kweichow and Hunan in an attack on northern Kwangsi. Li's forces captured Kweilin in the late summer of 1921, and the Kwangtung Army of Ch'en Chiung-ming (q.v.) conquered southern and central Kwangsi.

In December 1921 Sun Yat-sen arrived in Kweilin to direct the advance of the expeditionary forces into Hunan. Because of the obstructive tactics of Ch'en Chiung-ming in Canton, Sun withdrew his forces from Hunan in the spring of 1922, established field headquarters at Shaokuan in northern Kwangtung, and planned an advance into Kiangsi. In late May and early June the expeditionary forces, with Li Lieh-chün as chief of staff, advanced into southern Kiangsi, causing the Peiyang governor,

Ch'en Kuang-yuan, to resign and flee the province. The campaign came to an abrupt halt in mid-June when Ch'en Chiung-ming occupied Canton and took control of the government. Sun Yat-sen ordered Li's forces to return to Kwangtung and drive Ch'en from Canton. In July, the expeditionary forces were defeated and scattered by Ch'en's armies in northern Kwangtung. Li Lieh-chün fled to Hunan and made his way from there to Shanghai. After meeting with Sun Yat-sen in Shanghai, he went to Hong Kong and discussed plans for a campaign against Ch'en Chiung-ming with representatives of military leaders in Yunnan and Kwangsi.

After the defeat of Ch'en Chiung-ming by the Yunnan and Kwangsi armies and the return of Sun Yat-sen to Canton in February 1923, Li Lieh-chün was sent to Chaochow in eastern Kwangtung to reorganize units of Ch'en Chiung-ming's army which had declared allegiance to the Kuomintang. Li was recalled to Canton in June to serve as chief of general staff in Sun Yat-sen's military headquarters. At the First National Congress of the Kuomintang, held in January 1924, he was elected to the Central Executive Committee. Late in October, Sun Yat-sen accepted an invitation from the Peking government to explore the possibilities of forming a new national government. He sent Li to Japan to investigate the prospects of Japanese support for such a venture. After Sun arrived in Japan, Li joined his entourage and accompanied him to Tientsin and to Peking, where Sun died in March 1925.

Li Lieh-chün left Peking in the spring of 1925 and went to Kalgan, where he became an adviser to Feng Yü-hsiang (q.v.). After Feng's departure for Urga (Ulan Bator) in 1926, Li remained at Nank'ou with Feng's troops and accompanied them on their retreat to Suiyuan. He joined Feng at Urga, but left his service soon afterwards and went to Hong Kong.

By the time Li reached Hong Kong, the forces of the Northern Expedition, led by Chiang Kai-shek, had encountered stern resistance in Kiangsi from Li's old friend and classmate Sun Ch'uan-fang. Li corresponded with Sun and went to Shanghai in December in a futile effort to win him over to the Kuomintang cause. In January 1927, after arriving at Chiang Kai-shek's military headquarters in Nanchang, Li was appointed governor of Kiangsi.

When the Kuomintang split into two major factions early in 1927, Li Lieh-chün decided to support the conservative group led by Chiang Kai-shek. Accordingly, the left-Kuomintang government at Wuhan dismissed him as governor of Kiangsi on 2 April. Li joined Chiang's opposition government at Nanking as a member of the five-man government standing committee. After Chiang Kai-shek retired from office in August, Li Lieh-chün and Ts'ai Yuan-p'ei (q.v.), the only members of the standing committee who were still in Nanking, assumed responsibility for party and government affairs. They called a conference of party and military leaders, including Li Tsung-jen, Pai Ch'ung-hsi, and Ho Ying-ch'in (qq.v.), at which a political-military council was formed, with Li Lieh-chün as its chairman. Li worked with other party leaders to reunify the Kuomintang. They intensified their efforts after Sun Ch'uan-fang and Chang Tsung-ch'ang made an unexpected attack on Nanking in late August. Li played an important part in the formation of the chung-yang t'e-pieh wei-yuan-hui (Central Special Committee), which established a new National Government at Nanking. Li then became one of the five members of the new government standing committee.

On 22 November 1927 troops in Nanking fired on a crowd celebrating the victory of Li Tsung-jen over the Wuhan militarists who had opposed party reunification. The Central Special Committee was blamed for the incident, and after Chiang Kai-shek returned to Nanking in December, the committee was denounced for its alleged role in the incident and its members, including Li Lieh-chün, were dismissed from office. Li left Nanking early in 1928 and went to Shanghai. He was not reelected to the Central Executive Committee of the Kuomintang in 1929. Despite his estrangement from the central party leaders, he resisted all attempts by opponents of Chiang Kai-shek to enlist his support. Although his name appeared on lists of participants in the so-called enlarged conference of 1930 and in the secessionist government formed at Canton in 1931, he did not take part in these ventures. He was restored to membership on the Central Executive Committee in November 1931, but was dropped from that body and elected to the Central Supervisory Committee in 1935. Beginning in 1932, he also held advisory positions in the

National Government. However, he no longer wielded power in either the party or the government, and he lived quietly in Shanghai until 1937. After the Sian Incident of December 1936, he served as presiding judge at the trial of Chang Hsueh-liang (q.v.).

After the Sino-Japanese war began in the summer of 1937, Li Lieh-chün moved to Kunming and then to Chungking, where he served on the State Council of the National Government. He died in Chungking early in 1946, at the age of 65 sui.

Li Ming 李 銘
T. Fu-sun 馥 蓀

Li Ming (1887–22 October 1966), banker who was noted for his pioneering work in investment banking in China and for his efforts to promote Sino-foreign economic cooperation. He served on the board of directors of many banks and businesses and was general manager of the Chekiang Industrial Bank from 1922 to 1946.

The son of a silver merchant in Chekiang, Li Ming was born in Shaohsing. After receiving his primary education in the Chinese classics, he went to Hangchow in 1902 and enrolled at the Wayland Academy, which was operated by American Baptist missionaries. In 1905 he went to Japan to study at Yamaguchi Commercial College, where he majored in banking and commerce. He returned to China after graduation in 1910 and joined the Chekiang Provincial and Industrial Bank in Hangchow as an auditor. He became manager of the bank's Shanghai office in 1911 and soon proved his abilities by expanding the branch's business activities. He helped found the Chinese Bankers Association at Shanghai in 1917, and he was named to the board of directors of the Bank of China in 1920.

Because the Chekiang Provincial and Industrial Bank was a semi-governmental enterprise, it was unable to resist the frequent demands made on it by the provincial authorities. Because Li Ming believed that the bank could not prosper in such circumstances, he persuaded its private shareholders to allow him to negotiate with the provincial government for the creation of two banks to replace the Chekiang Provincial and Industrial Bank. A 1922 agreement resulted in the establishment of the Provincial Bank of Chekiang, solely owned by the provincial government, and the Chekiang Industrial Bank, a private banking firm with its head office at Shanghai. Li Ming became the general manager of the Chekiang Industrial Bank. The three chief features of his management policy were concentration, liquidity, and prudent investment. The Chekiang Industrial Bank maintained only two branches, one in Hankow and one in Hangchow, because Li believed that branches located in politically unstable areas were apt to become liabilities rather than assets. He followed a stringent loan policy, for he believed that, because China lacked a central banking system, it was necessary for commercial banks to maintain sufficient reserves to meet all of their obligations at any time. Under Li's guidance, the Chekiang Industrial Bank became one of the first Chinese banks to engage in foreign-exchange and international trade operations. Li Ming established a foreign-exchange department and employed a European expert to train his staff. The Chekiang Industrial Bank grew to become one of the five leading private banks in China.

In 1926 Li Ming became chairman of the Chinese Bankers Association at Shanghai, a post he held from 1926 to 1934 and from 1946 to 1949. Also in 1926 he was appointed liquidator of the Russo-Asiatic Bank, which had been established by the imperial governments of Russia and China and which was being liquidated as a result of the revolutions in both countries. In 1927 Li assumed the chairmanship, which he held until 1940, of the newly established National Bonds Sinking Fund Committee, which was charged with the custody and servicing of National Government treasury notes and domestic bonds. This committee, which was composed of bankers, other financiers, and government officials, was particularly important because the balancing of the National Government budget depended on the domestic bond issues. Because the committee undertook to act as a sort of trustee for bondholders, the National Government bonds won sufficient public confidence to be traded freely in Shanghai. However, the excessive number of bonds issued to meet the continued budget deficit, the frequent shortage of sinking funds, and the repeated attempts of the National Government to reorganize the loan services, defeated Li Ming's attempts to avoid a breakdown of national credit.

When the Bank of China was reorganized as a foreign-exchange bank in November 1928, Li Ming became chairman of its board of directors and Chang Kia-ngau (Chang Chia-ao, q.v.) became its general manager. Both men resigned from office when the bank was nationalized in 1935. Also in 1928 Li became a director of the Bank of Communications and chairman of the board of supervisors of the Central Bank of China, which he also helped to organize. He held these posts until 1949 and made every effort to modernize and strengthen the banking system of China.

In January 1932 fighting between Japanese and Chinese forces at Shanghai caused financial panic and runs on banks. Many Chinese banks had made large investments in real estate, and some bankers feared that they might have insufficient liquid assets to meet the emergency. Furthermore, land prices declined at this time. Li Ming took the lead in forming the Joint Reserve Board of the Chinese Bankers Association and served as its chairman. Real estate, securities, and other marketable properties with an aggregate value of CN$100 million were submitted by the various member banks to the reserve board. It then issued notes, which were mutually acceptable among the member banks as cash, and certificates, which could be used by banks with the power of issue as security reserves and by other banks for securing up to 40 percent of the face value of the certificates in bank notes from the banks of issue. The liquidity achieved by these measures ended the financial panic. In January 1933 Li Ming sponsored the establishment of the Shanghai Clearance House as a subsidiary organ of the Joint Reserve Board. He also made plans for the creation of the Shanghai Bankers Acceptance House, which finally came into being in March 1936 as a subsidiary of the Joint Reserve Board.

To further the economic development of China, Li Ming organized the National Industrial Syndicate in 1932, and this banking group purchased an electric company at Hangchow which it reorganized as the Hangchow Electricity Company. A new general station with modern equipment was constructed on the northern bank of the Ch'ientang River, and the transmission and distribution systems were overhauled and modernized. The new and efficient electric power system was a source of great pride and increased comfort for the Hangchow citizenry. Li Ming served as chairman of the board of the Hangchow Electricity Company until 1949.

Li Ming also worked to promote economic cooperation between Chinese and foreign interests. He believed that China needed foreign capital and technology to increase its rate of economic development and that only through joint investment could popular fears of imperialistic aggression be allayed. Accordingly, in the early 1930's he participated in the joint American-Chinese purchase of the electric power system in the International Settlement at Shanghai and of the Shanghai Mutual Telephone Company. The Shanghai Municipal Council had decided to sell its electric power system in 1929, and the American and Foreign Power Company, a New York holding company, had formed a syndicate to purchase it. Li Ming was one of the syndicate members representing Chinese interests. When the Shanghai Power Company, headed by Paul S. Hopkins, was established to operate the electric system, Li became the principal adviser to the company. This purchase involved about CN$120 million, and additional funds were needed for the rehabilitation and expansion of the utility. Because of the depression in the United States, the company had to turn to the Shanghai market. Li Ming helped form a group composed of Chinese banks, a British bank, an American bank, and the American brokerage firm of Swan, Culbertson, and Fritz to underwrite the issue of bonds and preferred stock of the Shanghai Power Company. This action marked the introduction into the Chinese banking system of such Western investment banking practices as investigating proposals, forming syndicates for underwriting, selling securities, and investment counseling. Soon afterwards, the Shanghai Mutual Telephone Company was sold to the International Telephone and Telegraph Company, which then created the Shanghai Telephone Company to operate the system. Once again, Li Ming and the brokerage firm of Swan, Culbertson, and Fritz underwrote a bond issue and rendered invaluable services to a joint Sino-foreign venture. Li served on the board of directors of the Shanghai Telephone Company from 1933 to 1949. In January 1934 the Western District Power Company, of which Li Ming was chairman of the board of directors and Paul S. Hopkins was president, received National Government permission to supply electricity to the western districts of Shanghai.

After the Sino-Japanese war began and a Japanese-sponsored government was established at Nanking (*see* Wang Ching-wei), Li Ming was threatened with arrest if he did not cooperate with the Nanking regime. In March 1941 Li suddenly left Shanghai and went to the United States, where he remained until the War in the Pacific ended in 1945. He became a New York director of the Shanghai Power Company in 1942 and a member of the New York board of trustees of Peking Union Medical College in 1944. He also served as an adviser to the Chinese delegation to the United Nations Monetary and Financial Conference at Bretton Woods, New Hampshire, and as a Chinese delegate to the International Business Conference, held at Rye, New York. In 1945 he played a leading role in the formation of China Industries, Inc., which was organized in conjunction with K. P. Ch'en (Ch'en Kuang-fu, q.v.), Lehman Brothers, Lazard Frères, and the Rockefeller interests to facilitate the financing of postwar Chinese industrial enterprises. The organization never became operative, however, because of the civil war that broke out in China: it was dissolved in 1949.

After returning to Shanghai in 1946, Li Ming resigned as general manager of the Chekiang Industrial Bank, but continued to control its operations as chairman of the board of directors. In 1947 he became a director of the China Foundation for the Promotion of Education and Culture and chairman of the National Bankers Association. For two months, he served as chairman of the Central Bank of China's import and export control board. The National Government passed a banking law in 1947 which classified banks according to their primary functions and which required that the names of banks reflect these functions. Accordingly, in 1948 the Chekiang Industrial Bank became the Chekiang First Bank of Commerce. When the Chinese Communist forces crossed the Yangtze in 1949, Li went to Hong Kong.

Li Ming raised a small amount of capital in Hong Kong and founded the Chekiang First Bank of Commerce, Ltd. Li was elected chairman of the board of directors, and his son Li

Te-chuan became manager of the bank. Li Ming died in Hong Kong on 22 October 1966, at the age of 78. He was survived by two sons, two daughters, ten grandchildren, and three great grandchildren. One of his daughters married Szeming Sze, a son of Sao-ke Alfred Sze (Shih Chao-chi, q.v.) who became medical director of the United Nations.

In the course of his career, Li Ming held more than 30 directorships in banks, industrial concerns, insurance companies, and public utilities. He was particularly noted for his pioneering work in investment banking and for promoting Sino-foreign economic cooperation.

Li Shih-tseng　　　　李 石 曾
Orig. Li Yü-ying　　　　李 煜 瀛

Li Shih-tseng (1881–), leader of the work-study movement in France who became known as one of the "four elder statesmen of the Kuomintang."

Although his native place was Kaoyang, Chihli (Hopei), Li Shih-tseng was born in Peking. He and his elder brother, Li Kun-ying, were the sons of Li Hung-tsao (ECCP, I, 471–72), who held such high offices in the Ch'ing government as those of Grand Councillor and tutor to Tsai-ch'ien (ECCP, II, 729–31), the T'ung-chih emperor. Li Shih-tseng was exposed to reformist ideas at an early age: his tutor, Ch'i Ling-ch'en, the father of Ch'i Ju-shan (q.v.), was a reformist as well as a distinguished scholar; and a frequent visitor to the Li home was Wang Chao (1859–1933), a supporter of the reform movement of K'ang Yu-wei (q.v.). After Li Hung-tsao died in 1897, the Ch'ing government awarded both of his sons the rank of lung-chang, which qualified them to hold posts on the level of a departmental head in a government board.

In 1901 Li Shih-tseng met Chang Jen-chieh (q.v.), with whom he established a life-long friendship. The two young men had many common interests, the most compelling of which was a desire to go abroad. Accordingly, when Sun Pao-ch'i (q.v.) was appointed minister to France in 1902, they joined his staff as attachés. On his way to France, Li stopped for a time in June at Shanghai, where he met Wu Chih-hui

and Ts'ai Yuan-p'ei (qq.v.), who also were to become his life-long friends. In later years, Li, Chang, Wu, and Ts'ai became known as the "four elder statesmen of the Kuomintang."

After arriving in Paris, Li Shih-tseng enrolled at the Pasteur Institute to study biology. He met Sun Yat-sen in 1905 and joined the French branch of the T'ung-meng-hui later that year. Wu Chih-hui arrived in Paris at the end of 1905 and joined with Li Shih-tseng and Chang Jen-chieh in founding the Shih-chieh-she [world society], a cultural and revolutionary publishing house with an affiliated printing establishment. Chang financed the establishment of the *Hsin shih-chi* [new century], which began publication in June 1907 and issued 121 numbers before suspending publication on 21 May 1910 because of heavy losses. Li and Wu, both of whom seem to have fallen under the spell of anarchism, wrote most of the articles for the magazine.

In 1907 Li Shih-tseng and Hsia Chien-chung founded the Far Eastern Biological Society. Li did considerable research on the soybean at the Pasteur Institute, and in 1908 he became a vegetarian. He also decided to establish an enterprise for the manufacture of soybean products, and in 1909, after a trip to China to obtain supplies and workers, he established the Usine Caseo Sojaine at Colombes. The more than 30 Chinese workers at the factory used their wages to pursue their studies in France. They were escorted to France by Ch'i Ju-shan, whose elder brother, Ch'i Chu-shan, managed the factory. Li Shih-tseng later published the results of his research on the soybean as *Le Soya: sa culture, ses usages alimentaires, therapique agricole et industrielles.*

When the news of the Wuchang revolt of October 1911 reached France, Li Shih-tseng and his associates, one of whom was Chang Chi (q.v.), hurried back to China. On arrival in Peking, Li was elected vice president, serving under Wang Ching-wei (q.v.), of the Peking-Tientsin branch of the T'ung-meng-hui. In January 1912 he and some fellow anarchists established the Chin-te hui [society to advance morality]. Its basic tenet was that social reform must accompany political change, and its members pledged that they would refrain from eating meat, drinking alcoholic beverages, visiting prostitutes, taking concubines, gambling, and accepting government office.

In April 1912 Li Shih-tseng joined with Wu Chih-hui, Chang Jen-chieh, Wang Ching-wei, Chang Chi, and Ch'i Ju-shan in founding the Liu-fa chien-hsueh hui [society for frugal study in France], also known as la Societé Rationelle des Etudiants Chinois en France. This group devised a plan, known as the thrift-study program, to enable Chinese students to study in France at an annual cost of China $600. A preparatory school, with Ch'i Ju-shan in charge, was set up in Peking to teach French to aspiring students for a six-month period. The first class included Li Shu-hua and Cheng Yü-hsiu (qq.v.). By the time the first group of 30 students reached France in January 1913, Li Shih-tseng had arranged for them to be admitted to the Collège de Montargis, south of Paris. In all, the thrift-study program enabled more than 100 students to study in France.

After the so-called second revolution collapsed in September 1913, most Kuomintang leaders were forced to flee China. Wu Chih-hui went to England; Ts'ai Yuan-p'ei took his family to Germany; and Wang Ching-wei, Tseng Chung-ming (q.v.), and Li Shih-tseng took their families to France. Wang lived with Li in Montargis and lectured to the thrift-study students. In the spring of 1915 Li, Wu, Ts'ai, and Wang met at Toulouse to discuss plans to establish some publications. Later that year, la Societé Franco-Chinois d'Education was organized in Paris, with Ts'ai Yuan-p'ei as the Chinese president. This group took advantage of the labor shortage in Europe by organizing the work-study movement, creating the Ch'in-kung chien-hsueh hui, or Societé Rationelle des Etudiants-Travailleurs Chinois en France. This program differed from the earlier thrift-study plan in that students worked in French factories and other businesses to finance their studies. More than 2,000 Chinese students, many of them from Hunan or Szechwan, participated in the program.

When Ts'ai Yuan-p'ei became chancellor of Peking University in 1916, he invited Li Shih-tseng to join its faculty as professor of biology. Li's soybean products business was forced by wartime conditions to suspend operations, and he returned to China in 1917. He devoted considerable attention to securing the return to China of the French portion of the Boxer Indemnity Fund for use in cultural and educational activities. After protracted negotiations,

a Sino-French agreement was signed in 1925. Li also sponsored the establishment in 1920 of the Sino-French University near Peking and the Institut Franco-Chinois de Lyon in France. Li served as chairman of the board of directors of the Sino-French University, with Ts'ai Yuan-p'ei as president. The Institut Franco-Chinois was housed in a fortress at Lyon which had been donated to it by the French government. The Chinese students then in France expected that they would be the first to be admitted to the Institut Franco-Chinois. However, Li and his associates, who had received financial support for this venture from the Canton government, chose a new group of about 100 students from Kwangtung and Kwangsi for the first class. Wu Chih-hui accompanied the students to Lyon and became president of the Institut Franco-Chinois. In September 1921 a group of about 100 work-study students, organized and led by Communist students, went to Lyon and forced their way into the Institut to protest their exclusion from the first class. About 103 of them, including Ch'en Yi, Ts'ai Ho-sen, and Li Li-san (qq.v.) were arrested and deported from France. The Institut prepared students for the University of Lyon and functioned as the overseas branch of the Sino-French University. It remained in existence until 1949, but came to serve as little more than a dormitory for Chinese students who were studying at various French universities.

At the First National Congress of the Kuomintang, held at Canton in January 1924, Li Shih-tseng and Wu Chih-hui were elected to the party's Central Supervisory Committee. By mid-1926 Chang Jen-chieh and Ts'ai Yuan-p'ei also had become full members of this important party organ.

After Feng Yü-hsiang (q.v.) occupied Peking in October 1924 and took control of the Peking government, he decided to expel P'u-yi (q.v.), the last Manchu emperor, from the Forbidden City. Li Shih-tseng was appointed the civilian representative to the eviction, which took place on 5 November. Li then was appointed chairman of the committee in charge of the inventory and custody of the palace treasures. In 1925 the Peking Palace Museum was founded, with Li as chairman of the board and Yi P'ei-chi (q.v.) as curator. Also in 1925, Li was created a Commandeur de la Legion d'Honneur in recognition of his efforts on behalf of Sino-French cultural cooperation. In the meantime, Sun Yat-sen, who had come to Peking for discussions with Tuan Ch'i-jui (q.v.) and his associates, had appointed Li to the Central Political Council. Sun died in Peking on 12 March 1925, and his remains were kept in temporary custody at the Pi-yun-ssu [temple] on the Sino-French University campus.

After the 8 March 1926 incident at the Taku harbor and the 18 March 1926 demonstration at Peking which resulted in the death of more than 40 people (for details, *see* Feng Yü-hsiang), Tuan Ch'i-jui ordered the arrest of Hsü Ch'ien, Li Ta-chao, Ku Meng-yü (qq.v.), Yi P'ei-chi, and Li Shih-tseng on charges of instigating the demonstration and disseminating Communist propaganda. Li took refuge in the French hospital and then escaped to Canton.

During the Kuomintang split of 1927, Li Shih-tseng, Wu Chih-hui, Ts'ai Yuan-p'ei, and Chang Jen-chieh staunchly supported the conservative faction of Chiang Kai-shek. They were among the members of the Central Supervisory Committee who met at Shanghai in April and adopted a resolution demanding the expulsion of all Communists from the Kuomintang and who supported the government established by Chiang Kai-shek at Nanking on 18 April in opposition to the Wuhan regime (*see* Wang Ching-wei).

Together with Ts'ai Yuan-p'ei and Wu Chih-hui, Li sponsored the creation of the Ta-hsueh-yuan [board of universities], with Ts'ai as its president, to replace the ministry of education. The new system, patterned on the French system, provided for the establishment of "university districts," and in 1928 three such districts were created. Li headed the Peiping district, with Li Shu-hua as his deputy. The system was found to be unsuited to China, however, and it was abolished by Chiang Monlin (Chiang Meng-lin, q.v.) after he assumed office as minister of education in 1929. Li Shih-tseng also was a sponsor of the Academia Sinica, established in 1928, and the National Peiping Research Academy, established in 1929. In October of that year, the new National Government at Nanking promulgated regulations for the Palace Museum and confirmed Li as chairman of the museum's board of directors. He held this office until November 1932.

Li Shih-tseng went to Geneva in 1932 to organize the Chinese delegation to the International Committee on Intellectual Cooperation sponsored by the League of Nations. While at Geneva, he established the Sino-International Library. After returning to China, Li commuted regularly between Shanghai, where he lived, and Nanking, where he participated in government and party affairs.

When the Sino-Japanese war began in July 1937, Li was in Europe, traveling between Paris and Geneva. He returned to China, but left the war-torn country in 1941 and went to New York. He cooperated with an American named Dolinet, who was the publisher of the magazine *Free World*, in establishing a Chinese edition of that journal. In 1943 he founded the Wood Shi-fee Institute to honor his long-time friend and associate Wu Chih-hui. Although he maintained residence in New York until mid-1945, Li made several trips to Chungking and Kunming during the war.

After returning to China in 1945, Li joined with Yang Chia-lo in compiling an encyclopedia, the first volume of which was published in 1946. In September 1948 he went to Peiping to celebrate the nineteenth anniversary of the National Peiping Research Academy. When the Chinese Communists began to threaten the old capital, he fled China and went to Geneva, where he remained until Switzerland recognized the People's Republic of China in 1950. Li then moved to Uruguay, taking the Sino-International Library collection with him, and established residence in Montevideo. After 1954, he maintained a second home in Taiwan and served as a national policy adviser to Chiang Kai-shek and a member of the Central Appraisal Committee, which superseded the Central Supervisory Committee.

Li Shih-tseng married three times. His first wife, *née* Yao T'ung-yi, died in Paris in 1941. On 14 February 1946 he married Lin Su-shan at Shanghai; she died in Montevideo in 1954. In 1957, at the age of 76, he married T'ien Pao-t'ien, who was some 40 years his junior, in Taipei. Li and his first wife had a son, Li Tsung-wei, and a daughter, Li Ya-mei.

Li Shu-hua   李 書 華
  T. Jun-chang   潤 章

Li Shu-hua (1890–), internationally known physicist and educator and vice president of the

National Peiping Research Academy from 1929 to 1948.

The son of Li Wan-k'uei, a landowning farmer, Li Shu-hua was born in Changli hsien, Chihli (Hopei). He had one younger brother, Li Shu-t'ien. Beginning in 1896, Li Shu-hua studied the Chinese classics under private tutors. Although he sat for the first level of imperial examinations in 1905 and did very well, his hopes of civil appointment were dashed in the autumn of that year when the examination system was abolished. In 1907 he studied at the Changli Higher Primary School, and in 1908 he went to Paoting and enrolled at the Chihli Higher Agricultural School. After the republican revolution of 1911, this school was renamed the Chihli Agricultural Technical Institute. As the top-ranking graduate of the institute in 1912, he was awarded a scholarship of China $500 by the provincial government for higher studies in Japan. At this time, Li Shih-tseng (q.v.) and others launched the program that was to become the work-study movement in France. Because this program cost about China $600 a year per student, Li applied for and received a scholarship increase of China $100.

After studying French in Peking for about six months, Li and his fellow students embarked on their journey to France, arriving in Paris in January 1913. They then went to Montargis, where Li Shih-tseng had arranged for them to be admitted to the Collège de Montargis. After the so-called second revolution collapsed in the autumn of 1913, many Kuomintang leaders who had opposed Yuan Shih-k'ai were forced to flee China. Wang Ching-wei (q.v.) came to Montargis, where he lectured to the Chinese students every Sunday morning.

In the autumn of 1915 Li Shu-hua enrolled at the agricultural institute of the University of Toulouse, from which he was graduated in 1918. By this time, he had become interested in physics, particularly in the electromagnetic theories of Gabriel Lippman and the radioactivity researches of Marie Curie. He enrolled at the University of Paris in 1919, obtained the degree of Licencié ès Sciences Physiques in 1920, and began work on his doctorate in the laboratory of Jean Perrin. After defending his dissertation, "Permeabilité selective des membranes polarisées," in June 1922, he became the first Chinese to receive the degree of Docteur ès

Sciences Physiques from the University of Paris. He then returned to China to become professor of physics at Peking University.

After arriving in Peking in August 1922, Li Shu-hua called on Ts'ai Yuan-p'ei (q.v.), the chancellor of Peking University, to arrange his courses. He made a brief trip to his native village to see his parents before assuming his academic duties. In addition to teaching physics at Peking University, he worked to develop the university's science curriculum.

When the National Government at Nanking experimented in 1928 with the organizing of institutions of higher education into "university districts" for administrative purposes, Li Shu-hua served under Li Shih-tseng as vice president of the Peiping university district. The new system proved unwieldy, and the experiment was terminated in the summer of 1929. In the meantime, the National Government had decided to establish the National Peiping Research Academy. The academy was inaugurated in September 1929, with Li Shu-hua as its vice president. He held this post until 1948.

In 1930 Chiang Kai-shek appointed Li Shu-hua political vice minister of education and a member of the Legislative Yuan. Li and Ch'en Pu-lei (q.v.), the administrative vice minister of education, assumed charge of the ministry because Chiang Kai-shek, who was acting as minister of education, had little time to devote to it. Early in 1931 Li also became a member of the newly established Sino-British Educational and Cultural Endowment Fund, the Sino-French Educational Endowment Fund, and the council of the Academia Sinica. He was appointed minister of education in February 1931, but he resigned after being blamed for the student demonstrations which followed the Japanese attack on Mukden on 18 September 1931.

Li Shu-hua returned to north China to devote his attention to the National Peiping Research Academy. Although Li Shih-tseng was its president, Li Shu-hua was responsible for its operation. Under his direction, the academy established research institutes in physics, chemistry, biology, zoology, botany, geology, history, and archaeology. In 1936 the academy began to transfer its equipment and personnel to Shansi because of the threat of war with the Japanese. When the Sino-Japanese war began in July 1937, Li and other educational leaders at Peiping announced their support of the united front against the Japanese. Li took refuge in the French hospital when the Japanese occupied Peiping, sent his wife and children to Tientsin, and went to Shanghai in October. After going to Wuhan, the temporary seat of the National Government, to arrange for the removal of the National Peiping Research Academy to Kunming, he established an academy office in Hong Kong. In mid-March, he led a group of about 20 staff members to Kunming. The institutes of physics, chemistry, zoology, and history were moved to Kunming soon afterwards. The institute of geology, which had been moved to Nanking in 1935, established headquarters at Changsha and then moved to Peip'ei in Szechwan. At Kunming, Li Shu-hua also served as acting chairman of the board of Sino-French University and performed a number of administrative services for the Academia Sinica.

In November 1945 Li Shu-hua went to London as a delegate to the inaugural session of the United Nations Educational, Scientific, and Cultural Organization (UNESCO). Before returning to China, he toured Europe and visited the United States, where he paid a call on Albert Einstein. Li also served as a delegate to later sessions of UNESCO, including those at Paris in 1946 and at Mexico City in 1947. In 1947 he visited important scientific institutions in the United States and Japan.

Li was elected to the new National Assembly, which convened in Nanking on 28 March 1948 and which assumed responsibility for the election of National Government officials. He went to Taiwan after the session ended and inspected the island's scientific organizations and institutions. The National Peiping Research Academy, which had returned to Peiping at war's end, celebrated its nineteenth anniversary on 9 September. Li Shu-hua remained in Peiping until mid-December, when the Chinese Communists surrounded the old capital. On 20 December, the National Government sent a plane to Peiping to rescue some prominent scholars marooned there. Although Mei Yi-ch'i, Yuan T'ung-li (qq.v.), Li Shu-hua, and a few other scholars left Peiping on that plane, many of the other educational leaders at the old capital elected to remain there.

Li Shu-hua went to Paris in July 1949, where he was created a Commandeur de la Legion d'Honneur. After serving on the Chinese delegation to the fourth session of UNESCO, he was offered research facilities by Pierre Girard, who also had studied under Jean Perrin and who had become head of the institute of physics, chemistry, and biology of the University of Paris. Li accepted this offer and did research on the properties of large molecules. In 1951–52 he gave lectures on Chinese language and literature at the University of Hamburg. After heading the Chinese delegation to the seventh session of UNESCO, held in Paris in November 1952, he went to New York. At the request of Mei Yi-ch'i, Li was given permission to use laboratory facilities at Columbia University. He also took up the study of the history of Chinese science and technology, using the facilities of the East Asian Library at Columbia, and in 1953 he wrote an article on the origin of the compass. The enthusiastic response to this article encouraged Li to write *The South Pointing Carriage and the Mariner's Compass*, which was published in both English and Chinese editions in Taipei. He also wrote articles on the history of paper making and printing, and his *Chung-kuo yin-shua-shu ch'i-yuan* was published in Hong Kong in 1962.

Li Shu-hua's first wife was Wan Chen-yuan. Their eldest child, Li Chi-chen, married Lung Yin, who became a professor of economics at Nankai University. Their second daughter, Li Yu-chen, married Lin T'ien-hui, who became a senior research scientist at the Smith, Kline, and French Laboratory in the United States. Their son, Li Hsiao-jun, became a senior research scientist at the Texas Research Center. In 1934 Wan Chen-yuan died in Tientsin, and in 1943 Li Shu-hua married Wang Wen-t'ien, who had studied economics at Berlin University and had taught at Honan University. During the Sino-Japanese war she served as acting dean of students at Nankai University.

Li Shu-t'ung
李 叔 同
Religious. Hung-i
弘 一

Li Shu-t'ung (1880–4 September 1942), pioneer of modern music and drama in China who became Hung-i, one of the most celebrated Buddhist clerics of his time.

Tientsin was the birthplace of Li Shu-t'ung, the son by a concubine of Li Hsiao-lou, a chinshih of 1847. The elder Li was an adept both of the philosophy of the Ming Neo-Confucian thinker Wang Yang-ming (1472–1529) and of Zen Buddhism. He died when Li Shu-t'ung was four, leaving the boy to be reared by his mother, then only in her twenties.

Li's education and upbringing were unexceptional for a boy of his class and era. Encouraged by his elder half-brothers, he began to study the Confucian classics and made rapid progress. He also learned painting and seal carving. At the same time, he gave evidence of pronounced religious preoccupation, as when he committed to memory the *Mahākaruṇādhāraṇī* and other liturgical texts recited by Buddhist monks at family memorial services or imitated monkish rituals of propitiation and exorcism. According to an account given to a friend in later years, the young Li was also given to fits of depression when he contemplated the transience, emptiness, and misery which even then seemed to him to characterize this world. Through the kindly attention of his elder half-brothers and the simple piety of the women members of his family, he achieved a command of the main elements of the Chinese classical tradition together with an understanding of Buddhism, at least as practiced by the devotees of the buddha Amitābha.

As a consequence of his family's high position, Li had been affianced at birth to a Miss Yü, whom he married in 1897. Two sons, born in 1900 and 1904 respectively, resulted from this union. Little more is known of either his wife or children, for, if Li in subsequent years did not precisely abandon them, he never regarded his marriage as having prior claims over filial piety, devotion to the arts, or religion. Also in 1897, Li became a partisan of the reform faction then seeking a voice in the operations of the Chinese government. To what extent he actually participated in the activities of the young men and junior officials who supported K'ang Yu-wei and Liang Ch'i-ch'ao (qq.v.) cannot be determined, but it is certain that he was considered a member of the reform party. He even carved a seal reading "Nan-hai K'ang-chün shih wu-shih" [K'ang Yu-wei is my teacher]. As a consequence, he was obliged to flee from Tientsin to Shanghai when, on 21–22 September 1898, the Empress Dowager Tz'u-hsi (ECCP, I, 295–300) launched the *coup d'état* which ended the Hundred Days Reform and which cost six of the reform leaders their lives. In his flight Li was accompanied only by his mother.

At Shanghai, Li thought it prudent to establish residence in the French concession. At the same time, he set about making the acquaintance of local literati. By winning three times in succession the prize offered for classical composition by the Hu-hsüeh-hui [Shanghai literary club], Li came to the favorable notice of the principal sponsor of the club, Hsü Huan-yuan. In 1899 Hsü invited Li and his mother to take up residence in his country villa south of Shanghai, initiating what Li himself later came to regard as the period of his secular life which came closest to perfection. Hsü's villa, surrounded by ancient willows and bordered by a meandering brook, was in a secluded suburb. Li was alloted a small house, where he lived contentedly with his mother and a few servants. Together with Hsü, and such friends of Hsü as Ts'ai Hsiao-hsiang, Chang Hsiao-lou, and Yuan Hsi-lien, Li spent six years at the villa painting and practicing the art of Chinese poetry in its various classical forms. These activities led eventually to the formation of the Shanghai shu-hua kung-hui [Shanghai association for calligraphy and painting], which for several years published the weekly *Shu-hua pao* [bulletin of calligraphy and painting]. The bulletin was edited by Li Shu-t'ung and was notable for the high quality of its plates and for exposing practitioners of traditional Chinese art to new artistic ideas. Li, whose own poetry, painting, calligraphy, and seal carving were attracting notice in Shanghai, shortly after 1900 published *Li-lu yin-p'u* [my book of seals], which contained impressions of rare and ancient seals from his own collection and of seals carved by himself. His next publication was *Li-lu shih-chung* [the bell], a collection of his own verse. Beginning in 1902, Li studied for a time at Nanyang University, where he and Shao Li-tzu (q.v.) were favorite pupils of Ts'ai Yuan-p'ei (q.v.).

While living at Hsü Huan-yuan's villa, Li Shu-t'ung made the acquaintance of a number of the most famous singsong girls of the time and down to the day of his ordination preserved in elaborate brocade mountings copies of poems and letters which he had exchanged with them. In 1901 Li's name was linked to that of Yang Ts'ui-hsi, a courtesan celebrated both for her abilities as a singer and for the minuteness of her bound feet. She later became the concubine of Ts'ai-chen, an important personage in his own right and the son of I-k'uang (ECCP, II, 964–65), who from 1903 until 1911 was the highest official in the Ch'ing government. A garbled and somewhat fictionalized account of their relationship appears in *Yang Ts'ui-hsi erh-san shih* [some incidents in the life of Yang Ts'ui-hsi].

In 1905 Li Shu-t'ung's mother died suddenly. Her death was a great shock to him, and, after seeing her coffin safely to its final resting place in Tientsin, he spent some time meditating on his future before deciding to go to Japan and to study Western art and music. During his years in Shanghai, Li had become interested in Western art and also in the adaptation of Western techniques to Chinese art. Another factor which influenced his decision was that a number of his old reformist acquaintances who had fled to Japan in 1898 were still living there.

After arriving in Japan late in 1905, Li Shu-t'ung entered the Ueno Bijutsu Semmon Gakkō [Ueno art academy], where his chief subject was oil painting. At the Ongaku Gakkō [academy of music] he studied music, concentrating on the piano. In both branches of study he made rapid progress and readily adapted himself to Western techniques. His charcoal study *Ch'ü-nü-hua* [portrait of a virgin] excited great interest, as much for its technique as for the spiritual expression of the model, and later became a part of the collection of Feng Tzu-k'ai (q.v.). After Li discovered that his age and the many hours needed for practice would effectively prevent him from obtaining first rank as a pianist, he began to study music theory and composition. Some of his songs were published years later under the title *Chung-wen ming-ko wu-shih-ch'ü* [fifty famous songs in Chinese]. In 1906 he began publication of *Yin-yüeh hsiao-tsa-chih* [the little magazine of music], a biannual devoted to the introduction of Western music theory to China and the first magazine devoted entirely to musical affairs to be published in China. The activity which won Li Shu-t'ung most fame during his years in Japan was neither painting nor music, however, but theater. Before going to Japan he had become a skilled amateur performer in Chinese opera, which he had studied in leisure moments while a student at Nanyang University. Li was profoundly impressed by the Western naturalistic drama which he saw presented on the Japanese stage. Accordingly, he joined with Ou-yang Yü-ch'ien (q.v.), and others in organizing the Ch'un-liu chü-she [spring willow drama club] for the presentation of Western plays in Chinese. In the course of the next several years the group put on successful productions of such plays as *La Dame aux camélias*, *Uncle Tom's Cabin*, and *Les Misérables*. Li specialized in women's roles, and his moving performance as Camille was acclaimed by both Chinese and Japanese critics.

In 1910 Li returned to China with a young Japanese girl who had been living with him for some months. Li established her in Shanghai and his wife and children in Tientsin and went to work as a teacher of drawing at the Chih-li mo-fan kung-hsüeh hsüeh-t'ang [Chihli academy of applied arts]. In 1912 Li's personal fortune, much of it invested in stocks, diminished considerably as a result of the revolution. He then moved to Shanghai, where he assumed the position of instructor in music at the Ch'eng-tung nü-hsüeh [east Shanghai girl's college]. At this time, revolutionary ardor was reflected in the formation of a number of literary societies dedicated to the cause of bringing new vitality to Chinese literature. Among these new groups was the Nan-she [southern society], led by Liu Ya-tzu (q.v.). Li Shu-t'ung attended its first meeting in April 1912 and became one of its more prominent members.

In Shanghai, Li also continued his career as a journalist and editor. When Ch'en Ch'i-mei (q.v.) started the *T'ai-p'ing-yang pao* [Pacific journal] in 1912, with Chu Shao-p'ing as editor in chief and Yeh Ch'u-ts'ang (q.v.) as chief editorial writer, he persuaded Li to assume the dual post of literary editor in chief and editor of the pictorial supplement, the *T'ai-p'ing-yang hua-pao*. The pictorial supplement, one of the first such features to be tried on a regular basis by a Chinese newspaper, succeeded largely because of Li's imaginative and tasteful direction. The literary section also flourished, and under Li's editorship a number of new young writers of merit were published, including Su Man-shu (q.v.), whose *Tuan-hung ling-yen* [a single goose] first appeared in this publication. Li also organized a new literary group, the Wen-mei hui [fine arts society] and assumed editorship of its journal, the *Wen-mei tsa-chih* [fine arts magazine]. Before long, however, both the *T'ai-p'ing-yang pao* and the

Wen-mei hui went bankrupt. As a result, Li left Shanghai for Hangchow.

Beginning in 1913 Li was employed as instructor in drawing and music at the Che-chiang liang-chi shih-fan hsüeh-hsiao [Chekiang dual level normal school], which subsequently became Che-chiang ti-i shih-fan ta-hsüeh [Chekiang first normal college]. In 1915 he also assumed the post of instructor in drawing at Nan-ching kao-teng shih-fan ta-hsueh [Nanking higher normal school]. Among Li's colleagues were Hsia K'ai-tsun, T'ien Chün-fu, and Ma Hsü-lun (q.v.), and his students included Feng Tzu-k'ai, Liu Chih-p'ing, Wu Meng-fei, and Ts'ao Chü-jen. As a teacher, Li was remembered by his students both for his clear, painstaking way of teaching and for his high example of seriousness and probity. In Hangchow he became increasingly sober and reflective and adopted a style of life which stressed the traditional Confucian simplicity appropriate to a teacher and scholar. In a remarkable way he was able to communicate his enthusiasm for drawing and music to students. His recognition and encouragement of Feng Tzu-k'ai's talent led directly to Feng's choice of art as a career.

Although Li Shu-t'ung had lived a full and sophisticated life, at least up to his return from Japan, he later confided to friends that he had never known real happiness and that as a layman he had never been without a depressing sense of the transience of all things. The death of his father in 1884, the failure of his political dreams in 1898, the death of his mother in 1905, his loveless marriage and complicated home life, and the political confusion and the loss of his fortune in 1912 eventually led him to a thoroughgoing reexamination of life and his place in it. Initially, he turned to Neo-Confucianism, a subject in which his father had acquired considerable learning. At the same time, he took up Taoism and went so far as to affect Taoist garb and to practice certain Taoist austerities. In January 1917 Li traveled to Ta-tz'u-shan and made his first extended fast, a 17-day effort involving gradual withdrawal from food, subsistence on water alone for one week, and gradual return to normal nutriment. The physical and spiritual effects of the fast were so pronounced that Li adopted a new personal name, "Ying" [newborn], and resolved to pursue to the end the new studies and disciplines that the experience of the fast

had opened up to him. At this stage, his religious interests were centered in Taoism, but he had begun to study related aspects of Buddhism. His conversion and decision to join the Buddhist clergy came about in the same apocalyptic way as had his wholehearted conversion to Taoism. When asked by a friend, Ma I-fu, to recommend a quiet district for meditation to a certain Mr. P'eng, a friend of Ma and a student of the *ching tso* [meditation], Li named Ta-tz'u-shan. As it happened, Li planned to be there at the same time, and he struck up an acquaintance with P'eng. When they arrived at Ta-tz'u-shan, P'eng conceived the desire to become a Buddhist monk. His decision so moved Li that he determined to follow suit, but he was able to take only the vows of a lay believer. At this time, Li became a disciple of the eminent monk Liao-wu, began public worship of the Buddha, gave up meat and spicy vegetables, and studied the Buddhist scriptures. On 15 April 1918, having given away all of his books, seals, clothes, scrolls, and paintings to his colleagues and students, he took his first vows of entrance into the Buddhist clergy. At this point he adopted his name in religion, "Hung-i" [vast unity]. It has been reported that Hung-i's wife, children, and Japanese concubine arrived in Ta-tz'u-shan shortly thereafter in hopes of dissuading him from becoming a monk. Their protests proved futile, however, and they departed—the wife and children for Tientsin, the Japanese concubine for Japan. Hung-i shaved his head and took final vows in July 1918.

As a monk, Hung-i continued to practice the austerities through which he had achieved his first insights into profound religious experience. His frequent fasts and rigorous life won him many lay admirers. Hung-i also became known for delivering simple, moving sermons. However, Hung-i's most notable contribution to modern Chinese Buddhism was not in evangelism nor in the investigation which he made into the doctrines of the ching-t'u [pure land] sect, but in reform of the Buddhist clergy. He believed that the decline of Buddhism had come about in large measure through the decay of the clergy and that moral reforms were needed. This view of the problem of a Buddhist renaissance centering on the clergy contrasted sharply with the views of Yin-kuang, who proclaimed a simplified version of ching-t'u teachings which stressed an unquestioning faith in the buddha Amitābha, and with those of Hsü-yün, who dispensed almost entirely with ecclesiastical apparatus and preached the Zen doctrine of the sudden enlightenment of the individual through meditation. T'ai-hsü (q.v.) attempted to bring the clergy back into the modern world by a synthesis of traditional doctrines with socialism, relativity theory, and other imports from the West, earning in passing the title "revolutionary monk," but Hung-i concentrated on the moral regeneration of the clergy.

In September 1918 Hung-i took a series of special vows known as chieh [prohibitions]. Finding that these vows were especially relevant to his own spiritual needs, Hung-i proceeded to make a special study of the tradition within Buddhism from which they emerged. This was the lü or "monastic discipline" sect, which flourished during T'ang times, but subsequently declined. The doctrines of the lü school had been codified and brought to completion by the eminent monk Tao-hsüan (596–667). The most important part of the canon consisted in carefully detailed "prohibitive precepts," 250 for monks and 348 for nuns, which effectively applied to all aspects of life. Because he was convinced that a national Buddhist renaissance would have to begin with a regenerated clergy and that he had discovered systems of "monastic discipline" through which such a regeneration could take place, Hung-i devoted the rest of his life to a reexamination and recodification of the doctrines of the lü school. In 1924 these studies culminated in his *Ssu-fen-lü pi-ch'iu chieh-hsiang piao-chi* [rules of monastic discipline in four sections]. In this synthesis of a large number of existing treatises on "monastic discipline," Hung-i set forth a simple, consistent system of behavior for clerics which, more than any other work published for hundreds of years, responded to the needs of the tens of thousands of Buddhist monks throughout China. The book was welcomed by Buddhist churchmen of almost all persuasions. Hung-i then wrote a series of treatises on related topics. Among these were biographical accounts of the sect's virtual founder, Tao-hsüan, which appeared as *Nan-shan Tao-hsüan lü-tsu lüeh-p'u* [a brief life of Tao-hsüan, founder of the "monastic discipline" school] and *Nan-shan nien-p'u* [chronological biography of Tao-hsüan]. For his efforts in reviving this branch of Buddhism, Hung-i

earned the designation ch'ung-hsing Nan-shan lü-tsung ti-shih-i-tai tsu-shih [eleventh patriarch and restorer of the "monastic discipline" school]. In 1929 Hung-i collaborated with his pupil Feng Tzu-k'ai on the first of a series of volumes entitled *Hu-sheng hua-chi*, a calligraphic text written by Hung-i in the form of fables with Buddhist morals. Feng produced 50 illustrations for the first volume. The second and third volumes appeared in 1940 and 1950.

Soon after the Sino-Japanese war began in 1937, Japanese forces occupied the area where Hung-i was living. Hung-i did not allow their presence to interrupt his life of preaching, traveling, and writing. By this time, Hung-i had reduced his personal needs to a minimum and traveled with little more than one battered straw mat for a bed and an extra robe. His endurance of want and suffering served as a much emulated example in the occupied areas through which he traveled. Typical of his spirit during his final years was his remark to Hsia K'ai-tsun after Hsia had accidently added too much salt to Hung-i's simple vegetable supper: "Let it be. Salt has the flavor of salt, and that is good too." Although a cleric and thus "dead to the world," Hung-i reacted patriotically to the Japanese invasion, resisting efforts to remove him to safer areas and responding to requests for samples of his calligraphy with such mottos as "nien-Fo pu-wang chiu-kuo" [in the worship of Buddha do not neglect the salvation of China]. Wartime privation combined with continued austerities and fasts soon began to weaken Hung-i's health. His condition became grave during the summer of 1942, and in September of that year he made a final gift of all his earthly possessions to Hsia K'ai-tsun and Liu Chih-p'ing. He died on 4 September 1942 at Ch'üanchou, Fukien.

Since his demise, the memory of Hung-i has been kept alive, largely through the efforts of his former colleagues and disciples. A memorial stele was raised at Ch'üanchou in 1952 on the tenth anniversary of his death. A year later a similar but larger monument was erected at Hangchow. Feng Tzu-k'ai and Yeh Sheng-t'ao (q.v.) were among the sponsors of the Hangchow column. In recent histories of Chinese music Hung-i has been commended for his pioneer efforts in introducing Western music to China. In 1958 a collection of his songs, edited and illustrated by Feng Tzu-k'ai, was published at

Peking under the title *Li Shu-t'ung ko-ch'ü chi* [songs of Li Shu-t'ung].

Li Ta 李 達
H. Ho-ming 鶴 鳴

Li Ta (1890–), scholar and founding member of the Chinese Communist party who became known as a leading spokesman on Marxist ideology. From 1953 until 1966, when he was criticized and removed from office, he held the presidency of Wuhan University.

The son of a tenant farmer in Lingling hsien, Hunan, Li Ta began his education in 1900 at a traditional private school and moved on to the Yungchou Middle School, a semi-modern institution, in 1905. Because he believed that education was the key to China's salvation, he decided to become a teacher. Accordingly, he entered the Peking Higher Normal School in 1909. He soon decided that industry, science, and technology were more important than education and transferred to a trade school in Hunan. In 1912 he passed the provincial scholarship examinations for study abroad and went to Japan to take courses in mining and metallurgy at Tokyo Imperial University. He soon became interested in political and social thought.

According to his own account, Li returned to China in 1918 having been influenced by the Russian Revolution and shocked by Japanese intervention in China and Siberia. He went to Peking to help organize protests by college students against Tuan Ch'i-jui (q.v.) and his negotiations with Japanese authorities. About this time, Li began to study Marxism. He returned to Japan for a brief period, and in 1920 he went to Shanghai as the representative of the Japanese branch of the Save China Association. He helped organize the Chinese Communist party, participated in its July 1921 founding meeting, and became head of its propaganda department. He also wrote articles on socialist thought for such magazines as the *Chieh-fang yü kai-tsao* [liberation and reform] and the *Hsin ch'ing-nien* [new youth], of which he became an editor. When the Shanghai group established the theoretical journal *Kung-ch'an-tang yüeh-k'an* [Communist party monthly] in November 1921 to educate party workers in the doctrines of Marxism-Leninism, Li became its editor. He also worked under Ch'en Tu-hsiu (q.v.) in administering a girls school established by the Communists at Shanghai.

In 1923 Li went to Changsha, where he became a lecturer at Hunan University. His lectures became the basis of his first important book, *Hsien-tai she-hui-hsueh* [modern sociology], a systematic exposition of Marxist theory which appeared in 1926. In the preface to the 1929 edition Li said that "the theories in this book are mostly directed at European, American, and Japanese capitalist society and cannot explain clearly much in 'semi-feudal' Chinese society." At some time during this period, Li served as a reporter for the Christian publication *I-shih pao* in Tientsin, and in 1926 he taught in Wuchang. After returning to Shanghai in 1928, he taught at Shanghai Law College, Chinan University, and Ta-lu University (*see* Ch'en Kung-po). After Ta-lu was closed by Nationalist police in May 1929, Li helped to found a publishing house, the K'un-lun shu-tien. Many of his later works, including his *Chung-kuo ch'an-yeh kai-ke kai-kuan* [general survey of China's industrial revolution], were published by this firm.

Little is known about Li Ta's activities or whereabouts during the 1930's and 1940's except that he reportedly taught at Hunan, Kwangtung, and Kwangsi universities. In 1949 he was identified as vice president of the Peking University of Political Science and Law. After the Central People's Government was established, he held posts on the Government Council committees for cultural, educational, and legal affairs and on the Central-South Military and Administrative Committee. He also was chairman of the first council of the Chinese Philosophical Society and vice chairman of the All-China Congress of Workers in the Social Sciences. After serving as president of Hunan University until 1953, he was transferred to Wuchang, where he became the president of Wuhan University. From 1961 to 1966 he also served as vice chairman of the central-south branch of the Chinese Academy of Sciences.

Li Ta's most important role after 1948 was as a spokesman on problems of Marxist ideology. His *Huo-pi hsueh kai-lun* [general discussion of finance] was published in 1949, and it was followed by a number of shorter accounts of the state of academic and ideological studies in the People's Republic of China. Li's later works also included interpretations of the writings of Mao Tse-tung. His party activities caused him to be criticized as a "dogmatic party leader" during the Hundred Flowers campaign. In the summer of 1966, however, Li reportedly was accused of being "an anti-party, anti-socialist, anti-Mao-Tse-tung-in-thought shock trooper, and a stubborn counterrevolutionary element." He allegedly had denied that the Thought of Mao Tse-tung represented the culmination of Marxism-Leninism. Li was removed from his posts soon after these accusations were made.

Li Ta-chao   李 大 釗
T. Shou-ch'ang   守 常

Li Ta-chao (1889–28 April 1927), founding member of the Chinese Communist party who, as librarian and professor at Peking University, strongly influenced the youth of China at the time of the May Fourth Movement. He was the principal director of Communist organizational and propaganda activities in north China until 1927, when Chang Tso-lin had him arrested and executed.

Born into a peasant family in Lot'ing in northeast Hopei province, Li Ta-chao was orphaned as a small child and was brought up by his grandparents. At the age of 16, he sold the family property and entered a middle school at Yungp'ing, near his native town. Two years later, he went to Tientsin to attend the Peiyang School of Law and Government (Pei-yang fa-cheng chuan-men hsueh-hsiao), from which he was graduated in 1913. Li came to the attention of Sun Hung-i (1870–1936; T. Po-lan), a well-known progressive leader in Tientsin who headed the Chihli (Hopei) provincial assembly during the final years of the Ch'ing dynasty. With the establishment of the republic early in 1912, Sun joined with Liang Ch'i-ch'ao, T'ang Hua-lung (qq.v.), and other leading proponents of parliamentary government in forming the Democratic party, which was reorganized as the Progressive party in 1913. Through Sun Hung-i, Li Ta-chao was introduced to T'ang Hua-lung, who became Li's sponsor and sent him to Japan to continue his education.

In the autumn of 1913 Li enrolled as a first-year student in political economy at Waseda University in Tokyo. In Japan he soon became acquainted with the journalist Chang Shih-chao (q.v.), and in the summer of 1914 he began to contribute articles on political science and economics to Chang's magazine, *Chia-yin tsa-chih* (*The Tiger Magazine*). When Yuan Shih-k'ai promulgated a new "constitutional compact," drafted for him by his political advisers Frank J. Goodnow and Ariga Nagao, Li Ta-chao wrote an article in which he refuted the contention of Yuan's foreign advisers that conditions in China were not favorable to a republican form of government and criticized the "constitutional compact," which concentrated government powers in Yuan's hands. In the following year, Li's opposition to Yuan's regime grew more pronounced, especially after the news of Japan's Twenty-one Demands reached students in Japan late in 1915. Li called on Chinese students throughout Japan to oppose the Twenty-one Demands. He also wrote an open letter from Chinese students in Japan to their countrymen at home, which was wired to China and widely circulated in an effort to arouse public opinion against Yuan's acceptance of these demands.

After returning to Peking in the summer of 1916, Li Ta-chao became a secretary to T'ang Hua-lung, who at that time was helping Liang Ch'i-ch'ao, Sun Hung-i, and others to organize the Hsien-fa yen-chiu hui [association for constitutional research], whose members became known as the Research clique. Probably through his connections with T'ang, Li became editor of a Peking daily backed by members of the Research clique, the *Ch'en-chung jih-pao*, which was reorganized late in 1918 as the *Ch'en-pao* [morning post]. Under Li's editorship, the paper increased its circulation and acquired a reputation for liberalism.

In February 1918 Li accepted an invitation from Ts'ai Yuan-p'ei (q.v.), the new chancellor of Peking University, to serve as head of the university library. As chief librarian and later (1920) as professor of history, economics, and political science, Li was to be associated with China's foremost institution of higher learning for a decade.

Li Ta-chao entered into the academic life of Peking University at a time of great intellectual ferment. The principal medium for the new literary and cultural movements was the *Hsin ch'ing-nien* [new youth], founded by Ch'en Tu-hsiu (q.v.). Early in 1916 Li became a member of the magazine's editorial staff, which also included Hu Shih (q.v.) and other Peking University professors. He also became an occasional contributor to the *Hsin ch'ing-nien*. In one article, "Ch'ing-ch'un" [youth], published in September 1916, he outlined a theory of cosmic change through gradually ascending cycles of birth, maturity, decay, and rebirth. A similar article, "Chin" [the present], appeared in the issue of April 1918.

Because the editors of the *Hsin ch'ing-nien* had been concerned primarily with social and ideological change, they had agreed at the outset on an editorial policy of non-involvement in contemporary political affairs. But when the policies of premier Tuan Ch'i-jui (q.v.) and his military supporters aroused the anger and dismay of many parliamentarians at Peking, Li Ta-chao and Ch'en Tu-hsiu found it increasingly difficult to refrain from airing their views on the political situation. In December 1918 the two men established the *Mei-chou p'ing-lun* [weekly critic], in which they criticized the Tuan government for its domestic policies and for its secret dealings with Japan. Through their writings in the new periodical, Li and Ch'en helped to stimulate a new interest in national affairs and to create a climate of opinion among China's youth which led to the patriotic student demonstrations of the May Fourth Movement of 1919.

Li Ta-chao's influence on the growing student movement was caused by his close personal contact with the students and his willingness to participate directly in their activities, as well as by his writings and lectures. In the summer of 1918 he had joined a small group of students and young intellectuals to discuss the formation of the Shao-nien Chung-kuo hsueh-hui [young China association], which would organize patriotic opposition to Tuan Ch'i-jui's pro-Japanese regime. When that association was formally established in July 1919, Li became a prominent member and a contributor to its magazine, *Shao-nien Chung-kuo* [young China]. He also gave aid to a number of other student organizations. For example, he secured financial assistance for the Peking University students who started the *Hsin-ch'ao* [renaissance] early in 1919 and gave editorial advice to a radical student society which began to publish the *Chueh-wu* [awakening] early in 1920. Li also lent a sympathetic ear to the personal problems of individual students. To help one young student in straitened circumstances—a Hunanese named Mao Tse-tung—Li arranged for his employment as a clerk in the university library. As a result of his active interest in the students and their activities, Li's office in the university library became a center for conferences and meetings of student leaders during and after the period of the May Fourth Movement.

It was while he was thus establishing himself as a popular and influential figure among the students at Peking University that Li Ta-chao began to give serious attention to the doctrines of Marxism. Although he had been exposed to Marxist ideas during his stay in Japan, his interest appears to have remained academic until the discouraging political situation in China and the success of the Russian Revolution suggested to him that Marxism might offer the solution to political and social problems in China. In an article in the October 1918 issue of *Hsin ch'ing-nien* entitled "The Victory of Bolshevism," Li expressed his enthusiasm for the creation of a new political order in Russia, organized on the basis of Marxist economic and social theories. In 1918 he also founded the Ma-k'e-shih chu-i yen-chiu-hui [Marxist research society]. He edited a special issue of *Hsin ch'ing-nien* devoted almost exclusively to Marxism in May 1919. Li himself contributed an important introductory article, "My Views on Marxism," which indicated that although he was far from convinced of the general validity of Marxism, he was sympathetic to its aims. By the end of 1919, his writings revealed that he had accepted the basic tenets of historical materialism, and by the middle of the following year he appears to have espoused the Marxist viewpoint completely.

Meanwhile, the events of the May Fourth Movement had strengthened Li's vision of a revitalized modern China, brought into being through the surging tide of China's youth, and the student demonstrations had convinced him that organization was the key to effective political action in China. However, in the course of his conversion to Marxism, Li came to the conclusion that further study of Marxist theories should be prompted among groups of students and young intellectuals before the work of political organization began. To this end, he established the Ma-k'o-ssu hsueh-shou yen-chiu-hui [society for the study of Marxism] in the summer of 1920. At its meetings he and other professors gave lectures on Marxism to students at Peking University.

Li's conviction that Marxist study should be given priority over political organization soon was altered through the influence of his former associate Ch'en Tu-hsiu, who had left Peking University for Shanghai in the autumn of 1919. Early in 1920 Li had been approached by Gregory Voitinsky, an agent of the Comintern who had recently arrived in Peking. Li had sent him to Ch'en Tu-hsiu with a letter of introduction. After several discussions with Voitinsky, Ch'en had decided to organize a Communist party nucleus in Shanghai in the summer of 1920. In September, one of Li Ta-chao's students, Chang Kuo-t'ao (q.v.), returned from a trip to Shanghai to inform Li of Ch'en's plans to set up a network of Communist cells in all major cities in preparation for the formal establishment of a Chinese Communist party. In response to Ch'en Tu-hsiu's requests, Li Ta-chao, with the help of Chang Kuo-t'ao, formed a small Communist group in Peking and, in accord with Ch'en's program, also organized a branch of the Socialist Youth Corps, to serve as a training ground for future cadres.

Li Ta-chao was able to turn the interests of many students in the direction of Marxism and to the new Communist organization. During the winter of 1920–21 he brought together a group of students, including Chang Kuo-t'ao and Teng Chung-hsia (q.v.), to carry the message of Marxism to the railroad workers in north China. As coordinator of the Peking nucleus, Li corresponded with other leaders in Shanghai and Canton, and they decided to convene a congress of Communist delegates in Shanghai in July 1921. Because Li was too busy with academic duties in Peking to attend the conference, the Peking group sent Chang Kuo-t'ao, who acted as chairman of the congress at which the Chinese Communist party was formally inaugurated.

A man of mild and amiable disposition, Li Ta-chao was able to move with ease among the many and varied political and cultural groups with which he had been associated since his pre-Communist days. He remained an active and influential member of the Shao-nien Chung-kuo hsueh-hsi until 1923, when he and other Communists formally withdrew from that organization. Through his former benefactor Sun Hung-i, he maintained cordial relations with the Research clique, and he continued to be friendly with Hu Shih and other liberal professors at Peking University, joining them in support of their efforts to promote "government by good men" in the spring and summer of 1922. He was, moreover, on good terms with members of the Kuomintang, and, through a former classmate at the Peiyang School of Law and Government who had become director of Wu P'ei-fu's political department, he also was able to communicate with the Chihli military clique, then the dominant military power in north China.

Li's wide range of acquaintances and his personal prestige among the students were political assets of no small importance during the first years of the Chinese Communist party, when its membership was tiny and its influence was insignificant. He was elected to the Central Committee at the party's Second National Congress, held in Shanghai in July 1922. Li was unable to attend the congress, but he attended a special plenum of the Central Committee which was convened at Hangchow in August by the Comintern representative Maring to discuss the new Comintern policy of cooperation with the Kuomintang. His colleagues on the Central Committee strongly opposed such policy, but, according to Chang Kuo-t'ao, Li not only supported Maring but also helped to win Ch'en Tu-hsiu, the party secretary, over to the Comintern position. At the Hangchow plenum, Li Ta-chao suggested that the principle of cooperation be extended to include Wu P'ei-fu (q.v.), then regarded with considerable favor by Li's liberal friends in Peking. Russian agents approached Wu, and Li worked hard to establish a harmonious relationship between the Chinese Communist party and Wu's subordinates in the Peking area. However, Wu P'ei-fu's suppression of the Peking-Hankow railway workers' strike in February 1923 ended all attempts to collaborate with the Chihli militarists and strengthened the resolve of Li and other Communist leaders to work enclusively with the Kuomintang.

Li Ta-chao was to play an active part in implementing the Communist-Kuomintang entente of 1922–26. Immediately after the Hangchow plenum, he went to visit Sun Yat-sen, who had just arrived in Shanghai from Canton, and was instrumental in persuading the Kuomintang leader to agree to a working relationship with both Russian and Chinese Communists. Sun consented to allow members of the Chinese Communist party to join the Kuomintang on an individual basis. In August 1922 Li became the first of the many Communists to be admitted to the Kuomintang. His membership was sponsored by Chang Chi (q.v.).

In the autumn of 1922 Li returned to his teaching duties at Peking University. With the help of Teng Chung-hsia and other members of the Chinese Communist party's north China bureau, he renewed his efforts to stimulate interest in Marxism among the students at various colleges in Peking. Among the campuses they visited was the Mongolian and Tibetan School, where they introduced the principles of Marxism-Leninism to such young Mongols as Ulanfu (q.v.), who later became a member of the Chinese Communist party and its leading activist in organizing the Inner Mongolian People's Revolutionary party. Late in 1923 Li Ta-chao left for Canton to attend the First National Congress of the Kuomintang as a delegate from the Peking municipal district. Li and two other Communists, T'an P'ing-shan (q.v.) and Yü Shu-te, were elected to the 24-man Central Executive Committee of the re-organized Kuomintang. At the close of the congress on 30 January 1924, Li was also chosen a member of the six-man central executive committee of the Peking branch of the Kuomintang.

In September 1924 Li returned to north China from a trip to the Soviet Union, where he had spent the summer touring the country and attending the Fifth Congress of the Comintern in Moscow. In Peking, Wu P'ei-fu was preparing the military forces of the Chihli clique for a renewed struggle for power against Chang Tso-lin (q.v.), Tuan Ch'i-jui, and Sun Yat-sen. Because of the massacre of the railway workers in February 1923, Li and Wu had become bitter enemies, and in 1924 Wu had issued orders for Li's arrest. To avoid capture, Li hid himself in a secluded temple in the hills of Ch'angli, not far from his native Lot'ing, where he remained until the conclusion of the Fengtien-Chihli war. With the overthrow of Wu P'ei-fu

and the Chihli clique by the armies of Chang Tso-lin and Feng Yü-hsiang (q.v.) and the establishment of Tuan Ch'i-jui as provisional chief executive in Peking, Li returned to Peking University to resume his teaching and political activities.

During the next two years, Li Ta-chao continued to enhance his prestige as an intellectual leader among the students in Peking and his reputation among political conservatives and the foreign community as a dangerous radical and agitator. His authority within the Kuomintang was reaffirmed at that party's Second National Congress in January 1926, at which he was reelected to the Central Executive Committee. As a prominent figure in both the Chinese Communist party and the Kuomintang, he worked to achieve closer cooperation between the two party organizations in Peking. His work was complicated by the open split of the Kuomintang into right- and left-wing factions following the death of Sun Yat-sen in March 1925. After the departure of the right-wing leaders from Peking toward the end of that year, Li and the Communists had been able to increase their influence in the Kuomintang left wing; and with the flight of the non-Communist left-wing leaders after the incident of 18 March 1926, the Kuomintang organization in Peking came under the control of its Communist members.

While Li Ta-chao and his Communist colleagues were strengthening their hold on the Kuomintang in Peking, the existence of both parties became increasingly precarious as a result of the military and political instability in north China. In 1925 a rift between Feng Yü-hsiang and Chang Tso-lin culminated in an open break between the two leaders. Li Ta-chao worked to encourage closer ties between the Kuomintang-Communist coalition and the Kuominchün of Feng Yü-hsiang against the power of Chang Tso-lin and his new ally Wu P'ei-fu. On 12 March 1925 units of Feng's Kuominchün blockading Taku, the port of Tientsin, were attacked by Chang Tso-lin's forces with the support of Japanese gunboats; and four days later, the ministers of Japan and the Western powers sent a joint ultimatum to the Tuan Ch'i-jui government in Peking demanding the removal of the blockade, in accordance with a provision of the Boxer Protocol of 1901. In response to this instance of "foreign imperialism," Hsü Ch'ien, Ku Meng-yü (qq.v.), Li Ta-chao, and other leaders of the left-Kuomintang called a mass meeting of students and citizens at the T'ien-an-men in Peking and led the demonstrators to the office of Tuan Ch'i-jui to demand immediate rejection of the ultimatum. The metropolitan police fired upon the demonstrators, killing or wounding more than 200, and Li narrowly escaped being trampled to death by the fleeing crowd.

On 19 March 1926 Tuan Ch'i-jui issued orders for the arrest of Li Ta-chao and other prominent leaders of the Kuomintang. Relying on the security provided by friendly Kuominchün forces in the area, Li remained in the vicinity of Peking. In articles published in a local paper, *Cheng-chih sheng-huo* [political life], he denounced Chang Tso-lin for collaborating with Japanese militarists at the expense of China's national interests. After the defeat of the Kuominchün forces in April 1926 and during the ensuing stalemate between the forces of Wu P'ei-fu and Chang Tso-lin in the north, the Communist and Kuomintang organizations in Peking continued to function, but they were forced to rely increasingly upon the protection afforded them by the Soviet embassy. And when the vigorously anti-Communist Chang Tso-lin moved his forces into Peking late in December 1926, Li and his comrades had to flee for their lives to the Soviet embassy compound. Li continued to direct party activities in north China until 6 April 1927, when Chang Tso-lin ordered a force composed of the Peking municipal police and his own gendarmes to raid the Soviet embassy. The raiding party arrested Li and several other Chinese revolutionaries and seized truckloads of documents in Chinese and Russian. More than 300 of these documents were collected and published in 1928 by the Peking municipal police headquarters as the *Su-lien yin-mou wen-cheng hui-pien* [compendium of documentary evidence of the Soviet conspiracy]. Following Li's arrest and imprisonment, more than 300 prominent friends and sympathizers in north China petitioned to obtain his release, but to no avail. On 28 April 1927, together with 19 of his comrades, Li died on the gallows at the age of 38. He was survived by his wife, a simple peasant woman whom he had married while in his teens, and by three sons and two daughters. His remains, kept for several years in a temple outside Peking, were finally buried in the spring of 1933 at Wan-an cemetery in the Western Hills.

Almost all of Li Ta-chao's writings were articles written for magazines and newspapers. A listing of some 280 of these articles written between 1912 and 1926 is included in the first volume of Chang Ching-lu's *Chung-kuo hsien-tai ch'u-pan shih-liao*, which was published at Peking in 1954. *Shou-ch'ang ch'üan-chi*, a collection of Li Ta-chao's most important writings, with a preface by Lu Hsün (Chou Shu-jen, q.v.), was published at Shanghai in 1939. It was reprinted as the *Shou-ch'ang wen-chi* in 1949 and again in 1950. *Li Ta-chao hsuan-chi* [selected works of Li Ta-chao] was published in Peking in 1962. Li's scholarly interest lay primarily in the fields of history and politics. He wrote a number of brief theoretical essays expounding the concept of dialectical materialism and its application to China's past, the best known being his *Shih-hsueh yao-lun* [essentials of historiography], published in 1924. As a student of politics, he was particularly interested in the concept of democracy as it related to socialist theory. In such articles and essays as *P'ing-min chu-i* [democracy], published in 1922, he distinguished between "bourgeois" democracy, which, according to Li, was actually an oligarchy of a privileged middle-class minority, and "proletarian" democracy or "ergatocracy" (kung-jen cheng-chih), in which all people who do useful work in a society participate equally in the conduct of its public affairs. Although Marxist theory heavily influenced all of Li's writings after 1919, his articles devoted to the interpretation of Marxism and its application to China reveal that his understanding of Communist doctrine was incomplete. Nevertheless, Chinese Communist historians have accorded Li's Marxist writings a certain historical value as part of the legacy of the early Communist movement in China. An important study of Li Ta-chao is Maurice Meisner's *Li Ta-chao and the Origins of Chinese Marxism*, which was published in the United States in 1967.

Li Ta-ming   李 大 明
  Orig. Li Ti-ming   李 帝 明
  West. Dai-ming Lee

Li Ta-ming (1904–18 March 1961), newspaper publisher and editor in China and the United

States and a leader of the Constitutionalist party. He succeeded his long-time associate Wu Hsien-tzu as editor of the *Chinese World* in San Francisco.

Soon after the birth of Li Ta-ming on the island of Kauai, Hawaii, his family moved to Honolulu, where they lived until Li was six sui. His father, Li Lin, was a merchant. Li Ta-ming had two living elder brothers (the first-born son in the family having died before 1904) and a sister. In 1909 the Li family left Honolulu and returned to Li Lin's native home at Shekki, Kwangtung, where the elder Li died two years later. After receiving his early education in Shekki, Li Ta-ming went to Honolulu in 1918, where he published a Chinese-language periodical *Ch'en-hsi* [dawn]. Although only 15 sui, he spent almost a year in Honolulu and wrote almost all of the articles for his magazine. He returned to China in 1919 and studied for two years in Canton and Hong Kong.

In 1921 Li Ta-ming helped to found the *Ta-t'ung jih-pao* [Ta-t'ung daily] at Hong Kong and made the acquaintance of Hsü Ch'in and Wu Hsien-tzu (q.v.), who were long-time associates of K'ang Yu-wei (q.v.). Through them he met and became a supporter of K'ang Yu-wei. Li continued to write for the *Ta-t'ung jih-pao* until 1926 and became known as an able political commentator. For a time, he and Ch'en Tu-hsiu (q.v.), one of the founders of the Chinese Communist party, engaged in heated debate on political matters.

In 1926, at the request of Hsü Ch'in, Li went to Hawaii, the United States, and Europe to assess the activities of Constitutionalist party branches and to direct anti-Kuomintang propaganda campaigns. After returning to Hong Kong in March 1927, he began to draft a plan for the reorganization of the Constitutionalist party for submission to K'ang Yu-wei, but he abandoned it when K'ang died at Tsingtao on 31 March. Li continued to work for the Constitutionalist party, and in 1928 he went to San Francisco to assist Wu Hsien-tzu in publishing the party newspaper *Chinese World*. Beginning in 1929, he also served as principal of the newly established Confucian School there.

Li Ta-ming returned to China in 1932 and founded the Oriental Press at Hong Kong. When this enterprise collapsed in 1934, he went to Shanghai, where he served as an adviser to a leading department store, the Sun Company. In 1936 he made a tour of north China and wrote the well-known *Pei-yu yin-hsiang* [impressions from a northern journey], which was published in Shanghai in 1937. He went to Hawaii in 1938 and became editor of the *New China Daily Press*, a Constitutionalist party newspaper. He also taught history and philosophy at the Mun Lun School in Honolulu. Soon after the Japanese attacked Pearl Harbor in December 1941, the American authorities in Honolulu prohibited the publishing of Chinese and Japanese newspapers in the area. Li protested the ban and caused it to be lifted.

At the request of the Constitutionalist party, Li Ta-ming went to San Francisco in 1944 to succeed Wu Hsien-tzu as the editor of *Chinese World*. At the time of the United Nations Conference on International Organization in 1945, he met with Carsun Chang (Chang Chia-sen, q.v.) to discuss the possibilities of combining the Constitutionalist party and the National Socialist party to form a new political group. The Constitutionalists met in November at Montreal, Canada, and renamed their organization the Chinese Democratic Constitutional party, with Wu Hsien-tzu as chairman and Li Ta-ming as his deputy and head of the American overseas headquarters. The new name proclaimed that the party had outgrown its royalist tendencies.

In 1946 Li Ta-ming returned to China and participated in the August meeting in Shanghai at which the Democratic Constitutional party and the National Socialist party combined to become the Democratic Socialist party, with Carsun Chang as chairman and Wu Hsien-tzu as vice chairman. At that time, the National Government was attempting to undercut Communist influence and to broaden its own structure by offering posts to members of minor political parties. Li Ta-ming was appointed minister without portfolio, but he refused the post. Li and other Constitutionalists soon became dissatisfied with the policies of the Democratic Socialist party and withdrew from it. Li went to Honolulu in 1947, but returned to Nanking the following year as a delegate to the new National Assembly. In 1949 he went to San Francisco and resumed management of the *Chinese World*, which then had the largest circulation of any Chinese-language daily in the United States. Under his direction, the

Chinese World became the first overseas Chinese newspaper to inaugurate an English-language section. Li launched a New York edition of the *Chinese World* in 1950, but it was not a success.

Because Wu Hsien-tzu retired from politics in the 1950's, Li Ta-ming became the leading spokesman for the Democratic Constitutional party. He continued to oppose the Chinese Communists and to criticize the Nationalists on Taiwan until his death on 18 March 1961. He was survived by his wife, Kuo Hsiu-ch'un (Lily Kwok), whom he had married in San Francisco in 1946, and by his two sons, Pao-lin (Paul) and Chün-ch'ao (John).

Li Te-ch'uan   李 德 全

Li Te-ch'uan (1 July 1896–), the wife of Feng Yü-hsiang (q.v.), became prominent in Chinese women's organizations during the Sino-Japanese war. From October 1949 to December 1964 she served the Central People's Government as minister of health.

Fuhsingchuang, Chihli (Hopei), a community of Chinese Christian survivors of the Boxer Rebellion, was the birthplace of Li Te-ch'uan. Her father was a well-to-do peasant who became a Christian minister, and she was baptized at the age of three months. Li is known to have had one brother and two younger sisters. After receiving her primary education at the Goodrich Fu Yü Girls School, she went to Peking about 1912 and enrolled at the Bridgman Girls Middle School, an institution run by American Congregational missionaries. Upon graduation, she received a loan from Bridgman that enabled her to enroll at North China Union Women's College.

After completing her studies, Li Te-ch'uan returned to the Bridgman Girls Middle School to teach biology. She later was employed on a part-time basis by the American Board of Commissioners for Foreign Missions and was given responsibility for women's activities at the Tengshihk'ou Church. In addition, she worked part-time as secretary of the students department of the Peking YWCA. Her YWCA responsibilities increased steadily in the next few years. In 1923 Robert Gailey, an All-American football center from Princeton who was serving as secretary of the Peking YMCA,

introduced Li to the man known as the Christian General, Feng Yü-hsiang (q.v.). She and Feng were married on 19 February 1924.

When Feng Yü-hsiang agreed in 1925 to permit Kuomintang political work in his Kuominchün in return for Russian instructors and military aid, Li Te-ch'uan helped draw up the programs for troop education and indoctrination. The resulting programs emphasized Christian teachings and devoted comparatively little time or attention to political matters. Li accompanied Feng to Urga (Ulan Bator) and Moscow in 1926. Upon their return to China, he issued a long statement on 16 September 1926 declaring allegiance to the Kuomintang.

After the so-called enlarged conference movement (*see* Yen Hsi-shan; Wang Ching-wei) against Chiang Kai-shek collapsed in the autumn of 1930, Feng went into retirement. He and Li lived in Kalgan until mid-1933 and in Shantung on the sacred mountain T'ai-shan until 1936, when they went to Nanking. After the Sino-Japanese war broke out and the National Government moved to Chungking, Feng held office as minister of water conservancy and a member of the Supreme National Defense Council. Li Te-ch'uan soon became a leading figure in women's organizations. She was active in the Chinese National Women's Association for War Relief, and she later became president of that body and of the Chinese Women's Christian Temperance Union, as well as executive director of the women's section of the Chungking Sino-Soviet Cultural Association. At war's end, she helped organize the Chinese Society for the Advancement of Cultural Welfare.

In January 1946 Li Te-ch'uan was elected to the military studies committee of the Political Consultative Conference. She also was elected to the National Assembly, but before it convened, the National Government announced that Feng Yü-hsiang would head a mission to the United States to study conservation and irrigation facilities. Feng and Li sailed from Shanghai in late September. Li attended the meetings of the International Assembly of Women in New York in October. She, Feng, and their two sons and three daughters established residence in California, and Feng followed about a third of the itinerary planned for him by the United States government before discontinuing his tour of conservation projects.

In 1947 he made speeches attacking Chiang Kai-shek and the National Government. He was recalled to China in December, but he refused to go, explaining publicly that his life would be forfeit if he returned to Chinese Nationalist territory. In January 1948 he was expelled from the Kuomintang for disloyalty. He soon became a registered agent of the Revolutionary Committee of the Kuomintang, founded by Li Chi-shen (q.v.) and other dissidents at Hong Kong.

In July 1948 Li Te-ch'uan and Feng Yü-hsiang boarded the Russian ship Pobeda for a trip to Odessa. Feng died on 1 September when a fire broke out on the ship in the Black Sea. After the ship landed at Odessa, Li Te-ch'uan traveled through the Soviet Union to Manchuria. In February 1949 she went to Peiping, which had been occupied by the Chinese Communists. She became vice president of the All-China Federation of Democratic Women in April and served as a delegate to the Congress of the Partisans of Peace at Prague. Upon her return to China, she became a member of the preparatory committee for the Chinese People's Political Consultative Conference and a central committee member of the Revolutionary Committee of the Kuomintang. In September, she served as a delegate from the All-China Federation of Democratic Women to the Chinese People's Political Consultative Conference and as a member of the conference's National Committee.

With the establishment of the Central People's Government on 1 October 1949, Li Te-ch'uan became minister of health. She received membership in the culture and education committee of the Government Administration Council, the national committee of the China Committee To Defend World Peace (later the China Peace Committee), and the executive board of the Sino-Soviet Friendship Association. In 1950 she became vice president of the People's Relief Administration and president of the Chinese Red Cross Society, and in 1951 she became a vice chairman of the Chinese People's Committee for the Protection of Children. In these capacities, she traveled extensively throughout the 1950's, representing the People's Republic of China at conferences of the International Red Cross and other health organizations and at meetings of the World Peace Council. She also led Chinese women's delegations to Pakistan, Italy, and Yugoslavia and to international women's conferences. In addition, she was a member of the Chinese delegation to the funeral of Josef Stalin in March 1953.

Li Te-ch'uan was elected to the Standing Committee of the Chinese People's Political Consultative Conference in 1953 and 1959. She participated in the National People's Congress of 1954 as a delegate from Hopei and as a member of the presidium. That year, she also was appointed a director of the Chinese People's Association for Cultural Relations with Foreign Countries and vice chairman of the Sino-Soviet Friendship Association. In 1956 she became vice chairman of the Asian Solidarity Committee of China (later the Afro-Asian Solidarity Committee), a member of the State Council's scientific planning committee, and a member of the presidium of the National Conference of Advanced Workers. She became head of the Sino-Korean Association when it was organized in 1958, and in December 1958 she joined the Chinese Communist party. In May 1962 Li Te-ch'uan was accorded the unusual honor of being appointed honorary president of the Cuban Red Cross. She continued to work with great energy and success in the field of public health in China until December 1964, when she was retired from the ministry of health. She then became one of the twenty-two vice chairmen of the Chinese People's Political Consultative Conference.

Li Tsung-jen   李 宗 仁
T. Te-lin   德 鄰

Li Tsung-jen (1890–), leader of the so-called Kwangsi clique, which also included Pai Ch'ung-hsi and Huang Shao-hung. He was elected to the vice presidency of the National Government in 1948, and he became acting President in 1949. He retired to the United States in December 1949, but went to live in the People's Republic of China in July 1965.

Kweilin, Kwangsi, was the birthplace of Li Tsung-jen. After completing his primary education, Li passed the competitive entrance examinations for the Kwangsi Army Primary School. Among his schoolmates were Pai Ch'ung-hsi, Huang Shao-hung (qq.v.), Hsia

Wei, Huang Hsü-ch'u, Li P'in-hsien, and Yeh Ch'i. About this time, Li joined the T'ung-meng-hui.

The Wuchang revolt of 1911 interrupted Li's studies, and he returned home. In 1912, when military schools throughout China resumed operations, he entered the Kwangsi Short-Course Military Academy at Kweilin. After being graduated in 1913, he spent six months at home before becoming a physical-training instructor for several educational institutions in the Kweilin area.

In 1916 Li joined the forces of Lin Hu as a platoon commander. Lin Hu's forces were under the over-all command of Lu Jung-t'ing (q.v.). Li fought in the so-called national protection and constitution protection movements. He was wounded twice on the battlefields of Kwangtung and Hunan, and his courage in battle won him a promotion to battalion commander in 1918. When Lu Jung-t'ing's forces were driven out of Kwangtung and back into Kwangsi in 1920, Li, whose forces had formed part of the rear guard, became deputy regimental commander.

When the Kwangtung Army invaded Kwangsi in 1921 and defeated Lu Jung-t'ing's army, most of the officers of Lin Hu's regiment defected to the Kwangtung side. Li Tsung-jen, however, led about 1,000 troops into the mountainous area around Yülin and began to build up an independent force in Peiliu. Later, he temporarily joined the Kwangtung Army of Ch'en Chiung-ming (q.v.). When Ch'en took action against Sun Yat-sen in 1922 and the Kwangtung Army was ordered back to Canton, Li left Ch'en's service and became commander of the Second Route of the Kwangsi Autonomous Army, and he moved his headquarters to Yülin. However, he soon broke with the Autonomous Army and declared his neutrality in the Kwangsi-Kwangtung conflict. Huang Shao-hung joined him at Yülin, and when Li accepted an appointment from Lu Jung-t'ing and reorganized his force as the 5th Independent Brigade, Huang received command of the 3rd Regiment. In the spring of 1923, when Huang accepted an appointment from Sun Yat-sen as commander of the Kwangsi Anti-Rebel Army, Li reorganized the 5th Independent Brigade as the Kwangsi-Settling Army, with Huang Hsü-ch'u as his chief of staff.

At the beginning of 1924 the chief contenders for political power in Kwangsi were Lu Jung-t'ing and Shen Hung-ying. Li Tsung-jen met with Huang Shao-hung and Pai Ch'ung-hsi, and they decided to ally themselves with Shen in a campaign to crush Lu Jung-t'ing's army and to unify Kwangsi. In June, their forces took Nanning. The following month, the two armies established the joint headquarters of the Kwangsi-Settling Anti-Rebel Army, with Li as commander in chief, Huang as his deputy, and Pai as chief of staff. In mid-July, Li demanded that Lu Jung-t'ing resign and disband his forces. Shen Hung-ying joined Li in a drive against Lu Jung-t'ing. They occupied Kweilin on 24 August and brought the campaign to an end in September.

In November 1924 Sun Yat-sen appointed Liu Chen-huan governor of Kwangsi, but Liu did not assume office. On 11 November, Li Tsung-jen proclaimed himself rehabilitation commissioner of Kwangsi, with Huang Shao-hung as his deputy, and declared his opposition to the appointment of Liu Chen-huan. Shortly afterwards, Hu Han-min and Hsü Ch'ung-chih invited Li to Canton to discuss the unification of Kwangtung and Kwangsi, and Li sent Huang to represent him. As a result of these talks, Li was appointed pacification commissioner of Kwangsi, with Huang as his deputy, and commander of the First Kwangsi Army. Li joined the Kuomintang and assumed office on 1 December.

In early 1925 Shen Hung-ying suddenly began to advance against Li along the West River line. Li, his forces outnumbered, requested the assistance of Li Chi-shen (q.v.), who controlled the Kwangtung 1st Division. Li Chi-shen sent Ch'en Chi-t'ang (q.v.) and his brigade to Kwangsi, and the combined forces drove Shen into Hunan in February. Soon afterwards, T'ang Chi-yao, the military governor of Yunnan, attempted to send forces through Kwangsi to Canton so that he could succeed Sun Yat-sen, who had died on 12 March. T'ang's forces drove into Kwangsi and took Nanning. Shen Hung-ying seized the opportunity to invade the northern part of the province with the aid of Fan Shih-sheng. T'ang's forces soon were defeated, and they retreated from Kwangsi with only a fraction of their original strength. By late 1925 all of Kwangsi was under the control of Li Tsung-jen, Huang Shao-hung, and Pai Ch'ung-hsi.

In March 1926, after several months of negotiation at Canton, the relationship between Kwangtung and Kwangsi was defined to the satisfaction of both sides, and the Kwangsi forces were designated the Seventh Army of the National Revolutionary Army, with Li Tsung-jen as commander, Pai Ch'ung-hsi as chief of staff, and Huang Shao-hung as party representative. On 24 March, Li formally assumed his new command. He had become an alternate member of the Central Supervisory Committee of the Kuomintang in January. Li had been among those who encouraged T'ang Sheng-chih (q.v.), who commanded the 4th Division in south Hunan, to break with Chao Heng-t'i (q.v.), the governor of Hunan, and join forces with the National Revolutionary Army. T'ang forced Chao from office in March, but Wu P'ei-fu (q.v.) soon drove T'ang out of Yochow. In April, T'ang had to retreat from Changsha to Hengshan. Li Tsung-jen urged the early launching of the Northern Expedition in support of T'ang, but the Russian adviser Borodin opposed this move. Units of the National Revolutionary Army were sent to Hunan in May, enabling T'ang to hold Hengyang. T'ang then became the commander of the Eighth Army of the National Revolutionary Army.

On 1 July 1926 Chiang Kai-shek issued orders for general mobilization, and the Northern Expedition began. On 17 July, Li Tsung-jen led Hsia Wei's unit into Changsha. Chiang Kai-shek arrived at Changsha on 11 August. After consulting with Li Tsung-jen and T'ang Sheng-chih, he decided to attack Wu P'ei-fu before dealing with Sun Ch'uan-fang (q.v.). On 15 August orders were issued for an attack on Wuhan. In that operation Li Tsung-jen commanded the right column, composed of his Seventh Army and the Fourth Army. Li's column and Liu Chih's 2nd Division participated in the military actions that resulted in the capture of Hengyang and Hankow. After Sun Ch'uan-fang issued an ultimatum demanding the withdrawal of the expeditionary forces to Kwangtung, Liu Chih's forces were moved to the Kiangsi front, and the Seventh Army soon joined them. After the surrender of Wuchang on 10 October, the Fourth Army also moved to the Kiangsi front. The Kiangsi campaign lasted 70 days, and Li's forces played an important role in it. Nationalist forces finally occupied Nanchang on 7 November.

The Northern Expedition was interrupted by the 1927 split between the left-wing Kuomintang regime at Wuhan and the supporters of Chiang Kai-shek at Nanchang. After Wang Ching-wei returned from Europe, Li Tsung-jen participated in the 5 April meeting in Shanghai at which it was decided that a conference should be convened at Nanking to resolve the differences that had split the Kuomintang. After Wang Ching-wei left Shanghai, another meeting was held. Its participants decided to purge the Kuomintang and the National Revolutionary Army of Communist and other leftist elements. On 18 April, Chiang Kai-shek set up a national government at Nanking. The support of Li Tsung-jen and Pai Ch'ung-hsi was essential to Chiang for the undertaking of both actions. Li, serving as commander in chief of the Third Route Army, participated in the capture of Hsuchow on 2 June. He also attended the 19–22 June meetings of Chiang Kai-shek and Feng Yü-hsiang (q.v.) which led to a measure of agreement between the two leaders. In August, Chiang Kai-shek announced his retirement in the interest of party unity and went to Japan, and Hu Han-min (q.v.) left Nanking for Shanghai. Thus, Li Tsung-jen, Pai Ch'ung-hsi, and Ho Ying-ch'in were left in control at Nanking. The three Nanking leaders then moved to defeat Sun Ch'uan-fang, who had sent his troops across the Yangtze at Lungt'ang in an attempt to recapture Nanking.

On 15 September 1927 the Nanking leaders, a number of Wuhan leaders, and representatives of the Western Hills faction decided to form the Central Special Committee of the Kuomintang to function as an interim government. T'ang Sheng-chih, in Wuhan, announced his opposition to the plans for reunification. In late October, Nanking launched a punitive expedition against him, with Li Tsung-jen as commander in chief and Pai Ch'ung-hsi as field commander. T'ang abandoned Wuhan, and Li's force, composed of the Seventh Army and the Nineteenth Army under Hu Tsung-to, took control there in mid-November. Li Tsung-jen became chairman of the Wuhan branch of the Political Council, and he had Hu Tsung-to made garrison commander of Wuhan. Li now controlled Hupeh and Hunan, thus extending Kwangsi power from the home province to the Yangtze. He also became a member of the Military Affairs Commission at Nanking.

The position of Wang Ching-wei and his supporters at Canton was weakened by the Canton Commune (*see* Chang T'ai-lei) of December 1927. Li Tsung-jen joined with others in inviting Chiang Kai-shek to resume office, and Chiang did so in January 1928. The following month, Li was appointed commander in chief of the Fourth Group Army, with Pai Ch'ung-hsi second in command. The Northern Expedition was resumed, and the Fourth Group Army participated in the final drive on Peking in June. Chiang Kai-shek, Li Tsung-jen, Feng Yü-hsiang, and Yen Hsi-shan met in July to discuss military reorganization, but finally decided to defer the matter.

When the new National Government was inaugurated at Nanking in October 1928, Li Tsung-jen became a member of the State Council. Li attended the troop-disbandment conference of January 1929, but Pai Ch'ung-hsi did not. By that time, the so-called Kwangsi clique of Li Tsung-jen, Pai Ch'ung-hsi, and Huang Shao-hung had spread its forces from Kwangsi to Hopei (Chihli) in the north and to Kiangsu in the east. The troop-disbandment conference ended inconclusively.

On 19 February 1929 the Wuhan branch of the Political Council issued an order relieving Lu Ti-p'ing (q.v.) of his post as governor of Hunan. Troops were sent into Hunan from Wuhan, and Lu was forced to retreat into Kiangsi. The Wuhan council named Ho Chien (q.v.) to succeed Lu. On 13 March, the Central Political Council ordered the dissolution of all branch councils within two days. On 15 March, the Third National Congress of the Kuomintang opened at Nanking. Almost simultaneously, a coup was staged against Pai Ch'ung-hsi in north China in which he lost his Fourth Group Army troops to T'ang Sheng-chih. On 21 March, Chiang Kai-shek made a statement condemning arbitrary actions by military men and the actions of the Wuhan council. That same day, Li Chi-shen, who had hoped to mediate the dispute between Chiang and the Kwangsi clique, was placed under detention. The National Government ordered a punitive expedition against Wuhan on 26 March, naming Li Tsung-jen and Pai Ch'ung-hsi as plotters against the government and relieving them of their posts. Li and Pai were expelled from the Kuomintang on 27 March.

Li Tsung-jen went to Hong Kong, where he was joined by Huang Shao-hung and Pai Ch'ung-hsi. The three men returned to Kwangsi in November 1929 and established the Party-Protecting National Salvation Army at Nanning, with Li as commander in chief, Huang as deputy commander and Kwangsi governor, and Pai as field commander. Li also became military affairs commissioner of Kwangsi.

The Kwangsi forces joined with the Fourth Army of Chang Fa-k'uei (q.v.) in January 1930 for an attack on Kwangtung, but they were defeated and forced back to Kwangsi within a month. The three Kwangsi generals and Chang Fa-k'uei then decided to support the northern coalition (*see* Feng Yü-hsiang; Yen Hsi-shan) by invading Hunan and capturing Wuhan. After initial successes in May, this attempt ended in defeat when Li and Chang turned back to extricate Huang at Hengyang, where his rear-guard forces had been cut off by Kwangtung troops. The entire Kwangsi force was defeated at Hungchiao, and the remnant forces returned to Kwangsi to regroup. Huang Shao-hung then broke with the Kwangsi clique because he opposed the policy of continuing the civil war.

The arrest of Hu Han-min at Nanking on 28 February 1931 opened the way for a reconciliation of Kwangsi and Kwangtung. In May, a number of political leaders opposed to Chiang Kai-shek, including Wang Ching-wei, Eugene Ch'en (qq.v.), and Ch'en Chi-t'ang, formed an opposition government at Canton. Li Tsung-jen went to Canton in mid-May to discuss the formation of a military alliance between Kwangsi and Kwangtung. Agreement was reached, and the Kwangsi-Kwangtung forces invaded southern Hunan in early September. After the Mukden Incident of 18 September, the National Government called for national unity and concerted action to meet the Japanese threat. The Canton regime insisted that Li Chi-shen and Hu Han-min be released and that Chiang Kai-shek resign from office before it would agree to dissolve itself. Both conditions were met. Although Chiang soon returned to power, the agreement remained in force. Li Tsung-jen and Ch'en Chi-t'ang were appointed to the Military Affairs Commission in March 1932. Huang Hsü-ch'u, who had assumed Huang Shao-hung's posts in Kwangsi, became governor of the province. Kwangsi continued to administer its affairs in virtual independence of the National Government. In April, Li was elected to the Central Executive Committee of the Kuomintang and was appointed pacification commissioner of Kwangsi, with Pai Ch'ung-hsi as his deputy.

From 1932 to July 1937 Li and Pai worked to reconstruct Kwangsi by putting into practice the san-tzu cheng-ts'e [three-self policy] of self-government, self-defense, and self-sufficiency and the san-yü cheng-ts'e [three-reservation policy] of building military power (for details, see Pai Ch'ung-hsi). Kwangsi became relatively free from crime and began to develop its industrial and educational capacities.

After Hu Han-min died in 1936, it seemed likely that the National Government would move to end the semi-independence of Kwangtung. Ch'en Chi-t'ang, with the support of Li Tsung-jen, attempted to forestall such action. In early June, Kwangsi forces under the overall command of Pai Ch'ung-hsi entered southern Hunan and issued an order for general mobilization of Kwangtung and Kwangsi forces. The force allegedly was an anti-Japanese expeditionary army, marching to the north to protect China because Chiang Kai-shek was not resisting the Japanese. Ch'en Chi-t'ang assumed the post of commander in chief of the First Anti-Japanese National Salvation Forces, and Li and Pai became his deputies. In early July, the revolt collapsed after the Kwangtung air force defected to the National Government.

On 25 July 1936 the National Government appointed Li Tsung-jen and Pai Ch'ung-hsi to posts outside of Kwangsi, but they refused to accept them. Five days later they organized a military government in Kwangsi, with Li Chi-shen as its chairman. However, the mediation efforts of Huang Shao-hung and Ch'eng Ch'ien led to an agreement between Li Tsung-jen and Chiang Kai-shek, and Kwangsi accepted the authority of the National Government. Li remained in Kwangsi as pacification commissioner and commander in chief of the Fifth Route Army (the new designation given to the Kwangsi forces).

In August 1937, a month after the Sino-Japanese war began, Li Tsung-jen was appointed commanding officer of the Fifth War Area, which was composed of northern Kiangsu, northern Anhwei, and southern Shantung. Li left Kwangsi on 10 October to take command of the war area and to assume office as governor of Anhwei. The Fifth Route Army was sent north and was split into two group armies. Li established headquarters in Hsuchow. Among the troops under his command were five Kwangsi divisions.

In early 1938 the Japanese launched an offensive near Hsuchow. On 25 March, two Japanese columns attacked Taierhchuang, a walled town northeast of Hsuchow. After five days of heavy fighting, the Chinese forces destroyed one of the Japanese columns. Both sides called for reinforcements, and, in mid-May, the fighting shifted to the perimeter of Hsuchow. On 19 May, the forces of Li abandoned Hsuchow and marched into western Anhwei and eastern Honan. Li then established headquarters at Laohokow in northern Hupeh. After the abandonment of Wuhan in October 1938, his chief task was to prevent the Japanese from advancing to the west. Li retained command of the Fifth War Area, but he was succeeded as governor of Anhwei by another Kwangsi general, Liao Lei.

In April 1939 the Japanese launched a drive from Hankow during which they captured Hsinyeh and Tangho. They then moved to surround six Chinese divisions based in the Tungpei mountains. Li sent his troops to counterattack, and the fighting began on 10 May. By 16 May they had extricated the Chinese divisions at Tungpei and had recovered Hsinyeh and Tangho.

Li Tsung-jen retained command of the Fifth War Area until early 1945, when he became director of the field headquarters of the Military Affairs Commission at Hanchung in southern Shensi. Soon after the war ended, he was appointed director of the presidential headquarters at Peiping. When the situation in Manchuria deteriorated and the possibility of a Chinese Communist victory over the Nationalists became stronger, Chiang Kai-shek unsuccessfully tried to persuade Li to assume direction of the Manchurian campaign. Li retained his Peiping office until 1948, when he announced his candidacy for the office of vice president. He was elected to the vice presidency on 29 April, defeating Chiang Kai-shek's candidate, Sun Fo. Thus, when Chiang retired from office on 21 January 1949, Li became acting President of China. Li, however, was not free to direct the National Government, for Chiang continued to issue orders as party leader (tsung-ts'ai) of the

Kuomintang, and many of the men in key governmental and military positions were loyal to him. Sun Fo, who had become premier, moved the Executive Yuan to Canton on 5 February without asking for Li's approval of the move. In effect, the National Government had been split into three parts, with Chiang, Li, and Sun all issuing orders. The situation was eased somewhat when Sun Fo resigned on 7 March and Ho Ying-ch'in became premier.

Li Tsung-jen and Pai Ch'ung-hsi, who was based in the Wuhan area, proposed to defend the Yangtze River line by having the air and naval forces deployed in support of the ground forces and having T'ang En-po's troops, then concentrated in the Shanghai sector, move westward to establish contact with Pai's command. Li asked Chiang Kai-shek to authorize this plan, but Chiang, who had already begun to move troops to the off-shore islands, refused.

Li, with Chiang's approval, made a final attempt to negotiate a peace settlement with the Chinese Communists. On 26 March 1949 the Communist leaders informed Nanking by radio that they had appointed a delegation headed by Chou En-lai to meet with National Government representatives at Peiping on 1 April. At the meetings, the Communists insisted on crossing the Yangtze and gave the Nationalists until 20 April to decide whether to accept this condition. Reportedly, they also offered Li a vice chairmanship in a new coalition government if he would sign the agreement. Li refused the offer, and, on 19 April, the National Government asked for an extension of the deadline date. On 20 April, the Chinese Communists attacked and crossed the Yangtze. The National Government abandoned Nanking on 23 April and moved to Canton. At this point, Li Tsung-jen, weary of battling both Chiang Kai-shek and the Communists, went to Kweilin. A delegation from the Central Executive Committee of the Kuomintang went there to urge him to return to office. Li finally allowed himself to be persuaded and went to Canton on 7 May.

Yunnan, Kweichow, and Szechwan were still held by the Nationalists and by Pai Ch'ung-hsi's forces. Li Tsung-jen now endeavored to evolve a strategy for holding Kwangtung and Hainan Island. On 14 July 1949 Chiang Kai-shek arrived at Canton to confer with Li and other officials. A special commission, with Chiang as chairman and Li as vice chairman, was established to effect a liaison between the Kuomintang and the National Government.

In October 1949 the National Government was forced to move to Chungking. On 11 November, Li Tsung-jen flew to Kweilin and met with Pai Ch'ung-hsi, Hsia Wei, Li P'in-hsin, and Huang Hsü-ch'u to make plans for the defense of Kwangsi. He then flew to Hainan to confer with Ch'en Chi-t'ang. After returning to Kwangsi a few days later, Li suffered a recurrence of an old stomach disorder. An operation seemed to be necessary, but proper medical facilities were not available in Kwangsi. On 20 November, Li flew to Hong Kong and began to make arrangements to go to the United States for medical treatment. On 22 November, Chiang Kai-shek sent a delegation headed by Chü Cheng and Chü Chia-hua to request that Li remain in China. Li refused, and the delegation withdrew. He also refused to be entrusted with any aid-seeking missions. On 5 December, he flew to the United States. After spending two months in a hospital in New York, he visited President Harry S. Truman at the White House on 2 March 1950. The previous day, Chiang Kai-shek, then in Taiwan, had announced that he was resuming the presidency. Li denounced the action, saying that it was illegal, but he could do nothing about it.

Li lived quietly in the United States for three years. Then, on 3 January 1954, he wrote an open letter to Chiang Kai-shek opposing Chiang's plan for reelection by the National Assembly in Taiwan. Li maintained that a new body should have been created in accordance with the provisions of the constitution. In Taiwan, impeachment proceedings were begun against Li, and he was voted out of office on 10 March 1954. On 22 March, Chiang Kai-shek was reelected President. Two days later, Ch'en Ch'eng was elected to succeed Li in the vice presidency.

In July 1965 Li Tsung-jen and his wife, Kuo Te-chieh, who was in very poor health, left the United States and went to the People's Republic of China. Their two sons, Li Yueh-lung and Jackson Li, remained in New York. Li was welcomed at Peking by an imposing delegation which included Chou En-lai. Two months later, on 26 September, after a tour of northeastern China, Li held a two-hour press conference for Chinese and foreign journalists in which he lauded the accomplishments of the Chinese people under the leadership of Mao Tse-tung, stressed that Taiwan was an inalienable part of China, attacked "Khrushchev revisionists" in the Soviet Union and "the reactionaries of various countries," and encouraged his former Kuomintang colleagues in Taiwan to follow his example and "return to the embrace of the motherland." Kuo Te-chieh died at Peking on 23 March 1966, and Li continued to live in the People's Republic of China.

Li Wei-han
Alt. Lo Mai

李維漢
羅邁

Li Wei-han (1897–), Chinese Communist administrator who became head of the party's united front work department in 1944 and thus was responsible for the political mobilization of non-Communist groups. From 1949 to 1954 he also headed the Commission on Nationalities Affairs, which was responsible for the supervision of non-Chinese minorities.

Born at Liling, southwest of Changsha, Li Wei-han received his early education in his native Hunan. At the age of about 20, he joined the Hsin-min hsueh-hui [new people's study society] organized by Ts'ai Ho-sen (q.v.) and Mao Tse-tung at Changsha. In 1919 he joined the work-study movement (see Li Shih-tseng) and went to France, where he studied, worked in factories, and participated in the formation of the French branch of the Chinese Communist party.

After returning to China in the early 1920's, Li Wei-han worked under Mao Tse-tung in the Chinese Communist organization in Hunan. In the spring of 1927, when he succeeded Mao as secretary of the Hunan provincial committee of the Chinese Communist party, he reportedly clashed with Mao on such issues as the effectiveness of Communist-led rural uprisings. On 21 May, Hsü K'o-hsiang, the commander of the 33rd Regiment of Ho Chien's Thirty-fifth Army, stationed at Changsha, turned on the Communists and their supporters there, fired on peasant militiamen, and arrested leading Communists. Peasant forces mobilized for an attack on the city, but Li Wei-han ordered them to disperse. He was censured for his "unrevolutionary"

actions at the Sixth National Congress of the Chinese Communist party, held at Moscow in June 1928, but he also was elected (in absentia) to alternate membership on the Central Committee.

Beginning in 1928, Li Wei-han worked for the central apparatus of the Chinese Communist party in Shanghai. He did propaganda work, conducted party training classes, and reportedly did intelligence work with K'ang Sheng (q.v.). About 1932 he went to the central soviet area in Kiangsi, where he became head of the Central Party School. He supported the policies of the so-called 28 Bolsheviks (see Ch'en Shao-yü), and in August 1933 he wrote an article for the Communist journal Tou-cheng [struggle] in which he criticized the policies of Lo Ming, who headed a small soviet area in western Fukien. Mao Tse-tung supported Lo Ming's policies, and he later criticized the "leftists" in the party for "erroneously advocating" opposition to Lo.

Li Wei-han and his Cantonese wife participated in the Long March in 1934–35. Although his influence on policy formation in the Chinese Communist party waned as Mao Tse-tung consolidated control of the party, he continued to play an active administrative role at Yenan. He headed the Central Party School from about 1937 to about 1940, and he served as secretary general of the Shensi-Kansu-Ninghsia Border Region government. Beginning in 1944 he headed the party's united front work department, which was responsible for political mobilization of non-Communist elements for Communist objectives. After the War in the Pacific ended, he participated in the meetings of the Political Consultative Conference at Chungking in January 1946. After the negotiations with the Nationalists collapsed, he guided organizational and propaganda programs which were designed to effect the political isolation of the Kuomintang in China.

When the Central People's Government was established in October 1949, Li Wei-han became secretary general of the Government Administration Council, secretary general and member of the Standing Committee of the National Committee of the Chinese People's Political Consultative Conference, and a member of several government committees in Peking. From 1949 to 1954 he also headed the Commission on Nationalities Affairs, which was responsible for the supervision of non-Chinese minorities. He served as Peking's chief delegate to the negotiations which resulted in the signing of an agreement on 23 May 1951 that brought Tibet under Chinese Communist control. With the reorganization of the government in 1954, he became secretary general of the National People's Congress and a vice chairman of its Standing Committee, as well as vice chairman of the National Committee of the Chinese People's Political Consultative Conference.

Despite his early rise in the Chinese Communist party and his years of service to the Communist cause, Li Wei-han was the only prominent leader who failed to be elected to the Central Committee at the Seventh National Congress in 1945. He was, however, elected to the Central Committee in 1956. In 1959 he served on the presidium of the Chinese People's Political Consultative Conference, and in 1960 he held the equivalent position at the National People's Congress. Although he participated in the 1964 meetings of the congress and the conference as a delegate from Sinkiang, he was dropped from their presidium.

Li Wei-han was an able administrator who was particularly important in Communist programs concerned with non-Communist groups. He summarized his work in this area in a June 1956 report to the National People's Congress, "The Democratic Front in China," and in a September 1956 report to the Eighth National Congress of the Chinese Communist party, "The United Front Work of the Party."

Li Yuan-hung   黎 元 洪
   T. Sung-ch'ing   宋 卿
   H. Huang-p'i   黃 陂

Li Yuan-hung (1864–3 June 1928), the only man to serve twice as president of the republican government at Peking (June 1916–July 1917; June 1922–June 1923).

Huangp'i, north of Hankow, was the birthplace of Li Yuan-hung. His ancestors, merchants from Anhwei, had settled in Hupeh as farmers. During the Taiping Rebellion Li's father, Li Chao-hsiang, had joined the government forces, and he had risen to the rank of captain. After retiring from the army and living on a government pension, Li Chao-hsiang went

north to join a military unit stationed near Tientsin. His family joined him at Tientsin soon afterwards. Li Yuan-hung began his formal education at a private school in 1879, and five years later he became a cadet at the Tientsin Naval Academy. Upon graduation in March 1889 he was sent on a six-month training cruise to Canton and back. After acquiring some naval experience, he was appointed early in 1894 to the post of chief engineer on the cruiser Kuang-chia, then stationed at Shanghai. The ship was ordered to Port Arthur soon after the Sino-Japanese war began in 1894, but before reaching its destination it struck a hidden coral reef. The crippled Kuang-chia then was shelled and sunk by the Japanese. Li, who could not swim, was washed ashore by the tide after floating in a life belt for three hours. He made his way to Port Arthur, where he remained for the rest of the war.

After the Japanese destroyed the Peiyang fleet in 1894–95, Li Yuan-hung abandoned all thoughts of a naval career. He went to Shanghai and took a position with Chang Chih-tung (ECCP, I, 27–32), the governor general of Liang-Kiang (Kiangsu, Kiangsi, and Anhwei). He was assigned responsibility for constructing fortifications at Nanking, and, under his direction, the task was completed within a year. When Chang Chih-tung was transferred to Wuchang in 1896 as governor general of Hu-Kwang (Hupeh and Hunan), he appointed Li to his staff of military advisers. Chang planned to organize and train a modern army, the Tzu-ch'iang chün [self-strengthening army], and he sent Li to Japan in 1897, 1899, and 1902 to observe and study military modernization. Li became one of Chang's most valued assistants in building up the new army in Hupeh, and he rose steadily in rank. In 1906 he received command of the newly created 21st Mixed Brigade.

In the years immediately preceding 1911 Hupeh became a principal center of revolutionary activity, with army units in the Wuhan area as primary targets of propaganda and infiltration. In the autumn of 1910, when Li discovered that his own brigade was being infiltrated by revolutionists, he took steps to break up the Chen-wu hsueh-she, a secret organization of army officers. Despite such efforts, the revolutionary movement in Hupeh continued to gain strength. In the autumn of

1911 the Wen-hsueh-she, headed by Chiang I-wu (d. 1913), and the Kung-chin-hui, headed by Sun Wu (d. 1940; Orig. Pao-jen; T. Yao-ching), secretly joined forces and planned a revolt at Wuchang for 6 October. The date was changed to 16 October, but the accidental explosion of a bomb on 9 October in a hidden T'ung-meng-hui arsenal in Hankow and the ensuing investigation by government authorities forced the revolutionaries to initiate the revolt on 10 October. The revolutionary forces soon succeeded in driving out Jui-cheng, the Manchu governor general, and Chang Piao, the senior military officer in the Wuhan area.

Because of the premature outbreak of the revolt, such recognized leaders of the movement as Sun Wu and Chiang I-wu were absent from Wuhan, leaving the revolutionaries disorganized and in desperate need of military leadership. On 11 October 1911 the revolutionaries met with the Hupeh provincial advisory council at Wuchang and named Li Yuan-hung, the senior officer remaining in Wuchang, to head the new revolutionary regime. Li, who had never been associated with the revolutionary movement and who did not wish to become involved in an anti-Manchu revolt, went into hiding. On being discovered by a search party, he consented to go with them to the provincial advisory council only after being threatened with violence. He reluctantly agreed to head a republican government at Wuchang and assumed the title of tutuh [military governor] of Hupeh. Five days later, on 16 October, he took the concurrent title of commander in chief of the Hupeh revolutionary army.

At first, Li Yuan-hung evinced little enthusiasm for the role forced upon him, and he contributed little to the new regime. The work of organizing the revolutionary government was left to such political leaders as T'ang Hua-lung and Chü Cheng (qq.v.) and the conduct of military operations was undertaken by the military bureau, headed by Sun Wu and Chiang I-wu and then by Chang Chen-wu (d. 1912; Orig. Yao-hsin; T. Ch'un-shan). After the arrival of Huang Hsing (q.v.) in the Wuhan area, Li retired in Huang's favor as commander in chief of the revolutionary army on 3 November 1911.

As it became apparent that the revolutionary movement was succeeding in other provinces and would probably succeed throughout China,

Li's willingness to commit his fortunes to the new regime seemed to increase. On 9 November 1911 he sent telegrams to revolutionary governments in other provinces in which he proposed that they send delegates to Wuchang to discuss the formation of a provisional central government. Provincial delegates began to gather in Wuchang late in November. By mid-December, because of the military situation at Wuchang, they had decided to move their conference to Nanking. They elected Sun Yat-sen to the provisional presidency on 29 December 1911 and Li Yuan-hung to the provisional vice presidency on 3 January 1912. After Sun Yat-sen's resignation in favor of Yuan Shih-k'ai, Li again was elected to the vice presidency on 20 February.

Li Yuan-hung remained at Wuchang as tutuh of Hupeh and did not join the government after it moved to Peking. Yuan Shih-k'ai, in an attempt to consolidate the new government's control of China, worked to reduce the power of revolutionary and regional leaders by separating them from their power bases in the provinces. Although some leaders left the provinces to accept attractive positions at Peking, Li Yuan-hung repeatedly refused to leave Hupeh and assume office at the new capital. In Hupeh, his relations with the local military chiefs, particularly the T'ung-meng-hui leader Chang Chen-wu, became increasingly strained. Li urged them to accept Yuan Shih-k'ai's invitation to serve as military advisers in Peking, and in the summer of 1912 Chang Chen-wu and other Hupeh military leaders departed for the capital. Soon afterwards, Li sent a confidential telegram to Yuan Shih-k'ai in which he accused Chang Chen-wu of fomenting revolt among the troops and recommended his execution. Yuan had Chang shot on 15 August and justified his action by publishing Li's telegram. This action undermined Li's popularity in Hupeh and weakened his relations with the Hupeh military and the newly formed Kuomintang.

Li Yuan-hung managed to maintain his position in Hupeh until the so-called second revolution of 1913 collapsed, but his waning prestige and inability to find allies made it increasingly difficult for him to resist the political and military pressures exerted on him by Yuan Shih-k'ai. Even before the outbreak of hostilities between Yuan's forces and the Kuomintang troops, he had bowed to Yuan's request for free passage through Hupeh to attack the Kuomintang forces in Hunan and Kiangsi. The expansion of Peiyang power to the Yangtze provinces after the second revolution made Li's position almost untenable. In December, Yuan Shih-k'ai dispatched his trusted lieutenant Tuan Ch'i-jui (q.v.) to Hankow to demand that Li assume office in Peking. On 9 December, Li boarded the private train which Tuan had provided for him and left for Peking.

On arrival at the capital, Li Yuan-hung was given a ceremonious welcome by Yuan Shih-k'ai and was accorded all the honors and courtesies due a vice president. Yuan also made him chief of general staff and arranged the marriage of one of his sons to Li's elder daughter. Despite these honors and courtesies, Li soon discovered that he had no real authority at Peking. In December 1913 his name was used to head a list of Yuan's military supporters who demanded the dissolution of the National Assembly. In May 1914 he was appointed to head the new but powerless Ts'an-cheng-yuan [council of state], which Yuan created as a replacement for the national assembly. He was created Wu-i ch'in-wang [Prince Wu-i] in Yuan's new imperial order in 1915. Throughout this period, Li repeatedly asked to be relieved of his offices and to be allowed to retire to his native province, but Yuan denied his requests. Because he could not extricate himself from Peking, Li adopted an attitude of passive non-cooperation.

Li Yuan-hung's political captivity appeared to be at an end when Yuan Shih-k'ai died on 6 June 1916. Li acceded to the presidency on 7 June. He soon found, however, that most of the real authority of the government had been assumed by Tuan Ch'i-jui as premier and that Tuan and his supporters in the Peiyang clique regarded him as little more than a figurehead. Li was at a disadvantage in opposing Tuan, for he lacked personal military backing and close relations with major factions in the National Assembly. His resentment of Tuan's monopoly of power led to considerable friction between the two men, and the situation was aggravated by the peremptory actions of Tuan's deputy Hsü Shu-cheng (q.v.). Tuan's enemies in the National Assembly, led by Sun Hung-i, the minister of interior, sought to use Li as a bridle for Tuan's power. Li's opposition to Tuan usually took the form of refusing to sign measures proposed by Tuan and his supporters.

A major issue which arose at Peking during this period was the question of whether China should enter the First World War on the side of the Allies. Li did not oppose the idea of declaring war on Germany, but he refused to accept Tuan Ch'i-jui's methods of achieving this end. In March 1917 Tuan submitted for Li's signature an official telegram to the Chinese minister in Japan which announced the Chinese government's decision to sever relations with Germany. Li refused to sign any such document without the approval of the National Assembly. As Tuan continued to press for China's entry into the war, his relations with Li and the National Assembly steadily deteriorated. In April, Tuan convened a meeting of Peiyang military leaders to ensure acceptance of his war policy, but this action and its implied threat of military coercion merely served to stiffen Li's opposition and to arouse such indignation in the National Assembly that its members demanded Tuan's resignation. On 23 May, emboldened by the expressed feelings of the National Assembly and by assurances of military support from Chang Hsün (q.v.), Li dismissed Tuan from the premiership.

In naming a new premier, Li made an effort to placate the Peiyang militarists. On 28 May 1917 he appointed Li Ching-hsi, a former associate of Yuan Shih-k'ai, to succeed Tuan Ch'i-jui. Almost immediately all of the northern military governors except Chang Hsün declared their provinces independent of the Peking government. Tuan Ch'i-jui and his associates planned this action in the hope that Li would turn to Chang for aid and that Chang, who dreamed of restoring the Ch'ing dynasty to power, would drive Li and the National Assembly from Peking. Li soon invited Chang to Peking to mediate the political crisis, and Chang advanced on the capital with a force of 5,000 men. After seizing control of Peking, Chang compelled Li on 12 June to issue an order dissolving the National Assembly. On 1 July, Li refused to sign an order restoring the Manchu monarchy. By this time, Li had come to believe that only Tuan Ch'i-jui could preserve the republic, and on 2 July he sent an order to Tientsin which reappointed Tuan premier and instructed him to raise an army against Chang Hsün. An order was sent to Feng Kuo-chang (q.v.), the vice president, instructing him to assume the duties of the presidency during the crisis. On 3 July, Li took refuge in the Japanese legation, where he remained until the monarchists were overthrown by Tuan Ch'i-jui on 14 July. Tuan soon induced him to resign from the presidency in favor of Feng Kuo-chang, and on 27 August 1917 Li left Peking for Tientsin.

According to his son, the years from August 1917 to April 1922 formed the most enjoyable period in Li Yuan-hung's life. He lived quietly at his estate in Tientsin and dissociated himself from all political activity. This idyllic life came to an end in mid-1922. After the Chihli leaders Wu P'ei-fu and Ts'ao K'un (qq.v.) triumphed over the Fengtien forces of Chang Tso-lin (q.v.), a number of political and military leaders joined together in a movement to achieve a peaceful unification of the northern and the southern governments by restoring the constitution of 1912 and the National Assembly of 1913 and by returning Li Yuan-hung to the presidency. Some of the supporters of this movement hoped to use it to enhance the prestige of the Chihli clique and to remove Hsü Shih-ch'ang (q.v.) from the presidency, but these aspirations were not apparent to Li Yuan-hung. He agreed to serve as president on two conditions: that the military leaders reduce the size of their armed forces and that the system of tuchün [military governors] be abolished. After receiving public assurances from the Chihli leaders that these conditions would be met, he went to Peking and assumed the presidency on 11 June 1922.

Despite the promises of the Chihli leaders, Li was little more than a figurehead at Peking. Both the cabinet and the National Assembly were dominated by the Chihli clique, and when Li tried to exercise his constitutional powers as president, he was either ignored or overridden by them. Ts'ao K'un and his supporters soon decided to oust Li and secure Ts'ao's election to the presidency. In June 1923 a hired "citizens corps" staged a demonstration against Li in Peking. Both the police and the soldiers of the Peking garrison, allegedly protesting arrears in their pay, surrounded Li's residence, severed the telephone and water lines, and then went on strike. These harassment tactics soon drove Li from Peking. On 13 June his train was halted near Tientsin by supporters of Ts'ao K'un, who detained him until he had signed a proclamation announcing his resignation from the presidency and had given them the presidential seal.

Li Yuan-hung left Tientsin for Shanghai on 8 September 1923 in the hope of uniting Chang Tso-lin, T'ang Chi-yao (q.v.), and other enemies of the Chihli clique in support of an opposition government. When this plan failed, Li, who was seriously ill with diabetes, sailed to Japan and rested for six months at the hot springs resort at Beppu. He returned to China in May 1924 to live in complete retirement at his Tientsin estate. On 3 June 1928 he died of a cerebral hemorrhage. He was survived by his wife, née Wu (d. 1929) and by his two sons, Shao-chi and Shao-yeh, and his two daughters, Shao-fang and Shao-fen. Li Shao-fang had married Yuan Shih-k'ai's son Yuan K'o-chin in 1914. Li Shao-chi, using the name Edward S. G. Li, had published *The Life of Li Yuan-hung* at Tientsin in 1925.

Several collections of Li Yuan-hung's papers and correspondence have been published. These include the *Li fu-tsung-t'ung shu-tu*, published in 1912; the *Li fu-tsung-t'ung shu-tu hui-pien* and the *Li fu-tsung-t'ung cheng-shu*, which appeared in 1914; the *Li ta-tsung-t'ung cheng-shu*, published at Shanghai in 1916; and the *Li ta-tsung-t'ung wen-tu lei-pien*, which first appeared in 1923 at Shanghai.

Liang Ch'i-ch'ao   梁 啓 超
T. Cho-ju, Jen-fu   卓 如, 任 甫
H. Jen-kung   任 公

Liang Ch'i-ch'ao (23 February 1873–19 January 1929), pupil of K'ang Yu-wei who became the foremost intellectual leader of the first two decades of twentieth-century China.

A native of Hsinhui, Kwangtung, Liang Ch'i-ch'ao was the eldest son in a family which had been farmers for ten generations. His grandfather, the first of the family to become a sheng-yuan, had served as a district director of studies. His grandfather and his father gave the young Liang his first instruction in the Chinese classics. He soon demonstrated his precocity by becoming a sheng-yuan at the age of 11. In 1887 he enrolled at the famous Hsueh-hai-t'ang, an academy which had been founded at Canton some 70 years earlier by Juan Yuan (ECCP, I, 399–402), where he studied philology and textual criticism of the classics and their commentaries. In 1889, at the age of only 16, he passed the provincial examinations in Canton and became a chü-jen. His performance so impressed one of the examiners, Li Tuan-fen (1833–1907), that Li arranged a marriage between his younger sister Li Hui-hsien and Liang. Liang went to Peking in 1890 and took the metropolitan examinations, but did not pass them. On his way back to Canton, he passed through Shanghai, where he came upon a copy of Hsü Chi-yu's world geography, the *Ying-huan chih-lüeh*, as well as translations of Western works published by the Kiangnan Arsenal. These books made a profound impression upon Liang, who soon became an enthusiastic advocate of "Western learning."

After his return to Canton, Liang went with a fellow student at the Hsueh-hai-t'ang to visit K'ang Yu-wei (q.v.), who had recently attracted notice as the author of a memorial to the throne urging far-reaching reforms in the imperial administration. Liang and his friend were awed by K'ang's learning. They became the first of many students at his school in Canton. According to Liang, his association with K'ang from 1890 to 1894 was of crucial importance to his intellectual development. He became thoroughly familiar with the many facets of K'ang's teaching, which included Buddhism and a philosophy of institutional reform based on the Kung-yang school of classical interpretation as well as on Western subjects. In 1893 he became an instructor at K'ang's school. He went to Peking in 1892 and 1894 to take the metropolitan examinations, but failed them both times.

In 1895 Liang went with his teacher to the capital, where he again failed the examinations. At that time, the war with Japan was being brought to an end by the Treaty of Shimonoseki, which compelled the Ch'ing government to pay a large war indemnity and to cede Taiwan to Japan. Liang organized vigorous opposition to treaty ratification among the Cantonese examination candidates in Peking and assisted K'ang Yu-wei in drafting the famous "Kung-ch'e shang-shu" [candidates' memorial], which urged the emperor to reject the peace terms and to institute a number of reforms in the Ch'ing government. During the summer of 1895, Liang served the reform movement as secretary to the Ch'iang-hsueh hui [society for the study of national strengthening], founded by K'ang Yu-wei and others, and as one of the chief

contributors to the society's reform newspaper *Chung-wai chi-wen*. When the Ch'ing government proscribed the Ch'iang-hsueh hui early in 1896, Liang's personal belongings were confiscated, and he was left penniless and homeless.

In the spring of 1896 Liang Ch'i-ch'ao left Peking for Shanghai, where he met Huang Tsun-hsien (ECCP, I, 530–31), Wang K'ang-nien (1860–1911), and other reform sympathizers. They agreed to finance a magazine, the *Shih-wu-pao*, with Wang as manager and Liang as editor. Liang's articles and editorials, which appeared regularly from the first issue (August 1896) until the autumn of 1897, were well received throughout China. In them he expressed his ideas on education, historical progress, and various aspects of reform and Westernization in China. Although generally echoing the views of K'ang Yu-wei, Liang's writings in the *Shih-wu-pao* reflected the influence of several other intellectuals, including T'an Ssu-t'ung (ECCP, II, 702–5) and the British missionary Timothy Richard, both of whom he had met in Peking; Huang Tsun-hsien, the brothers Ma Liang (q.v.) and Ma Chien-chung (1844–1900), with whom he was associated in Shanghai; and Yen Fu (q.v.), the editor of the *Kuo-wen pao* in Tientsin, with whom he frequently corresponded. Liang also collaborated with friends in Shanghai in organizing an anti-footbinding society, a school for girls, and a publishing company (the Ta-t'ung i-shu chü).

At the invitation of Ch'en Pao-chen (*see under* Ch'en San-li), the progressive governor of Hunan, Liang Ch'i-ch'ao went to Changsha in the autumn of 1897 to serve as chief lecturer at the newly established Shih-wu hsueh-t'ang [academy of current affairs]. In Hunan he met such reformers as T'ang Ts'ai-ch'ang (1867–1900), who was also a teacher at the academy, and Huang Tsun-hsien, the judicial commissioner of the province. Liang joined his friends in organizing a reform association, the Nan-hsueh-hui [southern study society]. However, he gave most of his time to the academy and its 40 students, among whom was the future military leader Ts'ai O (q.v.). Liang sought to imbue his students with such political concepts as constitutional monarchy and popular sovereignty, ideas which then were considered extremely radical. The teaching of such ideas soon brought violent protest from the conservative scholars of Hunan.

Early in 1898 Liang, who was in poor health, left Changsha for Shanghai. He went to Peking in March to assist K'ang Yu-wei in his efforts to promote reform. Liang worked to mobilize the examination candidates to protest the government's ceding of Dairen and Port Arthur to Russia, and he helped organize a new reform association, the Pao-kuo-hui [society for protecting the nation]. As the reform campaign gained momentum, he was recommended to the emperor and was granted an audience on 3 July 1898. The emperor conferred upon him the sixth official rank and placed him in charge of a newly authorized government translation bureau. During the Hundred Days Reform, Liang drew up a program for the translation of Western books and sought funds and personnel for the new bureau. When the empress dowager took control of the government and terminated the reform program on 21 September 1898, orders were issued for Liang's arrest. Japanese officials gave him refuge in the Japanese legation and helped him escape to Tokyo, where he was befriended by such prominent Japanese supporters of the reform movement as Inukai Tsuyoshi, the minister of education in the Okuma cabinet. In 1899 Liang began publishing a magazine, the *Ch'ing-i pao*, in which he urged the restoration to power of the imprisoned emperor and attacked the empress dowager and her supporters, including Jung-lu (ECCP, I, 405–9) and Yuan Shih-k'ai (q.v.). The new magazine quickly found favor among overseas Chinese. Despite the censorship efforts of the imperial authorities, copies of it were circulated in a number of cities in China.

Liang's writings of this period reveal changes in his political philosophy. He had begun to study Japanese and to read Western books in Japanese translation. The influence of such works as John Stuart Mill's *On Liberty* and Jean Jacques Rousseau's *Social Contract* soon became evident in his essays. His growing hospitality to the ideas of republicanism coincided with overtures from representatives of Sun Yat-sen, who hoped to win the reformers over to his cause. However, in the summer of 1899 Liang agreed to support K'ang Yu-wei's new monarchist society, the Pao-huang hui [society to protect the emperor], and he became completely estranged from the revolutionaries. During the next few years, he traveled extensively to raise funds for K'ang's organization among overseas

Chinese. In December 1899 he left Japan for Hawaii, where he remained until August 1900. He then hastened to Shanghai to take part in the Hankow uprising against the empress dowager's regime led by T'ang Ts'ai-ch'ang, but on learning that it had already been crushed, he left Shanghai to join K'ang Yu-wei in Singapore. From there he went to Australia on a fundraising tour, returning by way of the Philippines to Japan in the spring of 1901. Early in 1903, at the invitation of the American branches of the Pao-huang hui, Liang left Japan again for a tour of Canada and the United States. He lectured to Chinese groups in several major cities and visited President Theodore Roosevelt and Secretary of State John Hay in Washington. He returned to Japan in November.

Liang's observations of the American system of government and his impressions of the political behavior of Chinese both abroad and in China served to strengthen his developing conviction that China was quite unprepared for the freedoms guaranteed by a republican system and that the salvation of the Chinese lay less in a change of their political institutions than in their own renewal as a people. He had set forth these views for the first time in a periodical which he had founded in Yokohama in 1902, the famous *Hsin-min ts'ung-pao* [renovation of the people]. In his effort to bring new ideas before the Chinese people, Liang devoted many pages of the new journal to lucid and forceful articles on Western philosophers, historical figures, and political theories as well as discussions of China's traditional culture and its rejuvenation. The *Hsin-min ts'ung-pao*, which had a readership of more than 14,000 in 1906, came to exert considerable influence in overseas Chinese communities and in China.

Liang Ch'i-ch'ao's writings in the *Hsin-min ts'ung-pao* also indicated that his thinking had begun to diverge from that of K'ang Yu-wei. For example, K'ang emphasized the necessity of preserving Confucian doctrine as the basis of China's cultural integrity; Liang, however, began to view traditional reverence for that doctrine as an obstacle to freedom of thought and the development of new ideas in China. In spite of these differences, Liang continued to aid K'ang in defending the monarchist cause against mounting attacks in publications of the revolutionary party. After the Russo-Japanese war, some influential officials of the Ch'ing government favored reforms in China similar to those which had been instituted in Japan, and in 1905 a mission headed by Tuan-fang (ECCP, II, 780–82) was sent abroad to investigate the practice of constitutional government. Liang Ch'i-ch'ao secretly communicated with Tuan-fang and drafted several memorials for the mission. In the *Hsin-min ts'ung-pao* he intensified his campaign against the Chinese revolutionaries in Japan, who had organized themselves into the T'ung-meng-hui and had established the *Min-pao* [people's journal] as the organ of their party. Between 1905 and the summer of 1907, when Liang suspended publication of his journal, a prolonged and bitter battle of words took place between his magazine and the *Min-pao*.

After the Ch'ing court announced in 1906 that a constitution was in preparation, Liang organized a political society in Japan, the Cheng-wen-she (founded in the autumn of 1907) to foster the constitutional movement in China. Members of this society circulated mass petitions for the promulgation of a constitution and the convening of a parliament. Early in 1908 the Cheng-wen-she's headquarters was transferred to Shanghai, where the society, headed by Liang's old friend Ma Liang, published the political journal *Cheng-lun*, worked clandestinely with high officials at the imperial court, and planned the establishment of schools to train members in parliamentary government. These activities aroused the opposition of Yuan Shih-k'ai and other influential officials, who succeeded in having the Cheng-wen-she banned in the summer of 1908. Nevertheless, Liang's colleagues managed to establish contact with members of the newly created provincial assemblies in China by the end of 1909 and to promote the prompt convening of a national parliament in Peking. Early in 1910 Liang began to publish the *Kuo-feng pao*. He hoped to educate his countrymen in the workings of parliamentary government through articles which discussed representative political institutions in concrete terms.

After the Wuchang revolt of 10 October 1911, Liang Ch'i-ch'ao went to Mukden in an unsuccessful attempt to enlist the aid of military commanders in north China in putting pressure on the Ch'ing court to institute genuine constitutional monarchy. When that effort failed, he joined K'ang Yu-wei in supporting the idea of "a republican government with a titular monarch" [hsü-chün kung-ho]. However, the republican revolutionary movement was not to be denied.

With the establishment of the republic in 1912, Liang Ch'i-ch'ao ended his political alliance with K'ang Yu-wei, not only by accepting the new regime but also by taking an active part in its political affairs. Through his journalistic endeavors of the preceding 15 years, Liang had come to be regarded by many of his countrymen as one of the intellectual leaders of modern China. Many of the proponents of parliamentary government looked to him for guidance in establishing a republican national assembly, and on his return to China late in September 1912 he was invited by men of diverse political opinions to join their groups. A further indication of his popularity at this time was the fact that the entire printing (10,000 copies) of the first number of his new magazine, *Yung-yen* [justice], was sold out as soon as it appeared. Before returning to China, Liang had been in touch with several friends in China, including Carsun Chang (Chang Chia-sen), Lin Ch'ang-min, and T'ang Hua-lung (qq.v.), with regard to the organization of a political party, and in October 1912 he took part in the formation of the Min-chu-tang [democratic party]. In February 1913 he also joined the Kung-ho-tang [republican party], which had already hailed him as its intellectual leader.

In the parliamentary elections held early in 1913 Sun Yat-sen's Kuomintang emerged the victor, with the Kung-ho-tang as a poor second. With a view to forming an effective opposition to Sun's party in the National Assembly, Liang and his political colleagues arranged to merge the three other major parties, the Kung-ho-tang, the Min-chu-tang, and the T'ung-i-tang [united party], to form a larger organization, which they named the Chin-pu-tang [progressive party]. The new party supported Yuan Shih-k'ai in his struggle with the Kuomintang and supported his plans for a huge Reorganization Loan from an international banking consortium. After the so-called second revolution collapsed in the summer of 1913, the Chin-pu-tang replaced the Kuomintang as the most influential party in the National Assembly and Liang became minister of justice in a new cabinet headed by Hsiung Hsi-ling (q.v.), one of his old reform associates. Yuan Shih-k'ai soon dissolved not only the

Kuomintang (4 November 1913) but also the National Assembly (10 January 1914). Liang followed Hsiung Hsi-ling's example in resigning his cabinet post, but less than two months later he accepted an appointment as head of Yuan's new monetary bureau [pi-chih chü]. In June 1914 he also became a member of the council of state [ts'an-cheng yuan], an advisory body created by Yuan to take the place of the National Assembly.

After accepting these appointments, Liang was chagrined to discover that his cooperation with Yuan Shih-k'ai had turned public opinion against him. His enemies, including members of the banned Kuomintang, accused him of despicable opportunism, and his friends accused him of naivete and misguided idealism. Moreover, it soon became obvious to him that his cherished hopes for the reconstruction of China would not be realized through participation in Yuan's regime. His proposals for standardizing and stabilizing the currency and his plans for compulsory education and military service were either deemed unacceptable or ignored. Accordingly, Liang moved to Tientsin and early in 1915 accepted an invitation to be the chief contributor to the *Ta-Chung-hua*. In his articles for this magazine he worked to arouse public opinion against the acceptance of Japan's Twenty-one Demands by Yuan's government.

Liang remained a nominal member of Yuan Shih-k'ai's government until the summer of 1915, but well before that time he had begun to have misgivings about Yuan's ambitions. Early in the year he had been approached by Yang Tu (q.v.), one of Yuan's followers, who had sought to enlist his support of a plan to make Yuan emperor. After spending several months in south China in 1915, Liang went to Peking in June, where Yuan Shih-k'ai assured him that he had no imperial aspirations. However, a campaign to make Yuan emperor was publicly announced in August. Liang, who had returned to Tientsin, denounced the newly created Ch'ou-an-hui, a monarchist society, and attacked its aim of replacing the republic with a new monarchy. Liang had been in frequent contact with his former student Ts'ai O and had joined with Ts'ai in making plans for a revolt against the monarchists. Liang and Ts'ai were supported by Ts'ai's friend T'ang Chi-yao (q.v.), the governor of Yunnan province. In mid-September, some weeks after Ts'ai O had gone

to Yunnan, Liang Ch'i-ch'ao left Tientsin for Shanghai, where he spent the next two months attempting to induce other political and military leaders to join the revolt against Yuan Shih-k'ai. Early in March 1916 he traveled by way of Hong Kong and Haiphong to Kwangsi to win the support of Lu Jung-t'ing (q.v.), the governor of Kwangsi. On 15 March, Lu announced his decision to join the rebels. After Yuan Shih-k'ai relinquished the throne and resumed the title of president on 22 March 1916, Liang and his associates demanded the restoration of the 1913 National Assembly. When Yuan ignored this demand, Liang helped to organize the southwestern military leaders into a military council, which, on 8 May at Chaoching, Kwangtung, announced its intention to act as the legitimate government of the country until such time as Yuan retired from the presidency and public life. After Yuan's death in June 1916 and the succession of Li Yuan-hung (q.v.) to the presidency, the military council was dissolved, and Liang again turned his attention to the affairs of the Chin-pu-tang.

After the National Assembly convened in Peking, the Chin-pu-tang split into factions. Liang Ch'i-ch'ao and some of his associates organized the Hsien-fa yen-chiu hui [association for constitutional research], popularly known as the Yen-chiu hsi [research clique]. As the leader of this group, Liang hoped to play an influential role in determining constitutional revision, the formation of the cabinet, and foreign policy. In the spring of 1917 he lent his support to premier Tuan Ch'i-jui (q.v.) in Tuan's efforts to bring China into the First World War on the side of the Allies. He also backed Tuan's successful move in July to crush the Manchu restoration organized by K'ang Yu-wei and the militarist Chang Hsün (q.v.). Later in the same month, he joined Tuan's new cabinet as minister of finance and turned his attention once again to the problem of currency reform. However, the expenditures required to finance Tuan's domestic military policies, together with Tuan's secret loan negotiations with Japan, completely wrecked Liang's hopes for a stable currency. He resigned in mid-November with the rest of the cabinet. By this time, he had become convinced that seeking China's regeneration in the existing political milieu was both futile and foolish. Accordingly, he spent most of 1918 in retirement, devoting himself to study, writing, and planning various educational projects.

Liang Ch'i-ch'ao had long wished to improve his knowledge of the West, and shortly after the end of the First World War he went to Europe in the capacity of an unofficial delegate to the Paris Peace Conference, traveling in the company of such friends as Carsun Chang, Chiang Fang-chen, and V. K. Ting. He arrived in London in February 1919 and spent the remainder of the year visiting the capitals of Western Europe. One result of his travels was a revision of his earlier admiration for Western civilization. For Liang, the war in Europe and its aftermath afforded clear evidence of a basic social and intellectual malaise in the West which stemmed from its blind worship of science. He opposed Marxism, for he considered it to be as intellectually restricting as Confucianism. Because he believed that every individual should be free to develop his own thinking, he adopted the cause of "thought liberation" as one of his chief concerns.

While planning how best to achieve an intellectual and cultural regeneration in China, Liang and his friends in Europe and China organized the Hsin-hsueh-hui [new learning society] in September 1919. That group, which included Carsun Chang, Chang Tung-sun (q.v.), and Chiang Fang-chen, began publication of a periodical in Peking, the *Chieh-fang yü kai-tsao* [emancipation and reconstruction] (changed in September 1920 to *Kai-tsao*), which carried articles on a variety of new ideas from Western Europe and Russia by men of widely differing viewpoints.

In January 1920 Liang Ch'i-ch'ao left Europe. Upon his arrival in China two months later, he immediately embarked upon a number of cultural and educational projects. Among these were the Kung-hsueh-she [cooperative study society], formed to promote the translation and publication of important Western philosophical works, and the Chiang-hsueh-she [Chinese lecture association], organized for the purpose of inviting famous foreign thinkers, such as Bertrand Russell and Rabindranath Tagore, to lecture in China. These and other facets of his campaign for cultural reconstruction coincided with and to some extent contributed to the intellectual ferment of the May Fourth Movement, but they were not of central importance to it. Such younger men as Hu Shih and Ch'en

Tu-hsiu (qq.v.) had replaced Liang and his contemporaries as the leaders of students and other younger intellectuals.

In 1920 Liang accepted an invitation to teach Chinese history at Nankai University in Tientsin, thus embarking upon a new academic career which lasted, with interruptions, until a few months before his death. He also lectured at Tsinghua University, Yenching University, and Tung-nan University at Nanking and produced such scholarly works as the *Ch'ing-tai hsueh-shu kai-lun* (1920), the *Hsien-Ch'in cheng-chih ssu-hsiang shih* (1922), the *Chung-kuo li-shih yen-chiu fa* (1922), and the *Chung-kuo chin san pai-nien hsueh-shu shih* (1924), as well as several studies of individual philosophers and historical figures. Liang continued to teach and write until an increasingly serious kidney ailment forced him to stop. He died in the hospital of Peking Union Medical College early in 1929, at the age of 55.

The most comprehensive collection of Liang Ch'i-ch'ao's works is the *Yen-ping-shih ho-chi*, published by the Chung-hua Book Company in 1936. It is composed of 16 volumes of literary works and 24 volumes of monographic writings and testifies to his stature as the foremost intellectual figure of the first two decades of twentieth-century China.

Liang Ch'i-ch'ao and Li Hui-hsien had five children. The second son, Liang Ssu-ch'eng (q.v.), became a well-known architect. The third son, Liang Ssu-yung (q.v.) won renown as an archeologist. Li Hui-hsien died on 13 September 1924.

Liang Hung-chih 梁 鴻 志
T. Chung-i 衆 異

Liang Hung-chih (1883–9 November 1946), influential member of the Anhwei clique and the Anfu Club who became a prominent official in Japanese-sponsored regimes. He was executed for treason by the National Government in 1946.

A native of Ch'anglo, Fukien, Liang Hung-chih came from a prominent family of scholars and officials. His great-grandfather, Liang Chang-chu (ECCP, I, 499–501), was a distinguished scholar and an outstanding governor of Fukien. When Liang Hung-chih was six sui, his grandfather was assigned to the Chinese consulate at Nagasaki, and the entire family went to Japan for two years. Liang received his education in the Chinese classics in Japan and then in Ch'anglo. After passing the examinations for the chü-jen in 1903, he enrolled at the Imperial University of Peking. Little is known about his activities immediately after graduation. Some sources say that he served as an official in Shantung and then taught at the Fengtien Higher Normal School; others state that he joined the staff of Tuan Ch'i-jui (q.v.).

After the revolution of 1911, Liang Hung-chih served in the republican government at Peking as secretary, senior assistant, and then counselor in the bureau of laws, which drafted and examined government orders and legislation. About 1914 he was appointed to the Su-cheng chü, a predecessor of the Control Yuan.

The death of Yuan Shih-k'ai in June 1916 and the rise to power of Tuan Ch'i-jui advanced Liang Hung-chih's career. He became an influential member of the Anhwei clique and the Anfu Club (see Hsü Shu-cheng) and served as secretary general of the National Assembly in 1918. When Tuan was defeated by the Chihli faction of Ts'ao K'un and Wu P'ei-fu (qq.v.) in 1920, Liang sought refuge in the Japanese embassy. In 1922 he moved to Shanghai and then to Mukden. After the Chihli group was defeated by Chang Tso-lin and Feng Yü-hsiang in 1924 and Tuan Ch'i-jui became provisional chief executive of the Peking government, Liang returned to Peking to serve as secretary general of the chief executive's office. He resigned from office on 27 November 1925 and went to Tientsin.

In 1925 Liang joined the Japanese-sponsored General Committee on Eastern Cultural Affairs. His decision to move to Dairen about 1928 may have been the result of his pro-Japanese sentiments. However, he moved to Shanghai after the Japanese attack at Mukden on 18 September 1931. In the mid-1930's he published a collection of poems, the *Yuan-chu-ke shih-chi*. Liang remained in Shanghai after the Sino-Japanese war began in 1937. At the end of 1937, the Japanese army in central China, having organized several local puppet governments in areas which had come under its control, decided to establish a central puppet regime similar to the provisional government at Peiping sponsored by the Japanese army in north China. On 28 March 1938 the Wei-hsin, or reformed,

government, with jurisdiction over the Japanese-occupied areas of Kiangsu, Chekiang, and Anhwei, was established at Nanking. Liang Hung-chih was persuaded to head the new regime. The reformed government at Nanking was composed of three major organs: the executive yuan, headed by Liang Hung-chih; the legislative yuan, headed by Ch'en Ch'un; and the judicial yuan, headed by Wen Tsung-yao. The state council, composed of the presidents and vice presidents of the three yuan and the ministers of the executive yuan, was the highest policy-making body. The announced policies of the reformed government at Nanking were opposition to Communism, non-recognition of the National Government, and close cooperation with Japan.

In the autumn of 1938 representatives of the provisional government at Peiping and the reformed government at Nanking met in Dairen. On 22 September they agreed upon the establishment of a joint committee of the governments of China, to be composed of Wang K'o-min, Wang I-t'ang (qq.v.), and Chu Shen of the provisional government and Liang Hung-chih, Wen Tsung-yao, and Ch'en Ch'un of the reformed government. The committee, meeting alternately in Peiping and Nanking, was to be given control of transportation, communications, postal service, customs, education, and foreign affairs. After this conference ended, Liang Hung-chih went to Tokyo, where he met with Japanese officials on 15–17 November.

In the meantime, Wang Ching-wei (q.v.) had left Chungking and had gone to Hanoi, where, on 29 December 1938, he called for peace with Japan. In May 1939 he went to Shanghai for negotiations with the Japanese authorities. It was decided that Wang would head a central government of occupied China but that the provisional government at Peiping would retain its autonomy within the new framework. After Wang met with Liang Hung-chih and Wang K'o-min on 18–20 September, the joint committee of the governments of China issued a declaration supporting the establishment of a central government under the leadership of Wang Ching-wei. When the new regime was established at Nanking on 30 March 1940, Liang Hung-chih vacated the presidency of the executive yuan in favor of Wang Ching-wei and became the president of the control yuan, a position of little power.

Liang, an avid collector of rare books and paintings, took advantage of wartime conditions, which forced many families to sell their treasured collections, to assemble a group of 33 specimens of Sung painting and calligraphy. In 1940 he sponsored the publication of the *Ming-shih-la* [veritable records of the Ming dynasty], the manuscript having been discovered in a hidden wall niche at the Kiangsu Library of Chinese Studies.

When the War in the Pacific ended in 1945, Liang Hung-chih went into hiding in Soochow. He was discovered by Nationalist agents and was brought to Shanghai for trial. In prison he wrote two collections of poems, "Ju-yu chi" and "Tai-ssu chi," and an account of the Chihli-Anhwei war. These manuscripts, which he entrusted to his fellow prisoner Chin Hsiung-pai, later disappeared. Although testimony at his trial indicated that Liang had cooperated secretly with the National Government on several occasions during the war, he was sentenced to death as a traitor. He was executed in Shanghai on 9 November 1946.

Liang Shih-ch'iu　　梁 實 秋
　T.　Chih-hua　　治 華
　Pen. Ch'iu-lang　　秋 郎

Liang Shih-ch'iu (1902–), literary critic, teacher, and translator of Western literature who was a leading figure in the Crescent Moon Society, a group which upheld the individual and aesthetic purposes of literary expression in opposition to the cause of proletarian realism.

Although his ancestral home was in Hangchow, where his grandfather had amassed a modest fortune as a customs official, Liang Shih-ch'iu was born in Peking. His father, Liang Hsien-hsi, was employed by the Peking police force. Liang Shih-ch'iu completed his middle school and college preparatory work at Tsinghua Academy. In the summer of 1923 he went to the United States to enter Colorado College in Colorado Springs. Wen I-to (q.v.), a friend and schoolmate from Tsinghua, enrolled there at the same time. After being graduated the following summer, Liang moved to Cambridge, Massachusetts, to begin graduate work in English literature at Harvard University. He pursued the same field of study at Columbia University during his third and final year in the United States.

While at Harvard, Liang Shih-ch'iu came under the influence of Irving Babbitt, whose conservative views on the value of continuity and tradition in literature Liang adopted. In a paper written for Babbitt entitled "The Romantic Tendencies in Modern Chinese Literature," Liang scored contemporary Chinese writing for exhibiting all of the defects of nineteenth-century romantic literature at its worst. In its place, Liang proposed a national literature which would borrow its discipline from the literature of traditional China and its form from the classic literature of the West. Liang was particularly anxious that Chinese readers should be acquainted with the masterpieces of the European tradition. Accordingly, he devoted much of his time to translating Western classics.

Soon after returning to Peking in the summer of 1926, Liang Shih-ch'iu accepted a position at National Southeast University. The following spring he married Li Shu-fang. Because of the social and political turmoil accompanying the advance of the Nationalist armies northward during the summer, he moved to Shanghai, where he remained for the next three years, teaching at Chinan and other universities. Between 1930 and 1934, he taught at Tsingtao University in Shantung.

In the early years of the Nationalist period, Shanghai was a primary locus of cultural and literary activity. The doctrine of literature as an instrument of political action gained widespread acceptance, particularly in leftist circles. To combat the propaganda emphasis that such theories lent to literature, Hu Shih, Hsü Chih-mo (qq.v.), and Liang Shih-ch'iu in 1928 organized the Crescent Moon Society. In its official organ, *Hsin-yueh* [crescent moon], they sought to expound the ideal of a literature of liberation through which the Chinese people could achieve spiritual freedom. Liang argued strongly for the independent, individual, and aesthetic purposes of literary expression. His opposition to the cause of proletarian literature eventually brought him into sharp conflict with Lu Hsün (Chou Tso-jen, q.v.), among others, and secured for him a position of national prominence in the realm of letters.

Liang's involvement in the polemics of these years resulted in a number of volumes devoted to the discussion of literary questions and principles: *Lang-man-ti ku-tien-ti* [the romantic and the classic] published in 1927, an expansion of his Babbitt article; *Wen-hsueh ti chi-lü* [literary discipline], published in 1928; *Wen-i p'i-p'ing lun* [principles of literary criticism], published in 1934; and *P'ien-chien chi* [prejudices]. *Yueh-han-sun* [Dr. Samuel Johnson], also published in 1934, was a critical biography. Liang was also active as a translator. In 1928 he published *A-po-la yü Ai-lu-i-ssu ch'ing-shu* [the love letters of Abelard and Heloise] and in 1929, *P'an Pi-te* [Peter Pan]. He also translated *Silas Marner* and *Wuthering Heights*.

In 1934 Liang Shih-ch'iu left Tsingtao University to become head of the English department at National Peking University. His interest in translation continued, but its focus shifted to the plays of Shakespeare. Liang translated 20 of Shakespeare's plays into pai-hua [the vernacular]. Collected as *So-shih-pi-ya ming chü* [the famous plays by Shakespeare], the translations were published in Taipei between 1953 and 1957. Passages of plain prose and of blank verse are given simply as prose, but rhymed lines are translated into corresponding rhymed Chinese lines, to preserve the contrast.

From 1937 to 1946, Liang resided near Chungking. He lectured, served on the People's Political Council, and worked in the Kuo-li pien-i so [national institute of translation and compilation]. His collection of familiar essays, *Ya-she hsiao-p'in* [sketches by a cottager] published in 1949, was written at this time. From 1946 to 1949 Liang was a professor of English literature at National Peking Normal University. He moved to Taiwan in 1949. He was first chairman of the English language department of Taiwan Provincial Normal University and, subsequently, dean of its college of arts. In Taiwan, Liang published several books, including *Mei-kuo shih tsen-ma-yang-ti i-ko kuo-chia* [what America is like], *T'an Hsü Chih-mo* [a chat on Hsü Chih-mo], *Ch'ing-hua pa-nien* [eight years at Tsinghua], and *Wen-hsueh yuan-yin* [literary affinities]. He also edited the *Tsui-chin Ying-Han tz'u-tien* [current English-Chinese dictionary], which was published in Hong Kong in 1958.

Liang Shih-i   梁 士 詒
T. I-fu   翼 夫
H. Yen-sun   燕 孫

Liang Shih-i (5 May 1869–9 April 1933), government official and financier whose activities in the development of banking, railroads, and loan programs during the Peiyang period made him the recognized head of the so-called communications clique. His removal from the Peking government premiership in January 1922 was the immediate cause of the Chihli-Fengtien war.

Born in the Sanshui district of Kwangtung, Liang Shih-i was the elder son of Liang Chih-chien, who had been a disciple of the well-known Cantonese scholar Chu Tz'u-ch'i. He had a younger brother, Liang Shih-hsu, and four sisters. Liang Chih-chien supervised his son's education in the Chinese classics, and the younger Liang became a sheng-yuan in 1886 and a chü-jen in 1889. After failing the chin-shih examinations in 1890 and 1892, he passed them in 1894 and became a compiler in the Hanlin Academy at the age of 26 sui. His father took the chin-shih examinations in 1895 and 1896, but failed to pass them. Accordingly, Liang Chih-chien decided to abandon the idea of pursuing an official career at Peking. Liang Shih-i obtained leave from the Hanlin Academy and accompanied his father home. He remained in Sanshui until 1897, serving as head of the Feng-kang Academy. In 1897 he returned to Peking, where he held several scholarly offices in the imperial government until 1900, when he was forced to flee Peking because of the Boxer Uprising. He returned to Sanshui and reorganized the Feng-kang Academy as a modern school.

Liang Shih-i went to Peking in 1902 and sat for the special imperial examination on political economy in 1903. On the recommendation of T'ang Shao-yi (q.v.), Yuan Shih-k'ai, then the governor general of Chihli (Hopei), appointed Liang director general of the Peiyang pien-shu-shu [Peiyang publishing house], which published a series of military textbooks. Toward the end of 1904 Liang joined the staff of T'ang Shao-yi, who had been appointed minister to the Court of St. James's, and accompanied T'ang to Calcutta for negotiations with the British concerning the Lhasa Convention of 7 September 1904. They arrived in Calcutta in February 1905 and returned to Peking seven months later. The negotiations resumed at Peking soon afterwards, and a Sino-British agreement on the matter was signed on 27 April 1906. By this time, T'ang had been appointed director general of the Peking-Hankow and Nanking-Shanghai railways, and Liang Shih-i had become chief clerk of the railway administration. In November, T'ang was made vice president of the Board of Communications, and in 1907 the board created a directorate general of railways, with Liang as its head. Thus began Liang's association with the so-called communications clique, which he later was to lead. He was responsible for many of the Ch'ing government's railroad reform and development programs during the next few years and helped recover managerial rights to the Peking-Hankow railroad. He also helped to found the Chiao-t'ung yin-hang (Bank of Communications) in 1907 and became its assistant director. However, his interest in reform was confined to such areas as education, taxes, communications, and banking. He apparently had little interest in constitutional reform. Liang served as director general of railways until early 1911, when he was dismissed by the new president of the Board of Communications, Sheng Hsuan-huai (q.v.).

After the Wuchang revolt of October 1911, the Ch'ing government, in an attempt to save the monarchy, appointed Yuan Shih-k'ai premier. Liang Shih-i became vice president of the Board of Communications on 16 November. He was among the high officials at Peking who advised the Ch'ing government to abdicate in favor of a republican government. After the provisional republican government was inaugurated at Nanking on 1 January 1912, Liang, then president of the Board of Communications, joined with Hu Wei-te and Chao Ping-chün in submitting a memorial to the throne which called for the abdication of the emperor. He and the other members of Yuan Shih-k'ai's cabinet countersigned the abdication degree of 12 February.

When Yuan Shih-k'ai succeeded Sun Yat-sen as provisional president and moved the re-

publican government from Nanking to Peking, Liang Shih-i became chief secretary in the presidential office and general manager of the Bank of Communications. He supported Sun Yat-sen's plans to create a national rail network and participated in the discussions at Peking which led to Yuan Shih-k'ai's order of 9 September 1912 appointing Sun director of railroad development. In 1913 Liang and Chou Hsueh-hsi (q.v.), the finance minister, became the two senior commissioners of the newly established national finance commission. Chou resigned from office in May 1913, and Liang served as acting minister of finance until early 1915. In January 1914 he presided over a financial conference at which it was decided to reorganize the monetary system of China and to use a standard silver dollar.

After Yuan Shih-k'ai promulgated a new constitution on 1 May 1914, he created the post of Kuo-wu-ch'ing [secretary of state affairs] and abolished the secretarial office held by Liang Shih-i. He appointed Liang director general of the national revenue administration in May and gave him the concurrent post of director general of the domestic loan office in August. Liang's loan, tax, and monetary activities greatly improved the fiscal situation of the Peking regime. In 1915 he helped to sponsor the establishment of the Hsin-hua Savings Bank and the Yen-yeh Bank. He also negotiated with the American firm of Metherns and Son of Maryland for the establishment of a Sino-American shipping company to be known as the Eastern Pacific Steamship Company. The Peking government agreed to guarantee capital investment and interest in return for special tariff rates on Chinese cargo, but the project soon was abandoned because of the unsettled political situation in China. By this time, Yuan Shih-k'ai's monarchical movement had begun. Although Liang Shih-i's name was associated with the Ch'ou-an-hui [society for planning stability] and the Ch'uan-kuo ch'ing-yuan lien-ho-hui [national federation for appeal for a monarchy], he later claimed that he had not been a leader of the monarchical movement and that his name had been used by these organizations without his permission.

Liang Shih-i strongly advocated that China enter the First World War, and in 1915 he organized the Hui-min Corporation for the recruitment of Chinese laborers to serve with the Allies in Europe. In mid-1915 the company, which was managed by Yeh Kung-cho (q.v.) and Liang Su-ch'eng, entered into a contract with the French government under the terms of which more than 200,000 Chinese workers went to France during the war years. Although Liang Shih-i was criticized for undertaking this program, he later answered his critics by saying that the program was China's only active contribution to the war effort and, therefore, the sole justification for China's claim to a hearing at the Paris Peace Conference of 1919.

After Yuan Shih-k'ai died in June 1916, Liang Shih-i resigned from the national revenue administration. In July, he was named as one of the eight principal instigators of the monarchical plot, and an order for his arrest was issued. He immediately sought refuge in Hong Kong, where he continued his efforts to recruit Chinese workers for the war effort in France.

When Chang Hsün (q.v.) staged his July 1917 attempt to restore the Ch'ing dynasty, Liang Shih-i called for punitive measures against Chang and instructed Yeh Kung-cho, then in charge of the Bank of Communications in Tientsin, to give financial aid to Tuan Ch'i-jui (q.v.) for his campaign against Chang. The large sum of money raised by Yeh Kung-cho enabled Tuan to move swiftly in driving Chang from Peking.

At the end of November 1917, Liang Shih-i went to Japan, where he remained for two months. On returning to Hong Kong in February 1918 he discovered that the order for his arrest had been rescinded. Accordingly, he went to Peking in March to see Feng Kuo-chang (q.v.), who had become acting president. Liang was made chairman of the board of the Bank of Communications, and on 22 August he became speaker of the National Assembly.

In 1920 the Peking government reestablished the domestic loan bureau, with Liang as its director. That year, he joined with a group of bankers in founding a banking consortium, the Chung-hua yin kung-ssu [China financial corporation], and served as the chairman of its board of directors. When the Peking government created two official bureaus to assist industrial research, Liang was appointed to head the group concerned with the improvement of wool and leather industries.

In December 1921, at the behest of Chang Tso-lin (q.v.), Liang Shih-i was appointed premier by Hsü Shih-ch'ang (q.v.), who had become president. Wu P'ei-fu (q.v.) opposed the appointment, launched a vigorous campaign against Liang, and forced him to leave office on 19 January 1922. Chang Tso-lin regarded Wu's action as a personal affront, and the incident was the immediate cause of the Chihli-Fengtien war. In May, Hsü Shih-ch'ang, who held Liang responsible for the war, formally dismissed him from office and ordered his arrest. Liang fled to Japan and remained there until September 1922, when he returned to Hong Kong.

Liang Shih-i left Hong Kong in March 1924 for an extensive tour of Europe and the United States. After reaching London on 6 April, he was interviewed by representatives of Reuters and other wire services on the political situation in China and was received by King George V. He also met with British industrial and political leaders before moving on to France, Belgium, the Netherlands, Germany, Austria, Czechoslovakia, Switzerland, and Italy. While in Geneva, he met with Sir Eric Drummond, the Secretary General of the League of Nations. After completing his tour of Europe, Liang went to the United States, arriving in New York on 15 July. He called on J. P. Morgan, who entertained him at dinner, and then went to Washington and met with President Calvin Coolidge. After visiting the major cities of the United States, Liang returned to Hong Kong on 29 August 1924.

At the invitation of Tuan Ch'i-jui, who was serving as chief executive of the Peking government, Liang Shih-i went to Peking and participated in the national rehabilitation conference which met from 1 February through 21 April 1925. In May, he was appointed chairman of the national financial rehabilitation commission, which had been formed to plan a national conference on finances. Four months later, he was appointed to membership in the special tariff conference for the implementation of the decisions made at the Washington Conference of 1922. Both the national conference on finances and the special tariff conference convened in October.

In April 1926, following the ouster of Tuan Ch'i-jui, Liang Shih-i went to Mukden and helped Chang Tso-lin plan a reorganization of the local currency and financial structure. He went to Tientsin in June, paid a short visit to Hong Kong in August, and returned to Tientsin in October to establish residence there. When Chang Tso-lin took control of Peking in 1927, he asked Liang to form a cabinet, but Liang declined the offer. Chang then appointed him chairman of his political consultative committee. At the end of 1927 Liang became director general of the revenue administration and a member of the tariff autonomy commission. When the National Revolutionary Army reached Peking in June 1928 at the end of the Northern Expedition, he retired to Hong Kong. The Nationalists issued an order for his arrest, which was rescinded in 1931 at the request of Chang Hsueh-liang (q.v.), the son of Chang Tso-lin. Early in 1932 Liang accepted the invitation of the National Government to participate in the national crisis conference, which was held at Loyang in April. After the conference ended, he returned to Hong Kong.

Early in 1933 Liang Shih-i accepted an invitation from Tuan Ch'i-jui to visit him in Nanking. He reached Shanghai on 3 March, but became ill and had to abandon the journey. He died in Shanghai on 9 April 1933. He was survived by his wife, *née* Kao, whom he had married in 1897, and by three sons and five daughters. His daughters were Hao-yin (1896–), Huai-sheng (1900–), Yü-sheng (1900–), Tsang-sheng (1904–), and Yi-sheng (1909–). His sons were Ting-chi (1898–), who studied at Boston University and became a banker; Ting-shu (1907–), who went to Oxford University and became a railway technician; and Ting-min (1908–), who studied at the University of London and became a civil engineer.

A two-volume biography of Liang Shih-i, *San-shui Liang Yen-sun hsien-sheng nien-p'u*, was published in 1946 and reprinted in Taiwan in 1962. In addition to a detailed account of Liang's life, the book contains background material on economic and financial policies and politics in early republican China.

Liang Shu-ming   梁漱溟
H. Huan-ting   煥鼎

Liang Shu-ming (9 September 1893–), attempted a new formulation of Confucianism while teaching at Peking University in 1917–24. From 1927 to 1937 he was a leader in the rural reconstruction movement. Thereafter, he was active in "third force" politics and helped to form the coalition that became the China Democratic League. Although he lived in the People's Republic of China after 1949, he refused to accept Marxism-Leninism as a valid ideology for China.

A native of Kweilin, Kwangsi, Liang Shu-ming was born and raised in Peking. His father, Liang Chi, was a respected metropolitan official who established rehabilitation and vocational schools for convicts and poor children. Liang Shu-ming attended a modern primary school, where he learned English, the Shun-t'ien Middle School, and the Chihli Public Law School. During his student days, he was attracted to utilitarianism. On the eve of the revolution in 1911, he joined the Peking-Tientsin chapter of the T'ung-meng-hui and helped smuggle bombs and rifles to the revolutionaries. In 1912 he worked as a reporter for the Tientsin *Min-kuo pao* [republican newspaper]. In 1913 because of family disagreements and his own disillusionment with the republican cause, he turned to wei-shih, or "consciousness-only," Buddhism and spent three years in semiseclusion.

In 1916 Liang Shu-ming became the private secretary of his relative Chang Yao-tseng, who was serving as minister of judicial affairs at Peking. Ts'ai Yuan-p'ei (q.v.), who had been impressed by an article on Buddhism which Liang had contributed to the *Tung-fang tsa-chih* (*Eastern Miscellany*), soon invited him to join the faculty of Peking University. Liang accepted this offer in 1917, when Chang Yao-tseng was forced out of office by Chang Hsün (q.v.) during Chang Hsün's attempt to restore the Ch'ing dynasty to power.

Liang Shu-ming reexamined his beliefs in 1918 after his father committed suicide. He came to believe that thought must always vindicate itself by providing a view of life which is personally satisfying and a general explanation of society and social problems which can serve as a blueprint for action. He turned from both utilitarianism and Buddhism to his own version of Confucianism.

After formulating and presenting his Confucian ideas in lectures, Liang published *Tung-hsi wen-hua chi ch'i che-hsueh* [the cultures of East and West and their philosophies] in 1921.

Seeking to show that Chinese culture was relevant to the modern world, he identified the West, China, and India as three basic cultural types, ultimately differentiated from each other by the subjective attitude, or will, which informs and characterizes the attempts of each one to solve the problems posed by its environment. According to Liang, the Western will, the "attitude of struggle," seeks to wrest the satisfaction of its desires from the external world or from other people; the Chinese attitude is one of harmonization and satisfaction through adjustment; and the Indian attitude is escapist, recognizing the futility of desire and the search for satisfaction. Liang held that these cultural wills succeeded one another in dialectical sequence. Western culture was then in the ascendant, but it would give way to the Chinese, resulting in a higher world civilization which would mold the scientific and material successes of its predecessor to man's intuitional, moral, and ethical nature. In the distant future, the Indian attitude would displace the Chinese attitude, and another new era would begin.

Because the *Tung-hsi wen-hua chi ch'i che-hsueh* attempted to break through the iconoclasm of the Literary Revolution and the May Fourth Movement and to affirm the relevance of the past to the solution of contemporary Chinese problems, its publication resulted in heated controversies about the worth of traditional values, the function of religion, and the nature of culture and cultural change. However, Liang's views did not receive much support. He himself was dissatisfied with the book, and he later had it removed from circulation for three years. He planned an emended version of the work, but it never appeared.

Liang Shu-ming left Peking University in 1924 and became the principal of a middle school in Ts'aochou, Shantung. In accordance with his theories, he hoped to institute a new kind of education which would achieve ethical as well as intellectual development through the fellowship of faculty and students. He also hoped to found a university, but his plans soon foundered. He returned to Peking in 1925, where he spent two years living with a small group of students and seeking a worthwhile program in which to participate. He soon became interested in the rural reconstruction movement.

Liang worked for a time as head of the Kwangtung-Kwangsi reconstruction committee and visited the major reconstruction projects in China. Early in 1930 he resigned from office to join P'eng Yü-t'ing and Liang Chung-hua in establishing Honan Village Government College. He also edited the *Ts'un-chih yueh-k'an* [village government monthly]. The project collapsed soon after Han Fu-chü (q.v.), the governor of Honan, was transferred to Shantung. Han soon invited all of the men who had been associated with the Honan project to found a similar institution in Shantung. The Shantung Rural Reconstruction Research Institute was founded in 1931, and Liang Shu-ming served as its guiding spirit until 1937. Liang regarded the Shantung project, which exercised direct control over Tsoup'ing hsien and Hotse hsien and which operated in a lesser way throughout the province, as the necessarily small beginning of a nation-wide movement rather than as an experiment of limited scope.

By this time, Liang no longer believed in the cultural dialectic set forth in the *Tung-hsi wen-hua chi ch'i che-hsueh*. He now argued that because China was different from Western nations, it would be wrong to import such Western political systems as democracy and Communism. He denied the validity of applying Marxist class analysis to China and held that the derangement of Chinese society in the name of class struggle was the result of the irresponsible actions of men who were using Marxist theory to obtain power for themselves. Accordingly, he sought, through the Shantung program, to ameliorate social relations peacefully by creating through education an enlightened leadership of intellectuals and the peasant masses and integrated institutions which would combine the functions of local self-government with economic cooperation. He believed that education of the correct sort would obviate the need for revolution. However, Liang was unable to test his theories for any length of time because the outbreak of the Sino-Japanese war in 1937 forced the Shantung Rural Reconstruction Research Institute to close.

During the early war years, Liang served on the National Defense Advisory Council and its successor, the People's Political Council. After touring Communist-held and front-line areas, he became convinced that the Kuomintang-Communist united front was in jeopardy. Accordingly, in November 1939 he helped to found the T'ung-i chien-kuo t'ung-chih hui [united association of comrades for national construction] to act as a third force in politics and to maintain the united front. The organization was composed of representatives from such minor political parties as the China Youth party and the National Socialist party. In 1941 it was superseded by the League of Chinese Democratic Political Groups (*see* Chang Lan). Liang went to Hong Kong to establish and edit the league's newspaper, *Kuang-ming pao* [light], which began publication in September. Its staff included Huang Yen-p'ei, Hsü Fu-lin, and Shang Yen-ch'uan. When Hong Kong fell to the Japanese in December, the *Kuang-ming pao* was forced to suspend publication.

In January 1942 Liang Shu-ming took refuge in Kweilin, where he remained until a Japanese offensive in the summer of 1944 forced him to flee again. By October 1945 he had reached Chungking and had become secretary general of the China Democratic League, the successor of the League of Chinese Democratic Political Groups. He held this office until October 1946, by which time he had alienated the Chinese Communists by proposing National Government occupation of the main Manchurian rail lines and had angered the Kuomintang by investigating and writing a report on the assassination in Kunming of the prominent liberals Wen I-to (q.v.) and Li Kung-p'u. After retiring from office, Liang remained in Chungking, writing, teaching, and occasionally expressing his views in newspaper articles.

After declining to participate in the Chinese People's Political Consultative Conference of September 1949, held to establish the Central People's Government of the People's Republic of China, Liang Shu-ming emerged from retirement in January 1950 to accept nomination as a specially invited delegate to the National Committee of the conference. During the next few months he traveled extensively, observing rural work in Hopei, Shantung, and Szechwan. In October 1951 he published in the *Kuang-ming jih-pao* a lengthy statement entitled "Changes I Have Undergone in the Past Two Years," which was a recognition of Chinese Communist successes, a restatement of his earlier views, and an explanation of why his viewpoint had not changed. In answer to criticisms of this article, Liang said that he was open to persuasion but that his critics had not dealt substantively with any of the crucial issues on which he differed with the Chinese Communists.

In 1953, at a high-level meeting of Chinese Communist leaders, Liang strongly criticized the differences in the living standards of workers and peasants. He was hooted off the rostrum, and it was only because Ch'en Ming-shu (q.v.) intervened on his behalf that more serious steps against him were not taken. In the wake of the Communist-sponsored campaigns against Hu Feng and Hu Shih in 1955, Liang became the target of scores of articles, study meetings, and demonstrations. He was denounced as an outstanding example of feudal reaction and its philosophic handmaiden, subjective idealism, whose political function was to dull the consciousness of the masses. He also was identified as a partner and accomplice of Hu Shih. Liang remained silent until February 1956, when he announced that although he had welcomed criticism, he had experienced difficulty in subduing the urge to resist. He went on to say that his understanding of Marxism had improved and that he was continuing to study. He refrained from criticizing the government during the Hundred Flowers campaign, thus escaping criticism during the ensuing anti-rightist movement.

Among Liang Shu-ming's important works are the *Shu-ming su-ch'ien wen-lu* [Liang Shu-ming's essays: 1915–1922], the *Shu-ming su-hou wen-lu* [Liang Shu-ming's literary compositions written after the age of 30], the *Chung-kuo min-tsu tzu-chiu yün-tung chih tsui-hou chueh-wu* [the final awakening of the Chinese people's self-salvation movement], the *Hsiang-ts'un chien-she li-lun* [theory of rural reconstruction], the *Liang shu-ming chiao-yü lun-wen chi* [Liang Shu-ming's collected essays on education], and the *Chung-kuo wen-hua yao-i* [essentials of Chinese culture].

Little is known about Liang Shu-ming's personal life. He was married sometime after 1918 and is known to have had two sons.

Liang Ssu-ch'eng   梁 思 成

Liang Ssu-ch'eng (1901–), second son of Liang Ch'i-ch'ao who became an architect and a leading authority on the history of Chinese architecture. After 1945 he headed Tsinghua University's department of architecture, and after 1949 he served the People's Republic of China as a city planner and as vice president of the China Architecture Society.

Although his native place was Hsinhui, Kwangtung, Liang Ssu-ch'eng was born in Tokyo during the political exile of his father, Liang Ch'i-ch'ao (q.v.). He was the second of three brothers, the others being Liang Ssu-yung (q.v.), who became one of China's foremost archaeologists, and Liang Ssu-chung, who died in infancy. He also had two sisters. After the family returned to China, he attended the Hsing-hua Academy, entering in 1916, and Tsinghua College. In 1924 he went to the United States on a Boxer Indemnity Fund scholarship and studied first at Cornell University and then at the University of Pennsylvania, where he received a M.Arch. in 1927. After attending the Harvard Graduate School of Fine Arts in 1927–28, he returned to China to become a professor of architecture at National Northeastern University.

In 1931 Liang was appointed a research fellow of the Institute for Research in Chinese Architecture, where for the next decade he carried out pioneering studies of China's building traditions. In 1932–33 he taught at Peking University and Tsinghua College. Liang devoted much of his time to research on the history of Chinese architecture and the traditions of building in China. Among his publications of this period are *Ta-t'ung ku-chien-chu tiao-ch'a* [survey of old buildings in Ta-t'ung] of 1933 and *Ch'ing-tai ying-tsao tse-li* [the rules of building during the Ch'ing dynasty] of 1934. He became a research fellow of the Academia Sinica in 1941. Five years later, he was made chairman of the department of architecture at Tsinghua. He went to the United States in 1947 as a visiting professor at Yale University, and he received an honorary doctorate from Princeton before returning to China in 1948. He was elected a full member of Academia Sinica in 1948. During the early postwar years Liang also served as architectural consultant on the proposed United Nations building in New York. Liang remained in Peking when that city was captured by the Communist forces in 1949.

Three months after the capture of Peking in 1949, Liang was invited to take part in the drawing up of plans for redesigning the city. The rebuilding of the Huai-jen t'ang [hall of

cherished benevolence], where the Chinese Communist party was to hold major meetings, was also entrusted to him. From that time until 1955, Liang carried out many party commissions in architecture. All along, however, he believed that the Communist party did not really understand architecture. He was particularly disturbed by the 1953 slogan "utility, economy, and, if conditions allow, beauty" and openly disputed its wisdom. In 1955, following a speech by Nikita Khrushchev on architecture in the Soviet Union, Liang was subjected to severe criticism for his efforts to utilize traditional Chinese architectural concepts and methods in his designs for new buildings and in his college courses and for his attitude toward the Chinese Communist party's direction of architectural policy. He was also criticized for protesting the destruction of certain Peking landmarks, such as the T'ien-an-men [gate of heavenly peace] and the Yü-lu-chieh [the imperial road], as part of the reshaping of Peking in accordance with modern city planning principles. During most of 1955, Liang was hospitalized and therefore was unable to reply to his critics. When he recovered at the end of that year, the Communists organized special discussion meetings to convince him of his errors, and Liang wrote a confession early in 1956. In it he attacked bourgeois architecture and affirmed his belief that the art of architecture is "a superstructure dependent on the foundation, which is economic." Liang further stated that his criticism of urban planning in Peking had been faulty because he had failed to realize that politics, not aesthetics, should be the primary consideration of the architect. He went on to praise the new ceremonial buildings in Peking because they so well realized the party directive of "utility, economy, and, if conditions allow, beauty."

In 1957, during the Hundred Flowers movement, Liang spoke out for a more independent role for the architect, but he did not criticize the Chinese Communist party. In an article in the *Jen-min jih-pao* published on 8 June, he lauded the party as the prime force behind all of China's accomplishments since 1949, adding merely that he hoped that in the future the party, by heeding the well-intentioned advice of specialists, could accomplish even more and "come out with a clean new face, young and strong and even more lovable." Liang's article was in effect a defense of the party by an intellectual and a technical specialist. Coincidentally, the day after its publication, the Hundred Flowers policy was officially rescinded.

Liang wrote an article for the 14 July 1957 issue of *Jen-min jih-pao* in which he again reviewed his past error in failing to recognize party leadership in architecture and expressed his deep thanks that a long article linking him to Hu Shih and Hu Feng (qq.v.) had been considered unsuitable for publication by the *Jen-min jih-pao*. He added that he was a member of the China Democratic League and that his daughter, on becoming a member of the Chinese Communist party, had declared that she wanted to be the daughter of a party member too. This, asserted Liang, was the filial piety of a good daughter in the new China.

On 14 November 1957 Liang was among the signatories of a statement in the *Jen-min jih-pao* which expressed the gratitude of Chinese architects to Soviet experts. With regard to Peking, the article asserted that "the brilliant results of city planning and construction cannot be dissociated from the altruistic help of the Soviet Russian people, government, and experts."

In a 1959 article published in the *Kuang-ming jih-pao* Liang again expressed public gratitude to the party for correct leadership, adding that architects now understood "the line of the masses" and designed buildings accordingly. He reasserted his proposition in 1961 that although to a limited extent the effect of a building is achieved by the materials of its composition, the main factor is the artistic sense of social class. The discussions resulting from this statement centered around the questions of to what extent material determines form and how much deference should be granted in a socialist society to the wishes of technical specialists.

Liang Ssu-ch'eng also held political offices in the new Communist regime. In 1949 and 1955 he was elected to the Peking Municipal Council. When the China Architecture Society was formed in September 1953, he was elected one of the vice presidents of its executive board. He made an extended tour of the Soviet Union and visited Prague that year. He was a delegate to the First and Second National People's congresses. In May 1955 he was appointed to the department of technical sciences of the Academy of Science. He retained the chairmanship of the department of architecture at Tsinghua after that university was reorganized as a poly-technical university in 1952. In March 1959 Liang became a candidate member of the Chinese Communist party. His major contribution, however, lay in his careful study of the traditions of Chinese architecture, in which field he was a recognized authority. Many of Liang Ssu-ch'eng's former students held important posts as architects both in China and abroad.

Liang Ssu-yung   梁思永

Liang Ssu-yung (1904–2 April 1954), the youngest son of Liang Ch'i-ch'ao, became one of China's foremost archaeologists. From August 1950 until his death he was deputy director of the research institute of archaeology of the Chinese Academy of Science at Peking.

The youngest son of Liang Ch'i-ch'ao (q.v.) and Li Hui-hsien (d. 1924), Liang Ssu-yung was born in Shanghai, although his family had resided in Tokyo since 1901. His native place was Hsinhui, Kwangtung. Liang spent his early childhood in Japan and received a traditional education in the Chinese classics. After the family returned to China, he studied at the Hsing-hua Academy, entering in 1917, and at Tsinghua College. In 1921 he and his brother Liang Ssu-ch'eng (q.v.) joined with Hsü Tsung-shu in translating H. G. Wells's *Outline of History* into Chinese. Liang Ch'i-ch'ao took part in this undertaking by helping the boys polish their writing. The resulting work was published in four volumes by the Commercial Press at Shanghai. In 1923 the two brothers were struck by a car in Peking, but they escaped serious injury.

Liang Ssu-yung went to the United States in 1924 on a Boxer Indemnity Fund scholarship and enrolled at Dartmouth College, where he majored in history. After being graduated in 1927, he returned to China, arriving in July. He had hoped to join the Hsia-hsien archaeological expedition in Shansi, led by Li Chi (q.v.), but the expedition had ended by the time he returned. However, the Tsinghua Research Institute, which had sponsored the Hsia-hsien excavations, appointed him an assistant professor, thus enabling him to make a study of the prehistoric potsherds recovered by Li Chi's expedition.

In August 1928 Liang went to the United States to do graduate work in archaeology and anthropology at Harvard University. He also received valuable field training by participating in the Pecos excavations in the American southwest, which were directed by Alfred V. Kidder. After receiving an M.A. in archaeology, he returned to China in the summer of 1930 and joined the staff of the institute of history and philology of the Academia Sinica.

In the autumn of 1930 V. K. Ting (Ting Wen-chiang, q.v.), a close friend and biographer of Liang Ch'i-ch'ao and the director general of the Academia Sinica, received a letter from the French cleric and paleontologist Father Teilhard de Chardin which said that a Russian employee of the Chinese Eastern railway had discovered a neolithic site near Ang-ang-hsi, Heilungkiang. He told Liang Ssu-yung of the discovery, and the institute of history and philology sent Liang to the site to investigate. From 30 September to 3 October, Liang, with the help of Lukashkin, the railroad worker, excavated the site. They found about 300 specimens of stone, bone, and pottery remains and uncovered two burial pits. Liang studied these finds and about 700 other specimens previously excavated by Lukashkin and concluded that the Ang-ang-hsi culture was an eastern branch of the Mongolian and Jehol microlithic culture. He then decided to return to Peiping by way of Jehol so that he could study other prehistoric sites. Starting from T'ungliao on 21 October, he headed west to Linhsi, then south to Ch'ifeng and Ch'angte, and arrived in Peiping on 27 November. He then went to Ch'eng-tzu-yai to assist Li Chi and Wu Chin-ting in excavating the Lungshan culture site.

In 1931 Liang joined Li Chi at the Houkang diggings in Anyang. The fifth series of excavations at Houkang, which began on 7 November and ended on 9 December, revealed the stratigraphical sequence of the Yangshao, Lungshan, and Yin remains for the first time. Liang contracted pleurisy in the spring of 1932 and was forced to spend two years in bed. He returned to work in the autumn of 1934 as field director of the Hsi-pei-kang excavations at Hou-chia-chuang, Anyang. Between 3 October and 29 December, four large tombs were opened, and more than a thousand stone imple-

ments were discovered. Liang concluded that Hou-chia-chuang was the burial ground of the Yin capital unearthed at Hsiao-t'un, and Li Chi agreed with him. A large-scale excavation of the new site was ordered, and the digging continued well into 1935 (for details, see Li Chi). Liang spent most of 1936 digging at the Lungshan culture site in Liang-ch'eng-chen, Shantung, and supervising the excavation at Hsiao-t'un, Anyang.

After the Sino-Japanese war broke out in July 1937, Liang Ssu-yung helped evacuate the institute of history and philology and its records to Changsha, Kweilin, Kunming, and finally to Lichuang, a village in Nanch'i, Szechwan. Liang's strenuous activities during the war undermined his health, and in the early summer of 1941 he contracted tuberculosis. Thereafter, he was bedridden most of the time. In 1945 he underwent a major operation for the removal of several ribs. He went to Peiping in 1946 for an extended period of convalescence. In recognition of his contribution to Chinese archaeology, he was elected a fellow of the Academia Sinica. When the civil war between the Nationalists and the Chinese Communists approached its climax in 1949 and the institute of history and philology was evacuated to Taiwan, Liang chose to remain in Peiping.

In August 1950 the Central People's Government at Peking established the Chinese Academy of Science, with Liang Ssu-yung as deputy director of the research institute of archaeology. Despite his poor health, Liang planned most of the excavations and other research conducted by the institute. In September 1953 he took a six-month leave for health reasons. He decided to enter the hospital in February 1954 for a checkup before resuming his duties, but the medical examinations revealed that he had a serious heart disorder as well as tuberculosis. On 2 April 1954 he died at Peking.

Liang Ssu-yung was a brilliant scholar and a patient teacher. His major accomplishments include the introduction of the grid system of excavation to China, the identification of the royal tombs of Hsi-pei-kang, and the identification, with Li Chi, of the Hou-kang stratigraphy. His scholarly writings, though few, were significant. His description of the Ang-ang-hsi burials is considered a classic study of ancient cultures in Manchuria. He was the general editor of *Ch'eng-tzu-yai*, Li Chi's analysis of the Lung-shan culture, which many Chinese archaeologists used as a model. A collection of Liang's writings on archaeology, *Liang Ssu-yung k'ao-ku lun-wen chi*, was published in Peking in 1959.

Liao Ch'eng-chih 廖 承 志
Pseud. Ho Liu-hua 何 柳 華

Liao Ch'eng-chih (25 September 1908–), Chinese Communist official who was the son of Liao Chung-k'ai and Ho Hsiang-ning. After 1948 he played an increasingly important role in party and government organizations concerned with foreign affairs and the indoctrination of young people.

The son of Liao Chung-k'ai and Ho Hsiang-ning (qq.v.), Liao Ch'eng-chih was born in Tokyo. He had one sister, Liao Meng-hsing (Cynthia Liao), who was five years older than he. After receiving his primary education at a Roman Catholic school in Japan, he went to Canton in 1919 to attend middle school. He became active in left-wing student groups, and he joined the Kuomintang in 1924. After the May Thirtieth Incident of 1925 at Shanghai, when British police fired on labor demonstrators, he helped plan a sympathy strike at Canton. The assassination of his father, who had supported Sun Yat-sen's policies of alliance with Chinese and Russian Communists, on 20 August 1925 at Canton led the young Liao to redouble his efforts to organize student groups and demonstrations. After Chiang Kai-shek broke with the Communists in 1927 and began a vigorous campaign to eliminate radical elements in the areas under his control, Liao was forced to flee to Japan, where he enrolled at Waseda University. About this time, he joined the Chinese Communist party.

Liao Ch'eng-chih was forced to leave Japan in the spring of 1928 after participating in demonstrations held to protest the Japanese occupation of Shantung and the Tsinan Incident of 3 May 1928 (*see* Ho Yao-tsu). He participated in anti-Japanese demonstrations in Shanghai and then sailed for Europe, where he enrolled in political science and economics courses at Berlin University and the University of Hamburg. He went to Rotterdam and other ports to organize groups of Chinese seamen, but his activities came to the attention of the Dutch authorities in 1929, and they deported him. He returned to Hamburg only to be deported once again. He then went to the Soviet Union, where he spent three years.

Liao returned to China in 1932, but was arrested soon after his arrival in Shanghai. His mother managed to secure his release and that of Ch'en Keng (q.v.), who had been arrested with him. Liao then went to the O-yü-wan soviet area on the Hupeh-Honan-Anhwei border, where he served under Chang Kuo-t'ao and Hsü Hsiang-ch'ien (qq.v.). Nationalist troops forced the Chinese Communists to evacuate the O-yü-wan base on 25 November 1932 and retreat into northern Szechwan, where they established the Szechwan-Shensi border area in May 1933. In the spring of 1935 the Szechwan provincial forces drove them across the Chialing River. They moved along the Szechwan-Sikang border to establish a new base, and in June 1935 they were joined at Moukung by the Long March forces from the Kiangsi central soviet. Chang Kuo-t'ao and Mao Tse-tung soon came into conflict, and the Communist forces split. Chang and his adherents moved into Sikang, and Mao and his associates continued their march to the Communist base in Shensi, arriving there in October 1935. Liao Ch'eng-chih accompanied Mao on this journey, and, after arriving in Shensi, he was assigned to propaganda programs.

After the Sino-Japanese war broke out in July 1937, Liao went to Hong Kong to serve as purchasing agent for the Eighth Route Army and as Kwangtung provincial secretary of the Chinese Communist party. When the Japanese invaded Hong Kong in December 1941, he escaped to northern Kwangtung, where he was arrested and imprisoned by the Nationalists until January 1946, when the People's Political Council arranged for the release of Kuomintang political prisoners. In 1945 he was elected an alternate member of the Central Committee of the Chinese Communist party, and in 1946 he was elevated to full membership. After his release, Liao went to the East River district as the Communist member of one of the truce teams established to enforce the Kuomintang-Communist cease-fire agreement of 7 January 1946, which had been signed by the so-called Committee of Three—Chang Ch'ün, Chou En-lai (qq.v.), and General George C. Marshall. However, the agreement and the American mediation effort soon were undermined by the bitter mutual suspicion that divided the Kuomintang and the Chinese Communists. In 1947 Liao, then in Hong Kong, served as secretary of the Chinese Communist party's south China bureau.

After 1948, Liao Ch'eng-chih played an increasingly important role in the organizations created by the Chinese Communist party for the indoctrination of young people. He helped form the China New Democratic Youth League (later the Communist Youth League) in 1949, and from September 1951 to May 1957 he served as its second-ranking secretary. In May 1949 he became chairman of the All-China Federation of Democratic Youth, a post he held until April 1958. He also became a vice chairman and an executive committee member of the World Federation of Democratic Youth. Liao, who spoke English, Japanese, German, French, and Russian, often was chosen to represent the People's Republic of China at international conferences. In 1950 he was a delegate to the Second Congress of the International Union of Students, held in Prague in August, and to the First International Conference of the World Federation of Democratic Youth, held in Vienna in November. His work in the Communist international youth movements took him abroad every year after 1950. He participated in the international conferences held by the World Peace Council, of which he was a member, and attended executive committee meetings of the World Federation of Democratic Youth. In 1953 he chaired a Red Cross committee which discussed the repatriation of Japanese nationals in the People's Republic of China and served on the Chinese delegation to Josef Stalin's funeral. He participated in Chinese Red Cross missions to Japan in 1954 and 1957 and served as an adviser to the Chinese delegations to the Afro-Asian Conference at Bandung in April 1955 and to the Afro-Asian Solidarity Conference in Cairo in 1957.

Beginning in 1949, Liao Ch'eng-chih also held important posts in the Central People's Government. From 1949 to 1959 he was a vice chairman of the Overseas Chinese Affairs Commission, headed by his mother. He did much of the commission's administrative work. He assumed the chairmanship in 1959. From 1949 to 1954 he was a member of the National Commit-

tee of the Chinese People's Political Consultative Conference, the political and legal affairs committee of the Government Administration Council, and the executive board of the Sino-Soviet Friendship Association. In 1953–54 he served on the committee that drafted a new election law for the People's Republic of China. He was a delegate representing the overseas Chinese to the First and Second National People's congresses and a member of the Standing Committee of the First National People's Congress. After the government reorganization of 1954, he also became vice chairman of the Sino-Soviet Friendship Association's executive board. In March 1958 he was named one of the four vice chairmen of the State Council's newly created office in charge of foreign affairs.

Throughout this period, Liao also held important offices in the Chinese Communist party. He became deputy director of the united front work department in November 1951, and he was reelected to the Central Committee in 1956.

Liao Chung-k'ai
Orig. Liao En-hsü

See Winston Hsieh JAS Vol 31 No 3 (May '72)

廖 仲 愷 *p. 620*
廖 恩 煦

Liao Chung-k'ai (1878–20 August 1925), Kuomintang financial administrator and chief architect of the Kuomintang-Communist alliance that resulted in the reorganization of the party along Leninist lines. At the time of his assassination in 1925 he held such posts as minister of finance, governor and financial commissioner of Kwangtung, head of the Kuomintang workers department, and party representative to the Whampoa Military Academy and the party army.

Born into an overseas Chinese family in San Francisco, Liao Chung-k'ai received his early education in the United States. His father was a businessman, and the young Liao apparently grew up in comfortable surroundings. At the age of 17 sui, Liao accompanied his mother, who was ailing, to Hong Kong. There he married Ho Hsiang-ning (q.v.), whose father was a wealthy and prominent tea merchant. Financial assistance given the young couple by the Ho family enabled them to go to Japan in 1902 for further education. In Tokyo, Liao studied political economy at Waseda University.

Liao and Ho soon became interested in the anti-Manchu revolutionary movement of Sun Yat-sen, and, after meeting Sun in the summer of 1903, they became active supporters of his cause. Liao made a trip to Canton with Hu Han-min (q.v) in the summer of 1905 and joined the newly established T'ung-meng-hui soon after his return. By this time, Sun Yat-sen had become interested in the ideas of the American economist Henry George, and he asked Liao to translate part of George's *Progress and Poverty*. Liao's translation of the preface to that work appeared under the pen name T'u-fu in the first issue of the T'ung-meng-hui's *Min-pao* [people's journal], which began publication in November 1905. Other early writings of Liao reflect an interest in socialist and, to a lesser extent, anarchist ideas. A few months later, again at Sun's behest, he went to Tientsin, where he collaborated with a French military attaché named Boucopaix in gathering information about anti-Manchu activities in north China. At the conclusion of this mission, he returned to Japan, where he studied economics at Chuo (Central) University. After concentrating on his studies and graduating in 1909, he made another trip to China, where he took a special examination which gained him the title of chü-jen. He then served on the staff of Ch'en Chao-ch'ang, the Chinese border defense commissioner in Kirin province, who was negotiating with the Japanese for the recovery of the Yenki area on the Manchurian-Korean border.

When Kwangtung province declared itself independent of Manchu rule after the Wuchang revolt of October 1911, Hu Han-min became its military governor. Hu asked Liao Chung-k'ai to assume responsibility for the financial administration of the province. Liao accepted this offer and moved his family to Canton. He worked with great dedication and suggested many basic economic reform measures for Kwangtung province; but these had relatively little effect, as few reforms were actually carried out.

After the so-called second revolution of 1913 collapsed, Liao and other Kuomintang leaders sought refuge in Japan. Liao's wife and children accompanied him, and they maintained residence in Tokyo until 1923. After Sun Yat-sen reorganized the Kuomintang as the Chung-hua ko-ming-tang in 1914, Liao assisted him by managing the party's finances and by helping to plan party activities. He returned to China with Sun Yat-sen in March 1916. After the death of Yuan Shih-k'ai in June, Liao and Hu Han-min were sent by Sun to Peking to discuss national affairs with the authorities there. Liao followed Sun to Canton in 1917, where he was again placed in charge of the area's finances and consolidated his reputation as the Kuomintang's leading financial expert. Toward the end of 1918, when Sun Yat-sen became dissatisfied with his position at Canton, Liao and a few close supporters accompanied him to Shanghai.

In 1919 and 1920 Liao expounded and elaborated on Sun's economic theories in the new periodical *Chien-she tsa-chih* [reconstruction magazine], which first appeared in August 1919. A major theme of these articles was that China, which had been oppressed by industrial retardation and foreign imperialism, should develop its national economy along socialist lines. Liao argued that such a course would require economic controls to restrain private capitalism and to equalize land tenure and would necessitate the organizing of consumer cooperatives to alleviate the anarchy of production inherent in a *laissez-faire* economy. His writings on the subject of monetary revolution and reconstruction, which advocated the abandonment of hard currency for paper currency, foreshadowed China's currency reform of the 1930's. Liao also helped Sun Yat-sen to round out his political philosophy by translating Delos F. Wilcox's *Government by All the People* into Chinese as *Ch'üan-min cheng-chih*. Sun drew heavily on this material in formulating and developing his principle of min-ch'üan [people's democracy].

In May 1921, when Sun Yat-sen became president extraordinary at Canton, he named Liao Chung-k'ai vice minister of finance—the ministry being under the nominal headship of Wu T'ing-fang—and finance commissioner of Kwangtung province. Liao's primary responsibility was to raise sufficient funds to finance Sun Yat-sen's military campaigns. Although Liao was removed from his financial posts after Sun Yat-sen and Ch'en Chiung-ming (q.v.), the governor of Kwangtung, came into conflict about provincial administration, Sun restored him to his posts after dismissing Ch'en from the governorship in the spring of 1922. When supporters of Ch'en effected a coup at Canton in June 1922, forcing Sun Yat-sen to flee

Canton, Ch'en imprisoned Liao at Sheklung for two months.

For several years, Liao had been interested in socialism and the Russian Revolution. By 1922, Sun and Liao had begun to discuss the possibility of cooperating with the Soviet Union so that they could obtain aid from the Russians. In January 1923, following Sun's preliminary discussions in Shanghai with the Russian diplomat Adolf Joffe and the publication of the Sun-Joffee manifesto, Joffe went to Japan. Liao Chung-k'ai went to Japan about the same time on the pretext of visiting his brother Liao En-t'ao, who was a diplomat representing the Peking government in Tokyo. Liao Chung-k'ai and Joffe held discussions at the hot springs resort of Atami and apparently worked out a detailed plan of cooperation that included an agreement on the admission of Chinese Communists to the Kuomintang.

While Liao was in Japan, Ch'en Chiung-ming was ousted from Canton, and Sun Yat-sen returned to Kwangtung to establish a new military government. Liao returned to China with his family in May 1923 and assumed office as minister of finance and governor of Kwangtung. As plans were formulated for the reorganization of the Kuomintang along Leninist lines, his role in party affairs became increasingly important. In October he was appointed a member of the committee which was organized to carry out the party reorganization, and in November he went to Shanghai to confer with leaders of the various Kuomintang branch organizations. At the First National Congress of the reorganized Kuomintang, held at Canton in January 1924, he was elected to the Central Executive Committee and was appointed head of the workers department. Later in the year, he was also given a wide range of other major responsibilities: director of the Central Bank and head of the peasant department of the Kuomintang. In September he was given complete control of the finances of Kwangtung province.

In February 1924 Chiang Kai-shek had resigned as the head of a seven-man committee formed to establish a party military academy at Whampoa, and Liao Chung-k'ai had been chosen to replace him. When the Whampoa Military Academy was inaugurated in May, Liao became its party representative and Chiang

Kai-shek its commandant. As the senior political officer of the academy, Liao helped lay the foundations of the political commissar system used by the National Revolutionary Army on the Northern Expedition. This system later was used by both the Nationalist and the Communist armies in China.

By mid-1924 Liao, as a favorite of Sun Yat-sen and the chief architect of the Kuomintang-Communist alliance, had become one of the most powerful men in Canton. He was re-appointed governor of Kwangtung in June but was relieved of that office in September so that he could serve effectively as minister of finance, financial commissioner of Kwangtung, and quartermaster general of the central armies. He assisted Chiang Kai-shek in suppressing the Canton Merchants Corps in October 1924 and in planning the first eastern expedition against Ch'en Chiung-ming in March 1925. By the time the eastern campaign ended, Sun Yat-sen had died in Peking. Liao and Chiang then moved to defeat the armies of Yang Hsi-min and Liu Chen-huan at Canton. After the incident of 23 June at Canton, when British and French troops fired on Chinese workers and students who were protesting the May Thirtieth Incident at Shanghai and killed 52 of them, Liao, as head of the Kuomintang's workers department, played a leading role in organizing and directing a strike and a boycott of British goods which paralyzed economic activity in the Canton–Hong Kong area and enabled the Kuomintang to consolidate its strength in Kwangtung province.

When the National Government was inaugurated at Canton in July 1925, Liao Chung-k'ai became a member of the Government Council and one of three civilian members, the other two being Wang Ching-wei and C. C. Wu, of the Military Council, the highest military organ of the National Revolutionary Army. As the most influential supporter of Sun Yat-sen's policies of cooperation with both Russian and Chinese Communists, Liao had come to be identified as a leader of the left wing of the Kuomintang. Thus, his elevation to the Government and Military councils (he still retained his posts as minister of finance, governor and financial commissioner of Kwangtung, head of the Kuomintang workers department, and party representative to the Whampoa Military Academy and the party army) was regarded as a victory of the left wing of the Kuomintang over the right wing in the governmental reorganization of July 1925. This concentration of power in Liao's hands, and the firmness and energy with which he used his authority to further the revolutionary policies of Sun Yat-sen, won him the enmity of many Kuomintang conservatives. On 20 August 1925 Liao Chung-k'ai was assassinated as he stepped out of his automobile on his way to a meeting of the Central Executive Committee.

The persons responsible for Liao Chung-k'ai's death were never identified. A special investigating committee of Kuomintang leaders, including Wang Ching-wei, Hsü Ch'ung-chih, and Chiang Kai-shek, attributed the assassination plot to right-wing elements in the pay of the British. Also under suspicion were a cousin of Hu Han-min named Hu I-sheng and officers of the Kwangtung Army. Because of their connections with the suspects, Hu Han-min and Hsü Ch'ung-chih were obliged to leave Canton to escape public censure. Many other Kuomintang conservatives left Canton, and the left-wing leaders soon gained control of the National Government.

After his death, Liao Chung-k'ai was highly praised by many of his Kuomintang colleagues, including Chiang Kai-shek. He was particularly commended for his key role in the party reorganization of 1924, which prepared the way for the later Northern Expedition. Liao was also honored by Communist historians of the early republican period for his major contributions to the formulation of Sun Yat-sen's "Three Great Policies" of alliance with the Soviet Union, cooperation with the Chinese Communists, and organization of the worker and peasant masses.

Liao was survived by Ho Hsiang-ning and by their children, Liao Ch'eng-chih (q.v.) and Cynthia Liao (Liao Meng-hsing). His daughter later became a secretary to Madame Sun Yat-sen (Soong Ch'ing-ling) in Shanghai. After 1949, all three of them lived in the People's Republic of China.

A collection of Liao's correspondence, prefaces, and essays on economic and political topics was published in 1926 as *Liao Chung-k'ai chi*. A revised and enlarged edition appeared in Peking in 1963.

Liao P'ing   廖 平

Orig.	Liao Teng-t'ing	廖 登 廷
T.	Hsueh-chai	學 齋
	Chi-p'ing	季 平
H.	Hsü-kai	煦 陔
	Ssu-i	四 益

Liao P'ing (29 March 1852–6 June 1932), educator and controversial scholar of the Kung-yang school of classical interpretation, which supported the chin-wen [new text] versions of the Chinese classics. His writings influenced such scholars as K'ang Yu-wei and Ku Chieh-kang.

Chingyen, Szechwan, was the birthplace of Liao P'ing. His father tended cattle and later owned a small mill, but the family's financial situation remained such that all four children had to go to work. Because he was determined to acquire a classical education, Liao P'ing left home and went to live in a Buddhist monastery. He attended a local school and later went to Chengtu and studied under Wang K'ai-yün (q.v.) at the Tsun-ching Academy, where he was considered to be a brilliant student. He became a chü-jen in 1879 and a chin-shih in 1881. He refused an appointment as a magistrate because he wished to be near his ailing parents. After returning to Szechwan, he taught at a number of provincial schools before settling in Chengtu, where he headed the Academy of Chinese Studies (Kuo-hsueh-yuan) and taught at Chengtu Higher Normal College and West China Union University.

Liao, who was a scholar of the Kung-yang school of classical interpretation, believed that the officially recognized ku-wen [old text] versions of the Chinese classics were inferior to the chin-wen [new text] versions of the Former Han dynasty. He upheld the authenticity of the *Kung-yang* and the *Ku-liang* commentaries and denounced the *Tso-chuan* as a forgery of the Han dynasty scholar Liu Hsin. In 1886 his *Chin ku hsueh k'ao* [on the new text and the old text learning] was published, and it apparently came to the attention of K'ang Yu-wei (q.v.). This work later was revised and published as two books, *P'i Liu p'ien* [treatise rejecting Liu Hsin] and *Chih-sheng p'ien* [treatise on knowing the sage]. In the second book, Liao argued that the authentic chin-wen texts revealed Confucius as an advocate of institutional change. After meeting Liao in 1890, K'ang Yu-wei published the *Hsin-hsueh wei-ching k'ao* [the forged classics of the Wang Mang period], in which he claimed to have discovered the forgeries of Liu Hsin. K'ang's book enhanced his scholarly reputation and provoked a storm of controversy which resulted in the banning of the *Hsin-hsueh wei-ching k'ao* in 1894. In 1897 he published the *K'ung-tzu kai-chih k'ao* [Confucius as a reformer], which also adopted and developed Liao P'ing's ideas. Although Liao P'ing was distressed by K'ang's borrowings, he took no action against him.

According to Liao P'ing, his scholarly viewpoint passed through six stages. Accordingly, he called his studio the Liu-i-kuan [hall of six stages]. Even his close associates, however, had difficulty in understanding these changes. In general terms, he seems to have begun by accepting the theories of traditional scholars of the Latter Han dynasty, who made no attempt to challenge the *Wang-chih* [royal polity] or the *Chou-li* [rituals of Chou]. As evidenced by his *Ku-hsueh k'ao* of 1896, he came to regard the *Chou-li* as a fabrication of Liu Hsin. Later, in the *Wang-chih chi-shuo* [explanation of the Wang-chih] and *Huang-ti chiang-yü t'u-piao* [the imperial domain, with charts], he concluded that the *Wang-chih* and the *Chou-li* had been utilized by the earliest emperors of China both to govern China and to provide guidance for the control of all nations on earth. Finally, while reversing his earlier stand by acknowledging Confucius as the author of the classics, he nevertheless classified the *Li-chi* [book of rituals], the *Ch'un-ch'iu* [spring and autumn annals], and the *Shang-shu* [book of documents] as Jen-hsueh [humanistic studies] and the *Shih-ching* [book of songs], the *I-ching* [book of changes], and the *Yueh-ching* [book of music] as T'ien-hsueh [super-humanistic studies]. This classification aroused considerable controversy in the field of classical studies.

In addition to his classical studies, Liao P'ing wrote a number of books on geomancy and medicine. His works on the classics prior to 1897 were published in 14 volumes under the collective title *Ssu-i-kuan ching-hsueh ts'ung-shu*. In 1921 the *Hsin-ting Liu-i-kuan ts'ung-shu*, a greatly enlarged version of the earlier collection

which also included a number of medical articles, was published at Chengtu.

Liao P'ing retired from teaching in 1924. He died on 6 June 1932 at his home near Chiating, Szechwan.

Lieu, O. S.: *see* LIU HUNG-SHENG.

Lim Boon Keng: *see* LIN WEN-CH'ING.

Lim, Robert K. S.: *see* LIN K'O-SHENG.

Lin Ch'ang-min   林 長 民
T. Tsung-meng   宗 孟

Lin Ch'ang-min (16 July 1876–December 1925), scholar and government official who devoted his life to the development of constitutionalism and parliamentary government in China. He met an untimely end after joining Kuo Sung-ling at the time of Kuo's 1925 revolt against Chang Tso-lin.

Although he was born in Hangchow, Lin Ch'ang-min was a native of Fukien. He received his early education in a family school which had been founded by his father, Lin Hsiao-hsun, a Hanlin scholar and devotee of Western political theory. Among his teachers were Lin Shu (q.v.), who taught the Chinese classics, and Lin Wan-li, who taught Western subjects.

After passing the examinations for the sheng-yuan degree in 1897, Lin Ch'ang-min studied English and Japanese at the Hangchow Language School. In 1902 he made a brief trip to Japan, and after his graduation from the Hangchow Language School, he went to Japan to enroll at Waseda University. A classmate of such prominent Japanese as Nakano and Kazami Akira, he was graduated with honors in political economy in 1909. In Japan, Lin also served as president of the Fukien Students' Association. His circle of friends included Inukai Tsuyoshi and Ozaki Yukio, and he was acquainted with Chang Chien, Ts'en Ch'un-hsuan, Liu Ch'ung-yu, T'ang Hua-lung, Yang Tu, and Sung Chiao-jen. He had special respect for Sung Chiao-jen. Lin held the view that to be a statesman it is necessary to be magnanimous, and for the sake of the future of China he aligned himself even with those with whom he differed politically.

After returning to China in 1909, Lin Ch'ang-min refused to take the examination for returned students which would have earned for him the advanced degree of chin-shih. Liu Ch'ung-yu, then deputy speaker of the Fukien provincial assembly, recommended that Lin be appointed secretary general of the assembly, and Lin accepted the office. In the winter of 1909, representatives of various provincial assemblies converged on Shanghai to form an association of comrades to petition for parliamentary government. Lin served as secretary of the organization. He then went to Peking where, with Hsü Fo-su, an ardent constitutionalist, he advocated constitutional government in the *Kuo-min kung-pao*. In this way, he helped shape public opinion and so caused the Ch'ing government to shorten the period of preparation for constitutional government.

Lin Ch'ang-min also served as dean of Fukien Law School. However, he came in conflict with Cheng Yu-ch'i, a prominent local conservative who held the post of principal, and he was dismissed by the educational commissioner. With the help of his colleagues in the provincial assembly, Lin founded a law college of his own. He served and fostered this institution throughout his life.

Lin was on the staff of the *Shun-pao* [Shanghai news daily] in Shanghai when the Wuchang revolt erupted in 1911. That winter, delegates from various provinces met in Shanghai to discuss the organization of a government and the election of a commander in chief. Lin favored Li Yuan-hung, but Ch'en Ch'i-mei suggested Huang Hsing, and a heated debate ensued. Soon thereafter, at the behest of Sun Yat-sen, who had been elected provisional president, three delegates were dispatched from each province to form the provisional Senate. Lin Ch'ang-min was a Fukien delegate. When the provisional Senate was removed to Peking in the spring of 1912, Lin was elected its secretary general. In the ensuing year, an election was held for the National Assembly, and, curiously, Lin was elected a member representing San-yin-no-yen-han in Outer Mongolia. Upon the establishment of the National Assembly in April, he was elected to serve concurrently as its secretary general.

Lin Ch'ang-min was an eloquent speaker and was familiar with the intricacies of parliamentary procedures. In 1914, at Yuan Shih-k'ai's behest, a constitutional drafting committee was set up in the Ts'an-cheng-yuan [political council], and Lin was entrusted with its agenda, minutes, and general affairs. After Yuan's death in June 1916, Lin, with his friend Chang Kuo-kan and others, labored for the restoration of the provisional constitution and the first Parliament. These efforts caused Sun Yat-sen's campaigns and those of the National Protection Army, led by Tsai O and T'ang Chi-yao (qq.v.), to cease, thus bringing about a temporary unification of the southern and northern factions in China.

Lin was a member of the Progressive party [chin-pu-tang]. The Progressive party had a four-point platform: better government, respect for public opinion, maintenance of freedoms conferred by law, and greater welfare for the people. It advocated a certain amount of cooperation with the government in power, with the hope that China would be led to practice constitutional government through the power of persuasion rather than revolution. This approach was incompatible with that of the Kuomintang, and, although there was a period of cooperation between the Kuomintang and the Progressive party after the restoration of the first Parliament in August 1916 which culminated in the drafting of the *T'ien-t'an hsien-fa* [temple of heaven constitution]. However, a political battle began in May 1917 over the issue of China's declaration of war against Germany and led to the dissolution of Parliament.

When the constitution was being drafted, Lin had joined the Constitutional Research Association, and thereafter he had been regarded as a pillar of the so-called "research clique." In fact, however, being purely a constitutional study group, the association had neither a political nor a party platform, and it was never organized as a political body.

After the dissolution of the Parliament in 1917, Lin Ch'ang-min entered the service of Feng Kuo-chang (q.v.), then the vice president at Peking, as secretary general. Two months later, Tuan Ch'i-jui (q.v.) resumed power after defeating Chang Hsün (q.v.), who had plotted the restoration of P'u-yi as emperor. Leaders of the Progressive party were invited to join

Tuan's cabinet, and consequently, Lin, together with Liang Ch'i-ch'ao and T'ang Hua-lung, accepted the offer. Lin was made minister of justice. Three months later, the Progressive party decided to withdraw from the Tuan cabinet, and Lin resigned on the ground of partisan responsibility. During his incumbency in the judicial ministry, Lin was lauded for his refusal to take a bribe of 100,000 yuan from Chang Chen-fang, who was under sentence for his involvement in the restoration attempt and who tried to arrange special amnesty for himself.

At the conclusion of the First World War, Hsü Shih-ch'ang (q.v.), then the president, established a foreign affairs advisory committee with Wang Ta-hsieh as chairman and Lin Ch'ang-min as a member and executive director. Realizing that the Japanese delegates to the Paris Peace Conference would press Britain and France to allow Japan to seize German interests and rights in Shantung, Lin published an article entitled "Shantung is Finished" in the popular Peking paper Ch'en-pao [morning post] to warn his compatriots. This challenging article helped to awaken the public and gave impetus to the May Fourth Movement. At that time, Lin's committee also suggested the unification of all railways in China, with a view to countering the monopolistic designs of Japan in Manchuria. This advice was not accepted by Hsü, and the committee was abolished at its own request. From that time on, Lin Ch'ang-min was regarded as the leader of the anti-Japanese faction.

After the founding of the League of Nations, Lin, together with Ts'ai Yuan-p'ei and Wang Ch'ung-hui, launched the Chinese League of Nations Association, of which Lin became a director. Lin attended the League of Nations Association's general conference at Milan, Italy, accompanied by Wang Shih-chieh and Carsun Chang. Lin was also instrumental in founding the Asian Cultural Association and the Chiang-hsueh-she [Chinese lecture association]; the latter organization invited such scholars of world renown as John Dewey, Bertrand Russell, and Rabindranath Tagore to come to China and address students.

In the summer of 1920 Lin Ch'ang-min visited England. During this sojourn (1920–21), he became acquainted with the history and economic theories of socialism. He was par-ticularly attracted by the writings of Sidney and Beatrice Webb. After traveling in various countries in Europe, Lin became deeply impressed by the spread of postwar Bolshevism. After returning to China in October 1921, Lin, together with Liang Ch'i-ch'ao Ts'ai Yuan-p'ei, and Wang Ch'ung-hui, proposed that the first Parliament be restored to enact a constitution. Their proposal was well received, and under Li Yuan-hung's presidency the first Parliament and its constitutional drafting committee was revived. In mid-1922 Lin was elected to the drafting committee. Inspired by his observations in Europe, he recommended strongly that the structure of the labor system should be specified in constitutional provisions as a precautionary measure against the spread of Bolshevism. He admonished: "During the 19th century, the main struggle in various countries was for constitutional government, but in the 20th century peoples struggle for their livelihood .... Who can guarantee that Bolshevism will not become rampant in China?" During the deliberations on the provisions dealing with economic livelihood, Lin showed himself to be most resourceful and assiduous; accordingly, he was elected chief drafter and reporter by his colleagues. However, immediately after the economic section had gone through its third reading, the Chihli warlords under Ts'ao K'un (q.v.) successfully pressured and bribed the Parliament to elect Ts'ao to the presidency. The so-called Ts'ao K'un constitution was promulgated hurriedly and extralegally. The provisions on livelihood and on local self-government, which Lin believed to be of great importance, were deleted.

Lin was disheartened by this turn of events. He left Peking and issued a statement with some other members of the drafting committee, including Chang Shih-chao and Yang Yung-t'ai, censuring the Ts'ao K'un version of the constitution. They suggested 14 points for amending the constitution, among these a provision that would prohibit an incumbent military officer from election as president.

About that time (1923–24), there was general indignation in China over the Nishihara Loan, an instrument of the new Japanese "velvet glove" policy. Lin realized that such a policy would eventually prove detrimental to the mutual interests of China and Japan and thereby would threaten the general peace of Asia. He therefore wrote a pamphlet entitled *Ching-kao Jih-pen-jen shu* [respectful advice to the Japanese] to point out that this was a "suicidal policy." This pamphlet was translated into Japanese and attracted great attention in Japan and among the Japanese military leaders stationed in China.

In the winter of 1924 Tuan Ch'i-jui resumed power in Peking as chief executive. Lin was appointed a member of a rehabilitation conference and later was asked to make preparations for a national constitution drafting committee. That committee, with some of its 70-odd members appointed by the central government and others selected by various provinces, was supposed to complete its draft within three months. It met in August 1925 and elected Lin chairman. The committee held 47 meetings and drafted a constitution consisting of 14 chapters with 160 articles. The draft, which reflected Lin's beliefs, combined local self-government with a central federal power. It stipulated that the budget for education should not be less than 20 percent of the total disbursements of the government. It also provided for the establishment of a Kuo-shih fa-yuan [state court] to interpret the constitution.

Before the draft could be submitted to the government for consideration, a *coup d'état* took place in Peking. After ousting Ts'ao K'un in favor of Tuan Ch'i-jui, Feng Yü-hsiang (q.v.) plotted to reverse his policy by attempting to imprison Tuan. At that time, Feng succeeded in persuading Kuo Sung-ling (1887–1925), the field commander of one of the Fengtien armies and the favorite deputy of Chang Hsueh-liang (q.v.), to revolt against Chang Tso-lin. A subordinate of Feng who garrisoned Peking began to arrest Tuan's confidants and aides. All roads from Peking were closely guarded by Feng's soldiers to prevent any partisan of Tuan from fleeing. Because he was a supporter of Tuan, Lin was in danger of losing his life. However, he unexpectedly received a secret invitation from Kuo Sung-ling, who, having heard much about Lin's prestige and statesmanship, urged him to join the revolutionary cause. The secret message was delivered by Wang Nai-mo, then director of the Peking-Hankow railway and a supporter of Feng Yü-hsiang. To show his sincerity and urgency, Kuo, without awaiting Lin's reply, had dispatched a special train to Peking to fetch him.

The train had been waiting for Lin at the East Station in Peking for three days. Realizing the danger that a refusal of the secret invitation might incur, Lin availed himself of the opportunity to escape; he left Peking at midnight on 30 November 1925. Under the direction of Kuo's aide, the train did not stop until it arrived at Kou-pang-tzu, where Kuo and Lin met for the first time.

After seeing Kuo, Lin intended to cross the Liao River to reach Yin-k'ou as planned, but he found that the river had not frozen sufficiently to allow his cart to pass. Therefore, he was forced to accompany Kuo's army in its advance. Kuo's army scored some early victories, but was defeated by Heilungkiang cavalry, with Japanese help, at Pai-ch'i-pao. Kuo was captured and executed, and Lin was killed by a stray bullet at Shui-chu-chia-tun.

According to Liang Chin-tung, who was a close associate and confidant of Lin Ch'ang-min and who, with Lin's younger brother Tien-min (1867–1960), chief engineer of the Fukien Electric Company, went to Dairen to fetch Lin's remains, there was no political arrangement whatsoever between Lin and Kuo Sung-ling. Lin apparently left Peking merely to save himself from the possibility of political persecution. Kuo was interested in Lin's services because he had heard about Lin's prestige among the Japanese and presumed he could use Lin to negotiate with the Kwantung Army, which he expected to obstruct his military advance. However, Lin's adversaries and some of his friends ascribed Lin's motive in this misadventure to opportunism.

Lin was adept in calligraphy. He had considerable poetic talent in the classic idiom, and after the literary renaissance in China he sometimes wrote vernacular poems. Although he was by nature romantic and felt "an overwhelmingly amorous sentiment which he did not know how to fulfill," his marriage was not ideal. After his return from Europe, he gave lectures on love and marriage at Peking Normal College, in which he often cited indirectly his personal experience. His wife, *née* Yeh, died early. He was survived by two concubines, four sons, and two daughters. His elder daughter, Lin Hui-yin, married Liang Ssu-ch'eng, (q.v.), a son of Liang Ch'i-ch'ao. His second daughter was Lin Yeh-yu. His elder son, Lin Huan (Henry H. Lin), born in

1915, became a professor at Ohio University. Lin Heng was one year younger than Lin Huan; he became an air force pilot and was killed in Chungking during the Sino-Japanese war. Lin Ch'ang-min's two youngest sons, Lin Hsuan and Lin Hsung, both college graduates in engineering, lived in mainland China after 1949.

Lin Hsien-t'ang 林獻堂
T. Kuan-yuan 灌園

Lin Hsien-t'ang (22 December 1881–8 December 1956), prominent businessman, banker, and philanthropist in Taiwan, worked for many years before 1945 to secure better political and educational opportunities for the Chinese of Taiwan. From 1950 until his death he lived in Japan.

A native of Changchow, Fukien, Lin Hsien-t'ang was born into a wealthy gentry family in Changhua hsien, Taiwan. His father, Lin Wan-an, was a chü-jen who entered the camphor business after Taiwan was ceded to Japan. The young Lin received his education in the Chinese classics under private tutors. In 1895, because Taiwan was in turmoil as a result of the Sino-Japanese war, he and his family sought refuge in Ch'uanchou, Fukien, but they returned to Taiwan in 1896. After his father's death in 1900, Lin took over the family business and became the village head of Wufeng, where the family resided.

Lin Hsien-t'ang went to Japan on business in 1907 and met Liang Ch'i-ch'ao (q.v.), with whom he had corresponded. This meeting had considerable influence on Lin's political outlook and later career. Liang reportedly advised him that in struggling for their political rights the people of Taiwan should not resort to violence, but should use legal means. In dealing with the colonial government they should imitate the Irish. Direct association of the Taiwanese leaders with Japanese authorities in Japan would enhance their status and would serve as a counterbalance to the power of the Government General in Taiwan. Lin invited Liang Ch'i-ch'ao to visit him in Taiwan, and Liang finally made the trip in 1911. His visit seems to have strengthened Lin's emotional ties to China, for Lin made a trip to Peking in 1913.

Lin Hsien-t'ang played an active role in movements to secure better political and educational opportunities for the Chinese of Taiwan. In 1914 he helped finance the establishment of the Taichung Middle School (the predecessor of the Provincial Taichung First Middle School) and joined the Taiwan Society of Assimilation, founded by Itagaki Taisuke. The aim of this society was the achievement of integration and equal rights for the Chinese of Taiwan, but it was unsuccessful because the Government General and the Japanese residents of Taiwan opposed its programs. Lin Hsien-t'ang then strove for the repeal of a provisional law passed by the Japanese Diet in 1897 that authorized the governor of Taiwan to issue regulations which would have the full force of Japanese legislation. He made personal appeals to various officials and organized petition campaigns among Chinese students in Taiwan, but his efforts came to naught. In 1921 the provisional law achieved permanence. By that time, Lin also was engaged in a campaign to establish a representative assembly with a limited franchise. His speeches throughout the island were applauded enthusiastically, but his group's petitions to the Japanese Diet were ignored. In 1923 the Government General suppressed this movement, dismissing Lin from membership on its advisory committee and imprisoning other leaders of the movement.

During this period, Lin also engaged in cultural and commercial activities. When the Taiwan Culture Association (Tai-wan wen-hua hsueh-hui) was organized by students at the Taiwan Medical School in 1921, he was elected its general manager. In 1923 he became president of the *Taiwan Min-pao* [Taiwan people's journal], and in 1926 he joined the newly organized Ta-tung hsin-t'o hui-she [Ta-tung trust company], which had been established to protect the commercial interest of the Taiwanese people.

In 1927, partly because of disagreements with other leaders of the Taiwan Culture Association, Lin Hsien-t'ang left Taiwan and made a tour of Europe and the United States. He wrote a book about his travels, *Huan-ch'iu yu-chi* [a journey around the world]. After returning to Taiwan, he became president of the *Taiwan hsin-min-pao* Company, which incorporated the *Taiwan Min-pao* in 1930. However, the *Taiwan hsin-min-pao* Company was not permitted to publish its newspaper until 1932, by which time Lin no longer was its president.

When the Japanese government tried to restrict the exporting of Taiwan rice to Japan in 1932, Lin protested on behalf of the agrarian population of Taiwan. Because he owned a great deal of land and because he was a man of both wealth and prestige, the Government General frequently consulted him and asked his advice on local problems. In 1945, when Japan was facing defeat in the War in the Pacific, the Japanese government made Lin a member of the House of Peers in Tokyo.

When Taiwan was officially restored to China in the autumn of 1945, Lin Hsien-t'ang announced his support of the National Government. He served as chairman of the official ceremonies held on 25 October to celebrate the restoration and to welcome the new governor, Ch'en Yi (q.v.). In 1946 Lin was elected to the Taiwan provincial assembly, and in 1947 he became chairman of the board of trustees of the reorganized Chung-hua Bank. Public dissatisfaction with the inefficiency, arrogance, and brutality of Ch'en Yi and his associates increased steadily and reached a climax on 28 February 1947, when a huge demonstration took place in Taipei. Ch'en Yi's military police fired on the demonstrators, killing several and almost causing an island-wide revolt. Ch'en then launched a brutal suppression campaign, during which several thousand Taiwanese were massacred. He was removed from office and a regular provincial government (*see* Wei Tao-ming) was organized in April 1947. However, the damage had been done, and many Chinese in Taiwan, including Lin Hsien-t'ang, now had serious reservations about the National Government and its policies. In 1950, shortly after the Nationalist refugees from the mainland arrived in Taiwan, Lin moved to Japan, where he lived until his death on 8 September 1956. He was survived by his wife, Yang Shui-hsin, and by three sons and one daughter.

Lin Hsien-t'ang was also known for his poetry, written in the classical Chinese style. Three collections of his poems were published. He also organized several poetry societies and served as the director of the Taiwan Archives, founded in 1948.

Lin K'o-sheng   林 可 勝
West. Robert K. S. Lim

Lin K'o-sheng (15 October 1897–), known as Robert K. S. Lim, was the eldest son of Lim Boon Keng (Lin Wen-ch'ing). A renowned physiologist, he served as professor of physiology at Peking Union Medical College (1924–37), director of the Chinese Red Cross Medical Relief Corps (1937–42) and the emergency medical service training school (1938–42), and surgeon general of the Chinese army (1945–48). He went to the United States in 1949. In 1952 he joined Miles Laboratories, becoming director of medical sciences research in 1962.

The eldest son of Lim Boon Keng (Lin Wen-ch'ing, q.v.), Robert K. S. Lim was born in Singapore. His native place was Amoy, Fukien. After completing his secondary education in England, Robert Lim followed his father's example by entering the University of Edinburgh. He interrupted his studies during the First World War to serve in the British Army, attached to Indian troops. After returning to Edinburgh, he received the M.B. and Ch.B. degrees in 1919, became a lecturer in histology in the physiology department, and obtained the Ph.D. degree in 1920. That year, he was named a Goodsir Memorial Fellow. He remained at Edinburgh until 1923, when he was awarded a Rockefeller Foundation fellowship for a year's study at the University of Chicago. In 1924 he received the D.Sc. degree from the University of Edinburgh and returned to his native land to become professor of physiology at Peking Union Medical College, a post he was to hold until mid-1937.

Beginning in the 1920's, Robert Lim published reports of his research activities in Chinese, British, and American journals of physiology. He founded the Chung-kuo sheng-li hsueh-hsi [Chinese physiological society] and served as managing editor of its journal from 1927 until 1941, when it ceased publication. He was president of the Chung-kuo i-hsüeh hui [Chinese medical association] in 1928–30 and field director of the Chinese Red Cross Medical Relief Commission in north China in 1933. In 1936 he became chairman of the Hua-pei nung-yeh fu-hsing hui [north China council for agricultural reconstruction] and a counsellor of the Academia Sinica.

In the Autumn of 1937, Lim, who was on his way to Europe for a sabbatical year, was called to Nanking. When the National Government evacuated the city, he took charge of the remnants of the Chinese Red Cross and organized the Chinese Red Cross Medical Relief Corps. He served as its director until 1943 and, under his direction, the corps set up a medical supply system to assist the army, sent more than 100 medical units into the field, and created a unit of more than 200 ambulances which saw service on all fronts. In 1938 he established the Chan-shih wei-sheng-jen yüan hsün [emergency medical service training school] to train medical personnel for the civil relief services and the army. By 1942 the school had expanded to include a central school at Kweiyang and five branch schools in different war areas. It has been estimated that more than 13,000 people received training in these schools.

From 1942 to 1944 Robert Lim served under General Joseph Stilwell as medical inspector general of the Chinese expeditionary force in Burma. In May 1942 he led the remnants of Chinese military hospital staffs from Mogaung to Ledo. He became deputy surgeon general of the Chinese army in 1944 and surgeon general in 1945. After the war ended in 1945, he continued in this post so that he could rehabilitate the medical service. He organized the Kuo-fang i-hsueh yuan [national defense military center] and initiated a program which provided Chinese medical personnel with postgraduate training in the United States. In 1948 he was asked to become minister of health in the National Government, but he declined the offer and retired from his military post.

Robert Lim went to the United States in 1949 to become visiting research professor of clinical science at the University of Illinois in Chicago. From 1950 to 1952 he served as chairman of the department of physiology and pharmacology at Creighton University Medical School in Omaha, Nebraska. He then joined Miles Laboratories, Inc., in Elkhart, Indiana, as head of physiology and pharmacology research and became director of medical sciences research in 1962.

Among the many scientific papers published by Robert Lim are a number of special studies in gastric histology and pharmacology, including the results of extensive research on sedatives, hypotensives, and analgetics. As a military man, he was decorated by the Chinese, British, and American governments; as a scientist he was named to honorary membership in several foreign academic and professional societies. In 1961 the University of Hong Kong awarded him an honorary D.Sc. degree.

Robert Lim married twice. His first wife, Margaret (d.1936), was English. They had two children, Euphemia (1923–) and James (1927–). Lin married Chang Ch'ien-ying, the daughter of Chang Jen-chieh (q.v.), at Shanghai in 1946.

Lin Piao   林 彪

Lin Piao (1907–), Chinese Communist military leader who became a marshal of the People's Republic of China in 1955, minister of defense in 1959, and the second-ranking member of the party in 1966.

A native of Huangkang hsien, Hupeh, Lin Piao was the son of a small landholder (listed in Chinese Communist biographies of Lin Piao as a peasant) who owned a dye-works and who later worked as a purser on a steamer which sailed the Yangtze between Hankow and Shanghai. One of Lin Piao's elder cousins, Lin Yü-nan, was active in the Socialist Youth League in the 1920's and was arrested and executed by the Nationalists in the 1930's.

After attending primary school in his native village, Lin Piao went to Wuchang, where he studied at the Kung-chin Middle School from 1921 to 1924. The activities of Lin Yü-nan, who was about 20 years older than Lin Piao, and the programs of the Social Welfare Society, which had been established in Wuchang by Yün Tai-ying (q.v.) and others, soon aroused Lin Piao's interest in radical movements, and he began to participate in politically oriented student groups. In 1925, having been graduated from middle school, Lin went to Shanghai as a Hupeh delegate to the National Student Federation meeting held to discuss demonstrations protesting the May Thirtieth Incident. In Shanghai, Lin joined the Socialist Youth League; an elder brother belonged to this organization, and Yün Tai-ying was head of its propaganda apparatus.

In 1925, at the age of 18, Lin Piao went to Canton and enrolled at the Whampoa Military Academy, where Yün Tai-ying was serving as an instructor. Lin soon came to the attention of General Vasily K. Bluecher (known in China as Galin), the principal Soviet military adviser at Whampoa, and of Chou En-lai (q.v.), then deputy director of the academy's political department. While at Whampoa, Lin joined the Young Soldier's Association, a Communist-influenced organization at the academy (*see* Ho Chung-han). He later became a member of the Communist Youth League. After the fourth class, of which Lin was a member, was graduated from Whampoa, Lin was assigned to an independent regiment, commanded by Yeh T'ing, which was attached to the Fourth Army of Li Chi-shen (q.v.). He participated in the first phase of the Northern Expedition, which began with a drive into Hunan in July 1926 and ended with the capture of the Wuhan cities in the autumn of 1926, and rose in rank from platoon leader to company commander. He joined the Communist party in 1927.

On 1 August 1927 Yeh T'ing's forces, which had become the 24th Division of the Eleventh Army in the Second Front Army of Chang Fa-k'uei (q.v.), joined with the Twentieth Army of Ho Lung (q.v.) in staging an insurrection at Nanchang, later celebrated as the birth of the Chinese Communist army. When Nanchang proved untenable, the rebels marched southward to establish a base in Kwangtung. The Communist forces were defeated at Swatow in September. Lin Piao managed to save the supplies and equipment assigned to his unit, and he joined the forces of Chu Teh (q.v.) at Jaop'ing. By the end of 1927 these troops, with Chu Teh as commander and Ch'en Yi (1901–; q.v.) as political commissar, had moved into southern Hunan. In January 1928 they established a base at Ichang. Lin Piao, not yet 21, attracted Chu Teh's attention when he defeated a force much larger than his own at Laiyang. In April, Chu's group joined with a small band of Communists led by Mao Tse-tung in the Ching-kang mountains on the Hunan-Kiangsi border. They formed the Fourth Red Army, with Chu Teh as commander, and Mao Tse-tung as political commissar.

Chu Teh regarded Lin Piao as one of the most able and active young officers under his command and took a special interest in his career. When Chu became commander of the First Army Group of the Chinese Workers and Peasants Red Army, composed of the Third, Fourth, and Twelfth Red armies, Lin succeeded him as commander of the Fourth Red Army. Lin steadily rose in the military hierarchy as the Communists consolidated their central soviet base in Kiangsi from 1931 to 1934. He served as head of the Red Army Academy, the principal training center for guerrilla commanders at Juichin, until 1933, when he was succeeded by Ch'en Keng (q.v.). Lin played an important role in military actions against the forces of Chiang Kai-shek, which launched five campaigns to annihilate the Communists. After Chu Teh became commander in chief of the Chinese Workers and Peasants Red Army, Lin succeeded him once again, becoming commander of the First Army Group. Nieh Jung-chen (q.v.) was his political commissar, and Tso Ch'uan (q.v.) was his chief of staff.

Lin Piao accompanied Mao Tse-tung on the Long March, arriving at Paoan, Shensi, in October 1935. At Paoan, and later at the Chinese Communist wartime capital of Yenan, Lin devoted his attention to the training of Communist officers. He headed the Red Army Academy, which was renamed Anti-Japanese Military and Political University after the Sino-Japanese war began. When the Chinese Communist forces in northwest China were reorganized as the Eighth Route Army, with Chu Teh in command, Lin became the commander of its 115th Division, with Nieh Jung-chen as deputy commander and political commissar. His military reputation was enhanced in September 1937 by a decisive victory over a Japanese unit commanded by General Itagaki on the Hopei-Shansi border at the P'inghsing pass. Leaving Nieh Jung-chen to hold the Shansi-Chahar-Hopei border area, Lin Piao and the main force of the 115th Division moved into Honan and Shantung, where they won control of the territory that became the Communist Hopei-Shansi-Honan border region in May 1938. About this time, Lin Piao was wounded in action and was sent to the Soviet Union for medical treatment. Although some Communist sources state that he studied military medicine and Soviet military techniques, little is known about his activities during his three-year stay in the Soviet Union.

After returning to Yenan in February 1942, Lin was ordered to Chungking, the wartime capital of the National Government, where he represented the Eighth Route Army and served as a member of the Communist liaison mission headed by Chou En-lai. He returned to Yenan in 1943 to be deputy director of the Party School, headed by Mao Tse-tung. At the Seventh National Congress of the Chinese Communist party, held at Yenan in the spring of 1945, Lin was elected to the Central Committee.

As the War in the Pacific came to an end, both the Nationalists and the Communists recognized the crucial importance that Manchuria would assume in the approaching struggle for control of China. Lin Piao, who was serving in the headquarters of the Chinese Communist forces at Yenan, was assigned to field command as commander of the Shantung military district. However, he was not sent to Shantung. More than 100,000 troops and 50,000 political cadres were transferred to Manchuria from Shantung and other parts of north China, and Lin received over-all command of them, his mission being to accept the surrender of Japanese and Manchoukuo troops and to cooperate with the Soviet Red Army. He and his staff moved to Manchuria in October 1945, where he assumed command of the newly established Communist Northeast military district and responsibility for civil administration and party affairs. He then organized the Northeast Democratic Alliance Army, a force composed of anti-Japanese guerrilla units, and began training new recruits at Chiamussu.

In the meantime, the Nationalists attempted to send military forces to Manchuria, but Soviet units commanded by Marshal Rodion Ya. Malinovsky, which had moved into Manchuria in August 1945, refused them permission to land at Antung, Dairen, Yingkow, or Hualutao. By the time Nationalist units reached the principal cities of Manchuria, Lin Piao's forces had consolidated control of the surrounding areas, and the departing Soviet units had transferred much of the equipment taken from the Japanese Kwantung Army to the Chinese Communists. This equipment served to counterbalance the military aid given the Nationalists by the United States.

In May 1946 the Nationalists captured Ssu-p'ing-kai and forced Lin Piao to retreat to the area north of the Sungari River. However, the Nationalists were unable to maintain their position for long. Beginning in the summer of 1947, when Lin Piao ordered a counter-offensive, the Chinese Communist troops achieved victory after victory. The battle at Chinchow in October 1948 and the fall of Mukden on 1 November 1948 brought the Manchurian campaign to an end and ensured Communist control of the region.

Lin Piao's forces were reorganized as the Fourth Field Army, with Lin as commander and political commissar. He moved south of the Great Wall, captured Kalgan in December 1948, and occupied Tientsin and Peiping in January 1949. As commander of the Peiping-Tientsin front, he served on the delegation headed by Chou En-lai that held unsuccessful peace talks with a Nationalist delegation from February to April. Units of the Fourth Field Army captured Wuhan in May and then moved southward. Their advance was aided by a series of important Nationalist defections, including that of Ch'eng Ch'ien (q.v.), the governor of Hunan. Changsha, the provincial capital, fell to the Communists on 5 August. The occupation of Hengyang in October completed the conquest of the Hupeh-Hunan region. The Fourth Field Army then marched into Kwangtung and took Canton in October.

Lin Piao, who had remained at Hankow to supervise consolidation of his home region, became commander of the Central China Military District and first secretary of the Central Committee's bureau in that region. He was elected to the National Committee of the Chinese People's Political Consultative Conference, held at Peiping in September 1949, even though he was not a delegate to the conference.

When the Central People's Government of the People's Republic of China was inaugurated on 1 October 1949, Lin Piao became a member of the Government Council. In February 1950 he received command of the entire Central-South Military Region, which included six major provinces. In the autumn of that year, units of his Fourth Field Army formed the vanguard of the so-called Chinese People's Volunteers which crossed the Yalu River to participate in the Korean conflict. Many observers believed that Lin Piao did not assume field command of these units in Korea. His absence from an important meeting of the

Central-South Military and Administrative Committee in September was believed to have been the result of ill health rather than command responsibilities in Korea. On several occasions in the 1951–53 period Yeh Chien-ying (q.v.), one of Lin's subordinates, served as his surrogate without explanation.

In 1954 Lin Piao was elected a deputy, representing the People's Liberation Army, to the National People's Congress. The congress, which convened in September, adopted a constitution and restructured the government. Lin then became a vice premier of the State Council and a vice chairman of the National Defense Council. On 23 September 1955 he was awarded the three top military decorations and was made a marshal of the People's Republic of China. Four of the other nine military leaders who received this honor were close associates of Lin Piao: Chu Teh, Ch'en Yi, Nieh Jung-chen, and Yeh Chien-ying.

Lin also continued to rise in the party hierarchy. In April 1955 he was elected to the Political Bureau, and in May 1958 he was elected a vice chairman of the Central Committee, in which capacity he served as an *ex officio* member of the Standing Committee of the Political Bureau. At this point, he was the sixth-ranking leader of the Chinese Communist party, the first five being Mao Tse-tung, Liu Shao-ch'i, Chou En-lai, Chu Teh, and Ch'en Yun.

In September 1959 Lin Piao replaced P'eng Te-huai (q.v.) as minister of defense. He also became senior vice chairman of the National Defense Council and first vice chairman of the Chinese Communist party's military affairs committee, which determined military policy. Late in 1961 he generated a campaign known as the "Four Firsts" which consisted of four fundamental relationships—between weapons and men, political work and other work, routine political work and ideological work, and theory and practice—and which established the basis for political activity in the People's Liberation Army. During the early 1960's Lin Piao was a dominant figure in stressing the omnipotence of the Thought of Mao Tse-tung in the Chinese Communist military forces.

Lin Piao's political and military prominence was affirmed in September 1965, when he was chosen to make a major policy statement at the twentieth anniversary celebrations of the victory over Japan. "Long Live the Victory of People's War" appeared in the *Jen-min jih-pao* [people's daily] at Peking on 3 September. Lin argued that Mao Tse-tung's strategy, which stressed the necessity of establishing revolutionary bases in rural areas so that cities could be encircled and overcome, was of "universal practical importance for present revolutionary struggles." The cause of world revolution, then, depended on the successful transfer of Mao's doctrine to the international arena. With the gradual extension of "people's war" to and by Asian, African, and Latin American nations, the urban areas—Western Europe and North America—would be encircled and overcome. According to Lin, "everything is divisible, and so is this colossus of United States Imperialism. It can be split up and defeated. The peoples of Asia, Africa, Latin America, and other regions can destroy it piece by piece, some striking at its head and others at its feet."

Throughout the early and mid 1960's the influence of Lin Piao and of the military forces he controlled grew steadily. On 1 January 1964 the *Jen-min jih-pao* [people's daily], the official organ of the Chinese Communist party, called on the people of China to "learn from the political work experiences of the People's Liberation Army." Lin's forces played an important role in local, provincial, and national administration and politics. During the so-called Cultural Revolution, which began in 1966, major policy announcements on national affairs appeared regularly in the *Chieh-fang chün-pao* [liberation army daily] rather than in the *Jen-min jih-pao*. In June 1966, on the eve of the Cultural Revolution, articles in the theoretical journal *Hung-ch'i* [red flag] spoke of Lin Piao as an authoritative interpreter of Mao Tse-tung's doctrines. Lin Piao became the second-ranking member of the Chinese Communist party in August 1966, displacing Liu Shao-ch'i (q.v.).

Little is known about Lin Piao's personal life. In 1937 he married Liu Hsi-ming, and they reportedly had a son and a daughter.

Lin Po-ch'ü   林伯渠
  T. Tsu-han   祖涵

Lin Po-ch'ü (1882–29 May 1960), founding member of the Chinese Communist party who held important Kuomintang posts in 1924–26. From 1937 to 1948 he was chairman of the Shensi-Kansu-Ninghsia Border Region government, and from 1949 to 1954 he was secretary general of the Central People's Government Council.

Lingling hsien, Hunan, was the birthplace of Lin Po-ch'ü. His father, a teacher and landowner who hoped that the young Lin would become a scholar, guided his early schooling in the Chinese classics. After attending the Ch'angte Normal School in 1901–4, Lin went to Japan on a government scholarship. He studied at a higher normal school and later attended classes at Chuo University in Tokyo. In 1905, at the age of 20, he joined the newly founded T'ung-meng-hui. He returned to Hunan in 1908, where he taught school and worked to gain support for the anti-Manchu cause.

After the 1911 revolution, Lin Po-ch'ü served in the newly formed republican government of Hunan, in which T'an Yen-k'ai (q.v.) was tutuh [military governor] and Ch'eng Ch'ien (q.v.) was director of the military affairs bureau. Lin's elder brother Lin Hsiu-mei was a division commander under T'an, and his younger brother Lin Tsu-lieh courted and married one of Ch'eng Ch'ien's daughters. In the so-called second revolution of 1913, T'an Yen-k'ai deployed the Hunanese troops against the armies of Yuan Shih-k'ai, but they were defeated in August. Lin Po-ch'ü followed Ch'eng Ch'ien and other Kuomintang leaders to Japan. After Yuan Shih-k'ai's monarchical aspirations became apparent, Lin returned to China with Ch'eng in 1915 and served as his aide during the chaotic years from 1916 to 1919. Ch'eng and Lin attempted to win control of Hunan province for Sun Yat-sen, but their campaign failed after the northern government at Peking sent an overwhelming force against them in 1918. By mid-1919 they had been driven out of Hunan.

Lin went to Shanghai, where he soon became associated with a number of men who were studying the possible application of Marxism-Leninism to the problem of unifying China. Although he was a founding member of the Chinese Communist party in 1921, he remained loyal to Sun Yat-sen and was a staunch adherent of the view that Marxist economic doctrine was compatible with Sun Yat-sen's min-sheng [principle of the people's livelihood].

In 1922 Sun Yat-sen determined to reorganize and expand the Kuomintang, and he held a meeting at Shanghai on 4 September of some 50 prominent men, including Ch'eng Ch'ien and Ch'en Tu-hsiu (q.v.), who headed the infant Chinese Communist party. This group was augmented by six people, including Lin Po-ch'ü, for a second meeting, held on 15 November. A manifesto concerning party organization was issued on 1 January 1923.

Lin Po-ch'ü became prominent in the Kuomintang in 1923, when he served as deputy director of the general affairs department of the party headquarters in Shanghai. He thus became involved in the aspirations and ambiguities of the Comintern-inspired alliance between the Chinese Communist party and the Kuomintang. At the First National Congress of the newly reorganized Kuomintang, held in January 1924, he was one of six Chinese Communists elected to alternate membership on the Central Executive Committee. The following month, he became head of the peasant department of the Kuomintang central organization at Canton. When the Whampoa Military Academy was established in 1924, Lin became an instructor in the political department, headed by Chou En-lai. He was elevated to full membership on the Central Executive Committee of the Kuomintang at the party's Second National Congress, held in January 1926. As head of the party's peasant department, Lin assumed responsibility for supervising the Peasant Movement Training Institute at Canton, which was headed in 1926 by Mao Tse-tung.

When the Northern Expedition was launched in mid-1926, Lin Po-ch'ü was made party representative in the Sixth Army, the Hunanese forces commanded by Ch'eng Ch'ien. When this army occupied Nanking on 24 March 1927, violent anti-imperialist agitation was directed against Western residents of the city. Lin Po-ch'ü and the Communist political workers on his staff were blamed for the anti-Western riots, but it should be noted that Lin was not in Nanking at that time. He had gone to Wuhan, the new seat of the National Government, where he served as minister of finance in the new left-Kuomintang regime. When Wang Ching-wei (q.v.) broke with the Communists at Wuhan in July 1927, Lin fled to Nanchang, Kiangsi. On 1 August, Communist-led troops staged an insurrection and established a government in which Lin served as head of the finance committee and a member of the governing committee. Within a week, this government had fallen, and Lin had fled to Japan.

Lin Po-ch'ü went to the Soviet Union, arriving in Moscow in the spring of 1928, where he attended special classes at Sun Yat-sen University with such older Chinese Communists as Hsü T'e-li, Tung Pi-wu, and Wu Yü-chang (qq.v.). That summer, he took part in the Sixth National Congress of the Chinese Communist party, held in Moscow. Lin left Sun Yat-sen University in 1930 and went to Siberia, where he taught in schools for Chinese workers at Khabarovsk and Vladivostok.

In 1932 Lin Po-ch'ü returned to China to become commissar of finance in the central soviet government at Juichin, Kiangsi. After the retreat from Kiangsi late in 1934, he made the Long March to Shensi with Mao Tse-tung and Lin Piao. He soon emerged as part of the inner core of the party elite at Yenan, and he served as chairman of the Shensi-Kansu-Ninghsia Border Region government from 1937 to 1948. In October 1938 he became a member of the Central Committee of the Chinese Communist party. During the Sino-Japanese war, Lin also was prominent in Chinese Communist negotiations with the Nationalists. He had accompanied Chou En-lai and other Communist leaders to Sian during the Sian Incident (*see* Chang Hsueh-liang) of December 1936 and had participated in the negotiations that had resulted in the release of Chiang Kai-shek and the formation of a Kuomintang-Communist united front against the Japanese. In 1937 and 1938 he assisted Chou in negotiations with the Nationalists at Hankow concerning the practical workings of the alliance. After the National Government moved to Chungking, Lin served under Chou En-lai in the Communist liaison mission at the wartime capital, and he became a representative to the People's Political Council. He was the chief Chinese Communist delegate at Chungking when Chou En-lai was in Yenan from May to November 1944.

Lin Po-ch'ü's seniority in the Chinese Communist party was confirmed at the Seventh National Congress, held at Yenan in the spring of 1945. He was a member of the presidium of the congress, and he made one of the important opening speeches. At the conclusion of the congress in June, he was elected the fifth-ranking member of the Central Committee—following Mao Tse-tung, Chu Teh, Liu Shao-ch'i, and Jen Pi-shih—and was made a member of the Political Bureau. He remained in northern Shensi throughout the civil war that followed the breakdown of American mediation efforts in mid-1946.

When the Central People's Government of the People's Republic of China was established at Peking in October 1949, Lin Po-ch'ü assumed office as secretary general of the Government Council. He held this office until 1954, when the government was reorganized, after which he held such senior but less demanding positions as a vice chairmanship in the Standing Committee of the National People's Congress. In 1954 and 1959 he was elected vice president of the Sino-Soviet Friendship Association. He was reelected to the Central Committee and the Political Bureau of the Chinese Communist party in 1956, and he became senior vice chairman of the Standing Committee of the National People's Congress in 1959.

Lin Po-ch'ü, who had suffered from a heart ailment for some time, died in Peking on 29 May 1960. Mao Tse-tung, with whom Lin had been closely associated since 1932, was a member of his funeral committee. Liu Shao-ch'i headed the funeral committee and officiated at a memorial service held in Peking on 2 June at which Teng Hsiao-p'ing (q.v.), speaking on behalf of the Central Committee, eulogized Lin and his contributions to the liberation of the Chinese people. Lin's body was buried in the Cemetery of Revolutionary Heroes near Peking.

Lin Sen   林 森
  Alt. Lin Ch'ang-jen   林 長 仁
  T.   Tzu-ch'ao   子 超
  H.   Ch'ing-chih lao-jen 青 芝 老 人

Lin Sen (1868–1 August 1943), anti-Manchu revolutionary and a veteran leader of the Kuomintang, was the Chairman of the National Government from 1932 to 1943.

Minhsien (later Minhou hsien), Fukien, was the birthplace of Lin Sen. His father, a businessman, moved the family to Foochow when Lin

Sen was three sui. After receiving a traditional education in the Chinese classics, the young Lin entered a missionary school in 1877. In 1881 he enrolled at Anglo-Chinese College, a Methodist institution in Foochow. After graduation in 1883, he went to Taiwan, where he was employed by the Taipei Telegraph Office from 1884 to 1895. During this period, he returned to Foochow four times: in 1888 he went home to see his parents; in 1890 he got married; in 1892 he visited his wife, who had not accompanied him to Taipei and who was ill; and in 1895 he left Taiwan when it was ceded to the Japanese. In 1898 Lin went to Taiwan once again. By this time he had been converted to the anti-Manchu revolutionary cause, and he wanted to explore the possibility of wresting Taiwan from the Japanese and using it as a revolutionary base. However, he abandoned the project as impractical and returned to China in 1899.

Lin Sen went to Shanghai in 1902 and found employment with the Chinese Maritime Customs. Soon afterwards, he joined with other Fukienese in founding the Fukien Students Association, an anti-Manchu revolutionary group which came to have branch organizations in Fukien. Most of the members of this association joined the T'ung-meng-hui soon after its founding in 1905.

In 1909 Lin Sen was transferred to the customs station at Kiukiang. With the help of such supporters as Wu T'ieh-ch'eng (q.v.), he organized reading rooms to disseminate anti-Manchu literature and worked to win the support of officers and soldiers in the Newly Created Army. After the Wuchang revolt of October 1911 touched off the revolution, he helped persuade the Kiukiang military commander to support the revolutionaries and contributed greatly to the defection of the imperial naval forces (most of the naval officers were Fukienese) on the Yangtze. When a republican government was established at Kiukiang, he was elected chief of civil affairs, but he refused to assume office. He then went to Nanking as a member of the Kiangsi delegation to the assembly that elected Sun Yat-sen provisional president of the republic.

In 1912 Lin Sen was elected to the Senate at Peking, and he soon became its chairman. By early 1913 Yuan Shih-k'ai had begun to take action against the newly organized Kuomintang, and Lin Sen, realizing that the revolutionaries could not remain in Peking for long, secured a passport for travel abroad. After the collapse of the so-called second revolution, Yuan dissolved the Parliament in November 1913 and declared the Kuomintang an illegal organization. Because he possessed a passport, Lin Sen experienced no difficulty in leaving Peking in December and taking a ship to Japan on the first leg of a trip to the United States. In Japan he called on Sun Yat-sen, who was reorganizing the Kuomintang as the Chung-hua ko-ming-tang, and signed a pledge of personal obedience to him. When Sun learned of Lin's destination, he gave Lin a copy of the code he planned to use for future communications to take with him to the United States.

Lin then went to Hawaii, where he toured the islands for several months. When Feng Tzu-yu (q.v.) stopped in Honolulu on his way to the United States to assume direction of party affairs, he met with Lin and asked him to come to San Francisco. About two months later, Lin left Hawaii to join Feng. Before leaving, he recommended that his Kuomintang associates in Hawaii invite Wu T'ieh-ch'eng to aid them in publishing their party newspaper. By the time Lin arrived in San Francisco, Feng Tzu-yu had become acting chairman of the American branch of the Kuomintang, registered in the United States as the Chinese Nationalist league. Lin became acting vice chairman, and at the end of 1914 he was elected chairman, with Feng as vice chairman.

One of Lin Sen's major achievements in the United States was raising funds to finance the campaigns against Yuan Shih-k'ai in China. As chairman of the American Kuomintang's fund-raising organ, he toured the major cities of the United States and also went to Cuba. By the time of Yuan Shih-k'ai's death in June 1916, more than a million Japanese yen had been sent to Sun Yat-sen in Tokyo. Lin also initiated a program to train pilots for a Chinese air force. The first group of students selected for this program included Chan Hing-wan (Ch'en Ch'ing-yun) and Huang Kuang-jui (qq.v.).

Lin Sen returned to China in 1916 and went to Peking, where the Parliament was reconvened.

In 1917 the issue of China's participation in the First World War caused a parliamentary crisis, and Tuan Ch'i-jui (q.v.), the premier, dissolved the Parliament. This action resulted in the so-called constitution protection movement. A rump parliament, with Lin Sen as the speaker of its senate, convened at Canton and established a military government, with Sun Yat-sen as its commander in chief. Lin Sen remained in Canton until March 1919, by which time the government had been reorganized (*see* T'ang Chi-yao; Lu Jung-t'ing) and Sun Yat-sen had resigned from office and had gone to Shanghai. Lin then went to Shanghai with Wu T'ing-fang (q.v.). He returned to Canton with Sun Yat-sen in 1921. When the rump parliament elected Sun president extraordinary, Lin, as speaker of the senate, presented Sun with the election certificate and seal of office at the inauguration ceremony on 5 May 1921.

After Ch'en Chiung-ming (q.v.) took control of Canton on 16 June 1922, Sun Yat-sen went to Shanghai once again. Hsü Ch'ung-chih (q.v.) led his East Route Anti-Rebel Army into Fukien and captured Foochow in October. Lin Sen then became governor of Fukien, assuming office on 10 November. After Sun Yat-sen returned to Canton and resumed control of the southern government early in 1923, Lin Sen was ordered to Canton to assume charge of the construction of a monument to the 72 martyrs of the 1911 uprising at Huang-hua-kang. In July, he became minister of construction. Sun Yat-sen was proceeding with plans to reorganize the Kuomintang, and Lin Sen became a member of the nine-member provisional executive committee when it was established on 25 October. At the First National Congress of the Kuomintang, which was convened in January 1924, Lin Sen was one of twenty-four men elected to full membership on the Central Executive Committee. He also became the director of the overseas department in the central party headquarters.

After the death of Sun Yat-sen in March 1925 and the establishment of the National Government at Canton in July 1925, Lin Sen was elected to the 16-member State Council in the new government. At this time, Lin was in Peking, where he was closely associated with Tsou Lu (q.v.) in directing party activities in north China. In November, ten anti-Communist members of the Central Executive Committee, including Lin, held a meeting in the Western Hills near Peking. The Second National Congress of the Kuomintang, which met in January 1926, adopted a resolution calling for disciplinary action against the Western Hills group and threatening to dismiss its members from the party if they continued to work against the Kuomintang-Communist alliance. The Western Hills leaders convened an opposition second congress at Shanghai in April and elected an opposition central executive committee headed by Lin Sen. The situation was complicated by the 1927 split between the left-wing faction of the party led by Wang Ching-wei at Wuhan and the faction led by Chiang Kai-shek at Nanking. In September 1927 party unity was restored with the formation of a special committee composed of members of the Wuhan, Nanking, and Shanghai (Western Hills) factions. Lin Sen was the chief representative of the Shanghai faction on this committee. By this time, he and Teng Tse-ju (q.v.) had been appointed to supervise the construction of the memorial to Sun Yat-sen at Nanking.

When the National Government at Nanking was reorganized in October 1928 and the five-yuan system was initiated, Lin Sen became a member of the new State Council and vice president of the Legislative Yuan, which was headed by Hu Han-min (q.v.). By this time, he also had become a member of the Central Supervisory Committee of the Kuomintang. In 1930 he became a member of the committee established to compile and edit Kuomintang historical materials. That winter, he embarked on a tour of the Philippines, Australia, the United States, Europe, and Southeast Asia to inspect overseas branches of the Kuomintang and to solicit funds for the construction of a central party headquarters. On 28 February 1931 Chiang Kai-shek placed Hu Han-min under arrest and appointed the absent Lin president of the Legislative Yuan, with Shao Yuan-ch'ung (q.v.) as vice president. On 30 April, Lin joined with three other members of the Kuomintang Central Supervisory Committee—Hsiao Fo-ch'eng, Ku Ying-fen (qq.v.), and Teng Tse-ju—in proposing the impeachment of Chiang Kai-shek. This proposal resulted in the establishment of an opposition government at Canton. In addition to the four signers of the impeachment statement, supporters of the new regime included Ch'en Chi-t'ang, Wang Ching-wei, Sun Fo, Eugene Ch'en, and T'ang Shao-yi (qq.v.). Impending civil war was averted by the Mukden Incident of 18 September 1931, for the Japanese invasion restored unity to the Kuomintang. Lin Sen returned to Nanking in October from his trip abroad. In the governmental reorganization that took place soon after his arrival, he was elected Chairman of the National Government, a post he held until his death in 1943. Although he was the titular chief of state, he had few practical responsibilities and little power.

On 10 May 1943, while driving from his office in the wartime capital of Chungking to his residence, Lin had an automobile accident. Although shaken severely in the collision, he went to the government headquarters on 12 May to greet the new Norwegian minister to China. He suffered a stroke that day, and he died in Chungking on 1 August 1943. The National Government later honored him by changing the name of Minhou hsien to Lin-sen hsien.

The political scientist Ch'ien Tuan-sheng (q.v.) aptly summarized Lin Sen's later career: "Lin Sen was politically insignificant, but it is no exaggeration to say that seldom has a head of state in Republican China been so honored and loved by his countrymen. Physically he was of a dignified and stately demeanor. Politically he had been a veteran of the Kuomintang and active in parliamentary life. He had simple tastes, no personal ambitions, and practiced no nepotism, a thing from which Chinese politicians in power are seldom immune. He observed not only the letter of the law but its spirit as well. He never tried to assert the powers that were denied to him by the Organic Law of December 1931. But he was not passive. He had truly national interests at heart, and he was never hesitant to argue for them at the party's Political Council of which he was a member. Above all, he worked for national unity before the war began and for victory after it had come. He was a truly good president. If his benign influence was not more widely and deeply felt, it was only because his wise counsel was not as seriously sought as it should have been."

Lin Shu 林 紓
T. Ch'in-nan 琴 南
H. Wei-lu, Leng-hung-
   sheng 畏 盧, 冷 紅 生

Lin Shu (8 November 1852–9 October 1924), the first major Chinese translator of Western fiction and one of the last important prose writers in the Chinese classical style. He also was known for his outspoken opposition to the new literary movements of the May Fourth period.

Minhsien, Fukien, was the birthplace of Lin Shu. He came from a farming family which had become so impoverished that it often had to go without food for five or six days a month. By the time he was eight, the nine members of his family depended for support on the needlework done by Lin's mother and older sister. His mother, who came from a scholar-gentry family, soon discovered his unusual propensity for learning. An uncle finally obtained employment, and the small monthly allotment he sent enabled Lin to attend the nearby village school. When Lin was ten, his father obtained a position as private secretary to an official in Taiwan, and the family finances improved. Five years later, Lin joined his father in Taiwan, where, about 1864, he married a girl from Minhsien. His father died in 1870, and his father-in-law assumed part of the cost of his education.

After spending a brief period in Foochow at the Chih-yang Academy, Lin gave up his studies in 1872 and began to teach. By this time, he had contracted tuberculosis, and, although he eventually regained his health, he often was ill during the next eight years. In 1879, at the age of 27, he finally passed the examinations for the sheng-yuan degree. He improved his literary style by studying in the family library of a wealthy acquaintance, Li Tsung-yen, and passed the provincial examinations for the chü-jen degree in 1882. One of the other successful candidates at this examination was Cheng Hsiao-hsü (q.v.), who later became the prime minister of Manchoukuo; he and Lin became close friends. The chief examiner was Pao-t'ing (ECCP, II, 611–12), a Manchu nobleman known as a poet and reformer, whose son, Shou-fu, also became a friend of Lin.

After obtaining the chü-jen degree, Lin had no further success in the civil service examinations. Between 1883 and 1898 he failed the metropolitan examination in Peking seven times. These were years of personal sorrow for Lin Shu. In 1895, on returning home after his sixth attempt to pass the examinations, he found his mother gravely ill, and she died in December. His wife died of tuberculosis in 1897; his eldest daughter and his second son succumbed to the same disease in the next two years. To distract Lin from his grief, his friend Wang Tzu-jen, who had studied in France, suggested that they translate *La Dame aux camélias* by Alexandre Dumas *fils* into Chinese. Wang translated the work into vernacular Chinese, and Lin, who knew no French, then rendered it into classical Chinese. The resulting work, *Pa-li ch'a-hua-nü i-shih*, was published by Lin's friend Wang K'ang-nien (1860–1911; T. Jang-ch'ing). Thousands of copies were sold, and the story became very popular in literary circles.

By the spring of 1898 the reform movement led by K'ang Yu-wei (q.v.) and his associates was gaining strength in response to the German seizure of Kiaochow in Shantung and the appearance of Russian ships at Port Arthur. Although he did not join K'ang Yu-wei's group, Lin Shu, who was in Peking to take the metropolitan examinations for the seventh time, joined with Shou-fu and other friends in submitting a memorial to the emperor protesting the German invasion and suggesting political, financial, and military reforms. The memorial, which never reached the emperor, was rejected by court officials. Soon afterwards, Lin returned to Fukien, where he continued to advocate reforms, expressing his ideas in a series of 32 poems written in a semi-vernacular style. These poems proposed such reforms as education for women, the abolition of foot-binding, reduction of taxes, and the betterment of social conditions.

Near the end of 1898 Lin Shu went to Hangchow, where he taught school for three years. Much of his leisure time was spent in reading the Chinese classics and in observing the beautiful scenery for which Hangchow is famous and which was to provide motifs for his landscape paintings of later years. Some of his pai-hua [vernacular] poems of this period appeared in the *Hang-chou pai-hua pao* [Hangchow vernacular magazine].

Lin Shu went to Peking in 1901 to teach Chinese literature at the Wu-ch'eng Middle School. About this time, with the help of a collaborator named Wei Yi, he translated Harriet Beecher Stowe's *Uncle Tom's Cabin* into Chinese as *Hei-nu yü-t'ien lu*. Lin soon met Wu Ju-lun (ECCP, II, 870–72), who also was one of the last masters of the T'ung-ch'eng school of prose writing. When Wu became head of the faculty of Imperial University (later Peking University) in 1902, Lin joined the university's translation bureau, headed by Yen Fu (q.v.). About 1905 he also joined the faculty as a teacher of Chinese literature, and in 1909 he became dean of the school of letters.

Although he was by no means an advocate of the republican revolution of 1911, Lin Shu apparently had some sympathy for the young revolutionaries, as indicated by his 1914 novel, *Chin-ling ch'iu* [autumn in Nanking] and some of his stories. Before long, however, he found cause to resent the new order, particularly as it affected Peking University. Professors who were adherents of the T'ung-ch'eng school of writing, of which Lin Shu was considered to be a leader, gradually were replaced by such scholars as Chang Ping-lin (q.v.), who were interested in such fields as etymological studies and textual criticism. In 1913 Lin was forced to resign from the university.

In 1915 Lin Shu and Yao Yung-kai, a former colleague at Peking University and one of the leading literary men of the T'ung-ch'eng group, went to teach at the Cheng-chih Middle School on the invitation of Hsü Shu-cheng (q.v.), a close associate of Tuan Ch'i-jui (q.v.), who greatly admired Lin Shu. Lin then directed an institute which offered correspondence courses in Chinese literature and which boasted an enrollment of some 2,000 students from China and Southeast Asia.

In his later years, Lin Shu's influence and popularity declined rapidly as a result of the intellectual ferment that culminated in the May Fourth Movement of 1919. His pro-Manchu political sentiments and his friendship with the pro-Japanese Hsü Shu-cheng did little to enhance his reputation among Chinese youth. Moreover, Lin opposed the general use of pai-hua as a literary medium even though he had used it occasionally, and the pai-hua movement challenged his deepest literary convictions as well as lessening his prestige as a writer.

Lin Shu soon became one of the most outspoken critics of the new literary movements. In the spring of 1919 he wrote several articles attacking them and ridiculed Ch'en Tu-hsiu, Hu Shih (qq.v.), and others in short allegorical tales. On 18 March he wrote an open letter to Ts'ai Yuan-p'ei (q.v.), the chancellor of Peking University, in which he criticized the young intellectual leaders, many of whom taught at the university, for discarding classical literature and language. He accused them of seeking to destroy the traditional principles of Confucianism, maintaining that the deviation from traditional ethics and literature would not save China from decay and foreign domination, but would lead to disaster. Although Lin's 1919 writings on this subject and the rebuttals of Ts'ai Yuan-p'ei and others provoked considerable debate, his influence continued to decline. He soon withdrew to his residence in Peking, where he devoted his attention to translating and painting until his death on 9 October 1924, at the age of 72.

Lin Shu's personal life was characterized by his obstinate struggle to overcome physical frailty. In the last decade of his life, he was able to support his family on the income derived from the sale of his copyrights and his paintings. This income was the subject of jokes among his friends, who referred to his study as tsao-pi ch'ang, or the money factory. Little is known about Lin's family. He was survived by his second wife and by several children. His eldest son by his first wife became a magistrate in Hopei.

Lin's major work as a translator began in 1904 when, with the aid of collaborators, he translated Aesop's Fables (*I-so yü-yen*), H. Rider Haggard's *Joan Haste* (*Chia-yin hsiao-chuan*) and *Cleopatra* (*Ai-chi chin-t'a p'ou-shih chi*), and Charles Lamb's *Tales from Shakespeare* (*Yin pien yen yü*). The following year, he translated Sir Walter Scott's *Ivanhoe* (*Sa-k'o-hsün chieh-hou ying-hsiung lüeh*), Daniel Defoe's *Robinson Crusoe* (*Lu-pin-sun p'iao-liu chi*), Haggard's *Allan Quatermain* (*Fei-chou yen shui ch'ou-ch'eng lu*), and other adventure stories. The year 1906 saw the appearance of Swift's *Gulliver's Travels* (*Hai-wai hsien-ch'ü lu*), Washing-

ton Irving's *Tales of a Traveller* (*Lü-hsing shu-i*), A. Conan Doyle's *Micah Clarke* (*Chin-feng t'ieh-yü lu*), and four stories by Haggard. The following year, Lin translated about a dozen works, including Irving's *Alhambra* (*Ta-shih ku-kung yü tsai*) and part of *The Sketch Book* (*Fu-chang lu*), Scott's *The Talisman* (*Shih-tzu-chün ying-hsiung chi*) and *The Betrothed* (*Chien ti yüan-yang*), and Charles Dickens' *Nicholas Nickleby* (*Hua-chi wai-chih*). In 1908 he produced about 20 translations, among which were Dumas' *Le Chevalier de la Maison-Rouge* (*Yü-lou-hua-chieh ch'ien-hou-pien*), Robert Louis Stevenson's *The New Arabian Nights* (*Hsin t'ien-fang yeh-t'an*), and Dickens' *Oliver Twist* (*Tsei-shih*), *David Copperfield* (*K'uai-jou yü-sheng ch'ien-hou-pien*), and *Dombey and Son* (*Ping-hsüeh yin-yüan*).

Lin continued to produce important translations, and in 1914 he completed Chinese versions of several novels, including Dumas' *Comtesse de Charney* (*Hsieh-lien chün-chu chuan*), and some of Honoré de Balzac's short stories, which appeared in the *Hsiao-shuo yüeh-pao* [short story magazine]. Lin's 1916 translations included prose versions of four of Shakespeare's plays: *Richard II* (*Lei-ch'a-te chi*), *Henry IV* (*Heng-li ti-ssu chi*), *Henry VI* (*Heng-li ti-liu i-shih*), and *Julius Caesar* (*K'ai-sa i-shih*). At about this time, Lin also introduced his readers to the stories of Homer's *Iliad* and *Odyssey*. It is interesting to note that in 1917–19, before and during the rise of humanism in Chinese literature, Lin devoted his attention to Leo Tolstoy and translated (from their English versions) *The Death of Ivan Ilyitch* (*Jen-kuei kuan-t'ou*), *Russian Proprietor and Other Stories* (*She-hui sheng-ying lu*), *Childhood, Boyhood and Youth* (*Hsien-shen shuo-fa*), *The Kreutzer Sonata*, and *Family Happiness* (*Hen lü ch'ing ssu*).

Lin Shu was probably the most prolific Chinese translator in the history of China. At the time of his death he had rendered into Chinese some 180 works (published in about 281 volumes). In addition, more than 15 translations of short stories were published after his death, and some 17 translations of novels remained in manuscript form. In contrast to this facility in translating, he sometimes took several months to write a brief article.

Because he was unable to read any language but his own, Lin was forced to rely on collaborators. Although some—Wang Tzu-jen, Wei

Yi, Wang Ch'ing-t'ung, Wang Ch'ing-chi, Li Shih-chung, and two sons of Yen Fu—had literary talent, most of Lin's collaborators had insufficient training in literature. He was also dependent upon his collaborators for the selection of the works to be translated, and popular interest seems to have been the major consideration governing this selection. As a result, almost 100 of Lin's translations were of works by authors of little literary consequence, and about 30 more were adventure or detective stories by H. Rider Haggard or Arthur Conan Doyle, the latter's famous sleuth, Sherlock Holmes, being introduced to Chinese readers through Lin's version of *A Study in Scarlet* (*Hsieh-lo-k'o ch'i-an k'ai-ch'ang*). Nevertheless, Lin and his collaborators produced translations of some 40 important works, including in addition to those noted previously, Dickens' *The Old Curiosity Shop* (*Hsiao-nü Nai-erh chuan*), Goldsmith's *The Vicar of Wakefield* (*Shuang-yüan lü*), Hugo's *Quatre-vingt-treize* (*Shuang-hsiung i-ssu lu*), Montesquieu's *Lettres Persanes* (*Yü yen chüeh wei*), Bernardin de St. Pierre's *Paul et Virginie* (*Li hen t'ien*), Cervantes' *Don Quixote* (*Mo-hsia chuan*), Ibsen's *Ghosts* (*Mei nieh*), J. R. Wyss' *The Swiss Family Robinson* (*Ch'an-ch'ao chi ch'u, hsü pien*), tales from Edmund Spenser's *Faerie Queene* (*Huang-t'ang yen*), and a few other works by such authors as Henry Fielding and H. G. Wells.

Lin's prefaces and comments reflected the reaction of a traditional Chinese moralist and man of letters to Western literature. He frequently justified the selection for translation of love stories or even naturalistic novels by treating these as "cautionary tales" or "exemplary stories." An example is the Chinese title he gave to his translation of *The Old Curiosity Shop*, which he rendered as *Hsiao-nü Nai-erh chuan*, or "The Story of the Filial Girl Nell." In other instances, Lin regarded the stories he translated as examples for social, political, and educational reform or as works to inspire patriotism and the spirit of adventure.

Although Lin's total ignorance of foreign languages and his inability to check the accuracy or completeness of his collaborators' versions resulted in errors, distortions, and omissions in his translations, he possessed a mastery of the classical language and an ability to portray in rich and subtle language the mood and the setting of his characters which resulted in a

paradoxical situation: the alterations and omissions often had the effect of improving the text for Chinese readers, who were able to feel that they were reading an elegant classical Chinese tale which recounted the strange but interesting lives of the people of the West. In many cases, Lin's versions of Western literary works may be considered imaginative adaptations rather than closely worked translations.

The principal significance of Lin Shu as a translator was that he opened the eyes of Chinese readers to the achievements of Western literature and increased Chinese understanding of Western customs and society. He was the first Chinese of substantial literary prestige to attach importance to the literary merits of Western writers, deeming Charles Dickens, for example, an equal of the first-rank Chinese novelists of the past, and even of the traditional literary idol Ssu-ma Ch'ien. Lin was also the first Chinese writer to use the Chinese literary language as a medium for novels, and the influence of his writings brought about some changes in the technique of Chinese story-telling. Lin's translations were highly influential among the younger generation of China's writers, who were attracted to them despite their allegiance to the new vernacular language movement. Kuo Mo-jo wept over Haggard's *Joan Haste*, the first Western novel he had ever read, and admitted publicly that the single most significant influence on his writing was the romanticism of Walter Scott. Liu Fu (q.v.) was led by Lin's version of *La Dame aux camélias* to produce a stage version, a theatrical innovation which reinforced the romantic tendencies of his generation. And Lao She (Shu Ch'ing-ch'un, q.v.) derived much of his understanding of humor from Lin's translations of Dickens.

In 1914 a series of 50 of Lin's translations was published in 97 volumes by the Commercial Press as *Lin-i hsiao-shuo ts'ung-shu*; and several of his other translations appeared in three series of the *Shuo-pu ts'ung-shu* (1914–16), also published by the Commercial Press. In addition to his translations, Lin wrote eight novels, three old-style operas, six collections of short stories, three collections of articles and anecdotes, and three collections of poetry, one of which, the *Wei-lu shih-ts'un*, appeared in 1923. Collections of Lin's essays were published in 1910, 1916, and 1924 by the Commercial

Press as *Wei-lu wen-chi*, *Wei-lu hsü-chi*, and *Wei-lu san-chi*. More than ten textbooks on literature and ethics were either written or edited by him. Lin also maintained an active interest in painting: a volume of his essays on this subject, entitled *Ch'un-chüeh-chai lun-hua*, and a two-volume collection of photographic reproductions of his landscapes, *Wei-lu i-chi*, were published by the Commercial Press in 1935 and 1934, respectively.

Lin Wen-ch'ing 林文慶
West. Lim Boon Keng

Lin Wen-ch'ing (5 September 1869–1 January 1957), known as Lim Boon Keng, a successful doctor, entrepreneur, and public figure in Singapore who abandoned his lucrative career to serve as president of Amoy University from 1921 to 1937.

Born in Singapore to a family of Fukien ancestry, Lim Boon Keng displayed such academic brilliance as a youth that he became the first Chinese to win the Queen's Scholarship, which was awarded him at his graduation from secondary school in 1887. The scholarship provided a course of study at a British university, and Lim elected to study medicine at the University of Edinburgh. In 1891 he received the B.M. and C.M. degrees with first-class honors. After a year's additional study at Cambridge, he returned to Singapore in 1893 and established a medical practice. Lim was an immediate success, not only because of his medical skill but also because of his linguistic versatility. He had mastered Fukienese, Malay, and English, not to mention Cantonese, Swatow, and Tamil, and thus could talk to almost any patient in his native idiom. Lim's success was so pronounced that in 1895, at the age of only 26, he was named to the Legislative Council of Singapore.

In 1896 Lim married Margaret Huang. Her father was Huang Nai-shang, a Christian scholar and one-time civil governor of Fukien province who became an associate of Sun Yat-sen. Lim and Huang became close friends, and Lim appears to have aided his father-in-law in spreading the doctrines of revolution. In 1900 Lim rendered signal service to the anti-Manchu revolutionary movement. When Miyazaki Torazō, a Japanese friend of both Sun Yat-sen and K'ang Yu-wei (q.v.), visited K'ang in Singapore to promote cooperation between him and Sun, a misunderstanding led to his arrest by the local authorities. Sun Yat-sen hurried to Singapore to protest this action, and Lim Boon Keng soon managed to secure the release of Miyazaki. When Sun Yat-sen organized the Singapore branch of the T'ung-meng-hui in 1907, Lim immediately joined the new organization.

Lim Boon Keng was also known as one of the few Singapore-born Chinese who evinced genuine interest in the study and propagation of traditional Chinese culture. He and Song Ong Siong (1869–1941), who subsequently became the first Chinese in Malaya to receive the honor of knighthood, founded the English-language *Straits Chinese Magazine* and the Philomathic Society and established courses of instruction in the traditional Chinese classics. In addition to these activities, Lim took an active part in the founding of Chinese banks in Singapore and the development of Malay rubber production, and he became vice president of the Singapore Chamber of Commerce. For a time, he also served as a lecturer at the King Edward VII College of Medicine in Singapore. The British later recognized his achievements by creating him a member of the Order of the British Empire.

After the outbreak of the Wuchang revolt on 10 October 1911, Sun Yat-sen returned to China from Europe by way of Singapore. Sun later invited Lim to Nanking and appointed him chief of the department of health in the provisional republican government established early in 1912. When the government was moved to Peking after Sun's resignation as provisional president, Lim returned to Singapore, where he resumed his medical and educational activities.

In 1921 the entrepreneur Tan Kah Kee (Ch'en Chia-keng, q.v.) founded Amoy University in Fukien with an initial contribution of SS$1 million, and later in April he offered Lim Boon Keng the presidency of Amoy. Lim did not hesitate in sacrificing his lucrative medical practice to accept Tan's offer, for the post afforded him the opportunity to fulfill his lifelong ambition to promote good education for Fukienese youths living in both China and Southeast Asia. Lim was given the freedom to administer Amoy University as he chose, and he generally was considered to be an intelligent and progressive president. When Amoy University came under National Government jurisdiction in 1937, he resigned from office.

In spite of his many duties at Amoy, Lim did not abandon his other interests. He worked to foster the study of Confucian ethics and the activities of the Chinese Medical Association. In 1929 he completed an English translation of the poem *Li sao* by Ch'ü Yüan (c.338–288 B. C.) which he published as *The Li Sao, an Elegy on Encountering Sorrows*, with prefaces by H. A. Giles and Rabindranath Tagore. Although less accurate than the James Legge rendering of 1895 and equally unliterary, Lim's edition is distinguished because of the copiousness and usefulness of its annotations, especially the painstaking identification of flora and fauna. In 1930 Lim became the chief editor of the *Chinese Nation*, an English-language weekly published in Shanghai. In the next few years, he wrote many articles for this paper and several books, including *The Chinese Crisis from Within, Tragedies of Chinese Life*, and *The New China*. The University of Hong Kong awarded him an honorary LL.D. in recognition of his achievements in education and literature.

Soon after Lim Boon Keng's retirement in 1937, the Sino-Japanese war began. Because he was nearly 70, Lim chose to live quietly in Singapore during the war. He remained there during the Japanese occupation and was forced to serve as a member of the local "peace maintenance committee." However, he took no active part in committee operations, and the British authorities exonerated him from all blame. He died in Singapore in January 1957, at the age of 87.

Lim Boon Keng had five sons and one daughter. His eldest son was Robert K. S. Lim (Lin K'o-sheng, q.v.). His second son, Francis Lim, became a mechanical engineer, and his third son, Walter Lim, became a banker in Singapore. Lim Boon Keng was the brother-in-law of Wu Lien-te (q.v.), who married Ruth Huang.

Lin Yü-t'ang 　林 語 堂
Orig. Lin Yü-t'ang 　林 玉 堂

Lin Yü-t'ang (1895–), scholar, writer, and journalist. In the 1930's he was a leader of the movements to use social satire and to adapt Western newspaper prose to Chinese journalism. Beginning with the publication in 1935 of *My Country and My People*, he established an international reputation as a writer of popular books in English about China.

A native of Lunch'i, Changchow, in Amoy, Lin Yü-t'ang was a third-generation Christian and the son of a Chinese Presbyterian minister. He was brought up in a pleasant but strictly religious family atmosphere and at the age of 13 was sent to the Changchow Middle School. It was decided that he should enter the ministry, and, as a first step, he was sent from middle school to the Protestant College of Amoy. In 1911 he entered St. John's University in Shanghai. During his first 18 months at the university he studied at its institute of theology, but he became increasingly disinterested in his studies and finally decided to renounce Christianity. He was graduated from St. John's with a second-class degree, a precocious command of English, and a proportionately weaker foundation of classical Chinese. After leaving St. John's in 1916 he became professor of English at Tsinghua University and married Liao Tsuifeng.

In 1919 Lin decided to go to the United States for further study. He went to Cambridge, Massachusetts, where he studied at Harvard for one year and received the M.A. degree *in absentia* in 1922. In 1920 he went to France and worked for the French YMCA until 1921, when he went to Germany and attended the University of Jena for one term. At the beginning of the new academic year, he enrolled at Leipzig University, where he remained until 1923 and received his Ph.D. His thesis was entitled "Altchinesiche Lautlehre" [old Chinese phonetics].

After returning to China in 1923, Lin Yü-t'ang became a professor in the English department of Peking University; he also taught at Peking Normal University. He soon became associated with liberal intellectuals and in 1926 he and some 50 other professors were blacklisted by the authorities and ordered to leave Peking. During his last six months in Peking, Lin served as head of the English department of the National Normal University for Women.

Lin went to Amoy, where he became dean of the college of arts and letters in the university.

In the spring of 1927 he became secretary to the ministry of foreign affairs in the Wuhan government. When the new National Government was established at Nanking in 1928, Lin retired from politics. For a time, he helped edit an English-language magazine, *The People's Tribune*, which set forth the views of Wang Ching-wei and his followers. Lin then went to teach English in Soochow at Tung Wu University and at the Shanghai College of Law. He also became a director of the K'ai-ming Bookstore and, consequently, the editor of several English-language manuals. In 1930 he assumed direction of the foreign-language section of the Academia Sinica and took charge of philological research. It was probably during this period that he conceived of a tonal spelling system for Chinese, an idea subsequently developed by Y. R. Chao (Chao Yuen-ren, q.v.) into *Gwoyeu Romatzyh* [national romanization]. He also served as secretary to the Kuomintang veteran Wu Chih-hui. From 1924 to 1931 Lin was a regular contributor to the literary weekly *Yü-ssu* [fragments], edited by Lu Hsün and his brother Chou Tso-jen.

In 1932 Lin Yü-t'ang founded the *Lun-yü pan-yüeh-k'an* [analects fortnightly], which made his reputation in China. The magazine specialized in humor and satire and enjoyed considerable success, although Lin was attacked by rightists for mocking national sentiment and by leftists for trying to dull national conscience with ribaldry. Lin declared that the function of the magazine was to criticize, and he continued to publish it until 1935. During that period, his articles from the *Lun-yü pan-yüeh-k'an* appeared in English in the *China Critic*, a Shanghai weekly published by a group of Chinese intellectuals including Chang Hsin-hai, Quentin Pan, Hu Shih, and D. K. Lieu.

In the spring of 1934 Lin started his second magazine, *Jen-chien-shih hsiao-p'in-wen pan-yueh-k'an* [this human world], a semi-monthly magazine devoted to short essays. One aim of this publication was to develop a simple prose style for popular needs. In 1934 Lin launched the *Yü-chou feng* [cosmic wind], a fortnightly publication specializing in the American digest type of article. It was attacked by leftist intellectuals in the *Shun Pao* [Shanghai news daily] literary supplement and thereby received some profitable publicity. It continued publication until the end of 1935, and its contributors included Kuo Mo-jo, Lao She, and Chou Tso-jen.

In 1935 Lin became associated with *T'ien Hsia Monthly*, an English-language magazine published by the Sun Yat-sen Institute for the Advancement of Culture and Learning. This journal earned a high reputation for its quality and content, but it was forced to cease publication when the Sino-Japanese war broke out. Lin's first book in English, *My Country and My People*, was published in New York in 1935 and was an instant success in the West. It was translated into French in 1937, into Chinese in 1938, and into German in 1946.

Lin Yü-t'ang left China in 1936 and arrived with his family in New York to find himself in great demand as a writer. His second book, *The Importance of Living*, appeared in 1937. It was translated into French in 1948 and into German in 1955. In 1939 Lin published *The Birth of a New China*, a personal account of the Sino-Japanese war, and *Moment in Peking*, a novel of contemporary life which has affinities with the *Hung Lou Meng* tradition and is thought by critics to be one of his better books.

Lin left the United States in 1940 to return to China, but became ill in Hong Kong and had to return to the United States. He finally arrived in China in 1943. He lectured on Chinese culture at Central University and visited Kweilin, Hengyang, Changsha, Shaokuan, and Kunming. He became involved in a literary dispute with the writer Ts'ao Chü-jen, who was vigorously supported by the magazines *T'ai-pai* and *Mang-chung*. This dispute typified the uneasy relationship which developed between Lin and Chinese literary-academic circles in wartime China and which resulted in his return to the United States.

In the United States, Lin produced many English translations of Chinese works and wrote novels, essays, plays, and travel books. His novels include *A Leaf in the Storm* (1942), a novel of war-torn China; *Chinatown Family* (1948); *The Vermilion Gate* (1953); *Lady Wu* (1957); and *The Red Peony* (1961). Among his collections of essays are *Looking Beyond* (1955); *The Secret Name* (1958), studies in Communism; and *The Pleasures of a Non-Conformist* (1962). His tragicomedy, *Confucius Saw Nancy* was published in 1937. A study of the capital of Yuan, Ming, and Ch'ing China, *Imperial Peking*, appeared in 1961. Lin's translations constitute a large part of his literary production and are among his best achievements. Many of them appeared in the *Tien Hsia Monthly* and other Shanghai publications in the 1930's. His masterpiece of translation is *Six Chapters of a Floating Life*, a beautiful English rendering of the *Fu-sheng liu-chi* of Shen Fu (ECCP, II, 641–42), which appeared in 1935 in the *Tien Hsia Monthly*. In 1947 Lin edited and annotated a translation of Mao Tse-tung's *New Democracy* which appeared under the title *"Democracy," a Digest Bible of Chinese Communism*. In 1951 he published *Widow, Nun, and Courtesan*, a translation of three Chinese stories—Lao Hsiang's "Widow Chuan," Liu O's "A Nun of Taishan," and his own "Miss Tu." He published a collection of earlier translations in 1960 as *The Importance of Understanding: Translations from the Chinese*. Lin also compiled several "wisdom" books: *The Wisdom of China and India* (1942); *The Wisdom of Laotze* (1948); and *On the Wisdom of America* (1950). In 1967 he published *The Chinese Theory of Art*.

Lin accepted an invitation in 1954 to become chancellor of the new Nanyang University in Singapore, for which he recruited his own academic staff. The venture was not a success, and Lin became involved in a dispute with the authorities over policy and finance. He resigned with severance pay at the end of six months and returned to the United States by way of Europe. In New York, Lin joined the Madison Avenue Presbyterian Church, where his wife was active in church work, in December 1957. A year later he publicly announced his reconversion to Christianity, and in 1959 he published his testament entitled *From Pagan to Christian*.

In his earlier Chinese writings, Lin Yü-t'ang contributed to the development of new journalistic style. His witty use of English and droll exposition of Confucian philosophy blended with Laotzian passivity, endeared him to many Western readers. Lin's first two books remained the definitive interpretations of Chinese, society for more than a decade in the West. Although he earned a reputation as an Eastern philosopher abroad, Lin was never regarded as an original thinker in Chinese literary circles.

Lin Yü-t'ang and his wife had three daughters Ju-ssu (Adet), born in 1923; T'ai-i (Anor), born in 1926; and Hsiang-ju (Meimei). Using the names Adet and Anor Lin, the elder sisters wrote *Our Family* in 1939. In 1940 they produced a translation entitled *Girl Rebel, the Autobiography of a Woman Soldier*. And in 1941, together with Meimei Lin, they wrote *Dawn Over Chungking*. Adet Lin also published *The Milky Way, and Other Chinese Folk Tales*.

Liu Chan-en   劉湛恩
West. Herman C. E. Liu

Liu Chan-en (1896–7 April 1938), known as Herman Liu, prominent Baptist layman, educator, and civic leader in Shanghai. He served as educational secretary of the national committee of the YMCA in China from 1922 to 1928 and as president of the University of Shanghai from 1928 until his assassination in 1938.

Hanyang, where his parents were active members of the Northern Baptist mission, was the birthplace of Herman Liu. He received his primary and secondary education in mission schools, including the William Nast Academy at Kiukiang, and then entered Soochow University. After graduation in 1918, he went to the United States, where he received an M.A. from the University of Chicago and a Ph.D. from Teachers College, Columbia University. In 1922 he attended the Washington Conference, serving as secretary to the Chinese educational commission and representing the Chinese student organizations in the United States.

After returning to China in 1922, Herman Liu, then 26, was appointed educational secretary to the national committee of the YMCA. During the six years he held that post, he traveled extensively in China, giving particular attention to problems of vocational guidance. His special interest in this field led to his appointment as research director for the China Vocational Education Association, in which he was associated with China's foremost advocate of vocational education, Huang Yen-p'ei (q. v.). Herman Liu also served briefly as professor of education at both Ta-hsia (Great China) and Kuanghua universities in Shanghai. His professional writing during that period included pamphlets and books on citizenship training, vocational guidance, coeducation, and non-verbal tests for use in China. He was chief delegate from China to the world YMCA conference held at Helsingfors, Finland, in 1926. Following the conference, he traveled through Europe, observing educational problems and techniques.

In March 1928 Herman Liu was named president of the University of Shanghai, formerly Shanghai Baptist College. He assumed that position at a critical stage in China's struggle for political unification and in the adjustment of Christian education to the educational measures and controls instituted by the National Government. The requirements for registration with the government proved to be a complex issue not only in China but also within the supporting constituency of the university in the United States. In 1929 Liu traveled widely in the United States to explain to American supporters of the university that it had not compromised its principles by complying with the national registration requirements, which gave official recognition to Christian schools but which placed restrictions on the teaching of religion. That the University of Shanghai maintained good relations both with the National Government of China and with its American constituency during a period fraught with misunderstanding and ill will was attributed largely to Liu's tactful adminstration. The problems of administration were further complicated in 1931 and 1932 when Japanese attacks in Manchuria and at Shanghai led to strikes and disorder in the universities as patriotic students pressed their demands for war against Japan. During the ten years of Liu's administration, the University of Shanghai developed impressively in every respect— campus and buildings, staff, enrollment, and academic reputation. When the Sino-Japanese war broke out in 1937, Liu moved the university to the International Settlement in an attempt to ensure its uninterrupted operation.

During these years, Liu made several trips abroad. In 1929, in addition to his travels in the United States, he was the delegate from China to the World Education Conference in Geneva, after which he visited educational leaders throughout Europe. In 1933 Liu went to the United States and Canada. First, as a delegate and founding member of the Chinese Institute of Pacific Relations, he attended its conference at Banff, Canada; then, as a member of a team appointed by the Foreign Missions Conference of North America and led by Stanley Jones, an American missionary to India, he visited major American cities to promote interest in and support for overseas missions.

As one of the leading Baptist laymen in China, Herman Liu was chiefly responsible for the organization, in 1930, of the Chinese Baptist Alliance. In 1936 he inspired a "Forward Movement" in the alliance and played a leading part in organizing a Baptist convention in Kiangsu. Liu also served as a member and sometime acting chairman of the National Christian Council (see Ch'eng Ching-yi), a member of the executive committee of the Council of Higher Education of the Christian Colleges, chairman of the executive committee of the China Christian Education Association, Chairman of the War Relief Committee of the National Christian Council, a member of the International Red Cross, and president of the International Education Association. John E. Baker, chairman of the International Red Cross, described Liu as the "spark plug" of that agency's continuous efforts to raise and distribute funds in China.

When the Sino-Japanese war began in 1937, Herman Liu and three other public-spirited citizens voluntarily organized an "anti-enemy committee" to inform the foreign residents of Shanghai of the Chinese viewpoint regarding Japanese aggression. As a result of this action, Hollington Tong (Tung Hsien-kuang, q.v.), then vice minister of information in charge of international publicity, asked Liu to go to the United States to speak on behalf of the Chinese war effort. A few days later, on the morning of 7 April 1938, Liu was assassinated on a Shanghai street. His assassins were believed to be Japanese agents.

Herman Liu's wife, née Wang Li-ming, was a native of T'aihu, Anhwei, who studied in the United States. Upon returning to China, she became a vigorous supporter of the Women's Christian Temperance Union. After her husband's death she became increasingly critical of the Kuomintang, and in 1949 she attended the Chinese People's Political Consultative Conference as a delegate from the China Democratic League. She later served the Central People's Government as a leader of the China Women's Federation.

Liu Chih 劉峙
T. Ching-fu 經扶
H. T'ien-yueh 天嶽

Liu Chih (1892–), prominent Nationalist military commander. He served as governor of Honan from 1930 to 1935, reorganized troops in Kiangsu, Anhwei, and Honan after the Sian Incident, commanded the Chungking garrison district from 1939 to 1945, and served as field commander for the Hwai-Hai battle in late 1948. In 1952 he joined the National Government in Taiwan.

Born into a peasant family in Kian hsien, Kiangsi, Liu Chih received his early education at private schools in his native village. In the winter of 1905 he went to Japan to study, but he was forced to return to China after participating in a student strike. In 1907–10 he attended the Hunan Army Primary School, and in 1911 he entered the Wuchang Army Primary School. When the revolution began, the school suspended operations and the students were assigned to guard duty in Wuchang.

With the resumption of classes by the various military academies in July 1912, Liu Chih, who had been home to Kian and then had gone to Nanchang, entered the First Army Preparatory School at Chenghochen, near Peking. He and some of his schoolmates organized a secret society in support of the Kuomintang, and in the summer of 1913 they took leaves of absence from school so that they could participate in the so-called second revolution. However, the Peiyang forces of Yuan Shih-k'ai occupied Kiangsi and defeated the revolutionaries before the students reached the province. Liu returned to school, and he was graduated in June 1914. After spending about five months at Hsinminfu with the 39th Brigade of the 20th Division, he entered the Paoting Military Academy as a member of the second class, infantry division.

In May 1916 Liu Chih, having completed his studies, went south to join the headquarters of Ts'en Ch'un-hsuan (q.v.) as a staff officer. Soon afterwards he became a company commander in the 13th Mixed Brigade, commanded by Chu Teh (q.v.), of the 7th Division of the Yunnan Army in Szechwan. In February 1918 he participated in the campaign against Lung Chi-kuang (q.v.) in southern Kwangtung. By January 1920 he had become a battalion commander in the 1st Regiment of the Fourth Army for Reinforcement of Kiangsi. His unit moved in May to Fukien, where Ch'en Chiung-ming (q.v.) was building a base area, and became known as the Kiangsi Army. When Ch'en returned to Kwangtung in August to dislodge the Kwangsi warlords entrenched at Canton, Liu's unit was attached to the Second Army of Hsü Ch'ung-chih (q.v.). The campaign ended with the occupation of Canton on 26 October.

In May 1921, after Sun Yat-sen assumed office as president extraordinary in the new military government at Canton, Ch'en Chiung-ming, who had become governor of Kwangtung, appointed Liu Chih a staff officer, with the rank of major, in the Kwangtung Army headquarters. Liu was promoted to the rank of lieutenant colonel in June and was transferred to the Second Army as a staff officer. He led the vanguard troops of the Second Army into Kiangsi early in 1922. After Ch'en Chiung-ming's forces staged a coup at Canton on 16 June 1922, Liu's men moved back toward Canton, but they were defeated by the Kwangsi forces of Shen Hung-ying. Liu then went to Shanghai. When Hsü Ch'ung-chih became commander in chief of the East Route Anti-Rebel Army, Liu joined his headquarters as a staff officer. He later received command of the guard force.

Liu Chih continued to serve under Hsü Ch'ung-chih until the Whampoa Military Academy was established in 1924. He became an instructor, and then a section chief in the academy's headquarters. In the first eastern expedition against Ch'en Chiung-ming, in January 1925, he commanded the 2nd Battalion of the 1st Training Regiment. After the National Revolutionary Army was organized in the summer of 1925, he served successively as commander of the 1st Regiment, the 20th Division, and the 2nd Division of the First Army, then commanded by Chiang Kai-shek. During the Northern Expedition, Liu served under Ho Ying-ch'in (q.v.) and rose to become field commander of the First Route Army and a member of the Military Affairs Commission. In the military reorganization of January 1928 he became commander of the First Army Group of the First Group Army, which was commanded by Chiang Kai-shek, with Ho Ying-ch'in as chief of staff.

In August 1928, after the successful completion of the Northern Expedition, Liu Chih was appointed commander of the reorganized 1st Division and defense commander of Hsuchow-Haichow. At the Third National Congress of the Kuomintang, held in March 1929, he was elected to the party's Central Executive Committee. When the punitive expedition against the Kwangsi forces in the Wuhan area (*see* Li Tsung-jen) began, Liu assumed command of the Second Route Army and of the First Army of the punitive force. After the Kwangsi armies gave way in April, he became garrison commander of Wuhan and director of the second area for troop disbandment. In September, Chang Fa-k'uei (q.v.) announced his opposition to Chiang Kai-shek. Liu Chih marched to Ichang, Hupeh, to suppress Chang, but Chang moved into Hunan. Soon afterwards, Kuominchün (*see* Feng Yü-hsiang) generals in Honan, Shensi, and Kansu began to move against Chiang Kai-shek, and Liu Chih led the Second Route Army into battle on the Honan plain. In that operation, he served as field commander and as director of the Wuhan field headquarters. The campaign ended in November when the Kuominchün withdrew from Honan. Liu then joined other National Government troops in suppressing the rebellion of T'ang Sheng-chih (q.v.).

In March 1930 Liu Chih was transferred to the post of garrison commander of the Hsuchow-Pengpu sector. When the northern coalition of Feng Yü-hsiang and Yen Hsi-shan (qq. v.) moved against Chiang Kai-shek in May, Liu became commander of the Second Army Group of Nanking's punitive force. He directed operations on the Lunghai and Tientsin-Pukow rail lines, effected the capture of Tsinan, and participated in the final battles on the Peiping-Hankow rail line. On 6 October 1930, Liu was named governor of Honan.

Liu Chih also became director of Chiang Kai-shek's Kaifeng headquarters in January 1931. He cooperated with Chang Hsueh-liang (q.v.) in quashing the rebellion of Shih Yü-san that summer. When the Kaifeng headquarters was abolished late in 1931, Liu became special pacification commissioner of Honan. The importance of Honan in the National Government's defense arrangements was such that Liu

was also named to the State Council. Early in 1932 he helped expel the Communists from the Honan-Hupeh-Anhwei border area. He also campaigned against the Communists in eastern Kiangsi in the spring of 1933.

Late in 1935 Shang Chen (q.v.) succeeded Liu Chih as governor of Honan. Liu became pacification commissioner of both Honan and Anhwei, thus retaining the responsibility for the National Government's military authority in the Central Plains region. After the Sian Incident of December 1936 (*see* Chiang Kai-shek), he was appointed chairman of a commission established to reorganize troops in Kiangsu, Anhwei, and Honan.

When the Sino-Japanese war began in July 1937, Liu became commander in chief of the Second Army Group. In September, when hopes for a negotiated settlement had faded, he was named deputy commanding officer, under Chiang Kai-shek, of the First War Area. As commander in chief of the Chinese Nationalist forces on the north China front, he was responsible for checking the Japanese advance southward along the Peiping-Hankow rail line. Although the Nationalists concentrated more than 100,000 troops in the Shihchiachuang sector, they failed to halt the enemy advance. In October, Liu also assumed the post of director of training for the First War Area. The Japanese drive continued until the end of May 1938, when the Nationalists diverted them from Chengchow by breaching the Yellow River dikes.

Liu Chih became director of the Hunan-Hupeh-Szechwan-Kweichow border area and commander of the Fifth Reserve Army, with garrison station at Ichang, in the summer of 1938. When the Nationalist forces withdrew from Wuhan, he bore over-all responsibility for defensive action and the maintenance of order, reception and reorganization of troops, shipment of supplies, relief for refugees, and the defensive blocking of the river routes.

In the spring of 1939 Liu Chih became commander in chief of the garrison district and air defense commander at the National Government's wartime capital of Chungking. He held those difficult posts until February 1945, when he was appointed commander of the Fifth War Area. At war's end, he accepted the surrender of Japanese forces in Honan.

On 1 January 1946 Liu Chih was appointed director of the pacification headquarters at

Chengchow, with jurisdiction over Honan and Shensi. His primary task was to deal with the Chinese Communist forces that had disrupted rail communications in central China. His troops were defeated by the forces of Liu Po-ch'eng (q.v.) along the Lunghai rail line, and in September Liu Chih was replaced by Ku Chu-t'ung (q.v.). Liu, who had received the rank of general, then became a member of the Strategy Advisory Commission at Nanking. In June 1948 he was given charge of the so-called bandit-suppression headquarters for east China at Hsuchow. In November, the massive Hwai-Hai battle, centered on Hsuchow, began. Liu Chih was field commander of the half-million Nationalist troops involved in that battle, and his Communist opponents were Ch'en Yi, Ch'en Keng (qq.v.), and Liu Po-ch'eng. By late November, Liu Chih had been forced to move his headquarters to Pengpu, and by early January the battle had ended in disaster for the Nationalists. Liu was relieved of command on 15 January 1949.

Liu Chih went to Hong Kong and later visited Indonesia. In November 1952 he joined the National Government in Taiwan. In 1955–56 he held the post of national security adviser in the headquarters of Chiang Kai-shek. In 1961 his autobiography was published in mimeographed form in Taipei, and in 1962 an article, "Tzu yu t'an" [memoirs of an old soldier] was published, also in Taipei.

Liu Chih-tan 劉 志 丹
Orig. Liu Ching-kuei 劉 景 桂

Liu Chih-tan (1903–April 1936), Chinese Communist guerrilla leader who, with Kao Kang (q.v.), carved out the northern Shensi base that became the final destination of the Long March.

A native of Shensi, Liu Chih-tan was born into a landowning family in the Paoan district. After completing his primary education in the early 1920's, he enrolled at the Yülin Middle School, where one of his schoolmates was Kao Kang (q.v.). Some of Liu's teachers were former students of Li Ta-chao (q.v.) who had been sent to Shensi to stimulate interest in Marxism. Liu soon became interested in radical politics; he joined the Socialist Youth League in 1924 and the Chinese Communist party in 1925. He then went to Canton and enrolled at the Whampoa Military Academy. After being graduated from Whampoa in 1926, Liu returned to northwest China and joined the political department of the Kuominchün. He also became an instructor at the Chungshan Military Academy, which Feng Yü-hsiang had established at Sanyuan. One of his students at the academy was Kao Kang.

In 1927, after Feng Yü-hsiang agreed to support Chiang Kai-shek rather than the left-Kuomintang at Wuhan, all known Communists in the Kuominchün, including Liu Chih-tan, were relieved of their posts. Liu went to the Anhwei-Hupeh area and worked to foment peasant unrest. In the spring of 1928 he returned to Shensi and, supported by radical members of the Chungshan cadet brigade, led an insurrection in the Weinan-Huayin area which became known as the Wei-Hua uprising. After the revolt was suppressed, he went to Paoan and worked to strengthen Communist organization in northern Shensi. Late in 1929, on orders from Chinese Communist leaders in Shensi, he joined the Kansu military forces under a false name and became a regimental commander. His identity soon was discovered, however, and he was imprisoned; but friends and former teachers managed to secure his release.

In 1931 Liu Chih-tan and Hsieh Tzu-ch'ang organized Communist guerrilla units in the Sanshui area. After troops led by Kao Kang and remnants of the Twenty-fourth Red Army joined forces with Liu, a new army, the Anti-Imperialist Allied Army, was created. At the end of 1932 the combined force was designated the Twenty-sixth Red Army. At this point, Kao Kang, who had been serving as Liu's political commissar, left the army and began to organize a guerrilla band at Yuehhsien. The Twenty-sixth Red Army then moved into the Weinan region, but it soon was attacked, defeated, and shattered. Liu Chih-tan and a few other survivors of the debacle returned to central Shensi and rejoined Kao Kang. Liu and Kao established a base at Lung-chia-chai and built up a large force. By the end of 1933 they had created a new Twenty-sixth Red Army. In 1934 they decided to move to northern Shensi, which was loosely controlled by the unpopular warlord Ching Yueh-hsiu, rather than to attempt to wrest control of parts of central Shensi from more powerful generals. By the spring of 1935 they had established a Shensi-Kansu soviet regime at Wa-yao-pao and had organized a new unit, the Twenty-seventh Red Army. Nationalist units had encircled the area, but Liu's forces broke through their lines, defeated troops under Kao Kuei-tzu, and crushed the army of Ching Yueh-hsiu. Thus, Communist control was extended over six hsien—Yench'uan, Yench'ang, Paoan, Anchai, Anching, and Chengpien—and a safe base area was ready to receive the main Communist forces from Kiangsi which were working their way northward on the Long March.

In the summer of 1935 Liu Chih-tan's armies were combined with the newly arrived Twenty-fifth Red Army of Hsü Hai-tung (q.v.) to form the Fifteenth Group Army. The new force was placed under the over-all command of Hsü Hai-tung. A few senior party officials also arrived in Shensi that summer. In August, Liu Chih-tan, Kao Kang, and a number of Shensi cadres were arrested on charges of having "deviated from the party line" and imprisoned. They were released when Mao Tse-tung reached northern Shensi in October. An official Communist explanation of this episode blamed "sectarianism" within the party and the ambitions of some party leaders for the arrest of Liu and Kao. It also stated that Liu, Kao, and other leaders accepted the "order and sentence" without protest because they respected the need for party unity.

After his release, Liu Chih-tan served as vice chairman of the northwest military committee, garrison commander at Wa-yao-pao, commander of the Northern Route Army, and commander of the Twenty-eighth Army. In the spring of 1936 he led a strike eastward into Shansi province. In the course of his campaign against Nationalist forces on both sides of the Yellow River, he was severely wounded. He died in April 1936, at the age of 33. His exploits in the northwest during the early 1930's soon became legendary. The American journalist Edgar Snow, who visited Shensi in 1937, described him as a "modern Robin Hood."

Little is known about Liu Chih-tan's personal life. According to Edgar Snow, his widow and son were living at Paoan in 1937. His younger brother, Liu Ching-fan, became vice chairman of the Shensi-Kansu-Ninghsia Border Region government in 1947 and vice chairman of the Committee on People's Supervision in late 1949.

Liu Fu   劉復
T. Pan-nung   半農

Liu Fu (1891–14 July 1934), teacher, linguist, and man of letters. A devoted student of Chinese language and literature, he was an early advocate of the pai-hua [vernacular] movement. His writings proved that he was a master of the new literary style as well as an able theorist.

Born in Chiangyin, Kiangsu, Liu Fu came from a family which he came to describe as being ch'ing-p'in [poor but pure]. He and his younger brother, Liu T'ien-hua, received their early education at a local elementary school and then proceeded to the prefectural middle school in Ch'angchou, where Liu Fu began the study of Western languages. However, the school was forced to close as a consequence of the 1911 revolution. Liu immediately left Ch'angchou for Chinkiang, where he continued his language studies; his brother joined the revolutionary youth movement.

In 1912 the brothers were reunited. They went to Shanghai, where Liu was able to earn his living by writing and by translating works of Western literature. His brother pursued musical studies. In 1914 Liu T'ien-hua returned home to teach, but Liu Fu remained in Shanghai.

It was a contribution to Hsin ch'ing-nien [new youth] that first brought Liu Fu public notice. The editors, Ch'en Tu-hsiu and Ts'ai Yuan-p'ei (qq.v.), were so impressed that Ts'ai, then chancellor of Peking University, invited Liu to join his faculty. In 1917 Liu joined the faculty of Peking University as an instructor in Chinese.

Liu Fu soon became deeply involved in the debates then raging on the use of the vernacular language for serious, literary purposes. Several of his essays of this period were remarkable for the cogency with which he advanced and defended the new views. Particularly notable were his eloquent reply in Hsin ch'ing-nien to Wang Ching-hsuan's denunciation of the "new writing" and his able seconding of Hu Shih in an essay which stressed equally the need for reform in content and spirit of writing and for modernizing grammer and idiom. Like Hu Shih, Liu held that good writing had always been grounded in the vernacular. He applied this theory particularly to the study of the Shih-ching [book of odes] and Ch'u-tz'u [songs of the south], classic anthologies dating, for the most part, from late Chou times.

Liu was also a poet and became famous for his short lyrics. Several of the best of these, "Chih-pu" [weaving], "Chiao wo ju-ho pu-hsiang t'a" [tell me how to forget her], and "T'ing yü" [listening to the rain], were subsequently set to music by Y. R. Chao (Chao Yuen-ren, q.v.), and the songs enjoyed considerable popularity. In addition, Liu's varied language interests led in 1919 to the publication of *Chung-kuo wen-fa t'ung-lun* [an exposition of Chinese grammar].

In 1920 Liu went to Europe for advanced studies, ultimately obtaining a doctorate from the University of Paris in 1925 under Sylvain Lévi. His stay in Paris affected his intellectual interests; and, possibly under the influence of Paul Pelliot and his circle, he began to study the vernacular literature of T'ang times and earlier. The Pelliot collection of Tunhuang manuscripts at the Bibliothèque Nationale was an important source for such studies. Liu copied a number of the most interesting manuscripts by hand, and published them in 1926 under the title *Tun-huang to-so* [gleanings from Tun-huang]. In France, Liu also studied of the tones the Chinese language and published the results of his research in 1924 as *Ssu-sheng shih-yen lu* [record of experiments involving the four tones].

In late 1925 Liu returned to China. He was appointed a professor in the department of Chinese literature at Peking University. Soon, he gave up that post to became chairman of the department of Chinese literature at the Université Franco-Chinoise. During this period, Liu continued to write, producing in 1926 both a collection of poems, *Yang-pien chi* [the whip], and a version of Dumas' *La Dame aux camélias*. The same year, he also published an annotated edition of *Ho-tien* [what stories these ?], a collection of ghost tales by Chang Nan-chuang (fl.1800), and *T'ai-p'ing t'ien-kuo yu-ch'ü-wei wen-chien shih-liu-chung* [sixteen interesting documents of the Taiping], based on materials he had gathered in European libraries. In 1927 he published the anthology *Fa-kuo tuan-p'ien hsiao-shuo chi* [French short stories]. In July 1929 he became dean and director of studies at Fu-jen University, and in May 1930 he was appointed dean of the women's college at Peking University. In this last post, Liu's experiences were far from pleasant, and in July 1931 he was happy to accept one of the five new research professorships established at Peking University by the China Foundation for the Promotion of Education and Culture. The other appointees were Chou Tso-jen, T'ang Yung-t'ung, Ch'en Shou-i, and Hsü Chih-mo.

Liu then devoted himself to the study of linguistics. Problems of phonology and grammar engrossed him, as did analysis of the Tunhuang materials, especially the ballads and folk songs. During this period, Liu produced several important works of scholarship, including *Chung-kuo wen-fa chiang-hua* [lectures on Chinese grammar] of 1932. At the same time, he maintained a variety of other, non-academic interests. In 1929 he wrote a personal account of the Northern Expedition entitled *Liu-li* [adrift]. He was a devotee of Mei Lan-fang (q.v.) and of the classical operas in which Mei appeared. Liu also wrote essays on a wide variety of topics, and he was admired for his fluent, direct, and natural style. In 1930 he produced the valuable *Sung-Yuan i-lai su-tzu-p'u* [demotic characters of the Sung and Yuan periods and later]. He became increasingly concerned with national affairs and created a considerable stir in 1931 when he wrote the Kuomintang elder Chang Chi concerning the advisability of establishing a p'ei-tu [co-capital] at Sian.

In 1932 Liu produced the *Chung-kuo su-ch'ü tsung-mu* [catalogue of Chinese folk songs]. The same year, his brother, Liu T'ien-hua, who had become a successful musician and teacher, died at Peiping. In the summer of 1934 Liu Fu went on a field trip to Suiyuan province, where he hoped to collect typical ballads of the northwest frontier. Soon after reaching Suiyuan, however, he became ill and was rushed back to Peiping. He died at the hospital of Peking Union Medical College on 14 July 1934.

Liu, Herman: *see* LIU CHAN-EN.

Liu Hsiang　　　　　　劉 湘
　T. Fu-ch'eng　　　　　甫 澄

Liu Hsiang (1890–22 January 1938), Szechwanese militarist who sporadically held supreme authority in Szechwan in the 1920's and 1930's.

Little is known about Liu Hsiang's family background or early years except that he was born in Tayi, Szechwan. He was graduated in 1910 from the Szechwan Short-Term Military Academy, where one of his classmates was Yang Sen (q.v.), and he began his military career in 1912, when he joined the forces of Chang Lan (q.v.). By 1917 Liu had become a brigadier general and a company commander in the Szechwanese forces, and by mid-1918 he had received command of a division.

In May 1920 Hsiung K'o-wu (q.v.), the military governor of Szechwan, assumed leadership of the province's military commanders in demanding the evacuation of the Yunnan and Kweichow armies of T'ang Chi-yao (q.v.) from Szechwan. A long and bitter campaign began, and the "guest armies" finally were ejected from the province late that autumn. In December, the provincial military leaders declared Szechwan independent and autonomous, and Hsiung K'o-wu resigned the governorship. Liu Hsiang, who had been serving as commander of the Second Army, was elected commander in chief of all Szechwan armies at a rehabilitation conference. Yang Sen succeeded Liu as commander of the Second Army.

Liu Hsiang did not move quickly to consolidate control of Szechwan; rather, he allowed several militarists to retain jurisdiction over the areas they already dominated. This failure to act increased the already strong potential for civil strife in the province. In May 1921 Liu took action against Hsiung K'o-wu, forcing him to flee the province, and in July he assumed office as civil governor of Szechwan. Soon afterwards, he sent forces into western Hupeh in support of that province's drive for autonomy. However, this move was opposed by Wu P'ei-fu (q.v.), a more powerful warlord than Liu, and the Szechwan forces were defeated near Ichang in September. The campaign ended in October when Wu P'ei-fu, Chao Heng-t'i (q.v.), and Liu Hsiang made a peace agreement on the basis of the territorial *status quo*. The Szechwan forces returned home in November.

Civil war continued to threaten in Szechwan, and in May 1922 Liu Hsiang announced that he was resigning in favor of Wang Ling-chi. This announcement proved to be a smokescreen for his intended campaign against the commander of the First Army, Tan Mou-hsin. At the beginning of July, Yang Sen's Second Army

attacked Tan. In response, a coalition was formed which was headed by Liu Ch'eng-hsun and which included Tan Mou-hsin, Teng Hsi-hou, Lai Hsin-hui, T'ien Sung-yao, and Liu Pin. In mid-July their armies advanced on the Liu Hsiang–Yang Sen strongholds of Chungking and Luchow. By August, Liu and Yang had been driven out of Szechwan. They went to Hupeh, where Yang entered the service of Wu P'ei-fu, reorganized his remnant forces as a mixed brigade, and established headquarters at Ichang. Liu Hsiang served as his director of reorganization.

Liu and Yang did not have to wait long for an opportunity to return to Szechwan. Early in February 1923 strife developed between Liu Ch'eng-hsun, who had become civil governor of Szechwan, and Teng Hsi-hou. A week later, Yang and Liu, with the support of Wu P'ei-fu's forces, advanced into eastern Szechwan. The attackers made rapid progress, forcing Tan Mou-hsin out of Chungking in April. Tan called Yunnan and Kweichow forces to his aid, and Hsiung K'o-wu returned to Szechwan and occupied Chengtu in May and Chungking in October. Yang and Liu, now reinforced by Yuan Tsu-ming, recaptured Chungking in December 1923 and Chengtu in February 1924. Hsiung K'o-wu was driven into Kweichow. Soon afterwards, Liu Ts'un-hou, who had been military governor of Szechwan in 1917, resumed office.

In May 1924 Ts'ao K'un (q.v.), who then held the presidency at Peking, reorganized the Szechwan power structure. He abolished the military governorship and made Liu Ts'un-hou Szechwan-Shensi border defense commissioner. Liu Hsiang, who had been serving as pacification commissioner of Szechwan since July 1923, was made a full general and was given the post of Szechwan-Yunnan border defense commissioner. Yang Sen became Szechwan military rehabilitation commissioner. Yang's protector, Wu P'ei-fu, fell from power in Peking late in 1924, and in the spring of 1925 Liu Hsiang took steps to diminish Yang's power in Szechwan. In March, Liu's uncle Liu Wen-hui (q.v.), supported by Teng Hsi-hou and Lai Hsin-hui, clashed with Yang Sen. In May, Tuan Ch'i-jui (q.v.), then the chief executive at Peking, ordered Liu Hsiang to investigate and stabilize the Szechwan military situation. Liu recommended that Yang Sen be transferred to

Peking, and in mid-May he was appointed to succeed Yang as military rehabilitation commissioner. Yang resisted the proposed transfer of authority and undertook peace negotiations. When these broke down in mid-July, the anti-Yang forces organized an army under the over-all command of Yuan Tsu-ming and drove Yang from Szechwan. Liu Hsiang convened a conference in Chengtu in December at which it was decided that he should be tuchün [military governor] of Szechwan, with Liu Wen-hui as his deputy.

In February 1926 Liu Hsiang was confronted by the new alliance of Teng Hsi-hou and Yuan Tsu-ming, who supported the return of Yang Sen to Szechwan. Heavy fighting began in March and ended soon afterwards when Liu agreed to Yang's return to power. In May, Wu P'ei-fu, who had consolidated control in central China, appointed Yang Sen civil governor of Szechwan, with Teng Hsi-hou as tuchün and Yuan Tsu-ming as Szechwan-Kweichow border defense commissioner.

In the autumn of 1926 Liu Hsiang declared allegiance to the Nationalists, and in the spring of 1927 he and Yang Sen sided with Chiang Kai-shek against the Nationalist regime at Wuhan. He was appointed commander in chief of the Fifth Route Army in June, with Yang as field commander. After Chiang Kai-shek went into retirement later in 1927, Liu and Yang received command of the Sixth and Twentieth armies, respectively. When Chiang resumed office in January 1928, he ordered Liu Wen-hui and Liu Hsiang to take command of Yang Sen's forces.

In October 1928, the Northern Expedition having ended and a new National Government having been established at Nanking, Liu Wen-hui was appointed governor of Szechwan, with Liu Hsiang as a member of the provincial government and chairman of a Szechwan-Sikang military reorganization group that included Yang Sen (who had been restored as commander of the Twentieth Army), Teng Hsi-hou, Liu Ts'un-hou, T'ien Sung-yao, Lai Hsin-hui, and Kuo Ju-tung. On 20 December, Yang Sen and others issued a public telegram denouncing Liu Hsiang and Liu Wen-hui which was, in effect, a declaration of war. The first battle was fought by the forces of Liu Hsiang and Yang Sen. A few days later Liu requested that the National Government take action against

Yang, Lai Hsin-hui, and Lo Tse-chou. At the end of December, when the war was going badly for the two Lius, the situation was saved for them by the defection of Kuo Ju-tung to their side. Yang Sen was forced to evacuate his Wanhsien stronghold, and in mid-January 1929 he was dismissed from his offices by the National Government.

A long struggle between Liu Hsiang and Liu Wen-hui soon began. Late in 1932 Liu Hsiang, with the support of Yang Sen and Teng Hsi-hou, began a strong drive to win control of Szechwan. He was appointed commander in chief for bandit-suppression in Szechwan in July 1933, but he did not assume this post until October, by which time Liu Wen-hui had been driven into Sikang. In 1934 Liu Hsiang assumed office as governor of Szechwan. That November, he made his first trip outside Szechwan in an attempt to get aid from Chiang Kai-skek.

In his capacity as bandit-suppression commissioner, Liu was faced with combatting the activities of Communist units, especially those of Hsü Hsiang-ch'ien (q.v.). He forced Hsü to retreat into the Szechwan-Hupeh border region, but Hsü returned to Szechwan in February 1935 with a stronger force. At the same time, Chinese Communist forces on the Long March were approaching Szechwan from the south. Liu Hsiang was given the concurrent posts of peace preservation commissioner for Szechwan. Thanks to his efforts and those of Teng Hsi-hou, Szechwan weathered the critical year 1935, with the Chinese Communist forces passing on to the north.

The National Government had used the so-called bandit-suppression campaign of 1935 as an occasion for endeavoring to strengthen its influence in the loosely controlled provinces of west China, including Szechwan. Liu Hsiang, however, was less than willing to cooperate in the diminishing of his authority, although he accepted Nanking's commissions and assistance in overcoming local enemies. Because of other conflicts, the National Government was not in a position to force the issue until 1937. By that time, Liu Hsiang, having eliminated so many of his Szechwan rivals, lacked the means and local support to resist Nanking's pressures. Moreover, his province was in financial straits. Accordingly, agreement was reached for the "rehabilitation" of Szechwan in June 1937. The agreement provided for the withdrawal of Szechwan forces from their commanding positions at Ichang, Wanhsien, and Chungking, reorganization of these forces as Nationalist units, transfer to the National Government of "the training of the people," reorganization of provincial taxes, and the construction and control of highways by the National Government.

Ho Ying-ch'in (q.v.) was appointed chairman of the Szechwan-Sikang military rehabilitation commission, with Liu Hsiang as vice chairman. The first meeting of the commission was held at Chiang Kai-shek's provisional headquarters at Chungking on 7 July 1937, the day the Sino-Japanese war broke out. Because of the war, the commission held its closing session on 9 July, reaching the decision (authorized by Nanking) that no large-scale disbandment of Szechwan-Sikang forces should be undertaken at that time. Only old and unfit troops should be weeded out of the armies. Ho Ying-ch'in found it necessary to return to Nanking because of the national emergency, but he left Ku Chu-t'ung (q.v.) in Szechwan to work with Liu Hsiang in nationalizing the Szechwan-Sikang forces. Liu was made a member of the State Council, the Military Affairs Commission, and the Kuomintang Central Executive Committee.

Liu Hsiang led the Szechwan forces during the defense of Nanking against the Japanese. With the retreat from that sector in December 1937, he entered a hospital at Hankow. He died on 22 January 1938, and the National Government proceeded with actions designed to bring Szechwan fully under its authority as a wartime territorial base.

Liu Hung-sheng   劉 鴻 生
West. O. S. Lieu

Liu Hung-sheng (1888–1 October 1956), known as O. S. Lieu, one of the most prominent entrepreneurs of republican China, was particularly noted for his success in the match and wool industries. After 1949, he lived in the People's Republic of China as a "national industrialist."

Although his native place was Tinghai, Chekiang, O. S. Lieu was born in Shanghai. His father was a prosperous merchant, and Lieu received a good education in both the Chinese classics and modern subjects. He enrolled at St. John's College (later St. John's University) at about the age of 19, but he had to leave school because the family's financial position declined and his father died. For a time, Lieu worked as a translator for the Shanghai Municipal Council in the International Settlement.

In 1913, at the age of 25 sui, O. S. Lieu went to north China, where he found employment as a broker for the Kailan Mining Administration. His success in this job was such that he was able to start a small coal mining company of his own. He returned to Shanghai in 1920 as the area's general agent for the Kailan Mining Administration. He founded the China Coal Briquette Company, and in 1923 he established the Shanghai Cement Company.

By this time, O. S. Lieu had married the daughter of Yeh Ch'eng-chung (1840–1899), who had pioneered in the match industry in China and who had founded such companies as the Ying-chang Match Works in Shanghai. Although Lieu had never met his father-in-law, he became interested in Yeh's career and decided to establish a match factory. The Hung Sheng Match Company, founded in 1924, was very successful, and its profits enabled Lieu to develop his other interests. In 1927 he established the Hwa Foong Enamel Works and the China Woolen Works. That year, he also traveled to Europe and the United States to study Western business methods. After returning to China, he employed Lin Tien-chi to improve production methods and lower unit costs, and Lin instituted new methods for keeping the matches dry.

O. S. Lieu soon saw that the formation of a match combine would be advantageous to him. In 1930 he completed arrangements with the Ying-chang and the Chung-hua match factories to form the Great China Match Company. This combine produced about 200,000 cases of matches a year, about one-fourth of the total match production of China. In 1931 Lieu extended the combine arrangement throughout Kiangsu, and in 1936 he formed a national combine. The entire Chinese match industry set production quotas for all of its plants and agreed to refrain from building new factories for five years. The combine arrangement enabled the Chinese businesses to compete successfully with Japanese and Swedish match interests.

During this period, O. S. Lieu's brother, Liu Chi-sheng, attended to many of the administrative details of his enterprises, thus enabling Lieu to develop new interests. In 1931 he sponsored the establishment of the China Development Bank. He also served on the board of directors of the Shanghai Coal Merchants Bank, and the coal business continued to be an important part of his growing business empire. He became the chairman of two general development corporations and of the Shanghai Coal Godown Company, and he gradually created a chain of wharves and warehouses in various small ports. From 1931 to 1933 he served as a councillor of the Shanghai Municipal Council. He also was prominent in the newly founded Chinese Federation of Industries until 1936.

In November 1932 the government-owned China Merchants Steam Navigation Company was reorganized, and O. S. Lieu was appointed its general manager. Although he made many improvements in the operations of this shipping concern, he soon discovered that it had accumulated debts of such magnitude that the satisfactory servicing of its obligations was an impossibility. He resigned in 1934 and founded a small private shipping concern, the Chusan Steamship Company.

When Sino-Japanese relations threatened to deteriorate into war, O. S. Lieu made provisions for moving some of his factories to the interior areas. By 1936 he reportedly had built up a personal fortune of several million Chinese dollars, and St. John's University had recognized his achievements by awarding him an honorary LL.D degree. When the Sino-Japanese war began in 1937, Lieu established a match works in Hong Kong. He had been dependent on the Japanese for chemicals used in match making, but he now obtained the services of the chemist Chang T'ing-feng to produce electrolytic chemicals for him. In 1939 Lieu established factories for the production of raw materials for the match industry in Szechwan, Kweichow, Yunnan, and Kwangsi, selling many of their products to the National Government for distribution in the more remote areas of China. He moved the machinery from his China Woolen Works to Szechwan and established the China Woolen and Worsted

Works at Chungking in 1942. He undertook to supply enough material to make 10,000 suits per year to be sold to public functionaries at very low prices. In return, the National Government exempted his wool products from price control. Beginning in 1942 Lieu also served as director of the government monopolies bureau at Chungking. In 1944 Lieu, with the aid of the Bank of Communications and the ministry of finance, planned the establishment of the Northwest Woolen Works. One of its units processed the region's raw wool. A second unit established in 1944 was the China Hat Manufacturing Works.

After the Japanese surrender in 1945, O. S. Lieu returned to Shanghai and found that most of his enterprises had been preserved, thanks to the painstaking efforts of his younger brother, who had remained in the area throughout the Japanese occupation. In 1946, in addition to reconstructing his own business empire, Lieu served as chief executive officer of the Chinese National Relief and Rehabilitation Administration and director of its Shanghai regional office.

O. S. Lieu left Shanghai for Hong Kong on the eve of the Chinese Communist occupation in May 1949. After the People's Republic of China was established, the Chinese Communists announced their policy of protection for private industry and trade that was beneficial to the state and that provided for the living needs of the people. Because Lieu believed that his enterprises met these requirements and that he would be able to carry on his activities under the new regime, he returned to Shanghai as a "national industrialist." He became a member of the executive committee of the China Democratic National Construction Association, a committee member of the All-China Federation of Industry and Commerce, and a vice president of the China Red Cross Society. From December 1952 to June 1954 he also served on the East China Administrative Committee. In 1954 he was a delegate from Shanghai to the National People's Congress and a member of the National Committee of the Chinese People's Political Consultative Conference.

After 1951 O. S. Lieu and the eldest of his 12 sons, Liu Nien-i, came under attack as capitalists. The Central People's Government soon began to convert private enterprises into "state and private jointly operated enterprises" as the first step in the nationalization and socialist transformation of all industry and commerce. Like other capitalists in the People's Republic of China, O. S. Lieu was gradually forced into inactivity. He died in Shanghai on 1 October 1956, at the age of 68 sui. The official announcement of his death stated that he had "ardently supported and implemented the policy of the state on the socialist transformation of capitalist industry and commerce."

Liu I-cheng
T. I-mou

柳 詒 徵
翼 謀

Liu I-cheng (1879–), historian of the Tung-nan, school and librarian of the Chiang-su sheng-li t'u-shu-kuan at Nanking.

Tant'u, Kiangsi, was the birthplace of Liu I-cheng. His father died when Liu was only seven sui, and thereafter he lived in the home of his maternal grandfather, Pao Chung-ming. His mother tutored him in the Chinese classics, and he became a sheng-yuan in 1895 and began tutoring private students. In 1901 he went to Nanking, where he served as associate compiler at the Chiang-ch'u pien-i-chü [Kiangsu-Hupeh compilation and translation bureau], headed by Miao Ch'üan-sun (q.v.). In 1906 he taught for a short time in Peking and Mukden. He then returned to Nanking to become a professor of history at the Nanking Higher Normal School, which became Southeast University in 1923 and National Central University in 1927. One of his favorite students was Chang Ch'i-yün (q.v.), for whom he secured an appointment in 1927 as instructor in geography.

In 1924 Liu I-cheng also became the executive secretary of the *Hsüeh-heng* [critical review], which opposed the pai-hua [vernacular] movement of Hu Shih (q.v.) and his associates. Many of Liu's earlier writings were published in the *Hsüeh-heng*.

Liu I-cheng's scholarly activities reflected his dual role as historian and librarian. Between 1921 and 1929 he founded in Nanking the Society of History and Geography, which published the *Shih-ti hsüeh-pao* [journal for the study of historical geography], and the Historical Society, which published the *Shih-hsüeh*

tsa-chih [historiography magazine]. Among the frequent contributors to these magazines were Chang Ch'i-yün and Miao Feng-lin (1898–; T. Tsan-yü), who later joined with Liu in founding the Chung-shan shu-chü [Chung-shan book company] and publishing the *Kuo-feng pan-yueh k'an* [Kuo-feng semi-monthly]. These three magazines became the forum for the Tung-nan [southeastern] school of historical studies, which had some influence on Chinese scholarship in the 1920's and 1930's.

In 1927 Liu I-cheng was appointed librarian of the Chiang-su sheng-li t'u-shu-kuan [Kiangsu provincial library]. Formerly known as the Chin-ling Lung-p'an-li t'u-shu-kuan [library of the Lung-p'an quarter of Nanking], the library had been founded by Miao Ch'üan-sun and financed by Tuan-fang (ECCP, II, 780–82). Its valuable holdings of rare books and manuscripts were second only to those of the National Peking Library. Under Liu I-cheng's direction, a number of the library's rare books were photographically reproduced and published. These included the *Tsei-ch'ing hui-tsuan* [collected materials concerning the rebel-thieves] and a set of three works devoted to the study of Manchuria under the Ming dynasty. In 1936 a catalogue of the library's holdings was published; it had been compiled by Fan Hsi-tseng and Wang Huan-piao under the direction of Liu I-cheng.

Among Liu's articles in the *Hsüeh-heng* were "Wang Hsüan-ts'e shih-chi," which dealt with a Buddhist monk who visited India in 643, 648, and 657; "Han-kuan-i shih" [the history of debates among the bureaucracy of the Han dynasty]; "Hua-hua chien pei-shih" [studies in sinification], a study of Japan's search for and acceptance of Chinese culture; "Tu Mo wei-yen" [a note on Mo-tzu], proclaiming the supremacy of Mencius over Mo-tzu; "Wu-pai-nien ch'ien Nan-ching chih kuo-li ta-hsüeh" [a national university established 500 years ago in Nanking], a study of the Imperial Academy established during the Ming period; and the "T'ang-tai ping-shu k'ao" [the number of soldiers during the T'ang dynasty]. His *Chung-kuo wen-hua shih* [history of Chinese culture], which appeared in the *Hsüeh-heng* in 1929, was published as a book in 1932. That year also saw the appearance of his *Li-tai ping-shu mu-lu* [catalogue of military books through the dynasties].

Liu also published articles and bibliographical notes in the *Bulletin of the Kiangsu Provincial Library*. Among these articles were "Lu Pao-ching hsien-sheng nien-p'u" [chronological biography of Lu Pao-ching], a study of Lu Wen-ch'ao (ECCP, I, 549–50); "Nan-chien-shih t'an" [talks on the Nanking academy's recension of the twenty-one official dynastic histories]; "Tsu-p'u yen-chiu chü-li" [research in clan genealogies, with examples]; "Chiang-su shu-yüan chih ch'u-kao: li-su-pien" [draft history of Kiangsu society: section on local rites and customs]; and "Ming-tai Chiang-su wo-k'ou shih-chi" [collected accounts concerning the invasion of Kiangsu by Japanese pirates during Ming times], which appeared shortly after the Japanese attacked Mukden in September 1931.

In 1948 Liu I-cheng, who had become an official historian in the newly founded Kuo-shih kuan, was given the title of academician by the Academia Sinica. His *Kuo-shih yao-i* [the essence of Chinese history] was published in Shanghai in 1949.

Liu, J. Heng: *see* LIU JUI-HENG

Liu Jen-ching   劉 仁 靜

Liu Jen-ching (1899–), founding member of the Chinese Communist party who became a leading Trotskyist in the 1930's. He remained in China after 1949 and made a public statement regarding his earlier political errors.

Little is known about Liu Jen-ching's family background or early education except that he was born in Hupeh. At the time of the May Fourth Movement of 1919 he was a student at Peking University and a member of the student organization that published the magazine *Hsin-ch'ao* [new tide]. As information about the Russian Revolution and Marxism became available in north China, Liu developed a keen interest in the new doctrine. In the autumn of 1920 he joined a Marxist study group in Peking which was guided by Li Ta-chao (q.v.). Despite his youth, Liu attended the founding meeting of the Chinese Communist party, held at Shanghai in July 1921, as one of the two delegates from Peking, the other being Chang Kuo-t'ao

(q.v.). He also became a member of the Young China Association (*see* Chang Wen-t'ien) and the Peking branch of the Chinese Communist party.

In 1922 Liu accompanied Ch'en Tu-hsiu (q.v.) to Moscow to attend the Fourth Congress of the Comintern, which met in November-December 1922. That meeting stressed the need for the Communists in such under-developed countries as China to cooperate with nationalist groups to further the cause of revolution. At the Comintern congress, Liu Jen-ching, speaking on behalf of the Chinese Communists, accepted the Comintern directive ordering members of his party to join the Kuomintang. He stated that if the Chinese Communists joined the Kuomintang, they would be able to direct mass mobilization and to split the Kuomintang from within, and that if they did not ally themselves with the Kuomintang, they would run the risk of being isolated from the mainstream of Chinese nationalism and political action.

In the spring of 1923 Liu reportedly visited Paris as a representative of the Chinese Communist party, which then was holding its Third National Congress at Canton. Little is known about his activities from 1923 to 1927, but some sources indicate that he lived in Moscow, where he supported Trotsky's position in Soviet politics.

After the Nationalist-Communist split and the downfall of Ch'en Tu-hsiu as general secretary of the Chinese Communist party in 1927, Liu Jen-ching became dissatisfied with Communism in China. Although he returned to China, he had serious doubts about the position then articulated by Mao Tse-tung, namely, that a major social revolution could be based on the grievances of the Chinese peasantry. Liu believed that the Chinese Communists would only be able to gain state power after China had passed through a period of capitalist development, and he argued that the party, for the time being, should concentrate on political action in the cities.

In 1929 Liu Jen-ching went to Turkey to see Leon Trotsky, who, having been expelled from the Soviet Union, was living in Istanbul. After returning to China, Liu organized a small Trotskyist group in Shanghai called the Shih-yueh-she [October society]. In May 1931 Liu's group and two other small Trotskyist groups in Shanghai the Wo-men-ti-hua [our words] faction and the Chan-tou she [combat society], joined forces with the Wu-ch'an-che she [proletarian society] led by Ch'en-Tu'hsiu and P'eng Shu-chih (q.v.). Reportedly with the help of funds from Trotskyist groups in Europe, the squabbling Trotskyist groups in Shanghai then formed the Chinese Communist Party Left Opposition Faction (Chung-kuo kung-ch'an-tang tso-p'ai fan-tui-p'ai), also known as the Trotsky-Ch'en party (T'o-Ch'en p'ai). That year, Liu Jen-ching wrote an article advocating that the new Opposition party participate actively in the anti-Japanese patriotic movement, "Pei ya-p'o kuo ti wu-ch'an chieh-chi ying pu-ying ling-tao ai-kuo yun-tung?" Ch'en Tu-hsiu attempted for a time to influence the main body of the Chinese Communist party to accept the Trotskyist line, a task complicated by the fact that the new organization continued to be rent by bitter dissension. Liu Jen-ching continued to promote the Opposition party, and in 1934 he wrote numerous articles for a Trotskyist journal, *Hsiao-nei sheng-huo* [school life].

In 1937 Liu Jen-ching split with the Trotskyists for unknown reasons. He then joined the Kuomintang and went to work in the propaganda office of the San-min chu-i Youth Corps at Chungking. He later was assigned to the political department of the Tenth War Area and the special service training organization headed by Hu Tsung-nan (q.v.), who was responsible for containing the Communists in northwest China.

After the Japanese surrender in 1945, Liu Jen-ching returned to Shanghai, where he became an editor of a political journal called *Min-chu yü t'ung-i* [democracy and unity], in which he criticized and condemned the Chinese Communists. He later went to north China, where he reportedly joined the faculty of Peking Normal University under the assumed name Liu Yi-yü.

Despite his long-standing condemnation of the Communists under Mao Tse-tung, Liu Jen-ching remained in China at the time of the Communist takeover in 1949. He later made a public statement regarding his earlier political errors which was published in the Peking *Jen-min jih-pao* [people's daily] and reprinted in the Hong Kong *Ta Kung Pao* on 15 January 1951.

Liu Jui-heng   劉 瑞 恆
T.   Yueh-ju   月 如
West. J. Heng Liu

Liu Jui-heng (23 July 1890–28 August 1961), known as J. Heng Liu. As minister of health (1929–30) and director general of the National Health Administration (1931–37), he laid the foundations of the Chinese national public health service. In the 1940's he became associated with the American Bureau for Medical Aid to China, and in the 1950's he worked to coordinate the public health activities of various government agencies in Taiwan.

The son of Liu T'ung-hsuan, J. Heng Liu was born in Tientsin. After studying at Anglo-Chinese College from 1902 to 1904 and at Peiyang College from 1904 to 1906, J. Heng Liu went to the United States and enrolled at Harvard College. He was graduated in 1909, at the age of 18, with a B.S. degree. He then entered the Harvard Medical School, where he received the M.D. *cum laude* in 1913, after which he completed his training in surgery at Boston City Hospital.

Liu returned to China in 1915, where he spent three years teaching surgery at Shanghai under the auspices of the Harvard Medical School of China. In 1918 he joined the staff of the Peking Union Medical College (PUMC) as an associate in surgery. He went to the United States in 1920 to do cancer research with Dr. James B. Murphy at the Rockefeller Institute in New York and later spent several months studying under Dr. James C. Bloodgood of the medical school of the Johns Hopkins University in Baltimore. After returning to China in 1923, he was named superintendent and associate professor of surgery of the PUMC, which was the major teaching and research center of Western medical science in China. On 26 January 1925 he and Dr. Adrian S. Taylor performed exploratory surgery on Sun Yat-sen which revealed inoperable cancer of the liver and other organs. Sun died at Peking in March, and a Christian funeral service was held at the PUMC chapel.

J. Heng Liu believed and taught that public service was more important than private practice, however lucrative. In November 1928 he agreed to assume office as administrative vice minister of health in the National Government. A year later, he became minister of health and a director of the PUMC. He also served as vice chairman of the advisory committee in the Health Organization of the League of Nations beginning in 1930 and as surgeon general of the Chinese army after 1930. When the National Government was reorganized in April 1931, he became director general of the new National Health Administration, a cabinet-level post.

Between 1928 and 1937 J. Heng Liu laid the foundations of a national public health service. The year 1928 saw the publication of a national sanitary code and the compilation of a national register of Western medical practitioners. At a conference of the China Medical Association held at Nanking in 1929 Liu outlined his three-year plan for the ministry of health, which included the establishing of a central field health station at Nanking, a national quarantine service, and midwifery schools at Nanking and Canton. A national pharmacopeia was adopted in 1930 and published in 1931.

J. Heng Liu's executive ability enabled him to spread the knowledge and benefits of Western medicine in a country that previously had been ignorant of the principles and practices of public health and modern medical therapy. Under his direction, significant progress also was made in the field of preventive medicine. In October 1934 the ninth conference of the Far Eastern Association of Tropical Medicine was held at Nanking. Except for a plague conference held at Mukden in 1911 (*see* Wu Lien-te), this was the first international medical conference to be held in China. The meeting was held at the Central Field Health Station across from the Nanking Field Hospital, both of which had been founded under Liu's direction. Liu presided over the meeting, and he was able to point with some pride to the notable advances made during his term of office at Nanking. He praised his PUMC colleagues for their roles in these programs, particularly Dr. John B. Grant. Liu later said that he had "relied on Dr. Grant as adviser and collaborator" and that "many of the higher positions in the ministry, and in the newly created departments of health in the cities and provinces, were given to men and women trained by Dr. Grant."

The outbreak of the Sino-Japanese war in the summer of 1937 caused the suspension of most of the National Government's health programs, and in 1938 Liu moved to Hong Kong. He went to the United States in 1942, and in 1944 he became medical director of the China Defense Supplies Commission, which was responsible for the procurement and allocation of wartime aid to China. He also became associated with the American Bureau for Medical Aid to China (ABMAC).

After the Japanese surrender in 1945, Liu returned to China to supervise the medical aid program conducted under the auspices of the United Nations Relief and Rehabilitation Administration through its Chinese counterpart, the Chinese National Relief and Rehabilitation Administration. In 1946 he became field director for ABMAC, with headquarters at Shanghai, and he set about planning a gradual shift from postwar relief work to a peacetime program of medical reconstruction and education. In 1948, despite the Kuomintang-Communist civil war, he traveled extensively in China, visiting medical schools and hospitals.

After moving to Taiwan in 1949, J. Heng Liu worked in Taipei to help maintain a small body of trained medical personnel to form the nucleus of a government health service. He became vice president in charge of ABMAC field work in Taiwan and president of the Chinese Red Cross Society; and he worked to coordinate the public health activities of various government agencies until June 1959, when ill health forced him to resign from his offices and go to the United States for treatment and rest. In 1960 the National Government in Taiwan awarded him the Order of the Brilliant Star in recognition of his contributions to public health in China. Liu served as a director of ABMAC until July 1961, when he was hospitalized in New York after suffering a stroke. He died on 28 August 1961. He was survived by his wife, *née* Lucille Wang, whom he had married in 1915, and by their daughter, Irene, who was the wife of the economist Chi-ming Hou.

Liu Po-ch'eng 劉 伯 承

Liu Po-ch'eng (1892–), Chinese Communist general known for his expertise in the techniques of mobile warfare. Commander of the 129th

Division of the Eighth Route Army (1937–47) and of the Second Field Army (1948–49), he headed the general training department of the People's Liberation Army from 1954 to 1957 and became a marshal of the People's Republic of China in 1955.

The son of an itinerant musician, Liu Po-ch'eng was born in Kaihsien, Szechwan. After receiving his primary education in the Chinese classics, he enrolled at a military school in Chengtu. In 1911, having completed his military education, he joined a unit commanded by Hsiung K'o-wu (q.v.) and took part in anti-Manchu campaigns in Szechwan. He soon established a reputation for bravery in combat, and he was wounded several times in the course of these campaigns. After losing an eye in battle, he became known as the "One-eyed Dragon" [tu-yen lung].

In the 1920's Liu came under the influence of Wu Yü-chang (q.v.), a Szechwanese scholar and revolutionary who joined the Chinese Communist party in Peking about 1925. Liu joined the Chinese Communist party in May 1926 and, after a brief stint with guerrilla forces in Szechwan, went to Hankow to join the Northern Expedition. He became commander of the Fifteenth Army and a liaison officer with the Szechwan forces of Yang Sen (q.v.). After participating in the short-lived Communist takeover of Nanchang (see Ho Lung; Yeh T'ing) in August 1927, he fled to the Soviet Union, where he studied at the Military Institute in Moscow (1927) and the Frunze Military Academy (1928–30). Among the other Chinese Communist officers receiving military instruction in Moscow during this period were Tso Ch'uan and Yeh Chien-ying (qq.v.).

Liu Po-ch'eng returned to China in the summer of 1930 and went to Shanghai, where the Chinese Communist leaders appointed him to the staff group of the Central Committee's revolutionary military council. In 1931 he went to the central soviet base in Kiangsi, where he taught at the Red Army Academy and served as chief of staff of the Communist general military headquarters, headed by Chu Teh (q.v.). When the Chinese Communists were forced to evacuate their Kiangsi base and begin the Long March in October 1934, Liu commanded some of the vanguard units. He played an important role in the difficult trek through the remote hinterland of southwest China, supervising the crossing of the Tatu River in eastern Sikang and handling the negotiations with aboriginal tribesmen in that area. His knowledge of the Lolo language made it possible for the Long March forces to gain passage through the wild Lolo territory and thus to evade pursuing Nationalist forces. When the Communist forces split into two groups in July 1935, Chu Teh, Liu Po-ch'eng, and Chang Kuo-t'ao (q.v.) moved westward into Sikang, and Mao Tse-tung led the other group into Shensi. Liu and his associates eventually reached the Communist base at Yenan in October 1936.

After the Sino-Japanese war began in 1937, the Chinese Communist forces in north China were reorganized to form the Eighth Route Army. Liu Po-ch'eng received command of the 129th Division, with Teng Hsiao-p'ing (q.v.) as political commissar. The 129th Division, initially based in the Shansi-Hopei area, later extended its military-political operations to Shantung and Honan and created the wartime base which the Communists called the Shansi-Hopei-Shantung-Honan Border Liberated Area.

At the Seventh National Congress of the Chinese Communist party, held at Yenan in the spring of 1945, Liu Po-ch'eng and other prominent military men were elected to the Central Committee. He continued to command the Communist forces in the Shansi-Hopei-Shantung-Honan area after the War in the Pacific came to an end. These units, highly trained in mobile warfare, ranged along the Lunghai railway from Kaifeng to the Shantung coast and conducted probing actions in the areas south of the Yellow River. By 1947 they were fighting along the Peking-Hankow railway. Liu's forces were designated the Second Field Army in 1948. During the nation-wide Communist sweep to power in 1949 the Second Field Army fought from the Yellow River to the Yangtze, captured Nanking (April 1949), moved through the central Yangtze region, and fanned out into Kweichow, Szechwan, and Yunnan in the southwest. Liu Po-ch'eng represented the Second Field Army at the Chinese People's Political Consultative Conference in September 1949.

From 1950 to 1954 Liu Po-ch'eng held important regional positions at Chungking: chairman of the Southwest Military and

Administrative Committee and deputy secretary of the Chinese Communist party's southwest bureau. At the national level, he was a member of the Central People's Government Council and a vice chairman of the People's Revolutionary Military Council. He also served as president of the Military Academy of the People's Liberation Army at Nanking (1951–58). After the governmental reorganization of 1954, he became a vice chairman of the National Defense Council, a member of the Standing Committee of the National People's Congress, and director of the general training department of the People's Liberation Army. He became one of the ten marshals of the People's Republic of China in 1955 and a member of the Political Bureau of the Chinese Communist party in 1956. Hsiao K'o succeeded him as director of the general training department in 1957.

Liu Po-ch'eng was a serious student of the technical aspects of warfare. He absorbed Soviet military theories and tactics during his period of training at Moscow in the late 1920's and, upon his return to China, supervised the translation into Chinese of a number of Russian military manuals for use by the Chinese Red armies. In later years he became a leading exponent of the techniques of mobile warfare.

Liu Shao-ch'i   劉少奇
Pseud. Hu Fu   胡服

Liu Shao-ch'i (1900–), the Chinese Communist party's foremost expert on the theory and practice of organization and party structure, became Chairman of the People's Republic of China in April 1959. He was the second-ranking member of the party until 1966, when he became a principal target of the so-called Cultural Revolution.

Ninghsiang hsien, Hunan, was the native place of Liu Shao-ch'i. He was born in Yinshan, near Mao Tse-tung's native village of Shaoshan in Hsiangt'an hsien. The youngest of nine children, four boys and five girls, he was the son of a peasant landowner. After receiving his primary education in the Chinese classics, Liu went to Changsha in 1916 and enrolled at the Provincial First Normal School, where his schoolmates included Mao Tse-tung, Jen Pi-shih, and Li Li-san. At the school, Liu was

introduced to radical and nationalistic ideas. He hoped to go to France after graduation on the work-study program (*see* Li Shih-tseng), and he went to north China in the summer of 1918 to prepare for the journey by studying French. Liu did not go to Europe, however, but returned to Hunan. In the summer of 1919 he may have assisted Mao Tse-tung in editing the short-lived but influential *Hsiang-chiang p'ing-lun* [Hsiang river review].

Liu Shao-ch'i went to Shanghai in the summer of 1920 to seek funds for further education. He joined the Socialist Youth League when it was organized in August by Gregory Voitinsky, the Comintern representative in China, and his young Chinese assistant Yang Ming-chai (q.v.). Liu then returned to Hunan, where he was arrested by Chao Heng-t'i (q.v.), then the acting governor of Hunan. After being released on bail, Liu returned to Shanghai and began to study Russian. "At that time," he later attested, "I only knew that Socialism was good, heard about Marx and Lenin and the October Revolution and the Bolshevik party, but I was not clear what Socialism was or how it could be realized."

In the winter of 1920 the Comintern chose and sent a small group of Chinese students including Liu Shao-ch'i, Jen Pi-shih, Hsiao Ching-kuang, and P'eng Shu-chih (q.v.) to the Soviet Union. After arriving at Moscow in the spring of 1921, they were enrolled at the newly created Communist University for Toilers of the East, which had been established to train cadres from "eastern nationalities" of the Soviet Union and foreign students from the "colonial countries," especially the Asian countries. In 1921 the institution was not prepared to receive the Chinese students: there was no systematic course of study, and there were no interpreters to render lectures into Chinese. Until Ch'ü Ch'iu-pai (q.v.) was employed early in 1922 as a teaching assistant and interpreter, the Chinese students, whose knowledge of Russian was limited, could have absorbed little of the lecture material. After the First National Congress of the Chinese Communist party was held at Shanghai in July 1921, Liu joined the new party's branch at Moscow.

After returning to China in the spring of 1922, Liu Shao-ch'i was assigned to work in Shanghai under Chang Kuo-t'ao (q.v.), then a leader in Communist labor organization and chairman of the China Trade Union Secretariat. Several months later, he was sent to the Anyuan coal mines at P'inghsiang as the principal assistant labor organizer to Li Li-san (q.v.). The Anyuan colliery was part of the Han-yeh-p'ing iron and steel complex, which was composed of a steel mill at *Han*yang, iron mines at Ta*yeh*, and the coal mines at *P'ing*hsiang. In September 1922 Li and Liu organized a successful strike of the Anyuan miners; and they led a sympathy strike in February 1923 after Wu P'ei-fu (q.v.) executed railroad workers and Communist labor organizers on the Peking-Hankow rail line. When Li Li-san went to Peking early in 1923, Liu Shao-ch'i assumed charge of the Han-yeh-p'ing union activities.

In the winter of 1923 Liu Shao-ch'i went to Canton, where plans were being made for the creation of a Kuomintang-Communist alliance, and entered the Hsuan-ch'uan chiang-hsi so, a propaganda school established by the central headquarters of the Kuomintang. He was one of the first twelve graduates of the school. In April 1924 he worked with Teng Chung-hsia (q.v.) in preparing for the convening of the first National Labor Congress. In April 1925 he wrote an article eulogizing Sun Yat-sen for the *Chung-kuo kung-jen* [Chinese worker].

When the second National Labor Congress met at Canton at the beginning of May 1925, Liu Shao-ch'i participated in the meetings as a delegate from the Han-yeh-p'ing unions. At the congress, he was elected vice chairman of the newly created All-China Federation of Labor. He returned to Shanghai, where, after the May Thirtieth Incident, he helped organize anti-British agitation (for details, *see* Li Li-san). In May 1926 he was again in Canton, where he served as secretary general of the third National Labor Congress and delivered major reports on the status and development of the Chinese labor movement.

In October 1926, after the first stage of the Northern Expedition had ended with the capture of Wuhan and many Communist labor organizers had gathered in that important industrial area, Liu Shao-ch'i became secretary general of the Hupeh provincial labor union. In January 1927 he organized an anti-British demonstration at Hankow that led to a clash with marines guarding the British concession (for background, *see* Ch'en, Eugene). The Nationalists assumed control of the concession

by force, and a committee composed of T. V. Soong, Sun Fo (qq.v.), and Eugene Ch'en took charge of its administration. On 1 April, Liu spoke at a meeting honoring the Communist minister of labor in the Wuhan government, Su Chao-cheng (q.v.), who had arrived from Canton with an international delegation that included Jacques Doriot from France, Earl Browder from the United States, and Tom Mann from England.

The anti-Communist drive begun by Chiang Kai-shek and his associates on 12 April 1927 severely damaged the Chinese labor movement. Many members of labor unions in the Shanghai and Nanking areas were arrested and executed. Later that month, Liu Shao-ch'i was elected to the Central Committee of the Chinese Communist party, and in May he was one of three Chinese delegates, the other two being Li Li-san and Su Chao-cheng, to the Pan-Pacific Labor Conference at Hankow. He was appointed secretary general of the conference, and he gave a major report on the Chinese labor movement on 23 May. Also in May, he became general secretary of the All-China Federation of Labor. That summer, the Communist labor organizations were shattered when Feng Yü-hsiang and Wang Ching-wei (qq.v.) decided to purge the Communists in areas under their control.

After the Kuomintang-Communist split of 1927, Liu Shao-ch'i, like the Chinese Communist party he served, was faced with the basic problem of survival. Because Liu spent much of his time as an underground agent in Nationalist-controlled areas, little reliable information concerning his whereabouts during the next three years is available. At the Sixth National Congress of the Chinese Communist party, held at Moscow in 1928, he was named director of the workers department. In 1929 he was appointed provincial secretary of the party organization in Manchuria. About 1930 he returned to Shanghai, where he worked with Chou En-lai and others in reconstructing Communist labor unions. He organized a strike to protest the Japanese invasion of Manchuria on 18 September 1931.

In the autumn of 1932 Liu Shao-ch'i moved from Shanghai to the central Communist base in Kiangsi, where he organized rural workers for and in the primitive arsenals and workshops of the Chinese Workers and Peasants Red Army. He served as chairman of the All-China

Federation of Labor in 1933 and presented the summary report on the labor situation in the Communist areas at the second All-China Congress of Soviets in January 1934. His rising political status was confirmed when he was elected to membership on the Political Bureau of the Chinese Communist party at the fifth plenum of the sixth Central Committee in January 1934.

Although Liu Shao-ch'i accompanied the Communist forces when they began the Long March in October 1934, he later left them to resume political work in what the Communists termed the "White areas." Late in 1935 he was in Peiping, where he used the alias Hu Fu, a term used in ancient China to refer to the dress of northern barbarians. He was associated with the student demonstrations of 9 December 1935, which were prompted by Japanese attempts to create an autonomous regime in north China.

Between 1936 and 1942 Liu Shao-ch'i served successively as head of the north China, central plains, and central China bureaus of the Central Committee. In 1945 the Chinese Communist party praised him for his direction of underground work in these key areas. He shaped a political program that was essentially conservative, with long-range goals. He attempted to maintain the party apparatus despite stringent Nationalist controls and censorship, relying on the "utmost possible exploitation of overt, legitimate means" to increase Communist influence.

The Japanese military threat to China enabled Liu to direct nationalistic sentiments into anti-Kuomintang channels. In 1936, for example, anti-Japanese feeling ran strong in the major universities at Peiping and Tientsin. As head of the party's north China bureau, Liu worked to channel this tide of sentiment into the "Anti-Japanese National Salvation" movement. By taking advantage of the tensions created by Chiang Kai-shek's inaction with regard to north China and by enlisting the political support of patriotic young intellectuals who wanted a united front against the Japanese, the Communists came to have considerable influence in Nationalist-controlled north China. The underground work of Liu Shao-ch'i and other Communists in north China was rewarded after the outbreak of the Sino-Japanese war in 1937 when a considerable number of university students and graduates made their way to Communist-held areas.

During this period Liu also helped indirectly to present the Chinese Communist story to the Western world. Many years later, it was confirmed that he had authorized the "invisible ink" letter of introduction that had enabled the American journalist Edgar Snow to enter the Communist areas of northern Shensi in 1936.

Liu Shao-ch'i went to Yenan in 1937 to assume new responsibilities in the organization department. He reportedly helped Mao Tse-tung to undermine the prestige and authority of Chang Kuo-t'ao. At Yenan, Edgar Snow's wife, Nym Wales, interviewed Liu, whom she described as the Chinese Communist party's "leading expert on labor problems." Much of the information Liu provided was published in her 1945 book, *The Chinese Labor Movement*.

In July 1939 Liu Shao-ch'i delivered an important speech at the Institute of Marxism-Leninism in Yenan. This report, *Lun kung-ch'an-tang-yuan ti hsiu-yang (How To Be a Good Communist)* was the first of Liu's political statements to be published under his own name. After being presented as two lectures on 8 July, it appeared in three issues of *Chieh-fang* [liberation], published at Yenan by the Hsin-hua shu-tien [new China bookstore]. Liu argued that because many party members come from non-proletarian families and thus bring remnants of tainted ideologies into the party with them, they therefore must pass through an extended period of "steeling and self-cultivation" to acquire a proper proletarian outlook. Accordingly, each party member must train himself, through sustained study of Marxism-Leninism and direct participation in "revolutionary struggles," to be a model Communist, "honest, pure, and progressive."

Two of Liu's concepts merit special attention. First, he stressed that being a good Communist is essentially a matter of self-discipline, self-examination, self-criticism, and self-cultivation. The concept of self-cultivation, with its distinctly Confucian antecedents, is implicit in the term hsiu-yang, which Liu used in the Chinese title of this work. Second, Liu argued that being a good Communist is a function of one's state of mind rather than something determined by economic or social circumstances. Accordingly, a person may acquire a proletarian outlook regardless of his background. Thus, by combining these two ideas, the basic Marxist concept of the proletariat was expanded in Chinese Communist usage and freed from its socio-economic connotations. For a party which was by definition the vanguard of the proletariat, this approach had great potentialities in wartime China, where nationalism was at least as important as the class struggle in expanding Communist power.

After becoming secretary of the central China bureau of the Chinese Communist party in 1939, Liu worked to spur the formation of guerrilla units in Kiangsu and Anhwei, thus moving into new areas of organization and discipline. Following the so-called New Fourth Army Incident of January 1941 (*see* Yeh T'ing), Liu played a key role in the reconstruction of the New Fourth Army. On 22 January, Liu was named political commissar of the New Fourth Army, with Ch'en Yi (1901–; q.v.) as acting commander and Teng Tzu-hui (q.v.) as chief of its political department. Liu set policy guidelines in an article entitled "Present Conditions and Tasks in Central Kiangsu," which was published at Yench'eng in the New Fourth Army journal, *Chiang-Huai jih-pao* [Yangtze and Huai river daily]. He stressed Communist-directed mass education as a means of instilling national consciousness in the populace. His June 1941 statement, "On the Class Character of Man," reiterated basic Marxist-Leninist tenets, and his important speech of 2 July 1941, "On Inner Party Struggle" [Lun tang-nei tou-cheng], delivered at the Central Party School, defined "struggle" and commented on its nature and importance in the Chinese Communist party.

By the time of the cheng-feng [political rectification] movement of 1942 (for details, *see* Mao Tse-tung), Liu Shao-ch'i had achieved party recognition as a reliable spokesman on problems of organization and control and as a stern but realistic political moralist. After being recalled to Yenan in October 1942, arriving there early in 1943, he served as a vice chairman of the People's Revolutionary Military Council and as a member of the five-man Secretariat of the Central Committee, the other members being Mao Tse-tung, Chu Teh, Chou En-lai, and Jen Pi-shih. He was chosen to write the principal article for the twenty-second anniversary celebrations of the Chinese Communist party. This article, "Liquidate the Menshevist Ideology Within the Party" (Ch'ing-suan tang-nei ti meng-she-wei chu-i ssu-hsiang), appeared on 1 July 1943. In May 1944 Liu Shao-ch'i made a major speech at a conference of workers from factories and textile cooperatives in the Shensi-Kansu-Ninghsia Border Region; the meeting, at which Kao Kang and Teng Fa (qq.v.) also spoke, dealt with the problems faced by the Communists in achieving self-sufficiency in industrial production under wartime conditions.

While working to confirm and strengthen the Leninist nature of their party, the Chinese Communists also emphasized to American representatives in China the potential importance of American economic assistance to China's postwar reconstruction. This point was made by Liu Shao-ch'i and his associates at Yenan in conversations with American Foreign Service officer John S. Service in 1944.

The position of Liu Shao-ch'i as the Political Bureau member most concerned with problems of organization and party structure was confirmed on 14 May 1945, when he presented a lengthy report on revision of the party constitution at the Seventh National Congress of the Chinese Communist party. In this statement, usually known by its abridged English title, *On the Party* and often regarded as a tactical companion piece to Mao Tse-tung's "On Coalition Government," Liu confirmed the party's reliance on conventional "democratic centralism" and explicitly placed the Thought of Mao Tse-tung at the heart of its ideological structure. Liu also confirmed the Chinese Communist contention that political and ideological, rather than social, factors shaped the Chinese Communist party as the "political party of the proletariat." At this time, Liu became the third-ranking member of the Central Committee, following Mao Tse-tung and Chu Teh, and a vice chairman of the Political Bureau.

By the time of the Japanese surrender in 1945, Liu Shao-ch'i, though little known in the West, was one of the small group of men standing closest to Mao Tse-tung in authority at Yenan. When Mao flew to Chungking in the early autumn of 1945 for discussions with Chiang Kai-shek, Liu served as his surrogate at Yenan. In the spring of 1946, Liu told the American journalist Anna Louise Strong that Mao

Tse-tung had transformed traditional Marxism-Leninism into a practical creed for application in Asia. Mao's revolutionary theories, he stated, charted a path to power not only for the Chinese Communists but also for "the billion people who live in the colonial countries of Southeast Asia." He stressed that the Chinese Communists were building a "new capitalism" as a precursor to the socialist revolution and contrasted this with the "military communism" of the Soviet Union. Miss Strong later recounted this interview in "The Thought of Mao Tse-tung," which appeared in *Amerasia* in June 1947.

Liu remained in Yenan after the collapse of American mediation efforts in China in 1946 and after the outbreak of civil war between the Nationalists and the Chinese Communists. When a Nationalist drive forced the Communists to evacuate Yenan in March 1947, the high command separated; Mao Tse-tung, Jen Pi-shih, and Chou En-lai remained in northern Shensi, while Liu Shao-ch'i, Chu Teh, and an alternate working committee moved to the Shansi-Chahar-Hopei base area. The working committee, headed by Liu, was located in 1947 at Hsipo in P'ingshan hsien, Hopei. That September, Liu presided over a conference on agriculture which formulated and drafted a land law for application in Communist-controlled areas. This law, promulgated by the Chinese Communist party in October, served as the basis for national land reform legislation after 1949.

Although military operations and political planning were of primary importance during this period, the Chinese Communists did not neglect international issues. After the Tito apostasy in the summer of 1948, Liu Shao-ch'i, on behalf of the party leadership, released the statement *On Internationalism and Nationalism* (*Lun kuo-chi chu-i yü min-chu chu-i*) on 1 November. He criticized Belgrade's recalcitrance and condemned Tito, not for a breach of political discipline, but for the fundamental ideological error of "bourgeois nationalism." In contradistinction, Liu stressed "proletarian internationalism," interpreted by the Chinese Communists to mean a federation of national Communist parties allied on an equal and voluntary footing and united in a common ideology and a common allegiance to the Soviet Union.

Early in 1949 the Chinese Communist leaders gathered in southern Hopei for a Central Committee meeting, held from 16 to 23 March, at which the shifting of the revolution's center of gravity from the rural to the urban areas and the importance to China of industrialization were stressed. At the end of March, the senior party leaders moved to Peiping. In September, they convened the Chinese People's Political Consultative Conference to create a new government for China, and, on 1 October, Mao Tse-tung became Chairman of the Central People's Government of the People's Republic of China, with Chu Teh as the senior-ranking vice chairman and Liu Shao-ch'i as the second vice chairman. By this time, Liu also had become general secretary of the party Secretariat. In addition, he held top posts in what the Chinese Communists termed "people's organizations." Between 1949 and 1954 he headed the Sino-Soviet Friendship Association, and he was elected honorary chairman of the All-China Federation of Labor at its sixth congress in 1949 and its seventh congress in 1953.

When the Central People's Government was reorganized in 1954, Liu Shao-ch'i became chairman of the standing committee of the National People's Congress, the organ to which all other government organs theoretically were responsible. Changes were made in the top party hierarchy at the first session in September 1956 and the second session in May 1958 of the Eighth National Congress of the Chinese Communist party. Teng Hsiao-p'ing (q.v.) became general secretary of the Central Committee, thus assuming tasks that Liu had performed since 1945. The top decision-making organ of the party came to be the seven-man standing committee of the Political Bureau, on which Liu was the second-ranking member.

After an announcement was made in December 1958 that Mao Tse-tung intended to relinquish his governmental responsibilities, Liu Shao-ch'i was elected Chairman of the People's Republic of China in April 1959. At that time, he was described in official publications as Mao's "closest comrade in arms." Liu's election to this office appeared to raise him above possible rivals and thereby to ensure his later succession to the chairmanship of the Chinese Communist party.

Liu Shao-ch'i's public statements and activities after 1949 to some degree may be considered a guide to Peking's evolving policies on many domestic and international questions. In his November 1949 speech to the Trade Union Conference of Asian and Australasian Countries at Peking, he set forth basic Chinese Communist tenets on foreign relations, presented the process of creating the People's Republic of China as the model for all revolutionary movements in "colonial and semi-colonial countries," and set the tone of nationalistic militancy that characterized Peking's early pronouncements on foreign policy. Liu's two major speeches of 1950 set forth Peking's relatively moderate labor and agricultural policies. On 1 July 1951, the Chinese Communist party's thirtieth anniversary, Liu presented a report laced with adulation of "Chairman Mao's correct leadership" and stressed that Mao alone had consistently understood the correct application of Marxism-Leninism in China. Early in November of that year, Liu delivered a major speech on qualifications for Chinese Communist party members.

Liu Shao-ch'i went to Moscow in October 1952 to attend the Nineteenth Congress of the Communist party of the Soviet Union. He remained in Moscow until January 1953, three months after the congress closed, but the purpose of his mission was never explained. In February 1953 he delivered the principal speech on the occasion of the third anniversary of the Sino-Soviet Treaty of Friendship and Alliance.

After the death of Stalin in March 1953 and the signing of an armistice agreement in Korea in July of that year, Peking shifted its attention to problems of political consolidation and economic development. Soon afterwards, the top command of the party dealt sharply with a short-lived threat to its authority. Acting in accordance with a Political Bureau resolution of December 1953, the Central Committee met on 6–10 February 1954, and Liu Shao-ch'i delivered a slashing attack on dissidents and emphasized the need for "collective leadership" under Mao Tse-tung. This meeting was a prelude to the disclosures regarding the alleged "anti-party faction" of Kao Kang and Jao Shu-shih (q.v.).

In September 1954 Liu Shao-ch'i delivered an authoritative report on the draft constitution submitted to the National People's Congress. It later was adopted by that body as the formal framework of authority for the People's Republic of China. Two years later, Liu presented the principal political report to the Eighth National Congress of the Chinese Communist party. When Mao Tse-tung went to Moscow in 1957 for the fortieth anniversary celebrations of the Bolshevik Revolution, Liu remained in Peking as Mao's proxy and spoke to a rally on *The Significance of the October Revolution (Shih-yüeh ke-ming ti i-i)*. This speech was a significant indicator of Peking's awareness of changes in world political geography and interest in the developing nations of the Middle East, Africa, and Latin America. In May 1958, at the second session of the Eighth National Congress of the Chinese Communist party, Liu focused attention on the party's role in China's "socialist construction" and outlined a new development strategy that involved the mobilization of underemployed rural labor on an unprecedented scale. On 1 October 1959, when Nikita Khrushchev was in China for the tenth anniversary celebrations of the People's Republic of China, Liu's commemorative article, *The Victory of Marxism-Leninism in China (Ma-k'e-ssu Lieh-ning chu-i tsai Chung-kuo ti sheng-li)* was released in both Peking and Moscow. It vindicated the Great Leap Forward, supported the concept of "permanent revolution," and contained implied criticisms of the Soviet Union.

By 1960 increasing Sino-Soviet antagonism was becoming apparent. One key issue in the developing conflict within the Communist bloc was the problem of the international position and prestige of Mao Tse-tung. The Chinese Communists placed Mao in direct succession to the classical theorists of Communist revolution—Marx, Engels, and Lenin—as the principal arbiter of strategy for the emerging nations. Partly because other Communist bloc leaders did not accept this evaluation, Mao did not attend the forty-third anniversary celebrations of the Bolshevik Revolution, but sent Liu Shao-ch'i to Moscow in his stead.

As the second-ranking leader of the Chinese Communist party, Liu Shao-ch'i made the principal speech at the meeting celebrating its fortieth anniversary on 30 June 1961, by which time the party membership had grown to about 17,000,000. In August 1962 both the *Jen-min jih-pao* [people's daily] and the theoretical journal *Hung-ch'i* [red flag] reprinted his 1939 speech, *How to Be a Good Communist*. In political

terms, the reprinting of this statement constituted a high accolade which was normally
reserved for the writings of Mao Tse-tung and
seemed to confirm that Liu had been chosen
as Mao's successor. Although the fundamental
structure and argument of the 1962 edition was
unchanged, the phraseology differed considerably from the 1939 version. Comments
bearing on the Sino-Soviet conflict were added
to the text, as were new quotations from such
writings of Mao Tse-tung as *On Practice* and
On Contradiction. An English translation of
How To Be a Good Communist was published in
1964.

Liu Shao-ch'i made his first trip outside the
Communist orbit in 1963 when, accompanied
by Ch'en Yi, he traveled to Indonesia, Burma,
Cambodia, and North Viet Nam. In March
1966, again accompanied by the foreign
minister and a large official party, he made a
state visit to Pakistan, where he was greeted by
President Mohammed Ayub Khan. Liu emphasized China's friendship for Pakistan, which
had been made manifest in the backing given
Pakistan in the inconclusive conflict with India
in the autumn of 1965 and in the continued
flow of military supplies from the People's
Republic of China to Pakistan.

Beginning in 1966 Liu Shao-ch'i became a
target of severe public censure as the so-called
Cultural Revolution gained momentum in
China. At the eleventh plenum of the eighth
Central Committee, held in August 1966,
Lin Piao (q.v.) emerged as Mao Tse-tung's new
heir apparent. In late December the Japanese
press released a document purported to be a
political confession made by Liu Shao-ch'i at a
Central Committee meeting in the last week of
October. He allegedly admitted to political
errors extending back to 1946 and stated that
he had made particularly serious blunders in
the weeks prior to the Central Committee
meeting of August 1966. The leaders of the
Cultural Revolution singled out for attack many
of the bases of political power closely associated
with Liu Shao-ch'i—municipal party committees, propaganda organs, labor unions, and
official youth groups. The spring of 1967
brought mounting public demonstrations against
Liu in every major city of China, and the press
devoted major attention to his political sins.
On 1 July 1967, the forty-sixth anniversary of
the founding of the Chinese Communist party,

the ideological journal *Hung-ch'i* [red flag]
proclaimed the "overthrow" of Liu Shao-ch'i
and a "handful of party people" associated with
him.

Some outside observers estimated that the
Cultural Revolution in China reflected an
impatience on the part of Mao Tse-tung with
the Communist party structure as an apparatus
of control and a calculated intention to rely
increasingly on the "broad masses of the people"
to achieve long-range political goals. Liu
Shao-ch'i, as the party's foremost expert on the
theory and practice of organization and as a
proponent of strong organizational structure as
the basis of the party, represented an approach
to government and the socialist revolution that
conflicted with the stated aims of the new
movement.

Prior to the exposures of the Cultural
Revolution, little was known of Liu Shao-ch'i's
personal life. Before 1945, he had been married
and was known to have had children; one son
was entrusted to the care of Jen Pi-shih during
his father's absence for a period in 1947. In
the late 1940's Liu Shao-ch'i married Wang
Kuang-mei, a 1943 graduate of Fu-jen University in Peking and a member of a well-
known north China family with business and
industrial connections. Like her husband,
Wang Kuang-mei became a prominent target
of criticism during the Cultural Revolution.

Liu Shih-p'ei　　　　劉 師 培
　T. Shen-shu　　　　申 叔
　H. Tso-an　　　　　左 盦

Liu Shih-p'ei (2 May 1884–20 December 1919),
classical scholar and enthusiastic republican
revolutionary who, however, spent the last two
years of the imperial period in the service of the
Manchu authorities. After the 1911 revolution
Liu devoted himself to the preservation of
conservative scholarship and political institutions.

In three generations before him, Liu Shih-
p'ei's family had produced four noted scholars
of the Chinese classics: his great-grandfather,
Liu Wen-ch'i (ECCP, I, 534–35); his grandfather, Liu Yü-sung (ECCP, I, 535–36); his
father, Liu Kuei-tseng; and his uncle, Liu
Shou-tseng (ECCP, I, 536). Although their

ancestral home was in the Icheng district of Kiangsu, the family had lived in the city of Yangchow for several generations.

After receiving a traditional education in the Chinese classics, Liu Shih-p'ei became a sheng-yuan in 1901 and a chü-jen in 1902. He failed the metropolitan examinations at Peking in 1903 and went to Shanghai, where he met and became friendly with such young anti-Manchu revolutionaries as Chang Ping-lin and Ts'ai Yuan-p'ei (qq.v.). Liu joined them in their political activities and wrote articles advocating the overthrow of the Manchus. To show his revolutionary zeal, he changed his name to "Kuang-han" [restore China] to identify himself with the restoration of ethnic Chinese rule in opposition to the Manchus. Among his writings, the most representative of this period is the *Jang-shu* [on the expulsion], a title which in itself implies the driving out of the Manchus. In Shanghai, Liu also took part in establishing a monthly magazine, the *Kuo-ts'ui hsueh-pao*, and a school, the Kuo-ts'ui hsueh-t'ang. Both were devoted to the preservation of China's cultural heritage and were ardently nationalistic. In addition, Liu served as the editor of Ts'ai Yuan-p'ei's *O-shih ching-wen* [Russian menace warning bulletin], soon renamed the *Ching-chung jih-pao* [alarm bell daily bulletin]. He hoped to make his compatriots aware of the 1904 Russian advance into Manchuria. When the paper was closed by the imperial authorities in April 1905 because of its anti-Manchu stand, Liu escaped arrest by taking refuge in P'inghu, Chekiang. He then became a teacher in a middle school in Wuhu, Anhwei, where in 1906 he established the *Pai-hua pao* [vernacular paper].

After Chang Ping-lin became the editor of the republican *Min-pao* [people's journal] in Tokyo, he invited Liu Shih-p'ei to join his staff. Liu went to Japan in 1907, joined the *Min-pao* staff, and became a member of the T'ung-meng-hui, which had been organized by Sun Yat-sen in 1905. After being befriended and influenced by some of the more radical Japanese socialists, Liu began publishing the *T'ien-i pao* [natural law journal], which was one of the earliest Chinese periodicals devoted to socialism, and joined with Chang Chi (q.v.) in forming a club to study socialism. Another journal published by Liu Shih-p'ei in Tokyo during this period was the *Heng-pao* [journal of discussion]. In

addition to his interest in socialism, Liu's writings in Japan also indicate that he was attracted to anarchism.

In 1909 Liu Shih-p'ei suddenly changed his attitude toward the revolutionary movement, broke with his colleagues in Japan, and returned to China, where he joined the secretariat of Tuan-fang (ECCP, II, 780–82), then the Manchu viceroy of Liang-Kiang. The reasons for this abrupt change are not clear, but whatever the explanation, Liu spent the last two years of the imperial period in the service of the Manchu authorities.

After the Manchu government announced its plan to nationalize certain railways in 1911, Tuan-fang, who had become superintendent of the proposed Canton-Hankow-Chengtu railway, was ordered to Szechwan to suppress opposition to the program. The revolution broke out while Tuan-fang was on his way to Chengtu, and he was killed in November 1911. Liu Shih-p'ei, who had accompanied Tuan-fang on the trip, escaped to Chengtu, where he taught at the Szechwan Kuo-hsueh hsueh-hsiao [school for Chinese studies] and contributed to the Szechwan *Kuo-hsueh tsa-chih* [Chinese studies magazine], a journal issued by the school.

In 1913 Liu moved to Taiyuan, Shansi, where he started another journal of Chinese studies, the *Kuo-ku kou-ch'en* [from out of China's past]. He went to Peking in 1914, and he was appointed to the National Assembly by Yuan Shih-k'ai in 1915. Liu became one of the six original members (known collectively as the liu chün-tzu, or Six Gentlemen) of the Ch'ou-an-hui [society to plan for stability], who officially launched a movement to make Yuan Shih-k'ai monarch. Liu's chief contribution to the effort was his essay "Chün-cheng fu-ku lun" [on restoration of the monarchy]. After Yuan's death in 1916, Liu retired to Tientsin. At the invitation of Ts'ai Yuan-p'ei, then the chancellor of National Peking University, he joined the faculty of that institution in 1917 and remained there until his death from tuberculosis at the end of 1919. During his last years in Peking he wrote for the *Chung-kuo hsueh-pao* [China academic journal] and the *Kuo-ku tsa-chih* [national heritage magazine].

After Liu Shih-p'ei's death, at the age of 35, his friends and pupils collected and published seventy-four of his writings in seven volumes as the *Liu Shen-shu hsien-sheng i-shu* in 1936. This collection included studies of the Chinese classics, essays, poems, study notes, and textbooks on various subjects. The study notes included the "Tun-huang hsin-ch'u T'ang hsieh-pen t'i-yao," descriptive notes on 19 items of the T'ang manuscripts taken by Paul Pelliot from Tunhuang. Although Liu was acclaimed as a scholar, particularly of the *Ch'un-ch'iu tso-chuan* [Tso's commentary on the Spring and Autumn Annals], many of his writings lacked profundity and critical insight. As a prolific writer who communicated his opinions on a variety of subjects in periodicals established by himself or others, Liu Shih-p'ei helped pave the way for modern Chinese journalism.

Liu Ssu-fu   劉 思 復
Alt. Shih-fu   師 復

Liu Ssu-fu (1884–March 1915), founder and leader of the first anarchist societies to be established in China and publisher of the *Min-sheng* [voice of the people].

Born into a well-to-do family in Hsiangshan, Kwangtung, Liu Ssu-fu received a conventional education in the Chinese classics and became a sheng-yuan at the age of 15 sui. He then decided to study philology, mathematics, and the writings of the ancient Chinese philosophers. At the turn of the century, he and a group of friends organized a society to discuss the ideas of the reform leaders of the time. In 1904 he went to Japan to continue his studies, and the following year he became one of the founding members of the T'ung-meng-hui, headed by Sun Yat-sen.

Liu Ssu-fu returned to China in the summer of 1906 with a group of fellow revolutionaries and began to work on the staff of a Hong Kong newspaper, the *Tung-fang pao*. Liu also participated in the activities of a secret terrorist group organized by the T'ung-meng-hui which manufactured explosives for use in assassinating high Manchu officials in Canton. In the spring of 1907 plans were made to kill Li Chun, the naval commander in chief of Kwangtung, and Liu volunteered for the assignment. He went to Canton in June with a supply of explosives, but before he was able to complete his mission,

the bomb he was carrying exploded, blowing off all the fingers of his left hand. While being treated at a nearby hospital, he was arrested by the government authorities on suspicion of being a member of the revolutionary party. When the authorities finally established his identity, he was transferred from Canton to the prison in his native district of Hsiangshan. During his imprisonment he was able to read extensively and to write a number of books, including a study of Cantonese dialects, prison memoirs, and a tract on prison reform which made a favorable impression on the local authorities and was said to have caused the mitigation of his sentence. After being released in 1909, he went to Hong Kong, where he reestablished contact with his revolutionary associates.

Liu Ssu-fu is believed to have been attracted to the anarchist-communist movement when he was in prison. During that period two small Chinese anarchist groups had been formed abroad: one, organized by Chang Chi and Liu Shih-p'ei (qq.v.) in Tokyo, issued a propaganda periodical named *T'ien-i pao* in 1907–8; the other, established in Paris by Li Shih-tseng, Wu Chih-hui, and Chang Jen-chieh (qq.v.) as the Shih-chieh she [world society], published the *Hsin shih-chi* [new century] from 1907 to 1910. Although they were little known in China at that time, it was probably through issues of these publications, particularly the *Hsin shih-chi*, that Liu Ssu-fu was introduced to the ideas of Proudhon, Bakunin, Kropotkin, and other European anarchist leaders. In Hong Kong he studied the anarchist literature then available and became a convert to the anarchist faith in the ultimate freedom and equality of mankind through the destruction of such repressive institutions as government, property, the family, and religion. Translating these ideals into action, Liu organized an independent terrorist group in Hong Kong, the immediate aim of which was to eliminate the ruling class in China by assassinating its most prominent members. In August 1911 another unsuccessful attempt was made on the life of Li Chun, which was followed two months later by the assassination of the Manchu general at Canton, Feng-shan. Other intended victims included the Manchu regent, whom Wang Ching-wei (q.v.) had attempted to assassinate in 1910. Liu was on his way to Peking to carry out this project when the October revolt at Wuchang, resulting in the overthrow of the Manchus, rendered his task unnecessary.

Having proceeded as far as Shanghai, Liu Ssu-fu spent a month in Hangchow. While lodging at a small Buddhist temple on West Lake, he worked out plans for a full-fledged anarchist movement in China. After his return to Canton early in 1912, he and a group of comrades, as harbingers of brighter days to come, formed the Cock-Crow Society (Hui-ming hsueh-she) to propagate anarchism among the people. Some years earlier, several essays on anarchism and translations of the writings of European anarchists had appeared in Chinese in the *Hsin shih-chi* of Paris, but, because of rigid censorship under the Ch'ing dynasty, issues of this magazine had been extremely difficult to obtain in China at that time. To make these writings better known, Liu and his colleagues republished articles and translations from *Hsin shih-chi*, first as separate pamphlets and then, beginning in August 1913, in the pages of the Cock-Crow Society's periodical, *Hui-ming lu*. This magazine soon was renamed the *Min-sheng* [the voice of the people].

Liu Ssu fu was concerned with the importance of individual regeneration in the reformation of society along anarchist lines. Influenced, perhaps, by his studies of Tolstoy, he concluded that modern urban life was too complex and planned with a group of friends to retire to a rural area north of Hong Kong, where they could lead a simple, austere life of study and farming. Although this project soon was abandoned, it resulted in the formation of the Conscience Society (Hsin-she), founded by Liu and others in Canton in 1913. This anarchist association probably was modeled on the Society to Advance Morality (Chin-te hui), which had been organized in January 1912 by Li Shih-tseng, Wu Chih-hui, and other members of the earlier anarchist group in Paris. Membership in the Conscience Society required adherence to 12 rules of personal conduct which prohibited the consumption of meat, liquor, and tobacco, the employment of servants, riding in sedan chairs and rickshaws, marriage, family surnames, and participation in government, the parliament, political parties, the armed forces, or any religious organization. Another aspect of Liu's activities on behalf of anarchism at this time was his promotion of Esperanto as a universal language. He believed the establishing

of a universal language to be the first step in attaining a world brotherhood of man. Accordingly, he organized the Association for the Study of Esperanto (Shih-chieh-yü yen-chiu-hui), which claimed about 300 members, and became the Canton representative of the Universal Union of Esperantists.

Liu and his group were able to carry on their activities with little hindrance from the Canton authorities, and through their publications the anarchist movement attracted the attention of Chinese intellectuals. During the summer of 1913, however, as the struggle between the Kuomintang and Yuan Shih-k'ai (q.v.) erupted into the open warfare of the so-called second revolution, the anarchists ran into political difficulties. Liu Ssu-fu refused to support the Kuomintang, which he viewed as but one governmental organization seeking to overthrow another. Nevertheless, with the defeat of the Kuomintang in Canton by Yuan's adherent Lung Chi-kuang (q.v.), the Cock-Crow Society and its magazine were suppressed at Yuan's order; and when Liu moved the periodical to Macao, Yuan was able to secure its prohibition by the Portuguese authorities there. After several months of fugitive existence, Liu moved to the safety of the International Settlement in Shanghai, where he resumed publication of the *Min-sheng* in April 1914 and founded the Society of Anarchist-Communist Comrades (Wu-cheng-fu kung-ch'an chu-i t'ung-chih she) in July. To establish connections with the world anarchist movement, he sent a letter to the International Anarchist Congress reporting on the progress of anarchism in China, and he published news of foreign anarchist activities in the *Min-sheng*.

The ideals and aims of the new Society of Anarchist-Communist Comrades, drawn largely from the writings of Kropotkin, were set forth in a manifesto issued soon after the society came into being and thereafter in the pages of the *Min-sheng*. The purpose of the new society was to work toward the complete freedom of the people from political authority and economic exploitation. Of the existing forms of authority, the most powerful was that of the state, and thus it was the task of anarchists to overthrow all types of government. The major form of economic exploitation was capitalism, and hence anarchists were dedicated to the opposing principles of socialism. Liu distinguished between two types of socialism: collectivism, which called for state ownership of the means of production but private ownership of consumer products; and communism, which demanded communal ownership of *all* products as well as of the means of production. Anarchists favored socialism of the communist variety. To eliminate these existing forms of oppression, Liu recommended the propagation of anarchist ideas in the press, in public addresses, and in the schools, and resistance, both passive and active, to all forms of authority: refusal to pay taxes or to submit to military conscription and participation in strikes and assassinations. The final result of the ensuing world revolution, as outlined in the society's manifesto, would be a world "without landowners, capitalists, parasites, political leaders, officials, heads of families, armies, prisons, police, courts of justice, laws, and religion." It would be a classless society with public nurseries, schools, hospitals, and old-age homes. All the people would work together and share equally in the product of their labor.

Liu Ssu-fu made every effort to preserve the integrity of the anarchist doctrines. He castigated Chang Chi and other of the *Hsin shih-chi* group, saying that they had compromised their anarchist principles by belonging to the Kuomintang and by taking office in the Peking government. In emphasizing the revolutionary character of anarchist socialism, he took issue with "moderates" who, he said confused socialism with social reform. Thus he criticized Sun Yat-sen for adhering to the single-tax theory of Henry George, which, to Liu, was no more than a proposal for social reform. Liu's most bitter attacks, however, were reserved for Chiang K'ang-hu (q.v.), the founder of the Chinese Socialist party. He sharply contested Chiang's assertions that Marxist collectivism was the only form of socialism and claimed that the Socialist party leader had, in fact, only a limited understanding of socialism, particularly that of the anarchist-communist variety. Furthermore, Liu pointed to the political platform of the Socialist party, which called for nothing more than a few relatively moderate reforms of the existing system, to show that Chiang K'ang-hu, like Sun Yat-sen, could not be considered an authentic socialist.

Liu Ssu-fu continued to lead the anarchist movement in China until his untimely death from tuberculosis in March 1915, at the age of 30. From all accounts, he was a personally attractive man, completely dedicated to his ideals. Despite the wasting illness that kept him bed-ridden during his final years and despite his mangled left hand, he not only served as chief editor of the *Min-sheng*, but also acted as proofreader and typesetter for the magazine. Although he lived in dire poverty, he stubbornly refused to heed his comrades' suggestions that he sell the hand press used to print the *Min-sheng* in order to obtain funds for medical treatment. Although they eventually persuaded him to enter a hospital, he declined to follow medical instructions to build up his strength by eating meat, because that action would violate the code he had drawn up for the Conscience Society. According to his friends, Liu adhered strictly to the rules of this code, severing his ties with his family and adopting the simple pseudonym Shih-fu, and refusing to marry. However, some sources state that in 1906, before he became an anarchist, he had become engaged to Ting Hsiang-t'ien, a teacher in a Hong Kong school for girls, and that she shared his life during his early revolutionary years. In 1927 Liu's friends published a collection of his writings, the *Shih-fu wen-ts'un*.

The death of Liu Ssu-fu was a severe blow to the anarchist movement in China. The *Min-sheng* survived only until November 1916. Nevertheless, during the next few years, particularly at the time of the May Fourth Movement, anarchist thought enjoyed a considerable vogue among students and young intellectuals in Peking, Shanghai, and other cities. Such magazines as *Chin-hua* [progress], *Min-chung* [people's tocsin], and *Tzu-yu-jen* [freeman] continued to carry the message of anarchism, and anarchists were prominent during the 1920's in the labor movement in Canton, Changsha, and Shanghai.

In many ways the anarchist movement prepared the ground for the advent of Marxism-Leninism in China, and in 1920–21 several anarchist sympathizers were to be found among the organizers of the Chinese Communist party. But with the establishment and expansion of the Communist organization in the early 1920's, cooperation between anarchists and Communists changed to antagonism that was reflected in the protracted literary controversy between the anarchist Ou Sheng-pai and the head of the

Chinese Communist party, Ch'enTu-hsiu (q.v.). Thereafter, these two wings of the radical socialist movement began to vie with one another for the allegiance of intellectuals and labor unionists—a competition in which the anarchists were rapidly losing ground to the Communist party by the mid-1920's. The anarchist movement in China was on the decline, and in the 1930's its influence in political and intellectual circles dwindled into insignificance, although scattered anarchist groups and publications remained in existence until 1949.

Liu T'ing-fang   劉廷芳
West. Timothy Lew

Liu T'ing-fang (18 January 1890–1 August 1947), known as Timothy Lew, one of the most influential Chinese Protestant leaders of the republican period. He taught for many years at Yenching and Peking universities.

A native of Chekiang province, Timothy Lew studied in Wenchow and at St. John's University in Shanghai before going to the United States, where he received a B.A. degree from the University of Georgia in 1914, an M.A. degree from Columbia University in 1915, a B.D. degree from the Yale Divinity School in 1918, and a Ph.D. degree in education and psychology from Teachers College, Columbia University in 1920. During his years as a student in the United States he served as president of the Chinese Students Christian Association in North America and chairman of the board of representatives of the eastern section of the Chinese Students Alliance. He also was the editor of the *Liu-mei ch'ing-nien*, the quarterly journal of the Christian Association, and associate editor of the *Chinese Students' Monthly*. Beginning in 1918 he taught in the department of religious education at Union Theological Seminary in New York, thus becoming the first Chinese to teach a non-Chinese subject at an American theological school. He also became a member of the council of the Religious Education Association.

After returning to China in 1920, Timothy Lew became dean of the graduate school of education at Peking Normal College, professor of psychology at Peking University, and a professor of theology at Yenching University's school of religion. From 1921 to 1926 he was dean of the Yenching school of religion and assistant to the chancellor of the university, and he was one of several featured speakers at the National Christian Conference of 2–10 May 1922. At that time, in speaking of the type of Church desired by Chinese Christians, he said that "she shall teach her members to agree to differ, but resolve to love." He also continued to teach at Peking University and served as honorary pastor of the Mi-shih Chinese Independent Church in Peking. In March 1925, assisted by Y. Y. Tsu (q.v.), he conducted the Christian funeral service for Sun Yat-sen that was held at Peking Union Medical College. During this period Lew, who was a Congregationalist, participated in the activities of the World Student Christian Federation and helped organize the National Christian Council of China, which was established in 1922. He served as a member of the council's executive committee for more than a decade. He also was a director of the Peking YMCA and a member of the commission on literature of the YMCA's national committee.

Timothy Lew also exerted a significant influence on educational practices in China. He was a founder and a director of the Psychological Association in China, and in 1923 he became chairman of the committee on standardized tests of the China Christian Education Association. The tests produced by his committee were used in an extensive survey conducted in 1924 on behalf of the Chinese government and the Christian mission schools by the National Association for the Advancement of Education, of which Lew was executive secretary. From 1924 to 1927 Lew was president of the China Christian Education Association, the first Chinese to hold that office.

In 1926 Timothy Lew went to the United States, where he lectured at Yale Divinity School, Union Theological Seminary, and Hartford Theological Seminary. In 1927 he was awarded honorary degrees by Middlebury College and Oberlin College. That summer, he served as a delegate to the World Conference on Faith and Order at Lausanne, Switzerland and represented the National Christian Council of China at a meeting in Germany of the World Alliance for Promoting International Fellowship

Through the Churches. By this time, he had become known as one of the most articulate Protestant leaders of China. After he went to London as a guest preacher at the City Temple, the editors of *Punch* were so intrigued by his name, his personality, and his linguistic gifts (he spoke eight languages) that they published a verse, "Dr. Lew," to commemorate his visit. In the autumn of 1927, Liu returned to the United States to become a visiting professor at Boston University. In 1928 he delivered the Enoch Paul lectures at the Bangor Seminary in Maine and the Aldon Tuthill lectures at Chicago Theological Seminary.

After returning to China in the summer of 1928, Timothy Lew resumed his posts at Yenching and Peking universities. However, his many responsibilities forced him to reduce his teaching load. In 1930 he was elected unanimously to the chairmanship of the newly created China National Committee on Christian Higher Education, and he was returned to this office in the next five annual elections. He also was chairman of the Religious Education Fellowship of China, and he served on a number of committees which were investigating elementary-school conditions in China. He also served on committees that were trying to establish a standard scientific vocabulary for use in China.

Timothy Lew further contributed to the causes of education and Protestantism in China by editing such well-known journals as the *Life Journal* (1920–24), *Truth Weekly* (1924–26), the *Truth and Life Journal*, the *Amethyst Quarterly Journal*, and *Education for Tomorrow*. As chairman of a joint commission established in 1932 by six missionary societies, he wrote and translated hymns for and supervised the preparation and editing of the Chinese union hymnal, *Hymns of Universal Praise*. It was published in 1936 and was adopted enthusiastically by Protestant groups throughout China.

In 1936 Timothy Lew became a member of the Legislative Yuan. The following year, he was a delegate to the World Council of Churches' conferences at Oxford (Life and Work) and at Edinburgh (Faith and Order). He went to Tembarum, India, in 1938 to participate in the International Missionary Conference. By this time, the Sino-Japanese war had broken out, and it was not feasible for Lew to return to north China. Accordingly, he established

residence in Shanghai, where he remained until the end of 1941. Lew had always been slight and rather frail, and by the late 1930's his many years of prodigious labor had undermined his health. In 1942 he went to the United States to seek relief from the headaches, respiratory difficulties, and chronic fatigue that prevented him from working. He died of tuberculosis on 1 August 1947 at the Southwest Presbyterian Sanitorium in Albuquerque, New Mexico.

Timothy Lew was one of the most persuasive spokesmen for the Christian way of life in republican China. He defined the basic concepts of Protestant Christianity in terms that were both challenging and comprehensible, and he demonstrated their relevance to issues then current in China: democracy, the scientific revolution, and the problems involved in China's transition from its traditional past to modernity. Although some of his colleagues thought him too much of a heretic to be considered a great ecclesiastic, they all praised his strong influence on and efforts on behalf of generations of Chinese students.

Liu Wen-hui   劉 文 輝
T. Tzu-ch'ien   自 乾

Liu Wen-hui (1895–), Szechwanese militarist who served as commander of the Twenty-fourth Army (1927–45), commander in chief of Szechwan-Sikang border defense (1928–45), governor of Szechwan (1929–32), and governor of Sikang. After 1949 he held office in the People's Republic of China, becoming minister of forestry in 1959.

A native of Tayi hsien, Szechwan, Liu Wen-hui was schooled for a military career. He attended the Chengtu Army Primary School, the Shensi Army Middle School, the Peking Army Preparatory School, and the Paoting Military Academy. After graduation from Paoting in 1916, he returned to Szechwan, where he rose to become a brigade commander. His success in subduing the notorious bandit Ma Pu-yun resulted in his promotion to command of the 9th Division and then of the 31st Division.

In April 1925, on the orders of his nephew Liu Hsiang (q.v.), Liu Wen-hui spearheaded an attack on Yang Sen (q.v.). At year's end, when

Yang had been driven from the province, Liu Wen-hui became deputy military governor of Szechwan, serving under Liu Hsiang. However, the reconciliation of Liu Hsiang and Yang Sen in the late spring of 1926 resulted in Liu Wen-hui's retirement from office. At the end of 1926 he declared allegiance to the Nationalists, and his forces became the Twenty-fourth Army of the National Revolutionary Army. He held that command until 1946, and the Twenty-fourth Army became the foundation of his political power.

After Liu Ch'eng-hsun, the Sikang rehabilitation commissioner, announced his retirement from office in June 1927, southern Szechwan and part of Sikang came under Liu Wen-hui's control. In recognition of this fact, the National Government appointed Liu commander in chief of Szechwan-Sikang border defense in the summer of 1928.

On 31 October 1928 the new National Government at Nanking appointed Liu Wen-hui governor of Szechwan. Yang Sen and other commanders opposed his appointment and denounced Liu Wen-hui and Liu Hsiang. A civil war ensued, and the two Lius emerged victorious only after Kuo Ju-tung defected to their side at the end of December. Liu Wen-hui assumed office as governor of Szechwan in March 1929.

Liu retained his post as commander in chief of Szechwan-Sikang border defense. In mid-1930 a dispute began between the Ta Chin monastery and the t'ussu [tribal chieftain] of Paili. The Tibetan adversaries resisted Chinese mediation efforts, but Ma Su, the commander of the local garrison force, finally took sides and attacked the Ta Chin monastery. A protracted Chinese-Tibetan struggle ensued. By the end of May 1931, the Chinese had lost Kantzu, Paili, and Chanhua. A representative of the Mongolian and Tibetan Affairs Commission at Nanking, T'ang K'o-san, reached Chengtu soon afterwards and asked Liu Wen-hui for troops with which to back up his negotiations. Liu refused to provide them. After arriving in Sikang in July, T'ang sent a subordinate, Liu Tsan-t'ing, to Kantzu to negotiate with the Tibetans.

Liu Tsan-t'ing reached a provisional agreement with the Tibetans which favored them, but Nanking refused to approve it. Soon afterwards, in February 1932, Ma Su's troops revolted, killed him, and retreated from the front. At that juncture, the National Government gave Liu Wen-hui full authority to deal with the situation. Liu worked out a plan of attack with Ma Pu-fang (q.v.), then the garrison commander at Yüshu, Tsinghai, and recovered both Kantzu and Chanhua. He continued to advance, and by July 1932 he had reached the banks of the Chin Sha River. At the beginning of October, he signed a local agreement with the Tibetans which stabilized the front.

In the autumn of 1932 Liu Hsiang, Yang Sen, and Teng Hsi-hou began a strong campaign against Liu Wen-hui. The fighting halted in December, and the opposing sides met in conference at Neichiang. Liu Wen-hui returned to Chengtu and attempted to resign as provincial governor, but the National Government ignored his resignation. Civil strife resumed in May 1933 when fighting broke out between the forces of Liu Wen-hui and Teng Hsi-hou. In July, the National Government appointed Liu Hsiang bandit-suppression commissioner. That month, Liu Wen-hui again submitted his resignation as provincial governor. By the time Liu Hsiang assumed his new post in October, Liu Wen-hui had been forced to retreat into Sikang.

In December 1934 Liu Wen-hui was appointed chairman of a new commission for the formal establishment of Sikang province. Despite the intrusion of the retreating Communist forces into the region in 1935 and the unrest and fighting that resulted from a new Tibetan autonomy movement in 1936, Liu had brought sufficient stability to the area by November 1936 to begin the work of making Sikang an integral part of the Chinese republic. Liu received the concurrent position of deputy director of Chiang Kai-shek's Chungking headquarters in 1938. The importance of this post increased when the National Government moved to Chungking in October 1938. Liu continued to work in Sikang, and when the Sikang provincial government was inaugurated on 1 January 1939, he became the governor of the new province.

For a decade, Liu Wen-hui and his associates ruled Sikang as a virtually autonomous area. Liu's control of Sikang was in key respects personal and rested on his Twenty-fourth Army, headquartered at Yaan. The civil government of the province was located at Kangting, though Liu himself also maintained a residence at Chengtu in western Szechwan. Relations between Sikang and the National Government authorities were loose, and the province remained economically backward. However, Sikang did have some regional trading importance under Liu Wen-hui's rule, as it was the main gateway for trade between China and Tibet and a major source of opium for shipment to other parts of China.

After the War in the Pacific ended and the Kuomintang-Communist struggle resumed, the National Government removed Liu Wen-hui from command of the Twenty-fourth Army. In December 1949, as the Nationalists were preparing to abandon Szechwan, their last stronghold on the Chinese mainland, Liu Wen-hui, Teng Hsi-hou, and P'an Wen-hua declared allegiance to the Communists.

From 1950 to 1954 Liu Wen-hui served the Central People's Government of the People's Republic of China as vice chairman of the Southwest Military and Administrative Committee. In October 1951 he became a member of the National Committee of the Chinese People's Political Consultative Conference. In 1954 he represented Szechwan at the National People's Congress, became a member of the National Defense Council, and served as a specially invited delegate and Standing Committee member of the Chinese People's Political Consultative Conference. He became vice chairman of the conference's Szechwan provincial committee in January 1955. His last major appointment came in April 1959, when he was made minister of forestry.

Liu Wen-tao　　　劉文島
　T. Ch'en-su　　　塵蘇

Liu Wen-tao (3 April 1893–11 June 1967), served the National Government in such posts as minister to Germany and Austria (1931–33) and minister (ambassador after 1934) to Italy (1933–37).

Kwangchi hsien, Hupeh, was the birthplace of Liu Wen-tao. Little is known about his family background or early education. At the age of ten sui he tried to join the army, but was rejected because of his age and height. He persisted in his attempts to pursue a military career, and three years later he used documents belonging to a friend to gain admittance to the entrance examinations for the Hupeh Army Primary School. He passed the examinations, but his identity was discovered and he was brought before Hsiung Hsiang-sheng, the superintendent of the school, who allowed him to enroll under his own name. Liu did well in his studies, and he was promoted to the Wuchang Third Army Primary School. In 1909 he was admitted to the student-recruit corps of the Paoting Military Academy, and the following year he enrolled in the infantry course of the academy's first class.

With the outbreak of revolution in 1911, military schools suspended operations. Liu Wen-tao went south to Shanghai, where he served as a company commander in the forces of Ch'en Ch'i-mei (q.v.). After the republic was established, Liu returned to school in July 1912. Many of the students who had participated in the revolution became dissatisfied with the old-school Peiyang officers who had been running the academy. They elected representatives to present their demands for reform to the authorities. Liu headed this group, with T'ang Sheng-chih (q.v.) representing the infantry division and Ch'en Ming-shu (q.v.) representing the artillery division. In December, Chiang Fang-chen (q.v.) became president of the academy. Because Tuan Ch'i-jui (q.v.), the minister of war, supported the older officers, many of whom were his protégés, he ignored Chiang's applications for academy funds. In June 1913, after Chiang had attempted to kill himself, Liu left the academy with Chiang, rejecting the advice of colleagues to bear with the situation for the three months remaining before his graduation. Liu's schoolmates raised a collection to send him to Japan to study. He studied law at Tokyo Imperial University and political science at Waseda. Because he believed that Chinese lacked understanding of political organization, he wrote a monograph, "Cheng-tang cheng-chih lun" [an essay on party politics]. After graduation in the autumn of 1916, he returned to China, where he showed his monograph to Liang Ch'i-ch'ao (q.v.). Liang was impressed with Liu's abilities. When he and Chiang Fang-chen went to Europe in December 1918, they took Liu with them. Liu soon enrolled at the University of Paris.

In November 1920 Liu and his wife, Liao Shih-chao, translated into Chinese *L'armée nouvelle* by the French socialist Jean Jaurès, and their translation was published by the Commercial Press at Shanghai. Liu also published two articles, "National Defense and International Peace" and "China's Armament and World Peace," in the magazine *Kai-tsao* [reconstruction], edited by Chiang Fang-chen. After a brief trip to China in the summer of 1922 to raise funds to continue his education, Liu returned to France. He and his wife both received their doctorates in 1925.

Liu Wen-tao returned to China in the summer of 1925 to become a professor at Chung-hua University in Wuchang. Soon afterwards, his Paoting classmate Ch'en Ming-shu invited him to Canton to meet Chiang Kai-shek. Chiang and Ch'en jointly sponsored Liu's membership in the Kuomintang. Liu suggested that it would be best for him to go to Hunan and work among his former students who had joined the military establishment there. He went to Changsha that winter and, at the invitation of military governor Chao Heng-t'i, delivered a lecture to the officers of the Hunan Army. Liu elaborated on the theory advanced in *L'armée nouvelle* that an army should rely on a basic principle for victory, saying that the armies of China should rely on the Three People's Principles of Sun Yat-sen. The lecture was well received, and T'ang Sheng-chih later had it published.

After T'ang Sheng-chih supplanted Chao Heng-t'i and gave his support to the revolutionaries, Liu Wen-tao became party representative in T'ang's newly created Eighth Army. When the Northern Expedition was launched in July 1926, he also became chief of the political department in Chiang Kai-shek's field headquarters. After the occupation of the Wuhan cities that autumn, he was named mayor of Hankow, a member of the Hankow party executive committee, and an official of the Hupeh provincial government. He was dismissed from these posts in March 1927, after the Kuomintang had split into the left-wing faction, led by Wang Ching-wei, and the right-wing faction, led by Chiang Kai-shek. Liu and Ch'en Ming-shu were made deputy directors of the general political department in Chiang Kai-shek's headquarters at Nanking in May. Because Wu Chih-hui did not assume office as director, Liu soon came to serve as acting director. Although he retired from office with Chiang Kai-shek in August 1927, he remained active as a political agent for Chiang.

In the winter of 1928 Liu Wen-tao supported T'ang Sheng-chih's reemergence as a military leader. After T'ang recovered control of the Hunanese forces in north China, ousting Pai Ch'ung-hsi (q.v.) from power in that area, Liu again became mayor of Hankow, then a special municipality. In 1931 he received the concurrent post of commissioner of civil affairs for Hupeh.

On 16 September 1931 Liu Wen-tao was appointed minister to Germany and Austria. The Japanese attack on Mukden of 18 September gave new significance to his diplomatic mission. In 1932 he also served as a delegate to the World Disarmament Conference at Geneva. Liu was appointed minister to Italy on 13 September 1933. A year later, Nanking and Rome agreed to raise their missions to the status of embassies, and on 17 October 1934 Liu became the first Chinese ambassador to Italy. His principal task was to obtain Italian aid for China, and he had considerable success in this endeavor. The Italian government sent financial, naval, and aviation advisers to China, supplied the equipment for the construction and operation of China's first airplane factory, and offered training and housing facilities for Chinese military students in Italy.

In 1935 Liu Wen-tao was elected *in absentia* to the Central Executive Committee of the Kuomintang. He retained membership in that body until 1950. Also in 1935, diplomatic relations between China and Italy began to deteriorate after China voted with the majority of League of Nations members in October to impose sanctions on Italy for its aggression against Abyssinia. When Italy joined Germany and Japan in the Anti-Comintern Pact in November 1937 and extended formal diplomatic recognition to Manchoukuo, Liu Wen-tao, who previously had urged the continuance of diplomatic relations with Italy and Germany, resigned from office and returned to China.

After the National Government moved to its wartime capital of Chungking in 1938, Liu Wen-tao established residence at Chungking, where he served on the Supreme National Defense Council and on the standing committee of the Kuomintang Central Executive

Committee. He published *Hang-yeh tsu-ho lun* [on business combines] in 1941, *Hang-yeh tsu-ho yü chin-tai ssu-ch'ao* [business combines and recent thought trends] in 1943, and *I-ta-li shih ti* [history and geography of Italy] in 1944.

In May 1945, as the War in the Pacific came to an end, Liu became acting president of Chung-hua University, in anticipation of its return to Wuchang from its refugee campus in west China. At war's end, he was appointed commissioner of comfort missions for central China, in which capacity he visited Kiangsi, Hunan, and Hupeh. In 1947 Liu headed the Fukien-Taiwan commission which was established to investigate the brutal acts committed by the Taiwan governor Ch'en Yi (q.v.) and his subordinates. Upon the inauguration of the National Assembly in 1948, Liu was elected to the Legislative Yuan.

After 1950, Liu Wen-tao lived in retirement in Taiwan. He occasionally wrote articles for Chinese newspapers, and in 1954 he made a brief trip to the United States. After returning to Taipei, he wrote two books, *Chung-i kuan-hsi ti hui-i* [reminiscences of Sino-Italian relations] and *Jen-sheng che-hsueh* [philosophy of life]. He died at Taipei on 11 June 1967 at the age of 74. He was survived by his widow, *née* Lu Chi-shao; three sons, John Kung-fu Liu, David Kung-chan Liu, and Robert Kung-chan Liu; and two daughters, Mrs. Chia-kun Chu and Margaret Kung-ting Liu.

Liu Ya-tzu   柳 亞 子
  Orig. Liu Wei-kao   柳 慰 高
  T. Jen-ch'uan   人 權

Liu Ya-tzu (May 1887–June 1958), the last outstanding poet of the traditional school. He also was known as a scholar and as the founder of the Nan-she (Southern Society).

Born in the Wuchiang district of Soochow, Liu Ya-tzu came from a land-holding literary family whose property provided means to educate several generations of its male members in the scholar-gentry tradition. His father, Liu Nien-tseng (1866–1912), was a sheng-yuan, and his uncle was a scholar of mathematics and an expert calligrapher. Liu Ya-tzu began the study of the Confucian classics and T'ang poetry under his mother's guidance. By the

age of 11, he had begun to compose poetry and historical essays.

Having acquired a good classical education, Liu Ya-tzu distinguished himself by passing the sheng-yuan examination at the age of 15 (1902). Like many young men of his generation, he came under the influence of the reform movement led by K'ang Yu-wei and Liang Ch'i-ch'ao (qq.v.) and soon was swept into the revolutionary movement aimed at the overthrow of the Manchus and the establishment of a republican government in China. In 1902 Chang Ping-lin, Ts'ai Yuan-p'ei, Wu Chih-hui, and others organized the Chung-kuo chiao-yü hui [China education society] in Shanghai to promote modern education in China. The following year, the young Liu Ya-tzu joined this society and became a student at its new school, the Ai-kuo hsueh-she [patriotic institute], headed by Ts'ai Yuan-p'ei. In 1904–5 he was a student at the Tzu-chih hsueh-she [self-government academy] and an instructor at the Chien-hsing kung-hsueh [constant action public school]. In 1906 he joined the T'ung-meng-hui, founded by Sun Yat-sen, and became active in revolutionary work by writing patriotic essays and poems.

Liu Ya-tzu's most important activity in this early period, however, was the founding of the Nan-she (Southern Society), originally an association of southern Yangtze men of letters in the Soochow-Shanghai-Hangchow area. With such writers as Liu Ya-tzu, Ch'en Ch'ü-ping, and Kao Hsü as charter members, the group held its first meeting in Soochow on 13 November 1909. The society became nationwide in scope and attracted many well-known writers; its membership grew from about 20 to more than 1,000. The Southern Society, the last important rallying point of traditional literature in the republican period, was also known as a group of politically conscious writers with radical and nationalistic sentiments. Its members were not formally committed to any political ideology, but the participation of such men as Huang Hsing, Sung Chiao-jen, and Ch'en Ch'i-mei (qq.v.) lent a revolutionary hue to the society during the period of the anti-Manchu revolt of 1911 and the early years of the Chinese republic.

In 1911–12 Liu Ya-tzu was active as a journalist in Shanghai, editing several newspapers which supported the revolutionary cause, including the *T'ieh-pi pao*, the *T'ien-to pao*, the

Ming-sheng jih-pao, and the *T'ai-p'ing-yang pao*. He also served briefly as secretary in the office of Sun Yat-sen in Nanking, but soon left this position to return to journalism in Shanghai, where he wrote articles attacking the peace negotiations between the revolutionaries and Yuan Shih-k'ai. After Yuan's accession to the presidency in February 1912, Liu Ya-tzu abandoned his political activities in disgust and returned to Wuchiang.

Liu devoted himself for several years to a literary career, writing poems and essays and editing the publications of the Southern Society. The group held semi-annual meetings, usually in Shanghai, and regularly published collections of literary works by its members. Between 1910 and 1923, 22 collections of poems and essays written by Southern Society members were published in 23 volumes, in addition to a volume of stories in 1917. During this period, Liu Ya-tzu also assembled a comprehensive collection of the literature of the Wuchiang district. Hundreds of rare books and manuscripts had to be copied by hand, and Liu himself copied some of these.

As head of the Southern Society during most of the 14 years of its existence, Liu Ya-tzu associated with writers and political figures throughout China. The end of the Southern Society came ostensibly as the result of a controversy over the relative merits of T'ang and Southern Sung poetry. One group, represented by Liu Ya-tzu, favored the traditions of T'ang poetry, and, among modern writers, preferred the works of the nineteenth-century poet and reformer Kung Tzu-chen (ECCP, I, 431–34). Another group, represented by Ch'en San-li and Cheng Hsiao-hsü (qq.v.) favored the "T'ung-Kuang" (T'ung-chih and Kuang-hsü, 1862–1908) style, which traced its origins to the poetry of the Southern Sung period. The real reason for the controversy and subsequent end of the Southern Society, however, was Liu Ya-tzu's growing awareness of the inadequacy of the traditional Chinese literary language to express the ideas and aspirations of contemporary China. He was in full sympathy with the new movement, led by Ch'en Tu-hsiu and Hu Shih, which advocated the use of pai-hua [the modern vernacular] as a medium of literature. Liu himself changed to pai-hua in his prose writing, though he had to admit defeat in his attempts to write poetry in the vernacular.

This change in Liu Ya-tzu's literary views finally led to his resignation from the Southern Society. In 1923 he organized the Hsin Nan-she (New Southern Society), a group which hoped to create a new literature for China by introducing significant currents of world thought to China and by reevaluating classical Chinese literature. The New Southern Society, however, had only limited success.

Liu Ya-tzu was attracted to the new alignment of nationalist and revolutionary forces in south China. This was the period of the reorganization of the Kuomintang (1924) and the establishment of a new political regime in Canton. Liu, who had been promoting underground Kuomintang organizations in his native district, was made a member of the Kiangsu executive committee and head of the propaganda department. In 1926 he went to Canton to attend the Second National Congress of the Kuomintang; he was elected to the Central Supervisory Committee. However, he soon became disturbed by the attitude of Chiang Kai-shek, then military leader in Canton, toward the dispute between the party's left and right wings. A leftist member close to Liao Chung-k'ai, Liu Ya-tzu advocated the continuation of Sun Yat-sen's policies of admitting Communists to the Kuomintang as individuals and of alliance with the Soviet Union.

Liu returned home from Canton, but he did not stay long; almost immediately he was forced to flee by Sun Ch'uan-fang, who was then in control of Kiangsu and east China. He remained for a few months in Shanghai, but was forced to escape to Japan in May 1927 at the time of the purge of Communist and left-wing Kuomintang elements by Chiang Kai-shek. After almost a year of exile in Japan, Liu returned to Shanghai in April 1928. He refused to join the new National Government in Nanking, because he believed that its policies were at variance with those set forth by Sun Yat-sen in his final testament. Nevertheless, at the Fourth National Congress of the Kuomintang in 1931, he was reelected to the Central Supervisory Committee. In 1932 he was appointed head of the gazetteer office (T'ung-chih-kuan) of the Shanghai municipal government, and during the next few years he supervised the publication of several yearbooks and volumes of historical materials relating to Shanghai.

The outbreak of the Sino-Japanese war in mid-1937 cut short these activities. For about three years Liu Ya-tzu lived in Japanese-occupied Shanghai, where he severed all political ties and led a secluded life, devoting himself to research on the members of the Ming imperial household who had resisted the Manchu conquerors in the second half of the seventeenth century. Liu Ya-tzu hurriedly left Shanghai in December 1940 because he was afraid he would be coerced into serving the puppet regime that had been established in Nanking in March 1940 under the leadership of Wang Ching-wei, the former Kuomintang leftist leader and sometime member of the Southern Society. Liu went to Hong Kong. At the time of the New Fourth Army Incident in January 1941, Liu sent a telegram to Chungking condemning the action as a serious threat to the wartime united front. He was expelled from the Kuomintang.

In December 1941, when the Japanese occupied Hong Kong, Liu Ya-tzu had to flee to the interior, abandoning his carefully collected library of materials on the southern Ming period. After traveling to a guerrilla base at Haifeng in southern Kwangtung, Liu Ya-tzu reached Kweilin in June 1942. For the next two years, he devoted himself almost entirely to literature and produced a large number of works. In 1944 he went to Chungking and returned to politics. He joined the China Democratic League in 1945; he also became a founding member of the San Min Chu I Comrades Association and served as its chairman from 1946 to 1948.

Liu Ya-tzu returned to Shanghai in late 1945. When postwar Kuomintang-Communist political tensions deteriorated into civil war, he found that because he was a member of the Democratic League he was not safe in Shanghai. He fled to Hong Kong in 1947 and joined a group of anti-Kuomintang dissidents. He participated in January 1948 in the organization of the Kuomintang Revolutionary Committee under the chairmanship of Li Chi-shen. In addition to Liu Ya-tzu, other prominent members of this group included Feng Yü-hsiang, Ho Hsiang-ning (the widow of Liao Chung-k'ai), and T'an P'ing-shan. In 1949 Liu moved to Peking, where he spent the remaining years of his life. After the Central People's Government was established, he served on its

Government Council (1949–54). He also was a member of the standing committee of the National People's Congress (1954–58) and of the culture and education committee of the Government Administration Council. Because his health was poor, he avoided public functions and wrote very little, even cutting off family correspondence. He died of pneumonia in Peking in June 1958, at the age of 71.

Liu Ya-tzu's principal contributions were in the realm of literature, especially poetry. He was one of the last outstanding poets of the traditional school and one of the most prolific writers of his age. He compiled only a few incidental volumes of his own writings, notably *Ch'eng-fu chi* [the raft], written in 1927–28, and *Huai-chiu chi* [remembrance of things past] of 1947. Most of his early poems and essays can be found in the twenty-odd collections of the Southern Society. A selection of his poetry, *Liu Ya-tzu shih-tz'u hsuan*, edited by his two daughters, Liu Wu-fei and Liu Wu-kou, was published in Peking in 1959. A devoted bibliophile and book collector, Liu Ya-tzu was also an indefatigable editor of his friends' literary remains, notably those of Su Man-shu (q.v.), whose collected works he published in 1928. Liu also enjoyed a poetical friendship with Mao Tse-tung, exchanging traditional verses with him on several occasions; and Liu may have had a hand in the composition of several of Mao's most famous poems, including "Snow— to the melody *Ch'in-yuan-ch'un*," in which Mao by implication compares himself favorably with several major figures in Chinese history.

Impractical in everyday affairs, Liu Ya-tzu was greatly dependent upon his wife, *née* Cheng P'ei-i, whom he married in 1906. Throughout their long married life, she was his constant companion, accompanying him on his travels and sharing his misfortunes. A son, Liu Wu-chi (1907–), who was graduated from Tsinghua University, received a Ph.D. in English at Yale University in 1931 and later taught Chinese literature at Indiana University.

Lo Ch'ang-p'ei	羅 常 培
T. Hsin-t'ien	莘 田
H. T'ien-an	恬 庵

Lo Ch'ang-p'ei (9 August 1899–13 December 1958), scholar and educator who was known for his researches on historical phonology and Chinese dialects. After 1949 he was director of the institute of linguistics and philology of the Academy of Sciences at Peking.

Born in Peking, Lo Ch'ang-p'ei came from a family of Manchurian origin. The family name had been Sa-k'o-ta, and Lo's native place was Ning-ku-t'a, Kirin. He began his formal education in a modernized primary school, where one of his schoolmates was Shu Ch'ing-ch'un (q.v.), better known by his pen name, Lao She. The two became lifelong friends. According to Lao She, who later caricatured Lo in his short story "Wai-mao-erh," Lo was a bright, diligent, affable, but obstinate child.

After Lo's father died, the family's financial situation became straitened. Thus, at the age of 17, Lo became a stenographer in the Senate. However, he was able to enroll at Peking University to study Chinese literature. Lo's Senate job gave him the opportunity to hear and transcribe a number of dialects and heightened his interest in linguistics.

In 1919 Lo Ch'ang-p'ei was graduated from Peking University. Because he did not have the money to go abroad to study and because Peking University's philosophy department included such scholars and visiting scholars as Hu Shih, Liang Shu-ming, Chiang Monlin, John Dewey, and Bertrand Russell, Lo remained there. Among his fellow students in the department of philosophy were Chu Tzu-ch'ing and Ku Chieh-kang (qq.v.), both of whom became prominent scholars.

Lo Ch'ang-p'ei began his teaching career in the spring of 1921. While continuing his studies at Peking University, he took a part-time position teaching Chinese at the First Peking Municipal Middle School. That autumn, he went to Tientsin to teach full time at the Nankai Middle School. He returned to Peking in 1922 to become principal of the First Municipal Middle School. In 1923, at the age of 24, he was appointed to the faculty of Northwest University in Sian as professor of Chinese phonology. In 1928 he published his first scholarly articles, "*Ch'ieh-yün* hsü chiao-shih" [explication of the preface to *Ch'ieh-yün*, a rhyme book of c.600 A.D.], "*Ch'ieh-yün* t'an-i" [investigations in *Ch'ieh-yün*], and "Shuang-sheng tieh-yün shuo" [what is meant by "homorganic initials and reduplicated

finals"]. In these articles he discussed the traditional Chinese spelling and rhyming systems.

His research in Chinese historical phonology led Lo Ch'ang-p'ei to develop an interest in Chinese dialects. In 1926, while teaching at Amoy University, he started studying the Amoy dialect. His work was temporarily interrupted in 1927, when he went to teach at the Chung-shan University in Canton. In 1929 he joined the newly established Academia Sinica and worked under Y. R. Chao (Chao Yuen-ren, q.v.), who was in charge of the philology section. Inspired by Chao's knowledge, especially in the field of phonetics, Lo took up his study of the Amoy dialect again and published an important monograph entitled *Hsia-men yin-hsi* [the sound system of the Amoy dialect] in 1931. This monograph became the standard work on the Amoy dialect, which is one of the most important Chinese dialect groups; knowledge of it is of great value to the study of sounds in archaic Chinese.

In the autumn of 1934 Lo Ch'ang-p'ei became a professor of Chinese literature at Peking University, succeeding Liu Fu (q.v.), who had died in July of that year. Lo continued to work at the Academia Sinica and participated in the investigation of Chinese dialects under the direction of Chao Yuen-ren. He also collaborated with Chao and Li Fang-kuei (q.v.) in translating Bernhard Karlgren's *Etudes sur la phonologie Chinoise* into Chinese under the title *Chung-kuo yin-yün hsueh yen-chiu*. Meanwhile, he published such articles and books on Chinese historical phonology as *T'ang wu-tai hsi-pei fang-yin* [dialects in the northwest during T'ang and Five Dynasty times] of 1933, *Kuo-yin tzu-mu yen-chin shih* [history of the evolution of the national phonetic symbols] of 1934, and *Shih-yun hui-pien* [traditional phonology] of 1935, which was compiled by Lo and Liu Fu.

In the spring of 1937 Lo Ch'ang-p'ei left Peiping for Kunming. During the Sino-Japanese war, he was chairman of the Chinese department at Hsi-nan lien-ho ta-hsueh (National Southwest Associated University). He also continued to work for the Academia Sinica. Lo later recalled that in the beginning he and his colleagues were not enthusiastic about doing a systematic study of the dialects spoken in southwest China because they found the local languages to be similar to the mandarin. Later, he realized that investigation of Chinese dialects should do more than compare ancient and modern sounds or concentrate on the special vocabulary of a certain dialect. It was more important to draw an over-all map of Chinese dialects and to pinpoint significant isoglosses. Thus, he suggested that the institute of history and philology of the Academia Sinica should avail itself of the opportunity to make a general investigation of dialects throughout Yunnan province. His suggestion was accepted, and the work was carried out by the Academia Sinica during the war years. Among the dialects Lo investigated were those of Kun-ming, Lien-shan, Pai-i, Fu-kung, Li-su, Li-chiang, Kung-shan, Ch'ai-shan, Lang-shan, Lan-p'ing, La-ma, Ta-li, Pin-ch'uan, Teng-ch'uan, Erh-yuan, Yun-lung, and Lu-shui.

Though primarily a student of phonetics, Lo Ch'ang-p'ei did not limit himself to that field. During the war years, he developed an interest in the sociological and historical aspects of languages and became increasingly attracted to semantics. He tended to interpret cultural phenomena from a linguistic viewpoint. For instance, by examining the kinship terminology of the Tibetan-Burman speaking tribes he attempted to establish a historical relationship between them and the tribal peoples in south-west China. In his later work, he continued this tendency of using sociological and anthropological insights in the study of language. In this vein he completed his *Chung-kuo jen yü Chung-kuo wen-hua* [the Chinese people and Chinese culture].

From 1945 to 1948 Lo Ch'ang-p'ei was in the United States as a visiting professor of Chinese phonetics and literature, first at Pomona College and then at Yale University. During this period, he published several articles and read papers in English. These included "Indian Influence on the Study of Chinese Phonology," which was published in *Sino-Indian Studies* in March 1945; "A Preliminary Study on the Trung Language of Kung-shan," which appeared in the *Harvard Journal of Asiatic Studies* in March 1945; "Phonetic Substitution in Chinese Loanwords from Indic," read before the American Oriental Society in April 1947; "The Prefix *n–* in the Kachin Language," read before the American Linguistic Society in August 1947; and "Evidence on Amending Bernhard Karlgren's Ancient Chinese j– to rj–," read before the American Oriental Society in March 1948.

In the autumn of 1948 Lo Ch'ang-p'ei returned to Peiping to serve as a professor and as dean of the graduate school of humanities of Peking University. When the Communists besieged the city, he shut himself in his home and devoted his time to completing the manuscript of *Yü-yen yü wen-hua* [language and culture], which he had begun to write in 1943. Although it was not published until 1950, this work, except for the conclusion, was completed before the Communist takeover. *Yü-yen yü wen-hua* may be regarded as Lo's final major work in two senses. First, it is his last piece of non-political scholarly writing. Second, it synthesized his interests in many fields: phonology, philology, semasiology, literature, anthropology, and sociology. In this work, the influence of such prominent Western anthropologists and linguists as Edward Sapir, L. R. Palmer, E. B. Tylor, and Bronislaw Malinowski on Lo's conception of language can be seen clearly. Using the ideas of his Western preceptors, Lo stressed the fact that language and culture are inseparable and attempted to demonstrate the relationship between the two by presenting the results of his own studies. He suggested that linguistic studies in China should imitate Western scholarship in studying the language in the general context of its cultural background and that understanding of the cultural past could be enhanced by investigating the origin, infusion, and transformation of the language.

Lo Ch'ang-p'ei's writings before 1949 show no evidence of inclination toward any socialist doctrine. As a matter of fact, he was a member of the Kuomintang. He returned to Peiping in 1948, he later said, not because he was interested in the prospect of a new government, but because he wanted to rejoin his family and his manuscripts. His initial lack of enthusiasm for the Communist regime also was shown by the fact that, during the siege of Peiping in 1949, he remained secluded and devoted himself to the writing of *Yü-yen yü wen-hua*. In late 1949, however, Lo's attitudes began to change. He participated in the Chinese People's Political Consultative Conference. He applied for membership in the Chinese Communist party, but was rejected in 1950. Meanwhile, he engaged in a vigorous campaign of self-criticism and ardent advocacy of the Communist party line. These efforts brought him a series of appointments: director of the institute of linguistics and philology of the Chinese Academy of Sciences in Peking (1950), member of the Nationalities Affairs Commission (1951), member of the Committee for Reforming the Written Chinese Language (1954), and representative to the National People's Congress (1954). From July 1952 to March 1955 he also served as chief editor of the monthly journal *Chung-kuo yü-wen* [Chinese language], and from 1955 until his death he served on its editorial board.

Although he was plagued by high blood pressure, Lo continued to study and write almost until the day of his death. In 1957 he and Wang Chün published a major work, *P'u-t'ung yü-yen-hsüeh kang-yao* [outline of general linguistics]. Lo died on 13 December 1958. Several of his works were published post-humously. These include the first volume of *Han Wei Nan-pei-ch'ao yün-pu yen-pien yen-chiu* [the evolution of rhyme categories in the Han, Wei, and Nan-pei periods], written in collaboration with Chou Tsu-mo and published in 1958; *Pa-ssu-pa-tzu yü Yüan-tai Han-yü* [the hPags-pa script and the Chinese language of the Yüan period], published in 1959 and written with the help of Ts'ai Mei-piao; and *Han-yü yin-yün tao-lun* [guide to Chinese phonology] of 1962. A selection of Lo's writings on linguistics was published in 1963 under the title *Lo Ch'ang-p'ei yü-yen-hsüeh lun-wen hsüan-chi*. Eulogies of Lo as a great Communist and a great linguist, as well as a provisional bibliography of his writings, appeared shortly after his demise in *Chung-kuo yü-wen*.

Lo Chen-yü   羅 振 玉
   T. Shu-yün   叔 蘊
     Shu-yen   叔 言
   H. Hsüeh-t'ang   雪 堂

Lo Chen-yü (3 August 1866–19 June 1940), an important Chinese classical scholar, archaeologist, and bibliographer, was a Manchu loyalist and a supporter of the Japanese-sponsored regime in Manchoukuo.

Although his native place was Shangyü, Chekiang, Lo Chen-yü was born in Huaian, Kiangsu. His father, Lo Shu-hsün (1842–1905; T. Yao-chin), opened a pawnshop in 1875 with some friends, but this venture failed in 1881,

the year that Lo Chen-yü took the district examinations. Lo Shu-hsün, who had received an appointment as acting assistant magistrate of Chiangning, hastened to his official post and left his family to deal with his debts. Lo Chen-yü's mother, *née* Fan, paid off the last of the debts in 1902, after twenty years of toil and saving, during which time she raised her five sons and six daughters. She died in 1903. Lo Chen-yü, the third son, also worked to help support the family. In 1891 he took the provincial examinations, but failed them.

The defeat of China in the first Sino-Japanese war caused many young men to undertake new activities in the hope of building a stronger China. In 1896 Lo Chen-yü and a friend, Chiang Fu (1866–1911; T. Po-fu), went to Shanghai and founded the Nung-hsüeh she [agronomy society], an organization devoted to the translation of Japanese and Western literature on agriculture. The society's *Nung-hsüeh pao* [agronomy bulletin] began publication in 1897, and the *Nung-hsüeh ts'ung-shu* [agronomy collectanea] appeared in 1898. The two friends established a language school in 1898, the Tung-wen hsüeh-she [eastern culture society], which emphasized Japanese, but offered courses in English as well. Among the students at the school was Wang Kuo-wei (q.v.).

His work in Shanghai earned Lo Chen-yü a reputation as an expert in agricultural studies and modern education. In the winter of 1898 Lo accepted an invitation from Chang Chih-tung (ECCP, I, 27–32), the governor general of Hupeh and Hunan, to go to Wuchang. He gave advice to the Hupeh bureau of agriculture, served as dean of the agricultural school, and then worked at the Chiang-Ch'u i-shu chü [Kiangsu and Hupeh translation bureau]. In 1901 Chang sent him to Japan to study that country's educational system. After returning to China, he accepted an invitation in 1903 from Ts'en Ch'un-hsüan (q.v.), the governor general of Kwangtung and Kwangsi, to serve as a consultant on the reform of the educational system in those provinces. In Canton, he greatly enriched his book collection by purchasing the Yüeh-hsüeh-lou library of the K'ung family. Tuan-fang (ECCP, II, 780–82), the governor of Kiangsu, invited Lo to Soochow in the summer of 1904 for consultation on problems of education. Lo's efforts resulted in the establishing of the Kiangsu Normal School in Soochow.

In 1905 a new Board of Education was established at Peking. Lo Chen-yü was appointed to it, and he moved his family to Peking. Both the Nung-hsüeh she and the Tung-wen hsüeh-she were closed in 1906 because Lo was unable to supervise their operations from Peking. Lo served as field inspector of schools, touring Chihli (Hopei) and Shansi in 1907 and traveling through Shantung, Honan, Kiangsi, and Anhwei in 1908. He became an acting assistant secretary in the Board of Education and assistant examiner of students who had returned from abroad in 1908. The following year, he was appointed dean of the agricultural college at Imperial University in Peking.

After the revolution of 1911, Lo Chen-yü, Wang Kuo-wei, and Liu Ta-shen (Lo's son-in-law and a pioneer in the study of oracle bones) moved their families to Japan. Lo lived in Kyoto for eight years, making occasional trips to China. Lo published a number of archaeological studies during this period, and in 1915 he made a trip to the Yin-ch'ü excavation sites at Anyang, Honan, where the discovery of oracle bones in 1899 had opened new vistas to scholars of ancient Chinese history. When Lo returned to China in 1919, he established residence at Tientsin, where he continued to do research.

During the wedding celebration of P'u-yi (q.v.) in December 1922, Lo Chen-yü, along with many other Manchu loyalists, went to Peking to offer his congratulations to the former emperor. He joined P'u-yi's "court" in 1923 and worked to protect his safety and prerogatives in 1924, when P'u-yi was driven from the Forbidden City by Feng Yü-hsiang (q.v.). P'u-yi went to live in the Japanese concession at Tientsin, and Lo became one of his three principal advisers. At the end of 1928, after the idea of restoring P'u-yi to the throne had been broached to the Japanese, Lo moved to the Japanese-controlled city of Dairen. A feud between Cheng Hsiao-hsü (q.v.) and Lo Chen-yü developed during this period, and after P'u-yi moved to Port Arthur at the end of 1931, the two advisers came into conflict over the Japanese proposal that P'u-yi become head of a republic comprising Manchuria and Mongolia. Lo strongly urged insistence on the promised monarchy, while Cheng accepted the idea of a republic.

Manchoukuo, established on 1 March 1932, was a disappointment to Lo Chen-yü. P'u-yi became chief executive rather than emperor, and when he finally was enthroned in March 1934, the Japanese flooded Manchoukuo with Japanese nationals, making them citizens and important officials. After serving as president of the examination yuan from 1933 to 1938 Lo retired to his home in Dairen, where he lived until his death on 19 June 1940. In his autobiography, *Chi-liao pien*, Lo expressed regret that his loyalty to the Manchus had helped create Manchoukuo.

Lo Chen-yü's untiring efforts to collect, compile, and publish documents and studies constituted a major contribution to scholarship in China. He wrote on many subjects, but his best works were archaeological and historical studies. Typical of his writings are the *Tun-huang shih-shih chi* [the stone chambers of Tun-huang], of 1909; the *Yin-ch'ü shu-ch'i ch'ien-pien* [Anyang inscriptions], of 1911 (continued in 1933); and the *Yin-ch'ü wen-tzu lei-pien* [Anyang graphs, categorically arranged], of 1924. A complete list of his publications is to be found in *Lo Hsueh-t'ang chu-shu mu-lu erh-chuan*, which was reprinted in 1962 at Tokyo by Ching-chia in the journal *Tōhōgaku*. Lo also reprinted a number of bibliographical rarities at his own expense. His service in achieving publication of the *Ch'ing shih-lu* [veritable record of the Ch'ing dynasty], published in Tokyo in 1937 by the Manchoukuo government, would have been sufficient to earn him the gratitude of all students of modern Chinese history.

Lo Ch'i-yuan   羅綺園

Lo Ch'i-yuan (1893–1930), leader of the peasant movement during the 1924–28 period and head of the Chinese Communist party's peasant department in 1929–30. He was arrested and executed by Kuomintang authorities at Shanghai.

Little is known about Lo Ch'i-yuan's childhood or early life except that he was born into a family of wealthy landowners in Waichow (Huichou), Kwangtung, and that he was graduated from a middle school in Kwangtung. He joined the Socialist Youth League in

Canton about 1921, and he later joined the Kwangtung branch of the Chinese Communist party, headed by T'an P'ing-shan and Ch'en Kung-po (qq.v.). By 1924, when the Chinese Communist party and the Kuomintang established a formal alliance, Lo had become an important leader in the peasant movement. He became affiliated with the Peasant Movement Training Institute when it was established under the direction of P'eng P'ai (q.v.) in July 1924, and he served as director of its second class, which was graduated on 30 October 1924, and its fifth class, which was graduated on 8 December 1925. One of the lecturers for the fifth session was Mao Tse-tung. The purpose of the institute was to train cadres who would organize peasants in various provinces to aid the proposed Northern Expedition. Lo Ch'i-yuan also contributed to the peasant movement in 1925 by helping to organize a Kwangtung provincial peasants' congress, which met in May at Canton.

After the ex-Communist Ch'en Kung-po succeeded Liao Chung-k'ai (q.v.) as head of the Kuomintang's peasant department in 1925, Lo Ch'i-yuan became secretary of the department. Working with Lo in the department as secretaries in charge of organization work were P'eng P'ai, Juan Hsiao-hsien, and Tan Chih-t'ang. By this time, Lo, like many other Communists, had joined the Kuomintang. He and his associates worked to organize peasant associations and militia in the North River area of Kwangtung.

By the spring of 1927 Lo had become the commander of all peasant militia in Kwangtung, and when Ch'en Yen-nien (q.v.) went to Shanghai in April 1927, Lo succeeded him as secretary of the Kwangtung committee of the Chinese Communist party. In these two capacities, he attended the Fifth National Congress of the Chinese Communist party, at which he was elected to the Central Committee. Because Chiang Kai-shek had begun to purge Communists in the Shanghai area about two weeks before the congress began, a number of party leaders challenged the leadership of Ch'en Tu-hsiu (q.v.) at the congress, for he had followed the Comintern-determined policy of cooperation with the Kuomintang. The peasant movement was another subject of debate. Ch'en, heeding Comintern instructions of December 1926, advocated a policy of

"political confiscation" of land which allowed landlords with revolutionary ties to keep their land. Such peasant leaders as Lo Ch'i-yuan and P'eng P'ai fought for the more radical policy of immediate confiscation of all land, but Ch'en's proposal finally was approved by the congress.

When the left-wing Kuomintang regime at Wuhan also turned against the Communists and began to suppress peasant associations, Lo Ch'i-yuan withdrew from Kwangtung with part of his peasant militia, thus failing to coordinate his actions with those of P'eng P'ai, who was establishing the Hai-lu-feng soviet. Lo's troops soon were crushed, and he was forced to flee to Shanghai at the beginning of 1928.

At the Sixth National Congress of the Chinese Communist party, held in Moscow in the summer of 1928, Lo Ch'i-yuan was re-elected *in absentia* to the Central Committee. In 1929 he succeeded P'eng P'ai as head of the party's peasant department. Although the new party leader, Li Li-san (q.v.), regarded the peasant movement as an appendage of the labor movement, Lo occupied an important position in the central apparatus of the party. Lo's career was cut short when he and another Communist leader, Yang P'ao-an, were arrested in Shanghai in 1930. Soon afterwards, Lo was executed by the Kuomintang authorities in the Shanghai area.

Lo Chia-lun	羅 家 倫
T. Chih-hsi	志 希
Pen. Yi	毅

Lo Chia-lun (1896–), one of the principal leaders of the May Fourth Movement while a student at Peking University. He later was president of Tsinghua (1928–31) and National Central (1932–41) universities, and he served the National Government as Sinkiang supervisory commissioner and as ambassador to India (1946–49).

Although his native place was Shaohsing, Chekiang, Lo Chia-lun was born in Kiangsi, where his father, Lo Ch'uan-chen, was serving as a district magistrate. When he was only three sui, his mother began to teach him to read and write. Two years later, his father introduced him to poetry. Lo's mother died in 1904, leaving him and his four sisters to be brought up by their father. After the republic was established in 1912, Lo was sent to Shanghai for a modern education, and he enrolled at the Fu-tan School (Fu-tan Kung-hsueh). His exposure to new ideas and publications in Shanghai led him to begin writing essays for the school magazine.

In the summer of 1917 Lo Chia-lun passed the Peking University entrance examinations held at Shanghai; he matriculated that autumn, choosing foreign languages and literature as his major. Among his fellow students were Fu Ssu-nien and Tuan Hsi-p'eng (qq.v.). Lo and Fu often called on Hu Shih (q.v.), who was a leader of the movement to replace the classical written language with pai-hua [the vernacular]. After holding a number of discussions with Hu, who was teaching at Peking University, they decided to found a magazine. The inaugural issue of *Hsin-ch'ao* [new tide] appeared on 1 January 1919, with ten articles by Fu and three by Lo. Its three guiding principles were: a critical spirit, scientific thinking, and reformed rhetoric. By this time, Lo had become a frequent contributor to the *Tung-fang tsa-chih* (*Eastern Miscellany*), and his translation of one of Ibsen's plays had appeared in the *Hsin ch'ing-nien* (*New Youth*).

At the end of April 1919 Peking received the news that the Paris Peace Conference planned to accede to Japanese demands for the special rights formerly held by the Germans in Shantung. Peking University students responded by holding a meeting on the evening of 3 May; they decided to plan a demonstration for the following day. Lo Chia-lun was one of twenty students who were selected to contact students at other institutions and mobilize them for the demonstration. On 4 May, representatives of the various student groups met and prepared statements to be presented to foreign officials. The students assembled early in the afternoon and, despite the attempts of police and ministry of education officials to dissuade them, began their march. At the entrance to the Legation Quarter they were stopped by military and police officials. Because they could not proceed, they sent three representatives, one of whom was Lo Chia-lun, to call on the British, American, French, and Italian legations. It was a Sunday, and the ministers were not in, but members of their staffs received the student representatives.

After delivering their written statements, Lo and his fellow representatives hurried to rejoin the other students, only to discover that the demonstrators had grown impatient and had gone to the home of the pro-Japanese official Ts'ao Ju-lin (q.v.). They then had proceeded to wreck Ts'ao's home, thereby coming into conflict with the military and the police. The indignation of people throughout China was roused by the arrest of a number of the students. Thus, what had begun as a student demonstration developed into a national patriotic movement.

Lo Chia-lun continued to play a leading role in the movement. Under his pen name, Yi, he wrote in the *Mei-chou p'ing-lun* [weekly critic] of 26 May 1919 an important article, "The Spirit of the May Fourth Movement." For the first time, the term "May Fourth Movement" appeared in print, and it immediately was adopted as the official designation of the movement. Lo pointed out that the events of 4 May had revealed the spirit of sacrifice among Chinese students, the spirit of social sanction, and the spirit of national self-determination. Later, in the May 1920 issue of *Hsin-ch'ao*, Lo published a review of the movement entitled "The Successes and Failures of the Student Movement in the Past Year and Our Future Policy." This article, which advocated academic research to channel the movement properly and efforts to promote the welfare of the masses, gained wide circulation when it was reprinted in the Shanghai *Shun pao*.

In the autumn of 1920 Lo Chia-lun went to the United States, where he studied history and philosophy at Princeton University and Columbia University. He spent 1922 in England, studying at the University of London, and then spent two years in Germany at Berlin University. In 1925 he went to France and enrolled at the University of Paris.

After returning to China in the summer of 1926, Lo Chia-lun accepted a teaching position at Tung-nan (Southeastern) University. Soon afterwards, he joined the staff of Chiang Kai-shek and became chairman of the editorial committee of Chiang's military headquarters, which then was engaged in launching the Northern Expedition. In August 1927, when the Kuomintang established the Chung-yang tang-wu hsueh-hsiao (Central Party Affairs Institute) in Nanking, Lo became the deputy director of studies, serving under Tai Chi-t'ao (q.v.). He became a member and head of the education office of the newly established war area political affairs commission in March 1928, and in this capacity he traveled northward with the Northern Expedition forces. After the May Third Incident at Tsinan, Lo and Hsiung Shih-hui (q.v.) were dispatched on 9 May for negotiations with the Japanese, but the Japanese commander rejected them as envoys.

On 17 August 1928, the Northern Expedition having ended, Lo Chia-lun was appointed president of Tsinghua University. Because Tsinghua had been a college until the National Government had decided to transform it into a university in 1925, Lo was faced with such tasks as helping to formulate regulations for the university. After assuming office on 18 September, he announced the end of the old system of sending all graduates to the United States for further study and introduced a system of open examinations for the selection of a few outstanding students to study in the United States. He helped organize the colleges and departments of the university, admitted women for the first time, undertook a building program, appointed new professors, enlarged the library, caused the jurisdiction of the university to be transferred from the ministry of foreign affairs to the ministry of education, and had the funds of the university transferred from the ministry of foreign affairs to the China Foundation for the Promotion of Education and Culture. However, after the Peiping area came under the control of Yen Hsi-shan (q.v.) in May 1930, Lo's detractors among the Tsinghua alumni began a campaign to expel him from the presidency. On 23 May, Lo resigned and left Peiping. He decided to devote more of his time to research and accepted an appointment as professor of history at Wuhan University. In March 1931 his "Significance and Method of the Study of Modern Chinese History" was published in the *Wuhan University Social Science Quarterly*. In the meantime, Chiang Kai-shek had demanded that Lo either return to Tsinghua or go to Nanking. On 31 January 1931 Lo assumed office as dean of the Central Political School (formerly the Central Party Affairs Institute) at Nanking. He immediately announced his intention to convert the school into a four-year college.

In June 1932 Tuan Hsi-p'eng, the vice minister of education, was appointed acting president of National Central University in Nanking. This university had lacked a president for some time because of student opposition. When Tuan tried to assume office, the students assaulted him. The Executive Yuan then ordered the dissolution of the university, and the ministry of education took charge of the problem in early July. Lo Chia-lun was appointed to the committee charged with reorganizing the university, and he was appointed president of National Central University in August. After the students had been subjected to a screening process, the university resumed classes in October. Lo's measures to restore stability to the university were successful. In 1933, at the behest of the National Government, National Central University organized a military aviation department, which began classes in the autumn of 1934 with 28 students. Another new department, water conservation engineering, was added in 1935. During this period, Lo improved the equipment, courses, and personnel of the university. In 1936 he decided to expand the university and selected a site for the new campus, but the outbreak of the Sino-Japanese war forced him to abandon this project. The removal of the university to Chungking was ordered in August 1937, and Lo received permission to use funds that had been allocated to the new Nanking campus for the construction of university buildings in the Chungking area. Classes resumed at Chengtu (medical and dental) and Chungking in October and November 1937.

Lo continued to develop National Central University until September 1941, when he resigned from the presidency. In October, he was appointed head of the Yunnan-Kweichow inspection mission. Its task was to precede the expeditionary force that was being sent to Burma and to allay the fears of such provincial authorities as Lung Yün (q.v.), the governor of Yunnan, about the purpose of the expedition. Lo's efforts met with success, and he returned to Chungking in December.

Throughout 1942 Lo refused all appointments because his aged father was ill. On 1 March 1943 he was named Sinkiang supervisory commissioner and head of the northwest investigation mission. The following day, his father died in Kweiyang. After attending to the funeral arrangements, Lo returned to Chungking to prepare for the assumption of his new duties. He left Chungking in June and visited Shensi, Kansu, Ninghsia, and Tsinghai before reaching Urumchi in August. In September, on orders from the National Government, Lo accompanied Sheng Shih-ts'ai (q.v.), the governor of Sinkiang, to Chungking. He rejoined his colleagues at Lanchow in October, and they explored the upper reaches of the Yellow River. In November, they visited Tsinghai, where Lo composed the "Song of Tsinghai" for Ma Pu-fang (q.v.), the governor. The mission then retired to Tienshui, where it produced a 14-volume report in two months. At the end of March 1944 Lo and his colleagues returned to Chungking. Lo continued to serve as Sinkiang supervisory commissioner until January 1945, when he resigned because of a disagreement with Chang Chih-chung and Burhan (qq.v.) over the solution of the rebel problem in the Ili area.

After the War in the Pacific ended, Lo Chia-lun was appointed in October 1945 to a Chinese government mission that toured the battlefields of Burma, India, the Persian Gulf area, and the Mediterranean. He then went to London and took part in the UNESCO preparatory conference. He returned to Chungking in March 1946, by way of the United States, Hawaii, Guam, and the Philippines. After the National Government returned to Nanking, he became vice chairman, under Chang Chi (q.v.), of the Kuomintang's party history compilation committee.

In February 1947 Lo Chia-lun was appointed ambassador to India. Because India had not yet achieved independence, he presented his credentials to the British viceroy. Although his relations with the Indian leaders were cordial, Lo was not particularly successful in India because of the deterioration of China into civil war and the thorny issue of Tibet. Negotiations for a Sino-Indian treaty of commerce and trade failed because the Indian government refused to take a clear stand on the matter of Tibet. Moreover, Indian maps did not recognize any part of Tibet as being Chinese territory, and when the Tibetan authorities ordered Chinese representatives in Tibet to leave in July 1949, India supported and helped the Tibetans to achieve this end. Lo finally announced the National Government's recall of its represent-

atives in India after the Indian government recognized the Central People's Government of the People's Republic of China on 30 December 1949. He left New Delhi early in 1950 and went to Taiwan.

In Taipei, Lo Chia-lun succeeded Chang Chi as chairman of the Kuomintang party history compilation committee. In 1952–54 he was vice president of the Examination Yuan, and in 1953 he became editor of the *Ke-ming wen-hsien*, a multi-volume collection of documents from Kuomintang and Academia Historica archives. He wrote *Liu-shih-nien chih Chung-kuo Kuo-min-tang yü Chung-kuo* [the Kuomintang and China in the last sixty years], which was published in 1954. A revised version entitled *Ch'i-shih-nien chih Chung-kuo Kuo-min-tang yü Chung-kuo* appeared in 1964. Lo served as chief editor of the *Kuo-fu nien-p'u* [chronology of the life of Sun Yat-sen]. In 1958 he was appointed president of the Academia Historica. Lo Chia-lun was also known as a poet who wrote in both traditional and modern styles and as a calligrapher.

Lo Chia-lun married Djang Wei-djen (1898–) in November 1927; they had two daughters, Jiu-fong and Jiu-hwa.

Lo Fu: *see* CHANG WEN-T'IEN.

Lo-hua-sheng: *see* HSÜ TI-SHAN.

Lo I-nung　　　　羅亦農

Lo I-nung (1901–21 April 1928), leading figure in the Chinese Communist party at Shanghai in the mid-1920's. He was executed by the Nationalists in 1928.

Hsiangt'an, Hunan, was the birthplace of Lo I-nung. His father was a prosperous merchant and landowner, and Lo received a good education in the Chinese classics from tutors. At the age of 17, when his parents refused his request to study in Shanghai, he ran away from home and went to Shanghai. About the time of the May Fourth Movement, he became acquainted with a group of radical students and was exposed to Marxist ideas. He was among the first to join the Socialist Youth League when it was organized in August

1920 by Ch'en Tu-hsiu and Chang T'ai-lei. That winter, the Comintern selected a small group of students, including Jen Pi-shih, Liu Shao-ch'i (qq.v.), and Lo I-nung, for study at the Communist University for Toilers of the East in Moscow. They arrived in Moscow in the spring of 1921, by which time Lo had joined the Chinese Communist party. Lo became a leader of the Chinese students in Moscow. In 1923, when the number of Chinese students in Moscow increased, a special section was organized at the university to train Chinese cadres for work in their own country. Lo became the secretary of the Chinese section and an instructor in historical materialism. His many activities proved to be too much for his frail constitution, however, and he contracted tuberculosis.

In the spring of 1925 the Chinese Communist party recalled Lo I-nung to China. He was sent to Canton, a center of revolutionary political activity, to serve as party secretary at the second All-China Labor Congress, which was held in May. He also became an alternate member of the Kwangtung committee of the Chinese Communist party, in which capacity he participated in campaigns against the Kwangtung militarists, the Canton–Hong Kong general strike, and the investigation into the assassination of Liao Chung-k'ai (q.v.). In October 1925 he represented Kwangtung at an enlarged plenum of the Central Committee of the Chinese Communist party which met in Peking. Lo, because of his teaching experiences in Moscow, was given charge of a training program designed to produce more Communist cadres, and he remained in Peking for about two months to supervise the creation of a short-term but intensive training school.

Lo I-nung was appointed secretary of the Chinese Communist party's Kiangsu-Chekiang regional committee, with headquarters in Shanghai, in January 1926. Assisted by Chao Shih-yen, head of the regional committee's workers department, and by Chou En-lai (q.v.), head of the committee's departments of organization and military affairs, he worked to expand party organizations in the Shanghai factories and made plans for arming the workers. By 30 May 1926, the first anniversary of the May Thirtieth Incident, they had sufficient strength to stage a mass demonstration of laborers. They continued to organize strikes in Shanghai and to consolidate control of the Shanghai General Labor Union. In anticipation of the arrival of the Northern Expedition forces, they led two workers' uprisings. The first of these took place on 26 November 1926, during the war between Sun Ch'uan-fang (q.v.) and Hsia Ch'ao; and the second occurred on 22 February 1927. Finally, on 21 March 1927, as units of the National Revolutionary Army closed in on the city, Lo I-nung called a general strike to facilitate the seizure of Shanghai by the forces of Chiang Kai-shek.

By the time Chiang Kai-shek moved against the Communists in the Shanghai area on 12 April 1927, Lo I-nung had been replaced at Shanghai by Ch'en Yen-nien (q.v.) and had gone to Wuhan to attend the Fifth National Congress of the Chinese Communist party, at which he was elected to the Central Committee. Lo then went to Nanchang to serve as secretary of the party's Kiangsi provincial committee. In July 1927, after the left-wing faction of the Kuomintang at Wuhan also turned against the Communists, Lo was made secretary of the Hupeh provincial committee. In this capacity, he worked to reconstruct the Communist organizations in the province. On 7 August, the emergency conference convened by Ch'ü Ch'iu-pai (q.v.) at Kiukiang appointed Lo secretary of the Ch'ang-chiang (Yangtze) bureau of the party. He trained cadres for peasant mobilization in the rural areas of Hunan and Hupeh and, according to some sources, initiated the guerrilla activities in those two provinces that prepared the way for the establishment of Communist bases.

In November 1927 an enlarged plenum of the Central Committee elected Lo to the Political Bureau and the standing committee of the Central Committee and appointed him head of the party's organization department. He thus became one of the chief planners of the ill-fated Canton Commune (*see* Chang T'ai-lei) of December 1927.

After making an inspection trip through Hunan and Hupeh, Lo I-nung returned to Shanghai in April 1928. He was arrested on the morning of 15 April, extradited to the Nationalist authorities on 18 April, and executed on 21 April. The importance attached to his capture by the Kuomintang authorities was suggested by the Shanghai newspaper accounts of it, one of which stated that "the chief is caught; the Communist scourge will soon be extinguished."

Little is known about Lo I-nung's personal life. Indeed, the name Lo I-nung may well be a pseudonym adopted after he severed relations with his family.

Lo Jui-ch'ing   羅 瑞 卿

Lo Jui-ch'ing (1907–), political commissar in the Chinese Communist military forces who later held such posts in the Central People's Government as that of minister of public security (1949–58). In the 1950's he was the regime's principal organizer of public security programs and secret police operations. In 1959 he became vice premier of the State Council, vice minister of national defense, and chief of staff of the People's Liberation Army. He was removed from these posts in the mid-1960's and was accused of being a follower of P'eng Te-huai and Huang K'o-ch'eng.

Nanch'ung, Szechwan, was the birthplace of Lo Jui-ch'ing. Little is known about his family background or early education except that his father may have been a landowner. After being graduated from the Wuhan branch of the Whampoa Military Academy about 1927, he participated in the 1 August 1927 Communist uprising at Nanchang (*see* Ho Lung; Yeh T'ing). However, he did not become a member of the Chinese Communist party until 1928. He was sent to Moscow in 1929, allegedly to study law at Sun Yat-sen University, but actually to receive intelligence and police training. According to some reports, he worked for a time in a Russian intelligence organization before returning to China in 1930. He then joined the Fourth Red Army of Chu Teh (q.v.) and Mao Tse-tung as political commissar of the 11th Division. When Chu's force was reorganized as the First Army Group of the Chinese Workers and Peasants Red Army, Lo became the director of its political defense bureau. Wounds received by Lo during the second Nationalist campaign against the Communists in 1931 resulted in partial facial paralysis, giving him a rather sinister appearance.

At the second All-China Congress of Soviets, which met in January 1934, Lo Jui-ch'ing was elected to the executive committee of the central soviet government in Kiangsi. He accompanied Mao Tse-tung on the Long March to Shensi, and on arrival at Yenan in 1936 he became a vice chairman of the Red Army Academy, headed by Lin Piao (q.v.). When the Sino-Japanese war began in 1937, the academy became the Anti-Japanese Military and Political University, with Lo Jui-ch'ing as its acting head. From 1940 to 1945 Lo also served as director of the political department of the Eight Route Army's field headquarters and as a member of the Chinese Communist party's north China bureau. At the party's Seventh National Congress, held at Yenan in 1945, he was elected to alternate membership in the Central Committee.

After the War in the Pacific ended, Lo Jui-ch'ing became deputy political commissar of the Shansi-Chahar-Hopei military district. In 1946 he also became chief of staff to Yeh Chien-ying, who headed the Chinese Communist staff at the Peiping Executive Headquarters, where the Communists and the Nationalists were trying to come to an agreement and were working to implement the cease-fire agreement of January 1946. When the negotiations ended in failure, Lo returned to the Shansi-Chahar-Hopei military district to serve as political commissar of the Second Army Group of the North China People's Liberation Army. In 1948 he became political commissar of the Nineteenth Group Army and director of the political department of the north China military district, and in 1949 he became one of three vice chairmen of the Taiyuan municipal military control commission.

When the Central People's Government was established in Peking in October 1949, Lo Jui-ch'ing received membership in the Government Administration Council, the People's Revolutionary Military Council, the procurator general's office, and the executive board of the Sino-Soviet Friendship Association; he held these posts until 1954. Lo's most important office in the new regime, however, was that of minister of public security (1949–58). He apparently was the principal organizer of public security programs and secret police operations, although policy concerning these matters was the province of Li K'o-nung (q.v.). Lo was especially in evidence during the mass public purges of 1951, 1952, and 1956, when he organized suppression campaigns against "counter-revolutionaries" and made reports on their progress. In 1953 he became head of the Public Security Forces, a newly created branch of the People's Liberation Army. He also served as president of the Central People's Institute of Public Security (1955–58) and as director of the staff office of the State Council that dealt with public security. During this period, he also served the People's Republic of China as a delegate to the Chinese People's Political Consultative Conference, a member of the committee for drafting the election law, a member of the National Defense Council, a member of the administrative committee of the Central School of Administrative and Legal Cadres, and a delegate to the first three National People's congresses. In 1956 he was elevated to full membership on the Central Committee of the Chinese Communist party.

In 1959 Lo Jui-ch'ing became vice premier of the State Council, vice minister of national defense, and chief of staff of the People's Liberation Army. He was appointed secretary general of the party Central Committee's military affairs committee in 1961 and secretary of the Central Secretariat in 1962. He received the vice chairmanships of the National Defense Council and the National People's Congress in 1965. That year, he published an article in *Hung-ch'i* [red flag] entitled "Commemorate the Victory over German Fascism! Carry the Struggle against United States Imperialism to the End!" It was regarded by Western observers as a serious and systematic discussion of military doctrine. Toward the end of 1965, however, Lo Jui-ch'ing began to be absent from public occasions. When he had not been seen for several months, Western observers speculated that he had been removed from his posts because of his advocacy of professionalism in the armed forces, a policy at odds with the views of Mao Tse-tung and Lin Piao. These opinions were confirmed in the summer of 1967, when Lo was denounced publicly as a follower of P'eng Te-huai and Huang K'o-ch'eng (qq.v.), who had been purged in 1959.

Little is known about Lo Jui-ch'ing's personal life, partly because the nature of his work demanded that he maintain a degree of anonymity. In 1937 he married Liu Chueh-ts'an, and he remarried after her death in the 1940's.

Lo Jung-huan   羅 榮 桓

Lo Jung-huan (1906–16 December 1963), political commissar in Chinese Communist military forces during the 1930's and 1940's, was director of the general political department and the general cadres department of the People's Liberation Army from 1950 to 1956.

Hengshan, Hunan, was the birthplace of Lo Jung-huan. Little is known about his family background or early years except that his father may have been a grocer. After being graduated from a middle school in Changsha, Lo attended Sun Yat-sen University in Canton. In 1927 he joined the Young Communist League and the Chinese Communist party and went to the Wuhan area, where he participated in a Communist-led uprising in southern Hupeh. After this uprising failed, he joined a guerrilla band led by Mao Tse-tung and became a party representative in the Chinese Workers and Peasants Red Army. By mid-1930 he had become a political commissar in the Fourth Red Army of Lin Piao (q.v.). Lin and Lo continued to be close associates until the mid-1950's.

After Chu Teh (q.v.) became commander in chief of the Chinese Workers and Peasants Red Army, Lin Piao succeeded him as commander of the First Army Group, with Lo Jung-huan as director of the political department. In this capacity, Lo made the Long March to Shensi in 1934–35. When the Chinese Communist forces in northwest China were reorganized as the Eighth Route Army, Lo became political commissar in Lin Piao's 115th Division. He held this post until the Sino-Japanese war ended in 1945. When Chinese Communist armies moved into Shantung in 1939, Lo also became commander and political commissar of the Shantung military district and secretary of the Shantung branch of the Central Committee of the Chinese Communist party. In the final years of the war, when Lin Piao in effect had retired from active command of the 115th Division, Lo became its acting commander. At the Seventh National Congress of the Chinese Communist party, held in 1945, he was elected to the Central Committee. In 1946 Lo became deputy political commissar of Lin Piao's Northeast Democratic Alliance Army in

Manchuria. The army was redesignated the Fourth Field Army in 1948, and it moved into the Peiping area and then into central and south China in 1949.

In 1949 Lo Jung-huan became political commissar of the Peiping-Tientsin field head-quarters of the People's Liberation Army, political commissar (under Lin Piao) of the Central-South Military Region, and second secretary of that region's Communist party bureau. He served the Central People's Government as procurator general and as a member of the Government Council and the political and legal affairs committee of the Government Administration Council. Beginning in 1950, he was the director of the general political department and the general cadres department of the People's Liberation Army, and from 1950 to 1953 he was political commissar of the Chinese People's Volunteers in Korea. During this period, he also served on the executive board of the Sino-Soviet Friendship Association.

After the Central People's Government was reorganized in 1954, Lo continued to serve as director of the general political department and the general cadres department of the People's Liberation Army until December 1956. Also in 1954 he became a delegate to the National People's Congress, vice chairman of its Standing Committee, and vice chairman of the National Defense Council; he was reelected to these posts in 1958. Lo was one of the ten military leaders who received the rank of marshal of the People's Republic of China in September 1955. A year later, he served on the presidium of the Eighth National Congress of the Chinese Communist party, at which he was reelected to the Central Committee and elected to its Political Bureau. He died in Peking on 16 December 1963.

Lo Lung-chi   羅 隆 基
T. Nu-sheng   努 生

Lo Lung-chi (1896–7 December 1965), Western-educated political scientist who gained prominence in China as the editor of the *I-shih pao* and the Peking *Ch'en Pao*. During the Sino-Japanese war he became prominent in the China Democratic League. After 1949, he served the Central People's Government, becoming minister of timber industry in 1956. As a senior leader of the Democratic League he tried to create a loyal opposition at Peking, but in 1957 he and Chang Po-chün were accused of having formed a rightist coalition and were removed from all official posts.

The son of Lo Nien-tzu, a scholar, Lo Lung-chi was born in Anfu hsien, Kiangsi. After receiving a traditional education in the Chinese classics, he went to Peking in 1912 and entered Tsinghua College, where he became known for participating in student activities and for leading student movements. He was president of the Tsinghua Student Union and chief editor of the student magazine, the *Tsinghua Weekly*. He also took an active part in the May Fourth Movement of 1919. Because of these and other activities, it took him nine rather than the usual eight years to complete his course requirements.

In 1921, after graduation from Tsinghua, Lo Lung-chi went to the United States on a Boxer Indemnity Fund scholarship. He enrolled at the University of Wisconsin, receiving the B.A. in 1923 and the M.A. in 1925. After spending a year in England studying under Harold Laski at the London School of Economics, he returned to the United States and enrolled at Columbia University. He received a Ph.D. degree in 1928 after writing a dissertation entitled "Parliamentary Elections in England." During this period, Lo continued to be active in Chinese student activities. He served for a time as president of the Association of Chinese Students in America and editor of its *Chinese Students Quarterly*.

After returning to China in 1928 Lo Lung-chi became chairman of the department of political science at Kuang-hua University in Shanghai. He also assumed the editorship of the leading literary magazine *Hsin-yüeh* [the crescent moon] after its offices were moved from Peking to Shanghai. Articles on current politics and political ideas soon began to appear in the *Hsin-yüeh*. Until Hu Shih (q.v.) established the *Tu-li p'ing-lun* [independent critic] in 1932, his most important political essays were published in the *Hsin-yüeh*.

Lo Lung-chi's strong criticism of the National Government resulted in arrest, imprisonment, and dismissal from Kuang-hua University in November 1930. After being released early in 1931, he contributed an essay to and published a book entitled *Jen-ch'üan lun-chi* [on the rights of man]. He went to Tientsin and became a lecturer at Nankai University and editor of the *I-shih pao*, which had been founded by Father Vincent Lebbe (Lei Ming-yuan, q.v.), a Roman Catholic cleric. Because of its foreign sponsorship, the *I-shih pao* was relatively free from National Government control. As its editor, Lo soon became known as a crusading journalist.

In 1932 Lo Lung-chi became associated with a new political party headed by Carsun Chang (Chang Chia-sen, q.v.). Two years later, this group held a national meeting at Tientsin and formally established the National Socialist party [kuo-chia she-hui tang]. Because the formation of dissenting political parties had been forbidden by the National Government, the National Socialist party was a secret organization until 1938. Perhaps because of his association with Carsun Chang, Lo Lung-chi became editor in chief of the Peking *Ch'en Pao* [morning post] in 1936. Lo Lung-chi also participated in the activities of other organizations which stressed the threat to China posed by Japanese aggression. In 1936 he became a founding member of the National Salvation Association and an executive member of its Tientsin and Peiping branches. However, he differed from other leading members of the association in that he did not accept the Chinese Communist policy that called for the formation of a united front against the Japanese under the national leadership of Chiang Kai-shek. Lo, in the *I-shih pao* and the *Ch'en Pao*, called for opposition to Chiang in north China and resistance to the Japanese in south China. He later (1957, at Peiking) was criticized for this position on the grounds that opposition to Chiang in north China, where Sung Che-yuan (q.v.) was being pressed by the Japanese to turn the area into a special zone under their sponsorship, served only to aid the Japanese.

The Sian Incident of December 1936 (*see* Chiang Kai-shek) and the outbreak of the Sino-Japanese war in July 1937 led the National Government to invite leaders of all political parties and factions to assist in its resistance effort. Lo Lung-chi served as an adviser to the political department of the Military Affairs Commission (1937–38), a member of the People's Political Council (1938–41), and a member of the Chinese Political Science Society (1939–41). In 1939 he taught at Southwest Associated University, but he later was dismissed from its staff for criticizing the National Government and advocating that its executive powers be curtailed.

With the breakdown of the Kuomintang-Communist united front, leaders of some of the minority political parties joined together in 1941 to form the League of Chinese Democratic Political Groups. In October 1944, when this federation was reorganized as the China Democratic League, with Chang Lan (q.v.) as its chairman, Lo Lung-chi became head of its Kunming branch and a member of the standing committee of its central committee. Because membership was now on an individual rather than a party basis, Lo was able to form his own faction within the Democratic League. The question of cooperation with the major political parties brought him into conflict with Carsun Chang. Lo entertained the idea of cooperating with the Chinese Communists, while Chang thought the Kuomintang to be the lesser of two evils. In 1945, having become head of the Democratic League's propaganda department, Lo began publishing the *Democratic Weekly*.

In 1946, the War in the Pacific having ended, Lo Lung-chi represented the Democratic League at the Political Consultative Conference and served on the conference's constitution drafting committee. When the conference failed to reach an agreement on the formation of a coalition government, Lo went to Shanghai. He published the Democratic League's *Democratic Daily News* and served as the organization's Shanghai spokesman until it was declared illegal by the National Government in 1947. At that juncture, many of the league leaders went to Hong Kong, where they convened a plenary session in May 1948, pledged opposition to the United States and Chiang Kai-shek, and declared their support of the Chinese Communist party. Lo was unable to attend the meeting because he was convalescing in the Hung-ch'iao Sanatorium in Shanghai. However, he immediately voiced his opposition to the league's anti-American stand. Lo had come to know General George C. Marshall in 1946 and later had tried to influence the China policy of the United States by talking with J. Leighton Stuart, who had become American ambassador to China. Stuart and such other friends as the Kuomintang official Yang Hu had helped guarantee Lo's safety in Shanghai

after 1947. Lo hoped to gain American assistance in the formation of a government by the
democratic leaders of minority parties. He
also supported Li Tsung-jen (q.v.) as an alternative to Chiang Kai-shek. During the last
stages of Nationalist control of Shanghai, Lo
was virtually a prisoner in the sanitorium.
In the spring of 1949 he and Chang Lan
were spirited away and hidden by Chinese
Communist agents.

Lo Lung-chi went to Peiping in mid-1949
to help in the preparations for the Chinese
People's Political Consultative Conference. He
was one of sixteen Democratic League represent-
atives to the conference and a member of its
National Committee. When the Central
People's Government was inaugurated at
Peking on 1 October 1949, he was appointed to
the Government Administration Council. He
also became a member of the Sino-Soviet
Friendship Association and a director of the
Chinese People's Institute of Foreign Affairs.
When the Korean war broke out, he accepted
the directorship of the China Peace Committee.
In 1952 he was a delegate to the Asian and
Pacific Regions Peace Conference at Peking and
to the Peace Conference at Vienna. He
represented Kiangsi at the First National
People's Congress in 1954 and became a member
of the congress's Standing Committee. He
attended the World Peace Congress at Helsinki
in 1955 and became a member of the World
Peace Council, attending its special session at
Stockholm in April 1956. In May 1956 he was
named minister of timber industry in the Central
People's Government. Regarded as an expert
on foreign affairs, he became chairman of the
international affairs committee of the Chinese
People's Political Consultative Conference and
vice chairman of the Chinese People's Institute
of Foreign Affairs. He attempted to have these
two bodies serve as foreign policy study and
advisory groups to the ministry of foreign
affairs.

Throughout this period, Lo Lung-chi continued to be active in the China Democratic
League. In 1952 he became a member of the
administrative committee of the league's paper,
the *Kuang-ming jih-pao*, and began to influence
its editorial policy. He was elected a vice
chairman of the league in 1953. The death of
Chang Lan in 1955 and the virtual retirement
of Shen Chün-ju (q.v.) in March 1957 made

Lo and Chang Po-chün (q.v.) the senior leaders
of the Democratic League.

During the Hundred Flowers period in 1957
Lo Lung-chi and Chang Po-chün openly
criticized the Central People's Government.
Lo remarked that the main contradiction in the
Chinese intelligentsia at that time was the
contradiction in positions given to the high-
level intellectuals of bourgeois background and
the petty intellectuals of the proletarian class.
He decried the misuse of intellectual talent,
saying that "there are returned-students from
England who make their living as drag-coolies,
and returned-students from the United States
who run cigarette stalls." Several times he
professed support of the Chinese Communist
party as well as the democratic parties and love
for socialism as well as democracy. Lo saw
himself as a spokesman for a loyal opposition,
but his enemies interpreted his statements to
mean that he considered democracy and
socialism to be equally progressive and that he
considered socialism as practiced in the People's
Republic of China to be undemocratic.

Lo was attending a World Peace Council
meeting at Colombo, Ceylon, in June 1957
when the Hundred Flowers faded and an
"anti-rightist" campaign began. He and
Chang Po-chün were denounced and were
charged with having formed the "Chang-
Lo Anti-Party, Anti-Socialist, Anti-People
Alliance." The attack was led by Shih Liang,
a woman leader of the Democratic League.
Members of the league tried to force Lo's
wife, P'u Hsi-hsiu, to testify against him. His
brothers—Lo Yao-lin, Lo Mu-tseng, and Lo
Chao-jui—were attacked as exploiters of the
people. It seems that Lo, in trying to create a
loyal opposition, had convinced a number of
intellectuals to join the Democratic League
and had used the league and its publications to
propagate this concept. The Peking regime,
however, interpreted his aim as being the
creation of a party that opposed the Chinese
Communist party and advocated bourgeois
democracy. Lo requested that evidence of the
extent of his plotting with Chang be produced
to substantiate the allegations made against
them, and he denied any desire to see the
Chinese Communist party or the Central
People's Government overthrown. However,
he confessed to being "a guilty creature" and
admitted that he had "attempted to negate the

leadership . . . of the Party." By the end of 1958 he had been stripped of all his important posts. He died in Peking on 7 December 1965. At that time, the *Kuang-min jih-pao* identified him as a member of the National Committee of the Chinese People's Political Consultative Conference and a central committee member of the China Democratic League.

Lo Teng-hsien   羅 登 賢
Alt. Ta P'ing   達 平

Lo Teng-hsien (1904–July 1933), Chinese Communist labor organizer in south China who went to Manchuria in 1931 to organize anti-Japanese guerrilla units. After returning to Shanghai in 1933, he was arrested, extradited to Nanking, and executed by the Nationalists.

Born into a poor, working-class family in Kwangtung, Lo Teng-hsien was orphaned at an early age. He went to live with his elder sister in Hong Kong, and at the age of 11 he became an apprentice in the Butterfield and Swire shipyard.

By the time of the general strike in the Canton–Hong Kong area in 1925, Lo had been a journeyman in a metalworking establishment for six years. He participated in the strike, founded a union of Chinese metalworkers, and joined the Chinese Communist party. In 1926, having gained recognition as an able labor organizer, he was appointed to the Hong Kong municipal committee of the Chinese Communist party. After participating in the Canton Commune (*see* Chang T'ai-lei) of December 1927, he became a member of the party's Kwangtung committee. He later moved to Shanghai, where he led protests against the Japanese occupation of Tsinan, Shantung, in May 1928.

At the Sixth National Congress of the Chinese Communist party, held at Moscow in June 1928, Lo Teng-hsien was elected to the Central Committee and the Political Bureau. He also was made secretary of the party's. Kiangsu provincial committee. His proletarian background and his ability as a labor leader were important to the party, which had lost many labor organizers during the Kuomintang purges of 1927 (*see* Chiang Kai-shek). In 1930 he was transferred to the Central Secretariat. He became party secretary of the All-China

Federation of Labor in 1930 and chairman of that organization in 1931. Throughout the 1928–31 period he devoted himself to labor matters and paid little attention to the political controversies that raged within the Chinese Communist party.

After the Japanese attack on Mukden in September 1931, Lo Teng-hsien was sent to Manchuria as the representative of the party's Central Committee in that area and secretary of the party's Northeast branch. He held meetings with Communist cadres in Harbin to make plans for the creation of anti-Japanese guerrilla units, and he traveled between Harbin and Mukden for several months to organize and lead guerrilla units, thus laying the foundations of the Northeast Anti-Japanese United Army (Tung-pei k'ang-jih lien-chün). He directed workers and students in the cities of Manchuria to join the resistance forces of Ma Chan-shan (q.v.), and, after Ma's efforts collapsed, he supported the National Salvation Army (Chiu-kuo-chün). At that time, the Communist officer Chou Pao-chung (q.v.) was chief of staff of the National Salvation Army.

Lo Teng-hsien returned to Shanghai at the end of 1932 to become general secretary of the executive committee of the All-China Federation of Labor and to organize strikes in Japanese-owned factories in Shanghai. When the National Government launched a series of military campaigns against the Communists at the central soviet base in Kiangsi, he was assigned to organize a strike on the Hang-Chiang (Hanghsien to Chiangshan) railway in an effort to disrupt Nationalist transport and supply lines. Before he could complete the preparations for this strike, he was arrested by the International Settlement police in March 1933. He was extradited to Nanking, where he was executed in July 1933.

Lo Wen-kan   羅 文 幹
T. Chün-jen   鈞 任

Lo Wen-kan (1888–16 October 1941), Oxford-trained barrister who served the Peking government as minister of justice and chief justice of the Supreme Court and the National Government as minister of justice and minister of foreign affairs. He retired from public life in 1935.

Panyü, Kwangtung, was the birthplace of Lo Wen-kan. After receiving his primary and secondary education in his native province, he went to England and enrolled at Oxford in 1906. He was graduated from Oxford with an LL.M. degree in 1910, was called to the Inner Temple for final examination, and was admitted to the bar. In 1911 he returned to China and, in the final days of the Ch'ing period, became judicial commissioner in his native Kwangtung. He continued to hold that post until 1913, when he went to Peking to become metropolitan procurator general (shou-tu tsung-chien-ch'a-t'ing chien-ch'a chang). Although he resigned in the spring of 1916 as a protest against Yuan Shih-k'ai's monarchical attempt, he resumed office after Yuan died in June 1916 and Li Yuan-hung (q.v.) became president.

When the Law Codification Commission (hsiu-ting fa-lü kuan fu-tsung-ts'ai) was established in 1916, Lo Wen-kan was named to membership on it, and in July 1918 he became its vice chairman, serving under Wang Ch'ung-hui (q.v.). In the course of preparing a second revision of the criminal code, the two men became close friends. During this period, Lo also served as a professor of law at Peking University and as a lecturer at the Fa-kuan hsün-lien-so chiang-shih [training institute for judicial officers].

In August 1920 Wang Ch'ung-hui was appointed chief justice of the Supreme Court, with Lo Wen-kan as vice chief justice. When Liang Shih-i (q.v.) organized a cabinet in December 1921, he named Lo vice minister of justice. In April 1922 Lo became minister of justice, and on 15 June, after Li Yuan-hung resumed the presidency, he was appointed to the concurrent post of chief justice of the Supreme Court.

The appointment of Wang Ch'ung-hui as officiating premier on 20 September 1922 caused an abrupt change of course in Lo Wen-kan's career. Wang appointed Lo minister of finance in what became known as the "cabinet of able men" (hao-jen nei-ko), which also included V. K. Wellington Koo (Ku Wei-chün) and Hsü Ch'ien (qq.v.). Lo also became director of the salt administration and head of the currency bureau at this time. It was, of course, unusual for a chief justice to resign in order to fill a cabinet post, but Wang Ch'ung-hui prevailed upon Lo to do so

because he believed that the minister of finance had to be a man of high ability and unimpeachable integrity.

Because the chronic insolvency of the Peking government had brought it to the edge of disaster, Lo Wen-kan's post was of critical importance. The enormity of the task given him was indicated by the report he promptly prepared on the financial situation of China in 1922. The government's indebtedness in domestic and foreign loans totaled China $1,726,400,000, with payments due in the amount of China $480,000,000. Unpaid military and urban expenses amounted to China $180,000,000, and current monthly expenses averaged China $9,200,000. To service its debts and meet expenses the government had an average monthly income of slightly over China $200,000.

At this time, the Chihli clique, which supported the Peking government, was torn by a power struggle between Wu P'ei-fu and Ts'ao K'un (qq.v.) which centered on the premiership. Moreover, members of the Fengtien clique of Chang Tso-lin (q.v.) opposed the "cabinet of able men" because they believed that Wang Ch'ung-hui belonged to the Chihli clique, and they urged Wu Ching-lien, the speaker of the National Assembly, and Chang Po-lieh, the deputy speaker, to find a way to defeat the cabinet. Thus, the appointees of Wang Ch'ung-hui, who was a supporter of Wu P'ei-fu became targets of hostile political maneuvers by both the Fengtien clique and the Ts'ao K'un faction. In mid-November 1922 Wu Ching-lien charged that Lo Wen-kan had accepted a bribe in connection with the adjustment of an Austrian loan contract that had been signed before the First World War. Li Yuan-hung had both Lo and his treasury chief arrested on 18 November, and the entire cabinet resigned in protest on 21 November. The following day, Li Yuan-hung had Lo released and sent Sun Pao-ch'i (q.v.) to welcome him to the presidential office. Lo refused this invitation. Three days later, he returned to jail, demanding a fair investigation to determine his innocence or guilt. He spent eight months in jail, and on 29 July 1923 he was found innocent of the bribery charges and was freed. When his opponents in the Parliament appealed the decision, the appellate court withheld action on the case, and Lo was jailed again. Although Ts'ai Yuan-p'ei, the chancellor of Peking University, and Chiang Yung, the chairman of the Law Codification Commission, resigned from office to protest the illegal arrest of Lo Wen-kan, he remained in jail until the appeal was withdrawn in the spring of 1924. By this time, Lo had spent more than a year in jail on politically inspired and groundless charges.

From the spring of 1924 until the spring of 1926 Lo Wen-kan practiced law in Peking. After Tuan Ch'i-jui was forced from office by the resurgent power of Wu P'ei-fu, the minister of the navy, Tu Hsi-kuei, formed a so-called "regency cabinet" in June 1926, with Lo Wen-kan as minister of justice. Lo retained that portfolio for a year, despite several changes of cabinet. He also served as director general of the customs revenue administration, in which capacity he attended the 24 July 1926 meeting of Chinese and foreign delegates to the Special Customs Tariff Conference. In June 1927, when P'an Fu organized a new government at Peking to support Chang Tso-lin's claim to be Ta-yuan-shuai [generalissimo] of all China, Lo was made vice chairman of the treaty revision commission in the ministry of foreign affairs.

Chinese Nationalist plans for the unification of China through the Northern Expedition and Japanese plans for the development of East Asia effectively undermined Chang Tso-lin's government in 1928. When Chang left Peking on 3 June to return to his Manchurian realm, he ordered Lo and Shen Jui-lin, the minister of the interior, to assume charge of political affairs until the Northern Expedition arrived at Peking. With the death of Chang Tso-lin at the hands of the Japanese and the occupation of Peking by the Chinese Nationalists, Lo and Shen went to Mukden, where they became councillors in the headquarters of the Northeast Peace Preservation Forces under Chang Tso-lin's son and successor, Chang Hsueh-liang (q.v.).

In December 1931, after the Japanese had driven Chang Hsueh-liang from Manchuria, Lo Wen-kan, who had been acting as Chang's emissary to the southern Kuomintang leaders at Canton, joined Chang at Peiping and became a member of the North China Political Council. After Chiang Kai-shek retired from office and some of the southern leaders assumed control of the National Government at Nanking, Lo was appointed minister of justice on 1 January

1932. Sun Fo and Eugene Ch'en (qq.v.) were forced to resign from their respective posts as president of the Executive Yuan and minister of foreign affairs in late January, to be succeeded by Wang Ching-wei and Lo Wen-kan. On 1 February, Lo began his efforts to protect China from Japanese encroachment by informing Sir Eric Drummond, the Secretary General of the League of Nations, that reports of China's plans to declare war on Japan were false. Thereafter, Lo worked assiduously, if unsuccessfully, to obtain the intervention in China's favor of the League of Nations and of member countries.

Developments in Sinkiang province in 1933 led the National Government to enlist Lo's talents in yet another field, the adjustment of domestic political tangles. Sheng Shih-ts'ai (q.v.) had seized power at Urumchi in April and had clashed with the Muslim forces of Ma Chung-ying (q.v.). Huang Mu-sung (q.v.) had gone to Sinkiang in June as special pacification commissioner but had been arrested and held by Sheng on charges of plotting to overthrow the Sinkiang government. The price Sheng exacted for Huang's release was confirmation of his authority as border defense commissioner and of Liu Wen-lung's as acting governor. Nanking reluctantly agreed, and Huang returned to the capital on 21 July 1933. In mid-August, Wang Ching-wei sent Lo Wen-kan to Urumchi on a three-fold mission: to arrange a settlement between Sheng Shih-ts'ai and Ma Chung-ying; to balance Sheng's power with that of other leaders so that he could be brought under National Government control; and to achieve the cancellation, if possible, of the economic agreement between Sinkiang and the Soviet Union that had been signed in 1931 by Sheng's predecessor, Chin Shu-jen.

Lo Wen-kan arrived in Urumchi on 2 September 1933. Five days later, he administered oaths of office to Sheng Shih-ts'ai and Liu Wen-lung before going to Turfan to meet with Ma Chung-ying. Ma proved willing to accept Lo's proposal that he assume the post of garrison commander for eastern Sinkiang, but he demanded, as evidence of Sheng Shih-ts'ai's good faith, guarantees from Sheng concerning troop support. After Lo returned to Urumchi and reported on Ma's position, Sheng decided to resume the war against Ma. Lo left Urumchi and went to Ili, where he met with Chang

P'ei-yuan, another potential opponent of Sheng. After going to the Soviet Union to discuss the 1931 treaty with W. W. Yen (Yen Hui-ch'ing), Lo returned to China, having recognized that Nanking's authority did not reach Sinkiang and that Moscow was in a good position to expand its authority in Sinkiang.

Lo reached Nanking on 11 November 1933. A few days later, on the eve of his departure for Nanchang to report to Chiang Kai-shek, he announced that he intended to resign from both of his cabinet offices. On 29 November, the Kuomintang Central Political Council accepted Lo's resignation as foreign minister. Lo continued to serve as minister of justice until 3 October 1934, when the Central Political Council decided to transfer the ministry of justice from the Executive Yuan to the Judicial Yuan. Lo immediately resigned. A month later, he accepted a sinecure appointment as adviser to the ministry of foreign affairs, but in 1935 he retired to Kwangtung and embarked upon a mining enterprise. In 1938, having joined the National Socialist party of Carsun Chang (Chang Chia-sen, q.v.), Lo became a member of the People's Political Council at Chungking. On 16 October 1941 he died of malaria in Loting, Kwangtung, at the age of 53.

Lu Cheng-hsiang   陸徵祥
T. Tzu-hsin   子欣

Lu Cheng-hsiang (1871–15 January 1949), diplomat and cleric, entered the Chinese foreign service in 1892 as an interpreter assigned to the legation at St. Petersburg. He became minister to the Netherlands in 1908 and minister to Russia in 1911. After the republic was established, he served the Peking government at various times as minister of foreign affairs, premier, and minister to Switzerland. Following the death of his wife in 1926, he left Switzerland and went to Belgium, where he became a Benedictine monk.

Shanghai was the birthplace of Lu Cheng-hsiang. His father, Lu Ch'eng-an, who was an assistant in the London Missionary Society, raised him as a Protestant. His mother, *née* Wu Chen-chih, was striken with dropsy soon after her son's birth; she died in 1878. Lu was a sickly child, and he did not begin to receive a traditional education in the Chinese classics until he was 11 sui. Two years later, his father secured a place for him in the Kuang-fang Language School, which was associated with the Kiangnan Arsenal. Lu then began to study French language and literature under the direction of Alphonse Bottu. In 1888, at the age of 17, he was forced to withdraw from school for a year by ill health. After returning to school and completing his studies, he went to Peking and enrolled at the T'ung Wen Kuan, the language institute of the Tsungli Yamen, where he pursued French studies under Charles Vapereau and learned the elements of diplomacy and foreign relations.

In 1892, having been graduated from the T'ung Wen Kuan, Lu Cheng-hsiang was assigned by the Tsungli Yamen to St. Petersburg, where the Chinese minister to Russia, Germany, and Austria, Hsü Ching-ch'eng (ECCP, I, 312–13), had urgently requested an interpreter. In July 1893 Lu received a formal appointment as an interpreter, fourth grade. Hsü Ching-ch'eng took an interest in his new staff member and helped him prepare to become a career diplomat. Lu began to study Russian and English in his spare time, and, under Hsü's direction, he studied European diplomatic history of the nineteenth century. According to Lu's later account, Hsü Ching-ch'eng was "anguished by the corruption and decay of the Manchu government" and earnestly bade Lu to become "Europeanized" in his vocation: "Do not be afraid to become over-Europeanized, only be afraid that what is quintessential in Europe is not grasped." Lu became Hsü's protégé, and his colleagues began to refer to him as "Hsü Junior."

In March 1895 Lu Cheng-hsiang gained the rank of interpreter, third grade; later that year, he also became secretary of legation, in which capacity he served as chargé d'affaires during Hsü Ching-ch'eng's temporary absence from Russia. When Li Hung-chang (ECCP, I, 464-71) was appointed envoy extraordinary to the coronation of Nicholas II in the spring of 1896, Lu served as his interpreter and participated in Sino-Russian negotiations which led to the signing of a secret treaty of alliance in June. Lu then acted as Hsü Ching-ch'eng's interpreter in the negotiations which led to agreement on arrangements for the construction of the Chinese Eastern Railway across Manchuria.

After Hsü Ching-ch'eng was succeeded as minister to Russia by Yang Ju late in 1896, Lu Cheng-hsiang served as Yang's interpreter at the negotiations that resulted in the lease of Port Arthur and Dairen in 1898 and accompanied Yang to the First Hague Conference in 1899. On 12 February 1899 Lu married Berthe Bovy, the daughter of a Belgian general and a relative of the Belgian minister at St. Petersburg. Lu's superiors frowned upon the marriage because his wife was both a Catholic and a foreigner, but his career suffered no apparent ill effects. In 1900 he again served temporarily as chargé d'affaires at St. Petersburg and participated in negotiations concerning the evacuation of Russian troops sent into Manchuria during the Boxer Uprising.

When his father died on 26 January 1901, Lu Cheng-hsiang requested home leave, but he was given a minor promotion instead. After Wu Wei-te succeeded Yang Ju as Chinese minister to Russia in 1902, Lu was made counselor of legation, third grade. About this time, he cut off his queue, the traditional symbol of loyalty to the Manchus. He was granted home leave late in 1903, but was recalled to St. Petersburg when the Russo-Japanese conflict broke out in 1904. After serving a third time as chargé d'affaires in 1905, he was appointed Chinese minister to the Netherlands in 1906. Tsar Nicholas II granted him a special audience and awarded him a medal in recognition of his 14 years of service at St. Petersburg.

Lu Cheng-hsiang's first diplomatic task at The Hague was to negotiate an agreement for the establishing of Chinese consular offices in Dutch colonies, but he had no success. From June to October 1907 he represented China at the Second Hague Conference. He then went to Egypt for a vacation and remained there for several months. He returned to The Hague and resumed negotiations for a consular convention, but he was unable to make any progress. In 1908, on his recommendation, he was recalled to Peking as a protest.

In Peking, Lu Cheng-hsiang became acquainted with Yuan Shih-k'ai, then head of the Board of Foreign Affairs. Yuan strongly recommended that Lu be reappointed minister to the Netherlands, citing Lu's eloquent presentation of China's case at the Second Hague Conference. Lu's appointment was renewed in 1908, and he again attempted to negotiate a consular convention, this time with Beelaerts van Blokland, the Dutch minister at Peking. A Sino-Dutch consular convention finally was signed at Peking on 28 July 1911. Lu then went to The Hague and exchanged ratifications with the Dutch authorities. He then was ordered to St. Petersburg to negotiate a revision of the Sino-Russian treaty of 1881. Soon afterwards, he was appointed Chinese minister to Russia. On 23 October 1911 he joined the Roman Catholic Church.

When it became clear that the republican revolution in China would succeed, Lu Cheng-hsiang and other Chinese diplomats stationed abroad issued a joint telegram, received at Peking on 3 January 1912, urging the abdication of the Hsuan-t'ung emperor, P'u-yi (q.v.). On 13 February, the day after the abdication, Lu cabled his congratulations to Yuan Shih-k'ai and placed himself at the disposal of the republican government. In March, Lu was appointed minister of foreign affairs.

Lu Cheng-hsiang arrrived at Peking in May 1912 to assume office. He immediately began to transform the unwieldy foreign affairs structure into a modern ministry. He dismissed many beneficiaries of past nepotism, including one of Yuan Shih-k'ai's nephews, and caused the revision of a prior presidential mandate establishing an organic law for the ministry so that he could create a national foreign service based on merit alone. After T'ang Shao-yi (q.v.) resigned the premiership, Lu succeeded him on 29 June. He endeavored to form a non-partisan cabinet, but he encountered considerable opposition from the Parliament, then controlled by members of the T'ung-meng-hui. On 29 July, three days after the Parliament finally had approved the new slate of ministers, T'ung-meng-hui members introduced a bill impeaching Lu Cheng-hsiang for the delay and for alleged subservience to Yuan Shih-k'ai. The bill was not passed, but on 19 August Lu went on sick leave. On 18 September, he resigned as foreign minister in favor of Liang Ju-hao, and on 21 September, he resigned as premier.

Liang Ju-hao, faced with a Sino-Russian crisis centered on Outer Mongolia, resigned as minister of foreign affairs on 13 November 1912, and Lu Cheng-hsiang was reappointed to that office. Russia had signed an agreement with

Outer Mongolia and had recognized its autonomy. Lu began negotiations, and on 20 May 1913 a Sino-Russian agreement was signed which included recognition of Outer Mongolia as an integral part of China. Lu continued to serve as foreign minister after Tuan Ch'i-jui (q.v.) assumed the premiership in July 1913, but he suffered a new disappointment when the Senate, on 24 July, refused to ratify the Sino-Russian agreement. He resigned from office in September and accepted a sinecure post as adviser on foreign affairs in the presidential office. When Yuan Shih-k'ai, who had been serving as provisional president, formally assumed the presidency in October 1913, Lu acted as master of ceremonies at the inauguration. Soon afterwards, a new foreign minister, Sun Pao-ch'i (q.v.) negotiated a new agreement with Russia. In this agreement, signed on 5 November 1913, Russia recognized China's suzerainty over Outer Mongolia, and China recognized Outer Mongolia's autonomy.

In May 1914 Lu Cheng-hsiang became a member of the state council at Peking. Soon afterwards, he went to Switzerland. He returned to Peking in January 1915, just at the time when Japan presented Yuan Shih-k'ai's government with the Twenty-one Demands. Sun Pao-ch'i resigned, and Lu resumed office as foreign minister, this time in the cabinet of Hsü Shih-ch'ang (q.v.). Although Yuan Shih-k'ai and Ts'ao Ju-lin (q.v.), the vice minister of foreign affairs, conducted the ensuing negotiations with the Japanese, Lu was required to sign the final agreement on 25 May 1915. He protested to Yuan Shih-k'ai that the signing was "tantamount to signing my own death sentence" with respect to his place in Chinese diplomatic history.

June 1915 was marked by the signing of the tripartite—China, Russia, and Outer Mongolia—Treaty of Kiakhta (for details, *see* Ch'en Lu) and by the launching of Yuan Shih-k'ai's campaign to become monarch. After Hsü Shih-ch'ang retired to Hunan, Lu Cheng-hsiang succeeded him as Kuo-wu-ch'ing [secretary of state], a new office that was equivalent to the premiership. Although Lu later stated that he had not supported Yuan's ambitions, in 1915 he countersigned the letters of patent endowing titles of nobility that Yuan issued to various Chinese dignitaries. When Yuan abandoned his monarchical plans in March 1916, Hsü Shih-ch'ang resumed office as Kuo-

wu-ch'ing. In May, a month before Yuan Shih-k'ai's death, Lu resigned as minister of foreign affairs.

Early in 1917 Lu Cheng-hsiang became a member of a special foreign-affairs committee established by Tuan Ch'i-jui (q.v.), then the premier, to handle matters pertaining to the First World War. Lu represented Tuan in negotiations with foreign representatives at Peking in February concerning China's entry into the war on the side of the Allies. China declared war on Germany in August. After Feng Kuo-chang (q.v.) became president, with Wang Shih-chen (q.v.) as premier, Lu resumed office as minister of foreign affairs. He continued to hold office until December 1920, despite several upheavals in the Peking government.

Lu Cheng-hsiang headed the composite Chinese delegation to the Paris Peace Conference in January 1919. Because of the Shantung settlement, this delegation, which also included C. T. Wang (Wang Cheng-t'ing, q.v.) as a Canton representative, refused to sign the Treaty of Versailles. This refusal greatly enhanced Lu's reputation in China, where he had been unpopular since the signing of the Twenty-one Demands in 1915. On 4 May 1919, the day that Lu presented China's formal protest regarding the Shantung settlement to the Council of Three, the May Fourth Movement (*see* Lo Chia-lun) began in China. On 10 September, Lu and C. T. Wang signed the Treaty of St. Germain. With the ratification of that instrument, China became a member of the League of Nations. Lu then returned to China and resumed charge of the ministry of foreign affairs, which had been administered by Ch'en Lu in his absence.

Tuan Ch'i-jui and his supporters were toppled from power in August 1920, and W. W. Yen (Yen Hui-ch'ing, q.v.) became acting minister of foreign affairs in the new cabinet of Chin Yün-p'eng (q.v.). In October, Lu Cheng-hsiang assumed the nominal co-chairmanship of the National Famine Relief Commission. He addressed himself to family affairs in November and moved the coffins of his parents and his grandmother to Shihmen, on the outskirts of Peking. Then, in December, he formally resigned from office.

In May 1921 Lu was appointed chairman of the National Famine Relief Commission. By this time, his wife had become seriously ill;

and in 1922, acting on her physician's advice, he took her to Switzerland and established residence at their vacation home in Locarno. The Peking government offered Lu the post of minister to France. At his request, he became minister to Switzerland instead. He also represented China at the League of Nations Assembly in October 1922 and at several sessions of the International Labor Conference in 1922–24.

As his wife's health declined, Lu Cheng-hsiang increasingly sought solace in religion. He was granted an audience with Pope Pius XI in 1925. His wife died in April 1926, and on 5 July 1927 he entered the abbey of Saint André in Lophem-les-Bruges, Belgium, as a postulant in the Order of St. Benedict. He took the name Pierre Célestin. He was ordained in June 1935, at the age of 64. After the outbreak of the Sino-Japanese war in 1937, he collaborated with Bishop Paul Yu Pin in an attempt to win support for China's war effort. During the Second World War he preached to wounded Belgian soldiers. To the end of his days, he maintained contact with prominent Chinese officials, virtually remaining, as his abbot had remarked upon his entry into the abbey, "an envoy of China now as then." He assisted in the establishment of diplomatic relations between China and the Vatican in 1943. In May 1946, at the age of 75, Father Lu was made titular abbot of St. Peter's of Ghent. He found time to publish memoirs and essays, including *Ways of Confucius and of Christ*, which reflected the syncretism of his later thinking. Late in 1948 he became ill, and he died in the Clinique des Soeurs Noires at Bruges on 15 January 1949. His last words were recorded as being "All for China!"

Lu Chung-lin
T. Jui-po

鹿鍾麟
瑞伯

Lu Chung-lin (1884–), military officer and long-time subordinate of Feng Yü-hsiang who became minister of war at Nanking in 1929. When the northern coalition collapsed and the command structure of the Kuominchün disintegrated in 1930, he broke with Feng. He later served the National Government as minister of conscription and the Central People's Government as a member of the National Defense Council.

Tingchow, Chihli (Hopei), was the birthplace of Lu Chung-lin. Little is known about his background or his youth except that he was educated for a military career at the Military Staff College in Tientsin. After being graduated in 1915 he joined the 16th Mixed Brigade of Feng Yü-hsiang (q.v.) as a staff officer. Before long, he rose to become a battalion commander. Because of Lu's performance in the Shensi campaigns of 1921 and the Honan campaign of 1922, Feng developed a high appreciation of Lu's abilities. Accordingly, when Feng became military governor of Honan on 10 May 1922, he appointed Lu provincial director of police administration.

During the second Chihli-Fengtien war of 1924, Lu Chung-lin played an important role in Feng Yü-hsiang's conspiracy against Wu P'ei-fu (q.v.) and the resultant coup at Peking. He participated in the occupation of Peking on 23 October, the detention of Ts'ao K'un (q.v.) in his presidential headquarters, and the expulsion of the last Manchu emperor, P'u-yi, from the Forbidden City at Peking on 5 November. In rapid succession, Lu became commander of the 22nd Brigade, Peking garrison commander, and commander of the Temporary 1st Division of the Kuominchün. Early in 1925 he was appointed commander in chief of the metropolitan defense force and inspector general of the metropolitan police administration.

When Feng Yü-hsiang went to war against Chang Tso-lin (q.v.) and Wu P'ei-fu late in 1925, Lu Chung-lin took the field against the Fengtien forces in the Tientsin sector. Although the Kuominchün troops took Tientsin, the heavy casualty rate caused Feng Yü-hsiang to resign from his posts and go abroad in an attempt to reach a compromise settlement with Chang and Wu. Hostilities continued, however, and on 8 March 1926 the Kuominchün mined and blockaded the harbor at Taku, near Tientsin. This action resulted in the so-called 18 March incident (*see* Feng Yü-hsiang; Tuan Ch'i-jui). Lu Chung-lin, who had returned to Peking and had resumed command of the garrison, protected Hsü Ch'ien, Li Shih-tseng, Ku Meng-yü, Yi P'ei-chi, and Li Ta-chao (qq.v.) after Tuan Ch'i-jui ordered their arrest on charges of instigating the 18 March incident and disseminating Communist propaganda. However, Chang Tso-lin and Wu P'ei-fu continued to press their attack, and they forced Lu to evacuate his troops from Peking on 15 April.

After Feng Yü-hsiang resumed command of the Kuominchün at Wuyuan, Suiyuan, in September 1926, he declared allegiance to the Kuomintang. Feng received control of Honan in June 1927, and Lu Chung-lin became a member of the provincial government and chief of the Chengchow municipal council. When the Military Affairs Commission was established at Nanking in August, Lu was named to membership in that body. He also received command of the First Army of the Kuominchün, and he collaborated with the forces of Ho Ying-ch'in in the Nationalist capture of Hsuchow in December.

For the final stage of the Northern Expedition, Feng Yü-hsiang's armies were reorganized as the Second Army Group. In April 1928, Lu Chung-lin took the field against the Fengtien forces in northern Honan as commander in chief of the Northern Route Army of the Second Army Group. His troops played an important role in the final drive northward, winning a major battle at Changho and reaching the outskirts of Peking as it was being occupied by the forces of Yen Hsi-shan (q.v.) on 8 June 1928.

In October 1928, when the new National Government was established at Nanking, Lu Chung-lin became vice minister of war, serving under Feng Yü-hsiang. The troop disbandment conference of January 1929 resulted in a break between Feng and Chiang Kai-shek. Feng left Nanking and in effect declared his independence of the National Government on 20 May 1929. He was dismissed from all government and party offices, and Lu Chung-lin succeeded him as minister of war. Fighting between National Government forces and the Kuominchün in Honan in the autumn of 1929 led directly to a major challenge to Chiang Kai-shek's rule by the northern coalition of Feng Yü-hsiang and Yen Hsi-shan in 1930. The National Government authorities ordered the arrest of Lu Chung-lin and other Kuominchün leaders, but Lu evaded arrest and joined his chief. In the summer of 1930 Lu commanded the left wing of Feng's forces in the fighting along the Lunghai rail line. The northern coalition collapsed that autumn amid strong differences of opinion among the Kuominchün leaders with respect to strategy. The command structure of the Kuominchün disintegrated, and Lu Chung-

lin broke with his long-time leader and took refuge in Tientsin.

Lu Chung-lin was elected an alternate member of the Central Executive Committee of the Kuomintang during the governmental and party reorganization of December 1931. In 1935 he was elevated to full membership in the Central Executive Committee. After the Sino-Japanese war began in the summer of 1937, the National Government decided to make use of his services as a military man. In 1938 he was appointed governor of Hopei—the province having been occupied by the Japanese—and commander in chief of the Nationalist guerrilla forces in the Hopei-Chahar war zone. In November 1944 the National Government created a ministry of conscription at Chungking and appointed Lu minister. He continued to hold this post until the War in the Pacific ended. He became a member of the Military Strategy Advisory Committee in 1947 and received command of a Nationalist army group in 1948.

When the Chinese Communists won control of the mainland in 1949, Lu Chung-lin decided to remain there. In September 1954 he became a member of the National Defense Council in the Central People's Government at Peking; his appointment was renewed in April 1959.

Lu Han   盧 漢
   T. Yung-heng   永 衡

Lu Han (1891–), protégé, military subordinate, and close relative of Lung Yün who became governor of Yunnan in 1945 after Lung was ousted from that post. In December 1949 he declared allegiance to the People's Republic of China, and the Central People's Government rewarded him with appointments to nominally senior posts.

A close relative of Lung Yün (q.v.), Lu Han was a member of the ethnic minority known as the Lolo. Little is known about his family background or early years except that he was born in Chaot'ung, Yunnan, and that he was a graduate of the Yunnan Provincial Military School. He became a major in the Yunnan forces in 1924 and a colonel in 1926. After Lung Yün declared allegiance to the Nationalists in 1927, Lu received command of the 98th Division of the Thirty-eighth Army in the National Revolutionary Army.

In 1929, the Northern Expedition having ended, Lu Han was appointed commissioner of finance and then commissioner of construction in the Yunnan provincial government. He returned to the field in 1930 as commander of the Tenth Route Army of the anti-rebel forces that were organized to meet the threat to the National Government by Feng Yü-hsiang and Yen Hsi-shan (qq.v.) in alliance with the Kwangsi militarists Li Tsung-jen, Pai Ch'ung-hsi, and Huang Shao-hung (qq.v.). He retained command of these troops until 1937.

After the Sino-Japanese war broke out in July 1937, Lu Han received command of the Sixtieth Army. His unit participated in the 1938 battle of T'aierhchuang (*see* Li Tsung-jen), which ended in victory. Soon afterwards, he was promoted to commander of the Thirtieth Army Group and then to commander of the First Army Group. Beginning in 1940 he served under Hsueh Yueh (q.v.) as commander of the First Group Army in the Ninth War Area. The high command of the Ninth War Area in Changsha was noted for strategic planning and the direction of combat operations. Nevertheless, it was unable to resist the major Japanese offensive of 1944. Changsha was captured on 18 June 1944, and Hengyang fell on 8 August 1944. Lu Han then became commander of the Yunnan Peace Preservation forces. In 1945 he was appointed commanding officer of the regional command which had headquarters at Kunming.

Throughout this period, Lu Han had been the principal protégé and military subordinate of Lung Yün. At war's end, Lu and his forces were ordered to go to Indo-China to accept the surrender of Japanese troops in that area. In late August, he moved his force of about 160,000 men into Tonkin. His departure left Lung Yün with a guard force of about 9,000 men. Because the Nationalist authorities wished to bring Yunnan under their control, they seized the opportunity afforded by the absence of the Yunnan forces to oust Lung Yün from the governorship. In October, Tu Yü-ming (q.v.) staged a coup and overthrew Lung Yün. Soon afterwards, Lu Han was appointed governor of Yunnan. To prevent him from enjoying the political autonomy that had characterized Yunnan since the governorship of T'ang Chi-yao (q.v.), the Yunnanese forces later were sent to Manchuria. Lu served as a delegate

to the National Assembly in 1946 and as director of the Yunnan Industrial Corporation beginning in 1947. After Chiang Kai-shek retired from the presidency in January 1949 and Li Tsung-jen became acting President, Lu became head of the Kuomintang headquarters in Yunnan and, more importantly, director of the Yunnan-Kweichow pacification headquarters.

As the National Government's authority began to collapse in face of Chinese Communist successes in the civil war, Lu Han gradually moved to sever his military and financial ties with the Nationalists. Many observers believed that he was trying to establish a completely autonomous Yunnan. At the same time, Li Tsung-jen's efforts to preserve some measure of Nationalist control in south China were undercut by Chiang Kai-shek. Because the Nationalists were unsure of Lu Han's loyalty, Chiang Ching-kuo (q.v.) and Chiang Kai-shek went to Kunming in September 1949 to meet with him. The failure to win a firm commitment from Lu Han forced the Nationalists to abandon all hopes for a unified defense of southwest China. The Communist victories continued, and on 3 November Li Tsung-jen flew to Kunming to work out a plan with Lu Han for the defense of Szechwan, Kweichow, and Yunnan. He remained there until 11 November, when he flew to Kweilin to meet with other military leaders. The Communists continued to advance, and by the end of November, defeat in Szechwan and Kweichow had become inevitable. Yunnan was isolated.

Early in December 1949 Chiang Kai-shek made a final attempt to stop Lu Han from deserting the Nationalist cause. He sent Chang Ch'ün (q.v.) to Kunming for discussions with Lu. On 11 December, Lu declared allegiance to the People's Republic of China. He detained Chang Ch'ün and his associates until 23 December, by which time the last Nationalist resistance efforts in southwest China were coming to an end.

Lu Han soon received appointments from the Central People's Government as a member of the Southwest Military and Administrative Committee and as director of the military and administrative committee for Yunnan. In October 1951 he became a member of the National Committee of the Chinese People's Political Consultative Conference. In 1952 and 1953 he served as vice chairman of the

Southwest Military and Administrative Committee. However, in the governmental reorganization of 1954 he was removed from his posts in Yunnan and was relegated to sinecure positions. He became a member of the National Defense Council in October, vice chairman of the National Physical Culture and Sports Commission in November, and a member of the Standing Committee of the Chinese People's Political Consultative Conference in December. His services to the Communist cause in December 1949 were recognized in September 1955, when he was awarded the Order of Liberation, first class. In February 1956 he became a central committee member of the Kuomintang Revolutionary Committee and director of the nationalities affairs section of the National Committee of the Chinese People's Political Consultative Conference. He was a delegate from Yunnan to the National People's Congress in 1958. In April 1959 he was reelected to the Standing Committee of the Chinese People's Political Consultative Conference and reappointed to the National Defense Council.

Lu Hsün: *see* CHOU SHU-JEN.

Lu Jung-t'ing   陸 榮 廷
    T. Kan-hsing   幹 馨

Lu Jung-t'ing (1856–1927), Kwangsi warlord. He began his career as a bandit and later became army commander and deputy military governor of Kwangsi, a supporter and then an opponent of Yuan Shih-k'ai, inspector general of Kwangtung and Kwangsi, and a high official of the republican government at Canton. His public career ended in the early 1920's when his army was destroyed by the Kwangtung forces of Ch'en Chiung-ming.

Wuming hsien, Kwangsi, was the birthplace of Lu Jung-t'ing. He was orphaned at an early age and was left to fend for himself. After making his way to Langchow, the strategic city on the Kwangsi-Tonkin border, he was taken in by a salt smuggler named T'an. Lu took an active part in the family business and married T'an's daughter. He and the T'an family were forced to flee the area after Lu accidentally killed a Frenchman with whom he had been

arguing by throwing him into the river. They escaped into the mountains, where they lived for a time as woodcutters. After the Sino-French war of 1884, sentries were posted on both sides of the border. One day, Lu and his companions ambushed three French sentries and seized their rifles. Thus armed, they became brigands operating on the French side of the border.

Lu Jung-t'ing gradually built up an outlaw band of several hundred men which roamed the rural areas of French Indo-China. Whenever the French authorities pursued Lu and his men, they would escape to the Kwangsi side of the border. Because they never committed crimes in China, the Kwangsi authorities ignored their occasional presence. About 1904 Lu's band became such a menace that the French authorities complained to the Chinese imperial government at Peking. Soon afterwards, the Kwangsi authorities were ordered to bring Lu under control. Lu's friend Ch'en Ping-k'un, who served under Su Tzu-hsi, the commander in charge of the Kwangsi border area, suggested to Su that he pacify Lu by making him an officer in the Kwangsi forces. Su adopted the proposal, Lu accepted it, and the brigand band became a battalion under Lu's command. At this time, Lu also came to know Ts'en Ch'unhsuan (q.v.), the governor general of Kwangtung-Kwangsi.

By 1907 Lu Jung-t'ing had achieved the rank of tsan-chang [lieutenant colonel] and had received command of 12 more battalions of the border defense corps. In the autumn of 1907 a group of local revolutionaries led by Huang Ming-t'an captured the mountain fort at Chennan-kuan. Although Huang Hsing, Hu Hanmin (qq.v.), and Sun Yat-sen advanced into Kwangsi in an effort to assist the guerrillas, Lung Chi-kuang (q.v.), then the commandant for border defense, and Lu Jung-t'ing soon suppressed the uprising. Lung later was made ti-tu [army commander] of Kwangsi, with Lu Jung-t'ing as tsung-ping [brigadier]. When Lung was transferred to Kwangtung in 1911 as ti-tu, Lu became acting ti-tu of Kwangsi.

After the republican revolution began with the Wuchang revolt of 10 October 1911, Lu Jung-t'ing joined with Shen Ping-k'un and Wang Chih-hsiang, the governor and the treasurer of Kwangsi, in declaring the province independent. Shen Ping-k'un was elected tutuh [military governor] of Kwangsi, with Lu as deputy tutuh. In 1913, when the revolutionaries launched the so-called second revolution (*see* Li Lieh-chün) against Yuan Shih-k'ai, Lu supported Yuan and suppressed a large uprising at Liuchow. Lu also gave military aid to Lung Chi-kuang. Although Lu was considered one of Yuan Shih-k'ai's most loyal supporters, he broke with Yuan in 1916. The arrogance of the Peiyang clique and the granting of higher honors to such other commanders as Lung Chi-kuang had irritated Lu for more than a year. He had been mollified somewhat when Yuan had made his son a cadet in the Model Corps, a hand-picked unit commanded by Yuan himself. A few months later, however, the young Lu died from a sudden illness in Wuhan on his way from Peking to Kwangsi. Some of Lu's advisers suggested that the boy had been poisoned by Yuan—a far-fetched story—and Lu apparently believed them. By that time, the Yunnan uprising of December 1915, led by Ts'ai O and T'ang Chi-yao (qq.v.), had begun. The revolutionaries called on all Chinese to rise against Yuan, saying that he had betrayed the republic. Lu's friend and aide Ch'en Ping-k'un urged him to support the Yunnan leaders, as did Liang Ch'i-ch'ao (q.v.) and Ts'en Ch'un-hsuan. Early in 1916, at a meeting in Nanning, Lu informed his close associates of his decision to join the southwestern coalition against Yuan, telling them to keep his decision secret. He then sent Yuan Shih-k'ai a message requesting that Ch'en Ping-k'un replace him as tutuh so that he could lead an expedition against Kweichow, the destination of some revolutionary troops. Yuan appointed Lu pacification commissioner for Kweichow and sent him a large sum of money to finance the expedition. Yuan also ordered Lung Chi-kuang to lead an army to Yunnan by way of Kwangsi. Because Lung's son had married Lu's daughter, Yuan expected the two men to cooperate, but when Lung's forces reached Paishih, Lu's men disarmed them. On 15 March 1916 Lu declared Kwangsi independent. In April, he brought some of his men to Kwangtung, where an uneasy alliance had been formed between the revolutionaries and Lung Chi-kuang because neither of them could maintain order in the province alone.

On 1 May 1916 Lu Jung-t'ing established the headquarters of the National Protection Army of Kwangtung and Kwangsi at Chaoching, a river port between Canton and Wuchow. He asked Ts'en Ch'un-hsuan to become its commander. Soon afterwards, Liang Ch'i-ch'ao, who had played an important role in the Yunnan uprising, went to Kwangsi for discussions with Lu about organizing a military government. On 7 May 1916 a military council was established at Chaoching, with T'ang Chi-yao (q.v.), the governor of Yunnan, as its chairman, and Ts'en Ch'un-hsuan as vice chairman. It repudiated the authority of Yuan Shih-k'ai on the grounds that he had betrayed the republic and announced that, according to the provisional constitution of 1912, Li Yuan-hung (q.v.) was the legal chief of state. The council then stated that because Li was not yet in a position to exercise his legal authority, it was assuming the powers of the cabinet and the responsibility for directing operations against Yuan Shih-k'ai. After Yuan Shih-k'ai died in June 1916, Li Yuan-hung became president at Peking, with Tuan Ch'i-jui (q.v.) as premier. Ts'en Ch'un-hsuan and Lu Jung-t'ing then announced the dissolution of the southern military government. Because of growing agitation in Kwangtung for the removal of Lung Chi-kuang, Li Yuan-hung transferred Lung to Hainan Island as commissioner of mining development and appointed Lu Jung-t'ing tutuh of Kwangtung.

In March 1917 Lu Jung-t'ing went to Peking, where he was received and entertained by Li Yuan-hung, Tuan Ch'i-jui, and other officials. During Lu's absence from Canton his brother-in-law T'an Hao-ming served as acting tutuh of Kwangtung. Lu soon made arrangements with Tuan Ch'i-jui to have T'an appointed tutuh of Kwangsi and to have Ch'en Ping-k'un made tutuh of Kwangtung. Lu became inspector general of Kwangtung and Kwangsi, and his authority over these two important provinces made him the strongest warlord in south China. His prominence was such that during the restoration attempt of Chang Hsün (q.v.) in July 1917 Lu was named imperial viceroy of Kwangtung and Kwangsi in the hope of winning his support.

After Sun Yat-sen initiated the so-called constitution protection movement in the summer of 1917, he received assurances of cooperation from Lu Jung-t'ing and T'ang Chi-yao. On 31 August, the rump parliament at Canton established a military government, with Sun Yat-sen as commander in chief (ta-yuan-shuai) and with Lu Jung-t'ing and T'ang Chi-yao as commanders (yuan-shuai). Although Lu allowed the new government to exist at Canton and took part in it, he did not sever all links with the Peking government. The situation at Canton was an odd one—Sun Yat-sen had the support of the rump parliament, but he had no military forces; Lu Jung-t'ing had military power, but he did not enjoy popular support. Once Lu had consolidated his own authority and had won some territory in Hunan in October–November 1917, he began to lose interest in the constitution protection movement. He and the other Kwangsi militarists also attempted to prevent Sun from building up his own military establishment (*see* Ch'en Chiung-ming).

In the spring of 1918, having become dissatisfied with the military government, Lu and the other southern militarists caused the reorganization of the Canton regime. Supreme authority was given to a board of seven directors general: Ts'en Ch'un-hsuan (chairman), Lu Jung-t'ing, Sun Yat-sen, T'ang Shao-yi, Wu T'ing-fang, T'ang Chi-yao, and Lin Pao-tse. Sun Yat-sen withdrew from the government in May (although he did not resign formally until August) and went to Shanghai. T'ang Shao-yi and Wu T'ing-fang also left Canton; and T'ang Chi-yao, who had not come to Canton at the time of the reorganization, remained in Yunnan. With only Ts'en Ch'un-hsuan, Lu Jung-t'ing, and Lin Pao-tse in Canton, the board could not act, for it lacked a quorum. The rump parliament remedied the situation by appointing Hsiung K'o-wu, Liu Hsien-shih, and Wen Chung-yao to the board.

In August 1920 Ch'en Chiung-ming (q.v.), then at Changchow, Fukien, with his Kwangtung Army, decided to give active support to Sun Yat-sen's plan to establish a new national government at Canton. He advanced into Kwangtung at Sun's behest and, with the help of local militia, defeated the Kwangsi armies. On 24 October, Lu Jung-t'ing and Ts'en Ch'en-hsuan announced the dissolution of the military government. Lu departed for Kwangsi with his remnant forces, and Ts'en went to Shanghai. The Kwangtung Army occupied Canton on 26 October.

In December 1920 the Peking government

appointed Lu Jung-t'ing defense commissioner for the Kwangtung border area; a month later, he was made defense commissioner for the Kwangsi border area. Sun Yat-sen, on assuming office as president extraordinary of the new Canton government in May 1921, announced plans for a northern expedition and ordered Ch'en Chiung-ming to advance against the Kwangsi militarists. Lu's armies were unable to hold back Ch'en's Kwangtung Army; it captured Wuchow on 26 June and Nanning in July. Lu's armies had been destroyed and Kwangsi had been brought under the control of the Canton government by the end of September.

Because Lu Jung-t'ing's authority had been rooted in military power, the destruction of his army ended his career as a public figure, although he made a few attempts to return to power. In 1923 he asked T'ang Chi-yao for help, and T'ang sent a small force into Kwangsi. Ts'ao K'un (q.v.) appointed him military governor of Kwangsi in 1924, but Lu was unable to assume office because he had no military establishment. Lu spent the last years of his life in Tientsin and Shanghai, where he lived modestly. He died in Shanghai in 1927.

Lu Po-hung　　　陸伯鴻
West. Joseph Lo Pa Hong

Lu Po-hung (27 March 1875–30 December 1937), known as Lo Pa Hong, was a successful Shanghai industrialist and a prominent Roman Catholic layman.

Shanghai was the birthplace of Lo Pa Hong. His ancestors had come there from Szechwan in the early seventeenth century, had entered the shipbuilding industry and the cotton and silk trade, and had become Roman Catholics. During the nineteenth century Lo's family often served as hosts to Catholic missionaries, who learned from them the elements of Chinese and something of the customs of the country. In addition to a traditional Chinese education, Lo Pa Hong was given religious instruction at the Tung-chia-tu parochial school (his great-grandfather had given the funds to build the cathedral). He passed the examinations for the sheng-yuan degree in 1893. After two unsuccessful attempts to pass the examinations for the chü-jen degree, he began to study French under the guidance of a Chinese priest. Later in 1894 he became secretary to a French lawyer in Shanghai.

Lo Pa Hong married Marie Ngai Ki Tseng, who also came from a prominent and wealthy Catholic family, in 1896. In the course of time she bore him five sons. Her death in 1905 together with that of one of their sons affected Lo deeply and spurred him to undertake the philanthropic activities that characterized his later life. He began to make regular visits to hospitals and prisons, donating money to aid those people who were afflicted with incurable or contagious diseases.

Little is known about Lo Pa Hong's early years in business. In 1911 he was appointed general manager of the Nantao Electric Company, which was having serious financial problems. He secured British and Japanese loans to modernize and reorganize the company, repaying them with the help of the Congregation of the Mission. Thereafter, he often made financial arrangements with Catholic missionary organizations. In 1914, with the backing of the Siemens interests, he inaugurated a streetcar service between Shanghai and Nantao. This service later merged with the Nantao Electric Company, which became a highly successful business. In the meantime, Lo had founded the Ta Tung Sheng Chi Navigation Company. During the First World War the scarcity of iron and steel in China led Lo and a group of financiers to establish a foundry. At war's end, renewed competition from abroad forced the foundry to close, but aid from the Siemens interests enabled it to resume operations in 1925. Lo continued to be active in shipping and in developing public utilities in Shanghai. In 1923 he bought a section of the Whangpoo waterfront and established the Woohsing Wharf and Storage Company. The following year, he obtained control of the Chapei Electric and Waterworks Company. He became general manager of the Shanghai Inland Waterworks Company in 1928, and he founded the Ta Tseng Company, which engaged in river navigation, in 1929.

Throughout this period, Lo Pa Hong engaged in philanthropic activities, most of which also served to further the cause of Roman Catholicism in China. In 1911 he assumed charge of an old charity hospital, the P'u-yu-t'ang, which had been run by the Shanghai municipal authorities. He soon concluded that the hospital would have to be replaced and began raising money to buy land for a new hospital. He also obtained permission to use bricks from the old city walls in constructing the new building. The Hsin-p'u-yu-t'ang was opened in 1913, the year that Lo first was elected to the Shanghai Municipal Council. He built a chapel at the new hospital, and he often preached to the patients. The Hsin-p'u-yu-t'ang became a training center for members of the Catholic Action of China, established by Lo in 1913 to supplement missionary work with lay activity. This group later did missionary work in the rural areas near Shanghai. Lo also tried to interest educated Chinese in Roman Catholicism by means of public debates. He established a clinic in the Yang-tse borough of Shanghai in 1915 and a similar institution in Sungkiang, Kiangsu, in 1917. Also in 1917 he joined with several other philanthropists in establishing the Peking Central Hospital. In 1923 he founded the Blessed Heart Hospital in Shanghai and enlarged the Hsin-p'u-yu-t'ang; in 1934 he founded the Shanghai Mercy Hospital for mental diseases and the Nantao Isolation Hospital for contagious diseases. In addition to establishing these medical institutions, he made large contributions to all of them.

Education in the Shanghai area also benefitted from Lo Pa Hong's activities. He founded a primary school near the Tung-chia-tu cathedral in 1914 and another near the Yang-tse-poo clinic in 1916. He became interested in starting an English-language school in Shanghai which would be run by American Jesuits. He finally won support for this project after holding discussions in the United States in 1925, when visiting as a delegate from the Shanghai Chamber of Commerce to the International Foreign Trade Congress at Seattle, and in 1926, when attending the Eucharistic Congress at Chicago. He also went to Rome in 1926 and enlisted the support of Pope Pius XI. St. Luigi Gonzaga College opened in Shanghai in 1928. Lo also sponsored the establishment in 1928 of St. Gregory College, a primary and secondary school which was run by the Salesian Fathers. In 1937 he opened a Catholic girls school.

After the Sino-Japanese war began in 1937, Lo Pa Hong made his hospitals available to thousands of wounded soldiers and refugees. That year, he became the first Chinese to be appointed a papal chamberlain by the Vatican. During the Japanese occupation, he put religious charity before patriotism and defied National Government noncooperation orders by continuing to supervise his hospitals as a member of a Japanese-sponsored committee. Although he went into hiding when Nationalist pressure on him increased, he refused to leave Shanghai. On 30 December 1937 he was assassinated by two unknown terrorists.

Lo Pa Hong, like his forebears, combined business skill with religious devotion. The success of his eight major business enterprises, seven hospitals, and five schools, reflected his ingenuity as a financier and as a man of practical charity. A biography by a Jesuit, J. Masson, was published in Paris in 1950 as *Un millionnaire chinois au service des gueux: Joseph Lo Pa Hong.*

Lu Ti-p'ing   魯 滌 平
T. Yung-an   詠 安

Lu Ti-p'ing (1887–31 January 1935), Hunanese military officer who served as field commander of the Second Army of the National Revolutionary Army during the Northern Expedition. He later held the governorships of Hunan (1928), Kiangsi (1929–31), and Chekiang (1931–34).

The younger of two sons in a family of modest means, Lu Ti-p'ing was born in Ninghsiang, Hunan. In the final years of the Ch'ing period, he left his home and a routine education in the Chinese classics to attend the Pin-mu Academy, a junior military training school in Changsha which boasted a course in modern military science. Upon graduation, he joined the imperial forces, and by the time of the revolution of 1911 he had become a battalion commander in the Hunan New Army. Little is known about his career from 1912 to 1916 except that he resigned from the New Army soon after the revolution.

After T'an Yen-k'ai (q.v.) resumed office as tutuh [military governor] of Hunan in the summer of 1916, he appointed Lu Ti-p'ing commander of the 6th Regiment of the Hunan Army. Lu succeeded in retaining his post when T'an was ousted in August 1917. The following year, he received command of the 3rd Brigade. He participated in the expulsion of the Peking appointee Chang Ching-yao from the military governorship of Hunan in 1920, and he was appointed commander of the 2nd Division in the ensuing reorganization of the Hunan forces. Chao Heng-t'i (q.v.), the new military governor, ordered Lu to station his troops at Yochow.

When a revolt against Chao Heng-t'i's authority broke out in mid-1923, the southern government at Canton, hoping to exploit the situation, appointed T'an Yen-k'ai commander in chief of an expedition against Chao. The fighting proceeded in sporadic fashion until 1 September, when Chu Yao-hua, one of Lu Ti-p'ing's regimental commanders, staged a coup at Changsha and forced Chao to withdraw northward. Because Chao was now within reach of aid from Wu P'ei-fu (q.v.), Lu took the initiative in proposing and organizing a "peace conference" between Chao and T'an at Chiangch'a, near Hsiangtan. The conference broke down after two weeks, during which time Chao arranged for military aid from Wu P'ei-fu. Lu Ti-p'ing, his position with Chao Heng-t'i having been compromised by the action of his regimental commander and by his assumption of the role of neutral mediator at the conference, switched allegiance to T'an Yen-k'ai and received the title of commander of the Second Hunan Army (Lu's 2nd Division) in T'an's expeditionary force. By mid-November, Chao Hengt-t'i had driven T'an and Lu from Hunan. They reached the Canton area just in time to help beat back an attack by Ch'en Chiung-ming (q.v.).

In the autumn of 1924, when Sun Yat-sen proclaimed the launching of a northern expedition against Ts'ao K'un (q.v.) and Wu P'ei-fu, he designated the Hunanese troops and other forces under the over-all command of T'an Yen-k'ai the National Construction Army (Chien-kuo chün). With the death of Sun Yat-sen in March 1925 and the subsequent organization of the National Government and the National Revolutionary Army, the Hunanese forces became the Second Army, with T'an Yen-k'ai as commander and Lu Ti-p'ing as deputy commander. Lu assumed field command of the Second Army during the Northern Expedition because T'an's government posts kept him in Canton. The Second Army engaged the forces of Sun Ch'uan-fang (q.v.) in September 1926, with three of Lu's four divisions advancing across the Hunan border to Pinghsiang. Lu's forces captured Changshu on 5 October and Chinhsien on 23 October, thus weakening Sun's position at Nanchang. These and other victories in the Nanchang sector led to the surrender of that city on 8 November.

On 24 March 1927 the Second Army of Lu Ti-p'ing and the Sixth Army of Ch'eng Ch'ien (q.v.) occupied Nanking. The entry of these forces into Nanking was attended by anti-foreign actions that resulted in the loss of foreign lives and property. At first, Lu's 4th Division commander, Chang Hui-tsan, was blamed for the violence, and attention was called to the fact that Lu's political commissar, Li Fu-ch'un (q.v.), was a Communist; however, responsibility was finally attributed to elements of Ch'eng Ch'ien's Sixth Army, of which the Communist Lin Po-ch'ü (q.v.) was political commissar.

During the complicated political maneuvers that began in April 1927 with the break between the left-wing faction of the Kuomintang at Wuhan and Chiang Kai-shek's faction at Nanking and that ended in August 1927 with the temporary retirement of Chiang Kai-shek in the interests of party unity, Lu Ti-p'ing refused to take sides. When the National Government launched a campaign against T'ang Sheng-chih (q.v.) in October, the Second Army, then at Ichang, participated in it, but Lu, for reasons that are unclear, was in Shanghai. At any rate, he received full command of the Second Army that year, and in the spring of 1928 he became governor of Hunan and a member of the Wuhan branch of the Political Council. He introduced a system of civil-service examinations for the recruitment of hsien magistrates and revamped the province's financial structure. However, Lu soon came into conflict with the Kwangsi leaders Li Tsung-jen and Pai Ch'ung-hsi (qq.v.), who dominated the Wuhan branch of the Political Council; and on 21 February 1929 the council dismissed him from the governorship. Soon afterwards, Lu was appointed commander of the Fifth Anti-Rebel Army, and his troops cooperated with the military forces dispatched from Nanking in the campaign against the Kwangsi forces in the Wuhan area. With victory in early April, Lu was appointed garrison commander of the Wuhan area. By this time, he also had become an alternate member of the Kuomintang Central Executive Committee and a member of the Military Affairs Commission.

In September 1929 Lu Ti-p'ing was appointed governor of Kiangsi, which had become a center for Chinese Communists who had escaped the various purges of 1927. In mid-1930, while the National Government was heavily engaged in meeting the challenge of the northern coalition (see Feng Yü-hsiang; Yen Hsi-shan), the Communist P'eng Te-huai (q.v.) attacked and occupied Changsha, and other forces led by Chu Teh (q.v.) and Mao Tse-tung attacked near Nanchang. Lu was appointed commander in chief of the National Government's first so-called bandit-suppression campaign that autumn, and his units drove deeply into the mountains of Kiangsi. However, he pulled back after the 18th Division of Chang Hui-tsan was ambushed and crushed. Although left with about half of his forces, Lu also participated in the equally unsuccessful second campaign against the Communists, which took place in April-May 1931.

In the governmental reorganization that followed Chiang Kai-shek's temporary retirement at the end of 1931, Lu Ti-p'ing was appointed governor of Chekiang. He immediately undertook such tasks as the reinforcement of provincial defenses, the building of roads and telecommunications networks, the development of industry and commerce, and the improvement of the provincial administration. His long years of military and public life began to take their toll, and he suffered a stroke in 1933. Despite his continued ill health, the National Government did not accept his resignation from the governorship until December 1934. Lu then went to Nanking to assume the sinecure post of deputy chairman of the Military Advisory Council, but on 31 January 1935 he suffered another stroke and died.

Lu Ti-p'ing was survived by his wife, née Ting, by their son, Lu Cho-ch'ang, and by two small sons whose mother was his concubine, Miss Sha. All of them died, some naturally and some by execution, soon after the Communists came to power in 1949.

Lu Ting-yi   陸定一

Lu Ting-yi (1901–), leading Chinese Communist propagandist and long-time head of the party's propaganda department. In 1965 he became minister of culture at Peking.

The son of a landowner who also operated a textile factory, Lu Ting-yi was born in Wusih, Kiangsu. After receiving his primary and secondary education, he went to Shanghai, where he enrolled at Nanyang University. He participated in student activities during the May Fourth Movement of 1919. About 1924 he joined the Communist Youth League and the Chinese Communist party. After being graduated from Nanyang University, where he majored in engineering, he received a Peking government appointment to the Canton-Kowloon railway administration in 1925.

By mid-1926 Lu Ting-yi had returned to Shanghai and had become director of the propaganda department of the Communist Youth League, then headed by Jen Pi-shih (q.v.). He also served as editor of the league's magazine, *Chung-kuo ch'ing-nien* [China youth] until mid-1927, by which time the Kuomintang and the Chinese Communist party had split. In 1928 he went to Moscow, where he represented the Chinese Communist Youth League at the International Youth Congress and attended the Sixth National Congress of the Chinese Communist party, held at Moscow in June 1928.

Lu Ting-yi returned to Shanghai in 1929 to resume office as director of the Communist Youth League's propaganda department. In 1931, after the Nationalists executed Hsiang Chung-fa (q.v.), the general secretary of the Chinese Communist party, Communists in the Shanghai area were forced to suspend operations. Lu went to the central soviet area at Juichin, Kiangsi, where he edited the party newspaper *Hung-se chung-hua* [red China] and continued his work for the Communist Youth League. During the Long March to Shensi in 1934–35 he was a propaganda worker in the Chinese Workers and Peasants Red Army. In Shensi, he served as director of the Red Army's general political department in 1936 and as director of the propaganda department of the

First Front Army in 1937. The outbreak of the Sino-Japanese war and the formation of the Kuomintang-Communist united front against the Japanese resulted in the reorganization, in August 1937, of Chinese Communist troops in the northwest as the Eighth Route Army, with Chu Teh (q.v.) as commander in chief. Lu became deputy director and then director of the propaganda department in the Eighth Route Army's political department. His achievements in propaganda work were recognized by the Chinese Communist party at its Seventh National Congress in 1945, when he was elected to its Central Committee. In 1946, the War in the Pacific having ended, he served as a Communist member of the Political Consultative Conference and as a negotiator at the Peiping Executive Headquarters. The Kuomintang-Communist peace negotiations were unsuccessful, and full-scale civil war between the two contending factions soon broke out. Little is known about Lu's activities in the period between the beginning of 1947 and the autumn of 1949, when he participated in the Chinese People's Political Consultative Conference.

After the Central People's Government of the People's Republic of China was established in October 1949, Lu Ting-yi became director of the party propaganda department. He was demoted to deputy director in 1953, about the time that Kao Kang and Jao Shu-shih (qq.v.) were censured and accused of forming an anti-party alliance, but he was restored to the directorship in 1955. From 1949 to 1954 he also served as deputy chairman of the culture and education committee of the Government Administration Council. He was elected to the executive board of the Sino-Soviet Friendship Association in 1951, 1954, and 1959; and he served on the national committee of the China Peace Committee from 1950 to 1958. He represented Kiangsu at the first National People's Congress and became a member of the congress's Standing Committee. He also represented Kiangsu at the second and third National People's congresses.

Lu Ting-yi's importance in the Chinese Communist party was demonstrated on 26 May 1956, when he made the first public announcement of what became known as the Hundred Flowers Campaign. At a gathering of scientists, social scientists, doctors, writers, and artists he made a speech entitled "Let All Flowers Bloom

Together, Let Diverse Schools of Thought Contend." The text of this speech was published in the *Jen-min jih-pao* [people's daily] on 13 June. It presumably was derived from a speech given by Mao Tse-tung to a closed session of the Supreme State Conference on 2 May. However, Mao's speech never was published. Mao later elaborated on the policy of "letting a hundred flowers blossom and a hundred schools of thought contend" in his "The Correct Handling of Contradiction Among the People" of 27 February 1957, but it was Lu Ting-yi who publicly inaugurated the Hundred Flowers period.

In 1957 Lu Ting-yi served as vice chairman of a committee for the popularization of common spoken language and as a member of the Central People's Government delegation, headed by Mao Tse-tung, to the celebrations at Moscow marking the fortieth anniversary of the Russian Revolution. In 1965 he became minister of culture of the State Council.

Lu Ting-yi married twice. His first wife, who bore him two children, was killed by Nationalists in Fukien province about 1927. Lu remarried in 1941; he and his second wife reportedly had three children.

Lu Tso-fu   盧 作 孚

Lu Tso-fu (1894–8 February 1952), entrepreneur who founded such enterprises as the Ming-sung Industrial Company, a shipping firm. From 1938 to 1943 he served under Chang Kia-ngau as vice minister of communications in the National Government. He fled to Hong Kong in 1949, but returned to Chungking in response to Chinese Communist promises of financial aid to the Ming-sung Industrial Company. These promises were not kept, and Lu committed suicide in 1952.

A native of Hoch'uan, Szechwan, Lu Tso-fu was the son of an impoverished farmer. Little is known about his early years except that he managed to acquire sufficient education to become a mathematics teacher. After teaching at grade schools in Hoch'uan and at a high school in Kiangan, in 1919 he became a correspondent for a local newspaper. A few years later, he joined the provincial civil service

as a clerk in the education section of the southern Szechwan tao-t'ai's office. He rose to become chief of the section, in which capacity he was responsible for instituting educational reforms and for bringing such teachers as Yün Tai-ying (q.v.) to Szechwan. This achievement was particularly notable because Szechwan was constantly in the throes of civil strife during this era.

In 1925 Liu Hsiang (q.v.), then director general for military affairs in Szechwan, appointed Lu Tso-fu his adviser. With Liu Hsiang's backing, Lu founded a shipping company, the Ming-sung Industrial Company, in an attempt to challenge foreign domination of steam navigation on the Szechwan stretch of the Yangtze. When the Ming-sung Industrial Company was established at Hoch'uan in 1925 its capital was only CN$8,000. By mid-1926 it had collected an additional CN$52,000 and thus was able to procure a 70-ton steamer, christened the S. S. Ming Sung, to run between Hoch'uan and Chungking. In the interests of financial soundness, Lu served as ticket seller as well as the company's general manager. To learn management and operations techniques, he often traveled on steamers operated by Jardine, Matheson or Butterfield and Swire, both of which were British companies. He soon realized that to recover Chinese navigation rights in inland waters, it would be necessary to have ships traveling the difficult but profitable Chungking-Ichang region. In 1931 he moved the company's headquarters to Chungking. By 1935 about half of the steamers plying the Szechwan rivers had been acquired by the Ming-sung Industrial Company, and by the eve of the Sino-Japanese war in mid-1937, the company owned 46 vessels with an aggregate weight of 22,600 tons. After the war began in July 1937, the Ming-sung Industrial Company enjoyed a monopoly, for it assumed control of all foreign-operated steamers in Szechwan waters.

Even before the war began Lu Tso-fu suggested that closer ties between Szechwan and the National Government be established. In 1936 he persuaded Liu Hsiang, then the governor of Szechwan, to go to Nanking for discussions with Chiang Kai-shek. To implement some of the cooperation measures proposed in these discussions, Lu Tso-fu became commissioner of reconstruction in the Szechwan provincial government. Among the significant undertakings initiated by Lu was the building of the Chengtu–Chungking railway.

The Ming-sung Industrial Company played a vital role in aiding the transfer of the National Government to Chungking. Arsenals, industrial plants in the vulnerable seaboard provinces, essential commodities, and refugees all had to be evacuated with the government, first to Wuhan and then to Chungking. The company also carried 200,000 tons of industrial equipment from Shanghai to Chungking and other safe areas in the interior. Throughout the war, its ships purveyed food to armies on several fronts. Without the indispensable facilities provided by the Ming-sung Industrial Company under Lu Tso-fu's meticulous direction, the problems of efficient wartime transportation might have been insurmountable.

Lu Tso-fu served the National Government as vice minister of communications, under Chang Kia-ngau (Chang Chia-ao, q.v.), in 1938–42. From 1940 to 1942 he also held office as director of the National Food Administration, an onerous post which involved the procurement of grains and cereals for both civilian and military consumption. He continued to direct the Ming-sung Industrial Company as its importance increased through participation in wartime industrial enterprises. Among its major subsidiaries and affiliates were the Ta-ming Textile Company, the Ming-sung Machine Works, and the T'ien-fu Coal Mining Company. The machine works built 24 river steamers during the war, and by 1942 the Ming-sung Industrial Company had a capital of CN$7,000,000 and about 100 vessels which plied the waterways of Szechwan.

Long before he achieved prominence, Lu Tso-fu had cherished the ambition of transforming his native place into a model district. As director of the civil defense bureau of the Chialing River in 1926–31, he began to develop Peip'ei, near Hoch'uan. Over the years, Peip'ei came to compare with the model city of Nant'ung, which was the handiwork of Chang Chien (q.v.). To its natural advantages of scenic beauty and healthful hot springs were added such man-made assets as a power plant, schools, science museums, theaters, and attractive residential and office buildings. It became a showplace during the war, and one Chinese observer described it by saying that to the casual and unsuspecting tourist it would seem like a mirage in the desert.

As soon as the war ended, Lu Tso-fu, in keeping with the National Government's postwar policy of economic rehabilitation and development, undertook a massive program to expand the Ming-sung Industrial Company. To increase the company's tonnage, he bought some 16 landing ship tanks (LST) from the United States (these being 1,500-ton vessels), obtained a loan from the Canadian government for the building of nine river-navigation steamers, and joined with the Kincheng Banking Corporation in forming the Pacific Steamship Company to buy three ocean-going vessels. By 1948, the Ming-sung Industrial Company operated 111 vessels with an aggregate weight of 63,174 tons.

Lu Tso-fu fled to Hong Kong at the time of the Chinese Communist occupation of the mainland in 1949. He attempted to keep his company operating from his branch office in Hong Kong, for there were bank loans to be repaid as well as the Canadian loan. Because he was harrassed by these obligations, he accepted a Chinese Communist promise of financial aid and returned to Chungking. However, he discovered on arrival in Chungking that the Southwest Military and Administrative Committee had confiscated the "bureaucratic capital" of the company and had appointed official supervisors to manage its affairs. Lu was deprived of any voice in the company's operations, and the Canadian loan was left unserviced.

On 8 February 1952 Lu Tso-fu was elected to the presidium of a people's trial being held in Chungking. His secretary of many years, who was in the audience, accused Lu of several crimes, and the presidium decided that Lu should stand trial on the following day. On the evening of 8 February, Lu took an overdose of barbiturates and died.

Lung Chi-kuang 龍 濟 光
T. Tzu-ch'eng 子 誠

Lung Chi-kuang (1860–1921), Yunnanese military man who became military commander o Kwangsi in 1908 and of Kwangtung in 1911. A supporter of Yuan Shih-k'ai, he held control of Kwangtung from mid-1914 until mid-1916, when he was transferred to Hainan Island as commissioner of mining development. In December 1917, on orders from the Peking government, he attacked the forces of Sun Yat-sen, but his army was routed early in 1918.

A native of Mengtzu, Yunnan, Lung Chi-kuang was the second son to be born into a family of tu-shih [hereditary native chieftains]. When still a small child, Lung decided to pursue a military career, and he and his elder brother, Lung Chin-kuang, eventually joined the forces of Ts'en Yü-ying (ECCP, II, 742–46) in Yunnan. In 1905 the brothers went to Kwangsi to serve under their former commander's son, Ts'en Ch'un-hsuan (q.v.). Lung Chi-kuang soon became commandant for border defense on the Kwangsi–Indo-China border. One of his fellow officers was the former bandit Lu Jung-t'ing (q.v.). In the autumn of 1907 Lung and Lu suppressed an uprising by republican revolutionaries at Chen-nan-kuan despite the efforts of Huang Hsing, Hu Han-min (qq.v.), and Sun Yat-sen to assist the guerrillas by advancing into Kwangsi. For their services, Lung was promoted to acting ti-tu [army commander] of Kwangsi, and Lu was made tsung-ping [brigadier]. After the two men quelled an uprising at Hokow in 1908, Lung's appointment was confirmed.

In 1911 Chung Ming-ch'i, the acting governor general of Kwangtung, arranged for Lung Chi-kuang to take his men to Canton and appointed him ti-tu of Kwangtung. Before Lung could establish himself in Canton, however, the republican revolution broke out, and the revolutionaries took control of Kwangtung. Lung therefore stationed his men at Waichow (Huichou).

In the winter of 1912 Yuan Shih-k'ai appointed Ch'en Chiung-ming hu-chün-shih [military commissioner] of Kwangtung, with Lung Chi-kuang as his deputy. Lung and his army soon ran into financial difficulties, and Lung obtained the permission of Hu Han-min, then the tutuh [military governor] of Kwangtung, to move his men back to Kwangsi. When he arrived at Wuchow, Lung received a letter and a large sum of money from Yuan Shih-k'ai. He remained at Wuchow, awaiting further instructions. After the so-called second revolution began in the summer of 1914, Ch'en

Chiung-ming, who replaced Hu Han-min as tutuh on 14 June, declared Kwangtung's independence on 18 July. Yuan immediately appointed Lung Chi-kuang hu-chün-shih of Kwangtung and ordered him to march on Canton. Lung easily ousted Ch'en, replaced him as tutuh of Kwangtung, and occupied Canton on 13 August. At this point, Ts'en Ch'un-hsuan visited Canton in an attempt to persuade Lung to join the anti-Yuan movement, but had no success; in fact, he barely escaped arrest. The revolutionaries of the Canton area were driven underground, and they resorted to the tactics of terrorism. Trade-union members, under the leadership of Ma Ch'ao-chün (q.v.), organized an assassination team and waited for opportunities to harass Lung. They had no success until June 1914, when they attacked and killed Lung's deputy Ma Tsun-fa. Lung's spies traced the origin of the plot, and Ma Ch'ao-chün was forced to flee to Hong Kong. A few more bombings were staged by the revolutionaries in Canton, but none of them endangered Lung.

The acceptance by Yuan Shih-k'ai in May 1915 of the Twenty-one Demands and his plot to become monarch rallied republican forces throughout China and caused a new burst of anti-Yuan activity. Lung Chi-kuang, who had become one of Yuan's most trusted henchmen, further enraged the Kwangtung populace when he ordered a lantern procession in Canton to celebrate Yuan's diplomatic "success." When Lung went to visit his brother on 17 July, during a flood in Canton, Chung Ming-kuang, a member of the workers' assassination group, seized the opportunity to throw a bomb at him. It killed 17 members of Lung Chi-kuang's bodyguard and the assassin, but Lung received only a foot wound. This incident led Lung to take greater precautions and to intensify his search for the revolutionaries, but it did not weaken his support of Yuan Shih-k'ai. On 21 December 1915, when Yuan Shih-k'ai issued an elaborate honors list in preparation for the establishment of the new monarchy, Lung Chi-kuang was one of the few men to be created duke. He later was elevated to chun wang [prince of the second order].

By this time, the Yunnan uprising of December 1915, led by Ts'ai O and T'ang Chi-yao (qq.v.) had begun, and Yunnan had been declared independent. This declaration was the signal to revolutionaries all over the country to rise in defense of the republic. The ensuing anti-Yuan campaign was facilitated greatly when Lu Jung-t'ing joined the revolutionaries, declaring Kwangsi independent on 15 March 1916. Earlier that year, Yuan Shih-k'ai had ordered Lung Chi-kuang to send an army to Yunnan by way of Kwangsi. When Lung's forces, commanded by his brother, reached Paishih, Lu Jung-t'ing's men disarmed them. This action took Yuan by surprise; he had expected Lung and Lu to cooperate because Lung's son had married Lu's daughter. Although Yuan scotched his monarchical plans in March, the southwestern leaders continued to oppose him. They made overtures to Lung Chi-kuang, for Kwangtung was an area of strategic importance, but he resisted them. Revolutionary groups in Kwangtung assumed control of many important regions, the naval forces in Canton defected, and the clamor for independence increased.

By early April 1916 Lung Chi-kuang had decided that further open resistance to the revolutionaries would be useless. After receiving instructions from Yuan Shih-k'ai, he declared Kwangtung independent and invited the revolutionary leaders to a conference near Canton on 12 April—intending to arrest them during the meeting. Few of them accepted the invitation, but those who did attend were killed. This incident aroused the ire of the Kwangtung population and enraged Lu Jung-t'ing and Liang Ch'i-ch'ao (q.v.), whose representatives had been murdered. Lu Jung-t'ing decided to move some of his troops to Kwangtung. To avoid disaster, Lung made a scapegoat of Ts'ai Nai-huang, the official sent by Yuan Shih-k'ai to Canton to help Lung. Ts'ai was executed as the organizer of the assassination. Lung preserved his position in Canton, and he and the revolutionaries formed an alliance, for neither of them could maintain order in Kwangtung alone.

After Yuan Shih-k'ai died in June 1916 and Li Yuan-hung assumed the presidency at Peking, the southwestern military alliance was dissolved. Tuan Ch'i-jui (q.v.), the premier, who wanted to use Lung Chi-kuang to check the power of the revolutionaries, appointed Lung civil governor as well as tutuh of Kwangtung. Protests from southern leaders caused Li Yuan-hung to transfer Lung to Hainan Island

as commissioner of mining development and to appoint Lu Jung-t'ing tutuh of Kwangtung. Lung moved to Hainan with his army and took control of the island.

In December 1917, after Sun Yat-sen had initiated the so-called constitution protection movement and had established a military government at Canton, the Peking government appointed Lung Chi-kuang inspector general for Kwangtung and Kwangsi. He immediately moved his army across the Liuchow Strait to the mainland, but the campaigns against Sun's forces ended with the total route of his army. Lung took refuge in the French-leased territory of Kwangchowwan. He later went north to Peking, where, in July 1918, he attended a conference of provincial governors and other military leaders of the Peiyang clique. Having been deprived of his army and therefore having no further role to play in political or military affairs, he retired from public life and established residence in Shanghai. Shortly before his death in 1921, the Peking government conferred on him the rank of chiang-chün [general].

Lung Yün   龍 雲
Orig. Lung Teng-yün   龍 登 雲
T.   Chih-chou   志 舟

Lung Yün (1888–27 June 1962), governor of Yunnan from 1928 until 1945, when he was deposed. He spent 1945–48 in Chungking and Nanking as the unwilling guest of the National Government. After 1949 he held nominally senior posts in the Central People's Government. He came under censure as a rightist in 1957 and was dismissed from his official posts in February 1958.

A member of the minority group known as the Lolo, Lung Yün was born in the Chaot'ung district of Yunnan. Little is known about his early years except that he joined a number of secret societies in the Yunnan-Szechwan border area. He eventually came to the attention of T'ang Chi-yao (q.v.), who secured a place for him at the Yunnan Provincial Military Academy. After graduation in 1912, he joined T'ang's personal military staff. In this capacity, he participated in the Yunnan uprising of 1915, which resulted in the thwarting of Yuan

Shih-k'ai's monarchical ambitions and in the election of T'ang Chi-yao as military governor of an independent Yunnan. Lung continued to serve in T'ang's personal force until 1924, when he received command of the Fifth Army of the Yunnan forces.

By 1927 considerable opposition to the iron rule of T'ang Chi-yao had developed in Yunnan. In February 1927 Lung Yün, Hu Jo-yu, and two other military leaders staged a coup and presented T'ang with demands for reform. The Yunnan provincial government was reorganized so that Lung Yün held power, although T'ang Chi-yao received the post of director general. After T'ang Chi-yao's death in May, Lung Yün announced his support of the National Government and his readiness to commit troops to the Northern Expedition. He was appointed commander of the Thirty-eighth Army of the National Revolutionary Army. The National Government took further action in 1928, recognizing Lung Yün as governor of Yunnan and appointing him commander of the Thirteenth Route Army. By this time, Lung had consolidated his control of the province, and it was undisturbed by the civil wars that persisted in many provinces even after the national unification of China under the Kuomintang. He ran Yunnan as he wished, maintaining a loose alliance with the National Government. Lung was elected an alternate member of the Central Executive Committee of the Kuomintang in 1931 and a full member of the Central Supervisory Committee in 1935.

The outbreak of the Sino-Japanese war in July 1937 roused the people of Yunnan from their indifference to national affairs. Lung Yün joined other military leaders in answering Chiang Kai-shek's call to a conference in Nanking. The successful construction of the Burma Road in about a year's time was in some measure due to the efforts of Lung Yün. As the Japanese advanced, Yunnan came to have a special significance because it was a border province, a link with the outside world. The political climate of Yunnan also was disturbed by the influx of schools and universities, the faculties of which contained intellectuals of many political persuasions. Lung Yün's support was sought by all factions in the war, but he remained an ally of the National Government and worked to maintain the stability of Yunnan. However, neither he nor the National Govern-

ment authorities were oblivious to the delicate situation created by his entrenched position as governor of a semi-independent Yunnan.

After the War in the Pacific began, Lung Yün found it impossible to close his province to outside armies, for many units had to make use of the Burma Road. By this time, Chiang Kai-shek had established a Kunming headquarters, with Lung as director, thereby giving Lung some authority over the movements of outside forces. Although this appointment appeased Lung to some degree, he refused to allow Chinese or foreign combat troops into the city of Kunming.

In 1944 Ch'en Ming-shu and T'an P'ing-shan (qq.v.) began to form a group to oppose the ruling circles of the National Government. It was inaugurated in Chungking in 1945 as the San Min Chu I Comrades Association, and it advocated the restoration of the platform presented by Sun Yat-sen at the First National Congress of the Kuomintang. Lung Yün reportedly became a member of this group. However, at war's end, the Nationalist authorities moved quickly to bring Yunnan under their control. The Yunnan forces were sent to Indo-China to receive the surrender of the Japanese army in that area, and Tu Yü-ming (q.v.) staged a coup at Kunming in late 1945. Lung Yün was escorted to Chungking, where he was named head of the military council of the Military Affairs Commission. When the National Government returned to Nanking and the council was abolished, he was given a nominal post as a strategy adviser. His close relative and deputy commander, Lu Han (q.v.), succeeded him as governor of Yunnan. Throughout this period Lung was kept under a close surveillance that amounted to house arrest. Toward the end of 1948 he escaped from his supervisors, assumed a disguise, and took a plane to Hong Kong. Although he was associated with such dissidents as Li Chi-shen (q.v.) in Hong Kong, he did not accompany them to the Communist-occupied areas in north China in 1949. He refused an invitation to serve as a delegate at the Chinese People's Political Consultative Conference, but he nevertheless was made a member of the Central People's Government Council, a vice chairman of the National Defense Council, and a vice chairman of the Southwest Military and Administrative Committee.

Early in 1950 Lung Yün left Hong Kong and went to Peking to assume office. In 1954 he served as a delegate from Yunnan to the National People's Congress, at which he made a speech extolling the new constitution because of its provisions concerning the equality of various ethnic minorities in China. Two years later, he became a vice chairman of the Kuomintang Revolutionary Committee. In 1957, however, he was accused of being a rightist. He appeared before the National People's Congress in July 1957 and admitted that he had failed to remold his ideology, had criticized the Soviet Union, and had betrayed the love shown him by the Chinese Communist party. After confessing to wrong thinking, he was attacked by other leaders of the Kuomintang Revolutionary Committee, who accused him, among other things, of confiscating more than 3,000 mou of land from peasants. In February 1958 Lung Yün was dismissed from his official posts, which then included membership on the standing committee of the National People's Congress and a vice chairmanship of the National Defense Council, and was required to study and remold his ideas. Although he was removed from vice chairmanship of the Kuomintang Revolutionary Committee, he continued to serve on the standing committee of that organization.

Lung Yün died at Peking on 27 June 1962. He was survived by his wife, *née* Ku Ying-chiu, by his daughter, Kuo-pi, and by five of his six sons, Sheng-wu, Sheng-tsu, Sheng-wen, Sheng-hsun, and Sheng-te. Another son, Sheng-tseng, had been killed in Yunnan in 1950.

Ma Chan-shan   馬 占 山
T. Hsiu-fang   秀 芳

Ma Chan-shan (1885–29 November 1950), governor of Heilungkiang at the end of 1931. He and his Manchurian troops gained world-wide attention during the Nonni River battle of November 1931.

Little is known about Ma Chan-shan's family background or early years except that he was born in Huaiteh, Fengtien (Liaoning), and that he joined the Fengtien 2nd Cavalry Brigade about 1907. He rose to the rank of battalion commander before being transferred in 1927 to the army of Wu Chün-sheng, the military governor of Heilungkiang. After distinguishing himself in action against the "Little White Dragon" band and against Mongolian bandits, he was promoted to brigadier general and was given command of the 2nd Cavalry Division. When Wu Chün-sheng died in the bomb explosion that also killed Chang Tso-lin (q.v.) in June 1928 and the Northern Expedition forces captured Peking, Ma Chan-shan was assigned to bandit-suppression duties in Heilungkiang. In the summer of 1929, at the time when the National Government and Chang Hsueh-liang (q.v.) were planning anti-Soviet action in Manchuria, Ma was appointed garrison commander at Taheiho, across the Amur River from Blagoveskchensk.

When the Japanese invaded Manchuria on 18 September 1931, Chang Hsueh-liang and many of his Northeastern troops were absent from the area. Wan Fu-lin, the governor of Heilungkiang, had gone with Chang to Peiping, leaving the affairs of Heilungkiang in the hands of his feckless son, Wan Hai-p'eng. In the absence of strong provincial authority, Chang Hai-p'eng, the T'ao-Liao defense commissioner, reached agreement with the Japanese Kwantung Army, which gave him equipment and political support; and in early October, he proclaimed himself Mongolian border commissioner and advanced northward along the Taonan-Angangchi railway toward Tsitsihar, the capital. Ma Chan-shan resisted the advance of Chang's force and blew up several of the railway bridges, including the one that spanned the Nonni River. The two armies then camped on opposite banks of the river. On 12 October 1931, the National Government appointed Ma acting governor of Heilungkiang, and he assumed office at Tsitsihar ten days later.

The Japanese, who had provided the capital for the construction of the Taonan-Angangchi railway and who still held a lien on it, requested that Ma Chan-shan have the bridge over the Nonni repaired as soon as possible because the interruption of rail traffic interfered with the movement of supplies to Japanese-occupied Liaoning. Ma did not comply, and when a small group of railway workers tried to inspect the damage on 20 October, his troops fired on them. On 28 October, Major Hayashi, the Kwantung Army representative in Tsitsihar, demanded that repairs be completed by 3

November, failing which railway engineers would make the repairs under the protection of Japanese troops. As the deadline approached, Hayashi ordered both Ma and Chang Hai-p'eng to move their forces ten kilometers back from the river, and they complied. A small Japanese force and a group of engineers moved into the area, and repair work began on the morning of 4 November. However, a Japanese infantry company soon advanced beyond the bridge in the direction of the Tahsing station, still occupied by the Chinese. Ma's forces drove them back, and they advanced the next day only to be repulsed again. Such was the Nonni River battle. Two days of fighting had resulted in about 180 Japanese casualties and about 200 Chinese casualties, but because the League of Nations was investigating the Japanese presence in Manchuria and the area was much in the news, the battle gained world-wide attention.

Major Hayashi ordered reinforcements, and the Kwantung Army took Tahsing on 6 November. After a series of skirmishes accompanied by Japanese demands and Chinese refusals, the Japanese occupied Tsitsihar in November 1931. Ma Chan-shan withdrew to Hailun, regrouped his forces, and established a provincial government there. Soon afterwards, he was confirmed as governor of Heilungkiang.

By February 1932 Ma Chan-shan had been cut off completely from potential aid. Because he was isolated and without ammunition, his only recourse, as he later said, was to slow up the enemy advance, conserve his strength, and wait for an opportunity to act. On 14 February, he met at Harbin with the Kwantung 2nd Division commander and agreed to collaborate with the Japanese. He then attended several conferences regarding the creation of Manchoukuo and became minister of war in the new state when it was established in March. In return for his collaboration, the Japanese allowed him to retain office as Heilungkiang governor and conceded a delay of three months before assuming control of key bureaus in the provincial government. Ma bided his time, and then, on 1 April 1932, he left Tsitsihar before dawn with a convoy of trucks loaded with valuable supplies and a large sum of money from the newly replenished Heilungkiang treasury. By the time his departure was discovered at daybreak, he was miles away at Taianchen. He further confused the Japanese by sending them three contradictory telegrams explaining his departure. On 12 April he issued a public telegram from Taheiho in which he explained his seeming defection from the service of the National Government, reported some of his observations of Japanese activities, and announced his determination to resist Japanese encroachment.

Ma Chan-shan launched a general offensive against the Japanese near Hulan on 29 April 1932. As of 18 May, his troops reportedly were within five miles of Harbin, but they were forced to withdraw at the end of May by the Kwantung 14th Division. They then adopted guerrilla tactics and managed to hold their position near Tsitsihar until November, when the Japanese administered a series of defeats to loyalist forces throughout the Northeast. Ma Chan-shan and several other officers escaped to the Soviet Union, traveled through Germany, and arrived in Shanghai in June 1933. On 22 June, Ma was appointed to the Military Affairs Commission in recognition of his valiant efforts in Manchuria. However, he took up residence at Tientsin and avoided Nanking because he disapproved of the Tangku truce (*see* Ho Ying-ch'in).

After the Sino-Japanese war began in 1937, Ma Chan-shan was assigned to the Eighth War Area, under the over-all command of Chu Shao-liang (q.v.). Late in 1937 he was given the mission of helping to counter the Japanese offensive in Inner Mongolia west of Paotow. That winter, his forces engaged in a sharp action against the Japanese near Wuyuan in western Suiyuan which halted their drive and helped to preserve the flow of war supplies then coming to China overland from the Soviet Union. In 1941 he was reappointed governor of Heilungkiang; and he later became an alternate member of the Kuomintang's Central Executive Committee. After serving briefly as deputy commander of the Twelfth War Area just before the war ended in 1945, he returned to Manchuria as deputy commander of the Northeast Peace Preservation Corps. However, he and other natives of that region were not allowed by the Kuomintang to play significant roles in the ensuing Nationalist-Communist struggle for control of Manchuria. He moved to Peking after the Central People's Government of the People's Republic of China was established, and he died there on 29 November 1950.

Ma Ch'ao-chün   馬 超 俊
T. Hsing-ch'iao   星 樵

Ma Ch'ao-chün (1885–), republican revolutionary and follower of Sun Yat-sen who was a pioneer in the labor movement in China. He later held important administrative posts in both the Kuomintang and the National Government, and he served three terms as mayor of Nanking. After 1949, he lived in Taiwan.

The younger of two sons, Ma Ch'ao-chün was born into a poor family in Sunning (Toishan), Kwangtung. His father died when Ma was an infant, and Ma later had to herd cows and cut firewood to help earn money for the family. Nevertheless, he was able to start school at the age of eight sui. A few years later, his elder brother went to Canada and began sending money home for the support of Ma Ch'ao-chün and his mother, enabling Ma to devote all of his time to his education. He sat for the examinations for the sheng-yuan degree at the age of 15 sui and passed them, but he was excluded from the list of successful candidates because he refused to comply with the chief examiner's demands for money. Disgusted by this bribery attempt, Ma gave up the idea of becoming a scholar.

In 1900 Ma Ch'ao-chün became an apprentice at the Ma-hung-chi machinery workshop, which was located in a Kowloon dockyard. He spent his evenings studying Chinese and English at a school operated by the Shao-nien hsueh-she [juvenile institute], at which the chief instructor was Huang Shih-chung, the compiler of a history of the Taiping Rebellion, who interested Ma in revolutionary ideas. Ma completed his apprenticeship at the workshop in two years instead of the usual four, and he left Hong Kong for the United States in 1902.

After arriving in San Francisco, Ma Ch'ao-chün went to work at a dockyard and joined the Chih-kung-tang, which already had been converted into a revolutionary organization that advocated the overthrow of the Manchus. He learned about Sun Yat-sen from members of the Hsing-Chung-hui, and he met Sun in 1904. In the summer of 1905 he left San Francisco and went to Japan to rejoin Sun.

The revolutionary leader personally inducted Ma into his new organization, the T'ung-meng-hui, and sent him to study political economy at Meiji University.

Late in 1906 Sun Yat-sen sent Ma Ch'ao-chün to Hong Kong to organize workers and mobilize support for the republican cause. Ma began by seeking out his former colleagues from the machinery shop. They were impressed by his experiences in America and his education in Japan, and, after listening to his urgings concerning the revolutionary movement and the organization of workers for self-advancement, they decided to form the nucleus of a workers' group. After working to organize laborers in Hong Kong for a few months, Ma went to Canton, where his organizing efforts were aided by Huang Huan-t'ing; to Wuhan, where he established a group at the Hanyang Arsenal; and to Shanghai, where he had some success in organizing industrial workers. He then returned to Canton and joined with the workers at the Shih-ching Arsenal in forming a secret organization which pledged support to Sun Yat-sen. Having awakened the industrial workers (most of whom were Cantonese) in these cities to the potential of organization and revolution, Ma returned to Hong Kong. However, he continued to make trips to Canton to advise the local leaders of the labor movement. In December 1907 he and some of his workers were summoned from Hong Kong by Sun Yat-sen to take part in the Chen-nan-kuan uprising. When it failed, Ma returned to Hong Kong and established the Chung Hsing Company, which engaged in the export of human hair and, more importantly, served as a meeting place for revolutionaries.

Ma Ch'ao-chün and his Hong Kong workers shipped arms to Canton for the uprising in April 1911 (*see* Huang Hsing). While engaged in arranging these shipments, he met Shen Yen-chen, whom he later married. Some of Ma's men took part in the insurrection, and a few of them were among the 72 "revolutionary martyrs" who were buried at Huang-hua-kang after the uprising failed.

After the Wuchang revolt of October 1911 began, Huang Hsing ordered Ma Ch'ao-chün to bring a workers' force to the Wuhan area and to rouse workers in other parts of the country. Ma formed a corps of 70 workers and led them to Wuhan by way of Shanghai. When they arrived on 10 November, Huang Hsing assigned them to the Hanyang Arsenal. Feng Kuo-chang (q.v.) and his forces attacked Hanyang strongly on 20 November, but Ma and his volunteers managed to hold the arsenal for five days before being forced to withdraw.

When the republican government was established in 1912, Ma Ch'ao-chün became a member of the Parliament, but he left his post in 1913 when Yuan Shih-k'ai began to turn against the revolutionaries. At the time of the so-called second revolution in the summer of 1913, Kwangtung came under the control of Yuan's supporter Lung Chi-kuang (q.v.), and Ma responded by going to Canton and establishing the Hui-men Knitting Factory as a secret revolutionary base. Ma organized an assassination team, and in June 1914 a member of the team killed Lung's deputy Ma Tsun-fa. This act infuriated Lung, who intensified his search for the revolutionaries. Ma was forced to flee Canton. Late in 1914 he went to Japan, on orders from Sun Yat-sen. He studied aviation and, on completion of his course in 1916, joined the forces of Chü Cheng (q.v.) in Shantung. The anti-Yuan campaign ended with the death of Yuan Shih-k'ai in June 1916, and Ma then spent several months giving flying exhibitions and raising money to establish an aviation school.

In 1917, having formed a military government at Canton, Sun Yat-sen summoned Ma Ch'ao-chün and ordered him to assume respo... labor movement. After securing Sun's approval of an eight-point plan, Ma began working to implement his proposals. By the end of 1917 a National Mechanics Union, with headquarters at Canton, had been established, and International Labor Day had been observed by the workers in Canton. In 1919 the Canton mechanical workers staged a strike, and in 1920 the Hong Kong workers followed suit. Ma helped organize both strikes.

When Ch'en Chiung-ming (q.v.) brought the Kwangtung Army home from Fukien in 1920 to wrest control of the province from the Kwangsi warlords, Ma Ch'ao-chün led supporting guerrilla forces in the East River area against the rearguard troops of the Kwangsi armies. He was appointed a special assistant to Sun Fo (q.v.) when Sun became mayor of Canton in 1921, and the following year he was made a councillor in the municipal government. When Ch'en Chiung-ming moved against Sun Yat-sen in mid-1922, Ma mobilized workers to sabotage Ch'en's operations. He had to leave Canton when Ch'en issued an order for his arrest. In April 1923, after the ouster of Ch'en Chiung-ming from Canton, Ma was appointed deputy director of the Shih-ching Arsenal. After he successfully defended the arsenal against Ch'en Chiung-ming's army, he was promoted to director. The arsenal had suffered serious damage in 1922, but Ma soon restored it to normal operation. He left this post in 1924 and went to Shanghai to brief Kuomintang leaders and labor leaders on Sun Yat-sen's impending trip to Peking. He then joined Sun's entourage when it passed through Shanghai, and he accompanied Sun to Japan, Tientsin, and Peking. After Sun's death in March 1925, he returned to Canton.

By this time, Ma Ch'ao-chün had incurred the enmity of the Chinese Communists because of his consistent opposition to their cause. The National Mechanics Union and its affiliates reflected and supported Ma's beliefs. Thus, when the Communist-dominated National Labor Congress was held at Canton in 1925, Ma led a movement to boycott it. In one of the resolutions adopted at that congress, Ma was referred to as "a labor movement renegade." Moreover, Communist members of the Kuomintang presented a resolution at the Kuomintang's Second National Congress in 1926 calling for Ma's expulsion from the party, but the inter... (qq.v.) prevented its passage.

After traveling to the Americas in 1926 to study the labor movement and to acquaint overseas Kuomintang members with the political situation in China, Ma Ch'ao-chün returned to China in 1927 and joined the National Government as director of its labor bureau. He became a member of the Kwangtung government council and director of the province's department of industry and agriculture in 1928, and he resigned from his National Government post that December. In 1929 he represented Chinese workers at the Twelfth International Labor Conference in Geneva. That year, for the first time, the Chinese delegation included representatives of business and labor as well as representatives of the government. Upon his return to China, Ma was elected to the Legislative Yuan and to the Central Executive Committee of the Kuomintang. He also was made director of the central training department of the Kuomintang. He became mayor of Nanking in November 1931 and a member of the Government Council in 1935.

Ma Ch'ao-chün accompanied the National Government to Chungking after the Sino-Japanese war began, and he served as deputy director of the Kuomintang's social affairs department in 1938–40. He then became deputy director of the party's organization department. When the National Government returned to Nanking in 1945, he was elected to another term as mayor. In 1949, when the Chinese Communists won the civil war for the mainland, he went to Taiwan. He became a member of the committee formed to consider party reorganization and an adviser to Chiang Kai-shek in 1950, and he was appointed a supervisor of the Central Bank of China in 1961.

Ma Ch'ao-chün's publications include *Chung-kuo lao-kung yün-tung wen-t'i* [problems of the Chinese labor movement], which was published in 1927, and the first volume of *Chung-kuo lao-kung yün-tung shih* [a history of the Chinese labor movement]. He also served as chief editor of the five-volume *Chung-kuo lao-kung yün-tung shih*, which was published in Taipei in 1959.

Ma Chung-ying   馬 仲 英

Ma Chung-ying (1911– ?), Chinese Muslim military leader, took part in the 1931 rebellion of Muslims in Sinkiang against Chinese rule. In 1933 his cavalry forces again attempted to remove Chinese authority from the area, but were pushed into southern Sinkiang by White Russian forces. Ma entered the Soviet Union in July 1934 and disappeared.

Linhsia (Hochow), Kansu, was the native place of Ma Chung-ying. Ma Pu-fang, Ma Pu-ch'ing (qq.v.), and he had the same paternal great-grandfather. Little is known about Ma Chung-ying's early years except that he entered military service in 1924 and that in 1926, at the age of 17, he became a junior officer in the forces commanded by an uncle, Ma Ku-chung. In 1926 Liu Yü-fen, a subordinate of Feng Yü-hsiang (q.v.) who had become governor of

Kansu, took action against the Chinese Muslims of his province. In the ensuing fighting, Ma Chung-ying laid siege to and captured Linhsia on his own initiative. Liu Yü-fen ordered the forces of Ma Lin (a great-uncle of Ma Chung-ying) to suppress the young man, but Ma Chung-ying easily defeated them, thereby winning the nickname "Little Commander." Ma Ku-chung, however, refused to countenance his nephew's insubordination; he dismissed Ma Chung-ying from his army. The younger Ma then retired to the vicinity of Sining and began to build up his own forces.

After Feng Yü-hsiang decided to participate in the final stages of the Northern Expedition and moved many of his troops out of northwest China, the military situation in Kansu deteriorated rapidly. The lack of provincial unity was intensified by drought and famine and by the increasing friction between the Chinese and the Muslims of the province. Ma Chung-ying took advantage of this state of affairs by returning to Kansu during the late months of 1928 and initiating a series of military actions. In the spring of 1929, after several victories, he attempted to win official recognition by petitioning the National Government at Nanking to reorganize his force as a garrison unit to be stationed on the Ninghsia-Suiyuan border in western Inner Mongolia. About this time, Feng Yü-hsiang declared his independence of the National Government, and Han Fu-chü and Ma Chung-ying's relative Ma Hung-k'uei (q.v.) defected to the National Government side. Ma Hung-k'uei's action reinforced Ma Chung-ying's decision to align himself with the National Government. The execution of Ma Chung-ying's father by order of Liu Yü-fen in the winter of 1929 increased Ma's opposition to Feng Yü-hsiang, but his plans for revenge were curbed by the formation of an alliance between Feng and the Shansi leader Yen Hsi-shan (q.v.). Ma went to Nanking and enrolled at the Nanking Military Academy, but managed to return to his home area later in 1930 as garrison commander at Kanchow (Changyeh), Kansu. Because Ma soon began to recruit troops in an attempt to develop an autonomous base of power, Ku Chu-t'ung (q.v.), then the National Government's pacification commissioner for northwest China, attacked his base and forced him to retreat westward.

In 1931 Ma Chung-ying and his troops

challenged the authority of Chin Shu-jen (q.v.) in Sinkiang. With the death of the reigning prince of the khanate of Hami in November 1930, Chin had attempted to take control of this semi-independent Turki principality. The Turki natives rose in rebellion in March 1931 and sent representatives to Kansu to solicit the support of the T'ung-kans [Chinese Muslims], their coreligionists. Ma Chung-ying responded by thrusting into Sinkiang in June 1931 with a cavalry force. That autumn, the Sinkiang provincial forces, composed principally of White Russians who had fled to Sinkiang after the Russian Revolution, repelled Ma Chung-ying's attack on Hami after savage and bloody fighting. Ma turned southwest to attack Liaotun, where he was wounded in battle. He then withdrew to western Kansu, where Ma Pu-fang gave him control over four hsien, with headquarters at Suchow.

After reorganizing his forces, Ma Chung-ying returned to Sinkiang in the spring of 1933 with about 3,000 men. By this time, Chin Shu-jen had fled Sinkiang, and Sheng Shih-ts'ai (q.v.) had assumed power in the province. Ma's forces soon won control of some 13 districts in central Sinkiang, including the major oasis center of Turfan, which commanded the eastern approaches to Urumchi. At the beginning of June, Sheng Shih-ts'ai sent a delegation headed by Aitchen Wu to Ma's headquarters to discuss the possibility of holding peace talks. A few days later, Huang Mu-sung (q.v.), who had been appointed pacification commissioner of Sinkiang by the National Government, arrived in Urumchi. His efforts served only to aggravate the situation, and Sheng and Ma returned to the battlefield. In September, Lo Wen-kan, the minister of foreign affairs at Nanking, visited both Urumchi and Turfan in an unsuccessful attempt to restore peace to Sinkiang.

During the second half of 1933 Ma Chung-ying and his associates extended their operations in the Tarim basin of southern Sinkiang, where their troops aroused the antagonism of the Turki natives by looting and plundering. Ma launched an attack on Urumchi in December 1933 and pressed forward during the early weeks of 1934. However, Soviet military units entered Sinkiang to support the rule of Sheng Shih-ts'ai, and they easily overcame Ma's forces, causing them to flee westward to

Kashgar. In July 1934 Ma transferred command of his remaining troops to his brother-in-law Ma Hu-shan, crossed the border at Irkeshtam with several of his senior officers, and disappeared into the Soviet Union. His party reportedly was accompanied by Russian officials who had been stationed in Sinkiang. The circumstances of Ma's disappearance remained obscure. Press reports in the summer of 1934 stated that the Russians had interned him at Tashkent and had refused the Sinkiang government's extradition requests. In 1935 an article in the *Journal of the Royal Central Asian Society*, published in London, stated that Ma had "died on arrival at Moscow." Another story was that Sheng Shih-ts'ai, when visiting Stalin in 1938, demanded the liquidation of his former antagonist and that Ma was executed in the spring of 1939.

Descriptions of Ma Chung-ying and reports of his actions also vary widely. The Swedish explorer Sven Hedin, although he never met Ma, presented a vivid account of his actions and the devastation of eastern Sinkiang in *The Flight of Big Horse*, published in 1936. Other writers described Ma as a man of great personal bravery who was obsessed with the idea of creating a unified and independent Muslim state in northwest China and with dreams of foreign conquest.

Ma Fu-hsiang   馬 福 祥
T. Yün-t'ing   雲 亭

Ma Fu-hsiang (1876–19 August 1932), Chinese Muslim leader who ruled the district that later became Ninghsia (1913–20) and the Suiyuan special district (1921–24). He was appointed co-director with Feng Yü-hsiang of north-western border defense in 1924, but he left Feng's service in 1929. He then served the National Government as governor of Anhwei and chairman of the Mongolian and Tibetan Affairs Commission.

Hanchiachi, Taoho hsien, Kansu, was the birthplace of Ma Fu-hsiang. He belonged to the only Muslim sect in the region that had not taken part in the Muslim Rebellion of 1862–77, and his father reportedly had come to know Tso Tsung-t'ang (ECCP, II, 762–67) after Tso had established headquarters at Lanchow in

1872. The youngest of four brothers, Ma was trained for a military career from early childhood. He greatly admired his elder brother Ma Fu-lu and emulated him in mobilizing volunteer troops to aid the regular army at the time of the 1896 uprisings in the Hsunho region.

After passing the provincial military examinations in 1897, Ma Fu-hsiang joined the Kansu forces of Tung Fu-hsiang, serving in a cavalry company commanded by Ma Fu-lu. Tung's force soon moved to Chihli (Hopei) and became one of the five constituent armies of the Military Defense Army, under the over-all command of Jung-lu (ECCP, I, 405-9). During the Boxer Uprising of 1900 Tung's army moved to Nanyuan and then to Peking, where it fought foreign troops, attacked legations, and engaged in looting. The unit commanded by Ma Fu-lu participated in the fighting at Huangts'un, Liulin, and Yangts'un. After Ma Fu-lu was killed at Peking, Ma Fu-hsiang assumed command of the cavalry unit. When the emperor and the empress dowager fled the capital, Ma Fu-hsiang accompanied them to Sian as a member of their military escort. He then held a variety of commands at Sining, in the Kokonor district, and at Barkol. About 1910, having become a brigade commander, he was assigned to garrison duties at Lanchow.

At the time of the 1911 revolution, Ma Fu-hsiang collaborated with other provincial officials in announcing the neutrality of Kansu. In 1912 he accepted appointments as acting chief administrative officer of the Kokonor region and as guards commander of the Altai district. When Outer Mongolia declared its independence, the Mongols of the Ordos region became restless; and in September 1913 Ma was appointed to the Yinch'uan garrison as deputy military commissioner of Inner Mongolia and Kansu. He soon captured the Dalat Banner leader Wang-te-ni-ma at Paotow, and he was rewarded with promotion to the rank of lieutenant general and appointment as guards commander for the Yinch'uan region. Ma held command of the area that later became Ninghsia for seven years. Then, on 31 December 1920, the Peking government appointed him military governor of the special district of Suiyuan. He governed the district from the beginning of 1921 to the end of 1924. After Feng Yü-hsiang (q.v.) effected a coup at Peking

in November 1924, Ma was replaced as governor of Suiyuan by Li Ming-chung and was appointed co-director of northwestern border defense, the other director being Feng himself.

Little is known about Ma Fu-hsiang's activities in the 1925-27 period except that he continued to serve Feng Yü-hsiang. In 1928 he received membership in the Peiping and Kaifeng branches of the Political Council, in the Military Affairs Commission, and in the Kansu provincial government. When Feng Yü-hsiang turned against the National Government in 1929, Ma parted company with Feng and induced his son Ma Hung-k'uei (q.v.) to join with Han Fu-chü (q.v.) in defecting to the National Government side. Later in 1929, Ma Fu-hsiang became vice chairman of the Mongolian and Tibetan Affairs Commission and mayor of Tsingtao. In 1930 he succeeded Shih Yü-san as governor of Anhwei and became a member of the Central Executive Committee of the Kuomintang.

With the failure of the so-called enlarged conference movement (see Feng Yü-hsiang; Yen Hsi-shan) in 1930, Ma Fu-hsiang and Chang Chih-chiang (q.v.) assumed control of the remnant Kuominchün forces and began to reorganize them as National Government troops. From mid-1930 until late 1931 he served as chairman of the Mongolian and Tibetan Affairs Commission. During this period, he also worked to rearrange the power structure of Kansu (see Ma Hung-pin). He was made a member of the State Council in December 1931. A few months later, while visiting his son at the mountain resort of Chikungshan, Hupeh, he became seriously ill. He was put aboard a Peiping-bound express train in the hope that the staff of Peking Union Medical College could treat him successfully, but he died on the train at Liuliho, Hopei, on 19 August 1932.

Ma Hsiang-po: *see* MA LIANG.

Ma Hsü-lun   馬 叙 倫
    T. I-ch'u   夷 初

Ma Hsü-lun (27 April 1884-), educator, revolutionary, and government official, was a professor of Chinese philosophy at Peking

University in 1916–36. He became sympathetic to the Communist cause during the Sino-Japanese war, and he was named minister of education when the Central People's Government was established in 1949. From 1952 to 1954 he served as minister of higher education.

A native of Hangchow, Chekiang, Ma Hsü-lun was born into an impoverished scholarly family. He began the study of the Chinese classics under a local scholar, but the death of his father made it impossible for him to continue with a private tutor. In 1899 he entered the Yang-cheng School in Hangchow (later the First Chekiang Provincial High School), where he studied under the celebrated Chekiang savant Ch'en Chieh-shih, acquiring a solid grounding in philology and philosophy. He also joined with such schoolmates as T'ang Erh-ho, Chiang Fang-chen (qq.v.), Tu Shih-chen, and Hsü Shou-ch'ang in planning revolutionary activities. On the eve of their graduation in 1902 Ma, T'ang, and Tu were given scholarships for study in Japan, but these were rescinded when the provincial authorities discovered their revolutionary tendencies.

After spending some time in Shanghai, where he contributed writings to several revolutionary magazines, Ma Hsü-lun returned to Chekiang to become a teacher. In 1906 his former teacher Ch'en Chieh-shih took him to Canton to teach at a language school. At Canton, Ma soon met Chu Chih-hsin (q.v.) and other T'ung-meng-hui leaders. When Ch'en Chieh-shih returned to his native province in 1909 to become chairman of the Chekiang provincial advisory bureau, Ma accompanied him. Ma taught at the Hangchow Normal School and took part in local revolutionary activities. He and Hsia Tseng-yu maneuvered a meeting of the shareholders in the Shanghai-Hangchow-Ningpo railway into opposing the plan for its nationalization proposed by Sheng Hsuan-huai (q.v.), then head of the Board of Posts and Communications. In 1910 Ma joined the Nan-she [southern society], the poets' club founded by Liu Ya-tzu (q.v.). After the Wuchang revolt of 10 October 1911, Ma joined with Shen Chün-ju and Ts'ai Yuan-p'ei (qq.v.) in staging an uprising in Chekiang. When the revolutionaries assumed control of the province, T'ang Shou-ch'ien became governor, with Ma as his secretary. Ma soon left this post and

returned to teaching after a brief period in Shanghai as an editor of the *Ta-kung-ho jih pao*.

When T'ang Erh-ho founded National Peking Medical College in 1913, he invited Ma Hsü-lun to join its staff as an instructor in Chinese. Ma taught at the medical college until Yuan Shih-k'ai's monarchical aspirations became apparent, at which point he returned to Chekiang to take part in the anti-Yuan movement. He resumed his teaching duties after Yuan died in June 1916. About this time, Ts'ai Yuan-p'ei became the chancellor of Peking University. Ma soon joined its faculty as a professor of Chinese philosophy, lecturing principally on Chuang-tzu and the Cheng-Chu school of Confucian philosophy. Although his scholarship and his classroom eloquence made him a popular teacher, he was not well liked by his colleagues. He often came into conflict with Huang K'an, a disciple of Chang Ping-lin (q.v.), and with Hu Shih (q.v.). As a result of his differences with Hu Shih, Ma became a strong opponent of the pai-hua [vernacular] movement.

At the time of the May Fourth Movement of 1919, Ma Hsü-lun demonstrated his ability as a protest leader when, as secretary of the association of faculty members of secondary schools and institutions of higher learning in Peking, he led the teachers in a strike to show their support of the students. When the Peking authorities arrested the student leaders, Ts'ai Yuan-p'ei resigned from Peking University, and Chiang Monlin (Chiang Meng-lin, q.v.) became acting chancellor. It was proposed that the university move to Shanghai, but Ma Hsü-lun called a meeting of faculty members and students and convinced them that the move would turn the university into a second-rate institution. After Ts'ai Yuan-p'ei returned in September 1919, the university was reorganized and was placed under faculty control. Because his participation in the May Fourth demonstrations placed him in danger, Ma went to Chekiang early in 1921 and became principal of the Chekiang First Normal School. In 1922 he served as director of the province's department of education.

Ma Hsü-lun returned to Peking in September 1922 as vice minister of education in the cabinet of Wang Ch'ung-hui (q.v.). When this cabinet collapsed in November, he resumed his teaching duties at Peking University. After serving as vice minister of education in 1924 and as acting minister in 1925, he resigned again and returned to teaching. The reason for his resignation was that he had become director of propaganda in the Peking headquarters of the Kuomintang, and he no longer could serve the Peking government in good conscience. Following the incident of 18 March 1926 (*see* Feng Yü-hsiang; Tuan Ch'i-jui) concerning the blockade of Taku, Ma left Peking and went south after Tuan Ch'i-jui blamed the Kuomintang for the demonstrations.

When the Northern Expedition forces captured Chekiang early in 1927, Chang Jen-chieh (q.v.) became head of the provisional provincial government, with Ma Hsü-lun as director of the civil affairs department. Ma held this post until late 1928, when he became vice minister of education in the new National Government at Nanking. However, he soon came into conflict with the minister, Chiang Monlin, and he resigned at the end of 1929. In January 1931 he rejoined the faculty of Peking University only to serve under Chiang again after Chiang became chancellor later that year. As Japanese aggression in north China increased, Ma began to take part in demonstrations against the National Government's policy of nonresistance. During this period, his difficulties in getting along with his colleagues, particularly Hu Shih, also increased. Ma learned that the university no longer desired his services when, in 1936, he applied for a semester's leave and was granted a full year's leave instead.

Ma Hsü-lun moved to Shanghai in 1936 and remained there throughout the Sino-Japanese war. It was a difficult time for Ma. His oldest and closest friend, T'ang Erh-ho, joined the Japanese-sponsored regime in north China as minister of cultural affairs and offered him the presidency of Peking University. Ma refused the offer and terminated his friendship with T'ang. After his former student Ch'en Kung-po (q.v.) joined Wang Ching-wei's regime at Nanking in 1940, Ma refused to see him or to accept money from him. Ma finally agreed to see Ch'en Kung-po in February 1944 in the hope that he could persuade him to sever his connections with the Japanese. These and other demonstrations of personal integrity caused Ma's former colleagues to regard him with new respect, and some of them attempted to secure research grants for him. At war's end in 1945

many government leaders called on him to offer expressions of praise and comfort, but nobody thought of making provision for his support. The bitterness of Ma's feelings toward the Kuomintang had increased during the war, and the appointment of Hu Shih to the chancellorship of Peking University increased his dissatisfaction with the ruling party of China. He soon became an open opponent of the Kuomintang.

Toward the end of 1945 Ma Hsü-lun helped found the China Association for Promoting Democracy, and in 1946 he became the secretary of the China Committee of the International League for the Promotion of Human Rights. On 23 June 1946 he led a group from Shanghai to Nanking to demand an end to the civil war. At their destination, Ma and his colleagues were met by a group of "peasant representatives" who stopped them and asked some embarrassing questions. A free-for-all ensued, and Ma was so badly beaten that he had to take to his bed and remain there for over a month. When the National Government banned the various "democratic parties and groups" in 1947, Ma, as one of the most prominent leaders of such groups, fled to Hong Kong. He went to Peiping by way of the Communist-controlled Northeast early in 1949 and became a member of the standing committee of the higher education commission in the North China People's Government. He attended the Chinese People's Political Consultative Conference in September 1949 as the senior delegate representing the China Association for Promoting Democracy.

When the Central People's Government was established at Peking, Ma Hsü-lun was appointed minister of education, a member of the Government Council, and a member of the Government Administration Council. In 1952 the ministry of education was split into a ministry of higher education and a ministry of general education, and Ma became minister of higher education. He held this post until 1954. Ma was a delegate to the National People's Congress in 1954, 1959, and 1964, a vice chairman of the China Democratic League, a member of the third National Committee of the Chinese People's Political Consultative Conference, and a vice chairman of the Sino-Soviet Friendship Association. Ill health and old age forced him to give up most of his activities after

1960, but he continued to hold the chairmanship of the China Association for Promoting Democracy.

Ma Hsü-lun was well known for his research and writing on philosophical and philological problems. His philosophical researches resulted in the *Lao-tzu ho-ku* (1924), *Chuang-tzu i-cheng* (1930), and *Tu Lü-shih ch'un-ch'iu chi* (1931). He also produced such philological works as the *Shih-ku-wen su-chi* (1935), a study of ten individual stone drums of the Chou dynasty, with an interpretation of each inscription. In this field his major contribution lay in the study of the *Shuo-wen chieh-tzu* [analytical dictionary of characters] compiled by Hsü Shen (fl. 100 A.D.), notably in his *Shuo-wen chieh-tzu liu-shu su-cheng* [the six types of graphs in the *Shuo-wen chieh-tzu*], published in 1957. In 1958 a collection of Ma's learned articles appeared under the title *Ma Hsü-lun hsueh-shu lun-wen chi*.

Little is known about Ma Hsü-lun's personal life except that he married several times and that he is known to have had a daughter and a son, Ma K'e-hsiang.

Ma Hung-k'uei   馬 鴻 逵
T. Shao-yün   少 雲

Ma Hung-k'uei (1893–), son of Ma Fu-hsiang who served as governor of Ninghsia from 1933 to 1948.

The son of Ma Fu-hsiang (q.v.), Ma Hung-k'uei was a native of Hanchiachi in Taoho hsien, Kansu. He received a military education, completing his studies at the Kansu Military Academy at Lanchow in 1910. Beginning in 1913 he served under his father as a battalion commander and participated in battles against such marauders as the notorious White Wolf (Pai-lang). He was promoted to the post of bandit-suppression commissioner for the Kansu-Shensi-Mongolia border region in 1915. From 1922 to the end of 1924 he held command of the 5th Mixed Brigade of his father's forces.

Ma Hung-k'uei joined the military establishment of Feng Yü-hsiang (q.v.) in 1925 as bandit-suppression commander for western Suiyuan. His 5th Mixed Brigade was reorganized as the 7th Division of Feng's forces, and it later became the Fourth Army of the Kuominchün and then the 17th Temporary Division of the Second Group Army. As its commander, Ma participated in all of Feng's campaigns in 1926–28. After the Northern Expedition ended with the fall of Peking in June 1928, Ma and his division were placed under the over-all command of Han Fu-chü (q.v.) and were assigned to western Shantung for bandit-suppression work.

In May 1929, after Feng Yü-hsiang had decided to challenge the authority of Chiang Kai-shek, Ma Hung-k'uei joined with Han Fu-chü and Shih Yü-san in defecting from Feng's service with thousands of troops and declaring allegiance to the National Government. Ma was rewarded for his part in this action with appointments as commander of the Reorganized 64th Division, commander in chief of the Eleventh Army of the forces deployed against Feng Yü-hsiang and Yen Hsi-shan (q.v.), and member of the Honan provincial government. His Eleventh Army was redesignated the Fifteenth Route Army in 1930. Ma was named to succeed his cousin Ma Hung-pin (q.v.) as governor of Kansu in 1931, but he refused the appointment. His career came to resemble his father's with his appointment as a member of the Mongolian and Tibetan Affairs Commission in 1932 and as governor of Ninghsia in 1933.

The part of Ninghsia under the direct jurisdiction of the provincial government was composed of only 13 hsien, but was strategically important because it commanded the easiest and most direct route from western Suiyuan to Kansu. The remainder of the province was divided between two Mongol groups, the Etsingol Special Banner and the Alashan Special Banner. Ma began his governorship by assigning various military units to bandit-suppression duties, ordering the registration of all citizens and the issuance of identity cards, organizing a pao-chia system for the maintenance of public safety, and organizing civilian peace preservation units. His region of Ninghsia soon became a tightly controlled police state.

Early in 1934 Sun Tien-ying, a former officer in the Kuominchün, advanced on Ninghsia from Suiyuan. His forces soon clashed with those of Ma Hung-k'uei, and hostilities continued despite cease-fire orders from the Military Affairs Commission at Nanking. In February, troops from Suiyuan, Shansi, and Tsinghai, acting on National Government orders, joined the fight against Sun, who announced his retirement in March. His forces were disarmed and reorganized. When this threat to Ma Hung-k'uei's authority had been removed, he turned his attention to economic and social reconstruction. He also tried to strengthen his army by introducing a system whereby many young men were drafted and were forced to remain in the army for a decade or more. This system had adverse effects on agriculture in the province, for many of the farmers were older men who could not cultivate all of their land without the assistance of their sons. However, Ma's other programs partially offset these problems by reducing land taxes, expanding irrigation facilities, and undertaking reforestation. His programs, though on a smaller scale, were similar to those later introduced in Tsinghai by Ma Pu-fang. His achievements received official recognition in 1935, when he was elected an alternate member of the Central Executive Committee of the Kuomintang.

With the outbreak of the Sino-Japanese war in 1937 and the subsequent retreat of the National Government to Chungking, the strategic importance of northwest China increased. From 1938 to 1945 Ma Hung-k'uei, in addition to his duties as governor of Ninghsia, served as deputy commander of the Eighth War Area, which was commanded by Chu Shao-liang. Ma's troops became the Seventeenth Army Group. About this time, relations between the Alashan Banner government at Tingyuanying and the Ninghsia government became strained. Ma Hung-k'uei and Ta Wang, the ruling prince of the Alashan Banner, had maintained friendly relations before 1938, partly because their fathers had been friends. However, the establishment of a Japanese-sponsored Inner Mongolian government by Te Wang (Demchukdonggrub, q.v.) had caused Ma to fear that the Alashan Mongols might follow a similar course; and his suspicions increased when Colonel Doihara of the Kwantung Army paid a visit to Ta Wang. Accordingly, Ma sent troops to Tingyuanying, captured the city, and took Ta Wang into custody. Ta Wang was sent to Lanchow and was held there until 1944 even though no evidence was produced to show that he intended to collaborate with the Japanese. Ma stationed a battalion at Tingyuanying as "protection against bandits."

When the War in the Pacific ended, Ma Hung-k'uei became a deputy director of Chiang Kai-shek's northwest headquarters. In 1948, as the Kuomintang-Communist civil war was reaching its climax, he was transferred from the governorship of Ninghsia to the governorship of Kansu. The following year, he succeeded Ma Pu-fang as deputy director of the northwest military and political affairs administration when Ma Pu-fang became director of the northwest headquarters at Lanchow. The two Ma's flew to Canton to confer with acting President Li Tsung-jen (q.v.) about the defense of Kansu and Tsinghai. Soon after their return, Ma Pu-fang went to Hong Kong. By the middle of September, northwest China had come under Chinese Communist control. Ma Hung-k'uei left China for the United States, where he established residence in southern California and took up ranching and horse breeding.

Ma Hung-pin　　　　　　馬 鴻 賓
T. Tzu-yin　　　　　　　　子 寅

Ma Hung-pin (1883–21 October 1960), Chinese Muslim general who served as acting governor of Kansu in 1930–31 and as governor of Ninghsia in 1948–49. He declared allegiance to the Chinese Communists in September 1949 and was rewarded with administrative posts in the new regime.

A native of Linhsia (Hochow), Kansu, Ma Hung-pin was the son of Ma Fu-lu, an elder brother of Ma Fu-hsiang (q.v.). Little is known about his early years except that he was schooled for military life. About 1904 he became commander of a cavalry company at Sining, commissioner for wastelands development, and commissioner of mines. He received command of the Kansu West Route Cavalry Patrol Battalion in 1911. After the republic was established and the Mongol banners of the Ikechao and Ulanchab leagues grew restless because of Outer Mongolia's declaration of independence, Ma helped calm these groups by leading his forces into the Wuyuan-Linho sector of Inner Mongolia and announcing plans for a reform movement. In 1914 his assignment to that area was made official with his appointment as commander of the 7th Cavalry

Battalion, with responsibility for the defense of the Hotao area. He worked to rid the area of bandits, and in 1919 he defeated a large force led by the pretender to the Manchu throne, Ta-erh-liu-chi. In the winter of 1920, having risen to the rank of lieutenant general, Ma was appointed a defense commissioner.

Ma Hung-pin became commander in chief of bandit-suppression on the Shensi-Kansu border in 1926, and the following year, he entered the service of Feng Yü-hsiang (q.v.) as commander of the Temporary 22nd Division of the Second Army Group of the National Revolutionary Army. He continued to serve Feng until October 1929, by which time Feng's 1929 campaign against the forces of Chiang Kai-shek was limping to an end. Then he declared allegiance to the National Government, which rewarded him with the governorship of Ninghsia and command of the 7th Division. When the so-called enlarged conference movement, led by Feng Yü-hsiang and Yen Hsi-shan (q.v.), collapsed in 1930, Ma became a commissioner of the Kansu provincial government and acting governor of Kansu. In August 1931, however, the division commanders Ma Wen-chü and Lei Chung-t'ien effected a coup at Lanchow and placed Ma under house arrest. After being released at the time of Ma Wen-chü's arrest in September, Ma Hung-pin resigned the Kansu governorship. His cousin Ma Hung-k'uei (q.v.) was offered the post, but refused it. Eventually, Shao Li-tzu (q.v.) became governor of Kansu, and Ma Hung-pin received the post of Kanchow-Liangchow border defense commissioner, with headquarters at Suchow. In 1933 he participated in the defense of Ninghsia against the rebellious Sun Tien-ying, and in 1934 he was appointed commander of the 35th Division and was given responsibility for bandit suppression in the eastern Kansu region.

With the outbreak of the Sino-Japanese war in July 1937, Ma Hung-pin was appointed commander of the Eighty-first Army and vice commander of the Seventeenth Group Army. That winter, he also became defense commander of western Suiyuan. He led his forces northward to fight the Japanese and managed to hold the Kuyang-Anpei sector for more than a year. In 1940 he was appointed defense and conciliation commander for the Ikechao League and was assigned to the Paotow-Saratsi sector, then

held by the Japanese. Ma skirmished for several months in the upper Ordos region and recovered some territory on the south bank of the Yellow River. The National Government decorated him for his accomplishments in the field, but he received no new commands after his forces were transferred to the Kansu-Ninghsia border area in the spring of 1941. For the remainder of the war, his only office was that of member of the Kuomintang Central Supervisory Committee.

In 1948, as the Kuomintang-Communist battle for the mainland was nearing its end, Ma Hung-pin succeeded his cousin Ma Hung-k'uei as governor of Ninghsia when Ma Hung-k'uei became governor of Kansu. Ma Hung-pin declared allegiance to the Chinese Communists in mid-September 1949, thereby helping to undermine the attempts of Ma Hung-k'uei and Ma Pu-fang (q.v.) to defend the northwestern region. When the Central People's Government was established in October 1949, Ma Hung-pin became a member of the Northwest Military and Administrative Council, vice chairman of the Nationalities Affairs Commission, and deputy governor of Kansu. He was appointed vice chairman of the reorganized Northwest Administrative Council in 1953. He was a Kansu delegate to the National People's Congress in 1954 and was elected to the congress's nationalities commission. That year, he also was elected to the National Defense Council and was reelected deputy governor of Kansu. On 21 October 1960 Ma died in Lanchow, at the age of 77 sui.

Ma Liang   馬良
　T. Hsiang-po   相伯

Ma Liang (7 April 1840–4 November 1939), Jesuit priest, government official, and educator. He was a founder of the Aurora Academy, the Fu-tan Academy, and the Fu-jen School. Aurora and Fu-jen later became universities.

Born at Tanyang, Kiangsu, into a family which had embraced Roman Catholicism in the early 1600's, Ma Liang was the second son of Ma Sung-yen (d. 1872), who was known for his learning in Chinese herb medicine. At the age of five, Ma began to study the Bible, other Christian writings, and the Chinese classics. In 1851, at the age of 11, he entered the newly established Jesuit College of St. Ignatius at Shanghai, where he studied, among other things, Latin and French. Seven years later, he began to study Catholic theology. In 1862 Ma joined the Society of Jesus; in 1864 he completed his probationary term; and in 1870, at the age of 30, he was ordained a priest.

In 1871 Ma Liang was sent by the Society of Jesus as a missionary to Nanking. However, he disliked his work, and in 1872 he returned to Shanghai to become principal of the College of St. Ignatius. At this time, he became interested in Western science, and in 1874 he began to translate a Western mathematics textbook, which he entitled *Tu-shu ta-ch'üan*. Although the translation was completed two years later, his superiors refused to give Ma permission to publish it. He was also prohibited from doing missionary relief work at his own expense. Greatly upset by these two incidents, Ma Liang abandoned the priesthood in 1876 and returned to secular life.

Through the influence of his elder brother, Ma Chien-hsün, Ma Liang soon became an adviser on Western technology to Yü Tzu-huan, the provincial treasurer of Shantung. In 1877 he was appointed director of a machine factory at Lok'ou, Shantung. After resigning from his job a year later, he came to the attention of Li Hung-chang (ECCP, I, 464–71), who sent him to investigate mining affairs in Shantung. In 1880 Ma drafted a memorial to the Manchu throne in the name of Liu Ming-ch'uan (ECCP, I, 526-28) urging the construction of a railroad between Ch'ing-chiang-p'u (Huaiyin) and Peking as a means of defense against Russia.

Ma Liang became an adviser to Li Shu-ch'ang (ECCP, I, 483-84), newly appointed minister to Japan, and accompanied Li to Tokyo as councillor of the mission early in 1882. While in Tokyo, Ma met Prince Itō and other Japanese political leaders, and he studied Japanese. Although he was appointed consul to Kobe soon afterwards, he gave up the post to return to China, where he again served under Li Hung-chang. About this time, Ma's younger brother, Ma Chien-chung, was asked to assist the Korean government in reforming its administration and army. Because Li Hung-chang required Ma Chien-chung's services in China, Ma Liang was sent to Korea. After the Tai Wön Kun, the father of the Korean king, carried out a *coup d'état* on 23 July 1882, Wu Ch'ang-ch'ing, Ma Chien-chung, and Ting Ju-ch'ang commanded a naval expedition to Korea to help the Korean king suppress this rebellion. Also serving on Wu's staff was Yuan Shih-k'ai, then only 18 years old. Before returning to Peking in 1883, Ma Liang recommended the young Yuan for the post of shang-wu wei-yuan [commercial commissioner] in Korea.

After returning to China, Ma Liang resigned his posts and concentrated on the study of Western science. In 1884 Li Hung-chang appointed Ma Chien-chung the assistant manager of the China Merchants' Steam Navigation Company, and, at Li's suggestion, Ma Liang was sent on a tour of south China to inspect the company's operations. He also served as an auditor for the company.

In October 1885 the Ch'ing government established the office of governor of Taiwan and appointed Liu Ming-ch'uan to fill this post. At Liu's invitation, Ma became his adviser and soon joined him on Taiwan. Ma advanced a plan for the development of the island through foreign loans in 1886, but it was rejected by the Ch'ing authorities. A short time later he returned to Tientsin. Again in the employ of Li Hung-chang, he then was sent to the United States to negotiate a loan for the Ch'ing government. Although Ma was greeted enthusiastically in the United States as Li Hung-chang's secretary and although his negotiations were successful, the Ch'ing government refused to support Li's loan plan. Ma Liang left the United States for Europe, where he visited London and Paris and had an audience with Pope Leo XIII in Rome. He returned to China in 1887.

Little is known about Ma's activities between the years 1887 and 1896 except that he devoted himself largely to the study of science. Sometime after 1887 he married and had two children. His wife died in 1893. A year later, his mother died. She reportedly denounced him just before her death, saying: "My son is a Catholic priest; you are not a priest, therefore, you are not my son." Ma returned to the Roman Catholic Church in 1896 as a layman.

He sent his children to Catholic schools and requested that they thereafter refer to him as "uncle."

In 1896 Ma Liang became associated with Liang Ch'i-ch'ao (q.v.), then the editor of the *Shih-wu-pao*. At Ma's suggestion, Liang began to study Latin with Ma Chien-chung. At this time, the Ma brothers were writing a book on Chinese grammar and sentence construction, the *Ma-shih wen-t'ung*, which was published in 1904. Ma Liang and Ma Chien-chung were partially responsible for Liang Ch'i-ch'ao's rise to prominence, and they introduced him to such foreign-affairs and reform experts as Yen Fu, Ch'en Chi-t'ung, and Sheng Hsuan-huai. During the Hundred Days Reform of 1898, Liang recommended that an i-hsueh-kuan [translation bureau] be established in Shanghai and suggested that Ma Liang be appointed its director. The plan, however, was never put into effect because the reform movement was suppressed soon afterwards.

In 1901 Ma Liang went to the astronomical observatory at Hsü-chia-wei (Zicawei), Shanghai, where he began to teach Latin to small groups of students and to translate the Bible into Chinese. He soon transformed his informal academy into a regular institution of higher learning. Largely financed by Ma's personal contributions, the Aurora Academy (later a university) opened officially in 1903, with Ma as principal. Under his regulations, the students practiced self-rule through the election of officers. Literature, both Western and Oriental, and science were emphasized in the curriculum. In 1905 Ma arranged for Jesuit priests to assume teaching duties at the school. However, Ma Liang soon resigned as principal and left the academy because he felt that European priests were interfering in its administration. He and Yen Fu then established the Fu-tan hsueh-yuan [Fu-tan academy] at Wusung, with Ma as principal.

In 1906, at the invitation of the governor general of Kiangsu and Chekiang, Ma Liang lectured to provincial officials on monarchy, democracy (which he advocated), and constitutionalism. In the autumn of that year, after the Ch'ing government announced that a constitution was in preparation, Liang Ch'i-ch'ao founded the Cheng-wen-she in Japan to foster the constitutional movement in China. Although Liang wanted to make K'ang Yu-wei (q.v.) chairman of the new society, he made Ma Liang general manager because K'ang was out of favor with the Manchu throne. Ma soon went to Japan, where he received an enthusiastic welcome from Chinese students in Tokyo, Yokohama, Hakone, and Kyoto who shortly before had rioted against Ch'ing officials supervising Chinese student affairs. Ma's speeches reportedly helped to placate the students. In March 1908 the offices of the Cheng-wen-she were moved to Shanghai, where Ma continued to head the society. At this time, the Cheng-wen-she, whose members were working clandestinely with higher officials of the imperial court and planning the establishment of schools for training in parliamentary government, aroused the opposition of Yuan Shih-k'ai. As a result, several government officials who were sympathetic to the society were dismissed, and on 13 August 1908 the Cheng-wen-she was banned by imperial edict. Ma returned to his educational duties, but continued to serve as Liang Ch'i-ch'ao's representative in Shanghai.

In 1910, after resuming the principalship of the Fu-tan Academy, Ma Liang was elected a member of the Tzu-cheng-yuan [parliament] at Peking, and in 1911 he joined the Hsien-yu-hui. When the Wuchang revolt of 1911 broke out, the Fu-tan Academy was moved to Wusih, but it soon was returned to Wusung. Upon the establishment of the Republic in 1912, Ma was appointed fu-yin [chief magistrate] of Nanking. During October–November 1912 he served as acting president of Peking University. Also in 1912 he and Ying Hua (Ying Lien-chih, q.v.) petitioned Pope Pius X, requesting the establishment of a Catholic university in Peking. In 1913 the two men founded the Fu-jen School.

From 1913 to 1916 Ma Liang worked to block Yuan Shih-k'ai's monarchical aspirations. He advised Yuan against attempting to become monarch, and, as a result, his house was surrounded by Yuan's agents. However, in 1916, just before Yuan announced his accession to the throne, Ma, disguised as a vegetable seller, managed to flee Peking. After Yuan's death in June 1916, Ma returned to Peking, and in October of that year he published a pamphlet entitled "Objectives of the Constitution," in which he emphasized the importance of the rule of law for political and personal freedom and affirmed that sovereignty in the state must lie with the people. During this period, Ma also continued to pursue his educational and religious activities. In 1916 he sponsored a United Catholic Congress at Peking to oppose the adoption of Confucianism as China's national religion and published the *Hsin-shih ho-pien chih-chiang*, a translation of and commentary on the Four Gospels. His *Kuo-min chao-hsin ching* [a mirror for the people of the republic], a treatise which was similar to his "Objectives of the Constitution," was published in 1919. This work was notable for its analysis of the warlord problem and its advocacy of local self-government under a nationally elected democratic government.

In 1922 Ma Liang went to Nanking to head a committee created to investigate the financial administration of Han Kuo-chün, the governor of Kiangsu, who had just resigned from office. Ma returned to Shanghai when Sun Ch'uan-fang (q.v.) occupied Nanking. On the occasion of the fiftieth anniversary of the Shanghai *Shun-pao*, Ma wrote an article for the paper entitled "Religions of the World in the Past Fifty Years," in which he observed that religion and science were not mutually exclusive. Ying Hua invited Ma in 1925 to become chancellor of the newly established Fu-jen University, formerly the Fu-jen School. Ma declined the appointment, but he offered to help organize the administration of the university. The following year, Catholics in Shanghai founded a newspaper, the *T'ien-min pao*, with Ma as editor in chief.

From 1927 until his death in 1939, Ma Liang lived in retirement and devoted himself to scholarly, religious, and patriotic writing. In 1927, together with Father Hsü Yün-hsi, he translated into Chinese the autobiography of St. Theresa under the title *Ling-hsin hsiao-shih*. That year, the Academia Sinica was founded, and its creation was based partly on suggestions made by Ma in 1913–14. After the Mukden Incident of September 1931, Ma became concerned about the Japanese invasion of Manchuria and its implications; in 1931–32 he wrote several articles denouncing Japanese aggression, and he spoke on the radio to rally the Chinese people to protect their homeland. His articles on this subject were collected and published in 1933 as *Ma Hsiang-po hsien-sheng kuo-nan lun-wen chi* [the essays of Ma Hsiang-po written concerning the national emergency].

In 1934, on the three-hundredth anniversary of the death of the Ming prime minister and Catholic layman Hsü Kuang-ch'i (ECCP, I, 316-19), Ma wrote "Hsü Wen-ting-kung yü Chung-kuo k'o-hsüeh" [Hsü Kuang-ch'i and Chinese science] for the magazine *K'o-hsueh*. The Hsiang-po Library, to which he gave 8,700 Chinese and Western books, was dedicated to Ma Liang by the people of Tanyang in 1936. In the winter of that year, Archbishop Paul Yü Pin invited Ma to Nanking, where in March 1937 he was made a kuo-min cheng-fu wei-yüan [member of the national government]. After the Sino-Japanese war broke out in July 1937, Ma moved to Feng-tung-shan in Kweilin. He attained the age of 100 sui in January 1939, and in March and April of that year masses and celebrations were held throughout China in honor of his birthday. At the invitation of his former student Yü Yu-jen (q.v.), Ma began a journey to Kunming, but on the way he fell ill. On 4 November 1939 he died at Liangshan in Indo-China. Ma was survived by his daughter, Ma Tsung-wen (b. 1889).

Two collections of Ma's writings, *Ma Hsiang-po hsien-sheng wen-chi* and *Ma Hsiang-po hsien-sheng wen-chi hsü-pien*, were published at Peiping in 1947 and 1948 respectively.

Ma Pu-ch'ing   馬步青
T. Tzu-yün   子雲

Ma Pu-ch'ing (1898–), Chinese Muslim general. He was the elder brother of Ma Pu-fang.

The elder brother of Ma Pu-fang (q.v.), Ma Pu-ch'ing was born in Linhsia (Hochow), Kansu. After receiving his primary education in the Chinese classics, he enrolled at the Kansu First Provincial Middle School. About 1916 he entered military service as commander of the 1st Battalion of the Ninghai Army Cavalry Patrol. He subsequently became commander of the entire infantry and cavalry force of the Ninghai Army. In 1922 he became Fourth Route defense commissioner in Suiyuan province, and in 1923, having attained the rank of brigadier general, he received command of a cavalry regiment in the 5th Mixed Brigade. Then, as commander of the Ninghai Temporary Cavalry Brigade, he worked to suppress banditry and unrest in Kansu and the Kokonor region.

Ma Pu-ch'ing joined the National Revolutionary Army in 1928 as commander of the Temporary 77th Brigade of the 26th Division in the Second Group Army of Feng Yü-hsiang (q.v.). The following year, Feng appointed him commander of the 65th Brigade of the 22nd Division and garrison commander at Loyang. Although Ma participated in Feng's anti-Nanking campaigns of 1929 and 1930, he was not removed from command by the National Government during the 1931 reorganization of Feng's troops. Instead, he received command of the 26th Division, with the rank of lieutenant general. In 1932 he returned to his home province to take command of the Kansu 1st Cavalry Division. He again became concerned with bandit suppression and the maintenance of peace when that unit was reorganized as the Nationalist New 2nd Cavalry Division, with garrison station in the Hohsi region.

In 1936 Ma Pu-ch'ing became the commander of the Nationalist 5th Cavalry Division. He remained in the Hohsi area and prevented Chinese Communist forces from entering it later in 1936. In addition to military measures, he undertook such projects as reforestation and the expansion of educational facilities. He reportedly prohibited opium and wine production in the Hohsi region in 1937. About the time that the Sino-Japanese war broke out, his unit was reorganized as the Fifth Cavalry Army. Also in 1937 Ma became director of the Kansu–Sinkiang highway, with the task of transforming an ancient camel trail into a modern paved road to be used in the transport of war supplies from the Soviet Union. He accomplished this task in three years. Ma then was appointed reclamation commissioner of the Tsaidam region of Tsinghai province in 1942. His younger brother, Ma Pu-fang, was governor of Tsinghai, and they worked closely and well together. In 1943 Ma Pu-ch'ing became deputy commander in chief, serving under his brother, of the Fortieth Group Army and a member of the Mongolian and Tibetan Affairs Commission.

In the postwar period Ma Pu-ch'ing's fortunes declined. His Fifth Cavalry Army, which was ordered to Sinkiang in 1945 to fight rebellious Turki forces, was reorganized and removed from his command after its arrival in Sinkiang. The following year, the Fortieth Group Army was disbanded, leaving Ma without a military post. He accompanied the Nationalists to Taiwan in 1949 and became an adviser to the ministry of defense of the National Government in Taiwan.

Ma Pu-fang   馬 步 芳
  T. Tzu-hsiang   子 香

Ma Pu-fang (1903–), Chinese Muslim general who was governor of Tsinghai from 1938 until 1949. He later served the National Government in Taiwan as ambassador to Saudi Arabia, but he resigned in 1961.

Linhsia (Hochow), Kansu, was the birthplace of Ma Pu-fang. He was the younger brother of Ma Pu-ch'ing (q.v.) and the son of Ma Ch'i, who served as governor of Tsinghai from 1929 to 1931. Ma Ch'i was succeeded as governor by his brother, Ma Lin. Although Ma Pu-fang received a primary education designed to prepare him for a career as a Muslim Imam, he soon decided that he would rather be a military man. After being graduated from the Ninghai Officers Training Corps, he joined the Ninghai Army in 1920 as a deputy battalion commander. By the end of 1930 he had risen to become commander of the Provisional 1st Division (later the 9th Division) in the Nationalist forces of Ku Chu-t'ung (q.v.), then the pacification commissioner for northwest China. Ku appointed Ma garrison commander for all of southern Tsinghai and ordered him to march on Ma Chung-ying (q.v.) who had been attempting to consolidate an independent base of power in Kansu. Ma Pu-fang soon drove Ma Chung-ying westward, scattering his forces. He then returned to his garrison station at Yüshu in Tsinghai.

Early in 1932 Ma Pu-fang cooperated with Liu Wen-hui (q.v.) in working out a plan for ending the Chinese-Tibetan struggle that had begun with the Ta-chin-ssu affair of 1930, when Tibetan lamas and Chinese soldiers had clashed at Kantzu. They recovered Kantzu and Chanhua, and by July 1932 their forces had reached the Chin Sha River. Liu Wen-hui signed a local agreement with the Tibetans in October 1932, and Ma Pu-fang negotiated a Tsinghai-Tibetan peace treaty which was submitted for National Government approval in July 1933.

Although Ma Lin was the titular head of the Tsinghai government from 1931 to 1938, Ma Pu-fang was named acting governor of Tsinghai and commander of the 82nd Division. He was confirmed as governor in 1938, when Ma Lin received membership in the State Council. By this time, the Sino-Japanese war had broken out and the 82nd Division had been reorganized as the Eighty-second Army. The retreat of the National Government to Chungking greatly increased the strategic importance of northwest China. Ma Pu-fang, to strengthen his province and to block Japanese intrigue among the Chinese Muslims of the northwest, undertook what he termed "The Six Great Tasks"—the organization of a pao-chia system, the creation of a military reserve, the enforcement of prohibitions on opium, the improvement of literacy, the construction of provincial highways, and the development of forests.

Ma Pu-fang's administration was one of the most efficient in China. He introduced modern medicine to the province, initiated irrigation projects, and built factories for the manufacture of such goods as pottery, chemicals, and matches. By government order, everyone in the province—even officials, lamas, and students—had to plant several trees each year as part of the reforestation program. The citizens of Sining periodically had to meet a daily quota of dead flies, their contribution to Ma's sanitation program. Ma paid special attention to education. Citizens between the ages of 15 and 20 were taught 1,000 Chinese characters in special classes, and by 1942 almost 100,000 of them had learned to read. Ma's government established primary and secondary schools throughout the province and provided all Tsinghai students with uniforms, books, and other school supplies. Ma also gave strong moral and financial support to a private school system known as the K'unlun Schools, which provided comprehensive education for Muslim students. Although Ma's regime was highly authoritarian, it was a benevolent dictatorship. Furthermore, the reform and development programs did not place a heavy tax burden on the people, for the government supported itself mainly through industrial and commercial monopoly.

In 1943 Ma Pu-fang was appointed commander in chief of the Fortieth Group Army, with Ma Pu-ch'ing as deputy commander. Two years later, he became a deputy chairman of Chiang Kai-shek's northwest headquarters and a member of the Kuomintang's Central Executive Committee. The Fortieth Group Army was disbanded in 1946, just a few months after the War in the Pacific ended, and Ma was given the post of deputy director of the northwest military and political affairs administration at Lanchow. When Chang Chih-chung (q.v.) declared allegiance to the Chinese Communists in 1949, Ma succeeded him as director of the northwest headquarters. After returning from a conference at Canton with acting President Li Tsung-jen (q.v.) and other Nationalist leaders in July, Ma packed his possessions and moved to Hong Kong. Lanchow and Sining fell to the Chinese Communists soon after he left Tsinghai.

Ma Pu-fang went to Egypt in the early 1950's and remained there until that country recognized the People's Republic of China in 1957. He then accepted an appointment as Nationalist ambassador to Saudi Arabia. In May 1961 the National Government in Taiwan announced that he had been charged with corruption and incompetence and that his resignation had been accepted by the ministry of foreign affairs. Ma Pu-fang continued to live in the Middle East.

Ma Yin-ch'u   馬 寅 初
Orig. Ma Yuan-shan   馬 元 善

Ma Yin-ch'u (1882–), Western-trained economist who specialized in applied economics. A long-time critic of the National Government's economic policies, he later held office in the Central People's Government. He served as president of Peking University from 1951 to 1960, when he was dismissed because of the political unorthodoxy of his economic views.

A native of Ch'enghsien, Chekiang, Ma Yin-ch'u was the son of a well-to-do manufacturer of Shaohsing wine. After receiving a primary education in the Chinese classics in Ch'enghsien and a modern secondary education at a Christian school in Shanghai, he enrolled at Peiyang University in Tientsin to study metallurgy. Upon graduation in 1907 he went to the United States to become an undergraduate economics major at Yale University. He received a B.A. degree from Yale in

1910 and then did graduate work at Columbia University, specializing in applied economics and obtaining a Ph.D. degree in 1914. His thesis, entitled *The Finances of the City of New York*, was published in the same year.

Ma Yin-ch'u returned to China in 1915 and accepted an appointment as professor of economics at Peking University. He soon was invited by Chang Kia-ngau (Chang Chia-ao, q.v.) to become a member of the research department of the Bank of China, and he later became director of the bank's department of note issue. In 1920 Ma Yin-ch'u obtained a year's leave of absence from Peking University to investigate industrial and commercial activities in Shanghai. He established close ties with Shanghai businessmen and industrialists so that he could improve his understanding of conditions and practices in this economic center of China. As an applied economist interested professionally in money and banking, he deemed such understanding an essential precondition to the application of Western economic principles and methods to the development of the Chinese economy. Also in 1920 Ma helped Kuo Ping-wen (q.v.) establish the Shanghai College of Commerce and agreed to serve as an adviser to the National Commercial Bank.

In 1921 Ma Yin-ch'u returned to his teaching duties at Peking University. Before long Ma joined with the economist D. K. Lieu in founding the Chinese Economics Society in 1923 and became its first president. In 1923, 1925, 1926, and 1928 he published collections of lectures in which he severely criticized Marxist economic theories. He rejected the labor theory of value on the grounds of oversimplification and stated that Marxist theory, whatever its relevance to Western society, was not applicable to China because China lacked concentrated capital, developed forces of production, clear class demarcation, and a united urban proletariat. China's trouble, according to Ma, did not lie in capitalism, but in lack of capital. He supported the views of the German political economist Friedrich List, particularly as concerned the protection of young industries. Ma reiterated this point in such later works as *Chung-kuo kuan-shui wen-t'i* [China's tariff problems] of 1926 and *Chung-kuo ching-chi kai-tsao* [the economic reform of China] of 1935. The latter book, which dealt extensively with the theories of

Othmar Spann, argued that neither socialism nor liberalism was suited to China and proposed the adoption of the universalism propounded by some German and Austrian scholars.

After leaving Peking University in 1927, Ma Yin-ch'u returned to his native province to become professor of economics at Chekiang University and a member of the provincial government council. The following year, he joined the staff of Chiaotung University as professor of economics and head of its research institute. He also served as a professor and later dean of the Shanghai College of Commerce. In 1929 he published *Chung-hua yin-hang lun* [on banks in China]. About this time, Ma was appointed to the Legislative Yuan. He retained his membership in the yuan until 1947. In this capacity, he undertook the drafting of the Banking Law, and he frequently was called upon to lecture on economics at the Lu-chün ta-hsueh [war college]. With the deterioration of Sino-Japanese relations in the 1930's, Chiang Kai-shek convened two conferences at Lushan to discuss emergency measures in case of war. Ma attended both conferences. It was while the second meeting was in session that the Sino-Japanese war broke out in July 1937.

From 1938 to 1940 Ma Yin-ch'u was professor of economics and dean of the college of commerce at Chungking University. When the political department of the Military Affairs Commission undertook the compilation in 1938 of a series of textbooks for use in military schools during the war, Ma was commissioned to write a general work on economics. Ma became increasingly aware of the corruption and inefficiency that existed in some official circles, and in 1939 he launched attacks on the economic policies of the National Government, alleging that the "bureaucratic capitalism" of H. H. K'ung and T. V. Soong (qq.v.) was undermining the nation's economy. He delivered these criticisms in lectures at Chungking University and at meetings of the People's Political Council, and he published articles in such journals as the *Chung-shan yueh-k'an* and the *San-min-chu-i pan-yueh k'an*. Because he disregarded warnings from the National Government authorities, toward the end of 1940 he was sent to Hsifeng, Kweichow, and was held there under house arrest for almost two years. Although he was released and allowed to return to Chungking in 1942, he was forbidden by government order from teaching in any national university, speaking in public, or publishing articles that did not deal solely with economic theories.

At war's end Ma Yin-ch'u returned to Chekiang. He became a research fellow of the Academia Sinica in 1947 and joined the faculty of the Hsing-li School of Accounting and the Chung-hua Industrial and Commercial School in Shanghai. In 1948 he published the two-volume *Ts'ai-cheng hsueh yü Chung-kuo ts'ai-cheng: Li-lun yü hsien-shih* [the study of finance and Chinese financial affairs: theory and reality], and he made speeches predicting that the issuance of the new gold yuan currency would bring about the collapse of the Chinese economy. Later that year, he participated in student demonstrations in both Hangchow and Shanghai and then went to Hong Kong to escape the possibility of arrest.

Ma Yin-ch'u went to the Communist-controlled Northeast early in 1949 at the invitation of Chou En-lai (q.v.). He attended the World Peace Conference at Prague in April and returned to China to help plan the establishment of the New Economic Society at Peiping and to serve as a non-partisan delegate to the Chinese People's Political Consultative Conference in September. When the Central People's Government was established in October, Ma was made a member of the Government Council, vice chairman of the finance and economic affairs committee of the Government Administration Council, a director of the Sino-Soviet Friendship Association, and vice chairman of the China Peace Committee. In February 1950 he became a vice chairman of the East China Military and Administrative Committee. He also served as president of Chekiang University in 1950–51 and as a director representing government holdings of the Bank of China.

When Ma Yin-ch'u left Chekiang University to assume the presidency of Peking University in the summer of 1951, he announced a personal ten-year plan, saying that he would study Russian for four years and then would write for six years. In this manner, he hoped to reach a deeper understanding of Communism and to "communize" his own thinking. However, he did not allow this undertaking to interfere with his public duties. In 1952 he accepted appointments as a member of the

preparatory committee for the International Economic Conference, vice chairman of the China Committee for Promoting Foreign Trade, a director of the World Peace Council, a member of the Standing Committee of the Chinese People's Political Consultative Conference, and a member of the committee assigned to draft a constitution. He became a member of the Standing Committee of the National People's Congress and an executive director of the Bank of China in 1954, and the following year he was elected to the philosophy and social science department of the Chinese Academy of Sciences. During the early 1950's, Ma traveled frequently to Europe, usually to attend meetings of the World Peace Council; between 1950 and 1954 he visited Warsaw, Vienna, Berlin, Sofia, Stockholm, and other cities.

According to Ma's personal plan, 1955 was the year for him to start writing. In April of that year he completed an essay on "The Socialist Transformation of China's Capitalist Industry," but it was not published until 1957 because some people considered it a defense of capitalists. His "New Theory of Population," intended for presentation to the National People's Congress in July 1955, was withdrawn when it was criticized as being nothing more than an extension of Malthusian theory. Ma revised this treatise and presented it to the congress on 3 July 1957. In it he discussed the effects of overpopulation on capital accumulation, productivity of labor, and living standards, stressing the need for population control and proposing the regular registration of all data necessary for showing the movement of population increase. Ma devoted most of his energies to his "circular progression" and "spiral upward" theories to explain the achievement of "comprehensive balance," or general equilibrium, in the economy of China. His two articles on "The Theory of Comprehensive Balance and the Law of Proportional Development, Linked with Actual Conditions in China" appeared in the Peking *Jen-min jih-pao* [people's daily] in December 1956 and May 1957. In his 1958 book, *My Economic Theory, Philosophical Thought, and Political Stand*, he reprinted these two essays and his articles on population and private business and added new theoretical and anti-Keynesian material. He explained that everything is correlated in a circular movement because, according to dialectical materialism, these is an internal relation between everything in the universe. He diagrammed his theories as a rotating circle composed of a series of connected "links" which represent the various sectors of the economy. Between any two links there exists a correct quantitative ratio, and these ratios must be properly planned for all links if the various sectors of the economy are to be fully integrated. Ma also said that, in accordance with dialectical materialism, this circular movement is an ever mounting spiral reversion.

Between April 1958 and October 1959 more than 200 articles attacking Ma Yin-ch'u's theories appeared in China. He wrote a number of articles to disprove their criticisms, but it was not until November 1959 that he published a full-scale counterattack, "My Philosophical Thought and Economic Theories." In this article, which appeared in the November issue of *Hsin chien-she* [new construction] he also stated that although such friends as Chou En-lai had advised him to retract his statements to avoid jeopardizing his political position, he could not accept their advice because he considered the matter a purely academic problem and not a political one. "After writing articles, one should be brave enough to correct mistakes but must adhere to the truth and bear all consequences even if they are disadvantageous to his private interests or his life. I do not teach and have no direct contact with students, but I always want to educate them by means of action." The December 1959 and January 1960 issues of *Hsin chien-she* contained new attacks on Ma, and in April 1960 he was dismissed from the presidency of Peking University. However, he was elected to the Standing Committee of the National People's Congress in 1959 and retained his membership in the Standing Committee of the Chinese People's Political Consultative Conference, to which he was reelected in 1964.

GENERAL BIOGRAPHICAL
REFERENCE WORKS

Biographies of Prominent Chinese, ed. by A. R. Burt, J. B. Powell. and Carl Crow. Shanghai, no date.

Chang Yüeh-jui. *Chin-jen chuan-chi wen-hsüan*. Changsha, 1938.

張越瑞。近人傳記文選。

Chao Chia-chin and Chang Sheng-chih. *Ming-jen chuan-chi*. Hong Kong, 1947.

趙家緝。張聲智。名人傳記。

Chin-shih jen-wu chih, ed. by Chin Liang. Taipei, 1955.

近世人物志。金梁。

Chin-tai Chung-kuo ming-jen ku-shih, ed. by Yü Ling. Shanghai, 1949.

近代中國名人故事。俞凌。

Chin-tai ming-jen chuan-chi hsüan, ed. by Chu Te-chün. Shanghai, 1948.

近代名人傳記選。朱德君。

Chin-tai ming-jen hsiao-chuan, ed. by Wo-ch'iu chung-tzu (pseud.). 3 vols. No place, 1926.

近代名人小傳。沃丘仲子。

China Handbook, 1937–1945, with 1946 Supplement, ed. by the Chinese Ministry of Information. New York, 1947.

China Handbook, ed. by the China Handbook Editorial Board. Taipei, 1951–.

The China Year Book, ed. by N. G. W. Woodhead. Tientsin, 1921–39.

The Chinese Year Book, ed. by the Council on International Affairs, Ministry of Foreign Affairs. Shanghai, 1935–41.

Ch'ing-tai ch'i-pai ming-jen chuan, ed. by Ts'ai Kuan-lo. Kowloon, 1963.

清代七百名人傳。蔡冠洛。

Chuan-chi wen-hsüeh. Taipei, 1962–.

傳記文學。

Chūgoku bunkakai jimbutsu sōkan, ed. by Hashikawa Tokio. Peking, 1940.

中國文化界人物總鑑。橋川時雄。

Ch'un-ch'iu. Hong Kong, 1957–.

春秋。

Chung-hua min-kuo jen-shih lu. Taipei, 1953.

中華民國人事錄。

Chung-hua min-kuo ming-jen chuan, ed. by Chia I-chün. 2 vols. Peiping, 1932–33.

中華民國名人傳。賈逸君。

Chung-kung jen-ming tien, ed. by Chang Ta-chün. Kowloon, 1956.

中共人名典。張大軍。

Chung-kung jen-wu chih, ed. by *Jen-min nien-chien*. Hong Kong, 1951.

中共人物誌。人民年鑑。

Chung-kuo jen-wu hsin-chuan, ed. by Hsü Liang-chih. Hong Kong, 1954.

中國人物新傳。徐亮之。

Chung-kuo kung-ch'an-tang lieh-shih chuan, ed. by Hua Ying-shen. Hong Kong, 1949.

中國共產黨烈士傳。華應申。

Chung-kuo li-tai ming-jen nien-p'u mu-lu, ed. by Li Shih-t'ao. Shanghai, 1941.

中國歷代名人年譜目錄。李士濤。

Chung-kuo ming-jen chuan, ed. by T'ang Lu-feng. Shanghai, 1932.

中國名人傳。唐盧鋒。

Chung-kuo ming-jen tien, ed. by Li Hsi-keng and Fang Cheng-hsiang. Peking, 1949.

中國名人典。李希更。方正祥。

Chung-kuo pai-ming-jen chuan, ed. by Ch'en I-lin. Shanghai, 1937.

中國百名人傳。陳翊林。

Chung-kuo tang-tai ming-jen chuan, ed. by Fu Jun-hua. Shanghai, 1948.

中國當代名人傳。傅潤華。

Chung-kuo tang-tai ming-jen i-shih, ed. by Chang Hsing-fan. Shanghai, 1947.

中國當代名人逸事。張行帆。

Directory of Party and Government Officials of Communist China, ed. by the Bureau of Intelligence and Research, U.S. Department of State. 2 vols. Washington, 1960.

Eminent Chinese of the Ch'ing Period (1644–1912), ed. by Arthur W. Hummel. 2 vols. Washington, 1943–44.

Erh-shih chin-jen chih, ed. by *Jen-chien-shih* she. Shanghai, 1935.

二十今人志。人間世社。

Feng Tzu-yu. *Ko-ming i-shih*. Changsha, 1939.

馮自由。革命逸史。

Gendai Chūgoku Chōsen jimmei kan, ed. by Gaimushō Ajia-kyoku. Tokyo, 1953.

現代中國朝鮮人名鑑。アジア局。

Gendai Chūgoku jimmei jiten, ed. by Kasumigaseki-kai. Tokyo, 1962.

現代中國人名辭典。霞關會。

Gendai Chūgoku jiten, ed. by Chūgoku kenkyū-jo. Tokyo, 1950.

現代中國辭典。中國研究所。

Gendai Chūka minkoku Manshu teikoku jimmei kan, ed. by Gaimushō jōhōbu.

現代中華民國滿洲帝國人名鑑。
　　外務省情報部。

Gendai Shina jimmei jiten, ed. by Tairiku bunka kenkyū-jo. Tokyo, 1939.

現代支那人名辞典。大陸文化研究所。

Gendai Shina jimmei kan. Tokyo, 1928.

現代支那人名鑑。

Hatano Kenichi. *Gendai Shina no seiji to jimbutsu*. Tokyo, 1937.

波多野乾一。現代支那の政治と人物。

Hemmi Juro. *Chūkaminkoku kakumei nijishunen kinen shi*. Keijo, 1931.

逸見十郎。中華民國革命二十週年紀念史。

Hsien-tai shih-liao, ed. by Hai-t'ien ch'u-pan-she. 4 vols. Shanghai, 1935.

現代史料。海天出版社。

Hsin Chung-kuo fen-sheng jen-wu chih, ed. by Sonoda Ikki; tr. by Huang Hui-ch'uan and Tiao Ying-hua. Shanghai, 1930.

新中國分省人物誌。園田一龜。
　　黃惠泉。刁英華。

Hsin Chung-kuo jen-wu chih, ed. by Chou-mo pao. Hong Kong, 1950.

新中國人物誌。週末報。

Hsüeh Chün-tu. *The Chinese Communist Movement, 1921–1937*. Stanford, 1960.

———. *The Chinese Communist Movement, 1937–1949*. Stanford, 1962.

Hua-ch'iao hsing-shih hsien-hsien lieh-chuan, ed. by Hai-wai wen-k'u. Taipei. 1956.

華僑姓氏先賢列傳。海外文庫。

Huang Fen-sheng. *Pien-chiang jen-wu chih*. Chungking, 1945.

黃奮生。邊疆人物誌。

Huang Kung-wei. *Chung-kuo chin-tai jen-wu i-hua.* Taipei, 1949.

黃公偉。中國近代人物逸話。

Hu-nan ko-ming lieh-shih chuan, ed. by Chung-kung Hu-nan sheng-wei hsüan-ch'uan-pu. Changsha, 1952.

湖南革命烈士傳。中共湖南省委宣傳部。

I-chiang-shan hsün-chih chiang-shih chung-lieh lu, ed. by Tsung-ssu-ling-pu shih-cheng-ch'u. Taipei, 1959.

一江山殉職將士忠烈錄。總司令部史政處。

I-ching. Shanghai, 1936–37.

逸經。

Jen-chien-shih. Shanghai, 1934–35.

人間世。

Klein, Donald W. *Who's Who in Modern China*. New York, 1959.

Ko-ming hsien-lieh chuan-chi, ed. by Wang Shao-tzu. Shanghai, no date.

革命先烈傳記。王紹子。

Kuo-shih-kuan kuan-k'an. Nanking, 1947–49.

國史館館刊。

Liu Ts'un-jen. *Jen-wu t'an*. Hong Kong, 1952.

柳存仁。人物譚。

Lu Man-yen. *Shih-hsien pieh-chi*. Chungking, 1943.

陸曼炎。時賢別記。

Lu Tan-lin. *Tang-tai jen-wu chih*. Shanghai, 1947.

陸丹林。當代人物志。

Min-kuo ming-jen t'u-chien, ed. by Yang Chia-lo. 2 vols. Nanking, 1937.

民國名人圖鑑。楊家駱。

Ming-jen chuan, ed. by Hai-wai wen-k'u. Taipei, 1954.

名人傳。海外文庫。

Pei-chuan chi-pu, comp. by Min Erh-ch'ang. Peiping, 1932.

碑傳記補。閔爾昌。

Saishin Shina kanshin roku, ed. by Shina kenkyū-kai. Tokyo, 1919.

最新支那官紳錄。支那研究會。

Saishin Shina yōjin den, ed. by Tōa mondai chōsa-kai. Osaka, 1941.

最新支那要人傳。東亞問題調查會。

Sekai jimmei jiten: Tōyō-hen, ed. by Ōrui Noburu. Tokyo, 1952.

世界人名辭典:東洋篇。大類伸。

Shin Chūgoku jiten, ed. by Chūgoku kenkyū-jo. Tokyo, 1954.

新中國事典。中國研究所。

Shina jinshiroku, ed. by Sawamura Yukio and Ueda Toshio. Osaka, 1929.

支那人士錄。澤村幸夫。植田捷雄。

Shina mondai jiten, ed. by Fujita Chikamasa. Tokyo, 1942.

支那問題辭典。藤田親昌。

T'an-tang-tang-chai chu (pseud.). *Hsien-tai Chung-kuo ming-jen wai-shih*. Peiping, 1935.

坦蕩蕩齋主。現代中國名人外史。

Tang-tai Chung-kuo jen-wu chih, ed. by Chung-liu shu-chü. Shanghai, 1938.

當代中國人物誌。中流書局。

Tang-tai Chung-kuo ming-jen chih, ed. by Hsiao Hsiao. Shanghai, 1940.

當代中國名人誌。蕭瀟。

Tang-tai Chung-kuo ming-jen lu, ed. by Fan Yin-nan. Shanghai, 1931.

當代中國名人錄。樊蔭南。

Tang-tai Chung-kuo ming-jen tz'u-tien, ed. by Jen Chia-yao. Shanghai, 1947.
當代中國名人辭典。任嘉堯。

Tang-tai jen-wu, ed. by Su Chi-ch'ang. Chungking, 1947.
當代人物。蘇季常。

T'ang Tsu-p'ei. *Min-kuo ming-jen hsiao-chuan*. Hong Kong, 1953.
唐租培。民國名人小傳。

T'ao Chü-yin. *Chin-tai i-wen*. Shanghai, 1945.
陶菊隱。近代軼聞。

T'o Huang. *Chin-jih ti chiang-ling*. Shanghai, 1939.
拓荒。今日的將領。

Tso Shun-sheng. *Chung-kuo hsien-tai ming-jen i-shih*. Kowloon, 1951.
左舜生。中國現代名人軼事。

Tsui-chin kuan-shen lü-li hui-lü. Peking, 1920.
最近官紳履歷彙錄。

Tsurumi Yūsuke. *Danjō shijō gaijō no hito*. Tokyo, 1928.
鶴見祐輔。壇上紙上街上の人。

Tzu-yu Chung-kuo ming-jen chuan, ed. by Ting Ti-sheng. Taipei, 1952.
自由中國名人傳。丁滌生。

Wang Sen-jan. *Chin-tai erh-shih-chia p'ing-chuan*. Peiping, 1934.
王森然。近代二十家評傳。

Who's Who in China, ed. by the China Weekly Review. Shanghai, 1926-50.

Who's Who in Communist China, ed. by the Union Research Institute. Hong Kong, 1966.

Who's Who in Modern China, ed. by Max Perleberg. Hong Kong, 1954.

Who's Who of American Returned Students, ed. by Tsing Hua College. Peking, 1917.

Wu, Eugene. *Leaders of Twentieth-Century China*. Stanford, 1956.

Yü Hsüeh-lun. *Ch'i-ch'ing-lou tsa-chi*. 2 vols. Taipei, 1953, 1955.
喻血輪。綺情樓雜記。